# THE ROMANTIC TRIUMPH

# AMERICAN LITERATURE: A PERIOD ANTHOLOGY

OSCAR CARGILL, *General Editor*

---

THE ROOTS OF NATIONAL CULTURE: TO 1830

ROBERT E. SPILLER
*Swarthmore College*

THE ROMANTIC TRIUMPH: 1830-1860

TREMAINE McDOWELL
*University of Minnesota*

THE RISE OF REALISM: 1860-1888

LOUIS WANN
*University of Southern California*

THE SOCIAL REVOLT: 1888-1914

OSCAR CARGILL
*New York University*

CONTEMPORARY TRENDS: SINCE 1914

JOHN HERBERT NELSON
*University of Kansas*

# THE ROMANTIC TRIUMPH

## *American Literature*

FROM 1830 TO 1860

EDITED BY
TREMAINE McDOWELL
PROFESSOR OF ENGLISH
UNIVERSITY OF MINNESOTA



NEW YORK
THE MACMILLAN COMPANY

Set up and electrotyped. Published April, 1933.
Reprinted June, 1935; April, 1937; January, 1938.
April, 1939. March, 1940. June, 1940.
December, 1942. January, 1944. September, 1945

PRINTED IN THE UNITED STATES OF AMERICA
BY THE FERRIS PRINTING COMPANY

# PREFACE

The major purpose of this book is to give, from the prose and poetry of the American authors who flourished from 1830 to 1860, the most extensive readings which it is possible to print in a single volume of convenient size. Here, it is hoped, students of all persuasions will find material more than sufficient for their purposes. For those who concern themselves exclusively with the masters, there is a fuller representation of Poe, Emerson, and Hawthorne than can be found in similar collections; while for those who are interested also in general trends, there are passages from such symptomatic minors as Lydia Sigourney, T. H. Chivers, Bronson Alcott, and David Crockett. For those who view these years as a national period, a creative period, a New England period, a Romantic period—for each of these, provision has been made. In brief, thought has been given to the needs of all types of students—except those who would make American literature a stalking horse for the advancement of political, economic, or ethical programs.

Two shibboleths of editors are here ignored. Whenever possible, each work is given in its entirety; but where this ideal arrangement is impossible, extracts are presented without compunction or apology. No student, it is believed, should be deprived of all first-hand knowledge of the numerous and important books which cannot be included *in toto* in a classroom anthology. Again, it is hoped that the masterpieces of the period have been included in this volume; but its contents are not limited to "the best works" of the authors concerned. Rather, immature writings are occasionally introduced, to show an author's development; and imperfect later work is sometimes sampled, to reveal significant characteristics not otherwise to be illustrated.

Important authors are presented separately as individuals; less significant authors are grouped to exemplify tendencies and movements—an arrangement which may readily be ignored by those to whom it is unwelcome. Authors and groups are arranged approximately but not strictly in chronological order. Selections are given in the order of publication, the date of composition (if known) being indicated in parentheses at the left and the date of publication at the right. As a result of investigation of their periodical publication, several items are now given earlier dates than those hitherto accepted.

The notes are factual and historical, rather than critical, avoiding as far as possible all matters which are in dispute. A concise biographical sketch of each author is provided, primarily to relieve conscientious instructors from the labor of dictating facts, titles, and dates to their classes. The annotated bibliographies are designed to guide the uninitiated in their study and to aid them in avoiding the mass of inferior hack-work which unfortunately cannot be excluded from library shelves. To substantiate the dates given in the text, full details of publication of all items are included in the notes, as are also the sources of the texts followed—all of which matter may properly be ignored by every reader except the special student. The purpose of the notes on specific selections is to give students at least a hint of historical perspective. That they should approach the poetry of Longfellow or the prose of Melville exactly as did the contemporaries of those authors is as impossible as it is undesirable; but some attempt at bridging the decades is necessary if the literature of the Romantic Triumph is to be made human and vital to the present century.

The work of each author is presented without editing of any sort. Inconsistencies in spelling, capitalization, and punctuation within the text are therefore to be attributed to the idiosyncracies of the writers themselves—or of their original publishers. Titles and sub-titles of books, poems, and other items are likewise presented without change from the originals, save in instances where typographical considerations have led the present publisher to make alterations or additions.

The editor gratefully recognizes his obligations to the following persons who have generously assisted him: Mr. Nelson F. Adkins, Mr. Thomas Ollive Mabbott, Mr. J. H. Nelson, Mr. Charles W. Nichols, Mr. Robert E. Spiller, Mr. Louis Wann, Mr. Stanley T. Williams, and, above all, Mr. Oscar Cargill. The editor is also deeply indebted to his wife for her aid in the preparation of manuscript and the reading of proof.

TREMAINE McDOWELL

## ACKNOWLEDGMENTS

All extracts from Emerson, Thoreau, Hawthorne (with one exception), Whittier, Longfellow, Holmes, and Lowell are reprinted by permission of, and by arrangement with, Houghton Mifflin Company, the authorized publishers. Passages from *Love Letters of Nathaniel Hawthorne, 1839–1841* are used by permission of the late W. K. Bixby.

# CONTENTS

# THE ROMANTIC TRIUMPH

# THE ROMANTIC TRIUMPH
## (1830–1860)

"We are the pioneers of the world," Herman Melville declared of the American people. "God has predestined, mankind expects, great things from our race; and great things we feel in our souls. The most of the nations must soon be in our rear. We are . . . the advance guard, sent on through the wilderness of untried things." Because the establishment of the American republic was an experiment and an adventure, the faith and the aspiration thus voiced by Melville long animated its citizens and set them apart as a chosen race, destined to high achievement. This faith supported the rebellious colonists through weary and unheroic ordeals of the Revolution; and this aspiration finally guided the bickering, mutually suspicious states into a federal union. This spirit, likewise, shaped American literature during the late eighteenth and the early nineteenth century, while Royall Tyler, Brockden Brown, H. H. Brackenridge, and their contemporaries haltingly sought to transfer their literary allegiance from England to their native land; and Irving, Cooper, and Bryant unconsciously drew away from the outmoded Classicism of earlier generations, to move forward into the early phases of native Romanticism.

In the decades from 1830 to 1860, American idealism, now arrived at maturity, made itself felt in politics, religion, and letters in the form of self-reliant expansiveness. The emergence of this dynamic spirit is a familiar story. A necessary preliminary had been the second war with England, which gave the American people increased self-respect and self-confidence. Then began to appear the national temper and the national culture which vehement patriots had long but vainly attempted to create by decree. Then also came the conviction that the American experiment in republican government was at last crowned with triumphant success. Finally, in the 1840's and the 1850's, the cautious conservatism of earlier years succumbed to a new optimism; and the American people, fired by Utopian faith, gave themselves over to innovation and expansion. Abroad, Yankee ships entered every world-port; American trade touched every continent. At home, pioneers pushed across the plains into Oregon; forty-niners swept into California; imperialists laid violent hands on Texas. Meanwhile, self-trust and aspiration so dominated religious, social, and political theory that at last a president of the United States could declare: "I believe man can be elevated; man can become more and more endowed with divinity; and as he does, he becomes more God-like in character and capable of governing himself. Let us go on elevating our people, perfecting our institutions, until democracy shall reach such a point of perfection that we can acclaim with truth that the voice of the people is the voice of God."

The history of the Romantic Triumph in American literature is the record of the two-fold impact upon native authors of this same expansiveness. Positive and aggressive men of letters, fired by the new gospel, shared in the remaking of America as prophets, participants, and recorders. More aesthetic, less practical spirits turned away from these heated attempts to shape reality to fit aspiration, and deserted the American present for the solace of the distant or the past. Thus in the United States, as in Europe, Romanticists set out simultaneously for the two diverse goals of reformation and escape.

In the campaign to make the voice of the people truly the voice of God, autocracy in government was the first anachronism to be attacked. The assault came on two fronts—along the frontier and in the East. Western democracy in 1829 brought political absolutism to a violent pause by inaugurating as president an honest Indian fighter. While similar radicalism swept Europe and culminated in the spectacular events of '48, the Jacksonians, abhorred in New England as a "rank-rabble party . . . of barbarous robbers," struggled to reorganize the American state. But the actual rise of the common man was slow; and his triumphs were more evident at the polls than in the drawing-room or the library. Literature, therefore, permitted only a few glimpses of this unique battle for equalitarianism, in the writings of such primitive participants as Crockett and Longstreet and of such interested spectators from the saddle as Irving in *A Tour of the Prairies,* and Parkman in *The California and Oregon Trail.*

Meanwhile, the battle between the Eastern brand of individualism and the remnants of Tory autocracy was disrupting New England. There, in a region settled by non-conformists and separatists, there still persisted, in the midst of smug acquiescence, a small but rugged vein of self-trust. This, Emerson transmuted into the gospel of extreme individualism and self-reliance, whose inspired prophet he became. Making no attempt to reconcile the contradictory demands of humanity and the individual, he turned as resolutely from democracy as from autocracy. With the Concord seer, each citizen became the supreme judge before whom the statutes of commonwealth and nation are weighed and for whom no law has validity unless it corresponds with his own intuition. Announcing, "I have little esteem for governments," Emerson committed to his journals and occasionally presented to the public a series of pungent criticisms of public affairs. Here, despite his constant respect for fundamental law, he encouraged conduct as anarchistic as that of the most radical European Romantics. More easily recognized is the explosive individualism of Thoreau who, with his "dangerous frankness," lashed high and low alike for their conformity, and not only propounded but practised overt civil disobedience. Thus his *Walden* was adopted as a textbook by English liberals; and his essays served as one of the foundations for the Hindu doctrine of non-resistance. Meanwhile, Lowell defied the government in its despoiling of Mexico; and Melville burlesqued the rant and bombast of professional patriots. In those brave days, rebellion was ever in the air: "the

Abolitionists were dissolving the Union, while the Transcendentalists announced the nullification of unrighteous laws."

The older religious orthodoxy, already shaken by rationalism (first deistic and later unitarian), was now attacked by the great Romantic solvent, mysticism. West of the Alleghenies, the doctrine of predestination was found undemocratic; and the frontiersman substituted the emotional equalitarianism of the revival and the camp-meeting—a transformation of which there is no contemporary record in literature. In the East, two forms of mysticism made themselves felt. One was an early variety, namely, the devotion to "the inner light" long manifested by the Friends and now, for the first time in American poetry, given adequate literary expression by Whittier. Allies of the Friends ("I believe," declared Emerson, "I am more of a Quaker than anything else") were those powerful foes of both rationalism and orthodoxy, the Transcendentalists. Discarding historical Christianity, dogma (particularly any belief in human depravity), and all the restrictions imposed by logic and common sense, these new advocates of perfectibility relied wholly upon intuition, which to the Transcendentalist was the voice of the Over-Soul speaking directly to man. The emotional nature of this union of individual and universe is easily recognized in the orphic utterances of a rhapsodist like Alcott ("The blissful moments are those when a man abandons himself to the Spirit") or a mystical poet like Very; but the austere elevation of Emerson has caused many readers to forget that he too defined life as "an ecstacy" and repeatedly commanded: Trust your emotions. Despite his reliance on "the inner check," this "God-intoxicated Yankee" centered his conception of religion about the ecstatic moment, which he defined as the "saturnalian ecstacy of faith." Involved at least occasionally in this emotionalism were Margaret Fuller, Christopher Cranch, and the youthful Lowell, who dignified his early ecstatic experiences with the name of "revelations." And while Romantics thus reëstablished mysticism in religion, their rationalistic contemporary, Holmes, aided in the general assault upon Calvinism.

The Romantic generation, however, did not extensively modify the national preoccupation with conventional morality. Indeed, the demands of propriety were so powerful that native Romanticism was held to a decorum unparalleled abroad. No *Don Juan* and no *Mademoiselle de Maupin* are to be found in its annals; and the lives, like the works, of the New England Romanticists are without blemish. Thus commentators truthfully announced: "The chief characteristic of American literature is its moral purity;" and the didactic Longfellow became the household poet of the United States. Nevertheless, Hawthorne, contrary to popular misconception, actually freed himself from pietism by shifting much of his attention from the moral to the psychological aspects of evil; Poe, through his artist's detachment and his hatred for "the heresy of the didactic," approached the non-moral; and the skeptical Melville ventured into the realms of the anti-religious. This last arch-rebel even dared to suggest that there are fallacies in world-faiths, including Christianity, and to announce that man, like Captain Ahab in terrific grapple with

Moby Dick, whirls down at last to destruction and negation. But the work of lesser men was in the main so moral that, in the United States, Victorianism appears to have been superimposed on the Age of Romanticism.

Inevitably, the new idealists sought to remedy the ills of American society with the panaceas of radicalism. The West was instinctively inclined toward an idealistic view of society; but its citizens made themselves effectively heard only in support of one reform—the abolition of slavery. Slavery likewise was a constant challenge to Eastern liberals. In response, Longfellow, confined to his stateroom by a stormy sea, versified the woes of the negro in *Poems of Slavery;* and Lowell, as long as Maria White animated him to radicalism, applied humanitarianism to the problem. Thoreau, as a sharp individualist, centered his energy on the championing of John Brown. Emerson was stirred by slavery as by no other contemporary issue and of "that filthy enactment," the Fugitive Slave Law, he exclaimed: "I will not obey it, by God!" Only Whittier, however, reshaped his entire life that he might crusade for abolition. The steam-age likewise drew the wrath of Thoreau, who, damning its factories and its railways ("We do not ride on the railroad; it rides upon us"), proposed and exemplified as remedy a return to hand-labor. But Emerson, having preached the same gospel in his essays, had melancholy results when he attempted its application in his garden ("Papa," warned his young son, "I am afraid you will dig your leg"). The education of children was dramatically reconstructed by Alcott, with the approbation of Emerson; and such forward-looking innovations were made that educators have not yet reached all of Alcott's goals. Woman, also, was emancipated—in so far as Margaret Fuller could achieve that difficult feat. Other Romantics, dissatisfied with the whole fabric of contemporary life, sought not to ameliorate specific conditions, but entirely to reshape society. Now Ripley and Hawthorne, guided by Pantisocracy and Fouierism, strove to live the good life at Brook Farm; and Alcott sowed his "Transcendental wild oats" at Fruitlands. But communal enterprises could not long detain self-reliant individualists—and Hawthorne left Brook Farm to revel in the golden peace of a new Eden at the Old Manse. Emerson had consistently refused to go up to this reputed siege of Babylon, counting it wiser to continue the siege of his own hen-coop ("I have not yet conquered my own house"). As for Thoreau, he established beside Walden Pond his ideal community with a single citizen, insisting that he would prefer to keep bachelor's hall in hell rather than luxuriate in a boarding-house in heaven. And yet, although the Romantics never agreed as to whether the unit for ameliorating society should be the mass or the individual, they were unanimous in announcing the coming of a new day—hot reformers, each with the draft of a new Utopia in his waistcoat pocket.

As prophet and spokesman of the Romantic generation, Emerson had the high distinction of writing their declaration of independence. In vain had visions of the coming intellectual supremacy of America been revealed to Freneau, Dwight, and their brother poets. Unhappily, to none of these early enthusiasts had it been revealed exactly how native thought might be freed from foreign masters; and the American mind had remained "timid, imitative, tame." At length, after Channing had prepared the way, Emerson announced in "The American Scholar" his simple but effective, and universal, formula. Let Americans, he urged, bring to their thinking the stimulus of Romantic individualism, let them accept the gospel of self-reliance, and "our long day of dependence, our long apprenticeship to the learning of other lands" will draw to a close. Then followed the Romantic reformation of America, animated, on the frontier as in New England, by self-trust and expansiveness, rooted in equalitarianism, and devoted to the renovation of religion, the democratization of government, and the alleviation of social abuses.

No sharp line of demarcation can be drawn between the two wings of the Romanticists—between those who thus courageously attempted the transformation of America and those who sought not to change but to escape its actualities. For example, even Emerson and Thoreau in their gentler moments abandoned reform to seek brief solace from reality; and Hawthorne at times left his fantasies to voice the principles of democracy. Furthermore, all types of Romanticists were united by one common faith, namely, a belief in the supreme importance of emotion. Lesser authors, unfortunately, were not always able to transform the older sensibility into high Romantic passion. Sentimentalism, therefore, lingered in the gift-books, graced with the work of the indefatigable Mrs. Sigourney and the jaunty Willis; in such monthly repositories of emotion as *Godey's Lady's Book* and the *Gentleman's Magazine;* in such a perennial stimulus to tears as *Uncle Tom's Cabin;* and in the verse of later sentimentalists: Read, Foster, Parsons, Legaré, and the Cary sisters. On its higher levels, however, the literature of American Romanticism commonly transcended this easy tearfulness. Thus Longfellow, although sensibility overcame him in poems of childhood and death, affection and ethics, finally achieved noble intensity in his most mature lyrics, particularly the sonnets. The bachelor Whittier was betrayed into sentimentality whenever he dealt with young love; but his poems on abolition and on religion occasionally reached true elevation. The rationally minded Holmes was commonly saved from mawkishness by humor. Poe, who castigated sentimental authors in his criticism and satirized their confections in his burlesques, intensified their tearfulness into grim Romantic gloom and sublimated their decorous worship of femininity into the Romantic passion of his lyrics. Hawthorne, with his misleading self-depreciation, unjustly condemned his own tales, professing to find in them sentiment rather than emotion; but the observant reader discovers deep intensity in many a short story and in the major novels. In truth, the creator of Ethan Brand and Hester, of Colonel Pyncheon and Miriam had learned, even more surely than had Poe, how to transmute sensibility into elevated emotion. It remained for the serene Emerson, momentarily ignoring his self-centered essays on friendship and love ("Damn Consistency!" was Emerson's own pointed summary of his position), to find triumphant expression for the Romantic veneration of feeling in "Give All to Love."

The Romantics again met on common ground when they wrote of external nature, even though they sharply disagreed in its interpretation. Emerson announced that in nature, man finds ecstacy and discipline, symbols, beauty, and God—all that humanity knows or needs to know. Because there was much of Romantic passion in Thoreau's devotion to the external world, he came to woo Nature as his mistress. Then, in his last years, he faithlessly gave his heart also to the goddess of civil liberty; and Nature, alienated, thereafter granted him little save empty readings of bare and dusty fact. And yet to the youthful Thoreau, as to Emerson, nature was ever a stimulus to Romantic wonder and awe. Whittier, with something of "White of Selborne's loving view" but more of Wordsworth's reverence, discovered in mountain and plain both joy and healing; but there Poe found only the trappings of woe. Finally, when Lowell in maturity became a foe of naturalism, as in the essay on Thoreau, he modified his early sentimental delight in nature and rejected the pathetic fallacy. Divergent as are these attitudes toward the external world, the Romantics were often in agreement in their sensuous appreciation of its phenomena. Thus Emerson, like Rousseau, becomes a vegetable and exclaims, "I expand and live in the warm day like corn and melons;" while Thoreau "imbibes delight through every pore."

Sensitive spirits, who found nature too near their own doorsteps to afford Romantic escape, released themselves from actuality by turning to the past or to the distant. Some were content to remain in their native land. Longfellow and many a minor poetaster and romancer, securely insulated from the authentic frontier of Crockett and Parkman, delighted in a heroic realm of noble red men. Such sentimental Southerners as Kennedy built up the golden dream world of the Old Plantation. Patriots, North and South, reverted to a supposedly glamorous past: Prescott to the conquest of the new world; Simms and various dramatists and novelists to the Revolution; Whittier, Longfellow, and Hawthorne to the legends of early New England; and Longfellow to an idealized Acadia. In more rarefied moods, the Romantic generation, unsatisfied with any native theme, however distant, turned from America and escaped toward distant horizons. Many set out to build ivory towers of wonder in the Middle Ages; but only Longfellow in *The Golden Legend* and various ballads, Lowell in "The Vision of Sir Launfal," and Boker in *Francesca da Rimini* touched that alien epoch with genius. Others voyaged far among the legends and literatures of more recent civilizations and brought back to the New World rich cargoes of terror and beauty—most notably Poe from the shores of the Mediterranean, and Longfellow and Lowell from all Western Europe. In his desperate search for self-expression, Poe also paused momentarily in the Orient of "Tamerlane," while the restless Melville ploughed Atlantic and Pacific, and roamed through the South Sea isles.

At last, when the resources of the six continents and the seven seas were exhausted, there remained the boundless universe of the fantastic and the preternatural. Thither fled Poe and Chivers, Melville, and, with a difference, Hawthorne. In his tales of the grotesque, Poe, intent on emotional rather than intellectual effects, strode boldly through the realms of mad extravaganza and unabashed supernaturalism. Wandering at will in his Dream-Land, through his Valley of Many-Colored Grass, among his Ragged Mountains, and onward toward "ultimate, dim Thule," he made no effort either to rationalize or to moralize the nonreal and impossible. Melville likewise abandoned himself at times to utter unreality, but on a higher intellectual level. His brilliant fantasies remained, like Poe's, unexplained and inexplicable; but, because they were designed to stimulate thought rather than shudders or tears, they are always didactic or satiric. As for Hawthorne, the supernatural and the abnormal had a peculiar attraction for him, even in such feeble manifestations as contemporary spiritism and mesmerism. But he was too soundly skeptical to be misled by such follies, and in each of his tales he provided a formula for the reduction of all apparent supernaturalism to reality. His fantasy, furthermore, is even more purposeful than Melville's and rarely, if ever, does it lack allegorical significance.

American Romanticists, like their European fellows, hit upon various symbols to represent the object of their nebulous longing and aspiration. Most picturesque was the ethereal female, shaped of dreams, who had enchanted Novalis and Shelley, Rousseau and Hazlitt. This same charming but ever-fleeting object of desire moved through the pages of Melville's *Typee* and his *Mardi*. Eventually, however, no dream of fair women, not even of Fayaway or Yillah, could adequately body forth his tremendous aspiration; and his imagery expanded into the vast symbolism of the pursuit of the White Whale. Whittier and Poe, however, never renounced their youthful worship of femininity; and to the end Israfel pursued sweet female phantoms, "so vaporous, so transparent, so spectral." Interpreting in his own fashion Bacon's familiar dictum that "there is no exquisite beauty without some *strangeness* in the proportion," Poe intensified the charm of his goddesses by visiting upon them consumption, catalepsy, and death. Truthfully he remarked,

> I could not love have, except where Death
> Was mingling his with Beauty's breath.

Out of such mad pursuit there could come at last only frustration, pessimism, and despair. As it happened, certain of the New England Romantics early turned from their frantic search for the Blue Flower, and accepted reality. Lowell, during his years of *Sturm und Drang,* put a pistol to his head—but resolution thereupon left his trigger-finger and he became a humanitarian. Hawthorne in youthful solitude wrote wildly to his friend Bridge of suicide—but Sophia Peabody soon reconciled him to existence. Only Poe and Melville, incandescent in the fires of genius, were finally consumed by their own passions. At eighteen, Poe concluded that his "sear'd and blighted heart" had already left behind its happiest day, its happiest hour; in the years which followed, a "weary, way-worn wanderer," he reiterated this tragic pronouncement with increasing bitterness and melancholy. Melville found in the sea a temporary "substitute for pistol and ball," but eventually he too came to despair. At thirty-two, he announced: "I feel that I am now come to the inmost leaf of the bulb, and that shortly the flower must fall to the mould;" and five years later, he added: "I have pretty much made up my mind to be annihilated." That way madness lay; and to Melville came moments of the laughing pessimism of *Pierre:* "Ha! ha! how the demoniacs shout; how all skeletons grin; we all die with a rattle." Then followed, according to tradition, tragic experiences on the border-land of sanity and, thereafter, Melville's long years of silence, broken only by scattered minor utterances. Meanwhile, to Poe there came the hallucinations and despair which brought to his genius and to his work the "phosphoric radiance of decay," until at length he lay on a death-bed surrounded by "spectres that withered and loomed on the walls."

Fortunately for American letters, the Romantics rarely became so engrossed either in remoulding native society or in escaping from its rigors that they entirely forgot the demands of art. The history of the Romantic Revolt, therefore, is the story of literary as well as social, intellectual, and emotional expansion. Irving and Bryant had devoted themselves on occasion to aesthetic considerations; but the crassly unaesthetic, non-literary position of Cooper more nearly represented the general attitude of earlier American authors. Now, however, the range of the novel was broadened to include such a masterpiece of symmetry as *The Scarlet Letter* and such a Shandean triumph of intelligent wilfulness as *Moby Dick*. Lowell with his carefully molded phrases, Holmes with his neat, medicated wit, and Emerson with his almost sensuous love for words were conscious craftsmen in the essay. The revision given their poems by Longfellow and Lowell revealed their sound literary instincts; and Poe reworked his published poetry with a diligence and an intelligence almost without parallel in any literature. And thus, by creating fit forms to body forth their various dreams, this generation of seekers, these "pioneers of the world," gave to America its Golden Age of literature.

TREMAINE MCDOWELL

# EARLY SENTIMENTALISTS

## I. LYDIA HUNTLEY SIGOURNEY
(1791–1865)

### THE ALPINE FLOWERS

Meek dwellers mid yon terror-stricken cliffs!
With brows so pure, and incense-breathing lips,
Whence are ye? — Did some white-wing'd messenger
On Mercy's mission trust your timid germ
To the cold cradle of eternal snows?
Or breathing on the callous icicles,
Bid them with tear-drops nurse ye? —
— Tree nor shrub
Dare that drear atmosphere, — no polar pine
Uprears a veteran front, — yet there *ye* stand,
Leaning your cheeks against the thick-ribb'd ice,
And looking up with brilliant eyes to Him
Who bids you bloom unblanch'd amid the waste
Of desolation. Man, who panting toils
O'er slippery steeps, or trembling treads the verge
Of yawning gulfs, o'er which the headlong plunge
Is to Eternity, looks shuddering up,
And marks ye in your placid loveliness
Fearless, yet frail, and clasping his chill hands
Blesses your pencil'd beauty. Mid the pomp
Of mountain summits rushing on the sky,
And chaining the rapt soul in breathless awe,
He bows to bind you drooping to his breast,
Inhales your spirit from the frost-wing'd gale,
And freer dreams of heaven.

1827

## II. NATHANIEL PARKER WILLIS
(1806–1867)

### THE WHITE CHIP HAT

I pass'd her one day in a hurry,
When late for the Post with a letter —
I think near the corner of Murray —
And up rose my heart as I met her!
I ne'er saw a parasol handled
So like to a duchess's doing —
I ne'er saw a slighter foot sandall'd,
Or so fit to exhale in the shoeing —
Lovely thing!

Surprising! — one woman can dish us
So many rare sweets up together!
Tournure absolutely delicious —
Chip hat without flower or feather —
Well-gloved and enchantingly bodiced,
Her waist like the cup of a lily —
And an air, that, while daintily modest,
Repell'd both the saucy and silly —
Quite the thing!

For such a rare wonder you'll say, sir,
There's reason in straining one's tether —
And, to see her again in Broadway, sir,
Who would not be lavish of leather!
I met her again, and as *you* know
I'm sage as old Vòltaire at Ferney —
But I said a bad word — for my Juno
Look'd sweet on a sneaking attorney —
Horrid thing!

Away flies the dream I had nourish'd —
My castles like mockery fall, sir!
And, now, the fine airs that she flourish'd
Seem varnish and crockery all, sir!
The bright cup that angels might handle
Turns earthy when finger'd by asses —
And the star that "swaps" light with a candle
Thenceforth for a pennyworth passes! —
Not the thing!

1843

## UNSEEN SPIRITS

The shadows lay along Broadway,
'Twas near the twilight tide,
And slowly there a lady fair
Was walking in her pride.
Alone walked she; but, viewlessly,
Walked spirits at her side.

Peace charm'd the street beneath her feet,
And Honor charm'd the air;
And all astir look'd kind on her,
And call'd her good as fair —
For all God ever gave to her
She kept with chary care.

She kept with care her beauties rare
From lovers warm and true —
For her heart was cold to all but gold,
And the rich came not to woo —
But honor'd well are charms to sell
If priests the selling do.

Now walking there was one more fair —
A slight girl, lily-pale;
And she had unseen company
To make the spirit quail —
'Twixt Want and Scorn she walk'd forlorn,
And nothing could avail.

No mercy now can clear her brow
For this world's peace to pray;
For, as love's wild prayer dissolved in air,
Her woman's heart gave way! —
But the sin forgiven by Christ in heaven
By man is cursed alway!

1843

## [A BREAKFAST WITH CHARLES LAMB]

Invited to breakfast with a gentleman in the Temple to meet Charles Lamb and his sister,—"Elia and Bridget Elia." I never in my life had an invitation more to my taste. The essays of Elia are certainly the most charming things in the world, and it has been for the last ten years my highest compliment to the literary taste of a friend to present him with a copy. Who has not smiled over the humorous description of Mrs. Battle? Who that has read Elia would not give more to see him than all the other authors of his time put together?

Our host was rather a character. I had brought a letter of introduction to him from Walter Savage Landor, the author of "Imaginary Conversations," living at Florence, with a request that he would put me in a way of seeing one or two men about whom I had a curiosity, Lamb more particularly. I could not have been recommended to a better person. Mr. R. is a gentleman who, everybody says, *should have been* an author, but who never wrote a book. He is a profound German scholar, has travelled much, is the intimate friend of Southey, Coleridge, and Lamb, has breakfasted with Goëthe, travelled with Wordsworth through France and Italy, and spends part of every summer with him, and knows everything and everybody that is distinguished,—in short, is, in his bachelor's chambers in the Temple, the friendly nucleus of a great part of the talent of England.

I arrived a half-hour before Lamb, and had time to learn some of his peculiarities. He lives a little out of London, and is very much of an invalid. Some family circumstances have tended to depress him very much of late years, and unless excited by convivial intercourse, he scarce shows a trace of what he was. He was very much pleased with the American reprint of his Elia, though it contains several things which are not his—written so in his style, however, that it is scarce a wonder the editor should mistake them. If I remember right, they were "Valentine's Day," the "Nuns of Caverswell," and "Twelfth Night." He is excessively given to mystifying his friends, and is never so delighted as when he has persuaded some one into the belief of one of his grave inventions. His amusing biographical sketch of Liston was in this vein, and there was no doubt in anybody's mind that it was authentic, and written in perfectly good faith. Liston was highly enraged with it, and Lamb was delighted in proportion.

There was a rap at the door at last, and enter a gentleman in black small-clothes and gaiters, short and very slight in his person, his head set on his shoulders with a thoughtful forward bent, his hair just sprinkled with gray, a beautiful deep-set eye, aquiline nose, and a very indescribable mouth. Whether it expressed most humor or feeling, good-nature or a kind of whimsical peevishness, or twenty other things which passed over it by turns, I cannot in the least be certain.

His sister, whose literary reputation is associated very closely with her brother's, and who, as the original of "Bridget Elia," is a kind of object for literary affection, came in after him. She is a small, bent figure, evidently a victim to illness, and hears with difficulty. Her face has been, I should think, a fine and handsome one, and her bright gray eye is still full of intelligence and fire. They both seemed quite at home in our friend's chambers, and as there was to be no one else, we immediately drew round the breakfast-table. I had set a large arm-chair for Miss Lamb. "Don't take it, Mary," said Lamb, pulling it away from her very gravely: "it appears as if you were going to have a tooth drawn."

The conversation was very local. Our host and his guest had not met for some weeks, and they had a great deal to say of their mutual friends. Perhaps in this way, however, I saw more of the author; for his manner of speaking of them, and the quaint humor with which he complained of one, and spoke well of another, was so in the vein of his inimitable writings, that I could have fancied myself listening to an audible composition of a new Elia. Nothing could be more delightful than the kindness and affection between the brother and the sister, though Lamb was continually taking advantage of her deafness to mystify her with the most singular gravity upon every topic that was started. "Poor Mary!" said he, "she hears all of an epigram but the point."—"What are you saying of me, Charles?" she asked. "Mr. Willis," said he, raising his voice, "admires *your Confessions of a Drunkard very much;* and I was saying that it was no merit of yours, that you understood the subject." We had been speaking of this admirable essay (which is his own) half an hour before.

The conversation turned upon literature after a while; and our host, the Templar, could not express himself strongly enough in admiration of Webster's speeches, which he said were exciting the greatest attention among the politicians and lawyers of England. Lamb said, "I don't know much of American authors. Mary, there, devours Cooper's novels with a ravenous appetite, with which I have no sympathy. The only American book I ever read twice was the "Journal" of Edward [John] Woolman, a quaker preacher and tailor, whose character is one of the finest I ever met with. He tells a story or two about negro slaves, that brought the tears into my eyes. I can read no prose now, though Hazlitt sometimes, to be sure—but then, Hazlitt is worth all modern prose writers put together."

Mr. R. spoke of buying a book of Lamb's a few days before; and I mentioned my having bought a copy of "Elia" the last day I was in America, to send as a parting gift to one of the most lovely and talented women in our country.

"What did you give for it?" said Lamb.

"About seven and sixpence."

"Permit me to pay you that," said he, and with the utmost earnestness he counted out the money upon the table.

"I never yet wrote anything that would sell," he continued. "I am the publisher's ruin. My last poem won't sell a copy. Have you seen it, Mr. Willis?"

I had not.

"It's only eighteen pence, and I'll give you sixpence toward it;" and he described to me where I should find it sticking up in a shop-window in the Strand.

Lamb ate nothing, and complained in a querulous tone of the veal pie. There was a kind of potted fish (of which I forget the name at this moment) which he had expected our friend would procure for him. He inquired whether there was not a morsel left perhaps in the bottom of the last pot. Mr. R. was not sure.

"Send and see," said Lamb; "and if the pot has been cleaned, bring me the cover. I think the sight of it would do me good."

The cover was brought, upon which there was a picture of the fish. Lamb kissed it with a reproachful look at his friend, and then left the table, and began to wander round the room with a broken, uncertain step, as if he almost forgot to put one leg before the other. His sister rose after a while, and commenced walking up and down very much in the same manner on the opposite side of the table; and in the course of half an hour they took their leave.

To any one who loves the writings of Charles Lamb with but half my own enthusiasm, even these little particulars of an hour passed in his company will have an interest. To him who does not, they will seem dull and idle. Wreck as he certainly is, and must be, however, of what he was, I would rather have seen him for that single hour, than the hundred and one sights of London put together.

1835

## III. CHARLES FENNO HOFFMAN
(1806–1884)

### WHAT IS SOLITUDE?

Not in the shadowy wood,
 Not in the crag-hung glen,
Not where the echoes brood
 In caves untrod by men;
Not by the black seashore,
 Where barren surges break,
Not on the mountain hoar,
 Not by the breezeless lake;
Not on the desert plain
 Where man hath never stood,
Whether on isle or main —
 Not there is Solitude!

Birds are in woodland bowers;
 Voices in lonely dells;
Streams to the listening hours
 Talk in earth's secret cells;
Over the gray-ribbed sand
 Breathe Ocean's frothy lips;
Over the still lake's strand
 The wild flower toward it dips;
Pluming the mountain's crest
 Life tosses in its pines,
Coursing the desert's breast
 Life in the steed's mane shines.

Leave — if thou wouldst be lonely —
 Leave Nature for the crowd;
Seek there for one — one only
 With kindred mind endowed!
There — as with Nature erst
 Closely thou wouldst commune —
The deep soul-music nursed
 In either heart, attune!
Heart-wearied thou wilt own,
 Vainly that phantom wooed,
That thou at last hast known
 What is true Solitude!

1835

### ALGONQUIN DEATH SONG

"A BE TUH GE ZHIG"

 Under the hollow sky,
Stretch'd the Prairie lone,
 Centre of glory, I
Bleeding, disdain to groan,
 But like a battle cry
Peal forth thy thunder moan,
 *Baim-wa-wa!*

 Star — Morning Star, whose ray
Still with the dawn I see,
 Quenchless through half the day,
Gazing thou seest me;
 Yon birds of carnage, they
Fright not my gaze from thee!
 *Baim-wa-wa!*

 Bird, in thine airy rings
Over the foeman's line,
 Why do thy flapping wings
Nearer me thus incline?
 Blood of the dauntless brings
Courage, O Bird, to thine!
 *Baim-wa-wa!*

Hark to those Spirit-notes!
Ye high Heroes divine,
Hymned from your god-like throats
That song of Praise is mine!
Mine, whose grave pennon floats
Over the foeman's line!
*Baim-wa-wa!*

1845

## IV. THOMAS HOLLEY CHIVERS
### (1809–1858)

### *From* ISADORE

I

While the world lay round me sleeping,
I, alone, for ISADORE
Patient vigils lonely keeping —
Some one said to me while weeping,
"Why this grief forever more?"
And I answered, "I am weeping
For my blessed ISADORE!"

II

Then the VOICE again said: "Never
Shall thy soul see ISADORE!
God from thee thy love did sever—
He has damned thy soul forever!
Wherefore then her loss deplore?
Thou shalt live in Hell forever!
Heaven now holds thine ISADORE!

III

"She is dead — the world benighted —
Dark for want of ISADORE!
Have not all your hopes been blighted?
How can you be reunited?
Can mere words the dead restore?
Have not all your hopes been blighted?
Why then hope for ISADORE?"

IV

"Back to Hell, thou ghostly Horror!"
Thus I cried, dear ISADORE!
"Phantom of remorseless Sorrow!
Death might from thee pallor borrow —
Borrow leanness ever more!
Back to Hell again!—tomorrow
I will go to ISADORE!" * * *

1841?

### THE SHIP OF DEATH

By the shore of Time, now lying
On the inky flood beneath,
Patiently, thou soul undying!
Waits for thee the SHIP OF DEATH!

He who on that vessel starteth—
Sailing from the sons of men,
To the friends from whom he parteth,
Never more returns again!

From her mast no flag is flying,
To denote from whence she came;
She is known unto the dying—
AZRAEL is her captain's name.

Not a word was ever spoken,
On that dark, unfathomed sea;
Silence there is so unbroken,
She herself seems not to be!

Silent thus, in darkness lonely,
Doth the soul put forth alone,
While the wings of Angels only
Waft her to a LAND UNKNOWN.

1845

### *From* AVALON

I

Death's pale cold orb has turned to an eclipse
My Son of Love!
The worms are feeding on thy lily-lips,
My milk-white Dove!
Pale purple tinges thy soft finger-tips!
While nectar thy pure soul in glory sips,

As Death's cold frost mine own forever nips!
Where thou art lying
Beside the beautiful undying
In the valley of the pausing of the Moon,
Oh! AVALON! my son! my son!

II

Wake up, oh! AVALON! my son! my son!
And come from Death!
Heave off the clod that lies so heavy on
Thy breast beneath
In that cold grave, my more than Precious One!
And come to me! for I am here alone—
With none to comfort me!—my hopes are gone
Where thou art lying
Beside the beautiful undying
In the Valley of the pausing of the Moon,
Oh! AVALON! my son! my son!

III

Forever more must I, on this damp sod,
Renew and keep
My Covenant of Sorrows with my God,
And weep, weep, weep!
Writhing in pain beneath Death's iron rod!
Till I shall go to that DIVINE ABODE—
Treading the path that thy dear feet have trod—
Where thou art lying
Beside the beautiful undying
In the Valley of the pausing of the Moon,
Oh! AVALON! my son! my son!

IV

Oh! precious Saviour! gracious heavenly Lord!
Refresh my soul!
Here, with the healings of thy heavenly Word,
Make my heart whole!
My little Lambs are scattered now abroad
In Death's dark Valley, where they bleat unheard!
Dear Shepherd! give their Shepherd his reward
Where they are lying
Beside the beautiful undying
In the Valley of the pausing of the Moon,
With AVALON! my son! my son!

V

For thou didst tread with fire-ensandaled feet,
Star-crowned, forgiven,
The burning diapason of the stars so sweet,
To God in Heaven!
And, walking on the sapphire-paven street,
Didst take upon the highest Sill thy seat—
Waiting in glory there my soul to meet,
When I am lying
Beside the beautiful undying
In the Valley of the pausing of the Moon,
Oh! AVALON! my son! my son! * * *

1851

# EDGAR ALLAN POE
(1809–1849)

## TAMERLANE

Kind solace in a dying hour!
Such, father, is not (now) my theme—
I will not madly deem that power
Of Earth may shrive me of the sin
Unearthly pride hath revell'd in—
I have no time to dote or dream:
You call it hope—that fire of fire!
It is but agony of desire:
If I *can* hope—Oh, God! I can—
Its fount is holier—more divine—
I would not call thee fool, old man,
But such is not a gift of thine.

Know thou the secret of a spirit
Bow'd from its wild pride into shame.
O yearning heart! I did inherit
Thy withering portion with the fame,
The searing glory which hath shone
Amid the jewels of my throne,
Halo of Hell! and with a pain
Not Hell shall make me fear again—
O craving heart, for the lost flowers
And sunshine of my summer hours!
The undying voice of that dead time,
With its interminable chime,
Rings, in the spirit of a spell,
Upon thy emptiness—a knell.

I have not always been as now:
The fever'd diadem on my brow
I claim'd and won usurpingly—
Hath not the same fierce heirdom given
Rome to the Caesar—this to me?
The heritage of a kingly mind,
And a proud spirit which hath striven
Triumphantly with human kind.

On mountain soil I first drew life:
The mists of the Taglay have shed
Nightly their dews upon my head,
And, I believe, the winged strife
And tumult of the headlong air
Have nestled in my very hair.

So late from Heaven—that dew—it fell
('Mid dreams of an unholy night)
Upon me with the touch of Hell,
While the red flashing of the light
From clouds that hung, like banners, o'er,
Appeared to my half-closing eye
The pageantry of monarchy,
And the deep trumpet-thunder's roar
Came hurriedly upon me, telling
Of human battle, where my voice,
My own voice, silly child! was swelling
(O! how my spirit would rejoice,
And leap within me at the cry)
The battle-cry of Victory!

The rain came down upon my head
Unshelter'd—and the heavy wind
Rendered me mad and deaf and blind.
It was but man, I thought, who shed
Laurels upon me: and the rush,
The torrent of the chilly air
Gurgled within my ear the crush
Of empires—with the captive's prayer—
The hum of suitors—and the tone
Of flattery round a sovereign's throne.

My passions, from that hapless hour,
Usurp'd a tyranny which men
Have deem'd, since I have reach'd to power,
My innate nature—be it so:
But, father, there liv'd one who, then,
Then—in my boyhood—when their fire
Burn'd with a still intenser glow
(For passion must, with youth, expire)
E'en *then* who knew this iron heart
In woman's weakness had a part.

I have no words—alas!—to tell
The loveliness of loving well!
Nor would I now attempt to trace
The more than beauty of a face
Whose lineaments, upon my mind,
Are—shadows on th' unstable wind:
Thus I remember having dwelt
Some page of early lore upon,
With loitering eye, till I have felt
The letters—with their meaning—melt
To fantasies—with none.

O, she was worthy of all love!
Love—as in infancy was mine—
'Twas such as angel minds above
Might envy; her young heart the shrine
On which my every hope and thought
Were incense—then a goodly gift,
For they were childish and upright—
Pure—as her young example taught:
Why did I leave it, and, adrift,
Trust to the fire within, for light?

We grew in age—and love—together—
Roaming the forest and the wild;
My breast her shield in wintry weather—
And, when the friendly sunshine smil'd,
And she would mark the opening skies,
*I* saw no Heaven—but in her eyes.
Young Love's first lesson is—the heart:
For 'mid that sunshine and those smiles,
When, from our little cares apart,
And laughing at her girlish wiles,
I'd throw me on her throbbing breast,
And pour my spirit out in tears—
There was no need to speak the rest—
No need to quiet any fears
Of her—who ask'd no reason why,
But turn'd on me her quiet eye!

Yet *more* than worthy of the love
My spirit struggled with, and strove,
When, on the mountain peak, alone,
Ambition lent it a new tone—
I had no being—but in thee:
The world, and all it did contain
In the earth—the air—the sea—
Its joy—its little lot of pain
That was new pleasure—the ideal,
Dim vanities of dreams by night—
And dimmer nothings which were real—
(Shadows—and a more shadowy light!)
Parted upon their misty wings,
And, so, confusedly, became
Thine image and—a name—a name!
Two separate—yet most intimate things.

I was ambitious—have you known
The passion, father? You have not:
A cottager, I mark'd a throne
Of half the world as all my own,
And murmur'd at such lowly lot—
But, just like any other dream,
Upon the vapor of the dew
My own had past, did not the beam
Of beauty which did while it thro'
The minute—the hour—the day—oppress
My mind with double loveliness.

We walk'd together on the crown
Of a high mountain which look'd down

Afar from its proud natural towers
  Of rock and forest, on the hills—
The dwindled hills! begirt with bowers
  And shouting with a thousand rills.

I spoke to her of power and pride,
  But mystically—in such guise
That she might deem it nought beside
  The moment's converse; in her eyes
I read, perhaps too carelessly,
  A mingled feeling with my own—
The flush on her bright cheek, to me
  Seem'd to become a queenly throne
Too well that I should let it be
  Light in the wilderness alone.

I wrapp'd myself in grandeur then
  And donn'd a visionary crown—
    Yet it was not that Fantasy
    Had thrown her mantle over me—
But that, among the rabble—men,
    Lion ambition is chain'd down—
And crouches to a keeper's hand—
Not so in deserts where the grand—
The wild—the terrible conspire
With their own breath to fan his fire.

Look 'round thee now on Samarcand!—
  Is she not queen of Earth? her pride
Above all cities? in her hand
  Their destinies? in all beside
Of glory which the world hath known
Stands she not nobly and alone?
Falling—her veriest stepping-stone
Shall form the pedestal of a throne—
And who her sovereign? Timour—he
  Whom the astonished people saw
Striding o'er empires haughtily
  A diadem'd outlaw!

O, human love! thou spirit given,
On Earth, of all we hope in Heaven!
Which fall'st into the soul like rain
Upon the Siroc-wither'd plain,
And, failing in thy power to bless,
But leav'st the heart a wilderness!
Idea! which bindest life around
With music of so strange a sound
And beauty of so wild a birth—
Farewell! for I have won the Earth.
When Hope, the eagle that tower'd, could see
  No cliff beyond him in the sky,
His pinions were bent droopingly—
  And homeward turn'd his soften'd eye.
'Twas sunset: when the sun will part
There comes a sullenness of heart
To him who still would look upon
The glory of the summer sun.
That soul will hate the ev'ning mist
So often lovely, and will list
To the sound of the coming darkness (known
To those whose spirits harken) as one
Who, in a dream of night, *would* fly
But *cannot* from a danger nigh.

What tho' the moon—the white moon—
Shed all the splendor of her noon,
*Her* smile is chilly—and *her* beam,
In that time of dreariness, will seem
(So like you gather in your breath)
A portrait taken after death.
And boyhood is a summer sun
Whose waning is the dreariest one.
For all we live to know is known,
And all we seek to keep hath flown.
Let life, then, as the day-flower, fall
With the noon-day beauty—which is all.

I reach'd my home—my home no more—
  For all had flown who made it so.
I pass'd from out its mossy door,
  And, tho' my tread was soft and low,
A voice came from the threshold stone
Of one whom I had earlier known—
  O, I defy thee, Hell, to show
  On beds of fire that burn below,
  An humbler heart—a deeper wo.

Father, I firmly do believe—
I *know*—for Death who comes for me
From regions of the blest afar,
Where there is nothing to deceive,
Hath left his iron gate ajar,
And rays of truth you cannot see
Are flashing thro' Eternity—
I do believe that Eblis hath
A snare in every human path—
Else how, when in the holy grove
I wandered of the idol, Love,
Who daily scents his snowy wings
With incense of burnt offerings
From the most unpolluted things,
Whose pleasant bowers are yet so riven
Above with trellis'd rays from Heaven
No mote may shun—no tiniest fly—
The light'ning of his eagle eye—
How was it that Ambition crept,
Unseen, amid the revels there,
Till growing bold, he laughed and leapt
In the tangles of Love's very hair?
(1826?) 1827

## A DREAM WITHIN A DREAM

Take this kiss upon the brow!
And, in parting from you now,
Thus much let me avow:
You are not wrong, who deem
That my days have been a dream;
Yet if Hope has flown away
In a night, or in a day,
In a vision, or in none,
Is it therefore the less *gone?*
*All* that we see or seem
Is but a dream within a dream.

I stand amid the roar
Of a surf-tormented shore,
And I hold within my hand
Grains of the golden sand—
How few! yet how they creep
Through my fingers to the deep,
While I weep—while I weep!
O God! can I not grasp
Them with a tighter clasp?
O God! can I not save
*One* from the pitiless wave?
Is *all* that we see or seem
But a dream within a dream?
1827

## SONNET—TO SCIENCE

Science! true daughter of Old Time thou art!
Who alterest all things with thy peering eyes.
Why preyest thou thus upon the poet's heart,
Vulture, whose wings are dull realities?
How should he love thee, or how deem thee wise,
Who wouldst not leave him in his wandering
To seek for treasure in the jewelled skies,
Albeit he soared with an undaunted wing?
Hast thou not dragged Diana from her car,
And driven the Hamadryad from the wood
To seek a shelter in some happier star?
Hast thou not torn the Naiad from her flood,
The Elfin from the green grass, and from me
The summer dream beneath the tamarind tree?
(1829) 1829

## *From* AL AARAAF

" 'Neath blue-bell or streamer—
Or tufted wild spray
That keeps, from the dreamer
The moonbeam away—
Bright beings! that ponder,
With half closing eyes,
On the stars which your wonder
Hath drawn from the skies,

Till they glance thro' the shade, and
  Come down to your brow
Like —— eyes of the maiden
  Who calls on you now—
Arise! from your dreaming
  In violet bowers,
To duty beseeming
  These star-litten hours—
And shake from your tresses
  Encumber'd with dew
The breath of those kisses
  That cumber them too—
(O, how, without you, Love
  Could angels be blest?)
Those kisses of true love
  That lull'd ye to rest!
Up!—shake from your wing
  Each hindering thing:
The dew of the night—
  It would weight down your flight;
And true love caresses—
  O! leave them apart:
They are light on the tresses,
  But lead on the heart.

Ligeia! Ligeia!
  My beautiful one!
Whose harshest idea
  Will to melody run,
O! is it thy will
  On the breezes to toss?
Or, capriciously still,
  Like the lone Albatross
Incumbent on night
  (As she on the air)
To keep watch with delight
  On the harmony there?

Ligeia! wherever
  Thy image may be,
No magic shall sever
  Thy music from thee.
Thou hast bound many eyes
  In a dreamy sleep—
But the strains still arise
  Which *thy* vigilance keep—
The sound of the rain
  Which leaps down to the flower,
And dances again
  In the rhythm of the shower—
The murmur that springs
  From the growing of grass
Are the music of things—
  But are modell'd, alas!—
Away, then, my dearest,
  O! hie thee away
To springs that lie clearest
  Beneath the moon-ray—
To lone lake that smiles,
  In its dream of deep rest,
At the many star-isles
  That enjewel its breast—
Where wild flowers, creeping,
  Have mingled their shade,
On its margin is sleeping
  Full many a maid—
Some have left the cool glade, and
  Have slept with the bee—
Arouse them, my maiden,
  On moorland and lea—
Go! breathe on their slumber,
  All softly in ear,
The musical number
  They slumber'd to hear—
For what can awaken
  An angel so soon,
Whose sleep hath been taken
  Beneath the cold moon,
As the spell which no slumber
  Of witchery may test,
The rhythmical number
  Which lull'd him to rest?"
(1827–29) 1829

## ROMANCE

Romance, who loves to nod and sing,
With drowsy head and folded wing,
Among the green leaves as they shake
Far down within some shadowy lake,
To me a painted paroquet
Hath been—a most familiar bird—
Taught me my alphabet to say,
To lisp my very earliest word,
While in the wild wood I did lie,
A child—with a most knowing eye.

Of late, eternal Condor years
So shake the very Heaven on high

With tumult as they thunder by,
I have no time for idle cares
Through gazing on the unquiet sky.
And when an hour with calmer wings
Its down upon my spirit flings—
That little time with lyre and rhyme
To while away—forbidden things!
My heart would feel to be a crime
Unless it trembled with the strings.

1829

## TO HELEN

Helen, thy beauty is to me
  Like those Nicéan barks of yore,
That gently, o'er a perfumed sea,
  The weary, way-worn wanderer bore
  To his own native shore.

On desperate seas long wont to roam,
  Thy hyacinth hair, thy classic face,
Thy Naiad airs have brought me home
  To the glory that was Greece
And the grandeur that was Rome.

Lo! in yon brilliant window-niche
  How statue-like I see thee stand,
  The agate lamp within thy hand!
Ah, Psyche, from the regions which
  Are Holy Land!

1831

## ISRAFEL

> And the angel Israfel, whose heart-strings are a lute, and who has the sweetest voice of all God's creatures.
>
> —Koran.

In Heaven a spirit doth dwell
  "Whose heart-strings are a lute";
None sing so wildly well
As the angel Israfel,
And the giddy stars (so legends tell),
Ceasing their hymns, attend the spell
  Of his voice, all mute.

Tottering above
  In her highest noon,
  The enamored moon
Blushes with love,
  While, to listen, the red levin
  (With the rapid Pleiads, even,
  Which were seven,)
  Pauses in Heaven.

And they say (the starry choir
  And the other listening things)
That Israfeli's fire
Is owing to that lyre
  By which he sits and sings—
The trembling living wire
  Of those unusual strings.

But the skies that angel trod,
  Where deep thoughts are a duty,
Where Love's a grown-up God,
  Where the Houri glances are
Imbued with all the beauty
  Which we worship in a star.

Therefore, thou art not wrong,
  Israfeli, who despisest
An unimpassioned song;
To thee the laurels belong,
  Best bard, because the wisest!
Merrily live, and long!

The ecstasies above
  With thy burning measures suit—
Thy grief, thy joy, thy hate, thy love,
  With the fervour of thy lute—
  Well may the stars be mute!

Yes, Heaven is thine; but this
  Is a world of sweets and sours;
  Our flowers are merely—flowers,
And the shadow of thy perfect bliss
  Is the sunshine of ours.

If I could dwell
Where Israfel
  Hath dwelt, and he where I,
He might not sing so wildly well
  A mortal melody,
While a bolder note than this might
    swell
  From my lyre within the sky.

(1831) 1831

## THE CITY IN THE SEA

Lo! Death has reared himself a throne
In a strange city lying alone
Far down within the dim West,
Where the good and the bad and the worst and the best
Have gone to their eternal rest.
There shrines and palaces and towers
(Time-eaten towers that tremble not!)
Resemble nothing that is ours.
Around, by lifting winds forgot,
Resignedly beneath the sky
The melancholy waters lie.

No rays from the holy heaven come down
On the long night-time of that town;
But light from out the lurid sea
Streams up the turrets silently—
Gleams up the pinnacles far and free—
Up domes—up spires—up kingly halls—
Up fanes—up Babylon-like walls—
Up shadowy long-forgotten bowers
Of sculptured ivy and stone flowers—
Up many and many a marvelous shrine
Whose wreathèd friezes intertwine
The viol, the violet, and the vine.

Resignedly beneath the sky
The melancholy waters lie.
So blend the turrets and shadows there
That all seem pendulous in air,
While from a proud tower in the town
Death looks gigantically down.

There open fanes and gaping graves
Yawn level with the luminous waves;
But not the riches there that lie
In each idol's diamond eye—
Not the gayly-jewelled dead
Tempt the waters from their bed;
For no ripples curl, alas!
Along that wilderness of glass—
No swellings tell that winds may be
Upon some far-off happier sea—
No heavings hint that winds have been
On seas less hideously serene.

But lo, a stir is in the air!
The wave—there is a movement there!
As if the towers had thrust aside,
In slightly sinking, the dull tide—
As if their tops had feebly given
A void within the filmy Heaven.
The waves have now a redder glow—
The hours are breathing faint and low—
And when, amid no earthly moans,
Down, down that town shall settle hence,
Hell, rising from a thousand thrones,
Shall do it reverence.

1831

## THE SLEEPER

At midnight, in the month of June,
I stand beneath the mystic moon.
An opiate vapor, dewy, dim,
Exhales from out her golden rim,
And softly dripping, drop by drop,
Upon the quiet mountain top,
Steals drowsily and musically
Into the universal valley.
The rosemary nods upon the grave;
The lily lolls upon the wave;
Wrapping the fog about its breast,
The ruin molders into rest;
Looking like Lethe, see! the lake
A conscious slumber seems to take,
And would not, for the world, awake.
All Beauty sleeps!—and lo! where lies
Irene, with her Destinies!

Oh, lady bright! can it be right—
This window open to the night?
The wanton airs, from the tree-top,
Laughingly through the lattice drop—
The bodiless airs, a wizard rout,
Flit through thy chamber in and out,
And wave the curtain canopy
So fitfully—so fearfully—
Above the closed and fringèd lid

'Neath which thy slumb'ring soul lies hid,
That, o'er the floor and down the wall,
Like ghosts the shadows rise and fall!
Oh, lady dear, hast thou no fear?
Why and what art thou dreaming here?
Sure thou art come o'er far-off seas,
A wonder to these garden trees!
Strange is thy pallor! strange thy dress!
Strange, above all, thy length of tress,
And this all solemn silentness!
The lady sleeps! Oh, may her sleep,
Which is enduring, so be deep!
Heaven have her in its sacred keep!
This chamber changed for one more holy,
This bed for one more melancholy,
I pray to God that she may lie
Forever with unopened eye,
While the pale sheeted ghosts go by!

My love, she sleeps! Oh, may her sleep,
As it is lasting, so be deep!
Soft may the worms about her creep!
Far in the forest, dim and old,
For her may some tall vault unfold—
Some vault that oft hath flung its black
And wingèd panels fluttering back,
Triumphant, o'er the crested palls,
Of her grand family funerals—
Some sepulchre, remote, alone,
Against whose portal she hath thrown,
In childhood, many an idle stone—
Some tomb from out whose sounding door
She ne'er shall force an echo more,
Thrilling to think, poor child of sin!
It was the dead who groaned within.

1831

## LENORE

Ah, broken is the golden bowl! — the spirit flown forever!
Let the bell toll! — a saintly soul floats on the Stygian river:—
And, Guy De Vere, hast *thou* no tear? — weep now or never more!
See! on yon drear and rigid bier low lies thy love, Lenore!
Come, let the burial rite be read — the funeral song be sung! —
An anthem for the queenliest dead that ever died so young —
A dirge for her the doubly dead in that she died so young.

"Wretches, ye loved her for her wealth, and ye hated her for her pride;
And, when she fell in feeble health, ye blessed her — that she died:—
How *shall* the ritual, then, be read — the requiem how be sung
By you — by yours, the evil eye, — by yours, the slanderous tongue
That did to death the innocence that died, and died so young?"

*Peccavimus;* yet rave not thus! but let a Sabbath song
Go up to God so solemnly the dead may feel no wrong!
The sweet Lenore hath gone before, with Hope that flew beside,
Leaving thee wild for the dear child that should have been thy bride —
For her, the fair and debonair, that now so lowly lies,
The life upon her yellow hair, but not within her eyes —
The life still there, upon her hair, the death upon her eyes.

"Avaunt! — avaunt! from fiends below, the indignant ghost is riven —
From Hell unto a high estate within the utmost Heaven —
From moan and groan to a golden throne beside the King of Heaven: —
Let *no* bell toll, then, lest her soul, amid its hallowed mirth,
Should catch the note as it doth float up from the damnèd Earth!

And I — to-night my heart is light: — no dirge will I upraise,
But waft the angel on her flight with a Paean of old days."

(1830) 1831

## THE VALLEY OF UNREST

*Once* it smiled a silent dell
Where the people did not dwell;
They had gone unto the wars,
Trusting to the mild-eyed stars,
Nightly, from their azure towers,
To keep watch above the flowers,
In the midst of which all day
The red sun-light lazily lay.
*Now* each visitor shall confess
The sad valley's restlessness.
Nothing there is motionless—
Nothing save the airs that brood
Over the magic solitude.
Ah, by no wind are stirred those trees
That palpitate like the chill seas
Around the misty Hebrides!
Ah, by no wind those clouds are driven
That rustle through the unquiet Heaven
Uneasily, from morn till even,
Over the violets there that lie
In myriad types of the human eye—
Over the lilies there that wave
And weep above a nameless grave!
They wave:—from out their fragrant tops
Eternal dews come down in drops.
They weep:—from off their delicate stems
Perennial tears descend in gems.

1831

## THE COLISEUM

Type of the antique Rome! Rich reliquary
Of lofty contemplation left to Time
By buried centuries of pomp and power!
At length—at length—after so many days
Of weary pilgrimage and burning thirst
(Thirst for the springs of lore that in thee lie),
I kneel, an altered and an humble man,
Amid thy shadows, and so drink within
My very soul thy grandeur, gloom, and glory!

Vastness! and Age! and Memories of Eld!
Silence! and Desolation! and dim Night!
I feel ye now—I feel ye in your strength—
O spells more sure than e'er Judæan king
Taught in the gardens of Gethsemane!
O charms more potent than the rapt Chaldee
Ever drew down from out the quiet stars!
Here, where a hero fell, a column falls!
Here, where the mimic eagle glared in gold,
A midnight vigil holds the swarthy bat!
Here, where the dames of Rome their gilded hair
Waved to the wind, now wave the reed and thistle!
Here, where on golden throne the monarch lolled,
Glides, spectre-like, unto his marble home,
Lit by the wan light of the hornèd moon,
The swift and silent lizard of the stones!

But stay! these walls—these ivy-clad arcades—
These mouldering plinths—these sad and blackened shafts—
These vague entablatures—this crumbling frieze—
These shattered cornices—this wreck—this ruin—

These stones—alas! these gray stones—are they all—
All of the famed, and the colossal left
By the corrosive Hours to Fate and me?

"Not all"—the Echoes answer me—"not all!
Prophetic sounds and loud, arise forever
From us, and from all Ruin, unto the wise,
As melody from Memnon to the Sun.
We rule the hearts of mightiest men—we rule
With a despotic sway all giant minds.
We are not impotent—we pallid stones.
Not all our power is gone—not all our fame—
Not all the magic of our high renown—
Not all the wonder that encircles us—
Not all the mysteries that in us lie—
Not all the memories that hang upon
And cling around about us as a garment,
Clothing us in a robe of more than glory."

1833

## TO ONE IN PARADISE

Thou wast that all to me, love,
  For which my soul did pine—
A green isle in the sea, love,
  A fountain and a shrine,
All wreathed with fairy fruits and flowers,
  And all the flowers were mine.

Ah, dream too bright to last!
  Ah, starry Hope! that didst arise
But to be overcast!
  A voice from out the Future cries,
"On! on!"—but o'er the Past
  (Dim gulf!) my spirit hovering lies
Mute, motionless, aghast!

For, alas! alas! with me
  The light of Life is o'er!
  No more—no more—no more—
(Such language holds the solemn sea
  To the sands upon the shore)
Shall bloom the thunder-blasted tree,
  Or the stricken eagle soar!

And all my days are trances,
  And all my nightly dreams
Are where thy gray eye glances,
  And where thy footstep gleams—
In what ethereal dances,
  By what eternal streams.

(1833?) 1834

## SONNET—SILENCE

There are some qualities—some incorporate things,
  That have a double life, which thus is made
A type of that twin entity which springs
  From matter and light, evinced in solid and shade.
There is a two-fold *Silence*—sea and shore—
  Body and soul. One dwells in lovely places,
  Newly with grass o'ergrown; some solemn graces,
Some human memories and tearful lore,
Render him terrorless: his name's "No More."

He is the corporate Silence: dread him not!
  No power hath he of evil in himself;
But should some urgent fate (untimely lot!)
  Bring thee to meet his shadow (nameless elf,
That haunteth the lone regions where hath trod
No foot of man,) commend thyself to God!

1840

## DREAM-LAND

By a route obscure and lonely,
Haunted by ill angels only,
Where an Eidolon, named NIGHT,
On a black throne reigns upright,
I have reached these lands but newly
From an ultimate dim Thule—
From a wild weird clime that lieth, sublime,
Out of SPACE—out of TIME.

Bottomless vales and boundless floods,
And chasms, and caves, and Titan woods,
With forms that no man can discover
For the tears that drip all over;
Mountains toppling evermore
Into seas without a shore;
Seas that restlessly aspire,
Surging, unto skies of fire;
Lakes that endlessly outspread
Their lone waters—lone and dead,—
Their still waters—still and chilly
With the snows of the lolling lily.

By the lakes that thus outspread
Their lone waters, lone and dead,—
Their sad waters, sad and chilly
With the snows of the lolling lily,—
By the mountains—near the river
Murmuring lowly, murmuring ever,—
By the grey woods,—by the swamp
Where the toad and the newt encamp,—
By the dismal tarns and pools
Where dwell the Ghouls,—
By each spot the most unholy—
In each nook most melancholy,—
There the traveller meets, aghast,
Sheeted Memories of the Past—
Shrouded forms that start and sigh
As they pass the wanderer by—
White-robed forms of friends long given,
In agony, to the Earth—and Heaven.

For the heart whose woes are legion
'Tis a peaceful, soothing region—
For the spirit that walks in shadow
'Tis—oh 'tis an Eldorado!
But the traveller, travelling through it,
May not—dare not openly view it;
Never its mysteries are exposed
To the weak human eye unclosed;
So wills its King, who hath forbid
The uplifting of the fringèd lid;
And thus the sad Soul that here passes
Beholds it but through darkened glasses.

By a route obscure and lonely,
Haunted by ill angels only,
Where an Eidolon, named NIGHT,
On a black throne reigns upright,
I have wandered home but newly
From this ultimate dim Thule.

1844

## THE RAVEN

Once upon a midnight dreary, while I pondered, weak and weary,
Over many a quaint and curious volume of forgotten lore—
While I nodded, nearly napping, suddenly there came a tapping,
As of some one gently rapping, rapping at my chamber door.
" 'Tis some visitor," I muttered, "tapping at my chamber door—
Only this and nothing more."

Ah, distinctly I remember it was in the bleak December;
And each separate dying ember wrought its ghost upon the floor.
Eagerly I wished the morrow;—vainly I had sought to borrow
From my books surcease of sorrow—sorrow for the lost Lenore—
For the rare and radiant maiden whom the angels name Lenore—
Nameless *here* for evermore.

And the silken, sad, uncertain rustling of each purple curtain
Thrilled me—filled me with fantastic terrors never felt before;

So that now, to still the beating of my heart, I stood repeating,
"'Tis some visitor entreating entrance at my chamber door—
Some late visitor entreating entrance at my chamber door;—
This it is and nothing more."

Presently my soul grew stronger; hesitating then no longer,
"Sir," said I, "or Madam, truly your forgiveness I implore;
But the fact is I was napping, and so gently you came rapping,
And so faintly you came tapping, tapping at my chamber door,
That I scarce was sure I heard you"—here I opened wide the door;—
Darkness there and nothing more.

Deep into that darkness peering, long I stood there wondering, fearing,
Doubting, dreaming dreams no mortal ever dared to dream before;
But the silence was unbroken, and the stillness gave no token,
And the only word there spoken was the whispered word, "Lenore?"
This I whispered, and an echo murmured back the word, "Lenore!"
Merely this and nothing more.

Back into the chamber turning, all my soul within me burning,
Soon again I heard a tapping somewhat louder than before.
"Surely," said I, "surely that is something at my window lattice;
Let me see, then, what thereat is, and this mystery explore—
Let my heart be still a moment and this mystery explore;—
'Tis the wind and nothing more!"

Open here I flung the shutter, when, with many a flirt and flutter,
In there stepped a stately Raven of the saintly days of yore;
Not the least obeisance made he; not a minute stopped or stayed he;
But, with mien of lord or lady, perched above my chamber door—
Perched upon a bust of Pallas just above my chamber door—
Perched, and sat, and nothing more.

Then this ebony bird beguiling my sad fancy into smiling,
By the grave and stern decorum of the countenance it wore,
"Though thy crest be shorn and shaven, thou," I said, "art sure no craven,
Ghastly grim and ancient Raven wandering from the Nightly shore—
Tell me what thy lordly name is on the Night's Plutonian shore!"
Quoth the Raven, "Nevermore."

Much I marvelled this ungainly fowl to hear discourse so plainly,
Though its answer little meaning—little relevancy bore;
For we cannot help agreeing that no living human being
Ever yet was blessed with seeing bird above his chamber door—
Bird or beast upon the sculptured bust above his chamber door,
With such name as "Nevermore."

But the Raven, sitting lonely on the placid bust, spoke only
That one word, as if his soul in that one word he did outpour.
Nothing farther then he uttered—not a feather then he fluttered—
Till I scarcely more than muttered, "Other friends have flown before—
On the morrow *he* will leave me, as my Hopes have flown before."
Then the bird said, "Nevermore."

Startled at the stillness broken by reply so aptly spoken,
"Doubtless," said I, "what it utters is its only stock and store
Caught from some unhappy master whom unmerciful Disaster
Followed fast and followed faster till his songs one burden bore—
Till the dirges of his Hope that melancholy burden bore
Of 'Never—nevermore.'"

But the Raven still beguiling my sad fancy into smiling,
Straight I wheeled a cushioned seat in front of bird and bust and door;
Then, upon the velvet sinking, I betook myself to linking
Fancy unto fancy, thinking what this ominous bird of yore—
What this grim, ungainly, ghastly, gaunt, and ominous bird of yore
Meant in croaking "Nevermore."

This I sat engaged in guessing, but no syllable expressing
To the fowl whose fiery eyes now burned into my bosom's core;
This and more I sat divining, with my head at ease reclining
On the cushion's velvet lining that the lamplight gloated o'er,
But whose velvet-violet lining with the lamplight gloating o'er,
*She* shall press, ah, nevermore!

Then, methought, the air grew denser, perfumed from an unseen censer
Swung by seraphim whose foot-falls tinkled on the tufted floor.
"Wretch," I cried, "thy God hath lent thee—by these angels he hath sent thee
Respite—respite and nepenthe from thy memories of Lenore;
Quaff, oh, quaff this kind nepenthe and forget this lost Lenore!"
Quoth the Raven, "Nevermore."

"Prophet!" said I, "thing of evil!—prophet still, if bird or devil!—
Whether Tempter sent, or whether tempest tossed thee here ashore,
Desolate yet all undaunted, on this desert land enchanted—
On this home by Horror haunted—tell me truly, I implore—
Is there—*is* there balm in Gilead?—tell me—tell me, I implore!"
Quoth the Raven, "Nevermore."

"Prophet!" said I, "thing of evil!—prophet still, if bird or devil!
By that Heaven that bends above us—by that God we both adore—
Tell this soul with sorrow laden if, within the distant Aidenn,
It shall clasp a sainted maiden whom the angels name Lenore—
Clasp a rare and radiant maiden whom the angels name Lenore."
Quoth the Raven, "Nevermore."

"Be that word our sign of parting, bird or fiend!" I shrieked, upstarting—
"Get thee back into the tempest and the Night's Plutonian shore!
Leave no black plume as a token of that lie thy soul hath spoken!
Leave my loneliness unbroken!—quit the bust above my door!
Take thy beak from out my heart, and take thy form from off my door!"
Quoth the Raven, "Nevermore."

And the Raven, never flitting, still is sitting, *still* is sitting
On the pallid bust of Pallas just above my chamber door;
And his eyes have all the seeming of a demon's that is dreaming,
And the lamp-light o'er him streaming throws his shadow on the floor;

And my soul from out that shadow that lies floating on the floor
Shall be lifted—nevermore!

(1842–4) 1845

## ULALUME—A BALLAD

The skies they were ashen and sober;
The leaves they were crispéd and sere—
The leaves they were withering and sere:
It was night, in the lonesome October
Of my most immemorial year:
It was hard by the dim lake of Auber,
In the misty mid region of Weir—
It was down by the dank tarn of Auber,
In the ghoul-haunted woodland of Weir.

Here once, through an alley Titanic,
Of cypress, I roamed with my Soul—
Of cypress, with Psyche, my Soul.
These were days when my heart was volcanic
As the scoriac rivers that roll—
As the lavas that restlessly roll
Their sulphurous currents down Yaanek
In the ultimate climes of the Pole—
That groan as they roll down Mount Yaanek
In the realms of the Boreal pole.

Our talk had been serious and sober,
But our thoughts they were palsied and sere—
Our memories were treacherous and sere;
For we knew not the month was October,
And we marked not the night of the year
(Ah, night of all nights in the year!)—
We noted not the dim lake of Auber
(Though once we had journeyed down here)—
We remembered not the dank tarn of Auber,
Nor the ghoul-haunted woodland of Weir.

And now, as the night was senescent
And star-dials pointed to morn—
As the star-dials hinted of morn—
At the end of our path a liquescent
And nebulous luster was born,
Out of which a miraculous crescent
Arose with a duplicate horn—
Astarte's bediamonded crescent
Distinct with its duplicate horn.

And I said: "She is warmer than Dian;
She rolls through an ether of sighs—
She revels in a region of sighs.
She has seen that the tears are not dry on
These cheeks, where the worm never dies,
And has come past the stars of the Lion,
To point us the path to the skies—
To the Lethean peace of the skies—
Come up, in despite of the Lion,
To shine on us with her bright eyes—
Come up through the lair of the Lion,
With love in her luminous eyes."

But Psyche, uplifting her finger,
Said: "Sadly this star I mistrust—
Her pallor I strangely mistrust:
Ah, hasten!—ah, let us not linger!
Ah, fly!—let us fly!—for we must."
In terror she spoke, letting sink her
Wings till they trailed in the dust—
In agony sobbed, letting sink her
Plumes till they trailed in the dust—
Till they sorrowfully trailed in the dust.

I replied: "This is nothing but dreaming:

Let us on by this tremulous light!
Let us bathe in this crystalline light!
Its Sibyllic splendor is beaming
With Hope and in Beauty to-night:—
See! it flickers up the sky through the night!
Ah, we safely may trust to its gleaming,
And be sure it will lead us aright—
We surely may trust to a gleaming,
That cannot but guide us aright,
Since it flickers up to Heaven through the night."

Thus I pacified Psyche and kissed her,
And tempted her out of her gloom—
And conquered her scruples and gloom;
And we passed to the end of the vista,
But were stopped by the door of a tomb—
By the door of a legended tomb;
And I said: "What is written, sweet sister,
On the door of this legended tomb?"
She replied: "Ulalume—Ulalume!—
'Tis the vault of thy lost Ulalume!"

Then my heart it grew ashen and sober
As the leaves that were crispèd and sere—
As the leaves that were withering and sere;
And I cried: "It was surely October
On *this* very night of last year
That I journeyed—I journeyed down here!—
That I brought a dread burden down here—
On this night of all nights in the year,
Ah, what demon hath tempted me here?
Well I know, now, this dim lake of Auber—
This misty mid region of Weir—
Well I know, now, this dank tarn of Auber,
This ghoul-haunted woodland of Weir."

Said we, then—the two, then: "Ah, can it
Have been that the woodlandish ghouls—
The pitiful, the merciful ghouls—
To bar up our way and to ban it
From the secret that lies in these wolds—
From the thing that lies hidden in these wolds—
Have drawn up the specter of a planet
From the limbo of lunary souls—
This sinfully scintillant planet
From the Hell of the planetary souls?"

(1847?) 1847

## THE BELLS

I

Hear the sledges with the bells—
Silver bells!
What a world of merriment their melody foretells!
How they tinkle, tinkle, tinkle,
In the icy air of night!
While the stars that oversprinkle
All the heavens, seem to twinkle
With a crystalline delight;
Keeping time, time, time,
In a sort of Runic rhyme,
To the tintinnabulation that so musically wells
From the bells, bells, bells, bells,
Bells, bells, bells—
From the jingling and the tinkling of the bells.

II

Hear the mellow wedding bells—
Golden bells!
What a world of happiness their harmony foretells!
Through the balmy air of night

How they ring out their delight!—
From the molten-golden notes,
And all in tune,
What a liquid ditty floats
To the turtle-dove that listens, while she gloats
On the moon!
Oh, from out the sounding cells,
What a gush of euphony voluminously wells!
How it swells!
How it dwells
On the Future!—how it tells
Of the rapture that impels
To the swinging and the ringing
Of the bells, bells, bells—
Of the bells, bells, bells, bells,
Bells, bells, bells—
To the rhyming and the chiming of the bells!

III

Hear the loud alarum bells—
Brazen bells!
What a tale of terror, now, their turbulency tells!
In the startled ear of night
How they scream out their affright!
Too much horrified to speak,
They can only shriek, shriek,
Out of tune,
In a clamorous appealing to the mercy of the fire,
In a mad expostulation with the deaf and frantic fire,
Leaping higher, higher, higher,
With a desperate desire,
And a resolute endeavor
Now—now to sit, or never,
By the side of the pale-faced moon.
Oh, the bells, bells, bells!
What a tale their terror tells
Of Despair!
How they clang, and clash, and roar!
What a horror they outpour
On the bosom of the palpitating air!
Yet the ear, it fully knows,
By the twanging
And the clanging,
How the danger ebbs and flows;
Yet the ear distinctly tells,
In the jangling
And the wrangling,
How the danger sinks and swells,
By the sinking or the swelling in the anger of the bells—
Of the bells,—
Of the bells, bells, bells, bells,
Bells, bells, bells—
In the clamor and the clangor of the bells!

IV

Hear the tolling of the bells—
Iron bells!
What a world of solemn thought their monody compels!
In the silence of the night,
How we shiver with affright
At the melancholy menace of their tone!
For every sound that floats
From the rust within their throats
Is a groan.
And the people—ah, the people—
They that dwell up in the steeple,
All alone,
And who tolling, tolling, tolling,
In that muffled monotone,
Feel a glory in so rolling
On the human heart a stone—
They are neither man nor woman—
They are neither brute nor human—
They are Ghouls:—
And their king it is who tolls:—
And he rolls, rolls, rolls,
Rolls
A pæan from the bells!
And his merry bosom swells
With the pæan of the bells!
And he dances, and he yells;
Keeping time, time, time,
In a sort of Runic rhyme,

To the pæan of the bells—
Of the bells:
Keeping time, time, time,
In a sort of Runic rhyme,
To the throbbing of the bells—
Of the bells, bells, bells—
To the sobbing of the bells;
Keeping time, time, time,
As he knells, knells, knells,
In a happy Runic rhyme,
To the rolling of the bells—
Of the bells, bells, bells:—
To the tolling of the bells—
Of the bells, bells, bells, bells,
Bells, bells, bells—
To the moaning and the groaning of the bells.

(1848–9) 1849

## ELDORADO

Gayly bedight,
A gallant knight,
In sunshine and in shadow,
Had journeyed long,
Singing a song,
In search of Eldorado.

But he grew old—
This knight so bold—
And o'er his heart a shadow
Fell as he found
No spot of ground
That looked like Eldorado.

And, as his strength
Failed him at length,
He met a pilgrim shadow—
"Shadow," said he,
"Where can it be—
This land of Eldorado?"

"Over the Mountains
Of the Moon,
Down the Valley of the Shadow,
Ride, boldly ride,"
The shade replied,—
"If you seek for Eldorado!"

(1849) 1849

## FOR ANNIE

Thank Heaven! the crisis,
The danger, is past,
And the lingering illness
Is over at last—
And the fever called "Living"
Is conquered at last.

Sadly, I know
I am shorn of my strength,
And no muscle I move
As I lie at full length—
But no matter!—I feel
I am better at length.

And I rest so composedly,
Now, in my bed,
That any beholder
Might fancy me dead—
Might start at beholding me,
Thinking me dead.

The moaning and groaning,
The sighing and sobbing,
Are quieted now,
With that horrible throbbing
At heart:—ah, that horrible,
Horrible throbbing!

The sickness—the nausea—
The pitiless pain—
Have ceased, with the fever
That maddened my brain—
With the fever called "Living"
That burned in my brain.

And oh! of all tortures
*That* torture the worst
Has abated—the terrible
Torture of thirst
For the napthaline river
Of Passion accurst:—
I have drank of a water
That quenches all thirst:—

Of a water that flows,
With a lullaby sound,
From a spring but a very few
Feet under ground—

From a cavern not very far
Down under ground.

And ah! let it never
Be foolishly said
That my room it is gloomy
And narrow my bed;
For a man never slept
In a different bed—
And, to *sleep*, you must slumber
In just such a bed.

My tantalized spirit
Here blandly reposes,
Forgetting, or never
Regretting, its roses—
Its old agitations
Of myrtles and roses:

For now, while so quietly
Lying, it fancies
A holier odor
About it, of pansies—
A rosemary odor,
Commingled with pansies—
With rue and the beautiful
Puritan pansies.

And so it lies happily,
Bathing in many
A dream of the truth
And the beauty of Annie—
Drowned in a bath
Of the tresses of Annie.

She tenderly kissed me,
She fondly caressed,
And then I fell gently
To sleep on her breast—
Deeply to sleep
From the heaven of her breast.

When the light was extinguished,
She covered me warm,
And she prayed to the angels
To keep me from harm—
To the queen of the angels
To shield me from harm.

And I lie so composedly,
Now, in my bed
(Knowing her love),
That you fancy me dead—
And I rest so contentedly,
Now, in my bed
(With her love at my breast),
That you fancy me dead—
That you shudder to look at me,
Thinking me dead:—

But my heart it is brighter
Than all of the many
Stars in the sky,
For it sparkles with Annie—
It glows with the light
Of the love of my Annie—
With the thought of the light
Of the eyes of my Annie.

(1849) 1849

## TO MY MOTHER

Because I feel that, in the Heavens above,
The angels, whispering to one another,
Can find, among their burning terms of love,
None so devotional as that of "Mother,"
Therefore by that dear name I long have called you—
You who are more than mother unto me,
And fill my heart of hearts, where Death installed you,
In setting my Virginia's spirit free.
My mother—my own mother, who died early,
Was but the mother of myself; but you
Are mother to the one I loved so dearly,
And thus are dearer than the mother I knew
By that infinity with which my wife
Was dearer to my soul than its soul-life.

1849

## ANNABEL LEE

It was many and many a year ago,
In a kingdom by the sea,
That a maiden there lived whom you may know
By the name of Annabel Lee;—
And this maiden she lived with no other thought
Than to love and be loved by me.

*She* was a child and *I* was a child,
In this kingdom by the sea,
But we loved with a love that was more than love—
I and my Annabel Lee—
With a love that the wingéd seraphs of Heaven
Coveted her and me.

And this was the reason that, long ago,
In this kingdom by the sea,
A wind blew out of a cloud by night
Chilling my Annabel Lee;
So that her highborn kinsmen came
And bore her away from me,
To shut her up in a sepulchre
In this kingdom by the sea.

The angels, not half so happy in Heaven,
Went envying her and me:—
Yes! that was the reason (as all men know,
In this kingdom by the sea)
That the wind came out of the cloud, chilling
And killing my Annabel Lee.

But our love it was stronger by far than the love
Of those who were older than we—
Of many far wiser than we—
And neither the angels in Heaven above
Nor the demons down under the sea,
Can ever dissever my soul from the soul
Of the beautiful Annabel Lee:—

For the moon never beams without bringing me dreams
Of the beautiful Annabel Lee;
And the stars never rise but I see the bright eyes
Of the beautiful Annabel Lee;
And so, all the night-tide, I lie down by the side
Of my darling, my darling, my life and my bride,
In her sepulchre there by the sea—
In her tomb by the side of the sea.

1849

## THE DUC DE L'OMELETTE

And stepped at once into a cooler clime.
—COWPER.

Keats fell by a criticism. Who was it died of *The Andromache?* * Ignoble souls! — De L'Omelette perished of an ortolan. *L'histoire en est brève.* Assist me, Spirit of Apicius!

A golden cage bore the little winged wanderer, enamored, melting, indolent, to the *Chaussée D'Antin,* from its home in far Peru. From its queenly possessor La Bellissima, to the Duc De L'Omelette, six peers of the empire conveyed the happy bird.

That night the Duc was to sup alone. In the privacy of his bureau he reclined languidly on that ottoman for which he sacrificed his loyalty in outbidding his king, — the notorious ottoman of Cadêt.

*Montfleury. The author of the *Parnasse Réformé* makes him thus speak in Hades:—"*L' homme donc qu'il voudrait savoir ce dont je suis mort, qu il ne demande pas s'il fût de fievre ou de podagre ou d'autre chose, mais qu'il entende que ce fut de 'L'Andromache'.*" [Author's note.]

He buries his face in the pillow. The clock strikes! Unable to restrain his feelings, his Grace swallows an olive. At this moment the door gently opens to the sound of soft music, and lo! the most delicate of birds is before the most enamored of men! But what inexpressible dismay now overshadows the countenance of the Duc? — *"Horreur! — chien! — Baptiste! — l'oiseau! ah, bon Dieu! cet oiseau modeste que tu as deshabillé de ses plumes, et que tu as servi sans papier!"* It is superfluous to say more: — the Duc expired in a paroxysm of disgust. . . .

"Ha! ha! ha!", said his Grace on the third day after his decease.

"He! he! he!", replied the Devil faintly, drawing himself up with an air of *hauteur*.

"Why, surely you are not serious," retorted De L'Omelette. "I have sinned — *c'est vrai* — but, my good sir, consider! — you have no actual intention of putting such — such — barbarous threats into execution."

"No *what?"* said his majesty — "come, sir, strip!"

"Strip, indeed! — very pretty i' faith! — no, sir, I shall *not* strip. Who are you, pray, that I, Duc De L'Omelette, Prince de Foie-Gras, just come of age, author of the 'Mazurkiad,' and Member of the Academy, should divest myself at your bidding of the sweetest pantaloons ever made by Bourdon, the daintiest *robe-de-chambre* ever put together by Rombêrt — to say nothing of the taking my hair out of paper — not to mention the trouble I should have in drawing off my gloves?"

"Who am I? — ah, true! I am Baal-Zebub, Prince of the Fly. I took thee, just now, from a rose-wood coffin inlaid with ivory. Thou wast curiously scented, and labelled as per invoice. Belial sent thee, — my Inspector of Cemeteries. The pantaloons, which thou sayest were made by Bourdon, are an excellent pair of linen drawers, and thy *robe-de-chambre* is a shroud of no scanty dimensions."

"Sir!" replied the Duc, "I am not to be insulted with impunity! — Sir! I shall take the earliest opportunity of avenging this insult! — Sir! you shall hear from me! In the meantime *au revoir!"* — and the Duc was bowing himself out of the Satanic presence, when he was interrupted and brought back by a gentleman in waiting. — Hereupon his Grace rubbed his eyes, yawned, shrugged his shoulders, reflected. Having become satisfied of his identity, he took a bird's eye view of his whereabouts.

The apartment was superb. Even De L'Omelette pronounced it *bien comme il faut.* It was not its length nor its breadth, — but its height — ah, that was appalling! — There was no ceiling — certainly none — but a dense whirling mass of fiery-colored clouds. His Grace's brain reeled as he glanced upwards. From above, hung a chain of an unknown blood-red metal — its upper end lost, like the city of Boston, *parmi les nues.* From its nether extremity swung a large cresset. The Duc knew it to be a ruby; but from it there poured a light so intense, so still, so terrible, Persia never worshipped such — Gheber never imagined such — Mussulman never dreamed of such when, drugged with opium, he has tottered to a bed of poppies, his back to the flowers, and his face to the God Apollo. The Duc muttered a slight oath, decidedly approbatory.

The corners of the room were rounded into niches. — Three of these were filled with statues of gigantic proportions. Their beauty was Grecian, their deformity Egyptian, their *tout ensemble* French. In the fourth niche the statue was veiled; it was *not* colossal. But then there was a taper ankle, a sandalled foot. De L'Omelette pressed his hand upon his heart, closed his eyes, raised them, and caught his Satanic Majesty — in a blush.

But the paintings! — Kupris! Astarte! Astoreth! — a thousand and the same! And Rafaelle has beheld them! Yes, Rafaelle has been here; for did he not paint the —— ? and was he not consequently damned? The paintings! — the paintings! O luxury! O love! — who, gazing on those forbidden beauties, shall have eyes for the dainty devices of the golden frames that besprinkle, like stars, the hyacinth and the porphyry walls?

But the Duc's heart is fainting within him. He is not, however, as you suppose, dizzy with magnificence, nor drunk with the ecstatic breath of those innumerable censers. *C'est vrai que de toutes ces choses il a pensé beaucoup — mais!* The Duc De L'Omelette is terror-stricken; for, through the lurid vista which a single uncurtained window is affording, lo! gleams the most ghastly of all fires!

*Le pauvre Duc!* He could not help imagining that the glorious, the voluptuous, the never-dying melodies which pervaded that hall, as they passed filtered and transmuted through the alchemy of the enchanted window-panes, were the wailings and the howlings of the hopeless and the damned! And there, too! — there! — upon that ottoman! — who could *he* be? — he, the *petit-maitre* — no, the Deity — who sat as if carved in marble, *et qui sourit,* with his pale countenance, *si amérement?*

*Mais il faut agir,* — that is to say, a Frenchman never faints outright. Besides, his Grace hated a scene — De L'Omelette is himself again. There were some foils upon a table — some points also. The Duc had studied under B——; *il avait tué ses six hommes.* Now, then, *il peut s'échapper.* He measures two points, and, with a grace inimitable, offers his Majesty the choice. *Horreur!* his Majesty does not fence!

*Mais il joue!* — how happy a thought! — but his Grace had always an excellent memory. He had dipped in the "Diable" of the Abbé Gualtier. Therein it is said *"que le Diable n'ose pas refuser un jeu d'écarté."*

But the chances — the chances! True — desperate: but scarcely more desperate than the Duc. Besides, was he not in the secret? — had he not skimmed over Père Le Brun? — was he not a member of the Club Vingt-un? *"Si je perds,"* said he, *"je serai deux fois perdu* — I shall be doubly damned — *voila tout!* (Here his Grace shrugged his shoulders) *Si je gagne, je reviendrai à mes ortolans — que les cartes soient préparées!"*

His Grace was all care, all attention — his Majesty all confidence. A spectator would have thought of Francis and Charles. His Grace thought of his game. His Majesty did not think; he shuffled. The Duc cut.

The cards are dealt. The trump is turned — it is — it is — the king! No — it was the queen. His Majesty cursed her masculine habiliments. De L'Omelette placed his hand upon his heart.

They play. The Duc counts. The hand is out. His Majesty counts heavily, smiles, and is taking wine. The Duc slips a card.

*"C'est à vous à faire,"* said his Majesty, cutting. His Grace bowed, dealt, and arose from the table *en presentant le Roi.*

His Majesty looked chagrined.

Had Alexander not been Alexander, he would have been Diogenes; and the Duc assured his antagonist in taking leave, *"que s'il n'eût pas été De L'Omelette il n'aurait point d'objection d'être le Diable."*

1832

## SHADOW — A PARABLE

Yea! though I walk through the valley of the *Shadow.*
—PSALM OF DAVID.

Ye who read are still among the living: but I who write shall have long since gone my way into the region of shadows. For indeed strange things shall happen, and secret things be known, and many centuries shall pass away, ere these memorials be seen of men. And, when seen, there will be some to disbelieve, and some to doubt, and yet a few who will find much to ponder upon in the characters here graven with a stylus of iron.

The year had been a year of terror, and of feelings more intense than terror for which there is no name upon the earth. For many prodigies and signs had taken place, and far and wide, over sea and land, the black wings of the Pestilence were spread abroad. To those, nevertheless, cunning in the stars, it was not unknown that the heavens wore an aspect of ill; and to me, the Greek Oinos, among others, it was evident that now had arrived the alternation of that seven hundred and ninety-fourth year when, at the entrance of Aries, the planet Jupiter is conjoined with the red ring of the terrible Saturnus. The peculiar spirit of the skies, if I mistake not greatly, made itself manifest, not only in the physical orb of the earth, but in the souls, imaginations, and meditations of mankind.

Over some flasks of the red Chian wine, within the walls of a noble hall, in a dim city called Ptolemais, we sat, at night, a company of seven. And to our chamber there was no entrance save by a lofty door of brass: and the door was fashioned by the artizan Corinnos, and, being of rare workmanship, was fastened from within. Black draperies, likewise, in the gloomy room, shut out from our view the moon, the lurid stars, and the peopleless streets—but the boding and the memory of Evil, they would not be so excluded. There were things around us and about of which I can render no distinct account—things material and spiritual—heaviness in the atmosphere—a sense of suffocation—anxiety—and, above all, that terrible state of existence which the nervous experience when the senses are keenly living and awake, and meanwhile the powers of thought lie dormant. A dead weight hung upon us. It hung upon our limbs—upon the household furniture—upon the goblets from which we drank; and all things were depressed, and borne down thereby—all things save only the flames of the seven iron lamps which illumined our revel. Uprearing themselves in tall slender lines of light, they thus remained burning all pallid and motionless; and in the mirror which their lustre formed upon the round table of ebony at which we sat, each of us there assembled beheld the pallor of his own countenance, and the unquiet glare in the downcast eyes of his companions. Yet we laughed and were merry in our proper way—which was hysterical; and sang the songs of Anacreon—which are madness; and drank deeply—although the purple wine reminded us of blood. For there was yet another tenant of our chamber in the person of young Zoilus. Dead, and at full length he lay, enshrouded;—the genius and the demon of the scene. Alas! he bore no portion in our mirth, save that his countenance, distorted with the plague, and his eyes in which Death had but half extinguished the fire of the pestilence, seemed to take such interest in our merriment as the dead may haply take in the merriment of those who are to die. But although I, Oinos, felt that the eyes of the departed were upon me, still I forced myself not to perceive the bitterness of their expression, and, gazing down steadily into the depths of the ebony mirror, sang with a loud and sonorous voice the songs of the son of Teios. But gradually my songs they ceased, and their echoes, rolling afar off among the sable draperies of the chamber, became weak, and undistinguishable, and so faded away. And lo! from among those sable draperies where the sounds of the song departed, there came forth a dark and undefined shadow—a shadow such as the moon, when low in heaven, might fashion from the figure of a man: but it was the shadow neither of man, nor of God, nor of any familiar thing. And, quivering awhile among the draperies of the room, it at length rested in full view upon the surface of the door of brass. But the shadow was vague, and formless, and indefinite, and was the shadow neither of man nor of God—neither God of Greece, nor God of Chaldæa, nor any Egyptian God. And the shadow rested upon the brazen doorway, and under the arch of the entablature of the door, and moved not, nor spoke any word, but there became stationary and remained. And the door whereupon the shadow rested was, if I remember aright, over against the feet of the young Zoilus enshrouded. But we, the seven there assembled, having seen the shadow as it came out from among the draperies, dared not steadily behold it, but cast down our eyes, and gazed continually into the depths of the mirror of ebony. And at length I, Oinos, speaking some low words, demanded of the shadow its dwelling and its appellation. And the shadow answered, "I am SHADOW, and my dwelling is near to the Catacombs of Ptolemais, and hard by those dim plains of Helusion which border upon the foul Charonian canal." And then did we, the seven, start from our seats in horror, and stand trembling, and shuddering, and aghast: for the tones in the voice of the shadow were not the tones of any one being, but of a multitude of beings, and, varying in their cadences from syllable to syllable, fell duskily upon our ears in the well remembered and familiar accents of many thousand departed friends.

1835

## LIGEIA

> And the will therein lieth, which dieth not. Who knoweth the mysteries of the will, with its vigor? For God is but a great will pervading all things by nature of its intentness. Man doth not yield himself to the angels, nor unto death utterly, save only through the weakness of his feeble will.
>
> —JOSEPH GLANVILL.

I cannot, for my soul, remember how, when, or even precisely where, I first became acquainted with the lady Ligeia. Long years have since elapsed, and my memory is feeble through much suffering. Or, perhaps, I cannot *now* bring these points to mind, because, in truth, the character of my beloved, her rare learning, her singular yet placid cast of beauty, and the thrilling and enthralling eloquence of her low musical language, made their way into my heart by paces so steadily and stealthily progressive that they have been unnoticed and unknown. Yet I believe that I met her first and most frequently in some large, old, decaying city near the Rhine. Of her family—I have surely heard her speak. That it is of a remotely ancient date cannot be doubted. Ligeia! Ligeia! Buried in studies of a nature more than all else adapted to deaden impressions of the outward world, it is by that sweet word alone—by Ligeia—that I bring before mine eyes in fancy the image of her who is no more. And now, while I write, a recollection flashes upon me that I have *never known* the paternal name of her who was my friend and my betrothed, and who became the partner of my studies, and finally the wife of my bosom. Was it a playful charge on the part of my Ligeia? or was it a test of my strength of affection, that I should institute no inquiries upon this point? or was it rather a caprice of my own—a wildly romantic offering on the shrine of the most passionate devotion? I but indistinctly recall the fact itself—what wonder that I have utterly forgotten the circumstances which originated or attended it. And, indeed, if ever that spirit which is entitled *Romance*—if ever she, the wan and the misty-winged *Ashtophet* of idolatrous Egypt, presided, as they tell, over marriages ill-omened, then most surely she presided over mine.

There is one dear topic, however, on which my memory fails me not. It is the *person* of Ligeia. In stature she was tall, somewhat slender, and, in her latter days, even emaciated. I would in vain attempt to portray the majesty, the quiet ease, of her demeanor, or the incomprehensible lightness and elasticity of her footfall. She came and departed as a shadow. I was never made aware of her entrance into my closed study save by the dear music of her low sweet voice, as she placed her marble hand upon my shoulder. In beauty of face no maiden ever equalled her. It was the radiance of an opium dream—an airy and spirit-lifting vision more wildly divine than the phantasies which hovered about the slumbering souls of the daughters of Delos. Yet her features were not of that regular mould which we have been falsely taught to worship in the classical labors of the heathen. "There is no exquisite beauty," says Bacon, Lord Verulam, speaking truly of all the forms and *genera* of beauty, "without some *strangeness* in the proportion." Yet, although I saw that the features of

Ligeia were not of a classic regularity—although I perceived that her loveliness was indeed "exquisite," and felt that there was much of "strangeness" pervading it, yet I have tried in vain to detect the irregularity and to trace home my own perception of "the strange." I examined the contour of the lofty and pale forehead—it was faultless—how cold indeed that word when applied to a majesty so divine!—the skin rivalling the purest ivory, the commanding extent and repose, the gentle prominence of the regions above the temples; and then the raven-black, the glossy, the luxuriant and naturally-curling tresses, setting forth the full force of the Homeric epithet, "hyacinthine!" I looked at the delicate outlines of the nose—and nowhere but in the graceful medallions of the Hebrews had I beheld a similar perfection. There were the same luxurious smoothness of surface, the same scarcely perceptible tendency to the aquiline, the same harmoniously curved nostrils speaking the free spirit. I regarded the sweet mouth. Here was indeed the triumph of all things heavenly—the magnificent turn of the short upper lip—the soft, voluptuous slumber of the under—the dimples which sported, and the color which spoke—the teeth glancing back, with a brilliancy almost startling, every ray of the holy light which fell upon them in her serene and placid, yet most exultantingly radiant of all smiles. I scrutinized the formation of the chin—and here, too, I found the gentleness of breadth, the softness and the majesty, the fullness and the spirituality, of the Greek—the contour which the god Apollo revealed but in a dream, to Cleomenes, the son of the Athenian. And then I peered into the large eyes of Ligeia.

For eyes we have no models in the remotely antique. It might have been, too, that in these eyes of my beloved lay the secret to which Lord Verulam alludes. They were, I must believe, far larger than the ordinary eyes of our own race. They were even fuller than the fullest of the gazelle eyes of the tribe of the valley of Nourjahad. Yet it was only at intervals—in moments of intense excitement—that this peculiarity became more than slightly noticeable in Ligeia. And at such moments was her beauty—in my heated fancy thus it appeared perhaps—the beauty of beings either above or apart from the earth—the beauty of the fabulous Houri of the Turk. The hue of the orbs was the most brilliant of black, and, far over them, hung jetty lashes of great length. The brows, slightly irregular in outline, had the same tint. The "strangeness," however, which I found in the eyes, was of a nature distinct from the formation, or the color, or the brilliancy of the features, and must, after all, be referred to the *expression.* Ah, word of no meaning! behind whose vast latitude of mere sound we intrench our ignorance of so much of the spiritual. The expression of the eyes of Ligeia! How for long hours have I pondered upon it! How have I, through the whole of a midsummer night, struggled to fathom it! What was it—that something more profound than the well of Democritus—which lay far within the pupils of my beloved? What *was* it? I was possessed with a passion to discover. Those eyes! those large, those shining, those divine orbs! they became to me twin stars of Leda, and I to them devoutest of astrologers.

There is no point, among the many incomprehensible anomalies of the science of mind, more thrillingly exciting than the fact—never, I believe, noticed in the schools—that, in our endeavors to recall to memory something long forgotten, we often find ourselves *upon the very verge* of remembrance, without being able, in the end, to remember. And thus how frequently, in my intense scrutiny of Ligeia's eyes, have I felt approaching the full knowledge of their expression—felt it approaching—yet not quite be mine—and so at length entirely depart! And (strange, oh strangest mystery of all!) I found, in the commonest objects of the universe, a circle of analogies to that expression. I mean to say that, subsequently to the period when Ligeia's beauty passed into my spirit, there dwelling as in a shrine, I derived, from many existences in the material world, a sentiment such as I felt always aroused within me by her large and luminous orbs. Yet not the more could I define that sentiment, or analyze, or even steadily view it. I recognized it, let me repeat, sometimes in the survey of a rapidly-growing vine—in the contemplation of a moth, a butterfly, a chrysalis, a stream of running water. I have felt it in the ocean; in the falling of a meteor. I have felt it in the glances of unusually aged people. And there are one or two stars in heaven (one especially, a star of the sixth magnitude, double and changeable, to be found near the large star in Lyra) in a telescopic scrutiny of which I have been made aware of the feeling. I have been filled with it by certain sounds from stringed instruments, and not unfrequently by passages from books. Among innumerable other instances, I well remember something in a volume of Joseph Glanvill, which (perhaps merely from its quaintness—who shall say?) never failed to inspire me with the sentiment;—"And the will therein lieth, which dieth not. Who knoweth the mysteries of the will, with its vigor? For God is but a great will pervading all things by nature of its intentness. Man doth not yield him to the angels, nor unto death utterly, save only through the weakness of his feeble will."

Length of years, and subsequent reflection, have enabled me to trace, indeed, some remote connection between this passage in the English moralist and a portion of the character of Ligeia. An *intensity* in thought, action, or speech, was possibly, in her, a result, or at least an index, of that gigantic volition which, during our long intercourse, failed to give other and more immediate evidence of its existence. Of all the women whom I have ever known, she, the outwardly calm, the ever-placid Ligeia, was the most violently a prey to the tumultuous vultures of stern passion. And of such passion I could form no estimate, save by the miraculous expansion of those eyes which at once so delighted and appalled me—by the almost magical melody, modulation, distinctness and placidity of her very low voice—and by the fierce energy (rendered doubly effective by contrast with her manner of utterance) of the wild words which she habitually uttered.

I have spoken of the learning of

Ligeia: it was immense—such as I have never known in woman. In the classical tongues was she deeply proficient, and as far as my own acquaintance extended in regard to the modern dialects of Europe, I have never known her at fault. Indeed upon any theme of the most admired, because simply the most abstruse of the boasted erudition of the academy, have I *ever* found Ligeia at fault? How singularly—how thrillingly, this one point in the nature of my wife has forced itself, at this late period only, upon my attention! I said her knowledge was such as I have never known in woman—but where breathes the man who has traversed, and successfully, *all* the wide areas of moral, physical, and mathematical science? I saw not then what I now clearly perceive, that the acquisitions of Ligeia were gigantic, were astounding; yet I was sufficiently aware of her infinite supremacy to resign myself, with a child-like confidence, to her guidance through the chaotic world of metaphysical investigation at which I was most busily occupied during the earlier years of our marriage. With how vast a triumph—with how vivid a delight—with how much of all that is ethereal in hope—did I *feel,* as she bent over me in studies but little sought—but less known—that delicious vista by slow degrees expanding before me, down whose long, gorgeous, and all untrodden path, I might at length pass onward to the goal of a wisdom too divinely precious not to be forbidden!

How poignant, then, must have been the grief with which, after some years, I beheld my well-grounded expectations take wings to themselves and fly away! Without Ligeia I was but as a child groping benighted. Her presence, her readings alone, rendered vividly luminous the many mysteries of the transcendentalism in which we were immersed. Wanting the radiant lustre of her eyes, letters, lambent and golden, grew duller than Saturnian lead. And now those eyes shone less and less frequently upon the pages over which I pored. Ligeia grew ill. The wild eyes blazed with a too—too glorious effulgence; the pale fingers became of the transparent waxen hue of the grave, and the blue veins upon the lofty forehead swelled and sank impetuously with the tides of the most gentle emotion. I saw that she must die—and I struggled desperately in spirit with the grim Azrael. And the struggles of the passionate wife were, to my astonishment, even more energetic than my own. There had been much in her stern nature to impress me with the belief that, to her, death would have come without its terrors;—but not so. Words are impotent to convey any just idea of the fierceness of resistance with which she wrestled with the Shadow. I groaned in anguish at the pitiable spectacle. I would have soothed—I would have reasoned; but, in the intensity of her wild desire for life,—for life—*but* for life—solace and reason were alike the uttermost of folly. Yet not until the last instance, amid the most convulsive writhings of her fierce spirit, was shaken the external placidity of her demeanor. Her voice grew more gentle—grew more low—yet I would not wish to dwell upon the wild meaning of the quietly uttered words. My brain reeled as I hearkened entranced, to a melody more than mortal—to assumptions and aspirations which mortality had never before known.

That she loved me I should not have doubted; and I might have been easily aware that, in a bosom such as hers, love would have reigned no ordinary passion. But in death only, was I fully impressed with the strength of her affection. For long hours, detaining my hand, would she pour out before me the overflowing of a heart whose more than passionate devotion amounted to idolatry. How had I deserved to be so blessed by such confessions?—how had I deserved to be so cursed with the removal of my beloved in the hour of her making them? But upon this subject I cannot bear to dilate. Let me say only, that in Ligeia's more than womanly abandonment to a love, alas! all unmerited, all unworthily bestowed, I at length recognized the principle of her longing with so wildly earnest a desire for the life which was now fleeing so rapidly away. It is this wild longing—it is this eager vehemence of desire for life—*but* for life—that I have no power to portray—no utterance capable of expressing.

At high noon of the night in which she departed, beckoning me, peremptorily, to her side, she bade me repeat certain verses composed by herself not many days before. I obeyed her.—They were these:

Lo! 'tis a gala night
 Within the lonesome latter years!
An angel throng, bewinged, bedight
 In veils, and drowned in tears,
Sit in a theatre, to see
 A play of hopes and fears,
While the orchestra breathes fitfully
 The music of the spheres.

Mimes, in the form of God on high,
 Mutter and mumble low,
And hither and thither fly—
 Mere puppets they, who come and go
At bidding of vast formless things
 That shift the scenery to and fro,
Flapping from out their Condor wings
 Invisible Wo!

That motley drama!—oh, be sure
 It shall not be forgot!
With its Phantom chased forever more,
 By a crowd that seize it not,
Through a circle that ever returneth in
 To the self-same spot,
And much of Madness and more of Sin
 And Horror the soul of the plot.

But see, amid the mimic rout,
 A crawling shape intrude!
A blood-red thing that writhes from out
 The scenic solitude!
It writhes!—it writhes! with mortal pangs
 The mimes become its food,
And the seraphs sob at vermin fangs
 In human gore imbued.

Out—out are the lights—out all!
 And over each quivering form,
The curtain, a funeral pall,
 Comes down with the rush of a storm,
And the angels, all pallid and wan,
 Uprising, unveiling, affirm
That the play is the tragedy, "Man,"
 And its hero the Conqueror Worm.

"O God!" half shrieked Ligeia, leaping to her feet and extending her arms aloft with a spasmodic movement, as I made an end of these lines—"O God! O Divine Father!—shall these things be undeviatingly so?—shall this Conqueror be not once conquered? Are we not part and parcel in Thee? Who—who knoweth the mysteries of the will with its vigor? Man doth not yield him to the angels, *nor unto death utterly,* save only through the weakness of his feeble will."

And now, as if exhausted with emotion, she suffered her white arms to fall, and returned solemnly to her bed of Death. And as she breathed her last sighs, there came mingled with them a low murmur from her lips. I bent to them my ear and distinguished, again, the concluding words of the passage in Glanvill—*"Man doth not yield him to the angels, nor unto death utterly, save only through the weakness of his feeble will."*

She died;—and I, crushed into the very dust with sorrow, could no longer endure the lonely desolation of my dwelling in the dim and decaying city by the Rhine. I had no lack of what the world calls wealth. Ligeia had brought me far more, very far more than ordinarily falls to the lot of mortals. After a few months, therefore, of weary and aimless wandering, I purchased, and put in some repair, an abbey, which I shall not name, in one of the wildest and least frequented portions of fair England. The gloomy and dreary grandeur of the building, the almost savage aspect of the domain, the many melancholy and time-honored memories connected with both, had much in unison with the feelings of utter abandonment which had driven me into that remote and unsocial region of the country. Yet although the external abbey, with its verdant decay hanging about it, suffered but little alteration, I gave way, with a child-like perversity, and perchance with a faint hope of alleviating my sorrows, to a display of more than regal magnificence within.—For such follies, even in childhood, I had imbibed a taste and now they came back to me as if in the dotage of grief. Alas, I feel how much even of incipient madness might have been discovered in the gorgeous and fantastic draperies, in the solemn carvings of Egypt, in the wild cornices and furniture, in the Bedlam patterns of the carpets of tufted gold! I had become a bounden slave in the trammels of opium, and my labors and my orders had taken a coloring from my dreams. But these absurdities I must not pause to detail. Let me speak only of that one chamber, ever accursed, whither in a moment of mental alienation, I led from the altar as my bride—as the successor of the unforgotten Ligeia—the fair-haired and blue-eyed Lady Rowena Trevanion, of Tremaine.

There is no individual portion of the architecture and decoration of that bridal chamber which is not now visibly before me. Where were the souls of the haughty family of the bride, when, through thirst of gold, they permitted to pass the threshold of an apartment *so* bedecked, a maiden and a daughter so beloved? I have said that I minutely remember the details of the chamber—yet I am sadly forgetful on topics of deep moment—and here there was no system, no keeping, in the fantastic display, to take hold upon the memory. The room lay in a high turret of the castellated abbey, was pentagonal in shape, and of capacious size. Occupying the whole southern face of the pentagon was the sole window—an immense sheet of unbroken glass from Venice—a single pane, and tinted of a leaden hue, so that the rays of either the sun or moon, passing through it, fell with a ghastly lustre on the objects within. Over the upper portion of this huge window, extended the trellice-work of an aged vine, which clambered up the massy walls of the turret. The ceiling, of gloomy-looking oak, was excessively lofty, vaulted, and elaborately fretted with the wildest and most grotesque specimens of a semi-Gothic, semi-Druidical device. From out the most central recess of this melancholy vaulting, depended, by a single chain of gold with long links, a huge censer of the same metal, Saracenic in pattern, and with many perforations so contrived that there writhed in and out of them, as if endued with a serpent vitality, a continual succession of parti-colored fires.

Some few ottomans and golden candelabra, of Eastern figure, were in various stations about—and there was the couch, too—the bridal couch—of an Indian model, and low, and sculptured of solid ebony, with a pall-like canopy above. In each of the angles of the chamber stood on end a gigantic sarcophagus of black granite, from the tombs of the kings over against Luxor, with their aged lids full of immemorial sculpture. But in the draping of the apartment lay, alas! the chief phantasy of all. The lofty walls, gigantic in height—even unproportionably so—were hung from summit to foot, in vast folds, with a heavy and massive-looking tapestry—tapestry of a material which was found alike as a carpet on the floor, as a covering for the ottomans and the ebony bed, as a canopy for the bed, and as the gorgeous volutes of the curtains which partially shaded the window. The material was the richest cloth of gold. It was spotted all over, at irregular intervals, with arabesque figures, about a foot in diameter, and wrought upon the cloth in patterns of the most jetty black. But these figures partook of the true character of the arabesque only when regarded from a single point of view. By a contrivance now common, and indeed traceable to a very remote period of antiquity, they were made changeable in aspect. To one entering the room, they bore the appearance of simple monstrosities; but upon a farther advance, this appearance gradually departed; and step by step, as the visiter moved his station in the chamber, he saw himself surrounded by an endless succession of the ghastly forms which belong to the superstition of the Norman, or arise in the guilty slumbers of the monk. The phantasmagoric effect was vastly heightened by the artificial introduction of a strong continual current of wind behind the draperies—giving a hideous and uneasy animation to the whole.

In halls such as these—in a bridal chamber such as this—I passed, with the Lady of Tremaine, the unhallowed hours of the first month of our marriage—passed them with but little disquietude. That my wife dreaded the fierce moodiness of my temper—that she shunned me and loved me but little—I could not help perceiving; but it gave me rather pleasure than otherwise. I loathed her with a hatred belonging more to demon than to man. My memory flew back (oh, with what intensity of regret!) to Ligeia, the beloved, the august, the beautiful, the entombed. I revelled in recollections of her purity, of her wisdom, of her lofty, her ethereal nature, of her passionate, her idolatrous love. Now, then, did my spirit fully and freely burn with more than all the fires of her own. In the excitement of my opium dreams (for I was habitually fettered in the shackles of the drug)

I would call aloud upon her name, during the silence of the night, or among the sheltered recesses of the glens by day, as if, through the wild eagerness, the solemn passion, the consuming ardor of my longing for the departed, I could restore her to the pathway she had abandoned—ah, *could* it be forever?—upon the earth.

About the commencement of the second month of the marriage, the Lady Rowena was attacked with sudden illness, from which her recovery was slow. The fever which consumed her rendered her nights uneasy; and in her perturbed state of half-slumber, she spoke of sounds, and of motions, in and about the chamber of the turret, which I concluded had no origin save in the distemper of her fancy, or perhaps in the phantasmagoric influence of the chamber itself. She became at length convalescent—finally well. Yet but a brief period elapsed, ere a second more violent disorder again threw her upon a bed of suffering; and from this attack her frame, at all times feeble, never altogether recovered. Her illnesses were, after this epoch, of alarming character, and of more alarming recurrence, defying alike the knowledge and the great exertions of her physicians. With the increase of the chronic disease which had thus, apparently, taken too sure hold upon her constitution to be eradicated by human means, I could not fail to observe a similar increase in the nervous irritation of her temperament, and in her excitability by trivial causes of fear. She spoke again, and now more frequently and pertinaciously, of the sounds—of the slight sounds—and of the unusual motions among the tapestries, to which she had formerly alluded.

One night, near the closing in of September, she pressed this distressing subject with more than usual emphasis upon my attention. She had just awakened from an unquiet slumber, and I had been watching, with feelings half of anxiety, half of a vague terror, the workings of her emaciated countenance. I sat by the side of her ebony bed, upon one of the ottomans of India. She partly arose, and spoke, in an earnest low whisper, of sounds which she *then* heard, but which I could not hear—of motions which she *then* saw, but which I could not perceive. The wind was rushing hurriedly behind the tapestries, and I wished to show her (what, let me confess it, I could not *all* believe) that those almost inarticulate breathings, and those very gentle variations of the figures upon the wall, were but the natural effects of that customary rushing of the wind. But a deadly pallor, overspreading her face, had proved to me that my exertions to reassure her would be fruitless. She appeared to be fainting, and no attendants were within call. I remembered where was deposited a decanter of light wine which had been ordered by her physicians, and hastened across the chamber to procure it. But, as I stepped beneath the light of the censer, two circumstances of a startling nature attracted my attention. I had felt that some palpable although invisible object had passed lightly by my person; and I saw that there lay upon the golden carpet, in the very middle of the rich lustre thrown from the censer, a shadow—a faint, indefinite shadow of angelic aspect—such as might be fancied for the shadow of a shade. But I was wild with the excitement of an immoderate dose of opium, and heeded these things but little, nor spoke of them to Rowena. Having found the wine, I recrossed the chamber, and poured out a goblet-ful, which I held to the lips of the fainting lady. She had now partially recovered, however, and took the vessel herself, while I sank upon an ottoman near me, with my eyes fastened upon her person. It was then that I became distinctly aware of a gentle foot-fall upon the carpet, and near the couch; and in a second thereafter, as Rowena was in the act of raising the wine to her lips, I saw, or may have dreamed that I saw, fall within the goblet, as if from some invisible spring in the atmosphere of the room, three or four large drops of a brilliant and ruby colored fluid. If this I saw—not so Rowena. She swallowed the wine unhesitatingly, and I forbore to speak to her of a circumstance which must, after all, I considered, have been but the suggestion of a vivid imagination, rendered morbidly active by the terror of the lady, by the opium, and by the hour.

Yet I cannot conceal it from my own perception that, immediately subsequent to the fall of the ruby-drops, a rapid change for the worse took place in the disorder of my wife; so that, on the third subsequent night, the hands of her menials prepared her for the tomb, and on the fourth, I sat alone, with her shrouded body, in in that fantastic chamber which had received her as my bride.— Wild visions, opium-engendered, flitted, shadow-like, before me. I gazed with unquiet eye upon the sarcophagi in the angles of the room, upon the varying figures of the drapery, and upon the writhing of the parti-colored fires in the censer overhead. My eyes then fell, as I called to mind the circumstances of a former night, to the spot beneath the glare of the censer where I had seen the faint traces of the shadow. It was there, however, no longer; and breathing with greater freedom, I turned my glances to the pallid and rigid figure upon the bed. Then rushed upon me a thousand memories of Ligeia—and then came back upon my heart, with the turbulent violence of a flood, the whole of that unutterable wo with which I had regarded *her* thus enshrouded. The night waned; and still, with a bosom full of bitter thoughts of the one only and supremely beloved, I remained gazing upon the body of Rowena.

It might have been midnight, or perhaps earlier, or later, for I had taken no note of time, when a sob, low, gentle, but very distinct, startled me from my revery.— I *felt* that it came from the bed of ebony—the bed of death. I listened in an agony of superstitious terror—but there was no repetition of the sound. I strained my vision to detect any motion in the corpse—but there was not the slightest perceptible. Yet I could not have been deceived. I *had* heard the noise, however faint, and my soul was awakened within me. I resolutely and perseveringly kept my attention riveted upon the body. Many minutes elapsed before any circumstance occurred tending to throw light upon the mystery. At length it became evident that a slight, a very feeble, and barely noticeable tinge of color had flushed up within the cheeks, and along the sunken small veins of the eyelids. Through a species of unutterable horror and awe, for which the language of mortality has no sufficiently energetic expression, I felt my heart cease to beat, my limbs grow rigid where I sat. Yet a sense of duty finally operated to restore my self-possession. I could no longer doubt that we had been precipitate in our preparations—that Rowena still lived. It was necessary that some immediate exertion be made; yet the turret was altogether apart from the portion of the abbey tenanted by the servants—there were none within call—I had no means of summoning them to my aid without leaving the room for many minutes—and this I could not venture to do. I therefore struggled alone in my endeavors to call back the spirit still hovering. In a short period it was certain, however, that a relapse had taken place; the color disappeared from both eyelid and cheek, leaving a wanness even more than that of marble; the lips became doubly shrivelled and pinched up in the ghastly expression of death; a repulsive clamminess and coldness overspread rapidly the surface of the body; and all the usual rigorous stiffness immediately supervened. I fell back with a shudder upon the couch from which I had been so startlingly aroused, and again gave myself up to passionate waking visions of Ligeia.

An hour thus elapsed when (could it be possible?) I was a second time aware of some vague sound issuing from the region of the bed. I listened—in extremity of horror. The sound came again—it was a sigh. Rushing to the corpse, I saw—distinctly saw—a tremor upon the lips. In a minute afterward they relaxed, disclosing a bright line of the pearly teeth. Amazement now struggled in my bosom with the profound awe which had hitherto reigned there alone. I felt that my vision grew dim, that my reason wandered; and it was only by a violent effort that I at length succeeded in nerving myself to the task which duty thus once more had pointed out. There was now a partial glow upon the forehead and upon the cheek and throat; a perceptible warmth pervaded the whole frame; there was even a slight pulsation at the heart. The lady *lived;* and with redoubled ardor I betook myself to the task of restoration. I chafed and bathed the temples and the hands, and used every exertion which experience, and no little medical reading, could suggest. But in vain. Suddenly, the color fled, the pulsation ceased, the lips resumed the expression of the dead, and, in an instant afterward, the whole body took upon itself the icy chilliness, the livid hue, the intense rigidity, the sunken outline, and all the loathsome peculiarities of that which has been, for many days, a tenant of the tomb.

And again I sunk into visions of Ligeia—and again (what marvel that I shudder while I write?) *again* there reached my ears a low sob from the region of the ebony bed. But why shall I minutely detail the unspeakable horrors of that night? Why shall I pause to relate how, time after time, until near the period of the gray dawn, this hideous drama of revivification was repeated; how each terrific relapse was only into a sterner and apparently more irredeemable death; how each agony wore the aspect of a struggle with some invisible foe; and how each struggle was succeeded by I know not what of wild change in the personal appearance of the corpse? Let me hurry to a conclusion.

The greater part of the fearful night had worn away, and she who had been dead, once again stirred—and now more vigorously than hitherto, although arousing from a dissolution more appalling in its utter hopelessness than any. I had long ceased to struggle or to move, and remained sitting rigidly upon the ottoman, a helpless prey to a whirl of violent emotions, of which extreme awe was perhaps the least terrible, the least consuming. The corpse, I repeat, stirred, and now more vigorously than before. The hues of life flushed up with unwonted energy into the countenance—the limbs relaxed—and, save that the eyelids were yet pressed heavily together, and that the bandages and draperies of the grave still imparted their charnel character to the figure, I might have dreamed that Rowena had indeed shaken off, utterly, the fetters of Death. But if this idea was not, even then, altogether adopted, I could at least doubt no longer, when, arising from the bed, tottering, with feeble steps, with closed eyes, and with the manner of one bewildered in a dream, the thing that was enshrouded advanced boldly and palpably into the middle of the apartment.

I trembled not—I stirred not—for a crowd of unutterable fancies connected with the air, the stature, the demeanor of the figure, rushing hurriedly through my brain, had paralyzed—had chilled me into stone. I stirred not—but gazed upon the apparition. There was a mad disorder in my thoughts—a tumult unappeasable. Could it, indeed, be the *living* Rowena who confronted me? Could it indeed be Rowena *at all*—the fair-haired, the blue-eyed Lady Rowena Trevanion of Tremaine? Why, *why* should I doubt it? The bandage lay heavily about the mouth—but then might it not be the mouth of the breathing Lady of Tremaine? And the cheeks—there were the roses as in her noon of life—yes, these might indeed be the fair cheeks of the living Lady of Tremaine. And the chin, with its dimples, as in health, might it not be hers?—but *had she then grown taller since her malady?* What inexpressible madness seized me with that thought? One bound, and I had reached her feet! Shrinking from my touch, she let fall from her head, unloosened, the ghastly cerements which had confined it, and there streamed forth, into the rushing atmosphere of the chamber, huge masses of long and dishevelled hair; *it was blacker than the raven wings of the midnight!* And now slowly opened *the eyes* of the figure which stood before me. "Here then, at least," I shrieked aloud, "can I never—can I never be mistaken—these are the full, and the black, and the wild eyes—of my lost love—of the lady—of the LADY LIGEIA!"

1838

## THE FALL OF THE HOUSE OF USHER

Son cœur est un luth suspendu;
Sitôt qu'on le touche il résonne.
—DE BÉRANGER.

During the whole of a dull, dark, and soundless day in the autumn of the year, when the clouds hung oppressively low in the heavens, I had been passing alone, on horseback, through a singularly dreary tract of country; and at length found myself, as the shades of the evening drew on, within view of the melancholy House of Usher. I know not how it was—but, with the first glimpse of the building, a sense of insufferable gloom pervaded my spirit. I say insufferable; for the feeling was unrelieved by any of that half-pleasurable, because poetic, sentiment with which the mind usually receives even the sternest natural images of the desolate or terrible. I looked upon the scene before me—upon the mere house, and the simple landscape features of the domain, upon the bleak walls, upon the vacant eye-like windows, upon a few rank sedges, and upon a few white trunks of decayed trees—with an utter depression of soul which I can compare to no earthly sensation more properly than to the after-dream of the reveller upon opium; the bitter lapse into every-day life, the hideous dropping off of the veil. There was an iciness, a sinking, a sickening of the heart, an unredeemed dreariness of thought which no goading of the imagination could torture into aught of the sublime. What was it—I paused to think—what was it that so unnerved me in the contemplation of the House of Usher? It was a mystery all insoluble; nor could I grapple with the shadowy fancies that crowded upon me as I pondered. I was forced to fall back upon the unsatisfactory conclusion, that while, beyond doubt, there *are* combinations of very simple natural objects which have the power of thus affecting us, still the analysis of this power lies among considerations beyond our depth. It was possible, I reflected, that a mere different arrangement of the particulars of the scene, of the details of the picture, would be sufficient to modify, or perhaps to annihilate, its capacity for sorrowful impression; and, acting upon this idea, I reined my horse to the precipitous brink of a black and lurid tarn that lay in unruffled lustre by the dwelling, and gazed down—but with a shudder even more thrilling than before—upon the remodelled and inverted images of the gray sedge, and the ghastly tree-stems, and the vacant and eye-like windows.

Nevertheless, in this mansion of gloom I now proposed to myself a sojourn of some weeks. Its proprietor, Roderick Usher, had been one of my boon companions in boyhood; but many years had elapsed since our last meeting. A letter, however, had lately reached me in a distant part of the country—a letter from him—which, in its wildly importunate nature, had admitted of no other than a personal reply. The MS. gave evidence of nervous agitation. The writer spoke of acute bodily illness—of a mental disorder which oppressed him—and of an earnest desire to see me, as his best, and indeed his only personal friend, with a view of attempting, by the cheerfulness of my society, some alleviation of his malady. It was the manner in which all this, and much more, was said—it was the apparent *heart* that went with his request—which allowed me no room for hesitation; and I accordingly obeyed forthwith what I still considered a very singular summons.

Although, as boys, we had been even

intimate associates, yet I really knew little of my friend. His reserve had been always excessive and habitual. I was aware, however, that his very ancient family had been noted, time out of mind, for a peculiar sensibility of temperament, displaying itself, through long ages, in many works of exalted art, and manifested, of late, in repeated deeds of munificent yet unobtrusive charity, as well as in a passionate devotion to the intricacies, perhaps even more than to the orthodox and easily recognizable beauties, of musical science. I had learned, too, the very remarkable fact, that the stem of the Usher race, all time-honored as it was, had put forth, at no period, any enduring branch; in other words, that the entire family lay in the direct line of descent, and had always, with very trifling and very temporary variation, so lain. It was this deficiency, I considered, while running over in thought the perfect keeping of the character of the premises with the accredited character of the people, and while speculating upon the possible influence which the one, in the long lapse of centuries, might have exercised upon the other—it was this deficiency, perhaps, of collateral issue, and the consequent undeviating transmission, from sire to son, of the patrimony with the name, which had, at length, so identified the two as to merge the original title of the estate in the quaint and equivocal appellation of the "House of Usher"—an appellation which seemed to include, in the minds of the peasantry who used it, both the family and the family mansion.

I have said that the sole effect of my somewhat childish experiment—that of looking down within the tarn—had been to deepen the first singular impression. There can be no doubt that the consciousness of the rapid increase of my superstition—for why should I not so term it?—served mainly to accelerate the increase itself. Such, I have long known, is the paradoxical law of all sentiments having terror as a basis. And it might have been for this reason only, that, when I again uplifted my eyes to the house itself, from its image in the pool, there grew in my mind a strange fancy—a fancy so ridiculous, indeed, that I but mention it to show the vivid force of the sensations which oppressed me. I had so worked upon my imagination as really to believe that about the whole mansion and domain there hung an atmosphere peculiar to themselves and their immediate vicinity—an atmosphere which had no affinity with the air of heaven, but which had reeked up from the decayed trees, and the gray wall, and the silent tarn—a pestilent and mystic vapor, dull, sluggish, faintly discernible, and leaden-hued.

Shaking off from my spirit what *must* have been a dream, I scanned more narrowly the real aspect of the building. Its principal feature seemed to be that of an excessive antiquity. The discoloration of ages had been great. Minute fungi overspread the whole exterior, hanging in a fine tangled web-work from the eaves. Yet all this was apart from any extraordinary dilapidation. No portion of the masonry had fallen; and there appeared to be a wild inconsistency between its still perfect adaptation of parts, and the crumbling condition of the individual stones. In this there was much that reminded me of the specious totality of old wood-work which has rotted for long years in some neglected vault, with no disturbance from the breath of the external air. Beyond this indication of extensive decay, however, the fabric gave little token of instability. Perhaps the eye of a scrutinizing observer might have discovered a barely perceptible fissure, which, extending from the roof of the building in front, made its way down the wall in a zigzag direction, until it became lost in the sullen waters of the tarn.

Noticing these things, I rode over a short causeway to the house. A servant in waiting took my horse, and I entered the Gothic archway of the hall. A valet, of stealthy step, thence conducted me, in silence, through many dark and intricate passages in my progress to the *studio* of his master. Much that I encountered on the way contributed, I know not how, to heighten the vague sentiments of which I have already spoken. While the objects around me—while the carvings of the ceilings, the sombre tapestries of the walls, the ebon blackness of the floors, and the phantasmagoric armorial trophies which rattled as I strode, were but matters to which, or to such as which, I had been accustomed from my infancy—while I hesitated not to acknowledge how familiar was all this—I still wondered to find how unfamiliar were the fancies which ordinary images were stirring up. On one of the staircases, I met the physician of the family. His countenance, I thought, wore a mingled expression of low cunning and perplexity. He accosted me with trepidation and passed on. The valet now threw open a door and ushered me into the presence of his master.

The room in which I found myself was very large and lofty. The windows were long, narrow, and pointed, and at so vast a distance from the black oaken floor as to be altogether inaccessible from within. Feeble gleams of encrimsoned light made their way through the trellised panes, and served to render sufficiently distinct the more prominent objects around; the eye, however, struggled in vain to reach the remoter angles of the chamber, or the recesses of the vaulted and fretted ceiling. Dark draperies hung upon the walls. The general furniture was profuse, comfortless, antique, and tattered. Many books and musical instruments lay scattered about, but failed to give any vitality to the scene. I felt that I breathed an atmosphere of sorrow. An air of stern, deep, and irredeemable gloom hung over and pervaded all.

Upon my entrance, Usher arose from a sofa on which he had been lying at full length, and greeted me with a vivacious warmth which had much in it, I at first thought, of an overdone cordiality—of the constrained effort of the *ennuyé* man of the world. A glance, however, at his countenance, convinced me of his perfect sincerity. We sat down; and for some moments, while he spoke not, I gazed upon him with a feeling half of pity, half of awe. Surely, man had never before so terribly altered, in so brief a period, as had Roderick Usher! It was with difficulty that I could bring myself to admit the identity of the wan being before me with the companion of my early boyhood. Yet the character of his face had been at all times remarkable. A cadaverousness of complexion; an eye large, liquid, and luminous beyond comparison; lips somewhat thin and very pallid, but of a surpassingly beautiful curve; a nose of a delicate Hebrew model, but with a breadth of nostril unusual in similar formations; a finely moulded chin, speaking, in its want of prominence, of a want of moral energy; hair of a more than web-like softness and tenuity; these features, with an inordinate expansion above the regions of the temple, made up altogether a countenance not easily to be forgotten. And now in the mere exaggeration of the prevailing character of these features, and of the expression they were wont to convey, lay so much of change that I doubted to whom I spoke. The now ghastly pallor of the skin, and the now miraculous lustre of the eye, above all things startled and even awed me. The silken hair, too, had been suffered to grow all unheeded, and as, in its wild gossamer texture, it floated rather than fell about the face, I could not, even with effort, connect its Arabesque expression with any idea of simple humanity.

In the manner of my friend I was at once struck with an incoherence—an inconsistency; and I soon found this to arise from a series of feeble and futile struggles to overcome an habitual trepidancy—an excessive nervous agitation. For something of this nature I had indeed been prepared, no less by his letter, than by reminiscences of certain boyish traits, and by conclusions deduced from his peculiar physical conformation and temperament. His action was alternately vivacious and sullen. His voice varied rapidly from a tremulous indecision (when the animal spirits seemed utterly in abeyance) to that species of energetic concision—that abrupt, weighty, unhurried, and hollow-sounding enunciation—that leaden, self-balanced and perfectly modulated guttural utterance, which may be observed in the lost drunkard, or the irreclaimable eater of opium, during the periods of his most intense excitement.

It was thus that he spoke of the object of my visit, of his earnest desire to see me, and of the solace he expected me to afford him. He entered, at some length, into what he conceived to be the nature of his malady. It was, he said, a constitutional and a family evil, and one for which he despaired to find a remedy—a mere nervous affection, he immediately added, which would undoubtedly soon pass off. It displayed itself in a host of unnatural sensations. Some of these, as he detailed them, interested and bewildered me; although, perhaps, the terms, and the general manner of the narration had their weight. He suffered much from a morbid acuteness of the senses; the most insipid food was alone endurable; he could wear only garments of certain texture; the odors of all flowers were oppressive; his eyes were tortured by even a faint light; and there were but peculiar sounds, and these from stringed instruments, which did not inspire him with horror.

To an anomalous species of terror I found him a bounden slave. "I shall perish," said he, "I *must* perish in this deplorable folly. Thus, thus, and not otherwise, shall I be lost. I dread the events of the future, not in themselves, but in their results. I shudder at the thought of any, even the most trivial, incident, which many operate upon this intolerable agitation of soul. I have, indeed, no abhorrence of danger, except in its absolute effect—in terror. In this unnerved—in this pitiable condition—I feel that the period will sooner or later arrive when I must abandon life and reason together in some struggle with the grim phantasm, FEAR."

I learned, moreover, at intervals, and through broken and equivocal hints, another singular feature of his mental condition. He was enchained by certain superstitious impressions in regard to the dwelling which he tenanted, and whence, for many years, he had never ventured forth—in regard to an influence whose supposititious force was conveyed in terms too shadowy here to be re-stated—an influence which some peculiarities in the mere form and substance of his family mansion, had, by dint of long sufferance, he said, obtained over his spirit—an effect which the *physique* of the gray walls and turrets, and of the dim tarn into which they all looked down, had, at length, brought about upon the *morale* of his existence.

He admitted, however, although with hesitation, that much of the peculiar gloom which thus afflicted him could be traced to a more natural and far more palpable origin—to the severe and long-continued illness—indeed to the evidently approaching dissolution—of a tenderly beloved sister—his sole companion for long years—his last and only relative on earth. "Her decease," he said, with a bitterness which I can never forget, "would leave him (him the hopeless and the frail) the last of the ancient race of the Ushers." While he spoke, the lady Madeline (for so was she called) passed slowly through a remote portion of the apartment, and, without having noticed my presence, disappeared. I regarded her with an utter astonishment not unmingled with dread—and yet I found it impossible to account for such feelings. A sensation of stupor oppressed me, as my eyes followed her retreating steps. When a door, at length, closed upon her, my glance sought instinctively and eagerly the countenance of the brother—but he had buried his face in his hands, and I could only perceive that a far more than ordinary wanness had overspread the emaciated fingers through which trickled many passionate tears.

The disease of the lady Madeline had long baffled the skill of her physicians. A settled apathy, a gradual wasting away of the person, and frequent although transient affections of a partially cataleptical character, were the unusual diagnosis. Hitherto she had steadily borne up against the pressure of her malady, and had not betaken herself finally to bed; but, on the closing in of the evening of my arrival at the house, she succumbed (as her brother told me at night with inexpressible agitation) to the prostrating power of the destroyer; and I learned that the glimpse I had obtained of her person would thus probably be the last I should obtain—that the lady, at least while living, would be seen by me no more.

For several days ensuing, her name was unmentioned by either Usher or myself; and during this period I was busied in earnest endeavours to alleviate the melancholy of my friend. We painted and read together; or I listened, as if in a dream, to the wild improvisations of his speaking guitar.

And thus, as a closer and still closer intimacy admitted me more unreservedly into the recesses of his spirit, the more bitterly did I perceive the futility of all attempt at cheering a mind from which darkness, as if an inherent positive quality, poured forth upon all objects of the moral and physical universe, in one unceasing radiation of gloom.

I shall ever bear about me a memory of the many solemn hours I thus spent alone with the master of the House of Usher. Yet I should fail in any attempt to convey an idea of the exact character of the studies, or of the occupations, in which he involved me, or led me the way. An excited and highly distempered ideality threw a sulphureous lustre over all. His long improvised dirges will ring forever in my ears. Among other things, I hold painfully in mind a certain singular perversion and amplification of the wild air of the last waltz of Von Weber. From the paintings over which his elaborate fancy brooded, and which grew, touch by touch, into vaguenesses at which I shuddered the more thrillingly, because I shuddered knowing not why;—from these paintings (vivid as their images now are before me) I would in vain endeavor to educe more than a small portion which should lie within the compass of merely written words. By the utter simplicity, by the nakedness of his designs, he arrested and overawed attention. If ever mortal painted an idea, that mortal was Roderick Usher. For me at least—in the circumstances then surrounding me—there arose out of the pure abstractions which the hypochondriac contrived to throw upon his canvas, an intensity of intolerable awe, no shadow of which felt I ever yet in the contemplation of the certainly glowing yet too concrete reveries of Fuseli.

One of the phantasmagoric conceptions of my friend, partaking not so rigidly of the spirit of abstraction, may be shadowed forth, although feebly, in words. A small picture presented the interior of an immensely long and rectangular vault or tunnel, with low walls, smooth, white, and without interruption or device. Certain accessory points of the design served well to convey the idea that this excavation lay at an exceeding depth below the surface of the earth. No outlet was observed in any portion of its vast extent, and no torch, or other artificial source of light was discernible; yet a flood of intense rays rolled throughout, and bathed the whole in a ghastly and inappropriate splendor.

I have just spoken of that morbid condition of the auditory nerve which rendered all music intolerable to the sufferer, with the exception of certain effects of stringed instruments. It was, perhaps, the narrow limits to which he thus confined himself upon the guitar, which gave birth, in great measure, to the fantastic character of his performances. But the fervid *facility* of his *impromptus* could not be so accounted for. They must have been, and were, in the notes, as well as in the words of his wild fantasias (for he not unfrequently accompanied himself with rhymed verbal improvisations), the result of that intense mental collectedness and concentration to which I have previously alluded as observable only in particular moments of the highest artificial excitement. The words of one of these rhapsodies I have easily remembered. I was, perhaps, the more forcibly impressed with it, as he gave it, because, in the under or mystic current of its meaning, I fancied that I perceived, and for the first time, a full consciousness on the part of Usher, of the tottering of his lofty reason upon her throne. The verses, which were entitled "The Haunted Palace," ran very nearly, if not accurately, thus:

I

In the greenest of our valleys,
By good angels tenanted,
Once a fair and stately palace—
Radiant palace—reared its head.
In the monarch Thought's dominion—
It stood there!
Never seraph spread a pinion
Over fabric half so fair.

II

Banners yellow, glorious, golden,
On its roof did float and flow;
(This—all this—was in the olden
Time long ago)
And every gentle air that dallied,
In that sweet day,
Along the ramparts plumed and pallid,
A winged odor went away.

III

Wanderers in that happy valley
Through two luminous windows saw
Spirits moving musically
To a lute's well-tunèd law,
Round about a throne, where sitting
(Porphyrogene!)
In state his glory well befitting,
The ruler of the realm was seen.

IV

And all with pearl and ruby glowing
Was the fair palace door,
Through which came flowing, flowing, flowing
And sparkling evermore,
A troop of Echoes whose sweet duty
Was but to sing,
In voices of surpassing beauty,
The wit and wisdom of their king.

V

But evil things, in robes of sorrow,
Assailed the monarch's high estate;
(Ah, let us mourn, for never morrow
Shall dawn upon him, desolate!)
And, round about his home, the glory
That blushed and bloomed
Is but a dim-remembered story
Of the old time entombed.

VI

And travellers now within that valley,
Through the red-litten windows, see
Vast forms that move fantastically
To a discordant melody;
While, like a rapid ghastly river,
Through the pale door,
A hideous throng rush out forever,
And laugh—but smile no more.

I well remember that suggestions arising from this ballad, led us into a train of thought wherein there became manifest an opinion of Usher's which I mention not so much on account of its novelty, (for other men* have thought thus,) as on account of the pertinacity with which he maintained it. This opinion, in its general form, was that of the sentience of all vegetable things. But, in his disordered fancy, the idea had assumed a more daring character, and trespassed, under certain conditions, upon the kingdom of inorganization. I lack words to express the full extent, or the earnest *abandon* of his persuasion. The belief, however, was connected (as I have previously hinted) with the gray

*Watson, Dr. Percival, Spallanzani, and especially the Bishop of Landaff.—See "Chemical Essays," vol. v. [Author's note.]

stones of the home of his forefathers. The conditions of the sentience had been here, he imagined, fulfilled in the method of collocation of these stones —in the order of their arrangement, as well as in that of the many *fungi* which overspread them, and of the decayed trees which stood around—above all, in the long undisturbed endurance of this arrangement, and in its reduplication in the still waters of the tarn. Its evidence—the evidence of the sentience—was to be seen, he said (and I here started as he spoke), in the gradual yet certain condensation of an atmosphere of their own about the waters and the walls. The result was discoverable, he added, in that silent, yet importunate and terrible influence which for centuries had moulded the destinies of his family, and which made *him* what I now saw him—what he was. Such opinions need no comment, and I will make none.

Our books—the books which, for years, had formed no small portion of the mental existence of the invalid—were, as might be supposed, in strict keeping with this character of phantasm. We pored together over such works as the Ververt et Chartreuse of Gresset; the Belphegor of Machiavelli; the Heaven and Hell of Swedenborg; the Subterranean Voyage of Nicholas Klimm by Holberg; the Chiromancy of Robert Flud, of Jean D'Indaginé, and of De la Chambre; the Journey into the Blue Distance of Tieck; and the City of the Sun of Campanella. One favorite volume was a small octavo edition of the *Directorium Inquisitorium,* by the Dominican Eymeric de Gironne; and there were passages in Pomponius Mela, about the old African Satyrs and Œgipans, over which Usher would sit dreaming for hours. His chief delight, however, was found in the perusal of an exceedingly rare and curious book in quarto Gothic—the manual of a forgotten church—the *Vigiliae Mortuorum secundum Chorum Ecclesiae Maguntinae.*

I could not help thinking of the wild ritual of this work, and of its probable influence upon the hypochondriac, when, one evening, having informed me abruptly that the lady Madeline was no more, he stated his intention of preserving her corpse for a fortnight, (previously to its final interment), in one of the numerous vaults within the main walls of the building. The worldly reason, however, assigned for this singular proceeding, was one which I did not feel at liberty to dispute. The brother had been led to his resolution (so he told me) by consideration of the unusual character of the malady of the deceased, of certain obtrusive and eager inquiries on the part of her medical men, and of the remote and exposed situation of the burial-ground of the family. I will not deny that when I called to mind the sinister countenance of the person whom I met upon the staircase, on the day of my arrival at the house, I had no desire to oppose what I regarded as at best but a harmless, and by no means an unnatural, precaution.

At the request of Usher, I personally aided him in the arrangements for the temporary entombment. The body having been encoffined, we two alone bore it to its rest. The vault in which we placed it (and which had been so long unopened that our torches, half smothered in its oppressive atmosphere, gave us little opportunity for investigation) was small, damp, and entirely without means of admission for light; lying, at great depth, immediately beneath that portion of the building in which was my own sleeping apartment. It had been used, apparently, in remote feudal times, for the worst purposes of a donjon-keep, and, in later days, as a place of deposit for powder, or some other highly combustible substance, as a portion of its floor, and the whole interior of a long archway through which we reached it, were carefully sheathed with copper. The door, of massive iron, had been, also, similarly protected. Its immense weight caused an unusually sharp grating sound, as it moved upon its hinges.

Having deposited our mournful burden upon tressels within this region of horror, we partially turned aside the yet unscrewed lid of the coffin, and looked upon the face of the tenant. A striking similitude between the brother and sister now first arrested my attention; and Usher, divining, perhaps, my thoughts, murmured out some few words from which I learned that the deceased and himself had been twins, and that sympathies of a scarcely intelligible nature had always existed between them. Our glances, however, rested not long upon the dead—for we could not regard her unawed. The disease which had thus entombed the lady in the maturity of youth, had left, as usual in all maladies of a strictly cataleptical character, the mockery of a faint blush upon the bosom and the face, and that suspiciously lingering smile upon the lip which is so terrible in death. We replaced and screwed down the lid, and, having secured the door of iron, made our way, with toil, into the scarcely less gloomy apartments of the upper portion of the house.

And now, some days of bitter grief having elapsed, an observable change came over the features of the mental disorder of my friend. His ordinary manner had vanished. His ordinary occupations were neglected or forgotten. He roamed from chamber to chamber with hurried, unequal, and objectless step. The pallor of his countenance had assumed, if possible, a more ghastly hue—but the luminousness of his eye had utterly gone out. The once occasional huskiness of his tone was heard no more; and a tremulous quaver, as if of extreme terror, habitually characterized his utterance. There were times, indeed, when I thought his unceasingly agitated mind was laboring with some oppressive secret, to divulge which he struggled for the necessary courage. At times, again, I was obliged to resolve all into the mere inexplicable vagaries of madness, for I beheld him gazing upon vacancy for long hours, in an attitude of the profoundest attention, as if listening to some imaginary sound. It was no wonder that his condition terrified—that it infected me. I felt creeping upon me, by slow yet certain degrees, the wild influences of his own fantastic yet impressive superstitions.

It was, especially, upon retiring to bed late in the night of the seventh or eighth day after the placing of the lady Madeline within the donjon, that I experienced the full power of such feelings. Sleep came not near my couch—while the hours waned and waned away. I struggled to reason off the nervousness which had dominion over me. I endeavored to believe that much, if not all of what I felt, was due to the bewildering influence of the gloomy furniture of the room—of the dark and tattered draperies, which, tortured into motion by the breath of a rising tempest, swayed fitfully to and fro upon the walls, and rustled uneasily about the decorations of the bed. But my efforts were fruitless. An irrepressible tremor gradually pervaded my frame; and, at length, there sat upon my very heart an incubus of utterly causeless alarm. Shaking this off with a gasp and a struggle, I uplifted myself upon the pillows, and, peering earnestly within the intense darkness of the chamber, hearkened—I know not why, except that an instinctive spirit prompted me—to certain low and indefinite sounds which came, through the pauses of the storm, at long intervals, I knew not whence. Overpowered by an intense sentiment of horror, unaccountable yet unendurable, I threw on my clothes with haste (for I felt that I should sleep no more during the night), and endeavored to arouse myself from the pitiable condition into which I had fallen, by pacing rapidly to and fro through the apartment.

I had taken but few turns in this manner, when a light step on an adjoining staircase arrested my attention. I presently recognized it as that of Usher. In an instant afterward he rapped, with a gentle touch, at my door, and entered, bearing a lamp. His countenance was, as usual, cadaverously wan—but, moreover, there was a species of mad hilarity in his eyes—an evidently restrained *hysteria* in his whole demeanor. His air appalled me—but anything was preferable to the solitude which I had so long endured, and I even welcomed his presence as a relief.

"And you have not seen it?" he said abruptly, after having stared about him for some moments in silence—"you have not then seen it?—but, stay! you shall." Thus speaking, and having carefully shaded his lamp, he hurried to one of the casements, and threw it freely open to the storm.

The impetuous fury of the entering gust nearly lifted us from our feet. It was, indeed, a tempestuous yet sternly beautiful night, and one wildly singular in its terror and its beauty. A whirlwind had apparently collected its force in our vicinity; for there were frequent and violent alterations in the direction of the wind; and the exceeding density of the clouds (which hung so low as to press upon the turrets of the house) did not prevent our perceiving the life-like velocity with which they flew careering from all points against each other, without passing away into the distance. I say that even their exceeding density did not prevent our perceiving this—yet we had no glimpse of the moon or stars—nor was there any flashing forth of the lightning. But the under surfaces of the huge masses of agitated vapor, as well as all terrestrial objects immediately around us, were glowing in the unnatural light of a faintly luminous and distinctly visible gaseous exhalation which hung about and enshrouded the mansion.

"You must not—you shall not behold this!" said I, shudderingly, to Usher, as I led him, with a gentle violence, from the window to a seat. "These appearances, which bewilder you, are merely electrical phenomena not uncommon—or it may be that they have their ghastly origin in the rank miasma of the tarn. Let us close this casement;—the air is chilling and dangerous to your frame. Here is one of your favorite romances. I will read, and you shall listen;—and so we will pass away this terrible night together."

The antique volume which I had taken up was the "Mad Trist" of Sir Launcelot Canning; but I had called it a favorite of Usher's more in sad jest than in earnest; for, in truth, there is little in its uncouth and unimaginative prolixity which could have had interest for the lofty and spiritual ideality of my friend. It was, however, the only book immediately at hand; and I indulged a vague hope that the excitement which now agitated the hypochondriac, might find relief (for the history of mental disorder is full of similar anomalies) even in the extremeness of the folly which I should read. Could I have judged, indeed, by the wild overstrained air of vivacity with which he hearkened, or apparently hearkened, to the words of the tale, I might well have congratulated myself upon the success of my design.

I had arrived at that well-known portion of the story where Ethelred, the hero of the Trist, having sought in vain for peaceable admission into the dwelling of the hermit, proceeds to make good an entrance by force. Here, it will be remembered, the words of the narrative run thus:

"And Ethelred, who was by nature of a doughty heart, and who was now mighty withal, on account of the powerfulness of the wine which he had drunken, waited no longer to hold parley with the hermit, who, in sooth, was of an obstinate and maliceful turn, but, feeling the rain upon his shoulders, and fearing the rising of the tempest, uplifted his mace outright, and, with blows, made quickly room in the plankings of the door for his gauntleted hand; and now pulling therewith sturdily, he so cracked, and ripped, and tore all asunder, that the noise of the dry and hollow-sounding wood alarummed and reverberated throughout the forest."

At the termination of this sentence I started, and for a moment, paused; for it appeared to me (although I at once concluded that my excited fancy had deceived me)—it appeared to me that, from some very remote portion of the mansion, there came, indistinctly, to my ears, what might have been, in its exact similarity of character, the echo (but a stifled and dull one certainly) of the very cracking and ripping sound which Sir Launcelot had so particularly described. It was, beyond doubt, the coincidence alone which had arrested my attention; for, amid the rattling of the sashes of the casements, and the ordinary commingled noises of the still increasing storm, the sound, in itself, had nothing, surely, which should have interested or disturbed me. I continued the story:

"But the good champion Ethelred, now entering within the door, was sore enraged and amazed to perceive no signal of the maliceful hermit; but, in the stead thereof, a dragon of a scaly and prodigious demeanor, and of a fiery tongue, which sate in guard before a palace of gold, with a floor of silver; and upon the wall there hung a shield of shining brass with this legend enwritten—

Who entereth herein, a conqueror hath bin;
Who slayeth the dragon, the shield he shall win.

And Ethelred uplifted his mace, and struck upon the head of the dragon, which fell before him, and gave up his pesty breath, with a shriek so horrid and harsh, and withal so piercing, that Ethelred had fain to close his ears with his hands against the dreadful noise of it, the like whereof was never before heard."

Here again I paused abruptly, and now with a feeling of wild amazement—for there could be no doubt whatever that, in this instance, I did actually hear (although from what direction it proceeded I found it impossible to say) a low and apparently distant, but harsh, protracted, and most unusual screaming or grating sound—the exact counterpart of what my fancy had already conjured up for the dragon's unnatural shriek as described by the romancer.

Oppressed, as I certainly was, upon the occurrence of the second and most extraordinary coincidence, by a thousand conflicting sensations, in which wonder and extreme terror were predominant, I still retained sufficient presence of mind to avoid exciting, by any observation, the sensitive nervousness of my companion. I was by no means certain that he had noticed the sounds in question; although, assuredly, a strange alteration had, during the last few minutes, taken place in his demeanor. From a position fronting my own, he had gradually brought round his chair, so as to sit with his face to the door of the chamber; and thus I could but partially perceive his features, although I saw that his lips trembled as if he were murmuring inaudibly. His head had dropped upon his breast—yet I knew that he was not asleep, from the wide and rigid opening of the eye as I caught a glance of it in profile. The motion of his body, too, was at variance with this idea—for he rocked from side to side with a gentle yet constant and uniform sway. Having rapidly taken notice of all this, I resumed the narrative of Sir Launcelot, which thus proceeded:

"And now, the champion, having escaped from the terrible fury of the dragon, bethinking himself of the brazen shield, and of the breaking up of the enchantment which was upon it, removed the carcass from out of the way before him, and approached valorously over the silver pavement of the castle to where the shield was upon the wall; which in sooth tarried not for his full coming, but fell down at his feet upon the silver floor, with a mighty great and terrible ringing sound."

No sooner had these syllables passed my lips, than—as if a shield of brass had indeed, at the moment, fallen heavily upon a floor of silver—I became aware of a distinct, hollow, metallic, and clangorous, yet apparently muffled reverberation. Completely unnerved, I leaped to my feet; but the measured rocking movement of Usher was undisturbed. I rushed to the chair in which he sat. His eyes were bent fixedly before him, and throughout his whole countenance there reigned a stony rigidity. But, as I placed my hand upon his shoulder, there came a strong shudder over his whole person; a sickly smile quivered about his lips; and I saw that he spoke in a low, hurried, and gibbering murmur, as if unconscious of my presence. Bending closely over him, I at length drank in the hideous import of his words.

"Not hear it?—yes, I hear it, and *have* heard it. Long—long—long—many minutes, many hours, many days, have I heard it—yet I dared not—oh, pity me, miserable wretch that I am!—I dared not—I *dared* not speak! *We have put her living in the tomb!* Said I not that my senses were acute? I *now* tell you that I heard her first feeble movements in the hollow coffin. I heard them—many, many days ago—yet I dared not—*I dared not speak!* And now—to-night—Ethelred—ha! ha!—the breaking of the hermit's door, and the death-cry of the dragon, and the clangor of the shield!—say, rather, the rending of her coffin, and the grating of the iron hinges of her prison, and her struggles within the coppered archway of the vault! Oh whither shall I fly? Will she not be here anon? Is she not hurrying to upbraid me for my haste? Have I not heard her footstep on the stair? Do I not distinguish that heavy and horrible beating of her heart? Madman!" here he sprang furiously to his feet, and shrieked out his syllables, as if in the effort he were giving up his soul—*"Madman! I tell you that she now stands without the door!"*

As if in the superhuman energy of his utterance there had been found the potency of a spell—the huge antique panels to which the speaker pointed, threw slowly back, upon the instant, their ponderous and ebony jaws. It was the work of the rushing gust—but then without those doors there *did* stand the lofty and enshrouded figure of the lady Madeline of Usher. There was blood upon her white robes, and the evidence of some bitter struggle upon every portion of her emaciated frame. For a moment she remained trembling and reeling to and fro upon the threshold, then, with a low moaning cry, fell heavily inward upon the person of her brother, and in her violent and now final death-agonies, bore him to the floor a corpse, and a victim to the terrors he had anticipated.

From that chamber, and from that mansion, I fled aghast. The storm was still abroad in all its wrath as I found myself crossing the old causeway. Suddenly there shot along the path a wild light, and I turned to see whence a gleam so unusual could have issued; for the vast house and its shadows were alone behind me. The radiance was that of the full, setting, and blood-red moon which now shone vividly through that once barely-discernible fissure of which I have before spoken as extending from the roof of the building, in a zigzag direction, to the base. While I gazed, this fissure rapidly widened—there came a fierce breath of the whirlwind—the entire orb of the satellite burst at once upon my sight—my brain reeled as I saw the mighty walls rushing asunder—there was a long tumultuous shouting sound like the voice of a thousand waters—and the deep and dank tarn at my feet closed sullenly and silently over the fragments of the *"House of Usher."*

1839

# THE MURDERS IN THE RUE MORGUE

> What song the Syrens sang, or what name Achilles assumed when he hid himself among women, although puzzling questions, are not beyond *all* conjecture.
>
> —Sir Thomas Browne.

The mental features discoursed of as the analytical, are in themselves, but little susceptible of analysis. We appreciate them only in their effects. We know of them, among other things, that they are always to their possessor, when inordinately possessed, a source of the liveliest enjoyment. As the strong man exults in his physical ability, delighting in such exercises as call his muscles into action, so glories the analyst in that moral activity which *disentangles.* He derives pleasure from even the most trivial occupations bringing his talents into play. He is fond of enigmas, of conundrums, of hieroglyphics; exhibiting in his solutions of each a degree of *acumen* which appears to the ordinary apprehension præternatural. His results, brought about by the very soul and essence of method, have, in truth, the whole air of intuition.

The faculty of re-solution is possibly much invigorated by mathematical study, and especially by that highest branch of it which, unjustly, and merely on account of its retrograde operations, has been called, as if *par excellence,* analysis. Yet to calculate is not in itself to analyze. A chess-player, for example, does the one without effort at the other. It follows that the game of chess, in its effects upon mental character, is greatly misunderstood. I am not now writing a treatise, but simply prefacing a somewhat peculiar narrative by observations very much at random; I will, therefore, take occasion to assert that the higher powers of the reflective intellect are more decidedly and more usefully tasked by the unostentatious game of draughts than by all the elaborate frivolity of chess. In this latter, where the pieces have different and *bizarre* motions, with various and variable values, what is only complex is mistaken (a not unusual error) for what is profound. The *attention* is here called powerfully into play. If it flag for an instant, an oversight is committed, resulting in injury or defeat. The possible moves being not only manifold but involute, the chances of such oversights are multiplied; and in nine cases out of ten it is the more concentrative rather than the more acute player who conquers. In draughts, on the contrary, where the moves are *unique* and have but little variation, the probabilities of inadvertence are diminished, and the mere attention being left comparatively unemployed, what advantages are obtained by either party are obtained by superior *acumen.* To be less abstract—Let us suppose a game of draughts where the pieces are reduced to four kings, and where, of course, no oversight is to be expected. It is obvious that here the victory can be decided (the players being at all equal) only by some *recherché* movement, the result of some strong exertion of the intellect. Deprived of ordinary resources, the analyst throws himself into the spirit of his opponent, identifies himself therewith, and not unfrequently sees thus, at a glance, the sole methods (sometimes indeed absurdly simple ones) by which he may seduce into error or hurry into miscalculation.

Whist has long been noted for its influence upon what is termed the calculating power; and men of the highest order of intellect have been known to take an apparently unaccountable delight in it, while eschewing chess as frivolous. Beyond doubt there is nothing of a similar nature so greatly tasking the faculty of analysis. The best chess-player in Christendom *may* be little more than the best player of chess; but proficiency in whist implies capacity for success in all these more important undertakings where mind struggles with mind. When I say proficiency, I mean that perfection in the game which includes a comprehension of *all* the sources whence legitimate advantage may be derived. These are not only manifold but multiform, and lie frequently among recesses of thought altogether inaccessible to the ordinary understanding. To observe attentively is to remember distinctly; and, so far, the concentrative chess-player will do very well at whist; while the rules of Hoyle (themselves based upon the mere mechanism of the game) are sufficiently and generally comprehensible. Thus to have a retentive memory, and to proceed by "the book," are points commonly regarded as the sum total of good playing. But it is in matters beyond the limits of mere rule that the skill of the analyst is evinced. He makes, in silence, a host of observations and inferences. So, perhaps, do his companions; and the difference in the extent of the information obtained, lies not so much in the validity of the inference as in the quality of the observation. The necessary knowledge is that of *what* to observe. Our player confines himself not at all; nor, because the game is the object, does he reject deductions from things external to the game. He examines the countenance of his partner, comparing it carefully with that of each of his opponents. He considers the mode of assorting the cards in each hand; often counting trump by trump, and honor by honor, through the glances bestowed by their holders upon each. He notes every variation of face as the play progresses, gathering a fund of thought from the differences in the expression of certainty, of surprise, of triumph, or of chagrin. From the manner of gathering up a trick he judges whether the person taking it can make another in the suit. He recognises what is played through feint, by the air with which it is thrown upon the table. A casual or inadvertent word; the accidental dropping or turning of a card, with the accompanying anxiety or carelessness in regard to its concealment; the counting of the tricks, with the order of their arrangement; embarrassment, hesitation, eagerness or trepidation—all afford, to his apparently intuitive perception, indications of the true state of affairs. The first two or three rounds having been played, he is in full possession of the contents of each hand, and thenceforward puts down his cards with as absolute a precision of purpose as if the rest of the party had turned outward the faces of their own.

The analytical power should not be confounded with simple ingenuity; for while the analyst is necessarily ingenious, the ingenious man is often remarkably incapable of analysis. The constructive or combining power, by which ingenuity is usually manifested, and to which the phrenologists (I believe erroneously) have assigned a separate organ, supposing it a primitive faculty, has been so frequently seen in those whose intellect bordered otherwise upon idiocy, as to have attracted general observation among writers on morals. Between ingenuity and the analytic ability there exists a difference far greater, indeed, than between the fancy and the imagination, but of a character very strictly analogous. It will be found, in fact, that the ingenious are always fanciful, and the *truly* imaginative never otherwise than analytic.

The narrative which follows will appear to the reader somewhat in the light of a commentary upon the propositions just advanced.

Residing in Paris during the spring and part of the summer of 18—, I there became acquainted with a Monsieur C. Auguste Dupin. This young gentleman was of an excellent—indeed of an illustrious family, but, by a variety of untoward events, had been reduced to such poverty that the energy of his character succumbed beneath it, and he ceased to bestir himself in the world, or to care for the retrieval of his fortunes. By courtesy of his creditors, there still remained in his possession a small remnant of his patrimony; and, upon the income arising from this, he managed, by means of a rigorous economy, to procure the necessaries of life, without troubling himself about its superfluities. Books, indeed, were his sole luxuries, and in Paris these are easily obtained.

Our first meeting was at an obscure library in the Rue Montmartre, where the accident of our both being in search of the same very rare and very remarkable volume, brought us into closer communion. We saw each other again and again. I was deeply interested in the little family history which he detailed to me with all that candor which a Frenchman indulges whenever mere self is his theme. I was astonished, too, at the vast extent of his reading; and, above all, I felt my soul enkindled within me by the wild fervor, and the vivid freshness of his imagination. Seeking in Paris the objects I then sought, I felt that the society of such a man would be to me a treasure beyond price; and this feeling I frankly confided to him. It was at length arranged that we should live together during my stay in the city; and as my worldly circumstances were somewhat less embarrassed than his own, I was permitted to be at the expense of renting, and furnishing in a style which suited the rather fantastic gloom of our common temper, a time-eaten and grotesque mansion, long deserted through superstitions into which we did not inquire, and tottering to its fall in a retired and desolate portion of the Faubourg St. Germain.

Had the routine of our life at this place been known to the world, we should have been regarded as madmen—although, perhaps, as madmen of a harmless nature. Our seclusion was perfect. We admitted no visitors. Indeed the locality of our retirement had been carefully kept a secret from my own former associates; and it had been many years since Dupin had ceased to know or be known in Paris. We existed within ourselves alone.

It was a freak of fancy in my friend (for what else shall I call it?) to be enamored of the Night for her own sake; and into this *bizarrerie,* as into all his others, I quietly fell, giving myself up to his wild whims with a perfect *abandon.* The sable divinity would not herself dwell with us always; but we could counterfeit her presence. At the first dawn of the morning we closed all the massy shutters of our old building; lighting a couple of tapers which, strongly perfumed, threw out only the ghastliest and feeblest of rays. By the aid of these we then busied our souls in dreams—reading, writing, or conversing, until warned by the clock of the advent of the true Darkness. Then we sallied forth into the streets, arm and arm, continuing the topics of the day, or roaming far and wide until a late hour, seeking, amid the wild lights and shadows of the populous city, that infinity of mental excitement which quiet observation can afford.

At such times I could not help remarking and admiring (although from his rich ideality I had been prepared to expect it) a peculiar analytic ability in Dupin. He seemed, too, to take an eager delight in its exercise—if not exactly in its display—and did not hesitate to confess the pleasure thus derived. He boasted to me, with a low chuckling laugh, that most men, in respect to himself, wore windows in their bosoms, and was wont to follow up such assertions by direct and very startling proofs of his intimate knowledge of my own. His manner at these moments was frigid and abstract; his eyes were vacant in expression; while his voice, usually a rich tenor, rose into a treble which would have sounded petulantly but for the deliberateness and entire distinctness of the enunciation. Observing him in these moods, I often dwelt meditatively upon the old philosophy of the Bi-Part Soul, and amused myself with the fancy of a double Dupin—the creative and the resolvent.

Let it not be supposed, from what I have just said, that I am detailing any mystery, or penning any romance. What I have described in the Frenchman, was merely the result of an excited, or perhaps of a diseased intelligence. But of the character of his remarks at the periods in question an example will best convey the idea.

We were strolling one night down a long dirty street, in the vicinity of the Palais Royal. Being both, apparently, occupied with thought, neither of us had spoken a syllable for fifteen minutes at least. All at once Dupin broke forth with these words:—

"He is a very little fellow, that's true, and would do better for the *Théâtre des Variétés.*"

"There can be no doubt of that," I replied unwittingly, and not at first observing (so much had I been absorbed in reflection) the extraordinary manner in which the speaker had chimed in with my meditations. In an instant afterward I recollected myself, and my astonishment was profound.

"Dupin," said I, gravely, "this is beyond my comprehension. I do not hesitate to say that I am amazed, and can scarcely credit my senses. How was it possible you should know I was thinking of ——?" Here I paused, to ascertain beyond a doubt whether he really knew of whom I thought.

—— "of Chantilly," said he, "why do you pause? You were remarking to yourself that his diminutive figure unfitted him for tragedy."

This was precisely what had formed the subject of my reflections. Chantilly was a *quondam* cobbler of the Rue St. Denis, who, becoming stage-mad, had attempted the *rôle* of Xerxes, in Crébillon's tragedy so called, and been notoriously Pasquinaded for his pains.

"Tell me, for Heaven's sake," I exclaimed, "the method—if method there is—by which you have been enabled to fathom my soul in this matter." In fact I was even more startled than I would have been willing to express.

"It was the fruiterer," replied my friend, "who brought you to the conclusion that the mender of soles was not of sufficient height for Xerxes *et id genus omne*."

"The fruiterer!—you astonish me—I know no fruiterer whomsoever."

"The man who ran up against you as we entered the street—it may have been fifteen minutes ago."

I now remembered that, in fact, a fruiterer, carrying upon his head a large basket of apples, had nearly thrown me down, by accident, as we passed from the Rue C——— into the thoroughfare where we stood; but what this had to do with Chantilly I could not possibly understand.

There was not a particle of *charlatanerie* about Dupin. "I will explain," he said, "and that you may comprehend all clearly, we will first retrace the course of your meditations, from the moment in which I spoke to you until that of the *rencontre* with the fruiterer in question. The larger links of the chain run thus—Chantilly, Orion, Dr. Nichols, Epicurus, Stereotomy, the street stones, the fruiterer."

There are few persons who have not, at some period of their lives, amused themselves in retracing the steps by which particular conclusions of their own minds have been attained. The occupation is often full of interest; and he who attempts it for the first time is astonished by the apparently illimitable distance and incoherence between the starting-point and the goal. What, then, must have been my amazement when I heard the Frenchman speak what he had just spoken, and when I could not help acknowledging that he had spoken the truth. He continued:

"We had been talking of horses, if I remember aright, just before leaving the Rue C———. This was the last subject we discussed. As we crossed into this street, a fruiterer, with a large basket upon his head, brushing quickly past us, thrust you upon a pile of paving-stones collected at a spot where the causeway is undergoing repair. You stepped upon one of the loose fragments, slipped, slightly strained your ankle, appeared vexed or sulky, muttered a few words, turned to look at the pile, and then proceeded in silence. I was not particularly attentive to what you did; but observation has become with me, of late, a species of necessity.

"You kept your eyes upon the ground—glancing, with a petulant expression, at the holes and ruts in the pavement (so that I saw you were still thinking of the stones), until we reached the little alley called Lamartine, which has been paved, by way of experiment, with the overlapping and riveted blocks. Here your countenance brightened up, and, perceiving your lips move, I could not doubt that you murmured the word 'stereotomy,' a term very affectedly applied to this species of pavement. I knew that you could not say to yourself 'stereotomy' without being brought to think of atomies, and thus of the theories of Epicurus; and since, when we discussed this subject not very long ago, I mentioned to you how singularly, yet with how little notice, the vague guesses of that noble Greek had met with confirmation in the late nebular cosmogony, I felt that you could not avoid casting your eyes upward to the great *nebula* in Orion, and I certainly expected that you would do so. You did look up; and I was now assured that I had correctly followed your steps. But in that bitter *tirade* upon Chantilly, which appeared in yesterday's *Musée,* the satirist, making some disgraceful allusions to the cobbler's change of name upon assuming the buskin, quoted a Latin line about which we have often conversed. I mean the line

Perdidit antiquum litera prima sonum.

I had told you that this was in reference to Orion, formerly written Urion; and, from certain pungencies connected with this explanation, I was aware that you could not have forgotten it. It was clear, therefore, that you would not fail to combine the two ideas of Orion and Chantilly. That you did combine them I saw by the character of the smile which passed over your lips. You thought of the poor cobbler's immolation. So far, you had been stooping in your gait; but now I saw you draw yourself up to your full height. I was then sure that you reflected upon the diminutive figure of Chantilly. At this point I interrupted your meditations to remark that as, in fact, he *was* a very little fellow—that Chantilly—he would do better at the *Théâtre des Variétés.*"

Not long after this, we were looking over an evening edition of the "Gazette des Tribunaux," when the following paragraphs arrested our attention.

"EXTRAORDINARY MURDERS.—This morning, about three o'clock, the inhabitants of the Quartier St. Roch were aroused from sleep by a succession of terrific shrieks, issuing, apparently from the fourth story of a house in the Rue Morgue, known to be in the sole occupancy of one Madame L'Espanaye, and her daughter, Mademoiselle Camille L'Espanaye. After some delay, occasioned by a fruitless attempt to procure admission in the usual manner, the gateway was broken in with a crowbar, and eight or ten of the neighbors entered, accompanied by two *gendarmes.* By this time the cries had ceased; but as the party rushed up the first flight of stairs, two or more rough voices, in angry contention, were distinguished, and seemed to proceed from the upper part of the house. As the second landing was reached, these sounds, also, had ceased, and everything remained perfectly quiet. The party spread themselves, and hurried from room to room. Upon arriving at a large back chamber in the fourth story (the door of which, being found locked, with the key inside, was forced open), a spectacle presented itself which struck every one present not less with horror than with astonishment.

"The apartment was in the wildest disorder—the furniture broken and thrown about in all directions. There was only one bedstead; and from this the bed had been removed, and thrown into the middle of the floor. On a chair lay a razor, besmeared with blood. Upon the hearth were two or three long and thick tresses of grey human hair, also dabbled in blood, and seeming to have been pulled out by the roots. On the floor were found four Napoleons, an ear-ring of topaz, three large silver spoons, three smaller of *métal d'Alger,* and two bags, containing nearly four thousand francs in gold. The drawers of a *bureau,* which stood in one corner, were open, and had been, apparently, rifled, although many articles still remained in them. A small iron safe was discovered under the *bed* (not under the bedstead). It was open, with the key still in the door. It had no contents beyond a few old letters, and other papers of little consequence.

"Of Madame L'Espanaye no traces were here seen; but an unusual quantity of soot being observed in the fire-place, a search was made in the chimney, and (horrible to relate!) the corpse of the daughter, head downward, was dragged therefrom; it having been thus forced up the narrow aperture for a considerable distance. The body was quite warm. Upon examining it, many excoriations were perceived, no doubt occasioned by the violence with which it had been thrust up and disengaged. Upon the face were many severe scratches, and, upon the throat, dark bruises, and deep indentations of finger nails, as if the deceased had been throttled to death.

"After a thorough investigation of every portion of the house, without farther discovery, the party made its way into a small paved yard in the rear of the building, where lay the corpse of the old lady, with her throat so entirely cut that, upon an attempt to raise her, the head fell off. The body, as well as the head, was fearfully mutilated—the former so much so as scarcely to retain any semblance of humanity.

"To this horrible mystery there is not as yet, we believe, the slightest clew."

The next day's paper had these additional particulars.

"*The Tragedy in the Rue Morgue.* Many individuals have been examined in relation to this most extraordinary and frightful affair," [The word '*affaire*' has not yet, in France, that levity of import which it conveys with us] "but nothing whatever has transpired to throw light upon it. We give below all the material testimony elicited.

"*Pauline Dubourg,* laundress, deposes that she has known both the deceased for three years, having washed for them during that period. The old lady and her daughter seemed on good terms—very affectionate towards each other. They were excellent pay. Could not speak in regard to their mode or means of living. Believed that Madame L. told fortunes for a living. Was reputed to have money put by. Never met any persons in the house when she called for the clothes or took them home. Was sure that they had no servant in employ. There appeared to be no furniture in any part of the building except in the fourth story.

"*Pierre Moreau,* tobacconist, deposes that he has been in the habit of selling small quantities of tobacco and snuff to Madame L'Espanaye for nearly four years. Was born in the neighborhood, and has always resided there. The deceased and her daughter had occupied the house in which the corpses were found, for more than six years. It was formerly occupied by a jeweller, who under-let the upper rooms to various persons. The house was the property of Madame L. She became dissatisfied with the abuse of the premises by her tenant, and moved into them herself, refusing to let any portion. The old lady was childish. Witness had seen the daughter some five or six times during the six years. The two lived an exceedingly retired life—were reputed to have money. Had heard it said among the neighbors that Madame L. told fortunes—did not believe it. Had never seen any person enter the door except the old lady and her daughter, a porter once or twice, and a physician some eight or ten times.

" Many other persons, neighbors, gave evidence to the same effect. No one was spoken of as frequenting the house. It was not known whether there were any living connexions of Madame L. and her daughter. The shutters of the front windows were seldom opened. Those in the rear were always closed, with the exception of the large back room, fourth story. The house was a good house—not very old.

"*Isidore Musèt, gendarme,* deposes that he was called to the house about three o'clock in the morning, and found some twenty or thirty persons at the gateway, endeavoring to gain admittance. Forced it open, at length, with a bayonet—not with a crowbar. Had but little difficulty in getting it open, on account of its being a double or folding gate, and bolted neither at bottom nor top. The shrieks were continued until the gate was forced—and then suddenly ceased. They seemed to be screams of some person (or persons) in great agony—were loud and drawn out, not short and quick. Witness led the way up stairs. Upon reaching the first landing, heard two voices in loud and angry contention—the one a gruff voice, the other much shriller—a very strange voice. Could distinguish some words of the former, which was that of a Frenchman. Was positive that it was not a woman's voice. Could distinguish the words '*sacré*' and '*diable*.' The shrill voice was that of a foreigner. Could not be sure whether it was the voice of a man or of a woman. Could not make out what was said, but believed the language to be Spanish. The state of the room and of the bodies was described by this witness as we described them yesterday.

"*Henri Duval,* a neighbor, and by trade a silver-smith, deposes that he was one of the party who first entered the house. Corroborates the testimony of Musèt in general. As soon as they forced an entrance, they reclosed the door to keep out the crowd, which collected very fast, notwithstanding the lateness of the hour. The shrill voice this witness thinks, was that of an Italian. Was certain it was not French. Could not be sure that it was a man's voice. It might have been a woman's. Was not acquainted with the Italian language. Could not distinguish the words, but was convinced by the intonation that the speaker was an Italian. Knew Madame L. and her daughter. Had conversed with both frequently. Was sure that the shrill voice was not that of either of the deceased.

"——— *Odenheimer, restaurateur.* This witness volunteered his testimony. Not speaking French, was examined through an interpreter. Is a native of Amsterdam. Was passing the house at the time of the shrieks. They lasted for several minutes—probably ten. They were long and loud—very awful and distressing. Was one of those who entered the building. Corroborated the previous evidence in every respect but one. Was sure that the shrill voice was that of a man—of a Frenchman. Could not distinguish the words uttered. They were loud and quick—unequal—spoken apparently in fear as well as in anger. The voice was harsh—not so much shrill as harsh. Could not call it a shrill voice. The gruff voice said repeatedly '*sacré*,' '*diable*' and once '*mon Dieu.*'

"*Jules Mignaud,* banker, of the firm of Mignaud et Fils, Rue Deloraine. Is the elder Mignaud. Madame L'Espanaye had some property. Had opened an account with his banking house in the spring of the year —— (eight years previously). Made frequent deposits in small sums. Had checked for nothing until the third day before her death, when she took out in person the sum of 4000 francs. This sum was paid in gold, and a clerk sent home with the money.

"*Adolphe Le Bon,* clerk to Mignaud et Fils, deposes that on the day in question, about noon, he accompanied Madame L'Espanaye to her residence with the 4000 francs, put up in two bags. Upon the door being opened, Madamoiselle L. appeared and took from his hands one of the bags, while the old lady relieved him of the other. He then bowed and departed. Did not see any person in the street at the time. It is a bye-street—very lonely.

"*William Bird,* tailor, deposes that he was one of the party who entered the house. Is an Englishman. Has lived in Paris two years. Was one of the first to ascend the stairs. Heard the voices in contention. The gruff voice was that of a Frenchman. Could make out several words, but cannot now remember all. Heard distinctly '*sacré*' and '*mon Dieu.*' There was a sound at the moment as if of several persons struggling—a scraping and scuffling sound. The shrill voice was very loud—louder than the gruff one. Is sure that it was not the voice of an Englishman. Appeared to be that of a German. Might have been a woman's voice. Does not understand German.

"Four of the above-named witnesses, being recalled, deposed that the door of the chamber in which was found the body of Mademoiselle L. was locked on the inside when the party reached it. Everything was perfectly silent—no groans or noises of any kind. Upon forcing the door no person was seen. The windows, both of the back and front room, were down and firmly fastened from within. A door between the two rooms was closed, but not locked. The door leading from the front room into the passage was locked, with the key on the inside. A small room in the front of the house, on the fourth story, at the head of the passage, was open, the door being ajar. This room was crowded with old beds, boxes, and so forth. These were carefully removed and searched. There was not an inch of any portion of the house which was not carefully searched. Sweeps were sent up and down the chimneys. The house was a four story one, with garrets (*mansardes*). A trap-door on the roof was nailed down very securely—did not appear to have been opened for years. The time elapsing between the hearing of the voices in contention and the breaking open of the room door, was variously stated by the witnesses. Some made it as short as three minutes—some as long as five. The door was opened with difficulty.

"*Alfonzo Garcio*, undertaker, deposes that he resides in the Rue Morgue. Is a native of Spain. Was one of the party who entered the house. Did not proceed up stairs. Is nervous, and was apprehensive of the consequences of agitation. Heard the voices in contention. The gruff voice was that of a Frenchman. Could not distinguish what was said. The shrill voice was that of an Englishman—is sure of this. Does not understand the English language, but judges by the intonation.

"*Alberto Montani*, confectioner, deposes that he was among the first to ascend the stairs. Heard the voices in question. The gruff voice was that of a Frenchman. Distinguished several words. The speaker appeared to be expostulating. Could not make out the words of the shrill voice. Spoke quick and unevenly. Thinks it the voice of a Russian. Corroborates the general testimony. Is an Italian. Never conversed with a native of Russia.

"Several witnesses, recalled, here testified that the chimneys of all the rooms on the fourth story were too narrow to admit the passage of a human being. By 'sweeps' were meant cylindrical sweeping-brushes, such as are employed by those who clean chimneys. These brushes were passed up and down every flue in the house. There is no back passage by which anyone could have descended while the party proceeded up stairs. The body of Mademoiselle L'Espanaye was so firmly wedged in the chimney that it could not be got down until four or five of the party united their strength.

"*Paul Dumas*, physician, deposes that he was called to view the bodies about day-break. They were both then lying on the sacking of the bedstead in the chamber where Mademoiselle L. was found. The corpse of the young lady was much bruised and excoriated. The fact that it had been thrust up the chimney would sufficiently account for these appearances. The throat was greatly chafed. There were several deep scratches just below the chin, together with a series of livid spots which were evidently the impression of fingers. The face was fearfully discolored, and the eye-balls protruded. The tongue had been partially bitten through. A large bruise was discovered upon the pit of the stomach, produced, apparently, by the pressure of a knee. In the opinion of M. Dumas, Mademoiselle L'Espanaye had been throttled to death by some person or persons unknown. The corpse of the mother was horribly mutilated. All the bones of the right leg and arm were more or less shattered. The left *tibia* much splintered, as well as all the ribs of the left side. Whole body dreadfully bruised and discolored. It was not possible to say how the injuries had been inflicted. A heavy club of wood, or a broad bar of iron—a chair—any large, heavy, and obtuse weapon would have produced such results, if wielded by the hands of a very powerful man. No woman could have inflicted the blows with any weapon. The head of the deceased, when seen by witness, was entirely separated from the body, and was also greatly shattered. The throat had evidently been cut with some very sharp instrument—probably with a razor.

"*Alexandre Etienne,* surgeon, was called with M. Dumas to view the bodies. Corroborated the testimony, and the opinions of M. Dumas.

"Nothing farther of importance was elicited, although several other persons were examined. A murder so mysterious, and so perplexing in all its particulars, was never before committed in Paris—if indeed a murder has been committed at all. The police are entirely at fault—an unusual occurrence in affairs of this nature. There is not, however, the shadow of a clew apparent."

The evening edition of the paper stated that the greatest excitement still continued in the Quartier St. Roch—that the premises in question had been carefully re-searched, and fresh examinations of witnesses instituted, but all to no purpose. A postscript, however, mentioned that Adolphe Le Bon had been arrested and imprisoned—although nothing appeared to criminate him, beyond the facts already detailed.

Dupin seemed singularly interested in the progress of this affair—at least so I judged from his manner, for he made no comments. It was only after the announcement that Le Bon had been imprisoned, that he asked me my opinion respecting the murders.

I could merely agree with all Paris in considering them an insoluble mystery. I saw no means by which it would be possible to trace the murderer.

"We must not judge of the means," said Dupin, "by this shell of an examination. The Parisian police, so much extolled for *acumen,* are cunning, but no more. There is no method in their proceedings, beyond the method of the moment. They make a vast parade of measures; but, not unfrequently, these are so ill adapted to the objects proposed, as to put us in mind of Monsieur Jourdain's calling for his *robe-de-chambre—pour mieux entendre la musique.* The results attained by them are not unfrequently surprising, but, for the most part, are brought about by simple diligence and activity. When these qualities are unavailing, their schemes fail. Vidocq, for example, was a good guesser, and a persevering man. But, without educated thought, he erred continually by the very intensity of his investigations. He impaired his vision by holding the object too close. He might see, perhaps, one or two points with unusual clearness, but in so doing he, necessarily, lost sight of the matter as a whole. Thus there is such a thing as being too profound. Truth is not always in a well. In fact, as regards the more important knowledge, I do believe that she is invariably superficial. The depth lies in the valleys where we seek her, and not upon the mountain-tops where she is found. The modes and sources of this kind of error are well typified in the contemplation of the heavenly bodies. To look at a star by glances—to view it in a side-long way, by turning toward it the exterior portions of the *retina* (more susceptible of feeble impressions of light than the interior), is to behold the star distinctly—is to have the best appreciation of its lustre—a lustre which grows dim just in proportion as we turn our vision *fully* upon it. A greater number of rays actually fall upon the eye in the latter case, but, in the former, there is the more refined capacity for comprehension. By undue profundity we perplex and enfeeble thought; and it is possible to make even Venus herself vanish from the firmament by a scrutiny too sustained, too concentrated, or too direct.

"As for these murders, let us enter into some examinations for ourselves, before we make up an opinion respecting them. An inquiry will afford us amusement" [I thought this an odd term, so applied, but said nothing] "and, besides, Le Bon once rendered me a service for which I am not ungrateful. We will go and see the premises with our own eyes. I know G——, the Prefect of Police, and shall have no difficulty in obtaining the necessary permission."

The permission was obtained, and we proceeded at once to the Rue Morgue. This is one of those miserable thoroughfares which intervene between the Rue Richelieu and the Rue St. Roch. It was late in the afternoon when we reached it; as this quarter is at a great distance from that in which we resided. The house was readily found; for there were still many persons gazing up at the closed shutters, with an objectless curiosity, from the opposite side of the way. It was an ordinary Parisian house, with a gateway, on one side of which was a glazed watchbox, with a sliding panel in the window, indicating a *loge de concierge*. Before going in we walked up the street, turned down an alley, and then, again turning, passed in the rear of the building—Dupin, meanwhile, examining the whole neighborhood, as well as the house, with a minuteness of attention for which I could see no possible object.

Retracing our steps, we came again to the front of the dwelling, rang, and, having shown our credentials, were admitted by the agents in charge. We went up stairs—into the chamber where the body of Mademoiselle L'Espanaye had been found, and where both the deceased still lay. The disorders of the room had, as usual, been suffered to exist. I saw nothing beyond what had been stated in the "Gazette des Tribunaux." Dupin scrutinized every thing—not excepting the bodies of the victims. We then went into the other rooms, and into the yard; a *gendarme* accompanying us throughout. The examination occupied us until dark, when we took our departure. On our way home my companion stopped in for a moment at the office of one of the daily papers.

I have said that the whims of my friend were manifold, and that *Je les ménagais*:—for this phrase there is no English equivalent. It was his humor, now, to decline all conversation on the subject of the murder, until about noon the next day. He then asked me, suddenly, if I had observed any thing *peculiar* at the scene of the atrocity.

There was something in his manner of emphasizing the word "peculiar," which caused me to shudder, without knowing why.

"No, nothing *peculiar*," I said; "nothing more, at least, than we both saw stated in the paper."

"The 'Gazette,'" he replied, "has not entered, I fear, into the unusual horror of the thing. But dismiss the idle opinions of this print. It appears to me that this mystery is considered insoluble, for the very reason which should cause it to be regarded as easy of solution—I mean for the *outré* character of its features. The police are confounded by the seeming absence of motive—not for the murder itself—but for the atrocity of the murder. They are puzzled, too, by the seeming impossibility of reconciling the voices heard in contention, with the facts that no one was discovered upstairs but the assassinated Mademoiselle L'Espanaye, and that there were no means of egress without the notice of the party ascending. The wild disorder of the room; the corpse thrust, with the head downward, up the chimney; the frightful mutilation of the body of the old lady; these considerations, with those just mentioned, and others which I need not mention, have sufficed to paralyze the powers, by putting completely at fault the boasted *acumen,* of the government agents. They have fallen into the gross but common error of confounding the unusual with the abstruse. But it is by these deviations from the plane of the ordinary, that reason feels its way, if at all, in its search for the true. In investigations such as we are now pursuing, it should not be so much asked 'what has occurred,' as 'what has occurred that has never occurred before.' In fact, the facility with which I shall arrive, or have arrived, at the solution of this mystery, is in the direct ratio of its apparent insolubility in the eyes of the police."

I stared at the speaker in mute astonishment.

"I am now awaiting," continued he, looking toward the door of our apartment—"I am now awaiting a person who, although perhaps not the perpetrator of these butcheries, must have been in some measure implicated in their perpetration. Of the worst portion of the crimes committed, it is probable that he is innocent. I hope that I am right in this supposition; for upon it I build my expectation of reading the entire riddle. I look for the man here—in this room—every moment. It is true that he may not arrive; but the probability is that he will. Should he come, it will be necessary to detain him. Here are pistols; and we both know how to use them when occasion demands their use."

I took the pistols, scarcely knowing what I did, or believing what I heard, while Dupin went on, very much as if in a soliloquy. I have already spoken of his abstract manner at such times. His discourse was addressed to myself; but his voice, although by no means loud, had that intonation which is commonly employed in speaking to some one at a great distance. His eyes, vacant in expression, regarded only the wall.

"That the voices heard in contention," he said, "by the party upon the stairs, were not the voices of the women themselves, was fully proved by the evidence. This relieves us of all doubt upon the question whether the old lady could have first destroyed the daughter, and afterward have committed suicide. I speak of this point chiefly for the sake of method; for the strength of Madame L'Espanaye would have been utterly unequal to the task of thrusting her daughter's corpse up the chimney as it was found; and the nature of the wounds upon her own person entirely preclude the idea of self-destruction. Murder, then, has been committed by some third party; and the voices of this third party were those heard in contention. Let me now advert—not to the whole testimony respecting these voices—but to what was *peculiar* in that testimony. Did you observe any thing peculiar about it?"

I remarked that, while all the witnesses agreed in supposing the gruff voice to be that of a Frenchman, there was much disagreement in regard to the shrill, or, as one individual termed it, the harsh voice.

"That was the evidence itself," said Dupin, "but it was not the peculiarity of the evidence. You have observed nothing distinctive. Yet there *was* something to be observed. The witnesses, as you remark, agreed about the gruff voice; they were here unanimous. But in regard to the shrill voice, the peculiarity is—not that they disagreed—but that, while an Italian, an Englishman, a Spaniard, a Hollander, and a Frenchman attempted to describe it, each one spoke of it as that *of a foreigner*. Each is sure that it was not the voice of one of his own countrymen. Each likens it—not to the voice of an individual of any nation with whose language he is conversant—but the converse. The Frenchman supposes it the voice of a Spaniard, and 'might have distinguished some words *had he been acquainted with the Spanish*.' The Dutchman maintains it to have been that of a Frenchman; but we find it stated that '*not understanding French this witness was examined through an interpreter*.' The Englishman thinks it the voice of a German, and '*does not understand German*.' The Spaniard 'is sure' that it was that of an Englishman, but 'judges by the intonation' altogether, '*as he has no knowledge of the English*.' The Italian believes it the voice of a Russian, but '*has never conversed with a native of Russia*.' A second Frenchman differs, moreover, with the first, and is positive that the voice was that of an Italian; but, *not being cognizant of that tongue*, is like the Spaniard, 'convinced by the intonation.' Now, how strangely unusual must that voice have really been, about which such testimony as this *could* have been elicited!—in whose *tones*, even, denizens of the five great divisions of Europe could recognise nothing familiar! You will say that it might have been the voice of an Asiatic—of an African. Neither Asiatics nor Africans abound in Paris; but, without denying the inference, I will now merely call your attention to three points. The voice is termed by one witness 'harsh rather than shrill.' It is represented by two others to have been 'quick and *unequal*.' No words—no sounds resembling words—were by any witness mentioned as distinguishable.

"I know not," continued Dupin, "what impression I may have made, so far, upon your own understanding; but I do not hesitate to say that legitimate deductions even from this portion of the testimony—the portion respecting the gruff and shrill voices—are in themselves sufficient to engender a suspicion which should give direction to all farther progress in the investigation of the mystery. I said 'legitimate deductions;' but my meaning is not thus fully expressed. I designed to imply that the deductions are the *sole* proper ones, and that the suspicion arises *inevitably* from them as the single result. What the suspicion is, however, I will not say just yet. I merely wish you to bear in mind that, with myself, it was sufficiently forcible to give a definite form—a certain tendency—to my inquiries in the chamber.

"Let us now transport ourselves, in fancy, to this chamber. What shall we first seek here? The means of egress employed by the murderers. It is not too much to say that neither of us believes in præternatural events. Madame and Mademoiselle L'Espanaye were not destroyed by spirits. The doers of the deed were material, and escaped materially. Then how? Fortunately, there is but one mode of reasoning upon the point, and that mode *must* lead us to a definite decision.—Let us examine, each by each, the possible means of egress. It is clear that the assassins were in the room where Mademoiselle L'Espanaye was found, or at least in the room adjoining, when the party ascended the stairs. It is then only from these two apartments that we have to seek issues. The police have laid bare the floors, the ceilings, and the masonry of the walls, in every direction. No *secret* issues could have escaped their vigilance. But, not trusting to *their* eyes, I examined with my own. There were, then, *no* secret issues. Both doors leading from the rooms into the passage were securely locked, with the keys inside. Let us turn to the chimneys. These, although of ordinary width for some eight or ten feet above the hearths, will not admit, throughout their extent, the body of a large cat. The impossibility of egress, by means already stated, being thus absolute, we are reduced to the windows. Through those of the front room no one could have escaped without notice from the crowd in the street. The murderers *must* have passed, then, through those of the back room. Now, brought to this conclusion in so unequivocal a manner as we are, it is not our part, as reasoners, to reject it on account of apparent impossibilities. It is only left for us to prove that these apparent 'impossibilities' are, in reality, not such.

"There are two windows in the chamber. One of them is unobstructed by furniture, and is wholly visible. The lower portion of the other is hidden from view by the head of the unwieldy bedstead which is thrust close up against it. The former was found securely fastened from within. It resisted the utmost force of those who endeavored to raise it. A large gimlet-hole had been pierced in its frame to the left, and a very stout nail was found fitted therein, nearly to the head. Upon examining the other window, a similar nail was seen similarly fitted in it; and a vigorous attempt to raise this sash, failed also. The police were now entirely satisfied that egress had not been in these directions. And, *therefore*, it was thought a matter of supererogation to withdraw the nails and open the windows.

"My own examination was somewhat more particular, and was so for the reason I have just given—because here it was, I knew, that all apparent impossibilities *must* be proved to be not such in reality.

"I proceeded to think thus—*a posteriori.* The murderers *did* escape from one of these windows. This being so, they could not have re-fastened the sashes from the inside, as they were found fastened;—the consideration which put a stop, through its obviousness, to the scrutiny of the police in this quarter. Yet the sashes *were* fastened. They *must,* then, have the power of fastening themselves. There was no escape from this conclusion. I stepped to the unobstructed casement, withdrew the nail with some difficulty, and attempted to raise the sash. It resisted all my efforts, as I had anticipated. A concealed spring must, I now knew, exist; and this corroboration of my idea convinced me that my premises, at least, were correct, however mysterious still appeared the circumstances attending the nails. A careful search soon brought to light the hidden spring. I pressed it, and, satisfied with the discovery, forebore to upraise the sash.

"I now replaced the nail and regarded it attentively. A person passing out through this window might have reclosed it, and the spring would have caught—but the nail could not have been replaced. The conclusion was plain, and again narrowed in the field of my investigations. The assassins *must* have escaped through the other window. Supposing, then, the springs upon each sash to be the same, as was probable, there *must* be found a difference between the nails, or at least between the modes of their fixture. Getting upon the sacking of the bedstead, I looked over the head-board minutely at the second casement. Passing my hand down behind the board, I readily discovered and pressed the spring, which was, as I had supposed, identical in character with its neighbor. I now looked at the nail. It was as stout as the other, and apparently fitted in the same manner—driven in nearly up to the head.

"You will say that I was puzzled; but, if you think so, you must have misunderstood the nature of the inductions. To use a sporting phrase, I had not been once 'at fault.' The scent had never for an instant been lost. There was no flaw in any link of the chain. I had traced the secret to its ultimate result,—and that result was *the nail.* It had, I say, in every respect, the appearance of its fellow in the other window; but this fact was an absolute nullity (conclusive as it might seem to be) when compared with the consideration that here, at this point, terminated the clew. 'There *must* be something wrong,' I said, 'about the nail.' I touched it; and the head, with about a quarter of an inch of the shank, came off in my fingers. The rest of the shank was in the gimlet-hole, where it had been broken off. The fracture was an old one (for its edges were incrusted with rust), and had apparently been accomplished by the blow of a hammer, which had partially imbedded, in the top of the bottom sash, the head portion of the nail. I now carefully replaced this head portion in the indentation whence I had taken it, and the resemblance to a perfect nail was complete—the fissure was invisible. Pressing the spring, I gently raised the sash for a few inches; the head went up with it, remaining firm in its bed. I closed the window, and the semblance of the whole nail was again perfect.

"The riddle, so far, was now unriddled. The assassin had escaped through the window which looked upon the bed. Dropping of its own accord upon his exit (or perhaps purposely closed), it had become fastened by the spring; and it was the retention of this spring which had been mistaken by the police for that of the nail,—farther inquiry being thus considered unnecessary.

"The next question is that of the mode of descent. Upon this point I had been satisfied in my walk with you around the building. About five feet and a half from the casement in question there runs a lightning-rod. From this rod it would have been impossible for any one to reach the window itself, to say nothing of entering it. I observed, however, that the shutters of the fourth story were of the peculiar kind called by Parisian carpenters *ferrades*—a kind rarely employed at the present day, but frequently seen upon very old mansions at Lyons and Bordeaux. They are in the form of an ordinary door (a single, not a folding door), except that the upper half is latticed or worked in open trellis—thus affording an excellent hold for the hands. In the present instance these shutters are fully three feet and a half broad. When we saw them from the rear of the house, they were both about half open—that is to say, they stood off at right angles from the wall. It is probable that the police, as well as myself, examined the back of the tenement; but, if so, in looking at these *ferrades* in the line of their breadth (as they must have done), they did not perceive this great breadth itself, or, at all events, failed to take it into due consideration. In fact, having once satisfied themselves that no egress could have been made in this quarter, they would naturally bestow here a very cursory examination. It was clear to me, however, that the shutter belonging to the window at the head of the bed, would, if swung fully back to the wall, reach to within two feet of the lightning-rod. It was also evident that, by exertion of a very unusual degree of activity and courage, an entrance into the window, from the rod, might have been thus effected.—By reaching to the distance of two feet and a half (we now suppose the shutter open to its whole extent) a robber might have taken a firm grasp upon the trellis-work. Letting go, then, his hold upon the rod, placing his feet securely against the wall, and springing boldly from it, he might have swung the shutter so as to close it, and, if we imagine the window open at the time, might even have swung himself into the room.

"I wish you to bear especially in mind that I have spoken of a *very* unusual degree of activity as requisite to success in so hazardous and so difficult a feat. It is my design to show you, first, that the thing might possibly have been accomplished:—but, secondly and *chiefly*, I wish to impress upon your understanding the very *extraordinary*—the almost præternatural character of that agility which could have accomplished it.

"You will say, no doubt, using the language of the law, that 'to make out my case' I should rather undervalue, than insist upon a full estimation of the activity required in this matter. This may be the practice in law, but it is not the usage of reason. My ultimate object is only the truth. My immediate purpose is to lead you to place in juxta-position that *very unusual* activity of which I have just spoken, with that *very peculiar* shrill (or harsh) and *unequal* voice, about whose nationality no two persons could be found to agree, and in whose utterance no syllabification could be detected."

At these words a vague and half-formed conception of the meaning of Dupin flitted over my mind. I seemed to be upon the verge of comprehension, without power to comprehend—as men, at times, find themselves upon the brink of remembrance, without being able, in the end, to remember. My friend went on with his discourse.

"You will see," he said, "that I have shifted the question from the mode of egress to that of ingress. It was my design to convey the idea that both were effected in the same manner, at the same point. Let us now revert to the interior of the room. Let us survey the appearances here. The drawers of the bureau, it is said, had been rifled, although many articles of apparel still remained within them. The conclusion here is absurd. It is a mere guess—a very silly one—and no more. How are we to know that the articles found in the drawers were not all these drawers had originally contained? Madame L'Espanaye and her daughter lived an exceedingly retired life—saw no company—seldom went out—had little use for numerous changes of habiliment. Those found were at least of as good quality as any likely to be possessed by these ladies. If a thief had taken any, why did he not take the best—why did he not take all? In a word, why did he abandon four thousand francs in gold to encumber himself with a bundle of linen? The gold *was* abandoned. Nearly the whole sum mentioned by Monsieur Mignaud, the banker, was discovered, in bags, upon the floor. I wish you, therefore, to discard from your thoughts the blundering idea of *motive,* engendered in the brains of the police by that portion of the evidence which speaks of money delivered at the door of the house. Coincidences ten times as remarkable as this (the delivery of the money, and murder committed within three days upon the party receiving it), happen to all of us every hour of our lives, without attracting even momentary notice. Coincidences, in general, are great stumbling-blocks in the way of that class of thinkers who have been educated to know nothing of the theory of probabilities—that theory to which the most glorious objects of human research are indebted for the most glorious of illustration. In the present instance, had the gold been gone, the fact of its delivery three days before would have formed something more than a coincidence. It would have been corroborative of this idea of motive. But, under the real circumstances of the case, if we are to suppose gold the motive of this outrage, we must also imagine the perpetrator so vacillating an idiot as to have abandoned his gold and his motive together.

"Keeping now steadily in mind the points to which I have drawn your attention—that peculiar voice, that unusual agility, and that startling absence of motive in a murder so singularly atrocious as this—let us glance at the butchery itself. Here is a woman strangled to death by manual strength, and thrust up a chimney, head downward. Ordinary assassins employ no such modes of murder as this. Least of all, do they thus dispose of the murdered. In the manner of thrusting the corpse up the chimney, you will admit that there was something *excessively outré*—something altogether irreconcilable with our common notions of human action, even when we suppose the actors the most depraved of men. Think, too, how great must have been that strength which could have thrust the body *up* such an aperture so forcibly that the united vigor of several persons was found barely sufficient to drag it *down!*

"Turn, now, to other indications of the employment of a vigor most marvellous. On the hearth were thick tresses—very thick tresses—of grey human hair. These had been torn out by the roots. You are aware of the great force necessary in tearing thus from the head even twenty or thirty hairs together. You saw the locks in question as well as myself. Their roots (a hideous sight!) were clotted with fragments of the flesh of the scalp—sure token of the prodigious power which had been exerted in uprooting perhaps half a million of hairs at a time. The throat of the old lady was not merely cut, but the head absolutely severed from the body: the instrument was a mere razor. I wish you also to look at the *brutal* ferocity of these deeds. Of the bruises upon the body of Madame L'Espanaye I do not speak. Monsieur Dumas, and his worthy coadjutor Monsieur Etienne, have pronounced that they were inflicted by some obtuse instrument; and so far these gentlemen are very correct. The obtuse instrument was clearly the stone pavement in the yard, upon which the victim had fallen from the window which looked in upon the bed. This idea, however simple it may now seem, escaped the police for the same reason that the breadth of the shutters escaped them—because, by the affair of the nails, their perceptions had been hermetically sealed against the possibility of the windows having ever been opened at all.

"If now, in addition to all these things, you have properly reflected upon the odd disorder of the chamber, we have gone so far as to combine the ideas of an agility astounding, a strength superhuman, a ferocity brutal, a butchery without motive, a *grotesquerie* in horror absolutely alien from humanity, and a voice foreign in tone to the ears of men of many nations, and devoid of all distinct or intelligible syllabification. What result, then, has ensued? What impression have I made upon your fancy?"

I felt a creeping of the flesh as Dupin asked me the question. "A madman," I said, "has done this deed—some raving maniac, escaped from a neighboring *Maison de Santé*."

"In some respects," he replied, "your idea is not irrelevant. But the voices of madmen, even in their wildest paroxysms, are never found to tally with that peculiar voice heard upon the stairs. Madmen are of some nation and their language, however incoherent in its words, has always the coherence of syllabification. Besides, the hair of a madman is not such as I now hold in my hand. I disentangled this little tuft from the rigidly clutched fingers of Madame L'Espanaye. Tell me what you can make of it."

"Dupin!" I said, completely unnerved; "this hair is most unusual—this is no *human* hair."

"I have not asserted that it is," said he; "but, before we decide this point, I wish you to glance at the little sketch I have here traced upon this paper. It is a *fac-simile* drawing of what has been described in one portion of the testimony as 'dark bruises, and deep indentations of finger nails,' upon the throat of Mademoiselle L'Espanaye, and in another (by Messrs. Dumas and Etienne) as a 'series of livid spots, evidently the impression of fingers.'

"You will perceive," continued my friend, spreading out the paper upon the table before us, "that this drawing gives the idea of a firm and fixed hold. There is no *slipping* apparent. Each finger has retained—possibly until the death of the victim—the fearful grasp by which it originally imbedded itself. Attempt, now, to place all your fingers, at the same time, in the respective impressions as you see them."

I made the attempt in vain.

"We are possibly not giving this matter a fair trial," he said. "The paper is spread out upon a plane surface; but the human throat is cylindrical. Here is a billet of wood, the circumference of which is about that of the throat. Wrap the drawing around it, and try the experiment again."

I did so; but the difficulty was even more obvious than before.

"This," I said, "is the mark of no human hand."

"Read now," replied Dupin, "this passage from Cuvier."

It was a minute anatomical and generally descriptive account of the large fulvous Ourang-Outang of the East Indian Islands. The gigantic stature, the prodigious strength and activity, the wild ferocity, and the imitative propensities of these mammalia are sufficiently well known to all. I understood the full horrors of the murder at once.

"The description of the digits," said I, as I made an end of reading, "is in exact accordance with this drawing. I see that no animal but an Ourang-Outang, of the species here mentioned, could have impressed the indentations as you have traced them. This tuft of tawny hair, too, is identical in character with that of the beast of Cuvier. But I cannot possibly comprehend the particulars of this frightful mystery. Besides, there were *two* voices heard in contention, and one of them was unquestionably the voice of a Frenchman."

"True; and you will remember an expression attributed almost unanimously, by the evidence, to this voice,—the expression, '*mon Dieu!*' This, under the circumstances, has been justly characterized by one of the witnesses (Montani, the confectioner) as an expression of remonstrance or expostulation. Upon these two words, therefore, I have mainly built my hopes of a full solution of the riddle. A Frenchman was cognizant of the murder. It is possible—indeed it is far more than probable—that he was innocent of all participation in the bloody transactions which took place. The Ourang-Outang may have escaped from him. He may have traced it to the chamber; but, under the agitating circumstances which ensued, he could never have recaptured it. It is still at large. I will not pursue these guesses—for I have no right to call them more—since the shades of reflection upon which they are based are scarcely of sufficient depth to be appreciable by my own intellect, and since I could not pretend to make them intelligible to the understanding of another. We will call them guesses then, and speak of them as such. If the Frenchman in question is indeed, as I suppose, innocent of this atrocity, this advertisement, which I left last night, upon our return home, at the office of 'Le Monde' (a paper devoted to the shipping interest, and much sought by sailors) will bring him to our residence."

He handed me a paper, and I read thus:

CAUGHT—*In the Bois de Boulogne, early in the morning of the ——— inst.*, (the morning of the murder,) *a very large, tawny Ourang-Outang of the Bornese species. The owner (who is ascertained to be a sailor, belonging to a Maltese vessel) may have the animal again, upon identifying it satisfactorily, and paying a few charges arising from its capture and keeping. Call at No. ———, Rue ———, Faubourg St. Germain—au troisième.*

"How was it possible," I asked, "that you should know the man to be a sailor, and belonging to a Maltese vessel?"

"I do *not* know it," said Dupin. "I am not *sure* of it. Here, however, is a small piece of ribbon, which from its form, and from its greasy appearance, has evidently been used in tying the hair in one of those long *queues* of which sailors are so fond. Moreover, this knot is one which few besides sailors can tie, and is peculiar to the Maltese. I picked the ribbon up at the foot of the lightning-rod. It could not have belonged to either of the deceased. Now if, after all, I am wrong in my induction from this ribbon, that the Frenchman was a sailor belonging to a Maltese vessel, still I can have done no harm in saying what I did in the advertisement. If I am in error, he will merely suppose that I have been misled by some circumstance into which he will not take the trouble to inquire. But if I am right, a great point is gained. Cognizant although innocent of the murder, the Frenchman will naturally hesitate about replying to the advertisement—about demanding the Ourang-Outang. He will reason thus:—'I am innocent; I am poor; my Ourang-Outang is of great value—to one in my circumstances a fortune of itself—why should I lose it through idle apprehensions of danger? Here it is, within my grasp. It was found in the Bois de Boulogne—at a vast distance from the scene of that butchery. How can it ever be suspected that a brute beast should have done the deed? The police are at fault—they have failed to procure the slightest clew. Should they even trace the animal, it would be impossible to prove me cognizant of the murder, or to implicate me in guilt on account of that cognizance. Above all, *I am known*. The advertiser designates me as the possessor of the beast. I am not sure to what limit his knowledge may extend. Should I avoid claiming a property of so great value, which it is known that I possess, I will render the animal, at least, liable to suspicion. It is not my policy to attract attention either to myself or to the beast. I will answer the advertisement, get the Ourang-Outang, and keep it close until this matter has blown over.'"

At this moment we heard a step upon the stairs.

" Be ready," said Dupin, " with your pistols, but neither use them nor show them until at a signal from myself."

The front door of the house had been left open, and the visitor had entered, without ringing, and advanced several steps upon the staircase. Now, however, he seemed to hesitate. Presently we heard him descending. Dupin was moving quickly to the door, when we again heard him coming up. He did not turn back a second time, but stepped up with decision and rapped at the door of our chamber.

" Come in," said Dupin, in a cheerful and hearty tone.

A man entered. He was a sailor, evidently,—a tall, stout, and muscular-looking person, with a certain dare-devil expression of countenance, not altogether unprepossessing. His face, greatly sunburnt, was more than half hidden by whisker and *mustachio*. He had with him a huge oaken cudgel, but appeared to be otherwise unarmed. He bowed awkwardly, and bade us " good evening," in French accents, which, although somewhat Neufchatelish, were still sufficiently indicative of a Parisian origin.

" Sit down, my friend," said Dupin. " I suppose you have called about the Ourang-Outang. Upon my word, I almost envy you the possession of him; a remarkably fine, and no doubt a very valuable animal. How old do you suppose him to be?"

The sailor drew a long breath, with the air of a man relieved of some intolerable burden, and then replied, in an assured tone:

" I have no way of telling—but he can't be more than four or five years old. Have you got him here?"

" Oh no; we had no conveniences for keeping him here. He is at a livery stable in the Rue Dubourg, just by. You can get him in the morning. Of course you are prepared to identify the property?"

" To be sure I am, sir."

" I shall be sorry to part with him," said Dupin.

" I don't mean that you should be at all this trouble for nothing, sir," said the man. " Couldn't expect it. Am very willing to pay a reward for the finding of the animal—that is to say, any thing in reason."

" Well," replied my friend, " that is all very fair, to be sure. Let me think!—what should I have? Oh! I will tell you. My reward shall be this. You shall give me all the information in your power about these murders in the Rue Morgue."

Dupin said the last words in a very low tone, and very quietly. Just as quietly, too, he walked toward the door, locked it, and put the key in his pocket. He then drew a pistol from his bosom and placed it, without the least flurry, upon the table.

The sailor's face flushed up as if he were struggling with suffocation. He started to his feet and grasped his cudgel; but the next moment he fell back into his seat, trembling violently, and with the countenance of death itself. He spoke not a word. I pitied him from the bottom of my heart.

" My friend," said Dupin, in a kind tone, " you are alarming yourself unnecessarily—you are indeed. We mean you no harm whatever. I pledge you the honor of a gentleman, and of a Frenchman, that we intend you no injury. I perfectly well know that you are innocent of the atrocities in the Rue Morgue. It will not do, however, to deny that you are in some measure implicated in them. From what I have already said, you must know that I have had means of information about this matter—means of which you could never have dreamed. Now the thing stands thus. You have done nothing which you could have avoided—nothing, certainly, which renders you culpable. You were not even guilty of robbery, when you might have robbed with impunity. You have nothing to conceal. You have no reason for concealment. On the other hand, you are bound by every principle of honor to confess all you know. An innocent man is now imprisoned, charged with that crime of which you can point out the perpetrator."

The sailor had recovered his presence of mind, in a great measure, while Dupin uttered these words; but his original boldness of bearing was all gone.

"So help me God," said he, after a brief pause, "I *will* tell you all I know about this affair;—but I do not expect you to believe one half I say—I would be a fool indeed if I did. Still, I *am* innocent, and I will make a clean breast if I die for it."

What he stated was, in substance, this. He had lately made a voyage to the Indian Archipelago. A party, of which he formed one, landed at Borneo, and passed into the interior on an excursion of pleasure. Himself and a companion had captured the Ourang-Outang. This companion dying, the animal fell into his own exclusive possession. After great trouble, occasioned by the intractable ferocity of his captive during the home voyage, he at length succeeded in lodging it safely at his own residence in Paris, where, not to attract toward himself the unpleasant curiosity of his neighbors, he kept it carefully secluded, until such time as it should recover from a wound in the foot, received from a splinter on board ship. His ultimate design was to sell it.

Returning home from some sailors' frolic on the night, or rather in the morning of the murder, he found the beast occupying his own bed-room, into which it had broken from a closet adjoining, where it had been, as was thought, securely confined. Razor in hand, and fully lathered, it was sitting before a looking-glass, attempting the operation of shaving, in which it had no doubt previously watched its master through the key-hole of the closet. Terrified at the sight of so dangerous a weapon in the possession of an animal so ferocious, and so well able to use it, the man, for some moments, was at a loss what to do. He had been accustomed, however, to quiet the creature, even in its fiercest moods, by the use of a whip, and to this he now resorted. Upon sight of it, the Ourang-Outang sprang at once through the door of the chamber, down the stairs, and thence, through a window, unfortunately open, into the street.

The Frenchman followed in despair; the ape, razor still in hand, occasionally stopping to look back and gesticulate at its pursuer, until the latter had nearly come up with it. It then again made off. In this manner the chase continued for a long time. The streets were profoundly quiet, as it was nearly three o'clock in the morning. In passing down an alley in the rear of the Rue Morgue, the fugitive's attention was arrested by a light gleaming from the open window of Madame L'Espanaye's chamber, in the fourth story of her house. Rushing to the building, it perceived the lightning-rod, clambered up with inconceivable agility, grasped the shutter, which was thrown fully back against the wall, and, by its means, swung itself directly upon the headboard of the bed. The whole feat did not occupy a minute. The shutter was kicked open again by the Ourang-Outang as it entered the room.

The sailor, in the meantime, was both rejoiced and perplexed. He had strong hopes of now recapturing the brute, as it could scarcely escape from the trap into which it had ventured, except by the rod, where it might be intercepted as it came down. On the other hand, there was much cause for anxiety as to what it might do in the house. This latter reflection urged the man still to follow the fugitive. A lightning-rod is ascended without difficulty, especially by a sailor; but, when he had arrived as high as the window, which lay far to his left, his career was stopped; the most that he could accomplish was to reach over so as to obtain a glimpse of the interior of the room. At this glimpse he nearly fell from his hold through excess of horror. Now it was that those hideous shrieks arose upon the night, which had startled from slumber the inmates of the Rue Morgue. Madame L'Espanaye and her daughter, habited in their night clothes, had apparently been occupied in arranging some papers in the iron chest already mentioned, which had been wheeled into the middle of the room. It was open, and its contents lay beside it on the floor. The victims must have been sitting with their backs toward the window; and, from the time elapsing between the ingress of the beast and the screams, it seems probable that it was not immediately perceived. The flapping-to of the shutter would naturally have been attributed to the wind.

As the sailor looked in, the gigantic animal had seized Madame L'Espanaye by the hair (which was loose, as she had been combing it), and was flourishing the razor about her face, in imitation of the motions of a barber. The daughter lay prostrate and motionless; she had swooned. The screams and struggles of the old lady (during which the hair was torn from her head) had the effect of changing the probably pacific purposes of the Ourang-Outang into those of wrath. With one determined sweep of its muscular arm it nearly severed her head from her body. The sight of blood inflamed its anger into phrenzy. Gnashing its teeth, and flashing fire from its eyes, it flew upon the body of the girl, and imbedded its fearful talons in her throat, retaining its grasp until she expired. Its wandering and wild glances fell at this moment upon the head of the bed, over which the face of its master, rigid with horror, was just discernible. The fury of the beast, who no doubt bore still in mind the dreaded whip, was instantly converted into fear. Conscious of having deserved punishment, it seemed desirous of concealing its bloody deeds, and skipped about the chamber in an agony of nervous agitation; throwing down and breaking the furniture as it moved, and dragging the bed from the bedstead. In conclusion, it seized first the corpse of the daughter, and thrust it up the chimney, as it was found; then that of the old lady, which it immediately hurled through the window headlong.

As the ape approached the casement with its mutilated burden, the sailor shrank aghast to the rod, and rather gliding than clambering down it, hurried at once home—dreading the consequences of the butchery, and gladly abandoning, in his terror, all solicitude about the fate of the Ourang-Outang. The words heard by the party upon the staircase were the Frenchman's exclamations of horror and affright, commingled with the fiendish jabberings of the brute.

I have scarcely anything to add. The Ourang-Outang must have escaped from the chamber, by the rod, just before the breaking of the door. It must have closed the window as it passed through it. It was subsequently caught by the owner himself, who obtained for it a very large sum at the *Jardin des Plantes.* Le Bon was instantly released, upon our narration of the circumstances (with some comments from Dupin) at the *bureau* of the Prefect of Police. This functionary, however well disposed to my friend, could not altogether conceal his chagrin at the turn which affairs had taken, and was fain to indulge in a sarcasm or two, about the propriety of every person minding his own business.

"Let him talk," said Dupin, who had not thought it necessary to reply. "Let him discourse; it will ease his conscience. I am satisfied with having defeated him in his own castle. Nevertheless, that he failed in the solution of this mystery, is by no means that matter for wonder which he supposes it; for, in truth, our friend the Prefect is somewhat too cunning to be profound. In his wisdom is no *stamen.* It is all head and no body, like the picture of the Goddess Laverna,—or, at best, all head and shoulders, like a codfish. But he is a good creature after all. I like him especially for one master stroke of cant, by which he has attained his reputation for ingenuity. I mean the way he was '*de nier ce qui est, et d'expliquer ce qui n'est pas.*'"*

1841

## ELEONORA

Sub conservatione formae specificae salva anima.
—Raymond Lully.

I am come of a race noted for vigor of fancy and ardor of passion. Men have called me mad; but the question is not yet settled, whether madness is or is not the loftiest intelligence—whether much that is glorious—whether all that is profound—does not spring from disease of thought—from *moods* of mind exalted at the expense of the general intellect. They who dream by day are cognizant of many things which escape those who dream only by night. In their gray visions they obtain glimpses of eternity, and thrill, in waking, to find that they have been upon the verge of the great secret. In snatches, they learn something of the wisdom which is of good, and more of the mere knowledge which is of evil. They penetrate, however rudderless or compassless, into the

* Rousseau—Nouvelle Héloise. [Author's note.]

vast ocean of the "light ineffable," and again, like the adventurers of the Nubian geographer, "*aggressi sunt mare tenebrarum, quid in eo esset exploraturi.*"

We will say, then, that I am mad. I grant, at least, that there are two distinct conditions of my mental existence — the condition of a lucid reason, not to be disputed, and belonging to the memory of events forming the first epoch of my life — and a condition of shadow and doubt, appertaining to the present, and to the recollection of what constitutes the second great era of my being. Therefore what I shall tell of the earlier period, believe; and to what I may relate of the later time, give only such credit as may seem due; or doubt it altogether; or, if doubt it ye cannot, then play unto its riddle the Œdipus.

She whom I loved in youth, and of whom I now pen calmly and distinctly these remembrances, was the sole daughter of the only sister of my mother long departed. Eleonora was the name of my cousin. We had always dwelled together, beneath a tropical sun, in the Valley of the Many-Colored Grass. No unguided footstep ever came upon that vale; for it lay far away up among a range of giant hills that hung beetling around about it, shutting out the sunlight from its sweetest recesses. No path was trodden in its vicinity; and, to reach our happy home, there was need of putting back, with force, the foliage of many thousands of forest trees, and of crushing to death the glories of many millions of fragrant flowers. Thus it was that we lived all alone, knowing nothing of the world without the valley, — I, and my cousin, and her mother.

From the dim regions beyond the mountains at the upper end of our encircled domain, there crept out a narrow and deep river, brighter than all save the eyes of Eleonora; and, winding stealthily about in mazy courses, it passed away, at length, through a shadowy gorge, among hills still dimmer than those whence it had issued. We called it the "River of Silence;" for there seemed to be a hushing influence in its flow. No murmur arose from its bed, and so gently it wandered along, that the pearly pebbles upon which we loved to gaze, far down within its bosom, stirred not at all, but lay in a motionless content, each in its own old station, shining on gloriously forever.

The margin of the river, and of the many dazzling rivulets that glided, through devious ways, into its channel, as well as the spaces that extended from the margins away down into the depths of the streams until they reached the bed of pebbles at the bottom, — these spots, not less than the whole surface of the valley, from the river to the mountains that girdled it in, were carpeted all by a soft green grass, thick, short, perfectly even, and vanilla-perfumed, but so be-sprinkled throughout with the yellow buttercup, the white daisy, the purple violet, and the ruby-red asphodel, that its exceeding beauty spoke to our hearts, in loud tones, of the love and of the glory of God.

And, here and there, in groves about this grass, like wildernesses of dreams, sprang up fantastic trees, whose tall slender stems stood not upright, but slanted gracefully towards the light that peered at noon-day into the centre of the valley. Their bark was speckled with the vivid alternate splendor of ebony and silver, and was smoother than all save the cheeks of Eleonora; so that but for the brilliant green of the huge leaves that spread from their summits in long tremulous lines, dallying with the Zephyrs, one might have fancied them giant serpents of Syria doing homage to their Sovereign the Sun.

Hand in hand about this valley, for fifteen years, roamed I with Eleonora before Love entered within our hearts. It was one evening at the close of the third lustrum of her life, and of the fourth of my own, that we sat, locked in each other's embrace, beneath the serpent-like trees, and looked down within the waters of the River of Silence at our images therein. We spoke no words during the rest of that sweet day; and our words even upon the morrow were tremulous and few. We had drawn the god Eros from that wave, and now we felt that he had enkindled within us the fiery souls of our forefathers. The passions which had for centuries distinguished our race, came thronging with the fancies for which they had been equally noted, and together breathed a delirious bliss over the Valley of the Many-Colored Grass. A change fell upon all things. Strange, brilliant flowers, star-shaped, burst out upon the trees where no flowers had been known before. The tints of the green carpet deepened; and when, one by one, the white daisies shrank away, there sprang up, in place of them, ten by ten of the ruby-red asphodel. And life arose in our paths; for the tall flamingo, hitherto unseen, with all gay glowing birds, flaunted his scarlet plumage before us. The golden and silver fish haunted the river, out of the bosom of which issued, little by little, a murmur that swelled, at length, into a lulling melody more divine than that of the harp of Æolus — sweeter than all save the voice of Eleonora. And now, too, a voluminous cloud, which we had long watched in the regions of Hesper, floated out thence, all gorgeous in crimson and gold, and settling in peace above us, sank, day by day, lower and lower, until its edges rested upon the tops of the mountains, turning all their dimness into magnificence, and shutting us up, as if forever, within a magic prison-house of grandeur and of glory.

The loveliness of Eleonora was that of the Seraphim; but she was a maiden artless and innocent as the brief life she had led among the flowers. No guile disguised the fervor of love which animated her heart, and she examined with me its inmost recesses as we walked together in the Valley of the Many-Colored Grass, and discoursed of the mighty changes which had lately taken place therein.

At length, having spoken one day, in tears, of the last sad change which must befall Humanity, she thenceforward dwelt only upon this one sorrowful theme, interweaving it into all our converse, as, in the songs of the bard of Schiraz, the same images are found occurring, again and again, in every impressive variation of phrase.

She had seen that the finger of Death was upon her bosom — that, like the ephemeron, she had been made perfect in loveliness only to die; but the terrors of the grave, to her, lay solely in a consideration which she revealed to me, one evening at twilight, by the banks of the River of

Silence. She grieved to think that, having entombed her in the Valley of the Many-Colored Grass, I would quit forever its happy recesses, transferring the love which now was so passionately her own to some maiden of the outer and every-day world. And, then and there, I threw myself hurriedly at the feet of Eleonora, and offered up a vow to herself and to Heaven, that I would never bind myself in marriage to any daughter of Earth — that I would in no manner prove recreant to her dear memory, or to the memory of the devout affection with which she had blessed me. And I called the Mighty Ruler of the Universe to witness the pious solemnity of my vow. And the curse which I invoked of *Him* and of her, a saint in Helusion, should I prove traitorous to that promise, involved a penalty the exceeding great horror of which will not permit me to make record of it here. And the bright eyes of Eleonora grew brighter at my words; and she sighed as if a deadly burthen had been taken from her breast; and she trembled and very bitterly wept; but she made acceptance of the vow (for what was she but a child?), and it made easy to her the bed of her death. And she said to me, not many days afterwards, tranquilly dying, that, because of what I had done for the comfort of her spirit, she would watch over me in that spirit when departed, and, if so it were permitted her, return to me visibly in the watches of the night; but, if this thing were, indeed, beyond the power of the souls in Paradise, that she would, at least, give me frequent indications of her presence; sighing upon me in the evening winds, or filling the air which I breathed with perfume from the censers of the angels. And, with these words upon her lips, she yielded up her innocent life, putting an end to the first epoch of my own.

Thus far I have faithfully said. But as I pass the barrier in Time's path formed by the death of my beloved, and proceed with the second era of my existence, I feel that a shadow gathers over my brain, and I mistrust the perfect sanity of the record. But let me on. — Years dragged themselves along heavily, and still I dwelled within the Valley of the Many-Colored Grass; — but a second change had come upon all things. The star-shaped flowers shrank into the stems of the trees, and appeared no more. The tints of the green carpet faded; and, one by one, the ruby-red asphodels withered away; and there sprang up in place of them, ten by ten, dark, eye-like violets that writhed uneasily and were ever encumbered with dew. And Life departed from our paths; for the tall flamingo flaunted no longer his scarlet plumage before us, but flew sadly from the vale into the hills, with all the gay glowing birds that had arrived in his company. And the golden and silver fish swam down through the gorge at the lower end of our domain and bedecked the sweet river never again. And the lulling melody that had been softer than the wind-harp of Æolus and more divine than all save the voice of Eleonora, it died little by little away, in murmurs growing lower and lower, until the stream returned, at length, utterly, into the solemnity of its original silence. And then, lastly, the voluminous cloud uprose, and, abandoning the tops of the mountains to the dimness of old, fell back into the regions of Hesper, and took away all its manifold golden and gorgeous glories from the Valley of the Many-Colored Grass.

Yet the promises of Eleonora were not forgotten; for I heard the sounds of the swinging of the censers of the angels; and streams of a holy perfume floated ever and ever about the valley; and at lone hours, when my heart beat heavily, the winds that bathed my brow came unto me laden with soft sighs; and indistinct murmurs filled often the night air; and once — oh, but once only! I was awakened from a slumber like the slumber of death, by the pressing of spiritual lips upon my own.

But the void within my heart refused, even thus, to be filled. I longed for the love which had before filled it to overflowing. At length the valley *pained* me through it memories of Eleonora, and I left it forever for the vanities and the turbulent triumphs of the world.

. . . . . .

I found myself within a strange city, where all things might have served to blot from recollection the sweet dreams I had dreamed so long in the Valley of the Many-Colored Grass. The pomps and pageantries of a stately court, and the mad clangor of arms, and the radiant loveliness of woman, bewildered and intoxicated my brain. But as yet my soul had proved true to its vows, and the indications of the presence of Eleonora were still given me in the silent hours of the night. Suddenly, these manifestations they ceased; and the world grew dark before mine eyes; and I stood aghast at the burning thoughts which possessed — at the terrible temptations which beset me; for there came from some far, far distant and unknown land, into the gay court of the king I served, a maiden to whose beauty my whole recreant heart yielded at once — at whose footstool I bowed down without a struggle, in the most ardent, in the most abject worship of love. What indeed was my passion for the young girl of the valley in comparison with the fervor, and the delirium, and the spirit-lifting ecstasy of adoration with which I poured out my whole soul in tears at the feet of the ethereal Ermengarde? — Oh, bright was the seraph Ermengarde! and in that knowledge I had room for none other. — Oh, divine was the angel Ermengarde! and as I looked down into the depths of her memorial eyes I thought only of them — and *of her*.

I wedded; — nor dreaded the curse I had invoked; and its bitterness was not visited upon me. And once — but once again in the silence of the night, there came through my lattice the soft sighs which had forsaken me; and they modelled themselves into familiar and sweet voice, saying:

"Sleep in peace! — for the Spirit of Love reigneth and ruleth, and, in taking to thy passionate heart her who is Ermengarde, thou art absolved, for reasons which shall be made known to thee in Heaven, of thy vows unto Eleonora."

1841

## THE MASQUE OF THE RED DEATH

The "Red Death" had long devastated the country. No pestilence had ever been so fatal, or so hideous.

Blood was its Avatar and its seal—the redness and the horror of blood. There were sharp pains, and sudden dizziness, and then profuse bleeding at the pores, with dissolution. The scarlet stains upon the body and especially upon the face of the victim, were the pest ban which shut him out from the aid and from the sympathy of his fellow-men. And the whole seizure, progress and termination of the disease, were the incidents of half an hour.

But the Prince Prospero was happy and dauntless and sagacious. When his dominions were half depopulated, he summoned to his presence a thousand hale and light-hearted friends from among the knights and dames of his court, and with these retired to the deep seclusion of one of his castellated abbeys. This was an extensive and magnificent structure, the creation of the prince's own eccentric yet august taste. A strong and lofty wall girdled it in. This wall had gates of iron. The courtiers, having entered, brought furnaces and massy hammers and welded the bolts. They resolved to leave means neither of ingress or egress to the sudden impulses of despair or of frenzy from within. The abbey was amply provisioned. With such precautions the courtiers might bid defiance to contagion. The external world could take care of itself. In the meantime it was folly to grieve, or to think. The prince had provided all the appliances of pleasure. There were buffoons, there were improvisatori, there were ballet-dancers, there were musicians, there was Beauty, there was wine. All these and security were within. Without was the "Red Death."

It was toward the close of the fifth or sixth month of his seclusion, and while the pestilence raged most furiously abroad, that the Prince Prospero entertained his thousand friends at a masked ball of the most unusual magnificence.

It was a voluptuous scene, that masquerade. But first let me tell of the rooms in which it was held. There were seven—an imperial suite. In many palaces, however, such suites form a long and straight vista, while the folding doors slide back nearly to the walls on either hand, so that the view of the whole extent is scarcely impeded. Here the case was very different; as might have been expected from the duke's love of the *bizarre*. The apartments were so irregularly disposed that the vision embraced but little more than one at a time. There was a sharp turn at every twenty or thirty yards, and at each turn a novel effect. To the right and left, in the middle of each wall, a tall and narrow Gothic window looked out upon a closed corridor which pursued the windings of the suite. These windows were of stained glass whose color varied in accordance with the prevailing hue of the decorations of the chamber into which it opened. That at the eastern extremity was hung, for example, in blue—and vividly blue were its windows. The second chamber was purple in its ornaments and tapestries, and here the panes were purple. The third was green throughout, and so were the casements. The fourth was furnished and lighted with orange—the fifth with white—the sixth with violet. The seventh apartment was closely shrouded in black velvet tapestries that hung all over the ceiling and down the walls, falling in heavy folds upon a carpet of the same material and hue. But in this chamber only, the color of the windows failed to correspond with the decorations. The panes here were scarlet—a deep blood color. Now in no one of the seven apartments was there any lamp or candelabrum, amid the profusion of golden ornaments that lay scattered to and fro or depended from the roof. There was no light of any kind emanating from lamp or candle within the suite of chambers. But in the corridors that followed the suite, there stood, opposite to each window, a heavy tripod, bearing a brazier of fire that projected its rays through the tinted glass and so glaringly illumined the room. And thus were produced a multitude of gaudy and fantastic appearances. But in the western or black chamber the effect of the firelight that streamed upon the dark hangings through the blood-tinted panes, was ghastly in the extreme, and produced so wild a look upon the countenances of those who entered, that there were few of the company bold enough to set foot within its precincts at all.

It was in this apartment, also, that there stood against the western wall, a gigantic clock of ebony. Its pendulum swung to and fro with a dull, heavy, monotonous clang; and when the minute-hand made the circuit of the face, and the hour was to be stricken, there came from the brazen lungs of the clock a sound which was clear and loud and deep and exceedingly musical, but of so peculiar a note and emphasis that, at each lapse of an hour, the musicians of the orchestra were constrained to pause, momentarily, in their performance, to hearken to the sound; and thus the waltzers perforce ceased their evolutions; and there was a brief disconcert of the whole gay company; and, while the chimes of the clock yet rang, it was observed that the giddiest grew pale, and the more aged and sedate passed their hands over their brows as if in confused reverie or meditation. But when the echoes had fully ceased, a light laughter at once pervaded the assembly; the musicians looked at each other and smiled as if at their own nervousness and folly, and made whispering vows, each to the other, that the next chiming of the clock should produce in them no similar emotion; and then, after the lapse of sixty minutes (which embrace three thousand and six hundred seconds of the Time that flies), there came yet another chiming of the clock, and then were the same disconcert and tremulousness and meditation as before.

But, in spite of these things, it was a gay and magnificent revel. The tastes of the duke were peculiar. He had a fine eye for colors and effects. He disregarded the *decora* of mere fashion. His plans were bold and fiery, and his conceptions glowed with barbaric lustre. There are some who would have thought him mad. His followers felt that he was not. It was necessary to hear and see and touch him to be *sure* that he was not.

He had directed, in great part, the movable embellishments of the seven chambers, upon occasion of this great *fête;* and it was his own guiding taste which had given character to the masqueraders. Be sure they were grotesque. There were much glare and glitter and piquancy and phantasm—much of what has been since seen in "Hernani." There were arabesque figures with unsuited limbs and appointments. There were delirious fancies such as the madman fashions. There was much of the beautiful, much of the wanton, much of the *bizarre,* something of the terrible, and not a little of that which might have excited disgust. To and fro in the seven chambers there stalked, in fact, a multitude of dreams. And these—the dreams—writhed in and about, taking hue from the rooms, and causing the wild music of the orchestra to seem as the echo of their steps. And, anon, there strikes the ebony clock which stands in the hall of the velvet. And then, for a moment, all is still, and all is silent save the voice of the clock. The dreams are stiff-frozen as they stand. But the echoes of the chime die away—they have endured but an instant—and a light, half-subdued laughter floats after them as they depart. And now again the music swells, and the dreams live, and writhe to and fro more merrily than ever, taking hue from the many-tinted windows through which stream the rays from the tripods. But to the chamber which lies most westwardly of the seven, there are now none of the maskers who venture; for the night is waning away; and there flows a ruddier light through the blood-colored panes; and the blackness of the sable drapery appals; and to him whose foot falls upon the sable carpet, there comes from the near clock of ebony a muffled peal more solemnly emphatic than any which reaches *their* ears who indulge in the more remote gaieties of the other apartments.

But these other apartments were densely crowded, and in them beat feverishly the heart of life. And the revel went whirlingly on, until at length there commenced the sounding of midnight upon the clock. And then the music ceased, as I have told; and the evolutions of the waltzers were quieted; and there was an uneasy cessation of all things as before. But now there were twelve strokes to be sounded by the bell of the clock; and thus it happened, perhaps, that more of thought crept, with more of time, into the meditations of the thoughtful among those who revelled. And thus, too, it happened, perhaps, that before the last echoes of the last chime had utterly sunk into silence, there were many individuals in the crowd who had found leisure to become aware of the presence of a masked figure which had arrested the attention of no single individual before. And the rumor of this new presence having spread itself whisperingly around, there arose at length from the whole company a buzz, or murmur, expressive of disapprobation and surprise—then, finally, of terror, of horror, and of disgust.

In an assembly of phantasms such as I have painted, it may well be supposed that no ordinary appearance could have excited such sensation. In truth the masquerade license of the night was nearly unlimited; but the figure in question had out-Heroded Herod, and gone beyond the bounds of even the prince's indefinite decorum. There are chords in the hearts of the most reckless which cannot be touched without emotion. Even with the utterly lost, to whom life and death are equally jests, there are matters of which no jest can be made. The whole company, indeed, seemed now deeply to feel that in the costume and bearing of the stranger neither wit nor propriety existed. The figure was tall and gaunt, and shrouded from head to foot in the habiliments of the grave. The mask which concealed the visage was made so nearly to resemble the countenance of a stiffened corpse that the closest scrutiny must have had difficulty in detecting the cheat. And yet all this might have been endured, if not approved, by the mad revellers around. But the mummer had gone so far as to assume the type of the Red Death. His vesture was dabbled in *blood*—and his broad brow, with all the features of the face, was besprinkled with the scarlet horror.

When the eyes of Prince Prospero fell upon this spectral image (which with a slow and solemn movement, as if more fully to sustain its *rôle,* stalked to and fro among the waltzers) he was seen to be convulsed, in the first moment with a strong shudder either of terror or distaste; but, in the next, his brow reddened with rage.

"Who dares? " he demanded hoarsely of the courtiers who stood near him—" who dares insult us with this blasphemous mockery? Seize him and unmask him—that we may know whom we have to hang at sunrise, from the battlements! "

It was in the eastern or blue chamber in which stood the Prince Prospero as he uttered these words. They rang throughout the seven rooms loudly and clearly—for the prince was a bold and robust man, and the music had become hushed at the waving of his hand.

It was in the blue room where stood the prince, with a group of pale courtiers by his side. At first, as he spoke, there was a slight rushing movement of this group in the direction of the intruder, who at the moment was also near at hand, and now, with deliberate and stately step, made closer approach to the speaker. But from a certain nameless awe with which the mad assumptions of the mummer had inspired the whole party, there were found none who put forth hand to seize him ; so that, unimpeded, he passed within a yard of the prince's person; and, while the vast assembly, as if with one impulse, shrank from the centres of the rooms to the walls, he made his way uninterruptedly, but with the same solemn and measured step which had distinguished him from the first, through the blue chamber to the purple—through the purple to the green—through the green to the orange—through this again to the white—and even thence to the violet, ere a decided movement had been made to arrest him. It was then, however, that the Prince Prospero, maddening with rage and the shame of his own momentary cowardice, rushed hurriedly through the six chambers, while none followed him on account of a deadly terror that had seized upon all. He bore aloft a drawn dagger, and had approached, in rapid impetuosity, to within three or four feet of the retreating figure, when the latter, having attained the extremity of the velvet apartment, turned suddenly and confronted his pursuer. There was a sharp cry—and the dagger dropped gleaming upon the sable carpet, upon which, instantly afterwards, fell prostrate in death the Prince Prospero. Then, summoning the wild courage of despair, a throng of the revellers at once threw themselves into the black apartment, and, seizing the mummer, whose tall figure stood erect and motionless within the shadow of the ebony clock, gasped in unutterable horror at finding the grave-cerements and corpse-like mask which they handled with so violent a rudeness, untenanted by any tangible form.

And now was acknowledged the presence of the Red Death. He had come like a thief in the night. And one by one dropped the revellers in the blood-bedewed halls of their revel, and died each in the despairing posture of his fall. And the life of the ebony clock went out with that of the last of the gay. And the flames of the tripods expired. And Darkness and Decay and the Red Death held illimitable dominion over all.

1842

## THE BLACK CAT

For the most wild, yet most homely narrative which I am about to pen, I neither expect nor solicit belief. Mad indeed would I be to expect it, in a case where my very senses reject their own evidence. Yet, mad am I not—and very surely do I not dream. But to-morrow I die, and to-day I would unburthen my soul. My immediate purpose is to place before the world, plainly, succinctly, and without comment, a series of mere household events. In their consequences, these events have terrified—have tortured—have destroyed me. Yet I will not attempt to expound them. To me, they have presented little but Horror—to many they will seem less terrible than *barroques*. Hereafter, perhaps, some intellect may be found which will reduce my phantasm to the commonplace—some intellect more calm, more logical, and far less excitable than my own, which will perceive, in the circumstances I detail with awe, nothing more than an ordinary succession of very natural causes and effects.

From my infancy I was noted for the docility and humanity of my disposition. My tenderness of heart was even so conspicuous as to make me the jest of my companions. I was especially fond of animals, and was indulged by my parents with a great variety of pets. With these I spent most of my time, and never was so happy as when feeding and caressing them. This peculiarity of character grew with my growth, and, in my manhood, I derived from it one of my principal sources of pleasure. To those who have cherished an affection for a faithful and sagacious dog, I need hardly be at the trouble of explaining the nature or the intensity of the gratification thus derivable. There is something in the unselfish and self-sacrificing love of a brute, which goes directly to the heart of him who has had frequent occasion to test the paltry friendship and gossamer fidelity of mere *Man*.

I married early, and was happy to find in my wife a disposition not uncongenial with my own. Observing my partiality for domestic pets, she lost no opportunity of procuring those of the most agreeable kind. We had birds, gold-fish, a fine dog, rabbits, a small monkey, and *a cat*.

This latter was a remarkably large

and beautiful animal, entirely black, and sagacious to an astonishing degree. In speaking of his intelligence, my wife, who at heart was not a little tinctured with superstition, made frequent allusion to the ancient popular notion which regarded all black cats as witches in disguise. Not that she was ever *serious* upon this point—and I mention the matter at all for no better reason than that it happens, just now, to be remembered.

Pluto—this was the cat's name—was my favorite pet and playmate. I alone fed him, and he attended me wherever I went about the house. It was even with difficulty that I could prevent him from following me through the streets.

Our friendship lasted, in this manner, for several years, during which my general temperament and character—through the instrumentality of the Fiend Intemperance—had (I blush to confess it) experienced a radical alteration for the worse. I grew, day by day, more moody, more irritable, more regardless of the feelings of others. I suffered myself to use intemperate language to my wife. At length, I even offered her personal violence. My pets, of course, were made to feel the change in my disposition. I not only neglected, but ill-used them. For Pluto, however, I still retained sufficient regard to restrain me from maltreating him, as I made no scruple of maltreating the rabbits, the monkey, or even the dog, when by accident, or through affection, they came in my way. But my disease grew upon me—for what disease is like Alcohol!—and at length even Pluto, who was now becoming old, and consequently somewhat peevish—even Pluto began to experience the effects of my ill temper.

One night, returning home, much intoxicated, from one of my haunts about town, I fancied that the cat avoided my presence. I seized him; when, in his fright at my violence, he inflicted a slight wound upon my hand with his teeth. The fury of a demon instantly possessed me. I knew myself no longer. My original soul seemed, at once, to take its flight from my body; and a more than fiendish malevolence, gin-nurtured, thrilled every fibre of my frame. I took from my waistcoat-pocket a pen-knife, opened it, grasped the poor beast by the throat, and deliberately cut one of its eyes from the socket! I blush, I burn, I shudder, while I pen the damnable atrocity.

When reason returned with the morning—when I had slept off the fumes of the night's debauch—I experienced a sentiment half of horror, half of remorse, for the crime of which I had been guilty; but it was, at best, a feeble and equivocal feeling, and the soul remained untouched. I again plunged into excess, and soon drowned in wine all memory of the deed.

In the meantime the cat slowly recovered. The socket of the lost eye presented, it is true, a frightful appearance, but he no longer appeared to suffer any pain. He went about the house as usual, but, as might be expected, fled in extreme terror at my approach. I had so much of my old heart left, as to be at first grieved by this evident dislike on the part of a creature which had once so loved me.

But this feeling soon gave place to irritation. And then came, as if to my final and irrevocable overthrow, the spirit of PERVERSENESS. Of this spirit philosophy takes no account. Yet I am not more sure that my soul lives, than I am that perverseness is one of the primitive impulses of the human heart—one of the indivisible primary faculties, or sentiments, which give direction to the character of Man. Who has not, a hundred times, found himself committing a vile or a silly action, for no other reason than because he knows he should *not?* Have we not a perpetual inclination, in the teeth of our best judgment, to violate that which is *Law,* merely because we understand it to be such? This spirit of perverseness, I say, came to my final overthrow. It was this unfathomable longing of the soul *to vex itself*—to offer violence to its own nature—to do wrong for the wrong's sake only—that urged me to continue and finally to consummate the injury I had inflicted upon the unoffending brute. One morning, in cool blood, I slipped a noose about its neck and hung it to the limb of a tree;—hung it with the tears streaming from my eyes, and with the bitterest remorse at my heart; hung it *because* I knew that it had loved me, and *because* I felt it had given me no reason of offence;—hung it *because* I knew that in so doing I was committing a sin—a deadly sin that would so jeopardize my immortal soul as to place it—if such a thing were possible—even beyond the reach of the infinite mercy of the Most Merciful and Most Terrible God.

On the night of the day on which this cruel deed was done, I was aroused from sleep by the cry of fire. The curtains of my bed were in flames. The whole house was blazing. It was with great difficulty that my wife, a servant, and myself, made our escape from the conflagration. The destruction was complete. My entire worldly wealth was swallowed up, and I resigned myself thenceforward to despair.

I am above the weakness of seeking to establish a sequence of cause and effect, between the disaster and the atrocity. But I am detailing a chain of facts—and wish not to leave even a possible link imperfect. On the day succeeding the fire, I visited the ruins. The walls, with one exception, had fallen in. This exception was found in a compartment wall, not very thick, which stood about the middle of the house, and against which had rested the head of my bed. The plastering had here, in a great measure, resisted the action of the fire—a fact which I attributed to its having been recently spread. About this wall a dense crowd were collected, and many persons seemed to be examining a particular portion of it with very minute and eager attention. The words "strange!" "singular!" and other similar expressions, excited my curiosity. I approached and saw, as if graven in *bas relief* upon the white surface, the figure of a gigantic *cat.* The impression was given with an accuracy truly marvellous. There was a rope about the animal's neck.

When I first beheld this apparition—for I could scarcely regard it as less—my wonder and my terror were extreme. But at length reflection came to my aid. The cat, I remembered, had been hung in a garden adjacent to the house. Upon the alarm of fire, this garden had been immediately filled by the crowd—by some one of whom the animal must have been cut from the tree and thrown, through an open window, into my chamber. This had probably been done with the view of arousing me from sleep. The falling of other walls had compressed the victim of my cruelty into the substance of the freshly-spread plaster; the lime of which, with the flames, and the *ammonia* from the carcass, had then accomplished the portraiture as I saw it.

Although I thus readily accounted to my reason, if not altogether to my conscience, for the startling fact just detailed, it did not the less fail to make a deep impression upon my fancy. For months I could not rid myself of the phantasm of the cat; and, during this period, there came back into my spirit a half-sentiment that seemed, but was not, remorse. I went so far as to regret the loss of the animal, and to look about me, among the vile haunts which I now habitually frequented, for another pet of the same species, and of somewhat similar appearance, with which to supply its place.

One night as I sat, half stupified, in a den of more than infamy, my attention was suddenly drawn to some black object, reposing upon the head of one of the immense hogsheads of Gin, or of Rum, which constituted the chief furniture of the apartment. I had been looking steadily at the top of this hogshead for some minutes, and what now caused me surprise was the fact that I had not sooner perceived the object thereupon. I approached it, and touched it with my hand. It was a black cat—a very large one—fully as large as Pluto, and closely resembling him in every respect but one. Pluto had not a white hair upon any portion of his body; but this cat had a large, although indefinite splotch of white, covering nearly the whole region of the breast.

Upon my touching him, he immediately arose, purred loudly, rubbed against my hand, and appeared delighted with my notice. This, then, was the very creature of which I was in search. I at once offered to purchase it of the landlord; but this person made no claim to it—knew nothing of it—had never seen it before.

I continued my caresses, and, when I prepared to go home, the animal evinced a disposition to accompany me. I permitted it to do so; occasionally stooping and patting it as I proceeded. When it reached the house it domesticated itself at once, and became immediately a great favorite with my wife.

For my own part, I soon found a dislike to it arising within me. This was just the reverse of what I had anticipated; but—I know not how or why it was—its evident fondness for myself rather disgusted and annoyed. By slow degrees, these feelings of disgust and annoyance rose into the bitterness of hatred. I avoided the creature; a certain sense of shame, and the remembrance of my former deed of cruelty, preventing me from physically abusing it. I did not, for some weeks, strike, or otherwise violently ill use it; but gradually—very gradually—I came to look upon it with unutterable loathing, and to flee silently from its odious presence, as from the breath of a pestilence.

What added, no doubt, to my hatred of the beast, was the discovery, on the morning after I brought it home, that, like Pluto, it also had been deprived of one of its eyes. This circumstance, however, only endeared it to my wife, who, as I have already said, possessed, in a high degree, that humanity of feeling which had once been my distinguishing trait, and the source of many of my simplest and purest pleasures.

With my aversion to this cat, however, its partiality for myself seemed to increase. It followed my footsteps with a pertinacity which it would be difficult to make the reader comprehend. Whenever I sat, it would crouch beneath my chair, or spring upon my knees, covering me with its loathsome caresses. If I arose to walk it would get between my feet and thus nearly throw me down, or, fastening its long and sharp claws in my dress, clamber, in this manner, to my breast. At such times, although I longed to destroy it with a blow, I was yet withheld from so doing, partly by a memory of my former crime, but chiefly—let me confess it at once—by absolute *dread* of the beast.

This dread was not exactly a dread of physical evil—and yet I should be at a loss how otherwise to define it. I am almost ashamed to own—yes, even in this felon's cell, I am almost ashamed to own—that the terror and horror with which the animal inspired me, had been heightened by one of the merest chimæras it would be possible to conceive. My wife had called my attention, more than once, to the character of the mark of white hair, of which I have spoken, and which constituted the sole visible difference between the strange beast and the one I had destroyed. The reader will remember that this mark, although large, had been originally very indefinite; but, by slow degrees—degrees nearly imperceptible, and which for a long time my Reason struggled to reject as fanciful—it had, at length, assumed a rigorous distinctness of outline. It was now the representation of an object that I shudder to name—and for this, above all, I loathed, and dreaded, and would have rid myself of the monster *had I dared*—it was now, I say, the image of a hideous—of a ghastly thing—of the GALLOWS!—oh, mournful and terrible engine of Horror and of Crime—of Agony and of Death!

And now was I indeed wretched beyond the wretchedness of mere Humanity. And *a brute beast*—whose fellow I had contemptuously destroyed—*a brute beast* to work out for *me*—for me a man, fashioned in the image of the High God—so much of insufferable wo! Alas, neither by day nor by night knew I the blessing of Rest any more! During the former the creature left me no moment alone; and, in the latter, I started, hourly, from dreams of unutterable fear, to find the hot breath of *the thing* upon my face, and its vast weight—an incarnate Night-Mare that I had no power to shake off—incumbent eternally upon my *heart!*

Beneath the pressure of torments such as these, the feeble remnant of the good within me succumbed. Evil thoughts became my sole intimates—the darkest and most evil of thoughts. The moodiness of my usual temper increased to hatred of all things and of all mankind; while, from the sudden, frequent, and ungovernable outbursts of a fury to which I now blindly abandoned myself, my uncomplaining wife, alas! was the most usual and the most patient of sufferers.

One day she accompanied me, upon some household errand, into the cellar of the old building which our poverty compelled us to inhabit. The cat followed me down the steep stairs, and, nearly throwing me headlong, exasperated me to madness. Uplifting an axe, and forgetting, in my wrath, the childish dread which had hitherto stayed my hand, I aimed a blow at the animal which, of course, would have proved instantly fatal had it descended as I wished. But this blow was arrested by the hand of my wife. Goaded, by the interference, into a rage more than demoniacal, I withdrew my arm from her grasp and buried the axe in her brain. She fell dead upon the spot, without a groan.

This hideous murder accomplished, I set myself forthwith, and with entire deliberation, to the task of concealing the body. I knew that I could not remove it from the house, either by day or by night, without the risk of being observed by the neighbors. Many projects entered my mind. At one period I thought of cutting the corpse into minute fragments, and destroying them by fire. At another, I resolved to dig a grave for it in the floor of the cellar. Again, I deliberated about casting it in the well in the yard—about packing it in a box, as if merchandize, with the usual arrangements, and so getting a porter to take it from the house. Finally I hit upon what I considered a far better expedient than either of these. I determined to wall it up in the cellar—as the monks of the middle ages are recorded to have walled up their victims.

For a purpose such as this the cellar was well adapted. Its walls were loosely constructed, and had lately been plastered throughout with a rough plaster, which the dampness of the atmosphere had prevented from hardening. Moreover, in one of the walls was a projection, caused by a false chimney, or fireplace, that had been filled up, and made to resemble the rest of the cellar. I made no doubt that I could readily displace the bricks at this point, insert the corpse, and wall the whole up as before, so that no eye could detect any thing suspicious.

And in this calculation I was not deceived. By means of a crow-bar I easily dislodged the bricks, and, having carefully deposited the body against the inner wall, I propped it in that position, while, with little trouble, I re-laid the whole structure as it originally stood. Having procured mortar, sand, and hair, with every possible precaution, I prepared a plaster which could not be distinguished from the old, and with this I very carefully went over the new brick-work. When I had finished, I felt satisfied that all was right. The wall did not present the slightest appearance of having been disturbed. The rubbish on the floor was picked up with the minutest care. I looked around triumphantly, and said to myself—"Here at least, then, my labor has not been in vain."

My next step was to look for the beast which had been the cause of so much wretchedness; for I had, at length, firmly resolved to put it to death. Had I been able to meet with it, at the moment, there could have been no doubt of its fate; but it appeared that the crafty animal had been alarmed at the violence of my previous anger, and forebore to present itself in my present mood. It is impossible to describe, or to imagine, the deep, the blissful sense of relief which the absence of the detested creature occasioned in my bosom. It did not make its appearance during the night—and thus for one night at least, since its introduction into the house, I soundly and tranquilly slept; aye, *slept* even with the burden of murder upon my soul!

The second and the third day passed, and still my tormentor came not. Once again I breathed as a free man. The monster, in terror, had fled the premises forever! I should behold it no more! My happiness was supreme! The guilt of my dark deed disturbed me but little. Some few inquiries had been made, but these had been readily answered. Even a search had been instituted—but of course nothing was to be discovered. I looked upon my future felicity as secured.

Upon the fourth day after the assassination, a party of the police came, very unexpectedly, into the house, and proceeded again to make rigorous investigation of the premises. Secure, however, in the inscrutability of my place of concealment, I felt no embarrassment whatever. The officers bade me accompany them in their search. They left no nook or corner unexplored. At length, for the third or fourth time, they descended into the cellar. I quivered not in a muscle. My heart beat calmly as that of one who slumbers in innocence. I walked the cellar from end to end. I folded my arms upon my bosom, and roamed easily to and fro. The police were thoroughly satisfied and prepared to depart. The glee at my heart was too strong to be restrained. I burned to say if but one word, by way of triumph, and to render doubly sure their assurance of my guiltlessness.

"Gentlemen," I said at last, as the party ascended the steps, "I delight to have allayed your suspicions. I wish you all health, and a little more courtesy. By the bye, gentlemen, this—this is a very well constructed house." [In the rabid desire to say something easily, I scarcely knew what I uttered at all.] "I may say an *excellently* well constructed house. These walls—are you going, gentlemen?—these walls are solidly put together!" and here, through the mere phrenzy of bravado, I rapped heavily, with a cane which I held in my hand, upon that very portion of the brick-work behind which stood the corpse of the wife of my bosom.

But may God shield and deliver me from the fangs of the Arch-Fiend! No sooner had the reverberation of my blows sunk into silence, than I was answered by a voice from within the tomb!—by a cry, at first muffled and broken, like the sobbing of a child, and then quickly swelling into one long, loud, and continuous scream, utterly anomalous and inhuman—a howl—a wailing shriek, half of horror and half of triumph, such as might have arisen only out of hell, conjointly from the throats of the damned in their agony and of the demons that exult in the damnation.

Of my own thoughts it is folly to speak. Swooning, I staggered to the opposite wall. For one instant the party upon the stairs remained motionless, through extremity of terror and of awe. In the next, a dozen stout arms were toiling at the wall. It fell bodily. The corpse, already greatly decayed and clotted with gore, stood erect before the eyes of the spectators. Upon its head, with red extended mouth and solitary eye of fire, sat the hideous beast whose craft had seduced me into murder, and whose informing voice had consigned me to the hangman. I had walled the monster up within the tomb!

1843

## *From* HAWTHORNE'S *TWICE-TOLD TALES*

We said a few hurried words about Mr. Hawthorne in our last number, with the design of speaking more fully in the present. We are still, however, pressed for room, and must necessarily discuss his volumes more briefly and more at random than their high merits deserve.

The book professes to be a collection of *tales,* yet is, in two respects, misnamed. These pieces are now in their third republication, and, of course, are thrice-told. Moreover, they are by no means *all* tales, either in the ordinary or in the legitimate understanding of the term. Many of them are pure essays; for example, "Sights from a Steeple," "Sunday at Home," "Little Annie's Ramble," "A Rill from the Town-Pump," "The Toll-Gatherer's Day," "The Haunted Mind," "The Sister Years," "Snow-Flakes," "Night Sketches," and "Foot-Prints on the Sea-Shore." We mention these matters chiefly on account of their discrepancy with that marked precision and finish by which the body of the work is distinguished.

Of the Essays just named, we must be content to speak in brief. They are each and all beautiful, without being characterized by the polish and adaptation so visible in the tales proper. A painter would at once note their leading or predominant feature, and style it *repose.* There is no attempt at effect. All is quiet, thoughtful, subdued. Yet this repose may exist simultaneously with high originality of thought; and Mr. Hawthorne has demonstrated the fact. At every turn we meet with novel combinations; yet these combinations never surpass the limits of the quiet. We are soothed as we read; and withal is a calm astonishment that ideas so apparently obvious have never occurred or been presented to us before. Herein our author differs materially from Lamb or Hunt or Hazlitt—who, with vivid originality of manner and expression, have less of the true novelty of thought than is generally supposed, and whose originality, at best, has an uneasy and meretricious quaintness, replete with startling effects unfounded in nature, and inducing trains of reflection which lead to no satisfactory result. The Essays of Hawthorne have much of the character of Irving, with more of originality, and less of finish; while, compared with the Spectator, they have a vast superiority at all points. The Spectator, Mr. Irving, and Mr. Hawthorne have in common that tranquil and subdued manner which we have chosen to denominate *repose;* but, in the case of the two former, this repose is attained rather by the absence of novel combination.

or of originality, than otherwise, and consists chiefly in the calm, quiet, unostentatious expression of commonplace thoughts, in an unambitious, unadulterated Saxon. In them, by strong effort, we are made to conceive the absence of all. In the essays before us the absence of effort is too obvious to be mistaken, and a strong undercurrent of *suggestion* runs continuously beneath the upper stream of the tranquil thesis. In short, these effusions of Mr. Hawthorne are the product of a truly imaginative intellect, restrained, and in some measure repressed, by fastidiousness of taste, by constitutional melancholy and by indolence.

But it is of his tales that we desire principally to speak. The tale proper, in our opinion, affords unquestionably the fairest field for the exercise of the loftiest talent, which can be afforded by the wide domains of mere prose. Were we bidden to say how the highest genius could be most advantageously employed for the best display of its own powers, we should answer, without hesitation—in the composition of a rhymed poem, not to exceed in length what might be perused in an hour. Within this limit alone can the highest order of true poetry exist. We need only here say, upon this topic, that, in almost all classes of composition, the unity of effect or impression is a point of the greatest importance. It is clear, moreover, that this unity cannot be thoroughly preserved in productions whose perusal cannot be completed at one sitting. We may continue the reading of a prose composition, from the very nature of prose itself, much longer than we can persevere, to any good purpose, in the perusal of a poem. This latter, if truly fulfilling the demands of the poetic sentiment, induces an exaltation of the soul which cannot be long sustained. All high excitements are necessarily transient. Thus a long poem is a paradox. And, without unity of impression, the deepest effects cannot be brought about. Epics were the offspring of an imperfect sense of Art, and their reign is no more. A poem *too* brief may produce a vivid, but never an intense or enduring impression. Without a certain continuity of effort—without a certain duration or repetition of purpose—the soul is never deeply moved. There must be the dropping of the water upon the rock. De Béranger has wrought brilliant things—pungent and spirit-stirring—but, like all immassive bodies, they lack *momentum,* and thus fail to satisfy the Poetic Sentiment. They sparkle and excite, but, from want of continuity, fail deeply to impress. Extreme brevity will degenerate into epigrammatism; but the sin of extreme length is even more unpardonable. *In medio tutissimus ibis.*

Were we called upon, however, to designate that class of composition which, next to such a poem as we have suggested, should best fulfil the demands of high genius—should offer it the most advantageous field of exertion—we should unhesitatingly speak of the prose tale, as Mr. Hawthorne has here exemplified it. We allude to the short prose narrative, requiring from a half-hour to one or two hours in its perusal. The ordinary novel is objectionable, from its length, for reasons already stated in substance. As it cannot be read at one sitting, it deprives itself, of course, of the immense force derivable from *totality.* Worldly interests intervening during the pauses of perusal, modify, annul, or counteract, in a greater or less degree, the impressions of the book. But simple cessation in reading would, of itself, be sufficient to destroy the true unity. In the brief tale, however, the author is enabled to carry out the fulness of his intention, be it what it may. During the hour of perusal the soul of the reader is at the writer's control. There are no external or extrinsic influences—resulting from weariness or interruption.

A skilful literary artist has constructed a tale. If wise, he has not fashioned his thoughts to accommodate his incidents; but having conceived, with deliberate care, a certain unique or single *effect* to be wrought out, he then invents such incidents—he then combines such events as may best aid him in establishing this preconceived effect. If his very initial sentence tend not to the outbringing of this effect, then he has failed in his first step. In the whole composition there should be no word written, of which the tendency, direct or indirect, is not to the one pre-established design. And by such means, with such care and skill, a picture is at length painted which leaves in the mind of him who contemplates it with a kindred art, a sense of the fullest satisfaction. The idea of the tale has been presented unblemished, because undisturbed: and this is an end unattainable by the novel. Undue brevity is just as exceptionable here as in the poem; but undue length is yet more to be avoided.

We have said that the tale has a point of superiority even over the poem. In fact, while the *rhythm* of this latter is an essential aid in the development of the poem's highest idea—the idea of the Beautiful—the artificialities of this rhythm are an inseparable bar to the development of all points of thought or expression which have their basis in *Truth.* But Truth is often, and in very great degree, the aim of the tale. Some of the finest tales are tales of ratiocination. Thus the field of this species of composition, if not in so elevated a region on the mountain of Mind, is a tableland of far vaster extent than the domain of the mere poem. Its products are never so rich, but infinitely more numerous, and more appreciable by the mass of mankind. The writer of the prose tale, in short, may bring to his theme a vast variety of modes or inflections of thought and expression—(the ratiocinative, for example, the sarcastic, or the humorous) which are not only antagonistical to the nature of the poem, but absolutely forbidden by one of its most peculiar and indispensable adjuncts; we allude, of course, to rhythm. It may be added here, *par parenthèse,* that the author who aims at the purely beautiful in a prose tale is laboring at a great disadvantage. For Beauty can be better treated in the poem. Not so with terror, or passion, or horror, or a multitude of such other points. And here it will be seen how full of prejudice are the usual animadversions against those *tales of effect,* many fine examples of which were found in the earlier numbers of Blackwood. The impressions produced were wrought in a legitimate sphere of action, and constituted a legitimate although sometimes an exaggerated interest.

They were relished by every man of genius: although there were found many men of genius who condemned them without just ground. The true critic will but demand that the design intended be accomplished, to the fullest extent, by the means most advantageously applicable.

We have very few American tales of real merit—we may say, indeed, none, with the exception of "The Tales of a Traveler" of Washington Irving, and these "Twice-Told Tales" of Mr. Hawthorne. Some of the pieces of Mr. John Neal abound in vigor and originality; but, in general, his compositions of this class are excessively diffuse, extravagant, and indicative of an imperfect sentiment of Art. Articles at random are, now and then, met with in our periodicals which might be advantageously compared with the best effusions of the British Magazines; but, upon the whole, we are far behind our progenitors in this department of literature.

Of Mr. Hawthorne's Tales we would say, emphatically, that they belong to the highest region of Art—an Art subservient to genius of a very lofty order. We had supposed, with good reason for so supposing, that he had been thrust into his present position by one of the impudent *cliques* which beset our literature, and whose pretensions it is our full purpose to expose at the earliest opportunity; but we have been most agreeably mistaken. We know of few compositions which the critic can more honestly commend than these "Twice-Told Tales." As Americans, we feel proud of the book.

Mr. Hawthorne's distinctive trait is invention, creation, imagination, originality—a trait which, in the literature of fiction, is positively worth all the rest. But the nature of originality, so far as regards its manifestation in letters, is but imperfectly understood. The inventive or original mind as frequently displays itself in novelty of *tone* as in novelty of matter. Mr. Hawthorne is original at *all* points.

It would be a matter of some difficulty to designate the best of these tales; we repeat that, without exception, they are beautiful. "Wakefield" is remarkable for the skill with which an old idea—a well-known incident—is worked up or discussed. A man of whims conceives the purpose of quitting his wife and residing *incognito*, for twenty years, in her immediate neighborhood. Something of this kind actually happened in London. The force of Mr. Hawthorne's tale lies in the analysis of the motives which must or might have impelled the husband to such folly, in the first instance, with the possible causes of his perseverance. Upon this thesis a sketch of singular power has been constructed.

"The Wedding Knell" is full of the boldest imagination—an imagination fully controlled by taste. The most captious critic could find no flaw in this production.

"The Minister's Black Veil" is a masterly composition, of which the sole defect is that to the rabble its exquisite skill will be *caviare*. The *obvious* meaning of this article will be found to smother its insinuated one. The *moral* put into the mouth of the dying minister will be supposed to convey the *true* import of the narrative; and that a crime of dark dye (having reference to the "young lady") has been committed, is a point which only minds congenial with that of the author will perceive.

"Mr. Higginbotham's Catastrophe" is vividly original, and managed most dexterously.

"Dr. Heidegger's Experiment" is exceedingly well imagined, and executed with surpassing ability. The artist breathes in every line of it.

"The White Old Maid" is objectionable, even more than the "Minister's Black Veil," on the score of its mysticism. Even with the thoughtful and analytic, there will be much trouble in penetrating its entire import.

"The Hollow of the Three Hills" we would quote in full had we space; —not as evincing higher talent than any of the other pieces, but as affording an excellent example of the author's peculiar ability. The subject is commonplace. A witch subjects the Distant and the Past to the view of a mourner. It has been the fashion to describe, in such cases, a mirror in which the images of the absent appear; or a cloud of smoke is made to arise, and thence the figures are gradually unfolded. Mr. Hawthorne has wonderfully heightened his effect by making the ear, in place of the eye, the medium by which the fantasy is conveyed. The head of the mourner is enveloped in the cloak of the witch, and within its magic folds there arise sounds which have an all-sufficient intelligence. Throughout this article also, the artist is conspicuous—not more in positive than in negative merits. Not only is all done that should be done, but (what perhaps is an end with more difficulty attained) there is nothing done which should not be. Every word *tells,* and there is not a word which does not tell. * * *

In the way of objection we have scarcely a word to say of these tales. There is, perhaps, a somewhat too general or prevalent *tone*—a tone of melancholy and mysticism. The subjects are insufficiently varied. There is not so much of *versatility* evinced as we might well be warranted in expecting from the high powers of Mr. Hawthorne. But beyond these trivial exceptions we have really none to make. The style is purity itself. Force abounds. High imagination gleams from every page. Mr. Hawthorne is a man of the truest genius. We only regret that the limits of our Magazine will not permit us to pay him that full tribute of commendation, which, under other circumstances, we should be so eager to pay.

1842

## THE PHILOSOPHY OF COMPOSITION

Charles Dickens, in a note now lying before me, alluding to an examination I once made of the mechanism of "Barnaby Rudge," says—"By the way, are you aware that Godwin wrote his 'Caleb Williams' backwards? He first involved his hero in a web of difficulties, forming the second volume, and then, for the first, cast about him for some mode of accounting for what had been done."

I cannot think this the *precise* mode of procedure on the part of Godwin—and indeed what he himself acknowledges, is not altogether in accordance with Mr. Dickens' idea—but the author of "Caleb Williams" was too good an artist not to perceive the advantage derivable from at least a somewhat similar process. Nothing is more clear than that every plot, worth the name, must be elaborated to its *dénouement* before anything be attempted with the pen. It is only with the *dénouement* constantly in view that we can give a plot its indispensable air of consequence, or causation, by making the incidents, and especially the tone at all points, tend to the development of the intention.

There is a radical error, I think, in the usual mode of constructing a story. Either history affords a thesis—or one is suggested by an incident of the day—or, at best, the author sets himself to work in the combination of striking events to form merely the basis of his narrative—designing, generally, to fill in with description, dialogue, or autorial comment, whatever crevices of fact, or action, may, from page to page, render themselves apparent.

I prefer commencing with the consideration of an *effect*. Keeping originality *always* in view—for he is false to himself who ventures to dispense with so obvious and so easily attainable a source of interest—I say to myself, in the first place, "Of the innumerable effects, or impressions, of which the heart, the intellect, or (more generally) the soul is susceptible, what one shall I, on the present occasion, select?" Having chosen a novel, first, and secondly a vivid effect, I consider whether it can be best wrought by incident or tone—whether by ordinary incidents and peculiar tone, or the converse, or by peculiarity both of incident and tone—afterward looking about me (or rather within) for such combinations of event, or tone, as shall best aid me in the construction of the effect.

I have often thought how interesting a magazine paper might be written by any author who would—that is to say, who could—detail, step by step, the processes by which any one of his compositions attained its ultimate point of completion. Why such a paper has never been given to the world, I am much at a loss to say—but, perhaps, the autorial vanity has had more to do with the omission than any one other cause. Most writers—poets in especial—prefer having it understood that they compose by a species of fine frenzy—an ecstatic intuition—and would positively shudder at letting the public take a peep behind the scenes, at the elaborate and vacillating crudities of thougnt—at the true purposes seized only at the last moment—at the innumerable glimpses of idea that arrived not at the maturity of full view—at the fully matured fancies discarded in despair as unmanageable—at the cautious selections and rejections—at the painful erasures and interpolations—in a word, at the wheels and pinions—the tackle for scene-shifting—the step-ladders and demon-traps—the cock's feathers, the red paint and the black patches, which, in ninety-nine cases out of the hundred, constitute the properties of the literary *histrio*.

I am aware, on the other hand, that the case is by no means common, in which an author is at all in condition to retrace the steps by which his conclusions have been attained. In general, suggestions, having arisen pell-mell, are pursued and forgotten in a similar manner.

For my own part, I have neither

sympathy with the repugnance alluded to, nor, at any time, the least difficulty in recalling to mind the progressive steps of any of my compositions; and, since the interest of an analysis, or reconstruction, such as I have considered a *desideratum,* is quite independent of any real or fancied interest in the thing analyzed, it will not be regarded as a breach of decorum on my part to show the *modus operandi* by which some one of my own works was put together. I select "The Raven," as the most generally known. It is my design to render it manifest that no one point in its composition is referrible either to accident or intuition—that the work proceeded, step by step, to its completion with the precision and rigid consequence of a mathematical problem.

Let us dismiss, as irrelevant to the poem *per se,* the circumstance—or say the necessity—which, in the first place, gave rise to the intention of composing *a* poem that should suit at once the popular and the critical taste.

We commence, then, with this intention.

The initial consideration was that of extent. If any literary work is too long to be read at one sitting, we must be content to dispense with the immensely important effect derivable from unity of impression—for, if two sittings be required, the affairs of the world interfere, and every thing like totality is at once destroyed. But since, *ceteris paribus,* no poet can afford to dispense with *any thing* that may advance his design, it but remains to be seen whether there is, in extent, any advantage to counterbalance the loss of unity which attends it. Here I say no, at once. What we term a long poem is, in fact, merely a succession of brief ones—that is to say, of brief poetical effects. It is needless to demonstrate that a poem is such, only inasmuch as it intensely excites, by elevating, the soul; and all intense excitements are, through a psychal necessity, brief. For this reason, at least one half of the "Paradise Lost" is essentially prose—a succession of poetical excitements interspersed, *inevitably,* with corresponding depressions—the whole being deprived, through the extremeness of its length, of the vastly important artistic element, totality, or unity, of effect.

It appears evident, then, that there is a distinct limit, as regards length, to all works of literary art—the limit of a single sitting—and that, although in certain classes of prose composition, such as "Robinson Crusoe" (demanding no unity) this limit may be advantageously overpassed, it can never properly be overpassed in a poem. Within this limit, the extent of a poem may be made to bear mathematical relation to its merit—in other words, to the excitement or elevation—again in other words, to the degree of the true poetical effect which it is capable of inducing; for it is clear that the brevity must be in direct ratio of the intensity of the intended effect:—this, with one proviso—that a certain degree of duration is absolutely requisite for the production of any effect at all.

Holding in view these considerations, as well as that degree of excitement which I deemed not above the popular, while not below the critical, taste, I reached at once what I conceived the proper *length* for my intended poem—a length of about one hundred lines. It is, in fact, a hundred and eight.

My next thought concerned the choice of an impression, or effect, to be conveyed; and here I may as well observe that, throughout the construction, I kept steadily in view the design of rendering the work *universally* appreciable. I should be carried too far out of my immediate topic were I to demonstrate a point upon which I have repeatedly insisted, and which, with the poetical, stands not in the slightest need of demonstration—the point, I mean, that Beauty is the sole legitimate province of the poem. A few words, however, in elucidation of my real meaning, which some of my friends have evinced a disposition to misrepresent. That pleasure which is at once the most intense, the most elevating, and the most pure, is, I believe, found in the contemplation of the beautiful. When, indeed, men speak of Beauty, they mean, precisely, not a quality, as is supposed, but an effect—they refer, in short, just to that intense and pure elevation of *soul*—*not* of intellect, or of heart—upon which I have commented, and which is experienced in consequence of contemplating "the beautiful." Now I designate Beauty as the province of the poem, merely because it is an obvious rule of Art that effects should be made to spring from direct causes—that objects should be attained through means best adapted for their attainment—no one as yet having been weak enough to deny that the peculiar elevation alluded to is *most readily* attained in the poem. Now the object, Truth, or the satisfaction of the intellect, and the object Passion, or the excitement of the heart, are, although attainable, to a certain extent, in poetry, far more readily attainable in prose. Truth, in fact, demands a precision, and Passion a *homeliness* (the truly passionate will comprehend me) which are absolutely antagonistic to that Beauty which, I maintain, is the excitement, or pleasurable elevation, of the soul. It by no means follows from any thing here said, that passion, or even truth, may not be introduced, and even profitably introduced, into a poem—for they may serve in elucidation, or aid the general effect, as do discords in music, by contrast—but the true artist will always contrive, first, to tone them into proper subservience to the predominant aim, and, secondly, to enveil them, as far as possible, in that Beauty which is the atmosphere and the essence of the poem.

Regarding, then, Beauty as my province, my next question referred to the *tone* of its highest manifestation—and all experience has shown that this tone is one of *sadness*. Beauty of whatever kind, in its supreme development, invariably excites the sensitive soul to tears. Melancholy is thus the most legitimate of all the poetical tones.

The length, the province, and the tone, being thus determined, I betook myself to ordinary induction, with the view of obtaining some artistic piquancy which might serve me as a key-note in the construction of the poem—some pivot upon which the whole structure might turn. In carefully thinking over all the usual artistic effects—or more properly *points*, in the theatrical sense—I did not fail to perceive immediately that no one had been so universally employed as that of the *refrain*. The universality of its employment sufficed to assure me of its intrinsic value, and spared me the necessity of submitting it to analysis. I considered it, however, with regard to its susceptibility of improvement, and soon saw it to be in a primitive condition. As commonly used, the *refrain*, or burden, not only is limited to lyric verse, but depends for its impression upon the force of monotone—both in sound and thought. The pleasure is deduced solely from the sense of identity—of repetition. I resolved to diversify, and so vastly heighten, the effect, by adhering, in general, to the monotone of sound, while I continually varied that of thought: that is to say, I determined to produce continuously novel effects, by the variation *of the application* of the *refrain*—the *refrain* itself remaining, for the most part, unvaried.

These points being settled, I next bethought me of the *nature* of my *refrain*. Since its application was to be repeatedly varied, it was clear that the *refrain* itself must be brief, for there would have been an insurmountable difficulty in frequent variations of application in any sentence of length. In proportion to the brevity of the sentence, would, of course, be the facility of the variation. This led me at once to a single word as the best *refrain*.

The question now arose as to the *character* of the word. Having made up my mind to a *refrain*, the division of the poem into stanzas was, of course, a corollary: the *refrain* forming the close of each stanza. That such a close, to have force, must be sonorous and susceptible of protracted emphasis, admitted no doubt; and these considerations inevitably led me to the long *o* as the most sonorous vowel, in connection with *r* as the most producible consonant.

The sound of the *refrain* being thus determined, it became necessary to select a word embodying this sound, and at the same time in the fullest possible keeping with that melancholy which I had predetermined as the tone of the poem. In such a search it would have been absolutely impossible to overlook the word "Nevermore." In fact, it was the very first which presented itself.

The next *desideratum* was a pretext for the continuous use of the one word "nevermore." In observing the difficulty which I at once found in inventing a sufficiently plausible reason for its continuous repetition, I did not fail to perceive that this difficulty arose solely from the pre-assumption that the word was to be so continuously or monotonously spoken by *a human* being—I did not fail to perceive, in short, that the difficulty lay in the reconciliation of this monotony with the exercise of reason on the part of the creature repeating the word. Here, then, immediately arose the idea of a *non*-reasoning creature capable of speech; and very naturally, a parrot, in the first instance, suggested itself, but was superseded forthwith by a Raven, as equally capable of speech, and infinitely more in keeping with the intended *tone*.

I had now gone so far as the conception of a Raven—the bird of ill omen—monotonously repeating the one word, "Nevermore," at the conclusion of each stanza, in a poem of melancholy tone, and in length about one hundred lines. Now, never losing sight of the object *supremeness*, or perfection, at all points, I asked myself—"Of all melancholy topics, what, according to the *universal* understanding of mankind, is the *most* melancholy?" Death—was the obvious reply. "And when," I said, "is this most melancholy of topics most poetical?" From what I have already explained at some length, the answer, here also, is obvious—"When it most closely allies itself to *Beauty:* the death, then, of a beautiful woman is, unquestionably, the most poetical topic in the world—and equally is it beyond doubt that the lips best suited for such topic are those of a bereaved lover."

I had now to combine the two ideas, of a lover lamenting his deceased mistress, and a Raven continuously repeating the word "Nevermore." I had to combine these, bearing in mind my design of varying, at every turn, the *application* of the word repeated; but the only intelligible mode of such combination is that of imagining the Raven employing the word in answer to the queries of the lover. And here it was that I saw at once the opportunity afforded for the effect on which I had been depending—that is to say, the effect of the *variation of application.* I saw that I could make the first query propounded by the lover—the first query to which the Raven should reply "Nevermore"—that I could make this first query a commonplace one—the second less so—the third still less, and so on—until at length the lover, startled from his original *nonchalance* by the melancholy character of the word itself—by its frequent repetition—and by a consideration of the ominous reputation of the fowl that uttered it—is at length excited to superstition, and wildly propounds queries of a far different character—queries whose solution he has passionately at heart—propounds them half in superstition and half in that species of despair which delights in self-torture—propounds them not altogether because he believes in the prophetic or demoniac character of the bird (which, reason assures him, is merely repeating a lesson learned by rote) but because he experiences a phrenzied pleasure in so modeling his questions as to receive from the *expected* "Nevermore" the most delicious because the most intolerable of sorrow. Perceiving the opportunity thus afforded me—or, more strictly, thus forced upon me in the progress of the construction—I first established in mind the climax, or concluding query—that to which "Nevermore" should be in the last place an answer—that in reply to which this word "Nevermore" should involve the utmost conceivable amount of sorrow and despair.

Here then the poem may be said to have its beginning—at the end, where all works of art should begin—for it was here, at this point of my preconsiderations, that I first put pen to paper in the composition of the stanza:

"Prophet," said I, "thing of evil! prophet
still if bird or devil!
By that heaven that bends above us—by
that God we both adore,
Tell this soul with sorrow laden, if within
the distant Aidenn,
It shall clasp a sainted maiden whom the
angels name Lenore—
Clasp a rare and radiant maiden whom
the angels name Lenore."
Quoth the Raven, "Nevermore."

I composed this stanza, at this point, first, that by establishing the climax,

I might the better vary and graduate, as regards seriousness and importance, the preceding queries of the lover; and secondly, that I might definitely settle the rhythm, the metre, and the length and general arrangement of the stanza,—as well as graduate the stanzas which were to precede, so that none of them might surpass this in rhythmical effect. Had I been able, in the subsequent composition, to construct more vigorous stanzas, I should, without scruple, have purposely enfeebled them, so as not to interfere with the climacteric effect.

And here I may as well say a few words of the versification. My first object (as usual) was originality. The extent to which this has been neglected, in versification, is one of the most unaccountable things in the world. Admitting that there is little possibility of variety in mere *rhythm*, it is still clear that the possible varieties of metre and stanza are absolutely infinite—and yet, *for centuries, no man, in verse, has ever done, or ever seemed to think of doing, an original thing*. The fact is, originality (unless in minds of very unusual force) is by no means a matter, as some suppose, of impulse or intuition. In general, to be found, it must be elaborately sought, and although a positive merit of the highest class, demands in its attainment less of invention than negation.

Of course, I pretend to no originality in either the rhythm or metre of "The Raven." The former is trochaic—the latter is octameter acatalectic, alternating with heptameter catalectic repeated in the *refrain* of the fifth verse, and terminating with tetrameter catalectic. Less pedantically—the feet employed throughout (trochees) consist of a long syllable followed by a short: the first line of the stanza consists of eight of these feet—the second of seven and a half (in effect two-thirds)—the third of eight—the fourth of seven and a half—the fifth the same—the sixth three and a half. Now, each of these lines, taken individually has been employed before; and what originality "The Raven" has, is in their *combination into stanza;* nothing even remotely approaching this combination has ever been attempted. The effect of this originality of combination is aided by other unusual, and some altogether novel effects, arising from an extension of the application of the principles of rhyme and alliteration.

The next point to be considered was the mode of bringing together the lover and the Raven—and the first branch of this consideration was the *locale*. For this the most natural suggestion might seem to be a forest, or the fields—but it has always appeared to me that a close *circumscription of space* is absolutely necessary to the effect of insulated incident:—it has the force of a frame to a picture. It has an indisputable moral power in keeping concentrated the attention, and, of course, must not be confounded with mere unity of place.

I determined, then, to place the lover in his chamber—in a chamber rendered sacred to him by memories of her who had frequented it. The room is represented as richly furnished—this in mere pursuance of the ideas I have already explained on the subject of Beauty, as the sole true poetical thesis.

The *locale* being thus determined,

I had now to introduce the bird—and the thought of introducing him through the window, was inevitable. The idea of making the lover suppose, the first instance, that the flapping of the wings of the bird against the shutter, is a "tapping" at the door, originated in a wish to increase, by prolonging, the reader's curiosity, and in a desire to admit the incidental effect arising from the lover's throwing open the door, finding all dark, and thence adopting the half-fancy that it was the spirit of his mistress that knocked.

I made the night tempestuous, first, to account for the Raven's seeking admission, and secondly, for the effect of contrast with the (physical) serenity within the chamber.

I made the bird alight on the bust of Pallas, also for the effect of contrast between the marble and the plumage—it being understood that the bust was absolutely *suggested* by the bird—the bust of *Pallas* being chosen, first, as most in keeping with the scholarship of the lover, and secondly for the sonorousness of the word, *Pallas,* itself.

About the middle of the poem, also, I have availed myself of the force of contrast, with a view of deepening the ultimate impression. For example, an air of the fantastic—approaching as nearly to the ludicrous as was admissible—is given to the Raven's entrance. He comes in "with many a flirt and flutter."

Not the *least obeisance made he*—not a moment stopped or stayed he,
*But with mien of lord or lady,* perched above my chamber door.

In the two stanzas which follow, the design is more obviously carried out:—

Then this ebony bird beguiling my sad fancy into smiling
By the *grave and stern decorum of the countenance it wore,*
"Though thy *crest be shorn and shaven* thou," I said, "art sure no craven,
Ghastly grim and ancient Raven wandering from the nightly shore—
Tell me what thy lordly name is on the Night's Plutonian shore!"
Quoth the Raven, "Nevermore."

---

Much I marvelled *this ungainly fowl* to hear discourse so plainly,
Though its answer little meaning—little relevancy bore;
For we cannot help agreeing that no living human being
*Ever yet was blessed with seeing bird above his chamber door—*
*Bird or beast upon the sculptured bust above his chamber door,*
With such name as "Nevermore."

---

The effect of the *dénouement* being thus provided for, I immediately drop the fantastic for a tone of the most profound seriousness—this tone commencing in the stanza directly following the one last quoted, with the line,

But the Raven, sitting lonely on that placid bust, spoke only, etc.

From this epoch the lover no longer jests—no longer sees any thing even of the fantastic in the Raven's demeanor. He speaks of him as a "grim, ungainly, ghastly, gaunt, and ominous bird of yore," and feels the "fiery eyes" burning into his "bosom's core." This revolution of thought, or fancy, on the lover's part, is intended to induce a similar one on the part of the reader—to bring the mind into a proper frame for the *dénouement*—which is now brought about as rapidly and as *directly* as possible.

With the *dénouement* proper—with the Raven's reply, "Nevermore," to the lover's final demand if he shall meet his mistress in another world—the poem, in its obvious phase, that of a simple narrative, may be said to have its completion. So far, every thing is within the limits of the accountable—of the real. A raven, having learned by rote the single word "Nevermore," and having escaped from the custody of its owner, is driven at midnight, through the violence of a storm, to seek admission at a window from which a light still gleams—the chamber-window of a student, occupied half in poring over a volume, half in dreaming of a beloved mistress deceased. The casement being thrown open at the fluttering of the bird's wings, the bird itself perches on the most convenient seat out of the immediate reach of the student, who, amused by the incident and the oddity of the visitor's demeanor, demands of it, in jest and without looking for a reply, its name. The raven addressed, answers with its customary word, "Nevermore"—a word which finds immediate echo in the melancholy heart of the student, who, giving utterance aloud to certain thoughts suggested by the occasion, is again startled by the fowl's repetition of "Nevermore." The student now guesses the state of the case, but is impelled, as I have before explained, by the human thirst for self-torture, and in part by superstition, to propound such queries to the bird as will bring him, the lover, the most of the luxury of sorrow, through the anticipated answer "Nevermore." With the indulgence, to the utmost extreme, of this self-torture, the narration, in what I have termed its first or obvious phase, has a natural termination, and so far there has been no overstepping of the limits of the real.

But in subjects so handled, however skilfully, or with however vivid an array of incident, there is always a certain hardness or nakedness, which repels the artistical eye. Two things are invariably required—first, some amount of complexity, or more properly, adaptation; and, secondly, some amount of suggestiveness—some under current, however indefinite, of meaning. It is this latter, in especial, which imparts to a work of art so much of that *richness* (to borrow from colloquy a forcible term) which we are too fond of confounding with *the ideal.* It is the *excess* of the suggested meaning—it is the rendering this the upper instead of the under current of the theme—which turns into prose (and that of the very flattest kind) the so called poetry of the so called transcendentalists.

Holding these opinions, I added the two concluding stanzas of the poem—their suggestiveness being thus made to pervade all the narrative which has preceded them. The under current of meaning is rendered first apparent in the lines—

"Take thy beak from out *my heart,* and
take thy form from off my door!"
Quoth the Raven, "Nevermore!"

It will be observed that the words, "from out my heart," involve the first metaphorical expression in the poem. They, with the answer, "Nevermore," dispose the mind to seek a moral in all that has been previously narrated. The reader begins now to regard the Raven as emblematical—but it is not until the very last line of the very last stanza, that the intention of making him emblematical of *Mournful and Never-ending Remembrance* is permitted distinctly to be seen:

And the Raven, never flitting, still is sitting, still is sitting,
On the pallid bust of Pallas just above my chamber door;
And his eyes have all the seeming of a demon's that is dreaming,
And the lamplight o'er him streaming throws his shadow on the floor;
And my soul *from out that shadow* that lies floating on the floor
Shall be lifted—nevermore.

1846

## *From* THE POETIC PRINCIPLE

In speaking of the Poetic Principle, I have no design to be either thorough or profound. While discussing very much at random the essentiality of what we call Poetry, my principal purpose will be to cite for consideration some few of those minor English or American poems which best suit my own taste, or which, upon my own fancy, have left the most definite impression. By "minor poems" I mean, of course, poems of little length. And here, in the beginning, permit me to say a few words in regard to a somewhat peculiar principle, which, whether rightfully or wrongfully, has always had its influence in my own critical estimate of the poem. I hold that a long poem does not exist. I maintain that the phrase, "a long poem," is simply a flat contradiction in terms.

I need scarcely observe that a poem deserves its title only inasmuch as it excites, by elevating the soul. The value of the poem is in the ratio of this elevating excitement. But all excitements are, through a psychal necessity, transient. That degree of excitement which would entitle a poem to be so called at all, cannot be sustained throughout a composition of any great length. After the lapse of half an hour, at the very utmost, it flags—fails—a revulsion ensues—and then the poem is, in effect, and in fact, no longer such.

There are, no doubt, many who have found difficulty in reconciling the critical dictum that the "Paradise Lost" is to be devoutly admired throughout, with the absolute impossibility of maintaining for it, during perusal, the amount of enthusiasm which that critical dictum would demand. This great work, in fact, is to be regarded as poetical, only when, losing sight of that vital requisite in all works of Art, Unity, we view it merely as a series of minor poems. If, to preserve its Unity—its totality of effect or impression—we read it (as would be necessary) at a single sitting, the result is but a constant alternation of excitement and depression. After a passage of what we feel to be true poetry, there follows, inevitably, a passage of platitude which no critical pre-judgment can force us to admire; but if, upon completing the work we read it again, omitting the first book—that is to say, commencing with the second—we shall be surprised at now finding that admirable which we before condemned—that damnable which we had previously so much admired. It follows from all this that the ultimate, aggregate, or absolute effect of even the best epic under the sun, is a nullity:—and this is precisely the fact.

In regard to the Iliad, we have, if not positive proof, at least very good reason for believing it intended as a series of lyrics; but, granting the epic intention, I can say only that the work is based in an imperfect sense of art. The modern epic is, of the suppositititious ancient model, but an inconsiderate and blindfold imitation. But the day of these artistic anomalies is over. If, at any time, any very long poem *were* popular in reality—which I doubt—it is at least clear that no very long poem will ever be popular again.

That the extent of a poetical work is, *ceteris paribus,* the measure of its merit, seems undoubtedly, when we thus state it, a proposition sufficiently absurd—yet we are indebted for it to the Quarterly Reviews. Surely there can be nothing in mere *size,* abstractly considered—there can be nothing in mere *bulk,* so far as a volume is concerned, which has so continuously elicited admiration from these saturnine pamphlets! A mountain, to be sure, by the mere sentiment of physical magnitude which it conveys, *does* impress us with a sense of the sublime—but no man is impressed after *this* fashion by the material grandeur of even "The Columbiad." Even the Quarterlies have not instructed us to be so impressed by it. *As yet,* they have not *insisted* on our estimating Lamartine by the cubic foot, or Pollock by the pound—but what else are we to *infer* from their continued prating about "sustained effort"? If, by "sustained effort," any little gentleman has accomplished an epic, let us frankly commend him for the effort—if this indeed be a thing commendable—but let us forbear praising the epic on the effort's account. It is to be hoped that common sense, in the time to come, will prefer deciding upon a work of art rather by the impression it makes, by the effect it produces, than by the time it took to impress the effect, or by the amount of "sustained effort" which had been found necessary in effecting the impression. The fact is, that perseverance is one thing, and genius quite another; nor can all the Quarterlies in Christendom confound them. By and by, this proposition, with many which I have just been urging, will be received as self-evident. In the mean time, by being generally condemned as falsities, they will not be essentially damaged as truths.

On the other hand, it is clear that a poem may be improperly brief. Undue brevity degenerates into mere epigrammatism. A *very* short poem, while now and then producing a brilliant or vivid, never produces a profound or enduring effect. There must be the steady pressing down of the stamp upon the wax. De Béranger has wrought innumerable things, pungent and spirit-stirring; but in general they have been too imponderous to stamp themselves deeply into the public attention, and thus, as so many feathers of fancy, have been blown aloft only to be whistled down the wind. * * *

While the epic mania—while the idea that, to merit in poetry, prolixity is indispensable—has for some years past been gradually dying out of the public mind, by mere dint of its own absurdity—we find it succeeded by a heresy too palpably false to be long tolerated, but one which, in the brief period it has already endured, may be said to have accomplished more in the corruption of our Poetical Literature than all its other enemies combined. I allude to the heresy of *The Didactic.*

It has been assumed, tacitly and avowedly, directly and indirectly, that the ultimate object of all Poetry is Truth. Every poem, it is said, should inculcate a moral; and by this moral is the poetical merit of the work to be adjudged. We Americans, especially, have patronized this happy idea; and we Bostonians, very especially, have developed it in full. We have taken it into our heads that to write a poem simply for the poem's sake, and to acknowledge such to have been our design, would be to confess ourselves radically wanting in the true Poetic dignity and force:—but the simple fact is, that, would we but permit ourselves to look into our own souls, we should immediately there discover that under the sun there neither exists nor *can* exist any work more thoroughly dignified—more supremely noble than this very poem—this poem *per se*—this poem which is a poem and nothing more—this poem written solely for the poem's sake.

With as deep a reverence for the True as ever inspired the bosom of man, I would, nevertheless, limit, in some measure, its modes of inculcation. I would limit to enforce them. I would not enfeeble them by dissipation. The demands of Truth are severe. She has no sympathy with the myrtles. All *that* which is so indispensable in Song, is precisely all *that* with which *she* has nothing whatever to do. It is but making her a flaunting paradox, to wreathe her in gems and flowers. In enforcing a truth, we need severity rather than efflorescence of language. We must be simple, precise, terse. We must be cool, calm, unimpassioned. In a word, we must be in that mood which, as nearly as possible, is the exact converse of the poetical. *He* must be blind, indeed, who does not perceive the radical and chasmal differences between the truthful and the poetical modes of inculcation. He must be theory-mad beyond redemption who, in spite of these differences, shall still persist in attempting to reconcile the obstinate oils and waters of Poetry and Truth.

Dividing the world of mind into its three most immediately obvious distinctions, we have the Pure Intellect, Taste, and the Moral Sense. I place Taste in the middle, because it is just this position which, in the mind, it occupies. It holds intimate relations with either extreme; but from the Moral Sense is separated by so faint a difference that Aristotle has not hesitated to place some of its operations among the virtues themselves. Nevertheless, we find the *offices* of the trio marked with a sufficient distinction. Just as the Intellect concerns itself with Truth, so Taste informs us of the Beautiful, while the Moral Sense is regardful of Duty. Of this latter, while Conscience teaches the obligation, and Reason the expediency, Taste contents herself with displaying the charms:—waging war upon Vice solely on the ground of her deformity—her disproportion—her animosity to the fitting, to the appropriate, to the harmonious—in a word, to Beauty.

An immortal instinct, deep within the spirit of man, is thus, plainly, a sense of the Beautiful. This it is which administers to his delight in the manifold forms, and sounds, and odours, and sentiments, amid which he exists. And just as the lily is repeated in the lake, or the eyes of Amaryllis in the mirror, so is the mere oral or written repetition of these forms, and sounds, and colours, and odours, and sentiments, a duplicate source of delight. But this mere repetition is not poetry. He who shall simply sing, with however glowing enthusiasm, or with however vivid a truth of description, of the sights, and sounds, and odours, and colours, and sentiments, which greet *him* in common with all mankind—he, I say, has yet failed to prove his divine title. There is still a something in the distance which he has been unable to attain. We have still a thirst unquenchable, to allay which he has not shown us the crystal springs. This thirst belongs to the immortality of Man. It is at once a consequence and an indication of his perennial existence. It is the desire of the moth for the star. It is no mere appreciation of the Beauty before us—but a wild effort to reach the Beauty above. Inspired by an ecstatic prescience of the glories beyond the grave, we struggle, by multiform combinations among the things and thoughts of Time, to attain a portion of that Loveliness whose very elements, perhaps, appertain to eternity alone. And thus when by Poetry—or when by Music, the most entrancing of the Poetic moods—we find ourselves melted into tears, we weep then—not as the Abbaté Gravina supposes—through excess of pleasure, but through a certain, petulant, impatient sorrow at our inability to grasp *now,* wholly, here on earth, at once and for ever, those divine and rapturous joys, of which *through* the poem, or *through* the music, we attain to but brief and indeterminate glimpses.

The struggle to apprehend the supernal Loveliness—this struggle, on the part of souls fittingly constituted—has given to the world all *that* which it (the world) has ever been enabled at once to understand and to *feel* as poetic.

The Poetic Sentiment, of course, may develop itself in various modes—in Painting, in Sculpture, in Architecture, in the Dance—very especially in Music—and very peculiarly, and with a wide field, in the composition of the Landscape Garden. Our present theme, however, has regard only to its manifestation in words. And here let me speak briefly on the topic of rhythm. Contenting myself with the certainty that Music, in its various modes of metre, rhythm, and rhyme, is of so vast a moment in Poetry as never to be wisely rejected—is so vitally important an adjunct that he is simply silly who declines its assistance, I will not now pause to maintain its absolute essentiality. It is in Music, perhaps, that the soul most nearly attains the great end for which, when inspired by the Poetic Sentiment, it struggles—the creation of supernal Beauty. It *may* be, indeed, that here this sublime end is, now and then, attained *in fact.* We are often made to feel, with a shivering delight, that from an earthly harp are stricken notes which *cannot* have been unfamiliar to the angels. And thus there can be little doubt that in the union of Poetry with Music in its popular sense, we shall find the widest field for the Poetic development. The old Bards and Minnesingers had advantages which we do not possess—and Thomas Moore, singing his own songs, was, in the most legitimate manner, perfecting them as poems.

To recapitulate, then:—I would define, in brief, the Poetry of words as *The Rhythmical Creation of Beauty.* Its sole arbiter is Taste. With the Intellect or with the Conscience, it has only collateral relations. Unless incidentally, it has no concern whatever either with Duty or with Truth.

A few words, however, in explanation. *That* pleasure which is at once the most pure, the most elevating, and the most intense, is derived, I maintain, from the contemplation of the Beautiful. In the contemplation of Beauty we alone find it possible to attain that pleasurable elevation, or excitement, *of the soul,* which we recognize as the Poetic Sentiment, and which is so easily distinguished from Truth, which is the satisfaction of the Reason, or from Passion, which is the excitement of the heart. I make Beauty, therefore—using the word as inclusive of the sublime—I make Beauty the province of the poem, simply because it is an obvious rule of Art that effects should be made to spring as directly as possible from their causes:—no one as yet having been weak enough to deny that the peculiar elevation in question is at least *most readily* attainable in the poem. It by no means follows, however, that the incitements of Passion, or the precepts of Duty, or even the lessons of Truth, may not be introduced into a poem, and with advantage; for they may subserve, incidentally, in various ways, the general purposes of the work:—but the true artist will always contrive to tone them down in proper subjection to that *Beauty* which is the atmosphere and the real essence of the poem. * * *

1850

# RALPH WALDO EMERSON
## (1803–1882)

### From *JOURNALS*

*December 14, 1823.* I see no reason why I should bow my head to man, or cringe in my demeanour.

*February 20, 1824.* Material beauty perishes or palls. Intellectual beauty limits admiration to seasons and ages; hath its ebbs and flows of delight. . . . But moral beauty is lovely, imperishable, perfect. It is dear to the child and to the patriarch, to Heaven, Angel, Man.

*1826.* All things are double one against another, said Solomon. The whole of what we know is a system of compensations. Every defect in one manner is made up in another. Every suffering is rewarded; every sacrifice is made up; every debt is paid.

*1828.* I like to have a man's knowledge comprehend more than one class of topics, one row of shelves. I like a man who likes to see a fine barn as well as a good tragedy.

*March 4, 1831.* The Religion that is afraid of science dishonours God and commits suicide. It acknowledges that it is not equal to the whole of truth.

*April 3.* Trust to that prompting within you. No man ever got above it. Men have transgressed and hated and blasphemed it, but no man ever sinned but he felt it towering above him and threatening him with ruin.

*July 15.* The things taught in colleges and schools are not an education, but the means of education.

*Feb. 6, 1832.* Take nothing for granted. That strikes you in hearing the discourse of a wise man, that he has brought to the crucible and the analysis all that other people receive without question, as chemists are directed to select what manufacturers throw away.

*June 2.* I have sometimes thought that, in order to be a good minister, it was necessary to leave the ministry. The profession is antiquated. In an altered age, we worship in the dead forms of our forefathers. Were not a Socratic paganism better than an effete, superannuated Christianity?

*August 18.* To be genuine. Goethe, they say, was wholly so. The difficulty increases with the gifts of the individual. A plough-boy can be, but a minister, an orator, an ingenious thinker how hardly! George Fox was. "What I am in words," he said, "I am the same in life." Swedenborg was.

*September 1, 1833.* I thank the Great God who has led me through this European scene, this last schoolroom in which he has pleased to instruct me. . . . He has shown me the men I wished to see,— Landor, Coleridge, Carlyle, Wordsworth; he has thereby comforted and confirmed me in my convictions. Many things I owe to the sight of these men. I shall judge more justly, less timidly, of wise men forevermore.

*October 20.* God defend me from ever looking at a man as an animal.

*October 21.* I am sure of this, that by going much alone a man will get more of a noble courage in thought and word than from all the wisdom that is in books.

*January 22, 1834.* Luther and Napoleon are better treatises on the Will than Edwards's.

*July 18.* What is there of the divine in a load of bricks? What is there of the divine in a barber's shop? . . . Much. All.

*October 14.* Every involuntary repulsion that arises in your mind, give heed unto. It is the surface of a central truth.

*October 29.* We should hold to the usage until we are clear it is wrong.

*February 16, 1835.* If Milton, if Burns, if Bryant, is in the world, we have more tolerance, and more love for the changing sky, the mist, the rain, the bleak, overcast day, the indescribable sunrise and the immortal stars. If we believed no poet survived on the planet, nature would be tedious.

*November 6.* Charles says the nap is worn off the world.

(1823–35) 1909–14

## *NATURE*

A subtle chain of countless rings
The next unto the farthest brings;
The eye reads omens where it goes,
And speaks all languages the rose;
And, striving to be man, the worm
Mounts through all the spires of form.

### INTRODUCTION

Our age is retrospective. It builds the sepulchres of the fathers. It writes biographies, histories, and criticism. The foregoing generations beheld God and nature face to face; we, through their eyes. Why should not we also enjoy an original relation to the universe? Why should not we have a poetry and philosophy of insight and not of tradition, and a religion by revelation to us, and not the history of theirs? Embosomed for a season in nature, whose floods of life stream around and through us, and invite us, by the powers they supply, to action proportioned to nature, why should we grope among the dry bones of the past, or put the living generation into masquerade out of its faded wardrobe? The sun shines to-day also. There is more wool and flax in the fields. There are new lands, new men, new thoughts. Let us demand our own works and laws and worship.

Undoubtedly we have no questions to ask which are unanswerable. We must trust the perfection of the creation so far as to believe that whatever curiosity the order of things has awakened in our minds, the order of things can satisfy. Every man's condition is a solution in hieroglyphic to those inquiries he would put. He acts it as life, before he apprehends it as truth. In like manner, nature is already, in its forms and tendencies, describing its own design. Let us interrogate the great apparition that shines so peacefully around us. Let us inquire, to what end is nature?

All science has one aim, namely, to find a theory of nature. We have theories of races and of functions, but scarcely yet a remote approach to an idea of creation. We are now so far from the road to truth, that religious teachers dispute and hate each other, and speculative men are esteemed unsound and frivolous. But to a sound judgment, the most abstract truth is the most practical. Whenever a true theory appears, it will be its own evidence. Its test is, that it will explain all phenomena. Now many are thought not only unexplained but inexplicable; as language, sleep, madness, dreams, beasts, sex.

Philosophically considered, the universe is composed of Nature and the Soul. Strictly speaking, therefore, all that is separate from us, all which Philosophy distinguishes as the NOT ME, that is, both nature and art, all other men and my own body, must be ranked under this name, NATURE. In enumerating the values of nature and casting up their sum, I shall use the word in both senses;—in its common and in its philosophical import. In inquiries so general as our present one, the inaccuracy is not material; no confusion of thought will occur. *Nature,* in the common sense, refers to essences unchanged by man; space, the air, the river, the leaf. *Art* is applied to the mixture of his will with the same things, as in a house, a canal, a statue, a picture. But his operations taken together are so insignificant, a little chipping, baking, patching, and washing, that in an impression so grand as that of the world on the human mind, they do not vary the result.

## I. NATURE

To go into solitude, a man needs to retire as much from his chamber as from society. I am not solitary whilst I read and write, though nobody is with me. But if a man would be alone, let him look at the stars. The rays that come from those heavenly worlds will separate between him and what he touches. One might think the atmosphere was made transparent with this design, to give man, in the heavenly bodies, the perpetual presence of the sublime. Seen in the streets of cities, how great they are! If the stars should appear one night in a thousand years, how would men believe and adore; and preserve for many generations the remembrance of the city of God which had been shown! But every night come out these envoys of beauty, and light the universe with their admonishing smile.

The stars awaken a certain reverence, because though always present, they are inaccessible; but all natural objects make a kindred impression, when the mind is open to their influence. Nature never wears a mean appearance. Neither does the wisest man extort her secret, and lose his curiosity by finding out all her perfection. Nature never became a toy to a wise spirit. The flowers, the animals, the mountains, reflected the wisdom of his best hour, as much as they had delighted the simplicity of his childhood.

When we speak of nature in this manner, we have a distinct but most poetical sense in the mind. We mean the integrity of impression made by manifold natural objects. It is this which distinguishes the stick of timber of the wood-cutter, from the tree of the poet. The charming landscape which I saw this morning is indubitably made up of some twenty or thirty farms. Miller owns this field, Locke that, and Manning the woodland beyond. But none of them owns the landscape. There is a property in the horizon which no man has but he whose eye can integrate all the parts, that is, the poet. This is the best part of these men's farms, yet to this their warranty-deeds give no title.

To speak truly, few adult persons can see nature. Most persons do not see the sun. At least they have a very superficial seeing. The sun illuminates only the eye of the man, but shines into the eye and the heart of the child. The lover of nature is he whose inward and outward senses are still truly adjusted to each other; who has retained the spirit of infancy even into the era of manhood. His intercourse with heaven and earth becomes part of his daily food. In the presence of nature a wild delight runs through the man, in spite of real sorrows. Nature says,—he is my creature, and maugre all his impertinent griefs, he shall be glad with me. Not the sun or the summer alone, but every hour and season yields its tribute of delight; for every hour and change corresponds to and authorizes a different state of the mind, from breathless noon to grimmest midnight. Nature is a setting that fits equally well a comic or a mourning piece. In good health, the air is a cordial of incredible virtue. Crossing a bare common, in snow puddles, at twilight, under a clouded sky, without having in my thoughts any occurrence of special good fortune, I have enjoyed a perfect exhilaration. I am glad to the brink of fear. In the woods, too, a man casts off his years, as the snake his slough, and at what period soever of life, is always a child. In the woods is perpetual youth. Within these plantations of God, a decorum and sanctity reign, a perennial festival is dressed, and the guest sees not how he should tire of them in a thousand years. In the woods, we return to reason and faith. There I feel that nothing can befall me in life,—no disgrace, no calamity (leaving me my eyes), which nature cannot repair. Standing on the bare ground,—my head bathed by the blithe air, and uplifted into infinite space,—all mean egotism vanishes. I become a transparent eyeball; I am nothing; I see all; the currents of the Universal Being circulate through me; I am part or parcel of God. The name of the nearest friend sounds then foreign and accidental: to be brothers, to be acquaintances, master or servant, is then a trifle and a disturbance. I am the lover of uncontained and immortal beauty. In the wilderness, I find something more dear and connate than in streets or villages. In the tranquil landscape, and especially in the distant line of the horizon, man beholds somewhat as beautiful as his own nature.

The greatest delight which the fields and woods minister is the suggestion of an occult relation between man and the vegetable. I am not alone and unacknowledged. They nod to me, and I to them. The waving of the boughs in the storm is new to me and old. It takes me by surprise, and yet is not unknown. Its effect is like that of a higher thought or a better emotion coming over me, when I deemed I was thinking justly or doing right.

Yet it is certain that the power to produce this delight does not reside in nature, but in man, or in a harmony of both. It is necessary to use these pleasures with great temperance. For nature is not always tricked in holiday attire, but the same scene which yesterday breathed perfume and glittered as for the frolic of the nymphs, is overspread with melancholy to-day. Nature always wears the colors of the spirit. To a man laboring under calamity, the heat of his own fire hath sadness in it. Then there is a kind of contempt of the landscape felt by him who has just lost by death a dear friend. The sky is less grand as it shuts down over less worth in the population.

## II. COMMODITY

Whoever considers the final cause of the world will discern a multitude of uses that enter as parts into that result. They all admit of being thrown into one of the following classes: Commodity; Beauty; Language; and Discipline.

Under the general name of commodity, I rank all those advantages which our senses owe to nature. This, of course, is a benefit which is temporary and mediate, not ultimate, like its service to the soul. Yet although low, it is perfect in its kind, and is the only use of nature which all men apprehend. The misery of man appears like childish petulance, when we explore the steady and prodigal provision that has been made for his support and delight on this green ball which floats him through the heavens. What angels invented these splendid ornaments, these rich conveniences, this ocean of air above, this ocean of water beneath, this firmament of earth between? this zodiac of lights, this tent of dropping clouds, this striped coat of climates, this fourfold year? Beasts, fire, water, stones, and corn serve him. The field is at once his floor, his work-yard, his playground, his garden, and his bed.

> More servants wait on man
> Than he'll take notice of.

Nature, in its ministry to man, is not only the material, but is also the process and the result. All the parts incessantly work into each other's hands for the profit of man. The wind sows the seed; the sun evaporates the sea; the wind blows the vapor to the field; the ice, on the other side of the planet, condenses rain on this; the rain feeds the plant; the plant feeds the animal; and thus the endless circulations of the divine charity nourish man.

The useful arts are reproductions or new combinations by the wit of man, of the same natural benefactors. He no longer waits for favoring gales, but by means of steam, he realizes the fable of Æolus's bag, and carries the two and thirty winds in the boiler of his boat. To diminish friction, he paves the road with iron bars, and, mounting a coach with a ship-load of men, animals, and merchandise behind him, he darts through the country, from town to town, like an eagle or a swallow through the air. By the aggregate of these aids, how is the face of the world changed, from the era of Noah to that of Napoleon! The private poor man hath cities, ships, canals, bridges, built for him. He goes to the post-office, and the human race run on his errands; to the book-shop, and the human race read and write of all that happens, for him; to the court-house, and nations repair his wrongs. He sets his house upon the road, and the human race go forth every morning, and shovel out the snow, and cut a path for him.

But there is no need of specifying particulars in this class of uses. The catalogue is endless, and the examples so obvious, that I shall leave them to the reader's reflection, with the general remark, that this mercenary benefit is one which has respect to a farther good. A man is fed, not that he may be fed, but that he may work.

### III. BEAUTY

A nobler want of man is served by nature, namely, the love of Beauty.

The ancient Greeks called the world κόσμος, beauty. Such is the constitution of all things, or such the plastic power of the human eye, that the primary forms, as the sky, the mountain, the tree, the animal, give us a delight *in and for themselves;* a pleasure arising from outline, color, motion, and grouping. This seems partly owing to the eye itself. The eye is the best of artists. By the mutual action of its structure and of the laws of light, perspective is produced, which integrates every mass of objects, of what character soever, into a well colored and shaded globe, so that where the particular objects are mean and unaffecting, the landscape which they compose is round and symmetrical. And as the eye is the best composer, so light is the first of painters. There is no object so foul that intense light will not make beautiful. And the stimulus it affords to the sense, and a sort of infinitude which it hath, like space and time, make all matter gay. Even the corpse has its own beauty. But besides this general grace diffused over nature, almost all the individual forms are agreeable to the eye, as is proved by our endless imitations of some of them, as the acorn, the grape, the pine-cone, the wheat-ear, the egg, the wings and forms of most birds, the lion's claw, the serpent, the butterfly, sea-shells, flames, clouds, buds, leaves, and the forms of many trees, as the palm.

For better consideration, we may distribute the aspects of Beauty in a threefold manner.

1. First, the simple perception of natural forms is a delight. The influence of the forms and actions in nature is so needful to man, that, in its lowest functions, it seems to lie on the confines of commodity and beauty. To the body and mind which have been cramped by noxious work or company, nature is medicinal and restores their tone. The tradesman, the attorney comes out of the din and craft of the street and sees the sky and the woods, and is a man again. In their eternal calm, he finds himself. The health of the eye seems to demand a horizon. We are never tired, so long as we can see far enough.

But in other hours, Nature satisfies by its loveliness, and without any mixture of corporeal benefit. I see the spectacle of morning from the hill-top over against my house, from day-break to sun-rise, with emotions which an angel might share. The long slender bars of cloud float like fishes in the sea of crimson light. From the earth, as a shore, I look out into that silent sea. I seem to partake its rapid transformations; the active enchantment reaches my dust, and I dilate and conspire with the morning wind. How does Nature deify us with a few and cheap elements! Give me health and a day, and I will make the pomp of emperors ridiculous. The dawn is my Assyria; the sunset and moonrise my Paphos, and unimaginable realms of faerie; broad noon shall be my England of the senses and the understanding; the night shall be my Germany of mystic philosophy and dreams.

Not less excellent, except for our less susceptibility in the afternoon, was the charm, last evening, of a January sunset. The western clouds divided and subdivided themselves into pink flakes modulated with tints of unspeakable softness, and the air had so much life and sweetness that it was a pain to come within doors. What was it that nature would say? Was there no meaning in the live repose of the valley behind the mill, and which Homer or Shakespeare could not re-form for me in words? The leafless trees become spires of flame in the sunset, with the blue east for their background, and the stars of the dead calices of flowers, and every withered stem and stubble rimed with frost, contribute something to the mute music.

The inhabitants of cities suppose that the country landscape is pleasant only half the year. I please myself with the graces of the winter scenery, and believe that we are as much touched by it as by the genial influences of summer. To the attentive eye, each moment of the year has its own beauty, and in the same field, it beholds, every hour, a picture which was never seen before, and which shall never be seen again. The heavens change every moment, and reflect their glory or gloom on the plains beneath. The state of the crop in the surrounding farms alters the expression of the earth from week to week. The succession of native plants in the pastures and roadsides, which makes the silent clock by which time tells the summer hours, will make even the divisions of the day sensible to a keen observer. The tribes of birds and insects, like the plants punctual to their time, follow each other, and the year has room for all. By watercourses, the variety is greater. In July, the blue pontederia or pickerel-weed blooms in large beds in the shallow parts of our pleasant river, and swarms with yellow butterflies in continual motion. Art cannot rival this pomp of purple and gold. Indeed the river is a perpetual gala, and boasts each month a new ornament.

But this beauty of Nature which is seen and felt as beauty, is the least part. The shows of day, the dewy morning, the rainbow, mountains, orchards in blossom, stars, moonlight, shadows in still water, and the like, if too eagerly hunted, become shows merely, and mock us with their unreality. Go out of the house to see the moon, and 'tis mere tinsel; it will not please as when its light shines upon your necessary journey. The beauty that shimmers in the yellow afternoons of October, who ever could clutch it? Go forth to find it and it is gone; 'tis only a mirage as you look from the windows of diligence.

2. The presence of a higher, namely, of the spiritual element is essential to its perfection. The high and divine beauty which can be loved without effeminacy, is that which is found in combination with the human will. Beauty is the mark God sets upon virtue. Every natural action is graceful. Every heroic act is also decent, and

causes the place and the bystanders to shine. We are taught by great actions that the universe is the property of every individual in it. Every rational creature has all nature for his dowry and estate. It is his, if he will. He may divest himself of it; he may creep into a corner, and abdicate his kingdom, as most men do, but he is entitled to the world by his constitution. In proportion to the energy of his thought and will, he takes up the world into himself. "All those things for which men plough, build, or sail, obey virtue," said Sallust. "The winds and waves," said Gibbon, "are always on the side of the ablest navigators." So are the sun and moon and all the stars of heaven. When a noble act is done,—perchance in a scene of great natural beauty; when Leonidas and his three hundred martyrs consume one day in dying, and the sun and moon come each and look at them once in the steep defile of Thermopylæ; when Arnold Winkelried, in the high Alps, under the shadow of the avalanche, gathers in his side a sheaf of Austrian spears to break the line for his comrades; are not these heroes entitled to add the beauty of the scene to the beauty of the deed? When the bark of Columbus nears the shore of America;—before it, the beach lined with savages, fleeing out of all their huts of cane; the sea behind; and the purple mountains of the Indian Archipelago around, can we separate the man from the living picture? Does not the New World clothe his form with her palm-groves and savannahs as fit drapery? Ever does natural beauty steal in like air, and envelop great actions. When Sir Harry Vane was dragged up the Tower-hill, sitting on a sled, to suffer death as the champion of the English laws, one of the multitude cried out to him, "You never sate on so glorious a seat!" Charles II, to intimidate the citizens of London, caused the patriot Lord Russell to be drawn in an open coach through the principal streets of the city on his way to the scaffold. "But," his biographer says, "the multitude imagined they saw liberty and virtue sitting by his side." In private places, among sordid objects, an act of truth or heroism seems at once to draw to itself the sky as its temple, the sun as its candle. Nature stretches out her arms to embrace man, only let his thoughts be of equal greatness. Willingly does she follow his steps with the rose and the violet, and bend her lines of grandeur and grace to the decoration of her darling child. Only let his thoughts be of equal scope, and the frame will suit the picture. A virtuous man is in unison with her works, and makes the central figure of the visible sphere. Homer, Pindar, Socrates, Phocion, associate themselves fitly in our memory with the geography and climate of Greece. The visible heavens and earth sympathize with Jesus. And in common life whosoever has seen a person of powerful character and happy genius, will have remarked how easily he took all things along with him,—the persons, the opinions and the day, and nature became ancillary to a man.

3. There is still another aspect under which the beauty of the world may be viewed, namely, as it becomes an object of the intellect. Besides the relation of things to virtue, they have a relation to thought. The intellect searches out the absolute order of

things as they stand in the mind of God, and without the colors of affection. The intellectual and the active powers seem to succeed each other, and the exclusive activity of the one generates the exclusive activity of the other. There is something unfriendly in each to the other, but they are like the alternate periods of feeding and working in animals; each prepares and will be followed by the other. Therefore does beauty, which, in relation to actions, as we have seen, comes unsought, and comes because it is unsought, remain for the apprehension and pursuit of the intellect; and then again, in its turn, of the active power. Nothing divine dies. All good is eternally reproductive. The beauty of nature re-forms itself in the mind, and not for barren contemplation, but for new creation.

All men are in some degree impressed by the face of the world; some men even to delight. This love of beauty is Taste. Others have the same love in such excess, that, not content with admiring, they seek to embody it in new forms. The creation of beauty is Art.

The production of a work of art throws a light upon the mystery of humanity. A work of art is an abstract or epitome of the world. It is the result or expression of nature, in miniature. For although the works of nature are innumerable and all different, the result or the expression of them all is similar and single. Nature is a sea of forms radically alike and even unique. A leaf, a sunbeam, a landscape, the ocean, make an analogous impression on the mind. What is common to them all,—that perfectness and harmony, is beauty. The standard of beauty is the entire circuit of natural forms,—the totality of nature; which the Italians expressed by defining beauty "il più nell' uno." Nothing is quite beautiful alone; nothing but is beautiful in the whole. A single object is only so far beautiful as it suggests this universal grace. The poet, the painter, the sculptor, the musician, the architect, seek each to concentrate this radiance of the world on one point, and each in his several work to satisfy the love of beauty which stimulates him to produce. Thus is Art a nature passed through the alembic of man. Thus in art does Nature work through the will of a man filled with the beauty of her first works.

The world thus exists to the soul to satisfy the desire of beauty. This element I call an ultimate end. No reason can be asked or given why the soul seeks beauty. Beauty, in its largest and profoundest sense, is one expression for the universe. God is the all-fair. Truth, and goodness, and beauty, are but different faces of the same All. But beauty in nature is not ultimate. It is the herald of inward and eternal beauty, and is not alone a solid and satisfactory good. It must stand as a part, and not as yet the last or highest expression of the final cause of Nature.

## IV. LANGUAGE

Language is a third use which Nature subserves to man. Nature is the vehicle of thought, and in a simple, double, and three-fold degree.

1. Words are signs of natural facts.

2. Particular natural facts are symbols of particular spiritual facts.

3. Nature is the symbol of spirit.

1. Words are signs of natural facts. The use of natural history is to give us aid in supernatural history; the use of the outer creation, to give us language for the beings and changes of the inward creation. Every word which is used to express a moral or intellectual fact, if traced to its root, is found to be borrowed from some material appearance. *Right* means *straight; wrong* means *twisted. Spirit* primarily means *wind; transgression,* the crossing of a *line; supercilious,* the *raising of the eyebrow.* We say the *heart* to express emotion, the *head* to denote thought; and *thought* and *emotion* are words borrowed from sensible things, and now appropriated to spiritual nature. Most of the process by which this transformation is made, is hidden from us in the remote time when language was framed; but the same tendency may be daily observed in children. Children and savages use only nouns or names of things, which they convert into verbs, and apply to analogous mental acts.

2. But this origin of all words that convey a spiritual import,—so conspicuous a fact in the history of language,—is our least debt to nature. It is not words only that are emblematic; it is things which are emblematic. Every natural fact is a symbol of some spiritual fact. Every appearance in nature corresponds to some state of the mind, and that state of the mind can only be described by presenting that natural appearance as its picture. An enraged man is a lion, a cunning man is a fox, a firm man is a rock, a learned man is a torch. A lamb is innocence; a snake is subtle spite; flowers express to us the delicate affections. Light and darkness are our familiar expression for knowledge and ignorance; and heat for love. Visible distance behind and before us, is respectively our image of memory and hope.

Who looks upon a river in a meditative hour and is not reminded of the flux of all things? Throw a stone into the stream, and the circles that propagate themselves are the beautiful type of all influence. Man is conscious of a universal soul within or behind his individual life, wherein, as in a firmament, the natures of Justice, Truth, Love, Freedom, arise and shine. This universal soul he calls Reason: it is not mine, or thine, or his, but we are its; we are its property and men. And the blue sky in which the private earth is buried, the sky with its eternal calm, and full of everlasting orbs, is the type of Reason. That which intellectually considered we call Reason, considered in relation to nature, we call Spirit. Spirit is the Creator. Spirit hath life in itself. And man in all ages and countries embodies it in his language as the FATHER.

It is easily seen that there is nothing lucky or capricious in these analogies, but that they are constant, and pervade nature. These are not the dreams of a few poets, here and there, but man is an analogist, and studies relations in all objects. He is placed in the centre of beings, and a ray of relation passes from every other being to him. And neither can man be understood without these objects, nor these objects without man. All the facts in natural history taken by themselves, have no value, but are barren, like a single sex. But marry it to human history, and it is full of life. Whole floras, all Linnæus' and Buffon's volumes, are dry catalogues of facts; but the most trivial of these facts, the habit of a plant, the organs, or work, or noise of an insect, applied to the illustration of a fact in intellectual philosophy, or in any way associated to human nature, affects us in the most lively and agreeable manner. The seed of a plant,—to what affecting analogies in the nature of man is that little fruit made use of, in all discourse, up to the voice of Paul, who calls the human corpse a seed,—"It is sown a natural body; it is raised a spiritual body." The motion of the earth round its axis and round the sun, makes the day and the year. These are certain amounts of brute light and heat. But is there no intent of an analogy between man's life and the seasons? And do the seasons gain no grandeur or pathos from that analogy? The instincts of the ant are very unimportant considered as the ant's; but the moment a ray of relation is seen to extend from it to man, and the little drudge is seen to be a monitor, a little body with a mighty heart, then all its habits, even that said to be recently observed, that it never sleeps, become sublime.

Because of this radical correspondence between visible things and human thoughts, savages, who have only what is necessary, converse in figures. As we go back in history, language becomes more picturesque, until its infancy, when it is all poetry; or all spiritual facts are represented by natural symbols. The same symbols are found to make the original elements of all languages. It has moreover been observed, that the idioms of all languages approach each other in passages of the greatest eloquence and power. And as this is the first language, so is it the last. This immediate dependence of language upon nature, this conversion of an outward phenomenon into a type of somewhat in human life, never loses its power to affect us. It is this which gives that piquancy to the conversation of a strong-natured farmer or backwoodsman, which all men relish.

A man's power to connect his thought with its proper symbol, and so to utter it, depends on the simplicity of his character, that is, upon his love of truth and his desire to communicate it without loss. The corruption of man is followed by the corruption of language. When simplicity of character and the sovereignty of ideas is broken up by the prevalence of secondary desires,—the desire of riches, of pleasure, of power, and of praise,—and duplicity and falsehood take place of simplicity and truth, the power over nature as an interpreter of the will is in a degree lost; new imagery ceases to be created, and old words are perverted to stand for things which are not; a paper currency is employed, when there is no bullion in the vaults. In due time the fraud is manifest, and words lose all power to stimulate the understanding or the affections. Hundreds of writers may be found in every long-civilized nation who for a short time believe and make others believe that they see and utter truths, who do not of themselves clothe one thought in its natural garment, but who feed unconsciously on the language created by the primary writers of the country, those, namely, who hold primarily on nature.

But wise men pierce this rotten diction and fasten words again to visible things; so that picturesque language is at once a commanding certificate that he who employs it is a man in alliance with truth and God. The moment our discourse rises above the ground line of familiar facts and is inflamed with passion or exalted by thought, it clothes itself in images. A man conversing in earnest, if he watch his intellectual processes, will find that a material image more or less luminous arises in his mind, contemporaneous with every thought, which furnishes the vestment of the thought. Hence, good writing and brilliant discourse are perpetual allegories. This imagery is spontaneous. It is the blending of experience with the present action of the mind. It is proper creation. It is the working of the Original Cause through the instruments he has already made.

These facts may suggest the advantage which the country-life possesses, for a powerful mind, over the artificial and curtailed life of cities. We know more from nature than we can at will communicate. Its light flows into the mind evermore, and we forget its presence. The poet, the orator, bred in the woods, whose senses have been nourished by their fair and appeasing changes, year after year, without design and without heed,—shall not lose their lesson altogether, in the roar of cities or the broil of politics. Long hereafter, amidst agitation and terror in national councils,—in the hour of revolution,—these solemn images shall reappear in their morning lustre, as fit symbols and words of the thoughts which the passing events shall awaken. At the call of a noble sentiment, again the woods wave, the pines murmur, the river rolls and shines, and the cattle low upon the mountains, as he saw and heard them in his infancy. And with these forms, the spells of persuasion, the keys of power are put into his hands.

3. We are thus assisted by natural objects in the expression of particular meanings. But how great a language to convey such pepper-corn informations! Did it need such noble races of creatures, this profusion of forms, this host of orbs in heaven, to furnish man with the dictionary and grammar of his municipal speech? Whilst we use this grand cipher to expedite the affairs of our pot and kettle, we feel that we have not yet put it to its use, neither are able. We are like travellers using the cinders of a volcano to roast their eggs. Whilst we see that it always stands ready to clothe what we would say, we cannot avoid the question whether the characters are not significant of themselves. Have mountains, and waves, and skies, no significance but what we consciously give them when we employ them as emblems of our thoughts? The world is emblematic. Parts of speech are metaphors, because the whole of nature is a metaphor of the human mind. The laws of moral nature answer to those of matter as face to face in a glass. "The visible world and the relation of its parts, is the dial plate of the invisible." The axioms of physics translate the laws of ethics. Thus, "the whole is greater than its part;" "reaction is equal to action;" "the smallest weight may be made to lift the greatest, the difference of

weight being compensated by time;" and many the like propositions, which have an ethical as well as physical sense. These propositions have a much more extensive and universal sense when applied to human life, than when confined to technical use.

In like manner, the memorable words of history and the proverbs of nations consist usually of a natural fact, selected as a picture or parable of a moral truth. Thus: A rolling stone gathers no moss; A bird in the hand is worth two in the bush; A cripple in the right way will beat a racer in the wrong; Make hay while the sun shines; 'Tis hard to carry a full cup even; Vinegar is the son of wine; The last ounce broke the camel's back; Long-lived trees make roots first;—and the like. In their primary sense these are trivial facts, but we repeat them for the value of their analogical import. What is true of proverbs, is true of all fables, parables, and allegories.

This relation between the mind and matter is not fancied by some poet, but stands in the will of God, and so is free to be known by all men. It appears to men, or it does not appear. When in fortunate hours we ponder this miracle, the wise man doubts if at all other times he is not blind and deaf:

> Can such things be,
> And overcome us like a summer's cloud,
> Without our special wonder?

for the universe becomes transparent, and the light of higher laws than its own shines through it. It is the standing problem which has exercised the wonder and the study of every fine genius since the world began; from the era of the Egyptians and the Brahmins to that of Pythagoras, of Plato, of Bacon, of Leibnitz, of Swedenborg. There sits the Sphinx at the road-side, and from age to age, as each prophet comes by, he tries his fortune at reading her riddle. There seems to be a necessity in spirit to manifest itself in material forms; and day and night, river and storm, beast and bird, acid and alkali, pre-exist in necessary Ideas in the mind of God, and are what they are by virtue of preceding affections in the world of spirit. A Fact is the end or last issue of spirit. The visible creation is the terminus or the circumference of the invisible world. "Material objects," said a French philosopher, "are necessarily kinds of *scoriæ* of the substantial thoughts of the Creator, which must always preserve an exact relation to their first origin; in other words, visible nature must have a spiritual and moral side."

This doctrine is abstruse, and though the images of "garment," "scoriæ," "mirror," etc., may stimulate the fancy, we must summon the aid of subtler and more vital expositors to make it plain. "Every scripture is to be interpreted by the same spirit which gave it forth,"—is the fundamental law of criticism. A life in harmony with Nature, the love of truth and of virtue, will purge the eyes to understand her text. By degrees we may come to know the primitive sense of the permanent objects of nature, so that the world shall be to us an open book, and every form significant of its hidden life and final cause.

A new interest surprises us, whilst, under the view now suggested, we contemplate the fearful extent and multitude of objects; since "every object rightly seen, unlocks a new faculty of the soul." That which was unconscious truth, becomes, when interpreted and defined in an object, a part of the domain of knowledge,—a new weapon in the magazine of power.

### V. DISCIPLINE

In view of the significance of nature, we arrive at once at a new fact, that nature is a discipline. This use of the world includes the preceding uses, as parts of itself.

Space, time, society, labor, climate, food, locomotion, the animals, the mechanical forces, give us sincerest lessons, day by day, whose meaning is unlimited. They educate both the Understanding and the Reason. Every property of matter is a school for the understanding,—its solidity or resistance, its inertia, its extension, its figure, its divisibility. The understanding adds, divides, combines, measures, and finds nutriment and room for its activity in this worthy scene. Meantime, Reason transfers all these lessons into its own world of thought, by perceiving the analogy that marries Matter and Mind.

1. Nature is a discipline of the understanding in intellectual truths. Our dealing with sensible objects is a constant exercise in the necessary lessons of difference, of likeness, of order, of being and seeming, of progressive arrangement; of ascent from particular to general; of combination to one end of manifold forces. Proportioned to the importance of the organ to be formed, is the extreme care with which its tuition is provided,—a care pretermitted in no single case. What tedious training, day after day, year after year, never ending, to form the common sense; what continual reproductions of annoyances, inconveniences, dilemmas; what rejoicing over us of little men; what disputing of prices, what reckonings of interest,—and all to form the Hand of the mind;—to instruct us that "good thoughts are no better than good dreams, unless they be executed!"

The same good office is performed by property and its filial systems of debt and credit. Debt, grinding debt, whose iron face the widow, the orphan, and the sons of genius fear and hate;—debt, which consumes so much time, which so cripples and disheartens a great spirit with cares that seem so base, is a preceptor whose lessons cannot be foregone, and is needed most by those who suffer from it most. Moreover, property, which has been well compared to snow,—"if it fall level to-day, it will be blown into drifts to-morrow,"—is the surface action of internal machinery, like the index on the face of a clock. Whilst now it is the gymnastics of the understanding, it is hiving, in the foresight of the spirit, experience in profounder laws.

The whole character and fortune of the individual are affected by the least inequalities in the culture of the understanding; for example, in the perception of differences. Therefore is Space, and therefore Time, that man may know that things are not huddled and lumped, but sundered and individual. A bell and a plough have each their use, and neither can do the office of the other. Water is good to drink, coal to burn, wool to wear; but wool cannot be drunk, nor water spun, nor coal eaten. The wise man shows his wisdom in separation, in gradation, and his scale of creatures and of merits is as wide as nature. The foolish have no range in their scale, but suppose every man is as every other man. What is not good they call the worst, and what is not hateful, they call the best.

In like manner, what good heed Nature forms in us! She pardons no mistakes. Her yea is yea, and her nay, nay.

The first steps in Agriculture, Astronomy, Zoölogy (those first steps which the farmer, the hunter, and the sailor take), teach that Nature's dice are always loaded; that in her heaps and rubbish are concealed sure and useful results.

How calmly and genially the mind apprehends one after another the laws of physics! What noble emotions dilate the mortal as he enters into the councils of the creation, and feels by knowledge the privilege to BE! His insight refines him. The beauty of nature shines in his own breast. Man is greater that he can see this, and the universe less because Time and Space relations vanish as laws are known.

Here again we are impressed and even daunted by the immense Universe to be explored. "What we know is a point to what we do not know." Open any recent journal of science, and weigh the problems suggested concerning Light, Heat, Electricity, Magnetism, Physiology, Geology, and judge whether the interest of natural science is likely to be soon exhausted.

Passing by many particulars of the discipline of nature, we must not omit to specify two.

The exercise of the Will, or the lesson of power, is taught in every event. From the child's successive possession of his several senses up to the hour when he saith, "Thy will be done!" he is learning the secret that he can reduce under his will, not only particular events but great classes, nay, the whole series of events, and so conform all facts to his character. Nature is thoroughly mediate. It is made to serve. It receives the dominion of man as meekly as the ass on which the Savior rode. It offers all its kingdoms to man as the raw material which he may mold into what is useful. Man is never weary of working it up. He forges the subtile and delicate air into wise and melodious words, and gives them wing as angels of persuasion and command. One after another his victorious thought comes up with and reduces all things, until the world becomes at last only a realized will,—the double of the man.

2. Sensible objects conform to the premonitions of Reason and reflect the conscience. All things are moral; and in their boundless changes have an unceasing reference to spiritual nature. Therefore is nature glorious with form, color, and motion: that every globe in the remotest heaven, every chemical change from the rudest crystal up to the laws of life, every change of vegetation from the first principle of growth in the eye of a leaf, to the tropical forest and antediluvian coal-mine, every animal function from the sponge up to Hercules, shall hint or thunder to man the laws of right and wrong, and echo the Ten Commandments. Therefore is Nature ever the ally of Religion: lends all her pomp and riches to the religious sentiment. Prophet and priest, David,

Isaiah, Jesus, have drawn deeply from this source. This ethical character so penetrates the bone and marrow of nature, as to seem the end for which it was made. Whatever private purpose is answered by any member or part, this is its public and universal function, and is never omitted. Nothing in nature is exhausted in its first use. When a thing has served an end to the uttermost, it is wholly new for an ulterior service. In God, every end is converted into a new means. Thus the use of commodity, regarded by itself, is mean and squalid. But it is to the mind an education in the doctrine of Use, namely, that a thing is good only so far as it serves; that a conspiring of parts and efforts to the production of an end is essential to any being. The first and gross manifestation of this truth is our inevitable and hated training in values and wants, in corn and meat.

It has already been illustrated, that every natural process is a version of a moral sentence. The moral law lies at the centre of nature and radiates to the circumference. It is the pith and marrow of every substance, every relation, and every process. All things with which we deal, preach to us. What is a farm but a mute gospel? The chaff and the wheat, weeds and plants, blight, rain, insects, sun,—it is a sacred emblem from the first furrow of spring to the last stack which the snow of winter overtakes in the fields. But the sailor, the shepherd, the miner, the merchant, in their several resorts, have each an experience precisely parallel, and leading to the same conclusion: because all organizations are radically alike. Nor can it be doubted that this moral sentiment which thus scents the air, grows in the grain, and impregnates the waters of the world, is caught by man and sinks into his soul. The moral influence of nature upon every individual is that amount of truth which it illustrates to him. Who can estimate this? Who can guess how much firmness the sea-beaten rock has taught the fisherman? how much tranquillity has been reflected to man from the azure sky, over whose unspotted deeps the winds forevermore drive flocks of stormy clouds, and leave no wrinkle or stain? how much industry and providence and affection we have caught from the pantomime of brutes? What a searching preacher of self-command is the varying phenomenon of Health!

Herein is especially apprehended the unity of Nature,—the unity in variety,—which meets us everywhere. All the endless variety of things make an identical impression. Xenophanes complained in his old age that, look where he would, all things hastened back to Unity. He was weary of seeing the same entity in the tedious variety of forms. The fable of Proteus has a cordial truth. A leaf, a drop, a crystal, a moment of time, is related to the whole, and partakes of the perfection of the whole. Each particle is a microcosm, and faithfully renders the likeness of the world.

Not only resemblances exist in things whose analogy is obvious, as when we detect the type of the human hand in the flipper of the fossil saurus, but also in objects wherein there is great superficial unlikeness. Thus architecture is called "frozen music," by De Staël and Goethe. Vitruvius thought an architect should be a musician. "A Gothic church," said Coleridge, "is a petrified religion." Michael Angelo maintained that, to an architect, a knowledge of anatomy is essential. In Haydn's oratorios, the notes present to the imagination not only motions, as of the snake, the stag, and the elephant, but colors also; as the green grass. The law of harmonic sounds reappears in the harmonic colors. The granite is differenced in its laws only by the more or less of heat from the river that wears it away. The river, as it flows, resembles the air that flows over it; the air resembles the light which traverses it with more subtile currents; the light resembles the heat which rides with it through Space. Each creature is only a modification of the other; the likeness in them is more than the difference, and their radical law is one and the same. A rule of one art, or a law of one organization, holds true throughout nature. So intimate is this Unity that, it is easily seen, it lies under the undermost garment of Nature, and betrays its source in Universal Spirit. For it pervades Thought also. Every universal truth which we express in words, implies or supposes every other truth. *Omne verum vero consonat.* It is like a great circle on a sphere, comprising all possible circles; which, however, may be drawn and comprise it in like manner. Every such truth is the absolute Ens seen from one side. But it has innumerable sides.

The central Unity is still more conspicuous in actions. Words are finite organs of the infinite mind. They cannot cover the dimensions of what is in truth. They break, chop, and impoverish it. An action is the perfection and publication of thought. A right action seems to fill the eye, and to be related to all nature. "The wise man, in doing one thing, does all; or, in the one thing he does rightly, he sees the likeness of all which is done rightly."

Words and actions are not the attributes of brute nature. They introduce us to the human form, of which all other organizations appear to be degradations. When this appears among so many that surround it, the spirit prefers it to all others. It says, "From such as this have I drawn joy and knowledge; in such as this have I found and beheld myself; I will speak to it; it can speak again; it can yield me thought already formed and alive." In fact, the eye,—the mind,—is always accompanied by these forms, male and female; and these are incomparably the richest informations of the power and order that lie at the heart of things. Unfortunately every one of them bears the marks as of some injury; is marred and superficially defective. Nevertheless, far different from the deaf and dumb nature around them, these all rest like fountain-pipes on the unfathomed sea of thought and virtue whereto they alone, of all organizations, are the entrances.

It were a pleasant inquiry to follow into detail their ministry to our education, but where would it stop? We are associated in adolescent and adult life with some friends, who, like skies and waters, are coextensive with our idea; who, answering each to a certain affection of the soul, satisfy our desire on that side; whom we lack power to put at such focal distance from us, that we can mend or even analyze them. We cannot choose but love them. When much intercourse with a friend has supplied us with a standard of excellence, and has increased our respect for the resources of God who thus sends a real person to outgo our ideal; when he has, moreover, become an object of thought, and, whilst his character retains all its unconscious effect, is converted in the mind into solid and sweet wisdom,—it is a sign to us that his office is closing, and he is commonly withdrawn from our sight in a short time.

### VI. IDEALISM

Thus is the unspeakable but intelligible and practicable meaning of the world conveyed to man, the immortal pupil, in every object of sense. To this one end of Discipline, all parts of nature conspire.

A noble doubt perpetually suggests itself,—whether this end be not the Final Cause of the Universe; and whether nature outwardly exists. It is a sufficient account of that Appearance we call the World, that God will teach a human mind, and so makes it the receiver of a certain number of congruent sensations, which we call sun and moon, man and woman, house and trade. In my utter impotence to test the authenticity of the report of my senses, to know whether the impressions they make on me correspond with outlying objects, what difference does it make, whether Orion is up there in heaven, or some god paints the image in the firmament of the soul? The relations of parts and the end of the whole remaining the same, what is the difference, whether land and sea interact, and worlds revolve and intermingle without number or end,—deep yawning under deep, and galaxy balancing galaxy, throughout absolute space,—or whether, without relations of time and space, the same appearances are inscribed in the constant faith of man? Whether nature enjoy a substantial existence without, or is only in the apocalypse of the mind, it is alike useful and alike venerable to me. Be it what it may, it is ideal to me so long as I cannot try the accuracy of my senses.

The frivolous make themselves merry with the Ideal theory, as if its consequences were burlesque; as if it affected the stability of nature. It surely does not. God never jests with us, and will not compromise the end of nature by permitting any inconsequence in its procession. Any distrust of the permanence of laws would paralyze the faculties of man. Their permanence is sacredly respected, and his faith therein is perfect. The wheels and springs of man are all set to the hypothesis of the permanence of nature. We are not built like a ship to be tossed, but like a house to stand. It is a natural consequence of this structure, that so long as the active powers predominate over the reflective, we resist with indignation any hint that nature is more short-lived or mutable than spirit. The broker, the wheelwright, the carpenter, the tollman, are much displeased at the intimation.

But whilst we acquiesce entirely in the permanence of natural laws, the question of the absolute existence of nature still remains open. It is the uniform effect of culture on the human mind, not to shake our faith in the stability of particular phenomena, as of heat, water, azote; but to lead us to regard nature as phenomenon not a substance; to attribute necessary existence to spirit; to esteem nature as an accident and an effect.

To the senses and the unrenewed understanding, belongs a sort of instinctive belief in the absolute existence of nature. In their view man and nature are indissolubly joined. Things are ultimates, and they never look beyond their sphere. The presence of Reason mars this faith. The first effort of thought tends to relax this despotism of the senses which binds us to nature as if we were a part of it, and shows us nature aloof, and, as it were, afloat. Until this higher agency intervened, the animal eye sees, with wonderful accuracy, sharp outlines and colored surfaces. When the eye of Reason opens, to outline and surface are at once added grace and expression. These proceed from imagination and affection, and abate somewhat of the angular distinctness of objects. If the Reason be stimulated to more earnest vision, outlines and surfaces become transparent, and are no longer seen; causes and spirits are seen through them. The best moments of life are these delicious awakenings of the higher powers, and the reverential withdrawing of nature before its God.

Let us proceed to indicate the effects of culture.

1. Our first institution in the Ideal philosophy is a hint from Nature herself.

Nature is made to conspire with spirit to emancipate us. Certain mechanical changes, a small alteration in our local position, apprises us of a dualism. We are strangely affected by seeing the shore from a moving ship, from a balloon, or through the tints of an unusual sky. The least change in our point of view gives the whole world a pictorial air. A man who seldom rides, needs only to get into a coach and traverse his own town, to turn the street into a puppet-show. The men, the women,—talking, running, bartering, fighting,—the earnest mechanic, the lounger, the beggar, the boys, the dogs, are unrealized at once, or, at least, wholly detached from all relation to the observer, and seen as apparent, not substantial beings. What new thoughts are suggested by seeing a face of country quite familiar, in the rapid movement of the railroad car! Nay, the most wonted objects (make a very slight change in the point of vision) please us most. In a camera obscura, the butcher's cart, and the figure of one of our own family amuse us. So a portrait of a well-known face gratifies us. Turn the eyes upside down, by looking at the landscape through your legs, and how agreeable is the picture, though you have seen it any time these twenty years!

In these cases, by mechanical means, is suggested the difference between the observer and the spectacle,—between man and nature. Hence arises a pleasure mixed with awe; I may say, a low degree of the sublime is felt, from the fact, probably, that man is hereby apprised that whilst the world is a spectacle, something in himself is stable.

2. In a higher manner the poet communicates the same pleasure. By a few strokes he delineates, as on air, the sun, the mountain, the camp, the city, the hero, the maiden, not different from what we know them, but only lifted from the ground and afloat before the eye. He unfixes the land

and the sea, makes them revolve around the axis of his primary thought, and disposes them anew. Possessed himself by a heroic passion, he uses matter as symbols of it. The sensual man conforms thoughts to things; the poet conforms things to his thoughts. The one esteems nature as rooted and fast; the other, as fluid, and impresses his being thereon. To him, the refractory world is ductile and flexible; he invests dust and stones with humanity, and makes them the words of the Reason. The Imagination may be defined to be the use which the Reason makes of the material world. Shakspeare possesses the power of subordinating nature for the purposes of expression, beyond all poets. His imperial muse tosses the creation like a bauble from hand to hand, and uses it to embody any caprice of thought that is uppermost in his mind. The remotest spaces of nature are visited, and the farthest sundered things are brought together, by a subtile spiritual connection. We are made aware that magnitude of material things is relative, and all objects shrink and expand to serve the passion of the poet. Thus in his sonnets, the lays of birds, the scents and dyes of flowers he finds to be the *shadow* of his beloved; time, which keeps her from him, is his *chest;* the suspicion she has awakened, is her *ornament:*

The ornament of beauty is Suspect,
A crow which flies in heaven's sweetest air.

His passion is not the fruit of chance; it swells, as he speaks, to a city, or a state:

No, it was builded far from accident;
It suffers not in smiling pomp, nor falls
Under the brow of thralling discontent;
It fears not policy, that heretic,
That works on leases of short numbered hours,
But all alone stands hugely politic.

In the strength of his constancy, the Pyramids seem to him recent and transitory. The freshness of youth and love dazzles him with its resemblance to morning:

Take those lips away
Which so sweetly were forsworn;
And those eyes,—the break of day,
Lights that do mislead the morn.

The wild beauty of this hyperbole, I may say in passing, it would not be easy to match in literature.

This transfiguration which all material objects undergo through the passion of the poet,—this power which he exerts to dwarf the great, to magnify the small,—might be illustrated by a thousand examples from his plays. I have before me the Tempest and will cite only these few lines:

Ariel. The strong based promontory
Have I made shake, and by the spurs plucked up
The pine and cedar.

Prospero calls for music to soothe the frantic Alonzo, and his companions:

A solemn air, and the best comforter
To an unsettled fancy, cure thy brains
Now useless, boiled within thy skull.

Again:

The charm dissolves apace,
And, as the morning steals upon the night,
Melting the darkness, so their rising senses
Begin to chase the ignorant fumes that mantle
Their clearer reason.
Their understanding
Begins to swell: and the approaching tide

Will shortly fill the reasonable shores
That now lie foul and muddy.

The perception of real affinities between events (that is to say, of *ideal* affinities, for those only are real) enables the poet thus to make free with the most imposing forms and phenomena of the world, and to assert the predominance of the soul.

3. Whilst thus the poet animates nature with his own thoughts, he differs from the philosopher only herein, that the one proposes Beauty as his main end; the other Truth. But the philosopher, not less than the poet, postpones the apparent order and relations of things to the empire of thought. "The problem of philosophy," according to Plato, "is, for all that exists conditionally, to find a ground unconditioned and absolute." It proceeds on the faith that a law determines all phenomena, which being known, the phenomena can be predicted. That law, when in the mind, is an idea. Its beauty is infinite. The true philosopher and the true poet are one, and a beauty, which is truth, and a truth, which is beauty, is the aim of both. Is not the charm of one of Plato's or Aristotle's definitions strictly like that of the Antigone of Sophocles? It is, in both cases, that a spiritual life has been imparted to nature; that the solid seeming block of matter has been pervaded and dissolved by a thought; that this feeble human being has penetrated the vast masses of nature with an informing soul, and recognized itself in their harmony, that is, seized their law. In physics, when this is attained, the memory disburthens itself of its cumbrous catalogues of particulars, and carries centuries of observation in a single formula.

Thus even in physics, the material is degraded before the spiritual. The astronomer, the geometer, rely on their irrefragable analysis, and disdain the results of observation. The sublime remark of Euler on his law of arches, "This will be found contrary to all experience, yet is true," had already transferred nature into the mind, and left matter like an outcast corpse.

4. Intellectual science has been observed to beget invariably a doubt of the existence of matter. Turgot said, "He that has never doubted the existence of matter, may be assured he has no aptitude for metaphysical inquiries." It fastens the attention upon immortal necessary uncreated natures, that is, upon Ideas; and in their presence we feel that the outward circumstance is a dream and a shade. Whilst we wait in this Olympus of gods, we think of nature as an appendix to the soul. We ascend into their region, and know that these are the thoughts of the Supreme Being. "These are they who were set up from everlasting, from the beginning, or ever the earth was. When he prepared the heavens, they were there; when he established the clouds above, when he strengthened the fountains of the deep. Then they were by him, as one brought up with him. Of them took he counsel."

Their influence is proportionate. As objects of science they are accessible to few men. Yet all men are capable of being raised by piety or by passion into their region. And no man touches these divine natures, without becoming, in some degree, himself divine. Like a new soul, they renew the body. We become physically nimble and lightsome; we tread on air; life is no longer irksome, and we think it will never be so. No man fears age or misfortune or death in their serene company, for he is transported out of the district of change. Whilst we behold unveiled the nature of Justice and Truth, we learn the difference between the absolute and the conditional or relative. We apprehend the absolute. As it were, for the first time, *we exist*. We become immortal, for we learn that time and space are relations of matter; that with a perception of truth or a virtuous will they have no affinity.

5. Finally, religion and ethics, which may be fitly called the practice of ideas, or the introduction of ideas into life, have an analogous effect with all lower culture, in degrading nature and suggesting its dependence on spirit. Ethics and religion differ herein: that the one is the system of human duties commencing from man; the other, from God. Religion includes the personality of God; Ethics does not. They are one to our present design. They both put nature under foot. The first and last lesson of religion is, " The things that are seen, are temporal; the things that are unseen, are eternal." It puts an affront upon nature. It does that for the unschooled, which philosophy does for Berkeley and Viasa. The uniform language that may be heard in the churches of the most ignorant sects is,—" Contemn the unsubstantial shows of the world; they are vanities, dreams, shadows, unrealities; seek the realities of religion." The devotee flouts nature. Some theosophists have arrived at a certain hostility and indignation towards matter, as the Manichean and Plotinus. They distrusted in themselves any looking back to these flesh-pots of Egypt. Plotinus was ashamed of his body. In short, they might all say of matter, what Michael Angelo said of external beauty, " It is the frail and weary weed, in which God dresses the soul which he has called into time."

It appears that motion, poetry, physical and intellectual science, and religion, all tend to affect our convictions of the reality of the external world. But I own there is something ungrateful in expanding too curiously the particulars of the general proposition, that all culture tends to imbue us with idealism. I have no hostility to nature, but a child's love to it. I expand and live in the warm day like corn and melons. Let us speak her fair. I do not wish to fling stones at my beautiful mother, nor soil my gentle nest. I only wish to indicate the true position of nature in regard to man, wherein to establish man all right education tends; as the ground which to attain is the object of human life, that is, of man's connection with nature. Culture inverts the vulgar views of nature, and brings the mind to call that apparent which it uses to call real, and that real which it uses to call visionary. Children, it is true, believe in the external world. The belief that it appears only, is an afterthought, but with culture this faith will as surely arise on the mind as did the first.

The advantage of the ideal theory over the popular faith is this, that it presents the world in precisely that view which is most desirable to the mind. It is, in fact, the view which Reason, both speculative and practical, that is, philosophy and virtue, take. For seen in the light of thought, the world always is phenomenal; and virtue subordinates it to the mind. Idealism sees the world in God. It beholds the whole circle of persons and things, of actions and events, of country and religion, not as painfully accumulated, atom after atom, act after act, in an aged creeping Past, but as one vast picture which God paints on the instant eternity for the contemplation of the soul. Therefore the soul holds itself off from a too trivial and microscopic study of the universal tablet. It respects the end too much to immerse itself in the means. It sees something more important in Christianity than the scandals of ecclesiastical history or the niceties of criticism; and, very incurious concerning persons or miracles, and not at all disturbed by chasms of historical evidence, it accepts from God the phenomenon, as it finds it, as the pure and awful form of religion in the world. It is not hot and passionate at the appearance of what it calls its own good or bad fortune, at the union or opposition of other persons. No man is its enemy. It accepts whatsoever befalls, as part of its lesson. It is a watcher more than a doer, and it is a doer, only that it may the better watch.

### VII. SPIRIT

It is essential to a true theory of nature and of man, that it should contain somewhat progressive. Uses that are exhausted or that may be, and facts that end in the statement, cannot be all that is true of this brave lodging wherein man is harbored, and wherein all his faculties find appropriate and endless exercise. And all the uses of nature admit of being summed in one, which yields the activity of man an infinite scope. Through all its kingdoms, to the suburbs and outskirts of things, it is faithful to the cause whence it had its origin. It always speaks of Spirit. It suggests the absolute. It is a perpetual effect. It is a great shadow pointing always to the sun behind us.

The aspect of Nature is devout. Like the figure of Jesus, she stands with bended head, and hands folded upon the breast. The happiest man is he who learns from nature the lesson of worship.

Of that ineffable essence which we call Spirit, he that thinks most, will say least. We can foresee God in the coarse, and, as it were, distant phenomena of matter; but when we try to define and describe himself, both language and thought desert us, and we are as helpless as fools and savages. That essence refuses to be recorded in propositions, but when man has worshipped him intellectually, the noblest ministry of nature is to stand as the apparition of God. It is the organ through which the universal spirit speaks to the individual, and strives to lead back the individual to it.

When we consider Spirit, we see that the views already presented do not include the whole circumference of man. We must add some related thoughts.

Three problems are put by nature to the mind: What is matter? Whence is it? and Whereto? The first of these questions only, the ideal theory answers. Idealism saith: matter is a phenomenon, not a substance. Idealism acquaints us with the total disparity between the evidence of our own being and the evidence of the world's being. The one is perfect; the other, incapable of any assurance; the mind is a part of the nature of things; the world is a divine dream, from which we may presently awake to the glories and certainties of day. Idealism is a hypothesis to account for nature by other principles than those of carpentry and chemistry. Yet, if it only deny the existence of matter, it does not satisfy the demands of the spirit. It leaves God out of me. It leaves me in the splendid labyrinth of my perceptions, to wander without end. Then the heart resists it, because it balks the affections in denying substantive being to men and women. Nature is so pervaded with human life that there is something of humanity in all and in every particular. But this theory makes nature foreign to me, and does not account for that consanguinity which we acknowledge to it.

Let it stand then, in the present state of our knowledge, merely as a useful introductory hypothesis, serving to apprize us of the eternal distinction between the soul and the world.

But when, following the invisible steps of thought, we come to inquire, Whence is matter? and Whereto? many truths arise to us out of the recesses of consciousness. We learn that the highest is present to the soul of man; that the dread universal essence, which is not wisdom, or love, or beauty, or power, but all in one, and each entirely, is that for which all things exist, and that by which they are; that spirit creates; that behind nature, throughout nature, spirit is present; one and not compound, it does not act upon us from without, that is, in space and time, but spiritually, or through ourselves: therefore, that spirit, that is, the Supreme Being, does not build up nature around us but puts it forth through us, as the life of the tree puts forth new branches and leaves through the pores of the old. As a plant upon the earth, so a man rests upon the bosom of God; he is nourished by unfailing fountains, and draws at his need inexhaustible power. Who can set bounds to the possibilities of man? Once inhale the upper air, being admitted to behold the absolute natures of justice and truth, and we learn that man has access to the entire mind of the Creator, is himself the creator in the finite. This view, which admonishes me where the sources of wisdom and power lie, and points to virtue as to

> The golden key
> Which opes the palace of eternity,

carries upon its face the highest certificate of truth, because it animates me to create my own world through the purification of my soul.

The world proceeds from the same spirit as the body of man. It is a remoter and inferior incarnation of God, a projection of God in the unconscious. But it differs from the body in one important respect. It is not, like that, now subjected to the human will. Its serene order is inviolable by us. It is, therefore, to us, the present expositor of the divine mind. It is a fixed point whereby we may measure our departure. As we degenerate, the contrast between us and our house is more evident. We are as much strangers in nature as we are aliens from God. We do not understand the notes of birds. The fox and the deer run away from us; the bear and tiger rend us. We do not know the uses of more than a few plants, as corn and the apple, the potato and the vine. Is not the landscape, every glimpse of which hath a grandeur, a face of him? Yet this may show us what discord is between man and nature, for you cannot freely admire a noble landscape if laborers are digging in the field hard by. The poet finds something ridiculous in his delight until he is out of the sight of men.

## VIII. PROSPECTS

In inquiries respecting the laws of the world and the frame of things, the highest reason is always the truest. That which seems faintly possible, it is so refined, is often faint and dim because it is deepest seated in the mind among the eternal verities. Empirical science is apt to cloud the sight, and by the very knowledge of functions and processes to bereave the student of the manly contemplation of the whole. The savant becomes unpoetic. But the best read naturalist who lends an entire and devout attention to truth, will see that there remains much to learn of his relation to the world, and that it is not to be learned by any addition or subtraction or other comparison of known quantities, but is arrived at by untaught sallies of the spirit, by a continual self-recovery, and by entire humility. He will perceive that there are far more excellent qualities in the student than preciseness and infallibility; that a guess is often more fruitful than an indisputable affirmation, and that a dream may let us deeper into the secret of nature than a hundred concerted experiments.

For the problems to be solved are precisely those which the physiologist and the naturalist omit to state. It is not so pertinent to man to know all the individuals of the animal kingdom, as it is to know whence and whereto is this tyrannizing unity in his constitution, which evermore separates and classifies things, endeavoring to reduce the most diverse to one form. When I behold a rich landscape, it is less to my purpose to recite correctly the order and superposition of the strata, than to know why all thought of multitude is lost in a tranquil sense of unity. I cannot greatly honor minuteness in details, so long as there is no hint to explain the relation between things and thoughts; no ray upon the *metaphysics* of conchology, of botany, of the arts, to show the relation of the forms of flowers, shells, animals, architecture, to the mind, and build science upon ideas. In a cabinet of natural history, we become sensible of a certain occult recognition and sympathy in regard to the most unwieldy and eccentric forms of beast, fish, and insect. The American who has been confined, in his own country, to the sight of buildings designed after foreign models, is surprised on entering York Minster or St. Peter's at Rome, by the feeling that these structures are imitations also,—faint copies of an invisible archetype. Nor has science sufficient humanity, so long as the naturalist overlooks that wonderful congruity which subsists between man and the world; of which he is lord, not because he is the most subtile inhabitant, but because he is its head and heart, and finds something of himself in every great and small thing, in every mountain stratum, in every new law of color, fact of astronomy, or atmospheric influence which observation or analysis lays open. A perception of this mystery inspires the muse of George Herbert, the beautiful psalmist of the seventeenth century. The following lines are part of his little poem on Man.

Man is all symmetry,
Full of proportions, one limb to another,
And all to all the world besides.
Each part may call the farthest, brother;
For head with foot hath private amity,
And both with moons and tides.

Nothing hath got so far
But man hath caught and kept it as his prey;
His eyes dismount the highest star:
He is in little all the sphere.
Herbs gladly cure our flesh, because that they
Find their acquaintance there.

For us, the winds do blow,
The earth doth rest, heaven move, and fountains flow.
Nothing we see, but means our good,
As our delight, or as our treasure;
The whole is either our cupboard of food,
Or cabinet of pleasure.

The stars have us to bed:
Night draws the curtain; which the sun withdraws.
Music and light attend our head.
All things unto our flesh are kind,
In their descent and being; to our mind,
In their ascent and cause.

More servants wait on man
Than he'll take notice of. In every path,
He treads down that which doth befriend him
When sickness makes him pale and wan.
Oh mighty love! Man is one world, and hath
Another to attend him.

The perception of this class of truths makes the attraction which draws men to science, but the end is lost sight of in attention to the means. In view of this half-sight of science, we accept the sentence of Plato, that "poetry comes nearer to vital truth than history." Every surmise and vaticination of the mind is entitled to a certain respect, and we learn to prefer imperfect theories, and sentences which contain glimpses of truth, to digested systems which have no one valuable suggestion. A wise writer will feel that the ends of study and composition are best answered by announcing undiscovered regions of thought, and so communicating, through hope, new activity to the torpid spirit.

I shall therefore conclude this essay with some traditions of man and nature, which a certain poet sang to me; and which, as they have always been in the world, and perhaps reappear to every bard, may be both history and prophecy.

'The foundations of man are not in matter, but in spirit. But the element of spirit is eternity. To it, therefore, the longest series of events, the oldest chronologies are young and recent. In the cycle of the universal man, from whom the known individuals proceed, centuries are points, and all history is but the epoch of one degradation.

'We distrust and deny inwardly our sympathy with nature. We own and disown our relation to it, by turns. We are like Nebuchadnezzar, dethroned, bereft of reason, and eating grass like an ox. But who can set limits to the remedial force of spirit?

'A man is a god in ruins. When men are innocent, life shall be longer, and shall pass into the immortal as gently as we awake from dreams. Now, the world would be insane and rabid, if these disorganizations should last for hundreds of years. It is kept in check by death and infancy. Infancy is the perpetual Messiah, which comes into the arms of fallen men, and pleads with them to return to paradise.

'Man is the dwarf of himself. Once he was permeated and dissolved by spirit. He filled nature with his overflowing currents. Out from him sprang the sun and moon; from man the sun, from woman the moon. The laws of his mind, the periods of his actions externized themselves into day and night, into the year and the seasons. But, having made for himself this huge shell, his waters retired; he no longer fills the veins and veinlets; he is shrunk to a drop. He sees that the structure still fits him, but fits him colossally. Say, rather, once it fitted him, now it corresponds to him from far and on high. He adores timidly his own work. Now is man the follower of the sun, and woman the follower of the moon. Yet sometimes he starts in his slumber, and wonders at himself and his house, and muses strangely at the resemblance betwixt him and it. He perceives that if his law is still paramount, if still he have elemental power, if his word is sterling yet in nature, it is not conscious power, it is not inferior but superior to his will. It is instinct.' Thus my Orphic poet sang.

At present, man applies to nature but half his force. He works on the world with his understanding alone. He lives in it and masters it by a penny-wisdom; and he that works most in it is but a half-man, and whilst his arms are strong and his digestion good, his mind is imbruted, and he is a selfish savage. His relation to nature, his power over it, is through the understanding, as by manure; the economic use of fire, wind, water, and the mariner's needle; steam, coal, chemical agriculture; the repairs of the human body by the dentist and the surgeon. This is such a resumption of power as if a banished king should buy his territories inch by inch, instead of vaulting at once into his throne. Meantime, in the thick darkness, there are not wanting gleams of a better light,—occasional examples of the action of man upon nature with his entire force,—with reason as well as understanding. Such examples are: the traditions of miracles in the earliest antiquity of all nations; the history of Jesus Christ; the achievements of a principle, as in religious and political revolutions, and in the abolition of the slave-trade; the miracles of enthusiasm, as those reported of Swedenborg, Hohenlohe, and the Shakers; many obscure and yet contested facts, now arranged under the name of Animal Magnetism; prayer; eloquence; self-healing; and the wisdom of children. These are examples of Reason's momentary grasp of the scepter; the exertions of a power which exists not in time or space, but an instantaneous in-streaming causing power. The difference between the actual and the ideal force of man is happily figured by the schoolmen, in saying that the knowledge of man is an evening knowledge, *vespertina cognitio,* but that of God is a morning knowledge, *matutina cognitio.*

The problem of restoring to the world original and eternal beauty is solved by the redemption of the soul. The ruin or the blank that we see when we look at nature, is in our own eye. The axis of vision is not coincident with the axis of things, and so they appear not transparent but opaque. The reason why the world lacks unity, and lies broken and in heaps, is because man is disunited with himself. He cannot be a naturalist until he satisfies all the demands of the spirit. Love is as much its demand as perception. Indeed, neither can be perfect without the other. In the uttermost meaning of the words, thought is devout, and devotion is thought. Deep calls unto deep. But in actual life, the marriage is not celebrated. There are innocent men who worship God after the tradition of their fathers, but their sense of duty has not yet extended to the use of all their faculties. And there are patient naturalists, but they freeze their subject under the wintry light of the understanding. Is not prayer also a study of truth,—a sally of the soul into the unfound infinite? No man ever prayed heartily without learning something. But when a faithful thinker, resolute to detach every object from personal relations and see it in the light of thought, shall, at the same time, kindle science with the fire of the holiest affections, then will God go forth anew into the creation.

It will not need, when the mind is prepared for study, to search for objects. The invariable mark of wisdom is to see the miraculous in the common. What is a day? What is a year? What is summer? What is woman? What is a child? What is sleep? To our blindness, these things seem unaffecting. We make fables to hide the baldness of the fact and conform it, as we say, to the higher law of the mind. But when the fact is seen under the light of an idea, the gaudy fable fades and shrivels. We behold the real higher law. To the wise, therefore, a fact is true poetry, and the most beautiful of fables. These wonders are brought to our own door. You also are a man. Man and woman and their social life, poverty, labor, sleep, fear, fortune, are known to you. Learn that none of these things is superficial, but that each phenomenon has its roots in the faculties and affections of the mind. Whilst the abstract question occupies your intellect, nature brings it in the concrete to be solved by your hands. It were a wise inquiry for the closet, to compare, point by point, especially at remarkable crises in life, our daily history with the rise and progress of ideas in the mind.

So shall we come to look at the world with new eyes. It shall answer the endless inquiry of the intellect,—What is truth? and of the affections,—What is good? by yielding itself passive to the educated Will. Then shall come to pass what my poet said: 'Nature is not fixed but fluid. Spirit alters, molds, makes it. The immobility or bruteness of nature is the absence of spirit; to pure spirit it is fluid, it is volatile, it is obedient.

Every spirit builds itself a house and beyond its house a world and beyond its world a heaven. Know then that the world exists for you. For you is the phenomenon perfect. What we are, that only can we see. All that Adam had, all that Cæsar could, you have and can do. Adam called his house, heaven and earth; Cæsar called his house, Rome; you perhaps call yours, a cobbler's trade; a hundred acres of ploughed land; or a scholar's garret. Yet line for line and point for point your dominion is as great as theirs, though without fine names. Build therefore your own world. As fast as you conform your life to the pure idea in your mind, that will unfold its great proportions. A correspondent revolution in things will attend the influx of the spirit. So fast will disagreeable appearances, swine, spiders, snakes, pests, mad-houses, prisons, enemies, vanish; they are temporary and shall be no more seen. The sordor and filths of nature, the sun shall dry up and the wind exhale. As when the summer comes from the south the snow-banks melt and the face of the earth becomes green before it, so shall the advancing spirit create its ornaments along its path, and carry with it the beauty it visits and the song which enchants it; it shall draw beautiful faces, warm hearts, wise discourse, and heroic acts, around its way, until evil is no more seen. The kingdom of man over nature, which cometh not with observation,—a dominion such as now is beyond his dream of God,—he shall enter without more wonder than the blind man feels who is gradually restored to perfect sight.'

1836

# THE AMERICAN SCHOLAR

AN ORATION DELIVERED BEFORE THE PHI BETA KAPPA SOCIETY, AT CAMBRIDGE, AUGUST 31, 1837

Mr. President and Gentlemen:

I greet you on the recommencement of our literary year. Our anniversary is one of hope, and, perhaps, not enough of labor. We do not meet for games of strength or skill, for the recitation of histories, tragedies, and odes, like the ancient Greeks; for parliaments of love and poesy, like the Troubadours; nor for the advancement of science, like our contemporaries in the British and European capitals. Thus far, our holiday has been simply a friendly sign of the survival of the love of letters amongst a people too busy to give to letters any more. As such it is precious as the sign of an indestructible instinct. Perhaps the time is already come when it ought to be, and will be, something else; when the sluggard intellect of this continent will look from under its iron lids and fill the postponed expectation of the world with something better than the exertions of mechanical skill. Our day of dependence, our long apprenticeship to the learning of other lands, draws to a close. The millions that around us are rushing into life, cannot always be fed on the sere remains of foreign harvests. Events, actions arise, that must be sung, that will sing themselves. Who can doubt that poetry will revive and lead in a new age, as the star in the constellation Harp, which now flames in our zenith, astronomers announce, shall one day be the pole-star for a thousand years?

In this hope I accept the topic

which not only usage but the nature of our association seem to prescribe to this day,—the AMERICAN SCHOLAR. Year by year we come up hither to read one more chapter of his biography. Let us inquire what light new days and events have thrown on his character and his hopes.

It is one of those fables which out of an unknown antiquity convey an unlooked-for wisdom, that the gods, in the beginning, divided Man into men, that he might be more helpful to himself; just as the hand was divided into fingers, the better to answer its end.

The old fable covers a doctrine ever new and sublime; that there is One Man,—present to all particular men only partially, or through one faculty; and that you must take the whole society to find the whole man. Man is not a farmer, or a professor, or an engineer, but he is all. Man is priest, and scholar, and statesman, and producer, and soldier. In the *divided* or social state these functions are parcelled out to individuals, each of whom aims to do his stint of the joint work, whilst each other performs his. The fable implies that the individual, to possess himself, must sometimes return from his own labor to embrace all the other laborers. But, unfortunately, this original unit, this fountain of power, has been so distributed to multitudes, has been so minutely subdivided and peddled out, that it is spilled into drops, and cannot be gathered. The state of society is one in which the members have suffered amputation from the trunk, and strut about so many walking monsters,—a good finger, a neck, a stomach, an elbow, but never a man.

Man is thus metamorphosed into a thing, into many things. The planter, who is Man sent out into the field to gather food, is seldom cheered by any idea of the true dignity of his ministry. He sees his bushel and his cart, and nothing beyond, and sinks into the farmer, instead of Man on the farm. The tradesman scarcely ever gives an ideal worth to his work, but is ridden by the routine of his craft, and the soul is subject to dollars. The priest becomes a form; the attorney a statute-book; the mechanic a machine; the sailor a rope of the ship.

In this distribution of functions the scholar is the delegated intellect. In the right state he is *Man Thinking*. In the degenerate state, when the victim of society, he tends to become a mere thinker, or still worse, the parrot of other men's thinking.

In this view of him, as Man Thinking, the theory of his office is contained. Him Nature solicits with all her placid, all her monitory pictures; him the past instructs; him the future invites. Is not indeed every man a student, and do not all things exist for the student's behoof? And, finally, is not the true scholar the only true master? But the old oracle said, "All things have two handles; beware of the wrong one." In life, too often, the scholar errs with mankind and forfeits his privilege. Let us see him in his school, and consider him in reference to the main influences he receives.

I. The first in time and the first in importance of the influences upon the mind is that of nature. Every day, the sun; and, after sunset, Night and her stars. Ever the winds blow;

ever the grass grows. Every day, men and women, conversing, beholding and beholden. The scholar is he of all men whom this spectacle most engages. He must settle its value in his mind. What is nature to him? There is never a beginning, there is never an end, to the inexplicable continuity of this web of God, but always circular power returning into itself. Therein it resembles his own spirit, whose beginning, whose ending, he never can find,—so entire, so boundless. Far too as her splendors shine, system on system shooting like rays, upward, downward, without centre, without circumference,—in the mass and in the particle, Nature hastens to render account of herself to the mind. Classification begins. To the young mind every thing is individual, stands by itself. By and by, it finds how to join two things and see in them one nature; then three, then three thousand; and so, tyrannized over by its own unifying instinct, it goes on tying things together, diminishing anomalies, discovering roots running under ground whereby contrary and remote things cohere and flower out from one stem. It presently learns that since the dawn of history there has been a constant accumulation and classifying of facts. But what is classification but the perceiving that these objects are not chaotic, and are not foreign, but have a law which is also a law of the human mind? The astronomer discovers that geometry, a pure abstraction of the human mind, is the measure of planetary motion. The chemist finds proportions and intelligible method throughout matter; and science is nothing but the finding of analogy, identity, in the most remote parts. The ambitious soul sits down before each refractory fact; one after another reduces all strange constitutions, all new powers, to their class and their law, and goes on forever to animate the last fiber of organization, the outskirts of nature, by insight.

Thus to him, to this schoolboy under the bending dome of day, is suggested that he and it proceed from one root; one is leaf and one is flower; relation, sympathy, stirring in every vein. And what is that root? Is not that the soul of his soul? A thought too bold; a dream too wild. Yet when this spiritual light shall have revealed the law of more earthly natures,—when he has learned to worship the soul, and to see that the natural philosophy that now is, is only the first gropings of its gigantic hand, he shall look forward to an ever expanding knowledge as to a becoming creator. He shall see that nature is the opposite of the soul, answering to it part for part. One is seal and one is print. Its beauty is the beauty of his own mind. Its laws are the laws of his own mind. Nature then becomes to him the measure of his attainments. So much of nature as he is ignorant of, so much of his own mind does he not yet possess. And, in fine, the ancient precept, "Know thyself," and the modern precept, "Study nature," become at last one maxim.

II. The next great influence into the spirit of the scholar is the mind of the Past,—in whatever form, whether of literature, of art, of institutions, that mind is inscribed. Books are the best type of the influence of the past, and perhaps we shall get at the truth, —learn the amount of this influence more conveniently,—by considering their value alone.

The theory of books is noble. The scholar of the first age received into him the world around; brooded thereon; gave it the new arrangement of his own mind, and uttered it again. It came into him life; it went out from him truth. It came to him short-lived actions; it went out from him immortal thoughts. It came to him business; it went from him poetry. It was dead fact; now, it is quick thought. It can stand, and it can go. It now endures, it now flies, it now inspires. Precisely in proportion to the depth of mind from which it issued, so high does it soar, so long does it sing.

Or, I might say, it depends on how far the process had gone, of transmuting life into truth. In proportion to the completeness of the distillation, so will the purity and imperishableness of the product be. But none is quite perfect. As no air-pump can by any means make a perfect vacuum, so neither can any artist entirely exclude the conventional, the local, the perishable from his book, or write a book of pure thought, that shall be as efficient, in all respects, to a remote posterity, as to contemporaries, or rather to the second age. Each age, it is found, must write its own books; or rather, each generation for the next succeeding. The books of an older period will not fit this.

Yet hence arises a grave mischief. The sacredness which attaches to the act of creation, the act of thought, is transferred to the record. The poet chanting was felt to be a divine man: henceforth the chant is divine also. The writer was a just and wise spirit: henceforward it is settled the book is perfect; as love of the hero corrupts into worship of his statue. Instantly the book becomes noxious: the guide is a tyrant. The sluggish and perverted mind of the multitude, slow to open to the incursions of Reason, having once so opened, having once received this book, stands upon it, and makes an outcry if it is disparaged. Colleges are built on it. Books are written on it by thinkers, not by Man Thinking; by men of talent, that is, who start wrong, who set out from accepted dogmas, not from their own sight of principles. Meek young men grow up in libraries, believing it their duty to accept the views which Cicero, which Locke, which Bacon, have given; forgetful that Cicero, Locke, and Bacon were only young men in libraries when they wrote these books.

Hence, instead of Man Thinking, we have the bookworm. Hence the book-learned class, who value books, as such; not as related to nature and the human constitution, but as making a sort of Third Estate with the world and the soul. Hence the restorers of readings, the emendators, the bibliomaniacs of all degrees.

Books are the best of things, well used; abused, among the worst. What is the right use? What is the one end which all means go to effect? They are for nothing but to inspire. I had better never see a book than to be warped by its attraction clean out of my own orbit, and made a satellite instead of a system. The one thing in the world, of value, is the active soul. This every man is entitled to; this every man contains within him, although in almost all men obstructed, and as yet unborn. The soul active sees absolute truth and utters truth, or creates. In this action it is genius; not the privilege of here and there a favorite, but the sound estate of every man. In its essence it is progressive. The book, the college, the school of art, the institution of any kind, stop with some past utterance of genius. This is good, say they,—let us hold by this. They pin me down. They look backward and not forward. But genius looks forward: the eyes of man are set in his forehead, not in his hindhead: man hopes: genius creates. Whatever talents may be, if the man create not, the pure efflux of the Deity is not his;—cinders and smoke there may be, but not yet flame. There are creative manners, there are creative actions, and creative words; manners, actions, words, that is, indicative of no custom or authority, but springing spontaneous from the mind's own sense of good and fair.

On the other part, instead of being its own seer, let it receive from another mind its truth, though it were in torrents of light, without periods of solitude, inquest, and self-recovery, and a fatal disservice is done. Genius is always sufficiently the enemy of genius by over-influence. The literature of every nation bears me witness. The English dramatic poets have Shakspearized now for two hundred years.

Undoubtedly there is a right way of reading, so it be sternly subordinated. Man Thinking must not be subdued by his instruments. Books are for the scholar's idle times. When he can read God directly, the hour is too precious to be wasted in other men's transcripts of their readings. But when the intervals of darkness come, as come they must,—when the sun is hid and the stars withdraw their shining,—we repair to the lamps which were kindled by their ray, to guide our steps to the East again, where the dawn is. We hear, that we may speak. The Arabian proverb says, "A fig tree, looking on a fig tree, becometh fruitful."

It is remarkable, the character of the pleasure we derive from the best books. They impress us with the conviction that one nature wrote and the same reads. We read the verses of one of the great English poets, of Chaucer, of Marvell, of Dryden, with the most modern joy,—with a pleasure, I mean, which is in great part caused by the abstraction of all *time* from their verses. There is some awe mixed with the joy of our surprise, when this poet, who lived in some past world, two or three hundred years ago, says that which lies close to my own soul, that which I also had well-nigh thought and said. But for the evidence thence afforded to the philosophical doctrine of the identity of all minds, we should suppose some preestablished harmony, some foresight of souls that were to be, and some preparation of stores for their future wants, like the fact observed in insects, who lay up food before death for the young grub they shall never see.

I would not be hurried by any love of system, by any exaggeration of instincts, to underrate the Book. We all know, that as the human body can be nourished on any food, though it were boiled grass and the broth of shoes, so the human mind can be fed by any knowledge. And great and heroic men have existed who had almost no other information than by the printed page. I only would say that it needs a strong head to bear that diet. One must be an inventor to read well. As the proverb says, "He that would bring home the wealth of the Indies, must carry out the wealth of the Indies." There is then creative reading as well as creative writing. When the mind is braced by labor and invention, the page of whatever book we read becomes luminous with manifold allusion. Every sentence is doubly significant, and the sense of our author is as broad as the world. We then see, what is always true, that as the seer's hour of vision is short and rare among heavy days and months, so is its record, perchance, the least part of his volume. The discerning will read, in his Plato or Shakspeare, only that least part,—only the authentic utterances of the oracle;—all the rest he rejects, were it never so many times Plato's and Shakspeare's.

Of course there is a portion of reading quite indispensable to a wise man. History and exact science he must learn by laborious reading. Colleges, in like manner, have their indispensable office,—to teach elements. But they can only highly serve us when they aim not to drill, but to create; when they gather from far every ray of various genius to their hospitable halls, and by the concentrated fires, set the hearts of their youth on flame. Thought and knowledge are natures in which apparatus and pretension avail nothing. Gowns and pecuniary foundations, though of towns of gold, can never countervail the least sentence or syllable of wit. Forget this, and our American colleges will recede in their public importance, whilst they grow richer every year.

III. There goes in the world a notion that the scholar should be a recluse, a valetudinarian,—as unfit for any handiwork or public labor as a penknife for an axe. The so-called "practical men" sneer at speculative men, as if, because they speculate or *see,* they could do nothing. I have heard it said that the clergy,—who are always, more universally than any other class, the scholars of their day,—are addressed as women; that the rough, spontaneous conversation of men they do not hear, but only a mincing and diluted speech. They are often virtually disfranchised; and indeed there are advocates for their celibacy. As far as this is true of the studious classes, it is not just and wise. Action is with the scholar subordinate, but it is essential. Without it he is not yet man. Without it thought can never ripen into truth. Whilst the world hangs before the eye as a cloud of beauty, we cannot even see its beauty. Inaction is cowardice, but there can be no scholar without the heroic mind. The preamble of thought, the transition through which it passes from the unconscious to the conscious, is action. Only so much do I know, as I have lived. Instantly we know whose words are loaded with life, and whose not.

The world,—this shadow of the soul, or *other me,* lies wide around. Its attractions are the keys which unlock my thoughts and make me acquainted with myself. I run eagerly into this resounding tumult. I grasp the hands of those next me, and take my place in the ring to suffer and to work, taught by an instinct that so shall the dumb abyss be vocal with speech. I pierce its order; I dissipate its fear; I dispose of it within the circuit of my expanding life. So much only of life as I know by experience, so much of the wilderness have I vanquished and planted, or so far have I extended my being, my dominion. I do not see how any man can afford, for the sake of his nerves and his nap, to spare any action in which he can partake. It is pearls and rubies to his discourse. Drudgery, calamity, exasperation, want, are instructors in eloquence and wisdom. The true scholar grudges every opportunity of action past by, as a loss of power. It is the raw material out of which the intellect molds her splendid products. A strange process, too, this by which experience is converted into thought, as a mulberry leaf is converted into satin. The manufacture goes forward at all hours.

The actions and events of our childhood and youth are now matters of calmest observation. They lie like fair pictures in the air. Not so with our recent actions,—with the business which we now have in hand. On this we are quite unable to speculate. Our affections as yet circulate through it. We no more feel or know it than we feel the feet, or the hand, or the brain of our body. The new deed is yet a part of life,—remains for a time immersed in our unconscious life. In some contemplative hour it detaches itself from the life like a ripe fruit, to become a thought of the mind. Instantly it is raised, transfigured; the corruptible has put on incorruption. Henceforth it is an object of beauty, however base its origin and neighborhood. Observe too the impossibility of antedating this act. In its grub state, it cannot fly, it cannot shine, it is a dull grub. But suddenly, without observation, the selfsame thing unfurls beautiful wings, and is an angel of wisdom. So is there no fact, no event, in our private history, which shall not, sooner or later, lose its adhesive, inert form, and astonish us by soaring from our body into the empyrean. Cradle and infancy, school and playground, the fear of boys, and dogs, and ferules, the love of little maids and berries, and many another fact that once filled the whole sky, are gone already; friend and relative, profession and party, town and country, nation and world, must also soar and sing.

Of course, he who has put forth his total strength in fit actions has the richest return of wisdom. I will not shut myself out of this globe of action, and transplant an oak into a flower-pot, there to hunger and pine; nor trust the revenue of some single faculty, and exhaust one vein of thought, much like those Savoyards, who, getting their livelihood by carving shepherds, shepherdesses, and smoking Dutchmen, for all Europe, went out one day to the mountain to find stock, and discovered that they had whittled up the last of their pinetrees. Authors we have, in numbers, who have written out their vein, and who, moved by a commendable prudence, sail for Greece or Palestine, follow the trapper into the prairie, or ramble round Algiers, to replenish their merchantable stock.

If it were only for a vocabulary, the scholar would be covetous of action. Life is our dictionary. Years are well spent in country labors; in town; in the insight into trades and manufactures; in frank intercourse with many men and women; in science; in art; to the one end of mastering in all their facts a language by which to illustrate and embody our perceptions. I learn immediately from any speaker how much he has already lived, through the poverty or the splendor of his speech. Life lies behind us as the quarry from whence we get tiles and copestones for the masonry of to-day. This is the way to learn grammar. Colleges and books only copy the language which the field and the work-yard made.

But the final value of action, like that of books, and better than books, is that it is a resource. That great principle of Undulation in nature, that shows itself in the inspiring and expiring of the breath; in desire and satiety; in the ebb and flow of the sea; in day and night; in heat and cold; and, as yet more deeply ingrained in every atom and every fluid, is known to us under the name of Polarity,—these "fits of easy transmission and reflection," as Newton called them,—are the law of nature because they are the law of spirit.

The mind now thinks, now acts, and each fit reproduces the other. When the artist has exhausted his materials, when the fancy no longer paints, when thoughts are no longer apprehended and books are a weariness,—he has always the resource *to live.* Character is higher than intellect. Thinking is the function. Living is the functionary. The stream retreats to its source. A great soul will be strong to live, as well as strong to think. Does he lack organ or medium to impart his truths? He can still fall back on this elemental force of living them. This is a total act. Thinking is a partial act. Let the grandeur of justice shine in his affairs. Let the beauty of affection cheer his lowly roof. Those "far from fame," who dwell and act with him, will feel the force of his constitution in the doings and passages of the day better than it can be measured by any public and designed display. Time shall teach him that the scholar loses no hour which the man lives. Herein he unfolds the sacred germ of his instinct, screened from influence. What is lost in seemliness is gained in strength. Not out of those on whom systems of education have exhausted their culture, comes the helpful giant to destroy the old or to build the new, but out of unhandselled savage nature; out of terrible Druids and Berserkers come at last Alfred and Shakspeare.

I hear therefore with joy whatever is beginning to be said of the dignity and necessity of labor to every citizen. There is virtue yet in the hoe and the spade, for learned as well as for unlearned hands. And labor is everywhere welcome; always we are invited to work; only be this limitation observed, that a man shall not for the sake of wider activity sacrifice any opinion to the popular judgments and modes of action.

I have now spoken of the education of the scholar by nature, by books, and by action. It remains to say somewhat of his duties.

They are such as become Man Thinking. They may all be comprised in self-trust. The office of the scholar is to cheer, to raise, and to guide men by showing them facts amidst appearances. He plies the slow, unhonored, and unpaid task of observation. Flamsteed and Herschel, in their glazed observatories, may catalogue the stars with the praise of all men, and the results being splendid and useful, honor is sure. But he, in his private observatory, cataloguing obscure and nebulous stars of the human mind, which as yet no man has thought of as such,—watching days and months sometimes for a few facts; correcting still his old records; —must relinquish display and immediate fame. In the long period of his preparation he must betray often an ignorance and shiftlessness in popular arts, incurring the disdain of the able who shoulder him aside. Long he must stammer in his speech; often forgo the living for the dead. Worse yet, he must accept—how often!—poverty and solitude. For the ease and pleasure of treading the old road, accepting the fashions, the education, the religion of society, he takes the cross of making his own, and, of course, the self-accusation, the faint heart, the frequent uncertainty and loss of time, which are the nettles and tangling vines in the way of the self-relying and self-directed; and the state of virtual hostility in which he seems to stand to society, and especially to educated society. For all this loss and scorn, what offset? He is to find consolation in exercising the highest functions of human nature. He is one who raises himself from private considerations and breathes and lives on public and illustrious thoughts. He is the world's eye. He is the world's heart. He is to resist the vulgar prosperity that retrogrades ever to barbarism, by preserving and communicating heroic sentiments, noble biographies, melodious verse, and the conclusions of history. Whatsoever oracles the human heart, in all emergencies, in all solemn hours, has uttered as its commentary on the world of actions,—these he shall receive and impart. And whatsoever new verdict Reason from her inviolable seat pronounces on the passing men and events of to-day,—this he shall hear and promulgate.

These being his functions, it becomes him to feel all confidence in himself, and to defer never to the popular cry. He and he only knows the world. The world of any moment is the merest appearance. Some great decorum, some fetish of a government, some ephemeral trade, or war, or man, is cried up by half mankind and cried down by the other half, as if all depended on this particular up or down. The odds are that the whole question is not worth the poorest thought which the scholar has lost in listening to the controversy. Let him not quit his belief that a popgun is a popgun, though the ancient and honorable of the earth affirm it to be the crack of doom. In silence, in steadiness, in severe abstraction, let him hold by himself; add observation to observation, patient of neglect, patient of reproach, and bide his own time,—happy enough if he can satisfy himself alone that this day he has seen something truly. Success treads on every right step. For the instinct is sure, that prompts him to tell his brother what he thinks. He then learns that in going down into the secrets of his own mind he has descended into the secrets of all minds.

He learns that he who has mastered any law in his private thoughts, is master to that extent of all men whose language he speaks, and of all into whose language his own can be translated. The poet, in utter solitude remembering his spontaneous thoughts and recording them, is found to have recorded that which men in crowded cities find true for them also. The orator distrusts at first the fitness of his frank confessions, his want of knowledge of the persons he addresses, until he finds that he is the complement of his hearers;—that they drink his words because he fulfills for them their own nature; the deeper he dives into his privatest, secretest presentiment, to his wonder he finds this is the most acceptable, most public, and universally true. The people delight in it; the better part of every man feels, This is my music; this is myself.

In self-trust all the virtues are comprehended. Free should the scholar be,—free and brave. Free even to the definition of freedom, "without any hindrance that does not arise out of his own constitution." Brave; for fear is a thing which a scholar by his very function puts behind him. Fear always springs from ignorance. It is a shame to him if his tranquillity, amid dangerous times, arise from the presumption that like children and women his is a protected class; or if he seek a temporary peace by the diversion of his thoughts from politics or vexed questions, hiding his head like an ostrich in the flowering bushes, peeping into microscopes, and turning rhymes, as a boy whistles to keep his courage up. So is the danger a danger still; so is the fear worse. Manlike let him turn and face it. Let him look into its eye and search its nature, inspect its origin,—see the whelping of this lion,—which lies no great way back; he will then find in himself a perfect comprehension of its nature and extent; he will have made his hands meet on the other side, and can henceforth defy it and pass on superior. The world is his who can see through its pretension. What deafness, what stone-blind custom, what overgrown error you behold is there only by sufferance,—by your sufferance. See it to be a lie, and you have already dealt it its mortal blow.

Yes, we are the cowed,—we the trustless. It is a mischievous notion that we are come late into nature; that the world was finished a long time ago. As the world was plastic and fluid in the hands of God, so it is ever to so much of his attributes as we bring to it. To ignorance and sin, it is flint. They adapt themselves to it as they may; but in proportion as a man has any thing in him divine, the firmament flows before him and takes his signet and form. Not he is great who can alter matter, but he who can alter my state of mind. They are the kings of the world who give the color of their present thought to all nature and all art, and persuade men by the cheerful serenity of their carrying the matter, that this thing which they do is the apple which the ages have desired to pluck, now at last ripe, and inviting nations to the harvest. The great man makes the great thing. Wherever Macdonald sits, there is the head of the table. Linnæus makes botany the most alluring of studies, and wins it from the farmer and the herb-woman; Davy, chemistry; and Cuvier, fossils. The day is always his who works in it with serenity and great aims. The unstable estimates of men crowd to him whose mind is filled with a truth, as the heaped waves of the Atlantic follow the moon.

For this self-trust, the reason is deeper than can be fathomed,—darker than can be enlightened. I might not carry with me the feeling of my audience in stating my own belief. But I have already shown the ground of my hope, in adverting to the doctrine that man is one. I believe man has been wronged; he has wronged himself. He has almost lost the light that can lead him back to his prerogatives. Men are become of no account. Men in history, men in the world of to-day, are bugs, are spawn, and are called "the mass" and "the herd." In a century, in a millennium, one or two men; that is to say, one or two approximations to the right state of every man. All the rest behold in the hero or the poet their own green and crude being,—ripened; yes, and are content to be less, so *that* may attain to its full stature. What a testimony, full of grandeur, full of pity, is borne to the demands of his own nature, by the poor clansman, the poor partisan, who rejoices in the glory of his chief. The poor and the low find some amends to their immense moral capacity, for their acquiescence in a political and social inferiority. They are content to be brushed like flies from the path of a great person, so that justice shall be done by him to that common nature which it is the dearest desire of all to see enlarged and glorified. They sun themselves in the great man's light, and feel it to be their own element. They cast the dignity of man from their downtrod selves upon the shoulders of a hero, and will perish to add one drop of blood to make that great heart beat, those giant sinews combat and conquer. He lives for us, and we live in him.

Men such as they are, very naturally seek money or power; and power because it is as good as money,—the "spoils," so called, "of office." And why not? for they aspire to the highest, and this, in their sleep-walking, they dream is highest. Wake them and they shall quit the false good and leap to the true, and leave governments to clerks and desks. This revolution is to be wrought by the gradual domestication of the idea of Culture. The main enterprise of the world for splendor, for extent, is the upbuilding of a man. Here are the materials strewn along the ground. The private life of one man shall be a more illustrious monarchy, more formidable to its enemy, more sweet and serene in its influence to its friend, than any kingdom in history. For a man, rightly viewed, comprehendeth the particular natures of all men. Each philosopher, each bard, each actor has only done for me, as by a delegate, what one day I can do for myself. The books which once we valued more than the apple of the eye, we have quite exhausted. What is that but saying that we have come up with the point of view which the universal mind took through the eyes of one scribe; we have been that man, and have passed on. First, one, then another, we drain all cisterns, and waxing greater by all these supplies, we crave a better and more abundant food. The man has never lived that can feed us ever.

The human mind cannot be enshrined in a person who shall set a barrier on any one side to this unbounded, unboundable empire. It is one central fire, which flaming now out of the lips of Etna, lightens the capes of Sicily, and now out of the throat of Vesuvius, illuminates the towers and vineyards of Naples. It is one light which beams out of a thousand stars. It is one soul which animates all men.

But I have dwelt perhaps tediously upon this abstraction of the Scholar. I ought not to delay longer to add what I have to say of nearer reference to the time and to this country.

Historically, there is thought to be a difference in the ideas which predominate over successive epochs, and there are data for marking the genius of the Classic, of the Romantic, and now of the Reflective or Philosophical age. With the views I have intimated of the oneness or the identity of the mind through all individuals, I do not much dwell on these differences. In fact, I believe each individual passes through all three. The boy is a Greek; the youth, romantic; the adult, reflective. I deny not, however, that a revolution in the leading idea may be distinctly enough traced.

Our age is bewailed as the age of Introversion. Must that needs be evil? We, it seems, are critical; we are embarrassed with second thoughts; we cannot enjoy any thing for hankering to know whereof the pleasure consists; we are lined with eyes; we see with our feet; the time is infected with Hamlet's unhappiness,—

> Sicklied o'er with the pale cast of thought.

It is so bad then? Sight is the last thing to be pitied. Would we be blind? Do we fear lest we should outsee nature and God, and drink truth dry? I look upon the discontent of the literary class as a mere announcement of the fact that they find themselves not in the state of mind of their fathers, and regret the coming state as untried; as a boy dreads the water before he has learned that he can swim. If there is any period one would desire to be born in, is it not the age of Revolution; when the old and the new stand side by side and admit of being compared; when the energies of all men are searched by fear and by hope; when the historic glories of the old can be compensated by the rich possibilities of the new era? This time, like all times, is a very good one, if we but know what to do with it.

I read with some joy of the auspicious signs of the coming days, as they glimmer already through poetry and art, through philosophy and science, through church and state.

One of these signs is the fact that the same movement which effected the elevation of what was called the lowest class in the state, assumed in literature a very marked and as benign an aspect. Instead of the sublime and beautiful, the near, the low, the common, was explored and poetized. That which had been negligently trodden under foot by those who were harnessing and provisioning themselves for long journeys into far countries, is suddenly found to be richer than all foreign parts. The literature of the poor, the feelings of the child, the philosophy of the street, the meaning of household life, are the topics of the time. It is a great stride. It is a sign—is it not?—of new vigor when the extremities are made active, when currents of warm life run into the hands and the feet. I ask not for the great, the remote, the romantic; what is doing in Italy or Arabia; what is Greek art, or Provençal minstrelsy; I embrace the common, I explore and sit at the feet of the familiar, the low. Give me insight into to-day, and you may have the antique and future worlds. What would we really know the meaning of? The meal in the firkin; the milk in the pan; the ballad in the street; the news of the boat; the glance of the eye; the form and the gait of the body;—show me the ultimate reason of these matters; show me the sublime presence of the highest spiritual cause lurking, as always it does lurk, in these suburbs and extremities of nature; let me see every trifle bristling with the polarity that ranges it instantly on an eternal law; and the shop, the plough, and the ledger referred to the like cause by which light undulates and poets sing; —and the world lies no longer a dull miscellany and lumber-room, but has form and order; there is no trifle, there is no puzzle, but one design unites and animates the farthest pinnacle and the lowest trench.

This idea has inspired the genius of Goldsmith, Burns, Cowper, and, in a newer time, of Goethe, Wordsworth, and Carlyle. This idea they have differently followed and with various success. In contrast with their writing, the style of Pope, of Johnson, of Gibbon, looks cold and pedantic. This writing is blood-warm. Man is surprised to find that things near are not less beautiful and wondrous than things remote. The near explains the far. The drop is a small ocean. A man is related to all nature. This perception of the worth of the vulgar is fruitful in discoveries. Goethe, in this very thing the most modern of the moderns, has shown us, as none ever did, the genius of the ancients.

There is one man of genius who has done much for this philosophy of life, whose literary value has never yet been rightly estimated;—I mean Emanuel Swedenborg. The most imaginative of men, yet writing with the precision of a mathematician, he endeavored to engraft a purely philosophical Ethics on the popular Christianity of his time. Such an attempt of course must have difficulty which no genius could surmount. But he saw and showed the connection between nature and the affections of the soul. He pierced the emblematic or spiritual character of the visible, audible, tangible world. Especially did his shade-loving muse hover over and interpret the lower parts of nature; he showed the mysterious bond that allies moral evil to the foul material forms, and has given in epical parables a theory of insanity, of beasts, of unclean and fearful things.

Another sign of our times, also marked by an analogous political movement, is the new importance given to the single person. Every thing that tends to insulate the individual,—to surround him with barriers of natural respect, so that each man shall feel the world is his, and man shall treat with man as a sovereign state with a sovereign state,—tends to true union as well as greatness. "I learned," said the melancholy Pestalozzi, "that no man in God's wide earth is either willing or able to help any other man." Help must come from the bosom alone. The scholar is that man who must take up into himself all the ability of the time, all the contributions of the past, all the hopes of the future. He must be an university of knowledges. If there be one lesson more than another which should pierce his ear, it is, The world is nothing, the man is all; in yourself is the law of all nature, and you know not yet how a globule of sap ascends; in yourself slumbers the whole of Reason; it is for you to know all; it is for you to dare all. Mr. President and Gentlemen, this confidence in the unsearched might of man belongs, by all motives, by all prophecy, by all preparation, to the American Scholar. We have listened too long to the courtly muses of Europe. The spirit of the American freeman is already suspected to be timid, imitative, tame. Public and private avarice make the air we breathe thick and fat. The scholar is decent, indolent, complaisant. See already the tragic consequence. The mind of this country, taught to aim at low objects, eats upon itself. There is no work for any but the decorous and the complaisant. Young men of the fairest promise, who begin life upon our shores, inflated by the mountain winds, shined upon by all the stars of God, find the earth below not in unison with these, but are hindered from action by the disgust which the principles on which business is managed inspire, and turn drudges, or die of disgust, some of them suicides. What is the remedy? They did not yet see, and thousands of young men as hopeful now crowding to the barriers for the career do not yet see, that if the single man plant himself indomitably on his instincts, and there abide, the huge world will come round to him. Patience,—patience; with the shades of all the good and great for company; and for solace the perspective of your own infinite life; and for work the study and the communication of principles, the making those instincts prevalent, the conversion of the world. Is it not the chief disgrace in the world, not to be an unit;—not to be reckoned one character;—not to yield that peculiar fruit which each man was created to bear, but to be reckoned in the gross, in the hundred, or the thousand, of the party, the section, to which we belong; and our opinion predicted geographically, as the north, or the south? Not so, brothers and friends,—please God, ours shall not be so. We will walk on our own feet; we will work with our own hands; we will speak our own minds. The study of letters shall be no longer a name for pity, for doubt, and for sensual indulgence. The dread of man and the love of man shall be a wall of defence and a wreath of joy around all. A nation of men will for the first time exist, because each believes himself inspired by the Divine Soul which also inspires all men.

1837

## THE DIVINITY SCHOOL ADDRESS

DELIVERED BEFORE THE SENIOR CLASS IN DIVINITY COLLEGE, CAMBRIDGE, SUNDAY EVENING, JULY 15, 1838

In this refulgent summer, it has been a luxury to draw the breath of life. The grass grows, the buds burst, the meadow is spotted with fire and gold in the tint of flowers. The air is full of birds, and sweet with the breath of the pine, the balm-of-Gilead, and the new hay. Night brings no gloom to the heart with its welcome shade. Through the transparent darkness the stars pour their almost spiritual rays. Man under them seems a young child, and his huge globe a toy. The cool night bathes the world as with a river, and prepares his eyes again for the crimson dawn. The mystery of nature was never displayed more happily. The corn and the wine have been freely dealt to all creatures, and the never-broken silence with which the old bounty goes forward has not yielded yet one word of explanation. One is constrained to respect the perfection of this world in which our senses converse. How wide; how rich; what invitation from every property it gives to every faculty of man! In its fruitful soils; in its navigable sea; in its mountains of metal and stone; in its forests of all woods; in its animals; in its chemical ingredients; in the powers and path of light, heat, attraction and life, it is well worth the pith and heart of great men to subdue and enjoy it. The planters, the mechanics, the inventors, the astronomers, the builders of cities, and the captains, history delights to honor.

But when the mind opens, and reveals the laws which traverse the universe and make things what they are, then shrinks the great world at once into a mere illustration and fable of this mind. What am I? and What is? asks the human spirit with a curiosity new-kindled, but never to be quenched. Behold these outrunning laws, which our imperfect apprehension can see tend this way and that, but not come full circle. Behold these infinite relations, so like, so unlike; many, yet one. I would study, I would know, I would admire forever. These works of thought have been the entertainments of the human spirit in all ages.

A more secret, sweet, and overpowering beauty appears to man when his heart and mind open to the sentiment of virtue. Then he is instructed in what is above him. He learns that his being is without bound; that to the good, to the perfect, he is born, low as he now lies in evil and weakness. That which he venerates is still his own, though he has not realized it yet. *He ought.* He knows the sense of that grand word, though his analysis fails entirely to render account of it. When in innocency or when by intellectual perception he attains to say,—"I love the Right; Truth is beautiful within and without for evermore. Virtue, I am thine; save me; use me; thee will I serve, day and night, in great, in small, that I may be not virtuous, but virtue;"—then is the end of the creation answered, and God is well pleased.

The sentiment of virtue is a reverence and delight in the presence of certain divine laws. It perceives that this homely game of life we play, covers, under what seem foolish details, principles that astonish. The child amidst his baubles is learning the action of light, motion, gravity, muscular force; and in the game of human life, love, fear, justice, appetite, man, and God, interact. These laws refuse to be adequately stated. They will not be written out on paper, or spoken by the tongue. They elude our persevering thought; yet we read them hourly in each other's faces, in each other's actions, in our own remorse. The moral traits which are all globed into every virtuous act and thought, —in speech we must sever, and describe or suggest by painful enumeration of many particulars. Yet, as this sentiment is the essence of all religion, let me guide your eye to the precise objects of the sentiment, by an enumeration of some of those classes of facts in which this element is conspicuous.

The intuition of the moral sentiment is an insight of the perfection of the laws of the soul. These laws execute themselves. They are out of time, out of space, and not subject to circumstance. Thus in the soul of man there is a justice whose retributions are instant and entire. He who does a good deed is instantly ennobled. He who does a mean deed is by the action itself contracted. He who puts off impurity, thereby puts on purity. If a man is at heart just, then in so far is he God; the safety of God, the immortality of God, the majesty of God, do enter into that man with justice. If a man dissemble, deceive, he deceives himself, and goes out of acquaintance with his own being. A man in the view of absolute goodness, adores, with total humility. Every step so downward, is a step upward. The man who renounces himself, comes to himself.

See how this rapid intrinsic energy worketh everywhere, righting wrongs, correcting appearances, and bringing up facts to a harmony with thoughts. Its operation in life, though slow to the senses, is at last as sure as in the soul. By it a man is made the Providence to himself, dispensing good to his goodness, and evil to his sin. Character is always known. Thefts never enrich; alms never impoverish; murder will speak out of stone walls. The least admixture of a lie—for example, the taint of vanity, any attempt to make a good impression, a favorable appearance—will instantly vitiate the effect. But speak the truth, and all nature and all spirits help you with unexpected furtherance. Speak the truth, and all things alive or brute are vouchers, and the very roots of the grass underground there do seem to stir and move to bear you witness. See again the perfection of the Law as it applies itself to the affections, and becomes the law of society. As we are, so we associate. The good, by affinity, seek the good; the vile, by affinity, the vile. Thus of their own volition, souls proceed into heaven, into hell.

These facts have always suggested to man the sublime creed that the world is not the product of manifold power, but of one will, of one mind; and that one mind is everywhere active, in each ray of the star, in each wavelet of the pool; and whatever opposes that will is everywhere balked and baffled, because things are made so, and not otherwise. Good is positive. Evil is merely privative, not absolute: it is like cold, which is the privation of heat. All evil is so much death or nonentity. Benevolence is absolute and real. So much benevolence as a man hath, so much life hath he. For all things proceed out of this same spirit, which is differently named love, justice, temperance, in its different applications, just as the ocean receives different names on the several shores which it washes. All things proceed out of the same spirit, and all things conspire with it. Whilst a man seeks good ends, he is strong by the whole strength of nature. In so far as he roves from these ends, he bereaves himself of power, of auxiliaries; his being shrinks out of all remote channels, he becomes less and less, a mote, a point, until absolute badness is absolute death.

The perception of this law of laws awakens in the mind a sentiment which we call the religious sentiment, and which makes our highest happiness. Wonderful is its power to charm and to command. It is a mountain air. It is the embalmer of the world. It is myrrh and storax, and chlorine and rosemary. It makes the sky and the hills sublime, and the silent song of the stars is it. By it is the universe made safe and habitable, not by science or power. Thought may work cold and intransitive in things, and find no end or unity; but the dawn of the sentiment of virtue on the heart, gives and is the assurance that Law is sovereign over all natures; and the worlds, time, space, eternity, do seem to break out into joy.

This sentiment is divine and deifying. It is the beatitude of man. It makes him illimitable. Through it, the soul first knows itself. It corrects the capital mistake of the infant man, who seeks to be great by following the great, and hopes to derive advantages *from another,*—by showing the fountain of all good to be in himself, and that he, equally with every man, is an inlet into the deeps of Reason. When he says, "I ought;" when love warms him; when he chooses, warned from on high, the good and great deed; then, deep melodies wander through his soul from Supreme Wisdom. Then he can worship, and be enlarged by his worship; for he can never go behind this sentiment. In the sublimest flights of the soul, rectitude is never surmounted, love is never outgrown.

This sentiment lies at the foundation of society, and successively creates all forms of worship. The principle of veneration never dies out. Man fallen into superstition, into sensuality, is never quite without the visions of the moral sentiment. In like manner, all the expressions of this sentiment are sacred and permanent in proportion to their purity. The expressions of this sentiment affect us more than all other compositions. The sentences of the oldest time, which ejaculate this piety, are still fresh and fragrant. This thought dwelled always deepest in the minds of men in the devout and contemplative East; not alone in Palestine, where it reached its purest expression, but in Egypt, in Persia, in India, in China. Europe has always owed to oriental genius its divine impulses. What these holy bards said, all sane men found agreeable and true. And the unique impression of Jesus upon mankind, whose name is not so much written as ploughed into the history of this world, is proof of the subtle virtue of this infusion.

Meantime, whilst the doors of the temple stand open, night and day, before every man, and the oracles of this truth cease never, it is guarded by one stern condition; this namely; it is an intuition. It cannot be received at second hand. Truly speaking, it is not instruction, but provocation, that I can receive from another soul. What he announces, I must find true in me, or reject; and on his word, or as his second, be he who he may, I can accept nothing. On the contrary, the absence of this primary faith is the presence of degradation. As is the flood so is the ebb. Let this faith depart, and the very words it spake and the things it made become false and hurtful. Then falls the church, the state, art, letters, life. The doctrine of the divine nature being forgotten, a sickness infects and dwarfs the constitution. Once man was all; now he is an appendage, a nuisance. And because the indwelling Supreme Spirit cannot wholly be got rid of, the doctrine of it suffers this perversion, that the divine nature is attributed to one or two persons and denied to all the rest, and denied with fury. The doctrine of inspiration is lost; the base doctrine of the majority of voices usurps the place of the doctrine of the soul. Miracles, prophecy, poetry, the ideal life, the holy life, exist as ancient history merely; they are not in the belief, nor in the aspiration of society; but when suggested, seem ridiculous. Life is comic or pitiful as soon as the high ends of being fade out of sight, and man becomes near-sighted, and can only attend to what addresses the senses.

These general views, which, whilst they are general, none will contest, find abundant illustration in the history of religion, and especially in the history of the Christian church. In that, all of us have had our birth and nurture. The truth contained in that, you, my young friends, are now setting forth to teach. As the Cultus, or established worship of the civilized world, it has great historical interest for us. Of its blessed words, which have been the consolation of humanity, you need not that I should speak. I shall endeavor to discharge my duty to you on this occasion, by pointing out two errors in its administration, which daily appear more gross from the point of view we have just now taken.

Jesus Christ belonged to the true race of prophets. He saw with open eye the mystery of the soul. Drawn by its severe harmony, ravished with its beauty, he lived in it, and had his being there. Alone in all history he estimated the greatness of man. One man was true to what is in you and me. He saw that God incarnates himself in man, and evermore goes forth anew to take possession of his World. He said in this jubilee of sublime emotion, 'I am divine. Through me, God acts; through me, speaks. Would you see God, see me; or see thee, when thou also thinkest as I now think.' But what a distortion did his doctrine and memory suffer in the same, in the next, and the following ages! There is no doctrine of the Reason which will bear to be taught by the Understanding. The understanding caught this high chant from the poet's lips, and said, in the next age, 'This was Jehovah come down out of heaven. I will kill you, if you say he was a man.' The idioms of his language and the figures of his rhetoric have usurped the place of his truth; and churches are not built on his principles, but on his tropes. Christianity became a Mythus, as the poetic teaching of Greece and of Egypt, before. He spoke of miracles; for he felt that man's life was a miracle, and all that man doth, and he knew that this daily miracle shines as the character ascends. But the word Miracle, as pronounced by Christian churches, gives a false impression; it is Monster. It is not one with the blowing clover and the falling rain.

He felt respect for Moses and the prophets, but no unfit tenderness at postponing their initial revelations to the hour and the man that now is; to the eternal revelation in the heart. Thus was he a true man. Having seen that the law in us is commanding, he would not suffer it to be commanded. Boldly, with hand, and heart, and life, he declared it was God. Thus is he, as I think, the only soul in history who has appreciated the worth of man.

1. In this point of view we become sensible of the first defect of historical Christianity. Historical Christianity has fallen into the error that corrupts all attempts to communicate religion. As it appears to us, and as it has appeared for ages, it is not the doctrine of the soul, but an exaggeration of the personal, the positive, the ritual. It has dwelt, it dwells, with noxious exaggeration about the *person* of Jesus. The soul knows no persons. It invites every man to expand to the full circle of the universe, and will have no preferences but those of spontaneous love. But by this eastern monarchy of a Christianity, which indolence and fear have built, the friend of man is made the injurer of man. The manner in which his name is surrounded with expressions which were once sallies of admiration and love, but are now petrified into official titles, kills all generous sympathy and liking. All who hear me, feel that the language that describes Christ to Europe and America is not the style of friendship and enthusiasm to a good and noble heart, but is appropriated and formal,—paints a demigod, as the Orientals or the Greeks would describe Osiris or Apollo. Accept the injurious impositions of our early catechetical instruction, and even honesty and self-denial were but splendid sins, if they did not wear the Christian name. One would rather be

> A pagan, suckled in a creed outworn,

than to be defrauded of his manly right in coming into nature and finding not names and places, not land and professions, but even virtue and truth foreclosed and monopolized. You shall not be a man even. You shall not own the world; you shall not dare and live after the infinite Law that is in you, and in company with the infinite Beauty which heaven and earth reflect to you in all lovely forms; but you must subordinate your nature to Christ's nature; you must accept our interpretations, and take his portrait as the vulgar draw it.

That is always best which gives me to myself. The sublime is excited in me by the great stoical doctrine, Obey thyself. That which shows God in me, fortifies me. That which shows God out of me, makes me a wart and a wen. There is no longer a necessary reason for my being. Already the long shadows of untimely oblivion creep over me, and I shall decease forever.

The divine bards are the friends of my virtue, of my intellect, of my strength. They admonish me that the gleams which flash across my mind are not mine, but God's; that they had the like, and were not disobedient to the heavenly vision. So I love them. Noble provocations go out from them, inviting me to resist evil; to subdue the world; and to Be. And thus, by his holy thoughts, Jesus serves us, and thus only. To aim to convert a man by miracles, is a profanation of the soul. A true conversion, a true Christ, is now, as always, to be made by the reception of beautiful sentiments. It is true that a great and rich soul, like his, falling among the simple, does so preponderate, that, as his did, it names the world. The world seems to them to exist for him, and they have not yet drunk so deeply of his sense as to see that only by coming again to themselves, or to God in themselves, can they grow forevermore. It is a low benefit to give me something; it is a high benefit to enable me to do somewhat of myself. The time is coming when all men will see that the gift of God to the soul is not a vaunting, overpowering, excluding sanctity, but a sweet, natural goodness, a goodness like thine and mine, and that so invites thine and mine to be and to grow.

The injustice of the vulgar tone of preaching is not less flagrant to Jesus than to the souls which it profanes. The preachers do not see that they make his gospel not glad, and shear him of the locks of beauty and the attributes of heaven. When I see a majestic Epaminondas, or Washington; when I see among my contemporaries a true orator, an upright judge, a dear friend; when I vibrate to the melody and fancy of a poem; I see beauty that is to be desired. And so lovely, and with yet more entire consent of my human being, sounds in my ear the severe music of the bards that have sung of the true God in all ages. Now do not degrade the life and dialogues of Christ out of the circle of this charm, by insulation and peculiarity. Let them lie as they befell, alive and warm, part of human life and of the landscape and of the cheerful day.

2. The second defect of the traditionary and limited way of using the mind of Christ, is a consequence of the first; this, namely; that the Moral Nature, that Law of laws whose revelations introduce greatness,—yea, God himself,—into the open soul, is not explored as the fountain of the established teaching in society. Men have come to speak of the revelation as somewhat long ago given and done, as if God were dead. The injury to faith throttles the preacher; and the goodliest of institutions becomes an uncertain and inarticulate voice.

It is very certain that it is the effect of conversation with the beauty of the soul, to beget a desire and need to impart to others the same knowledge and love. If utterance is denied, the thought lies like a burden on the man. Always the seer is a sayer. Somehow his dream is told; somehow he publishes it with solemn joy; sometimes with pencil on canvas, sometimes with chisel on stone, sometimes in towers and aisles of granite, his soul's worship is builded; sometimes in anthems of indefinite music; but clearest and most permanent, in words.

The man enamored of this excellency becomes its priest or poet. The office is coeval with the world. But observe the condition, the spiritual limitation of the office. The spirit only can teach. Not any profane man, not any sensual, not any liar, not any slave can teach, but only he can give, who has; he only can create, who is. The man on whom the soul descends, through whom the soul speaks, alone can teach. Courage, piety, love, wisdom, can teach; and every man can open his door to these angels, and they shall bring him the gift of tongues. But the man who aims to speak as books enable, as synods use, as the fashion guides, and as interest commands, babbles. Let him hush.

To this holy office you propose to devote yourselves. I wish you may feel your call in throbs of desire and hope. The office is the first in the world. It is of that reality that it cannot suffer the deduction of any falsehood. And it is my duty to say to you that the need was never greater of new revelation than now. From the views I have already expressed, you will infer the sad conviction, which I share, I believe, with numbers, of the universal decay and now almost death of faith in society. The soul is not preached. The Church seems to totter to its fall, almost all life extinct. On this occasion, any complaisance would be criminal which told you, whose hope and commission it is to preach the faith of Christ, that the faith of Christ is preached.

It is time that this ill-suppressed murmur of all thoughtful men against the famine of our churches;—this moaning of the heart because it is bereaved of the consolation, the hope, the grandeur that come alone out of the culture of the moral nature,—should be heard through the sleep of indolence, and over the din of routine. This great and perpetual office of the preacher is not discharged. Preaching is the expression of the moral sentiment in application to the duties of life. In how many churches, by how many prophets, tell me, is man made sensible that he is an infinite Soul; that the earth and heavens are passing into his mind; that he is drinking forever the soul of God? Where now sounds the persuasion, that by its very melody imparadises my heart, and so affirms its own origin in heaven? Where shall I hear words such as in elder ages drew men to leave all and follow,—father and mother, house and land, wife and child? Where shall I hear these august laws of moral being so pronounced as to fill my ear, and I feel ennobled by the offer of my uttermost action and passion? The test of the true faith, certainly, should be its power to charm and command the soul, as the laws of nature control the activity of the hands,—so commanding that we find pleasure and honor in obeying. The faith should blend with the light of rising and of setting suns, with the flying cloud, the singing bird, and the breath of flowers. But now the priest's Sabbath has lost the splendor of nature; it is unlovely; we are glad when it is done; we can make, we do make, even sitting in our pews, a far better, holier, sweeter, for ourselves.

Whenever the pulpit is usurped by a formalist, then is the worshipper defrauded and disconsolate. We shrink as soon as the prayers begin, which do not uplift, but smite and offend us. We are fain to wrap our cloaks about us, and secure, as best we can, a solitude that hears not. I once heard a preacher who sorely tempted me to say I would go to church no more.

Men go, thought I, where they are wont to go, else had no soul entered the temple in the afternoon. A snow-storm was falling around us. The snow-storm was real, the preacher merely spectral, and the eye felt the sad contrast in looking at him, and then out of the window behind him into the beautiful meteor of the snow. He had lived in vain. He had no one word intimating that he had laughed or wept, was married or in love, had been commended, or cheated, or chagrined. If he had ever lived and acted, we were none the wiser for it. The capital secret of his profession, namely, to convert life into truth, he had not learned. Not one fact in all his experience had he yet imported into his doctrine. This man had ploughed and planted and talked and bought and sold; he had read books; he had eaten and drunken; his head aches, his heart throbs; he smiles and suffers; yet was there not a surmise, a hint, in all the discourse, that he had ever lived at all. Not a line did he draw out of real history. The true preacher can be known by this, that he deals out to the people his life,—life passed through the fire of thought. But of the bad preacher, it could not be told from his sermon what age of the world he fell in; whether he had a father or a child; whether he was a freeholder or a pauper; whether he was a citizen or a countryman; or any other fact of his biography. It seemed strange that the people should come to church. It seemed as if their houses were very unentertaining, that they should prefer this thoughtless clamor. It shows that there is a commanding attraction in the moral sentiment, that can lend a faint tint of light to dulness and ignorance coming in its name and place. The good hearer is sure he has been touched sometimes; is sure there is somewhat to be reached, and some word that can reach it. When he listens to these vain words, he comforts himself by their relation to his remembrance of better hours, and so they clatter and echo unchallenged.

I am not ignorant that when we preach unworthily, it is not always quite in vain. There is a good ear, in some men, that draws supplies to virtue out of very indifferent nutriment. There is poetic truth concealed in all the common-places of prayer and of sermons, and though foolishly spoken, they may be wisely heard; for each is some select expression that broke out in a moment of piety from some stricken or jubilant soul, and its excellency made it remembered. The prayers and even the dogmas of our church are like the zodiac of Denderah and the astronomical monuments of the Hindoos, wholly insulated from anything now extant in the life and business of the people. They mark the height to which the waters once rose. But this docility is a check upon the mischief from the good and devout. In a large portion of the community, the religious service gives rise to quite other thoughts and emotions. We need not chide the negligent servant. We are struck with pity, rather, at the swift retribution of his sloth. Alas for the unhappy man that is called to stand in the pulpit, and *not* give bread of life. Everything that befalls, accuses him. Would he ask contributions for the missions, foreign or domestic? Instantly his face is suffused with shame to propose to his parish that they should send money a hundred or a thousand miles, to furnish such poor fare as they have at home and would do well to go the hundred or the thousand miles to escape. Would he urge people to a godly way of living;—and can he ask a fellow-creature to come to Sabbath meetings, when he and they all know what is the poor uttermost they can hope for therein? Will he invite them privately to the Lord's Supper? He dares not. If no heart warm this rite, the hollow, dry, creaking formality is too plain, than that he can face a man of wit and energy and put the invitation without terror. In the street, what has he to say to the bold village blasphemer? The village blasphemer sees fear in the face, form, and gait of the minister.

Let me not taint the sincerity of this plea by any oversight of the claims of good men. I know and honor the purity and strict conscience of numbers of the clergy. What life the public worship retains, it owes to the scattered company of pious men, who minister here and there in the churches, and who, sometimes accepting with too great tenderness the tenet of the elders, have not accepted from others, but from their own heart, the genuine impulses of virtue, and so still command our love and awe, to the sanctity of character. Moreover, the exceptions are not so much to be found in a few eminent preachers, as in the better hours, the truer inspirations of all,—nay, in the sincere moments of every man. But, with whatever exception, it is still true that tradition characterizes the preaching of this country; that it comes out of the memory, and not out of the soul; that it aims at what is usual, and not at what is necessary and eternal; that thus historical Christianity destroys the power of preaching, by withdrawing it from the exploration of the moral nature of man; where the sublime is, where are the resources of astonishment and power. What a cruel injustice it is to that Law, the joy of the whole earth, which alone can make thought dear and rich; that Law whose fatal sureness the astronomical orbits poorly emulate;—that it is travestied and depreciated, that it is behooted and behowled, and not a trait, not a word of it articulated. The pulpit in losing sight of this Law, loses its reason, and gropes after it knows not what. And for want of this culture the soul of the community is sick and faithless. It wants nothing so much as a stern, high, stoical, Christian discipline, to make it know itself and the divinity that speaks through it. Now man is ashamed of himself; he skulks and sneaks through the world, to be tolerated, to be pitied, and scarcely in a thousand years does any man dare to be wise and good, and so draw after him the tears and blessings of his kind.

Certainly there have been periods when, from the inactivity of the intellect on certain truths, a greater faith was possible in names and persons. The Puritans in England and America found in the Christ of the Catholic Church, and in the dogmas inherited from Rome, scope for their austere piety, and their longings for civil freedom. But their creed is passing away, and none arises in its room. I think no man can go with his thoughts about him into one of our churches, without feeling that what hold the public worship had on men is gone, or going. It has lost its grasp on the affection of the good and the fear of the bad. In the country, neighborhoods, half parishes are *signing off*, to use the local term. It is already beginning to indicate character and religion to withdraw from the religious meetings. I have heard a devout person, who prized the Sabbath, say in bitterness of heart, "On Sundays, it seems wicked to go to church." And the motive that holds the best there is now only a hope and a waiting. What was once a mere circumstance, that the best and the worst men in the parish, the poor and the rich, the learned and the ignorant, young and old, should meet one day as fellows in one house, in sign of an equal right in the soul, has come to be a paramount motive for going thither.

My friends, in these two errors, I think, I find the causes of a decaying church and a wasting unbelief. And what greater calamity can fall upon a nation than the loss of worship? Then all things go to decay. Genius leaves the temple to haunt the senate or the market. Literature becomes frivolous. Science is cold. The eye of youth is not lighted by the hope of other worlds, and age is without honor. Society lives to trifles, and when men die we do not mention them.

And now, my brothers, you will ask, What in these desponding days can be done by us? The remedy is already declared in the ground of our complaint of the Church. We have contrasted the Church with the Soul. In the soul then let the redemption be sought. Wherever a man comes, there comes revolution. The old is for slaves. When a man comes, all books are legible, all things transparent, all religions are forms. He is religious. Man is the wonder-worker. He is seen amid miracles. All men bless and curse. He saith yea and nay, only. The stationariness of religion; the assumption that the age of inspiration is past, that the Bible is closed; the fear of degrading the character of Jesus by representing him as a man;—indicate with sufficient clearness the falsehood of our theology. It is the office of a true teacher to show us that God is, not was; that He speaketh, not spake. The true Christianity—a faith like Christ's in the infinitude of man—is lost. None believeth in the soul of man, but only in some man or person old and departed. Ah me! no man goeth alone. All men go in flocks to this saint or that poet, avoiding the God who seeth in secret. They cannot see in secret; they love to be blind in public. They think society wiser than their soul, and know not that one soul, and their soul, is wiser than the whole world. See how nations and races flit by on the sea of time and leave no ripple to tell where they floated or sunk, and one good soul shall make the name of Moses, or of Zeno, or of Zoroaster, reverend forever. None assayeth the stern ambition to be the Self of the nation and of nature, but each would be an easy secondary to some Christian scheme, or sectarian connection, or some eminent man. Once leave your own knowledge of God, your own sentiment, and take secondary knowledge, as St. Paul's or George Fox's or Swedenborg's, and you get wide from God with every year this secondary form lasts, and if, as now, for centuries,—the chasm yawns to that breadth, that men can scarcely be convinced there is in them anything divine.

Let me admonish you, first of all, to go alone; to refuse the good models, even those which are sacred in the imagination of men, and dare to love God without mediator or veil. Friends enough you shall find who will hold up to your emulation Wesleys and Oberlins, Saints and Prophets. Thank God for these good men, but say, 'I also am a man.' Imitation cannot go above its model. The imitator dooms himself to hopeless mediocrity. The inventor did it because it was natural to him, and so in him it has a charm. In the imitator something else is natural, and he bereaves himself of his own beauty, to come short of another man's.

Yourself a newborn bard of the Holy Ghost, cast behind you all conformity, and acquaint men at first hand with Deity. Look to it, first and only, that fashion, custom, authority, pleasure, and money, are nothing to you,—are not bandages over your eyes, that you cannot see,—but live with the privilege of the immeasurable mind. Not too anxious to visit periodically all families and each family in your parish connection,—when you meet one of these men or women, be to them a divine man; be to them thought and virtue; let their timid aspirations find in you a friend; let their trampled instincts be genially tempted out in your atmosphere; let their doubts know that you have doubted, and their wonder feel that you have wondered. By trusting your own heart, you shall gain more confidence in other men. For all our penny-wisdom, for all our soul-destroying slavery to habit, it is not to be doubted that all men have sublime thoughts; that all men value the few real hours of life; they love to be heard; they love to be caught up into the vision of principles. We mark with light in the memory the few interviews we have had, in the dreary years of routine and of sin, with souls that made our souls wiser; that spoke what we thought; that told us what we knew; that gave us leave to be what we inly were. Discharge to men the priestly office, and, present or absent, you shall be followed with their love as by an angel.

And, to this end, let us not aim at common degrees of merit. Can we not leave, to such as love it, the virtue that glitters for the commendation of society, and ourselves pierce the deep solitudes of absolute ability and worth? We easily come up to the standard of goodness in society. Society's praise can be cheaply secured, and almost all men are content with those easy merits; but the instant effect of conversing with God will be to put them away. There are persons who are not actors, not speakers, but influences; persons too great for fame, for display; who disdain eloquence; to whom all we call art and artist, seems too nearly allied to show and by-ends, to the exaggeration of the finite and selfish, and loss of the universal. The orators, the poets, the commanders encroach on us only as fair women do, by our allowance and homage. Slight them by preoccupation of mind, slight them, as you can well afford to do, by high and universal aims, and they instantly feel that you have right, and that it is in lower places that they must shine. They also feel your right; for they with you are open to the influx of the all-knowing Spirit, which annihilates before its broad noon the little shades and gradations of intelligence in the compositions we call wiser and wisest.

In such high communion let us study the grand strokes of rectitude; a bold benevolence, an independence of friends, so that not the unjust wishes of those who love us shall impair our freedom, but we shall resist for truth's sake the freest flow of kindness, and appeal to sympathies far in advance; and—what is the highest form in which we know this beautiful element—a certain solidity of merit, that has nothing to do with opinion, and which is so essentially and manifestly virtue, that it is taken for granted that the right, the brave, the generous step will be taken by it, and nobody thinks of commending it. You would compliment a coxcomb doing a good act, but you would not praise an angel. The silence that accepts merit as the most natural thing in the world, is the highest applause. Such souls, when they appear, are the Imperial Guard of Virtue, the perpetual reserve, the dictators of fortune. One needs not praise their courage,—they are the heart and soul of nature. O my friends, there are resources in us on which we have not drawn. There are men who rise refreshed on hearing a threat; men to whom a crisis which intimidates and paralyzes the majority,—demanding not the faculties of prudence and thrift, but comprehension, immovableness, the readiness of sacrifice,—comes graceful and beloved as a bride. Napoleon said of Massena, that he was not himself until the battle began to go against him; then, when the dead began to fall in ranks around him, awoke his powers of combination, and he put on terror and victory as a robe. So it is in rugged crises, in unweariable endurance, and in aims which put sympathy out of question, that the angel is shown. But these are heights that we can scarce remember and look up to without contrition and shame. Let us thank God that such things exist.

And now let us do what we can to rekindle the smouldering, nigh quenched fire on the altar. The evils of the church that now is are manifest. The question returns, What shall we do? I confess, all attempts to project and establish a Cultus with new rites and forms, seem to me vain. Faith makes us, and not we it, and faith makes its own forms. All attempts to contrive a system are as cold as the new worship introduced by the French to the goddess of Reason,—to-day, pasteboard and filigree, and ending to-morrow in madness and murder. Rather let the breath of new life be breathed by you through the forms already existing. For if once you are alive, you shall find they shall become plastic and new. The remedy to their deformity is first, soul, and second, soul, and evermore, soul. A whole popedom of forms one pulsation of virtue can uplift and vivify. Two inestimable advantages Christianity has given us: first, the Sabbath, the jubilee of the whole world, whose light dawns welcome alike into the closet of the philosopher, into the garret of toil, and into prison-cells, and everywhere suggests, even to the vile, the dignity of spiritual being. Let it stand forevermore, a temple, which new love, new faith, new sight shall restore to more than its first splendor to mankind. And secondly, the institution of preaching,—the speech of man to men,—essentially the most flexible of all organs, of all forms. What hinders that now, everywhere, in pulpits, in lecture-rooms, in houses, in fields, wherever the invitation of men or your own occasions lead you, you speak the very truth, as your life and conscience teach it, and cheer the waiting, fainting hearts of men with new hope and new revelation?

I look for the hour when that supreme Beauty which ravished the souls of those Eastern men, and chiefly of those Hebrews, and through their lips spoke oracles to all time, shall speak in the West also. The Hebrew and Greek Scriptures contain immortal sentences, that have been bread of life to millions. But they have no epical integrity, are fragmentary; are not shown in their order to the intellect. I look for the new Teacher that shall follow so far those shining laws that he shall see them come full circle; shall see their rounding complete grace; shall see the world to be the mirror of the soul; shall see the identity of the law of gravitation with purity of heart; and shall show that the Ought, that Duty, is one thing with Science, with Beauty, and with Joy.

1838

## SELF-RELIANCE

"Ne te quæsiveris extra."

Man is his own star; and the soul that can
Render an honest and a perfect man,
Commands all light, all influence, all fate;
Nothing to him falls early or too late.
Our acts our angels are, or good or ill,
Our fatal shadows that walk by us still.

—Epilogue to Beaumont and Fletcher's *Honest Man's Fortune.*

Cast the bantling on the rocks,
Suckle him with the she-wolf's teat,
Wintered with the hawk and fox,
Power and speed be hands and feet.

I read the other day some verses written by an eminent painter which were original and not conventional. The soul always hears an admonition in such lines, let the subject be what it may. The sentiment they instil is of more value than any thought they may contain. To believe your own thought, to believe that what is true for you in your private heart is true for all men,—that is genius. Speak your latent conviction, and it shall be the universal sense; for the inmost in due time becomes the outmost, and our first thought is rendered back to us by the trumpets of the Last Judgment. Familiar as the voice of the mind is to each, the highest merit we ascribe to Moses, Plato and Milton is that they set at naught books and traditions, and spoke not what men, but what *they* thought. A man should learn to detect and watch that gleam of light which flashes across his mind from within, more than the lustre of the firmament of bards and sages. Yet he dismisses without notice his thought, because it is his. In every work of genius we recognize our own rejected thoughts; they come back to us with a certain alienated majesty. Great works of art have no more affecting lesson for us than this. They teach us to abide by our spontaneous impression with good-humored inflexibility then most when the whole cry of voices is on the other side. Else to-morrow a stranger will say with masterly good sense precisely what we have thought and felt all the time, and we shall be forced to take with shame our own opinion from another.

There is a time in every man's education when he arrives at the conviction that envy is ignorance; that imitation is suicide; that he must take himself for better for worse as his portion; that though the wide universe is full of good, no kernel of nourishing corn can come to him but through his toil bestowed on that plot of ground which is given to him to till. The power which resides in him is new in nature, and none but he knows what that is which he can do, nor does he know until he has tried. Not for nothing one face, one character, one fact, makes much impression on him, and another none. This sculpture in the memory is not without preëstablished harmony. The eye was placed where one ray should fall, that it might testify of that particular ray. We but half express ourselves, and are ashamed of that divine idea which each of us represents. It may be safely trusted as proportionate and of good issues, so it be faithfully imparted, but God will not have his work made manifest by cowards. A man is relieved and gay when he has put his heart into his work and done his best; but what he has said or done otherwise shall give him no peace. It is a deliverance which does not deliver. In the attempt his genius deserts him; no muse befriends; no invention, no hope.

Trust thyself: every heart vibrates to that iron string. Accept the place the divine providence has found for you, the society of your contemporaries, the connection of events. Great men have always done so, and confided themselves childlike to the genius of their age, betraying their perception that the absolutely trustworthy was seated at their heart, working through their hands, predominating in all their being. And we are now men, and must accept in the highest mind the same transcendent destiny; and not minors and invalids in a protected corner, not cowards fleeing before a revolution, but guides, redeemers and benefactors, obeying the Almighty effort and advancing on Chaos and the Dark.

What pretty oracles nature yields us on this text in the face and behavior of children, babes, and even brutes! That divided and rebel mind, that distrust of a sentiment because our arithmetic has computed the strength and means opposed to our purpose, these have not. Their mind being whole, their eye is as yet unconquered, and when we look in their faces we are disconcerted. Infancy conforms to nobody; all conform to it; so that one babe commonly makes four or five out of the adults who prattle and play to it. So God has armed youth and puberty and manhood no less with its own piquancy and charm, and made it enviable and gracious and its claims not to be put by, if it will stand by itself. Do not think the youth has no force, because he cannot speak to you and me. Hark! in the next room his voice is sufficiently clear and emphatic. It seems he knows how to speak to his contemporaries. Bashful or bold then, he will know how to make us seniors very unnecessary.

The nonchalance of boys who are sure of a dinner, and would disdain as much as a lord to do or say aught to conciliate one, is the healthy attitude of human nature. A boy is in the parlor what the pit is in the playhouse; independent, irresponsible, looking out from his corner on such people and facts as pass by, he tries and sentences them on their merits, in the swift, summary way of boys, as good, bad, interesting, silly, eloquent, troublesome. He cumbers himself never about consequences, about interests; he gives an independent, genuine verdict. You must court him; he does not court you. But the man is as it were clapped into jail by his consciousness. As soon as he has once acted or spoken with *éclat* he is a committed person, watched by the sympathy or the hatred of hundreds, whose affections must now enter into his account. There is no Lethe for this. Ah, that he could pass again into his neutrality! Who can thus avoid all pledges and, having observed, observe again from the same unaffected, unbiased, unbribable, unaffrighted innocence,—must always be formidable. He would utter opinions on all passing affairs, which being seen to be not private but necessary, would sink like darts into the ear of men and put them in fear.

These are the voices which we hear in solitude, but they grow faint and inaudible as we enter into the world. Society everywhere is in conspiracy against the manhood of every one of its members. Society is a joint-stock company, in which the members agree, for the better securing of his bread to each shareholder, to surrender the liberty and culture of the eater. The virtue in most request is conformity. Self-reliance is its aversion. It loves not realities and creators, but names and customs.

Whoso would be a man, must be a noncomformist. He who would gather immortal palms must not be hindered by the name of goodness, but must explore if it be goodness. Nothing is at last sacred but the integrity of your own mind. Absolve you to yourself, and you shall have the suffrage of the world. I remember an answer which when quite young I was prompted to make to a valued adviser who was wont to importune me with the dear old doctrines of the church. On my saying, "What have I to do with the sacredness of traditions, if I live wholly from within?" my friend suggested,—"But these impulses may be from below, not from above." I replied, "They do not seem to me to be such; but if I am the Devil's child, I will live then from the Devil." No law can be sacred to me but that of my nature. Good and bad are but names very readily transferable to that or this; the only right is what is after my constitution; the only wrong what is against it. A man is to carry himself in the presence of all opposition as if everything were titular and ephemeral but he. I am ashamed to think how easily we capitulate to badges and names, to large societies and dead institutions. Every decent and well-spoken individual affects and sways me more than is right. I ought to go upright and vital, and speak the rude truth in all ways. If malice and vanity wear the coat of philanthropy, shall that pass? If an angry bigot assumes this bountiful cause of Abolition, and comes to me with his last news from Barbadoes, why should I not say to him, 'Go love thy infant; love thy wood-chopper; be good-natured and modest; have that grace; and never varnish your hard, uncharitable ambition with this incredible tenderness for black folk a thousand miles off. Thy love afar is spite at home.' Rough and graceless would be such greeting, but truth is handsomer than the affectation of love. Your goodness must have some edge to it, —else it is none. The doctrine of hatred must be preached, as the counteraction of the doctrine of love, when that pules and whines. I shun father and mother and wife and brother when my genius calls me. I would write on the lintels of the door-post, *Whim*. I hope it is somewhat better than whim at last, but we cannot spend the day in explanation. Expect me not to show cause why I seek or why I exclude company. Then again, do not tell me, as a good man did to-day, of my obligation to put all poor men in good situations. Are they *my* poor? I tell thee, thou foolish philanthropist, that I grudge the dollar, the dime, the cent I give to such men as do not belong to me and to whom I do not belong. There is a class of persons to whom by all spiritual affinity I am bought and sold; for them I will go to prison if need be; but your miscellaneous popular charities; the education at college of fools; the building of meeting-houses to the vain end to which many now stand; alms to sots, and the thousand-fold Relief Societies;—though I confess with shame I sometimes succumb and give the dollar, it is a wicked dollar, which by and by I shall have the manhood to withhold.

Virtues are, in the popular estimate, rather the exception than the rule. There is the man *and* his virtues. Men do what is called a good action, as some piece of courage or charity, much as they would pay a fine in expiation of daily non-appearance on parade. Their works are done as an apology or extenuation of their living in the world,—as invalids and the insane pay a high board. Their virtues are penances. I do not wish to expiate, but to live. My life is for itself and not for a spectacle. I much prefer that it should be of a lower strain, so it be genuine and equal, than that it should be glittering and unsteady. I wish it to be sound and sweet, and not to need diet and bleeding. I ask primary evidence that you are a man, and refuse this appeal from the man to his actions. I know that for myself it makes no difference whether I do or forbear those actions which are reckoned excellent. I cannot consent to pay for a privilege where I have intrinsic right. Few and mean as my gifts may be, I actually am, and do not need for my own assurance or the assurance of my fellows any secondary testimony.

What I must do is all that concerns me, not what the people think. This rule, equally arduous in actual and in intellectual life, may serve for the whole distinction between greatness and meanness. It is the harder because you will always find those who think they know what is your duty better than you know it. It is easy in the world to live after the world's opinion; it is easy in solitude to live after our own; but the great man is he who in the midst of the crowd keeps with perfect sweetness the independence of solitude.

The objection to conforming to usages that have become dead to you is that it scatters your force. It loses your time and blurs the impression of your character. If you maintain a dead church, contribute to a dead Bible-society, vote with a great party either for the government or against it, spread your table like base house-keepers,—under all these screens I have difficulty to detect the precise man you are: and of course so much force is withdrawn from all your proper life. But do your work, and I shall know you. Do your work, and you shall reinforce yourself. A man must consider what a blind-man's-buff is this game of conformity. If I know your sect I anticipate your argument. I hear a preacher announce for his text and topic the expediency of one of the institutions of his church. Do I not know beforehand that not possibly can he say a new and spontaneous word? Do I not know that with all this ostentation of examining the grounds of the institution he will do no such thing? Do I not know that he is pledged to himself not to look but at one side, the permitted side, not as a man, but as a parish minister? He is a retained attorney, and these airs of the bench are the emptiest affectation. Well, most men have bound their eyes with one or another handkerchief, and attached themselves to some one of these communities of opinion. This conformity makes them not false in a few particulars, authors of a few lies, but false in all particulars. Their every truth is not quite true. Their two is not the real two, their four not the real four; so that every word they say chagrins us and we know not where to begin to set them right. Meantime nature is not slow to equip us in the prison-uniform of the party to which we adhere. We come to wear one cut of face and figure, and acquire by degrees the gentlest asinine expression. There is a mortifying experience in particular, which does not fail to wreak itself also in the general history; I mean "the foolish face of praise," the forced smile which we put on in company where we do not feel at ease, in answer to conversation which does not interest us. The muscles, not spontaneously moved but moved by a low usurping wilfulness, grow tight about the outline of the face, with the most disagreeable sensation.

For nonconformity the world whips you with its displeasure. And therefore a man must know how to estimate a sour face. The by-standers look askance on him in the public street or in the friend's parlor. If this aversion had its origin in contempt and resistance like his own he might well go home with a sad countenance; but the sour faces of the multitude, like their sweet faces, have no deep cause, but are put on and off as the wind blows and a newspaper directs. Yet is the discontent of the multitude more formidable than that of the senate and the college. It is easy enough for a firm man who knows the world to brook the rage of the cultivated classes. Their rage is decorous and prudent, for they are timid, as being very vulnerable themselves. But when to their feminine rage the indignation of the people is added, when the ignorant and the poor are aroused, when the unintelligent brute force that lies at the bottom of society is made to growl and mow, it needs the habit of magnanimity and religion to treat it godlike as a trifle of no concernment.

The other terror that scares us from self-trust is our consistency; a reverence for our past act or word because the eyes of others have no other data for computing our orbit than our past acts, and we are loth to disappoint them.

But why should you keep your head over your shoulder? Why drag about this corpse of your memory, lest you contradict somewhat you have stated in this or that public place? Suppose you should contradict yourself; what then? It seems to be a rule of wisdom never to rely on your memory alone, scarcely even in acts of pure memory, but to bring the past for judgment into the thousand-eyed present, and live ever in a new day. In your metaphysics you have denied personality to the Deity, yet when the devout motions of the soul come, yield to them heart and life, though they should clothe God with shape and color. Leave your theory, as Joseph his coat in the hand of the harlot, and flee.

A foolish consistency is the hobgoblin of little minds, adored by little statesmen and philosophers and divines. With consistency a great soul has simply nothing to do. He may as well concern himself with his shadow on the wall. Speak what you think now in hard words and to-morrow speak what to-morrow thinks in hard words again, though it contradict every thing you said to-day.—'Ah, so you shall be sure to be misunderstood.'—Is it so bad then to be misunderstood? Pythagoras was misunderstood, and Socrates, and Jesus, and Luther, and Copernicus, and Galileo, and Newton, and every pure and wise spirit that ever took flesh. To be great is to be misunderstood.

I suppose no man can violate his nature. All the sallies of his will are rounded in by the law of his being, as the inequalities of Andes and Himmaleh are insignificant in the curve of the sphere. Nor does it matter how you gauge and try him. A character is like an acrostic or Alexandrian stanza,—read it forward, backward, or across, it still spells the same thing. In this pleasing contrite wood-life which God allows me, let me record day by day my honest thought without prospect or retrospect, and, I cannot doubt, it will be found symmetrical, though I mean it not and see it not. My book should smell of pines and resound with the hum of insects. The swallow over my window should interweave that thread or straw he carries in his bill into my web also. We pass for what we are. Character teaches above our wills. Men imagine that they communicate their virtue or vice only by overt actions, and do not see that virtue or vice emit a breath every moment.

There will be an agreement in whatever variety of actions, so they be each honest and natural in their hour. For of one will, the actions will be harmonious, however unlike they seem. These varieties are lost sight of at a little distance, at a little height of thought. One tendency unites them all. The voyage of the best ship is a zigzag line of a hundred tacks. See the line from a sufficient distance, and it straightens itself to the average tendency. Your genuine action will explain itself and will explain your other genuine actions. Your conformity explains nothing. Act singly, and what you have already done singly will justify you now. Greatness appeals to the future. If I can be firm enough to-day to do right and scorn eyes, I must have done so much right before as to defend me now. Be it how it will, do right now. Always scorn appearances and you always may. The force of character is cumulative. All the foregone days of virtue work their health into this. What makes the majesty of the heroes of the senate and the field, which so fills the imagination? The consciousness of a train of great days and victories behind. They shed a united light on the advancing actor. He is attended as by a visible escort of angels. That is it which throws thunder into Chatham's voice, and dignity into Washington's port, and America into Adams's eye. Honor is venerable to us because it is no ephemera. It is always ancient virtue. We worship it to-day because it is not of to-day. We love it and pay it homage because it is not a trap for our love and homage, but is self-dependent, self-derived, and therefore of an old immaculate pedigree, even if shown in a young prson.

I hope in these days we have heard the last of conformity and consistency. Let the words be gazetted and ridiculous henceforward. Instead of the gong for dinner, let us hear a whistle from the Spartan fife. Let us never bow and apologize more. A great man is coming to eat at my house. I do not wish to please him; I wish that he should wish to please me. I will stand here for humanity, and though I would make it kind, I would make it true. Let us affront and reprimand the smooth mediocrity and squalid contentment of the times, and hurl in the face of custom and trade and office, the fact which is the upshot of all history, that there is a great responsible Thinker and Actor working wherever a man works; that a true man belongs to no other time or place, but is the centre of things. Where he is there is nature. He measures you and all men and all events. Ordinarily, every body in society reminds us of somewhat else, or of some other person. Character, reality, reminds you of nothing else; it takes place of the whole creation. The man must be so much that he must make all circumstances indifferent. Every true man is a cause, a country, and an age; requires infinite spaces and numbers and time fully to accomplish his design;—and posterity seem to follow his steps as a train of clients. A man Cæsar is born, and for ages after we have a Roman Empire. Christ is born, and millions of minds so grow and cleave to his genius that he is confounded with virtue and the possible of man. An institution is the lengthened shadow of one man; as, Monachism, of the Hermit Antony; the Reformation, of Luther; Quakerism, of Fox; Methodism, of Wesley; Abolition, of Clarkson. Scipio, Milton called "the height of Rome;" and all history resolves itself very easily into the biography of a few stout and earnest persons.

Let a man then know his worth, and keep things under his feet. Let him not peep or steal, or skulk up and down with the air of a charity-boy, a bastard, or an interloper in the world which exists for him. But the man in the street, finding no worth in himself which corresponds to the force which built a tower or sculptured a marble god, feels poor when he looks on these. To him a palace, a statue, or a costly book have an alien and forbidding air, much like a gay equipage, and seem to say like that, "Who are you, Sir?" Yet they all are his, suitors for his notice, petitioners to his faculties that they will come out and take possession. The picture waits for my verdict; it is not to command me, but I am to settle its claims to praise. That popular fable of the sot who was picked up dead-drunk in the street, carried to the duke's house, washed and dressed and laid in the duke's bed, and, on his waking, treated with all obsequious ceremony like the duke, and assured that he had been insane, owes its popularity to the fact that it symbolizes so well the state of man, who is in the world a sort of sot, but now and then wakes up, exercises his reason and finds himself a true prince.

Our reading is mendicant and sycophantic. In history our imagination plays us false. Kingdom and lordship, power and estate, are a gaudier vocabulary than private John and Edward in a small house and common day's work; but the things of life are the same to both; the sum total of both is the same. Why all this deference to Alfred and Scanderbeg and Gustavus? Suppose they were virtuous; did they wear out virtue? As great a stake depends on your private act to-day as followed their public and renowned steps. When private men shall act with original views, the lustre will be transferred from the actions of kings to those of gentlemen.

The world has been instructed by its kings, who have so magnetized the eyes of nations. It has been taught by this colossal symbol the mutual reverence that is due from man to man. The joyful loyalty with which men have everywhere suffered the king, the noble, or the great proprietor to walk among them by a law of his own, make his own scale of men and things and reverse theirs, pay for benefits not with money but with honor, and represent the law in his person, was the hieroglyphic by which they obscurely signified their consciousness of their own right and comeliness, the right of every man.

The magnetism which all original action exerts is explained when we inquire the reason of self-trust. Who is the Trustee? What is the aboriginal Self, on which a universal reliance may be grounded? What is the nature and power of that science-baffling star, without parallax, without calculable elements, which shoots a ray of beauty even into trivial and impure actions, if the least mark of independence appear? The inquiry leads us to that source, at once the essence of genius, of virtue, and of life, which we call Spontaneity or Instinct. We denote this primary wisdom as Intuition, whilst all later teachings are tuitions. In that deep force, the last fact behind which analysis cannot go, all things find their common origin. For the sense of being which in calm hours rises, we know not how, in the soul, is not diverse from things, from space, from light, from time, from man, but one with them and proceeds obviously from the same source whence their life and being also proceed. We first share the life by which things exist and afterwards see them as appearances in nature and forget that we have shared their cause. Here is the fountain of action and of thought. Here are the lungs of that inspiration which giveth man wisdom and which cannot be denied without impiety and atheism. We lie in the lap of immense intelligence, which makes us receivers of its truth and organs of its activity. When we discern justice, when we discern truth, we do nothing of ourselves, but allow a passage to its beams. If we ask whence this comes, if we seek to pry into the soul that causes, all philosophy is at fault. Its presence or its absence is all we can affirm. Every man discriminates between the voluntary acts of his mind and his involuntary perceptions, and knows that to his involuntary perceptions a perfect faith is due. He may err in the expression of them, but he knows that these things are so, like day and night, not to be disputed. My wilful actions and acquisitions are but roving;—the idlest reverie, the faintest native emotion, command my curiosity and respect. Thoughtless people contradict as readily the statement of perceptions as of opinions, or rather much more readily; for they do not distinguish between perception and notion. They fancy that I choose to see this or that thing. But perception is not whimsical, but fatal. If I see a trait, my children will see it after me, and in course of time all mankind,—although it may chance that no one has seen it before me. For my perception of it is as much a fact as the sun.

The relations of the soul to the divine spirit are so pure that it is profane to seek to interpose helps. It must be that when God speaketh he should communicate, not one thing, but all things; should fill the world with his voice; should scatter forth light, nature, time, souls, from the centre of the present thought; and new date and new create the whole. Whenever a mind is simple and receives a divine wisdom, old things pass away,—means, teachers, texts, temples fall; it lives now, and absorbs past and future into the present hour. All things are made sacred by relation to it,—one as much as another. All things are dissolved to their centre by their cause, and in the universal miracle petty and particular miracles disappear. If therefore a man claims to know and speak of God and carries you backward to the phraseology of some old mouldered nation in another country, in another world, believe him not. Is the acorn better than the oak which is its fulness and completion? Is the parent better than the child into whom he has cast his ripened being? Whence then this worship of the past? The centuries are conspirators against the sanity and authority of the soul. Time and space are but physiological colors which the eye makes, but the soul is light: Where it is, is day; where it was, is night; and history is an impertinence and an injury if it be any thing more than a cheerful apologue or parable of my being and becoming.

Man is timid and apologetic; he is no longer upright; he dares not say 'I think,' 'I am,' but quotes some saint or sage. He is ashamed before the blade of grass or the blowing rose. These roses under my window make no reference to former roses or to better ones; they are for what they are; they exist with God to-day. There is no time to them. There is simply the rose; it is perfect in every moment of its existence. Before a leaf-bud has burst, its whole life acts; in the full-blown flower there is no more; in the leafless root there is no less. Its nature is satisfied and it satisfies nature in all moments alike. But man postpones or remembers; he does not live in the present, but with reverted eye laments the past, or, heedless of the riches that surround him, stands on tiptoe to foresee the future. He cannot be happy and strong until he too lives with nature in the present, above time.

This should be plain enough. Yet see what strong intellects dare not yet hear God himself unless he speak the phraseology of I know not what David, or Jeremiah, or Paul. We shall not always set so great a price on a few texts, on a few lives. We are like children who repeat by rote the sentences of grandames and tutors, and, as they grow older, of the men of talents and character they chance to see,—painfully recollecting the exact words they spoke; afterwards, when they come into the point of view which those had who uttered these sayings, they understand them and are willing to let the words go; for at any time they can use words as good when occasion comes. If we live truly, we shall see truly. It is as easy for the strong man to be strong, as it is for the weak to be weak. When we have new perception, we shall gladly disburden the memory of its hoarded treasures as old rubbish. When a man lives with God, his voice shall be as sweet as the murmur of the brook and the rustle of the corn.

And now at last the highest truth on this subject remains unsaid; probably cannot be said; for all that we say is the far-off remembering of the intuition. That thought by what I can now nearest approach to say it, is this. When good is near you, when you have life in yourself, it is not by any known or accustomed way; you shall not discern the footprints of any other; you shall not see the face of man; you shall not hear any name;—the way, the thought, the good, shall be wholly strange and new. It shall exclude example and experience. You take the way from man, not to man. All persons that ever existed are its forgotten ministers. Fear and hope are alike beneath it. There is somewhat low even in hope. In the hour of vision there is nothing that can be called gratitude, nor properly joy. The soul raised over passion beholds identity and eternal causation, perceives the self-existence of Truth and Right, and calms itself with knowing that all things go well. Vast spaces of nature, the Atlantic Ocean, the South Sea; long intervals of time, years, centuries, are of no account. This which I think and feel underlay every former state of life and circumstances, as it does underlie my present, and what is called life and what is called death.

Life only avails, not the having lived. Power ceases in the instant of repose; it resides in the moment of transition from a past to a new state, in the shooting of the gulf, in the darting to an aim. This one fact the world hates; that the soul *becomes;* for that forever degrades the past, turns all riches to poverty, all reputation to a shame, confounds the saint with the rogue, shoves Jesus and Judas equally aside. Why then do we prate of self-reliance? Inasmuch as the soul is present there will be power not confident but agent. To talk of reliance is a poor external way of speaking. Speak rather of that which relies because it works and is. Who has more obedience than I masters me, though he should not raise his finger. Round him I must revolve by the gravitation of spirits. We fancy it rhetoric when we speak of eminent virtue. We do not yet see that virtue is Height, and that a man or a company of men, plastic and permeable to principles, by the law of nature must overpower and ride all cities, nations, kings, rich men, poets, who are not.

This is the ultimate fact which we so quickly reach on this, as on every topic, the resolution of all into the ever-blessed ONE. Self-existence is the attribute of the Supreme Cause, and it constitutes the measure of good by the degree in which it enters into all lower forms. All things real are so by so much virtue as they contain. Commerce, husbandry, hunting, whaling, war, eloquence, personal weight, are somewhat, and engage my respect as examples of its presence and impure action. I see the same law working in nature for conservation and growth. Power is, in nature, the essential measure of right. Nature suffers nothing to remain in her kingdoms which cannot help itself. The genesis and maturation of a planet, its poise and orbit, the bended tree recovering itself from the strong wind, the vital resources of every animal and vegetable, are demonstrations of the self-sufficing and therefore self-relying soul.

Thus all concentrates: let us not rove; let us sit at home with the cause. Let us stun and astonish the intruding rabble of men and books and institutions by a simple declaration of the divine fact. Bid the invaders take the shoes from off their feet, for God is here within. Let our simplicity judge them, and our docility to our own law demonstrate the poverty of nature and fortune beside our native riches.

But now we are a mob. Man does not stand in awe of man, nor is his genius admonished to stay at home, to put itself in communication with the internal ocean, but it goes abroad to beg a cup of water of the urns of other men. We must go alone. I like the silent church before the service begins, better than any preaching. How far off, how cool, how chaste the persons look, begirt each one with a precinct or sanctuary! So let us always sit. Why should we assume the faults of our friend, or wife, or father, or child, because they sit around our hearth, or are said to have the same blood? All men have my blood and I all men's. Not for that will I adopt their petulance or folly, even to the extent of being ashamed of it. But your isolation must not be mechanical, but spiritual, that is, must be elevation. At times the whole world seems to be in conspiracy to importune you with emphatic trifles. Friend, climate, child, sickness, fear, want, charity, all knock at once at thy closet door and say,—'Come out unto us.' But keep thy state; come not into their confusion. The power men possess to annoy me I give them by a weak curiosity. No man can come near me but through my act. "What we love that we have, but by desire we bereave ourselves of the love."

If we cannot at once rise to the sanctities of obedience and faith, let us at least resist our temptations; let us enter into the state of war and wake Thor and Woden, courage and constancy, in our Saxon breasts. This is to be done in our smooth times by speaking the truth. Check this lying hospitality and lying affection. Live no longer to the expectation of these deceived and deceiving people with whom we converse. Say to them, 'O father, O mother, O wife, O brother, O friend, I have lived with you after appearances hitherto. Henceforward I am the truth's. Be it known unto you that henceforward I obey no law less than the eternal law. I will have no covenants but proximities. I shall endeavor to nourish my parents, to support my family, to be the chaste husband of one wife,—but these relations I must fill after a new and unprecedented way. I appeal from your customs. I must be myself. I cannot break myself any longer for you, or you. If you can love me for what I am, we shall be the happier. If you cannot, I will still seek to deserve that you should. I will not hide my tastes or aversions. I will so trust that what is deep is holy, that I will do strongly before the sun and moon whatever inly rejoices me and the heart appoints. If you are noble, I will love you; if you are not, I will not hurt you and myself by hypocritical attentions. If you are true, but not in the same truth with me, cleave to your companions; I will seek my own. I do this not selfishly but humbly and truly. It is alike your interest, and mine, and all men's, however long we have dwelt in lies, to live in truth. Does this sound harsh to-day? You will soon love what is dictated by your nature as well as mine, and if we follow the truth it will bring us out safe at last.'—But so may you give these friends pain. Yes, but I cannot sell my liberty and my power, to save their sensibility. Besids, all persons have their moments of reason, when they look out into the region of absolute truth; then will they justify me and do the same thing.

The populace think that your rejection of popular standards is a rejection of all standard, and mere antinomianism; and the bold sensualist will use the name of philosophy to gild his crimes. But the law of consciousness abides. There are two confessionals, in one or the other of which we must be shriven. You may fulfil your round of duties by clearing yourself in the *direct* or in the *reflex* way. Consider whether you have satisfied your relations to father, mother, cousin, neighbor, town, cat and dog—whether any of these can upbraid you. But I may also neglect this reflex standard and absolve me to myself. I have my own stern claims and perfect circle. It denies the name of duty to many offices that are called duties. But if I can discharge its debts it enables me to dispense with the popular code. If any one imagines that this law is lax, let him keep its commandment one day.

And truly it demands something godlike in him who has cast off the common motives of humanity and has ventured to trust himself for a taskmaster. High be his heart, faithful his will, clear his sight, that he may in good earnest be doctrine, society, law, to himself, that a simple purpose may be to him as strong as iron necessity is to others!

If any man consider the present aspects of what is called by distinction *society,* he will see the need of these ethics. The sinew and heart of man seem to be drawn out, and we are become timorous, desponding whimperers. We are afraid of truth, afraid of fortune, afraid of death, and afraid of each other. Our age yields no great and perfect persons. We want men and women who shall renovate life and our social state, but we see that most natures are insolvent, cannot satisfy their own wants, have an ambition out of all proportion to their practical force and do lean and beg day and night continually. Our housekeeping is mendicant, our arts, our occupations, our marriages, our religion we have not chosen, but society has chosen for us. We are parlor soldiers. We shun the rugged battle of fate, where strength is born.

If our young men miscarry in their first enterprises they lose all heart. If the young merchant fails, men say he is *ruined.* If the finest genius studies at one of our colleges and is not installed in an office within one year afterwards in the cities or suburbs of Boston or New York, it seems to his friends and to himself that he is right in being disheartened and in complaining the rest of his life. A sturdy lad from New Hampshire or Vermont, who in turn tries all the professions, who *teams it, farms it, peddles,* keeps a school, preaches, edits a newspaper, goes to Congress, buys a township, and so forth, in successive years, and always like a cat falls on his feet, is worth a hundred of these city dolls. He walks abreast with his days and feels no shame in not 'studying a profession,' for he does not postpone his life, but lives already. He has not one chance, but a hundred chances. Let a Stoic open the resources of man and tell men they are not leaning willows, but can and must detach themselves; that with the exercise of self-trust, new powers shall appear; that a man is the word made flesh, born to shed healing to the nations; that he should be ashamed of our compassion, and that the moment he acts from himself, tossing the laws, the books, idolatries, and customs out of the window, we pity him no more but thank and revere him;—and that teacher shall restore the life of man to splendor and make his name dear to all history.

It is easy to see that a greater self-reliance must work a revolution in all the offices and relations of men; in their religion; in their education; in their pursuits; their modes of living; their association; in their property; in their speculative views.

1. In what prayers do men allow themselves! That which they call a holy office is not so much as brave and manly. Prayer looks abroad and asks for some foreign addition to come through some foreign virtue, and loses itself in endless mazes of natural and supernatural, and mediatorial and miraculous. Prayer that craves a particular commodity, anything less than all good, is vicious. Prayer is the contemplation of the facts of life from the highest point of view. It is the soliloquy of a beholding and jubilant soul. It is the spirit of God pronouncing his works good. But prayer as a means to effect a private end is meanness and theft. It supposes dualism and not unity in nature and consciousness. As soon as the man is at one with God, he will not beg. He will then see prayer in all action. The

prayer of the farmer kneeling in his field to weed it, the prayer of the rower kneeling with the stroke of his oar, are true prayers heard throughout nature, though for cheap ends. Caratach, in Fletcher's "Bonduca," when admonished to inquire the mind of the god Audate, replies,—

His hidden meaning lies in our endeavors;
Our valors are our best gods.

Another sort of false prayers are our regrets. Discontent is the want of self-reliance; it is infirmity of will. Regret calamities if you can thereby help the sufferer; if not, attend your own work and already the evil begins to be repaired. Our sympathy is just as base. We come to them who weep foolishly and sit down and cry for company, instead of imparting to them truth and health in rough electric shocks, putting them once more in communication with their own reason. The secret of fortune is joy in our hands. Welcome evermore to gods and men is the self-helping man. For him all doors are flung wide; him all tongues greet, all honors crown, all eyes follow with desire. Our love goes out to him and embraces him because he did not need it. We solicitously and apologetically caress and celebrate him because he held on his way and scorned our disapprobation. The gods love him because men hated him. "To the persevering mortal," said Zoroaster, "the blessed Immortals are swift."

As men's prayers are a disease of the will, so are their creeds a disease of the intellect. They say with those foolish Israelites, 'Let not God speak to us, lest we die. Speak thou, speak any man with us, and we will obey.' Everywhere I am hindered of meeting God in my brother, because he has shut his own temple doors and recites fables merely of his brother's, or his brother's brother's God. Every new mind is a new classification. If it prove a mind of uncommon activity and power, a Locke, a Lavoisier, a Hutton, a Bentham, a Fourier, it imposes its classification on other men, and lo! a new system! In proportion to the depth of the thought, and so to the number of the objects it touches and brings within reach of the pupil, is his complacency. But chiefly is this apparent in creeds and churches, which are also classifications of some powerful mind acting on the elemental thought of duty and man's relation to the Highest. Such is Calvinism, Quakerism, Swedenborgism. The pupil takes the same delight in subordinating everything to the new terminology as a girl who has just learned botany in seeing a new earth and new seasons thereby. It will happen for a time that the pupil will find his intellectual power has grown by the study of his master's mind. But in all unbalanced minds the classification is idolized, passes for the end and not for a speedily exhaustible means, so that the walls of the system blend to their eye in the remote horizon with the walls of the universe; the luminaries of heaven seem to them hung on the arch their master built. They cannot imagine how you aliens have any right to see,—how you can see; 'It must be somehow that you stole the light from us.' They do not yet perceive that light, unsystematic, indomitable, will break into any cabin, even into theirs. Let them chirp awhile and call it their own. If they are honest and do well, presently their neat new pinfold will be too strait and low, will crack, will lean, will rot and vanish, and the immortal light, all young and joyful, million-orbed, million-colored, will beam over the universe as on the first morning.

2. It is for want of self-culture that the superstition of Travelling, whose idols are Italy, England, Egypt, retains its fascination for all educated Americans. They who made England, Italy, or Greece venerable in the imagination, did so by sticking fast where they were, like an axis of the earth. In manly hours we feel that duty is our place. The soul is no traveller; the wise man stays at home, and when his necessities, his duties, on any occasion call him from his house, or into foreign lands, he is at home still and shall make men sensible by the expression of his countenance that he goes, the missionary of wisdom and virtue, and visits cities and men like a sovereign and not like an interloper or a valet.

I have no churlish objection to the circumnavigation of the globe for the purposes of art, of study, and benevolence, so that the man is first domesticated, or does not go abroad with the hope of finding somewhat greater than he knows. He who travels to be amused, or to get somewhat which he does not carry, travels away from himself, and grows old even in youth among old things. In Thebes, in Palmyra, his will and mind have become old and dilapidated as they. He carries ruins to ruins.

Traveling is a fool's paradise. Our first journeys discover to us the indifference of places. At home I dream that at Naples, at Rome, I can be intoxicated with beauty and lose my sadness. I pack my trunk, embrace my friends, embark on the sea and at last wake up in Naples, and there beside me is the stern fact, the sad self, unrelenting, identical, that I fled from. I seek the Vatican and the palaces. I affect to be intoxicated with sights and suggestions, but I am not intoxicated. My giant goes with me wherever I go.

3. But the rage of travelling is a symptom of a deeper unsoundness affecting the whole intellectual action. The intellect is vagabond, and our system of education fosters restlessness. Our minds travel when our bodies are forced to stay at home. We imitate; and what is imitation but the travelling of the mind? Our houses are built with foreign taste; our shelves are garnished with foreign ornaments; our opinions, our tastes, our faculties lean, and follow the Past and the Distant. The soul created the arts wherever they have flourished. It was in his own mind that the artist sought his model. It was an application of his own thought to the thing to be done and the conditions to be observed. And why need we copy the Doric or the Gothic model? Beauty, convenience, grandeur of thought and quaint expression are as near to us as to any, and if the American artist will study with hope and love the precise thing to be done by him, considering the climate, the soil, the length of the day, the wants of the people, the habit and form of the government, he will create a house in which all these will find themselves fitted, and taste and sentiment will be satisfied also.

Insist on yourself; never imitate. Your own gift you can present every moment with the cumulative force of a whole life's cultivation; but of the adopted talent of another you have only an extemporaneous half possession. That which each can do best, none but his Maker can teach him. No man yet knows what it is, nor can, till that person has exhibited it. Where is the master who could have taught Shakspeare? Where is the master who could have instructed Franklin, or Washington, or Bacon, or Newton? Every great man is a unique. The Scipionism of Scipio is precisely that part he could not borrow. Shakspeare will never be made by the study of Shakspeare. Do that which is assigned you, and you cannot hope too much or dare too much. There is at this moment for you an utterance brave and grand as that of the colossal chisel of Phidias, or trowel of the Egyptians, or the pen of Moses or Dante, but different from all these. Not possibly will the soul, all rich, all eloquent, with thousand-cloven tongue, deign to repeat itself; but if you can hear what these patriarchs say, surely you can reply to them in the same pitch of voice; for the ear and the tongue are two organs of one nature. Abide in the simple and noble regions of thy life, obey thy heart, and thou shalt reproduce the Foreworld again.

4. As our Religion, our Education, our Art look abroad, so does our spirit of society. All men plume themselves on the improvement of society, and no man improves.

Society never advances. It recedes as fast on one side as it gains on the other. It undergoes continual changes; it is barbarous, it is civilized, it is christianized, it is rich, it is scientific; but this change is not amelioration. For every thing that is given something is taken. Society acquires new arts and loses old instincts. What a contrast between the well-clad, reading, writing, thinking American, with a watch, a pencil, and a bill of exchange in his pocket, and the naked New Zealander, whose property is a club, a spear, a mat, and an undivided twentieth of a shed to sleep under! But compare the health of the two men and you shall see that the white man has lost his aboriginal strength. If the traveller tell us truly, strike the savage with a broad-axe and in a day or two the flesh shall unite and heal as if you struck the blow into soft pitch, and the same blow shall send the white to his grave.

The civilized man has built a coach, but has lost the use of his feet. He is supported on crutches, but lacks so much support of muscle. He has a fine Geneva watch, but he fails of the skill to tell the hour by the sun. A Greenwich nautical almanac he has, and so being sure of the information when he wants it, the man in the street does not know a star in the sky. The solstice he does not observe; the equinox he knows as little; and the whole bright calendar of the year is without a dial in his mind. His note-books impair his memory; his libraries overload his wit; the insurance-office increases the number of accidents; and it may be a question whether machinery does not encumber; whether we have not lost by refinement some energy; by a Christianity, entrenched in establishments and forms, some vigor of wild virtue. For every Stoic was a Stoic; but in Christendom where is the Christian?

There is no more deviation in the

moral standard than in the standard of height or bulk. No greater men are now than ever were. A singular equality may be observed between the great men of the first and of the last ages; nor can all the science, art, religion, and philosophy of the nineteenth century avail to educate greater men than Plutarch's heroes, three or four and twenty centuries ago. Not in time is the race progressive. Phocion, Socrates, Anaxagoras, Diogenes, are great men, but they leave no class. He who is really of their class will not be called by their name, but will be his own man, and in his turn the founder of a sect. The arts and inventions of each period are only its costume and do not invigorate men. The harm of the improved machinery may compensate its good. Hudson and Behring accomplished so much in their fishing-boats as to astonish Parry and Franklin, whose equipment exhausted the resources of science and art. Galileo, with an opera-glass, discovered a more splendid series of celestial phenomena than any one since. Columbus found the New World in an undecked boat. It is curious to see the periodical disuse and perishing of means and machinery which were introduced with loud laudation a few years or centuries before. The great genius returns to essential man. We reckoned the improvements of the art of war among the triumphs of science, and yet Napoleon conquered Europe by the bivouac, which consisted of falling back on naked valor and disencumbering it of all aids. The Emperor held it impossible to make a perfect army, says Las Casas, "without abolishing our arms, magazines, commissaries and carriages, until, in imitation of the Roman custom, the soldier should receive his supply of corn, grind it in his hand-mill and bake his bread himself."

Society is a wave. The wave moves onward, but the water of which it is composed does not. The same particle does not rise from the valley to the ridge. Its unity is only phenomenal. The persons who make up a nation to-day, next year die, and their experience dies with them.

And so the reliance on Property, including the reliance on governments which protect it, is the want of self-reliance. Men have looked away from themselves and at things so long that they have come to esteem the religious, learned, and civil institutions as guards of property, and they deprecate assaults on these, because they feel them to be assaults on property. They measure their esteem of each other by what each has, and not by what each is. But a cultivated man becomes ashamed of his property, out of new respect for his nature. Especially he hates what he has if he see that it is accidental,—came to him by inheritance, or gift, or crime; then he feels that it is not having; it does not belong to him, has no root in him and merely lies there because no revolution or no robber takes it away. But that which a man is, does always by necessity acquire; and what the man acquires, is living property, which does not wait the beck of rulers, or mobs, or revolutions, or fire, or storm, or bankruptcies, but perpetually renews itself wherever the man breathes. "Thy lot or portion of life," said the Caliph Ali, "is seeking after thee; therefore be at rest from seeking after it." Our dependence on these foreign goods leads us to our slavish respect for numbers. The political parties meet in numerous conventions; the greater the concourse and with each new uproar of announcement, The Delegation from Essex! The Democrats from New Hampshire! The Whigs of Maine! the young patriot feels himself stronger than before by a new thousand of eyes and arms. In like manner the reformers summon conventions and vote and resolve in multitude. Not so, O friends! will the God deign to enter and inhabit you, but by a method precisely the reverse. It is only as a man puts off all foreign support and stands alone that I see him to be strong and to prevail. He is weaker by every recruit to his banner. Is not a man better than a town? Ask nothing of men, and, in the endless mutation, thou only firm column must presently appear the upholder of all that surrounds thee. He who knows that power is inborn, that he is weak because he has looked for good out of him and elsewhere, and, so perceiving, throws himself unhesitatingly on his thought, instantly rights himself, stands in the erect position, commands his limbs, works miracles; just as a man who stands on his feet is stronger than a man who stands on his head.

So use all that is called Fortune. Most men gamble with her, and gain all, and lose all, as her wheel rolls. But do thou leave as unlawful these winnings, and deal with Cause and Effect, the chancellors of God. In the Will work and acquire, and thou hast chained the wheel of Chance, and shall sit hereafter out of fear from her rotations. A political victory, a rise of rents, the recovery of your sick or the return of your absent friend, or some other favorable event raises your spirits, and you think good days are preparing for you. Do not believe it. Nothing can bring you peace but yourself. Nothing can bring you peace but the triumph of principles.

1841

## THE OVER-SOUL

But souls that of his own good life partake
He loves as his own self; dear as his eye
They are to Him: He'll never them forsake:
When they shall die, then God himself shall die:
They live, they live in blest eternity.

—Henry More.

Space is ample, east and west,
But two cannot go abreast,
Cannot travel in it two:
Yonder masterful cuckoo
Crowds every egg out of the nest,
Quick or dead, except its own;
A spell is laid on sod and stone,
Night and Day 've been tampered with,
Every quality and pith
Surcharged and sultry with a power
That works its will on age and hour.

There is a difference between one and another hour of life in their authority and subsequent effect. Our faith comes in moments; our vice is habitual. Yet there is a depth in those brief moments which constrains us to ascribe more reality to them than to all other experiences. For this reason the argument which is always forthcoming to silence those who conceive extraordinary hopes of man, namely the appeal to experience, is for ever invalid and vain. We give up the past to the objector, and yet we hope. He must explain this hope. We grant that human life is mean, but how did we find out that it was mean? What is the ground of this uneasiness of ours; of this old discontent? What is the universal sense of want and ignorance, but the fine innuendo by which the soul makes its enormous claim? Why do men feel that the natural history of man has never been written, but he is always leaving behind what you have said of him, and it becomes old, and books of metaphysics worthless? The philosophy of six thousand years has not searched the chambers and magazines of the soul. In its experiments there has always remained, in the last analysis, a residuum it could not resolve. Man is a stream whose source is hidden. Our being is descending into us from we know not whence. The most exact calculator has no prescience that somewhat incalculable may not balk the very next moment. I am constrained every moment to acknowledge a higher origin for events than the will I call mine.

As with events, so is it with thoughts. When I watch that flowing river, which, out of regions I see not, pours for a season its streams into me, I see that I am a pensioner; not a cause but a surprised spectator of this ethereal water; that I desire and look up and put myself in the attitude of reception, but from some alien energy the visions come.

The Supreme Critic on the errors of the past and the present, and the only prophet of that which must be, is that great nature in which we rest as the earth lies in the soft arms of the atmosphere; that Unity, that Over-Soul, within which every man's particular being is contained and made one with all other; that common heart of which all sincere conversation is the worship, to which all right action is submission; that overpowering reality which confutes our tricks and talents, and constrains every one to pass for what he is, and to speak from his character and not from his tongue, and which evermore tends to pass into our thought and hand and become wisdom and virtue and power and beauty. We live in succession, in division, in parts, in particles. Meantime within man is the soul of the whole; the wise silence; the universal beauty, to which every part and particle is equally related; the eternal ONE. And this deep power in which we exist and whose beatitude is all accessible to us, is not only self-sufficing and perfect in every hour, but the act of seeing and the thing seen, the seer and the spectacle, the subject and the object, are one. We see the world piece by piece, as the sun, the moon, the animal, the tree; but the whole, of which these are the shining parts, is the soul. Only by the vision of that Wisdom can the horoscope of the ages be read, and by falling back on our better thoughts, by yielding to the spirit of prophecy which is innate in every man, we can know what it saith. Every man's words who speaks from that life must sound vain to those who do not dwell in the same thought on their own part. I dare not speak for it. My words do not carry its august sense; they fall short and cold. Only itself can inspire whom it will, and behold! their speech shall be lyrical, and sweet, and universal as the rising of the wind. Yet I desire, even by profane words, if I may not use sacred, to indicate the heaven of this deity and to report what hints I have collected of the transcendent simplicity and energy of the Highest Law.

If we consider what happens in conversation, in reveries, in remorse, in times of passion, in surprises, in the instructions of dreams, wherein often we see ourselves in masquerade,—the droll disguises only magnifying and enhancing a real element and forcing it on our distant notice,—we shall catch many hints that will broaden and lighten into knowledge of the secret of nature. All goes to show that the soul in man is not an organ, but animates and exercises all the organs; is not a function, like the power of memory, of calculation, of comparison, but uses these as hands and feet; is not a faculty, but a light; is not the intellect or the will, but the master of the intellect and the will; is the background of our being, in which they lie,—an immensity not possessed and that cannot be possessed. From within or from behind, a light shines through us upon things and makes us aware that we are nothing, but the light is all. A man is the façade of a temple wherein all wisdom and all good abide. What we commonly call man, the eating, drinking, planting, counting man, does not, as we know him, represent himself, but misrepresents himself. Him we do not respect, but the soul, whose organ he is, would he let it appear through his action, would make our knees bend. When it breathes through his intellect, it is genius; when it breathes through his will, it is virtue; when it flows through his affection, it is love. And the blindness of the intellect begins when it would be something of itself. The weakness of the will begins when the individual would be something of himself. All reform aims in some one particular to let the soul have its way through us; in other words, to engage us to obey.

Of this pure nature every man is at some time sensible. Language cannot paint it with his colors. It is too subtile. It is undefinable, unmeasurable; but we know that it pervades and contains us. We know that all spiritual being is in man. A wise old proverb says, "God comes to see us without bell;" that is, as there is no screen or ceiling between our heads and the infinite heavens, so is there no bar or wall in the soul, where man, the effect, ceases, and God, the cause, begins. The walls are taken away. We lie open on one side to the deeps of spiritual nature, to the attributes of God. Justice we see and know, Love, Freedom, Power. These natures no man ever got above, but they tower over us, and most in the moment when our interests tempt us to wound them.

The sovereignty of this nature whereof we speak is made known by its independency of those limitations which circumscribe us on every hand. The soul circumscribes all things. As I have said, it contradicts all experience. In like manner it abolishes time and space. The influence of the senses has in most men overpowered the mind to that degree that the walls of time and space have come to look real and insurmountable; and to speak with levity of these limits is, in the world, the sign of insanity. Yet time and space are but inverse measures of the force of the soul. The spirit sports with time,—

> Can crowd eternity into an hour,
> Or stretch an hour to eternity.

We are often made to feel that there

is another youth and age than that which is measured from the year of our natural birth. Some thoughts always find us young, and keep us so. Such a thought is the love of the universal and eternal beauty. Every man parts from that contemplation with the feeling that it rather belongs to ages than to mortal life. The least activity of the intellectual powers redeems us in a degree from the conditions of time. In sickness, in languor, give us a strain of poetry or a profound sentence, and we are refreshed; or produce a volume of Plato or Shakspeare, or remind us of their names, and instantly we come into a feeling of longevity. See how the deep divine thought reduces centuries and milleniums, and makes itself present through all ages. Is the teaching of Christ less effective now than it was when first his mouth was opened? The emphasis of facts and persons in my thought has nothing to do with time. And so always the soul's scale is one, the scale of the senses and the understanding is another. Before the revelations of the soul, Time, Space, and Nature shrink away. In common speech we refer all things to time, as we habitually refer the immensely sundered stars to one concave sphere. And so we say that the Judgment is distant or near, that the Millennium approaches, that a day of certain political, moral, social reforms is at hand, and the like, when we mean that in the nature of things one of the facts we contemplate is external and fugitive, and the other is permanent and connate with the soul. The things we now esteem fixed shall, one by one, detach themselves like ripe fruit from our experience, and fall. The wind shall blow them none knows whither. The landscape, the figures, Boston, London, are facts as fugitive as any institution past, or any whiff of mist or smoke, and so is society, and so is the world. The soul looketh steadily forwards, creating a world before her, leaving worlds behind her. She has no dates, nor rites, nor persons, nor specialties, nor men. The soul knows only the soul; the web of events is the flowing robe in which she is clothed.

After its own law and not by arithmetic is the rate of its progress to be computed. The soul's advances are not made by gradation, such as can be represented by motion in a straight line, but rather by ascension of state, such as can be represented by metamorphosis,—from the egg to the worm, from the worm to the fly. The growths of genius are of a certain *total* character, that does not advance the elect individual first over John, then Adam, then Richard, and give to each the pain of discovered inferiority,—but by every throe of growth the man expands there where he works, passing, at each pulsation, classes, populations, of men. With each divine impulse the mind rends the thin rinds of the visible and finite, and comes out into eternity, and inspires and expires its air. It converses with truths that have always been spoken in the world, and becomes conscious of a closer sympathy with Zeno and Arrian than with persons in the house.

This is the law of moral and of mental gain. The simple rise as by specific levity not into a particular virtue, but into the region of all the virtues. They are in the spirit which contains them all. The soul requires purity, but purity is not it; requires justice, but justice is not that; requires beneficence, but is somewhat better; so that there is a kind of descent and accommodation felt when we leave speaking of moral nature to urge a virtue which it enjoins. To the well-born child all the virtues are natural, and not painfully acquired. Speak to his heart, and the man becomes suddenly virtuous.

Within the same sentiment is the germ of intellectual growth, which obeys the same law. Those who are capable of humility, of justice, of love, of aspiration, stand already on a platform that commands the sciences and arts, speech and poetry, action and grace. For whoso dwells in this moral beatitude already anticipates those special powers which men prize so highly. The lover has no talent, no skill, which passes for quite nothing with his enamored maiden, however little she may possess of related faculty; and the heart which abandons itself to the Supreme Mind finds itself related to all its works, and will travel a royal road to particular knowledges and powers. In ascending to this primary and aboriginal sentiment we have come from our remote station on the circumference instantaneously to the centre of the world, where, as in the closet of God, we see causes, and anticipate the universe, which is but a slow effect.

One mode of the divine teaching is the incarnation of the spirit in a form, —in forms, like my own. I live in society; with persons who answer to thoughts in my own mind, or express a certain obedience to the great instincts to which I live. I see its presence to them. I am certified of a common nature; and these other souls, these separated selves, draw me as nothing else can. They stir in me the new emotions we call passion; of love, hatred, fear, admiration, pity; thence come conversation, competition, persuasion, cities, and war. Persons are supplementary to the primary teaching of the soul. In youth we are mad for persons. Childhood and youth see all the world in them. But the larger experience of man discovers the identical nature appearing through them all. Persons themselves acquaint us with the impersonal. In all conversation between two persons tacit reference is made, as to a third party, to a common nature. That third party or common nature is not social; it is impersonal; is God. And so in groups where debate is earnest, and especially on high questions, the company become aware that the thought rises to an equal level in all bosoms, that all have a spiritual property in what was said, as well as the sayer. They all become wiser than they were. It arches over them like a temple, this unity of thought in which every heart beats with nobler sense of power and duty, and thinks and acts with unusual solemnity. All are conscious of attaining to higher self-possession. It shines for all. There is a certain wisdom of humanity which is common to the greatest men with the lowest, and which our ordinary education often labors to silence and obstruct. The mind is one, and the best minds, who love truth for its own sake, think much less of property in truth. They accept it thankfully everywhere, and do not label or stamp it with any man's name, for it is theirs long beforehand, and from eternity. The learned and the studious of thought have no monopoly of wisdom. Their violence of direction in some degree disqualifies them to think truly. We owe many valuable observations to people who are not very acute or profound, and who say the thing without effort which we want and have long been hunting in vain. The action of the soul is oftener in that which is felt and left unsaid than in that which is said in any conversation. It broods over every society, and they unconsciously seek for it in each other. We know better than we do. We do not yet possess ourselves, and we know at the same time that we are much more. I feel the same truth how often in my trivial conversation with my neighbors, that somewhat higher in each of us overlooks this by-play, and Jove nods to Jove from behind each of us.

Men descend to meet. In their habitual and mean service to the world, for which they forsake their native nobleness, they resemble those Arabian sheiks who dwell in mean houses and affect an external poverty, to escape the rapacity of the Pacha, and reserve all their display of wealth for their interior and guarded retirements.

As it is present in all persons, so it is in every period of life. It is adult already in the infant man. In my dealing with my child, my Latin and Greek, my accomplishments and my money stead me nothing; but as much soul as I have avails. If I am willful, he sets his will against mine, one for one, and leaves me, if I please, the degradation of beating him by my superiority of strength. But if I renounce my will and act for the soul, setting that up as umpire between us two, out of his young eyes looks the same soul; he reveres and loves with me.

The soul is the perceiver and revealer of truth. We know truth when we see it, let sceptic and scoffer say what they choose. Foolish people ask you, when you have spoken what they do not wish to hear, 'How do you know it is truth, and not an error of your own?' We know truth when we see it, from opinion, as we know when we are awake that we are awake. It was a grand sentence of Emanuel Swedenborg, which would alone indicate the greatness of that man's perception,—"It is no proof of a man's understanding to be able to affirm whatever he pleases; but to be able to discern that what is true is true, and that what is false is false,—this is the mark and character of intelligence." In the book I read, the good thought returns to me, as every truth will, the image of the whole soul. To the bad thought which I find in it, the same soul becomes a discerning, separating sword, and lops it away. We are wiser than we know. If we will not interfere with our thought, but will act entirely, or see how the thing stands in God, we know the particular thing, and every thing, and every man. For the Maker of all things and all persons stands behind us and casts his dread omniscience through us over things.

But beyond this recognition of its own in particular passages of the individual's experience, it also reveals truth. And here we should seek to reinforce ourselves by its very presence, and to speak with a worthier, loftier strain of that advent. For the soul's communication of truth is the highest event in nature, since it then does not give somewhat from itself, but it gives itself, or passes into and becomes that man whom it enlightens; or, in proportion to that truth he receives, it takes him to itself.

We distinguish the announcements of the soul, its manifestations of its own nature, by the term *Revelation.* These are always attended by the emotion of the sublime. For this communication is an influx of the Divine mind into our mind. It is an ebb of the individual rivulet before the flowing surges of the sea of life. Every distinct apprehension of this central commandment agitates men with awe and delight. A thrill passes through all men at the reception of new truth, or at the performance of a great action, which comes out of the heart of nature. In these communications the power to see is not separated from the will to do, but the insight proceeds from obedience, and the obedience proceeds from a joyful perception. Every moment when the individual feels himself invaded by it is memorable. By the necessity of our constitution a certain enthusiasm attends the individual's consciousness of that divine presence. The character and duration of this enthusiasm vary with the state of the individual, from an ecstasy and trance and prophetic inspiration,—which is its rarer appearance,—to the faintest glow of virtuous emotion, in which form it warms, like our household fires, all the families and associations of men, and makes society possible. A certain tendency to insanity has always attended the opening of the religious sense in men, as if they had been "blasted with excess of light." The trances of Socrates, the "union" of Plotinus, the vision of Porphyry, the conversion of Paul, the aurora of Behmen, the convulsions of George Fox and his Quakers, the illumination of Swedenborg, are of this kind. What was in the case of these remarkable persons a ravishment, has, in innumerable instances in common life, been exhibited in less striking manner. Everywhere the history of religion betrays a tendency to enthusiasm. The rapture of the Moravian and Quietist; the opening of the eternal sense of the Word, in the language of the New Jerusalem Church; the *revival* of the Calvinistic churches; the *experiences* of the Methodists, are varying forms of that shudder of awe and delight with which the individual soul always mingles with the universal soul.

The nature of these revelations is the same; they are perceptions of the absolute law. They are solutions of the soul's own questions. They do not answer the questions which the understanding asks. The soul answers never by words, but by the thing itself that is inquired after.

Revelation is the disclosure of the soul. The popular notion of a revelation is that it is a telling of fortunes. In past oracles of the soul the understanding seeks to find answers to sensual questions, and undertakes to tell from God how long men shall exist, what their hands shall do and who shall be their company, adding names and dates and places. But we must pick no locks. We must check this low curiosity. An answer in words is delusive; it is really no answer to the questions you ask. Do not require a description of the countries towards which you sail. The description does not describe them to you, and to-morrow you arrive there and know them by inhabiting them. Men ask concerning the immortality of the soul, the employments of heaven, the state of the sinner, and so forth. They even dream that Jesus has left replies to precisely these interrogatories. Never a moment did that sublime spirit speak in their *patois*. To truth, justice, love, the attributes of the soul, the idea of immutableness is essentially associated. Jesus, living in these moral sentiments, heedless of sensual fortunes, heeding only the manifestations of these, never made the separation of the idea of duration from the essence of these attributes, nor uttered a syllable concerning the duration of the soul. It was left to his disciples to sever duration from the moral elements, and to teach the immortality of the soul as a doctrine, and maintain it by evidences. The moment the doctrine of the immortality is separately taught, man is already fallen. In the flowing of love, in the adoration of humility, there is no question of continuance. No inspired man ever asks this question or condescends to these evidences. For the soul is true to itself, and the man in whom it is shed abroad cannot wander from the present, which is infinite, to a future which would be finite.

These questions which we lust to ask about the future are a confession of sin. God has no answer for them. No answer in words can reply to a question of things. It is not in an arbitrary "decree of God," but in the nature of man, that a veil shuts down on the facts of to-morrow; for the soul will not have us read any other cipher than that of cause and effect. By this veil which curtains events it instructs the children of men to live in to-day. The only mode of obtaining an answer to these questions of the senses is to forego all low curiosity, and, accepting the tide of being which floats us into the secret of nature, work and live, work and live, and all unawares the advancing soul has built and forged for itself a new condition, and the question and the answer are one.

By the same fire, vital, consecrating, celestial, which burns until it shall dissolve all things into the waves and surges of an ocean of light, we see and know each other, and what spirit each is of. Who can tell the grounds of his knowledge of the character of the several individuals in his circle of friends? No man. Yet their acts and words do not disappoint him. In that man, though he knew no ill of him, he put no trust. In that other, though they had seldom met, authentic signs had yet passed, to signify that he might be trusted as one who had an interest in his own character. We know each other very well,—which of us has been just to himself and whether that which we teach or behold is only an aspiration or is our honest effort also.

We are all discerners of spirits. That diagnosis lies aloft in our life or unconscious power. The intercourse of society, its trade, its religion, its friendships, its quarrels, is one wide judicial investigation of character. In full court, or in small committee, or confronted face to face, accuser and accused, men offer themselves to be judged. Against their will they exhibit those decisive trifles by which character is read. But who judges?

and what? Not our understanding. We do not read them by learning or craft. No; the wisdom of the wise man consists herein, that he does not judge them; he lets them judge themselves, and merely reads and records their own verdict.

By virtue of this inevitable nature, private will is overpowered, and, maugre our efforts or our imperfections, your genius will speak from you, and mine from me. That which we are, we shall teach, not voluntarily but involuntarily. Thoughts come into our minds by avenues which we never left open, and thoughts go out of our minds through avenues which we never voluntarily opened. Character teaches over our head. The infallible index of true progress is found in the tone the man takes. Neither his age, nor his breeding, nor company, nor books, nor actions, nor talents, nor all together can hinder him from being deferential to a higher spirit than his own. If he have not found his home in God, his manners, his forms of speech, the turn of his sentences, the build, shall I say, of all his opinions will involuntarily confess it, let him brave it out how he will. If he have found his centre, the Deity will shine through him, through all the disguises of ignorance, of ungenial temperament, of unfavorable circumstance. The tone of seeking is one, and the tone of having is another.

The great distinction between teachers sacred or literary,—between poets like Herbert, and poets like Pope,—between philosophers like Spinoza, Kant, and Coleridge, and philosophers like Locke, Paley, Mackintosh, and Stewart,—between men of the world who are reckoned accomplished talkers, and here and there a fervent mystic, prophesying half insane under the infinitude of his thought,—is that one class speak *from within,* or from experience, as parties and possessors of the fact; and the other class *from without,* as spectators merely, or perhaps as acquainted with the fact on the evidence of third persons. It is of no use to preach to me from without. I can do that too easily myself. Jesus speaks always from within, and in a degree that transcends all others. In that is the miracle. I believe beforehand that it ought so to be. All men stand continually in the expectation of the appearance of such a teacher. But if a man do not speak from within the veil, where the word is one with that it tells of, let him lowly confess it.

The same Omniscience flows into the intellect and makes what we call genius. Much of the wisdom of the world is not wisdom, and the most illuminated class of men are no doubt superior to literary fame, and are not writers. Among the multitude of scholars and authors we feel no hallowing presence; we are sensible of a knack and skill rather than of inspiration; they have a light and know not whence it comes and call it their own; their talent is some exaggerated faculty, some overgrown member, so that their strength is a disease. In these instances the intellectual gifts do not make the impression of virtue, but almost of vice; and we feel that a man's talents stand in the way of his advancement in truth. But genius is religious. It is a larger imbibing of the common heart. It is not anomalous, but more like and not less like other men. There is in all great poets a wisdom of humanity which is superior to any talents they exercise. The author, the wit, the partisan, the fine gentleman, does not take place of the man. Humanity shines in Homer, in Chaucer, in Spenser, in Shakspeare, in Milton. They are content with truth. They use the positive degree. They seem frigid and phlegmatic to those who have been spiced with the frantic passion and violent coloring of inferior but popular writers. For they are poets by the free course which they allow to the informing soul, which through their eyes beholds again and blesses the things which it hath made. The soul is superior to its knowledge, wiser than any of its works. The great poet makes us feel our own wealth, and then we think less of his compositions. His best communication to our mind is to teach us to despise all he has done. Shakspeare carries us to such a lofty strain of intelligent activity as to suggest a wealth which beggars his own; and we then feel that the splendid works which he has created, and which in other hours we extol as a sort of self-existent poetry, take no stronger hold of real nature than the shadow of a passing traveller on the rock. The inspiration which uttered itself in Hamlet and Lear could utter things as good from day to day for ever. Why then should I make account of Hamlet and Lear, as if we had not the soul from which they fell as syllables from the tongue?

This energy does not descend into individual life on any other condition than entire possession. It comes to the lowly and simple; it comes to whomsoever will put off what is foreign and proud; it comes as insight; it comes as serenity and grandeur. When we see those whom it inhabits, we are apprised of new degrees of greatness. From that inspiration the man comes back with a changed tone. He does not talk with men with an eye to their opinion. He tries them. It requires of us to be plain and true. The vain traveller attempts to embellish his life by quoting my lord and the prince and the countess, who thus said or did to *him*. The ambitious vulgar show you their spoons and brooches and rings, and preserve their cards and compliments. The more cultivated, in their account of their own experience, cull out the pleasing, poetic circumstance,—the visit to Rome, the man of genius they saw, the brilliant friend they know; still further on perhaps the gorgeous landscape, the mountain lights, the mountain thoughts they enjoyed yesterday,—and so seek to throw a romantic color over their life. But the soul that ascends to worship the great God is plain and true; has no rose-color, no fine friends, no chivalry, no adventures; does not want admiration; dwells in the hour that now is, in the earnest experience of the common day,—by reason of the present moment and the mere trifle having become porous to thought and bibulous of the sea of light.

Converse with a mind that is grandly simple, and literature looks like word-catching. The simplest utterances are worthiest to be written, yet are they so cheap and so things of course, that in the infinite riches of the soul it is like gathering a few pebbles off the ground, or bottling a little air in a phial, when the whole earth and the whole atmosphere are ours.

Nothing can pass there, or make you one of the circle, but the casting aside your trappings and dealing man to man in naked truth, plain confession and omniscient affirmation.

Souls such as these treat you as gods would, walk as gods in the earth, accepting without any admiration your wit, your bounty, your virtue even,—say rather your act of duty, for your virtue they own as their proper blood, royal as themselves, and over-royal, and the father of the gods. But what rebuke their plain fraternal bearing casts on the mutual flattery with which authors solace each other and wound themselves! These flatter not. I do not wonder that these men go to see Cromwell and Christina and Charles II and James I and the Grand Turk. For they are, in their own elevation, the fellows of kings, and must feel the servile tone of conversation in the world. They must always be a godsend to princes, for they confront them, a king to a king, without ducking or concession, and give a high nature the refreshment and satisfaction of resistance, of plain humanity, of even companionship, and of new ideas. They leave them wiser and superior men. Souls like these make us feel that sincerity is more excellent than flattery. Deal so plainly with man and woman as to constrain the utmost sincerity and destroy all hope of trifling with you. It is the highest compliment you can pay. Their "highest praising," said Milton, "is not flattery, and their plainest advice is a kind of praising."

Ineffable is the union of man and God in every act of the soul. The simplest person who in his integrity worships God, becomes God; yet for-ever and ever the influx of this better and universal self is new and unsearchable. It inspires awe and astonishment. How dear, how soothing to man, arises the idea of God, peopling the lonely place, effacing the scars of our mistakes and disappointments! When we have broken our god of tradition and ceased from our god of rhetoric, then may God fire the heart with his presence. It is the doubling of the heart itself, nay, the infinite enlargement of the heart with a power of growth to a new infinity on every side. It inspires in man an infallible trust. He has not the conviction, but the sight, that the best is the true, and may in that thought easily dismiss all particular uncertainties and fears, and adjourn to the sure revelation of time the solution of his private riddles. He is sure that his welfare is dear to the heart of being. In the presence of law to his mind he is overflowed with a reliance so universal that it sweeps away all cherished hopes and the most stable projects of mortal condition in its flood. He believes that he cannot escape from his good. The things that are really for thee gravitate to thee. You are running to seek your friend. Let your feet run, but your mind need not. If you do not find him, will you not acquiesce that it is best you should not find him? for there is a power, which, as it is in you, is in him also, and could therefore very well bring you together, if it were for the best. You are preparing with eagerness to go and render a service to which your talent and your taste invite you, the love of men and the hope of fame. Has it not occurred to you that you have no right to go, unless you are equally willing to be prevented from going? O, believe, as thou livest, that every sound that is spoken over the round world, which thou oughtest to hear, will vibrate on thine ear! Every proverb, every book, every byword that belongs to thee for aid or comfort, shall surely come home through open or winding passages. Every friend whom not thy fantastic will but the great and tender heart in thee craveth, shall lock thee in his embrace. And this because the heart in thee is the heart of all; not a valve, not a wall, not an intersection is there anywhere in nature, but one blood rolls uninterruptedly an endless circulation through all men, as the water of the globe is all one sea, and, truly seen, its tide is one.

Let man then learn the revelation of all nature and all thought to his heart; this, namely, that the Highest dwells with him; that the sources of nature are in his own mind, if the sentiment of duty is there. But if he would know what the great God speaketh, he must 'go into his closet and shut the door,' as Jesus said. God will not make himself manifest to cowards. He must greatly listen to himself, withdrawing himself from all the accents of other men's devotion. Even their prayers are hurtful to him, until he have made his own. Our religion vulgarly stands on numbers of believers. Whenever the appeal is made,—no matter how indirectly,—to numbers, proclamation is then and there made that religion is not. He that finds God a sweet enveloping thought to him never counts his company. When I sit in that presence, who shall dare to come in? When I rest in perfect humility, when I burn with pure love, what can Calvin or Swedenborg say?

It makes no difference whether the appeal is to numbers or to one. The faith that stands on authority is not faith. The reliance on authority measures the decline of religion, the withdrawal of the soul. The position men have given to Jesus, now for many centuries of history, is a position of authority. It characterizes themselves. It cannot alter the eternal facts. Great is the soul, and plain. It is no flatterer, it is no follower; it never appeals from itself. It believes in itself. Before the immense possibilities of man all mere experience, all past biography, however spotless and sainted, shrinks away. Before that heaven which our presentiments foreshow us, we cannot easily praise any form of life we have seen or read of. We not only affirm that we have few great men, but, absolutely speaking, that we have none; that we have no history, no record of any character or mode of living that entirely contents us. The saints and demigods whom history worships we are constrained to accept with a grain of allowance. Though in our lonely hours we draw a new strength out of their memory, yet, pressed on our attention, as they are by the thoughtless and customary, they fatigue and invade. The soul gives itself, alone, original, and pure, to the Lonely, Original, and Pure, who, on that condition, gladly inhabits, leads, and speaks through it. Then is it glad, young, and nimble. It is not wise, but it sees through all things. It is not called religious, but it is innocent. It calls the light its own, and feels that the grass grows and the stone falls by a law inferior to, and dependent on, its nature. Behold, it saith, I am born into the great, the universal mind. I, the imperfect, adore my own Perfect. I am somehow receptive of the great soul, and thereby I do overlook the sun and the stars and feel them to be the fair accidents and effects which change and pass. More and more the surges of everlasting nature enter into me, and I become public and human in my regards and actions. So come I to live in thoughts and act with energies which are immortal. Thus revering the soul, and learning, as the ancient said, that "its beauty is immense," man will come to see that the world is the perennial miracle which the soul worketh, and be less astonished at particular wonders; he will learn that there is no profane history; that all history is sacred; that the universe is represented in an atom, in a moment of time. He will weave no longer a spotted life of shreds and patches, but he will live with a divine unity. He will cease from what is base and frivolous in his life and be content with all places and with any service he can render. He will calmly front the morrow in the negligency of that trust which carries God with it and so hath already the whole future in the bottom of the heart.

1841

## THE POET

A moody child and wildly wise
Pursued the game with joyful eyes,
Which chose, like meteors, their way,
And rived the dark with private ray:
They overleapt the horizon's edge,
Searched with Apollo's privilege;
Through man, and woman, and sea, and star
Saw the dance of nature forward far;
Through worlds, and races, and terms, and time
Saw musical order, and pairing rhymes.

Olympian bards who sung
Divine ideas below,
Which always finds us young,
And always keep us so.

Those who are esteemed umpires of taste are often persons who have acquired some knowledge of admired pictures or sculptures, and have an inclination for whatever is elegant; but if you inquire whether they are beautiful souls, and whether their own acts are like fair pictures, you learn that they are selfish and sensual. Their cultivation is local, as if you should rub a log of dry wood in one spot to produce fire, all the rest remaining cold. Their knowledge of the fine arts is some study of rules and particulars, or some limited judgment of color or form, which is exercised for amusement or for show. It is a proof of the shallowness of the doctrine of beauty as it lies in the minds of our amateurs, that men seem to have lost the perception of the instant dependence of form upon soul. There is no doctrine of forms in our philosophy. We were put into our bodies, as fire is put into a pan to be carried about; but there is no accurate adjustment between the spirit and the organ, much less is the latter the germination of the former. So in regard to other forms, the intellectual men do not believe in any essential dependence of the material world on thought and volition. Theologians think it a pretty air-castle to talk of the spiritual meaning of a ship or a cloud, of a city or a contract, but they prefer to come again to the solid ground of historical evidence; and even the poets are contented with a civil and conformed manner of living, and to write poems from the fancy, at a safe distance from their own experience. But the highest minds of the world have never ceased to explore the double meaning, or, shall I say, the quadruple, or the centuple, or much more manifold meaning, of every sensuous fact: Orpheus, Empedocles, Heraclitus, Plato, Plutarch, Dante, Swedenborg, and the masters of sculpture, picture, and poetry. For we are not pans and barrows, nor even porters of the fire and torch-bearers, but children of the fire, made of it, and only the same divinity transmuted, and at two or three removes, when we know least about it. And this hidden truth, that the fountains whence all this river of Time, and its creatures, floweth, are intrinsically ideal and beautiful, draws us to the consideration of the nature and functions of the Poet, or the man of Beauty, to the means and materials he uses, and to the general aspect of his art in the present time.

The breadth of the problem is great, for the poet is representative. He stands among partial men for the complete man, and apprises us not of his wealth, but of the common wealth. The young man reveres men of genius, because, to speak truly, they are more himself than he is. They receive of the soul as he also receives, but they more. Nature enhances her beauty, to the eye of loving men, from their belief that the poet is beholding her shows at the same time. He is isolated among his contemporaries, by truth and by his art, but with this consolation in his pursuits, that they will draw all men sooner or later. For all men live by truth, and stand in need of expression. In love, in art, in avarice, in politics, in labor, in games, we study to utter our painful secret. The man is only half himself, the other half is his expression.

Notwithstanding this necessity to be published, adequate expression is rare. I know not how it is that we need an interpreter; but the great majority of men seem to be minors, who have not yet come into possession of their own, or mutes, who cannot report the conversation they have had with nature. There is no man who does not anticipate a supersensual utility in the sun and stars, earth and water. These stand and wait to render him a peculiar service. But there is some obstruction, or some excess of phlegm in our constitution, which does not suffer them to yield the due effect. Too feeble fall the impressions of nature on us to make us artists. Every touch should thrill. Every man should be so much an artist that he could report in conversation what had befallen him. Yet, in our experience, the rays or appulses have sufficient force to arrive at the senses, but not enough to reach the quick and compel the reproduction of themselves in speech. The poet is the person in whom these powers are in balance, the man without impediment, who sees and handles that which others dream of, traverses the whole scale of experience, and is representative of man, in virtue of being the largest power to receive and to impart.

For the Universe has three children, born at one time, which reappear, under different names, in every system of thought, whether they be called cause, operation, and effect; or, more poetically, Jove, Pluto, Neptune; or, theologically, the Father, the Spirit, and the Son; but which we will call here the Knower, the Doer, and the

Sayer. These stand respectively for the love of truth, for the love of good, and for the love of beauty. These three are equal. Each is that which he is essentially, so that he cannot be surmounted or analyzed, and each of these three has the power of the others latent in him, and his own, patent.

The poet is the sayer, the namer, and represents beauty. He is a sovereign, and stands on the centre. For the world is not painted or adorned, but is from the beginning beautiful; and God has not made some beautiful things, but Beauty is the creator of the universe. Therefore the poet is not any permissive potentate, but is emperor in his own right. Criticism is infested with a cant of materialism, which assumes that manual skill and activity is the first merit of all men, and disparages such as say and do not, overlooking the fact that some men, namely, poets, are natural sayers, sent into the world to the end of expression, and confounds them with those whose province is action, but who quit it to imitate the sayers. But Homer's words are as costly and admirable to Homer, as Agamemnon's victories are to Agamemnon. The poet does not wait for the hero or the sage, but, as they act and think primarily, so he writes primarily what will and must be spoken, reckoning the others, though primaries also, yet, in respect to him, secondaries and servants; as sitters or models in the studio of a painter, or as assistants who bring building-materials to an architect.

For poetry was all written before time was, and whenever we are so finely organized that we can penetrate into that region where the air is music, we hear those primal warblings, and attempt to write them down, but we lose ever and anon a word, or a verse, and substitute something of our own, and thus miswrite the poem. The men of more delicate ear write down these cadences more faithfully, and these transcripts, though imperfect, become the songs of the nations. For nature is as truly beautiful as it is good, or as it is reasonable, and must as much appear, as it must be done, or be known. Words and deeds are quite indifferent modes of the divine energy. Words are also actions, and actions are a kind of words.

The sign and credentials of the poet are, that he announces that which no man foretold. He is the true and only doctor; he knows and tells; he is the only teller of news, for he was present and privy to the appearance which he describes. He is a beholder of ideas, and an utterer of the necessary and causal. We do not speak now of men of poetical talents, or of industry and skill in metre, but of the true poet. I took part in a conversation the other day concerning a recent writer of lyrics, a man of subtle mind, whose head appeared to be a music-box of delicate tunes and rhythms, and whose skill, and command of language, we could not sufficiently praise. But when the question arose, whether he were not only a lyrist, but a poet, we were obliged to confess that he is plainly a contemporary, not an eternal man. He does not stand out of our low limitations, like a Chimborazo under the line, running up from a torrid base through all the climates of the globe, with belts of the herbage of every latitude on its high and mottled sides; but this genius is the landscape-garden of a modern house, adorned with fountains and statues, with well-bred men and women standing and sitting in the walks and terraces. We hear, through all the varied music, the ground-tone of conventional life. Our poets are men of talents who sing, and not the children of music. The argument is secondary, the finish of the verses is primary.

For it is not metres, but a metre-making argument, that makes a poem, — a thought so passionate and alive, that, like the spirit of a plant or an animal, it has an architecture of its own, and adorns nature with a new thing. The thought and the form are equal in the order of time, but in the order of genesis the thought is prior to the form. The poet has a new thought: he has a whole new experience to unfold; he will tell us how it was with him, and all men will be the richer in his fortune. The experience of each new age requires a new confession, and the world seems always waiting for its poet. I remember, when I was young, how much I was moved one morning by tidings that genius had appeared in a youth who sat near me at table. He had left his work, and gone rambling none knew whither, and had written hundreds of lines, but could not tell whether that which was in him was therein told; he could tell nothing but that all was changed — man, beast, heaven, earth, and sea. How gladly we listened! how credulous! Society seemed to be compromised. We sat in the aurora of a sunrise which was to put out all the stars. Boston seemed to be at twice the distance it had the night before, or was much farther than that. Rome, — what was Rome? Plutarch and Shakspeare were in the yellow leaf, and Homer no more should be heard of. It is much to know that poetry has been written this very day, under this very roof, by your side. What! that wonderful spirit has not expired! These stony moments are still sparkling and animated! I had fancied that the oracles were all silent, and nature had spent her fires; and behold! all night, from every pore, these fine auroras have been streaming. Every one has some interest in the advent of the poet, and no one knows how much it may concern him. We know that the secret of the world is profound, but who or what shall be our interpreter, we know not. A mountain ramble, a new style of face, a new person, may put the key into our hands. Of course, the value of genius to us is in the veracity of its report. Talent may frolic and juggle; genius realizes and adds. Mankind, in good earnest, have gone so far in understanding themselves and their work, and the foremost watchman on the peak announces his news. It is the truest word ever spoken, and the phrase will be the fittest, most musical, and the unerring voice of the world for that time.

All that we call sacred history attests that the birth of a poet is the principal event in chronology. Man, never so often deceived, still watches for the arrival of a brother who can hold him steady to a truth until he has made it his own. With what joy I begin to read a poem, which I confide in as an inspiration! And now my chains are to be broken; I shall mount above these clouds and opaque airs in which I live, — opaque, though they seem transparent, — and from the heaven of truth I shall see and comprehend my relations. That will reconcile me to life, and renovate nature, to see trifles animated by a tendency, and to know what I am doing. Life will no more be a noise; now I shall see men and women, and know the signs by which they may be discerned from fools and satans. This day shall be better than my birth-day: then I became an animal; now I am invited into the science of the real. Such is the hope, but the fruition is postponed. Oftener it falls that this winged man, who will carry me into the heaven, whirls me into mists, then leaps and frisks about with me as it were from cloud to cloud, still affirming that he is bound heavenward; and I, being myself a novice, am slow in perceiving that he does not know the way into the heavens, and is merely bent that I should admire his skill to rise, like a fowl or a flying-fish, a little way from the ground or the water; but the all-piercing, all-feeding, and ocular air of heaven, that man shall never inhabit. I tumble down again soon into my old nooks, and lead the life of exaggerations as before, and have lost my faith in the possibility of any guide who can lead me thither where I would be.

But, leaving these victims of vanity, let us, with new hope, observe how nature, by worthier impulses, has insured the poet's fidelity to his office of announcement and affirming, namely, by the beauty of things, which becomes a new and higher beauty when expressed. Nature offers all her creatures to him as a picture-language. Being used as a type, a second wonderful value appears in the object, far better than its old value, as the carpenter's stretched cord, if you hold your ear close enough, is musical in the breeze. "Things more excellent than every image," says Jamblichus, "are expressed through images." Things admit of being used as symbols, because nature is a symbol, in the whole, and in every part. Every line we can draw in the sand has expression; and there is no body without its spirit or genius. All form is an effort of character; all condition, of the quality of the life; all harmony, of health; and, for this reason, a perception of beauty should be sympathetic, or proper, only to the good. The beautiful rests on the foundations of the necessary. The soul makes the body, as the wise Spenser teaches: —

> So every spirit, as it is most pure,
> And hath in it the more of heavenly light,
> So it the fairer body doth procure
> To habit in, and it more fairly dight,
> With cheerful grace and amiable sight.
> For, of the soul, the body form doth take,
> For soul is form, and doth the body make.

Here we find ourselves, suddenly, not in a critical speculation, but in a holy place, and should go very warily and reverently. We stand before the secret of the world, — there where Being passes into Appearance, and Unity into Variety.

The Universe is the externization of the soul. Wherever the life is, that bursts into appearance around it. Our science is sensual, and therefore superficial. The earth and the heavenly bodies, physics and chemistry, we sensually treat, as if they were self-existent; but these are the retinue of that Being we have. "The mighty heaven," said Proclus, "exhibits, in its transfigurations, clear images of the splendor of intellectual perceptions; being moved in conjunction with the unapparent periods of intellectual natures." Therefore, science always goes abreast with the just elevation of the man, keeping step with religion and metaphysics; or, the state of science is an index of our self-knowledge. Since every thing in nature answers to a moral power, if any phenomenon remains brute and dark, it is because the corresponding faculty in the observer is not yet active.

No wonder, then, if these waters be so deep, that we hover over them with a religious regard. The beauty of the fable proves the importance of the sense, to the poet, and to all others; or, if you please, every man is so far a poet as to be susceptible of these enchantments of nature: for all men have the thoughts of which the universe is the celebration. I find that the fascination resides in the symbol. Who loves nature? Who does not? Is it only poets, and men of leisure and cultivation, who live with her? No; but also hunters, farmers, grooms, and butchers, though they express their affection in their choice of life, and not in their choice of words. The writer wonders what the coachman or the hunter values in riding, in horses, and dogs. It is not superficial qualities. When you talk with him, he holds these at as slight a rate as you. His worship is sympathetic: he has no definitions, but he is commanded in nature, by the living power which he feels to be there present. No imitation, or playing of these things, would content him; he loves the earnest of the north-wind, of rain, of stone and wood and iron. A beauty not explicable is dearer than a beauty which we can see to the end of. It is nature the symbol, nature certifying the supernatural, body overflowed by life, which he worships with coarse, but sincere rites.

The inwardness and mystery of this attachment drive men of every class to the use of emblems. The schools of poets and philosophers are not more intoxicated with their symbols, than the populace with theirs. In our political parties, compute the power of badges and emblems. See the great ball which they roll from Baltimore to Bunker Hill! In the political processions, Lowell goes in a loom, and Lynn in a shoe, and Salem in a ship. Witness the cider-barrel, the log-cabin, the hickory-stick, the palmetto, and all the cognizances of party. See the power of national emblems. Some stars, lilies, leopards, a crescent, a lion, an eagle, or other figure, which came into credit Gods know how, on an old rag of bunting, blowing in the wind on a fort at the ends of the earth, shall make the blood tingle under the rudest or the most conventional exterior. The people fancy they hate poetry, and they are all poets and mystics!

Beyond this universality of the symbolic language, we are apprised of the divineness of this superior use of things, whereby the world is a temple whose walls are covered with emblems, pictures, and commandments of the Deity — in this, that there is no fact in nature which does not carry the whole sense of nature; and the distinctions which we make in events and in affairs, of low and high, honest and base, disappear when nature is used as a symbol. Thought makes everything fit for use. The vocabulary of an omniscient man would embrace words and images excluded from polite conversation. What would be base, or even obscene, to the obscene, becomes illustrious, spoken in a new connection of thought. The piety of the Hebrew prophets purges their grossness. The circumcision is an example of the power of poetry to raise the low and offensive. Small and mean things serve as well as great symbols. The meaner the type by which a law is expressed, the more pungent it is, and the more lasting in the memories of men; just as we choose the smallest box or case in which any needful utensil can be carried. Bare lists of words are found suggestive to an imaginative and excited mind; as it is related of Lord Chatham, that he was accustomed to read in Bailey's Dictionary when he was preparing to speak in Parliament. The poorest experience is rich enough for all the purposes of expressing thought. Why covet a knowledge of new facts? Day and night, house and garden, a few books, a few actions, serve us as well as would all trades and all spectacles. We are far from having exhausted the significance of the few symbols we use. We can come to use them yet with a terrible simplicity. It does not need that a poem should be long. Every word was once a poem. Every new relation is a new word. Also, we use defects and deformities to a sacred purpose, so expressing our sense that the evils of the world are such only to the evil eye. In the old mythology, mythologists observe, defects are ascribed to divine natures, as lameness to Vulcan, blindness to Cupid, and the like, — to signify exuberances.

For as it is dislocation and detachment from the life of God that makes things ugly, the poet, who re-attaches things to nature and the Whole, — re-attaching even artificial things, and violations of nature, to nature, by a deeper insight, — disposes very easily of the most disagreeable facts. Readers of poetry see the factory-village and the railway, and fancy that the poetry of the landscape is broken up by these, — for these works of art are not yet consecrated in their reading; but the poet sees them fall within the great Order not less than the beehive or the spider's geometrical web. Nature adopts them very fast into her vital circles, and the gliding train of cars she loves like her own. Besides, in a centred mind, it signifies nothing how many mechanical inventions you exhibit. Though you add millions, and never so surprising, the fact of mechanics has not gained a grain's weight. The spiritual fact remains unalterable, by many or by few particulars; as no mountain is of any appreciable height to break the curve of the sphere. A shrewd country-boy goes to the city for the first time, and the complacent citizen is not satisfied with his little wonder. It is not that he does not see all the fine houses, and know that he never saw such before, but he disposes of them as easily as the poet finds place for the railway. The chief value of the new fact, is to enhance the great and constant fact of Life, which can dwarf any and every circumstance, and to which the belt of wampum, and the commerce of America, are alike.

The world being thus put under the mind for verb and noun, the poet is he who can articulate it. For though life is great, and fascinates, and absorbs, — and though all men are intelligent of the symbols through which it is named, — yet they cannot originally use them. We are symbols, and inhabit symbols; workmen, work, and tools, words and things, birth and death, all are emblems; but we sympathize with the symbols, and, being infatuated with the economical uses of things, we do not know that they are thoughts. The poet, by an ulterior intellectual perception, gives them a power which makes their old use forgotten, and puts eyes and a tongue into every dumb and inanimate object. He perceives the independence of the thought on the symbol, — the stability of the thought, the accidency and fugacity of the symbol. As the eyes of Lyncaeus were said to see through the earth, so the poet turns the world to glass, and shows us all things in their right series and procession. For, through that better perception, he stands one step nearer to things, and sees the flowing or metamorphosis; perceives that thought is multiform; that within the form of every creature is a force impelling it to ascend into a higher form: and, following with his eyes the life, uses the forms which express that life, and so his speech flows with the flowing of nature. All the facts of the animal economy, sex, nutriment, gestation, birth, growth, are symbols of the passage of the world into the soul of man, to suffer there a change, and reappear a new and higher fact. He uses forms according to the life, and not according to the form. This is true science. The poet alone knows astronomy, chemistry, vegetation, and animation; for he does not stop at these facts, but employs them as signs. He knows why the plain or meadow of space was strown with these flowers we call suns and moons and stars; why the great deep is adorned with animals, with men, and gods; for in every word he speaks he rides on them as the horses of thought.

By virtue of this science the poet is the Namer or Language-maker, naming things sometimes after their appearance, sometimes after their essence, and giving to every one its own name and not another's, thereby rejoicing the intellect, which delights in detachment or boundary. The poets made all the words, and therefore language is the archives of history, and, if we must say it, a sort of tomb of the muses. For, though the origin of most of our words is forgotten, each word was at first a stroke of genius, and obtained currency, because for the moment it symbolized the world to the first speaker and to the hearer. The etymologist finds the deadest word to have been once a brilliant picture. Language is fossil poetry. As the limestone of the continent consists of infinite masses of the shells of animalcules, so language is made up of images, or tropes, which now, in their secondary use, have long ceased to remind us of their poetic origin. But the poet names the thing because he sees it, or comes one step nearer to it than any other. This expression, or naming, is not art, but a second nature, grown out of the first, as a leaf out of a tree. What we call nature is a certain self-regulated motion or change; and nature does all things by her own hands, and does not leave another to baptize her, but baptizes herself; and this through the metamorphosis again. I remember that a certain poet described it to me thus: —

Genius is the activity which repairs the decays of things, whether wholly or partly of a material and finite kind. Nature, through all her kingdoms, insures herself. Nobody cares for planting the poor fungus: so she shakes down from the gills of one agaric countless spores, any one of which, being preserved, transmits new billions of spores to-morrow, or next day. The new agaric of this hour has a chance which the old one had not. This atom of seed is thrown into a new place, not subject to the accidents which destroyed its parent two rods off. She makes a man: and having brought him to ripe age, she will no longer run the risk of losing this wonder at a blow, but she detaches from him a new self, that the kind may be safe from accidents to which the individual is exposed. So when the soul of the poet has come to ripeness of thought, she detaches and sends away from it its poems or songs, — a fearless, sleepless, deathless progeny, which is not exposed to the accidents of the weary kingdom of time: a fearless, vivacious offspring, clad with wings (such was the virtue of the soul out of which they came), which carry them fast and far, and infix them irrevocably into the hearts of men. These wings are the beauty of the poet's soul. The songs, thus flying immortal from their mortal parent, are pursued by clamorous flights of censures, which swarm in far greater numbers, and threaten to devour them; but these last are not winged. At the end of a very short leap they fall plump down, and rot, having received from the souls out of which they came no beautiful wings. But the melodies of the poet ascend, and leap, and pierce into the deeps of infinite time.

So far the bard taught me, using his freer speech. But nature has a higher end, in the production of new individuals, than security, namely, *ascension,* or, the passage of the soul into higher forms. I knew, in my younger days, the sculptor who made the statue of the youth which stands in the public garden. He was, as I remember, unable to tell, directly, what made him happy, or unhappy, but by wonderful indirections he could tell. He rose one day, according to his habit, before the dawn, and saw the morning break, grand as the eternity out of which it came, and, for many days after, he strove to express this tranquillity, and, lo! his chisel had fashioned out of marble the form of a beautiful youth, Phosphorus, whose aspect is such that, it is said, all persons who look on it become silent. The poet also resigns himself to his mood, and that thought which agitated him is expressed, but *alter idem,* in a manner totally new. The expression is organic, or, the new type which things themselves take when liberated. As, in the sun, objects paint their images on the retina of the eye, so they, sharing the aspiration of the whole universe, tend to paint a far more delicate copy of their essence in his mind. Like the metamorphosis of things into higher organic forms, is their change into melodies. Over everything stands its dæmon, or soul, and as the form of the thing is reflected by the eye, so the soul of the thing is reflected by a melody. The sea, the mountain-ridge, Niagara, and every flower-bed, pre-exist, or super-exist, in pre-cantations, which sail like odors in the air, and when any man goes by with an ear sufficiently fine, he overhears them, and endeavors to write down the notes, without diluting or depraving them. And herein is the legitimation of criticism, in the mind's faith that the poems are a corrupt version of some text in nature, with which they ought to be made to tally. A rhyme in one of our sonnets should not be less pleasing than the iterated nodes of a sea-shell, or the resembling difference of a group of flowers. The pairing of the birds is an idyl, not tedious as our idyls are; a tempest is a rough ode without falsehood or rant; a summer, with its harvest sown, reaped, and stored, is an epic song, subordinating how many admirably executed parts. Why should not the symmetry and truth that modulate these, glide into our spirits, and we participate the invention of nature?

This insight, which expresses itself by what is called Imagination, is a very high sort of seeing, which does not come by study, but by the intellect being where and what it sees; by sharing the path, or circuit of things through forms, and so making them translucid to others. The path of things is silent. Will they suffer a speaker to go with them? A spy they will not suffer; a lover, a poet, is the transcendency of their own nature,—him they will suffer. The condition of true naming, on the poet's part, is his resigning himself to the divine *aura* which breathes through forms, and accompanying that.

It is a secret which every intellectual man quickly learns, that, beyond the energy of his possessed and conscious intellect, he is capable of a new energy (as of an intellect doubled on itself), by abandonment to the nature of things; that, beside his privacy of power as an individual man, there is a great public power, on which he can draw, by unlocking, at all risks, his human doors, and suffering the ethereal tides to roll and circulate through him: then he is caught up into the life of the Universe, his speech is thunder, his thought is law, and his words are universally intelligible as the plants and animals. The poet knows that he speaks adequately, then only when he speaks somewhat wildly, or, "with the flower of the mind;" not with the intellect, used as an organ, but with the intellect released from all service, and suffered to take its direction from its celestial life; or, as the ancients were wont to express themselves, not with intellect alone, but with the intellect inebriated by nectar. As the traveller who has lost his way, throws his reins on his horse's neck, and trusts to the instinct of the animal to find his road, so must we do with the divine animal who carries us through the world. For if in any manner we can stimulate this instinct, new passages are opened for us into nature, the mind flows into and through things hardest and highest, and the metamorphosis is possible.

This is the reason why bards love

wine, mead, narcotics, coffee, tea, opium, the fumes of sandal-wood and tobacco, or whatever other procurers of animal exhilaration. All men avail themselves of such means as they can, to add this extraordinary power to their normal powers; and to this end they prize conversation, music, pictures, sculpture, dancing, theatres, travelling, war, mobs, fires, gaming, politics, or love, or science, or animal intoxication, which are several coarser or finer *quasi*-mechanical substitutes for the true nectar, which is the ravishment of the intellect by coming nearer to the fact. These are auxiliaries to the centrifugal tendency of a man, to his passage out into free space, and they help him to escape the custody of that body in which he is pent up, and of that jail-yard of individual relations in which he is enclosed. Hence, a great number of such as were professionally expressers of Beauty, as painters, poets, musicians, and actors, have been more than others wont to lead a life of pleasure and indulgence; all but the few who received the true nectar; and, as it was a spurious mode of attaining freedom, as it was an emancipation not into the heavens, but into the freedom of baser places, they were punished for that advantage they won, by a dissipation and deterioration. But never can any advantage be taken of nature by a trick. The spirit of the world, the great calm presence of the Creator, comes not forth to the sorceries of opium or of wine. The sublime vision comes to the pure and simple soul in a clean and chaste body. That is not an inspiration, which we owe to narcotics, but some counterfeit excitement and fury. Milton says that the lyric poet may drink wine and live generously, but the epic poet, he who shall sing of the gods, and their descent unto men, must drink water out of a wooden bowl. For poetry is not 'Devil's wine,' but God's wine. It is with this as it is with toys. We fill the hands and nurseries of our children with all manner of dolls, drums, and horses, withdrawing their eyes from the plain face and sufficing objects of nature, the sun and moon, the animals, the water and stones, which should be their toys. So the poet's habit of living should be set on a key so low that the common influences should delight him. His cheerfulness should be the gift of the sunlight; the air should suffice for his inspiration, and he should be tipsy with water. That spirit which suffices quiet hearts, which seems to come forth to such from every dry knoll of sere grass, from every pine-stump and half-imbedded stone, on which the dull March sun shines, comes forth to the poor and hungry, and such as are of simple taste. If thou fill thy brain with Boston and New York, with fashion and covetousness, and wilt stimulate thy jaded senses with wine and French coffee, thou shalt find no radiance of wisdom in the lonely waste of the pine woods.

If the imagination intoxicates the poet, it is not inactive in other men. The metamorphosis excites in the beholder an emotion of joy. The use of symbols has a certain power of emancipation and exhilaration for all men. We seem to be touched by a wand, which makes us dance and run about happily, like children. We are like persons who come out of a cave or cellar into the open air. This is the effect on us of tropes, fables, oracles, and all poetic forms. Poets are thus liberating gods. Men have really got a new sense, and found within their world another world, or nest of worlds; for, the metamorphosis once seen, we divine that it does not stop. I will not now consider how much this makes the charm of algebra and the mathematics, which also have their tropes, but it is felt in every definition; as when Aristotle defines *space* to be an immovable vessel, in which things are contained; or when Plato defines a *line* to be a flowing point; or *figure* to be a bound of solid; and many the like. What a joyful sense of freedom we have, when Vitruvius announces the old opinion of artists that no architect can build any house well who does not know something of anatomy. When Socrates, in Charmides, tells us that the soul is cured of its maladies by certain incantations, and that these incantations are beautiful reasons, from which temperance is generated in souls; when Plato calls the world an animal, and Timaeus affirms that plants also are animals; or affirms a man to be a heavenly tree, growing with his root, which is his head, upward; and, as George Chapman, following him, writes, —

> So in our tree of man, whose nervie root
> Springs in his top;

when Orpheus speaks of hoariness as "that white flower which marks extreme old age;" when Proclus calls the universe the statue of the intellect; when Chaucer, in his praise of 'Gentilesse,' compares good blood in mean condition to fire, which, though carried to the darkest house betwixt this and the mount of Caucasus, will yet hold its natural office, and burn as bright as if twenty thousand men did it behold; when John saw, in the Apocalypse, the ruin of the world through evil, and the stars fall from heaven, as the fig-tree casteth her untimely fruit; when Æsop reports the whole catalogue of common daily relations through the masquerade of birds and beasts; — we take the cheerful hint of the immortality of our essence, and its versatile habits and escapes, as when the gypsies say of themselves "it is in vain to hang them, they cannot die."

The poets are thus liberating gods. The ancient British bards had for the title of their order, "Those who are free throughout the world." They are free, and they make free. An imaginative book renders us much more service at first, by stimulating us through its tropes, than afterward, when we arrive at the precise sense of the author. I think nothing is of any value in books, excepting the transcendental and extraordinary. If a man is inflamed and carried away by his thought, to that degree that he forgets the authors and the public, and heeds only this one dream, which holds him like an insanity, let me read his paper, and you may have all the arguments, and histories, and criticism. All the value which attaches to Pythagoras, Paracelsus, Cornelius Agrippa, Cardan, Kepler, Swedenborg, Schelling, Oken, or any other who introduces questionable facts into his cosmogony, as angels, devils, magic, astrology, palmistry, mesmerism, and so on, is the certificate we have of departure from routine, and that here is a new witness. That also is the best success in conversation, the magic of liberty, which puts the world, like a ball, in our hands. How cheap even the liberty then seems; how mean to study, when an emotion communicates to the intellect the power to sap and upheave nature: how great the perspective! nations, times, systems, enter and disappear, like threads in tapestry of large figure and many colors; dream delivers us to dream, and, while the drunkenness lasts, we will sell our bed, our philosophy, our religion, in our opulence.

There is good reason why we should prize this liberation. The fate of the poor shepherd, who, blinded and lost in the snow-storm, perishes in a drift within a few feet of his cottage door, is an emblem of the state of man. On the brink of the waters of life and truth, we are miserably dying. The inaccessibleness of every thought but that we are in, is wonderful. What if you come near to it, — you are as remote when you are nearest as when you are farthest. Every thought is also a prison; every heaven is also a prison. Therefore we love the poet, the inventor, who in any form, whether in an ode, or in an action, or in looks and behavior, has yielded us a new thought. He unlocks our chains, and admits us to a new scene.

This emancipation is dear to all men; and the power to impart it, as it must come from greater depth and scope of thought, is a measure of intellect. Therefore all books of the imagination endure, all which ascend to that truth, that the writer sees nature beneath him, and uses it as his exponent. Every verse or sentence, possessing this virtue, will take care of its own immortality. The religions of the world are the ejaculations of a few imaginative men.

But the quality of the imagination is to flow, and not to freeze. The poet did not stop at the color, or the form, but read their meaning; neither may he rest in this meaning, but he makes the same objects exponents of his new thought. Here is the difference betwixt the poet and the mystic, that the last nails a symbol to one sense, which was a true sense for a moment, but soon becomes old and false. For all symbols are fluxional; all language is vehicular and transitive, and is good, as ferries and horses are, for conveyance, not as farms and houses are, for homestead. Mysticism consists in the mistake of an accidental and individual symbol for an universal one. The morning-redness happens to be the favorite meteor to the eyes of Jacob Behmen, and comes to stand to him for truth and faith; and, he believes, it should stand for the same realities to every reader. But the first reader prefers as naturally the symbol of a mother and child, or a gardener and his bulb, or a jeweller polishing a gem. Either of these, or of a myriad more, are equally good to the person to whom they are significant. Only they must be held lightly, and be very willingly translated into the equivalent terms which others use. And the mystic must be steadily told, — All that you say is just as true without the tedious use of that symbol as with it. Let us have a little algebra, instead of this trite rhetoric, — universal signs, instead of these village symbols, — and we shall both be gainers. The history of hierarchies seems to show that all religious error consisted in making the symbol too stark and solid, and, at last, nothing but an excess of the organ of language.

Swedenborg, of all men in the recent ages, stands eminently for the translator of nature into thought. I do not know the man in history to whom things stood so uniformly for words. Before him the metamorphosis continually plays. Every thing on which his eye rests, obeys the impulses of moral nature. The figs become grapes whilst he eats them. When some of his angels affirmed a truth, the laurel twig which they held blossomed in their hands. The noise which at a distance appeared like gnashing and thumping, on coming nearer was found to be the voice of disputants. The men, in one of his visions, seen in heavenly light, appeared like dragons, and seemed in darkness; but to each other they appeared as men, and, when the light from heaven shone into their cabin, they complained of the darkness, and were compelled to shut the window that they might see.

There was this perception in him, which makes the poet or seer an object of awe and terror, namely, that the same man, or society of men, may wear one aspect to themselves and their companions, and a different aspect to higher intelligences. Certain priests, whom he describes as conversing very learnedly together, appeared to the children, who were at some distance, like dead horses; and many the like misappearances. And instantly the mind inquires, whether these fishes under the bridge, yonder oxen in the pasture, those dogs in the yard, are immutably fishes, oxen, and dogs, or only so appear to me, and perchance to themselves appear upright men; and whether I appear as a man to all eyes. The Brahmins and Pythagoras propounded the same question, and if any poet has witnessed the transformation, he doubtless found it in harmony with various experiences. We have all seen changes as considerable in wheat and caterpillars. He is the poet, and shall draw us with love and terror, who sees, through the flowing vest, the firm nature, and can declare it.

I look in vain for the poet whom I describe. We do not with sufficient plainness, or sufficient profoundness, address ourselves to life, nor dare we chaunt our own times and social circumstance. If we filled the day with bravery, we should not shrink from celebrating it. Time and nature yield us many gifts, but not yet the timely man, the new religion, the reconciler, whom all things await. Dante's praise is, that he dared to write his autobiography in colossal cipher, or into universality. We have yet had no genius in America, with tyrannous eye, which knew the value of our incomparable materials, and saw, in the barbarism and materialism of the times, another carnival of the same gods whose picture he so much admires in Homer; then in the Middle Age; then in Calvinism. Banks and tariffs, the newspaper and caucus, Methodism and Unitarianism, are flat and dull to dull people, but rest on the same foundations of wonder as the town of Troy and the temple of Delphi and are as swiftly passing away. Our log-rolling, our stumps and their politics, our fisheries, our Negroes and Indians, our boats, and our repudiations, the wrath of rogues, and the pusillanimity of honest men, the northern trade, the southern planting, the western clearing, Oregon and Texas, are yet unsung. Yet America is a poem in our eyes; its ample geography dazzles the imagination, and it will not wait long for metres. If I have not found that excellent combination of gifts in my countrymen which I seek, neither could I aid myself to fix the idea of the poet by reading now and then in Chalmers's collection of five centuries of English poets. These are wits more than poets, though there have been poets among them. But when we adhere to the ideal of the poet, we have our difficulties even with Milton and Homer. Milton is too literary, and Homer too literal and historical.

But I am not wise enough for a national criticism, and must use the old largeness a little longer, to discharge my errand from the muse to the poet concerning his art.

Art is the path of the creator to his work. The paths, or methods, are ideal and eternal, though few men ever see them, — not the artist himself, for years, or for a lifetime, unless he come into the conditions. The painter, the sculptor, the composer, the epic rhapsodist, the orator, all partake one desire, namely, to express themselves symmetrically and abundantly, not dwarfishly and fragmentarily. They found or put themselves in certain conditions, as, the painter and sculptor before some impressive human figures; the orator, into the assembly of the people; and the others, in such scenes as each has found exciting to his intellect; and each presently feels the new desire. He hears a voice, he sees a beckoning. Then he is apprised, with wonder, what herds of dæmons hem him in. He can no more rest; he says, with the old painter, "By God, it is in me, and must go forth of me." He pursues a beauty, half seen, which flies before him. The poet pours out verses in every solitude. Most of the things he says are conventional, no doubt; but by and by he says something which is original and beautiful. That charms him. He would say nothing else but such things. In our way of talking, we say, 'That is yours, this is mine;' but the poet knows well that it is not his; that it is as strange and beautiful to him as to you; he would fain hear the like eloquence at length. Once having tasted this immortal ichor, he cannot have enough of it, and, as an admirable creative power exists in these intellections, it is of the last importance that these things get spoken. What a little of all we know is said! What drops of all the sea of our science are baled up! and by what accident it is that these are exposed, when so many secrets sleep in nature! Hence the necessity of speech and song; hence these throbs and heart-beatings in the orator, at the door of the assembly, to the end, namely, that thought may be ejaculated as Logos, or Word.

Doubt not, O poet, but persist. Say, 'It is in me, and shall out.' Stand there, balked and dumb, stuttering and stammering, hissed and hooted, stand and strive, until, at last, rage draw out of thee that *dream*-power which every night shows thee is thine own; — a power transcending all limit and privacy, and by virtue of which a man is the conductor of the whole river of electricity. Nothing walks, or creeps, or grows, or exists, which must not in turn arise and walk before him as exponent of his meaning. Comes he to that power, his genius is no longer exhaustible. All the creatures, by pairs and by tribes, pour into his mind as into a Noah's ark, to come forth again to people a new world. This is like the stock of air for our respiration, or for the combustion of our fireplace; not a measure of gallons, but the entire atmosphere if wanted. And therefore the rich poets, as Homer, Chaucer, Shakspeare, and Raphael, have obviously no limits to their works, except the limits of their lifetime, and resemble a mirror carried through the street, ready to render an image of every created thing.

O poet! a new nobility is conferred in groves and pastures, and not in castles, or by the sword-blade, any longer. The conditions are hard, but equal. Thou shalt leave the world, and know the muse only. Thou shalt not know any longer the times, customs, graces, politics, or opinions of men, but shalt take all from the muse. For the time of towns is tolled from the world by funeral chimes, but in nature the universal hours are counted by succeeding tribes of animals and plants, and by growth of joy on joy. God wills also that thou abdicate a manifold and duplex life, and that thou be content that others speak for thee. Others shall be thy gentlemen, and shall represent all courtesy and worldly life for thee; others shall do the great and resounding actions also. Thou shalt lie close hid with nature, and canst not be afforded to the Capitol or the Exchange. The world is full of renunciations and apprenticeships, and this is thine; thou must pass for a fool and a churl for a long season. This is the screen and sheath in which Pan has protected his well-beloved flower, and thou shalt be known only to thine own, and they shall console thee with tenderest love. And thou shalt not be able to rehearse the names of thy friends in thy verse, for an old shame before the holy ideal. And this is the reward: that the ideal shall be real to thee, and the impressions of the actual world shall fall like summer rain, copious, but not troublesome, to thy invulnerable essence. Thou shalt have the whole land for thy park and manor, the sea for thy bath and navigation, without tax and without envy; the woods and the rivers thou shalt own; and thou shalt possess that wherein others are only tenants and boarders. Thou true land-lord! sea-lord! air-lord! Wherever snow falls, or water flows, or birds fly, wherever day and night meet in twilight, wherever the blue heaven is hung by clouds, or sown with stars, wherever are forms with transparent boundaries, wherever are outlets into celestial space, wherever is danger, and awe and love, there is Beauty, plenteous as rain, shed for thee, and though thou shouldst walk the world over, thou shalt not be able to find a condition inopportune or ignoble.

1844

## *From* EZRA RIPLEY, D.D.

Ezra Ripley was born May 1, 1751 (O.S.), at Woodstock, Connecticut. * * *

He was identified with the ideas

and forms of the New England Church, which expired about the same time with him, so that he and his coevals seemed the rear guard of the great camp and army of the Puritans, which, however, in its last days declining into formalism, in the heyday of its strength had planted and liberated America. It was a pity that his old meeting-house should have been modernized in his time. I am sure all who remember both will associate his form with whatever was grave and droll in the old, cold, unpainted, uncarpeted, square-pewed meeting-house, with its four iron-gray deacons in their little box under the pulpit,—with Watts's hymns, with long prayers, rich with the diction of ages; and not less with the report like musketry from the movable seats. He and his contemporaries, the old New England clergy, were believers in what is called a particular providence,—certainly, as they held it, a very particular providence,—following the narrowness of King David and the Jews, who thought the universe existed only or mainly for their church and congregation. Perhaps I cannot better illustrate this tendency than by citing a record from the diary of the father of his predecessor, the minister of Malden, written in the blank leaves of the almanac for the year 1735. The minister writes against January 31st: "Bought a shay for 27 pounds, 10 shillings. The Lord grant it may be a comfort and blessing to my family." In March following he notes: "Had a safe and comfortable journey to York." But April 24th, we find: "Shay overturned, with my wife and I in it, yet neither of us much hurt. Blessed be our gracious Preserver. Part of the shay, as it lay upon one side, went over my wife, and yet she was scarcely anything hurt. How wonderful the preservation." Then again, May 5th: "Went to the beach with three of the children. The beast, being frightened when we were all out of the shay, overturned and broke it. I desire (I hope I desire it) that the Lord would teach me suitably to resent this Providence, to make suitable remarks on it, and to be suitably affected with it. Have I done well to get me a shay? Have I not been proud or too fond of this convenience? Do I exercise the faith in the Divine care and protection which I ought to do? Should I not be more in my study and less fond of diversion? Do I not withhold more than is meet from pious and charitable uses?" Well, on 15th May we have this: "Shay brought home; mending cost thirty shillings. Favored in this respect beyond expectation." 16th May: "My wife and I rode together to Rumney Marsh. The beast frightened several times." And at last we have this record, June 4th: "Disposed of my shay to Rev. Mr. White."

The same faith made what was strong and what was weak in Dr. Ripley and his associates. He was a perfectly sincere man, punctual, severe, but just and charitable, and if he made his forms a strait-jacket to others, he wore the same himself all his years. Trained in this church, and very well qualified by his natural talent to work in it, it was never out of his mind. He looked at every person and thing from the parochial point of view. I remember, when a boy, driving about Concord with him, and in passing each house he told the story of the family that lived in it, and especially he gave me anecdotes of the nine church members who had made a division in the church in the time of his predecessor, and showed me how every one of the nine had come to bad fortune or to a bad end. His prayers for rain and against the lightning, "that it may not lick up our spirits;" and for good weather; and against sickness and insanity; "that we have not been tossed to and fro until the dawning of the day; that we have not been a terror to ourselves and others,"—are well remembered, and his own entire faith that these petitions were not to be overlooked, and were entitled to a favorable answer. Some of those around me will remember one occasion of severe drought in this vicinity, when the late Rev. Mr. Goodwin offered to relieve the Doctor of the duty of leading in prayer; but the Doctor suddenly remembering the season, rejected his offer with some humor, as with an air that said to all the congregation, "This is no time for you young Cambridge men; the affair, sir, is getting serious. I will pray myself." One August afternoon, when I was in his hayfield helping him with his man to rake up his hay, I well remember his pleading, almost reproachful looks at the sky, when the thunder-gust was coming up to spoil his hay. He raked very fast, then looked at the cloud, and said, "We are in the Lord's hand; mind your rake, George! We are in the Lord's hand;" and seemed to say, "You know me; this field is mine,—Dr. Ripley's,—thine own servant!"

He used to tell the story of one of his old friends, the minister of Sudbury, who, being at the Thursday lecture in Boston, heard the officiating clergyman praying for rain. As soon as the service was over, he went to the petitioner, and said, "You Boston ministers, as soon as a tulip wilts under your windows, go to church and pray for rain, until all Concord and Sudbury are under water." I once rode with him to a house at Nine Acre Corner to attend the funeral of the father of a family. He mentioned to me on the way his fears that the oldest son, who was now to succeed to the farm, was becoming intemperate. We presently arrived, and the Doctor addressed each of the mourners separately: "Sir, I condole with you." "Madam, I condole with you." "Sir, I knew your great-grandfather. When I came to this town, your great-grandfather was a substantial farmer in this very place, a member of the church, and an excellent citizen. Your grandfather followed him, and was a virtuous man. Now your father is to be carried to his grave, full of labors and virtues There is none of that large family left but you, and it rests with you to bear up the good name and usefulness of your ancestors. If you fail,—'Ichabod, the glory is departed.' Let us pray." Right manly he was, and the manly thing he could always say. I can remember a little speech he made to me, when the last tie of blood which held me and my brothers to his house was broken by the death of his daughter. He said, on parting, "I wish you and your brothers to come to this house as you have always done. You will not like to be excluded; I shall not like to be neglected."

When "Put" Merriam, after his release from the state prison, had the effrontery to call on the Doctor as an old acquaintance, in the midst of general conversation Mr. Frost came in, and the Doctor presently said, "Mr. Merriam, my brother and colleague, Mr. Frost, has come to take tea with me. I regret very much the causes (which you know very well) which make it impossible for me to ask you to stay and break bread with us." With the Doctor's views it was a matter of religion to say thus much. He had a reverence and love of society, and the patient, continuing courtesy, carrying out every respectful attention to the end, which marks what is called the manners of the old school. His hospitality obeyed Charles Lamb's rule, and "ran fine to the last." His partiality for ladies was always strong, and was by no means abated by time. He claimed privilege of years, was much addicted to kissing; spared neither maid, wife nor widow, and, as a lady thus favored remarked to me, "seemed as if he was going to make a meal of you."

He was very credulous, and as he was no reader of books or journals, he knew nothing beyond the columns of his weekly religious newspaper, the tracts of his sect, and perhaps the Middlesex Yeoman. He was the easy dupe of any tonguey agent, whether colonizationist or anti-papist, or charlatan of iron combs, or tractors, or phrenology, or magnetism, who went by. At the time when Jack Downing's letters were in every paper, he repeated to me at table some of the particulars of that gentleman's intimacy with General Jackson, in a manner that betrayed to me at once that he took the whole for fact. To undeceive him, I hastened to recall some particulars to show the absurdity of the thing, as the Major and the President going out skating on the Potomac, etc. "Why," said the Doctor with perfect faith, "it was a bright moonlight night;" and I am not sure that he did not die in the belief in the reality of Major Downing. Like other credulous men, he was opinionative, and, as I well remember, a great browbeater of the poor old fathers who still survive from the 19th of April, to the end that they should testify to his history as he had written it.

He was a man so kind and sympathetic, his character was so transparent, and his merits so intelligible to all observers, that he was very justly appreciated in this community. He was a natural gentleman, no dandy, but courtly, hospitable, manly and public-spirited; his nature social, his house open to all men. We remember the remark made by the old farmer who used to travel hither from Maine, that no horse from the Eastern country would go by the Doctor's gate. Travellers from the West and North and South bear the like testimony. His brow was serene and open to his visitor, for he loved men, and he had no studies, no occupations, which company could interrupt. His friends were his study, and to see them loosened his talents and his tongue. In his house dwelt order and prudence and plenty. There was no waste and no stint. He was open-handed and just and generous. Ingratitude and meanness in his beneficiaries did not wear out his compassion; he bore the insult, and the next day his basket for the beggar, his horse and chaise for the cripple, were at their door. Though he knew the value of a dollar as well as another man, yet he loved to buy dearer and sell cheaper than others. He subscribed to all charities, and it is no reflection on others to say that he was the most public-spirited man in the town. The late Dr. Gardiner, in a funeral sermon on some parishioner whose virtues did not readily come to mind, honestly said, "He was good at fires." Dr. Ripley had many virtues, and yet all will remember that even in his old age, if the firebell was rung, he was instantly on horseback with his buckets, and bag.

He showed even in his fireside discourse traits of that pertinency and judgment, softening ever and anon into elegancy, which make the distinction of the scholar, and which, under better discipline, might have ripened into a Bentley or a Porson. He had a foresight, when he opened his mouth, of all that he would say, and he marched straight to the conclusion. In debate, in the vestry of the Lyceum, the structure of his sentences was admirable; so neat, so natural, so terse, his words fell like stones; and often, though quite unconscious of it, his speech was a satire on the loose, voluminous, draggle-tail periods of other speakers. He sat down when he had done. A man of anecdote, his talk in the parlor was chiefly narrative. We remember the remark of a gentleman who listened with much delight to his conversation at the time when the Doctor was preparing to go to Baltimore and Washington, that "a man who could tell a story so well was company for kings and John Quincy Adams."

Sage and savage strove harder in him than in any of my acquaintances, each getting the mastery by turns, and pretty sudden turns: "Save us from the extremity of cold and these violent sudden changes." "The society will meet after the Lyceum, as it is difficult to bring people together in the evening,—and no moon." "Mr. N. F. is dead, and I expect to hear of the death of Mr. B. It is cruel to separate old people from their wives in this cold weather."

With a very limited acquaintance with books, his knowledge was an external experience, an Indian wisdom, the observation of such facts as country life for nearly a century could supply. He watched with interest the garden, the field, the orchard, the house and the barn, horse, cow, sheep and dog, and all the common objects that engage the thought of the farmer. He kept his eye on the horizon, and knew the weather like a sea-captain. The usual experiences of men, birth, marriage, sickness, death, burial; the common temptations; the common ambitions;—he studied them all, and sympathized so well in these that he was excellent company and counsel to all, even the most humble and ignorant. With extraordinary states of mind, with states of enthusiasm or enlarged speculation, he had no sympathy, and pretended to none. He was sincere, and kept to his point, and his mark was never remote. His conversation was strictly personal and apt to the party and the occasion. An eminent skill he had in saying difficult and unspeakable things; in delivering to a man or a woman that which all their other friends had abstained from saying, in uncovering the bandage from a sore place, and applying the surgeon's knife with a truly surgical spirit. Was a man a sot, or a spendthrift, or too long time a bachelor, or suspected of some hidden crime, or had he quarrelled with his wife, or collared his father, or was there any cloud or suspicious circumstances in his behavior, the good pastor knew his way straight to that point, believing himself entitled to a full explanation, and whatever relief to the conscience of both parties plain speech could effect was sure to be procured. In all such passages he justified himself to the conscience, and commonly to the love, of the persons concerned. He was the more competent to these searching discourses from his knowledge of family history. He knew everybody's grandfather, and seemed to address each person rather as the representative of his house and name, than as an individual. In him have perished more local and personal anecdotes of this village and vicinity than are possessed by any survivor. This intimate knowledge of families, and this skill of speech, and still more, his sympathy, made him incomparable in his parochial visits, and in his exhortations and prayers. He gave himself up to his feelings, and said on the instant the best things in the world. Many and many a felicity he had in his prayer, now forever lost, which defied all the rules of all the rhetoricians. He did not know when he was good in prayer or sermon, for he had no literature and no art; but he believed, and therefore spoke. He was eminently loyal in his nature, and not fond of adventure or innovation. By education, and still more by temperament, he was engaged to the old forms of the New England Church. Not speculative, but affectionate; devout, but with an extreme love of order, he adopted heartily, though in its mildest form, the creed and catechism of the fathers, and appeared a modern Israelite in his attachment to the Hebrew history and faith. He was a man very easy to read, for his whole life and conversation were consistent. All his opinions and actions might be securely predicted by a good observer on short acquaintance. My classmate at Cambridge, Frederick King, told me from Governor Gore, who was the Doctor's classmate, that in college he was called Holy Ripley.

And now, in his old age, when all the antique Hebraism and its customs are passing away, it is fit that he too should depart,—most fit that in the fall of laws a loyal man should die.

1841

## *From* NAPOLEON; OR, THE MAN OF THE WORLD

Among the eminent persons of the nineteenth century, Bonaparte is far the best known and the most powerful; and owes his predominance to the fidelity with which he expresses the tone of thought and belief, the aims of the masses of active and cultivated men. It is Swedenborg's theory that every organ is made up of homogeneous particles; or as it is sometimes expressed, every whole is made of similars; that is, the lungs are composed of infinitely small lungs; the liver, of infinitely small livers; the kidney, of little kidneys, etc. Following this analogy, if any man is found to carry with him the power and affections of vast numbers, if Napoleon is France, if Napoleon is Europe, it is because the people whom he sways are little Napoleons.

In our society there is a standing antagonism between the conservative and the democratic classes; between those who have made their fortunes, and the young and the poor who have fortunes to make; between the interests of dead labor,—that is, the labor of hands long ago still in the grave, which labor is now entombed in money stocks, or in land and buildings owned by idle capitalists,—and the interests of living labor, which seeks to possess itself of land and buildings and money stocks. The first class is timid, selfish, illiberal, hating innovation, and continually losing numbers by death. The second class is selfish also, encroaching, bold, self-relying, always outnumbering the other and recruiting its numbers every hour by births. It desires to keep open every avenue to the competition of all, and to multiply avenues: the class of business men in America, in England, in France and throughout Europe; the class of industry and skill. Napoleon is its representative. The instinct of active, brave, able men, throughout the middle class every where, has pointed out Napoleon as the incarnate Democrat. He had their virtues and their vices; above all, he had their spirit or aim. That tendency is material, pointing at a sensual success and employing the richest and most various means to that end; conversant with mechanical powers, highly intellectual, widely and accurately learned and skilful, but subordinating all intellectual and spiritual forces into means to a material success. To be the rich man is the end. "God has granted," says the Koran, "to every people a prophet in its own tongue." Paris and London and New York, the spirit of commerce, of money and material power, were also to have their prophet; and Bonaparte was qualified and sent.

Every one of the million readers of anecdotes or memoirs or lives of Napoleon delights in the page, because he studies in it his own history. Napoleon is thoroughly modern, and, at the highest point of his fortunes, has the very spirit of the newspapers. He is no saint,—to use his own word, "no capuchin," and he is no hero, in the high sense. The man in the street finds in him the qualities and powers of other men in the street. He finds him, like himself, by birth a citizen, who, by very intelligible merits, arrived at such a commanding position that he could indulge all those tastes which the common man possesses but is obliged to conceal and deny: good society, good books, fast travelling, dress, dinners, servants without number, personal weight, the execution of his ideas, the standing in the attitude of a benefactor to all persons about him, the refined enjoyments of pictures, statues, music, palaces, and conventional honors,—precisely what is agreeable to the heart of every man in the nineteenth century, this powerful man possessed. * * *

Bonaparte was the idol of common men because he had in transcendent degree the qualities and powers of common men. There is a certain satisfaction in coming down to the lowest ground of politics, for we get rid of cant and hypocrisy. Bonaparte wrought, in common with that great class he represented, for power and wealth,—but Bonaparte, specially, without any scruple as to the means. All the sentiments which embarrass men's pursuit of these objects, he set aside. The sentiments were for women and children. Fontanes, in 1804, expressed Napoleon's own sense, when in behalf of the Senate he addressed him,—"Sire, the desire of perfection is the worst disease that ever afflicted the human mind." The advocates of liberty and of progress are "ideologists;"—a word of contempt often in his mouth;—"Necker is an ideologist;" "Lafayette is an ideologist."

An Italian proverb, too well known, declares that "if you would succeed, you must not be too good." It is an advantage, within certain limits, to have renounced the dominion of the sentiments of piety, gratitude, and generosity; since what was an impassable bar to us, and still is to others, becomes a convenient weapon for our purposes; just as the river which was a formidable barrier, winter transforms into the smoothest of roads.

Napoleon renounced, once for all, sentiments and affections, and would help himself with his hands and his head. With him is no miracle and no magic. He is a worker in brass, in iron, in wood, in earth, in roads, in buildings, in money and in troops, and a very consistent and wise masterworkman. He is never weak and literary, but acts with the solidity and the precision of natural agents. He has not lost his native sense and sympathy with things. Men give way before such a man, as before natural events. To be sure there are men enough who are immersed in things, as farmers, smiths, sailors, and mechanics generally; and we know how real and solid such men appear in the presence of scholars and grammarians: but these men ordinarily lack the power of arrangement, and are like hands without a head. But Bonaparte superadded to this mineral and animal force, insight and generalization, so that men saw in him combined the natural and the intellectual power, as if the sea and land had taken flesh and begun to cipher. Therefore the land and sea seem to presuppose him. He came unto his own and they received him. This ciphering operative knows what he is working with and what is the product. He knew the properties of gold and iron, of wheels and ships, of troops and diplomatists, and required that each should do after its kind.

The art of war was the game in which he exerted his arithmetic. It consisted, according to him, in having always more forces than the enemy, on the point where the enemy is attacked, or where he attacks: and his whole talent is strained by endless manœuvre and evolution, to march always on the enemy at an angle, and destroy his forces in detail. It is obvious that a very small force, skillfully and rapidly manœuvring, so as always to bring two men against one at the point of engagement, will be an overmatch for a much larger body of men.

The times, his constitution, and his early circumstances combined to develop this pattern democrat. He had the virtues of his class and the conditions for their activity. That common-sense which no sooner respects any end than it finds the means to effect it; the delight in the use of means; in the choice, simplification, and combining of means; the directness and thoroughness of his work; the prudence with which all was seen and the energy with which all was done, make him the natural organ and head of what I may almost call, from its extent, the *modern* party.

Nature must have far the greatest share in every success, and so in his. Such a man was wanted, and such a man was born; a man of stone and iron, capable of sitting on horseback sixteen or seventeen hours, of going many days together without rest or food except by snatches, and with the speed and spring of a tiger in action; a man not embarrassed by any scruples; compact, instant, selfish, prudent, and of a perception which did not suffer itself to be baulked or misled by any pretences of others, or any superstition, or any heat or haste of his own. "My hand of iron," he said, "was not at the extremity of my arm, it was immediately connected with my head." He respected the power of nature and fortune, and ascribed to it his superiority, instead of valuing himself, like inferior men, on his opinionativeness, and waging war with nature. His favorite rhetoric lay in allusion to his star; and he pleased himself, as well as the people, when he styled himself the "Child of Destiny." "They charge me," he said, "with the commission of great crimes: men of my stamp do not commit crimes. Nothing has been more simple than my elevation, 'tis in vain to ascribe it to intrigue or crime; it was owing to the peculiarity of the times and to my reputation of having fought well against the enemies of my country. I have always marched with the opinion of great masses and with events. Of what use then would crimes be to me?" Again he said, speaking of his son, "My son cannot replace me; I could not replace myself. I am the creature of circumstances."

He had a directness of action never before combined with so much comprehension. He is a realist, terrific to all talkers and confused truth-obscuring persons. He sees where the matter hinges, throws himself on the precise point of resistance, and slights all other considerations. He is strong in the right manner, namely, by insight. He never blundered into victory, but won his battles in his head before he won them on the field. His principal means are in himself. He asks counsel of no other. In 1796 he writes to the Directory: "I have conducted the campaign without consulting any one. I should have done no good if I had been under the necessity of conforming to the notions of another person. I have gained some advantages over superior forces and when totally destitute of every thing, because, in the persuasion that your confidence was reposed in me, my actions were as prompt as my thoughts."

History is full, down to this day, of the imbecility of kings and governors. They are a class of persons much to be pitied, for they know not what they should do. The weavers strike for bread, and the king and his ministers, knowing not what to do, meet them with bayonets. But Napoleon understood his business. Here was a man who in each moment and emergency knew what to do next. It is an immense comfort and refreshment to the spirits, not only of kings, but of citizens. Few men have any next; they live from hand to mouth, without plan, and are ever at the end of their line, and after each action wait for an impulse from abroad. Napoleon had been the first man of the world, if his ends had been purely public. As he is, he inspires confidence and vigor by the extraordinary unity of his action. He is firm, sure, self-denying, self-postponing, sacrificing every thing,—money, troops, generals, and his own safety also, to his aim; not misled, like common adventurers, by the splendor of his own means. "Incidents ought not to govern policy," he said, "but policy, incidents." "To be hurried away by every event is to have no political system at all." His victories were only so many doors, and he never for a moment lost sight of his way onward, in the dazzle and uproar of the present circumstance. He knew what to do, and he flew to his mark. He would shorten a straight line to come at his object. Horrible anecdotes may no doubt be collected from his history, of the price at which he bought his successes; but he must not therefore be set down as cruel, but only as one who knew no impediment to his will; not bloodthirsty, not cruel, —but woe to what thing or person stood in his way! Not bloodthirsty, but not sparing of blood,—and pitiless. He saw only the object: the obstacle must give way. "Sire, General Clarke cannot combine with General Junot, for the dreadful fire of the Austrian battery."—"Let him carry the battery."—"Sire, every regiment that approaches the heavy artillery is sacrificed: Sire, what orders?"—"Forward, forward!" Seruzier, a colonel of artillery, gives in his "Military Memoirs" the following sketch of a scene after the battle of Austerlitz.—"At the moment in which the Russian army was making its retreat, painfully, but in good order, on the ice of the lake, the Emperor Napoleon came riding at full speed toward the artillery. 'You are losing time,' he cried; 'fire upon those masses; they must be engulfed: fire upon the ice!' The order remained unexecuted for ten minutes. In vain several officers and myself were placed on the slope of a hill to produce the effect: their balls and mine rolled upon the ice without breaking it up. Seeing that, I tried a simple method of elevating light howitzers. The almost perpendicular fall of the heavy projectiles produced the desired effect. My method was immediately followed by the adjoining batteries, and in less than no time we buried" some "thousands of Russians and Austrians under the waters of the lake."*

In the plenitude of his resources, every obstacle seemed to vanish. "There shall be no Alps," he said; and he built his perfect roads, climbing by graded galleries their steepest precipices, until Italy was as open to Paris as any town in France. He laid his bones to, and wrought for his crown. Having decided what was to be done, he did that with might and main. He put out all his strength. He risked every thing and spared

*As I quote at second hand, and cannot procure Seruzier, I dare not adopt the high figure I find. [Author's note.]

nothing, neither ammunition, nor money, nor troops, nor generals, nor himself.

We like to see every thing do its office after its kind, whether it be a milch-cow or a rattle-snake; and if fighting be the best mode of adjusting national differences (as large majorities of men seem to agree), certainly Bonaparte was right in making it thorough. The grand principle of war, he said, was that an army ought always to be ready, by day and by night and at all hours, to make all the resistance it is capable of making. He never economized his ammunition, but, on a hostile position, rained a torrent of iron,—shells, balls, grapeshot,—to annihilate all defence. On any point of resistance he concentrated squadron on squadron in overwhelming numbers until it was swept out of existence. To a regiment of horse-chasseurs at Lobenstein, two days before the battle of Jena, Napoleon said, "My lads, you must not fear death; when soldiers brave death, they drive him into the enemy's ranks." In the fury of assault, he no more spared himself. He went to the edge of his possibility. It is plain that in Italy he did what he could, and all that he could. He came, several times, within an inch of ruin; and his own person was all but lost. He was flung into the marsh at Arcola. The Austrians were between him and his troops, in the *mêlée,* and he was brought off with desperate efforts. At Lonato, and at other places, he was on the point of being taken prisoner. He fought sixty battles. He had never enough. Each victory was a new weapon. "My power would fall, were I not to support it by new achievements. Conquest has made me what I am, and conquest must maintain me." He felt, with every wise man, that as much life is needed for conservation as for creation. We are always in peril, always in a bad plight, just on the edge of destruction and only to be saved by invention and courage.

This vigor was guarded and tempered by the coldest prudence and punctuality. A thunderbolt in the attack, he was found invulnerable in his entrenchments. His very attack was never the inspiration of courage, but the result of calculation. His idea of the best defence consists in being still the attacking party. "My ambition," he says, "was great, but was of a cold nature." In one of his conversations with Las Casas, he remarked, "As to moral courage, I have rarely met with the two-o'clock-in-the-morning kind: I mean unprepared courage; that which is necessary on an unexpected occasion, and which, in spite of the most unforeseen events, leaves full freedom of judgment and decision:" and he did not hesitate to declare that he was himself eminently endowed with this two-o'clock-in-the-morning courage, and that he had met with few persons equal to himself in this respect.

Every thing depended on the nicety of his combinations, and the stars were not more punctual than his arithmetic. His personal attention descended to the smallest particulars. "At Montebello, I ordered Kellermann to attack with eight hundred horse, and with these he separated the six thousand Hungarian grenadiers, before the very eyes of the Austrian cavalry. This cavalry was half a league off, and required a quarter of an hour to arrive on the field of action, and I have observed that it is always these quarters of an hour that decide the fate of a battle." "Before he fought a battle, Bonaparte thought little about what he should do in case of success, but a great deal about what he should do in case of a reverse of fortune." The same prudence and good sense mark all his behavior. His instructions to his secretary at the Tuileries are worth remembering. "During the night, enter my chamber as seldom as possible. Do not awake me when you have any good news to communicate; with that there is no hurry. But when you bring bad news, rouse me instantly, for then there is not a moment to be lost." It was a whimsical economy of the same kind which dictated his practice, when general in Italy, in regard to his burdensome correspondence. He directed Bourrienne to leave all letters unopened for three weeks, and then observed with satisfaction how large a part of the correspondence had thus disposed of itself and no longer required an answer. His achievement of business was immense, and enlarges the known powers of man. There have been many working kings, from Ulysses to William of Orange, but none who accomplished a tithe of this man's performance. * * *

I call Napoleon the agent or attorney of the middle class of modern society; of the throng who fill the markets, shops, counting-houses, manufactories, ships, of the modern world, aiming to be rich. He was the agitator, the destroyer of prescription, the internal improver, the liberal, the radical, the inventor of means, the opener of doors and markets, the subverter of monopoly and abuse. Of course the rich and aristocratic did not like him. England, the centre of capital, and Rome and Austria, centres of tradition and genealogy, opposed him. The consternation of the dull and conservative classes, the terror of the foolish old men and old women of the Roman conclave, who in their despair took hold of any thing, and would cling to red-hot iron,—the vain attempts of statists to amuse and deceive him, of the emperor of Austria to bribe him; and the instinct of the young, ardent, and active men every where, which pointed him out as the giant of the middle class, make his history bright and commanding. He had the virtues of the masses of his constituents: he had also their vices. I am sorry that the brilliant picture has its reverse. But that is the fatal quality which we discover in our pursuit of wealth, that it is treacherous, and is bought by the breaking or weakening of the sentiments; and it is inevitable that we should find the same fact in the history of this champion, who proposed to himself simply a brilliant career, without any stipulation or scruple concerning the means.

Bonaparte was singularly destitute of generous sentiments. The highest-placed individual in the most cultivated age and population of the world,—he has not the merit of common truth and honesty. He is unjust to his generals; egotistic and monopolizing; meanly stealing the credit of their great actions from Kellermann, from Bernadotte; intriguing to involve his faithful Junot in hopeless bankruptcy, in order to drive him to a distance from Paris, because the familiarity of his manners offends the new pride of his throne. He is a boundless liar. The official paper, his "Moniteur," and all his bulletins, are proverbs for saying what he wished to be believed; and worse,—he sat, in his premature old age, in his lonely island, coldly falsifying facts and dates and characters, and giving to history a theatrical *éclat*. Like all Frenchmen he has a passion for stage effect. Every action that breathes of generosity is poisoned by this calculation. His star, his love of glory, his doctrine of the immortality of the soul, are all French. "I must dazzle and astonish. If I were to give the liberty of the press, my power could not last three days." To make a great noise is his favorite design. "A great reputation is a great noise: the more there is made, the farther off it is heard. Laws, institutions, monuments, nations, all fall; but the noise continues, and resounds in after ages." His doctrine of immortality is simply fame. His theory of influence is not flattering. "There are two levers for moving men,—interest and fear. Love is a silly infatuation, depend upon it. Friendship is but a name. I love nobody. I do not even love my brothers: perhaps Joseph a little, from habit, and because he is my elder; and Duroc, I love him too; but why?—because his character pleases me: he is stern and resolute, and I believe the fellow never shed a tear. For my part I know very well that I have no true friends. As long as I continue to be what I am, I may have as many pretended friends as I please. Leave sensibility to women; but men should be firm in heart and purpose, or they should have nothing to do with war and government." He was thoroughly unscrupulous. He would steal, slander, assassinate, drown, and poison, as his interest dictated. He had no generosity, but mere vulgar hatred; he was intensely selfish; he was perfidious; he cheated at cards; he was a prodigious gossip, and opened letters, and delighted in his infamous police, and rubbed his hands with joy when he had intercepted some morsel of intelligence concerning the men and women about him, boasting that "he knew everything;" and interfered with the cutting the dresses of the women; and listened after the hurrahs and the compliments of the street, incognito. His manners were coarse. He treated women with low familiarity. He had the habit of pulling their ears and pinching their cheeks when he was in good humor, and of pulling the ears and whiskers of men, and of striking and horse-play with them, to his last days. It does not appear that he listened at keyholes, or at least that he was caught at it. In short, when you have penetrated through all the circles of power and splendor, you were not dealing with a gentleman, at last; but with an impostor and a rogue; and he fully deserves the epithet of *Jupiter Scapin*, or a sort of Scamp Jupiter.

In describing the two parties into which modern society divides itself,—the democrat and the conservative,—I said, Bonaparte represents the democrat, or the party of men of business, against the stationary or conservative party. I omitted then to say, what is material to the statement, namely, that these two parties differ only as young and old. The democrat is a young conservative; the conservative is an old democrat. The aristocrat is the democrat ripe and gone to seed;—because both parties stand on the one ground of the supreme value of property, which one endeavors to get, and the other to keep. Bonaparte may be said to represent the whole history of this party, its youth and its age; yes, and with poetic justice its fate, in his own. The counter-revolution, the counter-party, still waits for its organ and representative, in a lover and a man of truly public and universal aims.

Here was an experiment, under the most favorable conditions, of the powers of intellect without conscience. Never was such a leader so endowed and so weaponed; never leader found such aids and followers. And what was the result of this vast talent and power, of these immense armies, burned cities, squandered treasures, immolated millions of men, of this demoralized Europe? It came to no result. All passed away like the smoke of his artillery, and left no trace. He left France smaller, poorer, feebler, than he found it; and the whole contest for freedom was to be begun again. The attempt was in principle suicidal. France served him with life and limb and estate, as long as it could identify its interest with him; but when men saw that after victory was another war; after the destruction of armies, new conscriptions; and they who had toiled so desperately were never nearer to the reward,—they could not spend what they had earned, nor repose on their down-beds, nor strut in their chateaux,—they deserted him. Men found that his absorbing egotism was deadly to all other men. It resembled the torpedo, which inflicts a succession of shocks on any one who takes hold of it, producing spasms which contract the muscles of the hand, so that the man cannot open his fingers; and the animal inflicts new and more violent shocks, until he paralyzes and kills his victim. So this exorbitant egotist narrowed, impoverished, and absorbed the power and existence of those who served him; and the universal cry of France and of Europe in 1814 was, "Enough of him;" "*Assez de Bonaparte.*"

It was not Bonaparte's fault. He did all that in him lay to live and thrive without moral principle. It was the nature of things, the eternal law of man and of the world which baulked and ruined him; and the result, in a million experiments, will be the same. Every experiment, by multitudes or by individuals, that has a sensual and selfish aim, will fail. The pacific Fourier will be as inefficient as the pernicious Napoleon. As long as our civilization is essentially one of property, of fences, of exclusiveness, it will be mocked by delusions. Our riches will leave us sick; there will be bitterness in our laughter, and our wine will burn our mouth. Only that good profits which we can taste with all doors open and which serves all men.

1850

## *ENGLISH TRAITS*

### VIII. CHARACTER

The English race are reputed morose. I do not know that they have sadder brows than their neighbors of northern climates. They are sad by comparison with the singing and dancing nations: not sadder, but slow and staid, as finding their joys at home. They, too, believe that where there is no enjoyment of life there can be no vigor and art in speech or thought; that your merry heart goes all the way, your sad one tires in a mile. This trait of gloom has been fixed on them by French travellers, who, from Froissart, Voltaire, Le Sage, Mirabeau, down to the lively journalists of the *feuilletons,* have spent their wit on the solemnity of their neighbors. The French say, gay conversation is unknown in their island. The Englishman finds no relief from reflection, except in reflection. When he wishes for amusement, he goes to work. His hilarity is like an attack of fever. Religion, the theatre and the reading the books of his country all feed and increase his natural melancholy. The police does not interfere with public diversions. It thinks itself bound in duty to respect the pleasures and rare gayety of this inconsolable nation; and their well-known courage is entirely attributable to their disgust of life.

I suppose their gravity of demeanor and their few words have obtained this reputation. As compared with the Americans, I think them cheerful and contented. Young people in our country are much more prone to melancholy. The English have a mild aspect and a ringing cheerful voice. They are large-natured and not so easily amused as the southerners, and are among them as grown people among children, requiring war, or trade, or engineering, or science, instead of frivolous games. They are proud and private, and even if disposed to recreation, will avoid an open garden. They sported sadly; *ils s'amusaient tristement, selon la coutume de leur pays,* said Froissart; and I suppose never nation built their party-walls so thick, or their garden-fences so high. Meat and wine produce no effect on them. They are just as cold, quiet and composed, at the end, as at the beginning of dinner.

The reputation of taciturnity they have enjoyed for six or seven hundred years; and a kind of pride in bad public speaking is noted in the House of Commons, as if they were willing to show that they did not live by their tongues, or thought they spoke well enough if they had the tone of gentlemen. In mixed company they shut their mouths. A Yorkshire mill-owner told me he had ridden more than once all the way from London to Leeds, in the first-class carriage, with the same persons, and no word exchanged. The club-houses were established to cultivate social habits, and it is rare that more than two eat together, and oftenest one eats alone. Was it then a stroke of humor in the serious Swedenborg, or was it only his pitiless logic, that made him shut up the English souls in a heaven by themselves?

They are contradictorily described as sour, splenetic, and stubborn,—and as mild, sweet, and sensible. The truth is they have great range and variety of character. Commerce sends abroad multitudes of different classes. The choleric Welshman, the fervid Scot, the bilious resident in the East or West Indies, are wide of the perfect behavior of the educated and dignified man of family. So is the burly farmer; so is the country squire, with his narrow and violent life. In every inn is the Commercial-Room, in which 'travellers,' or bagmen who carry patterns, and solicit orders for the manufacturers, are wont to be entertained. It easily happens that this class should characterize England to the foreigner, who meets them on the road and at every public house, whilst the gentry avoid the taverns, or seclude themselves whilst in them.

But these classes are the right English stock, and may fairly show the national qualities, before yet art and education have dealt with them. They are good lovers, good haters, slow but obstinate admirers, and in all things very much steeped in their temperament, like men hardly awaked from deep sleep, which they enjoy. Their habits and instincts cleave to nature. They are of the earth, earthy; and of the sea, as the sea-kinds, attached to it for what it yields them, and not from any sentiment. They are full of coarse strength, rude exercise, butcher's meat and sound sleep; and suspect any poetic insinuation or any hint for the conduct of life which reflects on this animal existence, as if somebody were fumbling at the umbilical cord and might stop their supplies. They doubt a man's sound judgment if he does not eat with appetite, and shake their heads if he is particularly chaste. Take them as they come, you shall find in the common people a surly indifference, sometimes gruffness and ill temper; and in minds of more power, magazines of inexhaustible war, challenging

The ruggedest hour that time and spite
 dare bring
To frown upon the enraged Northum-
 berland.

They are headstrong believers and defenders of their opinion, and not less resolute in maintaining their whim and perversity. Hezekiah Woodward wrote a book against the Lord's Prayer. And one can believe that Burton, the Anatomist of Melancholy, having predicted from the stars the hour of his death, slipped the knot himself round his own neck, not to falsify his horoscope.

Their looks bespeak an invincible stoutness: they have extreme difficulty to run away, and will die game. Wellington said of the young coxcombs of the Life-Guards, delicately brought up, "But the puppies fight well;" and Nelson said of his sailors, "They really mind shot no more than peas." Of absolute stoutness no nation has more or better examples. They are good at storming redoubts, at boarding frigates, at dying in the last ditch, or any desperate service which has daylight and honor in it; but not, I think, at enduring the rack, or any passive obedience, like jumping off a castle-roof at the word of a czar. Being both vascular and highly organized, so as to be very sensible of pain; and intellectual so as to see reason and glory in a matter.

Of that constitutional force which yields the supplies of the day, they have the more than enough; the excess which creates courage on fortitude, genius in poetry, invention in mechanics, enterprise in trade, magnificence in wealth, splendor in ceremonies, petulance and projects in youth. The young men have a rude health which runs into peccant humors. They drink brandy like water, cannot expend their quantities of waste strength on riding, hunting, swimming, and fencing, and run into absurd frolics with the gravity of the Eumenides. They stoutly carry into every nook and corner of the earth their turbulent sense; leaving no lie uncontradicted; no pretension unexamined. They chew hasheesh; cut themselves with poisoned creases; swing their hammock in the boughs of the Bohon Upas; taste every poison; buy every secret; at Naples they put St. Januarius's blood in an alembic; they saw a hole into the head of the "winking Virgin," to know why she winks; measure with an English footrule every cell of the Inquisition, every Turkish caaba, every Holy of holies; translate and send to Bentley the arcanum bribed and bullied away from shuddering Bramins; and measure their own strength by the terror they cause. These travellers are of every class, the best and the worst; and it may easily happen that those of rudest behavior are taken notice of and remembered. The Saxon melancholy in the vulgar rich and poor appears as gushes of ill-humor, which every check exasperates into sarcasm and vituperation. There are multitudes of rude young English who have the self-sufficiency and bluntness of their nation, and who, with their disdain of the rest of mankind and with this indigestion and choler, have made the English traveller a proverb for uncomfortable and offensive manners. It was no bad description of the Briton generically, what was said two hundred years ago of one particular Oxford scholar: "He was a very bold man, uttered anything that came into his mind, not only among his companions, but in public coffee-houses, and would often speak his mind of particular persons then accidentally present, without examining the company he was in; for which he was often reprimanded and several times threatened to be kicked and beaten."

The common Englishman is prone to forget a cardinal article in the bill of social rights, that every man has a right to his own ears. No man can claim to usurp more than a few cubic feet of the audibilities of a public room, or to put upon the company with the loud statement of his crotchets or personalities.

But it is in the deep traits of race that the fortunes of nations are written, and however derived,—whether a happier tribe or mixture of tribes, the air, or what circumstance that mixed for them the golden mean of temperament,—here exists the best stock in the world, broad-fronted, broad-bottomed, best for depth, range and equability; men of aplomb and reserves, great range and many moods, strong instincts, yet apt for culture; war-class as well as clerks; earls and tradesmen; wise minority, as well as foolish majority; abysmal temperament, hiding wells of wrath, and glooms on which no sunshine settles, alternated with a common sense and humanity which hold them fast to every piece of cheerful duty; making this temperament a sea to which all storms are superficial; a race to which their fortunes flow, as if they alone had the elastic organization at once fine and robust enough for dominion; as if the burly inexpressive, now mute and contumacious, now fierce and sharp-tongued dragon, which once made the island light with his fiery breath, had bequeathed his ferocity to his conqueror. They hide virtues under vices, or the semblance of them.

It is the misshapen hairy Scandinavian troll again, who lifts the cart out of the mire, or threshes

> The corn
> That ten day-laborers could not end,

but it is done in the dark, and with muttered maledictions. He is a churl with a soft place in his heart, whose speech is a brash of bitter waters, but who loves to help you at a pinch. He says no, and serves you, and your thanks disgust him. Here was lately a cross-grained miser, odd and ugly, resembling in countenance the portrait of Punch with the laugh left out; rich by his own industry; sulking in a lonely house; who never gave a dinner to any man and disdained all courtesies; yet as true a worshipper of beauty in form and color as ever existed, and profusely pouring over the cold mind of his countrymen creations of grace and truth, removing the reproach of sterility from English art, catching from their savage climate every fine hint, and importing into their galleries every tint and trait of sunnier cities and skies; making an era in painting; and when he saw that the splendor of one of his pictures in the Exhibition dimmed his rival's that hung next it, secretly took a brush and blackened his own.

They do not wear their heart in their sleeve for daws to peck at. They have that phlegm or staidness which it is a compliment to disturb. "Great men," said Aristotle, "are always of a nature originally melancholy." 'Tis the habit of a mind which attaches to abstractions with a passion which gives vast results. They dare to displease, they do not speak to expectation. They like the sayers of No, better than the sayers of Yes. Each of them has an opinion which he feels it becomes him to express all the more that it differs from yours. They are meditating opposition. This gravity is inseparable from minds of great resources.

There is an English hero superior to the French, the German, the Italian, or the Greek. When he is brought to the strife with fate, he sacrifices a richer material possession, and on more purely metaphysical grounds. He is there with his own consent, face to face with fortune, which he defies. On deliberate choice and from grounds of character, he has elected his part to live and die for, and dies with grandeur. This race has added new elements to humanity and has a deeper root in the world.

They have great range of scale, from ferocity to exquisite refinement. With larger scale, they have great retrieving power. After running each tendency to an extreme, they try another tack with equal heat. More intellectual than other races, when they live with other races they do not take their language, but bestow their own. They subsidize other nations, and are not subsidized. They proselyte, and are not proselyted. They assimilate other races to themselves, and are not assimilated. The English did not calculate the conquest of the Indies. It fell to their character. So they administer in different parts of the world, the codes of every empire and race; in Canada, old French law; in the Mauritius, the Code Napoléon; in the West Indies, the edicts of the Spanish Cortes; in the East Indies, the Laws of Menu; in the Isle of Man, of the Scandinavian Thing; at the Cape of Good Hope, of the old Netherlands; and in the Ionian Islands, the Pandects of Justinian.

They are very conscious of their advantageous position in history. England is the law-giver, the patron, the instructor, the ally. Compare the tone of the French and of the English press: the first querulous, captious, sensitive about English opinion; the English press never timorous about French opinion, but arrogant and contemptuous.

They are testy and headstrong through an excess of will and bias; churlish as men sometimes please to be who do not forget a debt, who ask no favors and who will do what they like with their own. With education and intercourse these asperities wear off and leave the good-will pure. If anatomy is reformed according to national tendencies, I suppose the spleen will hereafter be found in the Englishman, not found in the American, and differencing the one from the other. I anticipate another anatomical discovery, that this organ will be found to be cortical and caducous; that they are superficially morose, but at last tender-hearted, herein differing from Rome and the Latin nations. Nothing savage, nothing mean resides in the English heart. They are subject to panics of credulity and of rage, but the temper of the nation, however disturbed, settles itself soon and easily, as, in this temperate zone, the sky after whatever storms clears again, and serenity is its normal condition.

A saving stupidity masks and protects their perception, as the curtain of the eagle's eye. Our swifter Americans, when they first deal with English, pronounce them stupid; but, later, do them justice as people who wear well, or hide their strength. To understand the power of performance that is in their finest wits, in the patient Newton, or in the versatile transcendent poets, or in the Dugdales, Gibbons, Hallams, Eldons and Peels, one should see how English day-laborers hold out. High and low, they are of an unctuous texture. There is an adipocere in their constitution, as if they had oil also for their mental wheels and could perform vast amounts of work without damaging themselves.

Even the scale of expense on which people live, and to which scholars and professional men conform, proves the tension of their muscle, when vast numbers are found who can each lift this enormous load. I might even add, their daily feasts argue a savage vigor of body.

No nation was ever so rich in able men; "Gentlemen," as Charles I. said of Strafford, "whose abilities might make a prince rather afraid than ashamed in the greatest affairs of state;" men of such temper, that, like Baron Vere, "had one seen him returning from a victory, he would by his silence have suspected that he had lost the day; and, had he beheld him in a retreat, he would have collected him a conqueror by the cheerfulness of his spirit."

The following passage from the "Heimskringla" might almost stand as a portrait of the modern Englishman:—"Haldor was very stout and strong and remarkably handsome in appearances. King Harold gave him this testimony, that he, among all his men, cared least about doubtful circumstances, whether they betokened danger or pleasure; for whatever turned up, he was never in higher nor in lower spirits, never slept less nor more on account of them, nor ate nor drank but according to his custom. Haldor was not a man of many words, but short in conversation, told his opinion bluntly and was obstinate and hard: and this could not please the king, who had many clever people about him, zealous in his service. Haldor remained a short time with the king, and then came to Iceland, where he took up his abode in Hiardaholt and dwelt in that farm to a very advanced age."

The national temper, in the civil history, is not flashy or whiffling. The slow, deep English mass smoulders with fire, which at last sets all its borders in flame. The wrath of London is not French wrath, but has a long memory, and, in its hottest heat, a register and rule.

Half their strength they put not forth. They are capable of a sublime resolution, and if hereafter the war of races, often predicted, and making itself a war of opinions also (a question of despotism and liberty coming from Eastern Europe), should menace the English civilization, these sea-kings may take once again to their floating castles and find a new home and a second millennium of power in their colonies.

The stability of England is the security of the modern world. If the English race were as mutable as the French, what reliance? But the English stand for liberty. The conservative, money-loving, lord-loving English are yet liberty-loving; and so freedom is safe: for they have more personal force than any other people. The nation always resist the immoral action of their government. They think humanely on the affairs of France, of Turkey, of Poland, of Hungary, of Schleswig Holstein, though over-borne by the statecraft of the rulers at last.

Does the early history of each tribe show the permanent bias, which, though not less potent, is masked as the tribe spreads its activity into colonies, commerce, codes, arts, letters? The early history shows it, as the musician plays the air which he proceeds to conceal in a tempest of variations. In Alfred, in the Northmen, one may read the genius of the English society, namely, that private life is the place of honor. Glory, a career, and ambition, words familiar to the longitude of Paris, are seldom heard in English speech. Nelson wrote from their hearts his homely telegraph, "England expects every man to do his duty."

For actual service, for the dignity of a profession, or to appease diseased or inflamed talent, the army and navy may be entered (the worst boys doing well in the navy); and the civil service in departments where serious official work is done; and they hold in esteem the barrister engaged in the severer studies of the law. But the calm, sound and most British Briton shrinks from public life as charlatanism, and respects an economy founded on agriculture, coal-mines, manufactures or trade, which secures an independence through the creation of real values.

They wish neither to command nor obey, but to be kings in their own houses. They are intellectual and deeply enjoy literature; they like well to have the world served up to them in books, maps, models, and every mode of exact information, and, though not creators in art, they value its refinement. They are ready for leisure, can direct and fill their own day, nor need so much as others the constraint of a necessity. But the history of the nation discloses, at every turn, this original predilection for private independence, and however this inclination may have been disturbed by the bribes with which their vast colonial power has warped men out of orbit, the inclination endures, and forms and reforms the laws, letters, manners, and occupations. They choose that welfare which is compatible with the commonwealth, knowing that such alone is stable; as wise merchants prefer investments in the three per cents.

1856

## CONCORD HYMN

SUNG AT THE COMPLETION OF THE BATTLE MONUMENT, JULY 4, 1837

By the rude bridge that arched the flood,
  Their flag to April's breeze unfurled,
Here once the embattled farmers stood
  And fired the shot heard round the world.

The foe long since in silence slept;
  Alike the conqueror silent sleeps;
And Time the ruined bridge has swept
  Down the dark stream which seaward creeps.

On this green bank, by this soft stream,
  We set to-day a votive stone;
That memory may their deed redeem,
  When, like our sires, our sons are gone.

Spirit, that made those heroes dare
  To die, and leave their children free,
Bid Time and Nature gently spare
  The shaft we raise to them and thee.

(1837) 1837

## EACH AND ALL

Little thinks, in the field, yon red-cloaked clown
Of thee from the hill-top looking down;
The heifer that lows in the upland farm,
Far-heard, lows not thine ear to charm;
The sexton, tolling his bell at noon,
Deems not that great Napoleon
Stops his horse, and lists with delight,
Whilst his files sweep round yon Alpine height;
Nor knowest thou what argument
Thy life to thy neighbor's creed has lent.
All are needed by each one;
Nothing is fair or good alone.
I thought the sparrow's note from heaven,
Singing at dawn on the alder bough;
I brought him home, in his nest, at even;
He sings the song, but it cheers not now,
For I did not bring home the river and sky;—
He sang to my ear,—they sang to my eye.
The delicate shells lay on the shore;
The bubbles of the latest wave
Fresh pearls to their enamel gave,
And the bellowing of the savage sea
Greeted their safe escape to me.
I wiped away the weeds and foam,
I fetched my sea-born treasures home;
But the poor, unsightly, noisome things

Had left their beauty on the shore
With the sun and the sand and the
wild uproar.
The lover watched his graceful maid,
As 'mid the virgin train she strayed,
Nor knew her beauty's best attire
Was woven still by the snow-white
choir.
At last she came to his hermitage,
Like the bird from the woodlands to
the cage;—
The gay enchantment was undone,
A gentle wife, but fairy none.
Then I said, 'I covet truth;
Beauty is unripe childhood's cheat;
I leave it behind with the games of
youth:'—
As I spoke, beneath my feet
The ground-pine curled its pretty
wreath,
Running over the club-moss burrs;
I inhaled the violet's breath;
Around me stood the oaks and firs;
Pine-cones and acorns lay on the
ground;
Over me soared the eternal sky,
Full of light and of deity;
Again I saw, again I heard,
The rolling river, the morning bird;—
Beauty through my senses stole;
I yielded myself to the perfect whole.
(*c.* 1835) 1839

## THE HUMBLE-BEE

Burly, dozing humble-bee,
Where thou art is clime for me.
Let them sail for Porto Rique,
Far-off heats through seas to seek;
I will follow thee alone,
Thou animated torrid-zone!
Zigzag steerer, desert cheerer,
Let me chase thy waving lines;
Keep me nearer, me thy hearer,
Singing over shrubs and vines.

Insect lover of the sun,
Joy of thy dominion!
Sailor of the atmosphere;
Swimmer through the waves of air;
Voyager of light and noon;
Epicurean of June;
Wait, I prithee, till I come
Within earshot of thy hum,—
All without is martyrdom.

When the south wind, in May days,
With a net of shining haze
Silvers the horizon wall,
And with softness touching all,
Tints the human countenance
With a color of romance,
And infusing subtle heats,
Turns the sod to violets,
Thou, in sunny solitudes,
Rover of the underwoods,
The green silence dost displace
With thy mellow, breezy bass.

Hot midsummer's petted crone,
Sweet to me thy drowsy tone
Tells of countless sunny hours,
Long days, and solid banks of flowers;
Of gulfs of sweetness without bound
In Indian wildernesses found;
Of Syrian peace, immortal leisure,
Firmest cheer, and bird-like pleasure.

Aught unsavory or unclean
Hath my insect never seen;
But violets and bilberry bells,
Maple-sap and daffodels,
Grass with green flag half-mast high,
Succory to match the sky,
Columbine with horn of honey,
Scented fern, and agrimony,
Clover, catchfly, adder's-tongue
And brier-roses, dwelt among;
All beside was unknown waste,
All was picture as he passed.

Wiser far than human seer,
Yellow-breeched philosopher!
Seeing only what is fair,
Sipping only what is sweet,
Thou dost mock at fate and care,
Leave the chaff, and take the wheat.
When the fierce northwestern blast
Cools sea and land so far and fast,
Thou already slumberest deep;

Woe and want thou canst outsleep;
Want and woe, which torture us,
Thy sleep makes ridiculous.
(1837) 1839

## THE RHODORA:

### ON BEING ASKED, WHENCE IS THE FLOWER?

In May, when sea-winds pierced our solitudes,
I found the fresh Rhodora in the woods,
Spreading its leafless blooms in a damp nook,
To please the desert and the sluggish brook.
The purple petals, fallen in the pool,
Made the black water with their beauty gay;
Here might the red-bird come his plumes to cool,
And court the flower that cheapens his array.

Rhodora! if the sages ask thee why
This charm is wasted on the earth and sky,
Tell them, dear, that if eyes were made for seeing,
Then Beauty is its own excuse for being:
Why thou wert there, O rival of the rose!
I never thought to ask, I never knew:
But, in my simple ignorance, suppose
The self-same Power that brought me there brought you.
(1834) 1839

## THE PROBLEM

I like a church; I like a cowl;
I love a prophet of the soul;
And on my heart monastic aisles
Fall like sweet strains, or pensive smiles;
Yet not for all his faith can see
Would I that cowlèd churchman be.

Why should the vest on him allure,
Which I could not on me endure?

Not from a vain or shallow thought
His awful Jove young Phidias brought;
Never from lips of cunning fell
The thrilling Delphic oracle;
Out from the heart of nature rolled
The burdens of the Bible old;
The litanies of nations came,
Like the volcano's tongue of flame,
Up from the burning core below,—
The canticles of love and woe:
The hand that rounded Peter's dome
And groined the aisles of Christian Rome
Wrought in a sad sincerity;
Himself from God he could not free;
He builded better than he knew;—
The conscious stone to beauty grew.

Know'st thou what wove yon wood-bird's nest
Of leaves, and feathers from her breast?
Or how the fish outbuilt her shell,
Painting with morn each annual cell?
Or how the sacred pine-tree adds
To her old leaves new myriads?
Such and so grew these holy piles,
Whilst love and terror laid the tiles.
Earth proudly wears the Parthenon,
As the best gem upon her zone,
And Morning opes with haste her lids
To gaze upon the Pyramids;
O'er England's abbeys bends the sky,
As on its friends, with kindred eye;
For out of Thought's interior sphere
These wonders rose to upper air;
And Nature gladly gave them place,
Adopted them into her race,
And granted them an equal date
With Andes and with Ararat.

These temples grew as grows the grass;
Art might obey, but not surpass.
The passive Master lent his hand
To the vast soul that o'er him planned;

And the same power that reared the shrine
Bestrode the tribes that knelt within.
Ever the fiery Pentecost
Girds with one flame the countless host,
Trances the heart through chanting choirs,
And through the priest the mind inspires.
The word upon the prophet spoken
Was writ on tables yet unbroken;
The word by seers or sibyls told,
In groves of oak, or fanes of gold,
Still floats upon the morning wind,
Still whispers to the willing mind.
One accent of the Holy Ghost
The heedless world hath never lost.
I know what say the fathers wise,—
The Book itself before me lies,
Old *Chrysostom,* best Augustine,
And he who blent both in his line,
The younger *Golden Lips* or mines,
Taylor, the Shakspeare of divines,
His words are music in my ear,
I see his cowlèd portrait dear;
And yet, for all his faith could see,
I would not the good bishop be.
(1839) 1840

## *From* WOODNOTES

### I

#### 1

When the pine tosses its cones
To the song of its waterfall tones,
Who speeds to the woodland walks?
To birds and trees who talks?
Cæsar of his leafy Rome,
There the poet is at home.
He goes to the river-side,—
Not hook nor line hath he;
He stands in the meadows wide,—
Nor gun nor scythe to see.
Sure some god his eye enchants:
What he knows nobody wants.
In the wood he travels glad,
Without better fortune had,
Melancholy without bad.
Knowledge this man prizes best
Seems fantastic to the rest:
Pondering shadows, colors, clouds,
Grass-buds and caterpillar-shrouds,
Boughs on which the wild bees settle,
Tints that spot the violet's petal,
Why Nature loves the number five,
And why the star-form she repeats:
Lover of all things alive,
Wonderer at all he meets,
Wonderer chiefly at himself,
Who can tell him what he is?
Or how meet in human elf
Coming and past eternities?

#### 2

And such I knew, a forest seer,
A minstrel of the natural year,
Foreteller of the vernal ides,
Wise harbinger of spheres and tides,
A lover true, who knew by heart
Each joy the mountain dales impart;
It seemed that Nature could not raise
A plant in any secret place,
In quaking bog, on snowy hill,
Beneath the grass that shades the rill,
Under the snow, between the rocks,
In damp fields known to bird and fox.
But he would come in the very hour
It opened in its virgin bower,
As if a sunbeam showed the place,
And tell its long-descended race.
It seemed as if the breezes brought him,
It seemed as if the sparrows taught him;
As if by secret sight he knew
Where, in far fields, the orchis grew.
Many haps fall in the field
Seldom seen by wishful eyes,
But all her shows did Nature yield,
To please and win this pilgrim wise.
He saw the partridge drum in the woods;
He heard the woodcock's evening hymn;
He found the tawny thrushes' broods;
And the shy hawk did wait for him;
What others did at distance hear,

And guessed within the thicket's gloom,
Was shown to this philosopher,
And at his bidding seemed to come.

3

In unploughed Maine he sought the lumberers' gang
Where from a hundred lakes young rivers sprang;
He trode the unplanted forest floor, whereon
The all-seeing sun for ages hath not shone;
Where feeds the moose, and walks the surly bear,
And up the tall mast runs the woodpecker.
He saw beneath dim aisles, in odorous beds,
The slight Linnæa hang its twin-born heads,
And blessed the monument of the man of flowers,
Which breathes his sweet fame through the northern bowers.
He heard, when in the grove, at intervals,
With sudden roar the aged pine-tree falls,—
One crash, the death-hymn of the perfect tree,
Declares the close of its green century.
Low lies the plant to whose creation went
Sweet influence from every element;
Whose living towers the years conspired to build,
Whose giddy top the morning loved to gild.
Through these green tents, by eldest Nature dressed,
He roamed, content alike with man and beast.
Where darkness found him he lay glad at night;
There the red morning touched him with its light.
Three moons his great heart him a hermit made,
So long he roved at will the boundless shade.
The timid it concerns to ask their way,
And fear what foe in caves and swamps can stray,
To make no step until the event is known,
And ills to come as evils past bemoan.
Not so the wise; no coward watch he keeps
To spy what danger on his pathway creeps;
Go where he will, the wise man is at home,
His hearth the earth,—his hall the azure dome;
Where his clear spirit leads him, there's his road
By God's own light illumined and foreshowed.

4

'Twas one of the charmèd days
When the genius of God doth flow;
The wind may alter twenty ways,
A tempest cannot blow;
It may blow north, it still is warm;
Or south, it still is clear;
Or east, it smells like a clover-farm;
Or west, no thunder fear.
The musing peasant, lowly great,
Beside the forest water sate;
The rope-like pine-roots crosswise grown
Composed the network of his throne;
The wide lake, edged with sand and grass,
Was burnished to a floor of glass,
Painted with shadows green and proud
Of the tree and of the cloud.
He was the heart of all the scene;
On him the sun looked more serene;
To hill and cloud his face was known,—
It seemed the likeness of their own;
They knew by secret sympathy
The public child of earth and sky.
'You ask,' he said, 'what guide

Me through trackless thickets led,
Through thick-stemmed woodlands rough and wide.
I found the water's bed.
The watercourses were my guide;
I travelled grateful by their side,
Or through their channel dry;
They led me through the thicket damp,
Through brake and fern, the beavers' camp,
Through beds of granite cut my road,
And their resistless friendship showed.
The falling waters led me,
The foodful waters fed me,
And brought me to the lowest land,
Unerring to the ocean sand.
The moss upon the forest bark
Was pole-star when the night was dark;
The purple berries in the wood
Supplied me necessary food;
For Nature ever faithful is
To such as trust her faithfulness.
When the forest shall mislead me,
When the night and morning lie,
When sea and land refuse to feed me,
'T will be time enough to die;
Then will yet my mother yield
A pillow in her greenest field,
Nor the June flowers scorn to cover
The clay of their departed lover.'

1840

## THE SNOW-STORM

Announced by all the trumpets of the sky,
Arrives the snow, and, driving o'er the fields,
Seems nowhere to alight: the whited air
Hides hills and woods, the river, and the heaven,
And veils the farm-house at the garden's end.
The sled and traveller stopped, the courier's feet
Delayed, all friends shut out, the housemates sit
Around the radiant fireplace, enclosed
In a tumultuous privacy of storm.

Come see the north wind's masonry.
Out of an unseen quarry evermore
Furnished with tile, the fierce artificer
Curves his white bastions with projected roof
Round every windward stake, or tree, or door.
Speeding, the myriad-handed, his wild work
So fanciful, so savage, nought cares he
For number or proportion. Mockingly,
On coop or kennel he hangs Parian wreaths;
A swan-like form invests the hidden thorn;
Fills up the farmer's lane from wall to wall,
Maugre the farmer's sighs; and at the gate
A tapering turret overtops the work.
And when his hours are numbered, and the world
Is all his own, retiring, as he were not,
Leaves, when the sun appears, astonished Art
To mimic in slow structures, stone by stone,
Built in an age, the mad wind's night-work,
The frolic architecture of the snow.

1841

## COMPENSATION

The wings of Time are black and white,
Pied with morning and with night.
Mountain tall and ocean deep
Trembling balance duly keep.
In changing moon, in tidal wave,
Glows the feud of Want and Have.
Gauge of more and less through space,

Electric star or pencil plays,
The lonely Earth amid the balls
That hurry through the eternal halls,
A makeweight flying to the void,
Supplemental asteroid,
Or compensatory spark,
Shoots across the neutral Dark.

Man's the elm, and Wealth the vine;
Stanch and strong the tendrils twine:
Though the frail ringlets thee deceive,
None from its stock that vine can reave.
Fear not, then, thou child infirm,
There's no god dare wrong a worm;
Laurel crowns cleave to deserts,
And power to him who power exerts.
Hast not thy share? On winged feet,
Lo! it rushes thee to meet;
And all that Nature made thy own,
Floating in air or pent in stone,
Will rive the hills and swim the sea
And, like thy shadow, follow thee.

1841

## FORBEARANCE

Hast thou named all the birds without a gun?
Loved the wood-rose, and left it on its stalk?
At rich men's tables eaten bread and pulse?
Unarmed, faced danger with a heart of trust?
And loved so well a high behavior,
In man or maid, that thou from speech refrained,
Nobility more nobly to repay?
O, be my friend, and teach me to be thine!

1842

## POLITICS

Gold and iron are good
To buy iron and gold;
All earth's fleece and food
For their like are sold.
Boded Merlin wise,
Proved Napoleon great,
Nor kind nor coinage buys
Aught above its rate.
Fear, Craft and Avarice
Cannot rear a State.
Out of dust to build
What is more than dust,—
Walls Amphion piled
Phœbus stablish must.
When the Muses nine
With the Virtues meet,
Find to their design
An Atlantic seat,
By green orchard boughs
Fended from the heat,
Where the statesman plows
Furrow for the wheat,—
When the Church is social worth,
When the state-house is the hearth,
Then the perfect State is come,
The republican at home.

1844

## CHARACTER

The sun set, but set not his hope:
Stars rose; his faith was earlier up:
Fixed on the enormous galaxy,
Deeper and older seemed his eye;
And matched his sufferance sublime
The taciturnity of time.
He spoke, and words more soft than rain
Brought the Age of Gold again:
His action won such reverence sweet
As hid all measure of the feat.

1844

## FABLE

The mountain and the squirrel
Had a quarrel,
And the former called the latter 'Little Prig;'
Bun replied,
'You are doubtless very big;
But all sorts of things and weather

Must be taken in together,
To make up a year
And a sphere.
And I think it no disgrace
To occupy my place.
If I'm not so large as you,
You are not so small as I,
And not half so spry.
I'll not deny you make
A very pretty squirrel track;
Talents differ; all is well and wisely put;
If I cannot carry forests on my back,
Neither can you crack a nut.'

(*ca.* 1845) 1845

## URIEL

It fell in the ancient periods
 Which the brooding soul surveys,
Or ever the wild Time coined itself
 Into calendar months and days.

This was the lapse of Uriel,
Which in Paradise befell.
Once, among the Pleiads walking,
Seyd overheard the young gods talking;
And the treason, too long pent,
To his ears was evident.
The young deities discussed
Laws of form, and metre just,
Orb, quintessence, and sunbeams,
What subsisteth, and what seems.
One, with low tones that decide,
And doubt and reverend use defied,
With a look that solved the sphere,
And stirred the devils everywhere,
Gave his sentiment divine
Against the being of a line.
'Line in nature is not found;
Unit and universe are round;
In vain produced, all rays return;
Evil will bless, and ice will burn.'
As Uriel spoke with piercing eye,
A shudder ran around the sky;
The stern old war-gods shook their heads,
The seraphs frowned from myrtle-beds;
Seemed to the holy festival
The rash word boded ill to all;
The balance-beam of Fate was bent;
The bounds of good and ill were rent;
Strong Hades could not keep his own,
But all slid to confusion.

A sad self-knowledge, withering, fell
On the beauty of Uriel;
In heaven once eminent, the god
Withdrew, that hour, into his cloud;
Whether doomed to long gyration
In the sea of generation,
Or by knowledge grown too bright
To hit the nerve of feebler sight.
Straightway, a forgetting wind
Stole over the celestial kind,
And their lips the secret kept,
If in ashes the fire-seed slept.
But now and then, truth-speaking things
Shamed the angels' veiling wings;
And, shrilling from the solar course,
Or from fruit of chemic force,
Procession of a soul in matter,
Or the speeding change of water,
Or out of the good of evil born,
Came Uriel's voice of cherub scorn,
And a blush tinged the upper sky,
And the gods shook, they knew not why.

(1838) 1847

## HAMATREYA

Bulkeley, Hunt, Willard, Hosmer, Meriam, Flint,
Possessed the land which rendered to their toil
Hay, corn, roots, hemp, flax, apples, wool and wood.
Each of these landlords walked amidst his farm,
Saying, ''Tis mine, my children's and my name's.
How sweet the west wind sounds in my own trees!
How graceful climb those shadows on my hill!

I fancy these pure waters and the flags  
Know me, as does my dog: we sympathize;  
And, I affirm, my actions smack of the soil.'

Where are these men? Asleep beneath their grounds:  
And strangers, fond as they, their furrows plough.  
Earth laughs in flowers, to see her boastful boys  
Earth-proud, proud of the earth which is not theirs;  
Who steer the plough, but cannot steer their feet  
Clear of the grave.  
They added ridge to valley, brook to pond,  
And sighed for all that bounded their domain;  
'This suits me for a pasture; that's my park;  
We must have clay, lime, gravel, granite-ledge,  
And misty lowland, where to go for peat.  
The land is well,—lies fairly to the south.  
'Tis good, when you have crossed the sea and back,  
To find the sitfast acres where you left them.'  
Ah! the hot owner sees not Death, who adds  
Him to his land, a lump of mould the more.  
Hear what the Earth says:—

EARTH-SONG

'Mine and yours;  
Mine, not yours.  
Earth endures;  
Stars abide—  
Shine down in the old sea;  
Old are the shores;  
But where are old men?  
I who have seen much,  
Such have I never seen.

'The lawyer's deed  
Ran sure,  
In tail,  
To them, and to their heirs  
Who shall succeed,  
Without fail,  
Forevermore.

'Here is the land,  
Shaggy with wood,  
With its old valley,  
Mound and flood.  
But the heritors?—  
Fled like the flood's foam.  
The lawyer, and the laws,  
And the kingdom,  
Clean swept herefrom.

'They called me theirs,  
Who so controlled me;  
Yet every one  
Wished to stay, and is gone,  
How am I theirs,  
If they cannot hold me,  
But I hold them?'

When I heard the Earth-song  
I was no longer brave;  
My avarice cooled  
Like lust in the chill of the grave.

1847

## ODE

INSCRIBED TO W. H. CHANNING

Though loath to grieve  
The evil time's sole patriot,  
I cannot leave  
My honied thought  
For the priest's cant,  
Or statesman's rant.

If I refuse  
My study for their politique,  
Which at the best is trick,  
The angry Muse  
Puts confusion in my brain.

But who is he that prates  
Of the culture of mankind,

Of better arts and life?
Go, blindworm, go,
Behold the famous States
Harrying Mexico
With rifle and with knife!

Or who, with accent bolder,
Dare praise the freedom-loving mountaineer?
I found by thee, O rushing Contoocook!
And in thy valleys, Agiochook!
The jackals of the negro-holder.

The God who made New Hampshire
Taunted the lofty land
With little men;—
Small bat and wren
House in the oak:—
If earth-fire cleave
The upheaved land, and bury the folk,
The southern crocodile would grieve.
Virtue palters; Right is hence;
Freedom praised, but hid;
Funeral eloquence
Rattles the coffin-lid.

What boots thy zeal,
O glowing friend,
That would indignant rend
The northland from the south?
Wherefore? to what good end?
Boston Bay and Bunker Hill
Would serve things still;—
Things are of the snake.

The horseman serves the horse,
The neatherd serves the neat,
The merchant serves the purse,
The eater serves his meat;
'Tis the day of the chattel,
Web to weave, and corn to grind;
Things are in the saddle,
And ride mankind.

There are two laws discrete,
Not reconciled,—
Law for man, and law for thing;
The last builds town and fleet,
But it runs wild,
And doth the man unking.

'Tis fit the forest fall,
The steep be graded,
The mountain tunnelled,
The sand shaded,
The orchard planted,
The glebe tilled,
The prairie granted,
The steamer built.

Let man serve law for man;
Live for friendship, live for love,
For truth's and harmony's behoof;
The state may follow how it can,
As Olympus follows Jove.

Yet do not I implore
The wrinkled shopman to my sounding woods
Nor bid the unwilling senator
Ask votes of thrushes in the solitudes.
Every one to his chosen work;—
Foolish hands may mix and mar;
Wise and sure the issues are.
Round they roll till dark is light,
Sex to sex, and even to odd;—
The over-god
Who marries Right to Might,
Who peoples, unpeoples,—
He who exterminates
Races by stronger races,
Black by white faces,—
Knows to bring honey
Out of the lion;
Grafts gentlest scion
On pirate and Turk.

The Cossack eats Poland,
Like stolen fruit;
Her last noble is ruined,
Her last poet mute:
Straight, into double band
The victors divide;
Half for freedom strike and stand;—
The astonished Muse finds thousands at her side.

1847

## GIVE ALL TO LOVE

Give all to love;
Obey thy heart;

Friends, kindred, days,
Estate, good-fame,
Plans, credit and the Muse,—
Nothing refuse.

'Tis a brave master;
Let it have a scope:
Follow it utterly,
Hope beyond hope
High and more high
It dives into noon,
With wing unspent,
Untold intent;
But it is a god,
Knows its own path
And the outlets of the sky.

It was never for the mean;
It requireth courage stout.
Souls above doubt,
Valor unbending,
It will reward,—
They shall return
More than they were,
And ever ascending.

Leave all for love;
Yet, hear me, yet,
One word more thy heart behoved,
One pulse more of firm endeavor,—
Keep thee to-day,
To-morrow, forever,
Free as an Arab
Of thy beloved.

Cling with life to the maid;
But when the surprise,
First vague shadow of surmise
Flits across her bosom young,
Of a joy apart from thee,
Free be she, fancy-free;
Nor thou detain her vesture's hem,
Nor the palest rose she flung
From her summer diadem.

Though thou loved her as thyself,
As a self of purer clay,
Though her parting dims the day,
Stealing grace from all alive;
Heartily know,
When half-gods go,
The gods arrive.

1847

## THE APOLOGY

Think me not unkind and rude
That I walk alone in grove and glen;
I go to the god of the wood
To fetch his word to men.

Tax not my sloth that I
Fold my arms beside the brook;
Each cloud that floated in the sky
Writes a letter in my book.

Chide me not, laborious band,
For the idle flowers I brought;
Every aster in my hand
Goes home loaded with a thought.

There was never mystery
But 'tis figured in the flowers;
Was never secret history
But birds tell it in the bowers.

One harvest from thy field
Homeward brought the oxen strong;
A second crop thine acres yield,
Which I gather in a song.

(*ca.* 1835) 1847

## THRENODY

The South-wind brings
Life, sunshine and desire,
And on every mount and meadow
Breathes aromatic fire;
But over the dead he has no power,
The lost, the lost, he cannot restore;
And, looking over the hills, I mourn
The darling who shall not return.

I see my empty house,
I see my trees repair their boughs;
And he, the wondrous child,
Whose silver warble wild
Outvalued every pulsing sound

Within the air's cerulean round,—
The hyacinthine boy, for whom
Morn well might break and April bloom,
The gracious boy, who did adorn
The world whereinto he was born,
And by his countenance repay
The favor of the loving Day,—
Has disappeared from the Day's eye;
Far and wide she cannot find him;
My hopes pursue, they cannot bind him.
Returned this day, the South-wind searches,
And finds young pines and budding birches;
But finds not the budding man;
Nature, who lost, cannot remake him;
Fate let him fall, Fate can't retake him;
Nature, Fate, men, him seek in vain.

And whither now, my truant wise and sweet,
O, whither tend thy feet?
I had the right, few days ago,
Thy steps to watch, thy place to know:
How have I forfeited the right?
Hast thou forgot me in a new delight?
I hearken for thy household cheer,
O eloquent child!
Whose voice, an equal messenger,
Conveyed thy meaning mild.
What though the pains and joys
Whereof it spoke were toys
Fitting his age and ken,
Yet fairest dames and bearded men,
Who heard the sweet request,
So gentle, wise and grave,
Bended with joy to his behest
And let the world's affairs go by,
A while to share his cordial game,
Or mend his wicker wagon-frame,
Still plotting how their hungry ear
That winsome voice again might hear;
For his lips could well pronounce
Words that were persuasions.
Gentlest guardians marked serene
His early hope, his liberal mien;
Took counsel from his guiding eyes
To make this wisdom earthly wise.
Ah, vainly do these eyes recall
The school-march, each day's festival,
When every morn my bosom glowed
To watch the convoy on the road;
The babe in willow wagon closed,
With rolling eyes and face composed;
With children forward and behind,
Like Cupids studiously inclined;
And he the chieftain paced beside,
The centre of the troop allied,
With sunny face of sweet repose,
To guard the babe from fancied foes.
The little captain innocent
Took the eye with him as he went;
Each village senior paused to scan
And speak the lovely caravan.
From the window I look out
To mark thy beautiful parade,
Stately marching in cap and coat
To some tune by fairies played;—
A music heard by thee alone
To works as noble led thee on.
Now Love and Pride, alas! in vain,
Up and down their glances strain.
The painted sled stands where it stood;
The kennel by the corded wood;
His gathered sticks to stanch the wall
Of the snow-tower, when snow should fall;
The ominous hole he dug in the sand,
And childhood's castles built or planned;
His daily haunts I well discern,—
The poultry-yard, the shed, the barn,—
And every inch of garden ground
Paced by the blessed feet around,
From the roadside to the brook
Whereinto he loved to look.
Step the meek fowls where erst they ranged;
The wintry garden lies unchanged;
The brook into the stream runs on;
But the deep-eyed boy is gone.

On that shaded day,
Dark with more clouds than tempests are,
When thou didst yield thy innocent breath
In birdlike heavings unto death,
Night came, and Nature had not thee;
I said, 'We are mates in misery.'
The morrow dawned with needless glow;
Each snowbird chirped, each fowl must crow;
Each tramper started; but the feet
Of the most beautiful and sweet
Of human youth had left the hill
And garden,—they were bound and still.
There's not a sparrow or a wren,
There's not a blade of autumn grain,
Which the four seasons do not tend
And tides of life and increase lend;
And every chick of every bird,
And weed and rock-moss is preferred.
O ostrich-like forgetfulness!
O loss of larger in the less!
Was there no star that could be sent,
No watcher in the firmament,
No angel from the countless host
That loiters round the crystal coast,
Could stoop to heal that only child,
Nature's sweet marvel undefiled,
And keep the blossom of the earth,
Which all her harvests were not worth?
Not mine,—I never called thee mine,
But Nature's heir,—if I repine,
And seeing rashly torn and moved
Not what I made, but what I loved,
Grow early old with grief that thou
Must to the wastes of Nature go,—
'Tis because a general hope
Was quenched, and all must doubt and grope.
For flattering planets seemed to say
This child should ills of ages stay,
By wondrous tongue, and guided pen,
Bring the flown Muses back to men.
Perchance not he but Nature ailed,
The world and not the infant failed.
It was not ripe yet to sustain
A genius of so fine a strain,
Who gazed upon the sun and moon
As if he came unto his own,
And, pregnant with his grander thought,
Brought the old order into doubt.
His beauty once their beauty tried;
They could not feed him, and he died,
And wandered backward as in scorn,
To wait an æon to be born.
Ill day which made this beauty waste,
Plight broken, this high face defaced!
Some went and came about the dead;
And some in books of solace read;
Some to their friends the tidings say;
Some went to write, some went to pray;
One tarried here, there hurried one;
But their heart abode with none.
Covetous death bereaved us all,
To aggrandize one funeral.
The eager fate which carried thee
Took the largest part of me:
For this losing is true dying;
This is lordly man's down-lying,
This his slow but sure reclining,
Star by star his world resigning.
O child of paradise,
Boy who made dear his father's home,
In whose deep eyes
Men read the welfare of the times to come,
I am too much bereft.
The world dishonored thou hast left.
O truth's and nature's costly lie!
O trusted broken prophecy!
O richest fortune sourly crossed!
Born for the future, to the future lost!

The deep Heart answered, 'Weepest thou?
Worthier cause for passion wild
If I had not taken the child.
And deemest thou as those who pore,
With aged eyes, short way before,—
Think'st Beauty vanished from the coast
Of matter, and thy darling lost?

Taught he not thee—the man of eld,
Whose eyes within his eyes beheld
Heaven's numerous hierarchy span
The mystic gulf from God to man?
To be alone wilt thou begin
When worlds of lovers hem thee in?
To-morrow, when the masks shall fall
That dizen Nature's carnival,
The pure shall see by their own will,
Which overflowing Love shall fill,
'Tis not within the force of fate
The fate-conjoined to separate.
But thou, my votary, weepest thou?
I gave thee sight—where is it now?
I taught thy heart beyond the reach
Of ritual, bible, or of speech;
Wrote in thy mind's transparent table,
As far as the incommunicable;
Taught thee each private sign to raise
Lit by the supersolar blaze.
Past utterance, and past belief,
And past the blasphemy of grief,
The mysteries of Nature's heart;
And though no Muse can these impart,
Throb thine with Nature's throbbing breast,
And all is clear from east to west.

'I came to thee as to a friend;
Dearest, to thee I did not send
Tutors, but a joyful eye,
Innocence that matched the sky,
Lovely locks, a form of wonder,
Laughter rich as woodland thunder,
That thou might'st entertain apart
The richest flowering of all art:
And, as the great all-loving Day
Through smallest chambers takes its way,
That thou might'st break thy daily bread
With prophet, savior and head;
That thou might'st cherish for thine own
The riches of sweet Mary's Son,
Boy-Rabbi, Israel's paragon.
And thoughtest thou such guest
Would in thy hall take up his rest?
Would rushing life forget her laws,
Fate's glowing revolution pause?
High omens ask diviner guess;
Not to be conned to tediousness
And know my higher gifts unbind
The zone that girds the incarnate mind.
When the scanty shores are full
With Thought's perilous, whirling pool;
When frail Nature can no more,
Then the Spirit strikes the hour:
My servant Death, with solving rite,
Pours finite into infinite.
Wilt thou freeze love's tidal flow,
Whose streams through Nature circling go?
Nail the wild star to its track
On the half-climbed zodiac?
Light is light which radiates,
Blood is blood which circulates,
Life is life which generates,
And many-seeming life is one,—
Wilt thou transfix and make it none?
Its onward force too starkly pent
In figure, bone and lineament?
Wilt thou, uncalled, interrogate,
Talker! the unreplying Fate?
Nor see the genius of the whole
Ascendant in the private soul,
Beckon it when to go and come,
Self-announced its hour of doom?
Fair the soul's recess and shrine,
Magic-built to last a season;
Masterpiece of love benign,
Fairer that expansive reason
Whose omen 'tis, and sign.
Wilt thou not ope thy heart to know
What rainbows teach, and sunsets show?
Verdict which accumulates
From lengthening scroll of human fates,
Voice of earth to earth returned,
Prayers of saints that inly burned,—
Saying, *What is excellent,*
*As God lives, is permanent;*
*Hearts are dust, hearts' loves remain;*
*Heart's love will meet thee again.*
Revere the Maker; fetch thine eye

Up to his style, and manners of the
sky.
Not of adamant and gold
Built he heaven stark and cold;
No, but a nest of bending reeds,
Flowering grass and scented weeds;
Or like a traveller's fleeing tent,
Or bow above the tempest bent;
Built of tears and sacred flames,
And virtue reaching to its aims;
Built of furtherance and pursuing,
Not of spent deeds, but of doing.
Silent rushes the swift Lord
Through ruined systems still restored,
Broadsowing, bleak and void to bless,
Plants with worlds the wilderness;
Waters with tears of ancient sorrow
Apples of Eden ripe to-morrow.
House and tenant go to ground,
Lost in God, in Godhead found.'
(1842–44) 1847

## DAYS

Daughters of Time, the hypocritic
Days,
Muffled and dumb like barefoot dervishes,
And marching single in an endless file,
Bring diadems and fagots in their
hands.
To each they offer gifts after his will,
Bread, kingdoms, stars, and sky that
holds them all.
I, in my pleachèd garden, watched the
pomp,
Forgot my morning wishes, hastily
Took a few herbs and apples, and the
Day
Turned and departed silent. I, too
late,
Under her solemn fillet saw the scorn.
(1851–52) 1857

## BRAHMA

If the red slayer thinks he slays,
Or if the slain think he is slain,
They know not well the subtle ways
I keep, and pass, and turn again.

Far or forgot to me is near;
Shadow and sunlight are the same;
The vanished gods to me appear;
And one to me are shame and fame.

They reckon ill who leave me out;
When me they fly, I am the wings;
I am the doubter and the doubt,
And I the hymn the Brahmin sings.

The strong gods pine for my abode,
And pine in vain the sacred Seven;
But thou, meek lover of the good!
Find me, and turn thy back on
heaven.
(1856) 1857

## TWO RIVERS

Thy summer voice, Musketaquit,
Repeats the music of the rain;
But sweeter rivers pulsing flit
Through thee, as thou through Concord Plain.

Thou in thy narrow banks art pent:
The stream I love unbounded goes
Through flood and sea and firmament;
Through light, through life, it forward flows.

I see the inundation sweet,
I hear the spending of the stream
Through years, through men, through
Nature fleet,
Through love and thought, through
power and dream.

Musketaquit, a goblin strong,
Of shard and flint makes jewels gay;
They lose their grief who hear his
song,
And where he winds is the day of
day.

So forth and brighter fares my
stream,—
Who drink it shall not thirst again;

No darkness stains its equal gleam,
And ages drop in it like rain.
(1856) 1867

## TERMINUS

It is time to be old,
To take in sail:—
The god of bounds,
Who sets to seas a shore,
Came to me in his fatal rounds,
And said: 'No more!
No farther shoot
Thy broad ambitious branches, and thy root.
Fancy departs: no more invent;
Contract thy firmament
To compass of a tent.
There's not enough for this and that,
Make thy option which of two;
Economize the failing river,
Not the less revere the Giver,
Leave the many and hold the few.
Timely wise accept the terms,
Soften the fall with wary foot;
A little while
Still plan and smile,
And, fault of novel germs,
Mature the unfallen fruit.
Curse, if thou wilt, thy sires,
Bad husbands of their fires,
Who, when they gave thee breath,
Failed to bequeath
The needful sinew stark as once,
The Baresark marrow to thy bones,
But left a legacy of ebbing veins,
Inconstant heat and nerveless reins,—
Amid the Muses, left thee deaf and dumb,
Amid the gladiators, halt and numb.'

As the bird trims her to the gale,
I trim myself to the storm of time,
I man the rudder, reef the sail,
Obey the voice at eve obeyed at prime:
'Lowly faithful, banish fear,
Right onward drive unharmed;
The port, well worth the cruise, is near,
And every wave is charmed.'
(1866) 1867

# HENRY DAVID THOREAU
## (1817–1862)

### From *JOURNAL*

### [MISCELLANEOUS JOTTINGS]

*Oct. 22, 1837.* "What are you doing now?" he asked. "Do you keep a journal?" So I made my first entry to-day.

To be alone I find it necessary to escape the present, — I avoid myself. How could I be alone in the Roman emperor's chamber of mirrors? I seek a garret. The spiders must not be disturbed, nor the floor swept, nor the lumber arranged.

*Nov. 3.* If one would reflect, let him embark on some placid stream, and float with the current. He cannot resist the Muse. As we ascend the stream, plying the paddle with might and main, snatched and impetuous thoughts course through the brain. We dream of conflict, power, and grandeur. But turn the prow down stream, and rock, tree, kine, knoll, assuming new and varying positions, as wind and water shift the scene, favor the liquid lapse of thought, far-reaching and sublime, but ever calm and gently undulating.

*Sept. 3, 1838.* The only faith that men recognize is a creed. But the true creed which we unconsciously live by, and which rather adopts us than we it, is quite different from the written or preached one. Men anxiously hold fast to their creed, as to a straw, thinking this does them good service because their sheet anchor does not drag.

*Sept. 20.* It is a luxury to muse by a wall-side in the sunset of a September afternoon, — to cuddle down under a gray stone, and hearken to the siren song of the cricket. Day and night seem henceforth but accidents, and the time is a still eventide, and as the close of a happy day. Parched fields and mulleins gilded with the slanting rays are my diet. I know of no word so fit to express this disposition of Nature as Alma Natura.

*Oct. 22, 1839.* Nature will bear the closest inspection. She invites us to lay our eye level with her smallest leaf, and take an insect view of its plain.

*March 22, 1840.* While I bask in the sun on the shores of Walden Pond, by this heat and this rustle I am absolved from all obligation to the past. The council of nations may reconsider their votes; the grating of a pebble annuls them.

*July 26.* When I consider how, after sunset, the stars come out gradually in troops from behind the hills and woods, I confess that I could not have contrived a more curious and inspiring night.

*Jan. 30, 1841.* Here is the distinct trail of a fox stretching [a] quarter of a mile across the pond. Now I am curious to know what has determined its graceful curvatures, its greater or less spaces and distinctness, and how surely they were coincident with the fluctuations of some mind, why they now lead me two steps to the right, and then three to the left. If these things are not to be called up and accounted for in the Lamb's Book of Life, I shall set them down for careless accountants. Here was one expression of the divine mind this morning. The pond was his journal, and last night's snow made a *tabula rasa* for him. I know which way a mind wended this morning, what horizon it faced, by the setting of these tracks; whether it moved slowly or rapidly, by the greater or less intervals and distinctness, for the swiftest step leaves yet a lasting trace.

*April 4.* That cheap piece of tinkling brass which the farmer hangs about his cow's neck has been more to me than the tons of metal which are swung in the belfry.

*April 5.* This lament for a golden age is only a lament for golden men.

*Dec. 29.* I can at length stretch me when I come to Chaucer's breadth; and I think, "Well, I could be *that* man's acquaintance," for he walked in that low and retired way that I do, and was not too good to live.

[*Undated*] Emerson has special talents unequalled. The divine in man has had no more easy, methodically distinct expression. His personal influence upon young persons greater than any man's. In his world every man would be a poet, Love would reign, Beauty would take place, Man and Nature would harmonize.

(1837–41) 1906

## *From* CIVIL DISOBEDIENCE

I heartily accept the motto,—"That government is best which governs least;" and I should like to see it acted up to more rapidly and systematically. Carried out, it finally amounts to this, which also I believe,—"That government is best which governs not at all;" and when men are prepared for it, that will be the kind of government which they will have. Government is at best but an expedient; but most governments are usually, and all governments are sometimes, inexpedient. The objections which have been brought against a standing army, and they are many and weighty, and deserve to prevail, may also at last be brought against a standing government. The standing army is only an arm of the standing government. The government itself, which is only the mode which the people have chosen to execute their will, is equally liable to be abused and perverted before the people can act through it. Witness the present Mexican war, the work of comparatively a few individuals using the standing government as their tool; for, in the outset, the people would not have consented to this measure. * * *

How does it become a man to behave toward this American government to-day? I answer, that he cannot without disgrace be associated with it. I cannot for an instant recognize that political organization as *my* government which is the *slave's* government also.

All men recognize the right of revolution; that is, the right to refuse allegiance to, and to resist, the government, when its tyranny or its inefficiency are great and unendurable. But almost all say that such is not the case now. But such was the case, they think, in the Revolution of '75. If one were to tell me that this was a bad government because it taxed certain foreign commodities brought to its ports, it is most probable that I should not make an ado about it, for I can do without them. All machines have their friction; and possibly this does enough good to counterbalance the evil. At any rate, it is a great evil to make a stir about it. But when the friction comes to have its machine, and oppression and robbery are organized, I say, let us not have such a machine any longer. In other words, when a sixth of the population of a nation which has undertaken to be the refuge of liberty are slaves, and a whole country is unjustly overrun and conquered by a foreign army, and subjected to military law, I think that it is not too soon for honest men to rebel and revolutionize. What makes this duty the more urgent is the fact that the country so overrun is not our own, but ours is the invading army. * * *

Some years ago, the State met me in behalf of the Church, and commanded me to pay a certain sum toward the support of a clergyman whose preaching my father attended, but never I myself. "Pay," it said, "or be locked up in the jail." I declined to pay. But, unfortunately, another man saw fit to pay it. I did not see why the schoolmaster should be taxed to support the priest, and not the priest the schoolmaster; for I was not the State's schoolmaster, but I supported myself by voluntary subscription. I did not see why the lyceum should not present its tax-bill, and have the State to back its demand, as well as the Church. However, at the request of the selectmen, I condescended to make some such statement as this in writing: — "Know all men by these presents, that I, Henry Thoreau, do not wish to be regarded as a member of any incorporated society which I have not joined." This I gave to the town clerk; and he has it. The State, having thus learned that I did not wish to be regarded as a member of that church, has never made a like demand on me since; though it said that it must adhere to its original presumption that time. If I had known how to name them, I should then have signed off in detail from all the societies which I never signed on to; but I did not know where to find a complete list.

I have paid no poll-tax for six years. I was put into a jail once on this account, for one night; and, as I stood considering the walls of solid stone, two or three feet thick, the door of wood and iron, a foot thick, and the iron grating which strained the light, I could not help being struck with the foolishness of that institution which treated me as if I were mere flesh and blood and bones, to be locked up. I wondered that it should have concluded at length that this was the best use it could put me to, and had never thought to avail itself of my services in some way. I saw that, if there was a wall of stone between me and my townsmen, there was a still more difficult one to climb or break through before they could get to be as free as I was. I did not for a moment feel confined, and the walls seemed a great waste of stone and mortar. I felt as if I alone of all my townsmen had paid my tax. They plainly did not know how to treat me, but behaved like persons who are underbred. In every threat and in every compliment there was a blunder; for they thought that my chief desire was to stand the other side of that stone wall. I could not but smile to see how industriously they locked the door on my meditations, which followed them out again without let or hindrance, and *they* were really all that was dangerous. As they could not reach me, they had resolved to punish my body; just as boys, if they cannot come at some person against whom they have a spite, will abuse his dog. I saw that the State was half-witted, that it was timid as a lone woman with her silver spoons, and that it did not know its friends from its foes, and I lost all my remaining respect for it, and pitied it.

Thus the State never intentionally confronts a man's sense, intellectual or moral, but only his body, his senses. It is not armed with superior wit or honesty, but with superior physical strength. I was not born to be forced. I will breathe after my own fashion. Let us see who is the strongest. What force has a multitude? They only can force me who obey a higher law than I. They force me to become like themselves. I do not hear of *men* being *forced* to live this way or that by masses of men. What sort of life were that to live? When I meet a government which says to me, "Your money or your life," why should I be in haste to give it my money? It may be in a great strait, and not know what to do: I cannot help that. It must help itself; do as I do. It is not worth the while to snivel about it. I am not responsible for the successful working of the machinery of society. I am not the son of the engineer. I perceive that, when an acorn and a chestnut fall side by side, the one does not remain inert to make way for the other, but both obey their own laws, and spring and grow and flourish as best they can, till one, perchance, overshadows and destroys the other. If a plant cannot live according to its nature, it dies; and so a man.

The night in prison was novel and interesting enough. The prisoners in their shirt-sleeves were enjoying a chat and the evening air in the door-way, when I entered. But the jailer said, "Come, boys, it is time to lock up;" and so they dispersed, and I heard the sound of their steps returning into the hollow apartments. My room-mate was introduced to me by the jailer as "a first-rate fellow and a clever man." When the door was locked, he showed me where to hang my hat, and how he managed matters there. The rooms were whitewashed once a month; and this one, at least, was the whitest, most simply furnished, and probably the neatest apartment in the town. * * *

It was like traveling into a far country, such as I had never expected to behold, to lie there for one night. It seemed to me that I never had heard the town-clock strike before, nor the evening sounds of the village; for we slept with the windows open, which were inside the grating. It was to see my native village in the light of the Middle Ages, and our Concord was turned into a Rhine stream, and visions of knights and castles passed before me. They were the voices of old burghers that I heard in the streets. I was an involuntary spectator and auditor of whatever was done and said in the kitchen of the adjacent village-inn, — a wholly new and rare experience to me. It was a closer view of my native town. I was fairly inside of it. I never had seen its institutions before. This is one of its peculiar institutions; for it is a shire town. I began to comprehend what its inhabitants were about.

In the morning, our breakfasts were put through the hole in the door, in small oblong-square tin pans, made to fit, and holding a pint of chocolate, with brown bread, and an iron spoon. When they called for the vessels again, I was green enough to return what bread I had left; but my comrade seized it, and said that I should lay that up for lunch or dinner. Soon after he was let out to work at haying in a neighboring field, whither he went every day, and would not be back till noon; so he bade me good-day, saying that he doubted if he should see me again.

When I came out of prison, — for some one interfered, and paid that tax, — I did not perceive that great changes had taken place on the common, such as he observed who went in a youth and emerged a tottering and gray-headed man; and yet a change had to my eyes come over the scene, — the town, and State, and country, — greater than any that mere time could effect. I saw yet more distinctly the State in which I lived. I saw to what extent the people among whom I lived could be trusted as good neighbors and friends; that their friendship was for summer weather only; that they did not greatly propose to do right; that they were a distinct race from me by their prejudices and superstitions, as the Chinamen and Malays are; that in their sacrifices to humanity they ran no risks, not even to their property; that after all they were not so noble but they treated the thief as he had treated them, and hoped by a certain outward observance and a few prayers, and by walking in a particular straight though useless path from time to time, to save their souls. This may be to judge my neighbors harshly; for I believe that many of them are not aware that they have such an institution as the jail in their village.

It was formerly the custom in our village, when a poor debtor came out of jail, for his acquaintances to salute him, looking through their fingers which were crossed to represent the grating of a jail window, "How do ye do?" My neighbors did not thus salute me, but first looked at me, and then at one another, as if I had returned from a long journey. I was put into jail as I was going to the shoemaker's to get a shoe which was mended. When I was let out the next morning, I proceeded to finish my errand, and, having put on my mended shoe, joined a huckleberry party, who were impatient to put themselves under my conduct; and in half an hour, — for the horse was soon tackled, — was in the midst of a huckleberry field, on one of our highest hills, two miles off, and then the State was nowhere to be seen.

This is the whole history of "My Prisons." * * *

The authority of government, even such as I am willing to submit to,—for I will cheerfully obey those who know and can do better than I, and in many things even those who neither know nor can do so well,—is still an impure one: to be strictly just, it must have the sanction and consent of the governed. It can have no pure right over my person and property but what I concede to it. The progress from an absolute to a limited monarchy, from a limited monarchy to a democracy, is a progress toward a true respect for the individual. Even the Chinese philosopher was wise enough to regard the individual as the basis of the empire. Is a democracy, such as we know it, the last improvement possible in government? Is it not possible to take a step further towards recognizing and organizing the rights of man? There will never be a really free and enlightened State until the State comes to recognize the individual as a higher and independent power, from which all its own power and authority are derived, and treats him accordingly. I please myself with imagining a State at last which can afford to be just to all men, and to treat the individual with respect as a neighbor; which even would not think it inconsistent with its own repose if a few were to live aloof from it, not meddling with it, nor embraced by it, who fulfilled all the duties of neighbors and fellowmen. A State which bore this kind of fruit, and suffered it to drop off as fast as it ripened, would prepare the way for a still more perfect and glorious State, which also I have imagined, but not yet anywhere seen.

1849

## *WALDEN; OR, LIFE IN THE WOODS*

### *From* II. WHERE I LIVED, AND WHAT I LIVED FOR

At a certain season of our life we are accustomed to consider every spot as the possible site of a house. I have thus surveyed the country on every side within a dozen miles of where I live. In imagination I have bought all the farms in succession, for all were to be bought, and I knew their price. I walked over each farmer's premises, tasted his wild apples, discoursed on husbandry with him, took his farm at his price, at any price, mortgaging it to him in my mind; even put a higher price on it,—took everything but a deed of it,—took his word for his deed, for I dearly love to talk,—cultivated it, and him too to some extent, I trust, and withdrew when I had enjoyed it long enough, leaving him to carry it on. This experience entitled me to be regarded as a sort of real-estate broker by my friends. Wherever I sat, there I might live, and the landscape radiated from me accordingly. What is a house but a *sedes*, a seat?—better if a country seat. I discovered many a site for a house not likely to be soon improved, which some might have thought too far from the village, but to my eyes the village was too far from it. Well, there I might live, I said; and there I did live, for an hour, a summer and a winter life; saw how I could let the years run off, buffet the winter through, and see the spring come in. The future inhabitants of this region, wherever they may place their houses, may be sure that they have been anticipated. An afternoon sufficed to lay out the land into orchard, wood-lot, and pasture, and to decide what fine oaks or pines should be left to stand before the door, and whence each blasted tree could be seen to the best advantage; and then I let it lie, fallow perchance, for a man is rich in proportion to the number of things which he can afford to let alone.

My imagination carried me so far that I even had the refusal of several farms,—the refusal was all I wanted,—but I never got my fingers burned by actual possession. The nearest that I came to actual possession was when I bought the Hollowell place, and had begun to sort my seeds, and collected materials with which to make a wheelbarrow to carry it on or off with; but before the owner gave me a deed of it, his wife—every man has such a wife—changed her mind and wished to keep it, and he offered me ten dollars to release him. Now, to speak the truth, I had but ten cents in the world, and it surpassed my arithmetic to tell, if I was that man who had ten cents, or who had a farm, or ten dollars, or all together. However, I let him keep the ten dollars and the farm too, for I had carried it far enough; or rather, to be generous, I sold him the farm for just what I gave for it, and, as he was not a rich man, made him a present of ten dollars, and still had my ten cents, and seeds, and materials for a wheelbarrow left. I found thus that I had been a rich man without any damage to my poverty. But I retained the landscape, and I have since annually carried off what it yielded without a wheelbarrow. With respect to landscapes,—

> I am monarch of all I *survey*,
> My right there is none to dispute.

I have frequently seen a poet withdraw, having enjoyed the most valuable part of a farm, while the crusty farmer supposed that he had got a few wild apples only. Why, the owner does not know it for many years when a poet has put his farm in rhyme, the most admirable kind of invisible fence, has fairly impounded it, milked it, skimmed it, and got all the cream, and left the farmer only the skimmed milk.

The real attractions of the Hollowell farm, to me, were: its complete retirement, being about two miles from the village, half a mile from the nearest neighbor, and separated from the highway by a broad field; its bounding on the river, which the owner said protected it by its fogs from frosts in the spring, though that was nothing to me; the gray color and ruinous state of the house and barn, and the dilapidated fences, which put such an interval between me and the last occupant; the hollow and lichen-covered apple trees, gnawed by rabbits, showing what kind of neighbors I should have; but above all, the recollection I had of it from my earliest voyages up the river, when the house was concealed behind a dense grove of red maples, through which I heard the house-dog bark. I was in haste to buy it, before the proprietor finished getting out some rocks, cutting down the hollow apple trees, and grubbing up some young birches which had sprung up in the pasture, or, in short, had made any more of his improvements. To enjoy these advantages I was ready to carry it on; like Atlas, to take the world on my shoulders,—I never heard what compensation he received for that,—and do all those things which had no other motive or excuse but that I might pay for it and be unmolested in my possession of it; for I knew all the while that it would yield the most abundant crop of the kind I wanted, if I could only afford to let it alone. But it turned out as I have said.

All that I could say, then, with respect to farming on a large scale (I have always cultivated a garden) was, that I had had my seeds ready. Many think that seeds improve with age. I have no doubt that time discriminates between the good and the bad; and when at last I shall plant, I shall be less likely to be disappointed. But I would say to my fellows, once for all, As long as possible live free and uncommitted. It makes but little difference whether you are committed to a farm or the county jail.

Old Cato, whose "De Re Rusticâ" is my "Cultivator," says,—and the only translation I have seen makes sheer nonsense of the passage, "When you think of getting a farm turn it thus in your mind, not to buy greedily; nor spare your pains to look at it, and do not think it enough to go round it once. The oftener you go there the more it will please you, if it is good." I think I shall not buy greedily, but go round and round it as long as I live, and be buried in it first, that it may please me the more at last.

The present was my next experiment of this kind, which I purpose to describe more at length, for convenience putting the experience of two years into one. As I have said, I do not propose to write an ode to dejection, but to brag as lustily as chanticleer in the morning, standing on his roost, if only to wake my neighbors up.

When first I took up my abode in the woods, that is, began to spend my nights as well as days there, which, by accident, was on Independence Day, or the fourth of July, 1845, my house was not finished for winter, but was merely a defence against the rain, without plastering or chimney, the walls being of rough, weather-stained boards, with wide chinks, which made it cool at night. The upright white hewn studs and freshly planed door and window casings gave it a clean and airy look, especially in the morning, when its timbers were saturated with dew, so that I fancied that by noon some sweet gum would exude from them. To my imagination it retained throughout the day more or less of this auroral character, reminding me of a certain house on a mountain which I had visited a year before. This was an airy and unplastered cabin, fit to entertain a travelling god, and where a goddess might trail her garments. The winds which passed over my dwelling were such as sweep over the ridges of mountains, bearing the broken strains, or celestial parts only, of terrestrial music. The morning wind forever blows, the poem of creation is uninterrupted; but few are the ears that hear it. Olympus is but the outside of the earth everywhere.

The only house I had been the owner of before, if I except a boat, was a tent, which I used occasionally when making excursions in the summer, and this is still rolled up in my garret; but the boat, after passing from hand to hand, has gone down the stream of time. With this more substantial shelter about me, I had made some progress toward settling in the world. This frame, so slightly clad, was a sort of crystallization around me, and reacted on the builder. It was suggestive somewhat as a picture in outlines. I did not need to go outdoors to take the air, for the atmosphere within had lost none of its freshness. It was not so much within-doors as behind a door where I sat, even in the rainiest weather. The Harivansa says, "An abode without birds is like a meat without seasoning." Such was not my abode, for I found myself suddenly neighbor to the birds; not by having imprisoned one, but having caged myself near them. I was not only nearer to some of those which commonly frequent the garden and the orchard, but to those wilder and more thrilling songsters of the forest which never, or rarely, serenade a villager,—the wood-thrush, the veery, the scarlet tanager, the field-sparrow, the whippoorwill, and many others.

I was seated by the shore of a small pond, about a mile and a half south of the village of Concord and somewhat higher than it, in the midst of an extensive wood between that town and Lincoln, and about two miles south of that our only field known to fame, Concord Battle Ground; but I was so low in the woods that the opposite shore, half a mile off, like the rest, covered with wood, was my most distant horizon. For the first week, whenever I looked out on the pond it impressed me like a tarn high up on the side of a mountain, its bottom far above the surface of other lakes, and, as the sun arose, I saw it throwing off its nightly clothing of mist, and here and there, by degrees, its soft ripples or its smooth reflecting surface was revealed, while the mists, like ghosts, were stealthily withdrawing in every direction into the woods, as at the breaking up of some nocturnal conventicle. The very dew seemed to hang upon the trees later into the day than usual, as on the sides of mountains.

This small lake was of most value as a neighbor in the intervals of a gentle rain-storm in August, when, both air and water being perfectly still, but the sky overcast, mid-afternoon had all the serenity of evening, and the wood thrush sang around, and was heard from shore to shore. A lake like this is never smoother than at such a time; and the clear portion of the air above it being shallow and darkened by clouds, the water, full of light and reflections, becomes a lower heaven itself so much the more important. From a hill-top near by, where the wood had been recently cut off, there was a pleasing vista southward across the pond, through a wide indentation in the hills which form the shore there, where their opposite sides sloping toward each other suggested a stream flowing out in that direction through a wooded valley, but stream there was none. That way I looked between and over the near green hills to some distant and higher ones in the horizon, tinged with blue. Indeed, by standing on tiptoe I could catch a glimpse of some of the peaks of the still bluer and more distant mountain ranges in the northwest, those true-blue coins from heaven's own mint, and also of some portion of the village. But in other directions, even from this point, I could not see over or beyond the woods which surrounded me. It is well to have some water in your neighborhood, to give buoyancy to and float the earth. One value even of the smallest well is, that when you look into it you see that earth is not continent but insular. This is as important as that it keeps butter cool. When I looked across the pond from this peak toward the Sudbury meadows, which in time of flood I distinguished elevated perhaps by a mirage in their seething valley, like a coin in a basin, all the earth beyond the pond appeared like a thin crust insulated and floated even by this small sheet of intervening water, and I was reminded that this on which I dwelt was but *dry land*.

Though the view from my door was still more contracted, I did not feel crowded or confined in the least. There was pasture enough for my imagination. The low shrub oak plateau to which the opposite shore arose stretched away toward the prairies of the West and the steppes of Tartary, affording ample room for all the roving families of men. "There are none happy in the world but beings who enjoy freely a vast horizon,"—said Damodara, when his herds required new and larger pastures.

Both place and time were changed, and I dwelt nearer to those parts of the universe and to those eras in history which had most attracted me. Where I lived was as far off as many a region viewed nightly by astronomers. We are wont to imagine rare and delectable places in some remote and more celestial corner of the system, behind the constellation of Cassiopeia's Chair, far from noise and disturbance. I discovered that my house actually had its site in such a withdrawn, but forever new and unprofaned, part of the universe. If it were worth the while to settle in those parts near to the Pleiades or the Hyades, to Aldebaran or Altair, then I was really there, or at an equal remoteness from the life which I had left behind, dwindled and twinkling with as fine a ray to my nearest neighbor, and to be seen only in moonless nights by him. Such was that part of creation where I had squatted;—

There was a shepherd that did live,
  And held his thoughts as high
As were the mounts whereon his flocks
  Did hourly feed him by.

What should we think of the shepherd's life if his flocks always wandered to higher pastures than his thoughts?

Every morning was a cheerful invitation to make my life of equal simplicity, and I may say innocence, with Nature herself. I have been as sincere a worshipper of Aurora as the Greeks. I got up early and bathed in the pond; that was a religious exercise, and one of the best things which I did. They say that characters were engraven on the bathing tub of King Tching-thang to this effect: "Renew thyself completely each day; do it again, and again, and forever again." I can understand that. Morning brings back the heroic ages. I was as much affected by the faint hum of a mosquito making its invisible and unimaginable tour through my apartment at earliest dawn, when I was sitting with door and windows open, as I could be by any trumpet that ever sang of fame. It was Homer's requiem; itself an "Iliad" and "Odyssey" in the air, singing its own wrath and wanderings. There was something cosmical about it; a standing advertisement, till forbidden, of the everlasting vigor and fertility of the world. The morning, which is the most memorable season of the day, is the awakening hour. Then there is least somnolence in us; and for an hour, at least, some part of us awakes which slumbers all the rest of the day and night. Little is to be expected of that day, if it can be called a day, to which we are not awakened by our Genius, but by the mechanical nudgings of some servitor, are not awakened by our own newly acquired force and aspirations from within, accompanied by the undulations of celestial music, instead of factory bells, and a fragrance filling the air—to a higher life than we fell asleep from; and thus the darkness bear its fruit, and prove itself to be good, no less than the light. That man who does not believe that each day contains an earlier, more sacred, and auroral hour than he has yet profaned, has despaired of life, and is pursuing a descending and darkening way. After a partial cessation of his sensuous life, the soul of man, or its organs rather, are reinvigorated each day, and his Genius tries again what noble life it can make. All memorable events, I should say, transpire in morning time and in a morning atmosphere. The Vedas say, "All intelligences awake with the morning." Poetry and art, and the fairest and most memorable of the actions of men, date from such an hour. All poets and heroes, like Memnon, are the children of Aurora, and emit their music at sunrise. To him whose elastic and vigorous thought keeps pace with the sun, the day is a perpetual morning. It matters not what the clocks say or the attitudes and labors of men. Morning is when I am awake and there is a dawn in me. Moral reform is the effort to throw off sleep. Why is it that men give so poor an account of their day if they have not been slumbering? They are not such poor calculators. If they had not been overcome with drowsiness, they would have performed something. The millions are awake enough for physical labor; but only one in a million is awake enough for effective intellectual exertion, only one in a hundred millions to a poetic or divine life. To be awake is to be alive. I have never yet met a man who was quite awake. How could I have looked him in the face?

We must learn to reawaken and keep ourselves awake, not by mechanical aids, but by an infinite expectation of the dawn, which does not forsake us in our soundest sleep. I know of no more encouraging fact than the unquestionable ability of man to elevate his life by a conscious endeavor. It is something to be able to paint a particular picture, or to carve a statue, and so to make a few objects beautiful; but it is far more glorious to carve and paint the very atmosphere and medium through which we look, which morally we can do. To affect the quality of the day, that is the highest of arts. Every man is tasked to make his life, even in its details, worthy of the contemplation of his most elevated and critical hour. If we refused, or rather used up, such paltry information as we get, the oracles would distinctly inform us how this might be done.

I went to the woods because I wished to live deliberately, to front only the essential facts of life, and see if I could not learn what it had to teach, and not, when I came to die, discover that I had not lived. I did not wish to live what was not life, living is so dear; nor did I wish to practice resignation, unless it was quite necessary. I wanted to live deep and suck out all the marrow of life, to live so sturdily and Spartan-like as to put to rout all that was not life, to cut a broad swath and shave close, to drive life into a corner, and reduce it to its lowest terms, and, if it proved to be mean, why then to get the whole and genuine meanness of it, and publish its meanness to the world; or if it were sublime, to know it by experience, and be able to give a true account of it in my next excursion. For most men, it appears to me, are in a strange uncertainty about it, whether it is of the devil or of God, and have *somewhat hastily* concluded that it is the chief end of man here to "glorify God and enjoy him forever."

Still we live meanly, like ants; though the fable tells us that we were long ago changed into men; like pygmies we fight with cranes; it is error upon error, and clout upon clout, and our best virtue has for its occasion a superfluous and evitable wretchedness. Our life is frittered away by detail. An honest man has hardly need to count more than his ten fingers, or in extreme cases he may add his ten toes, and lump the rest. Simplicity, simplicity, simplicity! I say, let your affairs be as two or three, and not a hundred or a thousand; instead of a million count half a dozen, and keep your accounts on your thumb-nail. In the midst of this chopping sea of civilized life, such are the clouds and storms and quicksands and thousand-and-one items to be allowed for, that a man has to live, if he would not founder and go to the bottom and not make his port at all, by dead reckoning, and he must be a great calculator indeed who succeeds. Simplify, simplify. Instead of three meals a day, if it be necessary eat but one; instead of a hundred dishes, five; and reduce other things in proportion. Our life is like a German Confederacy, made up of petty states, with its boundary forever fluctuating, so that even a German cannot tell you how it is bounded at any moment. The nation itself, with all its so-called internal improvements, which, by the way, are all external and superficial, is just such an unwieldy and overgrown establishment, cluttered with furniture and tripped up by its own traps, ruined by luxury and heedless expense, by want of calculation and a worthy aim, as the million households in the land; and the only cure for it, as for them, is in a rigid economy, a stern and more than Spartan simplicity of life and elevation of purpose. It lives too fast. Men think that it is essential that the *Nation* have commerce, and export ice, and talk through a telegraph, and ride thirty miles an hour, without a doubt, whether *they* do or not; but whether we should live like baboons or like men, is a little uncertain. If we do not get out sleepers, and forge rails, and devote days and nights to the work, but go to tinkering upon our *lives* to improve *them,* who will build railroads? And if railroads are not built, how shall we get to heaven in season? But if we stay at home and mind our business, who will want railroads? We do not ride on the railroad; it rides upon us. Did you ever think what those sleepers are that underlie the railroad? Each one is a man, an Irishman, or a Yankee man. The rails are laid on them, and they are covered with sand, and the cars run smoothly over them. They are sound sleepers, I assure you. And every few years a new lot is laid down and run over; so that, if some have the pleasure of riding on a rail, others have the misfortune to be ridden upon. And when they run over a man that is walking in his sleep, a supernumerary sleeper in the wrong position, and wake him up, they suddenly stop the cars, and make a hue and cry about it, as if this were an exception. I am glad to know that it takes a gang of men for every five miles to keep the sleepers down and level in their beds as it is, for this is a sign that they may sometime get up again.

Why should we live with such hurry and waste of life? We are determined to be starved before we are hungry. Men say that a stitch in time saves nine, and so they take a thousand stitches to-day to save nine to-morrow. As for *work,* we haven't any of any consequence. We have the Saint Vitus' dance, and cannot possibly keep our heads still. If I should only give a few pulls at the parish bell-rope, as for a fire, that is, without setting the fire, there is hardly a man on his farm in the outskirts of Concord, notwithstanding that press of engagements which was his excuse so many times this morning, nor a boy, nor a woman, I might almost say, but would forsake all and follow that sound, not mainly to save property from the flames, but, if we will confess the truth, much more, to see it burn, since burn it must, and we, be it known, did not set it on fire,—or to see it put out, and have a hand in it, if that is done as handsomely; yes, even if it were the parish church itself. Hardly a man takes a half-hour's nap after dinner, but when he wakes he holds up his head and asks, "What's the news?" as if the rest of mankind had stood his sentinels. Some give directions to be waked every half-hour, doubtless for no other purpose; and then, to pay for it, they tell what they have dreamed. After a night's sleep the news is as indispensable as the breakfast. "Pray tell me anything new that has happened to a man anywhere on this globe,"—and he reads it over his coffee and rolls, that a man has had his eyes gouged out this morning on the Wachito River; never dreaming the while that he lives in the dark unfathomed mammoth cave of this world, and has but the rudiment of an eye himself.

For my part, I could easily do without the post-office. I think that there are very few important communications made through it. To speak critically, I never received more than one or two letters in my life—I wrote this some years ago—that were worth the postage. The penny-post is, commonly, an institution through which you seriously offer a man that penny for his thoughts which is so often safely offered in jest. And I am sure that I never read any memorable news in a newspaper. If we read of one man robbed, or murdered, or killed by accident, or one house burned, or one vessel wrecked, or one steamboat blown up, or one cow run over on the Western Railroad, or one mad dog killed, or one lot of grasshoppers in the winter,—we never need read of another. One is enough. If you are acquainted with the principle, what do you care for a myriad instances and applications? To a philosopher all *news,* as it is called, is gossip, and they who edit and read it are old women over their tea. Yet not a few are greedy after this gossip. There was such a rush, as I hear, the other day at one of the offices to learn the foreign news by the last arrival, that several large squares of plate glass belonging to the establishment were broken by the pressure,—news which I seriously think a ready wit might write a twelvemonth, or twelve years, beforehand with sufficient accuracy. * * *

Let us spend one day as deliberately as Nature, and not be thrown off the track by every nutshell and mosquito's wing that falls on the rails. Let us rise early and fast, or break fast, gently and without perturbation; let company come and let company go, let the bells ring and the children cry,—determined to make a day of it. Why should we knock under and go with the stream? Let us not be upset and overwhelmed in that terrible rapid and whirlpool called a dinner, situated in the meridian shallows. Weather this danger and you are safe, for the rest of the way is down hill. With unrelaxed nerves, with morning vigor, sail by it, looking another way, tied to the mast like Ulysses. If the engine whistles, let it whistle till it is hoarse for its pains. If the bell rings, why should we run? We will consider what kind of music they are like. Let us settle ourselves, and work and wedge our feet downward through the mud and slush of opinion, and prejudice, and tradition, and delusion, and appearance, that alluvion which covers the globe, through Paris and London, through New York and Boston and Concord, through Church and State, through poetry and philosophy and religion, till we come to a hard bottom and rocks in place, which we can call *reality,* and say, This is, and no mistake; and then begin, having a *point d' appui,* below freshet and frost and fire, a place where you might found a wall or a state, or set a lamp-post safely, or perhaps a gauge, not a Nilometer, but a Realometer, that future ages might know how deep a freshet of shams and appearances had gathered from time to time. If you stand right fronting and face to face to a fact, you will see the sun glimmer on both its surfaces, as if it were a scimitar, and feel its sweet edge dividing you through the heart and marrow, and so you will happily conclude your mortal career. Be it life or death, we crave only reality. If we are really dying, let us hear the rattle in our throats and feel cold in the extremities; if we are alive, let us go about our business.

Time is but the stream I go a-fishing in. I drink at it; but while I drink I see the sandy bottom and detect how shallow it is. Its thin current slides away, but eternity remains. I would drink deeper; fish in the sky, whose bottom is pebbly with stars. I cannot count one. I know not the first letter of the alphabet. I have always been regretting that I was not as wise as the day I was born. The intellect is a cleaver; it discerns and rifts its way into the secret of things. I do not wish to be any more busy with my hands than is necessary. My head is hands and feet. I feel all my best faculties concentrated in it. My instinct tells me that my head is an organ for burrowing, as some creatures use their snout and fore paws, and with it I would mine and burrow my way through these hills. I think that the richest vein is somewhere hereabouts; so by the divining-rod and thin rising vapors I judge; and here I will begin to mine.

## *From* XII. BRUTE NEIGHBORS

* * * Why do precisely these objects which we behold make a world? Why has man just these species of animals for his neighbors; as if nothing but a mouse could have filled this crevice? I suspect that Pilpay & Co. have put animals to their best use, for they are all beasts of burden, in a sense, made to carry some portion of our thoughts.

The mice which haunted my house were not the common ones, which are said to have been introduced into the country, but a wild native kind not found in the village. I sent one to a distinguished naturalist, and it interested him much. When I was building, one of these had its nest underneath the house, and before I had laid the second floor, and swept out the shavings, would come out regularly at lunch time and pick up the crumbs at my feet. It probably had never seen a man before; and it soon became quite familiar, and would run over my shoes and up my clothes. It could readily ascend the sides of the room by short impulses, like a squirrel, which it resembled in its motions. At length, as I leaned with my elbow on the bench one day, it ran up my clothes, and along my sleeve, and round and round the paper which held my dinner, while I kept the latter close, and dodged and played at bo-peep with it; and when at last I held still a piece of cheese between my thumb and finger, it came and nibbled it, sitting in my hand, and afterward cleaned its face and paws, like a fly, and walked away.

A phœbe soon built in my shed, and a robin for protection in a pine which grew against the house. In June the partridge, (*Tetrao umbellus,*) which is so shy a bird, led her brood past my windows, from the woods in the rear to the front of my house, clucking and calling to them like a hen, and in all her behavior proving herself the hen of the woods. The young suddenly disperse on your approach, at a signal from the mother, as if a whirlwind had swept them away, and they so exactly resemble the dried leaves and twigs that many a traveller has placed his foot in the midst of a brood, and heard the whir of the old bird as she flew off, and her anxious calls and mewing, or seen her trail her wings to attract his attention, without suspecting their neighborhood. The parent will sometimes roll and spin round before you in such a dishabille, that you cannot, for a few moments, detect what kind of creature it is. The young squat still and flat, often running their heads under a leaf, and mind only their mother's directions given from a distance, nor will your approach make them run again and betray themselves. You may even tread on them, or have your eyes on them for a minute, without discovering them. I have held them in my open hand at such a time, and still their only care, obedient to their mother and their instinct, was to squat there without fear or trembling. So perfect is this instinct, that once, when I had laid them on the leaves again, and one accidentally fell on its side, it was found with the rest in exactly the same position ten minutes afterward. They are not callow like the young of most birds, but more perfectly developed and precocious even than chickens. The remarkably adult yet innocent expression of their open and serene eyes is very memorable. All intelligence seems reflected in them. They suggest not merely the purity of infancy, but a wisdom clarified by experience. Such an eye was not born when the bird was, but is coeval with the sky it reflects. The woods do not yield another such a gem. The traveller does not often look into such a limpid well. The ignorant or reckless sportsman often shoots the parent at such a time, and leaves these innocents to fall a prey to some prowling beast or bird, or gradually mingle with the decaying leaves which they so much resemble. It is said that when hatched by a hen they will directly disperse on some alarm, and so are lost, for they never hear the mother's call which gathers them again. These were my hens and chickens.

It is remarkable how many creatures live wild and free though secret in the woods, and still sustain themselves in the neighborhood of towns, suspected by hunters only. How retired the otter manages to live here! He grows to be four feet long, as big as a small boy, perhaps without any human being getting a glimpse of him. I formerly saw the raccoon in the woods behind where my house is built, and probably still heard their whinnering at night. Commonly I rested an hour or two in the shade at noon, after planting, and ate my lunch, and read a little by a spring which was the source of a swamp and of a brook, oozing from under Brister's Hill, half a mile from my field. The approach to this was through a succession of descending grassy hollows, full of young pitch-pines, into a larger wood about the swamp. There, in a very secluded and shaded spot, under a spreading white-pine, there was yet a clean firm sward to sit on. I had dug out the spring and made a well of clear gray water, where I could dip up a pailful without roiling it, and thither I went for this purpose almost every day in midsummer, when the pond was warmest. Thither too the wood-cock led her brood, to probe the mud for worms, flying but a foot above them down the bank, while they ran in a troop beneath; but at last, spying me, she would leave her young and circle round and round me, nearer and nearer till within four or five feet, pretending broken wings and legs, to attract my attention, and get off her young, who would already have taken up their march, with faint wiry peep, single file through the swamp, as she directed. Or I heard the peep of the young when I could not see the parent bird. There too the turtle-doves sat over the spring, or fluttered from bough to bough of the soft white-pines over my head; or the red squirrel, coursing down the nearest bough, was particularly familiar and inquisitive. You only need sit still long enough in some attractive spot in the woods that all its inhabitants may exhibit themselves to you by turns.

I was witness to events of a less peaceful character. One day when I went out to my wood-pile, or rather my pile of stumps, I observed two large ants, the one red, the other much larger, nearly half an inch long, and black, fiercely contending with one another. Having once got hold they never let go, but struggled and wrestled and rolled on the chips incessantly. Looking farther, I was surprised to find that the chips were covered with such combatants, that it was not a *duellum*, but a *bellum*, a war between two races of ants, the red always pitted against the black, and frequently two red ones to one black. The legions of these Myrmidons covered all the hills and vales in my wood-yard, and the ground was already strewn with the dead and dying, both red and black. It was the only battle which I have ever witnessed, the only battle-field I ever trod while the battle was raging; internecine war; the red republicans on the one hand, and the black imperialists on the other. On every side they were engaged in deadly combat, yet without any noise that I could hear, and human soldiers never fought so resolutely. I watched a couple that were fast locked in each other's embraces, in a little sunny valley amid the chips, now at noonday prepared to fight till the sun went down, or life went out. The smaller red champion had fastened himself like a vice to his adversary's front, and through all the tumblings on that field never for an instant ceased to gnaw at one of his feelers near the root, having already caused the other to go by the board; while the stronger black one dashed him from side to side, and, as I saw on looking nearer, had already divested him of several of his members. They fought with more pertinacity than bull-dogs. Neither manifested the least disposition to retreat. It was evident that their battle-cry was "Conquer or die." In the meanwhile there came along a single red ant on the hill-side of this valley, evidently full of excitement, who either had despatched his foe, or had not yet taken part in the battle; probably the latter, for he had lost none of his limbs; whose mother had charged him to return with his shield or upon it. Or perchance he was some Achilles, who had nourished his wrath apart, and had now come to avenge or rescue his Patroclus. He saw this unequal combat from afar,—for the blacks were nearly twice the size of the red,—he drew near with rapid pace till he stood on his guard within half an inch of the combatants; then, watching his opportunity, he sprang upon the black warrior, and commenced his operations near the root of his right foreleg, leaving the foe to select among his own members; and so there were three united for life, as if a new kind of attraction had been invented which put all other locks and cements to shame. I should not have wondered by this time to find that they had their respective musical bands stationed on some eminent chip, and playing their national airs the while, to excite the slow and cheer the dying combatants. I was myself excited somewhat even as if they had been men. The more you think of it, the less the difference. And certainly there is not the fight recorded in Concord history, at least, if in the history of America, that will bear a moment's comparison with this, whether for the numbers engaged in it, or for the patriotism and heroism displayed. For numbers and for carnage it was an Austerlitz or Dresden. Concord Fight! Two killed on the patriots' side, and Luther Blanchard wounded! Why here every ant was a Buttrick,—"Fire! for God's sake fire!"—and thousands shared the fate of Davis and Hosmer. There was not one hireling there. I have no doubt that it was a principle they fought for, as much as our ancestors, and not to avoid a three-penny tax on their tea; and the results of this battle will be as important and memorable to those whom it concerns as those of the battle of Bunker Hill at least.

I took up the chip on which the three I have particularly described were struggling, carried it into my house, and placed it under a tumbler on my window-sill, in order to see the issue. Holding a microscope to the first-mentioned red ant, I saw that, though he was assiduously gnawing at the near fore-leg of his enemy, having severed his remaining feeler, his own breast was all torn away, exposing what vitals he had there to the jaws of the black warrior, whose breastplate was apparently too thick for him to pierce; and the dark carbuncles of the sufferer's eyes shone with ferocity such as war only could excite. They struggled half an hour longer under the tumbler, and when I looked again the black soldier had severed the heads of his foes from their bodies, and the still living heads were hanging on either side of him like ghastly trophies at his saddlebow, still apparently as firmly fastened as ever, and he was endeavoring with feeble struggles, being without feelers and with only the remnant of a leg, and I know not how many other wounds, to divest himself of them; which at length, after half an hour more, he accomplished. I raised the glass, and he went off over the window-sill in that crippled state. Whether he finally survived that combat, and spent the remainder of his days in some Hôtel des Invalides, I do not know; but I thought that his industry would not be worth much thereafter. I never learned which party was victorious, nor the cause of the war; but I felt for the rest of that day as if I had my feelings excited and harrowed by witnessing the struggle, the ferocity and carnage, of a human battle before my door. * * *

1854

## *From* WALKING

I wish to speak a word for Nature, for absolute freedom and wildness, as contrasted with a freedom and culture merely civil,—to regard man as an inhabitant, or a part and parcel of Nature, rather than a member of society. I wish to make an extreme statement, if so I may make an emphatic one, for there are enough champions of civilization: the minister and the school-committee and every one of you will take care of that.

I have met with but one or two

persons in the course of my life who understood the art of Walking, that is, of taking walks,—who had a genius, so to speak, for *sauntering:* which word is beautifully derived "from idle people who roved about the country, in the Middle Ages, and asked charity, under pretense of going *à la Sainte Terre,*" to the Holy Land, till the children exclaimed, "There goes a *Sainte-Terrer,*" a Saunterer, a Holy-Lander. They who never go to the Holy Land in their walks, as they pretend, are indeed mere idlers and vagabonds; but they who do go there are saunterers in the good sense, such as I mean. Some, however, would derive the word from *sans terre,* without land or a home, which, therefore, in the good sense, will mean, having no particular home, but equally at home everywhere. For this is the secret of successful sauntering. He who sits still in a house all the time may be the greatest vagrant of all; but the saunterer, in the good sense, is no more vagrant than the meandering river, which is all the while sedulously seeking the shortest course to the sea. But I prefer the first, which, indeed, is the most probable derivation. For every walk is a sort of crusade, preached by some Peter the Hermit in us, to go forth and reconquer this Holy Land from the hands of the Infidels.

It is true, we are but faint-hearted crusaders, even the walkers, nowadays, who undertake no persevering, never-ending enterprises. Our expeditions are but tours, and come round again at evening to the old hearth-side from which we set out. Half the walk is but retracing our steps. We should go forth on the shortest walk, perchance, in the spirit of undying adventure, never to return,—prepared to send back our embalmed hearts only as relics to our desolate kingdoms. If you are ready to leave father and mother, and brother and sister, and wife and child and friends, and never see them again,—if you have paid your debts, and made your will, and settled all your affairs, and are a free man, then you are ready for a walk.

To come down to my own experience, my companion and I, for I sometimes have a companion, take pleasure in fancying ourselves knights of a new, or rather an old, order,—not Equestrians or Chevaliers, not Ritters or Riders, but Walkers, a still more ancient and honorable class, I trust. The chivalric and heroic spirit which once belonged to the Rider seems now to reside in, or perchance to have subsided into, the Walker,—not the Knight, but Walker Errant. He is a sort of fourth estate, outside of Church and State and People.

We have felt that we almost alone hereabouts practiced this noble art; though, to tell the truth, at least, if their own assertions are to be received, most of my townsmen would fain walk sometimes, as I do, but they cannot. No wealth can buy the requisite leisure, freedom, and independence which are the capital in this profession. It comes only by the grace of God. It requires a direct dispensation from Heaven to become a walker. You must be born into the family of the Walkers. *Ambulator nascitur, non fit.* Some of my townsmen, it is true, can remember and have described to me some walks which they took ten years ago, in which they were so blessed as to lose themselves for half an hour in the woods; but I know very well that they have confined themselves to the highway ever since, whatever pretensions they may make to belong to this select class. No doubt they were elevated for a moment as by the reminiscence of a previous state of existence, when even they were foresters and outlaws.

When he came to grene wode,
  In a mery mornynge,
There he herde the notes small
  Of byrdes mery syngynge.

It is ferre gone, sayd Robyn,
  That I was last here;
Me lyste a lytell for to shote
  At the donne dere.

I think that I cannot preserve my health and spirits, unless I spend four hours a day at least,—and it is commonly more than that,—sauntering through the woods and over the hills and fields, absolutely free from all worldly engagements. You may safely say, A penny for your thoughts, or a thousand pounds. When sometimes I am reminded that the mechanics and shopkeepers stay in their shops not only all the forenoon, but all the afternoon too, sitting with crossed legs, so many of them,—as if the legs were made to sit upon, and not to stand or walk upon,—I think that they deserve some credit for not having all committed suicide long ago.

I, who cannot stay in my chamber for a single day without acquiring some rust, and when sometimes I have stolen forth for a walk at the eleventh hour or four o'clock in the afternoon, too late to redeem the day, when the shades of night were already beginning to be mingled with the daylight, have felt as if I had committed some sin to be atoned for,—I confess that I am astonished at the power of endurance, to say nothing of the moral insensibility, of my neighbors who confine themselves to shops and offices the whole day for weeks and months, aye, and years almost together. I know not what manner of stuff they are of,—sitting there now at three o'clock in the afternoon, as if it were three o'clock in the morning. Bonaparte may talk of the three-o'clock-in-the-morning courage, but it is nothing to the courage which can sit down cheerfully at this hour in the afternoon over against one's self whom you have known all the morning, to starve out a garrison to whom you are bound by such strong ties of sympathy. I wonder that about this time, or say between four and five o'clock in the afternoon, too late for the morning papers and too early for the evening ones, there is not a general explosion heard up and down the street, scattering a legion of antiquated and house-bred notions and whims to the four winds for an airing,—and so the evil cures itself. * * *

What is it that makes it so hard sometimes to determine whither we will walk? I believe that there is a subtle magnetism in Nature, which, if we unconsciously yield to it, will direct us aright. It is not indifferent to us which way we walk. There is a right way; but we are very liable from heedlessness and stupidity to take the wrong one. We would fain take that walk, never yet taken by us through this actual world, which is perfectly symbolical of the path which we love to travel in the interior and ideal world; and sometimes, no doubt, we find it difficult to choose our direction, because it does not yet exist distinctly in our idea.

When I go out of the house for a walk, uncertain as yet whither I will bend my steps, and submit myself to my instinct to decide for me, I find, strange and whimsical as it may seem, that I finally and inevitably settle southwest, toward some particular wood or meadow or deserted pasture or hill in that direction. My needle is slow to settle,—varies a few degrees, and does not always point due southwest, it is true, and it has good authority for this variation, but it always settles between west and south-southwest. The future lies that way to me, and the earth seems more unexhausted and richer on that side. The outline which would bound my walks would be, not a circle, but a parabola, or rather like one of those cometary orbits which have been thought to be non-returning curves, in this case opening westward, in which my house occupies the place of the sun. I turn round and round irresolute sometimes for a quarter of an hour, until I decide, for a thousandth time, that I will walk into the southwest or west. Eastward I go only by force; but westward I go free. Thither no business leads me. It is hard for me to believe that I shall find fair landscapes or sufficient wildness and freedom behind the eastern horizon. I am not excited by the prospect of a walk thither, but I believe that the forest which I see in the western horizon stretches uninterruptedly toward the setting sun, and there are no towns nor cities in it of enough consequence to disturb me. Let me live where I will, on this side is the city, on that the wilderness, and ever I am leaving the city more and more, and withdrawing into the wilderness. I should not lay so much stress on this fact, if I did not believe that something like this is the prevailing tendency of my countrymen. I must walk toward Oregon, and not toward Europe. And that way the nation is moving, and I may say that mankind progress from east to west. Within a few years we have witnessed the phenomenon of a southeastward migration, in the settlement of Australia; but this affects us as a retrograde movement, and, judging from the moral and physical character of the first generation of Australians, has not yet proved a successful experiment. The eastern Tartars think that there is nothing west beyond Thibet. "The world ends there," say they; "beyond there is nothing but a shoreless sea." It is unmitigated East where they live.

We go eastward to realize history and study the works of art and literature, retracing the steps of the race; we go westward as into the future, with a spirit of enterprise and adventure. The Atlantic is a Lethean stream, in our passage over which we have had an opportunity to forget the Old World and its institutions. If we do not succeed this time, there is perhaps one more chance for the race left before it arrives on the banks of the Styx; and that is in the Lethe of the Pacific, which is three times as wide.

I know not how significant it is, or how far it is an evidence of singularity, that an individual should thus consent in his pettiest walk with the general movement of the race; but I know that something akin to the migratory instinct in birds and quadrupeds,—which, in some instances, is known to have affected the squirrel tribe, impelling them to a general and mysterious movement, in which they were seen, say some, crossing the broadest rivers, each on its particular chip, with its tail raised for a sail, and bridging narrower streams with their dead,—that something like the *furor* which affects the domestic cattle in the spring, and which is referred to a worm in their tails,—affects both nations and individuals, either perennially or from time to time. Not a flock of wild geese cackles over our town, but it to some extent unsettles the value of real estate here, and, if I were a broker, I should probably take that disturbance into account.

Than longen folk to gon on pilgrimages,
And palmeres for to seken strange strondes.

Every sunset which I witness inspires me with the desire to go to a West as distant and as fair as that into which the sun goes down. He appears to migrate westward daily, and tempt us to follow him. He is the Great Western Pioneer whom the nations follow. We dream all night of those mountain-ridges in the horizon, though they may be of vapor only, which were last gilded by his rays. The island of Atlantis, and the islands and gardens of the Hesperides, a sort of terrestrial paradise, appear to have been the Great West of the ancients, enveloped in mystery and poetry. Who has not seen in imagination, when looking into the sunset sky, the gardens of the Hesperides, and the foundation of all those fables?

Columbus felt the westward tendency more strongly than any before. He obeyed it, and found a New World for Castile and Leon. The herd of men in those days scented fresh pastures from afar.

And now the sun had stretched out all the hills,
And now was dropped into the western bay;
At last *he* rose, and twitched his mantle blue;
To-morrow to fresh woods and pastures new.

Where on the globe can there be found an area of equal extent with that occupied by the bulk of our States, so fertile and so rich and varied in its productions, and at the same time so habitable by the European, as this is? Michaux, who knew but part of them, says that "the species of large trees are much more numerous in North America than in Europe; in the United States there are more than one hundred and forty species that exceed thirty feet in height; in France there are but thirty that attain this size." Later botanists more than confirm his observations. Humboldt came to America to realize his youthful dreams of a tropical vegetation, and he beheld it in its greatest perfection in the primitive forests of the Amazon, the most gigantic wilderness on the earth, which he has so eloquently described. The geographer Guyot, himself a European, goes farther,—farther than I am ready to follow him; yet not when he says: "As the plant is made for the animal, as the vegetable world is made for the animal world, America is made for the man of the Old World. . . . The man of the Old World sets out upon his way. Leaving the highlands of Asia, he descends from station to station towards

Europe. Each of his steps is marked by a new civilization superior to the preceding, by a greater power of development. Arrived at the Atlantic, he pauses on the shore of this unknown ocean, the bounds of which he knows not, and turns upon his footprints for an instant." When he has exhausted the rich soil of Europe, and reinvigorated himself, "then recommences his adventurous career westward as in the earliest ages." So far Guyot.

From this western impulse coming in contact with the barrier of the Atlantic sprang the commerce and enterprise of modern times. The younger Michaux, in his "Travels West of the Alleghanies in 1802," says that the common inquiry in the newly settled West was, "'From what part of the world have you come?' As if these vast and fertile regions would naturally be the place of meeting and common country of all the inhabitants of the globe."

To use an obsolete Latin word, I might say, *Ex Oriente lux; ex Occidente* FRUX. From the East light; from the West fruit. * * *

We had a remarkable sunset one day last November. I was walking in a meadow, the source of a small brook, when the sun at last, just before setting, after a cold gray day, reached a clear stratum in the horizon, and the softest, brightest morning sunlight fell on the dry grass and on the stems of the trees in the opposite horizon and on the leaves of the shrub-oaks on the hill-side, while our shadows stretched long over the meadow eastward, as if we were the only motes in its beams. It was such a light as we could not have imagined a moment before, and the air also was so warm and serene that nothing was wanting to make a paradise of that meadow. When we reflected that this was not a solitary phenomenon, never to happen again, but that it would happen forever and ever an infinite number of evenings, and cheer and reassure the latest child that walked there, it was more glorious still.

The sun sets on some retired meadow, where no house is visible, with all the glory and splendor that it lavishes on cities, and perchance as it has never set before,—where there is but a solitary marsh-hawk to have his wings gilded by it, or only a musquash looks out from his cabin, and there is some little black-veined brook in the midst of the marsh, just beginning to meander, winding slowly round a decaying stump. We walked in so pure and bright a light, gilding the withered grass and leaves, so softly and serenely bright, I thought I had never bathed in such a golden flood, without a ripple or a murmur to it. The west side of every wood and rising ground gleamed like the boundary of Elysium, and the sun on our backs seemed like a gentle herdsman driving us home at evening.

So we saunter toward the Holy Land, till one day the sun shall shine more brightly than ever he has done, shall perchance shine into our minds and hearts, and light up our whole lives with a great awakening light, as warm and serene and golden as on a bank-side in autumn.

1862

## *From* LIFE WITHOUT PRINCIPLE

* * * Let us consider the way in which we spend our lives.

This world is a place of business. What an infinite bustle! I am awaked almost every night by the panting of the locomotive. It interrupts my dreams. There is no sabbath. It would be glorious to see mankind at leisure for once. It is nothing but work, work, work. I cannot easily buy a blank-book to write thoughts in; they are commonly ruled for dollars and cents. An Irishman, seeing me making a minute in the fields, took it for granted that I was calculating my wages. If a man was tossed out of a window when an infant, and so made a cripple for life, or scared out of his wits by the Indians, it is regretted chiefly because he was thus incapacitated for—business! I think that there is nothing, not even crime, more opposed to poetry, to philosophy, ay, to life itself, than this incessant business.

There is a coarse and boisterous money-making fellow in the outskirts of our town, who is going to build a bank-wall under the hill along the edge of his meadow. The powers have put this into his head to keep him out of mischief, and he wishes me to spend three weeks digging there with him. The result will be that he will perhaps get some more money to hoard, and leave for his heirs to spend foolishly. If I do this, most will commend me as an industrious and hard-working man; but if I choose to devote myself to certain labors which yield more real profit, though but little money, they may be inclined to look on me as an idler. Nevertheless, as I do not need the police of meaningless labor to regulate me, and do not see anything absolutely praiseworthy in this fellow's undertaking any more than in many an enterprise of our own or foreign governments, however amusing it may be to him or them, I prefer to finish my education at a different school.

If a man walk in the woods for love of them half of each day, he is in danger of being regarded as a loafer; but if he spends his whole day as a speculator, shearing off those woods and making earth bald before her time, he is esteemed an industrious and enterprising citizen. As if a town had no interest in its forests but to cut them down!

Most men would feel insulted if it were proposed to employ them in throwing stones over a wall, and then in throwing them back, merely that they might earn their wages. But many are no more worthily employed now. For instance: just after sunrise, one summer morning, I noticed one of my neighbors walking beside his team, which was slowly drawing a heavy hewn stone swung under the axle, surrounded by an atmosphere of industry,—his day's work begun,—his brow commenced to sweat,—a reproach to all sluggards and idlers,—pausing abreast the shoulders of his oxen, and half turning round with a flourish of his merciful whip, while they gained their length on him. And I thought, Such is the labor which the American Congress exists to protect,—honest, manly toil,—honest as the day is long,—that makes his bread taste sweet, and keeps society sweet,—which all men respect and have consecrated; one of the sacred band, doing the needful but irksome drudgery. Indeed, I felt a slight reproach, because I observed this from a window, and was not abroad and stirring about a similar business. The day went by, and at evening I passed the yard of another neighbor, who keeps many servants, and spends much money foolishly, while he adds nothing to the common stock, and there I saw the stone of the morning lying beside a whimsical structure intended to adorn this Lord Timothy Dexter's premises, and the dignity forthwith departed from the teamster's labor, in my eyes. In my opinion, the sun was made to light worthier toil than this. I may add that his employer has since run off, in debt to a good part of the town, and, after passing through Chancery, has settled somewhere else, there to become once more a patron of the arts. * * *

It is remarkable that there is little or nothing to be remembered written on the subject of getting a living; how to make getting a living not merely honest and honorable, but altogether inviting and glorious; for if *getting* a living is not so, then living is not. One would think, from looking at literature, that this question had never disturbed a solitary individual's musings. Is it that men are too much disgusted with their experience to speak of it? The lesson of value which money teaches, which the Author of the Universe has taken so much pains to teach us, we are inclined to skip altogether. As for the means of living, it is wonderful how indifferent men of all classes are about it, even reformers, so called,—whether they inherit, or earn, or steal it. I think that Society has done nothing for us in this respect, or at least has undone what she has done. Cold and hunger seem more friendly to my nature than those methods which men have adopted and advise to ward them off.

The title *wise* is, for the most part, falsely applied. How can one be a wise man, if he does not know any better how to live than other men?—if he is only more cunning and intellectually subtle? Does Wisdom work in a treadmill? or does she teach how to succeed *by her example?* Is there any such thing as wisdom not applied to life? Is she merely the miller who grinds the finest logic? It is pertinent to ask if Plato got his *living* in a better way or more successfully than his contemporaries,—or did he succumb to the difficulties of life like other men? Did he seem to prevail over some of them merely by indifference, or by assuming grand airs? or find it easier to live, because his aunt remembered him in her will? The ways in which most men get their living, that is, live, are mere make-shifts, and a shirking of the real business of life,—chiefly because they do not know, but partly because they do not mean, any better.

The rush to California, for instance, and the attitude, not merely of merchants, but of philosophers and prophets, so called, in relation to it, reflect the greatest disgrace on mankind. That so many are ready to live by luck, and so get the means of commanding the labor of others less lucky, without contributing any value to society! And that is called enterprise! I know of no more startling development of the immorality of trade, and all the common modes of getting a living. The philosophy and poetry and religion of such a mankind are not worth the dust of a puff-ball. The hog that gets his living by rooting, stirring up the soil so, would be ashamed of such company. If I could command the wealth of all the worlds by lifting my finger, I would not pay *such* a price for it. Even Mahomet knew that God did not make this world in jest. It makes God to be a moneyed gentleman who scatters a handful of pennies in order to see mankind scramble for them. The world's raffle! A subsistence in the domains of Nature a thing to be raffled for! What a comment, what a satire, on our institutions! The conclusion will be that mankind will hang itself upon a tree. And have all the precepts in all the Bibles taught men only this? and is the last and most admirable invention of the human race only an improved muck-rake? Is this the ground on which Orientals and Occidentals meet? Did God direct us so to get our living, digging where we never planted,—and He would, perchance, reward us with lumps of gold?

God gave the righteous man a certificate entitling him to food and raiment, but the unrighteous man found a facsimile of the same in God's coffers, and appropriated it, and obtained food and raiment like the former. It is one of the most extensive systems of counterfeiting that the world has seen. I did not know that mankind was suffering for want of gold. I have seen a little of it. I know that it is very malleable, but not so malleable as wit. A grain of gold will gild a great surface, but not so much as a grain of wisdom.

The gold-digger in the ravines of the mountains is as much a gambler as his fellow in the saloons of San Francisco. What difference does it make whether you shake dirt or shake dice? If you win, society is the loser. The gold-digger is the enemy of the honest laborer, whatever checks and compensations there may be. It is not enough to tell me that you worked hard to get your gold. So does the Devil work hard. The way of transgressors may be hard in many respects. The humblest observer who goes to the mines sees and says that gold-digging is of the character of a lottery; the gold thus obtained is not the same thing with the wages of honest toil. But, practically, he forgets what he has seen, for he has seen only the fact, not the principle, and goes into trade there, that is, buys a ticket in what commonly proves another lottery, where the fact is not so obvious.

After reading Howitt's account of the Australian gold-diggings one evening, I had in my mind's eye, all night, the numerous valleys, with their streams, all cut up with foul pits, from ten to one hundred feet deep, and half a dozen feet across, as close as they can be dug, and partly filled with water,—the locality to which men furiously rush to probe for their fortunes,—uncertain where they shall break ground,—not knowing but the gold is under their camp itself,—sometimes digging one hundred and sixty feet before they strike the vein, or then missing it by a foot,—turned into demons, and regardless of each others' rights, in their thirst for riches,—whole valleys, for thirty miles, suddenly honeycombed by the pits of the miners so that even hundreds are drowned in them,—standing in water, and covered with mud and clay, they work night and day, dying of exposure and disease. Having read this, and partly forgotten it, I was thinking, accidentally, of my own unsatisfactory life, doing as others do; and with that vision of the diggings still before me, I asked myself why *I* might not be washing some gold daily, though it were only the finest particles,—why *I* might not sink a shaft down to the gold within me, and work that mine. *There* is a Ballarat, a Bendigo for you,—what though it were a sulky-gully? At any rate, I might pursue some path, however solitary and narrow and crooked, in which I could walk with love and reverence. Wherever a man separates from the multitude, and goes his own way in this mood, there indeed is a fork in the road, though ordinary travelers may see only a gap in the paling. His solitary path across-lots will turn out the *higher way* of the two.

Men rush to California and Australia as if the true gold were to be found in that direction; but that is to go to the very opposite extreme to where it lies. They go prospecting farther and farther away from the true lead, and are most unfortunate when they think themselves most successful. Is not our *native* soil auriferous? Does not a stream from the golden mountains flow through our native valley? and has not this for more than geologic ages been bringing down the shining particles and forming the nuggets for us? Yet, strange to tell, if a digger steal away, prospecting for this true gold, into the unexplored solitudes around us, there is no danger that any will dog his steps, and endeavor to supplant him. He may claim and undermine the whole valley even, both the cultivated and the uncultivated portions, his whole life long in peace, for no one will ever dispute his claim. They will not mind his cradles or his toms. He is not confined to a claim twelve feet square, as at Ballarat, but may mine anywhere, and wash the whole wide world in his tom.

Howitt says of the man who found the great nugget which weighed twenty-eight pounds, at the Bendigo diggings in Australia: "He soon began to drink; got a horse, and rode all about, generally at full gallop, and, when he met people, called out to inquire if they knew who he was, and then kindly informed them that he was 'the bloody wretch that had found the nugget.' At last he rode full speed against a tree, and nearly knocked his brains out." I think, however, there was no danger of that, for he had already knocked his brains out against the nugget. Howitt adds, "He is a hopelessly ruined man." But he is a type of the class. They are all fast men. Hear some of the names of the places where they dig: "Jackass Flat,"—"Sheep's-Head Gully,"—"Murderer's Bar," etc. Is there no satire in these names? Let them carry their ill-gotten wealth where they will, I am thinking it will still be "Jackass Flat," if not "Murderer's Bar," where they live. * * *

America is said to be the arena on which the battle of freedom is to be fought; but surely it cannot be freedom in a merely political sense that is meant. Even if we grant that the American has freed himself from a political tyrant, he is still the slave of an economical and moral tyrant. Now that the republic—the *res-publica*—has been settled, it is time to look after the *res-privata*,—

the private state,—to see, as the Roman senate charged its consuls, "*ne quid res*-PRIVATA *detrimenti caperet*," that the *private* state receive no detriment.

Do we call this the land of the free? What is it to be free from King George and continue the slaves of King Prejudice? What is it to be born free and not to live free? What is the value of any political freedom, but as a means to moral freedom? Is it a freedom to be slaves, or a freedom to be free, of which we boast? We are a nation of politicians, concerned about the outmost defenses only of freedom. It is our children's children who may perchance be really free. We tax ourselves unjustly. There is a part of us which is not represented. It is taxation without representation. We quarter troops, we quarter fools and cattle of all sorts upon ourselves. We quarter our gross bodies on our poor souls, till the former eat up all the latter's substance.

With respect to a true culture and manhood, we are essentially provincial still, not metropolitan,—mere Jonathans. We are provincial, because we do not find at home our standards; because we do not worship truth, but the reflection of truth; because we are warped and narrowed by an exclusive devotion to trade and commerce and manufactures and agriculture and the like, which are but means, and not the end.

So is the English Parliament provincial. Mere country bumpkins, they betray themselves, when any more important question arises for them to settle, the Irish question, for instance, —the English question why did I not say? Their natures are subdued to what they work in. Their "good breeding" respects only secondary objects. The finest manners in the world are awkwardness and fatuity when contrasted with a finer intelligence. They appear but as the fashions of past days,—mere courtliness, knee-buckles and small-clothes, out of date. It is the vice, but not the excellence of manners, that they are continually being deserted by the character; they are cast-off clothes or shells, claiming the respect which belonged to the living creature. You are presented with the shells instead of the meat, and it is no excuse generally, that, in the case of some fishes, the shells are of more worth than the meat. The man who thrusts his manners upon me does as if he were to insist on introducing me to his cabinet of curiosities, when I wished to see himself. It was not in this sense that the poet Decker called Christ "the first true gentleman that ever breathed." I repeat that in this sense the most splendid court in Christendom is provincial, having authority to consult about Transalpine interests only, and not the affairs of Rome. A prætor or proconsul would suffice to settle the questions which absorb the attention of the English Parliament and the American Congress.

Government and legislation! these I thought were respectable professions. We have heard of heaven-born Numas, Lycurguses, and Solons, in the history of the world, whose *names* at least may stand for ideal legislators; but think of legislating to *regulate* the breeding of slaves, or the exportation of tobacco! What have divine legislators to do with the exportation or the importation of tobacco? what humane ones with the breeding of slaves? Suppose you were to submit the question to any son of God,—and has He no children in the Nineteenth Century? is it a family which is extinct?—in what condition would you get it again? What shall a State like Virginia say for itself at the last day, in which these have been the principal, the staple productions? What ground is there for patriotism in such a State? I derive my facts from statistical tables which the States themselves have published.

A commerce that whitens every sea in quest of nuts and raisins, and makes slaves of its sailors for this purpose! I saw, the other day, a vessel which had been wrecked, and many lives lost, and her cargo of rags, juniper-berries, and bitter almonds were strewn along the shore. It seemed hardly worth the while to tempt the dangers of the sea between Leghorn and New York for the sake of a cargo of juniper-berries and bitter almonds. America sending to the Old World for her bitters! Is not the sea-brine, is not shipwreck, bitter enough to make the cup of life go down here? Yet such, to a great extent, is our boasted commerce; and there are those who style themselves statesmen and philosophers who are so blind as to think that progress and civilization depend on precisely this kind of interchange and activity, —the activity of flies about a molasses-hogshead. Very well, observes one, if men were oysters. And very well, answer I, if men were mosquitoes.

Lieutenant Herndon, whom our Government sent to explore the Amazon, and, it is said, to extend the area of slavery, observed that there was wanting there "an industrious and active population, who know what the comforts of life are, and who have artificial wants to draw out the great resources of the country." But what are the "artificial wants" to be encouraged? Not the love of luxuries, like the tobacco and slaves of, I believe, his native Virginia, nor the ice and granite and other material wealth of our native New England; nor are "the great resources of a country" that fertility or barrenness of soil which produces these. The chief want, in every State that I have been into, was a high and earnest purpose in its inhabitants. This alone draws out "the great resources" of Nature, and at last taxes her beyond her resources; for man naturally dies out of her. When we want culture more than potatoes, and illumination more than sugar-plums, then the great resources of a world are taxed and drawn out, and the result, or staple production, is, not slaves, nor operatives, but men,—those rare fruits called heroes, saints, poets, philosophers, and redeemers.

In short, as a snow-drift is formed where there is a lull in the wind, so, one would say, where there is a lull of truth, an institution springs up. But the truth blows right on over it, nevertheless, and at length blows it down.

What is called politics is comparatively something so superficial and inhuman, that practically I have never fairly recognized that it concerns me at all. The newspapers, I perceive, devote some of their columns specially to politics or government without charge; and this, one would say, is all that saves it; but as I love literature and to some extent the truth also, I never read those columns at any rate. I do not wish to blunt my sense of right so much. I have not got to answer for having read a single President's Message. A strange age of the world this, when empires, kingdoms, and republics come a-begging to a private man's door, and utter their complaints at his elbow! I cannot take up a newspaper but I find that some wretched government or other, hard pushed, and on its last legs, is interceding with me, the reader, to vote for it,—more importunate than an Italian beggar; and if I have a mind to look at its certificate, made, perchance, by some benevolent merchant's clerk, or the skipper that brought it over, for it cannot speak a word of English itself, I shall probably read of the eruption of some Vesuvius, or the overflowing of some Po, true or forged, which brought it into this condition. I do not hesitate, in such a case, to suggest work, or the almshouse; or why not keep its castle in silence, as I do commonly? The poor President, what with preserving his popularity and doing his duty, is completely bewildered. The newspapers are the ruling power. Any other government is reduced to a few marines at Fort Independence. If a man neglects to read the Daily Times, government will go down on its knees to him, for this is the only treason in these days.

Those things which now most engage the attention of men, as politics and the daily routine, are, it is true, vital functions of human society, but should be unconsciously performed, like the corresponding functions of the physical body. They are *infra*-human, a kind of vegetation. I sometimes awake to a half-consciousness of them going on about me, as a man may become conscious of some of the processes of digestion in a morbid state, and so have the dyspepsia, as it is called. It is as if a thinker submitted himself to be rasped by the great gizzard of creation. Politics is, as it were, the gizzard of society, full of grit and gravel, and the two political parties are its two opposite halves,—sometimes split into quarters, it may be, which grind on each other. Not only individuals, but states, have thus a confirmed dyspepsia, which expresses itself, you can imagine, by what sort of eloquence. Thus our life is not altogether a forgetting, but also, alas! to a great extent, a remembering, of that which we should never have been conscious of, certainly not in our waking hours. Why should we not meet, not always as dyspeptics, to tell our bad dreams, but sometimes as *eu*peptics, to congratulate each other on the ever-glorious morning? I do not make an exorbitant demand, surely.

1863

## SIC VITA

I am a parcel of vain strivings tied
By a chance bond together,
Dangling this way and that, their links
Were made so loose and wide,
Methinks,
For milder weather.

A bunch of violets without their roots,
And sorrel intermixed,

Encircled by a wisp of straw
Once coiled about their shoots,
The law
By which I'm fixed.

A nosegay which Time clutched from out
Those fair Elysian fields,
With weeds and broken stems, in haste,
Doth make the rabble rout
That waste
The day he yields.

And here I bloom for a short hour unseen,
Drinking my juices up,
With no root in the land
To keep my branches green,
But stand
In a bare cup.

Some tender buds were left upon my stem
In mimicry of life,
But ah! the children will not know
Till time has withered them,
The woe
With which they're rife.

But now I see I was not plucked for nought,
And after in life's vase
Of glass set while I might survive,
But by a kind hand brought
Alive
To a strange place.

That stock thus thinned will soon redeem its hours,
And by another year
Such as God knows, with freer air,
More fruits and fair flowers
Will bear,
While I droop here.

(1837) 1841

## A PRAYER

Great God, I ask thee for no meaner pelf
Than that I may not disappoint myself,
That in my action I may soar as high,
As I can now discern with this clear eye.
And next in value, which thy kindness lends,
That I may greatly disappoint my friends,
Howe'er they think or hope that it may be,
They may not dream how thou'st distinguished me.
That my weak hand may equal my firm faith,
And my life practise more than my tongue saith;
That my low conduct may not show,
Nor my relenting lines,
That I thy purpose did not know,
Or overrated thy designs.

1842

## SMOKE

Light-wingèd Smoke, Icarian bird,
Melting thy pinions in thy upward flight;
Lark without song, and messenger of dawn,
Circling above the hamlets as thy nest;
Or else, departing dream, and shadowy form
Of midnight vision, gathering up thy skirts;
By night star-veiling, and by day
Darkening the light and blotting out the sun;
Go thou, my incense, upward from this hearth,
And ask the Gods to pardon this clear flame.

1843

## HAZE

Woof of the fen, ethereal gauze,
Woven of Nature's richest stuffs,

Visible heat, air-water, and dry sea,
Last conquest of the eye;
Toil of the day displayed, sun-dust,
Aerial surf upon the shores of earth,
Etherial estuary, frith of light,
Breakers of air, billows of heat,
Fine summer spray on inland seas;
Bird of the sun, transparent-winged,
Owlet of noon, soft-pinioned,
From heath or stubble rising without song,—
Establish thy serenity o'er the fields.

1843

## INSPIRATION

If with light head erect I sing,
Though all the Muses lend their force,
From my poor love of any thing;
The verse is weak and shallow as its source.

But if with bended neck I grope,
Listening behind me for my wit,
With faith superior to hope,
More anxious to keep back than forward it;

Making my soul accomplice there
Unto the flame my heart hath lit,
Then will the verse forever wear,—
Time cannot bend the line which God hath writ.

I hearing get, who had but ears,
And sight, who had but eyes before;
I moments live, who lived but years,
And truth discern, who knew but learning's lore.

Now chiefly is my natal hour,
And only now my prime of life;
Of manhood's strength it is the flower,
'Tis peace's end and war's beginning strife.

It comes in summer's broadest noon,
By a gray wall, or some chance place,
Unseasoning time, insulting June,
And vexing day with its presuming face.

I will not doubt the love untold
Which not my worth nor want hath bought,
Which wooed me young, and wooes me old,
And to this evening hath me brought.

1863

# MINOR TRANSCENDENTALISTS

## I. AMOS BRONSON ALCOTT
(1799–1888)

### *From* ORPHIC SAYINGS

I

Thou art, my heart, a soul-flower, facing ever and following the motions of thy sun, opening thyself to her vivifying ray, and pleading thy affinity with the celestial orbs. Thou dost

the livelong day
Dial on time thine own eternity.

VII. MYSTICISM

Because the soul is herself mysterious, the saint is a mystic to the worldling. He lives to the soul; he partakes of her properties; he dwells in her atmosphere of light and hope. But the worldling, living to sense, is identified with the flesh; he dwells amidst the dust and vapors of his own lusts, which dim his vision, and obscure the heavens wherein the saint beholds the face of God.

X. APOTHEOSIS

Every soul feels at times her own possibility of becoming a God; she cannot rest in the human, she aspires after the Godlike. This instinctive tendency is an authentic augury of its own fulfilment. Men shall become Gods. Every act of admiration, prayer, praise, worship, desire, hope, implies and predicts the future apotheosis of the soul.

XIV. INSTINCT AND REASON

Innocent, the soul is quick with instincts of unerring aim; then she knows by intuition what lapsed reason defines by laborious inference; her appetites and affections are direct and trust-worthy. Reason is the left hand of instinct; it is tardy, awkward, but the right is ready and dextrous. By reasoning the soul strives to recover her lost intuitions; groping amidst the obscure darkness of sense, by means of the fingers of logic, for treasures present always and available to the eye of conscience. Sinners must needs reason: saints behold.

XXXIII. EACH AND ALL

Life eludes all scientific analysis. Each organ and function is modified in substance and varied in effect, by the subtile energy which pulsates throughout the whole economy of things, spiritual and corporeal. The each is instinct with the all; the all unfolds and reappears in each. Spirit is all in all. God, man, nature, are a divine synthesis, whose parts it is impiety to sunder. Genius must preside devoutly over all investigations, or analysis, with her murderous knife, will seek impiously to probe the vitals of being.

XXXVI. FLUX

Solidity is an illusion of the senses. To faith, nothing is solid: the nature of the soul renders such fact impossible. Modern chemistry demonstrates that nine tenths of the human body are fluid, and substances of inferior order in lesser proportion. Matter is ever pervaded and agitated by the omnipresent soul. All things are instinct with spirit.

### LII. REFORMERS

Reformers are metallic; they are sharpest steel; they pierce whatsoever of evil or abuse they touch. Their souls are attempered in the fires of heaven; they are mailed in the might of principles; God backs their purpose. They uproot institutions, erase traditions, revise usages, and renovate all things. They are the noblest of facts. Extant in time, they work for eternity; dwelling with men, they are with God.

1840, 1841

## MAN

He omnipresent is,
All round himself he lies,
Osiris spread abroad,
Upstaring in all eyes:
Nature his globed thought,
Without him she were not,
Cosmos from chaos were not spoken,
And God bereft of visible token.

1868

## MATTER

Out of chaos dawns in sight
The globe's full form in orbèd light;
Beam kindles beam, kind mirrors kind,
Nature's the eyeball of the Mind;
The fleeting pageant tells for nought
Till shaped in Mind's creative thought.

1877

---

# II. FREDERIC HENRY HEDGE

(1805–1890)

## QUESTIONINGS

Hath this world, without me wrought,
Other substance than my thought?
Lives it by my sense alone,
Or by essence of its own?
Will its life, with mine begun,
Cease to be when that is done,
Or another consciousness
With the self-same forms impress?

Doth yon fireball, poised in air,
Hang by my permission there?
Are the clouds that wander by,
But the offspring of mine eye,
Born with every glance I cast,
Perishing when that is past?
And those thousand, thousand eyes,
Scattered through the twinkling skies,
Do they draw their life from mine,
Or, of their own beauty shine?

Now I close my eyes, my ears,
And creation disappears;
Yet if I but speak the word,
All creation is restored.
Or — more wonderful — within,
New creations do begin;
Hues more bright and forms more rare,
Than reality doth wear,
Flash across my inward sense,
Born of the mind's omnipotence.

Soul! that all informest, say!
Shall these glories pass away?
Will those planets cease to blaze,
When these eyes no longer gaze?
And the life of things be o'er
When these pulses beat no more?

Thought! that in me works and lives, —
Life to all things living gives, —
Art thou not thyself, perchance,
But the universe in trance?
A reflection inly flung
By that world thou fanciedst sprung
From thyself — thyself a dream —
Of the world's thinking thou the theme.
Be it thus, or be thy birth
From a source above the earth —
Be thou matter, be thou mind,
In thee alone myself I find,
And through thee alone, for me,
Hath this world reality.
Therefore, in thee will I live,
To thee all myself will give,
Losing still, that I may find,
This bounded self in boundless Mind.

1841

## III. SARAH MARGARET FULLER OSSOLI (1810–1850)

### From *WOMAN IN THE NINETEENTH CENTURY*

### [MAN *vs.* WOMAN]

The growth of Man is two-fold, masculine and feminine.

So far as these two methods can be distinguished, they are so as

Energy and Harmony;
Power and Beauty;
Intellect and Love;

or by some such rude classification; for we have not language primitive and pure enough to express such ideas with precision.

These two sides are supposed to be expressed in Man and Woman, that is, as the more and the less, for the faculties have not been given pure to either, but only in preponderance. There are also exceptions in great number, such as men of far more beauty than power, and the reverse. But, as a general rule, it seems to have been the intention to give a preponderance on the one side, that is called masculine, and on the other, one that is called feminine.

There cannot be a doubt that, if these two developments were in perfect harmony, they would correspond to and fulfil one another, like hemispheres, or the tenor and the bass in music.

But there is no perfect harmony in human nature; and the two parts answer one another only now and then; or, if there be a persistent consonance, it can only be traced at long intervals, instead of discoursing an obvious melody.

What is the cause of this?

Man, in the order of time, was developed first; as energy comes before harmony; power before beauty.

Woman was therefore under his care as an elder. He might have been her guardian and teacher.

But, as human nature goes not straight forward, but by excessive action and then reaction in an undulated course, he misunderstood and abused his advantages, and became her temporal master instead of her spiritual sire.

On himself came the punishment. He educated Woman more as a servant than a daughter, and found himself a king without a queen.

The children of this unequal union

showed unequal natures, and, more and more, men seemed sons of the handmaid, rather than princess.

At last, there were so many Ishmaelites that the rest grew frightened and indignant. They laid the blame on Hagar, and drove her forth into the wilderness.

But there were none the fewer Ishmaelites for that.

At last men became a little wiser, and saw that the infant Moses was, in every case, saved by the pure instincts of Woman's breast. For, as too much adversity is better for the moral nature than too much prosperity, Woman, in this respect, dwindled less than Man, though in other respects still a child in leading-strings.

So Man did her more and more justice, and grew more and more kind.

But yet—his habits and his will corrupted by the past—he did not clearly see that Woman was half himself; that her interests were identical with his; and that, by the law of their common being, he could never reach his true proportions while she remained in any wise shorn of hers.

And so it has gone on to our day; both ideas developing, but more slowly than they would under a clearer recognition of truth and justice, which would have permitted the sexes their due influence on one another, and mutual improvement from more dignified relations.

Wherever there was pure love, the natural influences were, for the time, restored.

Wherever the poet or artist gave free course to his genius, he saw the truth, and expressed it in worthy forms, for these men especially share and need the feminine principle. The divine birds need to be brooded into life and song by mothers.

Wherever religion (I mean the thirst for truth and good, not the love of sect and dogma) had its course, the original design was apprehended in its simplicity, and the dove presaged sweetly from Dodona's oak. * * *

1844

## ASPIRATION

Foreseen, forespoken, not foredone,—
Ere the race be well begun,
The prescient soul is at the goal,
One little moment binds the whole;
Happy they themselves who call
To risk much, and to conquer all;
Happy are they who many losses,
Sore defeat or frequent crosses,
Though these may the heart dismay,
Cannot the sure faith betray;
Who in beauty bless the Giver;
Seek ocean on the loveliest river;
Or on desert island tossed,
Seeing Heaven, think naught lost.
May thy genius bring to thee
Of this life's experience free,
And the earth vine's mysterious cup,
Sweet and bitter yield thee up.
But should the now sparkling bowl
Chance to slip from thy control,
And much of the enchanted wine
Be spilt in sand, as 'twas in mine,
Let blessings lost bring consecration,
Change the pledge to a libation.
For the Power to whom we bow
Has given his pledge that, if not now,
They of pure and steadfast mind,
By faith exalted, truth refined,
Shall hear all music, loud and clear,

Whose first notes they ventured
here.
Then fear not thou to wind the horn
Though elf and gnome thy courage
scorn;
Ask for the castle's King and Queen;
Though rabble rout may come be-
tween,
Beat thee, senseless, to the ground,
In the dark beset thee round;
Persist to ask, and it will come.
Seek not for rest a humbler home,
So thou wilt see, what few have seen
The palace home of King and
Queen.

1859

## IV. JONES VERY
(1813–1880)

### THE PRESENCE

I sit within my room, and joy to find
That Thou who always lov'st, art
with me here,
That I am never left by Thee behind,
But by thyself Thou keep'st me ever
near;
The fire burns brighter when with
Thee I look,
And seems a kindlier servant sent
to me;
With gladder heart I read thy holy
book,
Because Thou art the eyes with which
I see;
This aged chair, that table, watch and
door
Around in ready service ever wait;
Nor can I ask of Thee a menial more
To fill the measure of my large estate,
For Thou thyself, with all a father's
care,
Where'er I turn, art ever with me
there.

1839

### THE DEAD

I see them,—crowd on crowd they
walk the earth
Dry leafless trees no autumn wind laid
bare;
And in their nakedness find cause for
mirth,
And all unclad would winter's rudeness dare.
No sap doth through their clattering
branches flow,
Whence springing leaves and blossoms
bright appear;
Their hearts the living God have
ceased to know
Who gives the spring time to th' expectant year.
They mimic life, as if from him to
steal
His glow of health to paint the livid
cheek;
They borrow words for thoughts they
cannot feel,
That with a seeming heart their tongue
may speak;
And in their show of life more dead
they live
Than those that to the earth with
many tears they give.

1839

### THE BARBERRY-BUSH

The bush that has most berries and
bitter fruit,—
Waits till the frost has turned its green
leaves red,
Its sweetened berries will thy palate
suit,
And thou may'st find e'en there a
homely bread.
Upon the hills of Salem, scattered
wide,
Their yellow blossoms gain the eye
in Spring;
And straggling e'en upon the turnpike's side,
Their ripened branches to your hand
they bring.

I've plucked them oft in boyhood's early hour,
That then I gave such name, and thought it true;
But now I know that other fruit as sour
Grows on what now thou callest *Me* and *You;*
Yet, wilt thou wait the autumn that I see,
Will sweeter taste than these red berries be.

1841?

### THE LIGHT FROM WITHIN

I saw on earth another light
Than that which lit my eye
Come forth as from my soul within,
And from a higher sky.

Its beams shone still unclouded on,
When in the farthest west
The sun I once had known had sunk
Forever to his rest.

And on I walked, though dark the night,
Nor rose his orb by day;
As one who by a surer guide
Was pointed out the way.

'Twas brighter far than noonday's beam;
It shone from God within,
And lit, as by a lamp from heaven,
The world's dark track of sin.

1886

## V. CHRISTOPHER PEARSE CRANCH (1813–1892)

### GNOSIS

Thought is deeper than all speech,
Feeling deeper than all thought;
Souls to souls can never teach
What unto themselves was taught.

We are spirits clad in veils;
Man by man was never seen;
All our deep communing fails
To remove the shadowy screen.

Heart to heart was never known;
Mind with mind did never meet;
We are columns left alone
Of a temple once complete.

Like the stars that gem the sky,
Far apart though seeming near,
In our light we scattered lie;
All is thus but starlight here.

What is social company
But a babbling summer stream?
What our wise philosophy
But the glancing of a dream?

Only when the sun of love
Melts the scattered stars of thought;
Only when we live above
What the dim-eyed world hath taught;

Only when our souls are fed
By the Fount which gave them birth,
And by inspiration led
Which they never drew from earth,

We like parted drops of rain
Swelling till they meet and run,
Shall be all absorbed again,
Melting, flowing into one.

1840

### THE PINES AND THE SEA

Beyond the low marsh-meadows and the beach,
Seen through the hoary trunks of windy pines,
The long blue level of the ocean shines.

The distant surf, with hoarse, complaining speech,
Out from its sandy barrier seems to reach;
And while the sun behind the woods declines,
The moaning sea with sighing boughs combines,
And waves and pines make answer, each to each.
O melancholy soul, whom far and near,
In life, faith, hope, the same sad undertone
Pursues from thought to thought! thou needs must hear
An old refrain, too much, too long thine own:
'Tis thy mortality infects thine ear;
The mournful strain was in thyself alone.

1875

## VI. WILLIAM ELLERY CHANNING
### (1818–1901)

### CONTENT

Within the unpainted cottage dwell
The spirits of serene content,
As clear as from its moss-grown well
Rises the crystal element.

Above, the elm, whose trunk is scarred
With many a dint of stormy weather,
Rises, a sumptuous screen, debarred
Of nothing that links life together.

Our common life may gratify
More feelings than the rarest art,
For nothing can aspire so high
As beatings of the human heart.

O! value then thy daily cheer,
Poor pensioner on nature's store,
And clasp the least, and hold most dear
What seemeth small, and add the more.

1843

### SONNET

I love the universe,—I love the joy
Of every living thing. Be mine the sure
Felicity, which ever shall endure;
While passion whirls the madmen, as they toy,
To hate, I would my simple being warm
In the calm pouring sun; and in that pure
And motionless silence, ever would employ
My best true powers, without a thought's annoy.

See and be glad! O high imperial race,
Dwarfing the common altitude of strength,
Learn that ye stand on an unshaken base;
Your powers will carry you to any length.
Up! earnestly feel the gentle sunset beams;
Be glad in woods, o'er sands,—by marsh, or streams.

1843

# NATHANIEL HAWTHORNE
(1804–1864)

## From *PASSAGES FROM THE AMERICAN NOTE-BOOKS*

### [MATERIALS FOR FICTIONS]

*June 15, 1835.* A walk down to the Juniper. The shore of the coves strewn with bunches of sea-weed, driven in by recent winds. Eel-grass, rolled and bundled up, and entangled with it—large marine vegetables, of olive color, with round, slender, snake-like stalks, four or five feet long, and nearly two feet broad; these are the herbage of the deep sea. Shoals of fishes, at a little distance from the shore, discernible by their fins out of water. Among the heaps of sea-weed there were sometimes small pieces of painted wood, bark, and other drift-age. * * *

[*1835.*] A change from a gay young girl to an old woman; the melancholy events, the effects of which have clustered around her character, and gradually imbued it with their influence, till she becomes a lover of sick-chambers, taking pleasure in receiving dying breaths and in laying out the dead; also having her mind full of funeral reminiscences, and possessing more acquaintances beneath the burial turf than above it.

The scene of a story or sketch to be laid within the light of a street-lantern; the time, when the lamp is near going out; and the catastrophe to be simultaneous with the last flickering gleam.

In an old house, a mysterious knocking might be heard on the wall, where had formerly been a doorway, now bricked up.

To make one's own reflection in a mirror the subject of a story.

It is a singular thing, that, at the distance, say, of five feet, the work of the greatest dunce looks just as well as that of the greatest genius—that little space being all the distance between genius and stupidity.

Four precepts: To break off customs; to shake off spirits ill-disposed; to meditate on youth; to do nothing against one's genius.

*September, 1836.* "Though we speak nonsense, God will pick out the meaning of it"—an extempore prayer by a New England divine.

A snake, taken into a man's stomach and nourished there from fifteen years to thirty-five, tormenting him most horribly. A type of envy or some other evil passion.

A Fancy Ball, in which the prominent American writers should appear, dressed in character.

Objects seen by a magic-lantern reversed. A street, or other location, might be presented, where there would be opportunity to bring forward all objects of worldly interest, and thus much pleasant satire might be the result.

A satirical article might be made out of the idea of an imaginary museum, containing such articles as

Aaron's rod, the petticoat of General Harrison, the pistol with which Benton shot Jackson—and then a diorama, consisting of political or other scenes, or done in wax-work. The idea to be wrought out and extended. Perhaps it might be the museum of a deceased old man.

*1837.* An idle man's pleasures and occupations and thoughts during a day spent by the sea-shore; among them, that of sitting on the top of a cliff, and throwing stones at his own shadow, far below.

The aromatic odor of peat smoke in the sunny autumnal air is very pleasant.

A person to be in the possession of something as perfect as mortal man has a right to demand; he tries to make it better, and ruins it entirely.

Meditations about the main gas-pipe of a great city—if the supply were to be stopped, what would happen? How many different scenes it sheds light on? It might be made emblematical of something.

A story to show how we are all wronged and wrongers, and avenge one another.

To poison a person or a party of persons with the sacramental wine.

Men of cold passions have quick eyes.

*1838.* A person to catch fire-flies, and try to kindle his household fire with them. It would be symbolical of something.

*July 29th.* Remarkable characters: a disagreeable figure, waning from middle age, clad in a pair of tow homespun pantaloons, and a very soiled shirt, barefoot, and with one of his feet maimed by an axe; also an arm amputated two or three inches below the elbow. His beard of a week's growth, grim and grisly, with a general effect of black; altogether a disgusting object.

"A story there passeth of an Indian king that sent unto Alexander a fair woman, fed with aconite and other poisons, with this intent complexionally to destroy him!"—*Sir T. Browne.*

*1839.* The semblance of a human face to be formed on the side of a mountain, or in the fracture of a small stone, by a *lusus naturæ.* The face is an object of curiosity for years or centuries, and by and by a boy is born, whose features gradually assume the aspect of that portrait. At some critical juncture, the resemblance is found to be perfect. A prophecy may be connected.

(1835–39) 1868

## SIGHTS FROM A STEEPLE

So! I have climbed high, and my reward is small. Here I stand, with wearied knees, earth, indeed, at a dizzy depth below, but heaven far, far beyond me still. Oh, that I could soar up into the very zenith, where man never breathed, nor eagle ever flew, and where the ethereal azure melts away from the eye, and appears only a deepened shade of nothingness! And yet I shiver at that cold and solitary thought. What clouds are gathering in the golden west, with direful intent against the brightness and warmth of this summer afternoon! They are ponderous air ships, black as death, and freighted with the tempest; and at intervals their thunder, the signal guns of that unearthly squadron, rolls distant along the deep of heaven.

These nearer heaps of fleecy vapor — methinks I could roll and toss upon them the whole day long! — seem scattered here and there for the repose of tired pilgrims through the sky. Perhaps — for who can tell? — beautiful spirits are disporting themselves there, and will bless my mortal eye with the brief appearance of their curly locks of golden light, and laughing faces, fair and faint as the people of a rosy dream. Or, where the floating mass so imperfectly obstructs the color of the firmament, a slender foot and fairy limb, resting too heavily upon the frail support, may be thrust through, and suddenly withdrawn, while longing fancy follows them in vain. Yonder again is an airy archipelago, where the sunbeams love to linger in their journeyings through space. Every one of those little clouds has been dipped and steeped in radiance, which the slightest pressure might disengage in silvery profusion, like water wrung from a sea-maid's hair. Bright they are as a young man's visions, and, like them, would be realized in chiliness, obscurity, and tears. I will look on them no more.

In three parts of the visible circle, whose centre is this spire, I discern cultivated fields, villages, white country-seats, the waving lines of rivulets, little placid lakes, and here and there a rising ground, that would fain be termed a hill. On the fourth side is the sea, stretching away towards a viewless boundary, blue and calm, except where the passing anger of a shadow flits across its surface, and is gone. Hitherward, a broad inlet penetrates far into the land; on the verge of the harbor, formed by its extremity, is a town; and over it am I, a watchman, all-heeding and unheeded. Oh, that the multitude of chimneys could speak, like those of Madrid, and betray, in smoky whispers, the secrets of all who, since their first foundation, have assembled at the hearths within! Oh, that the Limping Devil of Le Sage would perch beside me here, extend his wand over this contiguity of roofs, uncover every chamber, and make me familiar with their inhabitants! The most desirable mode of existence might be that of a spiritualized Paul Pry, hovering invisible round man and woman, witnessing their deeds, searching into their hearts, borrowing brightness from their felicity and shade from their sorrow, and retaining no emotion peculiar to himself. But none of these things are possible; and if I would know the interior of brick walls, or the mystery of human bosoms, I can but guess.

Yonder is a fair street, extending north and south. The stately mansions are placed each on its carpet of verdant grass, and a long flight of steps extends from every door to the pavement. Ornamental trees — the broad-leafed horse-chestnut, the elm so lofty and bending, the graceful but infrequent willow, and others whereof I know not the names — grow thrivingly among brick and stone. The oblique rays of the sun are intercepted by these green citizens, and by the houses, so that one side of the street is a shaded and pleasant walk. On its whole extent there is now but a single passenger, advancing from the upper end; and he, unless distance and the medium of a pocket spy-glass do him more than justice, is a fine young man of twenty. He saunters slowly forward, slapping his left hand with his folded gloves, bending his eyes upon the pavement, and sometimes raising them to throw a glance before him. Certainly, he has a pensive air. Is he in doubt, or in debt? Is he, if the question be allowable, in love? Does he strive to be melancholy and gentleman-like? Or, is he merely overcome by the heat? But I bid him farewell for the present. The door of one of the houses — an aristocratic edifice, with curtains of purple and gold waving from the windows, is now opened, and down the steps come two ladies, swinging their parasols, and lightly arrayed for a summer ramble. Both are young, both are pretty, but methinks the left-hand lass is the fairer of the twain; and, though she be so serious at this moment, I could swear that there is a treasure of gentle fun within her. They stand talking a little while upon the steps, and finally proceed up the street. Meantime, as their faces are now turned from me, I may look elsewhere.

Upon that wharf, and down the corresponding street, is a busy contrast to the quiet scene which I have just noticed. Business evidently has its center there, and many a man is wasting the summer afternoon in labor and anxiety, in losing riches or in gaining them, when he would be wiser to flee away to some pleasant country village, or shaded lake in the forest, or wild and cool sea-beach. I see vessels unloading at the wharf, and precious merchandise strewn upon the ground, abundantly as at the bottom of the sea, the market whence no goods return, and where there is no captain nor supercargo to render an account of sales. Here, the clerks are diligent with their paper and pencils, and sailors ply the block and tackle that hang over the hold, accompanying their toil with cries, long drawn and roughly melodious, till the bales and puncheons ascend to upper air. At a little distance a group of gentlemen are assembled round the door of a warehouse. Grave seniors be they, and I would wager — if it were safe in these times to be responsible for any one — that the least eminent among them might vie with the old Vicentio, that incomparable trafficker of Pisa. I can even select the wealthiest of the company. It is the elderly personage, in somewhat rusty black, with powdered hair, the superfluous whiteness of which is visible upon the cape of his coat. His twenty ships are wafted on some of their many courses by every breeze that blows, and his name — I will venture to say, though I know it not — is a familiar sound among the far separated merchants of Europe and the Indies.

But I bestow too much of my attention in this quarter. On looking again to the long and shady walk, I perceive that the two fair girls have encountered the young man. After a sort of shyness in the recognition, he turns back with them. Moreover, he has sanctioned my taste in regard to his companions by placing himself on the inner side of the pavement, nearest the Venus to whom I — enacting, on a steeple-top, the part of Paris on the top of Ida — adjudged the golden apple.

In two streets, converging at right angles towards my watchtower, I distinguish three different processions. One is a proud array of voluntary soldiers, in bright uniform, resembling, from the height whence I look down, the painted veterans that garrison the windows of a toyshop. And yet, it stirs my heart; their regular advance, their nodding plumes, the sun-flash on their bayonets and musket barrels, the roll of their drums ascending past me, and the fife ever and anon piercing through — these things have wakened a warlike fire, peaceful though I be. Close to their rear marches a battalion of schoolboys, ranged in crooked and irregular platoons, shouldering sticks, thumping a harsh and unripe clatter from an instrument of tin, and ridiculously aping the intricate manœuvres of the foremost band. Nevertheless, as slight differences are scarcely perceptible from a church spire, one might be tempted to ask, "Which are the boys?"— or rather, "Which the men?" But, leaving these, let us turn to the third procession, which, though sadder in outward show, may excite identical reflections in the thoughtful mind. It is a funeral. A hearse, drawn by a black and bony steed, and covered by a dusty pall; two or three coaches rumbling over the stones, their drivers half asleep; a dozen couple of careless mourners in their every-day attire; such was not the fashion of our fathers, when they carried a friend to his grave. There is now no doleful clang of the bell to proclaim sorrow to the town. Was the King of Terrors more awful in those days than in our own, that wisdom and philosophy have been able to produce this change? Not so. Here is a proof that he retains his proper majesty. The military men and the military boys are wheeling round the corner, and meet the funeral full in the face. Immediately the drum is silent, all but the tap that regulates each simultaneous footfall. The soldiers yield the path to the dusty hearse and unpretending train, and the children quit their ranks, and cluster on the sidewalks, with timorous and instinctive curiosity. The mourners enter the churchyard at the base of the steeple, and pause by an open grave among the burial stones; the lightning glimmers on them as they lower down the coffin, and the thunder rattles heavily while they throw the earth upon its lid. Verily, the shower is near, and I tremble for the young man and the girls, who have now disappeared from the long and shady street.

How various are the situations of the people covered by the roofs beneath me, and how diversified are the events at this moment befalling them! The new born, the aged, the dying, the strong in life, and the recent dead are in the chambers of these many mansions. The full of hope, the happy, the miserable, and the desperate dwell together within the circle of my glance. In some of the houses over which my eyes roam so coldly, guilt is entering into hearts that are still tenanted by a debased and trodden virtue,— guilt is on the very edge of commission, and the impending deed might be averted; guilt is done, and the criminal wonders if it be irrevocable. There are broad thoughts struggling in my mind, and, were I able to give them distinctness, they would make their way in eloquence. Lo! the raindrops are descending.

The clouds, within a little time, have gathered over all the sky, hanging heavily, as if about to drop in one unbroken mass upon the earth. At intervals, the lightning flashes from their brooding hearts, quivers, disappears, and then comes the thunder, travelling slowly after its twin-born flame. A strong wind has sprung up, howls through the darkened streets, and raises the dust in dense bodies, to rebel against the approaching storm. The disbanded soldiers fly, the funeral has already vanished like its dead, and all people hurry homeward — all that have a home; while a few lounge by the corners, or trudge on desperately, at their leisure. In a narrow lane, which communicates with the shady street, I discern the rich old merchant, putting himself to the top of his speed, lest the rain should convert his hair powder to a paste. Unhappy gentleman! By the slow vehemence and painful moderation wherewith he journeys, it is but too evident that Podagra has left its thrilling tenderness in his great toe. But yonder, at a far more rapid pace, come three other of my acquaintance, the two pretty girls and the young man, unseasonably interrupted in their walk. Their footsteps are supported by the risen dust,— the wind lends them its velocity,— they fly like three sea-birds driven landward by the tempestuous breeze. The ladies would not thus rival Atalanta, if they but knew that any one were at leisure to observe them. Ah! as they hasten onward, laughing in the angry face of nature, a sudden catastrophe has chanced. At the corner where the narrow lane enters the street, they come plump against the old merchant, whose tortoise motion has just brought him to that point. He likes not the sweet encounter; the darkness of the whole air gathers speedily upon his visage, and there is a pause on both sides. Finally, he thrusts aside the youth with little courtesy, seizes an arm of each of the two girls, and plods onward, like a magician with a prize of captive fairies. All this is easy to be understood. How disconsolate the poor lover stands! regardless of the rain that threatens an exceeding damage to his well-fashioned habiliments, till he catches a backward glance of mirth from a bright eye, and turns away with whatever comfort it conveys.

The old man and his daughters are safely housed, and now the storm lets loose its fury. In every dwelling I perceive the faces of the chambermaids as they shut down the windows, excluding the impetuous shower, and shrinking away from the quick, fiery glare. The large drops descend with force upon the slated roofs, and rise again in smoke. There is a rush and roar, as of a river through the air, and muddy streams bubble majestically along the pavement, whirl their dusky foam into the kennel, and disappear beneath iron grates. Thus did Arethusa sink. I love not my station here aloft, in the midst of the tumult which I am powerless to direct or quell, with the blue lightning wrinkling on my brow, and the thunder muttering its first awful syllables in my ear. I will descend. Yet let me give another glance to the sea, where the foam breaks out in long white lines upon a broad expanse of blackness, or boils up in far distant points, like snowy mountain-tops in the eddies of a flood; and let me look once more at the green plain and little hills of the country, over which the giant of the storm is striding in robes of mist, and at the town, whose obscured and desolate streets might beseem a city of the dead; and turning a single moment to the sky, now gloomy as an author's prospects, I prepare to resume my station on the lower earth. But stay! A little speck of azure has widened in the western heavens; the sunbeams find a passage, and go rejoicing through the tempest; and on yonder darkest cloud, born, like hallowed hopes, of the glory of another world and the troubles and tears of this, brightens forth the Rainbow!

1830

## YOUNG GOODMAN BROWN

Young Goodman Brown came forth at sunset into the street at Salem village; but put his head back, after crossing the threshold, to exchange a parting kiss with his young wife. And Faith, as the wife was aptly named, thrust her own pretty head into the street, letting the wind play with the pink ribbons of her cap while she called to Goodman Brown.

"Dearest heart," whispered she, softly and rather sadly, when her lips were close to his ear, "prithee put off your journey until sunrise and sleep in your own bed to-night. A lone woman is troubled with such dreams and such thoughts that she's afeard of herself sometimes. Pray tarry with me this night, dear husband, of all nights in the year."

"My love and my Faith," replied young Goodman Brown, "of all nights in the year, this one night must I tarry away from thee. My journey, as thou callest it, forth and back again, must needs be done 'twixt now and sunrise. What, my sweet, pretty wife, dost thou doubt me already, and we but three months married?"

"Then God bless you!" said Faith, with the pink ribbons; "and may you find all well when you come back."

"Amen!" cried Goodman Brown. "Say thy prayers, dear Faith, and go to bed at dusk, and no harm will come to thee."

So they parted; and the young man pursued his way until, being about to turn the corner by the meeting-house, he looked back and saw the head of Faith still peeping after him with a melancholy air, in spite of her pink ribbons.

"Poor little Faith!" thought he, for his heart smote him. "What a wretch am I to leave her on such an errand! She talks of dreams, too. Methought as she spoke there was trouble in her face, as if a dream had warned her what work is to be done to-night. But no, no; 't would kill her to think it. Well, she's a blessed angel on earth; and after this one night I'll cling to her skirts and follow her to heaven."

With this excellent resolve for the future, Goodman Brown felt himself justified in making more haste on his present evil purpose. He had taken a dreary road, darkened by all the gloomiest trees of the forest, which barely stood aside to let the narrow path creep through, and closed immediately behind. It was all as lonely as could be; and there is this peculiarity in such a solitude, that the traveller knows not who may be concealed by the innumerable trunks and the thick boughs overhead; so that with lonely footsteps he may yet be passing through an unseen multitude.

"There may be a devilish Indian behind every tree," said Goodman Brown to himself; and he glanced fearfully behind him as he added, "What if the devil himself should be at my very elbow!"

His head being turned back, he passed a crook of the road, and looking forward again, beheld the figure of a man, in grave and decent attire, seated at the foot of an old tree. He arose at Goodman Brown's approach and walked onward side by side with him.

"You are late, Goodman Brown," said he. "The clock of the Old South was striking as I came through Boston, and that is full fifteen minutes agone."

"Faith kept me back a while," replied the young man, with a tremor in his voice, caused by the sudden appearance of his companion, though not wholly unexpected.

It was now deep dusk in the forest, and deepest in that part of it where these two were journeying. As nearly as could be discerned, the second traveller was about fifty years old, apparently in the same rank of life as Goodman Brown, and bearing a considerable resemblance to him, though perhaps more in expression than features. Still they might have been taken for father and son. And yet, though the elder person was as simply clad as the younger, and as simple in manner too, he had an indescribable air of one who knew the world, and who would not have felt abashed at the governor's dinner table or in King William's court, were it possible that his affairs should call him thither. But the only thing about him that could be fixed upon as remarkable was his staff, which bore the likeness of a great black snake, so curiously wrought that it might almost be seen to twist and wriggle itself like a living serpent. This, of course, must have been an ocular deception, assisted by the uncertain light.

"Come, Goodman Brown," cried his fellow-traveller, "this is a dull pace for the beginning of a journey. Take my staff, if you are so soon weary."

"Friend," said the other, exchanging his slow pace for a full stop, "having kept covenant by meeting thee here, it is my purpose now to return whence I came. I have scruples touching the matter thou wot'st of."

"Sayest thou so?" replied he of the serpent, smiling apart. "Let us walk on, nevertheless, reasoning as we go; and if I convince thee not thou shalt turn back. We are but a little way in the forest yet."

"Too far! too far!" exclaimed the goodman, unconsciously resuming his walk. "My father never went into the woods on such an errand, nor his father before him. We have been a race of honest men and good Christians since the days of the martyrs; and shall I be the first of the name of Brown that ever took this path and kept"—

"Such company, thou wouldst say," observed the elder person, interpreting his pause. "Well said, Goodman Brown! I have been as well acquainted with your family as with ever a one among the Puritans; and that's no trifle to say. I helped your grandfather, the constable, when he lashed the Quaker woman so smartly through the streets of Salem; and it was I that brought your father a pitch-pine knot, kindled at my own hearth, to set fire to an Indian village, in King Philip's war. They were my good friends, both; and many a pleasant walk have we had along this path, and returned merrily after midnight. I would fain be friends with you for their sake."

"If it be as thou sayest," replied Goodman Brown, "I marvel they never spoke of these matters; or, verily, I marvel not, seeing that the least rumor of the sort would have driven them from New England. We are a people of prayer, and good works to boot, and abide no such wickedness."

"Wickedness or not," said the traveller with the twisted staff, "I have a very general acquaintance here in New England. The deacons of many a church have drunk the communion wine with me; the selectmen of divers towns make me their chairman; and a majority of the Great and General Court are firm supporters of my interest. The governor and I, too—but these are state secrets."

"Can this be so?" cried Goodman Brown, with a stare of amazement at his undisturbed companion. "Howbeit, I have nothing to do with the governor and council; they have their own ways, and are no rule for a simple husbandman like me. But, were I to go on with thee, how should I meet the eye of that good old man, our minister, at Salem village? Oh, his voice would make me tremble both Sabbath day and lecture day."

Thus far the elder traveller had listened with due gravity; but now burst into a fit of irrepressible mirth, shaking himself so violently that his snake-like staff actually seemed to wriggle in sympathy.

"Ha! ha! ha!" shouted he again and again; then composing himself, "Well, go on, Goodman Brown, go on; but, prithee, don't kill me with laughing."

"Well, then, to end the matter at once," said Goodman Brown, considerably nettled, "there is my wife, Faith. It would break her dear little heart; and I'd rather break my own."

"Nay, if that be the case," answered the other, "e'en go thy ways, Goodman Brown. I would not for twenty old women like the one hobbling before us that Faith should come to any harm."

As he spoke he pointed his staff at a female figure on the path, in whom Goodman Brown recognized a very pious and exemplary dame, who had taught him his catechism in youth, and was still his moral and spiritual adviser, jointly with the minister and Deacon Gookin.

"A marvel, truly, that Goody Cloyse should be so far in the wilderness at nightfall," said he. "But with your leave, friend, I shall take a cut through the woods until we have left this Christian woman behind. Being a stranger to you, she might ask whom I was consorting with and whither I was going."

"Be it so," said his fellow-traveller. "Betake you to the woods, and let me keep the path."

Accordingly the young man turned aside, but took care to watch his companion, who advanced softly along the road until he had come within a staff's length of the old dame. She, meanwhile, was making the best of her way, with singular speed for so aged a woman, and mumbling some indistinct words—a prayer, doubtless—as she went. The traveller put forth his staff and touched her withered neck with what seemed the serpent's tail.

"The devil!" screamed the pious old lady.

"Then Goody Cloyse knows her old friend?" observed the traveller, confronting her and leaning on his writhing stick.

"Ah, forsooth, and is it your worship indeed?" cried the good dame. "Yea, truly is it, and in the very image of my old gossip, Goodman Brown, the grandfather of the silly fellow that now is. But—would your worship believe it?—my broomstick hath strangely disappeared, stolen, as I suspect, by that unhanged witch, Goody Cory, and that, too, when I was all anointed with the juice of smallage, and cinquefoil, and wolf's bane"—

"Mingled with fine wheat and the fat of a new-born babe," said the shape of old Goodman Brown.

"Ah, your worship knows the recipe," cried the old lady, cackling aloud. "So, as I was saying, being all ready for the meeting, and no horse to ride on, I made up my mind to foot it; for they tell me there is a nice young man to be taken into communion to-night. But now your good worship will lend me your arm, and we shall be there in a twinkling."

"That can hardly be," answered her friend. "I may not spare you my arm, Goody Cloyse; but here is my staff, if you will."

So saying, he threw it down at her feet, where, perhaps, it assumed life, being one of the rods which its owner had formerly lent to the Egyptian magi. Of this fact, however, Goodman Brown could not take cognizance. He had cast up his eyes in astonishment, and, looking down again, beheld neither Goody Cloyse nor the serpentine staff, but his fellow-traveller alone, who waited for him as calmly as if nothing had happened.

"That old woman taught me my catechism," said the young man; and there was a world of meaning in this simple comment.

They continued to walk onward, while the elder traveller exhorted his companion to make good speed and persevere in the path, discoursing so aptly that his arguments seemed rather to spring up in the bosom of his auditor than to be suggested by himself. As they went, he plucked a branch of maple to serve for a walking stick, and began to strip it of the twigs and little boughs, which were wet with evening dew. The moment his fingers touched them they became strangely withered and dried up as with a week's sunshine. Thus the pair proceeded, at a good free pace, until suddenly, in a gloomy hollow of the road, Goodman Brown sat himself down on the stump of a tree and refused to go any farther.

"Friend," said he, stubbornly, "my mind is made up. Not another step will I budge on this errand. What if a wretched old woman do choose to go to the devil when I thought she was going to heaven: is that any reason why I should quit my dear Faith and go after her?"

"You will think better of this by and by," said his acquaintance, composedly. "Sit here and rest yourself a while; and when you feel like moving again, there is my staff to help you along."

Without more words, he threw his companion the maple stick, and was as speedily out of sight as if he had vanished into the deepening gloom. The young man sat a few moments by the roadside, applauding himself greatly, and thinking with how clear a conscience he should meet the minister in his morning walk, nor shrink from the eye of good old Deacon Gookin. And what calm sleep would be his that very night, which was to have been spent so wickedly, but so purely and sweetly now, in the arms of Faith! Amidst these pleasant and praiseworthy meditations, Goodman Brown heard the tramp of horses along the road, and deemed it advisable to conceal himself within the verge of the forest, conscious of the guilty purpose that had brought him thither, though now so happily turned from it.

On came the hoof tramps and the voices of the riders, two grave old voices, conversing soberly as they drew near. These mingled sounds appeared to pass along the road, within a few yards of the young man's hiding-place; but, owing doubtless to the depth of the gloom at that particular spot, neither the travellers nor their steeds were visible. Though their figures brushed the small boughs by the wayside, it could not be seen that they intercepted, even for a moment, the faint gleam from the strip of bright sky athwart which they must have passed. Goodman Brown alternately crouched and stood on tiptoe, pulling aside the branches and thrusting forth his head as far as he durst without discerning so much as a shadow. It vexed him the more, because he could have sworn, were such a thing possible, that he recognized the voices of the minister and Deacon Gookin, jogging along quietly, as they were wont to do, when bound to some ordination or ecclesiastical council. While yet within hearing, one of the riders stopped to pluck a switch.

"Of the two, reverend sir," said the voice like the deacon's, "I had rather miss an ordination dinner than to-night's meeting. They tell me that some of our community are to be here from Falmouth and beyond, and others from Connecticut and Rhode Island, besides several of the Indian powwows, who, after their fashion, know almost as much deviltry as the best of us. Moreover, there is a goodly young woman to be taken into communion."

"Mighty well, Deacon Gookin!" replied the solemn old tones of the minister. "Spur up, or we shall be late. Nothing can be done, you know, until I get on the ground."

The hoofs clattered again; and the voices, talking so strangely in the empty air, passed on through the forest, where no church had ever been gathered or solitary Christian prayed. Whither, then, could these holy men be journeying so deep into the heathen wilderness? Young Goodman Brown caught hold of a tree for support, being ready to sink down on the ground, faint and overburdened with the heavy sickness of his heart. He looked up to the sky, doubting whether there really was a heaven above him. Yet there was the blue arch, and the stars brightening in it.

"With heaven above and Faith below, I will yet stand firm against the devil!" cried Goodman Brown.

While he still gazed upward into the deep arch of the firmament and had lifted his hands to pray, a cloud, though no wind was stirring, hurried across the zenith and hid the brightening stars. The blue sky was still visible, except directly overhead, where this black mass of cloud was sweeping swiftly northward. Aloft in the air, as if from the depths of the cloud, came a confused and doubtful sound of voices. Once the listener fancied that he could distinguish the accents of towns-people of his own, men and women, both pious and ungodly, many of whom he had met at the communion table, and had seen others rioting at the tavern. The next moment, so indistinct were the sounds, he doubted whether he had heard aught but the murmur of the old forest, whispering without a wind. Then came a stronger swell of those familiar tones, heard daily in the sunshine at Salem village, but never until now from a cloud of night. There was one voice, of a young woman, uttering lamentations, yet with an uncertain sorrow, and entreating for some favor, which, perhaps it would grieve her to obtain; and all the unseen multitude, both saints and sinners, seemed to encourage her onward.

"Faith!" shouted Goodman Brown, in a voice of agony and desperation; and the echoes of the forest mocked him, crying, "Faith! Faith!" as if bewildered wretches were seeking her all through the wilderness.

The cry of grief, rage, and terror was yet piercing the night, when the unhappy husband held his breath for a response. There was a scream, drowned immediately in a louder murmur of voices, fading into far-off laughter, as the dark cloud swept away, leaving the clear and silent sky above Goodman Brown. But something fluttered lightly down through the air and caught on the branch of a tree. The young man seized it, and beheld a pink ribbon.

"My Faith is gone!" cried he, after one stupefied moment. "There is no good on earth; and sin is but a name. Come, devil; for to thee is this world given."

And, maddened with despair, so that he laughed loud and long, did Goodman Brown grasp his staff and set forth again, at such a rate that he seemed to fly along the forest path rather than to walk or run. The road grew wilder and drearier and more faintly traced, and vanished at length, leaving him in the heart of the dark wilderness, still rushing onward with the instinct that guides mortal man to evil. The whole forest was peopled with frightful sounds—the creaking of the trees, the howling of wild beasts, and the yell of Indians; while sometimes the wind tolled like a distant church bell, and sometimes gave a broad roar around the traveller, as if all Nature were laughing him to scorn. But he was himself the chief horror of the scene, and shrank not from its other horrors.

"Ha! ha! ha!" roared Goodman Brown when the wind laughed at him. "Let us hear which will laugh loudest. Think not to frighten me with your deviltry. Come witch, come wizard, come Indian powwow, come devil himself, and here comes Goodman Brown. You may as well fear him as he fear you."

In truth, all through the haunted forest there could be nothing more frightful than the figure of Goodman Brown. On he flew among the black pines, brandishing his staff with frenzied gestures, now giving vent to an inspiration of horrid blasphemy, and now shouting forth such laughter as set all the echoes of the forest laughing like demons around him. The fiend in his own shape is less hideous than when he rages in the breast of man. Thus sped the demoniac on his course, until, quivering among the trees, he saw a red light before him, as when the felled trunks and branches of a clearing have been set on fire, and throw up their lurid blaze against the sky, at the hour of midnight. He paused, in a lull of the tempest that had driven him onward, and heard the swell of what seemed a hymn, rolling solemnly from a distance with the weight of many voices. He knew the tune; it was a familiar one in the choir of the village meeting-house. The verse died heavily away, and was lengthened by a chorus, not of human voices, but of all the sounds of the benighted wilderness pealing in awful harmony together. Goodman Brown cried out, and his cry was lost to his own ear by its unison with the cry of the desert.

In the interval of silence he stole forward until the light glared full upon his eyes. At one extremity of an open space, hemmed in by the dark wall of the forest, arose a rock, bearing some rude, natural resemblance either to an altar or a pulpit, and surrounded by four blazing pines, their tops aflame, their stems untouched, like candles at an evening meeting. The mass of foliage that had overgrown the summit of the rock was all on fire, blazing high into the night and fitfully illuminating the whole field. Each pendent twig and leafy festoon was in a blaze. As the red light arose and fell, a numerous congregation alternately shone forth, then disappeared in shadow, and again grew, as it were, out of the darkness, peopling the heart of the solitary woods at once.

"A grave and dark-clad company," quoth Goodman Brown.

In truth they were such. Among them, quivering to and fro between gloom and splendor, appeared faces that would be seen next day at the council board of the province, and others which, Sabbath after Sabbath, looked devoutly heavenward, and benignantly over the crowded pews, from the holiest pulpits in the land. Some affirm that the lady of the governor was there. At least there were high dames well known to her, and wives of honored husbands, and widows, a great multitude, and ancient maidens, all of excellent repute, and fair young girls, who trembled lest their mothers should espy them. Either the sudden gleams of light flashing over the obscure field bedazzled Goodman Brown, or he recognized a score of the church members of Salem village famous for their especial sanctity. Good old Deacon Gookin had arrived, and waited at the skirts of that venerable saint, his revered pastor. But, irreverently consorting with these grave, reputable, and pious people, these elders of the church, these chaste dames and dewy virgins, there were men of dissolute lives and women of spotted fame, wretches given over to all mean and filthy vice, and suspected even of horrid crimes. It was strange to see that the good shrank not from the wicked, nor were the sinners abashed by the saints. Scattered also among their pale-faced enemies were the Indian priests, or powwows, who had often scared their native forest with more hideous incantations than any known to English witchcraft.

"But where is Faith?" thought Goodman Brown; and, as hope came into his heart, he trembled.

Another verse of the hymn arose, a slow and mournful strain, such as the pious love, but joined to words which expressed all that our nature can conceive of sin, and darkly hinted at far more. Unfathomable to mere mortals is the lore of fiends. Verse after verse was sung; and still the chorus of the desert swelled between like the deepest tone of a mighty organ; and with the final peal of that dreadful anthem there came a sound, as if the roaring wind, the rushing streams, the howling beasts, and every other voice of the unconcerted wilderness were mingling and according with the voice of guilty man in homage to the prince of all. The four blazing pines threw up a loftier flame, and obscurely discovered shapes and visages of horror on the smoke wreaths above the impious assembly. At the same moment the fire on the rock shot redly forth and formed a glowing arch above its base, where now appeared a figure. With reverence be it spoken, the figure bore no slight similitude, both in garb and manner, to some grave divine of the New England churches.

"Bring forth the converts!" cried a voice that echoed through the field and rolled into the forest.

At the word, Goodman Brown stepped forth from the shadow of the trees and approached the congregation, with whom he felt a loathful brotherhood by the sympathy of all that was wicked in his heart. He could have well-nigh sworn that the shape of his own dead father beckoned him to advance, looking downward from a smoke wreath, while a woman, with dim features of despair, threw out her hand to warn him back. Was it his mother? But he had no power to retreat one step, nor to resist, even in thought, when the minister and good old Deacon Gookin seized his arms and led him to the blazing rock. Thither came also the slender form of a veiled female, led between Goody Cloyse, that pious teacher of the catechism, and Martha Carrier, who had received the devil's promise to be queen of hell. A rampant hag was she. And there stood the proselytes beneath the canopy of fire.

"Welcome, my children," said the dark figure, "to the communion of your race. Ye have found thus young your nature and your destiny. My children, look behind you!"

They turned; and flashing forth, as it were, in a sheet of flame, the fiend worshippers were seen; the smile of welcome gleamed darkly on every visage.

"There," resumed the sable form, "are all whom ye have reverenced from youth. Ye deemed them holier than yourselves, and shrank from your own sin, contrasting it with their lives of righteousness and prayerful aspirations heavenward. Yet here are they all in my worshipping assembly. This night it shall be granted you to know their secret deeds; how hoary-bearded elders of the church have whispered wanton words to the young maids of their households; how many a woman, eager for widows' weeds, has given her husband a drink at bedtime and let him sleep his last sleep in her bosom; how beardless youths have made haste to inherit their fathers' wealth; and how fair damsels—blush not, sweet ones—have dug little graves in the garden, and bidden me, the sole guest, to an infant's funeral. By the sympathy of your human hearts for sin ye shall scent out all the places—whether in church, bed-chamber, street, field, or forest—where crime has been committed, and shall exult to behold the whole earth one stain of guilt, one mighty blood spot. Far more than this. It shall be yours to penetrate, in every bosom, the deep mystery of sin, the fountain of all wicked arts, and which inexhaustibly supplies more evil impulses than human power—than my power at its utmost—can make manifest in deeds. And now, my children, look upon each other."

They did so; and by the blaze of the hell-kindled torches, the wretched man beheld his Faith, and the wife her husband, trembling before that unhallowed altar.

"Lo, there ye stand, my children," said the figure, in a deep and solemn tone, almost sad with its despairing awfulness, as if his once angelic nature could yet mourn for our miserable race. "Depending upon one another's hearts, ye had still hoped that virtue were not all a dream. Now are ye undeceived. Evil is the nature of mankind. Evil must be your only happiness. Welcome again, my children, to the communion of your race."

"Welcome," repeated the fiend worshippers, in one cry of despair and triumph.

And there they stood, the only pair, as it seemed, who were yet hesitating on the verge of wickedness in this dark world. A basin was hollowed, naturally, in the rock. Did it contain water, reddened by the lurid light? or was it blood? or, perchance, a liquid flame? Herein did the shape of evil dip his hand and prepare to lay the mark of baptism upon their foreheads, that they might be partakers of the mystery of sin, more conscious of the secret guilt of others, both in deed and thought, than they could now be of their own. The husband cast one look at his pale wife, and Faith at him. What polluted wretches would the next glance show them to each other, shuddering alike at what they disclosed and what they saw!

"Faith! Faith!" cried the husband, "look up to heaven, and resist the wicked one."

Whether Faith obeyed he knew not. Hardly had he spoken when he found himself amid calm night and solitude, listening to a roar of the wind which died heavily away through the forest. He staggered against the rock, and felt it chill and damp; while a hanging twig, that had been all on fire, besprinkled his cheek with the coldest dew.

The next morning young Goodman Brown came slowly into the street of Salem village, staring around him like a bewildered man. The good old minister was taking a walk along the graveyard to get an appetite for breakfast and meditate his sermon, and bestowed a blessing, as he passed, on Goodman Brown. He shrank from the venerable saint as if to avoid an anathema. Old Deacon Gookin was at domestic worship, and the holy words of his prayer were heard through the open window. "What God doth the wizard pray to?" quoth Goodman Brown. Goody Cloyse, that excellent old Christian, stood in the early sunshine at her own lattice, catechizing a little girl who had brought her a pint of morning's milk. Goodman Brown snatched away the child as from the grasp of the fiend himself. Turning the corner by the meeting-house, he spied the head of Faith, with the pink ribbons, gazing anxiously forth, and bursting into such joy at sight of him that she skipped along the street and almost kissed her husband before the whole village. But Goodman Brown looked sternly and sadly into her face, and passed on without a greeting.

Had Goodman Brown fallen asleep in the forest and only dreamed a wild dream of a witch-meeting?

Be it so if you will; but, alas! it was a dream of evil omen for young Goodman Brown. A stern, a sad, a darkly meditative, a distrustful, if not a desperate man did he become from the night of that fearful dream. On the Sabbath day, when the congregation were singing a holy psalm, he could not listen because an anthem of sin rushed loudly upon his ear and drowned all the blessed strain. When the minister spoke from the pulpit with power and fervid eloquence, and, with his hand on the open Bible, of the sacred truths of our religion, and of saint-like lives and triumphant deaths, and of future bliss or misery unutterable, then did Goodman Brown turn pale, dreading lest the roof should thunder down upon the gray blasphemer and his hearers. Often, awaking suddenly at midnight, he shrank from the bosom of Faith; and at morning or eventide, when the family knelt down at prayer, he scowled and muttered to himself, and gazed sternly at his wife, and turned away. And when he had lived long, and was borne to his grave a hoary corpse, followed by Faith, an aged woman, and children and grandchildren, a goodly procession, besides neighbors not a few, they carved no hopeful verse upon his tombstone, for his dying hour was gloom.

1835

## THE WHITE OLD MAID

The moonbeams came through two deep and narrow windows, and showed a spacious chamber richly furnished in an antique fashion. From one lattice the shadow of the diamond panes was thrown upon the floor; the ghostly light, through the other, slept upon a bed, falling between the heavy silken curtains, and illuminating the face of a young man. But, how quietly the slumberer lay! how pale his features! and how like a shroud the sheet was wound about his frame! Yes; it was a corpse, in its burial clothes.

Suddenly, the fixed features seemed to move with dark emotion. Strange fantasy! It was but the shadow of the fringed curtain, waving betwixt the dead face and the moonlight, as the door of the chamber opened and a girl stole softly to the bedside. Was there delusion in the moonbeams, or did her gesture and her eye betray a gleam of triumph, as she bent over the pale corpse—pale as itself—and pressed her living lips to the cold ones of the dead? As she drew back from that long kiss, her features writhed as if a proud heart were fighting with its anguish. Again it seemed that the features of the corpse had moved responsive to her own. Still an illusion!

The silken curtain had waved, a second time, betwixt the dead face and the moonlight, as another fair young girl unclosed the door, and glided, ghost-like, to the bedside. There the two maidens stood, both beautiful, with the pale beauty of the dead between them. But she who had first entered was proud and stately, and the other a soft and fragile thing.

"Away!" cried the lofty one. "Thou hadst him living! The dead is mine!"

"Thine!" returned the other, shuddering. "Well hast thou spoken! The dead is thine!"

The proud girl started, and stared into her face with a ghastly look. But a wild and mournful expression passed across the features of the gentle one; and weak and helpless, she sank down on the bed, her head pillowed beside that of the corpse, and her hair mingling with his dark locks. A creature of hope and joy, the first draught of sorrow had bewildered her.

"Edith!" cried her rival.

Edith groaned, as with a sudden compression of the heart; and removing her cheek from the dead youth's pillow, she stood upright! fearfully encountering the eyes of the lofty girl.

"Wilt thou betray me?" said the latter, calmly.

"Till the dead bid me speak, I will be silent," answered Edith. "Leave us alone together! Go, and live many years, and then return, and tell me of thy life. He, too, will be here! Then, if thou tellest of sufferings more than death, we will both forgive thee."

"And what shall be the token?" asked the proud girl, as if her heart acknowledged a meaning in these wild words.

"This lock of hair," said Edith, lifting one of the dark, clustering curls, that lay heavily on the dead man's brow.

The two maidens joined their hands over the bosom of the corpse, and appointed a day and hour, far, far in time to come, for their next meeting in that chamber. The statelier girl gave one deep look at the motionless countenance, and departed—yet turned again and trembled, ere she closed the door, almost believing that her dead lover frowned upon her. And Edith, too! Was not her white form fading into the moonlight? Scorning her own weakness, she went forth, and perceived that a negro slave was waiting in the passage with a wax-light, which he held between her face and his own, and regarded her, as she thought, with an ugly expression of merriment. Lifting his torch on high, the slave lighted her down the staircase, and undid the portal of the mansion. The young clergyman of the town had just ascended the steps, and bowing to the lady, passed in without a word.

Years, many years, rolled on; the world seemed new again, so much older was it grown since the night when those pale girls had clasped their hands across the bosom of the corpse. In the interval, a lonely woman had passed from youth to extreme age, and was known by all the town, as the "Old Maid in the Winding Sheet." A taint of insanity had affected her whole life, but so quiet, sad, and gentle, so utterly free from violence, that she was suffered to pursue her harmless fantasies, unmolested by the world, with whose business or pleasures she had naught to do. She dwelt alone, and never came into the daylight, except to follow funerals. Whenever a corpse was borne along the street, in sunshine, rain, or snow, whether a pompous train of the rich and proud thronged after it, or few and humble were the mourners, behind them came the lonely woman, in a long white garment which the people called her shroud. She took no place among the kindred or the friends, but stood at the door to hear the funeral prayer, and walked in the rear of the procession, as one whose earthly charge it was to haunt the house of mourning, and be the shadow of affliction, and see that the dead were duly buried. So long had this been her custom, that the inhabitants of the town deemed her a part of every funeral, as much as the coffin pall, or the very corpse itself, and augured ill of the sinner's destiny unless the "Old Maid in the Winding Sheet" came gliding, like a ghost, behind. Once, it is said, she affrighted a bridal party with her pale presence, appearing suddenly in the illuminated hall, just as the priest was uniting a false maid to a wealthy man, before her lover had been dead a year. Evil was the omen to that marriage! Sometimes she stole forth by moonlight and visited the graves of venerable Integrity, and wedded Love, and virgin Innocence, and every spot where the ashes of a kind and faithful heart were mouldering. Over the hillocks of those favored dead would she stretch out her arms, with a gesture, as if she were scattering seeds; and many believed that she brought them from the garden of Paradise; for the graves which she had visited were green beneath the snow, and covered with sweet flowers from April to November. Her blessing was better than a holy verse upon the tombstone. Thus wore away her long, sad, peaceful, and fantastic life, till few were so old as she, and the people of later generations wondered how the dead had ever been buried, or mourners had endured their grief, without the "Old Maid in the Winding Sheet."

Still years went on, and still she followed funerals, and was not yet summoned to her own festival of death. One afternoon, the great street of the town was all alive with business and bustle, though the sun now gilded only the upper half of the church spire, having left the housetops and loftiest trees in shadow. The scene was cheerful and animated, in spite of the sombre shade between the high brick buildings. Here were pompous merchants, in white wigs and laced velvet; the bronzed faces of sea-captains; the foreign garb and air of Spanish creoles; and the disdainful port of natives of Old England; all contrasted with the rough aspect of one or two back settlers, negotiating sales of timber from forests where axe had never sounded. Sometimes a lady passed, swelling roundly forth in an embroidered petticoat, balancing her steps in high-heeled shoes, and courtesying with lofty grace to the punctilious obeisances of the gentlemen. The life of the town seemed to have its very centre not far from an old mansion that stood somewhat back from the pavement, surrounded by neglected grass, with a strange air of loneliness, rather deepened than dispelled by the throng so near it. Its site would have been suitably occupied by a magnificent Exchange or a brick block, lettered all over with various signs; or the large house itself might have made a noble tavern, with the "King's Arms" swinging before it, and guests in every chamber, instead of the present solitude. But, owing to some dispute about the right of inheritance, the mansion had been long without a tenant, decaying from year to year, and throwing the stately gloom of its shadow over the busiest part of the town. Such was the scene, and such the time, when a figure unlike any that have been described was observed at a distance down the street.

"I espy a strange sail yonder," remarked a Liverpool captain; "that woman in the long white garment!"

The sailor seemed much struck by the object, as were several others who, at the same moment, caught a glimpse of the figure that had attracted his notice. Almost immediately the various topics of conversation gave place to speculations, in an undertone, on this unwonted occurrence.

"Can there be a funeral so late this afternoon?" inquired some.

They looked for the signs of death at every door—the sexton, the hearse, the assemblage of black-clad relatives—all that makes up the woful pomp of funerals. They raised their eyes, also, to the sun-gilt spire of the church, and wondered that no clang proceeded from its bell, which had always tolled till now when this figure appeared in the light of day. But none had heard that a corpse was to be borne to its home that afternoon, nor was there any token of a funeral, except the apparition of the "Old Maid in the Winding Sheet."

"What may this portend?" asked each man of his neighbor.

All smiled as they put the question, yet with a certain trouble in their eyes, as if pestilence or some other wide calamity were prognosticated by the untimely intrusion among the living of one whose presence had always been associated with death and woe. What a comet is to the earth was that sad woman to the town. Still she moved on, while the hum of surprise was hushed at her approach, and the proud and the humble stood aside, that her white garment might not wave against them. It was a long, loose robe, of spotless purity. Its wearer appeared very old, pale, emaciated, and feeble, yet glided onward without the unsteady pace of extreme age. At one point of her course a little rosy boy burst forth from a door, and ran, with open arms, towards the ghostly woman, seeming to expect a kiss from her bloodless lips. She made a slight pause, fixing her eye upon him with an expression of no earthly sweetness, so that the child shivered and stood awe-struck, rather than affrighted, while the Old Maid passed on. Perhaps her garment might have been polluted even by an infant's touch; perhaps her kiss would have been death to the sweet boy within a year.

"She is but a shadow," whispered the superstitious. "The child put forth his arms and could not grasp her robe!"

The wonder was increased when the Old Maid passed beneath the porch of the deserted mansion, ascended the moss-covered steps, lifted the iron knocker, and gave three raps. The people could only conjecture that some old remembrance, troubling her bewildered brain, had impelled the poor woman hither to visit the friends of her youth; all gone from their home long since and for ever, unless their ghosts still haunted it—fit company for the "Old Maid in the Winding Sheet." An elderly man approached the steps and, reverently uncovering his gray locks, essayed to explain the matter.

"None, Madam," said he, "have dwelt in this house these fifteen years agone—no, not since the death of old Colonel Fenwicke, whose funeral you may remember to have followed. His heirs, being ill agreed among themselves, have let the mansion house go to ruin."

The Old Maid looked slowly round with a slight gesture of one hand, and a finger of the other upon her lip, appearing more shadow-like than ever in the obscurity of the porch. But again she lifted the hammer, and gave, this time, a single rap. Could it be that a footstep was now heard coming down the staircase of the old mansion, which all conceived to have been so long untenanted? Slowly, feebly, yet heavily, like the pace of an aged and infirm person, the step approached, more distinct on every downward stair, till it reached the portal. The bar fell on the inside; the door was opened. One upward glance towards the church spire, whence the sunshine had just faded, was the last that the people saw of the "Old Maid in the Winding Sheet."

"Who undid the door?" asked many.

This question, owing to the depth of shadow beneath the porch, no one could satisfactorily answer. Two or three aged men, while protesting against an inference which might be drawn, affirmed that the person within was a negro, and bore a singular resemblance to old Cæsar, formerly a slave in the house, but freed by death some thirty years before.

"Her summons has waked up a servant of the old family," said one half seriously.

"Let us wait here," replied another. "More guests will knock at the door, anon. But the gate of the graveyard should be thrown open!"

Twilight had overspread the town before the crowd began to separate, or the comments on this incident were exhausted. One after another was wending his way homeward, when a coach—no common spectacle in those days—drove slowly into the street. It was an old-fashioned equipage, hanging close to the ground, with arms on the panels, a footman behind, and a grave, corpulent coachman seated high in front—the whole giving an idea of solemn state and dignity. There was something awful in the heavy rumbling of the wheels. The coach rolled down the street, till, coming to the gateway of the deserted mansion, it drew up, and the footman sprang to the ground.

"Whose grand coach is this?" asked a very inquisitive body.

The footman made no reply, but ascended the steps of the old house, gave three raps with the iron hammer, and returned to open the coach-door. An old man, possessed of the heraldic lore so common in that day, examined the shield of arms on the panel.

"Azure, a lion's head erased, between three flower-de-luces," said he; then whispered the name of the family to whom these bearings belonged.

The last inheritor of its honors was recently dead, after a long residence amid the splendor of the British court, where his birth and wealth had given him no mean station. "He left no child," continued the herald, "and these arms, being in a lozenge, betoken that the coach appertains to his widow."

Further disclosures, perhaps, might have been made, had not the speaker suddenly been struck dumb by the stern eye of an ancient lady, who thrust forth her head from the coach, preparing to descend. As she emerged, the people saw that her dress was magnificent, and her figure dignified, in spite of age and infirmity—a stately ruin, but with a look, at once, of pride and wretchedness. Her strong and rigid features had an awe about them, unlike that of the white Old Maid, but as of something evil. She passed up the steps, leaning on a gold-headed cane; the door swung open as she ascended—and the light of a torch glittered on the embroidery of her dress, and gleamed on the pillars of the porch. After a momentary pause —a glance backwards—and then a desperate effort—she went in. The decipherer of the coat of arms had ventured up the lowest step, and shrinking back immediately, pale and tremulous, affirmed that the torch was held by the very image of old Cæsar.

"But such a hideous grin," added he, "was never seen on the face of mortal man, black or white! It will haunt me till my dying day."

Meantime, the coach had wheeled round, with a prodigious clatter on the pavement, and rumbled up the street, disappearing in the twilight, while the ear still tracked its course. Scarcely was it gone, when the people began to question whether the coach and attendants, the ancient lady, the spectre of old Cæsar, and the Old Maid herself, were not all a strangely combined delusion, with some dark purport in its mystery. The whole town was astir, so that, instead of dispersing, the crowd continually increased, and stood gazing up at the windows of the mansion, now silvered by the brightening moon. The elders, glad to indulge the narrative propensity of age, told of the long-faded splendor of the family, the entertainments they had given, and the guests, the greatest of the land, and even titled and noble ones from abroad, who had passed beneath that portal. These graphic reminiscences seemed to call up the ghosts of those to whom they referred. So strong was the impression on some of the more imaginative hearers, that two or three were seized with trembling fits, at one and the same moment, protesting that they had distinctly heard three other raps of the iron knocker.

"Impossible!" exclaimed others. "See! The moon shines beneath the porch, and shows every part of it, except in the narrow shade of that pillar. There is no one there!"

"Did not the door open?" whispered one of these fanciful persons.

"Didst thou see it, too?" said his companion, in a startled tone.

But the general sentiment was opposed to the idea that a third visitant had made application at the door of the deserted house. A few, however, adhered to this new marvel, and even declared that a red gleam like that of a torch had shone through the great front window, as if the negro were lighting a guest up the staircase. This, too, was pronounced a mere fantasy. But at once the whole multitude started, and each man beheld his own terror painted in the faces of all the rest.

"What an awful thing is this!" cried they.

A shriek too fearfully distinct for doubt had been heard within the mansion, breaking forth suddenly, and succeeded by a deep stillness, as if a heart had burst in giving it utterance. The people knew not whether to fly from the very sight of the house, or to rush trembling in, and search out the strange mystery. Amid their confusion and affright, they were somewhat reassured by the appearance of their clergyman, a venerable patriarch, and equally a saint, who had taught them and their fathers the way to Heaven for more than the space of an ordinary lifetime. He was a reverend figure, with long white hair upon his shoulders, a white beard upon his breast, and a back so bent over his staff that he seemed to be looking downward continually, as if to choose a proper grave for his weary frame. It was some time before the good old man, being deaf and of impaired intellect, could be made to comprehend such portions of the affair as were comprehensible at all. But, when possessed of the facts, his energies assumed unexpected vigor.

"Verily," said the old gentleman, "it will be fitting that I enter the mansion house of the worthy Colonel Fenwicke, lest any harm should have befallen that true Christian woman whom ye call the 'Old Maid in the Winding Sheet.'"

Behold, then, the venerable clergyman ascending the steps of the mansion, with a torch-bearer behind him. It was the elderly man who had spoken to the Old Maid, and the same who had afterwards explained the shield of arms and recognized the features of the negro. Like their predecessors, they gave three raps with the iron hammer.

"Old Cæsar cometh not," observed the priest. "Well I wot he no longer doth service in this mansion."

"Assuredly, then, it was something worse, in old Cæsar's likeness!" said the other adventurer.

"Be it as God wills," answered the clergyman. "See! my strength, though it be much decayed, hath sufficed to open this heavy door. Let us enter and pass up the staircase."

Here occurred a singular exemplification of the dreamy state of a very old man's mind. As they ascended the wide flight of stairs, the aged clergyman appeared to move with caution, occasionally standing aside, and oftener bending his head, as it were in salutation, thus practising all the gestures of one who makes his way through a throng. Reaching the head of the staircase, he looked around with sad and solemn benignity, laid aside his staff, bared his hoary locks, and was evidently on the point of commencing a prayer.

"Reverend Sir," said his attendant, who conceived this a very suitable prelude to their further search, "would it not be well that the people join with us in prayer?"

"Welladay!" cried the old clergyman, staring strangely around him. "Art thou here with me, and none other? Verily, past times were present to me, and I deemed that I was to make a funeral prayer, as many a time heretofore, from the head of this staircase. Of a truth, I saw the shades of many that are gone. Yea, I have prayed at their burials, one after another, and the 'Old Maid in the Winding Sheet' hath seen them to their graves!"

Being now more thoroughly awake to their present purpose, he took his staff and struck forcibly on the floor, till there came an echo from each deserted chamber, but no menial to answer their summons. They therefore walked along the passage, and again paused, opposite to the great front window through which was seen the crowd, in the shadow and partial moonlight of the street beneath. On their right hand was the open door of a chamber, and a closed one on their left. The clergyman pointed his cane to the carved oak panel of the latter.

"Within that chamber," observed he, "a whole lifetime since, did I sit by the death-bed of a goodly young man, who, being now at the last gasp"—

Apparently, there was some powerful excitement in the ideas which had now flashed across his mind. He snatched the torch from his companion's hand, and threw open the door with such sudden violence that the flame was extinguished, leaving them no other light than the moonbeams, which fell through two windows into the spacious chamber. It was sufficient to discover all that could be known. In a high-backed oaken armchair, upright, with her hands clasped across her breast, and her head thrown back, sat the "Old Maid in the Winding Sheet." The stately dame had fallen on her knees, with her forehead on the holy knees of the Old Maid, one hand upon the floor and the other pressed convulsively against her heart. It clutched a lock of hair, once sable, now discolored with a greenish mould. As the priest and layman advanced into the chamber, the Old Maid's features assumed such a semblance of shifting expression that they trusted to hear the whole mystery explained by a single word. But it was only the shadow of a tattered curtain waving betwixt the dead face and the moonlight.

"Both dead!" said the venerable man. "Then who shall divulge the secret? Methinks it glimmers to and fro in my mind, like the light and shadow across the Old Maid's face. And now 'tis gone!"

1835

## THE MINISTER'S BLACK VEIL

### A PARABLE *

The sexton stood in the porch of Milford meeting-house, pulling busily at the bell-rope. The old people of the village came stooping along the street. Children, with bright faces, tripped merrily beside their parents, or mimicked a graver gait, in the conscious dignity of their Sunday clothes. Spruce bachelors looked sidelong at the pretty maidens, and fancied that the Sabbath sunshine made them

*Another clergyman in New England, Mr. Joseph Moody, of York, Maine, who died about eighty years since, made himself remarkable by the same eccentricity that is here related of the Reverend Mr. Hooper. In his case, however, the symbol had a different import. In early life he had accidentally killed a beloved friend; and from that day till the hour of his own death, he hid his face from men. [Author's note.]

prettier than on week days. When the throng had mostly streamed into the porch, the sexton began to toll the bell, keeping his eye on the Reverend Mr. Hooper's door. The first glimpse of the clergyman's figure was the signal for the bell to cease its summons.

"But what has good Parson Hooper got upon his face?" cried the sexton in astonishment.

All within hearing immediately turned about, and beheld the semblance of Mr. Hooper, pacing slowly his meditative way towards the meeting-house. With one accord they started, expressing more wonder than if some strange minister were coming to dust the cushions of Mr. Hooper's pulpit.

"Are you sure it is our parson?" inquired Goodman Gray of the sexton.

"Of a certainty it is good Mr. Hooper," replied the sexton. "He was to have exchanged pulpits with Parson Shute, of Westbury; but Parson Shute sent to excuse himself yesterday, being to preach a funeral sermon."

The cause of so much amazement may appear sufficiently slight. Mr. Hooper, a gentlemanly person, of about thirty, though still a bachelor, was dressed with due clerical neatness, as if a careful wife had starched his band, and brushed the weekly dust from his Sunday's garb. There was but one thing remarkable in his appearance. Swathed about his forehead, and hanging down over his face, so low as to be shaken by his breath, Mr. Hooper had on a black veil. On a nearer view it seemed to consist of two folds of crape, which entirely concealed his features, except the mouth and chin, but probably did not intercept his sight, further than to give a darkened aspect to all living and inanimate things. With this gloomy shade before him, good Mr. Hooper walked onward, at a slow and quiet pace, stooping somewhat, and looking on the ground, as is customary with abstracted men, yet nodding kindly to those of his parishioners who still waited on the meeting-house steps. But so wonder-struck were they that his greeting hardly met with a return.

"I can't really feel as if good Mr. Hooper's face was behind that piece of crape," said the sexton.

"I don't like it," muttered an old woman, as she hobbled into the meeting-house. "He has changed himself into something awful, only by hiding his face."

"Our parson has gone mad!" cried Goodman Gray, following him across the threshold.

A rumor of some unaccountable phenomenon had preceded Mr. Hooper into the meeting-house, and set all the congregation astir. Few could refrain from twisting their heads towards the door; many stood upright, and turned directly about; while several little boys clambered upon the seats, and came down again with a terrible racket. There was a general bustle, a rustling of the women's gowns and shuffling of the men's feet, greatly at variance with that hushed repose which should attend the entrance of the minister. But Mr. Hooper appeared not to notice the perturbation of his people. He entered with an almost noiseless step, bent his head mildly to the pews on each side, and bowed as he passed his oldest parishioner, a white-haired great-grandsire, who occupied an arm-chair in the centre of the aisle. It was strange to observe how slowly this venerable man became conscious of something singular in the appearance of his pastor. He seemed not fully to partake of the prevailing wonder, till Mr. Hooper had ascended the stairs, and showed himself in the pulpit, face to face with his congregation, except for the black veil. That mysterious emblem was never once withdrawn. It shook with his measured breath, as he gave out the psalm; it threw its obscurity between him and the holy page, as he read the Scriptures; and while he prayed, the veil lay heavily on his uplifted countenance. Did he seek to hide it from the dread Being whom he was addressing?

Such was the effect of this simple piece of crape, that more than one woman of delicate nerves was forced to leave the meeting-house. Yet perhaps the pale-faced congregation was almost as fearful a sight to the minister, as his black veil to them.

Mr. Hooper had the reputation of a good preacher, but not an energetic one: he strove to win his people heavenward by mild, persuasive influences, rather than to drive them thither by the thunders of the Word. The sermon which he now delivered was marked by the same characteristics of style and manner as the general series of his pulpit oratory. But there was something, either in the sentiment of the discourse itself, or in the imagination of the auditors, which made it greatly the most powerful effort that they had ever heard from their pastor's lips. It was tinged, rather more darkly than usual, with the gentle gloom of Mr. Hooper's temperament. The subject had reference to secret sin, and those sad mysteries which we hide from our nearest and dearest, and would fain conceal from our own consciousness, even forgetting that the Omniscient can detect them. A subtle power was breathed into his words. Each member of the congregation, the most innocent girl, and the man of hardened breast, felt as if the preacher had crept upon them, behind his awful veil, and discovered their hoarded iniquity of deed or thought. Many spread their clasped hands on their bosoms. There was nothing terrible in what Mr. Hooper said, at least, no violence; and yet, with every tremor of his melancholy voice, the hearers quaked. An unsought pathos came hand in hand with awe. So sensible were the audience of some unwonted attribute in their minister, that they longed for a breath of wind to blow aside the veil, almost believing that a stranger's visage would be discovered, though the form, gesture, and voice were those of Mr. Hooper.

At the close of the services, the people hurried out with indecorous confusion, eager to communicate their pent-up amazement, and conscious of lighter spirits the moment they lost sight of the black veil. Some gathered in little circles, huddled closely together, with their mouths all whispering in the centre; some went homeward alone, wrapt in silent meditation; some talked loudly, and profaned the Sabbath day with ostentatious laughter. A few shook their sagacious heads, intimating that they could penetrate the mystery; while one or two affirmed that there was no mystery at all. but only that Mr. Hooper's eyes were so weakened by the midnight lamp, as to require a shade. After a brief interval, forth came good Mr. Hooper also, in the rear of his flock. Turning his veiled face from one group to another, he paid due reverence to the hoary heads, saluted the middle aged with kind dignity as their friend and spiritual guide, greeted the young with mingled authority and love, and laid his hands on the little children's heads to bless them. Such was always his custom on the Sabbath day. Strange and bewildered looks repaid him for his courtesy. None, as on former occasions, aspired to the honor of walking by their pastor's side. Old Squire Saunders, doubtless by an accidental lapse of memory, neglected to invite Mr. Hooper to his table, where the good clergyman had been wont to bless the food, almost every Sunday since his settlement. He returned, therefore, to the parsonage, and, at the moment of closing the door, was observed to look back upon the people, all of whom had their eyes fixed upon the minister. A sad smile gleamed faintly from beneath the black veil, and flickered about his mouth, glimmering as he disappeared.

"How strange," said a lady, "that a simple black veil, such as any woman might wear on her bonnet, should become such a terrible thing on Mr. Hooper's face!"

"Something must surely be amiss with Mr. Hooper's intellects," observed her husband, the physician of the village. "But the strangest part of the affair is the effect of this vagary, even on a sober-minded man like myself. The black veil, though it covers only our pastor's face, throws its influence over his whole person, and makes him ghost-like from head to foot. Do you not feel it so?"

"Truly do I," replied the lady; "and I would not be alone with him for the world. I wonder he is not afraid to be alone with himself!"

"Men sometimes are so," said her husband.

The afternoon service was attended with similar circumstances. At its conclusion, the bell tolled for the funeral of a young lady. The relatives and friends were assembled in the house, and the more distant acquaintances stood about the door, speaking of the good qualities of the deceased, when their talk was interrupted by the appearance of Mr. Hooper, still covered with his black veil. It was now an appropriate emblem. The clergyman stepped into the room where the corpse was laid, and bent over the coffin, to take a last farewell of his deceased parishioner. As he stooped, the veil hung straight down from his forehead, so that, if her eyelids had not been closed forever, the dead maiden might have seen his face. Could Mr. Hooper be fearful of her glance, that he so hastily caught back the black veil? A person who watched the interview between the dead and living, scrupled not to affirm, that, at the instant when the clergyman's features were disclosed, the corpse had slightly shuddered, rustling the shroud and muslin cap, though the countenance retained the composure of death. A superstitious old woman was the only witness of this prodigy. From the coffin Mr. Hooper passed into the chamber of the mourners, and thence to the head of the staircase, to make the funeral prayer. It was a tender and heart-dissolving prayer, full of sorrow, yet so imbued with celestial hopes, that the music of a heavenly harp, swept by the fingers of the dead, seemed faintly to be heard among the saddest accents of the minister. The people trembled, though they but darkly understood him when he prayed that they, and himself, and all of mortal race, might be ready, as he trusted this young maiden had been, for the dreadful hour that should snatch the veil from their faces. The bearers went heavily forth, and the mourners followed, saddening all the street, with the dead before them, and Mr. Hooper in his black veil behind.

"Why do you look back?" said one in the procession to his partner.

"I had a fancy," replied she, "that the minister and the maiden's spirit were walking hand in hand."

"And so had I, at the same moment," said the other.

That night, the handsomest couple in Milford village were to be joined in wedlock. Though reckoned a melancholy man, Mr. Hooper had a placid cheerfulness for such occasions, which often excited a sympathetic smile where livelier merriment would have been thrown away. There was no quality of his disposition which made him more beloved than this. The company at the wedding awaited his arrival with impatience, trusting that the strange awe, which had gathered over him throughout the day, would now be dispelled. But such was not the result. When Mr. Hooper came, the first thing that their eyes rested on was the same horrible black veil, which had added deeper gloom to the funeral, and could portend nothing but evil to the wedding. Such was its immediate effect on the guests that a cloud seemed to have rolled duskily from beneath the black crape, and dimmed the light of the candles. The bridal pair stood up before the minister. But the bride's cold fingers quivered in the tremulous hand of the bridegroom, and her deathlike paleness caused a whisper that the maiden who had been buried a few hours before was come from her grave to be married. If ever another wedding were so dismal, it was that famous one where they tolled the wedding knell. After performing the ceremony, Mr. Hooper raised a glass of wine to his lips, wishing happiness to the new-married couple in a strain of mild pleasantry that ought to have brightened the features of the guests, like a cheerful gleam from the hearth. At that instant, catching a glimpse of his figure in the looking-glass, the black veil involved his own spirit in the horror with which it overwhelmed all others. His frame shuddered, his lips grew white, he spilt the untasted wine upon the carpet, and rushed forth into the darkness. For the Earth, too, had on her Black Veil.

The next day, the whole village of Milford talked of little else than Parson Hooper's black veil. That, and the mystery concealed behind it, supplied a topic for discussion between acquaintances meeting in the street, and good women gossiping at their open windows. It was the first item of news that the tavernkeeper told to his guests. The children babbled of it on their way to school. One imitative little imp covered his face with an old black handkerchief, thereby so affrighting his playmates that the panic seized himself, and he well-nigh lost his wits by his own waggery.

It was remarkable that of all the busybodies and impertinent people in the parish, not one ventured to put the plain question to Mr. Hooper, wherefore he did this thing. Hitherto, whenever there appeared the slightest call for such interference, he had never lacked advisers, nor shown himself averse to be guided by their judgment. If he erred at all, it was by so painful a degree of self-distrust, that even the mildest censure would lead him to consider an indifferent action as a crime. Yet, though so well acquainted with this amiable weakness, no individual among his parishioners chose to make the black veil a subject of friendly remonstrance. There was a feeling of dread, neither plainly confessed nor carefully concealed, which caused each to shift the responsibility upon another, till at length it was found expedient to send a deputation of the church, in order to deal with Mr. Hooper about the mystery, before it should grow into a scandal. Never did an embassy so ill discharge its duties. The minister received them with friendly courtesy, but became silent, after they were seated, leaving to his visitors the whole burden of introducing their important business. The topic, it might be supposed, was obvious enough. There was the black veil swathed round Mr. Hooper's forehead, and concealing every feature above his placid mouth, on which, at times, they could perceive the glimmering of a melancholy smile. But that piece of crape, to their imagination, seemed to hang down before his heart, the symbol of a fearful secret between him and them. Were the veil but cast aside, they might speak freely of it, but not till then. Thus they sat a considerable time, speechless, confused, and shrinking uneasily from Mr. Hooper's eye, which they felt to be fixed upon them with an invisible glance. Finally, the deputies returned abashed to their constituents, pronouncing the matter too weighty to be handled, except by a council of the churches, if, indeed, it might not require a general synod.

But there was one person in the village unappalled by the awe with which the black veil had impressed all beside herself. When the deputies returned without an explanation, or even venturing to demand one, she, with the calm energy of her character, determined to chase away the strange cloud that appeared to be settling round Mr. Hooper, every moment more darkly than before. As his plighted wife, it should be her privilege to know what the black veil concealed. At the minister's first visit, therefore, she entered upon the subject with a direct simplicity, which made the task easier both for him and her. After he had seated himself, she fixed her eyes steadfastly upon the veil, but could discern nothing of the dreadful gloom that had so overawed the multitude: it was but a double fold of crape, hanging down from his forehead to his mouth, and slightly stirring with his breath.

"No," said she aloud, and smiling, "there is nothing terrible in this piece of crape, except that it hides a face which I am always glad to look upon. Come, good sir, let the sun shine from behind the cloud. First lay aside your black veil: then tell me why you put it on."

Mr. Hooper's smile glimmered faintly.

"There is an hour to come," said he, "when all of us shall cast aside our veils. Take it not amiss, beloved friend, if I wear this piece of crape till then."

"Your words are a mystery, too," returned the young lady. "Take away the veil from them, at least."

"Elizabeth, I will," said he, "so far as my vow may suffer me. Know, then, this veil is a type and a symbol, and I am bound to wear it ever, both in light and darkness, in solitude and before the gaze of multitudes, and as with strangers, so with my familiar friends. No mortal eye will see it withdrawn. This dismal shade must separate me from the world: even you, Elizabeth, can never come behind it!"

"What grievous affliction hath befallen you," she earnestly inquired, "that you should thus darken your eyes forever?"

"If it be a sign of mourning," replied Mr. Hooper, "I, perhaps, like most other mortals, have sorrows dark enough to be typified by a black veil."

"But what if the world will not believe that it is the type of an innocent sorrow?" urged Elizabeth. "Beloved and respected as you are, there may be whispers that you hide your face under the consciousness of secret sin. For the sake of your holy office, do away this scandal!"

The color rose into her cheeks as she intimated the nature of the rumors that were already abroad in the village. But Mr. Hooper's mildness did not forsake him. He even smiled again — that same sad smile, which always appeared like a faint glimmering of light, proceeding from the obscurity beneath the veil.

"If I hide my face for sorrow, there is cause enough," he merely replied; "and if I cover it for secret sin, what mortal might not do the same?"

And with this gentle, but unconquerable obstinacy did he resist all her entreaties. At length Elizabeth sat silent. For a few moments she appeared lost in thought, considering, probably, what new methods might be tried to withdraw her lover from so dark a fantasy, which, if it had no other meaning, was perhaps a symptom of mental disease. Though of a firmer character than his own, the tears rolled down her cheeks. But, in an instant, as it were, a new feeling took the place of sorrow: her eyes were fixed insensibly on the black veil, when, like a sudden twilight in the air, its terrors fell around her. She arose, and stood trembling before him.

"And do you feel it then, at last?" said he mournfully.

She made no reply, but covered her eyes with her hand, and turned to leave the room. He rushed forward and caught her arm.

"Have patience with me, Elizabeth!" cried he, passionately. "Do not desert me, though this veil must be between us here on earth. Be mine, and hereafter there shall be no veil over my face, no darkness between our souls! It is but a mortal veil — it is not for eternity! O! you know not how lonely I am, and how frightened, to be alone behind my black veil. Do not leave me in this miserable obscurity forever!"

"Lift the veil but once, and look me in the face," said she.

"Never! It cannot be!" replied Mr. Hooper.

"Then farewell!" said Elizabeth.

She withdrew her arm from his grasp, and slowly departed, pausing at the door, to give one long shuddering gaze, that seemed almost to penetrate the mystery of the black veil. But, even amid his grief, Mr. Hooper smiled to think that only a material emblem had separated him from happiness, though the horrors, which it shadowed forth, must be drawn darkly between the fondest of lovers.

From that time no attempts were made to remove Mr. Hooper's black veil, or, by a direct appeal, to discover the secret which it was supposed to hide. By persons who claimed a superiority to popular prejudice, it was reckoned merely an eccentric whim, such as often mingles with the sober actions of men otherwise rational, and tinges them all with its own semblance of insanity. But with the multitude, good Mr. Hooper was irreparably a bugbear. He could not walk the street with any peace of mind, so conscious was he that the gentle and timid would turn aside to avoid him, and that others would make it a point of hardihood to throw themselves in his way. The impertinence of the latter class compelled him to give up his customary walk at sunset to the burial ground; for when he leaned pensively over the gate, there would always be faces behind the gravestones, peeping at his black veil. A fable went the rounds that the stare of the dead people drove him thence. It grieved him, to the very depth of his kind heart, to observe how the children fled from his approach, breaking up their merriest sports, while his melancholy figure was yet afar off. Their instinctive dread caused him to feel more strongly than aught else, that a preternatural horror was interwoven with the threads of the black crape. In truth, his own antipathy to the veil was known to be so great, that he never willingly passed before a mirror, nor stooped to drink at a still fountain, lest, in its peaceful bosom, he should be affrighted by himself. This was what gave plausibility to the whispers, that Mr. Hooper's conscience tortured him for some great crime too horrible to be entirely concealed, or otherwise than so obscurely intimated. Thus, from beneath the black veil, there rolled a cloud into the sunshine, an ambiguity of sin or sorrow, which enveloped the poor minister, so that love or sympathy could never reach him. It was said that ghost and fiend consorted with him there. With self-shudderings and outward terrors, he walked continually in its shadow, groping darkly within his own soul, or gazing through a medium that saddened the whole world. Even the lawless wind, it was believed, respected his dreadful secret, and never blew aside the veil. But still good Mr. Hooper sadly smiled at the pale visages of the worldly throng as he passed by.

Among all its bad influences, the black veil had the one desirable effect, of making its wearer a very efficient clergyman. By the aid of his mysterious emblem — for there was no other apparent cause — he became a man of awful power over souls that were in agony for sin. His converts always regarded him with a dread peculiar to themselves, affirming, though but figuratively, that, before he brought them to celestial light, they had been with him behind the black veil. Its gloom, indeed, enabled him to sympathize with all dark affections. Dying sinners cried aloud for Mr. Hooper, and would not yield their breath till he appeared; though ever, as he stooped to whisper consolation, they shuddered at the veiled face so near their own. Such were the terrors of the black veil, even when Death had bared his visage! Strangers came long distances to attend service at his church, with the mere idle purpose of gazing at his figure, because it was forbidden them to behold his face. But many were made to quake ere they departed! Once, during Governor Belcher's administration, Mr. Hooper was appointed to preach the election sermon. Covered with his black veil, he stood before the chief magistrate, the council, and the representatives, and wrought so deep an impression, that the legislative measures of that year were characterized by all the gloom and piety of our earliest ancestral sway.

In this manner Mr. Hooper spent a long life, irreproachable in outward act, yet shrouded in dismal suspicions; kind and loving, though unloved, and dimly feared; a man apart from men, shunned in their health and joy, but ever summoned to their aid in mortal anguish. As years wore on, shedding their snows above his sable veil, he acquired a name throughout the New England churches, and they called him Father Hooper. Nearly all his parishioners, who were of mature age when he was settled, had been borne away by many a funeral: he had one congregation in the church, and a more crowded one in the churchyard; and having wrought so late into the evening, and done his work so well, it was now good Father Hooper's turn to rest.

Several persons were visible by the shaded candle-light, in the death chamber of the old clergyman. Natural connections he had none. But there was the decorously grave, though unmoved physician, seeking only to mitigate the last pangs of the patient whom he could not save. There were the deacons, and other eminently pious members of his church. There, also, was the Reverend Mr. Clark, of Westbury, a young and zealous divine, who had ridden in haste to pray by the bedside of the expiring minister. There was the nurse, no hired handmaiden of death, but one whose calm affection had endured thus long in secrecy, in solitude, amid the chill of age, and would not perish, even at the dying hour. Who, but Elizabeth! And there lay the hoary head of good Father Hooper upon the death pillow, with the black veil still swathed about his brow, and reaching down over his face, so that each more difficult gasp of his faint breath caused it to stir. All through life that piece of crape had hung between him and the world: it had separated him from cheerful brotherhood and woman's love, and kept him in that saddest of all prisons, his own heart; and still it lay upon his face, as if to deepen the gloom of his darksome chamber, and shade him from the sunshine of eternity.

For some time previous, his mind had been confused, wavering doubtfully between the past and the present, and hovering forward, as it were, at intervals, into the indistinctness of the world to come. There had been feverish turns, which tossed him from side to side, and wore away what little strength he had. But in his most convulsive struggles, and in the wildest vagaries of his intellect, when no other thought retained its sober influence, he still showed an awful solicitude lest the black veil should slip aside. Even if his bewildered soul could have forgotten, there was a faithful woman at his pillow, who, with averted eyes, would have covered that aged face, which she had last beheld in the comeliness of manhood. At length the death-stricken old man lay quietly in the torpor of mental and bodily exhaustion, with an imperceptible pulse, and breath that grew fainter and fainter, except when a long, deep, and irregular inspiration seemed to prelude the flight of his spirit.

The minister of Westbury approached the bedside.

"Venerable Father Hooper," said he, "the moment of your release is at hand. Are you ready for the lifting of the veil that shuts in time from eternity?"

Father Hooper at first replied merely by a feeble motion of his head; then, apprehensive, perhaps, that his meaning might be doubtful, he exerted himself to speak.

"Yea," said he, in faint accents, "my soul hath a patient weariness until that veil be lifted."

"And is it fitting," resumed the Reverend Mr. Clark, "that a man so given to prayer, of such a blameless example, holy in deed and thought, so far as mortal judgment may pronounce; is it fitting that a father in the church should leave a shadow on his memory, that may seem to blacken a life so pure? I pray you, my venerable brother, let not this thing be! Suffer us to be gladdened by your triumphant aspect as you go to your reward. Before the veil of eternity be lifted, let me cast aside this black veil from your face!"

And thus speaking, the Reverend Mr. Clark bent forward to reveal the mystery of so many years. But, exerting a sudden energy, that made all the beholders stand aghast, Father Hooper snatched both his hands from beneath the bedclothes, and pressed them strongly on the black veil, resolute to struggle, if the minister of Westbury would contend with a dying man.

"Never!" cried the veiled clergyman. "On earth, never!"

"Dark old man!" exclaimed the affrighted minister, "with what horrible crime upon your soul are you now passing to the judgment?"

Father Hooper's breath heaved; it rattled in his throat; but, with a mighty effort, grasping forward with his hands, he caught hold of life, and held it back till he should speak. He even raised himself in bed; and there he sat, shivering with the arms of death around him, while the black veil hung down, awful, at that last moment, in the gathered terrors of a lifetime. And yet the faint, sad smile, so often there, now seemed to glimmer from its obscurity, and linger on Father Hooper's lips.

"Why do you tremble at me alone?" cried he, turning his veiled face round the circle of pale spectators. "Tremble also at each other! Have men avoided me, and women shown no pity, and children screamed and fled, only for my black veil? What, but the mystery which it obscurely typifies, has made this piece of crape so awful? When the friend shows his inmost heart to his friend; the lover to his best beloved; when man does not vainly shrink from the eye of his Creator, loathsomely treasuring up the secret of his sin; then deem me a monster, for the symbol beneath which I have lived, and die! I look around me, and, lo! on every visage a Black Veil!"

While his auditors shrank from one another, in mutual affright, Father Hooper fell back upon his pillow, a veiled corpse, with a faint smile lingering on the lips. Still veiled, they laid him in his coffin, and a veiled corpse they bore him to the grave. The grass of many years has sprung up and withered on that grave, the burial stone is moss-grown, and good Mr. Hooper's face is dust; but awful is still the thought that it mouldered beneath the Black Veil!

1835

## ENDICOTT AND THE RED CROSS

At noon of an autumnal day, more than two centuries ago, the English colors were displayed by the standard-bearer of the Salem trainband, which had mustered for martial exercise under the orders of John Endicott. It was a period when the religious exiles were accustomed often to buckle on their armor, and practise the handling of their weapons of war. Since the first settlement of New England, its prospects had never been so dismal. The dissensions between Charles the First and his subjects were then, and for several years afterwards, confined to the floor of Parliament. The measures of the King and ministry were rendered more tyrannically violent by an opposition, which had not yet acquired sufficient confidence in its own strength to resist royal injustice with the sword. The bigoted and haughty primate, Laud, Archbishop of Canterbury, controlled the religious affairs of the realm, and was consequently invested with powers which might have wrought the utter ruin of the two Puritan colonies, Plymouth and Massachusetts. There is evidence on record that our forefathers perceived their danger, but were resolved that their infant country should not fall without a struggle, even beneath the giant strength of the King's right arm.

Such was the aspect of the times when the folds of the English banner, with the Red Cross in its field, were flung out over a company of Puritans. Their leader, the famous Endicott, was a man of stern and resolute countenance, the effect of which was heightened by a grizzled beard that swept the upper portion of his breastplate. This piece of armor was so highly polished that the whole surrounding scene had its image in the glittering steel. The central object in the mirrored picture was an edifice of humble architecture with neither steeple nor bell to proclaim it—what nevertheless it was—the house of prayer. A token of the perils of the wilderness was seen in the grim head of a wolf, which had just been slain within the precincts of the town, and according to the regular mode of claiming the bounty, was nailed on the porch of the meeting-house. The blood was still plashing on the doorstep. There happened to be visible, at the same noontide hour, so many other characteristics of the times and manners of the Puritans, that we must endeavor to represent them in a sketch, though far less vividly than they were reflected in the polished breastplate of John Endicott.

In close vicinity to the sacred edifice appeared that important engine of Puritanic authority, the whipping-post —with the soil around it well trodden by the feet of evil doers, who had there been disciplined. At one corner of the meeting-house was the pillory, and at the other the stocks; and, by a singular good fortune for our sketch, the head of an Episcopalian and suspected Catholic was grotesquely incased in the former machine; while a fellow-criminal, who had boisterously quaffed a health to the king, was confined by the legs in the latter. Side by side, on the meeting-house steps, stood a male and a female figure. The man was a tall, lean, haggard personification of fanaticism, bearing on his breast this label,—A WANTON GOSPELLER,—which betokened that he had dared to give interpretations of Holy Writ unsanctioned by the infallible judgment of the civil and religious rulers. His aspect showed no lack of zeal to maintain his heterodoxies, even at the stake. The woman wore a cleft stick on her tongue, in appropriate retribution for having wagged that unruly member against the elders of the church; and her countenance and gestures gave much cause to apprehend that, the moment the stick should be removed, a repetition of the offence would demand new ingenuity in chastising it.

The above-mentioned individuals had been sentenced to undergo their various modes of ignominy, for the space of one hour at noonday. But among the crowd were several whose punishment would be life-long; some, whose ears had been cropped, like those of puppy dogs; others, whose cheeks had been branded with the initials of their misdemeanors; one, with his nostrils slit and seared; and another, with a halter about his neck, which he was forbidden ever to take off, or to conceal beneath his garments. Methinks he must have been grievously tempted to affix the other end of the rope to some convenient beam or bough. There was likewise a young woman, with no mean share of beauty, whose doom it was to wear the letter A on the breast of her gown, in the eyes of all the world and her own children. And even her own children knew what that initial signified. Sporting with her infamy, the lost and desperate creature had embroidered the fatal token in scarlet cloth, with golden thread and the nicest art of needlework; so that the capital A might have been thought to mean Admirable, or anything rather than Adulteress.

Let not the reader argue, from any of these evidences of iniquity, that the times of the Puritans were more vicious than our own, when, as we pass along the very street of this sketch, we discern no badge of infamy on man or woman. It was the policy of our ancestors to search out even the most secret sins, and expose them to shame, without fear or favor, in the broadest light of the noonday sun. Were such the custom now, perchance we might find materials for a no less piquant sketch than the above.

Except the malefactors whom we have described, and the diseased or infirm persons, the whole male population of the town, between sixteen years and sixty, were seen in the ranks of the trainband. A few stately savages, in all the pomp and dignity of the primeval Indian, stood gazing at the spectacle. Their flint-headed arrows were but childish weapons compared with the matchlocks of the Puritans, and would have rattled harmlessly against the steel caps and hammered iron breastplates which inclosed each soldier in an individual fortress. The valiant John Endicott glanced with an eye of pride at his sturdy followers, and prepared to renew the martial toils of the day.

"Come, my stout hearts!" quoth he, drawing his sword. "Let us show these poor heathen that we can handle our weapons like men of might. Well for them, if they put us not to prove it in earnest!"

The iron-breasted company straightened their line, and each man drew the heavy butt of his matchlock close to his left foot, thus awaiting the orders of the captain. But, as Endicott glanced right and left along the front, he discovered a personage at some little distance with whom it behooved him to hold a parley. It was an elderly gentleman, wearing a black cloak and band, and a high-crowned hat, beneath which was a velvet skullcap, the whole being the garb of a Puritan minister. This reverend person bore a staff which seemed to have been recently cut in the forest, and his shoes were bemired as if he had been travelling on foot through the swamps of the wilderness. His aspect was perfectly that of a pilgrim, heightened also by an apostolic dignity. Just as Endicott perceived him he laid aside his staff, and stooped to drink at a bubbling fountain which gushed into the sunshine about a score of yards from the corner of the meeting-house. But, ere the good man drank, he turned his face heavenward in thankfulness, and then, holding back his gray beard with one hand, he scooped up his simple draught in the hollow of the other.

"What, ho! good Mr. Williams," shouted Endicott. "You are welcome back again to our town of peace. How does our worthy Governor Winthrop? And what news from Boston?"

"The Governor hath his health, worshipful Sir," answered Roger Williams, now resuming his staff, and drawing near. "And for the news, here is a letter, which, knowing I was to travel hitherward to-day, his Excellency committed to my charge. Belike it contains tidings of much import; for a ship arrived yesterday from England."

Mr. Williams, the minister of Salem and of course known to all the spectators, had now reached the spot where Endicott was standing under the banner of his company, and put the Governor's epistle into his hand. The broad seal was impressed with Winthrop's coat of arms. Endicott hastily unclosed the letter and began to read, while, as his eye passed down the page, a wrathful change came over his manly countenance. The blood glowed through it, till it seemed to be kindling with an internal heat; nor was it unnatural to suppose that his breastplate would likewise become redhot with the angry fire of the bosom which it covered. Arriving at the conclusion, he shook the letter fiercely in his hand, so that it rustled as loud as the flag above his head.

"Black tidings these, Mr. Williams," said he; "blacker never came to New England. Doubtless you know their purport?"

"Yea, truly," replied Roger Williams; "for the Governor consulted, respecting this matter, with my brethren in the ministry at Boston; and my opinion was likewise asked. And his Excellency entreats you by me, that the news be not suddenly noised abroad, lest the people be stirred up unto some outbreak, and thereby give the King and the Archbishop a handle against us."

"The Governor is a wise man—a wise man, and a meek and moderate," said Endicott, setting his teeth grimly. "Nevertheless, I must do according to my own best judgment. There is neither man, woman, nor child in New England, but has a concern as dear as life in these tidings; and if John Endicott's voice be loud enough, man, woman, and child shall hear them. Soldiers, wheel into a hollow square! Ho, good people! Here are news for one and all of you."

The soldiers closed in around their captain; and he and Roger Williams stood together under the banner of the Red Cross; while the women and the aged men pressed forward, and the mothers held up their children to look Endicott in the face. A few taps of the drum gave signal for silence and attention.

"Fellow-soldiers,—fellow-exiles," began Endicott, speaking under strong excitement, yet powerfully restraining it, "wherefore did ye leave your native country? Wherefore, I say, have we left the green and fertile fields, the cottages, or, perchance the old gray halls, where we were born and bred, the churchyards where our forefathers lie buried? Wherefore have we come hither to set up our own tombstones in a wilderness? A howling wilderness it is! The wolf and the bear meet us within halloo of our dwellings. The savage lieth in wait for us in the dismal shadow of the woods. The stubborn roots of the trees break our ploughshares, when we would till the earth. Our children cry for bread, and we must dig in the sands of the seashore to satisfy them. Wherefore, I say again, have we sought this country of a rugged soil and wintry sky? Was it not for the enjoyment of our civil rights? Was it not for liberty to worship God according to our conscience?"

"Call you this liberty of conscience?" interrupted a voice on the steps of the meeting-house.

It was the Wanton Gospeller. A sad and quiet smile flitted across the mild visage of Roger Williams. But Endicott, in the excitement of the moment, shook his sword wrathfully at the culprit—an ominous gesture from a man like him.

"What hast thou to do with conscience, thou knave?" cried he. "I said liberty to worship God, not license to profane and ridicule him. Break not in upon my speech, or I will lay thee neck and heels till this time tomorrow! Hearken to me, friends, nor heed that accursed rhapsodist. As I was saying, we have sacrificed all things, and have come to a land whereof the old world hath scarcely heard, that we might make a new world unto ourselves, and painfully seek a path from hence to heaven. But what think ye now? This son of a Scotch tyrant—this grandson of a

Papistical and adulterous Scotch woman whose death proved that a golden crown doth not always save an anointed head from the block"—

"Nay, brother, nay," interposed Mr. Williams; "thy words are not meet for a secret chamber, far less for a public street."

"Hold thy peace, Roger Williams!" answered Endicott, imperiously. "My spirit is wiser than thine for the business now in hand. I tell ye, fellow-exiles, that Charles of England, and Laud, our bitterest persecutor, arch-priest of Canterbury, are resolute to pursue us even hither. They are taking counsel, saith this letter, to send over a governor-general, in whose breast shall be deposited all the law and equity of the land. They are minded, also, to establish the idolatrous forms of English Episcopacy; so that, when Laud shall kiss the Pope's toe, as cardinal of Rome, he may deliver New England, bound hand and foot, into the power of his master!"

A deep groan from the auditors,—a sound of wrath, as well as fear and sorrow,—responded to this intelligence.

"Look ye to it, brethren," resumed Endicott, with increasing energy. "If this king and this arch-prelate have their will, we shall briefly behold a cross on the spire of this tabernacle which we have builded, and a high altar within its walls, with wax tapers burning round it at noonday. We shall hear the sacring bell, and the voices of the Romish priests saying the mass. But think ye, Christian men, that these abominations may be suffered without a sword drawn? without a shot fired? without blood spilt, yea, on the very stairs of the pulpit? No,—be ye strong of hand and stout of heart! Here we stand on our own soil, which we have bought with our goods, which we have won with our swords, which we have cleared with our axes, which we have tilled with the sweat of our brows, which we have sanctified with our prayers to the God that brought us hither! Who shall enslave us here? What have we to do with this mitred prelate,—with this crowned king? What have we to do with England?"

Endicott gazed round at the excited countenances of the people, now full of his own spirit, and then turned suddenly to the standard-bearer, who stood close behind him.

"Officer, lower your banner!" said he.

The officer obeyed; and, brandishing his sword, Endicott thrust it through the cloth, and, with his left hand, rent the Red Cross completely out of the banner. He then waved the tattered ensign above his head.

"Sacrilegious wretch!" cried the high-churchman in the pillory, unable longer to restrain himself, "thou hast rejected the symbol of our holy religion!"

"Treason, treason!" roared the royalist in the stocks. "He hath defaced the King's banner!"

"Before God and man, I will avouch the deed," answered Endicott. "Beat a flourish, drummer!—shout, soldiers and people!—in honor of the ensign of New England. Neither Pope nor Tyrant hath part in it now!"

With a cry of triumph, the people gave their sanction to one of the boldest exploits which our history records. And forever honored be the name of Endicott! We look back through the mist of ages, and recognize in the rending of the Red Cross from New England's banner the first omen of that deliverance which our fathers consummated after the bones of the stern Puritan had lain more than a century in the dust.

1837

## *From* FOOTPRINTS ON THE SEA-SHORE

It must be a spirit much unlike my own which can keep itself in health and vigor without sometimes stealing from the sultry sunshine of the world, to plunge into the cool bath of solitude. At intervals, and not infrequent ones, the forest and the ocean summon me—one with the roar of its waves, the other with the murmur of its boughs—forth from the haunts of men. But I must wander many a mile ere I could stand beneath the shadow of even one primeval tree, much less be lost among the multitude of hoary trunks, and hidden from earth and sky by the mystery of darksome foliage. Nothing is within my daily reach more like a forest than the acre or two of woodland near some suburban farmhouse. When, therefore, the yearning for seclusion becomes a necessity within me, I am drawn to the seashore, which extends its line of rude rocks and seldom-trodden sands for leagues around our bay. Setting forth, at my last ramble, on a September morning, I bound myself with a hermit's vow to interchange no thoughts with man or woman, to share no social pleasure, but to derive all that day's enjoyment from shore, and sea, and sky—from my soul's communion with these, and from fantasies, and recollections, or anticipated realities. Surely here is enough to feed a human spirit for a single day. Farewell, then, busy world! Till your evening lights shall shine along the street—till they gleam upon my sea-flushed face, as I tread homeward,—free me from your ties, and let me be a peaceful outlaw.

Highways and cross paths are hastily traversed; and, clambering down a crag, I find myself at the extremity of a long beach. How gladly does the spirit leap forth and suddenly enlarge its sense of being to the full extent of the broad, blue sunny deep! A greeting and a homage to the Sea! I descend to its margin, and dip my hand into the wave that meets me, and bathe my brow. That far-resounding roar is Ocean's voice of welcome. His salt breath brings a blessing along with it. Now let us pace together—the reader's fancy arm-in-arm with mine—this noble beach, which extends a mile or more from that craggy promontory to yonder rampart of broken rocks. In front, the sea; in the rear, a precipitous bank, the grassy verge of which is breaking away, year after year, and flings down its tufts of verdure upon the barrenness below. The beach itself is a broad space of sand, brown and sparkling, with hardly any pebbles intermixed. Near the water's edge there is a wet margin, which glistens brightly in the sunshine, and reflects objects like a mirror; and as we tread along the glistening border, a dry spot flashes around each footstep, but grows moist again as we lift our feet. In some spots the sand receives a complete impression of the sole—

square toe and all; elsewhere it is of such marble firmness that we must stamp heavily to leave a print even of the iron-shod heel. Along the whole of this extensive beach gambols the surf wave; now it makes a feint of dashing onward in a fury, yet dies away with a meek murmur, and does but kiss the strand; now, after many such abortive efforts, it rears itself up in an unbroken line, heightening as it advances, without a speck of foam on its green crest. With how fierce a roar it flings itself forward, and rushes far up the beach!

As I threw my eyes along the edge of the surf, I remember that I was startled, as Robinson Crusoe might have been, by the sense that human life was within the magic circle of my solitude. Afar off in the remote distance of the beach, appearing like sea-nymphs, or some airier things, such as might tread upon the feathery spray, was a group of girls. Hardly had I beheld them, when they passed into the shadow of the rocks and vanished. To comfort myself—for truly I would fain have gazed a while longer—I made acquaintance with a flock of beach birds. These little citizens of the sea and air preceded me by about a stone's throw along the strand, seeking, I suppose, for food upon its margin. Yet, with a philosophy which mankind would do well to imitate, they drew a continual pleasure from their toil for a subsistence. The sea was each little bird's great playmate. They chased it downward as it swept back, and again ran up swiftly before the impending wave, which sometimes overtook them and bore them off their feet. But they floated as lightly as one of their own feathers on the breaking crest. In their airy flutterings they seemed to rest on the evanescent spray. Their images—long-legged little figures, with gray backs and snowy bosoms—were seen as distinctly as the realities in the mirror of the glistening strand. As I advanced, they flew a score or two of yards, and, again alighting, recommenced their dalliance with the surf wave; and thus they bore me company along the beach, the types of pleasant fantasies, till at its extremity they took wing over the ocean, and were gone. After forming a friendship with these small surf spirits, it is really worth a sigh to find no memorial of them save their multitudinous little tracks in the sand.

When we have paced the length of the beach, it is pleasant, and not unprofitable, to retrace our steps, and recall the whole mood and occupation of the mind during the former passage. Our tracks, being all discernible, will guide us with an observing consciousness through every unconscious wandering of thought and fancy. Here we followed the surf in its reflux, to pick up a shell which the sea seemed loath to relinquish. Here we found a seaweed with an immense brown leaf, and trailed it behind us by its long snake-like stalk. Here we seized a live horseshoe by the tail, and counted the many claws of the queer monster. Here we dug into the sand for pebbles, and skipped them upon the surface of the water. Here we wet our feet while examining a jelly-fish, which the waves, having just tossed it up, now sought to snatch away again. Here we trod along the brink of a fresh-water brooklet which flows across the beach, becoming shallower and more shallow, till at last it sinks into the sand, and perishes in the effort to bear its little tribute to the main. Here some vagary appears to have bewildered us; for our tracks go round and round, and are confusedly intermingled, as if we had found a labyrinth upon the level beach. And here, amid our idle pastime, we sat down upon almost the only stone that breaks the surface of the sand, and were lost in an unlooked-for and overpowering conception of the majesty and awfulness of the great deep. Thus, by tracking our footprints in the sand, we track our own nature in its wayward course, and steal a glance upon it when it never dreams of being so observed. Such glances always make us wiser.

* * *

On the day of my last ramble (it was a September day, yet as warm as summer), what should I behold as I approached the above described basin but three girls sitting on its margin, and—yes, it is veritably so—laving their snowy feet in the sunny water! These, these are the warm realities of those three visionary shapes that flitted from me on the beach. Hark! their merry voices, as they toss up the water with their feet! They have not seen me. I must shrink behind this rock, and steal away again.

In honest truth, vowed to solitude as I am, there is something in this encounter that makes the heart flutter with a strangely pleasant sensation. I know these girls to be realities of flesh and blood, yet, glancing at them so briefly, they mingle like kindred creatures with the ideal beings of my mind. It is pleasant, likewise, to gaze down from some high crag, and watch a group of children, gathering pebbles and pearly shells, and playing with the surf, as with old Ocean's hoary beard. Nor does it infringe upon my seclusion to see yonder boat at anchor off the shore, swinging dreamily to and fro, and rising and sinking with the alternate swell; while the crew—four gentlemen in round-about jackets—are busy with their fishing-lines. But, with an inward antipathy and a headlong flight do I eschew the presence of any meditative stroller like myself, known by his pilgrim staff, his sauntering step, his shy demeanor, his observant yet abstracted eye. From such a man, as if another self had scared me, I scramble hastily over the rocks, and take refuge in a nook which many a secret hour has given me a right to call my own. I would do battle for it even with the churl that should produce the title deeds. Have not my musings melted into its rocky walls and sandy floor, and made them a portion of myself?

It is a recess in the line of cliffs, walled round by a rough, high precipice, which almost encircles and shuts in a little space of sand. In front, the sea appears as between the pillars of a portal. In the rear, the precipice is broken and intermixed with earth, which gives nourishment not only to clinging and twining shrubs, but to trees, that gripe the rock with their naked roots, and seem to struggle hard for footing and for soil enough to live upon. These are fir-trees; but oaks hang their heavy branches from above, and throw down acorns on the beach, and shed their withering foliage upon the waves. At this autumnal season the precipice is decked with variegated splendor; trailing wreaths of scarlet flaunt from the summit downward; tufts of yellow-flowering shrubs, and rose-bushes, with their reddened leaves and glossy seed-berries, sprout from each crevice; at every glance, I detect some new light or shade of beauty, all contrasting with the stern, gray rock. A rill of water trickles down the cliff and fills a little cistern near the base. I drain it at a draught, and find it fresh and pure. This recess shall be my dining hall. And what the feast? A few biscuits, made savory by soaking them in sea-water, a tuft of samphire gathered from the beach, and an apple for the dessert. By this time the little rill has filled its reservoir again; and, as I quaff it, I thank God more heartily than for a civic banquet, that He gives me the healthful appetite to make a feast of bread and water.

Dinner being over, I throw myself at length upon the sand, and, basking in the sunshine, let my mind disport itself at will. The walls of this my hermitage have no tongue to tell my follies, though I sometimes fancy that they have ears to hear them, and a soul to sympathize. There is a magic in this spot. Dreams haunt its precincts, and flit around me in broad sunlight, nor require that sleep shall blindfold me to real objects, ere these be visible. Here can I frame a story of two lovers, and make their shadows live before me, and be mirrored in the tranquil water, as they tread along the sand, leaving no footprints. Here, should I will it, I can summon up a single shade, and be myself her lover. Yes, dreamer,—but your lonely heart will be the colder for such fancies. Sometimes, too, the Past comes back and finds me here, and in her train come faces which were gladsome, when I knew them, yet seem not gladsome now. Would that my hiding-place were lonelier, so that the past might not find me! Get ye all gone, old friends, and let me listen to the murmur of the sea,—a melancholy voice, but less sad than yours. Of what mysteries is it telling? Of sunken ships, and whereabouts they lie? Of islands afar and undiscovered, whose tawny children are unconscious of other islands and of continents, and deem the stars of heaven their nearest neighbours? Nothing of all this. What then? Has it talked for so many ages, and meant nothing all the while? No; for those ages find utterance in the sea's unchanging voice, and warn the listener to withdraw his interest from mortal vicissitudes, and let the infinite idea of eternity pervade his soul. This is wisdom; and therefore will I spend the next half hour in shaping little boats of driftwood, and launching them on voyages across the cove, with the feather of a seagull for a sail. If the voice of ages tell me true, this is as wise an occupation as to build ships of five hundred tons, and launch them forth upon the main, bound to "far Cathay." Yet, how would the merchant sneer at me!

And, after all, can such philosophy be true? Methinks I could find a thousand arguments against it. Well, then, let yonder shaggy rock, mid-deep in the surf—see! he is somewhat wrathful,—he rages and roars and foams—let that tall rock be my antagonist, and let me exercise my oratory like him of Athens, who bandied words with an angry sea and got the victory. My maiden speech is a triumphant one; for the gentleman in sea-weed has nothing to offer in reply, save an immitigable roaring. His voice, indeed, will be heard a long while after mine is hushed. Once more I shout, and the cliffs reverberate the sound. Oh, what joy for a shy man to feel himself so solitary, that he may lift his voice to its highest pitch without hazard of a listener! But, hush!—be silent, my good friend!—whence comes that stifled laughter? It was musical,—but how should there be such music in my solitude? Looking upwards, I catch a glimpse of three faces, peeping from the summit of the cliff, like angels between me and their native sky. Ah, fair girls, you may make yourselves merry at my eloquence,—but it was my turn to smile when I saw your white feet in the pool! Let us keep each other's secrets.

The sunshine has now passed from my hermitage, except a gleam upon the sand just where it meets the sea. A crowd of gloomy fantasies will come and haunt me, if I tarry longer here, in the darkening twilight of these gray rocks. This is a dismal place in some moods of the mind. Climb we, therefore, the precipice, and pause a moment on the brink, gazing down into that hollow chamber by the deep, where we have been, what few can be, sufficient to our own pastime—yes, say the word outright!—self-sufficient to our own happiness. How lonesome looks the recess now, and dreary too,—like all other spots where happiness has been! There lies my shadow in the departing sunshine with its head upon the sea. I will pelt it with pebbles. A hit! a hit! I clap my hands in triumph, and see! my shadow clapping its unreal hands, and claiming the triumph for itself. What a simpleton must I have been all day, since my own shadow makes a mock of my fooleries!

Homeward! homeward! It is time to hasten home. It is time; it is time; for as the sun sinks over the western wave, the sea grows melancholy, and the surf has a saddened tone. The distant sails appear astray, and not of earth, in their remoteness amid the desolate waste. My spirit wanders forth afar, but finds no resting-place, and comes shivering back. It is time that I were hence. But grudge me not the day that has been spent in seclusion, which yet was not solitude, since the great sea has been my companion, and the little sea-birds my friends, and the wind has told me his secrets, and airy shapes have flitted around me in my hermitage. Such companionship works an effect upon a man's character, as if he had been admitted to the society of creatures that are not mortal. And when, at noontide, I tread the crowded streets, the influence of this day will still be felt; so that I shall walk among men kindly and as a brother, with affection and sympathy, but yet shall not melt into the indistinguishable mass of humankind. I shall think my own thoughts, and feel my own emotions, and possess my individuality unviolated.

But it is good, at the eve of such a day, to feel and know that there are men and women in the world. That feeling and that knowledge are mine at this moment; for, on the shore, far below me, the fishing party have landed from their skiff, and are cooking their scaly prey by a fire of driftwood, kindled in the angle of two rude rocks. The three visionary girls are likewise there. In the deepening twilight, while the surf is dashing near their hearth, the ruddy gleam of the fire throws a strange air of comfort over the wild cove, bestrewn as it is with pebbles and sea-weed, and exposed to the "melancholy main." Moreover, as the smoke climbs up the precipice, it brings with it a savoury smell from a pan of fried fish, and a black kettle of chowder, and reminds me that my dinner was nothing but bread and water, and a tuft of samphire, and an apple. Methinks the party might find room for another guest at that flat rock which serves them for a table; and if spoons be scarce, I could pick up a clamshell on the beach. They see me now; and—the blessing of a hungry man upon him!—one of them sends up a hospitable shout—Halloo, Sir Solitary! come down and sup with us! The ladies wave their handkerchiefs. Can I decline? No; and be it owned, after all my solitary joys, that this is the sweetest moment of a Day by the Sea-Shore.

1839

## THE BIRTHMARK

In the latter part of the last century there lived a man of science, an eminent proficient in every branch of natural philosophy, who not long before our story opens had made experience of a spiritual affinity more attractive than any chemical one. He had left his laboratory to the care of an assistant, cleared his fine countenance from the furnace smoke, washed the stain of acids from his fingers, and persuaded a beautiful woman to become his wife. In those days when the comparatively recent discovery of electricity and other kindred mysteries of Nature seemed to open paths into the region of miracle, it was not unusual for the love of science to rival the love of woman in its depth and absorbing energy. The higher intellect, the imagination, the spirit, and even the heart might all find their congenial aliment in pursuits which, as some of their ardent votaries believed, would ascend from one step of powerful intelligence to another, until the philosopher should lay his hand on the secret of creative force and perhaps make new worlds for himself. We know not whether Aylmer possessed this degree of faith in man's ultimate control over Nature. He had devoted himself, however, too unreservedly to scientific studies ever to be weaned from them by any second passion. His love for his young wife might prove the stronger of the two; but it could only be by intertwining itself with his love of science, and uniting the strength of the latter to his own.

Such a union accordingly took place, and was attended with truly remarkable consequences and a deeply impressive moral. One day, very soon after their marriage, Aylmer sat gazing at his wife with a trouble in his countenance that grew stronger until he spoke.

"Georgiana," said he, "has it never occurred to you that the mark upon your cheek might be removed?"

"No, indeed," said she, smiling; but

perceiving the seriousness of his manner, she blushed deeply. "To tell you the truth it has been so often called a charm that I was simple enough to imagine it might be so."

"Ah, upon another face perhaps it might," replied her husband; "but never on yours. No, dearest Georgiana, you came so nearly perfect from the hand of Nature that this slightest possible defect, which we hesitate whether to term a defect or a beauty, shocks me, as being the visible mark of earthly imperfection."

"Shocks you, my husband!" cried Georgiana, deeply hurt; at first reddening with momentary anger, but then bursting into tears. "Then why did you take me from my mother's side? You cannot love what shocks you!"

To explain this conversation it must be mentioned that in the centre of Georgiana's left cheek there was a singular mark, deeply interwoven, as it were, with the texture and substance of her face. In the usual state of her complexion — a healthy though delicate bloom — the mark wore a tint of deeper crimson, which imperfectly defined its shape amid the surrounding rosiness. When she blushed it gradually became more indistinct, and finally vanished amid the triumphant rush of blood that bathed the whole cheek with its brilliant glow. But if any shifting motion caused her to turn pale there was the mark again, a crimson stain upon the snow, in what Aylmer sometimes deemed an almost fearful distinctness. Its shape bore not a little similarity to the human hand, though of the smallest pygmy size. Georgiana's lovers were wont to say that some fairy at her birth hour had laid her tiny hand upon the infant's cheek, and left this impress there in token of the magic endowments that were to give her such sway over all hearts. Many a desperate swain would have risked life for the privilege of pressing his lips to the mysterious hand. It must not be concealed, however, that the impression wrought by this fairy sign manual varied exceedingly, according to the difference of temperament in the beholders. Some fastidious persons — but they were exclusively of her own sex — affirmed that the bloody hand, as they chose to call it, quite destroyed the effect of Georgiana's beauty, and rendered her countenance even hideous. But it would be as reasonable to say that one of those small blue stains which sometimes occur in the purest statuary marble would convert the Eve of Powers to a monster. Masculine observers, if the birthmark did not heighten their admiration, contented themselves with wishing it away, that the world might possess one living specimen of ideal loveliness without the semblance of a flaw. After his marriage,— for he thought little or nothing of the matter before,— Aylmer discovered that this was the case with himself.

Had she been less beautiful,— if Envy's self could have found aught else to sneer at,— he might have felt his affection heightened by the prettiness of this mimic hand, now vaguely portrayed, now lost, now stealing forth again and glimmering to and fro with every pulse of emotion that throbbed within her heart; but seeing her otherwise so perfect, he found this one defect grow more and more intolerable with every moment of their united lives. It was the fatal flaw of humanity which Nature, in one shape or another, stamps ineffaceably on all her productions, either to imply that they are temporary and finite, or that their perfection must be wrought by toil and pain. The crimson hand expressed the ineludible gripe in which mortality clutches the highest and purest of earthly mold, degrading them into kindred with the lowest, and even with the very brutes, like whom their visible frames return to dust. In this manner, selecting it as the symbol of his wife's liability to sin, sorrow, decay, and death, Aylmer's sombre imagination was not long in rendering the birthmark a frightful object, causing him more trouble and horror than ever Georgiana's beauty, whether of soul or sense, had given him delight.

At all the seasons which should have been their happiest, he invariably and without intending it, nay, in spite of a purpose to the contrary, reverted to this one disastrous topic. Trifling as it at first appeared, it so connected itself with innumerable trains of thought and modes of feeling that it became the central point of all. With the morning twilight Aylmer opened his eyes upon his wife's face and recognized the symbol of imperfection; and when they sat together at the evening hearth his eyes wandered stealthily to her cheek, and beheld, flickering with the blaze of the wood fire, the spectral hand that wrote mortality where he would fain have worshipped. Georgiana soon learned to shudder at his gaze. It needed but a glance with the peculiar expression that his face often wore to change the roses of her cheek into a deathlike paleness, amid which the crimson hand was brought strongly out, like a bas-relief of ruby on the whitest marble.

Late one night when the lights were growing dim, so as hardly to betray the stain on the poor wife's cheek, she herself, for the first time, voluntarily took up the subject.

"Do you remember, my dear Aylmer," said she, with a feeble attempt at a smile, "have you any recollection of a dream last night about this odious hand?"

"None! none whatever!" replied Aylmer, starting; but then he added, in a dry, cold tone, affected for the sake of concealing the real depth of his emotion, "I might well dream of it; for before I fell asleep it had taken a pretty firm hold of my fancy."

"And you did dream of it?" continued Georgiana, hastily; for she dreaded lest a gush of tears should interrupt what she had to say. "A terrible dream! I wonder that you can forget it. Is it possible to forget this one expression? — 'It is in her heart now; we must have it out!' Reflect, my husband; for by all means I would have you recall that dream."

The mind is in a sad state when Sleep, the all-involving, cannot confine her spectres within the dim region of her sway, but suffers them to break forth, affrighting this actual life with secrets that perchance belong to a deeper one. Aylmer now remembered his dream. He had fancied himself with his servant Aminadab, attempting an operation for the removal of the birthmark; but the deeper went the knife, the deeper sank the hand, until at length its tiny grasp appeared to have caught hold of Georgiana's heart; whence, however, her husband was inexorably resolved to cut or wrench it away.

When the dream had shaped itself perfectly in his memory, Aylmer sat in his wife's presence with a guilty feeling. Truth often finds its way to the mind close muffled in robes of sleep, and then speaks with uncompromising directness of matters in regard to which we practise an unconscious self-deception during our waking moments. Until now he had not been aware of the tyrannizing influence acquired by one idea over his mind, and of the lengths which he might find in his heart to go for the sake of giving himself peace.

"Aylmer," resumed Georgiana, solemnly, "I know not what may be the cost to both of us to rid me of this fatal birthmark. Perhaps its removal may cause cureless deformity; or it may be the stain goes as deep as life itself. Again: do we know that there is a possibility, on any terms, of unclasping the firm gripe of this little hand which was laid upon me before I came into the world?"

"Dearest Georgiana, I have spent much thought upon the subject," hastily interrupted Aylmer. "I am convinced of the perfect practicability of its removal."

"If there be the remotest possibility of it," continued Georgiana, "let the attempt be made at whatever risk. Danger is nothing to me; for life, while this hateful mark makes me the object of your horror and disgust,—life is a burden which I would fling down with joy. Either remove this dreadful hand, or take my wretched life! You have deep science. All the world bears witness of it. You have achieved great wonders. Cannot you remove this little, little mark, which I cover with the tips of two small fingers? Is this beyond your power, for the sake of your own peace, and to save your poor wife from madness?"

"Noblest, dearest, tenderest wife," cried Aylmer, rapturously, "doubt not my power. I have already given this matter the deepest thought — thought which might almost have enlightened me to create a being less perfect than yourself. Georgiana, you have led me deeper than ever into the heart of science. I feel myself fully competent to render this dear cheek as faultless as its fellow; and then, most beloved, what will be my triumph when I shall have corrected what Nature left imperfect in her fairest work! Even Pygmalion, when his sculptured woman assumed life, felt not greater ecstasy than mine will be."

"It is resolved, then," said Georgiana, faintly smiling. "And, Aylmer, spare me not, though you should find the birthmark take refuge in my heart at last."

Her husband tenderly kissed her cheek — her right cheek — not that which bore the impress of the crimson hand.

The next day Aylmer apprised his wife of a plan that he had formed whereby he might have opportunity for the intense thought and constant watchfulness which the proposed operation would require; while Georgiana, likewise, would enjoy the perfect repose essential to its success. They were to seclude themselves in the extensive apartments occupied by Aylmer as a laboratory, and where, during his toilsome youth, he had made discoveries in the elemental powers of Nature that had roused the admiration of all the learned societies in Europe. Seated calmly in this laboratory, the pale philosopher had investigated the secrets of the highest cloud region and of the profoundest mines; he had satisfied himself of the causes that kindled and kept alive the fires of the volcano; and had explained the mystery of fountains, and how it is that they gush forth, some so bright and pure, and others with such rich medicinal virtues, from the dark bosom of the earth. Here, too, at an earlier period, he had studied the wonders of the human frame, and attempted to fathom the very process by which Nature assimilates all her precious influences from earth and air, and from the spiritual world, to create and foster man, her masterpiece. The latter pursuit, however, Aylmer had long laid aside in unwilling recognition of the truth — against which all seekers sooner or later stumble — that our great creative Mother, while she amuses us with apparently working in the broadest sunshine, is yet severely careful to keep her own secrets, and, in spite of her pretended openness, shows us nothing but results. She permits us, indeed, to mar, but seldom to mend, and, like a jealous patentee, on no account to make. Now, however, Aylmer resumed these half-forgotten investigations; not, of course, with such hopes or wishes as first suggested them; but because they involved much physiological truth and lay in the path of his proposed scheme for the treatment of Georgiana.

As he led her over the threshold of the laboratory, Georgiana was cold and tremulous. Aylmer looked cheerfully into her face, with intent to reassure her, but was so startled with the intense glow of the birthmark upon the whiteness of her cheek that he could not restrain a strong convulsive shudder. His wife fainted.

"Aminadab! Aminadab!" shouted Aylmer, stamping violently on the floor.

Forthwith there issued from an inner apartment a man of low stature, but bulky frame, with shaggy hair hanging about his visage, which was grimed with the vapors of the furnace. This personage had been Aylmer's underworker during his whole scientific career, and was admirably fitted for that office by his great mechanical readiness, and the skill with which, while incapable of comprehending a single principle, he executed all the details of his master's experiments. With his vast strength, his shaggy hair, his smoky aspect, and the indescribable earthiness that incrusted him, he seemed to represent man's physical nature; while Aylmer's slender figure, and pale, intellectual face, were no less apt a type of the spiritual element.

"Throw open the door of the boudoir, Aminadab," said Aylmer, "and burn a pastil."

"Yes, master," answered Aminadab, looking intently at the lifeless form of Georgiana; and then he muttered to himself, "If she were my wife, I 'd never part with that birthmark."

When Georgiana recovered consciousness she found herself breathing an atmosphere of penetrating fragrance, the gentle potency of which had recalled her from her deathlike faintness. The scene around her looked like enchantment. Aylmer had converted those smoky, dingy, sombre rooms, where he had spent his brightest years in recondite pursuits, into a series of beautiful apartments not unfit to be the secluded abode of a lovely woman. The walls were hung with gorgeous curtains, which imparted the combination of grandeur and grace that no other species of adornment can achieve; and as they fell from the ceiling to the floor, their rich and ponderous folds, concealing all angles and straight lines, appeared to shut in the scene from infinite space. For aught Georgiana knew, it might be a pavilion among the clouds. And Aylmer, excluding the sunshine, which would have interfered with his chemical processes, had supplied its place with perfumed lamps, emitting flames of various hue, but all uniting in a soft, impurpled radiance. He now knelt by his wife's side, watching her earnestly, but without alarm; for he was confident in his science, and felt that he could draw a magic circle round her within which no evil might intrude.

"Where am I? Ah, I remember," said Georgiana, faintly; and she placed her hand over her cheek to hide the terrible mark from her husband's eyes.

"Fear not, dearest!" exclaimed he. "Do not shrink from me! Believe me, Georgiana, I even rejoice in this single imperfection, since it will be such a rapture to remove it."

"Oh, spare me!" sadly replied his wife. "Pray do not look at it again. I never can forget that convulsive shudder."

In order to soothe Georgiana, and, as it were, to release her mind from the burden of actual things, Aylmer now put in practice some of the light and playful secrets which science had taught him among its profounder lore. Airy figures, absolutely bodiless ideas, and forms of unsubstantial beauty came and danced before her, imprinting their momentary footsteps on beams of light. Though she had some indistinct idea of the method of these optical phenomena, still the illusion was almost perfect enough to warrant the belief that her husband possessed sway over the spiritual world. Then again, when she felt a wish to look forth from her seclusion, immediately, as if her thoughts were answered, the procession of external existence flitted across a screen. The scenery and the figures of actual life were perfectly represented, but with that bewitching, yet indescribable difference which always makes a picture, an image, or a shadow so much more attractive than the original. When wearied of this, Aylmer bade her cast her eyes upon a vessel containing a quantity of earth. She did so, with little interest at first; but was soon startled to perceive the germ of a plant shooting upward from the soil. Then came the slender stalk; the leaves gradually unfolded themselves; and amid them was a perfect and lovely flower.

"It is magical!" cried Georgiana. "I dare not touch it."

"Nay, pluck it," answered Aylmer, —"pluck it, and inhale its brief perfume while you may. The flower will wither in a few moments and leave nothing save its brown seed vessels;

but thence may be perpetuated a race as ephemeral as itself."

But Georgiana had no sooner touched the flower than the whole plant suffered a blight, its leaves turning coal-black as if by the agency of fire.

"There was too powerful a stimulus," said Aylmer, thoughtfully.

To make up for this abortive experiment, he proposed to take her portrait by a scientific process of his own invention. It was to be effected by rays of light striking upon a polished plate of metal. Georgiana assented; but, on looking at the result, was affrighted to find the features of the portrait blurred and indefinable; while the minute figure of a hand appeared where the cheek should have been. Aylmer snatched the metallic plate and threw it into a jar of corrosive acid.

Soon, however, he forgot these mortifying failures. In the intervals of study and chemical experiment he came to her flushed and exhausted, but seemed invigorated by her presence, and spoke in glowing language of the resources of his art. He gave a history of the long dynasty of the alchemists, who spent so many ages in quest of the universal solvent by which the golden principle might be elicited from all things vile and base. Aylmer appeared to believe that, by the plainest scientific logic, it was altogether within the limits of possibility to discover this long-sought medium; "but," he added, "a philosopher who should go deep enough to acquire the power would attain too lofty a wisdom to stoop to the exercise of it." Not less singular were his opinions in regard to the elixir vitæ. He more than intimated that it was at his option to concoct a liquid that should prolong life for years, perhaps interminably; but that it would produce a discord in Nature which all the world, and chiefly the quaffer of the immortal nostrum, would find cause to curse.

"Aylmer, are you in earnest?" asked Georgiana, looking at him with amazement and fear. "It is terrible to possess such power, or even to dream of possessing it."

"Oh, do not tremble, my love," said her husband. "I would not wrong either you or myself by working such inharmonious effects upon our lives; but I would have you consider how trifling, in comparison, is the skill requisite to remove this little hand."

At the mention of the birthmark, Georgiana, as usual, shrank as if a redhot iron had touched her cheek.

Again Aylmer applied himself to his labors. She could hear his voice in the distant furnace room giving directions to Aminadab, whose harsh, uncouth, misshapen tones were audible in response, more like the grunt or growl of a brute than human speech. After hours of absence, Aylmer reappeared and proposed that she should now examine his cabinet of chemical products and natural treasures of the earth. Among the former he showed her a small vial, in which, he remarked, was contained a gentle yet most powerful fragrance, capable of impregnating all the breezes that blow across the kingdom. They were of inestimable value, the contents of that little vial; and, as he said so, he threw some of the perfume into the air and filled the room with piercing and invigorating delight.

"And what is this?" asked Georgiana, pointing to a small crystal globe containing a gold-colored liquid. "It is so beautiful to the eye that I could imagine it the elixir of life."

"In one sense it is," replied Aylmer; "or, rather, the elixir of immortality. It is the most precious poison that ever was concocted in this world. By its aid I could apportion the lifetime of any mortal at whom you might point your finger. The strength of the dose would determine whether he were to linger out years, or drop dead in the midst of a breath. No king on his guarded throne could keep his life if I, in my private station, should deem that the welfare of millions justified me in depriving him of it."

"Why do you keep such a terrific drug?" inquired Georgiana in horror.

"Do not mistrust me, dearest," said her husband, smiling; "its virtuous potency is yet greater than its harmful one. But see! here is a powerful cosmetic. With a few drops of this in a vase of water, freckles may be washed away as easily as the hands are cleansed. A stronger infusion would take the blood out of the cheek, and leave the rosiest beauty a pale ghost."

"Is it with this lotion that you intend to bathe my cheek?" asked Georgiana, anxiously.

"Oh, no," hastily replied her husband; "this is merely superficial. Your case demands a remedy that shall go deeper."

In his interviews with Georgiana, Aylmer generally made minute inquiries as to her sensations and whether the confinement of the rooms and the temperature of the atmosphere agreed with her. These questions had such a particular drift that Georgiana began to conjecture that she was already subjected to certain physical influences, either breathed in with the fragrant air or taken with her food. She fancied likewise, but it might be altogether fancy, that there was a stirring up of her system — a strange, indefinite sensation creeping through her veins, and tingling, half painfully, half pleasurably, at her heart. Still, whenever she dared to look into the mirror, there she beheld herself pale as a white rose and with the crimson birthmark stamped upon her cheek. Not even Aylmer now hated it so much as she.

To dispel the tedium of the hours which her husband found it necessary to devote to the processes of combination and analysis, Georgiana turned over the volumes of his scientific library. In many dark old tomes she met with chapters full of romance and poetry. They were the works of the philosophers of the middle ages, such as Albertus Magnus, Cornelius Agrippa, Paracelsus, and the famous friar who created the prophetic Brazen Head. All these antique naturalists stood in advance of their centuries, yet were imbued with some of their credulity, and therefore were believed, and perhaps imagined themselves to have acquired from the investigation of Nature a power above Nature, and from physics a sway over the spiritual world. Hardly less curious and imaginative were the early volumes of the Transactions of the Royal Society, in which the members, knowing little of the limits of natural possibility, were continually recording wonders or proposing methods whereby wonders might be wrought.

But to Georgiana the most engrossing volume was a large folio from her husband's own hand, in which he had recorded every experiment of his scientific career, its original aim, the methods adopted for its development, and its final success or failure, with the circumstances to which either event was attributable. The book, in truth, was both the history and emblem of his ardent, ambitious, imaginative, yet practical and laborious life. He handled physical details as if there were nothing beyond them; yet spiritualized them all, and redeemed himself from materialism by his strong and eager aspiration towards the infinite. In his grasp the veriest clod of earth assumed a soul. Georgiana, as she read, reverenced Aylmer and loved him more profoundly than ever, but with a less entire dependence on his judgment than heretofore. Much as he had accomplished, she could not but observe that his most splendid successes were almost invariably failures, if compared with the ideal at which he aimed. His brightest diamonds were the merest pebbles, and felt to be so by himself, in comparison with the inestimable gems which lay hidden beyond his reach. The volume, rich with achievements that had won renown for its author, was yet as melancholy a record as ever mortal hand had penned. It was the sad confession and continual exemplification of the shortcomings of the composite man, the spirit burdened with clay and working in matter, and of the despair that assails the higher nature at finding itself so miserably thwarted by the earthly part. Perhaps every man of genius in whatever sphere might recognize the image of his own experience in Aylmer's journal.

So deeply did these reflections affect Georgiana that she laid her face upon the open volume and burst into tears. In this situation she was found by her husband.

"It is dangerous to read in a sorcerer's books," said he with a smile, though his countenance was uneasy and displeased. "Georgiana, there are pages in that volume which I can scarcely glance over and keep my senses. Take heed lest it prove as detrimental to you."

"It has made me worship you more than ever," said she.

"Ah, wait for this one success," rejoined he, "then worship me if you will. I shall deem myself hardly unworthy of it. But come, I have sought you for the luxury of your voice. Sing to me, dearest."

So she poured out the liquid music of her voice to quench the thirst of his spirit. He then took his leave with a boyish exuberance of gaiety, assuring her that her seclusion would endure but a little longer, and that the result was already certain. Scarcely had he departed when Georgiana felt irresistibly impelled to follow him. She had forgotten to inform Aylmer of a symptom which for two or three hours past had begun to excite her attention. It was a sensation in the fatal birthmark, not painful, but which induced a restlessness throughout her system. Hastening after her husband, she intruded for the first time into the laboratory.

The first thing that struck her eye was the furnace, that hot and feverish worker, with the intense glow of its fire, which by the quantities of soot clustered above it seemed to have been burning for ages. There was a distilling apparatus in full operation. Around the room were retorts, tubes, cylinders, crucibles, and other apparatus of chemical research. An electrical machine stood ready for immediate use. The atmosphere felt oppressively close, and was tainted with gaseous odors which had been tormented forth by the processes of science. The severe and homely simplicity of the apartment with its naked walls and brick pavement, looked strange, accustomed as Georgiana had become to the fantastic elegance of her boudoir. But what chiefly, indeed almost solely, drew her attention, was the aspect of Aylmer himself.

He was pale as death, anxious and absorbed, and hung over the furnace as if it depended upon his utmost watchfulness whether the liquid which it was distilling should be the draught of immortal happiness or misery. How different from the sanguine and joyous mien that he had assumed for Georgiana's encouragement!

"Carefully now, Aminadab; carefully, thou human machine; carefully, thou man of clay!" muttered Aylmer, more to himself than his assistant. "Now, if there be a thought too much or too little, it is all over."

"Ho! ho!" mumbled Aminadab. "Look, master! look!"

Aylmer raised his eyes hastily, and at first reddened, then grew paler than ever, on beholding Georgiana. He rushed towards her and seized her arm with a gripe that left the print of his fingers upon it.

"Why do you come hither? Have you no trust in your husband?" cried he, impetuously. "Would you throw the blight of that fatal birthmark over my labors? It is not well done. Go, prying woman, go!"

"Nay, Aylmer," said Georgiana with the firmness of which she possessed no stinted endowment, "it is not you that have a right to complain. You mistrust your wife; you have concealed the anxiety with which you watch the development of this experiment. Think not so unworthily of me, my husband. Tell me all the risk we run, and fear not that I shall shrink; for my share in it is far less than your own."

"No, no, Georgiana!" said Aylmer, impatiently; "it must not be."

"I submit," replied she calmly. "And, Aylmer, I shall quaff whatever draught you bring me; but it will be on the same principle that would induce me to take a dose of poison if offered by your hand."

"My noble wife," said Aylmer, deeply moved; "I knew not the height and depth of your nature until now. Nothing shall be concealed. Know, then, that this crimson hand, superficial as it seems, has clutched its grasp into your being with a strength of which I had no previous conception. I have already administered agents powerful enough to do aught except to change your entire physical system. Only one thing remains to be tried. If that fail us we are ruined."

"Why did you hesitate to tell me this?" asked she.

"Because, Georgiana," said Aylmer, in a low voice, "there is danger."

"Danger? There is but one danger — that this horrible stigma shall be left upon my cheek!" cried Georgiana. " Remove it, remove it, whatever be the cost, or we shall both go mad! "

" Heaven knows your words are too true," said Aylmer, sadly. " And now, dearest, return to your boudoir. In a little while all will be tested."

He conducted her back and took leave of her with a solemn tenderness which spoke far more than his words how much was now at stake. After his departure Georgiana became rapt in musings. She considered the character of Aylmer, and did it completer justice than at any previous moment. Her heart exulted, while it trembled, at his honorable love — so pure and lofty that it would accept nothing less than perfection nor miserably make itself contented with an earthlier nature than he had dreamed of. She felt how much more precious was such a sentiment than that meaner kind which would have borne with the imperfection for her sake, and have been guilty of treason to holy love by degrading its perfect idea to the level of the actual; and with her whole spirit she prayed that, for a single moment, she might satisfy his highest and deepest conception. Longer than one moment she well knew it could not be; for his spirit was ever on the march, ever ascending, and each instant required something that was beyond the scope of the instant before.

The sound of her husband's footsteps aroused her. He bore a crystal goblet containing a liquor colorless as water, but bright enough to be the draught of immortality. Aylmer was pale; but it seemed rather the consequence of a highly-wrought state of mind and tension of spirit than of fear or doubt.

" The concoction of the draught has been perfect," said he, in answer to Georgiana's look. " Unless all my science have deceived me, it cannot fail."

" Save on your account, my dearest Aylmer," observed his wife, " I might wish to put off this birthmark of mortality by relinquishing mortality itself in preference to any other mode. Life is but a sad possession to those who have attained precisely the degree of moral advancement at which I stand. Were I weaker and blinder it might be happiness. Were I stronger, it might be endured hopefully. But, being what I find myself, methinks I am of all mortals the most fit to die."

" You are fit for heaven without tasting death! " replied her husband. " But why do we speak of dying? The draught cannot fail. Behold its effect upon this plant."

On the window seat there stood a geranium diseased with yellow blotches, which had overspread all its leaves. Aylmer poured a small quantity of the liquid upon the soil in which it grew. In a little time, when the roots of the plant had taken up the moisture, the unsightly blotches began to be extinguished in a living verdure.

" There needed no proof," said Georgiana, quietly. " Give me the goblet. I joyfully stake all upon your word."

" Drink, then, thou lofty creature! " exclaimed Aylmer, with fervid admiration. " There is no taint of imperfection on thy spirit. Thy sensible frame, too, shall soon be all perfect."

She quaffed the liquid and returned the goblet to his hand.

" It is grateful," said she with a

placid smile. "Methinks it is like water from a heavenly fountain; for it contains I know not what of unobtrusive fragrance and deliciousness. It allays a feverish thirst that had parched me for many days. Now, dearest, let me sleep. My earthly senses are closing over my spirit like the leaves around the heart of a rose at sunset."

She spoke the last words with a gentle reluctance, as if it required almost more energy than she could command to pronounce the faint and lingering syllables. Scarcely had they loitered through her lips ere she was lost in slumber. Aylmer sat by her side, watching her aspect with the emotions proper to a man the whole value of whose existence was involved in the process now to be tested. Mingled with this mood, however, was the philosophic investigation characteristic of the man of science. Not the minutest symptom escaped him. A heightened flush of the cheek, a slight irregularity of breath, a quiver of the eyelid, a hardly perceptible tremor through the frame,— such were the details which, as the moments passed, he wrote down in his folio volume. Intense thought had set its stamp upon every previous page of that volume, but the thoughts of years were all concentrated upon the last.

While thus employed, he failed not to gaze often at the fatal hand, and not without a shudder. Yet once, by a strange and unaccountable impulse, he pressed it with his lips. His spirit recoiled, however, in the very act; and Georgiana, out of the midst of her deep sleep, moved uneasily and murmured as if in remonstrance. Again Aylmer resumed his watch. Nor was it without avail. The crimson hand, which at first had been strongly visible upon the marble paleness of Georgiana's cheek, now grew more faintly outlined. She remained not less pale than ever; but the birthmark, with every breath that came and went, lost somewhat of its former distinctness. Its presence had been awful; its departure was more awful still. Watch the stain of the rainbow fading out of the sky, and you will know how that mysterious symbol passed away.

"By Heaven! it is well-nigh gone!" said Aylmer to himself, in almost irrepressible ecstasy. "I can scarcely trace it now. Success! success! And now it is like the faintest rose color. The lightest flush of blood across her cheek would overcome it. But she is so pale!"

He drew aside the window curtain and suffered the light of natural day to fall into the room and rest upon her cheek. At the same time he heard a gross, hoarse chuckle, which he had long known as his servant Aminadab's expression of delight.

"Ah, clod! ah, earthly mass!" cried Aylmer, laughing in a sort of frenzy, "you have served me well! Matter and spirit — earth and heaven — have both done their part in this! Laugh, thing of the senses! You have earned the right to laugh."

These exclamations broke Georgiana's sleep. She slowly unclosed her eyes and gazed into the mirror which her husband had arranged for that purpose. A faint smile flitted over her lips when she recognized how barely perceptible was now that crimson hand which had once blazed forth with such disastrous brilliancy as to scare away all their happiness. But then her eyes sought Aylmer's face with a trouble and anxiety that he could by no means account for.

"My poor Aylmer!" murmured she.

"Poor? Nay, richest, happiest, most favored!" exclaimed he. "My peerless bride, it is successful! You are perfect!"

"My poor Aylmer," she repeated, with a more than human tenderness, "you have aimed loftily; you have done nobly. Do not repent that with so high and pure a feeling, you have rejected the best the earth could offer. Aylmer, dearest Aylmer, I am dying!"

Alas! it was too true! The fatal hand had grappled with the mystery of life, and was the bond by which an angelic spirit kept itself in union with a mortal frame. As the last crimson tint of the birthmark — that sole token of human imperfection — faded from her cheek, the parting breath of the now perfect woman passed into the atmosphere, and her soul, lingering a moment near her husband, took its heavenward flight. Then a hoarse, chuckling laugh was heard again! Thus ever does the gross fatality of earth exult in its invariable triumph over the immortal essence which, in this dim sphere of half development, demands the completeness of a higher state. Yet, had Aylmer reached a profounder wisdom, he need not thus have flung away the happiness which would have woven his mortal life of the selfsame texture with the celestial. The momentary circumstance was too strong for him; he failed to look beyond the shadowy scope of time, and living once for all in eternity, to find the perfect future in the present.

1843

## *From* THE OLD MANSE

### THE AUTHOR MAKES THE READER ACQUAINTED WITH HIS ABODE

Between two tall gateposts of rough-hewn stone (the gate itself having fallen from its hinges at some unknown epoch) we beheld the gray front of the old parsonage, terminating the vista of an avenue of black ash trees. It was now a twelvemonth since the funeral procession of the venerable clergyman, its last inhabitant, had turned from that gateway towards the village burying-ground. The wheel-track leading to the door as well as the whole breadth of the avenue, was almost overgrown with grass, affording dainty mouthfuls to two or three vagrant cows, and an old white horse who had his own living to pick up along the roadside. The glimmering shadows that lay half asleep between the door of the house and the public highway, were a kind of spiritual medium, seen through which the edifice had not quite the aspect of belonging to the material world. Certainly it had little in common with those ordinary abodes which stand so imminent upon the road that every passer-by can thrust his head, as it were, into the domestic circle. From these quiet windows the figures of passing travellers looked too remote and dim to disturb the sense of privacy. In its near retirement and accessible seclusion it was the very spot for the residence of a clergyman,—a man not estranged from human life, yet enveloped, in the midst of it, with a veil woven of intermingled gloom and brightness. It was worthy to have been one of the time-honored parsonages of England in which, through many generations, a succession of holy occupants pass from youth to age, and bequeath each an inheritance of sanctity to pervade the house and hover over it as with an atmosphere.

Nor, in truth, had the Old Manse ever been profaned by a lay occupant until that memorable summer afternoon when I entered it as my home. A priest had built it; a priest had succeeded to it; other priestly men from time to time had dwelt in it; and children born in its chambers had grown up to assume the priestly character. It was awful to reflect how many sermons must have been written there. The latest inhabitant alone—he by whose translation to paradise the dwelling was left vacant—had penned nearly three thousand discourses, besides the better, if not the greater, number that gushed living from his lips. How often, no doubt, had he paced to and fro along the avenue, attuning his meditations to the sighs and gentle murmurs and deep and solemn peals of the wind among the lofty tops of the trees! In that variety of natural utterances he could find something accordant with every passage of his sermon, were it of tenderness or reverential fear. The boughs over my head seemed shadowy with solemn thoughts as well as with rustling leaves. I took shame to myself for having been so long a writer of idle stories, and ventured to hope that wisdom would descend upon me with the falling leaves of the avenue, and that I should light upon an intellectual treasure in the Old Manse well worth those hoards of long-hidden gold which people seek for in moss-grown houses. Profound treatises of morality; a layman's unprofessional, and therefore unprejudiced, views of religion; histories (such as Bancroft might have written had he taken up his abode here as he once purposed) bright with picture, gleaming over a depth of philosophic thought,—these were the works that might fitly have flowed from such a retirement. In the humblest event, I resolved at least to achieve a novel that should evolve some deep lesson, and should possess physical substance enough to stand alone.

In furtherance of my design, and as if to leave me no pretext for not fulfilling it, there was in the rear of the house the most delightful little nook of a study that ever afforded its snug seclusion to a scholar. It was here that Emerson wrote Nature; for he was then an inhabitant of the Manse, and used to watch the Assyrian dawn and Paphian sunset and moonrise from the summit of our eastern hill. When I first saw the room its walls were blackened with the smoke of unnumbered years, and made still blacker by the grim prints of Puritan ministers that hung around. These worthies looked strangely like bad angels, or at least like men who had wrestled so continually and so sternly with the devil that somewhat of his sooty fierceness had been imparted to their own visages. They had all vanished now; a cheerful coat of paint and golden-tinted paper-hangings lighted up the small apartment; while the shadow of a willow tree that swept against the overhanging eaves attempered the cheery western sunshine. In place of the grim prints there was the sweet and lovely head of one of Raphael's Madonnas and two pleasant little pictures of the Lake of Como. The only other decorations were a purple vase of flowers, always fresh, and a bronze one containing graceful ferns. My books (few, and by no means choice; for they were chiefly such waifs as chance had thrown in my way) stood in order about the room, seldom to be disturbed.

The study had three windows, set with little old-fashioned panes of glass, each with a crack across it. The two on the western side looked, or rather peeped between the willow branches, down into the orchard, with glimpses of the river through the trees. The third, facing northward, commanded a broader view of the river, at a spot where its hitherto obscure waters gleam forth into the light of history. It was at this window that the clergyman who then dwelt in the Manse stood watching the outbreak of a long and deadly struggle between two nations; he saw the irregular array of his parishioners on the farther side of the river and the glittering line of the British on the hither bank. He awaited, in an agony of suspense, the rattle of the musketry. It came; and there needed but a gentle wind to sweep the battle smoke around this quiet house.

Perhaps the reader, whom I cannot help considering as my guest in the Old Manse and entitled to all courtesy in the way of sight-showing,—perhaps he will choose to take a nearer view of the memorable spot. We stand now on the river's brink. It may well be called the Concord, the river of peace and quietness; for it is certainly the most unexcitable and sluggish stream that ever loitered imperceptibly towards its eternity—the sea. Positively I had lived three weeks beside it before it grew quite clear to my perception which way the current flowed. It never has a vivacious aspect except when a northwestern breeze is vexing its surface on a sunshiny day. From the incurable indolence of its nature, the stream is happily incapable of becoming the slave of human ingenuity, as is the fate of so many a wild, free mountain torrent. While all things else are compelled to subserve some useful purpose, it idles its sluggish life away in lazy liberty, without turning a solitary spindle or affording even water power enough to grind the corn that grows upon its banks. The torpor of its movement allows it nowhere a bright, pebbly shore, nor so much as a narrow strip of glistening sand, in any part of its course. It slumbers between broad prairies, kissing the long meadow grass, and bathes the overhanging boughs of elder bushes and willows, or the roots of elms and ash trees and clumps of maples. Flags and rushes grow along its plashy shore; the yellow water-lily spreads its broad, flat leaves on the margin; and the fragrant white pond-lily abounds, generally selecting a position just so far from the river's brink that it cannot be grasped save at the hazard of plunging in.

It is a marvel whence this perfect flower derives its loveliness and perfume, springing as it does from the black mud over which the river sleeps, and where lurk the slimy eel, and speckled frog, and the mud turtle, whom continual washing cannot cleanse. It is the very same black mud out of which the yellow lily sucks its obscene life and noisome odor. Thus we see too in the world, that some persons assimilate only what is ugly and evil from the same moral circumstances which supply good and beautiful results—the fragrance of celestial flowers—to the daily life of others.

The reader must not, from any testimony of mine, contract a dislike towards our slumberous stream. In the light of a calm and golden sunset it becomes lovely beyond expression; the more lovely for the quietude that so well accords with the hour, when even the wind, after blustering all day long, usually hushes itself to rest. Each tree and rock and every blade of grass is distinctly imaged, and, however unsightly in reality, assumes ideal beauty in the reflection. The minutest things of earth and the broad aspect of the firmament are pictured equally without effort and with the same felicity of success. All the sky glows downward at our feet; the rich clouds float through the unruffled bosom of the stream like heavenly thoughts through a peaceful heart. We will not, then, malign our river as gross and impure while it can glorify itself with so adequate a picture of the heaven that broods above it; or, if we remember its tawny hue and the muddiness of its bed, let it be a symbol that the earthliest human soul has an infinite spiritual capacity and may contain the better world within its depths. But, indeed, the same lesson might be drawn out of any mud puddle in the streets of a city; and, being taught us everywhere, it must be true.

Come, we have pursued a somewhat devious track in our walk to the battle-ground. Here we are, at the point where the river was crossed by the old bridge, the possession of which was the immediate object of the contest. On the hither side grow two or three elms, throwing a wide circumference of shade, but which must have been planted at some period within the threescore years and ten that have passed since the battle day. On the farther shore, overhung by a clump of elder bushes, we discern the stone abutment of the bridge. Looking down into the river, I once discovered some heavy fragments of the timbers, all green with half a century's growth of water moss; for during that length of time the tramp of horses and human footsteps has ceased along this ancient highway. The stream has here about the breadth of twenty strokes of a swimmer's arm,—a space not too wide when the bullets were whistling across. Old people who dwell hereabouts will point out the very spots on the western bank where our countrymen fell down and died; and on this side of the river an obelisk of granite has grown up from the soil that was fertilized with British blood. The monument, not more than twenty feet in height, is such as it befitted the inhabitants of a village to erect in illustration of a matter of local interest rather than what was suitable to commemorate an epoch of national history. Still, by the fathers of the village this famous deed was done; and their descendants might rightfully claim the privilege of building a memorial.

A humbler token of the fight, yet a more interesting one than the granite obelisk, may be seen close under the stone wall which separates the battle-ground from the precincts of the parsonage. It is the grave—marked by a small, mossgrown fragment of stone at the head and another at the foot—the grave of two British soldiers who were slain in the skirmish, and have ever since slept peacefully where Zechariah Brown and Thomas Davis buried them. Soon was their warfare ended; a weary night march from Boston, a rattling volley of musketry across the river, and then these many years of rest. In the long procession of slain invaders who passed into eternity from the battle-fields of the revolution, these two nameless soldiers led the way.

Lowell, the poet, as we were once standing over this grave, told me a tradition in reference to one of the inhabitants below. The story has something deeply impressive, though its circumstances cannot altogether be reconciled with probability. A youth in the service of the clergyman happened to be chopping wood, that April morning, at the back door of the Manse, and when the noise of battle rang from side to side of the bridge he hastened across the intervening field to see what might be going forward. It is rather strange, by the way, that this lad should have been so diligently at work when the whole population of town and country were startled out of their customary business by the advance of the British troops. Be that as it might, the tradition says that the lad now left his task and hurried to the battle-field with the axe still in his hand. The British had by this time retreated. the Americans were in pursuit; and the late scene of strife was thus deserted by both parties. Two soldiers lay on the ground—one was a corpse; but, as the young New Englander drew nigh, the other Briton raised himself painfully upon his hands and knees and gave a ghastly stare into his face. The boy,—it must have been a nervous impulse, without purpose, without thought, and betokening a sensitive and impressible nature rather than a hardened one,—the boy uplifted his axe and dealt the wounded soldier a fierce and fatal blow upon the head.

I could wish that the grave might be opened; for I would fain know whether either of the skeleton soldiers has the mark of an axe in his skull. The story comes home to me like truth. Oftentimes, as an intellectual and moral exercise, I have sought to follow that poor youth through his subsequent career, and observe how his soul was tortured by the blood stain, contracted as it had been before the long custom of war had robbed human life of its sanctity and while it still seemed murderous to slay a brother man. This one circumstance has borne more fruit for me than all that history tells us of the fight. * * *

The Old Manse! We had almost forgotten it, but will return thither through the orchard. This was set out by the last clergyman, in the decline of his life, when the neighbors laughed at the hoary-headed man for planting trees from which he could have no prospect of gathering fruit. Even had that been the case, there was only so much the better motive for planting them, in the pure and unselfish hope of benefiting his successors,—an end so seldom achieved by more ambitious efforts. But the old minister, before reaching his patriarchal age of ninety, ate the apples from this orchard during many years, and added silver and gold to his annual stipend by disposing of the superfluity. It is pleasant to think of him walking among the trees in the quiet afternoons of early autumn and picking up here and there a windfall, while he observes how heavily the branches are weighed down, and computes the number of empty flour barrels that will be filled by their burden. He loved each tree, doubtless, as if it had been his own child. An orchard has a relation to mankind, and readily connects itself with matters of the heart. The trees possess a domestic character; they have lost the wild nature of their forest kindred, and have grown humanized by receiving the care of man as well as by contributing to his wants. There is so much individuality of character, too, among apple trees that it gives them an additional claim to be the objects of human interest. One is harsh and crabbed in its manifestations; another gives us fruit as mild as charity. One is churlish and illiberal, evidently grudging the few apples that it bears; another exhausts itself in freehearted benevolence. The variety of grotesque shapes into which apple trees contort themselves has its effect on those who get acquainted with them: they stretch out their crooked branches, and take such hold of the imagination that we remember them as humorists and odd fellows. And what is more melancholy than the old apple trees that linger about the spot where once stood a homestead, but where there is now only a ruined chimney rising out of a grassy and weedgrown cellar? They offer their fruit to every wayfarer,—apples that are bitter sweet with the moral of Time's vicissitude.

I have met with no other such pleasant trouble in the world as that of finding myself, with only the two or three mouths which it was my privilege to feed, the sole inheritor of the old clergyman's wealth of fruits. Throughout the summer there were cherries and currants; and then came autumn, with his immense burden of apples, dropping them continually from his overladen shoulders as he trudged along. In the stillest afternoon, if I listened, the thump of a great apple was audible, falling without a breath of wind, from the mere necessity of perfect ripeness. And, besides, there were pear trees, that flung down bushels upon bushels of heavy pears; and peach trees, which, in a good year, tormented me with peaches, neither to be eaten nor kept, nor, without labor and perplexity, to be given away. The idea of an infinite generosity and exhaustless bounty on the part of our Mother Nature was well worth obtaining through such cares as these. That feeling can be enjoyed in perfection only by the natives of summer islands where the bread-fruit, the cocoa, the palm, and the orange grow spontaneously and hold forth the ever-ready meal; but likewise almost as well by a man long habituated to city life, who plunges into such a solitude as that of the Old Manse, where he plucks the fruit of trees that he did not plant, and which therefore, to my heterodox taste, bear the closest resemblance to those that grew in Eden. It has been an apothegm these five thousand years, that toil sweetens the bread it earns. For my part, (speaking from hard experience, acquired while belaboring the rugged furrows of Brook Farm), I relish best the free gifts of Providence.

Not that it can be disputed that the light toil requisite to cultivate a moderately-sized garden imparts such zest to kitchen vegetables as is never found in those of the market gardener. Childless men, if they would know something of the bliss of paternity, should plant a seed,—be it squash, bean, Indian corn, or perhaps a mere flower or worthless weed,—should plant it with their own hands, and nurse it from infancy to maturity altogether by their own care. If there be not too many of them, each individual plant becomes an object of separate interest. My garden, that skirted the avenue of the Manse, was of precisely the right extent. An hour or two of morning labor was all that it required. But I used to visit and revisit it a dozen times a day, and stand in deep contemplation over my vegetable progeny with a love that nobody could share or conceive of, who had never taken part in the process of creation. It was one of the most bewitching sights in the world to observe a hill of beans thrusting aside the soil, or a row of early peas just peeping forth sufficiently to trace a line of delicate green. Later in the season the humming-birds were attracted by the blossoms of a peculiar variety of bean; and they were a joy to me, those little spiritual visitants, for deigning to sip airy food out of my nectar cups. Multitudes of bees used to bury themselves in the yellow blossoms of the summer squashes. This, too, was a deep satisfaction; although, when they had laden themselves with sweets, they flew away to some unknown hive, which would give back nothing in requital of what my garden had contributed. But I was glad thus to fling a benefaction upon the passing breeze with the certainty that somebody must profit by it, and that there would be a little more honey in the world to allay the sourness and bitterness which mankind is always complaining of. Yes, indeed; my life was the sweeter for that honey.

Speaking of summer squashes, I must say a word of their beautiful and varied forms. They presented an endless diversity of urns and vases, shallow or deep, scalloped or plain, moulded in patterns which a sculptor would do well to copy, since Art has never invented any thing more graceful. A hundred squashes in the garden were worthy, in my eyes at least, of being rendered indestructible in marble. If ever Providence (but I know it never will) should assign me a superfluity of gold, part of it shall be expended for a service of plate, or most delicate porcelain, to be wrought into the shapes of summer squashes gathered from vines which I will plant with my own hands. As dishes for containing vegetables, they would be peculiarly appropriate.

But not merely the squeamish love of the beautiful was gratified by my toil in the kitchen garden. There was a hearty enjoyment, likewise, in observing the growth of the crook-necked winter squashes, from the first little bulb, with the withered blossom adhering to it, until they lay strewn upon the soil, big, round fellows, hiding their heads beneath the leaves, but turning up their great yellow rotundities to the noontide sun. Gazing at them, I felt that by my agency something worth living for had been done. A new substance was born into the world. They were real and tangible existences which the mind could seize hold of and rejoice in. A cabbage, too,—especially the early Dutch cabbage, which swells to a monstrous circumference, until its ambitious heart often bursts asunder,—is a matter to be proud of when we can claim a share with the earth and sky in producing it. But, after all, the hugest pleasure is reserved until these vegetable children of ours are smoking on the table, and we, like Saturn, make a meal of them.

What with the river, the battle-field, the orchard and the garden, the reader begins to despair of finding his way back into the Old Manse. But in agreeable weather it is the truest hospitality to keep him out-of-doors. I never grew quite acquainted with my habitation till a long spell of sulky rain had confined me beneath its roof. There could not be a more sombre aspect of external Nature than as then seen from the windows of my study. The great willow-tree had caught and retained among its leaves a whole cataract of water, to be shaken down at intervals by the frequent gusts of wind. All day long, and for a week together, the rain was drip-drip-dripping and splash-splash-splashing from the eaves and bubbling and foaming into the tubs beneath the spouts. The old unpainted shingles of the house and outbuildings were black with moisture; and the mosses of ancient growth upon the walls looked green and fresh as if they were the newest things and after-thought of time. The usually mirrored surface of the river was blurred by an infinity of raindrops; the whole landscape had a completely water-soaked appearance, conveying the impression that the earth was wet through like a sponge; while the summit of a wooded hill about a mile distant was enveloped in a dense mist, where the demon of the tempest seemed to have his abiding-place and to be plotting still direr inclemencies. * * *

Happy the man who in a rainy day can betake himself to a huge garret, stored, like that of the Manse, with lumber that each generation has left behind it from a period before the revolution. Our garret was an arched hall, dimly illuminated through small and dusty windows; it was but a twilight at the best, and there were nooks, or rather caverns, of deep obscurity, the secrets of which I never learned, being too reverent of their dust and cobwebs. The beams and rafters roughly hewn and with strips of bark still on them and the rude masonry of the chimneys, made the garret look wild and uncivilized,—an aspect unlike what was seen elsewhere in the quiet and decorous old house. But on one side there was a little whitewashed apartment, which bore the traditionary title of the Saint's Chamber, because holy men in their youth had slept, and studied, and prayed there. With its elevated retirement, its one window, its small fireplace, and its closet convenient for an oratory, it was the very spot where a young man might inspire himself with solemn enthusiasm and cherish saintly dreams. The occupants, at various epochs, had left brief records and ejaculations inscribed upon the walls. There, too, hung a tattered and shrivelled roll of canvas, which on inspection proved to be the forcibly wrought picture of a clergyman, in wig, band, and gown, holding a Bible in his hand. As I turned his face towards the light he eyed me with an air of authority such as men of his profession seldom assume in our days. The original had been pastor of the parish more than a century ago, a friend of Whitefield, and almost his equal in fervid eloquence. I bowed before the effigy of the dignified divine, and felt as if I had now met face to face with the ghost by whom, as there was reason to apprehend, the Manse was haunted.

Houses of any antiquity in New England are so invariably possessed with spirits that the matter seems hardly worth alluding to. Our ghost used to heave deep sighs in a particular corner of the parlor, and sometimes rustled paper, as if he were turning over a sermon in the long upper entry,—where nevertheless he was invisible in spite of the bright moonshine that fell through the eastern window. Not improbably he wished me to edit and publish a selection from a chest full of manuscript discourses that stood in the garret. Once, while Hillard and other friends sat talking with us in the twilight, there came a rustling noise as of a minister's silk gown, sweeping through the very midst of the company, so closely as almost to brush against the chairs. Still there was nothing visible. A yet stranger business was that of a ghostly servant maid, who used to be heard in the kitchen at deepest midnight, grinding coffee, cooking, ironing,—performing, in short, all kinds of domestic labor,—although no traces of anything accomplished could be detected the next morning. Some neglected duty of her servitude—some ill-starched ministerial band—disturbed the poor damsel in her grave and kept her at work without any wages.

But to return from this digression. A part of my predecessor's library was stored in the garret,—no unfit receptacle indeed for such dreary trash as comprised the greater number of volumes. The old books would have been worth nothing at an auction. In this venerable garret, however, they possessed an interest, quite apart from their literary value, as heirlooms, many of which had been transmitted down through a series of consecrated hands from the days of the mighty Puritan divines. Autographs of famous names were to be seen in faded ink on some of their flyleaves; and there were marginal observations or interpolated pages closely covered with manuscript in illegible shorthand, perhaps concealing matter of profound truth and wisdom. The world will never be the better for it. A few of the books were Latin folios, written by Catholic authors; others demolished Papistry, as with a sledge-hammer, in plain English. A dissertation on the book of Job—which only Job himself could have had patience to read—filled at least a score of small, thickset quartos, at the rate of two or three volumes to a chapter. Then there was a vast folio body of divinity—too corpulent a body, it might be feared, to comprehend the spiritual element of religion. Volumes of this form dated back two hundred years or more, and were generally bound in black leather, exhibiting precisely such an appearance as we should attribute to books of enchantment. Others equally antique were of a size proper to be carried in the large waistcoat pockets of old times,—diminutive, but as black as their bulkier brethren, and abundantly interfused with Greek and Latin quotations. These little old volumes impressed me as if they had been intended for very large ones, but had been unfortunately blighted at an early stage of their growth.

The rain pattered upon the roof and the sky gloomed through the dusty garret windows while I burrowed among these venerable books in search of any living thought which should burn like a coal of fire or glow like an inextinguishable gem, beneath the dead trumpery that had long hidden it. But I found no such treasure; all was dead alike; and I could not but muse deeply and wonderingly upon the humiliating fact that the works of man's intellect decay like those of his hands. Thought grows moldy. What was good and nourishing food for the spirits of one generation affords no sustenance for the next. Books of religion, however, cannot be considered a fair test of the enduring and vivacious properties of human thought, because such books so seldom really touch upon their ostensible subject, and have, therefore, so little business to be written at all. So long as an unlettered soul can attain to saving grace there would seem to be no deadly error in holding theological libraries to be accumulations of, for the most part, stupendous impertinence. * * *

If ever my readers should decide to give up civilized life, cities, houses, and whatever moral or material enormities in addition to these the perverted ingenuity of our race has contrived, let it be in the early autumn. Then Nature will love him better than at any other season, and will take him to her bosom with a more motherly tenderness. I could scarcely endure the roof of the old house above me in those first autumnal days. How early in the summer, too, the prophecy of autumn comes! Earlier in some years than in others; sometimes even in the first weeks of July. There is no other feeling like what is caused by this faint, doubtful, yet real perception—if it be not rather a foreboding—of the year's decay, so blessedly sweet and sad in the same breath.

Did I say that there was no feeling like it? Ah, but there is a half-acknowledged melancholy like to this when we stand in the perfected vigor of our life and feel that Time has now given us all his flowers, and that the next work of his never idle fingers must be to steal them one by one away.

I have forgotten whether the song of the cricket be not as early a token of autumn's approach as any other,—that song which may be called an audible stillness; for though very loud and heard afar, yet the mind does not take note of it as a sound, so completely is its individual existence merged among the accompanying characteristics of the season. Alas for the pleasant summer time! In August the grass is still verdant on the hills and in the valleys; the foliage of the trees is as dense as ever and as green; the flowers gleam forth in richer abundance along the margin of the river and by the stone walls and deep among the woods; the days, too, are as fervid now as they were a month ago; and yet in every breath of wind and in every beam of sunshine we hear the whispered farewell and behold the parting smile of a dear friend. There is a coolness amid all the heat, a mildness in the blazing noon. Not a breeze can stir but it thrills us with the breath of autumn. A pensive glory is seen in the far golden gleams, among the shadows of the trees. The flowers—even the brightest of them, and they are the most gorgeous of the year—have this gentle sadness wedded to their pomp, and typify the character of the delicious time each within itself. The brilliant cardinal flower has never seemed gay to me.

Still later in the season Nature's tenderness waxes stronger. It is impossible not to be fond of our mother now; for she is so fond of us! At other periods she does not make this impression on me, or only at rare intervals; but in those genial days of autumn, when she has perfected her harvests and accomplished every needful thing that was given her to do, then she overflows with a blessed superfluity of love. She has leisure to caress her children now. It is good to be alive at such times. Thank Heaven for breath—yes, for mere breath—when it is made up of a heavenly breeze like this! It comes with a real kiss upon our cheeks; it would linger fondly around us if it might; but, since it must be gone, it embraces us with its whole kindly heart and passes onward to embrace likewise the next thing that it meets. A blessing is flung abroad and scattered far and wide over the earth, to be gathered up by all who choose. I recline upon the still unwithered grass and whisper to myself, "O perfect day! O beautiful world! O beneficent God!" And it is the promise of a blessed eternity; for our Creator would never have made such lovely days and have given us the deep hearts to enjoy them, above and beyond all thought, unless we were meant to be immortal. This sunshine is the golden pledge thereof. It beams through the gates of paradise and shows us glimpses far inward.

By and by, in a little time, the outward world puts on a drear austerity. On some October morning there is a heavy hoar-frost on the grass and along the tops of the fences; and at sunrise the leaves fall from the trees of our avenue without a breath of wind, quietly descending by their own weight. All summer long they have murmured like the noise of waters; they have roared loudly while the branches were wrestling with the thunder gust; they have made music both glad and solemn; they have attuned my thoughts by their quiet sound as I paced to and fro beneath the arch of intermingling boughs. Now they can only rustle under my feet. Henceforth the gray parsonage begins to assume a larger importance, and draws to its fireside,—for the abomination of the air-tight stove is reserved till wintry weather,—draws closer and closer to its fireside the vagrant impulses that had gone wandering about through the summer.

When summer was dead and buried the Old Manse became as lonely as a hermitage. Not that ever—in my time at least—it had been thronged with company; but, at no rare intervals, we welcomed some friend out of the dusty glare and tumult of the world and rejoiced to share with him the transparent obscurity that was floating over us. In one respect our precincts were like the Enchanted Ground through which the pilgrim travelled on his way to the Celestial City! The guests, each and all, felt a slumberous influence upon them; they fell asleep in chairs, or took a more deliberate siesta on the sofa, or were seen stretched among the shadows of the orchard, looking up dreamily through the boughs. They could not have paid a more acceptable compliment to my abode nor to my own qualities as a host. I held it as a proof that they left their cares behind them as they passed between the stone gateposts at the entrance of our avenue, and that the so powerful opiate was the abundance of peace and quiet within and all around us. Others could give them pleasure and amusement or instruction—these could be picked up anywhere; but it was for me to give them rest—rest in a life of trouble. What better could be done for those weary and world-worn spirits?—for him whose career of perpetual action was impeded and harassed by the rarest of his powers and the richest of his acquirements?—for another who had thrown his ardent heart from earliest youth into the strife of politics, and now, perchance, began to suspect that one lifetime is too brief for the accomplishment of any lofty aim?—for her on whose feminine nature had been imposed the heavy gift of intellectual power, such as a strong man might have staggered under, and with it the necessity to act upon the world? —in a word, not to multiply instances, what better could be done for anybody who came within our magic circle than to throw the spell of a tranquil spirit over him? And when it had wrought its full effect, then we dismissed him, with but misty reminiscences, as if he had been dreaming of us. * * *

And now I begin to feel—and perhaps should have sooner felt—that we have talked enough of the Old Manse. Mine honored reader, it may be, will vilify the poor author as an egotist for babbling through so many pages about a mossgrown country parsonage, and his life within its walls and on the river and in the woods, and the influences that wrought upon him from all these sources. My conscience, however, does not reproach me with betraying anything too sacredly individual to be revealed by a human spirit to its brother or sister spirit. How narrow—how shallow and scanty too—is the stream of thought that has been flowing from my pen, compared with the broad tide of dim emotions, ideas, and associations which swell around me from that portion of my existence! How little have I told! and of that little, how almost nothing is even tinctured with any quality that makes it exclusively my own! Has the reader gone wandering, hand in hand with me, through the inner passages of my being? and have we groped together into all its chambers and examined their treasures or their rubbish? Not so. We have been standing on the greensward, but just within the cavern's mouth, where the common sunshine is free to penetrate, and where every footstep is therefore free to come. I have appealed to no sentiment or sensibilities save such as are diffused among us all. So far as I am a man of really individual attributes I veil my face; nor am I, nor have I ever been, one of those supremely hospitable people who serve up their own hearts, delicately fried, with brain sauce, as a tidbit for their beloved public.

Glancing back over what I have written, it seems but the scattered reminiscences of a single summer. In fairyland there is no measurement of time; and, in a spot so sheltered from the turmoil of life's ocean, three years hastened away with a noiseless flight, as the breezy sunshine chases the cloud shadows across the depths of a still valley. Now came hints, growing more and more distinct, that the owner of the old house was pining for his native air. Carpenters next appeared making a tremendous racket among the out-buildings, strewing the green grass with pine shavings and chips of chestnut joists and vexing the whole antiquity of the place with their discordant renovations. Soon, moreover, they divested our abode of the veil of woodbine which had crept over a large portion of its southern face. All the aged mosses were cleared unsparingly away; and there were horrible whispers about brushing up the external walls with a coat of paint—a purpose as little to my taste as might be that of rouging the venerable cheeks of one's grandmother. But the hand that renovates is always more sacrilegious than that which destroys. In fine, we gathered up our household goods, drank a farewell cup of tea in our pleasant little breakfast room,—delicately fragrant tea, an unpurchasable luxury, one of the many angel gifts that had fallen like dew upon us,—and passed forth between the tall stone gate-posts as uncertain as the wandering Arabs where our tent might next be pitched. Providence took me by the hand, and—an oddity of dispensation which, I trust, there is no irreverence in smiling at—has led me, as the newspapers announce while I am writing, from the Old Manse into a custom house. As a story teller, I have often contrived strange vicissitudes for my imaginary personages, but none like this.

1846

## ETHAN BRAND:

### A CHAPTER FROM AN ABORTIVE ROMANCE

Bartram the lime-burner, a rough, heavy-looking man, begrimed with charcoal, sat watching his kiln at nightfall, while his little son played at building houses with the scattered fragments of marble, when, on the hillside below them, they heard a roar of laughter, not mirthful, but slow, and even solemn, like a wind shaking the boughs of the forest.

"Father, what is that?" asked the little boy, leaving his play, and pressing betwixt his father's knees.

"Oh, some drunken man, I suppose," answered the lime-burner; "some merry fellow from the barroom in the village, who dared not laugh loud enough within doors lest he should blow the roof of the house off. So here he is, shaking his jolly sides at the foot of Graylock."

"But, father," said the child, more

sensitive than the obtuse, middle-aged clown, "he does not laugh like a man that is glad. So the noise frightens me!"

"Don't be a fool, child!" cried his father, gruffly. "You will never make a man, I do believe; there is too much of your mother in you. I have known the rustling of a leaf to startle you. Hark! Here comes the merry fellow now. You shall see that there is no harm in him."

Bartram and his little son, while they were talking thus, sat watching the same lime-kiln that had been the scene of Ethan Brand's solitary and meditative life, before he began his search for the Unpardonable Sin. Many years, as we have seen, had now elapsed, since that portentous night when the IDEA was first developed. The kiln, however, on the mountain-side, stood unimpaired, and was in nothing changed since he had thrown his dark thoughts into the intense glow of its furnace, and melted them, as it were, into the one thought that took possession of his life. It was a rude, round, tower-like structure about twenty feet high, heavily built of rough stones, and with a hillock of earth heaped about the larger part of its circumference; so that the blocks and fragments of marble might be drawn by cart-loads, and thrown in at the top. There was an opening at the bottom of the tower, like an oven-mouth, but large enough to admit a man in a stooping posture, and provided with a massive iron door. With the smoke and jets of flame issuing from the chinks and crevices of this door, which seemed to give admittance into the hillside, it resembled nothing so much as the private entrance to the infernal regions, which the shepherds of the Delectable Mountains were accustomed to show to pilgrims.

There are many such lime-kilns in that tract of country, for the purpose of burning the white marble which composes a large part of the substance of the hills. Some of them, built years ago, and long deserted, with weeds growing in the vacant round of the interior, which is open to the sky, and grass and wild-flowers rooting themselves into the chinks of the stones, look already like relics of antiquity, and may yet be overspread with the lichens of centuries to come. Others, where the lime-burner still feeds his daily and night-long fire, afford points of interest to the wanderer among the hills, who seats himself on a log of wood or a fragment of marble, to hold a chat with the solitary man. It is a lonesome, and, when the character is inclined to thought, may be an intensely thoughtful occupation; as it proved in the case of Ethan Brand, who had mused to such strange purpose, in days gone by, while the fire in this very kiln was burning.

The man who now watched the fire was of a different order, and troubled himself with no thoughts save the very few that were requisite to his business. At frequent intervals, he flung back the clashing weight of the iron door, and, turning his face from the insufferable glare, thrust in huge logs of oak, or stirred the immense brands with a long pole. Within the furnace were seen the curling and riotous flames, and the burning marble, almost molten with the intensity of heat; while without, the reflection of the fire quivered on the dark intricacy of the surrounding forest, and showed in the foreground a bright and ruddy little picture of the hut, the spring beside its door, the athletic and coal-begrimed figure of the lime-burner, and the half-frightened child, shrinking into the protection of his father's shadow. And when again the iron door was closed, then reappeared the tender light of the half-full moon, which vainly strove to trace out the indistinct shapes of the neighboring mountains; and, in the upper sky, there was a flitting congregation of clouds, still faintly tinged with the rosy sunset, though thus far down into the valley the sunshine had vanished long and long ago.

The little boy now crept still closer to his father, as footsteps were heard ascending the hillside, and a human form thrust aside the bushes that clustered beneath the trees.

"Halloo! who is it?" cried the lime-burner, vexed at his son's timidity, yet half infected by it. "Come forward, and show yourself, like a man, or I'll fling this chunk of marble at your head!"

"You offer me a rough welcome," said a gloomy voice, as the unknown man drew nigh. "Yet I neither claim nor desire a kinder one, even at my own fireside."

To obtain a distincter view, Bartram threw open the iron door of the kiln, whence immediately issued a gush of fierce light, that smote full upon the stranger's face and figure. To a careless eye there appeared nothing very remarkable in his aspect, which was that of a man in a coarse, brown, country-made suit of clothes, tall and thin, with the staff and heavy shoes of a wayfarer. As he advanced, he fixed his eyes — which were very bright — intently upon the brightness of the furnace, as if he beheld, or expected to behold, some object worthy of note within it.

"Good evening, stranger," said the lime-burner; "whence come you, so late in the day?"

"I come from my search," answered the wayfarer; "for, at last, it is finished."

"Drunk! — or crazy!" muttered Bartram to himself. "I shall have trouble with the fellow. The sooner I drive him away, the better."

The little boy, all in a tremble, whispered to his father, and begged him to shut the door of the kiln, so that there might not be so much light; for that there was something in the man's face which he was afraid to look at, yet could not look away from. And, indeed, even the lime-burner's dull and torpid sense began to be impressed by an indescribable something in that thin, rugged, thoughtful visage, with the grizzled hair hanging wildly about it, and those deeply sunken eyes, which gleamed like fires within the entrance of a mysterious cavern. But, as he closed the door, the stranger turned towards him, and spoke in a quiet, familiar way, that made Bartram feel as if he were a sane and sensible man, after all.

"Your task draws to an end, I see," said he. "This marble has already been burning three days. A few hours more will convert the stone to lime."

"Why, who are you?" exclaimed the lime-burner. "You seem as well acquainted with my business as I am myself."

"And well I may be," said the

stranger; "for I followed the same craft many a long year, and here, too, on this very spot. But you are a new-comer in these parts. Did you never hear of Ethan Brand?"

"The man that went in search of the Unpardonable Sin?" asked Bartram, with a laugh.

"The same," answered the stranger. "He has found what he sought, and therefore he comes back again."

"What! then you are Ethan Brand himself?" cried the lime-burner, in amazement. "I am a new-comer here, as you say, and they call it eighteen years since you left the foot of Graylock. But, I can tell you, the good folks still talk about Ethan Brand, in the village yonder, and what a strange errand took him away from his lime-kiln. Well, and so you have found the Unpardonable Sin?"

"Even so!" said the stranger, calmly.

"If the question is a fair one," proceeded Bartram, "where might it be?"

Ethan Brand laid his finger on his own heart.

"Here!" replied he.

And then, without mirth in his countenance, but as if moved by an involuntary recognition of the infinite absurdity of seeking throughout the world for what was the closest of all things to himself, and looking into every heart, save his own, for what was hidden in no other breast, he broke into a laugh of scorn. It was the same slow, heavy laugh, that had almost appalled the lime-burner when it heralded the wayfarer's approach.

The solitary mountain-side was made dismal by it. Laughter, when out of place, mistimed, or bursting forth from a disordered state of feeling, may be the most terrible modulation of the human voice. The laughter of one asleep, even if it be a little child, — the madman's laugh, — the wild, screaming laugh of a born idiot, — are sounds that we sometimes tremble to hear, and would always willingly forget. Poets have imagined no utterance of fiends or hobgoblins so fearfully appropriate as a laugh. And even the obtuse lime-burner felt his nerves shaken, as this strange man looked inward at his own heart, and burst into laughter that rolled away into the night, and was indistinctly reverberated among the hills.

"Joe," said he to his little son, "scamper down to the tavern in the village, and tell the jolly fellows there that Ethan Brand has come back, and that he has found the Unpardonable Sin!"

The boy darted away on his errand, to which Ethan Brand made no objection, nor seemed hardly to notice it. He sat on a log of wood, looking steadfastly at the iron door of the kiln. When the child was out of sight, and his swift and light footsteps ceased to be heard treading first on the fallen leaves and then on the rocky mountain-path, the lime-burner began to regret his departure. He felt that the little fellow's presence had been a barrier between his guest and himself, and that he must now deal, heart to heart, with a man who, on his own confession, had committed the one only crime for which Heaven could afford no mercy. That crime, in its indistinct blackness, seemed to overshadow him. The lime-burner's own sins rose up within him, and made his memory riotous with a throng of evil shapes that asserted their kindred with the Master Sin, whatever it might be, which it was within the scope of man's corrupted nature to conceive and cherish. They were all of one family; they went to and fro between his breast and Ethan Brand's, and carried dark greetings from one to the other.

Then Bartram remembered the stories which had grown traditionary in reference to this strange man, who had come upon him like a shadow of the night, and was making himself at home in his old place, after so long absence that the dead people, dead and buried for years, would have had more right to be at home, in any familiar spot, than he. Ethan Brand, it was said, had conversed with Satan himself in the lurid blaze of this very kiln. The legend had been matter of mirth heretofore, but looked grisly now. According to this tale, before Ethan Brand departed on his search, he had been accustomed to evoke a fiend from the hot furnace of the lime-kiln, night after night, in order to confer with him about the Unpardonable Sin; the man and the fiend each laboring to frame the image of some mode of guilt which could neither be atoned for nor forgiven. And, with the first gleam of light upon the mountain-top, the fiend crept in at the iron door, there to abide the intensest element of fire, until again summoned forth to share in the dreadful task of extending man's possible guilt beyond the scope of Heaven's else infinite mercy.

While the lime-burner was struggling with the horror of these thoughts, Ethan Brand rose from the log, and flung open the door of the kiln. The action was in such accordance with the idea in Bartram's mind, that he almost expected to see the Evil One issue forth, red-hot, from the raging furnace.

"Hold! hold!" cried he, with a tremulous attempt to laugh; for he was ashamed of his fears, although they overmastered him. "Don't, for mercy's sake, bring out your Devil now!"

"Man!" sternly replied Ethan Brand, "what need have I of the Devil? I have left him behind me, on my track. It is with such half-way sinners as you that he busies himself. Fear not, because I open the door. I do but act by old custom, and am going to trim your fire, like a lime-burner, as I was once."

He stirred the vast coals, thrust in more wood, and bent forward to gaze into the hollow prison-house of the fire, regardless of the fierce glow that reddened upon his face. The lime-burner sat watching him, and half suspected this strange guest of a purpose, if not to evoke a fiend, at least to plunge bodily into the flames, and thus vanish from the sight of man. Ethan Brand, however, drew quietly back, and closed the door of the kiln.

"I have looked," said he, "into many a human heart that was seven times hotter with sinful passions than yonder furnace is with fire. But I found not there what I sought. No, not the Unpardonable Sin!"

"What is the Unpardonable Sin?" asked the lime-burner; and then he shrank farther from his companion, trembling lest his question should be answered.

"It is a sin that grew within my own breast," replied Ethan Brand, standing erect, with a pride that distinguishes all enthusiasts of his stamp.

"A sin that grew nowhere else! The sin of an intellect that triumphed over the sense of brotherhood with man and reverence for God, and sacrificed everything to its own mighty claims! The only sin that deserves a recompense of immortal agony! Freely, were it to do again, would I incur the guilt. Unshrinkingly I accept the retribution!"

"The man's head is turned," muttered the lime-burner to himself. "He may be a sinner like the rest of us, — nothing more likely, — but, I'll be sworn, he is a madman too."

Nevertheless, he felt uncomfortable at his situation, alone with Ethan Brand on the wild mountain-side, and was right glad to hear the rough murmur of tongues, and the footsteps of what seemed a pretty numerous party, stumbling over the stones and rustling through the underbrush. Soon appeared the whole lazy regiment that was wont to infest the village tavern, comprehending three or four individuals who had drunk flip beside the bar-room fire through all the winters, and smoked their pipes beneath the stoop through all the summers, since Ethan Brand's departure. Laughing boisterously, and mingling all their voices together in unceremonious talk, they now burst into the moonshine and narrow streaks of firelight that illuminated the open space before the lime-kiln. Bartram set the door ajar again, flooding the spot with light, that the whole company might get a fair view of Ethan Brand, and he of them.

There, among other old acquaintances, was a once ubiquitous man, now almost extinct, but whom we were formerly sure to encounter at the hotel of every thriving village throughout the country. It was the stage-agent. The present specimen of the genus was a wilted and smoke-dried man, wrinkled and red-nosed, in a smartly cut, brown, bob-tailed coat, with brass buttons, who, for a length of time unknown, had kept his desk and corner in the bar-room, and was still puffing what seemed to be the same cigar that he had lighted twenty years before. He had great fame as a dry joker, though, perhaps, less on account of any intrinsic humor than from a certain flavor of brandy-toddy and tobacco-smoke, which impregnated all his ideas and expressions, as well as his person. Another well-remembered though strangely altered face was that of Lawyer Giles, as people still called him in courtesy; an elderly ragamuffin, in his soiled shirt-sleeves and tow-cloth trousers. This poor fellow had been an attorney, in what he called his better days, a sharp practitioner, and in great vogue among the village litigants; but flip, and sling, and toddy, and cocktails, imbibed at all hours, morning, noon, and night, had caused him to slide from intellectual to various kinds and degrees of bodily labor, till at last, to adopt his own phrase, he slid into a soap-vat. In other words, Giles was now a soap-boiler, in a small way. He had come to be but the fragment of a human being, a part of one foot having been chopped off by an axe, and an entire hand torn away by the devilish grip of a steam-engine. Yet, though the corporeal hand was gone, a spiritual member remained; for, stretching forth the stump, Giles steadfastly averred that he felt an invisible thumb and fingers with as vivid a sensation as before the real ones were amputated. A maimed and miserable wretch he was; but one, nevertheless, whom the world could not trample on, and had no right to scorn, either in this or any previous stage of his misfortunes, since he had still kept up the courage and spirit of a man, asked nothing in charity, and with his one hand — and that the left one — fought a stern battle against want and hostile circumstances.

Among the throng, too, came another personage, who, with certain points of similarity to Lawyer Giles, had many more of difference. It was the village doctor; a man of some fifty years, whom, at an earlier period of his life, we introduced as paying a professional visit to Ethan Brand during the latter's supposed insanity. He was now a purple-visaged, rude, and brutal, yet half-gentlemanly figure, with something wild, ruined, and desperate in his talk, and in all the details of his gesture and manners. Brandy possessed this man like an evil spirit, and made him as surly and savage as a wild beast, and as miserable as a lost soul; but there was supposed to be in him such wonderful skill, such native gifts of healing, beyond any which medical science could impart, that society caught hold of him, and would not let him sink out of its reach. So, swaying to and fro upon his horse, and grumbling thick accents at the bedside, he visited all the sick-chambers for miles about among the mountain towns, and sometimes raised a dying man, as it were, by miracle, or quite as often, no doubt, sent his patient to a grave that was dug many a year too soon. The doctor had an everlasting pipe in his mouth, and, as somebody said, in allusion to his habit of swearing, it was always alight with hell-fire.

These three worthies pressed forward, and greeted Ethan Brand each after his own fashion, earnestly inviting him to partake of the contents of a certain black bottle, in which, as they averred, he would find something far better worth seeking for than the Unpardonable Sin. No mind, which has wrought itself by intense and solitary meditation into a high state of enthusiasm, can endure the kind of contact with low and vulgar modes of thought and feeling to which Ethan Brand was now subjected. It made him doubt — and, strange to say, it was a painful doubt — whether he had indeed found the Unpardonable Sin, and found it within himself. The whole question on which he had exhausted life, and more than life, looked like a delusion.

"Leave me," he said bitterly, "ye brute beasts, that have made yourselves so, shrivelling up your souls with fiery liquors! I have done with you. Years and years ago, I groped into your hearts, and found nothing there for my purpose. Get ye gone!"

"Why, you uncivil scoundrel," cried the fierce doctor, "is that the way you respond to the kindness of your best friends? Then let me tell you the truth. You have no more found the Unpardonable Sin than yonder boy Joe has. You are but a crazy fellow, — I told you so twenty years ago, — neither better nor worse than a crazy fellow, and the fit companion of old Humphrey, here!"

He pointed to an old man, shabbily dressed, with long white hair, thin visage, and unsteady eyes. For some years past this aged person had been wandering about among the hills, inquiring of all travellers whom he met for his daughter. The girl, it seemed, had gone off with a company of circus-performers; and occasionally tidings of her came to the village, and fine stories were told of her glittering appearance as she rode on horseback in the ring, or performed marvelous feats on the tight-rope.

The white-haired father now approached Ethan Brand, and gazed unsteadily into his face.

"They tell me you have been all over the earth," said he, wringing his hands with earnestness. "You must have seen my daughter, for she makes a grand figure in the world, and everybody goes to see her. Did she send any word to her old father, or say when she was coming back?"

Ethan Brand's eye quailed beneath the old man's. That daughter, from whom he so earnestly desired a word of greeting, was the Esther of our tale, the very girl whom, with such cold and remorseless purpose, Ethan Brand had made the subject of a psychological experiment, and wasted, absorbed, and perhaps annihilated her soul, in the process.

"Yes," murmured he, turning away from the hoary wanderer; "it is no delusion. There is an Unpardonable Sin!"

While these things were passing, a merry scene was going forward in the area of cheerful light, beside the spring and before the door of the hut. A number of the youth of the village, young men and girls, had hurried up the hillside, impelled by curiosity to see Ethan Brand, the hero of so many a legend familiar to their childhood. Finding nothing, however, very remarkable in his aspect, — nothing but a sunburnt wayfarer, in plain garb and dusty shoes, who sat looking into the fire as if he fancied pictures among the coals, — these young people speedily grew tired of observing him. As it happened, there was other amusement at hand. An old German Jew, travelling with a diorama on his back, was passing down the mountain-road towards the village just as the party turned aside from it, and, in hopes of eking out the profits of the day, the showman had kept them company to the lime-kiln.

"Come, old Dutchman," cried one of the young men, "let us see your pictures, if you can swear they are worth looking at!"

"Oh, yes, Captain," answered the Jew, — whether as a matter of courtesy or craft, he styled everybody Captain, — "I shall show you, indeed, some very superb pictures!"

So, placing his box in a proper position, he invited the young men and girls to look through the glass orifices of the machine, and proceeded to exhibit a series of the most outrageous scratchings and daubings, as specimens of the fine arts, that ever an itinerant showman had the face to impose upon his circle of spectators. The pictures were worn out, moreover, tattered, full of cracks and wrinkles, dingy with tobacco-smoke, and otherwise in a most pitiable condition. Some purported to be cities, public edifices, and ruined castles in Europe; others represented Napoleon's battles and Nelson's sea-fights; and in the midst of these would be seen a gigantic, brown, hairy hand, — which might have been mistaken for the Hand of Destiny, though, in truth, it was only the showman's, — pointing its forefinger to various scenes of the conflict, while its owner gave historical illustrations. When, with much merriment at its abominable deficiency of merit, the exhibition was concluded, the German bade little Joe put his head into the box. Viewed through the magnifying-glasses, the boy's round, rosy visage assumed the strangest imaginable aspect of an immense Titanic child, the mouth grinning broadly, and the eyes and every other feature overflowing with fun at the joke. Suddenly, however, that merry face turned pale, and its expression changed to horror, for this easily impressed and excitable child had become sensible that the eye of Ethan Brand was fixed upon him through the glass.

"You make the little man to be afraid, Captain," said the German Jew, turning up the dark and strong outline of his visage, from his stooping posture. "But look again, and, by chance, I shall cause you to see somewhat that is very fine, upon my word!"

Ethan Brand gazed into the box for an instant, and then starting back, looked fixedly at the German. What had he seen? Nothing, apparently; for a curious youth, who had peeped in almost at the same moment, beheld only a vacant space of canvas.

"I remember you now," muttered Ethan Brand to the showman.

"Ah, Captain," whispered the Jew of Nuremberg, with a dark smile, "I find it to be a heavy matter in my show-box, — this Unpardonable Sin! By my faith, Captain, it has wearied my shoulders, this long day, to carry it over the mountain."

"Peace," answered Ethan Brand, sternly, "or get thee into the furnace yonder!"

The Jew's exhibition had scarcely concluded, when a great, elderly dog — who seemed to be his own master, as no person in the company laid claim to him — saw fit to render himself the object of public notice. Hitherto, he had shown himself a very quiet, well-disposed old dog, going round from one to another, and, by way of being sociable, offering his rough head to be patted by any kindly hand that would take so much trouble. But now, all of a sudden, this grave and venerable quadruped, of his own mere motion, and without the slightest suggestion from anybody else, began to run round after his tail, which, to heighten the absurdity of the proceeding, was a great deal shorter than it should have been. Never was seen such headlong eagerness in pursuit of an object that could not possibly be attained; never was heard such a tremendous outbreak of growling, snarling, barking, and snapping, — as if one end of the ridiculous brute's body were at deadly and most unforgivable enmity with the other. Faster and faster, round about went the cur; and faster and still faster fled the unapproachable brevity of his tail; and louder and fiercer grew his yells of rage and animosity; until, utterly exhausted, and as far from the goal as ever, the foolish old dog ceased his performance as suddenly as he had begun it. The next moment he was as mild, quiet, sensible, and respectable in his deportment, as when he first scraped acquaintance with the company.

As may be supposed, the exhibition

was greeted with universal laughter, clapping of hands, and shouts of encore, to which the canine performer responded by wagging all that there was to wag of his tail, but appeared totally unable to repeat his very successful effort to amuse the spectators.

Meanwhile, Ethan Brand had resumed his seat upon the log, and moved, it might be, by a perception of some remote analogy between his own case and that of this self-pursuing cur, he broke into the awful laugh, which, more than any other token, expressed the condition of his inward being. From that moment, the merriment of the party was at an end; they stood aghast, dreading lest the inauspicious sound should be reverberated around the horizon, and that mountain would thunder it to mountain, and so the horror be prolonged upon their ears. Then, whispering one to another that it was late, — that the moon was almost down, — that the August night was growing chill, — they hurried homewards, leaving the lime-burner and little Joe to deal as they might with their unwelcome guest. Save for these three human beings, the open space on the hillside was a solitude, set in a vast gloom of forest. Beyond that darksome verge, the firelight glimmered on the stately trunks and almost black foliage of pines, intermixed with the lighter verdure of sapling oaks, maples, and poplars, while here and there lay the gigantic corpses of dead trees, decaying on the leaf-strewn soil. And it seemed to little Joe — a timorous and imaginative child — that the silent forest was holding its breath until some fearful thing should happen.

Ethan Brand thrust more wood into the fire, and closed the door of the kiln; then looking over his shoulder at the lime-burner and his son, he bade, rather than advised, them to retire to rest.

"For myself, I cannot sleep," said he. "I have matters that it concerns me to meditate upon. I will watch the fire, as I used to do in the old time."

"And call the Devil out of the furnace to keep you company, I suppose," muttered Bartram, who had been making intimate acquaintance with the black bottle above mentioned. "But watch, if you like, and call as many devils as you like! For my part, I shall be all the better for a snooze. Come, Joe!"

As the boy followed his father into the hut, he looked back at the wayfarer, and the tears came into his eyes, for his tender spirit had an intuition of the bleak and terrible loneliness in which this man had enveloped himself.

When they had gone, Ethan Brand sat listening to the crackling of the kindled wood, and looking at the little spirits of fire that issued through the chinks of the door. These trifles, however, once so familiar, had but the slightest hold of his attention, while deep within his mind he was reviewing the gradual but marvelous change that had been wrought upon him by the search to which he had devoted himself. He remembered how the night dew had fallen upon him, — how the dark forest had whispered to him, — how the stars had gleamed upon him, — a simple and loving man, watching his fire in the years gone by, and ever musing as it burned. He remembered with what tenderness, with what love and sympathy for mankind, and what pity for human guilt and woe, he had first begun to contemplate those ideas which afterwards became the inspiration of his life; with what reverence he had then looked into the heart of man, viewing it as a temple originally divine, and, however desecrated, still to be held sacred by a brother; with what awful fear he had deprecated the success of his pursuit, and prayed that the Unpardonable Sin might never be revealed to him. Then ensued that vast intellectual development, which, in its progress, disturbed the counterpoise between his mind and heart. The Idea that possessed his life had operated as a means of education; it had gone on cultivating his powers to the highest point of which they were susceptible; it had raised him from the level of an unlettered laborer to stand on a star-lit eminence, whither the philosophers of the earth, laden with the lore of universities, might vainly strive to clamber after him. So much for the intellect! But where was the heart? That, indeed, had withered, — had contracted, — had hardened, — had perished! It had ceased to partake of the universal throb. He had lost his hold of the magnetic chain of humanity. He was no longer a brother-man, opening the chambers or the dungeons of our common nature by the key of holy sympathy, which gave him a right to share in all its secrets; he was now a cold observer, looking on mankind as the subject of his experiment, and, at length, converting man and woman to be his puppets, and pulling the wires that moved them to such degrees of crime as were demanded for his study.

Thus Ethan Brand became a fiend. He began to be so from the moment that his moral nature had ceased to keep the pace of improvement with his intellect. And now, as his highest effort and inevitable development, — as the bright and gorgeous flower, and rich, delicious fruit of his life's labor, — he had produced the Unpardonable Sin!

"What more have I to seek? what more to achieve?" said Ethan Brand to himself. "My task is done, and well done!"

Starting from the log with a certain alacrity in his gait and ascending the hillock of earth that was raised against the stone circumference of the lime-kiln, he thus reached the top of the structure. It was a space of perhaps ten feet across, from edge to edge, presenting a view of the upper surface of the immense mass of broken marble with which the kiln was heaped. All these innumerable blocks and fragments of marble were red-hot and vividly on fire, sending up great spouts of blue flame, which quivered aloft and danced madly, as within a magic circle, and sank and rose again, with continual and multitudinous activity. As the lonely man bent forward over this terrible body of fire, the blasting heat smote up against his person with a breath that, it might be supposed, would have scorched and shrivelled him up in a moment.

Ethan Brand stood erect, and raised his arms on high. The blue flames played upon his face, and imparted the wild and ghastly light which alone could have suited its expression; it was that of a fiend on the verge of plunging into his gulf of intensest torment.

"O Mother Earth," cried he, "who art no more my Mother, and into whose bosom this frame shall never be resolved! O mankind, whose brotherhood I have cast off, and trampled thy great heart beneath my feet! O stars of heaven, that shone on me of old, as if to light me onward and upward! — farewell all, and forever. Come, deadly element of Fire, — henceforth my familiar friend! Embrace me, as I do thee!"

That night the sound of a fearful peal of laughter rolled heavily through the sleep of the lime-burner and his little son; dim shapes of horror and anguish haunted their dreams, and seemed still present in the rude hovel, when they opened their eyes to the daylight.

"Up, boy, up!" cried the lime-burner, staring about him. "Thank Heaven, the night is gone, at last; and rather than pass such another, I would watch my lime-kiln, wide awake, for a twelvemonth. This Ethan Brand, with his humbug of an Unpardonable Sin, has done me no such mighty favor, in taking my place!"

He issued from the hut, followed by little Joe, who kept fast hold of his father's hand. The early sunshine was already pouring its gold upon the mountain-tops, and though the valleys were still in shadow, they smiled cheerfully in the promise of the bright day that was hastening onward. The village, completely shut in by hills, which swelled away gently about it, looked as if it had rested peacefully in the hollow of the great hand of Providence. Every dwelling was distinctly visible; the little spires of the two churches pointed upwards, and caught a fore-glimmering of brightness from the sun-gilt skies upon their gilded weathercocks. The tavern was astir, and the figure of the old, smoke-dried stage-agent, cigar in mouth, was seen beneath the stoop. Old Graylock was glorified with a golden cloud upon his head. Scattered likewise over the breasts of the surrounding mountains, there were heaps of hoary mist, in fantastic shapes, some of them far down into the valley, others high up towards the summits, and still others, of the same family of mist or cloud, hovering in the gold radiance of the upper atmosphere. Stepping from one to another of the clouds that rested on the hills, and thence to the loftier brotherhood that sailed in air, it seemed almost as if a mortal man might thus ascend into the heavenly regions. Earth was so mingled with sky that it was a day-dream to look at it.

To supply that charm of the familiar and homely, which Nature so readily adopts into a scene like this, the stage coach was rattling down the mountain-road, and the driver sounded his horn, while Echo caught up the notes, and intertwined them into a rich and varied and elaborate harmony, of which the original performer could lay claim to little share. The great hills played a concert among themselves, each contributing a strain of airy sweetness.

Little Joe's face brightened at once.

"Dear father," cried he, skipping cheerily to and fro, "that strange man is gone, and the sky and the mountains all seem glad of it!"

"Yes," growled the lime-burner, with an oath, "but he has let the fire go down, and no thanks to him if five hundred bushels of lime are not spoiled. If I catch the fellow hereabouts again, I shall feel like tossing him into the furnace!"

With his long pole in his hand, he ascended to the top of the kiln. After a moment's pause, he called to his son.

"Come up here, Joe!" said he.

So little Joe ran up the hillock, and stood by his father's side. The marble was all burnt into perfect, snow-white lime. But on its surface, in the midst of the circle, — snow-white too, and thoroughly converted into lime, — lay a human skeleton, in the attitude of a person who, after long toil, lies down to long repose. Within the ribs — strange to say — was the shape of a human heart.

"Was the fellow's heart made of marble?" cried Bartram, in some perplexity at this phenomenon. "At any rate, it is burnt into what looks like special good lime; and, taking all the bones together, my kiln is half a bushel the richer for him."

So saying, the rude lime-burner lifted his pole, and, letting it fall upon the skeleton, the relics of Ethan Brand were crumbled into fragments.

(1848?) 1850

## From *LOVE LETTERS OF NATHANIEL HAWTHORNE, 1839–1841*

### [HAWTHORNE AT BROOK FARM]

*Oak Hill* [*Brook Farm*],
April 13th, 1841

*Ownest love,*

Here is thy poor husband in a polar Paradise! I know not how to interpret this aspect of Nature — whether it be of good or evil omen to our enterprise. But I reflect that the Plymouth pilgrims arrived in the midst of storm and stepped ashore upon mountain snow-drifts; and nevertheless they prospered, and became a great people — and doubtless it will be the same with us. I laud my stars, however, that thou wilt not have thy first impressions of our future home from such a day as this. Thou wouldst shiver all thy life afterwards, and never realize that there could be bright skies, and green hills and meadows, and trees heavy with foliage, when now the whole scene is a great snow-bank, and the sky full of snow likewise. Through faith, I persist in believing that spring and summer will come in their due season; but the unregenerated man shivers within me, and suggests a doubt whether I may not have wandered within the precincts of the Arctic circle, and chosen my heritage among everlasting snows. Dearest, provide thyself with a good stock of furs; and if thou canst obtain the skin of a polar bear, thou wilt find it a very suitable summer dress for this region. Thou must not hope to walk abroad, except upon snowshoes, nor to find any warmth, save in thy husband's heart.

Belovedest, I have not yet taken my first lesson in agriculture, as thou mayest well suppose — except that I went to see our cows foddered, yesterday afternoon. We have eight of our own; and the number is now increased by a transcendental heifer, belonging to Miss Margaret Fuller. She is very fractious, I believe, and apt to kick over the milk-pail. Thou knowest best, whether in these traits of character, she resembles her mistress. Thy husband intends to convert himself into a milk-maid this evening; but I pray heaven that Mr. Ripley may be moved to assign him the kindliest cow in the herd — otherwise he shall perform his duty with fear and trembling.

Ownest wife, I like my brethren in affliction very well; and, couldst thou see us sitting round our table, at meal-times, before the great kitchen fire, thou wouldst call it a cheerful sight. Mrs. Parker is a most comfortable woman to behold; she looks as if her ample person were stuffed full of tenderness — indeed, as if she were all one great, kind heart.

April 14th, 10 A.M.

Sweetest, I did not milk the cows last night, because Mr. Ripley was afraid to trust them to my hands, or me to their horns — I know not which. But this morning I have done wonders. Before breakfast, I went out to the barn, and began to chop hay for the cattle, and with such 'righteous vehemence' (as Mr. Ripley says) did I labor, that in the space of ten minutes, I broke the machine. Then I brought wood and replenished the fires; and finally went down to breakfast, and ate up a huge mound of buckwheat cakes. After breakfast, Mr. Ripley put a four-pronged instrument into my hands, which he gave me to understand was called a pitch-fork; and he and Mr. Farley being armed with similar weapons, we all then commenced a gallant attack upon a heap of manure. This office being concluded, and thy husband having purified himself, he sits down to finish this letter to his most beloved wife. Dearest, I will never consent that thou come within half a mile of me, after such an encounter as that of this morning. Pray Heaven that his letter retain nothing of the fragrance with which the writer was imbued. As for thy husband himself, he is particularly partial to the odor; but that whimsical little nose of thine might chance to quarrel with it.

Belovedest, Miss Fuller's cow hooks the other cows, and has made herself ruler of the herd, and behaves in a very tyrannical manner. . . . Dearest, I shall make an excellent husbandman. I feel the original Adam reviving within me.

*Oak Hill*, April 16th, ½ past 6 A.M.

. . . Dearest, since I last wrote thee, there has been an addition to our community of four gentlemen in sables, who promise to be among our most useful and respectable members. They arrived yesterday about noon. Mr. Ripley had proposed to them to join us, no longer ago than that very morning. I had some conversation with them in the afternoon, and was glad to hear them express much satisfaction with their new abode and all the arrangements. They do not appear to be very communicative, however, — or perhaps it may be merely an external reserve, like my own, to shield their delicacy. Several of their prominent characteristics, as well as their black attire, lead me to believe that they are members of the clerical profession; but I have not yet ascertained from their own lips what has been the nature of their past lives. I trust to have much pleasure in their society, and, sooner or later, that we shall all of us derive great strength from our intercourse with them. I cannot too highly applaud the readiness with which these four gentlemen in black have thrown aside all the fopperies and flummeries which have their origin in a false state of society. When I last saw them, they looked as heroically regardless of the stains and soils incident to our profession as I did when I emerged from the gold-mine.

Ownest wife, thy husband has milked a cow! ! !

. . . Belovedest, the herd has rebelled against the usurpation of Miss Fuller's heifer; and, whenever they are turned out of the barn, she is compelled to take refuge under our protection. So much did she impede thy husband's labors by keeping close to him, that he found it necessary to give her two or three gentle pats with a shovel; but still she preferred to trust herself to my tender mercies, rather than venture among the horns of the herd. She is not an amiable cow; but she has a very intelligent face, and seems to be of a reflective cast of character. I doubt not that she will soon perceive the expediency of being on good terms with the rest of the sisterhood. I have not yet been twenty yards from our house and barn; but I begin to perceive that this is a beautiful place. The scenery is of a mild and placid character, with nothing bold in its aspect; but I think its beauties will grow upon us, and make us love it the more, the longer we live here. There is a brook, so near the house that we shall [be] able to hear its ripple in the summer evenings, but for agricultural purposes, it has been made to flow in a straight and rectangular fashion, which does it infinite damage, as a picturesque object.

Naughtiest, it was a moment or two before I could think whom you meant by Mr. Dismal View. Why, he is one of the best of the brotherhood, so far as cheerfulness goes; for, if he do not laugh himself, he makes the rest of us laugh continually. He is the quaintest and queerest personage thou ever didst see — full of dry jokes, the humor of which is so incorporated with the strange twistifications of his physiognomy, that his sayings ought to be written down, accompanied with illustrations by Cruikshank. Then he keeps quoting innumerable scraps of Latin, and makes classical allusions, while we are turning over the gold-mine; and the contrast between the nature of his employment and the character of his thoughts is irresistibly ludicrous.

Sweetest, I have written this epistle in the parlor, while Farmer Ripley, and Farmer Farley, and Farmer Dismal View were talking about their agricultural concerns. So you will not wonder if it is not a classical piece of composition, either in point of thought or expression.

*Brook Farm,* Aug. 13th, 1841

Belovedest, I am very well, and not at all weary; for yesterday's rain gave us a holiday and moreover the labors of the farm are not so pressing as they have been. And — joyful thought! — in little more than a fortnight, thy husband will be free from his bondage — free to think of his Dove — free to enjoy Nature — free to think and feel! I do think that a greater weight will then be removed from me, than when Christian's burthen fell at the foot of the Cross. Even my Custom-House experience was not such a thraldom and weariness; my mind and heart were freer. Oh, belovedest, labor is the curse of the world, and nobody can meddle with it without becoming proportionably brutified. Dost thou think it is a praiseworthy matter that I have spent five golden months in providing food for cows and horses? Dearest, it is not so. Thank God, my soul is not utterly buried under a dungheap. I shall yet retain it, somewhat defiled, to be sure, but not utterly unsusceptible of purification.

*Brook Farm,* Aug. 22nd, 1841

Most dear wife, it seems a long time since I have written to thee. Dost thou love me at all? I should have been reprehensible in not writing, the last time Mr. and Mrs. Ripley went to town; but I had an indispensable engagement in the bean-field — whither indeed I was glad to betake myself, in order to escape a parting scene with poor Mr. Farley. He was quite out of his wits, the night before, and thy husband sat up with him till long past midnight. The farm is pleasanter now that he is gone; for his unappeasable wretchedness threw a gloom over everything. Since I last wrote to thee, we have done haying; and the remainder of my bondage will probably be light. It will be a long time, however, before I shall know how to make a good use of leisure, either as regards enjoyment or literary occupation. . . .

Dearest wife, it is extremely doubtful whether Mr. Ripley will succeed in locating his community on this farm. He can bring Mr. Ellis to no terms; and the more they talk about the matter, the farther they appear to be from a settlement. Thou and I must form other plans for ourselves; for I can see few or no signs that Providence purposes to give us a home here. I am weary, weary, thrice weary of waiting so many ages. Yet what can be done? Whatever may be thy husband's gifts, he has not hitherto shown a single one that may avail to gather gold. I confess that I have strong hopes of good from this arrangement with Monroe; but when I look at the scanty avails of my past literary efforts, I do not feel authorized to expect much from the future. Well; we shall see. Other persons have bought large estates and built splendid mansions with such little books as I mean to write; so that it is perhaps not unreasonable to hope that mine may enable me to build a little cottage — or, at least, to buy or hire one. But I am becoming more and more convinced that we must not lean upon the community. Whatever is to be done must be done by thy husband's own undivided strength. Most beloved, I shall not remain here through the winter, unless with an absolute certainty that there will be a house ready for us in the spring. Otherwise, I shall return to Boston — still, however, considering myself an associate of the community, so that we may take advantage of any more favorable aspect of affairs. Dearest, how much depends on these little books! Methinks, if any thing could draw out my whole strength, it would be the motives that now press upon me. Yet, after all, I must keep these considerations out of my mind, because an external pressure always disturbs instead of assisting me. . . .

*Salem,* Sep. 3d, 1841 — 4 o'clock P.M.

. . . Dearest, I have been out only once, in the day time, since my arrival. How immediately and irrevocably (if thou didst not keep me out of the abyss) should I relapse into the way of life in which I spent my youth! Were it not for my Dove, this present world would see no more of me forever. The sunshine would never fall on me, no more than on a ghost. Once in a while, people might discern my figure gliding stealthily through the dim evening — that would be all. I should be only a shadow of the night; it is thou that givest me reality, and makest all things real for me. If, in the interval since I quitted this lonely old chamber, I had found no woman (and thou wast the only possible one) to impart reality and significance to life, I should have come back hither ere now, with the feeling that all was a dream and a mockery. Dost thou rejoice that thou hast saved me from such a fate? Yes; it is a miracle worthy even of thee, to have converted a life of shadows into the deepest truth, by thy magic touch. . . .

*Brook Farm,* Septr. 29th, 1841 — A.M.

. . . Dearest love, thy husband was elected to two high offices, last night, viz., to be a Trustee of the Brook Farm estate, and Chairman of the Committee on Finance! ! ! ! Now dost thou not blush to have formed so much lower an opinion of my business talents, than is entertained by other discerning people? From the nature of my office, I shall have the chief direction of all the money affairs of the community — the making of bargains — the supervision of receipts and expenditures, &c. &c. &c. Thou didst not think of this, when thou didst pronounce me unfit to make a bargain with that petty knave of a publisher. A prophet has no honor among those of his own kindred, nor a financier in the judgment of his wife.

Belovedest, my accession to these august offices does not at all decide the question of my remaining here permanently. I told Mr. Ripley, that I could not spend the winter at the farm, and that it was quite uncertain whether I returned in the spring. . . .

*Brook Farm,* October 21st, 1841
—Noon

. . . What atrocious weather! In all this month, we have not had a single truly October day; it has been a real November month, and of the most disagreeable kind. I came to this place in one snowstorm, and shall probably leave it in another; so that my reminiscences of Brook Farm are like to be the coldest and dreariest imaginable. . . .

1907

# HERMAN MELVILLE
## (1819–1891)

### *TYPEE: A PEEP AT POLYNESIAN LIFE*

*From* CHAPTER XVIII

### SWIMMING IN COMPANY WITH THE GIRLS OF THE VALLEY

Returning health and peace of mind gave a new interest to everything around me. I sought to diversify my time by as many enjoyments as lay within my reach. Bathing in company with troops of girls, formed one of my chief amusements. We sometimes enjoyed the recreation in the waters of a miniature lake, into which the central stream of the valley expanded. This lovely sheet of water was almost circular in figure, and about three hundred yards across. Its beauty was indescribable. All around its banks waved luxuriant masses of tropical foliage, soaring high above which were seen, here and there, the symmetrical shaft of the cocoa-nut tree, surmounted by its tuft of graceful branches, drooping in the air like so many waving ostrich plumes.

The ease and grace with which the maidens of the valley propelled themselves through the water, and their familiarity with the element, were truly astonishing. Sometimes they might be seen gliding along, just under the surface, without apparently moving hand or foot—then throwing themselves on their sides, they darted through the water, revealing glimpses of their forms, as, in the course of their rapid progress, they shot for an instant partly into the air—at one moment they dived deep down into the water and the next they rose bounding to the surface.

I remember upon one occasion plunging in among a parcel of these river-nymphs, and counting vainly on my superior strength, sought to drag some of them under the water, but I quickly repented my temerity. The amphibious young creatures swarmed about me like a shoal of dolphins, and seizing hold of my devoted limbs, tumbled me about and ducked me under the surface, until from the strange noises which rang in my ears, and the supernatural visions dancing before my eyes, I thought I was in the land of spirits. I stood indeed as little chance among them as a cumbrous whale attacked on all sides by a legion of sword-fish. When at length they relinquished their hold of me, they swam away in every direction, laughing at my clumsy endeavours to reach them.

There was no boat on the lake; but at my solicitation and for my special use, some of the young men attached to Marheyo's household, under the direction of the indefatigable Kory-Kory, brought up a light and tastefully-carved canoe from the sea. It was launched upon the sheet of water, and floated there as gracefully as a swan. But, melancholy to relate, it produced an effect I had not anticipated. The sweet nymphs, who had sported with me before in the lake, now all fled its vicinity. The prohibited craft, guarded by the edicts of the "taboo," extended the prohibition to the waters in which it lay.

For a few days, Kory-Kory, with one or two other youths, accompanied me in my excursions to the lake, and while I paddled about in my light canoe, would swim after me shouting and gambolling in pursuit. But I was ever partial to what is termed in 'The Young Man's Own Book'—"the society of virtuous and intelligent young ladies;" and in the absence of the mermaids, the amusement became dull and insipid. One morning I expressed to my faithful servitor my desire for the return of the nymphs. The honest fellow looked at me bewildered for a moment, and then shook his head solemnly, and murmured "*taboo! taboo!*" giving me to understand that unless the canoe was removed, I could not expect to have the young ladies back again. But to this procedure I was averse; I not only wanted the canoe to stay where it was, but I wanted the beauteous Fayaway to get into it, and paddle with me about the lake. This latter proposition completely horrified Kory-Kory's notions of propriety. He inveighed against it, as something too monstrous to be thought of. It not only shocked their established notions of propriety, but was at variance with all their religious ordinances.

However, although the "taboo" was a ticklish thing to meddle with, I determined to test its capabilities of resisting an attack. I consulted the chief Mehevi, who endeavoured to persuade me from my object: but I was not to be repulsed; and accordingly increased the warmth of my solicitations. At last he entered into a long, and I have no doubt a very learned and eloquent exposition of the history and nature of the "taboo" as affecting this particular case; employing a variety of most extraordinary words, which, from their amazing length and sonorousness, I have every reason to believe were of a theological nature. But all that he said failed to convince me: partly, perhaps, because I could not comprehend a word that he uttered; but chiefly, that for the life of me, I could not understand why a woman should not have as much right to enter a canoe as a man. At last he became a little more rational, and intimated that, out of the abundant love he bore me, he would consult with the priests and see what could be done.

How it was that the priesthood of Typee satisfied the affair with their consciences, I know not; but so it was, and Fayaway's dispensation from this portion of the taboo was at length procured. Such an event, I believe, never before had occurred in the valley; but it was high time the islanders should be taught a little gallantry, and I trust that the example I set them may produce beneficial effects. Ridiculous, indeed, that the lovely creatures should be obliged to paddle about in the water, like so many ducks, while a parcel of great strapping fellows skimmed over its surface in their canoes.

The first day after Fayaway's emancipation I had a delightful little party on the lake—the damsel, Kory-Kory, and myself. My zealous body-servant brought from the house a calabash of poe-poe, half a dozen young cocoa-nuts—stripped of their husks—three pipes, as many yams, and me on his back a part of the way. Something of a load; but Kory-Kory was a very strong man for his size, and by no means brittle in the spine. We had a very pleasant day; my trusty valet plied the paddle and swept us gently along the margin of the water, beneath the shades of the overhanging thickets. Fayaway and I reclined in the stern of the canoe, on the very best possible terms with one another; the gentle nymph occasionally placing her pipe to her lip, and exhaling the mild fumes of the tobacco, to which her rosy breath added a fresh perfume. Strange as it may seem, there is nothing in which a young and beautiful female appears to more advantage than in the act of smoking. How captivating is a Peruvian lady, swinging in her gaily-woven hammock of grass, extended between two orange-trees, and inhaling the fragrance of a choice cigarro! But Fayaway, holding in her delicately-formed olive hand the long yellow reed of her pipe, with its quaintly carved bowl, and every few moments languishingly giving forth light wreaths of vapour from her mouth and nostrils, looked still more engaging.

We floated about thus for several hours, when I looked up to the warm, glowing, tropical sky, and then down into the transparent depths below; and when my eye, wandering from the bewitching scenery around, fell upon the grotesquely-tattooed form of Kory-Kory, and finally encountered the pensive gaze of Fayaway, I thought I had been transported to some fairy region, so unreal did everything appear.

This lovely piece of water was the coolest spot in all the valley, and I now made it a place of continual resort during the hottest period of the day. One side of it lay near the termination of a long gradually expanding gorge, which mounted to the heights that environed the vale. The strong trade wind, met in its course by these elevations, circled and eddied about their summits, and was sometimes driven down the steep ravine and swept across the valley, ruffling in its passage the otherwise tranquil surface of the lake.

One day, after we had been paddling about for some time, I disembarked Kory-Kory, and paddled the canoe to the windward side of the lake. As I turned the canoe, Fayaway, who was with me, seemed all at once to be struck with some happy idea. With a wild exclamation of delight, she disengaged from her person the ample robe of tappa which was knotted over her shoulder (for the purpose of shielding her from the sun), and spreading it out like a sail, stood erect with upraised arms in the head of the canoe. We American sailors pride ourselves upon our straight clean spars, but a prettier little mast than Fayaway made was never shipped a-board of any craft.

In a moment the tappa was distended by the breeze—the long brown tresses of Fayaway streamed in the air—and the canoe glided rapidly through the water, and shot towards the shore. Seated in the stern, I directed its course with my paddle until it dashed up the soft sloping bank, and Fayaway, with a light spring, alighted on the ground; whilst Kory-Kory, who had watched our manœuvres with admiration, now clapped his hands in transport, and shouted like a madman. Many a time afterwards was this feat repeated. * * *

*From* CHAPTER XXXII

## FRIGHTFUL DISCOVERIES

* * * I have already mentioned that from the ridge-pole of Marheyo's house were suspended a number of packages enveloped in tappa. Many of these I had often seen in the hands of the natives, and their contents had been examined in my presence. But there were three packages hanging very nearly over the place where I lay, which from their remarkable appearance had often excited my curiosity. Several times I had asked Kory-Kory to show me their contents; but my servitor, who in almost every other particular had acceded to my wishes, always refused to gratify me in this.

One day, returning unexpectedly from the "Ti," my arrival seemed to throw the inmates of the house into the greatest confusion. They were seated together on the mats, and by the lines which extended from the roof to the floor I immediately perceived that the mysterious packages were for some purpose or other under inspection. The evident alarm the savages betrayed filled me with forebodings of evil, and with an uncontrollable desire to penetrate the secret so jealously guarded. Despite the efforts of Marheyo and Kory-Kory to restrain me, I forced my way into the midst of the circle, and just caught a glimpse of three human heads, which others of the party were hurriedly enveloping in the coverings from which they had been taken.

One of the three I distinctly saw. It was in a state of perfect preservation, and, from the slight glimpse I had of it, seemed to have been subjected to some smoking operation which had reduced it to the dry, hard, and mummy-like appearance it presented. The two long scalp-locks were twisted up into balls upon the crown of the head, in the same way that the individual had worn them during life. The sunken cheeks were rendered yet more ghastly by the rows of glistening teeth which protruded from between the lips, while the sockets of the eyes—filled with oval bits of mother-of-pearl shell, with a black spot in the centre—heightened the hideousness of its aspect.

Two of the three were heads of the islanders; but the third, to my horror, was that of a white man. Although it had been quickly removed from my sight, still the glimpse I had of it was enough to convince me that I could not be mistaken.

Gracious God! what dreadful thoughts entered my mind! In solving this mystery perhaps I had solved another, and the fate of my lost companion might be revealed in the shocking spectacle I had just witnessed. I longed to have torn off the folds of cloth, and satisfied the awful doubts under which I laboured. But before I had recovered from the consternation into which I had been thrown, the fatal packages were hoisted aloft and once more swung over my head.

The natives now gathered round me tumultuously, and laboured to convince me that what I had just seen were the heads of three Happar warriors, who had been slain in battle. This glaring falsehood added to my alarm, and it was not until I reflected that I had observed the packages swinging from their elevation before Toby's disappearance, that I could at all recover my composure.

But although this horrible apprehension had been dispelled, I had discovered enough to fill me, in my present state of mind, with the most bitter reflections. It was plain that I had seen the last relic of some unfortunate wretch, who must have been massacred on the beach by the savages, in one of those perilous trading adventures which I have before described.

It was not, however, alone the murder of the stranger that overcame me with gloom. I shuddered at the idea of the subsequent fate his inanimate body might have met with. Was the same doom reserved for me? Was I destined to perish like him—like him, perhaps, to be devoured, and my head to be preserved as a fearful memento of the event? My imagination ran riot in these horried speculations, and I felt certain that the worst possible evils would befal me. But whatever were my misgivings, I studiously concealed them from the islanders, as well as the full extent of the discovery I had made. * * *

The next morning, shortly after sunrise, the same thundering sounds which had awakened me from sleep on the second day of the Feast of Calabashes, assured me that the savages were on the eve of celebrating another, and, as I fully believed, a horrible solemnity.

All the inmates of the house, with the exception of Marheyo, his son, and Tinor, after assuming their gala dresses, departed in the direction of the Taboo Groves.

Although I did not anticipate a compliance with my request, still, with a view of testing the truth of my suspicions, I proposed to Kory-Kory that, according to our usual custom in the morning, we should take a stroll to the Ti: he positively refused; and when I renewed the request, he evinced his determination to prevent my going there; and, to divert my mind from the subject, he offered to accompany me to the stream. We accordingly went, and bathed. On our coming back to the house, I was surprised to find that all its inmates had returned, and were lounging upon the mats as usual, although the drums still sounded from the groves.

The rest of the day I spent with Kory-Kory and Fayaway, wandering about a part of the valley situated in an opposite direction from the Ti, and whenever I so much as looked towards that building, although it was hidden from view by intervening trees, and at the distance of more than a mile, my attendant would exclaim, "taboo, taboo!"

At the various houses where we stopped, I found many of the inhabitants reclining at their ease, or pursuing some light occupation, as if nothing unusual were going forward; but amongst them all I did not perceive a single chief or warrior. When I asked several of the people why they were not at the "Hoolah Hoolah" (the feast), they uniformly answered the question in a manner which implied that it was not intended for them, but for Mehevi, Narmonee, Mow Mow, Kolor, Womonoo, Kalow—running over in their desire to make me comprehend their meaning, the names of all the principal chiefs.

Everything, in short, strengthened my suspicions with regard to the nature of the festival they were now celebrating; and which amounted almost to a certainty. While in Nukuheva I had frequently been informed that the whole tribe were never present at these cannibal banquets, but the chiefs and priests only; and everything I now observed agreed with the account.

The sound of the drums continued, without intermission, the whole day, and falling continually upon my ear, caused me a sensation of horror which I am unable to describe. On the following day hearing none of those noisy indications of revelry, I concluded that the inhuman feast was terminated; and feeling a kind of morbid curiosity to discover whether the Ti might furnish any evidence of what had taken place there, I proposed to Kory-Kory to walk there. To this proposition he replied by pointing with his finger to the newly risen sun, and then up to the zenith, intimating that our visit must be deferred until noon. Shortly after that hour we accordingly proceeded to the Taboo Groves, and as soon as we entered their precincts, I looked fearfully round in quest of some memorial of the scene which had so lately been acted there; but everything appeared as usual. On reaching the Ti, we found Mehevi and a few chiefs reclining on the mats, who gave me as friendly a reception as ever. No allusions of any kind were made by them to the recent events; and I refrained, for obvious reasons, from referring to them myself.

After staying a short time, I took my leave. In passing along the piazza, previously to descending from the pi-pi, I observed a curiously carved vessel of wood, of considerable size, with a cover placed over it, of the same material, and which resembled in shape a small canoe. It was surrounded by a low railing of bamboos, the top of which was scarcely a foot from the ground. As the vessel had been placed in its present position since my last visit, I at once concluded that it must have some connexion with the recent festival; and, prompted by a curiosity I could not repress, in passing it I raised one end of the cover; at the same moment the chiefs, perceiving my design, loudly ejaculated, "Taboo! taboo!" But the slight glimpse sufficed; my eyes fell upon the disordered members of a human skeleton, the bones still fresh with moisture, and with particles of flesh clinging to them here and there!

Kory-Kory, who had been a little in advance of me, attracted by the exclamations of the chiefs, turned round in time to witness the expression of horror on my countenance. He now hurried towards me, pointing at the same time to the canoe, and exclaiming, rapidly, "Puarkee! puarkee!" (Pig, pig.) I pretended to yield to the deception, and repeated the words after him several times, as though acquiescing in what he said. The other savages, either deceived by my conduct, or unwilling to manifest their displeasure at what could not now be remedied, took no further notice of the occurrence, and I immediately left the Ti.

All that night I lay awake, revolving in my mind the fearful situation in which I was placed. The last horrid revelation had now been made, and the full sense of my condition rushed upon my mind with a force I had never before experienced.

Where, thought I, desponding, is there the slightest prospect of escape? The only person who seemed to possess the ability to assist me was the stranger, Marnoo; but would he ever return to the valley? and if he did, should I be permitted to hold any communication with him? It seemed as if I were cut off from every source of hope, and that nothing remained but passively to await whatever fate was in store for me. A thousand times I endeavoured to account for the mysterious conduct of the natives. For what conceivable purpose did they thus retain me a captive? What could be their object in treating me with such apparent kindness, and did it not cover some treacherous scheme? Or, if they had no other design than to hold me a prisoner, how should I be able to pass away my days in this narrow valley, deprived of all intercourse with civilized beings, and for ever separated from friends and home?

One only hope remained to me. The French could not long defer a visit to the bay, and if they should permanently locate any of their troops in the valley, the savages could not for any length of time conceal my existence from them. But what reason had I to suppose that I should be spared until such an event occurred—an event which might be postponed by a hundred different contingencies?

1846

## *MARDI: AND A VOYAGE THITHER*

### CHAPTER CXII

### THEY MEET THE PILGRIMS AT THE TEMPLE OF ORO

Deep, deep, in deep groves, we found the great temple of Oro, Spreader-of-the-Sky, and deity supreme.

While here we silently stood eyeing this Mardi-renowned image, there entered the fane a great multitude of its attendants, holding pearl-shells on their heads, filled with a burning incense. And ranging themselves in a crowd round Oro, they began a long-rolling chant, a sea of sounds; and the thick smoke of their incense went up to the roof.

And now approached Pani and the pilgrims; followed at a distance by the wilful boy.

"Behold great Oro," said the guide.

"We see naught but a cloud," said the chief Divino.

"My ears are stunned by the chanting," said the blind pilgrim.

"Receive more gifts, oh guide!" said Fanna the matron.

"Oh, Oro! invisible Oro! I kneel," slow murmured the sad-eyed maid.

But now a current of air swept aside the eddying incense; and the wilful boy, all eagerness to behold the image, went hither and thither; but the gathering of attendants was great; and at last he exclaimed, "Oh Oro! I cannot see thee, for the crowd that stands between thee and me."

"Who is this babbler?" cried they with the censers, one and all turning upon the pilgrim; "let him speak no more; but bow down, and grind the dust where he stands; and declare himself the vilest creature that crawls. So Oro and Alma command."

"I feel nothing in me so utterly vile," said the boy, "and I cringe to none. But I would as lief *adore* your image, as that in my heart, for both mean the same; but more, how can I? I love great Oro, though I comprehend him not. I marvel at his works, and feel as nothing in his sight; but because he is thus omnipotent, and I a mortal, it follows not that I am vile. Nor so doth he regard me. We do ourselves degrade ourselves, not Oro us. Hath not Oro made me? And therefore am I not worthy to stand erect before him? Oro is almighty but no despot. I wonder; I hope; I love; I weep; I have in me a feeling nigh to fear, that is not fear; but wholly vile I am not; nor can we love and cringe. But Oro knows my heart, which I cannot speak."

"Impious boy," cried they with the censers, "we will offer thee up, before the very image thou contemnest. In the name of Alma, seize him." And they bore him away unresisting.

"Thus perish the ungodly," said Pani to the shuddering pilgrims.

And they quitted the temple, to journey towards the Peak of Ofo.

"My soul bursts!" cried Yoomy. "My lord, my lord, let us save the boy."

"Speak not," said Media. "His fate is fixed. Let Mardi stand."

"Then let us away from hence, my lord; and join the pilgrims; for, in these inland vales, the lost one may be found, perhaps at the very base of Ofo."

"Not there; not there," cried Babbalanja; "Yillah may have touched these shores; but long since she must have fled."

## CHAPTER CXIII

## THEY DISCOURSE OF ALMA

Sailing to and fro in the lake, to view its scenery, much discourse took place concerning the things we had seen; and far removed from the censer-bearers, the sad fate that awaited the boy was now the theme of all.

A good deal was then said of Alma, to whom the guide, the pilgrims, and the censer-bearers had frequently alluded, as to some paramount authority.

Called upon to reveal what his chronicles said on this theme, Braid-Beard complied; at great length narrating what now follows condensed.

Alma, it seems, was an illustrious prophet, and teacher divine; who, ages ago, at long intervals, and in various islands, had appeared to the Mardians under the different titles of Brami, Manko, and Alma. Many thousands of moons had elapsed since his last and most memorable avatar, as Alma on the isle of Maramma. Each of his advents had taken place in a comparatively dark and benighted age. Hence, it was devoutly believed, that he came to redeem the Mardians from their heathenish thrall; to instruct them in the ways of truth, virtue, and happiness; to allure them to good by promises of beatitude hereafter; and to restrain them from evil by denunciations of woe. Separated from the impurities and corruptions which in a long series of centuries had become attached to every thing originally uttered by the prophet, the maxims, which as Brami he had taught, seemed similar to those inculcated by Manko. But as Alma, adapting his lessons to the improved condition of humanity, the divine prophet had more completely unfolded his scheme; as Alma, he had made his last revelation.

This narration concluded, Babbalanja mildly observed, "Mohi, without seeking to accuse you of uttering falsehoods, since what you relate rests not upon testimony of your own; permit me to question the fidelity of your account of Alma. The prophet came to dissipate errors, you say; but superadded to many that have survived the past, ten thousand others have originated in various constructions of the principles of Alma himself. The prophet came to do away with all gods but one; but since the days of Alma, the idols of Maramma have more than quadrupled. The prophet came to make us Mardians more virtuous and happy; but along with all previous good, the same wars, crimes, and miseries, which existed in Alma's day, under various modifications, are yet extant. Nay: take from your chronicles, Mohi, the history of those horrors, one way or other, resulting from the doings of Alma's nominal followers, and your chronicles would not so frequently make mention of blood. The prophet came to guarantee our eternal felicity; but according to what is held in Maramma, that felicity rests on so hard a proviso, that to a thinking mind, but very few of our sinful race may secure it. For one, then, I wholly reject your Alma; not so much, because of all that is hard to be understood in his histories; as because of obvious and undeniable things all round us; which, to me, seem at war with an unreserved faith in his doctrines as promulgated here in Maramma. Besides; everything in this isle strengthens my incredulity; I never was so thorough a disbeliever as now."

"Let the winds be laid," cried Mohi, "while your rash confession is being made in this sacred lake."

Said Media, "Philosopher, remember the boy, and they that seized him."

"Ah! I do indeed remember him. Poor youth! in his agony, how my heart yearned towards his. But that very prudence which you deny me, my lord, prevented me from saying aught in his behalf. Have you not observed that until now, when we are completely by ourselves, I have refrained from freely discoursing of what we have seen in this island? Trust me, my lord, there is no man that bears more in mind the necessity of being either a believer or a hypocrite in Maramma, and the imminent peril of being honest here, than I, Babbalanja. And have I not reason to be wary, when in my boyhood, my own sire was burnt for his temerity; and in this very isle? Just Oro! it was done in the name of Alma; what wonder, then, that at times I almost hate that sound. And from those flames, they devoutly swore he went to others—horrible fable!"

Said Mohi, "Do you deny, then, the everlasting torments?"

" 'Tis not worth a denial. Nor by

formally denying it, will I run the risk of shaking the faith of thousands, who in that pious belief find infinite consolation for all they suffer in Mardi."

"How?" said Media; "are there those who soothe themselves with the thought of everlasting flames?"

"One would think so, my lord, since they defend that dogma more resolutely than any other. Sooner will they yield you the isles of Paradise than it. And in truth, as liege followers of Alma, they would seem but right in clinging to it as they do; for, according to all one hears in Maramma, the great end of the prophet's mission seems to have been the revealing to us Mardians the existence of horrors, most hard to escape. But better we were all annihilated, than that one man should be damned."

Rejoined Media, "But think you not that possibly Alma may have been misconceived? Are you certain that doctrine is his?"

"I know nothing more than that such is the belief in this land. And in these matters, I know not where else to go for information. But, my lord, had I been living in those days when certain men are said to have been actually possessed by spirits from hell, I had not let slip the opportunity —as our forefathers did—to cross-question them concerning the place they came from."

"Well, well," said Media, "your Alma's faith concerns not me; I am a king, and a demi-god; and leave vulgar torments to the commonality."

"But it concerns me," muttered Mohi; "yet I know not what to think."

"For me," said Yoomy, "I reject it. Could I, I would not believe it. It is at variance with the dictates of my heart; instinctively my heart turns from it, as a thirsty man from gall."

"Hush; say no more," said Mohi; "again we approach the shore."

*From* CHAPTER CXLV

## CHIEFLY OF KING BELLO

* * * Indeed, did the old chronicler Braid-Beard speak truth, there were some tribes in Mardi that accounted this king of Dominora a testy, quarrelsome, rapacious old monarch; the indefatigable breeder of contentions and wars; the elder brother of this household of nations, perpetually essaying to lord it over the juveniles; and though his patrimonial dominions were situated to the north of the lagoon, not the slightest misunderstanding took place between the rulers of the most distant islands, than this doughty old cavalier on a throne, forthwith thrust his insolent spear into the matter, though it in no wise concerned him, and fell to irritating all parties by his gratuitous interference.

Especially was he officious in the concerns of Porpheero, a neighbouring island, very large and famous, whose numerous broad valleys were divided among many rival kings—the king of Franko, a small-framed, poodle-haired, fine fiery gallant; finical in his tattooing; much given to the dance and glory;—the king of Ibeereea, a tall and stately cavalier, proud, generous, punctilious, temperate in wine; one hand for ever on his javelin, the other, in superstitious homage, lifted to his gods; his limbs all over marks of stakes and crosses; —the king of Luzianna, a slender, dark-browed chief; at times wrapped in a moody robe, beneath which he fumbled something, as if it were a dagger; but otherwise a sprightly troubadour, given to serendades and moonlight; —the many chiefs of sunny Latianna; minstrel monarchs, full of song and sentiment; fiercer in love than war; glorious bards of freedom; but rendering tribute while they sang;—the priest-king of Vatikanna; his chest marked over with antique tattooings; his crown, a cowl; his rusted scepter swaying over falling towers, and crumbling mounds; full of the superstitious past; askance, eyeing the suspicious time to come;—the king of Hapzaboro; portly pleasant; a lover of wild boar's meat; a frequent quaffer from the can; in his better moods, much fancying solid comfort;—the eight-and-thirty banded kings, chieftains, seigniors, and oligarchies of the broad hill and dale of Tutoni; clubbing together their domains that one might wrest his neighbor's; an earnest race; deep thinkers, deeper drinkers; long pipes, long heads; their wise ones given to mystic cogitations, and consultations with the devil;—the twin kings of Zandinavia; hardy, frugal mountaineers; upright of spine and heart; clad in skins of bears;—the king of Jutlanda; much like their Highnesses of Zandinavia; a sealskin cap his crown; a fearless sailor of his frigid seas;—the king of Muzkovi; a shaggy, icicled White-bear of a despot in the north; said to reign over millions of acres of glaciers; had vast provinces of snow-drifts, and many flourishing colonies among the floating icebergs. Absolute in his rule as Predestination in metaphysics, did he command all his people to give up the ghost, it would be held treason to die last. Very precise and foppish in his imperial tastes was this monarch. Disgusted with the want of uniformity in the stature of his subjects, he was said to nourish thoughts of killing off all those below his prescribed standard—six feet, long measure. Immortal souls were of no account in his fatal wars; since, in some of his serf-breeding estates, they were daily manufactured to order.

Now, to all the above-mentioned monarchs, old Bello would frequently dispatch heralds; announcing, for example, his unalterable resolution, to espouse the cause of this king against that; at the very time, perhaps, that their Serene Superfluities, instead of crossing spears, were touching flagons. And upon these occasions, the kings would often send back word to old Bello that instead of troubling himself with their concerns, he might far better attend to his own; which, they hinted, were in a sad way, and much needed reform.

The royal old warrior's pretext for these and all similar proceedings was the proper adjustment in Porpheero, of what he facetiously styled the "Equipoise of Calabashes;" which he stoutly swore was essential to the security of the various tribes in that country.

"But who put the balance into thy hands, King Bello?" cried the indignant nations.

"Oro!" shouted the hump-backed king, shaking his javelin.

Superadded to the paternal interest which Bello betrayed in the concerns of the kings of Porpheero, according to our chronicler, he also manifested no less interest in those of the remotest islands. Indeed, where he found a rich country, inhabited by a people deemed by him barbarous and incapable of wise legislation, he sometimes relieved them from their political anxieties, by assuming the dictatorship over them. And if incensed at his conduct, they flew to their spears, they were accounted rebels, and treated accordingly. But as old Mohi very truly observed, herein Bello was not alone; for throughout Mardi, all strong nations, as well as all strong men, loved to govern the weak. And those who most taunted King Bello for his political rapacity, were open to the very same charge. So with Vivenza, a distant island, at times very loud in denunciations of Bello, as a great national brigand. Not yet wholly extinct in Vivenza were its aboriginal people, a race of wild Nimrods and hunters, who year by year were driven further and further into remoteness, till as one of their sad warriors said, after continual removes along the log, his race was on the point of being remorselessly pushed off the end.

Now, Bello was a great geographer, and land surveyor, and gauger of the seas. Terraqueous Mardi, he was continually exploring in quest of strange empires. Much he loved to take the altitude of lofty mountains, the depth of deep rivers, the breadth of broad isles. Upon the highest pinnacles of commanding capes and promontories, he loved to hoist his flag. He circled Mardi with his watch-towers; and the distant voyager passing wild rocks in the remotest waters, was startled by hearing the tattoo, or the reveille, beating from hump-backed Bello's omnipresent drum. Among Antarctic glaciers his shrill bugle calls mingled with the scream of the gulls; and so impressed seemed universal nature with the sense of his dominion, that the very clouds in heaven never sailed over Dominora without rendering the tribute of a shower; whence the air of Dominora was more moist than that of any other clime.

In all his grand undertakings, King Bello was marvellously assisted by his numerous fleets of war-canoes; his navy being the largest in Mardi. Hence his logicians swore that the entire Lagoon was his; and that all prowling whales, prowling keels, and prowling sharks were invaders. And with this fine conceit to inspire them, his poets-laureat composed some glorious old salt-water odes, enough to make your very soul sing to hear them.

But though the rest of Mardi much delighted to list to such noble minstrelsy, they agreed not with Bello's poets in deeming the lagoon their old monarch's hereditary domain. * * *

## CHAPTER CLVIII

## THEY VISIT THE GREAT CENTRAL TEMPLE OF VIVENZA

The throng that greeted us upon landing were exceedingly boisterous.

"Whence came ye?" they cried. "Whither bound? Saw ye ever such a land as this? Is it not a great and extensive republic? Pray, observe how tall we are; just feel of our thighs; are we not a glorious people? Here, feel of our beards. Look round; look round; be not afraid. Behold those palms; swear now, that this land surpasses all others. Old

Bello's mountains are mole-hills to ours; his rivers, rills; his empires, villages; his palm-trees, shrubs."

"True," said Babbalanja. "But great Oro must have had some hand in making your mountains and streams. Would ye have been as great in a desert?"

"Where is your king?" asked Media, drawing himself up in his robe, and cocking his crown.

"Ha, ha, my fine fellow! We are all kings here; royalty breathes in the common air. But come on, come on. Let us show you our great Temple of Freedom."

And so saying, irreverently grasping his sacred arm, they conducted us toward a lofty structure, planted upon a bold hill, and supported by thirty pillars of palm; four quite green; as if recently added; and beyond these, an almost interminable vacancy, as if the palms in Mardi were, at some future time, to aid in upholding that fabric.

Upon the summit of the temple was a staff; and as we drew nigh, a man with a collar round his neck, and the red marks of stripes upon his back, was just in the act of hoisting a tappa standard—correspondingly striped. Other collared menials were going in and out of the temple.

Near the porch, stood an image like that on the top of the arch we had seen. Upon its pedestal, were pasted certain hieroglyphical notices; according to Mohi, offering rewards for missing men, so many hands high.

Entering the temple, we beheld an amphitheatrical space, in the middle of which, a great fire was burning. Around it, were many chiefs, robed in long togas, and presenting strange contrasts in their style of tattooing.

Some were sociably laughing, and chatting; others diligently making excavations between their teeth with slivers of bamboo; or turning their heads into mills, were grinding up leaves and ejecting their juices. Some were busily inserting the down of a thistle into their ears. Several stood erect, intent upon maintaining striking attitudes; their javelins tragically crossed upon their chests. They would have looked very imposing were it not, that in rear their vesture was sadly disordered. Others, with swelling fronts, seemed chiefly indebted to their dinners for their dignity. Many were nodding and napping. And, here and there, were sundry indefatigable worthies, making a great show of imperious and indispensable business; sedulously folding banana leaves into scrolls, and recklessly placing them into the hands of little boys, in gay turbans and trim little girdles; who thereupon fled as if with salvation for the dying.

It was a crowded scene; the dusky chiefs here and there, grouped together, and their fantastic tattooings showing like the carved work on quaint old chimney-stacks seen from afar. But one of their number overtopped all the rest. As when, drawing nigh unto old Rome, amid the crowd of sculptured columns and gables, St. Peter's grand dome soars far aloft, serene in the upper air; so, showed one calm grand forehead among those of this mob of chieftains. That head was Saturnina's. Gall and Spurzheim! saw you ever such a brow?—poised like an avalanche, under the shadow of a forest! woe betide the devoted valleys below! Lavater!

behold those lips, like mystic scrolls! Those eyes, like panthers' caves at the base of Popocatepetl!

"By my right hand, Saturnina!" cried Babbalanja, "but thou wert made in the image of thy Maker! Yet, have I beheld men, to the eye as commanding as thou; and surmounted by heads globe-like as thine, who never had thy caliber. We must measure brains, not heads, my lord; else, the sperm-whale, with his tun of an occiput, would transcend us all."

Near by, were arched ways, leading to subterranean places, whence issued a savoury steam, and an extraordinary clattering of calabashes, and smacking of lips, as if something were being eaten down there by the fattest of fat fellows, with the heartiest of appetites, and the most irresistible of relishes. It was a quaffing, guzzling, gobbling noise. Peeping down, we beheld a company, breasted up against a board, groaning under numerous viands. In the middle of all, was a mighty great gourd, yellow as gold, and jolly round like a pumpkin in October, and so big it must have grown in the sun. Thence flowed a tide of red wine. And before it, stood plenty of paunches being filled therewith like portly stone jars at a fountain. Melancholy to tell, before that fine flood of old wine, and among those portly old topers, was a lean man; who occasionally ducked in his bill. He looked like an ibis standing in the Nile at flood tide; among a tongue-lapping herd of hippopotami.

They were jolly as the jolliest; and laughed so uproariously, that their hemispheres all quivered and shook, like vast provinces in an earthquake. Ha! ha! ha! how they laughed, and they roared. A deaf man might have heard them; and no milk could have soured within a forty-two-pounder ball shot of that place.

Now; the smell of good things is no very bad thing in itself. It is the savor of good things beyond; proof positive of a glorious good meal. So snuffing up those zephyrs from Araby the blest, those boisterous gales, blowing from out the mouths of baked boars, stuffed with bread-fruit, bananas, and sage, we would fain have gone down and partaken.

But this could not be; for we were told that those worthies below were a club in secret conclave; very busy in settling certain weighty state affairs upon a solid basis. They were all chiefs of immense capacity—how many gallons, there was no finding out.

Be sure, now, a most riotous noise came up from those catacombs, which seemed full of the ghosts of fat Lamberts; and this uproar it was, that heightened the din above-ground.

But, heedless of all, in the midst of the amphitheater, stood a tall, gaunt warrior, ferociously tattooed, with a beak like a buzzard; long dusty locks, and his hands full of headless arrows. He was laboring under violent paroxysms; three benevolent individuals essaying to hold him. But repeatedly breaking loose, he burst anew into his delirium; while with an absence of sympathy, distressing to behold, the rest of the assembly seemed wholly engrossed with themselves; nor did they appear to care how soon the unfortunate lunatic might demolish himself by his frantic proceedings.

Toward one side of the amphitheatrical space, perched high upon an elevated dais, sat a white-headed old man with a tomahawk in his hand, earnestly engaged in overseeing the tumult, though not a word did he say. Occasionally, however, he was regarded by those present with a mysterious sort of deference; and when they chanced to pass between him and the crazy man, they invariably did so in a stooping position; probably to elude the atmospheric grape and canister continually flying from the mouth of the lunatic.

"What mob is this?" cried Media.

" 'Tis the grand council of Vivenza," cried a bystander. "Hear ye not Alanno?" and he pointed to the lunatic.

Now coming close to Alanno, we found, that with incredible volubility, he was addressing the assembly upon some all-absorbing subject connected with King Bello, and his presumed encroachments towards the northwest of Vivenza.

One hand smiting his hip, and the other his head, the lunatic thus proceeded; roaring like a wild beast, and beating the air like a windmill:—

"I have said it! the thunder is flashing, the lightning is crashing! already there's an earthquake in Dominora! Full soon will old Bello discover that his diabolical machinations against this ineffable land must soon come to naught. Who dare not declare, that we are not invincible? I repeat it, we are. Ha! ha! Audacious Bello must bite the dust! Hair by hair, we will trail his gory gray beard at the end of our spears! Ha! ha! I grow hoarse, but would mine were a voice like the wild bulls of Bullorom, that I might be heard from one end of this great and gorgeous land to its farthest zenith; ay, to the uttermost diameter of its circumference. Awake! oh, Vivenza. The signs of the times are portentous; nay, extraordinary; I hesitate not to add, peculiar! Up! up! Let us not descend to the bathos, when we should soar to the climax! Does not all Mardi wink and look on? Is the great sun itself a frigid spectator? Then let us double up our mandibles to the deadly encounter. Methinks I see it now. Old Bello is crafty, and his oath is recorded to obliterate us! Across this wide lagoon he casts his serpent eyes; whets his insatiable bill; mumbles his barbarous tusks; licks his forked tongues; and who knows when we shall have the shark in our midst? Yet be not deceived; for though as yet Bello has forborne molesting us openly, his emissaries are at work; his infernal sappers, and miners, and wet-nurses and midwives, and gravediggers, are busy! His canoe-yards are all in commotion! In navies his forests are being launched upon the wave; and ere long typhoons, zephyrs, white squalls, balmy breezes, hurricanes, and besoms will be raging round us!"

His philippic concluded, Alanno was conducted from the place; and being now quite exhausted, cold cobblestones were applied to his temples, and he was treated to a bath in a stream.

This chieftain, it seems, was from a distant western valley, called Hio-Hio, one of the largest and most fertile in Vivenza, though but recently settled. Its inhabitants and those of the vales adjoining—a right sturdy set of fellows—were accounted the most dogmatically democratic and ultra of all the tribes in Vivenza; ever seeking to push on their brethren to the uttermost; and especially were they bitter against Bello. But they were a fine young tribe, nevertheless. Like strong new wine they worked violently in becoming clear. Time, perhaps, would make them all right.

An interval of greater uproar than ever now ensued; during which, with his tomahawk, the white-headed old man repeatedly thumped and pounded the seat where he sat, apparently to augment the din, though he looked anxious to suppress it.

At last, tiring of his posture, he whispered in the ear of a chief, his friend; who, approaching a portly warrior present, prevailed upon him to rise and address the assembly. And no sooner did this one do so, than the whole convocation dispersed, as if to their yams; and with a grin, the little old man leaped from his seat, and stretched his legs on a mat.

The fire was now extinguished, and the temple deserted.

1849

## *MOBY DICK; OR, THE WHALE*

### CHAPTER XL

### MIDNIGHT, FORECASTLE

HARPOONEERS AND SAILORS

(*Foresail rises and discovers the watch standing, lounging, leaning, and lying in various attitudes, all singing in chorus.*)

Farewell and adieu to you, Spanish
ladies!
Farewell and adieu to you, ladies of
Spain!
Our captain's commanded.—

1ST NANTUCKET SAILOR

Oh, boys, don't be sentimental; it's bad for the digestion! Take a tonic, follow me!

(*Sings, and all follow.*)

Our captain stood upon the deck,
A spy-glass in his hand,
A viewing of those gallant whales
That blew at every strand.
Oh, your tubs in your boats, my boys,
And by your braces stand,
And we'll have one of those fine whales,
Hand, boys, over hand!
So, be cheery, my lads! may your hearts
never fail!
While the bold harpooneer is striking the
whale!

MATE'S VOICE FROM THE QUARTER-DECK

Eight bells there, forward!

2D NANTUCKET SAILOR

Avast the chorus! Eight bells there! d'ye hear, bell-boy? Strike the bell eight, thou Pip! thou blackling! and let me call the watch. I've the sort of mouth for that—the hogshead mouth. So, so (*thrusts his head down the scuttle*), Star—bo-l-e-e-n-s, a-h-o-y! Eight bells there below! Tumble up!

DUTCH SAILOR

Grand snoozing to-night, maty; fat night for that. I mark this in our old Mogul's wine; it's quite as deadening to some as filliping to others. We sing; they sleep—ay, lie down there, like ground-tier butts. At 'em again! There, take this copper-pump, and hail 'em through it. Tell 'em to avast dreaming of their lasses. Tell 'em it's the resurrection; they must kiss their last, and come to judgment. That's the way—*that's* it; thy throat ain't spoiled with eating Amsterdam butter.

FRENCH SAILOR

Hist, boys! let's have a jig or two before we ride to anchor in Blanket Bay. What say ye? There comes the other watch. Stand by all legs! Pip! little Pip! hurrah with your tambourine!

PIP

(*Sulky and sleepy.*)

Don't know where it is.

FRENCH SAILOR

Beat thy belly, then, and wag thy ears. Jig it, men, I say; merry's the word; hurrah! Damn me, won't you dance? Form, now, Indian-file, and gallop into the double-shuffle! Throw yourselves! Legs! legs!

ICELAND SAILOR

I don't like your floor, maty; it's too springy to my taste. I'm used to ice-floors. I'm sorry to throw cold water on the subject; but excuse me.

MALTESE SAILOR

Me too; where's your girls? Who but a fool would take his left hand by his right, and say to himself, how d'ye do? Partners! I must have partners!

SICILIAN SAILOR

Aye; girls and a green!—then I'll hop with ye; yea, turn grasshopper!

LONG-ISLAND SAILOR

Well, well, ye sulkies, there's plenty more of us. Hoe corn when you may, say I. All legs go to harvest soon. Ah! here comes the music; now for it!

AZORE SAILOR

(*Ascending, and pitching the tambourine up the scuttle.*)

Here you are, Pip; and there's the windlass-bits; up you mount! Now, boys!

(*The half of them dance to the tambourine; some go below; some sleep or lie among the coils of rigging. Oaths a-plenty.*)

AZORE SAILOR

(*Dancing.*)

Go it, Pip! Bang it, bell-boy! Rig it, dig it, stig it, quig it, bell-boy! Make fireflies; break the jinglers!

PIP

Jinglers, you say?—there goes another, dropped off; I pound it so.

CHINA SAILOR

Rattle thy teeth, then, and pound away; make a pagoda of thyself.

FRENCH SAILOR

Merry-mad! Hold up thy hoop, Pip, till I jump through it! Split jibs! tear yourselves!

TASHTEGO

(*Quietly smoking.*)

That's a white man; he calls that fun: humph! I save my sweat.

OLD MANX SAILOR

I wonder whether those jolly lads bethink them of what they are dancing over. I'll dance over your grave, I will—that's the bitterest threat of your night-women, that beat headwinds round corners. O Christ! to think of the green navies and the green-skulled crews! Well, well; belike the whole world's a ball, as you scholars have it; and so 'tis right to make one ball-room of it. Dance on, lads, you're young; I was once.

3D NANTUCKET SAILOR

Spell oh!—whew! this is worse than pulling after whales in a calm—give us a whiff, Tash.

(*They cease dancing, and gather in clusters. Meantime the sky darkens—the wind rises.*)

LASCAR SAILOR

By Brahma! boys, it'll be douse sail soon. The sky-born, high-tide Ganges turned to wind! Thou showest thy black brow, Seeva!

MALTESE SAILOR
(*Reclining and shaking his cap.*)

It's the waves—the snow's caps turn to jig it now. They'll shake their tassels soon. Now would all the waves were women, then I'd go drown, and chassee with them evermore! There's naught so sweet on earth—heaven may not match it!—as those swift glances of warm, wild bosoms in the dance, when the overarboring arms hide such ripe, bursting grapes.

SICILIAN SAILOR
(*Reclining.*)

Tell me not of it! Hark ye, lad—fleet interlacings of the limbs—lithe swayings—coyings—flutterings! lip! heart! hip! all graze: unceasing touch and go! not taste, observe ye, else come satiety. Eh, Pagan? (*Nudging.*)

TAHITAN SAILOR
(*Reclining on a mat.*)

Hail, holy nakedness of our dancing girls!—the Heeva-Heeva! Ah! low veiled, high palmed Tahiti! I still rest me on thy mat, but the soft soil has slid! I saw thee woven in the wood, my mat! green the first day I brought ye thence; now worn and wilted quite. Ah me!—not thou nor I can bear the change! How then, if so be transplanted to yon sky? Hear I the roaring streams from Pirohitee's peak of spears, when they leap down the crags and drown the villages?—The blast! the blast! Up, spine, and meet it! (*Leaps to his feet.*)

PORTUGUESE SAILOR

How the sea rolls swashing 'gainst the side! Stand by for reefing, hearties! the winds are just crossing swords, pell-mell they'll go lunging presently.

DANISH SAILOR

Crack, crack, old ship! so long as thou crackest, thou holdest! Well done! the mate there holds ye to it stiffly. He's no more afraid than the isle fort at Cattegat, put there to fight the Baltic with storm-lashed guns, on which the sea-salt cakes!

4TH NANTUCKET SAILOR

He has his orders, mind ye that. I heard old Ahab tell him he must always kill a squall, something as they burst a waterspout with a pistol—fire your ship right into it!

ENGLISH SAILOR

Blood! but that old man's a grand old cove! We are the lads to hunt him up his whale!

ALL

Aye! aye!

OLD MANX SAILOR

How the three pines shake! Pines are the hardest sort of tree to live when shifted to any other soil, and here there's none but the crew's cursed clay. Steady, helmsman! steady. This is the sort of weather when brave hearts snap ashore, and keeled hulls split at sea. Our captain has his birth-mark; look yonder, boys, there's another in the sky—lurid-like, ye see, all else pitch black.

DAGGOO

What of that? Who's afraid of black's afraid of me! I'm quarried out of it!

SPANISH SAILOR

(*Aside.*) He wants to bully, ah!—the old grudge makes me touchy. (*Advancing.*) Aye, harpooneer, thy race is the undeniable dark side of mankind—devilish dark at that. No offense.

DAGGOO
(*Grimly.*)

None.

ST. JAGO'S SAILOR

That Spaniard's mad or drunk. But that can't be, or else in his one case our old Mogul's fire-waters are somewhat long in working.

5TH NANTUCKET SAILOR

What's that I saw—lightning? Yes.

SPANISH SAILOR

No; Daggoo showing his teeth.

DAGGOO
(*Springing.*)

Swallow thine, manikin! White skin, white liver!

SPANISH SAILOR
(*Meeting him.*)

Knife thee heartily! big frame, small spirit!

ALL

A row! a row! a row!

TASHTEGO
(*With a whiff.*)

A row a'low, and a row aloft—gods and men—both brawlers! Humph!

BELFAST SAILOR

A row! arrah, a row! The Virgin be blessed, a row! Plunge in with ye!

ENGLISH SAILOR

Fair play! Snatch the Spaniard's knife! A ring, a ring!

OLD MANX SAILOR

Ready formed. There! the ringed horizon. In that ring Cain struck Abel. Sweet work, right work! No? Why then, God, mad'st thou the ring?

MATE'S VOICE FROM THE QUARTER-DECK

Hands by the halyards! in top-gallant sails! Stand by to reef topsails!

ALL

The squall! the squall! jump, my jollies! (*They scatter.*)

PIP
(*Shrinking under the windlass.*)

Jollies? Lord help such jollies! Crish, crash! there goes the jib-stay! Blang-whang! God! Duck lower, Pip, here comes the royal yard! It's worse than being in the whirled woods, the last day of the year! Who'd go climbing after chestnuts now? But there they go, all cursing, and here I don't. Fine prospects to 'em; they're on the road to heaven. Hold on hard! Jimmini, what a squall! But those chaps there are worse yet—they are your white squalls, they. White squalls? white whale, shirr! shirr! Here have I heard all their chat just now, and the white whale—shirr! shirr!—but spoken of once! and only this evening—it makes me jingle all over like my tambourine—that anaconda of an old man swore 'em in to hunt him! Oh, thou big white God aloft there somewhere in yon darkness, have mercy on this small black boy down here; preserve him from all men that have no bowels to feel fear!

CHAPTER CXXXIII

## THE CHASE—FIRST DAY

That night, in the mid-watch, when the old man—as his wont at intervals—stepped forth from the scuttle in which he leaned, and went to his pivot-hole, he suddenly thrust out his face fiercely, snuffing up the sea air as a sagacious ship's dog will, in drawing nigh to some barbarous isle. He declared that a whale must be near. Soon that peculiar odor, sometimes to a great distance given forth by the living sperm whale, was palpable to all the watch; nor was any mariner surprised when, after inspecting the compass, and then the dog-vane, and then ascertaining the precise bearing of the odor as nearly as possible, Ahab rapidly ordered the ship's course to be slightly altered, and the sail to be shortened.

The acute policy dictating these movements was sufficiently vindicated at daybreak by the sight of a long sleek on the sea directly and lengthwise ahead, smooth as oil, and resembling in the pleated watery wrinkles bordering it, the polished metallic-like marks of some swift tide-rip, at the mouth of a deep, rapid stream.

"Man the mast-heads! Call all hands!"

Thundering with the butts of three clubbed handspikes on the forecastle deck, Daggoo roused the sleepers with such judgment claps that they seemed to exhale from the scuttle, so instantaneously did they appear with their clothes in their hands.

"What d'ye see?" cried Ahab, flattening his face to the sky.

"Nothing, nothing, sir!" was the sound hailing down in reply.

"T'gallant-sails! stunsails! alow and aloft, and on both sides!"

All sail being set, he now cast loose the life-line, reserved for swaying him to the main-royal mast-head; and in a few moments they were hoisting him thither, when, while but two-thirds of the way aloft, and while peering ahead through the horizontal vacancy between the main-top-sail and top-gallant-sail, he raised a gull-like cry in the air, "There she blows!—there she blows! A hump like a snow-hill! It is Moby Dick!"

Fired by the cry which seemed simultaneousy taken up by the three look-outs, the men on deck rushed to the rigging to behold the famous whale they had so long been pursuing. Ahab had now gained his final perch, some feet above the other look-outs, Tashtego standing just beneath him on the cap of the top-gallant-mast, so that the Indian's head was almost on a level with Ahab's heel. From this height the whale was now seen some mile or so ahead, at every roll of the sea revealing his high sparkling hump, and regularly jetting his silent spout into the air. To the credulous mariners it seemed the same silent spout they had so long ago beheld in the moonlit Atlantic and Indian Oceans.

"And did none of ye see it before?" cried Ahab, hailing the perched men all around him.

"I saw him almost that same instant, sir, that Captain Ahab did, and I cried out," said Tashtego.

"Not the same instant; not the same—no, the doubloon is mine, Fate reserved the doubloon for me. *I* only; none of ye could have raised the White Whale first. There she blows! there she blows!—there she blows! There again!—there again!" he cried, in long-drawn, lingering, methodic tones, attuned to the gradual prolongings of the whale's visible jets. "He's going to sound! In stunsails! Down top-gallant-sails! Stand by three boats. Mr. Starbuck, remember, stay on board, and keep the ship. Helm there! Luff, luff a point! So; steady, man, steady! There go flukes! No, no; only black water! All ready the boats there? Stand by, stand by! Lower me, Mr. Starbuck; lower, lower,—quick, quicker!" and he slid through the air to the deck.

"He is heading straight to leeward, sir," cried Stubb; "right away from us; cannot have seen the ship yet."

"Be dumb, man! Stand by the braces! Hard down the helm!—brace up! Shiver her!—shiver her! So; well that! Boats, boats!"

Soon all the boats but Starbuck's were dropped; all the boat-sails set—all the paddles plying; with rippling swiftness, shooting to leeward; and Ahab heading the onset. A pale, death-glimmer lit up Fedallah's sunken eyes; a hideous motion gnawed his mouth.

Like noiseless nautilus shells, their light prows sped through the sea; but only slowly they neared the foe. As they neared him, the ocean grew still more smooth; seemed drawing a carpet over its waves; seemed a noon-meadow, so serenely it spread. At length the breathless hunter came so nigh his seemingly unsuspecting prey, that his entire dazzling hump was distinctly visible, sliding along the sea as if an isolated thing, and continually set in a revolving ring of finest, fleecy, greenish foam. He saw the vast involved wrinkles of the slightly projecting head beyond. Before it, far out on the soft Turkish-rugged waters, went the glistening white shadow from his broad, milky forehead, a musical rippling playfully accompanying the shade; and behind, the blue waters interchangeably flowed over into the moving valley of his steady wake; and on either hand bright bubbles arose and danced by his side. But these were broken again by the light toes of hundreds of gay fowls softly feathering the sea, alternate with their fitful flight; and like to some flag-staff rising from the painted hull of an argosy, the tall but shattered pole of a recent lance projected from the white whale's back; and at intervals one of the cloud of soft-toed fowls hovering, and to and fro skimming like a canopy over the fish, silently perched and rocked on this pole, the long tail feathers streaming like pennons.

A gentle joyousness—a mighty mildness of repose in swiftness, invested the gliding whale. Not the white bull Jupiter swimming away with ravished Europa clinging to his graceful horns; his lovely, leering eyes sideways intent upon the maid; with smooth bewitching fleetness, rippling straight for the nuptial bower in Crete; not Jove, not that great majesty Supreme! did surpass the glorified White Whale as he so divinely swam.

On each soft side—coincident with the parted swell, that but once laving him, then flowed so wide away—on each bright side, the whale shed off enticings. No wonder there had been some among the hunters who, namelessly transported and allured by all this serenity, had ventured to assail it; but had fatally found that quietude but the vesture of tornadoes. Yet calm, enticing calm, oh, whale! thou glidest on, to all who for the first time eye thee, no matter how many in that same way thou may'st have bejuggled and destroyed before.

And thus, through the serene tranquillities of the tropical sea, among waves whose handclappings were suspended by exceeding rapture, Moby Dick moved on, still withholding from sight the full terrors of his submerged trunk, entirely hiding the wrenched hideousness of his jaw. But soon the fore part of him slowly rose from the water; for an instant his whole marbleized body formed a high arch, like Virginia's Natural Bridge, and warningly waving his bannered flukes in the air, the grand god revealed himself, sounded, and went out of sight. Hoveringly halting, and dipping on the wing, the white seafowls longingly lingered over the agitated pool that he left.

With oars apeak, and paddles down, the sheets of their sails adrift, the three boats now stilly floated, awaiting Moby Dick's reappearance.

"An hour," said Ahab, standing rooted in his boat's stern; and he gazed beyond the whale's place, towards the dim blue spaces and wide wooing vacancies to leeward. It was only an instant; for again his eyes seemed whirling round in his head as he swept the watery circle. The breeze now freshened; the sea began to swell.

"The birds!—the birds!" cried Tashtego.

In long Indian file, as when herons take wing, the white birds were now all flying towards Ahab's boat; and when within a few yards began fluttering over the water there, wheeling round and round, with joyous, expectant cries. Their vision was keener than man's; Ahab could discover no sign in the sea. But suddenly as he peered down and down into its depths, he profoundly saw a white living spot no bigger than a white weasel, with wonderful celerity uprising, and magnifying as it rose, till it turned, and then there were plainly revealed two long crooked rows of white, glistening teeth, floating up from the undiscoverable bottom. It was Moby Dick's open mouth and scrolled jaw; his vast, shadowed bulk still half blending with the blue of the sea. The glittering mouth yawned beneath the boat like an open-doored marble tomb; and giving one sidelong sweep with his steering oar, Ahab whirled the craft aside from this tremendous apparition. Then, calling upon Fedallah to change places with him, went forward to the bows, and seizing Perth's harpoon, commanded his crew to grasp their oars and stand by to stern.

Now, by reason of this timely spinning round the boat upon its axis, its bow, by anticipation, was made to face the whale's head while yet under water. But as if perceiving this stratagem, Moby Dick, with that malicious intelligence ascribed to him, sidelingly transplanted himself, as it were, in an instant, shooting his pleated head lengthwise beneath the boat.

Through and through; through every plank and each rib, it thrilled for an instant, the whale obliquely lying on his back, in the manner of a biting shark, slowly and feelingly taking its bows full within his mouth, so that the long, narrow, scrolled lower jaw curled high up into the open air, and one of the teeth caught in a row-lock. The bluish pearl-white of the inside of the jaw was within six inches of Ahab's head, and reached higher than that. In this attitude the White Whale now shook the slight cedar as a mildly cruel cat her mouse. With unastonished eyes Fedallah gazed, and crossed his arms; but the tiger-yellow crew were tumbling over each other's heads to gain the uttermost stern.

And now, while both elastic gunwales were springing in and out, as the whale dallied with the doomed craft in this devilish way; and from his body being submerged beneath the boat, he could not be darted at from the bows, for the bows were almost inside of him, as it were; and while the other boats involuntarily paused, as before a quick crisis impossible to withstand, then it was that monomaniac Ahab, furious with this tantalizing vicinity of his foe, which placed him all alive and helpless in the very jaws he hated; frenzied with all this, he seized the long bone with his naked hands, and wildly strove to wrench it from its gripe. As now he thus vainly strove, the jaw slipped from him; the frail gunwales bent in, collapsed, and snapped, as both jaws, like an enormous shears, sliding further aft, bit the craft completely in twain, and locked themselves fast again in the sea, midway between the two floating wrecks. These floated aside, the broken ends drooping, the crew at the stern-wreck clinging to the gunwales, and striving to hold fast to the oars to lash them across.

At that preluding moment, ere the boat was yet snapped, Ahab, the first to perceive the whale's intent, by the crafty upraising of his head, a movement that loosed his hold for the time; at that moment his hand had made one final effort to push the boat out of the bite. But only slipping further into the whale's mouth, and tilting over sideways as it slipped, the boat had shaken off his hold on the jaw; spilled him out of it, as he leaned to the push; and so he fell flat-faced upon the sea.

Ripplingly withdrawing from his prey, Moby Dick now lay at a little distance, vertically thrusting his oblong white head up and down in the billows; and at the same time slowly revolving his whole spindled body; so that when his vast wrinkled forehead rose—some twenty or more feet out of the water—the now rising swells, with all their confluent waves, dazzlingly broke against it; vindictively tossing their shivered spray still higher into the air.* So, in a gale, the but half baffled Channel billows only recoil from the base of the Eddystone, triumphantly to overleap its summit with their scud.

But soon resuming his horizontal attitude, Moby Dick swam swiftly round and round the wrecked crew; sideways churning the water in his vengeful wake, as if lashing himself up to still another and more deadly assault. The sight of the splintered boat seemed to madden him, as the blood of grapes and mulberries cast before Antiochus's elephants in the book of Maccabees. Meanwhile Ahab half smothered in the foam of the whale's insolent tail and too much of a cripple to swim,—though he could still keep afloat, even in the heart of such a whirlpool as that; helpless Ahab's head was seen, like a tossed bubble which the least chance shock might burst. From the boat's fragmentary stern, Fedallah incuriously and mildly eyed him; the clinging crew, at the other drifting end, could not succor him; more than enough was it for them to look to themselves. For so revolvingly appalling was the White Whale's aspect, and so planetarily swift the ever-contracting circles he made, that he seemed horizontally swooping upon them. And though the other boats, unharmed, still hovered hard by, still they dared not pull into the eddy to strike, lest that should be the signal for the instant destruction of the jeopardized castaways, Ahab and all; nor in that case could they themselves hope to escape. With straining eyes, then, they remained on the outer edge of the direful zone, whose center had now become the old man's head.

Meantime, from the beginning all this had been descried from the ship's mastheads; and squaring her yards, she had borne down upon the scene; and was now so nigh, that Ahab in the water hailed her:—"Sail on the"—but that moment a breaking sea dashed on him from Moby Dick, and whelmed him for the time. But struggling out of it again, and chancing to rise on a towering crest, he shouted,—"Sail on the whale!—Drive him off!"

The Pequod's prows were pointed; and breaking up the charmed circle, she effectually parted the White Whale from his victim. As he sullenly swam off, the boats flew to the rescue.

Dragged into Stubb's boat with bloodshot, blinded eyes, the white brine caking in his wrinkles; the long tension of Ahab's bodily strength did crack, and helplessly he yielded to his body's doom for a time, lying all crushed in the bottom of Stubb's boat, like one trodden under foot of herds of elephants. Far inland, nameless wails came from him, as desolate sounds from out ravines.

But this intensity of his physical prostration did but so much the more abbreviate it. In an instant's compass, great hearts sometimes condense to one deep pang, the sum total of those shallow pains kindly diffused through feebler men's whole lives. And so, such hearts, though summary

*This motion is peculiar to the sperm whale. It receives its designation (pitchpoling) from its being likened to that preliminary up-and-down poise of the whale-lance, in the exercise called pitchpoling, previously described. By this motion the whale must best and most comprehensively view whatever objects may be encircling him. [Author's note.]

in each one suffering; still, if the gods decree it, in their lifetime aggregate a whole age of woe, wholly made up of instantaneous intensities; for even in their pointless centers, those noble natures contain the entire circumferences of inferior souls.

"The harpoon," said Ahab, half way rising, and draggingly leaning on one bended arm—"is it safe?"

"Aye, sir, for it was not darted; this is it," said Stubb, showing it.

"Lay it before me;—any missing men?"

"One, two, three, four, five;—there were five oars, sir, and here are five men."

"That's good.—Help me, man; I wish to stand. So, so, I see him! there! there! going to leeward still; what a leaping spout!—Hands off from me! The eternal sap runs up in Ahab's bones again! Set the sail; out oars; the helm!"

It is often the case that when a boat is stove, its crew, being picked up by another boat, help to work that second boat; and the chase is thus continued with what is called double-banked oars. It was thus now. But the added power of the boat did not equal the added power of the whale, for he seemed to have treble-banked his every fin; swimming with a velocity which plainly showed, that if now, under these circumstances, pushed on, the chase would prove an indefinitely prolonged, if not a hopeless one; nor could any crew endure for so long a period, such an unintermitted, intense straining at the oar; a thing barely tolerable only in some one brief vicissitude. The ship itself, then, as it sometimes happens, offered the most promising intermediate means of overtaking the chase. Accordingly, the boats now made for her, and were soon swayed up to their cranes—the two parts of the wrecked boat having been previously secured by her—and then hoisting everything to her side, and stacking her canvas high up, and sideways outstretching it with stun-sails, like the double-jointed wings of an albatross; the Pequod bore down in the leeward wake of Moby-Dick. At the well known, methodic intervals, the whale's glittering spout was regularly announced from the manned mast-heads; and when he would be reported as just gone down, Ahab would take the time, and then pacing the deck, binnacle-watch in hand, so soon as the last second of the allotted hour expired, his voice was heard.—"Whose is the doubloon now? D'ye see him?" and if the reply was, No, sir! straightway he commanded them to lift him to his perch. In this way the day wore on; Ahab, now aloft and motionless; anon, unrestingly pacing the planks.

As he was thus walking, uttering no sound, except to hail the men aloft, or to bid them hoist a sail still higher, or to spread one to a still greater breadth—thus to and fro pacing, beneath his slouched hat, at every turn he passed his own wrecked boat, which had been dropped upon the quarter-deck, and lay there reversed; broken bow to shattered stern. At last he paused before it; and as in an already over-clouded sky fresh troops of clouds will sometimes sail across, so over the old man's face there now stole some such added gloom as this.

Stubb saw him pause; and perhaps intending, not vainly, though, to evince his own unabated fortitude, and thus keep up a valiant place in his Captain's mind, he advanced, and eyeing the wreck exclaimed—"The thistle the ass refused; it pricked his mouth too keenly, sir; ha! ha!"

"What soulless thing is this that laughs before a wreck? Man, man! did I not know thee brave as fearless fire (and as mechanical) I could swear thou wert a poltroon. Groan nor laugh should be heard before a wreck."

"Aye, sir," said Starbuck, drawing near, " 'tis a solemn sight; an omen, and an ill one."

"Omen? omen?—the dictionary! If the gods think to speak outright to man, they will honorably speak outright; not shake their heads, and give an old wives' darkling hint.—Begone! Ye two are the opposite poles of one thing; Starbuck is Stubb reversed, and Stubb is Starbuck; and ye two are all mankind; and Ahab stands alone among the millions of the peopled earth, nor gods nor men his neighbors! Cold, cold—I shiver!—How now? Aloft there! D'ye see him? Sing out for every spout, though he spout ten times a second!"

The day was nearly done; only the hem of his golden robe was rustling. Soon, it was almost dark, but the look-out men still remained unset.

"Can't see the spout now, sir;—too dark"—cried a voice from the air.

"How heading when last seen?"

"As before, sir,—straight to leeward."

"Good! he will travel slower now 'tis night. Down royals and top-gallant stun-sails, Mr. Starbuck. We must not run over him before morning; he's making a passage now, and may heave-to a while. Helm there! Keep her full before the wind!—Aloft! come down!—Mr. Stubb, send a fresh hand to the foremast head, and see it manned till morning."—Then advancing towards the doubloon in the mainmast—"Men, this gold is mine, for I earned it; but I shall let it abide here till the White Whale is dead; and then, whosoever of ye first raises him, upon the day he shall be killed, this gold is that man's; and if on that day I shall again raise him, then, ten times its sum shall be divided among all of ye! Away now!—the deck is thine, sir."

And so saying, he placed himself half-way within the scuttle, and slouching his hat, stood there till dawn, except when at intervals rousing himself to see how the night wore on.

## CHAPTER CXXXIV

## THE CHASE—SECOND DAY

At day-break, the three mast-heads were punctually manned afresh.

"D'ye see him?" cried Ahab, after allowing a little space for the light to spread.

"See nothing, sir."

"Turn up all hands and make sail! he travels faster than I thought for;—the top-gallant sails!—aye, they should have been kept on her all night. But no matter—'tis but resting for the rush."

Here be it said, that this pertinacious pursuit of one particular whale, continued through day into night, and through night into day, is a thing by no means unprecedented in the South Sea fishery. For such is the wonderful skill, prescience of experience, and invincible confidence acquired by some great natural geniuses among the Nantucket commanders; that from the simple observation of a whale when last descried, they will, under certain given circumstances, pretty accurately foretell both the direction in which he will continue to swim for a time, while out of sight, as well as his probable rate of progression during that period. And in these cases, somewhat as a pilot, when about losing sight of a coast, whose general trending he well knows, and which he desires shortly to return to again, but at some further point; like as this pilot stands by his compass, and takes the precise bearing of the cape at present visible, in order the more certainly to hit aright the remote, unseen headland, eventually to be visited: so does the fisherman, at his compass, with the whale; for after being chased, and diligently marked, through several hours of daylight, then, when night obscures the fish, the creature's future wake through the darkness is almost as established to the sagacious mind of the hunter, as the pilot's coast is to him. So that to this hunter's wondrous skill, the proverbial evanescence of a thing writ in water, a wake, is to all desired purposes well-nigh as reliable as the steadfast land. And as the mighty iron Leviathan of the modern railway is so familiarly known in its every pace, that, with watches in their hands, men time his rate as doctors that of a baby's pulse; and lightly say of it, the up train or the down train will reach such or such a spot, at such or such an hour, even so, almost, there are occasions when these Nantucketers time that other Leviathan of the deep, according to the observed humor of his speed; and say to themselves, so many hours hence this whale will have gone two hundred miles, will have about reached this or that degree of latitude or longitude. But to render this acuteness at all successful in the end, the wind and the sea must be the whaleman's allies; for of what present avail to the becalmed or windbound mariner is the skill that assures him he is exactly ninety-three leagues and a quarter from his port? Inferable from these statements are many collateral subtile matters touching the chase of whales.

The ship tore on; leaving such a furrow in the sea as when a cannon-ball, missent, becomes a plough-share and turns up the level field.

"By salt and hemp!" cried Stubb, "but this swift motion of the deck creeps up one's legs and tingles at the heart. This ship and I are two brave fellows!—Ha! ha! Some one take me up, and launch me, spine-wise, on the sea,—for by live-oaks! my spine's a keel. Ha, ha! we go the gait that leaves no dust behind!"

"There she blows—she blows!—she blows!—right ahead!" was now the masthead cry.

"Aye, aye!" cried Stubb; "I knew it—ye can't escape—blow on and split your spout, O whale! the mad fiend himself is after ye! blow your trump—blister your lungs!—Ahab will dam off your blood, as a miller shuts his water-gate upon the stream!"

And Stubb did but speak out for well-nigh all that crew. The frenzies of the chase had by this time worked them bubblingly up, like old wine worked anew. Whatever pale fears and forebodings some of them might have felt before; these were not only now kept out of sight through the growing awe of Ahab, but they were broken up, and on all sides routed, as timid prairie hares that scatter before the bounding bison. The hand of Fate had snatched all their souls; and by the stirring perils of the previous day; the rack of the past night's suspense; the fixed, unfearing, blind, reckless way in which their wild craft went plunging towards its flying mark; by all these things, their hearts were bowled along. The wind that made great bellies of their sails, and rushed the vessel on by arms invisible as irresistible; this seemed the symbol of that unseen agency which so enslaved them to the race.

They were one man, not thirty. For as the one ship that held them all; though it was put together of all contrasting things—oak, and maple, and pine wood; iron, and pitch, and hemp—yet all these ran into each other in the one concrete hull, which shot on its way, both balanced and directed by the long central keel; even so, all the individualities of the crew, this man's valor, that man's fear; guilt and guiltiness, all varieties were welded into oneness, and were all directed to that fatal goal which Ahab their one lord and keel did point to.

The rigging lived. The mast-heads, like the tops of tall palms, were outspreadingly tufted with arms and legs. Clinging to a spar with one hand, some reached forth the other with impatient wavings; others, shading their eyes from the vivid sunlight, sat far out on the rocking yards; all the spars in full bearing of mortals, ready and ripe for their fate. Ah! how they still strove through that infinite blueness to seek out the thing that might destroy them!

"Why sing ye not out for him, if ye see him?" cried Ahab, when, after the lapse of some minutes since the first cry, no more had been heard. "Sway me up, men; ye have been deceived; not Moby Dick casts one odd jet that way, and then disappears."

It was even so; in their headlong eagerness, the men had mistaken some other thing for the whale-spout, as the event itself soon proved; for hardly had Ahab reached his perch; hardly was the rope belayed to its pin on deck, when he struck the key-note to an orchestra, that made the air vibrate as with the combined discharges of rifles. The triumphant halloo of thirty buckskin lungs was heard, as—much nearer to the ship than the place of the imaginary jet, less than a mile ahead—Moby Dick bodily burst into view! For not by any calm and indolent spoutings; not by the peaceable gush of that mystic fountain in his head, did the White Whale now reveal his vicinity; but by the far more wondrous phenomenon of breaching. Rising with his utmost velocity from the furthest depths, the Sperm Whale thus booms his entire bulk into the pure element of air, and piling up a mountain of dazzling foam, shows his place to the distance of seven miles and more. In those moments, the torn, enraged waves he shakes off, seem his mane; in some cases this breaching is his act of defiance.

"There she breaches! there she breaches!" was the cry, as in his immeasurable bravadoes the White Whale tossed himself salmon-like to Heaven. So suddenly seen in the blue plain of the sea, and relieved against the still bluer margin of the sky, the spray that he raised, for the moment, intolerably glittered and glared like a glacier; and stood there gradually fading and fading away from its first sparkling intensity, to the dim mistiness of an advancing shower in a vale.

"Aye, breach your last to the sun, Moby Dick!" cried Ahab, "thy hour and thy harpoon are at hand!—Down! down all of ye, but one man at the fore. The boats!—stand by!"

Unmindful of the tedious rope-ladders of the shrouds, the men, like shooting stars, slid to the deck, by the isolated back-stays and halyards; while Ahab, less dartingly, but still rapidly was dropped from his perch.

"Lower away," he cried, so soon as he had reached his boat—a spare one, rigged the afternoon previous. "Mr. Starbuck, the ship is thine—keep away from the boats, but keep near them. Lower, all!"

As if to strike a quick terror into them, by this time being the first assailant himself, Moby Dick had turned, and was now coming for the three crews. Ahab's boat was central; and cheering his men, he told them he would take the whale head-and-head,—that is, pull straight up to his forehead,—a not uncommon thing; for when within a certain limit, such a course excludes the coming onset from the whale's sidelong vision. But ere that close limit was gained, and while yet all three boats were plain as the ship's three masts to his eye; the White Whale churning himself into furious speed, almost in an instant as it were, rushing among the boats with open jaws, and a lashing tail, offered appalling battle on every side; and heedless of the irons darted at him from every boat, seemed only intent on annihilating each separate plank of which those boats were made. But skillfully manœuvred, incessantly wheeling like trained chargers in the field, the boats for a while eluded him; though, at times, but by a plank's breadth; while all the time, Ahab's unearthly slogan tore every other cry but his to shreds.

But at last in his untraceable evolutions, the White Whale so crossed and recrossed, and in a thousand ways entangled the slack of the three lines now fast to him, that they foreshortened, and, of themselves, warped the devoted boats towards the planted irons in him; though now for a moment the whale drew aside a little, as if to rally for a more tremendous charge. Seizing that opportunity, Ahab first paid out more line: and then was rapidly hauling and jerking in upon it again—hoping that way to disencumber it of some snarls—when lo!—a sight more savage than the embattled teeth of sharks!

Caught and twisted—corkscrewed in the mazes of the line, loose harpoons and lances, with all their bristling barbs and points, came flashing and dripping up to the chocks in the bows of Ahab's boat. Only one thing could be done. Seizing the boat-knife, he critically reached within—through—and then, without—the rays of steel; dragged in the line beyond, passed it, inboard, to the bowsman, and then, twice sundering the rope near the chocks—dropped the intercepted fagot of steel into the sea; and was all fast again. That instant, the White Whale made a sudden rush among the remaining tangles of the other lines; by so doing, irresistibly dragged the more involved boats of Stubb and Flask towards his flukes; dashed them together like two rolling husks on a surf-beaten beach, and then, diving down into the sea, disappeared in a boiling maelstrom, in which, for a space, the odorous cedar chips of the wrecks danced round and round, like the grated nutmeg in a swiftly stirred bowl of punch.

While the two crews were yet circling in the waters, reaching out after the revolving line-tubs, oars, and other floating furniture, while aslope little Flask bobbed up and down like an empty vial, twitching his legs upwards to escape the dreaded jaws of sharks; and Stubb was lustily singing out for some one to ladle him up; and while the old man's line—now parting—admitted of his pulling into the creamy pool to rescue whom he could;—in that wild simultaneousness of a thousand concerted perils,—Ahab's yet unstricken boat seemed drawn up towards Heaven by invisible wires,—as, arrow-like, shooting perpendicularly from the sea, the White Whale dashed his broad forehead against its bottom, and sent it, turning over and over, into the air; till it fell again—gunwale downwards—and Ahab and his men struggled out from under it, like seals from a sea-side cave.

The first uprising momentum of the whale—modifying its direction as he struck the surface—involuntarily launched him along it, to a little distance from the center of the destruction he had made; and with his back to it, he now lay for a moment slowly feeling with his flukes from side to side; and whenever a stray oar, bit of plank, the least chip or crumb of the boats touched his skin, his tail swiftly drew back, and came sideways, smiting the sea. But soon, as if satisfied that his work for that time was done, he pushed his pleated forehead through the ocean, and trailing after him the intertangled lines, continued his leeward way at a traveler's methodic pace.

As before, the attentive ship having descried the whole fight, again came bearing down to the rescue, and dropping a boat, picked up the floating mariners, tubs, oars, and whatever else could be caught at, and safely landed them on her decks. Some sprained shoulders, wrists, and ankles; livid contusions; wrenched harpoons and lances; inextricable intricacies of rope; shattered oars and planks; all these were there; but no fatal or even serious ill seemed to have befallen any one. As with Fedallah the day before, so Ahab was now found grimly clinging to his boat's broken half, which afforded a comparatively easy float; nor did it so exhaust him as the previous day's mishap.

But when he was helped to the deck, all eyes were fastened upon him; as instead of standing by himself he still half-hung upon the shoulder of Starbuck, who had thus far been the foremost to assist him. His ivory leg had been snapped off, leaving but one short sharp splinter.

"Aye, aye, Starbuck, 'tis sweet to lean sometimes, be the leaner who he will; and would old Ahab had leaned oftener than he has."

"The ferrule has not stood, sir," said the carpenter, now coming up; "I put good work into that leg."

"But no bones broken, sir, I hope," said Stubb with true concern.

"Aye! and all splintered to pieces, Stubb!—d'ye see it.—But even with a broken bone, old Ahab is untouched; and I account no living bone of mine one jot more me, than this dead one that's lost. Nor white whale, nor man, nor fiend, can so much as graze old Ahab in his own proper and inaccessible being. Can any lead touch yonder floor, any mast scrape yonder roof?—Aloft there! which way?"

"Dead to leeward, sir."

"Up helm, then; pile on the sail again, ship-keepers! down the rest of the spare boats and rig them—Mr. Starbuck away, and muster the boats' crews."

"Let me first help thee towards the bulwarks, sir."

"Oh, oh, oh! how this splinter gores me now! Accursed fate! that the unconquerable captain in the soul should have such a craven mate!"

"Sir?"

"My body, man, not thee. Give me something for a cane—there, that shivered lance will do. Muster the men. Surely I have not seen him yet. By heaven, it cannot be!—missing?—quick! call them all."

The old man's hinted thought was true. Upon mustering the company, the Parsee was not there.

"The Parsee!" cried Stubb—"he must have been caught in——"

"The black vomit wrench thee!—run all of ye above, alow, cabin, forecastle—find him—not gone—not gone!"

But quickly they returned to him with the tidings that the Parsee was nowhere to be found.

"Aye, sir," said Stubb—"caught among the tangles of your line—I thought I saw him dragging under."

"*My* line? *my* line? Gone?—gone?—What means that little word? What death-knell rings in it, that old Ahab shakes as if he were the belfry. The harpoon, too!—toss over the litter there,—d'ye see it?—the forged iron, men, the white whale's—no, no, no,—blistered fool! this hand did dart it!—'tis in the fish!—Aloft there! Keep him nailed—Quick!—all hands to the rigging of the boats—collect the oars—harpooneers! the irons, the irons!—hoist the royals higher—a pull on all the sheets!—helm there! steady, steady for your life! I'll ten times girdle the unmeasured globe; yea and dive straight through it, but I'll slay him yet!"

"Great God! but for one single instant show thyself," cried Starbuck; "never, never wilt thou capture him, old man.—In Jesus' name no more of this, that's worse than devil's madness. Two days chased; twice stove to splinters; thy very leg once more snatched from under thee; thy evil shadow gone—all good angels mobbing thee with warnings:—what more wouldst thou have?—Shall we keep chasing this murderous fish till he swamps the last man? Shall we be dragged by him to the bottom of the sea? Shall we be towed by him to the infernal world? Oh, oh!—Impiety and blasphemy to hunt him more!"

"Starbuck, of late I've felt strangely moved to thee; ever since that hour we both saw—thou know'st what, in one another's eyes. But in this matter of the whale, be the front of thy face to me as the palm of this hand—a lipless, unfeatured blank. Ahab is for ever Ahab, man. This whole act's immutably decreed. 'Twas rehearsed by thee and me a billion years before this ocean rolled. Fool! I am the Fates' lieutenant; I act under orders. Look thou, underling! that thou obeyest mine.—Stand round me, men. Ye see an old man cut down to the stump; leaning on a shivered lance; propped up on a lonely foot. 'Tis Ahab—his body's part; but Ahab's soul's a centipede, that moves upon a hundred legs. I feel strained, half stranded, as ropes that tow dismasted frigates in a gale; and I may look so. But ere I break, ye'll hear me crack; and till ye hear *that,* know that Ahab's hawser tows his purpose yet. Believe ye, men, in the things called omens? Then laugh aloud, and cry encore! For ere they drown, drowning things will twice rise to the surface; then rise again, to sink for evermore. So with Moby Dick—two days he's floated—to-morrow will be the third. Aye, men, he'll rise once more—but only to spout his last! D'ye feel brave men, brave?"

"As fearless fire," cried Stubb.

"And as mechanical," muttered Ahab. Then as the men went forward, he muttered on:—"The things called omens! And yesterday I talked the same to Starbuck there, concerning my broken boat. Oh! how valiantly I seek to drive out of others' hearts what's clinched so fast in mine! —The Parsee—the Parsee!—gone, gone? and he was to go before:—but still was to be seen again ere I could perish—How's that?—There's a riddle now might baffle all the lawyers backed by the ghosts of the whole line of judges:—like a hawk's beak it pecks my brain. *I'll, I'll* solve it, though!"

When dusk descended, the whale was still in sight to leeward.

So once more the sail was shortened, and everything passed nearly as on the previous night; only, the sound of hammers, and the hum of the grindstone was heard till nearly daylight, as the men toiled by lanterns in the complete and careful rigging of the spare boats and sharpening their fresh weapons for the morrow. Meantime, of the broken keel of Ahab's wrecked craft the carpenter made him another leg; while still as on the night before, slouched Ahab stood fixed within his scuttle; his hid, heliotrope glance anticipatingly gone backward on its dial; set due eastward for the earliest sun.

## CHAPTER CXXXV

## THE CHASE—THIRD DAY

The morning of the third day dawned fair and fresh, and once more the solitary night-man at the fore-mast-head was relieved by crowds of the daylight look-outs, who dotted every mast and almost every spar.

"D'ye see him?" cried Ahab; but the whale was not yet in sight.

"In his infallible wake, though; but follow that wake, that's all. Helm there; steady, as thou goest, and hast been going. What a lovely day again! were it a new-made world, and made for a summer-house to the angels, and this morning the first of its throwing open to them, a fairer day could not dawn upon that world. Here's food for thought, had Ahab time to think; but Ahab never thinks; he only feels, feels, feels, *that's* tingling enough for mortal man! to think's audacity. God only has that right and privilege.

Thinking is, or ought to be, a coolness and a calmness; and our poor hearts throb, and our poor brains beat too much for that. And yet, I've sometimes thought my brain was very calm—frozen calm, this old skull cracks so, like a glass in which the contents turn to ice, and shiver it. And still this hair is growing now; this moment growing, and heat must breed it; but no, it's like that sort of common grass that will grow anywhere, between the earthly clefts of Greenland ice or in Vesuvius lava. How the wild winds blow it; they whip it about me as the torn shreds of split sails lash the tossed ship they cling to. A vile wind that has no doubt blown ere this through prison corridors and cells, and wards of hospitals, and ventilated them, and now comes blowing hither as innocent as fleeces. Out upon it!—it's tainted. Were I the wind, I'd blow no more on such a wicked, miserable world. I'd crawl somewhere to a cave, and slink there. And yet, 'tis a noble and heroic thing, the wind! who ever conquered it? In every fight it has the last and bitterest blow. Run tilting at it, and you but run through it. Ha! a coward wind that strikes stark naked men, but will not stand to receive a single blow. Even Ahab is a braver thing—a nobler thing than *that*. Would now the wind but had a body; but all the things that most exasperate and outrage mortal man, all these things are bodiless, but only bodiless as objects, not as agents. There's a most special, a most cunning, oh, a most malicious difference! And yet, I say again, and swear it now, that there's something all glorious and gracious in the wind. These warm Trade Winds, at least, that in the clear heavens blow straight on, in strong and steadfast, vigorous mildness; and veer not from their mark, however the baser currents of the sea may turn and tack, and mightiest Mississippis of the land swift and swerve about, uncertain where to go at last. And by the eternal Poles! these same Trades that so directly blow my good ship on; these Trades, or something like them—something so unchangeable, and full as strong, blow my keeled soul along! To it! Aloft there! What d'ye see?"

"Nothing, sir."

"Nothing! and noon at hand! The doubloon goes a-begging! See the sun! Aye, aye, it must be so. I've oversailed him. How, got the start? Aye, he's chasing *me* now; not I, *him*—that's bad; I might have known it, too. Fool! the lines—the harpoons he's towing. Aye, aye, I have run him by last night. About! about! Come down, all of ye, but the regular lookouts! Man the braces!"

Steering as she had done, the wind had been somewhat on the Pequod's quarter, so that now being pointed in the reverse direction, the braced ship sailed hard upon the breeze as she rechurned the cream in her own white wake.

"Against the wind he now steers for the open jaw," murmured Starbuck to himself, as he coiled the new-hauled main-brace upon the rail. "God keep us, but already my bones feel damp within me, and from the inside wet my flesh. I misdoubt me that I disobey my God in obeying him!"

"Stand by to sway me up!" cried Ahab, advancing to the hempen basket. "We should meet him soon."

"Aye, aye, sir," and straightway

Starbuck did Ahab's bidding, and once more Ahab swung on high.

A whole hour now passed; gold-beaten out to ages. Time itself now held long breaths with keen suspense. But at last, some three points off the weather-bow, Ahab descried the spout again, and instantly from the three mast-heads three shrieks went up as if the tongues of fire had voiced it.

"Forehead to forehead I meet thee, this third time, Moby Dick! On deck there!—brace sharper up; crowd her into the wind's eye. He's too far off to lower yet, Mr. Starbuck. The sails shake! Stand over that helmsman with a top-maul! So, so; he travels fast, and I must down. But let me have one more good round look aloft here at the sea; there's time for that. An old, old sight, and yet somehow so young; aye, and not changed a wink since I first saw it, a boy, from the sandhills of Nantucket! The same!—the same!—the same to Noah as to me. There's a soft shower to leeward. Such lovely leewardings! They must lead somewhere—to something else than common land, more palmy than the palms. Leeward! the white whale goes that way; look to windward, then; the better if the bitterer quarter. But good bye, good bye, old mast-head! What's this?—green? ay, tiny mosses in these warped cracks. No such green weather stains on Ahab's head! There's the difference now between man's old age and matter's. But aye, old mast, we both grow old together; sound in our hulls, though, are we not, my ship? Aye, minus a leg, that's all. By heaven this dead wood has the better of my live flesh every way. I can't compare with it; and I've known some ships made of dead trees outlast the lives of men made of the most vital stuff of vital fathers. What's that he said? he should still go before me, my pilot; and yet to be seen again? But where? Shall I have eyes at the bottom of the sea, supposing I descend those endless stairs? and all night I've been sailing from him, wherever he did sink to. Aye, aye, like many more thou told'st direful truth as touching thyself, O Parsee; but, Ahab, there thy shot fell short. Good-bye, mast-head—keep a good eye upon the whale, the while I'm gone. We'll talk to-morrow, nay, to-night, when the white whale lies down there, tied by head and tail."

He gave the word; and still gazing round him, was steadily lowered through the cloven blue air to the deck.

In due time the boats were lowered; but as standing in his shallop's stern, Ahab just hovered upon the point of the descent, he waved to the mate,—who held one of the tackle-ropes on deck—and bade him pause.

"Starbuck!"

"Sir?"

"For the third time my soul's ship starts upon this voyage, Starbuck."

"Aye, sir, thou wilt have it so."

"Some ships sail from their ports, and ever afterwards are missing, Starbuck!"

"Truth, sir: saddest truth."

"Some men die at ebb tide; some at low water; some at the full of the flood;—and I feel now like a billow that's all one crested comb, Starbuck. I am old;—shake hands with me, man."

Their hands met; their eyes fastened; Starbuck's tears the glue.

"Oh, my captain, my captain!—

noble heart—go not—go not!—see, it's a brave man that weeps; how great the agony of the persuasion then!"

"Lower away!"—cried Ahab, tossing the mate's arm from him. "Stand by the crew!"

In an instant the boat was pulling round close under the stern.

"The sharks! the sharks!" cried a voice from the low cabin-window there; "O master, my master, come back!"

But Ahab heard nothing; for his own voice was high-lifted then; and the boat leaped on.

Yet the voice spake true; for scarce had he pushed from the ship, when numbers of sharks, seemingly rising from out the dark waters beneath the hull, maliciously snapped at the blades of the oars, every time they dipped in the water; and in this way accompanied the boat with their bites. It is a thing not uncommonly happening to the whale-boats in those swarming seas; the sharks at times apparently following them in the same prescient way that vultures hover over the banners of marching regiments in the east. But these were the first sharks that had been observed by the Pequod since the White Whale had been first descried; and whether it was that Ahab's crew were all such tiger-yellow barbarians, and therefore their flesh more musky to the senses of the sharks—a matter sometimes well known to affect them,—however it was, they seemed to follow that one boat without molesting the others.

"Heart of wrought steel!" murmured Starbuck, gazing over the side, and following with his eyes the receding boat—"canst thou yet ring boldly to that sight?—lowering thy keel among ravening sharks, and followed by them, open-mouthed to the chase; and this the critical third day?—For when three days flow together in one continuous intense pursuit; be sure the first is the morning, the second the noon, and the third the evening and the end of that thing—be that end what it may. Oh! my God! what is this that shoots through me, and leaves me so deadly calm, yet expectant,—fixed at the top of a shudder! Future things swim before me, as in empty outlines and skeletons; all the past is somehow grown dim. Mary, girl! thou fadest in pale glories behind me; boy! I seem to see but thy eyes grown wondrous blue Strangest problems of life seem clearing; but clouds sweep between—Is my journey's end coming? My legs feel faint; like his who has footed it all day. Feel thy heart,—beats it yet?—Stir thyself, Starbuck!—stave it off—move, move! speak aloud!—Mast-head there! See ye my boy's hand on the hill?—Crazed;—aloft there!—keep thy keenest eye upon the boats:—mark well the whale!—Ho! again!—drive off that hawk! see! he pecks—he tears the vane"—pointing to the red flag flying at the main-truck—"Ha! he soars away with it—Where's the old man now? sees't thou that sight, oh Ahab!—shudder, shudder!"

The boats had not gone very far, when by a signal from the mast-heads—a downward pointed arm, Ahab knew that the whale had sounded; but intending to be near him at the next rising, he held on his way a little sideways from the vessel; the becharmed crew maintaining the profoundest silence, as the head-beat waves hammered and hammered against the opposing bow.

"Drive, drive in your nails, oh ye waves! to their uttermost heads drive them in! ye but strike a thing without a lid; and no coffin and no hearse can be mine:—and hemp only can kill me! Ha! ha!"

Suddenly the waters around them slowly swelled in broad circles; then quickly upheaved, as if sideways sliding from a submerged berg of ice, swiftly rising to the surface. A low rumbling sound was heard; a subterraneous hum; and then all held their breaths; as bedraggled with trailing ropes, and harpoons, and lances, a vast form shot lengthwise, but obliquely from the sea. Shrouded in a thin drooping veil of mist, it hovered for a moment in the rainbowed air; and then fell swamping back into the deep. Crushed thirty feet upwards, the waters flashed for an instant like heaps of fountains, then brokenly sank in a shower of flakes, leaving the circling surface creamed like new milk round the marble trunk of the whale.

"Give way!" cried Ahab to the oarsmen and the boats darted forward to the attack; but maddened by yesterday's fresh irons that corroded in him, Moby Dick seemed combinedly possessed by all the angels that fell from heaven. The wide tiers of welded tendons overspreading his broad white forehead, beneath the transparent skin, looked knitted together; as head on, he came churning his tail among the boats; and once more flailed them apart; spilling out the irons and lances from the two mates' boats, and dashing in one side of the upper part of their bows, but leaving Ahab's almost without a scar.

While Daggoo and Queequeg were stopping the strained planks; and as the whale swimming out from them, turned, and showed one entire flank as he shot by them again; at that moment a quick cry went up. Lashed round and round to the fish's back; pinioned in the turns upon turns in which, during the past night, the whale had reeled the involutions of the lines around him, the half torn body of the Parsee was seen; his sable raiment frayed to shreds; his distended eyes turned full upon old Ahab.

The harpoon dropped from his hand.

"Befooled, befooled!"—drawing in a long lean breath—"Aye, Parsee! I see thee again.—Aye, and thou goest before; and this, *this* then is the hearse that thou didst promise. But I hold thee to the last letter of thy word. Where is the second hearse? Away, mates, to the ship! those boats are useless now; repair them if ye can in time, and return to me; if not, Ahab is enough to die—Down, men! the first thing that but offers to jump from this boat I stand in, that thing I harpoon. Ye are not other men, but my arms and my legs; and so obey me.—Where's the whale? gone down again?"

But he looked too nigh the boat; for as if bent upon escaping with the corpse he bore, and as if the particular place of the last encounter had been but a stage in his leeward voyage, Moby Dick was now again steadily swimming forward; and had almost passed the ship,—which thus far had been sailing in the contrary direction to him, though for the present her headway had been stopped. He seemed swimming with his utmost velocity, and now only intent upon pursuing his own straight path in the sea.

"Oh! Ahab," cried Starbuck, "not too late is it, even now, the third day, to desist. See! Moby Dick seeks thee not. It is thou, thou, that madly seekest him!"

Setting sail to the rising wind, the lonely boat was swiftly impelled to leeward, by both oars and canvas. And at last when Ahab was sliding by the vessel, so near as plainly to distinguish Starbuck's face as he leaned over the rail, he hailed him to turn the vessel about, and follow him, not too swiftly, at a judicious interval. Glancing upwards, he saw Tashtego, Queequeg, and Daggoo, eagerly mounting to the three mast-heads; while the oarsmen were rocking in the two staved boats which had just been hoisted to the side, and were busily at work in repairing them. One after the other, through the port-holes, as he sped, he also caught flying glimpses of Stubb and Flask, busying themselves on deck among bundles of new irons and lances. As he saw all this; as he heard the hammers in the broken boats; far other hammers seemed driving a nail into his heart. But he rallied. And now marking that the vane or flag was gone from the main-mast-head, he shouted to Tashtego, who had just gained that perch, to descend again for another flag, and a hammer and nails, and so nail it to the mast.

Whether fagged by the three days' running chase, and the resistance to his swimming in the knotted hamper he bore; or whether it was some latent deceitfulness and malice in him: whichever was true, the White Whale's way now began to abate, as it seemed, from the boat so rapidly nearing him once more; though indeed the whale's last start had not been so long a one as before. And still as Ahab glided over the waves the unpitying sharks accompanied him; and so pertinaciously stuck to the boat; and so continually bit at the plying oars, that the blades became jagged and crunched, and left small splinters in the sea, at almost every dip.

"Heed them not! those teeth but give new rowlocks to your oars. Pull on! 'tis the better rest, the shark's jaw than the yielding water."

"But at every bite, sir, the thin blades grow smaller and smaller!"

"They will last long enough! pull on!—But who can tell"—he muttered—"whether these sharks swim to feast on the whale or on Ahab?—But pull on! Aye, all alive, now—we near him. The helm! take the helm; let me pass,"—and so saying, two of the oarsmen helped him forward to the bows of the still flying boat.

At length as the craft was cast to one side, and ran ranging along with the White Whale's flank, he seemed strangely oblivious of its advance—as the whale sometimes will—and Ahab was fairly within the smoky mountain mist, which, thrown off from the whale's spout, curled round his great, Monadnock hump. He was even thus close to him; when, with body arched back, and both arms lengthwise high-lifted to the poise, he darted his fierce iron, and his far fiercer curse into the hated whale. As both steel and curse sank to the socket, as if sucked into a morass, Moby Dick sideways writhed; spasmodically rolled his nigh flank against the bow, and, without staving a hole in it, so suddenly canted the boat over, that had it not been for the elevated part of the gunwale to which he then clung, Ahab would once more have been tossed into the sea. As it was, three of the oarsmen—who foreknew not the precise instant of the dart, and were therefore unprepared for its effects—these were flung out; but so fell, that, in an instant two of them clutched the gunwale again, and rising to its level on a combing wave, hurled themselves bodily inboard again; the third man helplessly dropping astern, but still afloat and swimming.

Almost simultaneously, with a mighty volition of ungraduated, instantaneous swiftness, the White Whale darted through the weltering sea. But when Ahab cried out to the steersman to take new turns with the line, and hold it so; and commanded the crew to turn round on their seats, and tow the boat up to the mark; the moment the treacherous line felt that double strain and tug, it snapped in the empty air!

"What breaks in me? Some sinew cracks!—'tis whole again; oars! oars! Burst in upon him!"

Hearing the tremendous rush of the sea-crashing boat, the whale wheeled round to present his blank forehead at bay; but in that evolution, catching sight of the nearing black hull of the ship; seemingly seeing in it the source of all his persecutions; bethinking it—it may be—a larger and nobler foe; of a sudden, he bore down upon its advancing prow, smiting his jaws amid fiery showers of foam.

Ahab staggered; his hand smote his forehead. "I grow blind; hands! stretch out before me that I may yet grope my way. Is't night?"

"The whale! The ship!" cried the cringing oarsmen.

"Oars! oars! Slope downwards to thy depths, O sea, that ere it be for ever too late, Ahab may slide this last, last time upon his mark! I see: the ship! the ship! Dash on, my men! Will ye not save my ship?"

But as the oarsmen violently forced their boat through the sledge-hammering seas, the before whale-smitten bow-ends of two planks burst through, and in an instant almost, the temporarily disabled boat lay nearly level with the waves; its half-wading, splashing crew, trying hard to stop the gap and bale out the pouring water.

Meantime, for that one beholding instant, Tashtego's masthead hammer remained suspended in his hand; and the red flag, half-wrapping him as with a plaid, then streamed itself straight out from him, as his own forward-flowing heart; while Starbuck and Stubb, standing upon the bowsprit beneath, caught sight of the down-coming monster just as soon as he.

"The whale, the whale! Up helm, up helm! Oh, all ye sweet powers of air, now hug me close! Let not Starbuck die, if die he must, in a woman's fainting fit. Up helm, I say—ye fools, the jaw! the jaw! Is this the end of all my bursting prayers? all my life-long fidelities? Oh, Ahab, Ahab, lo, thy work. Steady! helmsman, steady. Nay, nay! Up helm again! He turns to meet us! Oh, his unappeasable brow drives on towards one, whose duty tells him he cannot depart. My God, stand by me now!"

"Stand not by me, but stand under me, whoever you are that will now help Stubb; for Stubb, too, sticks here. I grin at thee, thou grinning whale! Who-ever helped Stubb, or kept Stubb awake, but Stubb's own unwinking eye? And now poor Stubb goes to bed upon a mattress that is all too soft; would it were stuffed with brushwood! I grin at thee, thou grinning whale! Look ye, sun, moon, and stars! I call ye assassins of as good a fellow as ever spouted up his ghost. For all that, I would yet ring glasses with ye, would ye but hand the cup! Oh, oh, oh, oh! thou grinning whale, but there'll be plenty of gulping soon! Why fly ye not, O Ahab? For me, off shoes and jacket to it; let Stubb die in his drawers! A most moldy and over salted death, though;—cherries! cherries! cherries! Oh, Flask, for one red cherry ere we die!"

"Cherries? I only wish that we were where they grow. Oh, Stubb, I hope my poor mother's drawn my part-pay ere this; if not, few coppers will come to her now, for the voyage is up."

From the ship's bows, nearly all the seamen now hung inactive; hammers, bits of plank, lances, and harpoons, mechanically retained in their hands, just as they had darted from their various employments; all their enchanted eyes intent upon the whale, which from side to side strangely vibrating his predestinating head, sent a broad band of overspreading semicircular foam before him as he rushed. Retribution, swift vengeance, eternal malice were in his whole aspect, and spite of all that mortal man could do, the solid white buttress of his forehead smote the ship's starboard bow, till men and timbers reeled. Some fell flat upon their faces. Like dislodged trucks, the heads of the harpooneers aloft shook on their bull-like necks. Through the breach, they heard the waters pour, as mountain torrents down a flume.

"The ship! The hearse!—the second hearse!" cried Ahab from the boat; "its wood could only be American!"

Diving beneath the settling ship, the Whale ran quivering along its keel; but turning under water, swiftly shot to the surface again, far off the other bow, but within a few yards of Ahab's boat, where, for a time, he lay quiescent.

"I turn my body from the sun. What ho, Tashtego! let me hear thy hammer. Oh! ye three unsurrendered spires of mine; thou uncracked keel; the only god-bullied hull; thou firm deck, and haughty helm, and Pole-pointed prow,—death-glorious ship! must ye then perish, and without me? Am I cut off from the last fond pride of meanest ship-wrecked captains? Oh, lonely death on lonely life! Oh, now I feel my topmost greatness lies in my topmost grief. Ho, ho! from all your furthest bounds, pour ye now in, ye bold billows of my whole foregone life, and top this one piled comber of my death! Towards thee I roll, thou all-destroying but unconquering whale; to the last I grapple with thee; from hell's heart I stab at thee; for hate's sake I spit my last breath at thee. Sink all coffins and all hearses to one common pool! and since neither can be mine let me then tow to pieces, while still chasing thee, though tied to thee, thou damned whale! *Thus*, I give up the spear!"

The harpoon was darted; the stricken whale flew forward; with igniting velocity the line ran through the groove;—ran foul. Ahab stooped to clear it; he did clear; but the flying turn caught him round the neck, and voicelessly as Turkish mutes bowstring their victim, he was shot out of the boat, ere the crew knew he was gone. Next instant, the heavy eye-splice in the rope's final end flew out of the stark-empty tub, knocked down an oarsman, and smiting the sea, disappeared in its depths.

For an instant, the tranced boat's crew stood still; then turned. "The ship? Great God, where is the ship?" Soon they through dim, bewildering mediums saw her sidelong fading phantom, as in the gaseous Fata Morgana; only the uppermost masts out of water; while fixed by infatuation, or fidelity, or fate, to their once lofty perches, the pagan harpooneers still maintained their sinking lookouts on the sea. And now, concentric circles seized the lone boat itself, and all its crew, and each floating oar, and every lance-pole, and spinning, animate and inanimate, all round and round in one vortex, carried the smallest chip of the Pequod out of sight.

But as the last whelmings intermixingly poured themselves over the sunken head of the Indian at the mainmast, leaving a few inches of the erect spar yet visible, together with long streaming yards of the flag, which calmly undulated, with ironical coincidings, over the destroying billows they almost touched;—at that instant, a red arm and a hammer hovered backwardly uplifted in the open air, in the act of nailing the flag faster and yet faster to the subsiding spar. A sky-hawk that tauntingly had followed the main-truck downwards from its natural home among the stars, pecking at the flag, and incommoding Tashtego there; this bird now chanced to intercept its broad fluttering wing between the hammer and the wood; and simultaneously feeling that ethereal thrill, the submerged savage beneath, in his death-gasp, kept his hammer frozen there; and so the bird of heaven, with archangelic shrieks, and his imperial beak thrust upwards, and his whole captive form folded in the flag of Ahab, went down with his ship, which, like Satan, would not sink to hell till she had dragged a living part of heaven along with her, and helmeted herself with it.

Now small fowls flew screaming over the yet yawning gulf; a sullen white surf beat against its steep sides; then all collapsed, and the great shroud of the sea rolled on as it rolled five thousand years ago.

1851

# THE CONQUEST OF THE NEW WORLD

## I. WILLIAM HICKLING PRESCOTT
(1796–1859)

### *HISTORY OF THE CONQUEST OF MEXICO*

*From* BOOK III, CHAPTER IX

### INTERVIEW WITH MONTEZUMA

With the first faint streak of dawn, the Spanish general was up, mustering his followers. They gathered, with beating hearts, under their respective banners as the trumpet sent forth its spirit-stirring sounds across water and woodland, till they died away in distant echoes among the mountains. The sacred flames on the altars of numberless *teocallis,* dimly seen through the grey mists of morning, indicated the site of the capital, till temple, tower, and palace were fully revealed in the glorious illumination which the sun, as he rose above the eastern barrier, poured over the beautiful valley. It was the eighth of November, 1519; a conspicuous day in history, as that on which the Europeans first set foot in the capital of the Western World.

Cortés with his little body of horse formed a sort of advanced guard to the army. Then came the Spanish infantry, who in a summer's campaign had acquired the discipline and the weather-beaten aspect of veterans. The baggage occupied the centre; and the rear was closed by the dark files of Tlascalan warriors. The whole number must have fallen short of seven thousand; of which less than four hundred were Spaniards.

For a short distance, the army kept along the narrow tongue of land that divides the Tezcucan from the Chalcan waters, when it entered on the great dike, which, with the exception of an angle near the commencement, stretches in a perfectly straight line across the salt floods of Tezcuco to the gates of the capital. It was the same causeway, or rather the basis of that, which still forms the great southern avenue of Mexico. The Spaniards had occasion more than ever to admire the mechanical science of the Aztecs, in the geometrical precision with which the work was executed, as well as the solidity of its construction. It was composed of huge stones well laid in cement; and wide enough, throughout its whole extent, for ten horsemen to ride abreast.

They saw, as they passed along, several large towns, resting on piles, and reaching far into the water, — a kind of architecture which found great favor with the Aztecs, being in imitation of that of their metropolis. The busy population obtained a good subsistence from the manufacture of salt, which they extracted from the waters of the great lake. The duties on the traffic in this article were a considerable source of revenue to the crown.

Everywhere the Conquerors beheld the evidence of a crowded and thriving population, exceeding all they had yet seen. The temples and principal buildings of the cities were covered with a hard white stucco, which glistened like enamel in the level beams of the morning. The margin of the great basin was more thickly gemmed, than that of Chalco, with towns and hamlets. The water was darkened by swarms of canoes filled with Indians, who clambered up the sides of the causeway, and gazed with curious astonishment on the strangers. And here, also, they beheld those fairy islands of flowers, overshadowed occasionally by trees of considerable size, rising and falling with the gentle undulation of the billows. At the distance of half a league from the capital, they encountered a solid work or curtain of stone, which traversed the dike. It was twelve feet high, was strengthened by towers at the extremities, and in the centre was a battlemented gate-way, which opened a passage to the troops. It was called the Fort of Xoloc, and became memorable in after times as the position occupied by Cortés in the famous siege of Mexico.

Here they were met by several hundred Aztec chiefs, who came out to announce the approach of Montezuma, and to welcome the Spaniards to his capital. They were dressed in the fanciful gala costume of the country, with the *maxtlatl,* or cotton sash, around their loins, and a broad mantle of the same material, or of the brilliant feather-embroidery, flowing gracefully down their shoulders. On their necks and arms they displayed collars and bracelets of turquoise mosaic, with which delicate plumage was curiously mingled, while their ears, under-lips, and occasionally their noses, were garnished with pendants formed of precious stones, or crescents of fine gold. As each cacique made the usual formal salutation of the country separately to the general, the tedious ceremony delayed the march more than an hour. After this, the army experienced no further interruption till it reached a bridge near the gates of the city. It was built of wood, since replaced by one of stone, and was thrown across an opening of the dike, which furnished an outlet to the waters, when agitated by the winds, or swollen by a sudden influx in the rainy season. It was a draw-bridge; and the Spaniards, as they crossed it, felt how truly they were committing themselves to the mercy of Montezuma, who, by thus cutting off their communications with the country, might hold them prisoners in his capital.

In the midst of these unpleasant reflections, they beheld the glittering retinue of the emperor emerging from the great street which led then, as it still does, through the heart of the city. Amidst a crowd of Indian nobles, preceded by three officers of state, bearing golden wands, they saw the royal palanquin blazing with burnished gold. It was borne on the shoulders of nobles, and over it a canopy of gaudy feather-work, powdered with jewels, and fringed with silver, was supported by four attendants of the same rank. They were barefooted, and walked with a slow, measured pace, and with eyes bent on the ground. When the train had come within a convenient distance, it halted, and Montezuma, descending from his litter, came forward leaning on the arms of the lords of Tezcuco and Iztapalapan, his nephew and brother, both of whom, as we have seen, had already been made known to the Spaniards. As the monarch advanced under the canopy, the obsequious attendants strewed the ground with cotton tapestry, that his imperial feet might not be contaminated by the rude soil. His subjects of high and low degree, who lined the sides of the causeway, bent forward with their eyes fastened on the ground as he passed, and some of the humbler class prostrated themselves before him. Such was the homage paid to the Indian despot, showing that the slavish forms of Oriental adulation were to be found among the rude inhabitants of the Western World.

Montezuma wore the girdle and ample square cloak, *tilmatli,* of his nation. It was made of the finest cotton, with the embroidered ends gathered in a knot round his neck. His feet were defended by sandals having soles of gold, and the leathern thongs which bound them to his ankles were embossed with the same metal. Both the cloak and sandals were sprinkled with pearls and precious stones, among which the emerald and the *chalchivitl* — a green stone of higher estimation than any other among the Aztecs — were conspicuous. On his head he wore no other ornament than a *panache* of plumes of the royal green, which floated down his back, the badge of military, rather than of regal, rank.

He was at this time about forty years of age. His person was tall and thin, but not ill-made. His hair, which was black and straight, was not very long; to wear it short was considered unbecoming persons of rank. His beard was thin; his complexion somewhat paler than is often found in his dusky, or rather copper-coloured race. His features, though serious in their expression, did not wear the look of melancholy, indeed, of dejection, which characterises his portrait, and which may well have settled on them at a later period. He moved with dignity, and his whole demeanour, tempered by an expression of benignity not to have been anticipated from the reports circulated of his character, was worthy of a great prince. — Such is the portrait left to us of the celebrated Indian emperor, in this his first interview with the white men.

The army halted as he drew near. Cortés, dismounting, threw his reins to a page, and, supported by a few of the principal cavaliers, advanced to meet him. The interview must have been one of uncommon interest to both. In Montezuma, Cortés beheld the lord of the broad realms he had traversed, whose magnificence and power had been the burden of every tongue. In the Spaniard, on the other hand, the Aztec prince saw the strange being whose history seemed to be so mysteriously connected with his own; the predicted one of his oracles; whose achievements proclaimed him something more than human. But, whatever may have been the monarch's feelings, he so far suppressed them as to receive his guest with princely courtesy, and to express his satisfaction at personally seeing him in his capital. Cortés responded by the most profound expressions of respect, while he made ample acknowledgments for the substantial proofs which the emperor had given the Spaniards of his munificence. He then hung round Montezuma's neck a sparkling chain of coloured crystal, accompanying this with a movement as if to embrace him, when he was restrained by the two Aztec lords, shocked at the menaced profanation of the sacred person of their master. After the interchange of these civilities, Montezuma appointed his brother to conduct the Spaniards to their residence in the capital, and again entering his litter, was borne off amidst prostrate crowds in the same state in which he had come. The Spaniards quickly followed, and with colours flying and music playing soon made their entrance into the southern quarter of Tenochtitlan.

Here, again, they found fresh cause for admiration in the grandeur of the city, and the superior style of its architecture. The dwellings of the poorer class were, indeed, chiefly of reeds and mud. But the great avenue through which they were now marching was lined with the houses of the nobles, who were encouraged by the emperor to make the capital their residence. They were built of a red porous stone drawn from quarries in the neighbourhood, and, though they rarely rose to a second story, often covered a large space of ground. The flat roofs, *azoteas,* were protected by stone parapets, so that every house was a fortress. Sometimes these roofs resembled parterres of flowers, so thickly were they covered with them, but more frequently these were cultivated in broad terraced gardens, laid out between the edifices. Occasionally a great square or market-place intervened, surrounded by its porticoes of stone and stucco; or a pyramidal temple reared its colossal bulk, crowned with its tapering sanctuaries, and altars blazing with inextinguishable fires. The great street facing the southern causeway, unlike most others in the place, was wide, and extended some miles in nearly a straight line, as before noticed, through the centre of the city. A spectator standing at one end of it, as his eye ranged along the deep vista of temples, terraces, and gardens, might clearly discern the other, with the blue mountains in the distance, which, in the transparent atmosphere of the table-land, seemed almost in contact with the buildings.

But what most impressed the Spaniards was the throngs of people who swarmed through the streets and on the canals, filling every door-way and window, and clustering on the roofs of the buildings. "I well remember the spectacle," exclaims Bernal Diaz; "it seems now, after so many years, as present to my mind as if it were but yesterday." But what must have been the sensations of the Aztecs themselves, as they looked on the portentous pageant! as they heard, now for the first time, the well-cemented pavement ring under the iron tramp of the horses,—the strange animals which fear had clothed in such supernatural terrors; as they gazed on the children of the East, revealing their celestial origin in their fair complexions; saw the bright falchions and bonnets of steel, a metal to them unknown, glancing like meteors in the sun, while sounds of unearthly music—at least, such as their rude instruments had never wakened — floated in the air! But every other emotion was lost in that of deadly hatred, when they beheld their detested enemy, the Tlascalan, stalking in defiance as it were, through their streets, and staring around with looks of ferocity and wonder, like some wild animal of the forest, who had strayed by chance from his native fastnesses into the haunts of civilisation.

As they passed down the spacious street, the troops repeatedly traversed bridges suspended above canals, along which they saw the Indian barks gliding swiftly with their little cargoes of fruits and vegetables for the markets of Tenochtitlan. At length, they halted before a broad area near the centre of the city, where rose the huge pyramidal pile dedicated to the patron war-god of the Aztecs, second only in size, as well as sanctity, to the temple of Cholula, and covering the same ground now in part occupied by the great cathedral of Mexico.

Facing the western gate of the inclosure of the temple stood a low range of stone buildings, spreading over a wide extent of ground, the palace of Axayacatl, Montezuma's father, built by that monarch about fifty years before. It was appropriated as the barracks of the Spaniards. The emperor himself was in the courtyard, waiting to receive them. Approaching Cortés, he took from a vase of flowers, borne by one of his slaves, a massy collar, in which the shell of a species of craw-fish, much prized by the Indians, was set in gold, and connected by heavy links of the same metal. From this chain depended eight ornaments, also of gold, made in resemblance of the same shell-fish, a span in length each, and of delicate workmanship; for the Aztec goldsmiths were confessed to have shown skill in their craft, not inferior to their brethren of Europe. Montezuma, as he hung the gorgeous collar round the general's neck, said, "This palace belongs to you, Malinche" (the epithet by which he always addressed him), "and your brethren. Rest after your fatigues, for you have much need to do so, and in a little while I will visit you again." So saying, he withdrew with his attendants, evincing, in this act, a delicate consideration not to have been expected in a barbarian. * * *

1843

## *HISTORY OF THE CONQUEST OF PERU*

*From* BOOK III, CHAPTER V

### [THE MASSACRE AT CAXAMALCA]

The clouds of the evening had passed away, and the sun rose bright on the following morning, the most memorable epoch in the annals of Peru. It was Saturday, the 16th of November, 1532. The loud cry of the trumpet called the Spaniards to arms with the first streak of dawn; and Pizarro, briefly acquainting them with the plan of the assault, made the necessary dispositions.

The *plaza,* as mentioned in the preceding chapter, was defended on its three sides by low ranges of buildings, consisting of spacious halls with wide doors or vomitories opening into the square. In these halls he stationed his cavalry in two divisions, one under his brother Hernando, the other under De Soto. The infantry he placed in another of the buildings, reserving twenty chosen men to act with himself as occasion might require. Pedro de Candia, with a few soldiers and the artillery,—comprehending under this imposing name two small pieces of ordnance, called falconets,—he established in the fortress. All received orders to wait at their posts till the arrival of the Inca. After his entrance into the great square, they were still to remain under cover, withdrawn from observation, till the signal was given by the discharge of a gun, when they were to cry their war-cries, to rush out in a body from their covert, and, putting the Peruvians to the sword, bear off the person of the Inca. The arrangement of the immense halls, opening on a level with the *plaza,* seemed to be contrived on purpose for a *coup de théâtre.* Pizarro particularly inculcated order and implicit obedience, that in the hurry of the moment there should be no confusion. Everything depended on their acting with concert, coolness, and celerity.

The chief next saw that their arms were in good order; and that the breastplates of their horses were garnished with bells, to add by their noise to the consternation of the Indians. Refreshments were also liberally provided, that the troops should be in condition for the conflict. These arrangements being completed, mass was performed with great solemnity by the ecclesiastics who attended the expedition; the God of battles was invoked to spread his shield over the soldiers who were fighting to extend the empire of the Cross; and all joined with enthusiasm in the chant, *"Exsurge Domine,"* "Rise, O Lord! and judge thine own cause." One might have supposed them a company of martyrs, about to lay down their lives in defence of their faith, instead of a licentious band of adventurers, meditating one of the most atrocious acts of perfidy on the record of history! Yet, whatever were the vices of the Castilian cavalier, hypocrisy was not among the number. He felt that he was battling for the Cross, and under this conviction, exalted as it was at such a moment as this into predominant impulse, he was blind to the baser motives which mingled with the enterprise. With feelings thus kindled to a flame of religious ardour, the soldiers of Pizarro looked forward with renovated spirits to the coming conflict; and the chieftain saw with satisfaction, that in the hour of trial his men would be true to their leader and themselves.

It was late in the day before any movement was visible in the Peruvian camp, where much preparation was making to approach the Christian quarters with due state and ceremony. A message was received from Atahuallpa, informing the Spanish commander that he should come with his warriors fully armed, in the same manner as the Spaniards had come to his quarters the night preceding. This was not an agreeable intimation to Pizarro, though he had no reason, probably, to expect the contrary. But to object might imply distrust, or, perhaps, disclose, in some measure, his own designs. He expressed his satisfaction, therefore, at the intelligence, assuring the Inca, that, come as he would, he would be received by him as a friend and brother.

It was noon before the Indian procession was on its march, when it was seen occupying the great causeway for a long extent. In front came a large body of attendants, whose office seemed to be to sweep away every particle of rubbish from the road. High above the crowd appeared the Inca, borne on the shoulders of his principal nobles, while others of the same rank marched by the sides of his litter, displaying such a dazzling show of ornaments on their persons, that, in the language of one of the Conquerors, "they blazed like the sun." But the greater part of the Inca's forces mustered along the fields that lined the road, and were spread over the broad meadows as far as the eye could reach.

When the royal procession had arrived within half a mile of the city, it came to a halt; and Pizarro saw, with surprise, that Atahuallpa was preparing to pitch his tents, as if to encamp there. A messenger soon after arrived, informing the Spaniards that the Inca would occupy his present station the ensuing night, and enter the city on the following morning.

This intelligence greatly disturbed Pizarro, who had shared in the general impatience of his men at the tardy movements of the Peruvians. The troops had been under arms since daylight, the cavalry mounted, and the infantry at their post, waiting in silence the coming of the Inca. A profound stillness reigned throughout the town, broken only at intervals by the cry of the sentinel from the summit of the fortress, as he proclaimed the movements of the Indian army. Nothing, Pizarro well knew, was so trying to the soldier as prolonged suspense, in a critical situation like the present; and he feared lest his ardor might evaporate, and be succeeded by that nervous feeling natural to the bravest soul at such a crisis, and which, if not fear, is near akin to it. He returned an answer, therefore, to Atahuallpa, deprecating his change of purpose; and adding, that he had provided everything for his entertainment, and expected him that night to sup with him.

This message turned the Inca from his purpose; and, striking his tents again, he resumed his march, first advising the general that he should leave the greater part of his warriors behind, and enter the place with only a few of them, and without arms, as he preferred to pass the night at Caxamalca. At the same time he ordered accommodation to be provided for himself and his retinue in one of the large stone buildings, called, from a serpent sculptured on the walls, "the House of the Serpent." No tidings could have been more grateful to the Spaniards. It seemed as if the Indian monarch was eager to rush into the snare that had been spread for him! The fanatical cavalier could not fail to discern in it the immediate finger of Providence. * * *

As the leading files of the procession entered the great square, larger, says an old chronicler, than any square in Spain, they opened to the right and left for the royal retinue to pass. Everything was conducted with admirable order. The monarch was permitted to traverse the *plaza* in silence, and not a Spaniard was to be seen. When some five or six thousand of his people had entered the place, Atahuallpa halted, and, turning round with an inquiring look, demanded, "Where are the strangers?"

At this moment Fray Vicente de Valverde, a Dominican friar, Pizarro's chaplain, and afterwards Bishop of Cuzco, came forward with his breviary, or, as other accounts say, a Bible, in one hand, and a crucifix in the other, and, approaching the Inca, told him that he came by order of his commander to expound to him the doctrines of the true faith, for which purpose the Spaniards had come from a great distance to his country. * * * The friar concluded with beseeching the Peruvian monarch to receive him kindly; to abjure the errors of his own faith, and embrace that of the Christians now proffered to him, the only one by which he could hope for salvation; and, furthermore, to acknowledge himself a tributary of the Emperor Charles the Fifth, who, in that event, would aid and protect him as his loyal vassal. * * *

The eyes of the Indian monarch flashed fire, and his dark brow grew darker as he replied, "I will be no man's tributary. I am greater than any prince upon earth. Your emperor may be a great prince; I do not doubt it, when I see that he has sent his subjects so far across the waters; and I am willing to hold him as a brother. As for the Pope of whom you speak, he must be crazy to talk of giving away countries which do not belong to him. For my faith," he continued, "I will not change it. Your own God, as you say, was put to death by the very men whom he created. But mine," he concluded, pointing to his deity,—then alas! sinking in glory behind the mountains, —"my God still lives in the heavens, and looks down on his children."

He then demanded of Valverde by what authority he had said these things. The friar pointed to the book which he held, as his authority. Atahuallpa, taking it, turned over the pages a moment, then, as the insult he had received probably flashed across his mind, he threw it down with vehemence, and exclaimed,—"Tell your comrades that they shall give me an account of their doings in my land. I will not go from here, till they have made me full satisfaction for all the wrongs they have committed."

The friar, greatly scandalized by the indignity offered to the sacred volume, stayed only to pick it up, and, hastening to Pizarro, informed him of what had been done, exclaiming, at the same time,—"Do you not see, that, while we stand here wasting our breath in talking with this dog, full of pride as he is, the fields are filling with Indians! Set on, at once; I absolve you." Pizarro saw that the hour had come. He waved a white scarf in the air, the appointed signal. The fatal gun was fired from the fortress. Then, springing into the square, the Spanish captain and his followers shouted the old war-cry of "St. Jago and at them." It was answered by the battle-cry of every Spaniard in the city, as, rushing from the avenues of the great halls in which they were concealed, they poured into the *plaza,* horse and foot, each in his own dark column, and threw themselves into the midst of the Indian crowd. The latter, taken by surprise, stunned by the report of artillery and muskets, the echoes of which reverberated like thunder from the surrounding buildings, and blinded by the smoke which rolled in sulphurous volumes along the square, were seized with a panic. They knew not whither to fly for refuge from the coming ruin. Nobles and commoners,—all were trampled down under the fierce charge of the cavalry, who dealt their blows, right and left, without sparing; while their swords, flashing through the thick gloom, carried dismay into the hearts of the wretched natives, who now, for the first time, saw the horse and his rider in all their terrors. They made no resistance,—as, indeed, they had no weapons with which to make it. Every avenue to escape was closed, for the entrance to the square was choked up with the dead bodies of men who had perished in vain efforts to fly; and, such was the agony of the survivors under the terrible pressure of their assailants, that a large body of Indians, by their convulsive struggles, burst through the wall of stone and dried clay which formed part of the boundary of the *plaza!* It fell, leaving an opening of more than a hundred paces, through which multitudes now found their way into the country, still hotly pursued by the cavalry, who, leaping the fallen rubbish, hung on the rear of the fugitives, striking them down in all directions.

Meanwhile the fight, or rather massacre, continued hot around the Inca, whose person was the great object of the assault. His faithful nobles, rallying about him, threw themselves in the way of the assailants, and strove, by tearing them from their saddles, or, at least, by offering their own bosoms as a mark for their vengeance, to shield their beloved master. It is said by some authorities, that they carried weapons concealed under their clothes. If so, it availed them little, as it is not pretended that they used them. But the most timid animal will defend itself when at bay. That they did not do so in the present instance is proof that they had no weapons to use. Yet they still continued to force back the cavaliers, clinging to their horses with dying grasp, and, as one was cut down, another taking the place of his fallen comrade with a loyalty truly affecting.

The Indian monarch, stunned and bewildered, saw his faithful subjects falling round him without fully comprehending his situation. The litter on which he rode heaved to and fro, as the mighty press swayed backwards and forwards; and he gazed on the overwhelming ruin, like some forlorn mariner, who, tossed about in his bark by the furious elements, sees the lightning's flash and hears the thunder bursting around him with the consciousness that he can do nothing to avert his fate. At length, weary with the work of destruction, the Spaniards, as the shades of evening grew deeper, felt afraid that the royal prize might, after all, elude them; and some of the cavaliers made a desperate attempt to end the affray at once by taking Atahuallpa's life. But Pizarro, who was nearest his person, called out with Stentorian voice, "Let no one, who values his life, strike at the Inca;" and, stretching out his arm to shield him, received a wound on the hand from one of his own men,—the only wound received by a Spaniard in the action.

The struggle now became fiercer

than ever round the royal litter. It reeled more and more, and at length several of the nobles who supported it having been slain, it was overturned, and the Indian prince would have come with violence to the ground, had not his fall been broken by the efforts of Pizarro and some other of the cavaliers, who caught him in their arms. The imperial *borla* was instantly snatched from his temples by a soldier named Estete, and the unhappy monarch, strongly secured, was removed to a neighbouring building, where he was carefully guarded.

All attempt at resistance now ceased. The fate of the Inca soon spread over town and country. The charm which might have held the Peruvians together was dissolved. Every man thought only of his own safety. Even the soldiery encamped on the adjacent fields took the alarm, and, learning the fatal tidings, were seen flying in every direction before their pursuers, who in the heat of triumph showed no touch of mercy. At length night, more pitiful than man, threw her friendly mantle over the fugitives, and the scattered troops of Pizarro rallied once more at the sound of the trumpet in the bloody square of Caxamalca.

The number of slain is reported, as usual, with great discrepancy. Pizarro's secretary says two thousand natives fell. A descendant of the Incas—a safer authority than Garcilasso—swells the number to ten thousand. Truth is generally found somewhere between the extremes. The slaughter was incessant, for there was nothing to check it. That there should have been no resistance will not appear strange, when we consider the fact, that the wretched victims were without arms, and that their senses must have been completely overwhelmed by the strange and appalling spectacle which burst on them so unexpectedly. "What wonder was it," said an ancient Inca to a Spaniard, who repeats it, "what wonder that our countrymen lost their wits, seeing blood run like water, and the Inca, whose person we all of us adore, seized and carried off by a handful of men?" Yet though the massacre was incessant, it was short in duration. The whole time consumed by it, the brief twilight of the tropics, did not much exceed half an hour; a short period indeed,—yet long enough to decide the fate of Peru, and to subvert the dynasty of the Incas.

That night Pizarro kept his engagement with the Inca, since he had Atahuallpa to sup with him.

1847

## II. FRANCIS PARKMAN
(1823–1893)

### *MONTCALM AND WOLFE*

*From* CHAPTER XXVII

1750

### THE HEIGHTS OF ABRAHAM

* * * At last the time for action came. On Wednesday, the twelfth, the troops at St. Nicolas were embarked again, and all were told to hold themselves in readiness. Wolfe, from the flagship "Sutherland," issued his last general orders. "The enemy's force is now divided, great scarcity of provisions in their camp, and universal discontent among the Canadians.

Our troops below are in readiness to join us; all the light artillery and tools are embarked at the Point of Levi; and the troops will land where the French seem least to expect it. The first body that gets on shore is to march directly to the enemy and drive them from any little post they may occupy; the officers must be careful that the succeeding bodies do not by any mistake fire on those who go before them. The battalions must form on the upper ground with expedition, and be ready to charge whatever presents itself. When the artillery and troops are landed, a corps will be left to secure the landing-place, while the rest march on and endeavor to bring the Canadians and French to a battle. The officers and men will remember what their country expects from them, and what a determined body of soldiers inured to war is capable of doing against five weak French battalions mingled with a disorderly peasantry."

The spirit of the army answered to that of its chief. The troops loved and admired their general, trusted their officers, and were ready for any attempt. "Nay, how could it be otherwise," quaintly asks honest Sergeant John Johnson, of the fifty-eighth regiment, "being at the heels of gentlemen whose whole thirst, equal with their general, was for glory? We had seen them tried, and always found them sterling. We knew that they would stand by us to the last extremity."

Wolfe had thirty-six hundred men and officers with him on board the vessels of Holmes; and he now sent orders to Colonel Burton at Point Levi to bring to his aid all who could be spared from that place and the Point of Orleans. They were to march along the south bank, after nightfall, and wait further orders at a designated spot convenient for embarkation. Their number was about twelve hundred, so that the entire force destined for the enterprise was at the utmost forty-eight hundred. With these, Wolfe meant to climb the heights of Abraham in the teeth of an enemy who, though much reduced, were still twice as numerous as their assailants.

Admiral Saunders lay with the main fleet in the Basin of Quebec. This excellent officer, whatever may have been his views as to the necessity of a speedy departure, aided Wolfe to the last with unfailing energy and zeal. It was agreed between them that while the General made the real attack, the admiral should engage Montcalm's attention by a pretended one. As night approached, the fleet ranged itself along the Beauport shore; the boats were lowered and filled with sailors, marines, and the few troops that had been left behind; while ship signalled to ship, cannon flashed and thundered, and shot ploughed the beach, as if to clear a way for assailants to land. In the gloom of the evening, the effect was imposing. Montcalm, who thought that the movements of the English above the town were only a feint, that their main force was still below it, and that their real attack would be made there, was completely deceived, and massed his troops in front of Beauport to repel the expected landing. But while in the fleet of Saunders all was uproar and ostentatious menace, the danger was ten miles away, where the squadron of Holmes lay tranquil and silent at its anchorage off Cap-Rouge.

It was less tranquil than it seemed. All on board knew that a blow would be struck that night, though only a few high officers knew where. Colonel Howe, of the light infantry, called for volunteers to lead the unknown and desperate venture, promising, in the words of one of them, " that if any of us survived we might depend on being recommended to the General." As many as were wanted—twenty-four in all—soon came forward. Thirty large bateaux and some boats belonging to the squadron lay moored alongside the vessels; and late in the evening the troops were ordered into them, the twenty-four volunteers taking their place in the foremost. They held in all about seventeen hundred men. The rest remained on board.

Bougainville could discern the movement, and misjudged it, thinking that he himself was to be attacked. The tide was still flowing; and, the better to deceive him, the vessels and boats were allowed to drift upward with it for a little distance, as if to land above Cap-Rouge.

The day had been fortunate for Wolfe. Two deserters came from the camp of Bougainville with intelligence that, at ebb tide on the next night, he was to send down a convoy of provisions to Montcalm. The necessities of the camp at Beauport, and the difficulties of transportation by land, had before compelled the French to resort to this perilous means of conveying supplies; and their boats, drifting in darkness under the shadows of the northern shore, had commonly passed in safety. Wolfe saw at once that, if his own boats went down in advance of the convoy, he could turn the intelligence of the deserters to good account.

He was still on board the " Sutherland." Every preparation was made, and every order given; it only remained to wait the turning of the tide. Seated with him in the cabin was the commander of the sloop-of-war " Porcupine," his former schoolfellow, John Jervis, afterwards Earl St. Vincent. Wolfe told him that he expected to die in the battle of the next day; and taking from his bosom a miniature of Miss Lowther, his betrothed, he gave it to him with a request that he would return it to her if the presentiment should prove true.

Towards two o'clock the tide began to ebb, and a fresh wind blew down the river. Two lanterns were raised into the maintop shrouds of the " Sutherland." It was the appointed signal; the boats cast off and fell down with the current, those of the light infantry leading the way. The vessels with the rest of the troops had orders to follow a little later. * * *

For full two hours the procession of boats, borne on the current, steered silently down the St. Lawrence. The stars were visible, but the night was moonless and sufficiently dark. The general was in one of the foremost boats, and near him was a young midshipman, John Robison, afterwards professor of natural philosophy in the University of Edinburgh. He used to tell in his later life how Wolfe, with a low voice, repeated Gray's Elegy in a Country Churchyard to the officers about him. Probably it was to relieve the intense strain of his thoughts. Among the rest was the verse which his own fate was soon to illustrate,—

The paths of glory lead but to the grave.

"Gentlemen," he said, as his recital ended, "I would rather have written those lines than take Quebec." None were there to tell him that the hero is greater than the poet.

As they neared their destination, the tide bore them in towards the shore, and the mighty wall of rock and forest towered in darkness on their left. The dead stillness was suddenly broken by the sharp *Qui vive!* of a French sentry, invisible in the thick gloom. *France!* answered a Highland officer of Fraser's regiment from one of the boats of the light infantry. He had served in Holland, and spoke French fluently.

*À quel régiment?*

*De la Reine,* replied the Highlander. He knew that a part of that corps was with Bougainville. The sentry, expecting the convoy of provisions, was satisfied, and did not ask for the password.

Soon after, the foremost boats were passing the heights of Samos, when another sentry challenged them, and they could see him through the darkness running down to the edge of the water, within range of a pistol-shot. In answer to his questions, the same officer replied, in French: "Provision-boats. Don't make a noise; the English will hear us." In fact, the sloop-of-war "Hunter" was anchored in the stream not far off. This time, again, the sentry let them pass. In a few moments they rounded the headland above the Anse du Foulon. There was no sentry there. The strong current swept the boats of the light infantry a little below the intended landing-place. They disembarked on a narrow strand at the foot of heights as steep as a hill covered with trees can be. The twenty-four volunteers led the way, climbing with what silence they might, closely followed by a much larger body. When they reached the top they saw in the dim light a cluster of tents at a short distance, and immediately made a dash at them. Vergor leaped from bed and tried to run off, but was shot in the heel and captured. His men, taken by surprise, made little resistance. One or two were caught, and the rest fled.

The main body of troops waited in their boats by the edge of the strand. The heights near by were cleft by a great ravine choked with forest trees; and in its depths ran a little brook called Ruisseau St.-Denis, which, swollen by the late rains, fell plashing in the stillness over a rock. Other than this no sound could reach the strained ear of Wolfe but the gurgle of the tide and the cautious climbing of his advance-parties as they mounted the steeps at some little distance from where he sat listening. At length from the top came a sound of musket-shots, followed by loud huzzas, and he knew that his men were masters of the position. The word was given; the troops leaped from the boats and scaled the heights, some here, some there, clutching at trees and bushes, their muskets slung at their backs. Tradition still points out the place, near the mouth of the ravine, where the foremost reached the top. Wolfe said to an officer near him: "You can try it, but I don't think you'll get up." He himself, however, found strength to drag himself up with the rest. The narrow slanting path on the face of the heights had been made impassable by trenches and abattis; but all obstructions were soon cleared away, and then the ascent was easy. In the gray of the morning the long file of red-coated soldiers moved quickly upward, and formed in order on the plateau above.

Before many of them had reached the top, cannon were heard close on the left. It was the battery at Samos firing on the boats in the rear and the vessels descending from Cap-Rouge. A party was sent to silence it; this was soon effected, and the more distant battery at Sillery was next attacked and taken. As fast as the boats were emptied they returned for the troops left on board the vessels and for those waiting on the southern shore under Colonel Burton.

The day broke in clouds and threatening rain. Wolfe's battalions were drawn up along the crest of the heights. No enemy was in sight, though a body of Canadians had sallied from the town and moved along the strand towards the landing-place, whence they were quickly driven back. He had achieved the most critical part of his enterprise; yet the success that he coveted placed him in imminent danger. On one side was the garrison of Quebec and the army of Beauport, and Bougainville was on the other. Wolfe's alternative was victory or ruin; for if he should be overwhelmed by a combined attack, retreat would be hopeless. His feelings no man can know; but it would be safe to say that hesitation or doubt had no part in them.

He went to reconnoitre the ground, and soon came to the Plains of Abraham, so called from Abraham Martin, a pilot known as Maître Abraham, who had owned a piece of land here in the early times of the colony. The Plains were a tract of grass, tolerably level in most parts, patched here and there with cornfields, studded with clumps of bushes, and forming a part of the high plateau at the eastern end of which Quebec stood. On the south it was bounded by the declivities along the St. Lawrence; on the north, by those along the St. Charles, or rather along the meadows through which that lazy stream crawled like a writhing snake. At the place that Wolfe chose for his battle-field the plateau was less than a mile wide.

Thither the troops advanced, marched by files till they reached the ground, and then wheeled to form their line of battle, which stretched across the plateau and faced the city. It consisted of six battalions and the detached grenadiers from Louisbourg, all drawn up in ranks three deep. Its right wing was near the brink of the heights along the St. Lawrence; but the left could not reach those along the St. Charles. On this side a wide space was perforce left open, and there was danger of being outflanked. To prevent this, Brigadier Townshend was stationed here with two battalions, drawn up at right angles with the rest, and fronting the St. Charles. The battalion of Webb's regiment, under Colonel Burton, formed the reserve; the third battalion of Royal Americans was left to guard the landing; and Howe's light infantry occupied a wood far in the rear. Wolfe, with Monckton and Murray, commanded the front line, on which the heavy fighting was to fall, and which, when all the troops had arrived, numbered less than thirty-five hundred men.

Quebec was not a mile distant, but they could not see it; for a ridge of broken ground intervened, called Buttes-à-Neveu, about six hundred paces off. The first division of troops had scarcely come up when, about six o'clock, this ridge was suddenly thronged with white uniforms. It was the battalion of Guienne, arrived at the eleventh hour from its camp by the St. Charles. Some time after there was hot firing in the rear. It came from a detachment of Bougainville's command attacking a house where some of the light infantry were posted. The assailants were repulsed, and the firing ceased. Light showers fell at intervals, besprinkling the troops as they stood patiently waiting the event.

Montcalm had passed a troubled night. Through all the evening the cannon bellowed from the ships of Saunders, and the boats of the fleet hovered in the dusk off the Beauport shore, threatening every moment to land. Troops lined the intrenchments till day, while the General walked the field that adjoined his headquarters till one in the morning, accompanied by the Chevalier Johnstone and Colonel Poulariez. Johnstone says that he was in great agitation, and took no rest all night. At daybreak he heard the sound of cannon above the town. It was the battery at Samos firing on the English ships. He had sent an officer to the quarters of Vaudreuil, which were much nearer Quebec, with orders to bring him word at once should anything unusual happen. But no word came, and about six o'clock he mounted and rode thither with Johnstone. As they advanced, the country behind the town opened more and more upon their sight; till at length, when opposite Vaudreuil's house, they saw across the St. Charles, some two miles away, the red ranks of British soldiers on the heights beyond. "This is a serious business," Montcalm said; and sent off Johnstone at full gallop to bring up the troops from the centre and left of the camp. Those of the right were in motion already, doubtless by the Governor's order. Vaudreuil came out of the house. Montcalm stopped for a few words with him; then set spurs to his horse, and rode over the bridge of the St. Charles to the scene of danger. He rode with a fixed look, uttering not a word.

The army followed in such order as it might, crossed the bridge in hot haste, passed under the northern rampart of Quebec, entered at the Palace Gate, and pressed on in headlong march along the quaint narrow streets of the warlike town: troops of Indians in scalp-locks and war-paint, a savage glitter in their deep-set eyes; bands of Canadians whose all was at stake,—faith, country, and home; the colony regulars; the battalions of Old France, a torrent of white uniforms and gleaming bayonets, La Sarre, Languedoc, Roussillon, Béarn,—victors of Oswego, William Henry, and Ticonderoga. So they swept on, poured out upon the plain, some by the gate of St. Louis, and some by that of St. John, and hurried, breathless, to where the banners of Guienne still fluttered on the ridge.

Montcalm was amazed at what he saw. He had expected a detachment, and he found an army. Full in sight before him stretched the lines of Wolfe: the close ranks of the English infantry, a silent wall of red, and the wild array of the Highlanders, with their waving tartans, and bagpipes screaming defiance. Vaudreuil had not come; but not the less was felt the evil of a divided authority and the jealousy of the rival chiefs. Montcalm waited long for the forces he had ordered to join him from the left wing of the army. He waited in vain. It is said that the governor had detained them, lest the English should attack the Beauport shore. Even if they did so, and succeeded, the French might defy them, could they but put Wolfe to rout on the Plains of Abraham. Neither did the garrison of Quebec come to the aid of Montcalm. He sent to Ramesay, its commander, for twenty-five field-pieces which were on the Palace battery. Ramesay would give him only three, saying that he wanted them for his own defence. There were orders and counter-orders, misunderstanding, haste, delay, perplexity.

Montcalm and his chief officers held a council of war. It is said that he and they alike were for immediate attack. His enemies declare that he was afraid lest Vaudreuil should arrive and take command; but the Governor was not a man to assume responsibility at such a crisis. Others say that his impetuosity overcame his better judgment; and of this charge it is hard to acquit him. Bougainville was but a few miles distant, and some of his troops were much nearer; a messenger sent by way of Old Lorette could have reached him in an hour and a half at most, and a combined attack in front and rear might have been concerted with him. If, moreover, Montcalm could have come to an understanding with Vaudreuil, his own force might have been strengthened by two or three thousand additional men from the town and the camp of Beauport; but he felt that there was no time to lose, for he imagined that Wolfe would soon be reinforced, which was impossible, and he believed that the English were fortifying themselves, which was no less an error. He has been blamed not only for fighting too soon, but for fighting at all. In this he could not choose. Fight he must, for Wolfe was now in a position to cut off all his supplies. His men were full of ardor, and he resolved to attack before their ardor cooled. He spoke a few words to them in his keen, vehement way. "I remember very well how he looked," one of the Canadians, then a boy of eighteen, used to say in his old age; "he rode a black or dark bay horse along the front of our lines, brandishing his sword, as if to excite us to do our duty. He wore a coat with wide sleeves, which fell back as he raised his arm, and showed the white linen of the wristband."

The English waited the result with a composure which, if not quite real, was at least well feigned. The three field-pieces sent by Ramesay plied them with canister-shot, and fifteen hundred Canadians and Indians fusilladed them in front and flank. Over all the plain, from behind bushes and knolls and the edge of cornfields, puffs of smoke sprang incessantly from the guns of these hidden marksmen. Skirmishers were thrown out before the lines to hold them in check, and the soldiers were ordered to lie on the grass to avoid the shot. The firing was liveliest on the English left, where bands of sharpshooters got under the edge of the declivity, among thickets, and behind scattered houses, whence they killed and wounded a considerable number of Townshend's men. The light infantry were called up from the rear. The houses were taken and retaken, and one or more of them was burned.

Wolfe was everywhere. How cool he was, and why his followers loved him, is shown by an incident that happened in the course of the morning. One of his captains was shot through the lungs; and on recovering consciousness he saw the General standing at his side. Wolfe pressed his hand, told him not to despair, praised his services, promised him early promotion, and sent an aide-de-camp to Monckton to beg that officer to keep the promise if he himself should fall.

It was towards ten o'clock when, from the high ground on the right of the line, Wolfe saw that the crisis was near. The French on the ridge had formed themselves into three bodies, regulars in the centre, regulars and Canadians on right and left. Two field-pieces, which had been dragged up the heights at Anse du Foulon, fired on them with grape-shot, and the troops, rising from the ground, prepared to receive them. In a few moments more they were in motion. They came on rapidly, uttering loud shouts, and firing as soon as they were within range. Their ranks, ill ordered at the best, were further confused by a number of Canadians who had been mixed among the regulars, and who, after hastily firing, threw themselves on the ground to reload. The British advanced a few rods; then halted and stood still. When the French were within forty paces the word of command rang out, and a crash of musketry answered all along the line. The volley was delivered with remarkable precision. In the battalions of the centre, which had suffered least from the enemy's bullets, the simultaneous explosion was afterwards said by the French officers to have sounded like a cannon-shot. Another volley followed, and then a furious clattering fire that lasted but a minute or two. When the smoke rose, a miserable sight was revealed: the ground cumbered with dead and wounded, the advancing masses stopped short and turned into a frantic mob, shouting, cursing, gesticulating. The order was given to charge. Then over the field rose the British cheer, mixed with the fierce yell of the Highland slogan. Some of the corps pushed forward with the bayonet; some advanced firing. The clansmen drew their broadswords and dashed on, keen and swift as bloodhounds. At the English right, though the attacking column was broken to pieces, a fire was still kept up, chiefly, it seems, by sharpshooters from the bushes and cornfields, where they had lain for an hour or more. Here Wolfe himself led the charge, at the head of the Louisbourg grenadiers. A shot shattered his wrist. He wrapped his handkerchief about it and kept on. Another shot struck him, and he still advanced, when a third lodged in his breast. He staggered, and sat on the ground. Lieutenant Brown, of the grenadiers, one Henderson, a volunteer in the same company, and a private soldier, aided by an officer of artillery who ran to join them, carried him in their arms to the rear. He begged them to lay him down. They did so, and asked if he would have a surgeon. "There's no need," he answered; "it's all over with me." A moment after, one of them cried out: "They run; see how they run!" "Who run?" Wolfe demanded, like a man roused from sleep. "The enemy, sir. Egad, they give way everywhere!" "Go, one of you, to Colonel Burton," returned the dying man; "tell him to march Webb's regiment down to Charles River, to cut off their retreat from the bridge." Then, turning on his side, he murmured, "Now, God be praised, I will die in peace!" and in a few moments his gallant soul had fled.

Montcalm, still on horseback, was borne with the tide of fugitives towards the town. As he approached the walls a shot passed through his body. He kept his seat; two soldiers supported him, one on each side, and led his horse through the St. Louis Gate. On the open space within, among the excited crowd, were several women, drawn, no doubt, by eagerness to know the result of the fight. One of them recognized him, saw the streaming blood, and shrieked, *"O mon Dieu! mon Dieu! le Marquis est tué!"* "It's nothing, it's nothing," replied the death-stricken man; "don't be troubled for me, my good friends." (*"Ce n'est rien, ce n'est rien; ne vous affligez pas pour moi, mes bonnes amies."*)

1884

# INDIAN AND PIONEER

## I. FRANCIS PARKMAN
### (1823–1893)

### *THE CALIFORNIA AND OREGON TRAIL*

*From* CHAPTER IX

### SCENES AT FORT LARAMIE

'Tis true they are a lawless brood,
But rough in form, nor mild in mood.
—THE BRIDE OF ABYDOS.

Looking back, after the expiration of a year, upon Fort Laramie and its inmates, they seem less like a reality than like some fanciful picture of the olden time; so different was the scene from any which this tamer side of the world can present. Tall Indians, enveloped in their white buffalo-robes, were striding across the area or reclining at full length on the low roofs of the buildings which inclosed it. Numerous squaws, gayly bedizened, sat grouped in front of the apartments they occupied; their mongrel offspring, restless and vociferous, rambled in every direction through the fort; and the trappers, traders and *engagés* of the establishment were busy at their labor or their amusements.

We were met at the gate, but by no means cordially welcomed. Indeed, we seemed objects of some distrust and suspicion, until Henry Chatillon explained that we were not traders, and we, in confirmation, handed to the *bourgeois* a letter of introduction from his principals. He took it, turned it upside down, and tried hard to read it; but his literary attainments not being adequate to the task, he applied for relief to the clerk, a sleek, smiling Frenchman, named Montalon. The letter read, Bordeaux (the *bourgeois*) seemed gradually to awaken to a sense of what was expected of him. Though not deficient in hospitable intentions, he was wholly unaccustomed to act as master of ceremonies. Discarding all formalities of reception, he did not honor us with a single word, but walked swiftly across the area, while we followed in some admiration to a railing and a flight of steps opposite the entrance. He signed to us that we had better fasten our horses to the railing; then he walked up the steps, tramped along a rude balcony, and kicking open a door, displayed a large room, rather more elaborately finished than a barn. For furniture it had a rough bedstead, but no bed; two chairs, a chest of drawers, a tin-pail to hold water, and a board to cut tobacco upon. A brass crucifix hung on the wall, and close at hand a recent scalp, with hair full a yard long, was suspended from a nail. I shall again have occasion to mention this dismal trophy, its history being connected with that of our subsequent proceedings.

This apartment, the best in Fort Laramie, was that usually occupied by the legitimate *bourgeois,* Papin; in whose absence the command devolved upon Bordeaux. The latter, a stout, bluff little fellow, much inflated by a sense of his new authority, began to roar for buffalo-robes. These being brought and spread upon the floor, formed our beds; much better ones than we had of late been accustomed to. Our arrangements made, we stepped out to the balcony to take a more leisurely survey of the long looked-for haven at which we had arrived at last. Beneath us was the square area surrounded by little rooms, or rather cells, which opened upon it. These were devoted to various purposes, but served chiefly for the accommodation of the men employed at the fort, or of the equally numerous squaws whom they were allowed to maintain in it. Opposite to us rose the blockhouse above the gateway; it was adorned with a figure which even now haunts my memory; a horse at full speed, daubed upon the boards with red paint, and exhibiting a degree of skill that might rival that displayed by the Indians in executing similar designs upon their robes and lodges. A busy scene was enacting in the area. The wagons of Vaskiss, an old trader, were about to set out for a remote post in the mountains, and the Canadians were going through their preparations with all possible bustle, while here and there an Indian stood looking on with imperturbable gravity. * * *

We did not long enjoy our new quarters undisturbed. The door was silently pushed open, and two eyeballs and a visage as black as night looked in upon us; then a red arm and shoulder intruded themselves, and a tall Indian, gliding in, shook us by the hand, grunted his salutation, and sat down on the floor. Others followed, with faces of the natural hue; and letting fall their heavy robes from their shoulders, they took their seats, quite at ease, in a semi-circle before us. The pipe was now to be lighted and passed round from one to another; and this was the only entertainment that at present they expected from us. These visitors were fathers, brothers, or other relatives of the squaws in the fort, where they were permitted to remain, loitering about in perfect idleness. All those who smoked with us were men of standing and repute. Two or three others dropped in also; young fellows who neither by their years nor their exploits were entitled to rank with the old men and warriors, and who, abashed in the presence of their superiors, stood aloof, never withdrawing their eyes from us. Their cheeks were adorned with vermilion, their ears with pendants of shell, and their necks with beads. Never yet having signalized themselves as hunters, or performed the honorable exploit of killing a man, they were held in slight esteem, and were diffident and bashful in proportion. Certain formidable inconveniences attended this influx of visitors. They were bent on inspecting everything in the room; our equipments and our dress alike underwent their scrutiny; for though the contrary has been carelessly asserted, few beings have more curiosity than Indians in regard to subjects within their ordinary range of thought. As to other matters, indeed, they seem utterly indifferent. They will not trouble themselves to inquire into what they cannot comprehend, but are quite contented to place their hands over their mouths in token of wonder, and exclaim that it is 'great medicine.' With this comprehensive solution, an Indian never is at a loss. He never launches forth into speculation and conjecture; his reason moves in its beaten track. His soul is dormant; and no exertions of the missionaries, Jesuit or Puritan, of the old world or of the new, have as yet availed to rouse it.

As we were looking, at sunset, from the wall, upon the wild and desolate plains that surround the fort, we observed a cluster of strange objects, like scaffolds, rising in the distance against the red western sky. They bore aloft some singular-looking burdens; and at their foot glimmered something white, like bones. This was the place of sepulture of some Dahcotah chiefs, whose remains their people are fond of placing in the vicinity of the fort, in the hope that they may thus be protected from violation at the hands of their enemies. Yet it has happened more than once, and quite recently, that war parties of the Crow Indians, ranging through the country, have thrown the bodies from the scaffolds, and broken them to pieces, amid the yells of the Dahcotahs, who remained pent up in the fort, too few to defend the honored relics from insult. The white objects upon the ground were buffalo-skulls, arranged in the mystic circle commonly seen at Indian places of sepulture upon the prairie.

We soon discovered, in the twilight, a band of fifty or sixty horses approaching the fort. These were the animals belonging to the establishment; who having been sent out to feed, under the care of armed guards, in the meadows below, were now being driven into the *corral* for the night. A little gate opened into this inclosure: by the side of it stood one of the guards, an old Canadian, with gray bushy eyebrows, and a dragoon-pistol stuck into his belt; while his comrade, mounted on horseback, his rifle laid across the saddle in front of him, and his long hair blowing before his swarthy face, rode at the rear of the disorderly troop, urging them up the ascent. In a moment the narrow *corral* was thronged with the half-wild horses, kicking, biting, and crowding restlessly together.

The discordant jingling of a bell, rung by a Canadian in the area, summoned us to supper. This sumptuous repast was served on a rough table in one of the lower apartments of the fort, and consisted of cakes of bread and dried buffalo-meat—an excellent thing for strengthening the teeth. At this meal were seated the *bourgeois* and superior dignitaries of the establishment, among whom Henry Chatillon was worthily included. No sooner was it finished than the table was spread a second time (the luxury of bread being now, however, omitted) for the benefit of certain hunters and trappers of an inferior standing; while the ordinary Canadian *engagés* were regaled on dried meat in one of their lodging rooms. * * *

We were sitting, on the following morning, in the passageway between the gates, conversing with the traders Vaskiss and May. These two men, together with our sleek friend, the clerk Montalon, were, I believe, the only persons then in the fort who could read and write. May was telling a curious story about the traveller Catlin, when an ugly, diminutive Indian, wretchedly mounted, came up at a gallop, and rode past us into the fort. On being questioned, he said that Smoke's village was close at hand. Accordingly only a few minutes elapsed before the hills beyond the river were covered with a disorderly swarm of savages, on horseback and on foot. May finished his story; and by that time the whole array had descended to Laramie Creek, and commenced crossing it in a mass. I walked down to the bank. The stream is wide, and was then between three and four feet deep, with a very swift current. For several rods the water was alive with dogs, horses, and Indians. The long poles used in erecting the lodges are carried by the horses, being fastened by the heavier end, two or three on each side, to a rude sort of pack-saddle, while the other end drags on the ground. About a foot behind the horse a kind of large basket or pannier is suspended between the poles, and firmly lashed in its place. On the back of the horse are piled various articles of luggage; the basket also is well filled with domestic utensils, or, quite as often, with a litter of puppies, a brood of small children, or a superannuated old man. Numbers of these curious vehicles, called, in the bastard language of the country, *travaux,* were now splashing together through the stream. Among them swam countless dogs, often burdened with miniature *travaux;* and dashing forward on horseback through the throng came the superbly formed warriors, the slender figure of some lynx-eyed boy clinging fast behind them. The women sat perched on the pack-saddles, adding not a little to the load of the already over-burdened horses. The confusion was prodigious. The dogs yelled and howled in chorus; the puppies in the *travaux* set up a dismal whine as the water invaded their comfortable retreat; the little black-eyed children, from one year of age upward, clung fast with both hands to the edge of their baskets, and looked over in alarm at the water rushing so near them, sputtering and making wry mouths as it splashed against their faces. Some of the dogs, encumbered by their load, were carried down by the current, yelping piteously; and the old squaws would rush into the water, seize their favorites by the neck and drag them out. As each horse gained the bank he scrambled up as he could. Stray horses and colts came among the rest, often breaking away at full speed through the crowd, followed by the old hags, screaming, after their fashion, on all occasions of excitement. Buxom young squaws, blooming in all the charms of vermilion, stood here and there on the bank, holding aloft their master's lance as a signal to collect the scattered portions of his household. In a few moments the crowd melted away; each family, with its horses and equipage, filing off to the plain at the rear of the fort; and here, in the space of half an hour, arose sixty or seventy of their tapering lodges. Their horses were feeding by hundreds over the surrounding prairie, and their dogs were roaming everywhere. The fort was full of men, and the children were whooping and yelling incessantly under the walls.

These new-comers were scarcely arrived, when Bordeaux was running across the fort, shouting to his squaw to bring him his spy-glass. The obedient Marie, the very model of a squaw, produced the instrument, and Bordeaux hurried with it up to the wall. Pointing it to the eastward, he exclaimed, with an oath, that the families were coming. But a few moments elapsed before the heavy caravan of the emigrant wagons could be seen, steadily advancing from the hills. They gained the river, and without turning or pausing plunged in; they passed through, and slowly ascending the opposing bank, kept directly on their way past the fort and the Indian village, until, gaining a spot a quarter of a mile distant, they wheeled into a circle. For some time our tranquillity was undisturbed. The emigrants were preparing their encampment; but no sooner was this accomplished, than Fort Laramie was fairly taken by storm. A crowd of broad-brimmed hats, thin visages, and staring eyes appeared suddenly at the gate. Tall, awkward men, in brown homespun; women with cadaverous faces and long lank figures, came thronging in together, and, as if inspired by the very demon of curiosity, ransacked every nook and corner of the fort. Dismayed at this invasion, we withdrew in all speed to our chamber, vainly hoping that it might prove an inviolable sanctuary. The emigrants prosecuted their investigations with untiring vigor. They penetrated the rooms, or rather dens, inhabited by the astonished squaws. They explored the apartments of the men, and even that of Marie and the *bourgeois*. At last a numerous deputation appeared at our door, but were immediately expelled. Being totally devoid of any sense of delicacy or propriety, they seemed resolved to search every mystery to the bottom.

Having at length satisfied their curiosity, they next proceeded to business. The men occupied themselves in procuring supplies for their onward journey; either buying them with money or giving in exchange superfluous articles of their own.

The emigrants felt a violent prejudice against the French Indians, as they called the trappers and traders. They thought, and with some justice, that these men bore them no good will. Many of them were firmly persuaded that the French were instigating the Indians to attack and cut them off. On visiting the encampment we were at once struck with the extraordinary perplexity and indecision that prevailed among the emigrants. They seemed like men totally out of their element; bewildered and amazed, like a troop of schoolboys lost in the woods. It was impossible to be long among them without being conscious of the high and bold spirit with which most of them were animated. But the *forest* is the home of the backwoodsman. On the remote prairie he is totally at a loss. He differs as much from the genuine 'mountain-man,' the wild prairie hunter, as a Canadian voyageur, paddling his canoe on the rapids of the Ottawa, differs from an American sailor among the storms of Cape Horn. Still my companion and I were somewhat at a loss to account for this perturbed state of mind. It could not be cowardice: these men were of the same stock with the volunteers of Monterey and Buena Vista. Yet, for the most part, they were the rudest and most ignorant of the frontier population; they knew absolutely nothing of the country and its inhabitants; they had already experienced much misfortune and apprehended more; they had seen nothing of mankind, and had never put their own resources to the test.

A full proportion of suspicion fell upon us. Being strangers, we were looked upon as enemies. Having occasion for a supply of lead and a few other necessary articles, we used to go over to the emigrant camps to obtain them. After some hesitation, some dubious glances, and fumbling of the hands in the pockets, the terms would be agreed upon, the price tendered, and the emigrant would go off to bring the article in question. After waiting until our patience gave out, we would go in search of him, and find him seated on the tongue of his wagon.

"Well, stranger," he would observe, as he saw us approach, "I reckon I won't trade!"

Some friend of his had followed him from the scene of the bargain, and suggested in his ear that clearly we meant to cheat him, and he had better have nothing to do with us.

This timorous mood of the emigrants was doubly unfortunate, as it exposed them to real danger. Assume, in the presence of Indians, a bold bearing, self-confident yet vigilant, and you will find them tolerably safe neighbors. But your safety depends on the respect and fear you are able to inspire. If you betray timidity or indecision, you convert them from that moment into insidious and dangerous enemies. The Dahcotah saw clearly enough the perturbation of the emigrants, and instantly availed themselves of it. They became extremely insolent and exacting in their demands. It has become an established custom with them to go to the camp of every party, as it arrives in succession at the fort, and demand a feast. Smoke's village had come with this express design, having made several days' journey with no other object than that of enjoying a cup of coffee and two or three biscuits. So the 'feast' was demanded, and the emigrants dared not refuse it.

One evening, about sunset, the village was deserted. We met old men, warriors, squaws, and children in gay attire, trooping off to the encampment, with faces of anticipation; and, arriving here, they seated themselves in a semicircle. Smoke occupied the centre, with his warriors on either hand; the young men and boys next succeeded, and the squaws and children formed the horns of the crescent. The biscuit and coffee were most promptly dispatched, the emigrants staring open-mouthed at their savage guests. With each emigrant party that arrived at Fort Laramie this scene was renewed; and every day the Indians grew more rapacious and presumptuous. One evening they broke to pieces, out of mere wantonness, the cups from which they had been feasted; and this so exasperated the emigrants that many of them seized their rifles and could scarcely be restrained from firing on the insolent mob of Indians. Before we left the country this dangerous spirit on the part of the Dahcotah had mounted to a yet higher pitch. They began openly to threaten the emigrants with destruction, and actually fired upon one or two parties of whites. A military force and military law are urgently called for in that perilous region; and unless troops are speedily stationed at Fort Laramie, or elsewhere in the neighborhood, both the emigrants and other travellers will be exposed to most imminent risks. * * *

But to glance at the interior of a lodge. Shaw and I used often to visit them. Indeed we spent most of our evenings in the Indian village; Shaw's assumption of the medical character giving us a fair pretext. As a sample of the rest I will describe one of these visits. The sun had just set, and the horses were driven into the *corral.* The Prairie Cock, a noted beau, came in at the gate with a bevy of young girls, with whom he began a dance in the area, leading them round and round in a circle, while he jerked up from his chest a succession of monotonous sounds, to which they kept time in a rueful chant. Outside the gate boys and young men were idly frolicking; and close by, looking grimly upon them, stood a warrior in his robe, with his face painted jet-black, in token that he had lately taken a Pawnee scalp. Passing these, the tall dark lodges rose between us and the red western sky. We repaired at once to the lodge of Old Smoke himself. It was by no means better than the others; indeed, it was rather shabby; for in this democratic community the chief never assumes superior state. Smoke sat cross-legged on a buffalo-robe, and his grunt of salutation as we entered was unusually cordial, out of respect no doubt to Shaw's medical character. Seated around the lodge were several squaws, and an abundance of children. The complaint of Shaw's patients was, for the most part, a severe inflammation of the eyes, occasioned by exposure to the sun, a species of disorder which he treated with some success. He had brought with him a homœopathic medicine-chest, and was, I presume, the first who introduced that harmless system of treatment among the Ogillallah. No sooner had a robe been spread at the head of the lodge for our accommodation, and we had seated ourselves upon it, than a patient made her appearance; the chief's daughter herself, who, to do her justice, was the best-looking girl in the village. Being on excellent terms with the physician, she placed herself readily under his hands, and submitted with a good grace to his applications, laughing in his face during the whole process, for a squaw hardly knows how to smile. This case dispatched, another of a different kind succeeded. A hideous, emaciated old woman sat in the darkest corner of the lodge, rocking to and fro with pain, and hiding her eyes from the light by pressing the palms of both hands against her face. At Smoke's command she came forward very unwillingly, and exhibited a pair of eyes that had nearly disappeared from excess of inflammation. No sooner had the doctor fastened his gripe upon her than she set up a dismal moaning, and writhed so in his grasp that he lost all patience, but being resolved to carry his point, he succeeded at last in applying his favorite remedies.

"It is strange," he said, when the operation was finished, "that I forgot to bring any Spanish flies with me; we must have something here to answer for a counter-irritant!"

So, in the absence of better, he seized upon a red-hot brand from the fire, and clapped it against the temple of the old squaw, who set up an unearthly howl, at which the rest of the family broke out into a laugh.

During these medical operations Smoke's eldest squaw entered the lodge with a sort of stone mallet in her hand. I had observed some time before a litter of well-grown black puppies comfortably nestled among some buffalo-robes at one side, but this new-comer speedily disturbed their enjoyment; for, seizing one of them by the hind paw, she dragged him out, and carrying him to the entrance of the lodge, hammered him on the head till she killed him. Being quite conscious to what this preparation tended, I looked through a hole in the back of the lodge to see the next steps of the process. The squaw, holding the puppy by the legs, was swinging him to and fro through the blaze of a fire, until the hair was singed off. This done, she unsheathed her knife and cut him into small pieces, which she dropped into a kettle to boil. In a few moments a large wooden dish was set before us, filled with this delicate preparation. We felt conscious of the honor. A dog-feast is the greatest compliment a Dahcotah can offer to his guest; and knowing that to refuse eating would be an affront, we attacked the little dog, and devoured him before the eyes of his unconscious parent. Smoke in the meantime was preparing his great pipe. It was lighted when we had finished our repast, and we passed it from one to another till the bowl was empty. This done, we took our leave without farther ceremony, knocked at the gate of the fort, and after making ourselves known, were admitted.

1847–8

# II. DAVID CROCKETT
## (1786–1836)

## *A NARRATIVE OF THE LIFE OF DAVID CROCKETT*

### [INDIAN FIGHTING UNDER ANDREW JACKSON]

In a few days afterwards, we heard of some Indians in a town about eight miles off. So we mounted our horses, and put out for that town, under the direction of two friendly Creeks we had taken for pilots. We had also a Cherokee colonel, Dick Brown, and some of his men with us. When we got near the town we divided; one of our pilots going with each division. And so we passed on each side of the town, keeping near to it, until our lines met on the far side. We then closed up at both ends, so as to surround it completely; and then we sent Captain Hammond's company of rangers to bring on the affray. He had advanced near the town, when the Indians saw him, and they raised the yell, and came running at him like so many red devils. The main army was now formed in a hollow square around the town, and they pursued Hammond till they came in reach of us. We then gave them a fire, and they returned it, and then ran back into their town. We began to close on the town by making our files closer and closer, and the Indians soon saw they were our property. So most of them wanted us to take them prisoners; and their squaws and all would run and take hold of any of us they could, and give themselves up. I saw seven squaws have hold of one man, which made me think of the Scriptures. So I hollered out the Scriptures was fulfilling; that there was seven women holding to one man's coat tail. But I believe it was a hunting shirt all the time. We took them all prisoners that came out to us in this way; but I saw some warriors run into a house, until I counted forty-six of them. We pursued them until we got near the house, when we saw a squaw sitting in the door, and she placed her feet against the bow she had in her hand, and then took an arrow, and, raising her feet, she drew with all her might, and let fly at us, and she killed a man, whose name, I believe, was Moore. He was a lieutenant, and his death so enraged us all, that she was fired on, and had at least twenty balls blown through her. This was the first man I ever saw killed with a bow and arrow. We now shot them like dogs; and then set the house on fire, and burned it up with the forty-six warriors in it. I recollect seeing a boy who was shot down near the house. His arm and thigh was broken, and he was so near the burning house that the grease was stewing out of him. In this situation he was still trying to crawl along; but not a murmur escaped him, though he was only about twelve years old. So sullen is the Indian, when his dander is up, that he had sooner die than make a noise, or ask for quarters.

The number that we took prisoners, being added to the number we killed, amounted to one hundred and eighty-six; though I don't remember the exact number of either. We had five of our men killed. We then returned to our camp, at which our fort was erected, and known by the name of Fort Strother. No provisions had yet reached us, and we had now been for several days on half rations. However we went back to our Indian town on the next day, when many of the carcasses of the Indians were still to be seen. They looked very awful, for the burning had not entirely consumed them, but given them a very terrible appearance, at least what was left of them. * * * We then again returned to the army, and remained there several days half starving, as all our beef was gone. We commenced eating the beef-hides, and continued to eat every scrap we could lay our hands on.

## [ELECTIONEERING ON THE FRONTIER]

I went first into Heckman county, to see what I could do among the people as a candidate. Here they told me that they wanted to move their town nearer to the centre of the county, and I must come out in favour of it. There's no devil if I knowed what this meant, or how the town was to be moved; and so I kept dark, going on the identical same plan that I now find is called *"non-committal."* About this time there was a great squirrel hunt on Duck river, which was among my people. They were to hunt two days: then to meet and count the scalps, and have a big barbecue, and what might be called a tip-top country frolic. The dinner, and a general treat, was all to be paid for by the party having taken the fewest scalps. I joined one side, taking the place of one of the hunters, and got a gun ready for the hunt. I killed a great many squirrels, and when we counted scalps, my party was victorious.

The company had every thing to

eat and drink that could be furnished in so new a country, and much fun and good humour prevailed. But before the regular frolic commenced, I mean the dancing, I was called on to make a speech as a candidate; which was a business I was as ignorant of as an outlandish negro.

A public document I had never seen, nor did I know there were such things; and how to begin I couldn't tell. I made many apologies, and tried to get off, for I know'd I had a man to run against who could speak prime, and I know'd, too, that I wa'n't able to shuffle and cut with him. He was there, and knowing my ignorance as well as I did myself, he also urged me to make a speech. The truth is, he thought my being a candidate was a mere matter of sport; and didn't think, for a moment, that he was in any danger from an ignorant backwoods bear hunter. But I found I couldn't get off, and so I determined just to go ahead, and leave it to chance what I should say. I got up and told the people, I reckoned they know'd what I come for, but if not, I could tell them. I had come for their votes, and if they didn't watch mighty close, I'd get them too. But the worst of all was, that I couldn't tell them any thing about government. I tried to speak about something, and I cared very little what, until I choaked up as bad as if my mouth had been jam'd and cram'd chock full of dry mush. There the people stood, listening all the while, with their eyes, mouths, and years all open, to catch every word I would speak.

At last I told them I was like a fellow I had heard of not long before. He was beating on the head of an empty barrel near the road-side, when a traveler, who was passing along, asked him what he was doing that for? The fellow replied, that there was some cider in that barrel a few days before, and he was trying to see if there was any then, but if there was he couldn't get at it. I told them that there had been a little bit of speech in me a while ago, but I believed I couldn't get it out. They all roared out in a mighty laugh, and I told some other anecdotes, equally amusing to them, and believing I had them in a first-rate way, I quit and got down, thanking the people for their attention. But I took care to remark that I was dry as a powder horn and that I thought it was time for us to wet our whistles a little; and so I put off to the liquor stand, and was followed by the greater part of the crowd.

I felt certain this was necessary, for I knowed my competitor could open government matters to them as easy as he pleased. He had, however, mighty few left to hear him, as I continued with the crowd, now and then taking a horn, and telling good humoured stories, till he was done speaking. I found I was good for the votes at the hunt.

## [BEAR HUNTING IN TENNESSEE]

* * * I found, when I got there, they had treed the bear in a large forked poplar, and it was setting in the fork.

I could see the lump, but not plain enough to shoot with any certainty, as there was no moonlight; and so I set in to hunting for some dry brush to make me a light; but I could find none, though I could find that the ground was torn mightily to pieces by the cracks.

At last I thought I could shoot by guess, and kill him; so I pointed as near the lump as I could, and fired away. But the bear didn't come; he only clomb up higher, and got out on a limb, which helped me to see him better. I now loaded up again and fired, but this time he didn't move at all. I commenced loading for a third fire, but the first thing I knowed, the bear was down among my dogs, and they were fighting all around me. I had my big butcher in my belt, and I had a pair of dressed buckskin breeches on. So I took out my knife, and stood, determined, if he should get hold of me, to defend myself in the best way I could. I stood there for some time, and could now and then see a white dog I had, but the rest of them, and the bear, which were dark coloured, I couldn't see at all, it was so miserable dark. They still fought around me, and sometimes within three feet of me; but, at last, the bear got down into one of the cracks, that the earthquakes had made in the ground, about four feet deep, and I could tell the biting end of him by the hollering of my dogs. So I took my gun and pushed the muzzle of it about, till I thought I had it against the main part of his body, and fired; but it happened to be only the fleshy part of his foreleg. With this, he jumped out of the crack, and he and the dogs had another hard fight around me, as before. At last, however, they forced him back into the crack again, as he was when I had shot.

I had laid down my gun in the dark, and I now began to hunt for it; and, while hunting, I got hold of a pole, and I concluded I would punch him awhile with that. I did so, and when I would punch him, the dogs would jump in on him, when he would bite them badly, and they would jump out again. I concluded, as he would take punching so patiently, it might be that he would lie still enough for me to get down in the crack, and feel slowly along till I could find the right place to give him a dig with my butcher. So I got down, and my dogs got in before him and kept his head towards them, till I got along easily up to him; and placing my hand on his rump, felt for his shoulder, just behind which I intended to stick him. I made a lounge with my long knife, and fortunately stuck him right through the heart; at which he just sank down, and I crawled out in a hurry. In a little time my dogs all come out too, and seemed satisfied, which was the way they always had of telling me that they had finished him.

I suffered very much that night with cold, as my leather breeches, and everything else I had on, was wet and frozen. But I managed to get my bear out of this crack after several hard trials, and so I butchered him, and laid down to try to sleep.

## [CROCKETT IN POLITICS]

I can say, on my conscience, that I was, without disguise, the friend and supporter of General Jackson, upon his principles as he laid them down, and as *"I understood them,"* before his election as president. During my two first sessions in Congress, Mr.

Adams was president, and I worked along with what was called the Jackson party pretty well. I was re-elected to Congress, in 1829, by an overwhelming majority; and soon after the commencement of this second term, I saw, or thought I did, that it was expected of me that I was to bow to the name of Andrew Jackson, and follow him in all his motions, and mindings, and turnings, even at the expense of my conscience and judgment. Such a thing was new to me, and a total stranger to my principles. I know'd well enough, though, that if I didn't "hurra" for his name, the hue and cry was to be raised against me, and I was to be sacrificed, if possible. His famous, or rather I should say his in-*famous* Indian bill was brought forward, and I opposed it from the purest motives in the world. Several of my colleagues got around me, and told me how well they loved me, and that I was ruining myself. They said this was a favourite measure of the president, and I ought to go for it. I told them I believed it was a wicked, unjust measure, and that I should go against it, let the cost to myself be what it might; that I was willing to go with General Jackson in every thing that I believed was honest and right; but, further than this, I wouldn't go for him, or any other man in the whole creation; that I would sooner be honestly and politically d—nd, than hypocritically immortalized. I had been elected by a majority of three thousand five hundred and eighty-five votes, and I believed they were honest men, and wouldn't want me to vote for any unjust notion, to please Jackson or any one else; at any rate, I was of age, and was determined to trust them. I voted against this Indian bill, and my conscience yet tells me that I gave a good honest vote, and one that I believe will not make me ashamed in the day of judgment. I served out my term, and though many amusing things happened, I am not disposed to swell my narrative by inserting them.

When it closed, and I returned home, I found the storm had raised against me sure enough; and it was echoed from side to side, and from end to end of my district, that I had turned against Jackson. This was considered the unpardonable sin. I was hunted down like a wild varment, and in this hunt every little newspaper in the district, and every little pin-hook lawyer was engaged. Indeed, they were ready to print any and every thing that the ingenuity of man could invent against me. Each editor was furnished with the journals of Congress from head-quarters; and hunted out every vote I had missed in four sessions, whether from sickness or not, no matter, and each one was charged against me at *eight* dollars. In all I had missed about *seventy* votes, which they made amount to five hundred and sixty dollars; and they contended I had swindled the government out of this sum, as I had received my pay, as other members do. I was now again a candidate in 1830, while all the attempts were making against me; and every one of these little papers kept up a constant war on me, fighting with every scurrilous report they could catch.

Over all I should have been elected, if it hadn't been, that but a few weeks before the election, the little fourpence-ha'penny limbs of the law fell on a plan to defeat me, which had the desired effect. They agreed to spread out over the district, and make appointments for me to speak, almost everywhere, to clear up the Jackson question. They would give me no notice of these appointments, and the people would meet in great crowds to hear what excuse Crockett had for quitting Jackson.

But instead of Crockett's being there, this small-fry of lawyers would be there, with their saddle-bags full of the little newspapers and their journals of Congress, and would get up and speak, and read their scurrilous attacks on me, and would then tell the people that I was afraid to attend; and in this way would turn many against me. All this intrigue was kept a profound secret from me, until it was too late to counteract it; and when the election came, I had a majority in seventeen counties, putting all their votes together, but the eighteenth beat me; and so I was left out of Congress during those two years. The people of my district were induced, by these tricks, to take a stay on me for that time; but they have since found out that they were imposed on, and on re-considering my case, have reversed the decision; which, as the Dutchman said, "is as fair a ding as eber was." * * *

After all this, the reader will perceive that I am now here in Congress, this 28th day of January, in the year of our Lord one thousand eight hundred and thirty-four; and that, what is more agreeable to my feelings as a freeman, I am at liberty to vote as my conscience and judgment dictates to be right, without the yoke of any party on me, or the driver at my heels, with his whip in hand, commanding me to ge-wo-haw, just at his pleasure. Look at my arms, you will find no party hand-cuff on them! Look at my neck, you will not find there any collar, with the engraving

> MY DOG.
>
> ANDREW JACKSON.

But you will find me standing up to my rack, as the people's faithful representative, and the public's most obedient, very humble servant,

DAVID CROCKETT.

1834

## III. AUGUSTUS BALDWIN LONGSTREET
(1790–1870)

### THE HORSE SWAP

During the session of the Superior Court, in the village of ——, about three weeks ago, when a number of people were collected in the principal street of the village, I observed a young man riding up and down the street, as I supposed, in a violent passion. He galloped this way, then that, and then the other. Spurred his horse to one group of citizens, then to another. Then dashed off at half speed, as if fleeing from danger; and suddenly checking his horse, returned —first in a pace, then in a trot, and then in a canter. While he was performing these various evolutions, he cursed, swore, whooped, screamed, and tossed himself in every attitude which man could assume on horse back. In short, he *cavorted* most magnanimously, (a term which, in our tongue, expresses all that I have described, and a little more) and seemed to be setting all creation at defiance. As I like to see all that is passing, I determined to take a position a little nearer to him, and to ascertain if possible, what it was that affected him so sensibly. Accordingly I approached a crowd before which he had stopt for a moment, and examined it with the strictest scrutiny.—But I could see nothing in it, that seemed to have any thing to do with the cavorter. Every man appeared to be in a good humor, and all minding their own business. Not one so much as noticed the principal figure. Still he went on. After a semicolon pause, which my appearance seemed to produce, (for he eyed me closely as I approached) he fetched a whoop, and swore that "he could out-swap any live man, woman or child, that ever walked these hills, or that ever straddled horse flesh since the days of old daddy Adam." "Stranger," said he to me, "did you ever see the *Yallow* Blossom from Jasper?"

"No," said I, "but I have often heard of him."

"I'm the boy," continued he; "perhaps a *leetle*—jist a *leetle* of the best man, at a horse swap, that ever trod shoe-leather."

I began to feel my situation a little awkward, when I was relieved by a man somewhat advanced in years, who stept up and began to survey the "*Yallow Blossom's*" horse with much apparent interest. This drew the rider's attention, and he turned the conversation from me to the stranger.

"Well, my old coon," said he, "do you want to swap *hosses?*"

"Why, I don't know," replied the stranger; "I believe I've got a beast I'd trade with you for that one, if you like him."

"Well, fetch up your nag, my old cock; you're jist the lark I wanted to get hold of. I am perhaps a *leetle,* jist a *leetle,* of the best man at a horse swap, that ever stole *cracklins* out of his mammy's fat gourd. Where's your *hoss?*"

"I'll bring him presently; but I want to examine your horse a little."

"Oh! look at him," said the Blossom, alighting and hitting him a cut—"look at him. He's the best piece of *hoss* flesh in the thirteen united universal worlds. There's no sort o' mistake in little Bullet. He can pick up miles on his feet and fling 'em behind him as fast as the next man's *hoss,* I don't care where he comes from.—And he can keep at it as long as Sun can shine without resting."

During this harangue, little Bullet looked as if he understood it all, believed it, and was ready at any moment to verify it. He was a horse of goodly countenance, rather expressive of vigilance than fire; though an unnatural appearance of fierceness was thrown into it, by the loss of his ears, which had been cropt pretty close to his head. Nature had done but little for Bullet's head and neck; but he managed, in a great measure, to hide their defects, by bowing perpetually. He had obviously suffered severely for corn; but if his ribs and hip bones had not disclosed the fact, *he* never would have done it; for he was in all respects, as cheerful and happy, as if he commanded all the corn-cribs and fodder stacks in Georgia. His height was about twelve hands; but as his shape partook somewhat of that of the Giraffe, his haunches stood much lower. They were short, strait, peaked, and concave. Bullet's tail, however, made amends for all his defects. All that the artist could do to beautify it, had been done; and all that horse could do to compliment the artist, Bullet did. His tail was nicked in superior style, and exhibited the line of beauty in so many directions, that it could not fail to hit the most fastidious taste in some of them. From the root it dropt into a graceful festoon; then rose in a handsome curve; then resumed its first direction; and then mounted suddenly upwards like a cypress knee to a perpendicular of about two and a half inches. The whole had a careless and bewitching inclination to the right. Bullet obviously knew where his beauty lay, and took all occasions to display it to the best advantage. If a stick cracked, or if any one moved suddenly about him, or coughed, or hawked, or spoke a little louder than common, up went Bullet's tail like lightning; and if the *going up* did not please, the *coming down* must of necessity, for it was as different from the other movement, as was its direction. The first, was a bold and rapid flight upward; usually to an angle of forty-five degrees. In this position he kept his interesting appendage, until he satisfied himself that nothing in particular was to be done; when he commenced dropping it by half inches, in second beats—then in triple time—then faster and shorter, and faster and shorter still; until it finally died away imperceptibly into its natural position. If I might compare sights to sounds, I should say, its *settling*, was more like the note of a locust than any thing else in nature.

Either from native sprightliness of disposition, from uncontrolable activity, or from an unconquerable habit of removing flies by the stamping of the feet, Bullet never stood still; but always kept up a gentle fly-scaring movement of his limbs, which was peculiarly interesting.

"I tell you, man," proceeded the Yellow Blossom, "he's the best live hoss that ever trod the grit of Georgia. Bob Smart knows the hoss. Come here, Bob, and mount this hoss and show Bullet's motions." Here, Bullet bristled up, and looked as if he had been hunting for Bob all day long, and had just found him. Bob sprang on his back. "Boo-oo-oo!" said Bob, with a fluttering noise of the lips; and away went Bullet, as if in a quarter race, with all his beauties spread in handsome style.

"Now fetch him back," said Blossom. Bullet turned and came in pretty much as he went out.

"Now trot him by." Bullet reduced his tail to "*customary*"—sidled to the right and left airily, and exhibited at least three varieties of trot, in the short space of fifty yards.

"Make him pace!" Bob commenced twitching the bridle and kicking at the same time. These inconsistent movements obviously (and most naturally) disconcerted Bullet; for it was impossible for him to learn, from them, whether he was to proceed or stand still. He started to trot—and was told that wouldn't do. He attempted a canter—and was checked again. He stopt—and was urged to go on. Bullet now rushed into the wide field of experiment, and struck out a gait of his own, that completely turned the tables upon his rider, and certainly deserved a patent. It seemed to have derived its elements from the jig, the minuet and the cotillon. If it was not a pace, it certainly had *pace* in it; and no man would venture to call it any thing else; so it passed off to the satisfaction of the owner.

"Walk him!" Bullet was now at home again; and he walked as if money was staked on him.

The stranger, whose name I afterwards learned was Peter Ketch, having examined Bullet to his heart's content, ordered his son Neddy to go and bring up Kit. Neddy soon appeared upon Kit; a well formed sorrel of the middle size, and in good order. His *tout ensemble* threw Bullet entirely in the shade; though a glance was sufficient to satisfy any one, that Bullet had the decided advantage of him in point of intellect.

"Why man," said Blossom, "do you bring such a hoss as that to trade for Bullet? Oh, I see you're no notion of trading."

"Ride him off, Neddy!" said Peter. Kit put off at a handsome lope.

"Trot him back!" Kit came in at a long, sweeping trot, and stopt suddenly at the crowd.

"Well," said Blossom, "let me look at him; may be he'll do to plough."

"Examine him!" said Peter, taking hold of the bridle close to the mouth; "He's nothing but a tacky. He an't as *pretty* a horse as Bullet, I know; but he'll do. Start 'em together for a hundred and fifty *mile;* and if Kit an't twenty mile ahead of him at the coming out, any man may take Kit for nothing. But he's a monstrous mean horse, gentlemen; any man may see that. He's the scariest horse, too, you ever saw. He won't do to hunt on, no how. Stranger, will you let Neddy have your rifle to shoot off him? Lay the rifle between his ears, Neddy, and shoot at the blaze in that stump. Tell me when his head is high enough."

Ned fired, and hit the blaze; and Kit did not move a hair's breadth.

"Neddy, take a couple of sticks and beat on that hogshead at Kit's tail."

Ned made a tremendous rattling; at which *Bullet* took fright, broke his bridle and dashed off in grand style; and would have stopt all farther negotiations, by going home in disgust, had not a traveller arrested him and brought him back; but Kit did not move.

"I tell you, gentlemen," continued Peter, "he's the scariest horse you ever saw. He an't as gentle as Bullet; but he won't do any harm if you watch him. Shall I put him in a cart, gig, or wagon for you, stranger? He'll cut the same capers there he does here. He's a monstrous mean horse."

During all this time, Blossom was examining him with the nicest scrutiny. Having examined his frame and limbs, he now looked at his eyes.

"He's got a curious look out of his eyes," said Blossom.

"Oh yes, sir," said Peter, "just as blind as a bat. Blind horses always have clear eyes. Make a motion at his eyes, if you please, sir."

Blossom did so, and Kit threw up his head rather as if something pricked him under the chin, than as if fearing a blow. Blossom repeated the experiment, and Kit jirked back in considerable astonishment.

"Stone blind, you see, gentlemen," proceeded Peter; "but he's just as good to travel of a dark night as if he had eyes."

"Blame my buttons," said Blossom, "if I like them eyes."

"No," said Peter, "nor I neither. I'd rather have 'em made of diamonds; but they'll do, if they don't show as much white as Bullet's."

"Well," said Blossom, "make a pass at me."

"No," said Peter; "you made the banter; now make your pass."

"Well I'm never afraid to price my hosses. You must give me twenty-five dollars boot."

"Oh, certainly; say fifty, and my saddle and bridle in. Here, Neddy, my son, take away daddy's horse."

"Well," said Blossom, "I've made my pass; now you make yours."

"I'm for short talk in a horse swap; and therefore always tell a gentleman, at once, what I mean to do. You must give me ten dollars."

Blossom swore absolutely, roundly and profanely, that he never would give boot. .

"Well," said Peter, "I didn't care about trading; but you cut such high shines, that I thought I'd like to back you out; and I've done it. Gentlemen, you see I've brought him to a hack."

"Come, old man," said Blossom, "I've been joking with you. I begin to think you do want to trade; therefore, give me five dollars and take Bullet. I'd rather lose ten dollars, any time, than not make a trade; though I hate to fling away a good hoss."

"Well," said Peter, "I'll be as clever as you are. Just put the five dollars on Bullet's back and hand him over, it's a trade."

Blossom swore again, as roundly as before, that he would not give boot; and, said he, "Bullet wouldn't hold five dollars on his back, no how. But as I bantered you, if you say an even swap, here's at you."

"I told you," said Peter, "I'd be as clever as you; therefore, here goes two dollars more, just for trade sake. Give me three dollars, and it's a bargain."

Blossom repeated his former assertion; and here the parties stood for a long time, and the by-standers (for many were now collected,) began to taunt both parties. After some time, however, it was pretty unanimously decided that the old man had backed Blossom out.

At length Blossom swore he "never would be backed out, for three dollars, after bantering a man;" and accordingly they closed the trade.

"Now," said Blossom, as he handed Peter the three dollars, "I'm a man, that when he makes a bad trade, makes the most of it until he can make a better. I'm for no rues and after-claps."

"That's just my way," said Peter; "I never goes to law to mend my bargains."

"Ah, you're the kind of boy I love to trade with. Here's your hoss, old man. Take the saddle and bridle off him, and I'll strip yours; but lift up the blanket easy from Bullet's back, for he's a mighty tenderbacked hoss."

The old man removed the saddle, but the blanket stuck fast. He attempted to raise it, and Bullet bowed himself, switched his tail, danced a little, and gave signs of biting.

"Don't hurt him, old man," said Blossom archly; "take it off easy. I am, perhaps, a leetle of the best man at a horse-swap that ever catched a coon."

Peter continued to pull at the blanket more and more roughly; and Bullet became more and more *cavortish:* in so much, that when the blanket came off, he had reached the *kicking* point in good earnest.

The removal of the blanket, disclosed a sore on Bullet's back-bone, that seemed to have defied all medical skill. It measured six full inches in length, and four in breadth; and had as many features as Bullet had motions. My heart sickened at the sight; and I felt that the brute who had been riding him in that situation, deserved the halter.

The prevailing feeling, however, was that of mirth. The laugh became loud and general, at the old man's expense; and rustic witticisms were liberally bestowed upon him and his late purchase. These, Blossom continued to provoke by various remarks. He asked the old man, "if he thought Bullet would let five dollars lie on his back." He declared most seriously, that he had owned that horse three months, and had never discovered before, that he had a sore back, "or he never should have thought of trading him," &c. &c.

The old man bore it all with the most philosophic composure. He evinced no astonishment at his late discovery, and made no replies. But his son, Neddy, had not disciplined his feelings quite so well. His eyes opened, wider and wider, from the first to the last pull of the blanket; and when the whole sore burst upon his view, astonishment and fright seemed to contend for the mastery of his countenance. As the blanket disappeared, he stuck his hands in his breeches pockets, heaved a deep sigh, and lapsed into a profound reverie; from which he was only roused by the cuts at his father. He bore them as long as he could; and when he could contain himself no longer, he began, with a certain wildness of expression, which gave a peculiar interest to what he uttered: "His back's mighty bad off; but dod drot my soul, if he's put it to daddy as bad as he thinks he has, for old Kit's both blind and *deef,* I'll be dod drot if he eint."

"The devil he is," said Blossom.

"Yes, dod drot my soul if he eint. You walk him and see if he *eint.* His eyes don't look like it; but he *jist as live go agin* the house with you, or in a ditch, as any how. Now you go try him." The laugh was now turned on Blossom; and many rushed to test the fidelity of the little boy's report. A few experiments established its truth, beyond controversy.

"Neddy," said the old man, "you oughtn't to try and make people discontented with their things." "Stranger, don't mind what the little boy says. If you can only get Kit rid of them little failings, you'll find him all sorts of a horse. You are a *leetle* the best man, at a horse swap, that ever I got hold of; but don't fool away Kit. Come, Neddy, my son, let's be moving; the stranger seems to be getting snappish."

1835

# IV. WILLIAM GILMORE SIMMS
## (1806–1870)

## *THE YEMASSEE*

### CHAPTER XXV

### [THE DEATH OF OCCONESTOGA]

The pain of death is nothing. To the chief,
The forest warrior, it is good to die—
To die as he has lived, battling and hoarse,
Shouting a song of triumph. But to live
Under such doom as this, were far beyond
Even his stoic, cold philosophy.

It was a gloomy amphitheatre in the deep forests to which the assembled multitude bore the unfortunate Occonestoga. The whole scene was unique in that solemn grandeur, that sombre hue, that deep spiritual repose, in which the human imagination delights to invest the region which has been rendered remarkable for the deed of punishment or crime. A small swamp or morass hung upon one side of the wood, from the rank bosom of which, in numberless millions, the flickering fire-fly perpetually darted upwards, giving a brilliance and animation to the spot, which at that moment, no assemblage of light or life could possibly enliven. The ancient oak, a bearded Druid, was there to contribute to the due solemnity of all associations—the green but gloomy cedar, the ghostly cypress, and here and there, the over-grown pine,—all rose up in their primitive strength, and with an undergrowth around them of shrub and flower, that scarcely, at any time, in that sheltered and congenial habitation, had found it necessary to shrink from winter. In the center of the area thus invested, rose a high and venerable mound, the tumulus of many preceding ages, from the washed sides of which might now and then be seen protruding the bleached bones of some ancient warrior or sage. A circle of trees at a little distance hedged it in,—made secure and sacred by the performance there of many of their religious rites and offices,—themselves, as they bore the broad arrow of the Yemassee, being free from all danger of overthrow or desecration by Indian hands.

Amid the confused cries of the multitude, they bore the captive to the foot of the tumulus, and bound him backward, half reclining upon a tree. An hundred warriors stood around, armed according to the manner of the nation, each with a tomahawk, and knife, and bow. They stood up as for battle, but spectators simply, and took no part in a proceeding which belonged entirely to the priesthood. In a wider and denser circle, gathered hundreds more—not the warriors, but the people—the old, the young, the women, and the children, all fiercely excited, and anxious to see a ceremony, so awfully exciting to an Indian imagination; involving, as it did, not only the perpetual loss of human caste and national consideration, but the eternal doom, the degradation, the denial of, and the exile from, their simple forest heaven. Interspersed with this latter crowd, seemingly at regular intervals, and with an allotted labour assigned them, came a number of old women, not unmeet representatives, individually, for either of the weird sisters of the Scottish Thane,

So withered and so wild in their attire—

and, regarding their cries and actions,

of whom we may safely affirm that they looked like anything but inhabitants of earth! In their hands they bore, each of them, a flaming torch, of the rich and gummy pine; and these they waved over the heads of the multitude in a thousand various evolutions, accompanying each movement with a fearful cry, which, at regular periods, was chorused by the assembled mass. A bugle, a native instrument of sound, five feet or more in length, hollowed out from the commonest timber—the cracks and breaks of which were carefully sealed up with the resinous gum oozing from their burning torches, and which to this day, borrowed from the natives, our negroes employ on the southern waters with a peculiar compass and variety of note—was carried by one of the party, and gave forth at intervals, timed with much regularity, a long protracted, single blast, adding greatly to the wild and picturesque character of the spectacle. At the articulation of these sounds, the circles continued to contract, though slowly; until at length but a brief space lay between the armed warriors, the crowd, and the unhappy victim.

The night grew dark of a sudden, and the sky was obscured by one of the brief tempests that usually usher in the summer, and mark the transition, in the south, of one season to the other. A wild gust rushed along the wood. The leaves were whirled over the heads of the assemblage, and the trees bent downwards, until they cracked and groaned again beneath the wind. A feeling of natural superstition crossed the minds of the multitude, as the hurricane, though common enough in that region, passed hurriedly along; and a spontaneous and universal voice of chaunted prayer rose from the multitude, in their own wild and emphatic language, to the evil deity whose presence they beheld in its progress:

"Thy wing, Opitchi-Manneyto,
It o'erthrows the tall trees—
Thy breath, Opitchi-Manneyto,
Makes the waters tremble—
Thou art in the hurricane,
When the wigwam tumbles—
Thou art in the arrow-fire,
When the pine is shiver'd—
But upon the Yemassee,
Be thy coming gentle—
Are they not thy well-beloved?
Bring they not a slave to thee?
Look! the slave is bound for thee,
'Tis the Yemassee that brings him.
Pass, Opitchi-Manneyto—
Pass, black spirit, pass from us—
Be thy passage gentle."

And as the uncouth strain rose at the conclusion into a diapason of unanimous and contending voices, of old and young, male and female, the brief summer tempest had gone by. A shout of self-gratulation, joined with warm acknowledgments, testified the popular sense and confidence in that especial Providence, which even the most barbarous nations claim as for ever working in their behalf.

At this moment, surrounded by the chiefs, and preceded by the great prophet or high-priest, Enoree-Mattee, came Sanutee, the well-beloved of the Yemassee, to preside over the destinies of his son. There was a due and becoming solemnity, but nothing of the peculiar feelings of the father, visible in his countenance. Blocks of wood were placed around as seats for the chiefs, but Sanutee and the prophet threw themselves, with more of imposing veneration in the proceeding, upon the edge of the tumulus, just where an overcharged spot, bulging out with the crowding bones of its inmates, had formed an elevation answering the purpose of couch or seat. They sat, directly looking upon the prisoner, who reclined, bound securely upon his back to a decapitated tree, at a little distance before them. A signal having been given, the women ceased their clamours, and approaching him they waved their torches so closely above his head as to make all his features distinctly visible to the now watchful and silent multitude. He bore the examination with stern, unmoved features, which the sculptor in brass or marble might have been glad to transfer to his statue in the block. While the torches waved, one of the women now cried aloud, in a barbarous chant, above him:—

"Is not this a Yemassee?
Wherefore is he bound thus—
Wherefore, with the broad arrow
On his right arm growing,
Wherefore is he bound thus—
Is not this a Yemassee?"

A second woman now approached him, waving her torch in like manner, seeming closely to inspect his features, and actually passing her fingers over the emblem upon his shoulder, as if to ascertain more certainly the truth of the image. Having done this, she turned about to the crowd, and in the same barbarous sort of strain with the preceding, replied as follows:—

"It is not the Yemassee,
But a dog that runs away.
From his right arm take the arrow,
He is not the Yemassee."

As these words were uttered, the crowd of women and children around cried out for the execution of the judgment thus given, and once again flamed the torches wildly, and the shoutings were general among the multitude. When they had subsided, a huge Indian came forward, and sternly confronted the prisoner. This man was Malatchie, the executioner; and he looked the horrid trade which he professed. His garments were stained and smeared with blood and covered with scalps, which, connected together by slight strings, formed a loose robe over his shoulders. In one hand he carried a torch, in the other a knife. He came forward, under the instructions of Enoree-Mattee, the prophet, to claim the slave of Opitchi-Manneyto,—that is, in our language, the slave of hell. This he did in the following strain:—

"'Tis Opitchi-Manneyto
In Malatchie's ear that cries,
This is not the Yemassee—
And the woman's word is true—
He's a dog that should be mine,
I have hunted for him long.
From his master he had run,
With the stranger made his home,
Now I have him, he is mine—
Hear Opitchi-Manneyto."

And, as the besmeared and malignant executioner howled his fierce demand in the very ears of his victim, he hurled the knife which he carried, upwards with such dexterity into the air, that it rested point downward and sticking fast, on its descent into the tree and just above the head of the doomed Occonestoga. With his hand, the next instant, he laid a resolute gripe upon the shoulder of the victim, as if to confirm and strengthen his claim by actual possession; while, at the same time, with a sort of malignant pleasure, he thrust his besmeared and distorted visage close into the face of his prisoner. Writhing against the ligaments which bound him fast, Occonestoga strove to turn his head aside from the disgusting and obtrusive presence; and the desperation of his effort, but that he had been too carefully secured, might have resulted in the release of some of his limbs; for the breast heaved and laboured, and every muscle of his arms and legs was wrought, by his severe action, into so many ropes, hard, full, and indicative of prodigious strength.

There was one person in that crowd who sympathized with the victim. This was Hiwassee, the maiden in whose ears he had uttered a word, which, in her thoughtless scream and subsequent declaration of the event, when she had identified him, had been the occasion of his captivity. Something of self-reproach for her share in his misfortune, and an old feeling of regard for Occonestoga, who had once been a favourite with the young of both sexes among his people, was at work in her bosom; and turning to Echotee, her newly-accepted lover, as soon as the demand of Malatchie had been heard, she prayed him to resist the demand. In such cases, all that a warrior had to do was simply to join issue upon the claim, and the popular will then determined the question. Echotee could not resist an application so put to him, and by one who had just listened to a prayer of his own, so all-important to his own happiness; and being himself a noble youth, one who had been a rival of the captive in his better days, a feeling of generosity combined with the request of Hiwassee, and he boldly leaped forward. Seizing the knife of Malatchie, which stuck in the tree, he drew it forth and threw it upon the ground, thus removing the sign of property which the executioner had put up in behalf of the evil deity.

"Occonestoga is the brave of the Yemassee," exclaimed the young Echotee, while the eyes of the captive looked what his lips could not have said. "Occonestoga is a brave of Yemassee—he is no dog of Malatchie. Wherefore is the cord upon the limbs of a free warrior? Is not Occonestoga a free warrior of Yemassee? The eyes of Echotee have looked upon a warrior like Occonestoga when he took many scalps. Did not Occonestoga lead the Yemassee against the Savannahs? The eyes of Echotee saw him slay the red-eyed Suwannee, the great chief of the Savannahs. Did not Occonestoga go on the war-path with our young braves against the Edistoes, the brown-foxes that came out of the swamp? The eyes of Echotee beheld him. Occonestoga is a brave, and a hunter of Yemassee—he is not the dog of Malatchie. He knows not fear. He hath an arrow with wings, and the panther he runs down in the chase. His tread is the tread of a sly serpent that comes, so that he hears him not, upon the track of the red deer, feeding down in the valley. Echotee knows the warrior—Echotee knows the hunter—he knows Occonestoga, but he knows no dog of Opitchi-Manneyto."

"He hath drunk of the poison drink of the pale-faces—his feet are gone from the good path of the Yemassee—he would sell his people to the English for a painted bird. He is the slave of Opitchi-Manneyto," cried Malatchie in reply. Echotee was not satisfied to yield the point so soon, and he responded accordingly.

"It is true. The feet of the young warrior have gone away from the good paths of the Yemassee, but I see not the weakness of the chief, when my eye looks back upon the great deeds of the warrior. I see nothing but the shrinking body of Suwannee under the knee, under the knife of the Yemassee. I hear nothing but the war-whoop of the Yemassee, when he broke through the camp of the brown-foxes, and scalped them where they skulked in the swamp. I see this Yemassee strike the foe and take the scalp, and I know Occonestoga—Occonestoga, the son of the well-beloved—the great chief of the Yemassee."

"It is good—Occonestoga has thanks for Echotee—Echotee is a brave warrior!" murmured the captive to his champion, in tones of melancholy acknowledgment. The current of public feeling began to set somewhat in behalf of the victim, and an occasional whisper to that effect might be heard here and there among the multitude. Even Malatchie himself looked for a moment as if he thought it not improbable that he might be defrauded of his prey; and, while a free shout from many attested the compliment which all were willing to pay to Echotee for his magnanimous defense of one who had once been a rival—and not always successful—in the general estimation, the executioner turned to the prophet and to Sanutee, as if doubtful whether or not to proceed farther in his claim. But all doubt was soon quieted, as the stern father rose before the assembly. Every sound was stilled in expectation of his words on this so momentous an occasion to himself. They waited not long. The old man had tasked all the energies of the patriot, not less than of the stoic, and having once determined upon the necessity of the sacrifice, he had no hesitating fears or scruples palsying his determination. He seemed not to regard the imploring glance of his son, seen and felt by all besides in the assembly; but, with a voice entirely unaffected by the circumstances of his position, he spoke forth the doom of the victim in confirmation with that originally expressed.

"Echotee has spoken like a brave warrior with a tongue of truth, and a soul that has birth with the sun. But he speaks out of his own heart—and does not speak to the heart of the traitor. The Yemassee will all say for Echotee, but who can say for Occonestoga when Sanutee himself is silent? Does the Yemassee speak with a double tongue? Did not the Yemassee promise Occonestoga to Opitchi-Manneyto with the other chiefs? Where are they? They are gone into the swamp, where the sun shines not, and the eyes of Opitchi-Manneyto are upon them. He knows them for his slaves. The arrow is gone from their shoulders, and the Yemassee knows them no longer. Shall the dog escape who led the way to the English—who brought the poison drink to the chiefs, which made them dogs to the English and slaves to Opitchi-Manneyto? Shall he escape the doom the Yemassee hath put upon them? Sanutee speaks the voice of the Manneyto. Occonestoga is a dog, who would sell his father—who would make our women to carry water for the pale-faces. He is not the son of Sanutee

—Sanutee knows him no more. Look, —Yemassees—the well-beloved has spoken!"

He paused, and turning away, sank down silently upon the little bank on which he had before rested; while Malatchie, without further opposition —for the renunciation of his own son, by one so highly esteemed as Sanutee, was conclusive against the youth—advanced to execute the terrible judgment upon his victim.

"Oh! father, chief, Sanutee, the well-beloved!" was the cry that now, for the first time, burst convulsively from the lips of the prisoner—"hear me, father,—Occonestoga will go on the warpath with thee, and with the Yemassee—against the Edisto, against the Spaniard—hear, Sanutee—he will go with thee against the English." But the old man bent not—yielded not, and the crowd gathered nigher in the intensity of their interest.

"Wilt thou have no ear, Sanutee? —it is Occonestoga—it is the son of Matiwan that speaks to thee." Sanutee's head sank as the reference was made to Matiwan, but he showed no other sign of emotion. He moved not —he spoke not—and bitterly and hopelessly the youth exclaimed—

"Oh! thou art colder than the stonehouse of the adder—and deafer than his ears. Father, Sanutee, wherefore wilt thou lose me, even as the tree its leaf, when the storm smites it in summer? Save me, my father."

And his head sank in despair, as he beheld the unchanging look of stern resolve with which the unbending sire regarded him. For a moment he was unmanned: until a loud shout of derision from the crowd, as they beheld the show of his weakness, came to the support of his pride. The Indian shrinks from humiliation, where he would not shrink from death; and, as the shout reached his ears, he shouted back his defiance, raised his head loftily in air, and with the most perfect composure, commenced singing his song of death, the song of many victories.

"Wherefore sings he his death-song?" was the cry from many voices, —"he is not to die!"

"Thou art the slave of Opitchi-Manneyto," cried Malatchie to the captive—"thou shalt sing no lie of thy victories in the ear of Yemassee. The slave of Opitchi-Manneyto has no triumph"—and the words of the song were effectually drowned, if not silenced, in the tremendous clamour which they raised about him. It was then that Malatchie claimed his victim—the doom had been already given, but the ceremony of expatriation and outlawry was yet to follow, and under the direction of the prophet, the various castes and classes of the nation prepared to take a final leave of one who could no longer be known among them. First of all came a band of young marriageable women, who, wheeling in a circle three times about him, sang together a wild apostrophe containing a bitter farewell, which nothing in our language could perfectly embody.

"Go,—thou hast no wife in Yemassee—thou hast given no lodge to the daughter of Yemassee—thou hast slain no meat for thy children. Thou hast no name—the women of Yemassee know thee no more. They know thee no more."

And the final sentence was reverberated from the entire assembly—

"They know thee no more—they know thee no more."

Then came a number of the ancient men—the patriarchs of the nation, who surrounded him in circular mazes three several times, singing as they did so a hymn of like import.

"Go—thou sittest not in the council of Yemassee—thou shalt not speak wisdom to the boy that comes. Thou hast no name in Yemassee—the fathers of Yemassee, they know thee no more."

And again the whole assembly cried out, as with one voice—"They know thee no more—they know thee no more."

These were followed by the young warriors, his old associates, who now, in a solemn band, approached him to go through a like performance. His eyes were shut as they came—his blood was chilled in his heart, and the articulated farewell of their wild chant failed seemingly to reach his ear. Nothing but the last sentence he heard—

"Thou that wast a brother,
Thou art nothing now—
The young warriors of Yemassee,
They know thee no more."

And the crowd cried with them—"they know thee no more."

"Is no hatchet sharp for Occonestoga?" moaned forth the suffering savage. But his trials were only then begun. Enoree-Mattee now approached him with the words, with which, as the representative of the good Manneyto, he renounced him,—with which he denied him access to the Indian heaven, and left him a slave and an outcast, a miserable wanderer amid the shadows and the swamps, and liable to all the dooms and terrors which come with the service of Opitchi-Manneyto.

"Thou wast a child of Manneyto—" sung the high priest in a solemn chant, and with a deep-toned voice that thrilled strangely amid the silence of the scene.

"Thou wast a child of Manneyto,
He gave thee arrows and an eye,—
Thou wast the strong son of Manneyto,
He gave thee feathers and a wing—
Thou wast a young brave of Manneyto,
He gave thee scalps and a war-song—
But he knows thee no more—he knows thee no more."

And the clustering multitude again gave back the last line in wild chorus. The prophet continued his chant:

"That Opitchi-Manneyto!—
He commands thee for his slave—
And the Yemassee must hear him,
Hear, and give thee for his slave—
They will take from thee the arrow,
The broad arrow of thy people—
Thou shalt see no blessed valley,
Where the plum-groves always bloom—
Thou shalt hear no song of valour,
From the ancient Yemassee—
Father, mother, name, and people,
Thou shalt lose with that broad arrow,
Thou art lost to the Manneyto—
He knows thee no more, he knows thee no more."

The despair of hell was in the face of the victim, and he howled forth, in a cry of agony, that for a moment silenced the wild chorus of the crowd around, the terrible consciousness in his mind of that privation which the doom entailed upon him. Every feature was convulsed with emotion; and the terrors of Opitchi-Manneyto's dominion seemed already in strong exercise upon the muscles of his heart, when Sanutee, the father, silently approached him, and with a pause of a few moments, stood gazing upon the son from whom he was to be separated eternally—whom not even the uniting, the restoring hand of death could possibly restore to him. And he—his once noble son—the pride of his heart, the gleam of his hope, the triumphant warrior, who was even to increase his own glory, and transmit the endearing title of well-beloved, which the Yemassee had given him, to a succeeding generation—he was to be lost for-ever! These promises were all blasted, and the father was now present to yield him up eternally—to deny him—to forfeit him in fearful penalty, to the nation whose genius he had wronged, and whose rights he had violated. The old man stood for a moment, rather, we may suppose, for the recovery of his resolution, than with any desire for the contemplation of the pitiable form before him. The pride of the youth came back to him,—the pride of the strong mind in its desolation—as his eye caught the inflexible gaze of his unswerving father; and he exclaimed bitterly and loud:—

"Wherefore art thou come—thou hast been my foe, not my father—away—I would not behold thee!" and he closed his eyes after the speech, as if to relieve himself from a disgusting presence.

"Thou has said well, Occonestoga—Sanutee is thy foe—he is not thy father. To say this in thy ears has he come. Look on him, Occonestoga—look up, and hear thy doom. The young and the old of the Yemassee—the warrior and the chief—they have all denied thee—all given thee up to the Opitchi-Manneyto! Occonestoga is no name for the Yemassee. The Yemassee gives it to his dog. The prophet of Manneyto has forgotten thee—thou art unknown to those who were thy people. And I, thy father—with this speech, I yield thee to Opitchi-Manneyto. Sanutee is no longer thy father—thy father knows thee no more."

And once more came to the ears of the victim, the melancholy chorus of the multitude—"He knows thee no more, he knows thee no more." Sanutee turned quickly away as he had spoken; and, as if he suffered more than he was willing to show, the old man rapidly hastened to the little mound where he had been previously sitting, his eyes averted from the further spectacle. Occonestoga, goaded to madness by these several incidents, shrieked forth the bitterest execrations, until Enoree-Mattee, preceding Malatchie, again approached. Having given some directions in an under-tone to the latter, he retired, leaving the executioner alone with his victim. Malatchie, then, while all was silence in the crowd—a thick silence, in which even respiration seemed to be suspended—proceeded to his duty; and lifting the feet of Occonestoga carefully from the ground, he placed a log under them—then addressing him, as he again bared his knife which he stuck in the tree above his head, he sung—

"I take from thee the earth of Yemassee—
I take from thee the water of Yemassee—
I take from thee the arrow of Yemassee—
Thou art no longer a Yemassee—
The Yemassee knows thee no more."

"The Yemassee knows thee no more," cried the multitude, and their universal shout was deafening upon the ear. Occonestoga said no word now—he could offer no resistance to the unnerving hands of Malatchie, who now bared the arm more completely of its covering. But his limbs were convulsed with the spasms of that dreadful terror of the future which was racking and raging in every pulse of his heart. He had full faith in the superstitions of his people. His terrors acknowledged the full horrors of their doom. A despairing agony, which no language could describe, had possession of his soul. Meanwhile, the silence of all indicated the general anxiety; and Malatchie prepared to seize the knife and perform the operation, when a confused murmur arose from the crowd around; the mass gave way and parted, and, rushing wildly into the area, came Matiwan, his mother—the long black hair streaming—the features, an astonishing likeness to his own, convulsed like his; and her action that of one reckless of all things in the way of the forward progress she was making to the person of her child. She cried aloud as she came, with a voice that rang like a sudden death-bell through the ring—

"Would you keep the mother from her boy, and he be lost to her for ever? Shall she have no parting with the young brave she bore in her bosom? Away, keep me not back—I will look upon, I will love him. He shall have the blessing of Matiwan, though the Yemassee and the Manneyto curse."

The victim heard, and a momentary renovation of mental life, perhaps a renovation of hope, spoke out in the simple exclamation which fell from his lips—

"Oh, Matiwan—oh, mother!"

She rushed towards the spot where she heard his appeal, and thrusting the executioner aside, threw her arms desperately about his neck.

"Touch him not, Matiwan," was the general cry from the crowd—"Touch him not, Matiwan—Manneyto knows him no more."

"But Matiwan knows him—the mother knows her child, though the Manneyto denies him. Oh, boy—oh, boy, boy, boy." And she sobbed like an infant on his neck.

"Thou art come, Matiwan—thou art come, but wherefore?—to curse like the father—to curse like the Manneyto?" mournfully said the captive.

"No, no, no! Not to curse—not to curse! When did mother curse the child she bore? Not to curse, but to bless thee.—To bless thee and forgive."

"Tear her away," cried the prophet; "let Opitchi-Manneyto have his slave."

"Tear her away, Malatchie," cried the crowd, now impatient for the execution. Malatchie approached.

"Not yet—not yet," appealed the woman. "Shall not the mother say farewell to the child she shall see no more?" and she waved Malatchie back, and in the next instant drew hastily from the drapery of her dress a small hatchet, which she had carefully concealed.

"What wouldst thou do, Matiwan?" asked Occonestoga, as his eye caught the glare of the weapon.

"Save thee, my boy—save thee for thy mother, Occonestoga—save thee for the happy valley."

"Wouldst thou slay me, mother?—wouldst strike the heart of thy son?" he asked, with a something of reluctance to receive death from the hands of a parent.

"I strike thee but to save thee, my son:—since they cannot take the totem from thee after the life is gone. Turn away from me thy head—let me not look upon thine eyes as I strike, lest my hands grow weak and tremble. Turn thine eyes away—I will not lose thee."

His eyes closed, and the fatal instrument, lifted above her head, was now visible in the sight of all. The executioner rushed forward to interpose, but he came too late. The tomahawk was driven deep into the skull, and but a single sentence from his lips preceded the final insensibility of the victim.

"It is good, Matiwan, it is good—thou hast saved me—the death is in my heart." And back he sank as he spoke, while a shriek of mingled joy and horror from the lips of the mother announced the success of her effort to defeat the doom, the most dreadful in the imagination of the Yemassee.

"He is not lost—he is not lost! They may not take the child from his mother. They may not keep him from the valley of Manneyto. He is free—he is free!" And she fell back in a deep swoon into the arms of Sanutee, who by this time had approached. She had defrauded Opitchi-Manneyto of his victim, for they may not remove the badge of the nation from any but the living victim.

1835

# PLANTATION AND SLAVE

## I. JOHN PENDLETON KENNEDY
(1795–1870)

### *SWALLOW BARN; OR A SOJOURN IN THE OLD DOMINION*

CHAPTER I

### SWALLOW BARN

Swallow Barn is an aristocratical old edifice which sits, like a brooding hen, on the southern bank of the James River. It looks down upon a shady pocket or nook, formed by an indentation of the shore, from a gentle acclivity thinly sprinkled with oaks whose magnificent branches afford habitation to sundry friendly colonies of squirrels and woodpeckers.

This time-honored mansion was the residence of the family of Hazards. But in the present generation, the spells of love and mortgage have translated the possession to Frank Meriwether, who having married Lucretia, the eldest daughter of my late Uncle Walter Hazard, and lifted some gentlemanlike incumbrances which had been sleeping for years upon the domain, was thus inducted into the proprietary rights. The adjacency of his own estate gave a territorial feature to this alliance, of which the fruits were no less discernible in the multiplication of negroes, cattle, and poultry, than in a flourishing clan of Meriwethers.

The main building is more than a century old. It is built with thick brick walls, but one story in height, and surmounted by a double-faced or hipped roof, which gives the idea of a ship bottom upwards. Later buildings have been added to this, as the wants or ambition of the family have expanded. These are all constructed of wood, and seem to have been built in defiance of all laws of congruity, just as convenience required. But they form altogether an agreeable picture of habitation, suggesting the idea of comfort in the ample space they fill, and in their conspicuous adaptation to domestic uses.

The hall door is an ancient piece of walnut, which has grown too heavy for its hinges, and by its daily travel has furrowed the floor in a quadrant, over which it has an uneasy journey. It is shaded by a narrow porch, with a carved pediment upheld by massive columns of wood, somewhat split by the sun. An ample court-yard, inclosed by a semicircular paling, extends in front of the whole pile, and is traversed by a gravel road leading from a rather ostentatious iron gate, which is swung between two pillars of brick surmounted by globes of cut stone. Between the gate and the house a large willow spreads its arched and pendent drapery over the grass. A bridle rack stands within the inclosure, and near it a ragged horse-nibbled plum-tree—the current belief being that a plum-tree thrives on ill usage—casts its skeleton shadow on the dust.

Some Lombardy poplars, springing above a mass of shrubbery, partially screen various supernumerary buildings at a short distance in the rear of the mansion. Amongst these is to be seen the gable end of a stable, with the date of its erection stiffly emblazoned in black bricks near the upper angle, in figures set in after the fashion of the work on a girl's sampler. In the same quarter a pigeon-box, reared on a post and resembling a huge tee-totum, is visible, and about its several doors and windows a family of pragmatical pigeons are generally strutting, bridling, and bragging at each other from sunrise until dark.

Appendant to this homestead is an extensive tract of land which stretches some three or four miles along the river, presenting alternately abrupt promontories mantled with pine and dwarf oak, and small inlets terminating in swamps. Some sparse portions of forest vary the landscape, which, for the most part, exhibits a succession of fields clothed with Indian corn, some small patches of cotton or tobacco plants, with the usual varieties of stubble and fallow grounds. These are inclosed by worm fences of shrunken chestnut, where lizards and ground-squirrels are perpetually running races along the rails.

A few hundred steps from the mansion, a brook glides at a snail's pace towards the river, holding its course through a wilderness of laurel and alder, and creeping around islets covered with green mosses. Across this stream is thrown a rough bridge, which it would delight a painter to see; and not far below it an aged sycamore twists its roots into a grotesque framework to the pure mirror of a spring, which wells up its cool waters from a bed of gravel and runs gurgling to the brook. There it aids in furnishing a cruising ground to a squadron of ducks who, in defiance of all nautical propriety, are incessantly turning up their sterns to the skies. On the grass which skirts the margin of the spring, I observe the family linen is usually spread out by some three or four negro women, who chant shrill music over their wash-tubs, and seem to live in ceaseless warfare with sundry little besmirched and bow-legged blacks, who are never tired of making somersets, and mischievously pushing each other on the clothes laid down to dry.

Beyond the bridge, at some distance, stands a prominent object in the perspective of this picture,—the most venerable appendage to the establishment—a huge barn with an immense roof hanging almost to the ground, and thatched a foot thick with sunburnt straw, which reaches below the eaves in ragged flakes. It has a singularly drowsy and decrepit aspect. The yard around it is strewed knee-deep with litter, from the midst of which arises a long rack resembling a chevaux de frise, which is ordinarily filled with fodder. This is the customary lounge of half a score of oxen and as many cows, who sustain an imperturbable companionship with a sickly wagon, whose parched tongue and drooping swingle-trees, as it stands in the sun, give it a most forlorn and invalid character; whilst some sociable carts under the sheds, with their shafts perched against the walls, suggest the idea of a set of gossiping cronies taking their ease in a tavern porch. Now and then a clownish hobble-de-hoy colt, with long fetlocks and disordered mane, and a thousand burs in his tail, stalks through this company. But as it is forbidden ground to all his tribe, he is likely very soon to encounter a shower of corn-cobs from some of the negro men; upon which contingency he makes a rapid retreat across the bars which imperfectly guard the entrance to the yard, and with an uncouth display of his heels bounds away towards the brook, where he stops and looks back with a saucy defiance; and after affecting to drink for a moment, gallops away with a braggart whinny to the fields.

*From* CHAPTER XLVI

## THE QUARTER

Having despatched these important matters at the stable, we left our horses in charge of the servants, and walked towards the cabins, which were not more than a few hundred paces distant. These hovels, with their appurtenances, formed an exceedingly picturesque landscape. They were scattered, without order, over the slope of a gentle hill; and many of them were embowered under old and majestic trees. The rudeness of their construction rather enhanced the attractiveness of the scene. Some few were built after the fashion of the better sort of cottages; but age had stamped its heavy traces upon their exterior: the green moss had gathered upon the roofs, and the coarse weatherboarding had broken, here and there, into chinks. But the more lowly of these structures, and the most numerous, were nothing more than plain log-cabins, compacted pretty much on the model by which boys build partridge-traps; being composed of the trunks of trees, still clothed with their bark, and knit together at the corners with so little regard to neatness that the timbers, being of unequal lengths, jutted beyond each other, sometimes to the length of a foot. Perhaps, none of these latter sort were more than twelve feet square, and not above seven in height. A door swung upon wooden hinges, and a small window of two narrow panes of glass were, in general, the only openings in the front. The intervals between the logs were filled with clay; and the roof, which was constructed of smaller timbers, laid lengthwise along it and projecting two or three feet beyond the side or gable walls, heightened, in a very marked degree, the rustic effect. The chimneys communicated even a droll expression to these habitations. They were, oddly enough, built of billets of wood, having a broad foundation of stone, and growing narrower as they rose, each receding gradually from the house to which it was attached, until it reached the height of the roof. These combustible materials were saved from the access of the fire by a thick coating of mud; and the whole structure, from its tapering form, might be said to bear some resemblance to the spout of a tea kettle; indeed, this domestic implement would furnish no unapt type of the complete cabin.

From this description, which may serve to illustrate a whole species of habitations very common in Virginia, it will be seen, that on the score of accommodation, the inmates of these dwellings were furnished according to a very primitive notion of comfort.

Still, however, there were little garden-patches attached to each, where cymblings, cucumbers, sweet potatoes, water-melons and cabbages flourished in unrestrained luxuriance. Add to this, that there were abundance of poultry domesticated about the premises, and it may be perceived that, whatever might be the inconveniences of shelter, there was no want of what, in all countries, would be considered a reasonable supply of luxuries.

Nothing more attracted my observation than the swarms of little negroes that basked on the sunny sides of these cabins, and congregated to gaze at us as we surveyed their haunts. They were nearly all in that costume of the golden age which I have heretofore described; and showed their slim shanks and long heels in all varieties of their grotesque natures. Their predominant love of sunshine, and their lazy, listless postures, and apparent content to be silently looking abroad, might well afford a comparison to a set of terrapins luxuriating in the genial warmth of summer, on the logs of a mill-pond.

And there, too, were the prolific mothers of this redundant brood,—a number of stout negro-women who thronged the doors of the huts, full of idle curiosity to see us. And, when to these are added a few reverend, wrinkled, decrepit old men, with faces shortened as if with drawing-strings, noses that seemed to have run all to nostril, and with feet of the configuration of a mattock, my reader will have a tolerably correct idea of this negro-quarter, its population, buildings, external appearance, situation and extent.

Meriwether, I have said before, is a kind and considerate master. It is his custom frequently to visit his slaves, in order to inspect their condition, and, where it may be necessary, to add to their comforts or relieve their wants. His coming amongst them, therefore, is always hailed with pleasure. He has constituted himself into a high court of appeal, and makes it a rule to give all their petitions a patient hearing, and to do justice in the premises. This, he tells me, he considers as indispensably necessary;—he says, that no overseer is entirely to be trusted: that there are few men who have the temper to administer wholesome laws to any population, however small, without some omissions or irregularities; and that this is more emphatically true of those who administer them entirely at their own will. On the present occasion, in almost every house where Frank entered, there was some boon to be asked; and I observed, that in every case, the petitioner was either gratified or refused in such a tone as left no occasion or disposition to murmur. Most of the women had some bargains to offer, of fowls or eggs or other commodities of household use, and Meriwether generally referred them to his wife, who, I found, relied almost entirely on this resource, for the supply of such commodities; the negroes being regularly paid for whatever was offered in this way.

One old fellow had a special favour to ask,—a little money to get a new padding for his saddle, which, he said, "galled his cretur's back." Frank, after a few jocular passages with the veteran, gave him what he desired, and sent him off rejoicing.

"That, sir," said Meriwether, "is

no less a personage than Jupiter. He is an old bachelor, and has his cabin here on the hill. He is now near seventy, and is a kind of King of the Quarter. He has a horse, which he extorted from me last Christmas; and I seldom come here without finding myself involved in some new demand, as a consequence of my donation. Now he wants a pair of spurs which, I suppose, I must give him. He is a preposterous coxcomb, and Ned has administered to his vanity by a present of a *chapeau de bras*—a relic of my military era, which he wears on Sundays with a conceit that has brought upon him as much envy as admiration—the usual condition of greatness."

The air of contentment and good humor and kind family attachment, which was apparent throughout this little community, and the familiar relations existing between them and the proprietor struck me very pleasantly. I came here a stranger, in great degree, to the negro character, knowing but little of the domestic history of these people, their duties, habits or temper, and somewhat disposed, indeed, from prepossessions, to look upon them as severely dealt with, and expecting to have my sympathies excited towards them as objects of commiseration. I have had, therefore, rather a special interest in observing them. The contrast between my preconceptions of their condition and the reality which I have witnessed, has brought me a most agreeable surprise. I will not say that, in a high state of cultivation and of such self-dependence as they might possibly attain in a separate national existence, they might not become a more respectable people; but I am quite sure they never could become a happier people than I find them here. Perhaps they are destined, ultimately, to that national existence, in the clime from which they derive their origin—that this is a transition state in which we see them in Virginia. If it be so, no tribe of people have ever passed from barbarism to civilization whose middle stage of progress has been more secure from harm, more genial to their character, or better supplied with mild and beneficent guardianship, adapted to the actual state of their intellectual feebleness, than the negroes of Swallow Barn. And, from what I can gather, it is pretty much the same on the other estates in this region. I hear of an unpleasant exception to this remark now and then; but under such conditions as warrant the opinion that the unfavorable case is not more common than that which may be found in a survey of any other department of society. The oppression of apprentices, of seamen, of soldiers, of subordinates, indeed, in every relation, may furnish elements for a bead-roll of social grievances quite as striking, if they were diligently noted and brought to view.

What the negro is finally capable of, in the way of civilization, I am not philosopher enough to determine. In the present stage of his existence, he presents himself to my mind as essentially parasitical in his nature. I mean that he is, in his moral constitution, a dependant upon the white race; dependant for guidance and direction even to the procurement of his most indispensable necessaries. Apart from this protection he has the helplessness of a child,—without foresight, without faculty of contrivance, without thrift of any kind. We have instances, in the neighborhood of this estate, of individuals of the tribe falling into the most deplorable destitution from the want of that constant supervision which the race seems to require. This helplessness may be the due and natural impression which two centuries of servitude have stamped upon the tribe. But it is not the less a present and insurmountable impediment to that most cruel of all projects —the direct, broad emancipation of these people;—an act of legislation in comparison with which the revocation of the edict of Nantes would be entitled to be ranked among political benefactions. Taking instruction from history, all organized slavery is inevitably but a temporary phase of human condition. Interest, necessity and instinct, all work to give progression to the relations of mankind, and finally to elevate each tribe or race to its maximum of refinement and power. We have no reason to suppose that the negro will be an exception to this law.

At present, I have said, he is parasitical. He grows upward, only as the vine to which nature has supplied the sturdy tree as a support. He is extravagantly imitative. The older negroes here have—with some spice of comic mixture in it—that formal, grave and ostentatious style of manners, which belonged to the gentlemen of former days; they are profuse of bows and compliments, and very aristocratic in their way. The younger ones are equally to be remarked for aping the style of the present time, and especially for such tags of dandyism in dress as come within their reach. Their fondness for music and dancing is a predominant passion. I never meet a negro man—unless he is quite old—that he is not whistling; and the women sing from morning till night. And as to dancing, the hardest day's work does not restrain their desire to indulge in such pastime. During the harvest, when their toil is pushed to its utmost—the time being one of recognized privileges—they dance almost the whole night. They are great sportsmen, too. They angle and haul the seine, and hunt and tend their traps, with a zest that never grows weary. Their gayety of heart is constitutional and perennial, and when they are together they are as voluble and noisy as so many blackbirds. In short, I think them the most good-natured, careless, light-hearted, and happily-constructed human beings I have ever seen. Having but few and simple wants, they seem to me to be provided with every comfort which falls within the ordinary compass of their wishes; and, I might say, that they find even more enjoyment, —as that word may be applied to express positive pleasures scattered through the course of daily occupation —than any other laboring people I am acquainted with. * * *

1832

## II. JOHN CALDWELL CALHOUN
### (1782–1850)

### *From* SPEECH ON THE SLAVERY QUESTION, DELIVERED IN THE SENATE, MARCH 4, 1850

* * * The result of the whole of these causes combined is, that the

North has acquired a decided ascendancy over every department of this Government, and through it a control over all the powers of the system. A single section governed by the will of the numerical majority, has now, in fact, the control of the Government and the entire powers of the system. What was once a constitutional federal Republic, is now converted, in reality, into one as absolute as that of the Autocrat of Russia, and as despotic in its tendency, as any absolute government that ever existed.

As, then, the North has the absolute control over the Government, it is manifest that on all questions between it and the South, where there is a diversity of interests, the interest of the latter will be sacrificed to the former, however oppressive the effects may be; as the South possesses no means by which it can resist, through the action of the Government. But if there was no question of vital importance to the South, in reference to which there was a diversity of views between the two sections, this state of things might be endured, without the hazard of destruction to the South. But such is not the fact. There is a question of vital importance to the Southern section, in reference to which the views and feelings of the two sections are as opposite and hostile as they can possibly be.

I refer to the relation between the two races in the Southern section, which constitutes a vital portion of her social organization. Every portion of the North entertains views and feelings more or less hostile to it. Those most opposed and hostile, regard it as a sin, and consider themselves under the most sacred obligation to use every effort to destroy it. Indeed, to the extent that they conceive that they have power, they regard themselves as implicated in the sin, and responsible for not suppressing it by the use of all and every means. Those less opposed and hostile, regard it as a crime—an offence against humanity, as they call it; and although not so fanatical, feel themselves bound to use all efforts to effect the same object; while those who are least opposed and hostile, regard it as a blot and a stain on the character of what they call the Nation, and feel themselves accordingly bound to give it no countenance or support. On the contrary, the Southern section regards the relation as one which cannot be destroyed without subjecting the two races to the greatest calamity, and the section to poverty, desolation, and wretchedness; and accordingly they feel bound, by every consideration of interest and safety, to defend it.

This hostile feeling on the part of the North towards the social organization of the South long lay dormant; but it only required some cause to act on those who felt most intensely that they were responsible for its continuance, to call it into action. The increasing power of this Government, and of the control of the Northern section over all its departments, furnished the cause. It was this which made an impression on the minds of many, that there was little or no restraint to prevent the Government from doing whatever it might choose to do. This was sufficient of itself to put the most fanatical portion of the North in action, for the purpose of destroying the existing relation between the two races in the South.

The first organized movement towards it commenced in 1835. Then, for the first time, societies were organized, presses established, lecturers sent forth to excite the people of the North, and incendiary publications scattered over the whole South through the mail. The South was thoroughly aroused. Meetings were held everywhere, and resolutions adopted, calling upon the North to apply a remedy to arrest the threatened evil, and pledging themselves to adopt measures for their own protection if it was not arrested. At the meeting of Congress, petitions poured in from the North, calling upon Congress to abolish slavery in the District of Columbia, and to prohibit what they called the internal slave trade between the States—announcing at the same time, that their ultimate object was to abolish slavery, not only in the District, but in the States and throughout the Union. At this period, the number engaged in the agitation was small, and possessed little or no personal influence.

Neither party in Congress had, at that time, any sympathy with them or their cause. The members of each party presented their petitions with great reluctance. Nevertheless, small and contemptible as the party then was, both of the great parties of the North dreaded them. They felt that though small, they were organized in reference to a subject which had a great and a commanding influence over the Northern mind. Each party, on that account, feared to oppose their petitions, lest the opposite party should take advantage of the one who might do so, by favoring them. The effect was that both united in insisting that the petitions should be received, and that Congress should take jurisdiction over the subject. To justify their course, they took the extraordinary ground that Congress was bound to receive petitions on every subject, however objectionable they might be, and whether they had or had not jurisdiction over the subject. These views prevailed in the House of Representatives, and partially in the Senate; and thus the party succeeded, in their first movements, in gaining what they proposed—a position in Congress from which agitation could be extended over the whole Union. This was the commencement of the agitation, which has ever since continued, and which, as is now acknowledged, has endangered the Union itself.

As for myself, I believed at that early period, if the party who got up the petitions should succeed in getting Congress to take jurisdiction, that agitation would follow; and that it would in the end, if not arrested, destroy the Union. I then so expressed myself in debate, and called upon both parties to take grounds against assuming jurisdiction; but in vain. Had my voice been heeded, and had Congress refused to take jurisdiction, by the united votes of all parties, the agitation which followed would have been prevented; and the fanatical zeal that gives impulse to the agitation, and which has brought us to our present perilous condition, would have become extinguished from the want of fuel to feed the flame. *That* was the time for the North to have shown her devotion to the Union; but, unfortunately, both of the great parties of that section were so intent on obtaining or retaining party ascendancy, that all other considerations were overlooked or forgotten.

What has since followed are but natural consequences. With the success of their first movement, this small fanatical party began to acquire strength; and with that, to become an object of courtship to both the great parties. The necessary consequence was a further increase of power, and a gradual tainting of the opinions of both of the other parties with their doctrines, until the infection has extended over both; and the great mass of the population of the North, who, whatever may be their opinion of the original abolition party, which still preserves its distinctive organization, hardly ever fail, when it comes to acting, to co-operate in carrying out their measures. With the increase of their influence, they extended the sphere of their action. In a short time after the commencement of their first movement, they had acquired sufficient influence to induce the Legislatures of most of the Northern States to pass acts which in effect abrogated the clause of the Constitution that provides for the delivery up of fugitive slaves. Not long after, petitions followed to abolish slavery in forts, magazines, and dockyards, and all other places where Congress had exclusive power of legislation. This was followed by petitions and resolutions of Legislatures of the Northern States, and popular meetings, to exclude the Southern States from all Territories acquired, or to be acquired; and to prevent the admission of any State hereafter into the Union, which, by its Constitution, does not prohibit slavery. And Congress is invoked to do all this, expressly with the view to the final abolition of slavery in the States. That has been avowed to be the ultimate object from the beginning of the agitation until the present time; and yet the great body of both parties of the North, with the full knowledge of the fact, although disavowing the abolitionists, have co-operated with them in almost all their measures.

Such is a brief history of the agitation, as far as it has yet advanced. Now I ask, Senators, what is there to prevent its further progress, until it fulfils the ultimate end proposed, unless some decisive measure should be adopted to prevent it? Has any one of the causes, which had added to its increase from its original small and contemptible beginning until it has attained its present magnitude, diminished in force? Is the original cause of the movement—that slavery is a sin, and ought to be suppressed—weaker now than at the commencement? Or is the Abolition party less numerous or influential, or have they less influence with, or control over, the two great parties of the North in elections? Or has the South greater means of influencing or controlling the movements of this Government now, than it had when the agitation commenced? To all these questions but one answer can be given: No—no—no. The very reverse is true. Instead of being weaker, all the elements in favor of agitation are stronger now than they were in 1835, when it first commenced; while all the elements of influence on the part of the South are weaker. Unless something decisive is done, I again ask, what is to stop this agitation, before the great and final object at which it aims—the abolition of slavery in the States—is consummated? Is it, then, not certain, that if something is not done to arrest it, the South will be forced to choose between abolition and secession? Indeed, as events are now moving, it will not require the South to secede, in order to dissolve the Union. Agitation will of itself effect it, of which its past history furnishes abundant proof—as I shall next proceed to show.

It is a great mistake to suppose that disunion can be effected by a single blow. The cords which bind these states together in one common Union, are far too numerous and powerful for that. Disunion must be the work of time. It is only through a long process, and successively, that the cords can be snapped, until the whole fabric falls asunder. Already the agitation of the slavery question has snapped some of the most important, and has greatly weakened all the others, as I shall proceed to show.

The cords that bind the States together are not only many, but various in character. Some are spiritual or ecclesiastical; some political; others social. Some appertain to the benefit conferred by the Union, and others to the feeling of duty and obligation.

The strongest of those of a spiritual and ecclesiastical nature, consisted in the unity of the great religious denominations, all of which originally embraced the whole Union. All these denominations, with the exception, perhaps, of the Catholics, were organized very much upon the principle of our political institutions. Beginning with smaller meetings, corresponding with the political divisions of the country, their organization terminated in one great central assemblage, corresponding very much with the character of Congress. At these meetings the principal clergymen and lay members of the respective denominations, from all parts of the Union, met to transact business relating to their common concerns. It was not confined to what appertained to the doctrines and discipline of the respective denominations, but extended to plans for disseminating the Bible—establishing missions, distributing tracts—and of establishing presses for the publication of tracts, newspapers, and periodicals, with a view of diffusing religious information—and for the support of their respective doctrines and creeds. All this combined contributed greatly to strengthen the bonds of the Union. The ties which held each denomination together formed a strong cord to hold the whole Union together; but, powerful as they were, they have not been able to resist the explosive effect of slavery agitation.

The first of these cords which snapped, under its explosive force, was that of the powerful Methodist Episcopal Church. The numerous and strong ties which held it together are all broken, and its unity gone. They now form separate churches; and, instead of that feeling of attachment and devotion to the interests of the whole church which was formerly felt, they are now arrayed into two hostile bodies, engaged in litigation about what was formerly their common property.

The next cord that snapped was that of the Baptists—one of the largest and most respectable of the denominations. That of the Presbyterian is not entirely snapped, but some of its strands have given way. That of the Episcopal Church is the only one of the four great Protestant denominations which remains unbroken and entire.

The strongest cord of a political character, consists of the many and powerful ties that have held together the two great parties which have, with some modifications, existed from the beginning of the Government. They both extended to every portion of the Union, and strongly contributed to hold all its parts together. But this powerful cord has fared no better than the spiritual. It resisted, for a long time, the explosive tendency of the agitation, but has finally snapped under its force—if not entirely, in a great measure. Nor is there one of the remaining cords which has not been greatly weakened. To this extent the Union has already been destroyed by agitation, in the only way it can be, by sundering and weakening the cords which bind it together.

If the agitation goes on, the same force, acting with increased intensity, as has been shown, will finally snap every cord, when nothing will be left to hold the States together except force. But, surely that can with no propriety of language be called a Union, when the only means by which the weaker is held connected with the stronger portion is *force*. It may, indeed, keep them connected; but the connection will partake much more of the character of subjugation, on the part of the weaker to the stronger, than the union of free, independent, and sovereign States, in one confederation, as they stood in the early stages of the Government, and which only is worthy of the sacred name of Union.

* * * How can the Union be saved? There is but one way by which it can with any certainty; and that is, by a full and final settlement, on the principle of justice, of all the questions at issue between the two sections. The South asks for justice, simple justice; and less she ought not to take. She has no compromise to offer but the Constitution; and no concession or surrender to make. She has already surrendered so much that she has little left to surrender. Such a settlement would go to the root of the evil, and remove all cause of discontent, by satisfying the South that she could remain honorably and safely in the Union, and thereby restore the harmony and fraternal feelings between the sections, which existed anterior to the Missouri agitation. Nothing else can, with any certainty, finally and for ever settle the questions at issue, terminate agitation, and save the Union.

But can this be done? Yes, easily; not by the weaker party, for it can of itself do nothing—not even protect itself—but by the stronger. The North has only to will it to accomplish it, to do justice by conceding to the South an equal right in the acquired Territory, and to do her duty by causing the stipulations relative to fugitive slaves to be faithfully fulfilled; to cease the agitation of the slave question, and to provide for the insertion of a provision in the Constitution, by an amendment, which will restore to the South, in substance, the power she possessed of protecting herself, before the equilibrium between the sections was destroyed by the action of this Government. There will be no difficulty in devising such a provision: one that will protect the South, and which, at the same time, will improve and strengthen the Government, instead of impairing and weakening it.

But will the North agree to this? —It is for her to answer the question. But, I will say, she cannot refuse, if she has half the love of the Union which she professes to have, or with out justly exposing herself to the charge that her love of power and aggrandizement is far greater than her love of the Union. At all events, the responsibility of saving the Union rests on the North, and not on the South. The South cannot save it by any act of hers, and the North may save it without any sacrifice whatever, unless to do justice, and to perform her duties under the Constitution, should be regarded by her as a sacrifice.

It is time, Senators, that there should be an open and manly avowal on all sides, as to what is intended to be done. If the question is not now settled, it is uncertain whether it ever can hereafter be; and we, as the representatives of the States of this Union, regarded as Governments, should come to a distinct understanding as to our respective views, in order to ascertain whether the great questions at issue can be settled or not. If you, who represent the stronger portion, cannot agree to settle them on the broad principle of justice and duty, say so; and let the States we both represent agree to separate and part in peace. If you are unwilling we should part in peace, tell us so; and we shall know what to do, when you reduce the question to submission or resistance. If you remain silent, you will compel us to infer by your acts what you intend. In that case, California will become the test question. If you admit her, under all the difficulties that oppose her admission, you compel us to infer that you intend to exclude us from the whole of the acquired Territories; with the intention of destroying, irretrievably, the equilibrium between the two sections. We would be blind not to perceive in that case, that your real objects are power and aggrandizement, and infatuated not to act accordingly.

I have now, Senators, done my duty in expressing my opinions fully, freely, and candidly, on this solemn occasion. In doing so, I have been governed by the motives which have governed me in all stages of the agitation of the slavery question since its commencement. I have exerted myself, during the whole period, to arrest it, with the intention of saving the Union, if it could be done; and if it could not, to save the section where it has pleased Providence to cast my lot, and which I sincerely believe has justice and the Constitution on its side. Having faithfully done my duty to the best of my ability, both to the Union and my section, throughout this agitation, I shall have the consolation, let what will come, that I am free from all responsibility.

1850

## III. DANIEL WEBSTER
(1782–1852)

### *From* SPEECH ON THE CONSTITUTION AND THE UNION, MARCH 7, 1850

* * * Mr. President, in the excited times in which we live, there is found to exist a state of crimination and recrimination between the North and the South. There are lists of grievances produced by each; and those grievances, real or supposed, alienate the minds of one portion of the country from the other, exasperate the feelings, and subdue the sense of fraternal affection, patriotic love, and mutual regard. I shall bestow a little attention, Sir, upon these various grievances existing on the one side and on the other. I begin with complaints of the South. I will not answer, further than I have, the general statements of the honorable Senator from South Carolina, that the North has prospered at the expense of the South in consequence of the manner of administering this Government, in the collecting of its revenues, and so forth. These are disputed topics, and I have no inclination to enter into them. But I will allude to other complaints of the South, and especially to one which has in my opinion just foundation; and that is, that there has been found at the North, among individuals and among legislators, a disinclination to perform fully their constitutional duties in regard to the return of persons bound to service who have escaped into the free States. In that respect, the South, in my judgment, is right, and the North is wrong. Every member of every Northern Legislature is bound by oath, like every other officer in the country, to support the Constitution of the United States; and the article of the Constitution which says to these States that they shall deliver up fugitives from service is as binding in honor and conscience as any other article. No man fulfils his duty in any legislature who sets himself to find excuses, evasions, escapes from this constitutional obligation. I have always thought that the Constitution addressed itself to the Legislatures of the States or to the States themselves. It says that those persons escaping to other States shall be delivered up, and I confess I have always been of the opinion that it was an injunction upon the States themselves. When it is said that a person escaping into another State, and coming therefore within the jurisdiction of that State, shall be delivered up, it seems to me the import of the clause is, that the State itself, in obedience to the Constitution, shall cause him to be delivered up. That is my judgment. I have always entertained that opinion, and I entertain it now. But when the subject, some years ago, was before the Supreme Court of the United States, the majority of the judges held that the power to cause fugitives from service to be delivered up was a power to be exercised under the authority of this Government. I do not know, on the whole, that it may not have been a fortunate decision. My habit is to respect the result of judicial deliberations and the solemnity of judicial decisions. As it now stands, the business of seeing that these fugitives are delivered up resides in the power of Congress and the national judicature, and my friend

at the head of the Judiciary Committee has a bill on the subject now before the Senate, which, with some amendments to it, I propose to support, with all its provisions, to the fullest extent. And I desire to call the attention of all sober-minded men at the North, of all conscientious men, of all men who are not carried away by some fanatical idea or some false impression, to their constitutional obligations. I put it to all the sober and sound minds at the North as a question of morals and a question of conscience. What right have they, in their legislative capacity or any other capacity, to endeavor to get round this Constitution, or to embarrass the free exercise of the rights secured by the Constitution to the persons whose slaves escape from them? None at all; none at all. Neither in the forum of conscience, nor before the face of the Constitution, are they, in my opinion, justified in such an attempt. Of course it is a matter for their consideration. They probably, in the excitement of the times, have not stopped to consider of this. They have followed what seemed to be the current of thought and of motives, as the occasion arose, and they have neglected to investigate fully the real question, and to consider their constitutional obligations; which, I am sure, if they did consider, they would fulfil with alacrity. I repeat, therefore, Sir, that here is a well-founded ground of complaint against the North, which ought to be removed, which it is now in the power of the different departments of this government to remove; which calls for the enactment of proper laws authorizing the judicature of this government, in the several States, to do all that is necessary for the recapture of fugitive slaves and for their restoration to those who claim them. Wherever I go, and whenever I speak on the subject, and when I speak here I desire to speak to the whole North, I say that the South has been injured in this respect, and has a right to complain; and the North has been too careless of what I think the Constitution peremptorily and emphatically enjoins upon her as a duty. * * *

Then, Sir, there are the abolition societies, of which I am unwilling to speak, but in regard to which I have very clear notions and opinions. I do not think them useful. I think their operations for the last twenty years have produced nothing good or valuable. At the same time, I believe thousands of their members to be honest and good men, perfectly well-meaning men. They have excited feelings; they think they must do something for the cause of liberty; and, in their sphere of action, they do not see what else they can do than to contribute to an abolition press, or an abolition society, or to pay an abolition lecturer. I do not mean to impute gross motives even to the leaders of these societies, but I am not blind to the consequences of their proceedings. I cannot but see what mischiefs their interference with the South has produced. And is it not plain to every man? Let any gentleman who entertains doubts on this point recur to the debates in the Virginia House of Delegates in 1832, and he will see with what freedom a proposition made by Mr. Jefferson Randolph for the gradual abolition of slavery was discussed in that body.

Every one spoke of slavery as he thought; very ignominious and disparaging names and epithets were applied to it. The debates in the House of Delegates on that occasion, I believe, were all published. They were read by every colored man who could read, and to those who could not read, those debates were read by others. At that time Virginia was not unwilling or afraid to discuss this question, and to let that part of her population know as much of the discussion as they could learn. That was in 1832. As has been said by the honorable member from South Carolina, these abolition societies commenced their course of action in 1835. It is said, I do not know how true it may be, that they sent incendiary publications into the slave States; at any rate, they attempted to arouse, and did arouse, a very strong feeling; in other words, they created great agitation in the North against Southern slavery. Well, what was the result? The bonds of the slaves were bound more firmly than before, their rivets were more strongly fastened. Public opinion, which in Virginia had begun to be exhibited against slavery, and was opening out for the discussion of the question, drew back and shut itself up in its castle. I wish to know whether any body in Virginia can now talk openly as Mr. Randolph, Governor McDowell, and others talked openly, and sent their remarks to the press, in 1832? We all know the fact, and we all know the cause; and every thing that these agitating people have done has been, not to enlarge, but to restrain, not to set free, but to bind faster, the slave population of the South. That is my judgment. Sir, as I have said, I know many abolitionists in my own neighbourhood, very honest, good people, misled, I think, by strange enthusiasm; but they wish to do something, and they are called on to contribute, and they do contribute; and it is my firm opinion this day, that within the last twenty years as much money has been collected and paid to abolition societies, abolition presses, and abolition lectures, as would purchase the freedom of every slave, man, woman, and child, in the State of Maryland, and send them to Liberia. But I have yet to learn that the benevolence of these abolition societies has at any time taken that particular turn.

Again, Sir, the violence of the Northern press is complained of. The press violent! Why, Sir, the press is violent everywhere. There are outrageous reproaches in the North against the South, and there are reproaches as vehement in the South against the North. Sir, the extremists of both parts of this country are violent; they mistake loud and violent talk for eloquence and for reason. They think that he who talks loudest reasons best. And this we must expect, when the press is free, as it is here, and I trust always will be; for, with all its licentiousness and all its evil, the entire and absolute freedom of the press is essential to the preservation of government on the basis of a free constitution. Wherever it exists there will be foolish and violent paragraphs in the newspapers, as there are, I am sorry to say, foolish and violent speeches in both houses of Congress. In truth, Sir, I must say that, in my opinion, the vernacular tongue of the country has become greatly vitiated, depraved, and corrupted by the style of our Congressional debates. And if it were possible for those debates to vitiate the principles of the people as much as they have depraved their tastes, I should cry out, "God save the Republic!"

Well, in all this I see no solid grievance, no grievance presented by the South, within the redress of the government, but the single one to which I have referred; and that is, the want of a proper regard to the injunction of the Constitution for the delivery of fugitive slaves.

There are also complaints of the North against the South. I need not go over them particularly. The first and gravest is, that the North adopted the Constitution, recognizing the existence of slavery in the States, and recognizing the right, to a certain extent, of the representation of slaves in Congress, under a state of sentiment and expectation which does not now exist; and that, by events, by circumstances, by the eagerness of the South to acquire territory and extend her slave population, the North finds itself, in regard to the relative influence of the South and the North, of the free States and the slave States, where it never did expect to find itself when they agreed to the compact of the Constitution. They complain, therefore, that instead of slavery being regarded as an evil, as it was then, an evil which all hoped would be extinguished gradually, it is now regarded by the South as an institution to be cherished, and preserved, and extended; an institution which the South has already extended to the utmost of her power by the acquisition of new territory.

Well, then, passing from that, every body in the North reads; and every body reads whatsoever the newspapers contain; and the newspapers, some of them, especially those presses to which I have alluded, are careful to spread about among the people every reproachful sentiment uttered by any Southern man bearing at all against the North; every thing that is calculated to exasperate and to alienate; and there are many such things, as every body will admit, from the South, or some portion of it, which are disseminated among the reading people; and they do exasperate, and alienate, and produce a most mischievous effect upon the public mind at the North. Sir, I would not notice things of this sort appearing in obscure quarters; but one thing has occurred in this debate which struck me very forcibly. An honorable member from Louisiana addressed us the other day on this subject. I suppose there is not a more amiable and worthy gentleman in this chamber, nor a gentleman who would be more slow to give offence to any body, and he did not mean in his remarks to give offence. But what did he say? Why, Sir, he took pains to run a contrast between the slaves of the South and the laboring people of the North, giving the preference, in all points of condition, and comfort, and happiness, to the slaves of the South. The honorable member, doubtless, did not suppose that he gave any offence, or did any injustice. He was merely expressing his opinion. But does he know how remarks of that sort will be received by the laboring people of the North? Why, who are the laboring people of the North? They are the whole

North. They are the people who till their own farms with their own hands; freeholders, educated men, independent men. Let me say, Sir, that five-sixths of the whole property of the North is in the hands of the laborers of the North; they cultivate their farms, they educate their children, they provide the means of independence; if they are not freeholders, they earn wages; these wages accumulate, are turned into capital, into new freeholds, and small capitalists are created. That is the case, and such the course of things, among the industrious and frugal. And what can these people think when so respectable and worthy a gentleman as the member from Louisiana undertakes to prove that the absolute ignorance and the abject slavery of the South are more in conformity with the high purposes and destiny of immortal, rational human beings, than the educated, the independent, free labor of the North?

There is a more tangible and irritating cause of grievance at the North. Free blacks are constantly employed in the vessels of the North, generally as cooks or stewards. When the vessel arrives at a Southern port, these free colored men are taken on shore, by the police or municipal authority, imprisoned, and kept in prison till the vessel is again ready to sail. This is not only irritating, but exceedingly unjustifiable and oppressive. Mr. Hoar's mission, some time ago, to South Carolina, was a well-intended effort to remove this cause of complaint. The North thinks such imprisonments illegal and unconstitutional; and as the cases occur constantly and frequently, they regard it as a great grievance.

Now, Sir, so far as any of these grievances have their foundation in matters of law, they can be redressed, and ought to be redressed; and so far as they have their foundation in matters of opinion, in sentiment, in mutual crimination and recrimination, all that we can do is to endeavor to allay the agitation, and cultivate a better feeling and more fraternal sentiments between the South and the North.

Mr. President, I should much prefer to have heard from every member on this floor declarations of opinion that this Union could never be dissolved, than the declaration of opinion by any body, that, in any case, under the pressure of any circumstances, such a dissolution was possible. I hear with distress and anguish the word "secession," especially when it falls from the lips of those who are patriotic, and known to the country, and known all over the world, for their political services. Secession! Peaceable secession! Sir, your eyes and mine are never destined to see that miracle. The dismemberment of this vast country without convulsion! The breaking up of the fountains of the great deep without ruffling the surface! Who is so foolish, I beg every body's pardon, as to expect to see any such thing? Sir, he who sees these States, now revolving in harmony around a common centre, and expects to see them quit their places and fly off without convulsion, may look the next hour to see the heavenly bodies rush from their spheres, and jostle against each other in the realms of space, without causing the wreck of the universe. There can be no such thing as a peaceable secession. Peaceable secession is an utter impossibility. Is the great Constitution under which we live, covering this whole country, is it to be thawed and melted away by secession, as the snows on the mountain melt under the influence of a vernal sun, disappear almost unobserved and run off? No, Sir! No, Sir! I will not state what might produce the disruption of the Union; but, Sir, I see as plainly as I see the sun in heaven what that disruption itself must produce; I see that it must produce war, and such a war as I will not describe, *in its twofold character.*

Peaceable secession! peaceable secession! The concurrent agreement of all the members of this great republic to separate! A voluntary separation, with alimony on one side and on the other! Why, what would be the result? Where is the line to be drawn? What States are to secede? What is to remain American? What am I to be? An American no longer? Am I to become a sectional man, a local man, a separatist, with no country in common with the gentlemen who sit around me here, or who fill the other house of Congress? Heaven forbid! Where is the flag of the republic to remain? Where is the eagle still to tower? Or is he to cower, and shrink, and fall to the ground? Why, Sir, our ancestors—our fathers and our grandfathers, those of them that are yet living amongst us with prolonged lives, would rebuke and reproach us; and our children and our grandchildren would cry out shame upon us, if we of this generation should dishonor these ensigns of the power of the Government and the harmony of that Union which is every day felt among us with so much joy and gratitude. What is to become of the army? What is to become of the navy? What is to become of the public lands? How is each of the thirty States to defend itself? I know, although the idea has not been stated distinctly, there is to be, or it is supposed possible that there will be, a Southern Confederacy. I do not mean, when I allude to this statement, that any one seriously contemplates such a state of things. I do not mean to say that it is true, but I have heard it suggested elsewhere, that the idea has been entertained, that, after the dissolution of this Union, a Southern Confederacy might be formed. I am sorry, Sir, that it has ever been thought of, talked of, or dreamed of, in the wildest flights of human imagination. But the idea, so far as it exists, must be of a separation, assigning the slave States to one side and the free States to the other. Sir, I may express myself too strongly, perhaps, but there are impossibilities in the natural as well as in the physical world, and I hold the idea of a separation of these States, those that are free to form one government, and those that are slave-holding to form another, as such an impossibility. We could not separate the States by any such line, if we were to draw it. We could not sit down here to-day and draw a line of separation that would satisfy any five men in the country. There are natural causes that would keep and tie us together, and there are social and domestic relations which we could not break if we would, and which we should not if we could. Sir, nobody can look over the face of this country at the present moment, nobody can see where its population is the most dense and growing without being ready to admit, and compelled to admit, that ere long the strength of America will be in the Valley of the Mississippi.

Well, now, Sir, I beg to inquire what the wildest enthusiast has to say on the possibility of cutting that river in two, and leaving free States at its source and on its branches, and slave States down near its mouth, each forming a separate Government? Pray, Sir, let me say to the people of this country, that these things are worthy of their pondering and of their consideration. Here, Sir, are five millions of freemen in the free States north of the river Ohio. Can any body suppose that this population can be severed, by a line that divides them from the territory of a foreign and an alien government, down somewhere, the Lord knows where, upon the lower banks of the Mississippi? What would become of Missouri? Will she join the *arrondissement* of the slave States? Shall the man from the Yellow-Stone and the Platte be connected, in the new republic, with the man who lives on the southern extremity of the Cape of Florida? Sir, I am ashamed to pursue this line of remark. I dislike it, I have an utter disgust for it. I would rather hear of natural blasts and mildews, war, pestilence, and famine, than to hear gentlemen talk of secession. To break up! to break up this great Government, to dismember this glorious country, to astonish Europe with an act of folly such as Europe for two centuries has never beheld in any government or any people! No, Sir! no, Sir! There will be no secession! Gentlemen are not serious when they talk of secession.

Sir, I hear there is to be a Convention held at Nashville. I am bound to believe that, if worthy gentlemen meet at Nashville in convention, their object will be to adopt conciliatory counsels; to advise the South to forbearance and moderation, and to advise the North to forbearance and moderation; and to inculcate principles of brotherly love and affection, and attachment to the Constitution of the country as it now is. I believe, if the convention meet at all, it will be for this purpose; for certainly, if they meet for any purpose hostile to the Union, they have been singularly inappropriate in their selection of a place. I remember, Sir, that, when the treaty of Amiens was concluded between France and England, a sturdy Englishman and a distinguished orator, who regarded the conditions of the peace as ignominious to England, said in the House of Commons, that, if King William could know the terms of that treaty, he would turn in his coffin! Let me commend this saying of Mr. Windham, in all its emphasis and in all its force, to any persons who shall meet at Nashville for the purpose of concerting measures for the overthrow of this Union over the bones of Andrew Jackson!

Sir, I wish now to make two remarks, and hasten to a conclusion. I wish to say, in regard to Texas, that if it should be hereafter, at any time, the pleasure of the Government of Texas to cede to the United States a portion, larger or smaller, of her territory which lies adjacent to New Mexico, and north of 36° 30′ of north latitude, to be formed into free

States, for a fair equivalent in money or in the payment of her debt, I think it an object well worthy the consideration of Congress, and I shall be happy to concur in it myself, if I should have a connection with the government at that time.

I have one other remark to make. In my observations upon slavery as it has existed in this country, and as it now exists, I have expressed no opinion of the mode of its extinguishment or melioration. I will say, however, though I have nothing to propose, because I do not deem myself so competent as other gentlemen to take any lead on this subject, that if any gentleman from the South shall propose a scheme, to be carried on by this Government upon a large scale, for the transportation of free colored people to any colony or any place in the world, I should be quite disposed to incur almost any degree of expense to accomplish that object. Nay, Sir, following an example set more than twenty years ago by a great man, then a Senator from New York, I would return to Virginia, and through her to the whole South, the money received from the lands and territories ceded by her to this Government, for any such purpose as to remove, in whole or in part, or in any way to diminish or deal beneficially with, the free colored population of the Southern States. I have said that I honor Virginia for her cession of this territory. There have been received into the treasury of the United States eighty millions of dollars, the proceeds of the sales of the public lands ceded by her. If the residue should be sold at the same rate, the whole aggregate will exceed two hundred millions of dollars. If Virginia and the South see fit to adopt any proposition to relieve themselves from the free people of color among them, or such as may be made free, they have my full consent that the government shall pay them any sum of money out of the proceeds of that cession which may be adequate to the purpose.

And now, Mr. President, I draw these observations to a close. I have spoken freely, and I meant to do so. I have sought to make no display. I have sought to enliven the occasion by no animated discussion, nor have I attempted any train of elaborate argument. I have wished only to speak my sentiments, fully and at length; being desirous, once and for all, to let the Senate know, and to let the country know, the opinions and sentiments which I entertain on all these subjects. These opinions are not likely to be suddenly changed. If there be any future service that I can render to the country, consistently with these sentiments and opinions, I shall cheerfully render it. If there be not, I shall still be glad to have had an opportunity to disburden myself from the bottom of my heart, and to make known every political sentiment that therein exists.

And now, Mr. President, instead of speaking of the possibility or utility of secession, instead of dwelling in those caverns of darkness, instead of groping with those ideas so full of all that is horrid and horrible, let us come out into the light of day; let us enjoy the fresh air of Liberty and Union; let us cherish those hopes which belong to us; let us devote ourselves to those great objects that are fit for our consideration and our action; let us raise our conceptions to the magnitude and the importance of the duties that devolve upon us; let our comprehension be as broad as the country for which we act, our aspirations as high as its certain destiny; let us not be pigmies in a case that calls for men. Never did there devolve on any generation of men higher trusts than now devolve upon us, for the preservation of this Constitution and the harmony and peace of all who are destined to live under it. Let us make our generation one of the strongest and brightest links in that golden chain which is destined, I fondly believe, to grapple the people of all the States to this Constitution for ages to come. We have a great, popular, constitutional government, guarded by law and by judicature, and defended by the affections of the whole people. No monarchical throne presses the States together, no iron chain of military power encircles them; they live and stand upon a Government popular in its form, representative in its character, founded upon principles of equality, and so constructed, we hope, as to last for ever. In all its history it has been beneficent; it has trodden down no man's liberty; it has crushed no State. Its daily respiration is liberty and patriotism; its yet youthful veins are full of enterprise, courage, and honorable love of glory and renown. Large before, the country has now, by recent events, become vastly larger. This republic now extends, with a vast breadth, across the whole continent. The two great seas of the world wash the one and the other shore. We realize, on a mighty scale, the beautiful description of the ornamental border of the buckler of Achilles—

Now the broad shield complete, the artist crown'd
With his last band, and poured the ocean round;
In living silver seem'd the waves to roll,
And beat the buckler's verge, and bound the whole.

1850

## IV. HARRIET BEECHER STOWE
(1811–1896)

### *UNCLE TOM'S CABIN: OR LIFE AMONG THE LOWLY*

*From* CHAPTER XX

### TOPSY

One morning, while Miss Ophelia was busy in some of her domestic cares, St. Clare's voice was heard calling her at the foot of the stairs.

"Come down here, Cousin; I've something to show you."

"What is it?" said Miss Ophelia, coming down, with her sewing in her hand.

"I've made a purchase for your department—see here," said St. Clare; and, with the word, he pulled along a little negro girl, about eight or nine years of age.

She was one of the blackest of her race; and her round shining eyes, glittering as glass beads, moved with quick and restless glances over everything in the room. Her mouth, half open with astonishment at the wonders of the new Mas'r's parlour, displayed a white and brilliant set of teeth. Her woolly hair was braided in sundry little tails, which stuck out in every direction. The expression of the face was an odd mixture of shrewdness and cunning, over which was oddly drawn, like a kind of veil, an expression of the most doleful gravity and solemnity. She was dressed in a single filthy, ragged garment, made of bagging; and stood with her hands demurely folded before her. Altogether, there was something odd and goblin-like about her appearance, —something, as Miss Ophelia afterwards said, "so heathenish," as to inspire that good lady with utter dismay; and, turning to St. Clare, she said,

"Augustine, what in the world have you brought that thing here for?"

"For you to educate, to be sure, and train in the way she should go. I thought she was rather a funny specimen in the Jim Crow line. Here, Topsy," he added, giving a whistle, as a man would to call the attention of a dog, "give us a song, now, and show us some of your dancing."

The black, glassy eyes glittered with a kind of wicked drollery, and the thing struck up, in a clear shrill voice, an odd negro melody, to which she kept time with her hands and feet, spinning round, clapping her hands, knocking her knees together, in a wild, fantastic sort of time, and producing in her throat all those odd guttural sounds which distinguish the native music of her race; and finally, turning a summerset or two, and giving a prolonged closing note, as odd and unearthly as that of a steam-whistle, she came suddenly down on the carpet, and stood with her hands folded, and a most sanctimonious expression of meekness and solemnity over her face, only broken by the cunning glances which she shot askance from the corners of her eyes.

Miss Ophelia stood silent, perfectly paralysed with amazement. * * *

Sitting down before her, she began to question her.

"How old are you, Topsy?"

"Dun no, Missis," said the image, with a grin that showed all her teeth.

"Don't know how old you are? Didn't anybody ever tell you? Who was your mother?"

"Never had none!" said the child with another grin.

"Never had any mother! What do you mean? Where were you born?"

"Never was born!" persisted Topsy, with another grin, that looked so goblin-like, that, if Miss Ophelia had been at all nervous, she might have fancied that she had got hold of some sooty gnome from the land of Diablerie; but Miss Ophelia was not nervous, but plain and business-like, and she said, with some sternness,

"You mustn't answer me in that way, child; I'm not playing with you. Tell me where you were born, and who your father and mother were."

"Never was born," reiterated the creature, more emphatically; "never had no father nor mother, nor nothin'. I was raised by a speculator, with lots of others. Old Aunt Sue used to take car on us."

The child was evidently sincere; and Jane, breaking into a short laugh, said,

"Laws, Missis, there's heaps of 'em. Speculators buys 'em up cheap, when they's little, and gets 'em raised for market."

"How long have you lived with your master and mistress?"

"Dun no, Missis."

"Is it a year, or more, or less?"

"Dun no, Missis."

"Laws, Missis, those low negroes, they can't tell,—they don't know anything about time," said Jane; "they don't know what a year is; they don't know their own ages."

"Have you ever heard anything about God, Topsy?"

The child looked bewildered, but grinned as usual.

"Do you know who made you?"

"Nobody, as I knows on," said the child, with a short laugh.

The idea appeared to amuse her considerably; for her eyes twinkled, and she added.

"I 'spect I growed. Don't think nobody never made me."

"Do you know how to sew?" said Miss Ophelia, who thought she would turn her inquiries to something more tangible.

"No, Missis."

"What can you do?—what did you do for your master and mistress?"

"Fetch water, and wash dishes, and rub knives, and wait on folks."

"Were they good to you?"

"'Spect they was," said the child, scanning Miss Ophelia cunningly.

Miss Ophelia rose from this encouraging colloquy; St. Clare was leaning over the back of her chair.

"You find virgin soil there, Cousin; put in your own ideas,—you won't find many to pull up." * * *

Miss Ophelia began with Topsy by taking her into her chamber the first morning, and solemnly commencing a course of instruction in the art and mystery of bed-making.

Behold, then, Topsy, washed and shorn of all the little braided tails wherein her heart had delighted, arrayed in a clean gown, with well-starched apron, standing reverently before Miss Ophelia, with an expression of solemnity well befitting a funeral.

"Now, Topsy, I'm going to show you just how my bed is to be made. I am very particular about my bed. You must learn exactly how to do it."

"Yes, ma'am," says Topsy, with a deep sigh, and a face of woful earnestness.

"Now, Topsy, look here;—this is the hem of the sheet,—this is the right side of the sheet, and this is the wrong;—will you remember?"

"Yes, ma'am," says Topsy, with another sigh.

"Well, now, the under sheet you must bring over the bolster,—so,—and tuck it clear down under the mattress nice and smooth,—so, do you see?"

"Yes, ma'am," said Topsy, with profound attention.

"But the upper sheet," said Miss Ophelia, "must be brought down in this way, and tucked firm and smooth at the foot,—so,—the narrow hem at the foot."

"Yes, ma'am," said Topsy, as before;—but we will add, what Miss Ophelia did not see, that, during the time when the good lady's back was turned, in the zeal of her manipulations, the young disciple had contrived to snatch a pair of gloves and a ribbon, which she had adroitly slipped into her sleeves, and stood with her hands dutifully folded, as before.

"Now, Topsy, let's see *you* do this," said Miss Ophelia, pulling off the clothes, and seating herself.

Topsy, with great gravity and adroitness, went through the exercise completely to Miss Ophelia's satisfaction; smoothing the sheets, patting out every wrinkle, and exhibiting, through the whole process, a gravity and seriousness with which her instructress was greatly edified. By an unlucky slip, however, a fluttering fragment of the ribbon hung out of one of her sleeves, just as she was finishing, and caught Miss Ophelia's attention. Instantly she pounced upon it. "What's this? You naughty, wicked child,—you've been stealing this!"

The ribbon was pulled out of Topsy's own sleeve, yet was she not in the least disconcerted; she only looked at it with an air of the most surprised and unconscious innocence.

"Laws! why that ar's Miss Feely's ribbon, an't it? How could it a got caught in my sleeve?"

"Topsy, you naughty girl, don't you tell me a lie,—you stole that ribbon!"

"Missis, I declar for't, I didn't;—never seed it till dis yer blessed minnit."

"Topsy," said Miss Ophelia, "don't you know it's wicked to tell lies?"

"I never tells no lies, Miss Feely," said Topsy, with virtuous gravity; "it's jist the truth I've been a tellin' now, and an't nothin' else."

"Topsy, I shall have to whip you, if you tell lies so."

"Law, Missis, if you's to whip all day, couldn't say no other way," said Topsy, beginning to blubber. "I never seed dat ar,—it must a got caught in my sleeve. Miss Feely must have left it on the bed, and it got caught in the clothes, and so got in my sleeve."

Miss Ophelia was so indignant at the barefaced lie, that she caught the child and shook her.

"Don't you tell me that again!"

The shake brought the gloves on to the floor, from the other sleeve.

"There, you!" said Miss Ophelia, "will you tell me now you didn't steal the ribbon?"

Topsy now confessed to the gloves, but still persisted in denying the ribbon.

"Now, Topsy," said Miss Ophelia, "if you'll confess all about it, I won't whip you this time." Thus adjured, Topsy confessed to the ribbon and gloves, with woful protestations of penitence.

"Well, now, tell me. I know you must have taken other things since you have been in the house, for I let you run about all day yesterday. Now, tell me if you took anything, and I shan't whip you."

"Laws, Missis! I took Miss Eva's red thing she wars on her neck."

"You did, you naughty child!—Well, what else?"

"I took Rosa's yer-rings,—them red ones."

"Go bring them to me this minute, both of 'em."

"Laws, Missis, I can't—they's burnt up!"

"Burnt up?—what a story! Go get 'em, or I'll whip you."

Topsy, with loud protestations, and tears, and groans, declared that she *could* not. "They's burnt up,—they was."

"What did you burn 'em up for?" said Miss Ophelia.

"Cause I's wicked,—I is. I's mighty wicked, any-how. I can't help it."

Just at this moment Eva came innocently into the room, with the identical coral necklace on her neck.

" Why, Eva, where did you get your necklace? " said Miss Ophelia.

" Get it? Why, I've had it on all day," said Eva.

" Did you have it on yesterday? "

" Yes; and what is funny, Aunty, I had it on all night. I forgot to take it off when I went to bed."

Miss Ophelia looked perfectly bewildered; the more so as Rosa at that instant came into the room, with a basket of newly-ironed linen poised on her head, and the coral ear-drops shaking in her ears!

" I'm sure I can't tell anything what to do with such a child! " she said, in despair. " What in the world did you tell me you took those things for, Topsy? "

" Why, Missis said I must 'fess; and I couldn't think of nothin' else to 'fess," said Topsy, rubbing her eyes.

" But, of course, I didn't want you to confess things you didn't do," said Miss Ophelia; " that's telling a lie, just as much as the other."

" Laws, now, is it? " said Topsy, with an air of innocent wonder.

" La, there an't any such thing as truth in that limb," said Rosa, looking indignantly at Topsy. " If I was Mas'r St. Clare, I'd whip her till the blood run. I would,—I'd let her catch it! "

" No, no, Rosa," said Eva, with an air of command, which the child could assume at times; " you mustn't talk so, Rosa. I can't bear to hear it."

" La, sakes! Miss Eva, you's so good, you don't know nothin how to get along with niggers. There's no way but cut 'em well up, I tell ye."

" Rosa," said Eva, " hush! Don't you say another word of that sort," and the eye of the child flashed, and her cheek deepened in colour.

Rosa was cowed in a moment.

" Miss Eva has got the St. Clare blood in her, that's plain. She can speak for all the world just like her papa," she said, as she passed out of the room.

Eva stood looking at Topsy.

There stood the two children, representatives of the two extremes of society. The fair, high-bred child, with her golden hair, her deep eyes, her spiritual, noble brow, and prince-like movements; and her black, keen, subtle, cringing, yet acute neighbor. They stood the representatives of their races. The Saxon, born of ages of cultivation, command, education, physical and moral eminence; the Afric, born of ages of oppression, ignorance, toil, and vice!

*From* CHAPTER XL

## THE MARTYR

* * * The hunt [for Cassy and Emmeline] was long, animated, and thorough, but unsuccessful; and, with grave, ironic exultation, Cassy looked down on Legree as, weary and dispirited, he alighted from his horse.

" Now, Quimbo," said Legree, as he stretched himself down in the sitting-room, " you just go and walk that Tom up here, right away! The old cuss is at the bottom of this yer whole matter; and I'll have it out of his old black hide, or I'll know the reason why! "

Sambo and Quimbo, both, though hating each other, were joined in one mind by a no less cordial hatred of Tom. Legree had told them, at first, that he had bought him for a general overseer in his absence; and this had begun an ill-will, on their part, which had increased in their debased and servile natures, as they saw him becoming obnoxious to their master's displeasure. Quimbo, therefore, departed with a will to execute his orders.

Tom heard the message with a forewarning heart; for he knew all the plan of the fugitives' escape, and the place of their present concealment;—he knew the deadly character of the man he had to deal with, and his despotic power. But he felt strong in God to meet death, rather than betray the helpless.

He set his basket down by the row, and, looking up, said, "Into Thy hands I commend my spirit! Thou hast redeemed me, Oh Lord God of truth!" and then quietly yielded himself to the rough, brutal grasp with which Quimbo seized him.

"Ay, ay!" said the giant, as he dragged him along, "ye'll cotch it, now! I'll boun' Mas'r's back's up *high!* No sneaking out, now! Tell ye ye'll get it, and no mistake! See how ye'll look now, helpin' Mas'r's niggers to run away! See what ye'll get!"

The savage words, none of them reached that ear!—a higher voice there was saying, "Fear not them that kill the body, and after that have no more that they can do." Nerve and bone of that poor man's body vibrated to those words, as if touched by the finger of God; and he felt the strength of a thousand souls in one. As he passed along, the trees and bushes, the huts of his servitude, the whole scene of his degradation, seemed to whirl by him, as the landscape by the rushing car. His soul throbbed,—his home was in sight,—and the hour of release seemed at hand.

"Well, Tom," said Legree, walking up and seizing him grimly by the collar of his coat, and speaking through his teeth, in a paroxysm of determined rage, "do you know I've made up my mind to KILL you?"

"It's very likely, Mas'r," said Tom, calmly.

"I *have,*" said Legree, with grim, terrible calmness, "*done—just—that—thing,* Tom, unless you tell me what you know about these yer gals!"

Tom stood silent.

"D'ye hear?" said Legree, stamping, with a roar like that of an incensed lion. "Speak!"

"*I ha'nt got nothing to tell, Mas'r,*" said Tom, with a slow, firm, deliberate utterance.

"Do you dare to tell me, ye old black Christian, ye don't *know?*" said Legree.

Tom was silent.

"Speak!" thundered Legree, striking him furiously. "Do you know anything?"

"I know, Mas'r; but I can't tell anything. *I can die!*"

Legree drew in a long breath; and, suppressing his rage, took Tom by the arm, and, approaching his face almost to his, said, in a terrible voice, "Hark'e, Tom—ye think, 'cause I've let you off before, I don't mean what I say; but this time I've *made up my mind,* and counted the cost. You've always stood it out agin' me: now I'll *conquer ye, or kill ye!*—one or t'other. I'll count every drop of blood there is in you, and take 'em one by one, till ye give up!"

Tom looked up to his master, and answered, "Mas'r, if you was sick, or in trouble, or dying, and I could save ye, I'd *give* ye my heart's blood; and, if taking every drop of blood in this poor old body would save your precious soul, I'd give 'em freely, as the Lord gave His for me. O, Mas'r, don't bring this great sin on your soul! It will hurt you more than 'twill me! Do the worst you can, my troubles 'll be over soon; but if ye don't repent, yours won't *never* end!"

Like a strange snatch of heavenly music, heard in the lull of a tempest, this burst of feeling made a moment's blank pause. Legree stood aghast, and looked at Tom; and there was such a silence that the tick of the old clock could be heard, measuring, with silent touch, the last moments of mercy and probation to that hardened heart.

It was but a moment. There was one hesitating pause,—one irresolute, relenting thrill,—and the spirit of evil came back, with sevenfold vehemence; and Legree, foaming with rage, smote his victim to the ground.

. . . . . . .

Scenes of blood and cruelty are shocking to our ear and heart. What man has nerve to do, man has not nerve to hear. What brother-man and brother-Christian must suffer cannot be told us, even in our secret chamber, it so harrows up the soul. And yet, O my country! these things are done under the shadow of thy laws! O, Christ! thy Church sees them, almost in silence!

But, of old, there was One whose suffering changed an instrument of torture, degradation and shame, into a symbol of glory, honor, and immortal life; and where His spirit is, neither degrading stripes, nor blood, nor insults, can make the Christian's last struggle less than glorious.

Was he alone, that long night, whose brave, loving spirit was bearing up, in that old shed, against buffeting and brutal stripes?

Nay! There stood by him, ONE,—seen by him alone,—"like unto the Son of God."

The tempter stood by him, too,—blinded by furious, despotic will,—every moment pressing him to shun that agony by the betrayal of the innocent. But the brave, true heart was firm on the Eternal Rock. Like his Master, he knew that, if he saved others, himself he could not save; nor could utmost extremity wring from him words, save of prayer and holy trust.

"He's most gone, Mas'r," said Sambo, touched, in spite of himself, by the patience of his victim.

"Pay away till he gives up! Give it to him!—give it to him!" shouted Legree. "I'll take every drop of blood he has, unless he confesses."

Tom opened his eyes, and looked upon his master. "Ye poor, miserable critter!" he said, "there an't no more ye can do! I forgive ye, with all my soul!" and he fainted entirely away.

"I b'lieve my soul he's done for, finally," said Legree, stepping forward to look at him. "Yes, he is! Well, his mouth's shut up at last, that's one comfort!"

Yes, Legree; but who shall shut up that voice in thy soul—that soul, past repentance, past prayer, past hope, in whom the fire that never shall be quenched is already burning!

Yet Tom was not quite gone. His wondrous words and pious prayers had struck upon the hearts of the imbruted blacks, who had been the instruments of cruelty upon him; and the instant Legree withdrew they took him down, and in their ignorance, sought to call him back to life—as if *that* were any favor to him.

"Sartin, we's been doin' a drefful wicked thing!" said Sambo; "hopes Mas'r'll have to 'count for it, and not we."

They washed his wounds,—they provided a rude bed of some refuse cotton for him to lie down on; and one of them, stealing up to the house, begged a drink of brandy of Legree, pretending that he was tired, and wanted it for himself. He brought it back, and poured it down Tom's throat.

"O Tom!" said Quimbo, "we's been awful wicked to ye!"

"I forgive ye, with all my heart!" said Tom, faintly.

"O Tom! do tell us who is *Jesus*, anyhow!" said Sambo, "Jesus, that's been a standin' by you so, all this night.—Who is he?"

The word roused the failing, fainting spirit. He poured forth a few energetic sentences of that wondrous One—his life, his death, his everlasting presence, and power to save.

They wept,—both the savage men.

"Why didn't I never hear this before?" said Sambo; "but I do believe!—I can't help it! Lord Jesus, have mercy on us!"

"Poor critters!" said Tom, "I'd be willing to bar' all I have, if it'll only bring ye to Christ! O Lord! give me these two more souls, I pray."

That prayer was answered!

1851–2

# JOHN GREENLEAF WHITTIER
(1807–1892)

## THE MORAL WARFARE

When Freedom, on her natal day,
Within her war-rocked cradle lay,
An iron race around her stood,
Baptized her infant brow in blood;
And, through the storm which round her swept,
Their constant ward and watching kept.

Then, where our quiet herds repose,
The roar of baleful battle rose,
And brethren of a common tongue
To mortal strife as tigers sprung,
And every gift on Freedom's shrine
Was man for beast, and blood for wine!

Our fathers to their graves have gone;
Their strife is past, their triumph won;
But sterner trials wait the race
Which rises in their honored place;
A moral warfare with the crime
And folly of an evil time.

So let it be. In God's own might
We gird us for the coming fight,
And, strong in Him whose cause is ours
In conflict with unholy powers,
We grasp the weapons He has given,—
The Light, and Truth, and Love of Heaven.

(1836) 1838

## SONG OF SLAVES IN THE DESERT

Where are we going? where are we going,
Where are we going, Rubee?
Lord of peoples, lord of lands,
Look across these shining sands,
Through the furnace of the noon,
Through the white light of the moon.
Strong the Ghiblee wind is blowing,
Strange and large the world is growing!
Speak and tell us where we are going,
Where are we going, Rubee?

Bornou land was rich and good,
Wells of water, fields of food,
Dourra fields, and bloom of bean,
And the palm-tree cool and green:
Bornou land we see no longer,
Here we thirst and here we hunger,
Here the Moor-man smites in anger:
Where are we going, Rubee?

When we went from Bornou land,
We were like the leaves and sand,
We were many, we are few;
Life has one, and death has two:
Whitened bones our path are showing,
Thou All-seeing, thou All-knowing!
Hear us, tell us, where are we going,
Where are we going, Rubee?

Moons of marches from our eyes
Bornou land behind us lies;
Stranger round us day by day
Bends the desert circle gray;
Wild the waves of sand are flowing,
Hot the winds above them blowing,—
Lord of all things! where are we going?
Where are we going, Rubee?

We are weak, but Thou art strong;
Short our lives, but Thine is long;
We are blind, but Thou hast eyes;
We are fools, but Thou art wise!
Thou, our morrow's pathway knowing

Through the strange world round us growing,  
Hear us, tell us where are we going,  
Where are we going, Rubee?

(1847) 1847

## PROEM

I love the old melodious lays  
Which softly melt the ages through,  
The songs of Spenser's golden days,  
Arcadian Sidney's silvery phrase,  
Sprinkling our noon of time with freshest morning dew.

Yet, vainly in my quiet hours  
To breathe their marvellous notes I try;  
I feel them, as the leaves and flowers  
In silence feel the dewy showers,  
And drink with glad, still lips the blessing of the sky.

The rigor of a frozen clime,  
The harshness of an untaught ear,  
The jarring words of one whose rhyme  
Beat often Labor's hurried time,  
Or Duty's rugged march through storm and strife, are here.

Of mystic beauty, dreamy grace,  
No rounded art the lack supplies;  
Unskilled the subtle lines to trace,  
Or softer shades of Nature's face,  
I view her common forms with unanointed eyes.

Nor mine the seer-like power to show  
The secrets of the heart and mind;  
To drop the plummet-line below  
Our common world of joy and woe,  
A more intense despair or brighter hope to find.

Yet here at least an earnest sense  
Of human right and weal is shown;  
A hate of tyranny intense,  
And hearty in its vehemence,  
As if my brother's pain and sorrow were my own.

O Freedom! if to me belong  
Nor mighty Milton's gift divine,  
Nor Marvell's wit and graceful song,  
Still with a love as deep and strong  
As theirs, I lay, like them, my best gifts on thy shrine!

(1847) 1849

## ICHABOD

So fallen! so lost! the light withdrawn  
Which once he wore!  
The glory from his gray hairs gone  
Forevermore!

Revile him not, the Tempter hath  
A snare for all;  
And pitying tears, not scorn and wrath,  
Befit his fall!

Oh, dumb be passion's stormy rage,  
When he who might  
Have lighted up and led his age,  
Falls back in night.

Scorn! would the angels laugh, to mark  
A bright soul driven,  
Fiend-goaded, down the endless dark,  
From hope and heaven!

Let not the land once proud of him  
Insult him now,  
Nor brand with deeper shame his dim,  
Dishonored brow.

But let its humbled sons, instead,  
From sea to lake,  
A long lament, as for the dead,  
In sadness make.

Of all we loved and honored, naught
Save power remains;
A fallen angel's pride of thought,
Still strong in chains.

All else is gone; from those great eyes
The soul has fled:
When faith is lost, when honor dies,
The man is dead!

Then, pay the reverence of old days
To his dead fame;
Walk backward, with averted gaze,
And hide the shame!

(1850) 1850

## WORDSWORTH

WRITTEN ON A BLANK LEAF OF HIS MEMOIRS

Dear friends, who read the world aright,
And in its common forms discern
A beauty and a harmony
The many never learn!

Kindred in soul of him who found
In simple flower and leaf and stone
The impulse of the sweetest lays
Our Saxon tongue has known,—

Accept this record of a life
As sweet and pure, as calm and good,
As a long day of blandest June
In green field and in wood.

How welcome to our ears, long pained
By strife of sect and party noise,
The brook-like murmur of his song
Of nature's simple joys!

The violet by its mossy stone,
The primrose by the river's brim,
And chance-sown daffodil, have found
Immortal life through him.

The sunrise on his breezy lake,
The rosy tints his sunset brought,
World-seen, are gladdening all the vales
And mountain-peaks of thought.

Art builds on sand; the works of pride
And human passion change and fall;
But that which shares the life of God
With Him surviveth all.

(1851) 1851

## FIRST-DAY THOUGHTS

In calm and cool and silence, once again
I find my old accustomed place among
My brethren, where, perchance, no human tongue
Shall utter words; where never hymn is sung,
Nor deep-toned organ blown, nor censer swung,
Nor dim light falling through the pictured pane!
There, syllabled by silence, let me hear
The still small voice which reached the prophet's ear;
Read in my heart a still diviner law
Than Israel's leader on his tables saw!
There let me strive with each besetting sin,
Recall my wandering fancies, and restrain
The sore disquiet of a restless brain;
And, as the path of duty is made plain,
May grace be given that I may walk therein,
Not like the hireling, for his selfish gain,
With backward glances and reluctant tread,
Making a merit of his coward dread,
But, cheerful, in the light around me thrown,
Walking as one to pleasant service led;

Doing God's will as if it were my own,
Yet trusting not in mine, but in his strength alone!
(1852) 1853

## BURNS

### ON RECEIVING A SPRIG OF HEATHER IN BLOSSOM

No more these simple flowers belong
To Scottish maid and lover;
Sown in the common soil of song,
They bloom the wide world over.

In smiles and tears, in sun and showers,
The minstrel and the heather,
The deathless singer and the flowers
He sang of live together.

Wild heather-bells and Robert Burns!
The moorland flower and peasant!
How, at their mention, memory turns
Her pages old and pleasant!

The gray sky wears again its gold
And purple of adorning,
And manhood's noonday shadows hold
The dews of boyhood's morning.

The dews that washed the dust and soil
From off the wings of pleasure,
The sky, that flecked the ground of toil
With golden threads of leisure.

I call to mind the summer day,
The early harvest mowing,
The sky with sun and clouds at play,
And flowers with breezes blowing.

I hear the blackbird in the corn,
The locust in the haying;
And, like the fabled hunter's horn,
Old tunes my heart is playing.

How oft that day, with fond delay,
I sought the maple's shadow,
And sang with Burns the hours away,
Forgetful of the meadow!

Bees hummed, birds twittered, overhead
I heard the squirrels leaping,
The good dog listened while I read,
And wagged his tail in keeping.

I watched him while in sportive mood
I read "*The Twa Dogs'*" story,
And half believed he understood
The poet's allegory.

Sweet day, sweet songs! The golden hours
Grew brighter for that singing,
From brook and bird and meadow flowers
A dearer welcome bringing.

New light on home-seen Nature beamed,
New glory over Woman;
And daily life and duty seemed
No longer poor and common.

I woke to find the simple truth
Of fact and feeling better
Than all the dreams that held my youth
A still repining debtor:

That Nature gives her handmaid, Art,
The themes of sweet discoursing;
The tender idyls of the heart
In every tongue rehearsing.

Why dream of lands of gold and pearl,
Of loving knight and lady,
When farmer boy and barefoot girl
Were wandering there already?

I saw through all familiar things
The romance underlying;
The joys and griefs that plume the wings
Of Fancy skyward flying.

I saw the same blithe day return,
The same sweet fall of even,

That rose on wooded Craigie-burn,
  And sank on crystal Devon.

I matched with Scotland's heathery hills
  The sweetbrier and the clover;
With Ayr and Doon, my native rills,
  Their wood-hymns chanting over.

O'er rank and pomp, as he had seen,
  I saw the Man uprising;
No longer common or unclean,
  The child of God's baptizing!

With clearer eyes I saw the worth
  Of life among the lowly;
The Bible at his Cotter's hearth
  Had made my own more holy.

And if at times an evil strain,
  To lawless love appealing,
Broke in upon the sweet refrain
  Of pure and healthful feeling,

It died upon the eye and ear,
  No inward answer gaining;
No heart had I to see or hear
  The discord and the staining.

Let those who never erred forget
  His worth, in vain bewailings;
Sweet Soul of Song! I own my debt
  Uncancelled by his failings!

Lament who will the ribald line
  Which tells his lapse from duty,
How kissed the maddening lips of wine
  Or wanton ones of beauty;

But think, while falls that shade between
  The erring one and Heaven,
That he who loved like Magdalen,
  Like her may be forgiven.

Not his the song whose thunderous chime
  Eternal echoes render;
The mournful Tuscan's haunted rhyme,
  And Milton's starry splendor!

But who his human heart has laid
  To Nature's bosom nearer?
Who sweetened toil like him, or paid
  To love a tribute dearer?

Through all his tuneful art, how strong
  The human feeling gushes!
The very moonlight of his song
  Is warm with smiles and blushes!

Give lettered pomp to teeth of Time,
  So "Bonnie Doon" but tarry;
Blot out the Epic's stately rhyme,
  But spare his Highland Mary!
(1854) 1854

## THE BAREFOOT BOY

Blessings on thee, little man,
Barefoot boy, with cheek of tan!
With thy turned-up pantaloons,
And thy merry whistled tunes;
With thy red lip, redder still
Kissed by strawberries on the hill;
With the sunshine on thy face,
Through thy torn brim's jaunty grace;
From my heart I give thee joy,—
I was once a barefoot boy!
Prince thou art,—the grown-up man
Only is republican.
Let the million-dollared ride!
Barefoot, trudging at his side,
Thou hast more than he can buy
In the reach of ear and eye,—
Outward sunshine, inward joy:
Blessings on thee, barefoot boy!

Oh for boyhood's painless play,
Sleep that wakes in laughing day,
Health that mocks the doctor's rules,
Knowledge never learned of schools,
Of the wild bee's morning chase,
Of the wild-flower's time and place,
Flight of fowl and habitude
Of the tenants of the wood;
How the tortoise bears his shell,
How the woodchuck digs his cell,
And the ground-mole sinks his well;
How the robin feeds her young;

How the oriole's nest is hung;
Where the whitest lilies blow,
Where the freshest berries grow,
Where the ground-nut trails its vine,
Where the wood-grape's clusters shine;
Of the black wasp's cunning way,
Mason of his walls of clay,
And the architectural plans
Of gray hornet artisans!
For, eschewing books and tasks,
Nature answers all he asks;
Hand in hand with her he walks,
Face to face with her he talks,
Part and parcel of her joy,—
Blessings on the barefoot boy!

Oh for boyhood's time of June,
Crowding years in one brief moon,
When all things I heard or saw,
Me, their master, waited for.
I was rich in flowers and trees,
Humming-birds and honey-bees;
For my sport the squirrel played,
Plied the snouted mole his spade;
For my taste the blackberry cone
Purpled over hedge and stone;
Laughed the brook for my delight
Through the day and through the night,
Whispering at the garden wall,
Talked with me from fall to fall;
Mine the sand-rimmed pickerel pond,
Mine the walnut slopes beyond,
Mine, on bending orchard trees,
Apples of Hesperides!
Still as my horizon grew,
Larger grew my riches too;
All the world I saw or knew
Seemed a complex Chinese toy,
Fashioned for a barefoot boy!

Oh for festal dainties spread,
Like my bowl of milk and bread;
Pewter spoon and bowl of wood,
On the door-stone, gray and rude!
O'er me, like a regal tent,
Cloudy-ribbed, the sunset bent,
Purple-curtained, fringed with gold,
Looped in many a wind-swung fold;
While for music came the play
Of the pied frogs' orchestra;
And, to light the noisy choir,
Lit the fly his lamp of fire.
I was monarch: pomp and joy
Waited on the barefoot boy!

Cheerily, then, my little man,
Live and laugh, as boyhood can!
Though the flinty slopes be hard,
Stubble-speared the new-mown sward,
Every morn shall lead thee through
Fresh baptisms of the dew;
Every evening from thy feet
Shall the cool wind kiss the heat:
All too soon these feet must hide
In the prison cells of pride,
Lose the freedom of the sod,
Like a colt's for work be shod,
Made to tread the mills of toil,
Up and down in ceaseless moil:
Happy if their track be found
Never on forbidden ground;
Happy if they sink not in
Quick and treacherous sands of sin.
Ah! that thou couldst know thy joy,
Ere it passes, barefoot boy!
(1855) 1856

## SKIPPER IRESON'S RIDE

Of all the rides since the birth of time,
Told in story or sung in rhyme,—
On Apuleius's Golden Ass,
Or one-eyed Calender's horse of brass,
Witch astride of a human back,
Islam's prophet on Al-Borák,—
The strangest ride that ever was sped
Was Ireson's, out from Marblehead!
  Old Floyd Ireson, for his hard heart,
  Tarred and feathered and carried in a cart
  By the women of Marblehead!

Body of turkey, head of owl,
Wings a-droop like a rained-on fowl,
Feathered and ruffled in every part,
Skipper Ireson stood in the cart.
Scores of women, old and young,

Strong of muscle, and glib of tongue,
Pushed and pulled up the rocky lane,
Shouting and singing the shrill refrain:
"Here's Flud Oirson, fur his horrd horrt,
Torr'd an' futherr'd an' corr'd in a corrt
By the women o' Morble'ead!"

Wrinkled scolds with hands on hips,
Girls in bloom of cheek and lips,
Wild-eyed, free-limbed, such as chase
Bacchus round some antique vase,
Brief of skirt, with ankles bare,
Loose of kerchief and loose of hair,
With conch-shells blowing and fish-horns' twang,
Over and over the Mænads sang:
"Here's Flud Oirson, fur his horrd horrt,
Torr'd an' futherr'd an' corr'd in a corrt
By the women o' Morble'ead!"

Small pity for him!—He sailed away
From a leaking ship in Chaleur Bay,—
Sailed away from a sinking wreck,
With his own town's-people on her deck!
"Lay by! lay by!" they called to him.
Back he answered, "Sink or swim!
Brag of your catch of fish again!"
And off he sailed through the fog and rain!
Old Floyd Ireson, for his hard heart,
Tarred and feathered and carried in a cart
By the women of Marblehead!

Fathoms deep in dark Chaleur
That wreck shall lie forevermore.
Mother and sister, wife and maid,
Looked from the rocks of Marblehead
Over the moaning and rainy sea,—
Looked for the coming that might not be!
What did the winds and the sea-birds say
Of the cruel captain who sailed away?—
Old Floyd Ireson, for his hard heart,
Tarred and feathered and carried in a cart
By the women of Marblehead!

Through the street, on either side,
Up flew windows, doors swung wide;
Sharp-tongued spinsters, old wives gray,
Treble lent the fish-horn's bray.
Sea-worn grandsires, cripple-bound,
Hulks of old sailors run aground,
Shook head, and fist, and hat, and cane,
And cracked with curses the hoarse refrain:
"Here's Flud Oirson, fur his horrd horrt,
Torr'd an' futherr'd an' corr'd in a corrt
By the women o' Morble'ead!"

Sweetly along the Salem road
Bloom of orchard and lilac showed.
Little the wicked skipper knew
Of the fields so green and the sky so blue.
Riding there in his sorry trim,
Like an Indian idol glum and grim,
Scarcely he seemed the sound to hear
Of voices shouting, far and near:
"Here's Flud Oirson, fur his horrd horrt,
Torr'd an' futherr'd an' corr'd in a corrt
By the women o' Morble'ead!"

"Hear me, neighbors!" at last he cried,—
"What to me is this noisy ride?
What is the shame that clothes the skin
To the nameless horror that lives within?
Waking or sleeping, I see a wreck,
And hear a cry from a reeling deck!
Hate me and curse me,—I only dread
The hand of God and the face of the dead!"
Said old Floyd Ireson, for his hard heart,

Tarred and feathered and carried in a cart
By the women of Marblehead!

Then the wife of the skipper lost at sea
Said, "God has touched him! why should we?"
Said an old wife mourning her only son,
"Cut the rogue's tether and let him run!"
So with soft relentings and rude excuse,
Half scorn, half pity, they cut him loose,
And gave him a cloak to hide him in,
And left him alone with his shame and sin.
Poor Floyd Ireson, for his hard heart,
Tarred and feathered and carried in a cart
By the women of Marblehead!

(1857) 1857

## TELLING THE BEES

Here is the place; right over the hill
Runs the path I took;
You can see the gap in the old wall still,
And the stepping-stones in the shallow brook.

There is the house, with the gate red-barred,
And the poplars tall;
And the barn's brown length, and the cattleyard,
And the white horns tossing above the wall.

There are the beehives ranged in the sun;
And down by the brink
Of the brook are her poor flowers, weed-o'errun,
Pansy and daffodil, rose and pink.

A year has gone, as the tortoise goes,
Heavy and slow;
And the same rose blows, and the same sun glows,
And the same brook sings of a year ago.

There's the same sweet clover-smell in the breeze;
And the June sun warm
Tangles his wings of fire in the trees,
Setting, as then, over Fernside farm.

I mind me how with a lover's care
From my Sunday coat
I brushed off the burrs, and smoothed my hair,
And cooled at the brookside my brow and throat.

Since we parted, a month had passed,—
To love, a year;
Down through the beeches I looked at last
On the little red gate and the well-sweep near.

I can see it all now,—the slantwise rain
Of light through the leaves,
The sundown's blaze on her window-pane,
The bloom of her roses under the eaves.

Just the same as a month before,—
The house and the trees,
The barn's brown gable, the vine by the door,—
Nothing changed but the hives of bees.

Before them, under the garden wall,
Forward and back,
Went drearily singing the chore-girl small,
Draping each hive with a shred of black.

Trembling, I listened: the summer sun
Had the chill of snow;
For I knew she was telling the bees of one
Gone on the journey we all must go!

Then I said to myself, "My Mary weeps
For the dead to-day:
Haply her blind old grandsire sleeps
The fret and the pain of his age away."

But her dog whined low; on the door-way sill,
With his cane to his chin,
The old man sat; and the chore-girl still
Sung to the bees stealing out and in.

And the song she was singing ever since
In my ear sounds on:—
"Stay at home, pretty bees, fly not hence!
Mistress Mary is dead and gone!"

(1858) 1858

## MY PLAYMATE

The pines were dark on Ramoth hill,
Their song was soft and low;
The blossoms in the sweet May wind
Were falling like the snow.

The blossoms drifted at our feet,
The orchard birds sang clear;
The sweetest and the saddest day
It seemed of all the year.

For, more to me than birds or flowers,
My playmate left her home,
And took with her the laughing spring,
The music and the bloom.

She kissed the lips of kith and kin,
She laid her hand in mine:
What more could ask the bashful boy
Who fed her father's kine?

She left us in the bloom of May:
The constant years told o'er
Their seasons with as sweet May morns,
But she came back no more.

I walk, with noiseless feet, the round
Of uneventful years;
Still o'er and o'er I sow the spring
And reap the autumn ears.

She lives where all the golden year
Her summer roses blow;
The dusky children of the sun
Before her come and go.

There haply with her jewelled hands
She smooths her silken gown,—
No more the homespun lap wherein
I shook the walnuts down.

The wild grapes wait us by the brook,
The brown nuts on the hill,
And still the May-day flowers make sweet
The woods of Follymill.

The lilies blossom in the pond,
The bird builds in the tree,
The dark pines sing on Ramoth hill
The slow song of the sea.

I wonder if she thinks of them,
And how the old time seems,—
If ever the pines of Ramoth wood
Are sounding in her dreams.

I see her face, I hear her voice;
Does she remember mine?
And what to her is now the boy
Who fed her father's kine?

What cares she that the orioles build
For other eyes than ours,—
That other hands with nuts are filled,
And other laps with flowers?

O playmate in the golden time!
Our mossy seat is green,
Its fringing violets blossom yet,
The old trees o'er it lean.

The winds so sweet with birch and fern
A sweeter memory blow;
And there in spring the veeries sing
The song of long ago.

And still the pines of Ramoth wood
Are moaning like the sea,—
The moaning of the sea of change
Between myself and thee!
(1860) 1860

## LAUS DEO!

It is done!
Clang of bell and roar of gun
Send the tidings up and down.
How the belfries rock and reel!
How the great guns, peal on peal,
Fling the joy from town to town!

Ring, O bells!
Every stroke exulting tells
Of the burial hour of crime.
Loud and long, that all may hear,
Ring for every listening ear
Of Eternity and Time!

Let us kneel:
God's own voice is in that peal,
And this spot is holy ground.
Lord, forgive us! What are we,
That our eyes this glory see,
That our ears have heard the sound!

For the Lord
On the whirlwind is abroad;
In the earthquake He has spoken;
He has smitten with His thunder
The iron walls asunder,
And the gates of brass are broken!

Loud and long
Lift the old exulting song;
Sing with Miriam by the sea,
He has cast the mighty down;
Horse and rider sink and drown;
"He hath triumphed gloriously!"

Did we dare,
In our agony of prayer,
Ask for more than He has done?
When was ever His right hand
Over any time or land
Stretched as now beneath the sun?

How they pale,
Ancient myth and song and tale,
In this wonder of our days,
When the cruel rod of war
Blossoms white with righteous law,
And the wrath of man is praise!

Blotted out!
All within and all about
Shall a fresher life begin;
Freer breathe the universe
As it rolls its heavy curse
On the dead and buried sin!

It is done!
In the circuit of the sun
Shall the sound thereof go forth.
It shall bid the sad rejoice,
It shall give the dumb a voice,
It shall belt with joy the earth!

Ring and swing,
Bells of joy! On morning's wing
Send the song of praise abroad!
With a sound of broken chains
Tell the nations that He reigns,
Who alone is Lord and God!
(1865) 1865

## SNOW-BOUND, A WINTER IDYL

**TO THE MEMORY OF THE HOUSEHOLD IT DESCRIBES THIS POEM IS DEDICATED BY THE AUTHOR**

As the Spirits of Darkness be stronger in the dark, so Good Spirits, which be Angels of Light, are augmented not only by the Divine light of the Sun, but also by our common VVood Fire: and as the Celestial Fire drives away dark spirits, so also this our Fire of VVood doth the same.

—COR. AGRIPPA, *Occult Philosophy,* Book I. ch. v.

Announced by all the trumpets of the sky,
Arrives the snow, and, driving o'er the fields,
Seems nowhere to alight: the whited air
Hides hills and woods, the river and the heaven,
And veils the farm-house at the garden's end.
The sled and traveller stopped, the courier's feet
Delayed, all friends shut out, the housemates sit
Around the radiant fireplace, enclosed
In a tumultuous privacy of storm.

—EMERSON, *The Snow Storm.*

The sun that brief December day
Rose cheerless over hills of gray,
And, darkly circled, gave at noon
A sadder light than waning moon.
Slow tracing down the thickening sky
Its mute and ominous prophecy,
A portent seeming less than threat,
It sank from sight before it set.
A chill no coat, however stout,
Of homespun stuff could quite shut out,
A hard, dull bitterness of cold,
That checked, mid-vein, the circling race
Of life-blood in the sharpened face,
The coming of the snow-storm told.
The wind blew east; we heard the roar
Of Ocean on his wintry shore,
And felt the strong pulse throbbing there
Beat with low rhythm our inland air.

Meanwhile we did our nightly chores,—
Brought in the wood from out of doors,
Littered the stalls, and from the mows
Raked down the herd's-grass for the cows:
Heard the horse whinnying for his corn;
And, sharply clashing horn on horn,
Impatient down the stanchion rows
The cattle shake their walnut bows;
While, peering from his early perch
Upon the scaffold's pole of birch,
The cock his crested helmet bent
And down his querulous challenge sent.

Unwarmed by any sunset light
The gray day darkened into night,
A night made hoary with the swarm
And whirl-dance of the blinding storm,
As zigzag, wavering to and fro,
Crossed and recrossed the wingèd snow;
And ere the early bedtime came
The white drift piled the window-frame,
And through the glass the clothes-line posts
Looked in like tall and sheeted ghosts.

So all night long the storm roared on:
The morning broke without a sun;
In tiny spherule traced with lines
Of Nature's geometric signs,
In starry flake, and pellicle,
All day the hoary meteor fell;
And, when the second morning shone,
We looked upon a world unknown,
On nothing we could call our own.
Around the glistening wonder bent
The blue walls of the firmament,
No cloud above, no earth below,—
A universe of sky and snow!
The old familiar sights of ours
Took marvellous shapes; strange domes and towers
Rose up where sty or corn-crib stood,
Or garden-wall, or belt of wood;
A smooth white mound the brush-pile showed,
A fenceless drift what once was road;
The bridle-post an old man sat
With loose-flung coat and high cocked hat;
The well-curb had a Chinese roof;
And even the long sweep, high aloof,
In its slant splendor, seemed to tell
Of Pisa's leaning miracle.

A prompt, decisive man, no breath
Our father wasted: "Boys, a path!"
Well pleased, (for when did farmer boy
Count such a summons less than joy?)
Our buskins on our feet we drew;

With mittened hands, and caps drawn
low,
To guard our necks and ears from
snow,
We cut the solid whiteness through.
And, where the drift was deepest,
made
A tunnel walled and overlaid
With dazzling crystal: we had read
Of rare Aladdin's wondrous cave,
And to our own his name we gave,
With many a wish the luck were ours
To test his lamp's supernal powers.
We reached the barn with merry din,
And roused the prisoned brutes within.
The old horse thrust his long head out,
And grave with wonder gazed about;
The cock his lusty greeting said,
And forth his speckled harem led;
The oxen lashed their tails, and
hooked,
And mild reproach of hunger looked;
The hornèd patriarch of the sheep,
Like Egypt's Amun roused from
sleep,
Shook his sage head with gesture mute,
And emphasized with stamp of foot.

All day the gusty north-wind bore
The loosening drift its breath before;
Low circling round its southern zone,
The sun through dazzling snow-mist
shone.
No church-bell lent its Christian tone
To the savage air, no social smoke
Curled over woods of snow-hung oak.
A solitude made more intense
By dreary-voicèd elements,
The shrieking of the mindless wind,
The moaning tree-boughs swaying
blind,
And on the glass the unmeaning beat
Of ghostly finger-tips of sleet.
Beyond the circle of our hearth
No welcome sound of toil or mirth
Unbound the spell, and testified
Of human life and thought outside.
We minded that the sharpest ear
The buried brooklet could not hear,
The music of whose liquid lip
Had been to us companionship,
And, in our lonely life, had grown
To have an almost human tone.

As night drew on, and, from the crest
Of wooded knolls that ridged the west,
The sun, a snow-blown traveller, sank
From sight beneath the smothering
bank,
We piled, with care, our nightly
stack
Of wood against the chimney-back,—
The oaken log, green, huge, and thick,
And on its top the stout back-stick;
The knotty forestick laid apart,
And filled between with curious art
The ragged brush; then, hovering near,
We watched the first red blaze appear,
Heard the sharp crackle, caught the
gleam
On whitewashed wall and sagging
beam,
Until the old, rude-furnished room
Burst, flower-like, into rosy bloom;
While radiant with a mimic flame
Outside the sparkling drift became,
And through the bare-boughed lilac-
tree
Our own warm hearth seemed blazing
free.
The crane and pendent trammels
showed,
The Turks' heads on the andirons
glowed;
While childish fancy, prompt to tell
The meaning of the miracle,
Whispered the old rhyme: *"Under the
tree,*
*When fire outdoors burns merrily,*
*There the witches are making tea."*

The moon above the eastern wood
Shone at its full; the hill-range stood
Transfigured in the silver flood,
Its blown snows flashing cold and keen,
Dead white, save where some sharp
ravine
Took shadow, or the sombre green
Of hemlocks turned to pitchy black

Against the whiteness at their back.
For such a world and such a night
Most fitting that unwarming light,
Which only seemed where'er it fell
To make the coldness visible.

Shut in from all the world without,
We sat the clean-winged hearth about,
Content to let the north-wind roar
In baffled rage at pane and door,
While the red logs before us beat
The frost-line back with tropic heat;
And ever, when a louder blast
Shook beam and rafter as it passed,
The merrier up its roaring draught
The great throat of the chimney laughed;
The house-dog on his paws outspread
Laid to the fire his drowsy head,
The cat's dark silhouette on the wall
A couchant tiger's seemed to fall;
And, for the winter fireside meet,
Between the andirons' straddling feet,
The mug of cider simmered slow,
The apples sputtered in a row,
And, close at hand, the basket stood
With nuts from brown October's wood.

What matter how the night behaved?
What matter how the north-wind raved?
Blow high, blow low, not all its snow
Could quench our hearth-fire's ruddy glow.
O Time and Change!—with hair as gray
As was my sire's that winter day,
How strange it seems, with so much gone
Of life and love, to still live on!
Ah, brother! only I and thou
Are left of all that circle now,—
The dear home faces whereupon
That fitful firelight paled and shone.
Henceforward, listen as we will,
The voices of that hearth are still;
Look where we may, the wide earth o'er
Those lighted faces smile no more.
We tread the paths their feet have worn,
We sit beneath their orchard trees,
We hear, like them, the hum of bees
And rustle of the bladed corn;
We turn the pages that they read,
Their written words we linger o'er,
But in the sun they cast no shade,
No voice is heard, no sign is made,
No step is on the conscious floor!
Yet Love will dream, and Faith will trust
(Since He who knows our need is just),
That somehow, somewhere, meet we must.
Alas for him who never sees
The stars shine through his cypress-trees!
Who, hopeless, lays his dead away,
Nor looks to see the breaking day
Across the mournful marbles play!
Who hath not learned, in hours of faith,
The truth to flesh and sense unknown,
That Life is ever lord of Death,
And Love can never lose its own!

We sped the time with stories old,
Wrought puzzles out, and riddles told,
Or stammered from our school-book lore
"The Chief of Gambia's golden shore."
How often since, when all the land
Was clay in Slavery's shaping hand,
As if a far-blown trumpet stirred
The languorous sin-sick air, I heard:
"*Does not the voice of reason cry,*
*Claim the first right which Nature gave,*
*From the red scourge of bondage fly,*
*Nor deign to live a burdened slave!*"
Our father rode again his ride
On Memphremagog's wooded side;
Sat down again to moose and samp
In trapper's hut and Indian camp;

Lived o'er the old idyllic ease
Beneath St. François' hemlock-trees;
Again for him the moonlight shone
On Norman cap and bodiced zone;
Again he heard the violin play
Which led the village dance away,
And mingled in its merry whirl
The grandam and the laughing girl.
Or, nearer home, our steps he led
Where Salisbury's level marshes spread
Mile-wide as flies the laden bee;
Where merry mowers, hale and strong,
Swept, scythe on scythe, their swaths along
The low green prairies of the sea.
We shared the fishing off Boar's Head,
And round the rocky Isles of Shoals
The hake-broil on the drift-wood coals;
The chowder on the sand-beach made,
Dipped by the hungry, steaming hot,
With spoons of clam-shell from the pot.
We heard the tales of witchcraft old,
And dream and sign and marvel told
To sleepy listeners as they lay
Stretched idly on the salted hay,
Adrift along the winding shores,
When favoring breezes deigned to blow
The square sail of the gundelow
And idle lay the useless oars.

Our mother, while she turned her wheel
Or run the new-knit stocking-heel,
Told how the Indian hordes came down
At midnight on Cocheco town,
And how her own great-uncle bore
His cruel scalp-mark to fourscore.
Recalling, in her fitting phrase,
So rich and picturesque and free,
(The common unrhymed poetry
Of simple life and country ways,)
The story of her early days,—
She made us welcome to her home;
Old hearths grew wide to give us room;
We stole with her a frightened look
At the gray wizard's conjuring-book,
The fame whereof went far and wide
Through all the simple country-side;
We heard the hawks at twilight play,
The boat-horn on Piscataqua,
The loon's weird laughter far away;
We fished her little trout-brook, knew
What flowers in wood and meadow grew,
What sunny hillsides autumn-brown
She climbed to shake the ripe nuts down,
Saw where in sheltered cove and bay
The ducks' black squadron anchored lay,
And heard the wild-geese calling loud
Beneath the gray November cloud.

Then, haply, with a look more grave,
And soberer tone, some tale she gave
From painful Sewel's ancient tome,
Beloved in every Quaker home,
Of faith fire-winged by martyrdom,
Or Chalkley's Journal, old and quaint,—
Gentlest of skippers, rare sea-saint!—
Who, when the dreary calms prevailed,
And water-butt and bread-cask failed,
And cruel, hungry eyes pursued
His portly presence mad for food,
With dark hints muttered under breath
Of casting lots for life or death,
Offered, if Heaven withheld supplies,
To be himself the sacrifice.
Then, suddenly, as if to save
The good man from his living grave,
A ripple on the water grew,
A school of porpoise flashed in view.
"Take, eat," he said, "and be content;
These fishes in my stead are sent
By Him who gave the tangled ram
To spare the child of Abraham."

Our uncle, innocent of books,
Was rich in lore of fields and brooks,

The ancient teachers never dumb
Of Nature's unhoused lyceum.
In moons and tides and weather wise,
He read the clouds as prophecies,
And foul or fair could well divine,
By many an occult hint and sign,
Holding the cunning-warded keys
To all the woodcraft mysteries;
Himself to Nature's heart so near
That all her voices in his ear
Of beast or bird had meanings clear,
Like Apollonius of old,
Who knew the tales the sparrows told,
Or Hermes, who interpreted
What the sage cranes of Nilus said;
A simple, guileless, childlike man,
Content to live where life began;
Strong only on his native grounds,
The little world of sights and sounds
Whose girdle was the parish bounds,
Whereof his fondly partial pride
The common features magnified,
As Surrey hills to mountains grew
In White of Selborne's loving view,—
He told how teal and loon he shot,
And how the eagle's eggs he got,
The feats on pond and river done,
The prodigies of rod and gun;
Till, warming with the tales he told,
Forgotten was the outside cold,
The bitter wind unheeded blew,
From ripening corn the pigeons flew,
The partridge drummed i' the wood, the mink
Went fishing down the river-brink.
In fields with bean or clover gay,
The woodchuck, like a hermit gray,
Peered from the doorway of his cell;
The muskrat plied the mason's trade,
And tier by tier his mud-walls laid;
And from the shagbark overhead
The grizzled squirrel dropped his shell.

Next, the dear aunt, whose smile of cheer
And voice in dreams I see and hear,—
The sweetest woman ever Fate
Perverse denied a household mate,
Who, lonely, homeless, not the less
Found peace in love's unselfishness,
And welcome whereso'er she went,
A calm and gracious element,
Whose presence seemed the sweet income
And womanly atmosphere of home,—
Called up her girlhood memories,
The huskings and the apple-bees,
The sleigh-rides and the summer sails,
Weaving through all the poor details
And homespun warp of circumstance
A golden woof-thread of romance.
For well she kept her genial mood
And simple faith of maidenhood;
Before her still a cloud-land lay,
The mirage loomed across her way;
The morning dew, that dries so soon
With others, glistened at her noon;
Through years of toil and soil and care,
From glossy tress to thin gray hair,
All unprofaned she held apart
The virgin fancies of the heart.
Be shame to him of woman born
Who hath for such but thought of scorn.

There, too, our elder sister plied
Her evening task the stand beside;
A full, rich nature, free to trust,
Truthful and almost sternly just,
Impulsive, earnest, prompt to act,
And make her generous thought a fact,
Keeping with many a light disguise
The secret of self-sacrifice.
O heart sore-tried! thou hast the best
That Heaven itself could give thee,—rest,
Rest from all bitter thoughts and things!
How many a poor one's blessing went
With thee beneath the low green tent
Whose curtain never outward swings!

As one who held herself a part
Of all she saw, and let her heart
Against the household bosom lean,
Upon the motley-braided mat
Our youngest and our dearest sat,
Lifting her large, sweet, asking eyes,
Now bathed in the unfading green
And holy peace of Paradise.
Oh, looking from some heavenly hill,
Or from the shade of saintly palms,
Or silver reach of river calms,
Do those large eyes behold me still?
With me one little year ago:—
The chill weight of the winter snow
For months upon her grave has lain;
And now, when summer south-winds blow
And brier and harebell bloom again,
I tread the pleasant paths we trod,
I see the violet-sprinkled sod
Whereon she leaned, too frail and weak
The hillside flowers she loved to seek,
Yet following me where'er I went
With dark eyes full of love's content.
The birds are glad; the brier-rose fills
The air with sweetness; all the hills
Stretch green to June's unclouded sky;
But still I wait with ear and eye
For something gone which should be nigh,
A loss in all familiar things,
In flower that blooms, and bird that sings.
And yet, dear heart! remembering thee,
Am I not richer than of old?
Safe in thy immortality,
What change can reach the wealth I hold?
What chance can mar the pearl and gold
Thy love hath left in trust with me?
And while in life's late afternoon,
Where cool and long the shadows grow,
I walk to meet the night that soon
Shall shape and shadow overflow,
I cannot feel that thou art far,
Since near at need the angels are;
And when the sunset gates unbar,
Shall I not see thee waiting stand,
And, white against the evening star,
The welcome of thy beckoning hand?

Brisk wielder of the birch and rule,
The master of the district school
Held at the fire his favored place,
Its warm glow lit a laughing face
Fresh-hued and fair, where scarce appeared
The uncertain prophecy of beard.
He teased the mitten-blinded cat,
Played cross-pins on my uncle's hat,
Sang songs, and told us what befalls
In classic Dartmouth's college halls.
Born the wild Northern hills among,
From whence his yeoman father wrung
By patient toil subsistence scant,
Not competence and yet not want,
He early gained the power to pay
His cheerful, self-reliant way;
Could doff at ease his scholar's gown
To peddle wares from town to town;
Or through the long vacation's reach
In lonely lowland districts teach,
Where all the droll experience found
At stranger hearths in boarding round,
The moonlit skater's keen delight,
The sleigh-drive through the frosty night,
The rustic-party, with its rough
Accompaniment of blind-man's-buff,
And whirling-plate, and forfeits paid,
His winter task a pastime made.
Happy the snow-locked homes wherein
He tuned his merry violin,
Or played the athlete in the barn,
Or held the good dame's winding-yarn,
Or mirth-provoking versions told
Of classic legends rare and old,
Wherein the scenes of Greece and Rome
Had all the commonplace of home,
And little seemed at best the odds
'Twixt Yankee pedlers and old gods;
Where Pindus-born Arachthus took
The guise of any grist-mill brook,

And dread Olympus at his will
Became a huckleberry hill.

A careless boy that night he seemed;
But at his desk he had the look
And air of one who wisely schemed,
And hostage from the future took
In trainèd thought and lore of book.
Large-brained, clear-eyed, of such as he
Shall Freedom's young apostles be,
Who, following in War's bloody trail,
Shall every lingering wrong assail;
All chains from limb and spirit strike,
Uplift the black and white alike;
Scatter before their swift advance
The darkness and the ignorance,
The pride, the lust, the squalid sloth,
Which nurtured Treason's monstrous growth,
Made murder pastime, and the hell
Of prison-torture possible;
The cruel lie of caste refute,
Old forms remold, and substitute
For Slavery's lash the freeman's will,
For blind routine, wise-handed skill;
A school-house plant on every hill,
Stretching in radiate nerve-lines thence
The quick wires of intelligence;
Till North and South together brought
Shall own the same electric thought,
In peace a common flag salute,
And, side by side in labor's free
And unresentful rivalry,
Harvest the fields wherein they fought.

Another guest that winter night
Flashed back from lustrous eyes the light.
Unmarked by time, and yet not young,
The honeyed music of her tongue
And words of meekness scarcely told
A nature passionate and bold,
Strong, self-concentered, spurning guide,
Its milder features dwarfed beside
Her unbent will's majestic pride.
She sat among us, at the best,
A not unfeared, half-welcome guest,
Rebuking with her cultured phrase
Our homeliness of words and ways.
A certain pard-like, treacherous grace
Swayed the lithe limbs and dropped the lash,
Lent the white teeth their dazzling flash;
And under low brows, black with night,
Rayed out at times a dangerous light;
The sharp heat-lightnings of her face
Presaging ill to him whom Fate
Condemned to share her love or hate.
A woman tropical, intense
In thought and act, in soul and sense,
She blended in a like degree
The vixen and the devotee,
Revealing with each freak or feint
The temper of Petruchio's Kate,
The raptures of Siena's saint.
Her tapering hand and rounded wrist
Had facile power to form a fist;
The warm, dark languish of her eyes
Was never safe from wrath's surprise.
Brows saintly calm and lips devout
Knew every change of scowl and pout;
And the sweet voice had notes more high
And shrill for social battle-cry.

Since then what old cathedral town
Has missed her pilgrim staff and gown,
What convent-gate has held its lock
Against the challenge of her knock!
Through Smyrna's plague-hushed thoroughfares,
Up sea-set Malta's rocky stairs,
Gray olive slopes of hills that hem
Thy tombs and shrines, Jerusalem,
Or startling on her desert throne
The crazy Queen of Lebanon
With claims fantastic as her own,
Her tireless feet have held their way;
And still, unrestful, bowed, and gray,
She watches under Eastern skies,

With hope each day renewed and fresh,
The Lord's quick coming in the flesh,
Whereof she dreams and prophesies!

Where'er her troubled path may be,
The Lord's sweet pity with her go!
The outward wayward life we see,
The hidden springs we may not know.
Nor is it given us to discern
What threads the fatal sisters spun,
Through what ancestral years has run
The sorrow with the woman born,
What forged her cruel chain of moods,
What set her feet in solitudes,
And held the love within her mute,
What mingled madness in the blood,
A life-long discord and annoy,
Water of tears with oil of joy,
And hid within the folded bud
Perversities of flower and fruit.
It is not ours to separate
The tangled skein of will and fate,
To show what metes and bounds should stand
Upon the soul's debatable land,
And between choice and Providence
Divide the circle of events;
But He who knows our frame is just,
Merciful and compassionate,
And full of sweet assurances
And hope for all the language is,
That He remembereth we are dust!

At last the great logs, crumbling low,
Sent out a dull and duller glow,
The bull's-eye watch that hung in view,
Ticking its weary circuit through,
Pointed with mutely warning sign
Its black hand to the hour of nine.
That sign the pleasant circle broke:
My uncle ceased his pipe to smoke,
Knocked from its bowl the refuse gray,
And laid it tenderly away;
Then roused himself to safely cover
The dull red brands with ashes over.
And while, with care, our mother laid
The work aside, her steps she stayed
One moment, seeking to express
Her grateful sense of happiness
For food and shelter, warmth and health,
And love's contentment more than wealth,
With simple wishes (not the weak,
Vain prayers which no fulfilment seek,
But such as warm the generous heart,
O'er-prompt to do with Heaven its part)
That none might lack, that bitter night,
For bread and clothing, warmth and light.

Within our beds awhile we heard
The wind that round the gables roared,
With now and then a ruder shock,
Which made our very bedsteads rock.
We heard the loosened clapboards tost,
The board-nails snapping in the frost;
And on us, through the unplastered wall,
Felt the light sifted snow-flakes fall.
But sleep stole on, as sleep will do
When hearts are light and life is new;
Faint and more faint the murmurs grew,
Till in the summer-land of dreams
They softened to the sound of streams,
Low stir of leaves, and dip of oars,
And lapsing waves on quiet shores.

Next morn we wakened with the shout
Of merry voices high and clear;
And saw the teamsters drawing near
To break the drifted highways out.
Down the long hillside treading slow
We saw the half-buried oxen go,
Shaking the snow from heads up-tost,

Their straining nostrils white with frost.
Before our door the straggling train
Drew up, an added team to gain.
The elders threshed their hands a-cold,
  Passed, with the cider-mug, their jokes
  From lip to lip; the younger folks
Down the loose snow-banks, wrestling, rolled,
Then toiled again the cavalcade
  O'er windy hill, through clogged ravine,
  And woodland paths that wound between
Low drooping pine-boughs winter-weighed.
From every barn a team afoot,
At every house a new recruit,
Where, drawn by Nature's subtlest law,
Haply the watchful young men saw
Sweet doorway pictures of the curls
And curious eyes of merry girls,
Lifting their hands in mock defense
Against the snow-ball's compliments,
And reading in each missive tossed
The charm with Eden never lost.

We heard once more the sleigh-bells sound;
  And, following where the teamsters led,
The wise old Doctor went his round,
Just pausing at our door to say,
In the brief autocratic way
Of one who, prompt at Duty's call,
Was free to urge her claim on all,
  That some poor neighbor sick abed
At night our mother's aid would need.
For, one in generous thought and deed,
  What mattered in the sufferer's sight
  The Quaker matron's inward light,
The Doctor's mail of Calvin's creed?
All hearts confess the saints elect
  Who, twain in faith, in love agree,
And melt not in an acid sect
  The Christian pearl of charity!

So days went on: a week had passed
Since the great world was heard from last.
The Almanac we studied o'er,
Read and reread our little store
Of books and pamphlets, scarce a score;
One harmless novel, mostly hid
From younger eyes, a book forbid,
And poetry (or good or bad,
A single book was all we had),
Where Ellwood's meek, drab-skirted Muse,
  A stranger to the heathen Nine,
  Sang, with a somewhat nasal whine,
The wars of David and the Jews.
At last the floundering carrier bore
The village paper to our door.
Lo! broadening outward as we read,
To warmer zones the horizon spread;
In panoramic length unrolled
We saw the marvels that it told.
Before us passed the painted Creeks,
  And daft McGregor on his raids
  In Costa Rica's everglades.
And up Taygetos winding slow
Rode Ypsilanti's Mainote Greeks,
A Turk's head at each saddle-bow!
Welcome to us its week-old news,
Its corner for the rustic Muse,
  Its monthly gauge of snow and rain,
Its record, mingling in a breath
The wedding bell and dirge of death:
Jest, anecdote, and love-lorn tale,
The latest culprit sent to jail;
Its hue and cry of stolen and lost,
Its vendue sales and goods at cost,
  And traffic calling loud for gain.
We felt the stir of hall and street,
The pulse of life that round us beat;
The chill embargo of the snow
Was melted in the genial glow;
Wide swung again our ice-locked door,
And all the world was ours once more!
Clasp, Angel of the backward look

And folded wings of ashen gray
And voice of echoes far away,
The brazen covers of thy book;
The weird palimpsest old and vast,
Wherein thou hid'st the spectral past;
Where, closely mingling, pale and glow
The characters of joy and woe;
The monographs of outlived years,
Or smile-illumed or dim with tears,
Green hills of life that slope to death,
And haunts of home, whose vistaed trees
Shade off to mournful cypresses
With the white amaranths underneath.
Even while I look, I can but heed
The restless sands' incessant fall,
Importunate hours that hours succeed,
Each clamorous with its own sharp need,
And duty keeping pace with all.
Shut down and clasp the heavy lids;
I hear again the voice that bids
The dreamer leave his dream midway
For larger hopes and graver fears;
Life greatens in these later years,
The century's aloe flowers to-day!

Yet, haply, in some lull of life,
Some Truce of God which breaks its strife,
The worldling's eyes shall gather dew,
Dreaming in throngful city ways
Of winter joys his boyhood knew;
And dear and early friends—the few
Who yet remain—shall pause to view
These Flemish pictures of old days;
Sit with me by the homestead hearth,
And stretch the hands of memory forth
To warm them at the wood-fire's blaze!
And thanks untraced to lips unknown
Shall greet me like the odors blown
From unseen meadows newly mown,
Or lilies floating in some pond,
Wood-fringed, the wayside gaze beyond;
The traveller owns the grateful sense
Of sweetness near, he knows not whence,
And, pausing, takes with forehead bare
The benediction of the air.
(1866) 1866

## THE ETERNAL GOODNESS

O Friends! with whom my feet have trod
The quiet aisles of prayer,
Glad witness to your zeal for God
And love of man I bear.

I trace your lines of argument;
Your logic linked and strong
I weigh as one who dreads dissent,
And fears a doubt as wrong.

But still my human hands are weak
To hold your iron creeds:
Against the words ye bid me speak
My heart within me pleads.

Who fathoms the Eternal Thought?
Who talks of scheme and plan?
The Lord is God! He needeth not
The poor device of man.

I walk with bare, hushed feet the ground
Ye tread with boldness shod;
I dare not fix with mete and bound
The love and power of God.

Ye praise His justice; even such
His pitying love I deem:
Ye seek a king; I fain would touch
The robe that hath no seam.

Ye see the curse which overbroods
A world of pain and loss;
I hear our Lord's beatitudes
And prayer upon the cross.

More than your schoolmen teach, within
Myself, alas! I know:

Too dark ye cannot paint the sin,
Too small the merit show.

I bow my forehead to the dust,
I veil mine eyes for shame,
And urge, in trembling self-distrust,
A prayer without a claim.

I see the wrong that round me lies,
I feel the guilt within;
I hear, with groan and travail-cries,
The world confess its sin.

Yet, in the maddening maze of things,
And tossed by storm and flood,
To one fixed trust my spirit clings;
I know that God is good!

Not mine to look where cherubim
And seraphs may not see,
But nothing can be good in Him
Which evil is in me.

The wrong that pains my soul below
I dare not throne above,
I know not of His hate,—I know
His goodness and His love.

I dimly guess from blessings known
Of greater out of sight,
And, with the chastened Psalmist, own
His judgments too are right.

I long for household voices gone,
For vanished smiles I long,
But God hath led my dear ones on,
And He can do no wrong.

I know not what the future hath
Of marvel or surprise,
Assured alone that life and death
His mercy underlies.

And if my heart and flesh are weak
To bear an untried pain,
The bruisèd reed He will not break,
But strengthen and sustain.

No offering of my own I have,
Nor works my faith to prove;
I can but give the gifts He gave,
And plead His love for love.

And so beside the Silent Sea
I wait the muffled oar;
No harm from Him can come to me
On ocean or on shore.

I know not where His islands lift
Their fronded palms in air;
I only know I cannot drift
Beyond His love and care.

O brothers! if my faith is vain,
If hopes like these betray,
Pray for me that my feet may gain
The sure and safer way.

And Thou, O Lord! by whom are seen
Thy creatures as they be,
Forgive me if too close I lean
My human heart on Thee!
(1865) 1867

## THE FRIEND'S BURIAL

My thoughts are all in yonder town,
Where, wept by many tears,
To-day my mother's friend lays down
The burden of her years.

True as in life, no poor disguise
Of death with her is seen,
And on her simple casket lies
No wreath of bloom and green.

Oh, not for her the florist's art,
The mocking weeds of woe;
Dear memories in each mourner's heart
Like heaven's white lilies blow.

And all about the softening air
Of new-born sweetness tells,
And the ungathered May-flowers wear
The tints of ocean shells.

The old, assuring miracle
Is fresh as heretofore;

And earth takes up its parable
  Of life from death once more.

Here organ-swell and church-bell toll
  Methinks but discord were;
The prayerful silence of the soul
  Is best befitting her.

No sound should break the quietude
  Alike of earth and sky;
O wandering wind in Seabrook wood,
  Breathe but a half-heard sigh!

Sing softly, spring-bird, for her sake;
  And thou not distant sea,
Lapse lightly as if Jesus spake,
  And thou wert Galilee!

For all her quiet life flowed on
  As meadow streamlets flow,
Where fresher green reveals alone
  The noiseless ways they go.

From her loved place of prayer I see
  The plain-robed mourners pass,
With slow feet treading reverently
  The graveyard's springing grass.

Make room, O mourning ones, for me,
  Where, like the friends of Paul,
That you no more her face shall see
  You sorrow most of all.

Her path shall brighten more and more
  Unto the perfect day;
She cannot fail of peace who bore
  Such peace with her away.

O sweet, calm face that seemed to wear
  The look of sins forgiven!
O voice of prayer that seemed to bear
  Our own needs up to heaven!

How reverent in our midst she stood,
  Or knelt in grateful praise!
What grace of Christian womanhood
  Was in her household ways!

For still her holy living meant
  No duty left undone;
The heavenly and the human blent
  Their kindred loves in one.

And if her life small leisure found
  For feasting ear and eye,
And Pleasure, on her daily round,
  She passed unpausing by,

Yet with her went a secret sense
  Of all things sweet and fair,
And Beauty's gracious providence
  Refreshed her unaware.

She kept her line of rectitude
  With love's unconscious ease;
Her kindly instincts understood
  All gentle courtesies.

An inborn charm of graciousness
  Made sweet her smile and tone,
And glorified her farm-wife dress
  With beauty not its own.

The dear Lord's best interpreters
  Are humble human souls;
The Gospel of a life like hers
  Is more than books or scrolls.

From scheme and creed the light goes out,
  The saintly fact survives;
The blessed Master none can doubt
  Revealed in holy lives.

(1873) 1874

## SUNSET ON THE BEARCAMP

A gold fringe on the purpling hem
  Of hills the river runs,
As down its long, green valley falls
  The last of summer's suns.
Along its tawny gravel-bed
  Broad-flowing, swift, and still,
As if its meadow levels felt
  The hurry of the hill,
Noiseless between its banks of green
  From curve to curve it slips;
The drowsy maple-shadows rest
  Like fingers on its lips.

A waif from Carroll's wildest hills,
Unstoried and unknown;
The ursine legend of its name
Prowls on its banks alone.
Yet flowers as fair its slopes adorn
As ever Yarrow knew,
Or, under rainy Irish skies,
By Spenser's Mulla grew;
And through the gaps of leaning trees
Its mountain cradle shows:
The gold against the amethyst,
The green against the rose.

Touched by a light that hath no name,
A glory never sung,
Aloft on sky and mountain wall
Are God's great pictures hung.
How changed the summits vast and old!
No longer granite-browed,
They melt in rosy mist; the rock
Is softer than the cloud;
The valley holds its breath; no leaf
Of all its elms is twirled:
The silence of eternity
Seems falling on the world.

The pause before the breaking seals
Of mystery is this;
Yon miracle-play of night and day
Makes dumb its witnesses.
What unseen altar crowns the hills
That reach up stair on stair?
What eyes look through, what white wings fan
These purple veils of air?
What Presence from the heavenly heights
To those of earth stoops down?
Not vainly Hellas dreamed of gods
On Ida's snowy crown!

Slow fades the vision of the sky,
The golden water pales,
And over all the valley-land
A gray-winged vapor sails.
I go the common way of all;
The sunset fires will burn,
The flowers will blow, the river flow,
When I no more return.
No whisper from the mountain pine
Nor lapsing stream shall tell
The stranger, treading where I tread,
Of him who loved them well.

But beauty seen is never lost,
God's colors all are fast;
The glory of this sunset heaven
Into my soul has passed,
A sense of gladness unconfined
To mortal date or clime;
As the soul liveth, it shall live
Beyond the years of time.
Beside the mystic asphodels
Shall bloom the home-born flowers,
And new horizons flush and glow
With sunset hues of ours.

Farewell! these smiling hills must wear
Too soon their wintry frown,
And snow-cold winds from off them shake
The maple's red leaves down.
But I shall see a summer sun
Still setting broad and low;
The mountain slopes shall blush and bloom,
The golden water flow.
A lover's claim is mine on all
I see to have and hold,—
The rose-light of perpetual hills,
And sunsets never cold!

(1876) 1878

# HENRY WADSWORTH LONGFELLOW
## (1807–1882)

### A PSALM OF LIFE

WHAT THE HEART OF THE YOUNG MAN SAID TO THE PSALMIST

Tell me not, in mournful numbers,
Life is but an empty dream!—
For the soul is dead that slumbers,
And things are not what they seem.

Life is real! Life is earnest!
And the grave is not its goal;
Dust thou art, to dust returnest,
Was not spoken of the soul.

Not enjoyment, and not sorrow,
Is our destined end or way;
But to act, that each tomorrow
Find us farther than today.

Art is long, and Time is fleeting,
And our hearts, though stout and brave,
Still, like muffled drums, are beating
Funeral marches to the grave.

In the world's broad field of battle,
In the bivouac of Life,
Be not like dumb, driven cattle!
Be a hero in the strife!

Trust no Future, howe'er pleasant!
Let the dead Past bury its dead!
Act,—act in the living Present!
Heart within, and God o'erhead!

Lives of great men all remind us
We can make our lives sublime,
And, departing, leave behind us,
Footprints on the sands of time;

Footprints, that perhaps another,
Sailing o'er life's solemn main,
A forlorn and shipwrecked brother,
Seeing, shall take heart again.

Let us, then, be up and doing,
With a heart for any fate;
Still achieving, still pursuing,
Learn to labor and to wait.

(1838) 1838

### FOOTSTEPS OF ANGELS

When the hours of Day are numbered,
And the voices of the Night
Wake the better soul, that slumbered,
To a holy, calm delight;

Ere the evening lamps are lighted,
And, like phantoms grim and tall,
Shadows from the fitful firelight
Dance upon the parlor wall;

Then the forms of the departed
Enter at the open door;
The beloved, the true-hearted,
Come to visit me once more;

He, the young and strong, who cherished
Noble longings for the strife,
By the roadside fell and perished,
Weary with the march of life!

They, the holy ones and weakly,
Who the cross of suffering bore,
Folded their pale hands so meekly,
Spake with us on earth no more!

And with them the Being Beauteous,
Who unto my youth was given,
More than all things else to love me,
And is now a saint in heaven.

With a slow and noiseless footstep
  Comes that messenger divine,
Takes the vacant chair beside me,
  Lays her gentle hand in mine.

And she sits and gazes at me
  With those deep and tender eyes,
Like the stars, so still and saint-like,
  Looking downward from the skies.

Uttered not, yet comprehended,
  Is the spirit's voiceless prayer,
Soft rebukes, in blessings ended,
  Breathing from her lips of air.

Oh, though oft depressed and lonely,
  All my fears are laid aside,
If I but remember only
  Such as these have lived and died!

(1837–9) 1839

## THE BELEAGUERED CITY

I have read, in some old, marvellous tale,
  Some legend strange and vague,
That a midnight host of spectres pale
  Beleaguered the walls of Prague.

Beside the Moldau's rushing stream,
  With the wan moon overhead,
There stood, as in an awful dream,
  The army of the dead.

White as a sea-fog, landward bound,
  The spectral camp was seen,
And, with a sorrowful, deep sound,
  The river flowed between.

No other voice nor sound was there,
  No drum, nor sentry's pace;
The mist-like banners clasped the air
  As clouds with clouds embrace.

But when the old cathedral bell
  Proclaimed the morning prayer,
The white pavilions rose and fell
  On the alarmèd air.

Down the broad valley fast and far
  The troubled army fled;
Up rose the glorious morning star,
  The ghastly host was dead.

I have read, in the marvellous heart of man,
  That strange and mystic scroll,
That an army of phantoms vast and wan
  Beleaguer the human soul.

Encamped beside Life's rushing stream,
  In Fancy's misty light,
Gigantic shapes and shadows gleam
  Portentous through the night.

Upon its midnight battle-ground
  The spectral camp is seen,
And, with a sorrowful, deep sound,
  Flows the River of Life between.

No other voice nor sound is there,
  In the army of the grave;
No other challenge breaks the air,
  But the rushing of Life's wave.

And when the solemn and deep church-bell
  Entreats the soul to pray,
The midnight phantoms feel the spell,
  The shadows sweep away.

Down the broad Vale of Tears afar
  The spectral camp is fled;
Faith shineth as a morning star,
  Our ghastly fears are dead.

(1839) 1839

## HYMN TO THE NIGHT

'Ασπασίη, τρίλλιστος

I heard the trailing garments of the Night
  Sweep through her marble halls!
I saw her sable skirts all fringed with light
  From the celestial walls!

I felt her presence, by its spell of might,
Stoop o'er me from above;
The calm, majestic presence of the Night,
As of the one I love.

I heard the sounds of sorrow and delight,
The manifold, soft chimes,
That fill the haunted chambers of the Night,
Like some old poet's rhymes.

From the cool cisterns of the midnight air
My spirit drank repose;
The fountain of perpetual peace flows there,—
From those deep cisterns flows.

O holy Night! from thee I learn to bear
What man has borne before!
Thou layest thy finger on the lips of Care,
And they complain no more.

Peace! Peace! Orestes-like I breathe this prayer!
Descend with broad-winged flight,
The welcome, the thrice-prayed for, the most fair,
The best-beloved Night!

(1839) 1839

## THE SKELETON IN ARMOR

"Speak! speak! thou fearful guest!
Who, with thy hollow breast
Still in rude armor drest,
Comest to daunt me!
Wrapt not in Eastern balms,
But with thy fleshless palms
Stretched, as if asking alms,
Why dost thou haunt me?"

Then from those cavernous eyes
Pale flashes seemed to rise,
As when the Northern skies
Gleam in December;
And, like the water's flow
Under December's snow,
Came a dull voice of woe
From the heart's chamber.

"I was a Viking old!
My deeds, though manifold,
No Skald in song has told,
No Saga taught thee!
Take heed, that in thy verse
Thou dost the tale rehearse,
Else dread a dead man's curse;
For this I sought thee.

"Far in the Northern Land,
By the wild Baltic's strand,
I, with my childish hand,
Tamed the gerfalcon;
And, with my skates fast-bound,
Skimmed the half-frozen Sound,
That the poor whimpering hound
Trembled to walk on.

"Oft to his frozen lair
Tracked I the grisly bear,
While from my path the hare
Fled like a shadow;
Oft through the forest dark
Followed the were-wolf's bark
Until the soaring lark
Sang from the meadow.

"But when I older grew,
Joining a corsair's crew,
O'er the dark sea I flew
With the marauders.
Wild was the life we led;
Many the souls that sped,
Many the hearts that bled,
By our stern orders.

"Many a wassail-bout
Wore the long winter out;
Often our midnight shout
Set the cocks crowing,
As we the Berserk's tale
Measured in cups of ale,
Draining the oaken pail
Filled to o'erflowing.

"Once as I told in glee
Tales of the stormy sea,
Soft eyes did gaze on me,
  Burning yet tender;
And as the white stars shine
On the dark Norway pine,
On that dark heart of mine
  Fell their soft splendor.

"I wooed the blue-eyed maid,
Yielding, yet half afraid,
And in the forest's shade
  Our vows were plighted.
Under its loosened vest
Fluttered her little breast,
Like birds within their nest
  By the hawk frighted.

"Bright in her father's hall
Shields gleamed upon the wall,
Loud sang the minstrels all,
  Chanting his glory;
When of old Hildebrand
I asked his daughter's hand,
Mute did the minstrels stand
  To hear my story.

"While the brown ale he quaffed,
Loud then the champion laughed,
And as the wind-gusts waft
  The sea-foam brightly,
So the loud laugh of scorn
Out of those lips unshorn,
From the deep drinking-horn
  Blew the foam lightly.

"She was a Prince's child,
I but a Viking wild,
And though she blushed and smiled,
  I was discarded!
Should not the dove so white
Follow the sea-mew's flight?
Why did they leave that night
  Her nest unguarded?

"Scarce had I put to sea,
Bearing the maid with me,
Fairest of all was she
  Among the Norsemen!
When on the white sea-strand,
Waving his armèd hand,
Saw we old Hildebrand,
  With twenty horsemen.

"Then launched they to the blast,
Bent like a reed each mast,
Yet we were gaining fast,
  When the wind failed us;
And with a sudden flaw
Came round the gusty Skaw,
So that our foe we saw
  Laugh as he hailed us.

"And as to catch the gale
Round veered the flapping sail,
'Death!' was the helmsman's hail,
  'Death without quarter!'
Midships with iron keel
Struck we her ribs of steel;
Down her black hulk did reel
  Through the black water!

"As with his wings aslant,
Sails the fierce cormorant,
Seeking some rocky haunt,
  With his prey laden,—
So toward the open main,
Beating to sea again,
Through the wild hurricane,
  Bore I the maiden.

"Three weeks we westward bore,
And when the storm was o'er,
Cloud-like we saw the shore
  Stretching to leeward;
There for my lady's bower
Built I the lofty tower,
Which, to this very hour,
  Stands looking seaward.

"There lived we many years;
Time dried the maiden's tears;
She had forgot her fears,
  She was a mother;
Death closed her mild blue eyes;
Under that tower she lies;
Ne'er shall the sun arise
  On such another!

"Still grew my bosom then,
Still as a stagnant fen!
Hateful to me were men,
The sunlight hateful!
In the vast forest here,
Clad in my warlike gear,
Fell I upon my spear,
Oh, death was grateful!

"Thus, seamed with many scars,
Bursting these prison bars
Up to its native stars
My soul ascended!
There from the flowing bowl
Deep drinks the warrior's soul,
*Skoal!* to the Northland! *skoal!*"
Thus the tale ended.
(1840) 1841

## THE SLAVE'S DREAM

Beside the ungathered rice he lay,
His sickle in his hand;
His breast was bare, his matted hair
Was buried in the sand.
Again, in the mist and shadow of sleep,
He saw his Native Land.

Wide through the landscape of his dreams
The lordly Niger flowed;
Beneath the palm-trees on the plain
Once more a king he strode;
And heard the tinkling caravans
Descend the mountain road.

He saw once more his dark-eyed queen
Among her children stand;
They clasped his neck, they kissed his cheeks,
They held him by the hand! —
A tear burst from the sleeper's lids
And fell into the sand.

And then at furious speed he rode
Along the Niger's bank;
His bridle-reins were golden chains,
And, with a martial clank,
At each leap he could feel his scabbard of steel
Smiting his stallion's flank.

Before him, like a blood-red flag,
The bright flamingoes flew;
From morn till night he followed their flight,
O'er plains where the tamarind grew,
Till he saw the roofs of Caffre huts,
And the ocean rose to view.

At night he heard the lion roar,
And the hyena scream,
And the river-horse, as he crushed the reeds
Beside some hidden stream;
And it passed, like a glorious roll of drums,
Through the triumph of his dream.

The forests, with their myriad tongues,
Shouted of liberty;
And the Blast of the Desert cried aloud,
With a voice so wild and free,
That he started in his sleep and smiled
At their tempestuous glee.

He did not feel the driver's whip,
Nor the burning heat of day;
For Death had illumined the Land of Sleep,
And his lifeless body lay
A worn-out fetter, that the soul
Had broken and thrown away!
(1842) 1842

## THE BELFRY OF BRUGES

### CARILLON

In the ancient town of Bruges,
In the quaint old Flemish city,
As the evening shades descended,
Low and loud and sweetly blended,
Low at times and loud at times,
And changing like a poet's rhymes,
Rang the beautiful wild chimes
From the Belfry in the market
Of the ancient town of Bruges.

Then, with deep sonorous clangor
Calmly answering their sweet anger,

When the wrangling bells had ended,
Slowly struck the clock eleven,
And, from out the silent heaven,
Silence on the town descended.
Silence, silence everywhere,
On the earth and in the air,
Save that footsteps here and there
Of some burgher home returning,
By the street lamps faintly burning,
For a moment woke the echoes
Of the ancient town of Bruges.

But amid my broken slumbers
Still I heard those magic numbers,
As they loud proclaimed the flight
And stolen marches of the night;
Till their chimes in sweet collision
Mingled with each wandering vision,
Mingled with the fortune-telling
Gypsy-bands of dreams and fancies,
Which amid the waste expanses
Of the silent land of trances
Have their solitary dwelling;
All else seemed asleep in Bruges,
In the quaint old Flemish city.

And I thought how like these chimes
Are the poet's airy rhymes,
All his rhymes and roundelays,
His conceits, and songs, and ditties,
From the belfry of his brain,
Scattered downward, though in vain,
On the roofs and stones of cities!
For by night the drowsy ear
Under its curtains cannot hear,
And by day men go their ways,
Hearing the music as they pass,
But deeming it no more, alas!
Than the hollow sound of brass.

Yet perchance a sleepless wight,
Lodging at some humble inn
In the narrow lanes of life,
When the dusk and hush of night
Shut out the incessant din
Of daylight and its toil and strife,
May listen with a calm delight
To the poet's melodies,
Till he hears, or dreams he hears,
Intermingled with the song,
Thoughts that he has cherished long;
Hears amid the chime and singing
The bells of his own village ringing,
And wakes, and finds his slumberous
eyes
Wet with most delicious tears.

Thus dreamed I, as by night I lay
In Bruges, at the Fleur-de-Blé,
Listening with a wild delight
To the chimes that, through the night,
Rang their changes from the Belfry
Of that quaint old Flemish city.
(1842) 1843

## THE ARSENAL AT SPRINGFIELD

This is the Arsenal. From floor to
ceiling,
Like a huge organ, rise the burnished arms;
But from their silent pipes no anthem
pealing
Startles the villages with strange
alarms.

Ah! what a sound will rise, how wild
and dreary,
When the death-angel touches those
swift keys!
What loud lament and dismal Mise-
rere
Will mingle with their awful sym-
phonies!

I hear even now the infinite fierce
chorus,
The cries of agony, the endless
groan,
Which, through the ages that have
gone before us,
In long reverberations reach our
own.

On helm and harness rings the Saxon
hammer,
Through Cimbric forest roars the
Norseman's song,

And loud, amid the universal clamor,
O'er distant deserts sounds the Tartar gong.

I hear the Florentine, who from his palace
Wheels out his battle-bell with dreadful din,
And Aztec priests upon their teocallis
Beat the wild war-drum made of serpent's skin;

The tumult of each sacked and burning village;
The shout that every prayer for mercy drowns;
The soldiers' revels in the midst of pillage;
The wail of famine in beleaguered towns;

The bursting shell, the gateway wrenched asunder,
The rattling musketry, the clashing blade;
And ever and anon, in tones of thunder,
The diapason of the cannonade.

Is it, O man, with such discordant noises,
With such accursed instruments as these,
Thou drownest Nature's sweet and kindly voices,
And jarrest the celestial harmonies?

Were half the power that fills the world with terror,
Were half the wealth bestowed on camps and courts,
Given to redeem the human mind from error,
There were no need of arsenals nor forts:

The warrior's name would be a name abhorrèd!
And every nation, that should lift again
Its hand against a brother, on its forehead
Would wear forevermore the curse of Cain!

Down the dark future, through long generations,
The echoing sounds grow fainter and then cease;
And like a bell, with solemn, sweet vibrations,
I hear once more the voice of Christ say, "Peace!"

Peace! and no longer from its brazen portals
The blast of War's great organ shakes the skies!
But beautiful as songs of the immortals,
The holy melodies of love arise.

1844

## NUREMBERG

In the valley of the Pegnitz, where across broad meadow-lands
Rise the blue Franconian mountains, Nuremberg, the ancient, stands.

Quaint old town of toil and traffic, quaint old town of art and song,
Memories haunt thy pointed gables, like the rooks that round them throng:

Memories of the Middle Ages, when the emperors, rough and bold,
Had their dwelling in thy castle, time-defying, centuries old;

And thy brave and thrifty burghers boasted, in their uncouth rhyme,
That their great imperial city stretched its hand through every clime.

In the court-yard of the castle, bound with many an iron band,
Stands the mighty linden planted by Queen Cunigunde's hand;

On the square the oriel window, where in old heroic days
Sat the poet Melchior singing Kaiser Maximilian's praise.

Everywhere I see around me rise the wondrous world of Art:
Fountains wrought with richest sculpture standing in the common mart;

And above cathedral doorways saints and bishops carved in stone,
By a former age commissioned as apostles to our own.

In the church of sainted Sebald sleeps enshrined his holy dust,
And in bronze the Twelve Apostles guard from age to age their trust;

In the church of sainted Lawrence stands a pix of sculpture rare,
Like the foamy sheaf of fountains, rising through the painted air.

Here, when Art was still religion, with a simple, reverent heart,
Lived and labored Albrecht Dürer, the Evangelist of Art;

Hence in silence and in sorrow, toiling still with busy hand,
Like an emigrant he wandered, seeking for the Better Land.

*Emigravit* is the inscription on the tombstone where he lies;
Dead he is not, but departed, — for the artist never dies.

Fairer seems the ancient city, and the sunshine seems more fair,
That he once has trod its pavement, that he once has breathed its air!

Through these streets so broad and stately, these obscure and dismal lanes,
Walked of yore the Mastersingers, chanting rude poetic strains.

From remote and sunless suburbs came they to the friendly guild,
Building nests in Fame's great temple, as in spouts the swallows build.

As the weaver plied the shuttle, wove he too the mystic rhyme,
And the smith his iron measures hammered to the anvil's chime;

Thanking God, whose boundless wisdom makes the flowers of poesy bloom
In the forge's dust and cinders, in the tissues of the loom.

Here Hans Sachs, the cobbler-poet, laureate of the gentle craft,
Wisest of the Twelve Wise Masters, in huge folios sang and laughed.

But his house is now an ale-house, with a nicely sanded floor,
And a garland in the window, and his face above the door;

Painted by some humble artist, as in Adam Puschman's song,
As the old man gray and dove-like, with his great beard white and long.

And at night the swart mechanic comes to drown his cark and care,
Quaffing ale from pewter tankards, in the master's antique chair.

Vanished is the ancient splendor, and before my dreamy eye
Wave these mingled shapes and figures, like a faded tapestry.

Not thy Councils, not thy Kaisers, win for thee the world's regard;
But thy painter, Albrecht Dürer, and Hans Sachs thy cobbler bard.

Thus, O Nuremberg, a wanderer from a region far away,
As he paced thy streets and courtyards, sang in thought his careless lay:

Gathering from the pavement's crevice, as a floweret of the soil,
The nobility of labor, — the long pedigree of toil.

(1844) 1844

## SEAWEED

When descends on the Atlantic
The gigantic
Storm-wind of the equinox,
Landward in his wrath he scourges
The toiling surges,
Laden with seaweed from the rocks:

From Bermuda's reefs; from edges
Of sunken ledges,
In some far-off, bright Azore;
From Bahama, and the dashing,
Silver-flashing
Surges of San Salvador;

From the tumbling surf, that buries
The Orkneyan skerries,
Answering the hoarse Hebrides;
And from wrecks of ships, and drifting
Spars, uplifting
On the desolate, rainy seas; —

Ever drifting, drifting, drifting
On the shifting
Currents of the restless main;
Till in sheltered coves, and reaches
Of sandy beaches,
All have found repose again.

So when storms of wild emotion
Strike the ocean
Of the poet's soul, erelong
From each cave and rocky fastness,
In its vastness,
Floats some fragment of a song:

From the far-off isles enchanted,
Heaven has planted
With the golden fruit of Truth;
From the flashing surf, whose vision
Gleams Elysian
In the tropic clime of Youth;

From the strong Will, and the Endeavor
That forever
Wrestle with the tides of Fate;
From the wreck of Hopes far-scattered,
Tempest-shattered,
Floating waste and desolate; —

Ever drifting, drifting, drifting
On the shifting
Currents of the restless heart;
Till at length in books recorded,
They, like hoarded
Household words, no more depart.

(1844) 1845

## *EVANGELINE: A TALE OF ACADIE*

### PART THE FIRST

### I

### [THE PEACE OF GRAND-PRÉ]

In the Acadian land, on the shores of the Basin of Minas,
Distant, secluded, still, the little village of Grand-Pré
Lay in the fruitful valley. Vast meadows stretched to the eastward,
Giving the village its name, and pasture to flocks without number.
Dikes, that the hands of the farmers had raised with labor incessant,
Shut out the turbulent tides; but at stated seasons the flood-gates
Opened, and welcomed the sea to wander at will o'er the meadows.
West and south there were fields of flax, and orchards and cornfields

Spreading afar and unfenced o'er the plain; and away to the northward
Blomidon rose and the forests old, and aloft on the mountains
Sea-fogs pitched their tents, and mists from the mighty Atlantic
Looked on the happy valley but ne'er from their station descended.
There, in the midst of its farms, reposed the Acadian village.
Strongly built were the houses, with frames of oak and of hemlock,
Such as the peasants of Normandy built in the reign of the Henries.
Thatched were the roofs, with dormer-windows; and gables projecting
Over the basement below protected and shaded the door-way.
There in the tranquil evenings of summer, when brightly the sunset
Lighted the village street and gilded the vanes on the chimneys,
Matrons and maidens sat, in snow-white caps and in kirtles
Scarlet and blue and green, with distaffs spinning the golden
Flax for the gossiping looms, whose noisy shuttles within doors
Mingled their sound with the whir of the wheels and the songs of the maidens.
Solemnly down the street came the parish priest, and the children
Paused in their play to kiss the hand he extended to bless them:
Reverend walked he among them; and up rose matrons and maidens,
Hailing his slow approach with words of affectionate welcome.
Then came the laborers home from the field; and serenely the sun sank
Down to his rest, and twilight prevailed. Anon from the belfry
Softly the Angelus sounded, and over the roofs of the village
Columns of pale blue smoke, like clouds of incense ascending,
Rose from a hundred hearths, the homes of peace and contentment.
Thus dwelt together in love these simple Acadian farmers,
Dwelt in the love of God and of man. Alike were they free from
Fear, that reigns with the tyrant, and envy, the vice of republics.
Neither locks had they to their doors nor bars to their windows,
But their dwellings were open as day and the hearts of the owners;
There the richest was poor, and the poorest lived in abundance.

Somewhat apart from the village, and nearer the Basin of Minas,
Benedict Bellefontaine, the wealthiest farmer of Grand-Pré,
Dwelt on his goodly acres; and with him, directing his household,
Gentle Evangeline lived, his child, and the pride of the village.
Stalworth and stately in form was the man of seventy winters;
Hearty and hale was he, an oak that is covered with snow-flakes;
White as the snow were his locks, and his cheeks as brown as the oak-leaves.
Fair was she to behold, that maiden of seventeen summers.
Black were her eyes as the berry that grows on the thorn by the way-side—
Black, yet how softly they gleamed beneath the brown shade of her tresses!
Sweet was her breath as the breath of kine that feed in the meadows.
When in the harvest heat she bore to the reapers at noontide
Flagons of home-brewed ale, ah! fair in sooth was the maiden.
Fairer was she when, on Sunday morn, while the bell from its turret
Sprinkled with holy sounds the air, as the priest with his hyssop
Sprinkles the congregation and scatters blessings upon them,

Down the long street she passed with her chaplet of beads and her missal,
Wearing her Norman cap, and her kirtle of blue, and the ear-rings
Brought in the olden time from France, and since, as an heirloom,
Handed down from mother to child, through long generations.
But a celestial brightness, a more ethereal beauty,
Shone on her face and encircled her form, when after confession,
Homeward serenely she walked with God's benediction upon her.
When she had passed, it seemed like the ceasing of exquisite music.

Firmly builded with rafters of oak, the house of the farmer
Stood on the side of a hill commanding the sea; and a shady
Sycamore grew by the door, with a woodbine wreathing around it.
Rudely carved was the porch, with seats beneath; and a footpath
Led through an orchard wide, and disappeared in the meadow.
Under the sycamore-tree were hives overhung by a penthouse,
Such as the traveller sees in regions remote by the road-side,
Built o'er a box for the poor, or the blessed image of Mary.
Farther down, on the slope of the hill, was the well with its moss-grown
Bucket, fastened with iron, and near it a trough for the horses.
Shielding the house from storms, on the north, were the barns and the farm-yard.
There stood the broad-wheeled wains and the antique ploughs and the harrows;
There were the folds for the sheep; and there, in his feathered seraglio,
Strutted the lordly turkey, and crowed the cock with the self-same
Voice that in ages of old had startled the penitent Peter.
Bursting with hay were the barns, themselves a village. In each one
Far o'er the gable projected a roof of thatch; and a staircase,
Under the sheltering eaves, led up to the odorous corn-loft.
There too the dove-cot stood, with its meek and innocent inmates
Murmuring ever of love, while above in the variant breezes
Numberless noisy weathercocks rattled and sang of mutation.

Thus, at peace with God and the world, the farmer of Grand-Pré
Lived on his sunny farm, and Evangeline governed his household.
Many a youth, as he knelt in church and opened his missal,
Fixed his eyes upon her, as the saint of his deepest devotion;
Happy was he who might touch her hand or the hem of her garment!
Many a suitor came to her door, by the darkness befriended,
And as he knocked and waited to hear the sound of her footsteps,
Knew not which beat the louder, his heart or the knocker of iron;
Or at the joyous feast of the Patron Saint of the village,
Bolder grew, and pressed her hand in the dance as he whispered
Hurried words of love, that seemed a part of the music.
But among all who came young Gabriel only was welcome,
Gabriel Lajeunesse, the son of Basil the blacksmith,
Who was a mighty man in the village, and honored of all men—
For since the birth of time, throughout all ages and nations,
Has the craft of the smith been held in repute by the people.
Basil was Benedict's friend. Their children from earliest childhood
Grew up together as brother and sister; and Father Felician.

Priest and pedagogue both in the village, had taught them their letters
Out of the selfsame book, with the hymns of the church and the plain-song.
But when the hymn was sung, and the daily lesson completed,
Swiftly they hurried away to the forge of Basil the blacksmith.
There at the door they stood, with wondering eyes to behold him
Take in his leathern lap the hoof of the horse as a plaything,
Nailing the shoe in its place; while near him the tire of the cartwheel
Lay like a fiery snake, coiled round in a circle of cinders.
Oft on autumnal eves, when without in the gathering darkness
Bursting with light seemed the smithy through every cranny and crevice,
Warm by the forge within they watched the laboring bellows;
And as its panting ceased, and the sparks expired in the ashes,
Merrily laughed, and said they were nuns going into the chapel.
Oft on sledges in winter, as swift as the swoop of the eagle,
Down the hill-side bounding, they glided away o'er the meadow.
Oft in the barns they climbed to the populous nests on the rafters,
Seeking with eager eyes that wondrous stone which the swallow
Brings from the shore of the sea to restore the sight of its fledglings,
Lucky was he who found that stone in the nest of the swallow!
Thus passed a few swift years, and they no longer were children.
He was a valiant youth; and his face, like the face of the morning,
Gladdened the earth with its light, and ripened thought into action.
She was a woman now, with the heart and hopes of a woman.
"Sunshine of Saint Eulalie" was she called; for that was the sunshine
Which, as the farmers believed, would load their orchards with apples:
She, too, would bring to her husband's house delight and abundance,
Filling it with love and the ruddy faces of children.

(1845–47) 1847

## *THE SONG OF HIAWATHA*

### XX

### THE FAMINE

Oh, the long and dreary Winter!
Oh, the cold and cruel Winter!
Ever thicker, thicker, thicker
Froze the ice on lake and river,
Ever deeper, deeper, deeper
Fell the snow o'er all the landscape,
Fell the covering snow, and drifted
Through the forest, round the village.
Hardly from his buried wigwam
Could the hunter force a passage;
With his mittens and his snow-shoes
Vainly walked he through the forest,
Sought for bird or beast and found none,
Saw no track of deer or rabbit,
In the snow beheld no footprints,
In the ghastly, gleaming forest
Fell, and could not rise from weakness,
Perished there from cold and hunger.
Oh the famine and the fever!
Oh the wasting of the famine!
Oh the blasting of the fever!
Oh the wailing of the children!
Oh the anguish of the women!
All the earth was sick and famished;
Hungry was the air around them,
Hungry was the sky above them,
And the hungry stars in heaven
Like the eyes of wolves glared at them!
Into Hiawatha's wigwam
Came two other guests as silent
As the ghosts were, and as gloomy,
Waited not to be invited,
Did not parley at the doorway,
Sat there without word of welcome

In the seat of Laughing Water;
Looked with haggard eyes and hollow
At the face of Laughing Water.
  And the foremost said: "Behold me!
I am Famine, Bukadawin!"
And the other said: "Behold me!
I am Fever, Ahkosewin!"
  And the lovely Minnehaha
Shuddered as they looked upon her,
Shuddered at the words they uttered,
Lay down on her bed in silence,
Hid her face, but made no answer:
Lay there trembling, freezing, burning
At the looks they cast upon her,
At the fearful words they uttered.
  Forth into the empty forest
Rushed the maddened Hiawatha;
In his heart was deadly sorrow,
In his face a stony firmness;
On his brow the sweat of anguish
Started, but it froze and fell not.
  Wrapped in furs and armed for hunting,
With his mighty bow of ash-tree,
With his quiver full of arrows,
With his mittens, Minjekahwun,
Into the vast and vacant forest
On his snow-shoes strode he forward.
  "Gitche Manito, the Mighty!"
Cried he with his face uplifted
In that bitter hour of anguish,
"Give your children food, O father!
Give us food, or we must perish!
Give me food for Minnehaha,
For my dying Minnehaha!"
  Through the far-resounding forest,
Through the forest vast and vacant
Rang that cry of desolation,
But there came no other answer
Than the echo of his crying,
Than the echo of the woodlands,
"Minnehaha! Minnehaha!"
  All day long roved Hiawatha
In that melancholy forest,
Through the shadow of whose thickets,
In the pleasant days of Summer,
Of that ne'er forgotten Summer,
He had brought his young wife homeward
From the land of the Dacotahs;
When the birds sang in the thickets,
And the streamlets laughed and glistened,
And the air was full of fragrance,
And the lovely Laughing Water
Said with voice that did not tremble,
"I will follow you, my husband!"
  In the wigwam with Nokomis,
With those gloomy guests that watched her,
With the Famine and the Fever,
She was lying, the Beloved,
She the dying Minnehaha.
  "Hark!" she said; "I hear a rushing,
Hear a roaring and a rushing,
Hear the Falls of Minnehaha
Calling to me from a distance!"
"No, my child!" said old Nokomis,
"'Tis the night-wind in the pine-trees!"
  "Look!" she said; "I see my father
Standing lonely at his doorway,
Beckoning to me from his wigwam
In the land of the Dacotahs!"
"No, my child!" said old Nokomis,
"'Tis the smoke, that waves and beckons!"
  "Ah!" said she, "the eyes of Pauguk
Glare upon me in the darkness,
I can feel his icy fingers
Clasping mine amid the darkness!
Hiawatha! Hiawatha!"
  And the desolate Hiawatha,
Far away amid the forest,
Miles away among the mountains,
Heard that sudden cry of anguish,
Heard the voice of Minnehaha
Calling to him in the darkness,
"Hiawatha! Hiawatha!"
  Over snow-fields waste and pathless,
Under snow-encumbered branches,
Homeward hurried Hiawatha,
Empty-handed, heavy-hearted,
Heard Nokomis moaning, wailing:
"Wahonowin! Wahonowin!
Would that I had perished for you,
Would that I were dead as you are!
Wahonowin! Wahonowin!"

And he rushed into the wigwam,
Saw the old Nokomis slowly
Rocking to and fro and moaning,
Saw his lovely Minnehaha
Lying dead and cold before him,
And his bursting heart within him
Uttered such a cry of anguish,
That the forest moaned and shuddered,
That the very stars in heaven
Shook and trembled with his anguish.
Then he sat down, still and speechless,
On the bed of Minnehaha,
At the feet of Laughing Water,
At those willing feet, that never
More would lightly run to meet him,
Never more would lightly follow.
With both hands his face he covered,
Seven long days and nights he sat there,
As if in a swoon he sat there,
Speechless, motionless, unconscious
Of the daylight or the darkness.
Then they buried Minnehaha;
In the snow a grave they made her,
In the forest deep and darksome,
Underneath the moaning hemlocks;
Clothed her in her richest garments,
Wrapped her in her robes of ermine,
Covered her with snow, like ermine;
Thus they buried Minnehaha.
And at night a fire was lighted,
On her grave four times was kindled,
For her soul upon its journey
To the Islands of the Blessed.
From his doorway Hiawatha
Saw it burning in the forest,
Lighting up the gloomy hemlocks;
From his sleepless bed uprising,
From the bed of Minnehaha,
Stood and watched it at the doorway,
That it might not be extinguished,
Might not leave her in the darkness.
"Farewell!" said he, "Minnehaha!
Farewell, O my Laughing Water!
All my heart is buried with you,
All my thoughts go onward with you!
Come not back again to labor,
Come not back again to suffer,
Where the Famine and the Fever
Wear the heart and waste the body.
Soon my task will be completed,
Soon your footsteps I shall follow
To the Islands of the Blessed,
To the Kingdom of Ponemah,
To the Land of the Hereafter!"
(1854–55) 1855

## MY LOST YOUTH

Often I think of the beautiful town
That is seated by the sea;
Often in thought go up and down
The pleasant streets of that dear old town,
And my youth comes back to me.
And a verse of a Lapland song
Is haunting my memory still:
"A boy's will is the wind's will,
And the thoughts of youth are long, long thoughts."

I can see the shadowy lines of its trees,
And catch, in sudden gleams,
The sheen of the far-surrounding seas,
And islands that were the Hesperides
Of all my boyish dreams.
And the burden of that old song,
It murmurs and whispers still:
"A boy's will is the wind's will,
And the thoughts of youth are long, long thoughts."

I remember the black wharves and the slips,
And the sea-tides tossing free;
And Spanish sailors with bearded lips,
And the beauty and mystery of the ships,
And the magic of the sea.
And the voice of that wayward song
Is singing and saying still:
"A boy's will is the wind's will,
And the thoughts of youth are long, long thoughts."

I remember the bulwarks by the shore,
And the fort upon the hill;
The sunrise gun, with its hollow roar,
The drum-beat repeated o'er and o'er,
And the bugle wild and shrill.
And the music of that old song
Throbs in my memory still:
"A boy's will is the wind's will,
And the thoughts of youth are long, long thoughts."

I remember the sea-fight far away,
How it thundered o'er the tide!
And the dead captains, as they lay
In their graves, o'erlooking the tranquil bay
Where they in battle died.
And the sound of that mournful song
Goes through me with a thrill:
"A boy's will is the wind's will,
And the thoughts of youth are long, long thoughts."

I can see the breezy dome of groves,
The shadows of Deering's Woods;
And the friendships old and the early loves
Come back with a Sabbath sound, as of doves
In quiet neighborhoods.
And the verse of that sweet old song,
It flutters and murmurs still:
"A boy's will is the wind's will,
And the thoughts of youth are long, long thoughts."

I remember the gleams and glooms that dart
Across the school-boy's brain;
The song and the silence in the heart,
That in part are prophecies, and in part
Are longings wild and vain.
And the voice of that fitful song
Sings on, and is never still:
"A boy's will is the wind's will,
And the thoughts of youth are long, long thoughts."

There are things of which I may not speak;
There are dreams that cannot die;
There are thoughts that make the strong heart weak,
And bring a pallor into the cheek,
And a mist before the eye.
And the words of that fatal song
Come over me like a chill:
"A boy's will is the wind's will,
And the thoughts of youth are long, long thoughts."

Strange to me now are the forms I meet
When I visit the dear old town;
But the native air is pure and sweet,
And the trees that o'ershadow each well-known street,
As they balance up and down,
Are singing the beautiful song,
Are sighing and whispering still:
"A boy's will is the wind's will,
And the thoughts of youth are long, long thoughts."

And Deering's Woods are fresh and fair,
And with joy that is almost pain
My heart goes back to wander there,
And among the dreams of the days that were,
I find my lost youth again.
And the strange and beautiful song,
The groves are repeating it still:
"A boy's will is the wind's will,
And the thoughts of youth are long, long thoughts."

(1855) 1855

## *TALES OF A WAYSIDE INN*

### THE SAGA OF KING OLAF

#### XIX. KING OLAF'S WAR-HORNS

"Strike the sails!" King Olaf said;
"Never shall men of mine take flight;

Never away from battle I fled,
Never away from my foes!
Let God dispose
Of my life in the fight!"

"Sound the horns!" said Olaf the King;
And suddenly through the drifting brume
The blare of the horns began to ring,
Like the terrible trumpet shock
Of Regnarock,
On the Day of Doom!

Louder and louder the war-horns sang
Over the level floor of the flood;
All the sails came down with a clang,
And there in the midst overhead
The sun hung red
As a drop of blood.

Drifting down on the Danish fleet
Three together the ships were lashed,
So that neither should turn and retreat;
In the midst, but in front of the rest,
The burnished crest
Of the Serpent flashed.

King Olaf stood on the quarter-deck,
With bow of ash and arrows of oak;
His gilded shield was without a fleck,
His helmet inlaid with gold,
And in many a fold
Hung his crimson cloak.

On the forecastle Ulf the Red
Watched the lashing of the ships;
"If the Serpent lie so far ahead,
We shall have hard work of it here,"
Said he with a sneer
On his bearded lips.

King Olaf laid an arrow on string,
"Have I a coward on board?" said he.
"Shoot it another way, O King!"
Sullenly answered Ulf,
The old sea-wolf;
"You have need of me!"

In front came Svend, the King of the Danes,
Sweeping down with his fifty rowers;
To the right, the Swedish king with his thanes;
And on board of the Iron Beard
Earl Eric steered
To the left with his oars.

"These soft Danes and Swedes," said the King,
"At home with their wives had better stay,
Than come within reach of my Serpent's sting:
But where Eric the Norseman leads
Heroic deeds
Will be done to-day!"

Then as together the vessels crashed,
Eric severed the cables of hide,
With which King Olaf's ships were lashed,
And left them to drive and drift
With the currents swift
Of the outward tide.

Louder the war-horns growl and snarl,
Sharper the dragons bite and sting!
Eric the son of Hakon Jarl
A death-drink salt as the sea
Pledges to thee,
Olaf the King!

### XX. EINAR TAMBERSKELVER

It was Einar Tamberskelver
Stood beside the mast;
From his yew-bow, tipped with silver,
Flew the arrows fast;
Aimed at Eric unavailing,
As he sat concealed,
Half behind the quarter-railing,
Half behind his shield.

First an arrow struck the tiller,
Just above his head;
"Sing, O Eyvind Skaldaspiller,"
Then Earl Eric said.
"Sing the song of Hakon dying,
Sing his funeral wail!"

And another arrow flying
  Grazed his coat of mail.

Turning to a Lapland yeoman,
  As the arrow passed,
Said Earl Eric, "Shoot that bowman
  Standing by the mast."
Sooner than the word was spoken
  Flew the yeoman's shaft;
Einar's bow in twain was broken,
  Einar only laughed.

"What was that?" said Olaf, standing
  On the quarter-deck.
"Something heard I like the stranding
  Of a shattered wreck."
Einar then, the arrow taking
  From the loosened string,
Answered, "That was Norway break-
  ing
  From thy hand, O King!"

"Thou art but a poor diviner,"
  Straightway Olaf said;
"Take my bow, and swifter, Einar,
  Let thy shafts be sped."
Of his bows the fairest choosing,
  Reached he from above;
Einar saw the blood-drops oozing
  Through his iron glove.

But the bow was thin and narrow;
  At the first essay,
O'er its head he drew the arrow,
  Flung the bow away;
Said, with hot and angry temper
  Flushing in his cheek,
"Olaf! for so great a Kämper
  Are thy bows too weak!"

Then, with smile of joy defiant
  On his beardless lip,
Scaled he, light and self-reliant,
  Eric's dragon-ship.
Loose his golden locks were flowing,
  Bright his armor gleamed;
Like Saint Michael overthrowing
  Lucifer he seemed.

### XXI. KING OLAF'S DEATH-DRINK

All day has the battle raged,
All day have the ships engaged,
But not yet is assuaged
  The vengeance of Eric the Earl.

The decks with blood are red,
The arrows of death are sped,
The ships are filled with the dead,
  And the spears the champions hurl.

They drift as wrecks on the tide,
The grappling-irons are plied,
The boarders climb up the side,
  The shouts are feeble and few.

Ah! never shall Norway again
See her sailors come back o'er the
  main;
They all lie wounded or slain,
  Or asleep in the billows blue!

On the deck stands Olaf the King,
Around him whistle and sing
The spears that the foemen fling,
  And the stones they hurl with their
    hands.

In the midst of the stones and the
  spears,
Kolbiorn, the marshal, appears,
His shield in the air he uprears,
  By the side of King Olaf he stands.

Over the slippery wreck
Of the Long Serpent's deck
Sweeps Eric with hardly a check,
  His lips with anger are pale;

He hews with his axe at the mast,
Till it falls, with the sails overcast,
Like a snow-covered pine in the vast
  Dim forests of Orkadale.

Seeking King Olaf then,
He rushes aft with his men,
As a hunter into the den
  Of the bear, when he stands at bay.

"Remember Jarl Hakon!" he cries;
When lo! on his wondering eyes,
Two kingly figures arise,
Two Olafs in warlike array!

Then Kolbiorn speaks in the ear
Of King Olaf a word of cheer,
In a whisper that none may hear,
With a smile on his tremulous lip;

Two shields raised high in the air,
Two flashes of golden hair,
Two scarlet meteors' glare,
And both have leaped from the ship.

Earl Eric's men in the boats
Seize Kolbiorn's shield as it floats,
And cry, from their hairy throats,
"See! it is Olaf the King!"

While far on the opposite side
Floats another shield on the tide,
Like a jewel set in the wide
Sea-current's eddying ring.

There is told a wonderful tale,
How the King stripped off his mail,
Like leaves of the brown sea-kale,
As he swam beneath the main;

But the young grew old and gray,
And never, by night or by day,
In his kingdom of Norroway
Was King Olaf seen again!

(1859–60) 1863

## DIVINA COMMEDIA

### I

Oft have I seen at some cathedral door
A laborer, pausing in the dust and heat,
Lay down his burden, and with reverent feet
Enter, and cross himself, and on the floor
Kneel to repeat his paternoster o'er;
Far off the noises of the world retreat;
The loud vociferations of the street
Become an undistinguishable roar.
So, as I enter here from day to day,
And leave my burden at this minster gate,
Kneeling in prayer, and not ashamed to pray,
The tumult of the time disconsolate
To inarticulate murmurs dies away,
While the eternal ages watch and wait.

(1864) 1864

### II

How strange the sculptures that adorn these towers!
This crowd of statues, in whose folded sleeves
Birds build their nests; while canopied with leaves
Parvis and portal bloom like trellised bowers,
And the vast minster seems a cross of flowers!
But fiends and dragons on the gargoyled eaves
Watch the dead Christ between the living thieves,
And, underneath, the traitor Judas lowers!
Ah! from what agonies of heart and brain,
What exultations trampling on despair,
What tenderness, what tears, what hate of wrong,
What passionate outcry of a soul in pain,
Uprose this poem of the earth and air,
This mediæval miracle of song!

(1864) 1866

### III

I enter, and I see thee in the gloom
Of the long aisles, O poet saturnine!
And strive to make my steps keep pace with thine.
The air is filled with some unknown perfume;

The congregation of the dead make room
  For thee to pass; the votive tapers shine;
  Like rooks that haunt Ravenna's groves of pine
  The hovering echoes fly from tomb to tomb.
From the confessionals I hear arise
  Rehearsals of forgotten tragedies,
  And lamentations from the crypts below;
And then a voice celestial that begins
  With the pathetic words, "Although your sins
  As scarlet be," and ends with "as the snow."

(1865) 1866

IV

With snow-white veil and garments as of flame,
  She stands before thee, who so long ago
  Filled thy young heart with passion and the woe
  From which thy song and all its splendors came;
And while with stern rebuke she speaks thy name,
  The ice about thy heart melts as the snow
  On mountain heights, and in swift overflow
  Comes gushing from thy lips in sobs of shame.
Thou makest full confession; and a gleam,
  As of the dawn on some dark forest cast,
  Seems on thy lifted forehead to increase;
Lethe and Eunoë—the remembered dream
  And the forgotten sorrow—bring at last
  That perfect pardon which is perfect peace.

(1867) 1867

V

I lift mine eyes, and all the windows blaze
  With forms of Saints and holy men who died,
  Here martyred and hereafter glorified;
  And the great Rose upon its leaves displays
Christ's Triumph, and the angelic roundelays,
  With splendor upon splendor multiplied;
  And Beatrice again at Dante's side
  No more rebukes, but smiles her words of praise.
And then the organ sounds, and unseen choirs
  Sing the old Latin hymns of peace and love,
  And benedictions of the Holy Ghost;
And the melodious bells among the spires
  O'er all the house-tops and through heaven above
  Proclaim the elevation of the Host!

(1866) 1866

VI

O star of morning and of liberty!
  O bringer of the light, whose splendor shines
  Above the darkness of the Apennines,
  Forerunner of the day that is to be!
The voices of the city and the sea,
  The voices of the mountains and the pines,
  Repeat thy song, till the familiar lines
  Are footpaths for the thought of Italy!
Thy fame is blown abroad from all the heights,
  Through all the nations, and a sound is heard,
  As of a mighty wind, and men devout,

Strangers of Rome, and the new proselytes,
In their own language hear thy wondrous word,
And many are amazed, and many doubt.
(1866) 1866

## CHAUCER

An old man in a lodge within a park;
The chamber walls depicted all around
With portraitures of huntsman, hawk, and hound,
And the hurt deer. He listeneth to the lark,
Whose song comes with the sunshine through the dark
Of painted glass in leaden lattice bound;
He listeneth and he laugheth at the sound,
Then writeth in a book like any clerk.
He is the poet of the dawn, who wrote
The Canterbury Tales, and his old age
Made beautiful with song; and as I read
I hear the crowing cock, I hear the note
Of lark and linnet, and from every page
Rise odors of ploughed field or flowery mead.
(1873) 1875

## SHAKESPEARE

A vision as of crowded city streets,
With human life in endless overflow;
Thunder of thoroughfares; trumpets that blow
To battle; clamor, in obscure retreats,
Of sailors landed from their anchored fleets;
Tolling of bells in turrets, and below
Voices of children, and bright flowers that throw
O'er garden-walls their intermingled sweets!
This vision comes to me when I unfold
The volume of the Poet paramount,
Whom all the Muses loved, not one alone; —
Into his hands they put the lyre of gold,
And, crowned with sacred laurel at their fount,
Placed him as Musagetes on their throne.
(1873) 1875

## MILTON

I pace the sounding sea-beach and behold
How the voluminous billows roll and run,
Upheaving and subsiding, while the sun
Shines through their sheeted emerald far unrolled,
And the ninth wave, slow gathering fold by fold
All its loose-flung garments into one,
Plunges upon the shore, and floods the dun
Pale reach of sands, and changes them to gold.
So in majestic cadence rise and fall
The mighty undulations of thy song,
O sightless bard, England's Mæonides!
And ever and anon, high over all
Uplifted, a ninth wave superb and strong,
Floods all the soul with its melodious seas.
(1873) 1875

## THE SOUND OF THE SEA

The sea awoke at midnight from its sleep,
And round the pebbly beaches far and wide
I heard the first wave of the rising tide
Rush onward with uninterrupted sweep;
A voice out of the silence of the deep,
A sound mysteriously multiplied
As of a cataract from the mountain's side,
Or roar of winds upon a wooded steep.
So comes to us at times, from the unknown
And inaccessible solitudes of being,
The rushing of the sea-tides of the soul;
And inspirations, that we deem our own,
Are some divine foreshadowing and foreseeing
Of things beyond our reason or control.

(1874) 1875

## THE TIDE RISES, THE TIDE FALLS

The tide rises, the tide falls,
The twilight darkens, the curlew calls;
Along the sea-sands damp and brown
The traveller hastens toward the town,
And the tide rises, the tide falls.

Darkness settles on roofs and walls,
But the sea, the sea in the darkness calls;
The little waves, with their soft, white hands,
Efface the footprints in the sands,
And the tide rises, the tide falls.

The morning breaks; the steeds in their stalls
Stamp and neigh, as the hostler calls;
The day returns, but nevermore
Returns the traveller to the shore,
And the tide rises, the tide falls.

(1879) 1880

## NIGHT

Into the darkness and the hush of night
Slowly the landscape sinks, and fades away,
And with it fade the phantoms of the day,
The ghosts of men and things, that haunt the light.
The crowd, the clamor, the pursuit, the flight,
The unprofitable splendor and display,
The agitations, and the cares that prey
Upon our hearts, all vanish out of sight.
The better life begins; the world no more
Molests us; all its records we erase
From the dull commonplace book of our lives,
That like a palimpsest is written o'er
With trivial incidents of time and place,
And lo! the ideal, hidden beneath, revives.

(1879) 1880

## *KAVANAGH: A TALE*

### [AN AMERICAN LITERATURE]

One evening, as he [Mr. Churchill] was sitting down to begin, for at least the hundredth time, the great Romance,— subject of so many resolves and so much remorse, so often determined upon but never begun,— a loud knock at the street-door, which stood wide open, announced a visitor. Unluckily, the study-door was likewise open; and consequently, being in full view, he found it impossible to refuse himself; nor, in fact, would have done so, had all the doors been shut and bolted,— the art of refusing one's self being at that time but imperfectly understood at Fairmeadow. Accordingly, the visitor was shown in.

He announced himself as Mr. Hathaway. Passing through the village, he could not deny himself the pleasure of calling on Mr. Churchill, whom he knew by his writings in the periodicals, though not personally. He wished, moreover, to secure the coöperation of one already so favorably known to the literary world in a new Magazine he was about to establish, in order to raise the character of American literature, which, in his opinion, the existing reviews and magazines had entirely failed to accomplish. A daily increasing want of something better was felt by the public, and the time had come for the establishment of such a periodical as he proposed. After explaining in a rather florid and exuberant manner his plans and prospects, he entered more at large into the subject of American literature, which it was his design to foster and patronize.

"I think, Mr. Churchill," said he, "that we want a national literature commensurate with our mountains and rivers,— commensurate with Niagara and the Alleghanies, and the Great Lakes."

"Oh!"

"We want a national epic that shall correspond to the size of the country; that shall be to all other epics what Banvard's Panorama of the Mississippi is to all other paintings,— the largest in the world."

"Ah!"

"We want a national drama in which scope enough shall be given to our gigantic ideas and to the unparalleled activity and progress of our people!"

"Of course."

"In a word, we want a national literature altogether shaggy and unshorn, that shall shake the earth, like a herd of buffaloes thundering over the prairies."

"Precisely," interrupted Mr. Churchill; "but excuse me! — are you not confounding things that have no analogy? Great has a very different meaning when applied to a river and when applied to a literature. Large and shallow may perhaps be applied to both. Literature is rather an image of the spiritual world, than of the physical, is it not? — of the internal, rather than the external. Mountains, lakes, and rivers are, after all, only its scenery and decorations, not its substance and essence. A man will not necessarily be a great poet because he lives near a great mountain. Nor, being a poet, will he necessarily write better poems than another, because he lives nearer Niagara."

"But, Mr. Churchill, you do not

certainly mean to deny the influence of scenery on the mind?"

"No, only to deny that it can create genius. At best, it can only develop it. Switzerland has produced no extraordinary poet; nor, as far as I know, have the Andes, or the Himalaya Mountains, or the Mountains of the Moon in Africa."

"But, at all events," urged Mr. Hathaway, "let us have our literature national. If it is not national, it is nothing."

"On the contrary, it may be a great deal. Nationality is a good thing to a certain extent, but universality is better. All that is best in the great poets of all countries is not what is national in them, but what is universal. Their roots are in their native soil; but their branches wave in the unpatriotic air, that speaks the same language unto all men, and their leaves shine with the illimitable light that pervades all lands. Let us throw all the windows open; let us admit the light and air on all sides; that we may look toward the four corners of the heavens, and not always in the same direction."

"But you admit nationality to be a good thing?"

"Yes, if not carried too far; still, I confess, it rather limits one's views of truth. I prefer what is natural. Mere nationality is often ridiculous. Every one smiles when he hears the Icelandic proverb, 'Iceland is the best land the sun shines upon.' Let us be natural, and we shall be national enough. Besides, our literature can be strictly national only so far as our character and modes of thought differ from those of other nations. Now, as we are very like the English,— are, in fact, English under a different sky,— I do not see how our literature can be very different from theirs. Westward from hand to hand we pass the lighted torch, but it was lighted at the old domestic fireside of England."

"Then you think our literature is never to be anything but an imitation of the English?"

"Not at all. It is not an imitation, but, as some one has said, a continuation."

"It seems to me that you take a very narrow view of the subject."

"On the contrary, a very broad one. No literature is complete until the language in which it is written is dead. We may well be proud of our task and of our position. Let us see if we can build in any way worthy of our forefathers."

"But I insist on originality."

"Yes, but without spasms and convulsions. Authors must not, like Chinese soldiers, expect to win victories by turning somersets in the air."

"Well, really, the prospect from your point of view is not very brilliant. Pray, what do you think of our national literature?"

"Simply, that a national literature is not the growth of a day. Centuries must contribute their dew and sunshine to it. Our own is growing slowly but surely, striking its roots downward and its branches upward, as is natural; and I do not wish, for the sake of what some people call originality, to invert it, and try to make it grow with its roots in the air. And as for having it so savage and wild as you want it, I have only to say, that all literature, as well as all art, is the result of culture and intellectual refinement."

"Ah! we do not want art and refinement; we want genius,— untutored, wild, original, free."

"But if this genius is to find any expression it must employ art, for art is the external expression of our thoughts. Many have genius, but, wanting art, are forever dumb. The two must go together to form the great poet, painter, or sculptor."

"In that sense, very well."

"I was about to say also that I thought our literature would finally not be wanting in a kind of universality. As the blood of all nations is mingling with our own, so will their thoughts and feelings finally mingle in our literature. We shall draw from the Germans, tenderness; from the Spaniards, passion; from the French, vivacity,— to mingle more and more with our English solid sense. And this will give us universality, so much to be desired."

1849

# OLIVER WENDELL HOLMES
(1809–1894)

## THE HEIGHT OF THE RIDICULOUS

I wrote some lines once on a time
In wondrous merry mood,
And thought, as usual, men would say
They were exceeding good.

They were so queer, so very queer,
I laughed as I would die;
Albeit, in the general way,
A sober man am I.

I called my servant, and he came;
How kind it was of him
To mind a slender man like me,
He of the mighty limb!

"These to the printer," I exclaimed,
And, in my humorous way,
I added (as a trifling jest),
"There'll be the devil to pay."

He took the paper, and I watched,
And saw him peep within;
At the first line he read, his face
Was all upon the grin.

He read the next; the grin grew broad,
And shot from ear to ear;
He read the third; a chuckling noise
I now began to hear.

The fourth; he broke into a roar;
The fifth; his waistband split;
The sixth; he burst five buttons off,
And tumbled in a fit.

Ten days and nights, with sleepless eye,
I watched that wretched man,
And since, I never dare to write
As funny as I can.

(1830) 1830

## THE BALLAD OF THE OYSTERMAN

It was a tall young oysterman lived by the river-side,
His shop was just upon the bank, his boat was on the tide;
The daughter of a fisherman, that was so straight and slim,
Lived over on the other bank, right opposite to him.

It was the pensive oysterman that saw a lovely maid,
Upon a moonlight evening, a-sitting in the shade;
He saw her wave her handkerchief, as much as if to say,
"I'm wide awake, young oysterman, and all the folks away."

Then up arose the oysterman, and to himself said he,
"I guess I'll leave the skiff at home, for fear that folks should see;
I read it in the story-book, that, for to kiss his dear,
Leander swam the Hellespont, — and I will swim this here."

And he has leaped into the waves, and crossed the shining stream,
And he has clambered up the bank, all in the moonlight gleam;
Oh there were kisses sweet as dew, and words as soft as rain, —
But they have heard her father's step, and in he leaps again!

Out spoke the ancient fisherman, —
"Oh, what was that, my daughter?"

"'Twas nothing but a pebble, sir, I threw into the water."
"And what is that, pray tell me, love, that paddles off so fast?"
"It's nothing but a porpoise, sir, that's been a-swimming past."

Out spoke the ancient fisherman,—
"Now bring me my harpoon!
I'll get into my fishing-boat, and fix the fellow soon."
Down fell that pretty innocent, as falls a snow-white lamb,
Her hair drooped round her pallid cheeks, like seaweed on a clam.

Alas for those two loving ones! she waked not from her swound,
And he was taken with the cramp, and in the waves was drowned;
But Fate has metamorphosed them, in pity of their woe,
And now they keep an oyster-shop for mermaids down below.

(1830) 1830

## OLD IRONSIDES

Ay, tear her tattered ensign down!
Long has it waved on high,
And many an eye has danced to see
That banner in the sky;
Beneath it rung the battle shout,
And burst the cannon's roar;—
The meteor of the ocean air
Shall sweep the clouds no more.

Her deck, once red with heroes' blood,
Where knelt the vanquished foe,
When winds were hurrying o'er the flood,
And waves were white below,
No more shall feel the victor's tread,
Or know the conquered knee;—
The harpies of the shore shall pluck
The eagle of the sea!

Oh, better that her shattered hulk
Should sink beneath the wave;
Her thunders shook the mighty deep,
And there should be her grave;
Nail to the mast her holy flag,
Set every threadbare sail,
And give her to the god of storms,
The lightning and the gale!

(1830) 1830

## THE LAST LEAF

I saw him once before,
As he passed by the door,
And again
The pavement stones resound
As he totters o'er the ground
With his cane.

They say that in his prime,
Ere the pruning-knife of Time
Cut him down,
Not a better man was found
By the Crier on his round
Through the town.

But now he walks the streets,
And he looks at all he meets
Sad and wan,
And he shakes his feeble head,
That it seems as if he said,
"They are gone."

The mossy marbles rest
On the lips that he has prest
In their bloom,
And the names he loved to hear
Have been carved for many a year
On the tomb.

My grandmamma has said—
Poor old lady, she is dead
Long ago—
That he had a Roman nose,
And his cheek was like a rose
In the snow.

But now his nose is thin,
And it rests upon his chin
Like a staff,
And a crook is in his back,
And a melancholy crack
In his laugh.

I know it is a sin
For me to sit and grin
At him here;
But the old three-cornered hat,
And the breeches, and all that,
Are so queer!

And if I should live to be
The last leaf upon the tree
In the spring,
Let them smile, as I do now,
At the old forsaken bough
Where I cling.

(1831) 1831

## MY AUNT

My aunt! my dear unmarried aunt!
Long years have o'er her flown;
Yet still she strains the aching clasp
That binds her virgin zone;
I know it hurts her,—though she looks
As cheerful as she can;
Her waist is ampler than her life,
For life is but a span.

My aunt! my poor deluded aunt!
Her hair is almost gray;
Why will she train that winter curl
In such a spring-like way?
How can she lay her glasses down,
And say she reads as well,
When, through a double convex lens,
She just makes out to spell?

Her father—grandpapa! forgive
This erring lip its smiles—
Vowed she should make the finest girl
Within a hundred miles;
He sent her to a stylish school;
'Twas in her thirteenth June;
And with her, as the rules required,
"Two towels and a spoon."

They braced my aunt against a board,
To make her straight and tall;
They laced her up, they starved her down,
To make her light and small;
They pinched her feet, they singed her hair,
They screwed it up with pins;—
Oh, never mortal suffered more
In penance for her sins.

So, when my precious aunt was done,
My grandsire brought her back;
(By daylight, lest some rabid youth
Might follow on the track;)
"Ah!" said my grandsire, as he shook
Some powder in his pan,
"What could this lovely creature do
Against a desperate man!"

Alas! nor chariot, nor barouche,
Nor bandit cavalcade,
Tore from the trembling father's arms
His all-accomplished maid.
For her how happy had it been!
And Heaven had spared to me
To see one sad, ungathered rose
On my ancestral tree.

(1831) 1831

## NON-RESISTANCE

Perhaps too far in these considerate days
Has patience carried her submissive ways;
Wisdom has taught us to be calm and meek,
To take one blow, and turn the other cheek;
It is not written what a man shall do
If the rude caitiff smite the other too!

Land of our fathers, in thine hour of need
God help thee, guarded by the passive creed!
As the lone pilgrim trusts to beads and cowl,
When through the forest rings the gray wolf's howl;
As the deep galleon trusts her gilded prow
When the black corsair slants athwart her bow;

As the poor pheasant, with his peaceful mien,
Trusts to his feathers, shining golden-green,
When the dark plumage with the crimson beak
Has rustled shadowy from its splintered peak,—
So trust thy friends, whose babbling tongues would charm
The lifted sabre from thy foeman's arm,
Thy torches ready for the answering peal
From bellowing fort and thunder-freighted keel!
(1850) 1850

## THE CHAMBERED NAUTILUS

This is the ship of pearl, which, poets feign,
  Sails the unshadowed main,—
  The venturous bark that flings
On the sweet summer wind its purpled wings
In gulfs enchanted, where the siren sings,
  And coral reefs lie bare,
Where the cold sea-maids rise to sun their streaming hair.

Its webs of living gauze no more unfurl;
  Wrecked is the ship of pearl!
  And every chambered cell
Where its dim dreaming life was wont to dwell,
As the frail tenant shaped his growing shell,
  Before thee lies revealed,—
Its irised ceiling rent, its sunless crypt unsealed!

Year after year beheld the silent toil
  That spread his lustrous coil;
  Still, as the spiral grew,
He left the past year's dwelling for the new,
Stole with soft step its shining archway through,
  Built up its idle door,
Stretched in his last-found home, and knew the old no more.

Thanks for the heavenly message brought by thee,
  Child of the wandering sea,
  Cast from her lap forlorn!
From thy dead lips a clearer note is born
Than ever Triton blew from wreathèd horn!
  While on mine ear it rings
Through the deep caves of thought I hear a voice that sings:—

Build thee more stately mansions, O my soul,
  As the swift seasons roll!
  Leave thy low-vaulted past!
Let each new temple, nobler than the last,
Shut thee from heaven with a dome more vast,
  Till thou at length art free,
Leaving thine outgrown shell by life's unresting sea!
1858

## THE LIVING TEMPLE

Not in the world of light alone,
Where God has built his blazing throne,
Nor yet alone in earth below,
With belted seas that come and go,
And endless isles of sunlit green,
Is all thy Maker's glory seen:
Look in upon thy wondrous frame,—
Eternal wisdom still the same!

The smooth, soft air with pulse-like waves
Flows murmuring through its hidden caves,
Whose streams of brightening purple rush,

Fired with a new and livelier blush.
While all their burden of decay
The ebbing current steals away,
And red with Nature's flame they start
From the warm fountains of the heart.

No rest that throbbing slave may ask,
Forever quivering o'er his task,
While far and wide a crimson jet
Leaps forth to fill the woven net
Which in unnumbered crossing tides
The flood of burning life divides,
Then, kindling each decaying part,
Creeps back to find the throbbing heart.

But warmed with that unchanging flame
Behold the outward moving frame,
Its living marbles jointed strong
With glistening band and silvery thong,
And linked to reason's guiding reins
By myriad rings in trembling chains,
Each graven with the threaded zone
Which claims it as the master's own.

See how yon beam of seeming white
Is braided out of seven-hued light,
Yet in those lucid globes no ray
By any chance shall break astray.
Hark how the rolling surge of sound,
Arches and spirals circling round,
Wakes the hushed spirit through thine ear
With music it is heaven to hear.

Then mark the cloven sphere that holds
All thought in its mysterious folds;
That feels sensation's faintest thrill,
And flashes forth the sovereign will;
Think on the stormy world that dwells
Locked in its dim and clustering cells!
The lightning gleams of power it sheds
Along its hollow glassy threads!

O Father! grant thy love divine
To make these mystic temples thine!
When wasting age and wearying strife
Have sapped the leaning walls of life,
When darkness gathers over all,
And the last tottering pillars fall,
Take the poor dust thy mercy warms,
And mold it into heavenly forms!

1858

## THE DEACON'S MASTERPIECE

### OR, THE WONDERFUL "ONE-HOSS SHAY"

#### A LOGICAL STORY

Have you heard of the wonderful one-hoss shay,
That was built in such a logical way
It ran a hundred years to a day,
And then, of a sudden, it—ah, but stay,
I'll tell you what happened without delay,
Scaring the parson into fits,
Frightening people out of their wits,—
Have you ever heard of that, I say?

Seventeen hundred and fifty-five.
*Georgius Secundus* was then alive,—
Snuffy old drone from the German hive.
That was the year when Lisbon-town
Saw the earth open and gulp her down,
And Braddock's army was done so brown,
Left without a scalp to its crown.
It was on the terrible Earthquake-day
That the Deacon finished the one-hoss shay.

Now in building of chaises, I tell you what
There is always *somewhere* a weakest spot,—
In hub, tire, felloe, in spring or thill,
In panel, or crossbar, or floor, or sill,
In screw, bolt, thoroughbrace,—lurking still,
Find it somewhere you must and will,—
Above or below, or within or without,—

And that's the reason, beyond a doubt,
That a chaise *breaks down,* but doesn't *wear out.*

But the Deacon swore (as Deacons do,
With an "I dew vum," or an "I tell *yeou,*")
He would build one shay to beat the taown
'N' the keounty 'n' all the kentry raoun';
It should be so built that it *couldn'* break daown:
"Fur," said the Deacon, " 't's mighty plain
Thut the weakes' place mus' stan' the strain;
'N' the way t' fix it, uz I maintain,
Is only jest
T' make that place uz strong uz the rest."

So the Deacon inquired of the village folk
Where he could find the strongest oak,
That couldn't be split nor bent nor broke,—
That was for spokes and floor and sills;
He sent for lancewood to make the thills;
The crossbars were ash, from the straightest trees;
The panels of white-wood, that cuts like cheese,
But lasts like iron for things like these;
The hubs of logs from the "Settler's ellum,"—
Last of its timber,—they couldn't sell 'em,
Never an axe had seen their chips,
And the wedges flew from between their lips,
Their blunt ends frizzled like celery-tips;
Step and prop-iron, bolt and screw,
Spring, tire, axle, and linchpin too,
Steel of the finest, bright and blue;
Thoroughbrace bison-skin, thick and wide;
Boot, top, dasher, from tough old hide
Found in the pit when the tanner died.
That was the way he "put her through."
"There!" said the Deacon, "naow she'll dew!"

Do! I tell you, I rather guess
She was a wonder, and nothing less!
Colts grew horses, beards turned gray,
Deacon and deaconess dropped away,
Children and grandchildren—where were they?
But there stood the stout old one-hoss shay
As fresh as on Lisbon-earthquake-day!

EIGHTEEN HUNDRED;—it came and found
The Deacon's masterpiece strong and sound.
Eighteen hundred increased by ten;—
"Hahnsum kerridge" they called it then.
Eighteen hundred and twenty came;—
Running as usual; much the same.
Thirty and forty at last arrive,
And then come fifty, and FIFTY-FIVE.

Little of all we value here
Wakes on the morn of its hundredth year
Without both feeling and looking queer.
In fact, there's nothing that keeps its youth,
So far as I know, but a tree and truth.
(This is a moral that runs at large;
Take it.—You're welcome.—No extra charge.)

FIRST OF NOVEMBER,—the Earthquake-day.—
There are traces of age in the one-hoss shay,
A general flavor of mild decay,
But nothing local, as one may say.

There couldn't be,—for the Deacon's art
Had made it so like in every part
That there wasn't a chance for one to start.
For the wheels were just as strong as the thills,
And the floor was just as strong as the sills,
And the panels just as strong as the floor,
And the whipple-tree neither less nor more,
And the back crossbar as strong as the fore,
And spring and axle and hub *encore*.
And yet, *as a whole*, it is past a doubt
In another hour it will be *worn out!*

First of November, 'Fifty-five!
This morning the parson takes a drive.
Now, small boys, get out of the way!
Here comes the wonderful one-horse shay,
Drawn by a rat-tailed, ewe-necked bay.
"Huddup!" said the parson.—Off went they.
The parson was working his Sunday's text,—
Had got to *fifthly*, and stopped perplexed
At what the—Moses—was coming next.
All at once the horse stood still,
Close by the meet'n'-house on the hill.
First a shiver, and then a thrill,
Then something decidedly like a spill,—
And the parson was sitting upon a rock,
At half-past nine by the meet'n'-house clock,—
Just the hour of the Earthquake shock!
What do you think the parson found,
When he got up and stared around?
The poor old chaise in a heap or mound,
As if it had been to the mill and ground!
You see, of course, if you're not a dunce,
How it went to pieces all at once,—
All at once and nothing first,—
Just as bubbles do when they burst.

End of the wonderful one-hoss shay.
Logic is logic. That's all I say.

1858

## THE BOYS

Has there any old fellow got mixed with the boys?
If there has, take him out, without making a noise.
Hang the Almanac's cheat and the Catalogue's spite!
Old Time is a liar! We're twenty to-night!

We're twenty! We're twenty! Who says we are more?
He's tipsy,—young jackanapes!—show him the door!
"Gray temples at twenty?"—Yes! *white*, if we please;
Where the snow-flakes fall thickest there's nothing can freeze!

Was it snowing I spoke of? Excuse the mistake!
Look close,—you will see not a sign of a flake;
We want some new garlands for those we have shed,—
And these are white roses in place of the red!

We've a trick, we young fellows, you may have been told,
Of talking (in public) as if we were old:—
That boy we call "Doctor," and this we call "Judge;"
It's a neat little fiction,—of course it's all fudge.

That fellow's the "Speaker,"—the one on the right;

"Mr. Mayor," my young one, how are you tonight?
That's our "Member of Congress," we say when we chaff;
There's the "Reverend" What's his name?—don't make me laugh.

That boy with the grave mathematical look
Made believe he had written a wonderful book,
And the ROYAL SOCIETY thought it was *true!*
So they chose him right in; a good joke it was, too!

There's a boy, we pretend, with a three-decker-brain,
That could harness a team with a logical chain;
When he spoke for our manhood in syllabled fire,
We called him "The Justice," but now he's "The Squire."

And there's a nice youngster of excellent pith,—
Fate tried to conceal him by naming him Smith;
But he shouted a song for the brave and the free,—
Just read on his medal, "My country, of thee!"

You hear that boy laughing?—You think he's all fun;
But the angels laugh, too, at the good he has done;
The children laugh loud as they troop to his call,
And the poor man that knows him laughs loudest of all!

Yes, we're boys,—always playing with tongue or with pen,—
And I sometimes have asked,—Shall we ever be men?
Shall we always be youthful and laughing and gay,
Till the last dear companion drops smiling away?

Then here's to our boyhood, its gold and its gray!
The stars of its winter, the dews of its May!
And when we have done with our life-lasting toys,
Dear Father, take care of thy children, THE BOYS!

1859

## A HYMN OF TRUST

O Love Divine, that stooped to share
Our sharpest pang, our bitterest tear,
On Thee we cast each earth-born care,
We smile at pain while Thou art near!

Though long the weary way we tread,
And sorrow crown each lingering year,
No path we shun, no darkness dread,
Our hearts still whispering, Thou art near!

When drooping pleasure turns to grief,
And trembling faith is changed to fear,
The murmuring wind, the quivering leaf
Shall softly tell us, Thou art near!

On Thee we fling our burdening woe,
O Love Divine, forever dear,
Content to suffer while we know,
Living and dying, Thou art near!

1859

## DOROTHY Q.

### A FAMILY PORTRAIT

Grandmother's mother: her age, I guess,
Thirteen summers, or something less;
Girlish bust, but womanly air;
Smooth, square forehead with uprolled hair;

Lips that lover has never kissed;
Taper fingers and slender wrist;
Hanging sleeves of stiff brocade;
So they painted the little maid.

On her hand a parrot green
Sits unmoving and broods serene.
Hold up the canvas full in view,—
Look! there's a rent the light shines through,
Dark with a century's fringe of dust,—
That was a Red-Coat's rapier-thrust!
Such is the tale the lady old,
Dorothy's daughter's daughter, told.

Who the painter was none may tell,—
One whose best was not over well;
Hard and dry, it must be confessed,
Flat as a rose that has long been pressed;
Yet in her cheek the hues are bright,
Dainty colors of red and white,
And in her slender shape are seen
Hint and promise of stately mien.

Look not on her with eyes of scorn,—
Dorothy Q. was a lady born!
Ay! since the galloping Normans came,
England's annals have known her name;
And still to the three-hilled rebel town
Dear is that ancient name's renown,
For many a civic wreath they won,
The youthful sire and the gray-haired son.

O Damsel Dorothy! Dorothy Q.!
Strange is the gift that I owe to you;
Such a gift as never a king
Save to daughter or son might bring,—
All my tenure of heart and hand,
All my title to house and land;
Mother and sister and child and wife
And joy and sorrow and death and life!

What if a hundred years ago
Those close-shut lips had answered No,
When forth the tremulous question came
That cost the maiden her Norman name,
And under the folds that look so still
The bodice swelled with the bosom's thrill?
Should I be I, or would it be
One tenth another, to nine tenths me?

Soft is the breath of a maiden's YES:
Not the light gossamer stirs with less;
But never a cable that holds so fast
Through all the battles of wave and blast,
And never an echo of speech or song
That lives in the babbling air so long!
There were tones in the voice that whispered then
You may hear to-day in a hundred men.

O lady and lover, how faint and far
Your images hover,—and here we are,
Solid and stirring in flesh and bone,—
Edward's and Dorothy's—all their own,—
A goodly record for Time to show
Of a syllable spoken so long ago!—
Shall I bless you, Dorothy, or forgive
For the tender whisper that bade me live?

It shall be a blessing, my little maid!
I will heal the stab of the Red-Coat's blade,
And freshen the gold of the tarnished frame,
And gild with a rhyme your household name;
So you shall smile on us brave and bright
As first you greeted the morning's light,
And live untroubled by woes and fears
Through a second youth of a hundred years.

(1871) 1871

## AT THE SATURDAY CLUB

This is our place of meeting; opposite
That towered and pillared building: look at it;
*King's* Chapel in the Second George's day,
Rebellion stole its regal name away, —
*Stone* Chapel sounded better; but at last
The poisoned name of our provincial past
Had lost its ancient venom; then once more
Stone Chapel was King's Chapel as before.
(So let rechristened North Street, when it can,
Bring back the days of Marlborough and Queen Anne!)

Next the old church your wandering eye will meet —
A granite pile that stares upon the street —
Our civic temple; slanderous tongues have said
Its shape was modelled from St. Botolph's head,
Lofty, but narrow; jealous passers-by
Say Boston always held her head too high.

Turn half-way round, and let your look survey
The white façade that gleams across the way, —
The many-windowed building, tall and wide,
The palace-inn that shows its northern side
In grateful shadow when the sunbeams beat
The granite wall in summer's scorching heat.
This is the place; whether its name you spell
Tavern, or caravansera, or hotel.
Would I could steal its echoes! you should find
Such store of vanished pleasures brought to mind:
Such feasts! the laughs of many a jocund hour
That shook the mortar from King George's tower;
Such guests! What famous names its record boasts,
Whose owners wander in the mob of ghosts!
Such stories! Every beam and plank is filled
With juicy wit the joyous talkers spilled,
Ready to ooze, as once the mountain pine
The floors are laid with oozed its turpentine!

A month had flitted since The Club had met;
The day came round; I found the table set,
The waiters lounging round the marble stairs,
Empty as yet the double row of chairs.
I was a full half hour before the rest,
Alone, the banquet-chamber's single guest.
So from the table's side a chair I took,
And having neither company nor book
To keep me waking, by degrees there crept
A torpor over me, — in short, I slept.

Loosed from its chain, along the wreck-strown track
Of the dead years my soul goes travelling back;
My ghosts take on their robes of flesh; it seems
Dreaming is life; nay, life less life than dreams,
So real are the shapes that meet my eyes.
They bring no sense of wonder, no surprise,
No hint of other than an earth-born source;
All seems plain daylight, everything of course.

How dim the colors are, how poor and faint
This palette of weak words with which I paint!
Here sit my friends; if I could fix them so
As to my eyes they seem, my page would glow
Like a queen's missal, warm as if the brush
Of Titian or Velasquez brought the flush
Of life into their features. *Ay de mi!*
If syllables were pigments, you should see
Such breathing portraitures as never man
Found in the Pitti or the Vatican.

Here sits our POET, Laureate, if you will.
Long has he worn the wreath, and wears it still.
*Dead?* Nay, not so; and yet they say his bust
Looks down on marbles covering royal dust,
Kings by the Grace of God, or Nature's grace;
*Dead!* No! Alive! I see him in his place,
Full-featured, with the bloom that heaven denies
Her children, pinched by cold New England skies,
Too often, while the nursery's happier few
Win from a summer cloud its roseate hue.
Kind, soft-voiced, gentle, in his eye there shines
The ray serene that filled Evangeline's.
Modest he seems, not shy; content to wait
Amid the noisy clamor of debate
The looked-for moment when a peaceful word
Smooths the rough ripples louder tongues have stirred.
In every tone I mark his tender grace
And all his poems hinted in his face;
What tranquil joy his friendly presence gives!
How could I think him dead? He lives! He lives!

There, at the table's further end I see
In his old place our Poet's *vis-à-vis,*
The great PROFESSOR, strong, broad-shouldered, square,
In life's rich noontide, joyous, debonair.
His social hour no leaden care alloys,
His laugh rings loud and mirthful as a boy's, —
That lusty laugh the Puritan forgot, —
What ear has heard it and remembers not?
How often, halting at some wide crevasse
Amid the windings of his Alpine pass,
High up the cliffs, the climbing mountaineer,
Listening the far-off avalanche to hear,
Silent, and leaning on his steel-shod staff,
Has heard that cheery voice, that ringing laugh,
From the rude cabin whose nomadic walls
Creep with the moving glacier as it crawls!

How does vast Nature lead her living train
In ordered sequence through that spacious brain,
As in the primal hour when Adam named
The new-born tribes that young creation claimed! —
How will her realm be darkened, losing thee,
Her darling, whom we call *our* AGASSIZ!

But who is he whose massive frame belies

The maiden shyness of his downcast
eyes?
Who broods in silence till, by questions pressed,
Some answer struggles from his laboring breast?
An artist Nature meant to dwell apart,
Locked in his studio with a human heart,
Tracking its caverned passions to their lair,
And all its throbbing mysteries laying bare.

Count it no marvel that he broods alone
Over the heart he studies, — 'tis his own;
So in his page, whatever shape it wear,
The Essex wizard's shadowed self is there, —
The great ROMANCER, hid beneath his veil
Like the stern preacher of his sombre tale;
Virile in strength, yet bashful as a girl,
Prouder than Hester, sensitive as Pearl.

From his mild throng of worshippers released,
Our Concord Delphi sends its chosen priest,
Prophet or poet, mystic, sage, or seer,
By every title always welcome here.
Why that ethereal spirit's frame describe?
You know the race-marks of the Brahmin tribe, —
The spare, slight form, the sloping shoulder's droop,
The calm, scholastic mien, the clerkly stoop,
The lines of thought the sharpened features wear,
Carved by the edge of keen New England air.

List! for he speaks! As when a king would choose
The jewels for his bride, he might refuse
This diamond for its flaw, — find that less bright
Than those, its fellows, and a pearl less white
Than fits her snowy neck, and yet at last,
The fairest gems are chosen, and made fast
In golden fetters; so, with light delays
He seeks the fittest word to fill his phrase;
Nor vain nor idle his fastidious quest,
His chosen word is sure to prove the best.

Where in the realm of thought, whose air is song,
Does he, the Buddha of the West, belong?
He seems a wingèd Franklin, sweetly wise,
Born to unlock the secrets of the skies;
And which the nobler calling, — if 'tis fair
Terrestrial with celestial to compare, —
To guide the storm-cloud's elemental flame,
Or walk the chambers whence the lightning came,
Amidst the sources of its subtile fire,
And steal their effluence for his lips and lyre?

If lost at times in vague aerial flights,
None treads with firmer footstep when he lights;
A soaring nature, ballasted with sense,
Wisdom without her wrinkles or pretence,
In every Bible he has faith to read,
And every altar helps to shape his creed.
Ask you what name this prisoned spirit bears
While with ourselves this fleeting breath it shares?

Till angels greet him with a sweeter one
In heaven, on earth we call him Emerson.

I start; I wake; the vision is withdrawn;
Its figures fading like the stars at dawn;
Crossed from the roll of life their cherished names,
And memory's pictures fading in their frames;
Yet life is lovelier for these transient gleams
Of buried friendships; blest is he who dreams!

(1883) 1884

## THE AUTOCRAT OF THE BREAKFAST-TABLE

### [ESSAY] I

I was just going to say, when I was interrupted, that one of the many ways of classifying minds is under the heads of arithmetical and algebraical intellects. All economical and practical wisdom is an extension or variation of the following arithmetical formula: $2 + 2 = 4$. Every philosophical proposition has the more general character of the expression $a + b = c$. We are mere operatives, empirics, and egotists, until we learn to think in letters instead of figures.

They all stared. There is a divinity student lately come among us to whom I commonly address remarks like the above, allowing him to take a certain share in the conversation, so far as assent or pertinent questions are involved. He abused his liberty on this occasion by presuming to say that Leibnitz had the same observation.—No, sir, I replied, he has not. But he said a mighty good thing about mathematics, that sounds something like it, and you found it, *not in the original,* but quoted by Dr. Thomas Reid. I will tell the company what he did say, one of these days.

—If I belong to a Society of Mutual Admiration?—I blush to say that I do not at this present moment. I once did, however. It was the first association to which I ever heard the term applied; a body of scientific young men in a great foreign city* who admired their teacher, and to some extent each other. Many of them deserved it; they have become

*The "body of scientific young men in a great foreign city" was the Société d'Observation Medicalé, of Paris, of which M. Louis was president, and MM. Barth, Grisotte, and our own Dr. Bowditch were members. They agreed in admiring their justly-honored president, and thought highly of some of their associates, who have since made good their promise of distinction.

About the time when these papers were published, the Saturday Club was founded, or, rather, found itself in existence, without any organization, almost without parentage. It was natural enough that such men as Emerson, Longfellow, Agassiz, Peirce, with Hawthorne, Motley, Sumner, when within reach, and others who would be good company for them, should meet and dine together once in a while, as they did, in point of fact, every month, and as some who are still living, with other and newer members, still meet and dine. If some of them had not admired each other they would have been exceptions in the world of letters and science. The club deserves being remembered for having no constitution or by-laws, for making no speeches, reading no papers, observing no ceremonies, coming and going at will without remark, and acting out, though it did not proclaim the motto, "Shall I not take mine ease in mine inn?" There was and is nothing of the Bohemian element about this club, but it has had many good times and not a little good talking. [Author's note.]

famous since. It amuses me to hear the talk of one of those beings described by Thackeray—

Letters four do form his name—

about a social development which belongs to the very noblest stage of civilization. All generous companies of artists, authors, philanthropists, men of science, are, or ought to be, Societies of Mutual Admiration. A man of genius, or any kind of superiority, is not debarred from admiring the same quality in another, nor the other from returning his admiration. They may even associate together and continue to think highly of each other. And so of a dozen such men, if any one place is fortunate enough to hold so many. The being referred to above assumes several false premises. First, that men of talent necessarily hate each other. Secondly, that intimate knowledge or habitual association destroys our admiration of persons whom we esteemed highly at a distance. Thirdly, that a circle of clever fellows, who meet together to dine and have a good time, have signed a constitutional compact to glorify themselves and to put down him and the fraction of the human race not belonging to their number. Fourthly, that it is an outrage that he is not asked to join them.

Here the company laughed a good deal, and the old gentleman who sits opposite said: "That's it! that's it!"

I continued, for I was in the talking vein. As to clever people's hating each other, I think *a little* extra talent does sometimes make people jealous. They become irritated by perpetual attempts and failures, and it hurts their tempers and dispositions. Unpretending mediocrity is good, and genius is glorious; but a weak flavor of genius in an essentially common person is detestable. It spoils the grand neutrality of a commonplace character, as the rinsings of an unwashed wineglass spoil a draught of fair water. No wonder the poor fellow we spoke of, who always belongs to this class of slightly flavored mediocrities, is puzzled and vexed by the strange sight of a dozen men of capacity working and playing together in harmony. He and his fellows are always fighting. With them familiarity naturally breeds contempt. If they ever praise each other's bad drawings, or broken-winded novels, or spavined verses, nobody ever supposed it was from admiration; it was simply a contract between themselves and a publisher or dealer.

If the Mutuals have really nothing among them worth admiring, that alters the question. But if they are men with noble powers and qualities, let me tell you that, next to youthful love and family affections, there is no human sentiment better than that which unites the Societies of Mutual Admiration. And what would literature or art be without such associations? Who can tell what we owe to the Mutual Admiration Society of which Shakespeare, and Ben Jonson, and Beaumont and Fletcher were members? Or to that of which Addison and Steele formed the centre, and which gave us the Spectator? Or to that where Johnson, and Goldsmith, and Burke, and Reynolds, and Beauclerk, and Boswell, most admiring among all admirers, met together? Was there any great harm in the fact that the Irvings and Paulding wrote in company? or any unpardonable cabal in the literary union of Verplanck and Bryant and Sands, and as many more as they chose to associate with them?

The poor creature does not know what he is talking about when he abuses this noblest of institutions. Let him inspect its mysteries through the knot-hole he has secured, but not use that orifice as a medium for his popgun. Such a society is the crown of a literary metropolis; if a town has not material for it, and spirit and good feeling enough to organize it, it is a mere caravansary, fit for a man of genius to lodge in, but not to live in. Foolish people hate and dread and envy such an association of men of varied powers and influence, because it is lofty, serene, impregnable, and, by the necessity of the case, exclusive. Wise ones are prouder of the title M. S. M. A. than of all their other honors put together.

—All generous minds have a horror of what are commonly called "facts." They are the brute beasts of the intellectual domain. Who does not know fellows that always have an ill-conditioned fact or two which they lead after them into decent company like so many bulldogs, ready to let them slip at every ingenious suggestion, or convenient generalization, or pleasant fancy? I allow no "facts" at this table. What! Because bread is good and wholesome, and necessary and nourishing, shall you thrust a crumb into my windpipe while I am talking? Do not these muscles of mine represent a hundred loaves of bread? and is not my thought the abstract of ten thousand of these crumbs of truth with which you would choke off my speech?

[The above remark must be conditioned and qualified for the vulgar mind. The reader will, of course, understand the precise amount of seasoning which must be added to it before he adopts it as one of the axioms of his life. The speaker disclaims all responsibility for its abuse in incompetent hands.]

This business of conversation is a very serious matter. There are men whom it weakens one to talk with an hour more than a day's fasting would do. Mark this which I am going to say, for it is as good as a working professional man's advice, and costs you nothing: It is better to lose a pint of blood from your veins than to have a nerve tapped. Nobody measures your nervous force as it runs away, nor bandages your brain and marrow after the operation.

There are men of *esprit* who are excessively exhausting to some people. They are the talkers who have what may be called *jerky* minds. Their thoughts do not run in the natural order of sequence. They say bright things on all possible subjects, but their zigzags rack you to death. After a jolting half-hour with one of these jerky companions, talking with a dull friends affords great relief. It is like taking the cat in your lap after holding a squirrel.

What a comfort a dull but kindly person is, to be sure, at times! A ground-glass shade over a gas-lamp does not bring more solace to our dazzled eyes than such a one to our minds.

"Do not dull people bore you?" said one of the lady-boarders,—the same who sent me her autograph-book last week with a request for a few original stanzas, not remembering that "The Pactolian" pays me five dollars a line for every thing I write in its columns.

"Madam," said I (she and the century were in their teens together), "all men are bores, except when we want them. There never was but one man whom I would trust with my latch-key."

"Who might that favored person be?"

"Zimmermann." *

—The men of genius that I fancy most, have erectile heads like the cobra-di-capello. You remember what they tell of William Pinkney, the great pleader; how in his eloquent paroxysms the veins of his neck would swell and his face flush and his eyes glitter, until he seemed on the verge of apoplexy. The hydraulic arrangements for supplying the brain with blood are only second in importance to its own organization. The bulbous-headed fellows who steam well when they are at work are the men that draw big audiences and give us marrowy books and pictures. It is a good sign to have one's feet grow cold when he is writing. A great writer and speaker once told me that he often wrote with his feet in hot water; but for this, *all* his blood would have run into his head, as the mercury sometimes withdraws into the ball of a thermometer.

—You don't suppose that my remarks made at this table are like so many postage-stamps, do you,—each to be only once uttered? If you do, you are mistaken. He must be a poor creature who does not often repeat himself. Imagine the author of the excellent piece of advice, "Know thyself," never alluding to that sentiment again during the course of a protracted existence! Why, the truths a man carries about with him are his tools; and do you think a carpenter is bound to use the same plane but once to smooth a knotty board with, or to hang up his hammer after it has driven its first nail? I shall never repeat a conversation, but an idea often. I shall use the same types when I like, but not commonly the same stereotypes. A thought is often original, though you have uttered it a hundred times. It has come to you over a new route, by a new and express train of associations.

Sometimes, but rarely, one may be caught making the same speech twice over, and yet be held blameless. Thus, a certain lecturer, after performing in an inland city, where dwells a *Littératrice* of note, was invited to meet her and others over the social teacup. She pleasantly referred to his many wanderings in his new occupation. "Yes," he replied, "I am like the Huma,* the bird that never lights, being always in the cars, as he is always on the wing."—Years elapsed. The lecturer visited the same place once more for the same purpose. Another social cup after the lecture, and a second meet-

*The *"Treatise on Solitude"* is not so frequently seen lying about on library tables as in our younger days. I remember that I always respected the title and let the book alone. [Author's note.]

*It was an agreeable incident of two consecutive visits to Hartford, Conn., that I met there the late Mrs. Sigourney. The second meeting recalled the first, and with it the allusion to the Huma, which bird is the subject of a short poem by another New England authoress, which may be found in Mr. Griswold's collection. [Author's note.]

ing with the distinguished lady. "You are constantly going from place to place," she said.—"Yes," he answered, "I am like the Huma,"—and finished the sentence as before.

What horrors, when it flashed over him that he had made this fine speech, word for word, twice over! Yet it was not true, as the lady might perhaps have fairly inferred, that he had embellished his conversation with the Huma daily during that whole interval of years. On the contrary, he had never once thought of the odious fowl until the recurrence of precisely the same circumstances brought up precisely the same idea. He ought to have been proud of the accuracy of his mental adjustments. Given certain factors, and a sound brain should always evolve the same fixed product with the certainty of Babbage's calculating machine.

—What a satire, by the way, is that machine on the mere mathematician! A Frankenstein-monster, a thing without brains and without heart, too stupid to make a blunder; which turns out results like a corn-sheller, and never grows any wiser or better, though it grind a thousand bushels of them!

I have an immense respect for a man of talents *plus* "the mathematics." But the calculating power alone should seem to be the least human of qualities, and to have the smallest amount of reason in it; since a machine can be made to do the work of three or four calculators, and better than any one of them. Sometimes I have been troubled that I had not a deeper intuitive apprehension of the relations of numbers. But the triumph of the ciphering hand-organ has consoled me. I always fancy I can hear the wheels clicking in a calculator's brain. The power of dealing with numbers is a kind of "detached lever" arrangement, which may be put into a mighty poor watch. I suppose it is about as common as the power of moving the ears voluntarily, which is a moderately rare endowment.

—Little localized powers, and little narrow streaks of specialized knowledge, are things men are very apt to be conceited about. Nature is very wise; but for this encouraging principle how many small talents and little accomplishments would be neglected! Talk about conceit as much as you like, it is to human character what salt is to the ocean; it keeps it sweet, and renders it endurable. Say rather it is like the natural unguent of the sea-fowl's plumage, which enables him to shed the rain that falls on him and the wave in which he dips. When one has had *all* his conceit taken out of him, when he has lost *all* his illusions, his feathers will soon soak through, and he will fly no more.

"So you admire conceited people, do you?" said the young lady who has come to the city to be finished off for —the duties of life.

I am afraid you do not study logic at your school, my dear. It does not follow that I wish to be pickled in brine because I like a salt-water plunge at Nahant. I say that conceit is just as natural a thing to human minds as a centre is to a circle. But little-minded people's thoughts move in such small circles that five minutes' conversation gives you an arc long enough to determine their whole curve. An arc in the movement of a large intellect does not sensibly differ from a straight line. Even if it have the third vowel as its centre, it does not soon betray it. The highest thought, that is, is the most seemingly impersonal; it does not obviously imply any individual centre.

Audacious self-esteem, with good ground for it, is always imposing. What resplendent beauty that must have been which could have authorized Phryne to "peel" in the way she did! What fine speeches are those two: *"Non omnis moriar,"* and "I have taken all knowledge to be my province"! Even in common people, conceit has the virtue of making them cheerful; the man who thinks his wife, his baby, his house, his horse, his dog, and himself severally unequalled, is almost sure to be a good-humored person, though liable to be tedious at times.

—What are the great faults of conversation? Want of ideas, want of words, want of manners, are the principal ones, I suppose you think. I don't doubt it, but I will tell you what I have found spoil more good talks than anything else;—long arguments on special points between people who differ on the fundamental principles upon which these points depend. No men can have satisfactory relations with each other until they have agreed on certain *ultimata* of belief not to be disturbed in ordinary conversation, and unless they have sense enough to trace the secondary questions depending upon these ultimate beliefs to their source. In short, just as a written constitution is essential to the best social order, so a code of finalities is a necessary condition of profitable talk between two persons. Talking is like playing on the harp; there is as much in laying the hand on the strings to stop their vibrations as in twanging them to bring out their music.

—Do you mean to say the pun-question is not clearly settled in your minds? Let me lay down the law upon the subject. Life and language are alike sacred. Homicide and *verbicide*—that is, violent treatment of a word with fatal results to its legitimate meaning, which is its life—are alike forbidden. Manslaughter, which is the meaning of the one, is the same as man's laughter, which is the end of the other. A pun is *primâ facie* an insult to the person you are talking with. It implies utter indifference to or sublime contempt for his remarks, no matter how serious. I speak of total depravity, and one says all that is written on the subject is deep raving. I have committed my self-respect by talking with such a person. I should like to commit him, but cannot, because he is a nuisance. Or I speak of geological convulsions, and he asks me what was the cosine of Noah's ark; also, whether the Deluge was not a deal huger than any modern inundation.

A pun does not commonly justify a blow in return. But if a blow were given for such cause, and death ensued, the jury would be judges both of the facts and of the pun, and might, if the latter were of an aggravated character, return a verdict of justifiable homicide. Thus, in a case lately decided before Miller, J., Doe presented Roe a subscription paper, and urged the claims of suffering humanity. Roe replied by asking, When charity was like a top? It was in evidence that Doe preserved a dignified silence. Roe then said, "When it begins to hum." Doe then—and not till then—struck Roe, and his head happening to hit a bound volume of the Monthly Rag-Bag and Stolen Miscellany, intense mortification ensued, with a fatal result. The chief laid down his notions of the law to his brother justices, who unanimously replied, "Jest so." The chief rejoined, that no man should jest so without being punished for it, and charged for the prisoner, who was acquitted, and the pun ordered to be burned by the sheriff. The bound volume was forfeited as a deodand, but not claimed.

People that make puns are like wanton boys that put coppers on the railroad tracks. They amuse themselves and other children, but their little trick may upset a freight train of conversation for the sake of a battered witticism.

I will thank you, B. F., to bring down two books, of which I will mark the places on this slip of paper. (While he is gone, I may say that this boy, our landlady's youngest, is called BENJAMIN FRANKLIN, after the celebrated philosopher of that name. A highly merited compliment.)

I wished to refer to two eminent authorities. Now be so good as to listen. The great moralist says: "To trifle with the vocabulary which is the vehicle of social intercourse is to tamper with the currency of human intelligence. He who would violate the sanctities of his mother tongue would invade the recesses of the paternal till without remorse, and repeat the banquet of Saturn without an indigestion."

And, once more, listen to the historian. "The Puritans hated puns The Bishops were notoriously addicted to them. The Lords Temporal carried them to the verge of license. Majesty itself must have its Royal quibble. 'Ye be burly, my Lord of Burleigh,' said Queen Elizabeth, 'but ye shall make less stir in our realm than my Lord of Leicester.' The gravest wisdom and the highest breeding lent their sanction to the practice. Lord Bacon playfully declared himself a descendant of 'Og, the King of Bashan. Sir Philip Sidney, with his last breath, reproached the soldier who brought him water, for wasting a casque full upon a dying man. A courtier, who saw Othello performed at the Globe Theatre, remarked, that the blackamoor was a brute, and not a man. 'Thou hast reason,' replied a great Lord, 'according to Plato his saying; for this be a two-legged animal *with* feathers.' The fatal habit became universal. The language was corrupted. The infection spread to the national conscience. Political double-dealings naturally grew out of verbal double meanings. The teeth of the new dragon were sown by the Cadmus who introduced the alphabet of equivocation. What was levity in the time of the Tudors grew to regicide and revolution in the age of the Stuarts."

Who was that boarder that just whispered something about the Macaulay-flowers of literature?—There was a dead silence.—I said calmly, I shall henceforth consider any interruption by a pun as a hint to change my boarding-house. Do not plead my example. If *I* have used any such, it has been only as a Spartan father would show up a drunken helot. We have done with them.

—If a logical mind ever found out anything with its logic?—I should say that its most frequent work was to build a *pons asinorum* over chasms which shrewd people can bestride without such a structure. You can hire logic, in the shape of a lawyer, to prove anything that you want to prove. You can buy treatises to show that Napoleon never lived, and that no battle of Bunker-hill was ever fought. The great minds are those with a wide span,* which couple truths related to, but far removed from, each other. Logicians carry the surveyor's chain over the track of which these are the true explorers. I value a man mainly for his primary relations with truth, as I understand truth,—not for any secondary artifice in handling his ideas. Some of the sharpest men in argument are notoriously unsound in judgment. I should not trust the counsel of a clever debater, any more than that of a good chess-player. Either may of course advise wisely, but not necessarily because he wrangles or plays well.

The old gentleman who sits opposite got his hand up, as a pointer lifts his forefoot, at the expression, "his relations with truth, as I understand truth," and when I had done, sniffed audibly, and said I talked like a transcendentalist. For his part, common sense was good enough for him.

Precisely so, my dear sir, I replied; common sense, *as you understand it.* We all have to assume a standard of judgment in our own minds, either of things or persons. A man who is willing to take another's opinion has to exercise his judgment in the choice of whom to follow, which is often as nice a matter as to judge of things for one's self. On the whole, I had rather judge men's minds by comparing their thoughts with my own, than judge of thoughts by knowing who utter them. I must do one or the other. It does not follow, of course, that I may not recognize another man's thoughts as broader and deeper than my own; but that does not necessarily change my opinion, otherwise this would be at the mercy of every superior mind that held a different one. How many of our most cherished beliefs are like those drinking-glasses of the ancient pattern, that serve us well so long as we keep them in our hand, but spill all if we attempt to set them down! I have sometimes compared conversation to the Italian game of *mora,* in which one player lifts his hand with so many fingers extended, and the other gives the number if he can. I show my thought, another his; if they agree, well; if they differ, we find the largest common factor, if we can, but at any rate avoid disputing about remainders and fractions, which is to real talk what tuning an instrument is to playing on it.

—What if, instead of talking this morning, I should read you a copy of verses, with critical remarks by the author? Any of the company can retire that like.

ALBUM VERSES

When Eve had led her lord away,
  And Cain had killed his brother,
The stars and flowers, the poets say,
  Agreed with one another.

*There is something like this in J. H. Newman's *Grammar of Assent.* See *Characteristics,* arranged by W. S. Lilly, p. 81. [Author's note.]

To cheat the cunning tempter's art,
  And teach the race its duty,
By keeping on its wicked heart
  Their eyes of light and beauty.

A million sleepless lids, they say,
  Will be at least a warning;
And so the flowers would watch by day,
  The stars from eve to morning.

On hill and prairie, field and lawn,
  Their dewy eyes upturning,
The flowers still watch from reddening dawn
  Till western skies are burning.

Alas! each hour of daylight tells
  A tale of shame so crushing,
That some turn white as sea-bleached shells,
  And some are always blushing.

But when the patient stars look down
  On all their light discovers,
The traitor's smile, the murderer's frown,
  The lips of lying lovers,

They try to shut their saddening eyes,
  And in the vain endeavor
We see them twinkling in the skies,
  And so they wink forever.

What do *you* think of these verses, my friends?—Is that piece an impromptu? said my landlady's daughter. (Aet. 19 +. Tender-eyed blonde. Long ringlets. Cameo pin. Gold pencil-case on a chain. Locket. Bracelet. Album. Autograph book. Accordeon. Reads Byron, Tupper, and Sylvanus Cobb, Junior, while her mother makes the puddings. Says "Yes?" when you tell her anything.) —*Oui et non, ma petite,*—Yes and no, my child. Five of the seven verses were written off-hand; the other two took a week,—that is, were hanging round the desk in a ragged, forlorn, unrhymed condition as long as that. All poets will tell you just such stories. *C'est le* DERNIER *pas qui coûte.* Don't you know how hard it is for some people to get out of a room after their visit is really over? They want to be off, and you want to have them off, but they don't know how to manage it. One would think they had been built in your parlor or study, and were waiting to be launched. I have contrived a sort of ceremonial inclined plane for such visitors, which being lubricated with certain smooth phrases, I back them down, metaphorically speaking, stern-foremost, into their "native element," the great ocean of out-doors. Well, now, there are poems as hard to get rid of as these rural visitors. They come in glibly, use up all the serviceable rhymes, *day, ray, beauty, duty, skies, eyes, other, brother, mountain, fountain,* and the like; and so they go on until you think it is time for the wind-up, and the wind-up won't come on any terms. So they lie about until you get sick of the sight of them, and end by thrusting some cold scrap of a final couplet upon them, and turning them out of doors. I suspect a good many "impromptus" could tell just such a story as the above.—Here turning to our landlady, I used an illustration which pleased the company much at the time, and has since been highly commended. "Madam," I said, "you can pour three gills and three quarters of honey from that pint jug, if it is full, in less than one minute; but, Madam, you could not empty that last quarter of a gill, though you were turned into a marble Hebe, and held the vessel upside down for a thousand years."

One gets tired to death of the old, old rhymes, such as you see in that copy of verses,—which I don't mean to abuse, or to praise either. I always feel as if I were a cobbler, putting new top-leathers to an old pair of boot-soles and bodies, when I am fitting sentiments to these venerable jingles.

. . . . . . . youth<br>
. . . . . . . morning<br>
. . . . . . . truth<br>
. . . . . . . warning.

Nine tenths of the "Juvenile Poems" written spring out of the above musical and suggestive coincidences.

"Yes?" said our landlady's daughter.

I did not address the following remark to her, and I trust, from her limited range of reading, she will never see it; I said it softly to my next neighbor.

When a young female wears a flat circular side-curl, gummed on each temple,—when she walks with a male, not arm in arm, but his arm against the back of hers,—and when she says "Yes?" with the note of interrogation, you are generally safe in asking her what wages she gets, and who the "feller" was you saw her with.

"What were you whispering?" said the daughter of the house, moistening her lips, as she spoke, in a very engaging manner.

"I was only laying down a principle of social diagnosis."

"Yes?"

—It is curious to see how the same wants and tastes find the same implements and modes of expression in all times and places. The young ladies of Otaheite, as you may see in Cook's Voyages, had a sort of crinoline arrangement fully equal in radius to the largest spread of our own lady-baskets. When I fling a Bay-State shawl over my shoulders, I am only taking a lesson from the climate which the Indian had learned before me. A *blanket*-shawl we call it, and not a plaid; and we wear it like the aborigines, and not like the Highlanders.

—We are the Romans of the modern world,—the great assimilating people. Conflicts and conquests are of course necessary accidents with us, as with our prototypes. And so we come to their style of weapon. Our army sword is the short, stiff, pointed *gladius* of the Romans; and the American bowie-knife is the same tool, modified to meet the daily wants of civil society. I announce at this table an axiom not to be found in Montesquieu or the journals of Congress:—

The race that shortens its weapons lengthens its boundaries.

*Corollary.* It was the Polish *lance* that left Poland at last with nothing of her own to bound.

Dropped from her nerveless grasp the
*shattered spear!*

What business had Sarmatia to be fighting for liberty with a fifteen-foot pole between her and the breasts of her enemies? If she had but clutched the old Roman and young American weapon, and come to close quarters, there might have been a chance for her; but it would have spoiled the best passage in "The Pleasures of Hope."

—Self-made men?—Well, yes. Of course every body likes and respects self-made men. It is a great deal better to be made in that way than not to be made at all. Are any of you younger people old enough to remember that Irishman's house on the marsh at Cambridge-port, which house he built from drain to chimney-top with his own hands? It took him a good many years to build it, and one could see that it was a little out of plumb, and a little wavy in outline, and a little queer and uncertain in general aspect. A regular hand could certainly have built a better house; but it was a very good house for a "self-made" carpenter's house, and people praised it, and said how remarkably well the Irishman had succeeded. They never thought of praising the fine blocks of houses a little farther on.

Your self-made man, whittled into shape with his own jack-knife, deserves more credit, if that is all, than the regular engine-turned article, shaped by the most approved pattern, and French-polished by society and travel. But as to saying that one is every way the equal of the other, that is another matter. The right of strict social discrimination of all things and persons, according to their merits, native or acquired, is one of the most precious republican privileges. I take the liberty to exercise it when I say that, *other things being equal,* in most relations of life I prefer a man of family.

What do I mean by a man of family?—O, I'll give you a general idea of what I mean. Let us give him a first-rate fit out; it costs us nothing.

Four or five generations of gentlemen and gentlewomen; among them a member of his Majesty's Council for the Province, a Governor or so, one or two Doctors of Divinity, a member of Congress, not later than the time of long boots with tassels.

Family portraits.* The member of the Council, by Smibert. The great merchant-uncle, by Copley, full length, sitting in his arm-chair, in a velvet cap and flowered robe, with a globe by him, to show the range of his commercial transactions, and letters with large red seals lying round, one directed conspicuously to The Honorable, etc., etc. Great-grandmother, by

*The full-length pictures by Copley I was thinking of are such as may be seen in the Memorial Hall of Harvard University, but many are to be met with in different parts of New England, sometimes in the possession of the poor descendants of the rich gentlefolks in lace ruffles and glistening satins, grandees and grand dames of the ante-Revolutionary period. I remember one poor old gentleman who had nothing left of his family possessions but the full-length portraits of his ancestors, the Counsellor and his lady, saying, with a gleam of the pleasantry which had come down from the days of Mather Byles, and "Balch the Hatter," and Sigourney, that he fared not so badly after all, for he had a pair of *canvas-backs* every day through the whole year.

The mention of these names, all of which are mere traditions to myself and my contemporaries, reminds me of the long succession of wits and humorists whose companionship has been the delight of their generation, and who leave nothing on record by which they will be remembered; Yoricks who set the table in a roar, story-tellers who gave us scenes of life in monologue better than the stilted presentments of the stage, and those always welcome friends with social interior furnishings, whose smile provoked the wit of others and whose rich, musical laughter was its abundant reward. Who among us in my earlier days ever told a story or carolled a rippling *chanson* so gayly, so easily, so charmingly as John Sullivan, whose memory is like the breath of a long bygone summer? Mr. Arthur Gilman has left his monument in the stately structures he planned; Mr. James T. Fields in the pleasant volumes full of precious recollections; but twenty or thirty years from now old men will tell their boys that the Yankee story-teller died with the first, and that the chief of our literary reminiscents, whose ideal portrait gallery reached from Wordsworth to Swinburne, left us when the second bowed his head and "fell on sleep," no longer to delight the guests whom his hospitality gathered around him with the pictures to which his lips gave life and action. [Author's note.]

the same artist; brown satin, lace very fine, hands superlative; grand old lady, stiffish, but imposing. Her mother, artist unknown; flat, angular, hanging sleeves; parrot on fist. A pair of Stuarts, viz., 1. A superb, full-blown, mediæval gentleman, with a fiery dash of Tory blood in his veins, tempered down with that of a fine old rebel grandmother, and warmed up with the best of old India Madeira; his face is one flame of ruddy sunshine; his ruffled shirt rushes out of his bosom with an impetuous generosity, as if it would drag his heart after it; and his smile is good for twenty thousand dollars to the Hospital, besides ample bequests to all relatives and dependants. 2. Lady of the same; remarkable cap; high waist, as in time of Empire; bust *à la Josephine;* wisps of curls, like celery-tips, at sides of forehead; complexion clear and warm, like rose-cordial. As for the miniatures by Malbone, we don't count them in the gallery.

Books, too, with the names of old college-students in them, — family names;—you will find them at the head of their respective classes in the days when students took rank on the catalogue from their parents' condition. Elzevirs, with the Latinized appellations of youthful progenitors, and *Hic liber est meus* on the title-page. A set of Hogarth's original plates. Pope, original edition, 15 volumes, London, 1717. Barrow on the lower shelves, in folio. Tillotson on the upper, in a little dark platoon of octodecimos.

Some family silver; a string of wedding and funeral rings; the arms of the family curiously blazoned; the same in worsted, by a maiden aunt.

If the man of family has an old place to keep these things in, furnished with claw-footed chairs and black mahogany tables, and tall bevel-edged mirrors, and stately upright cabinets, his outfit is complete.

No, my friends, I go (always, other things being equal) for the man who inherits family traditions and the cumulative humanities of at least four or five generations. Above all things, as a child, he should have tumbled about in a library. All men are afraid of books, who have not handled them from infancy. Do you suppose our dear *didascalos* * over there ever read *Poli Synopsis,* or consulted *Castelli Lexicon,* while he was growing up to their stature? Not he; but virtue passed through the hem of their parchment and leather garments whenever he touched them, as the precious drugs sweated through the bat's handle in the Arabian story. I tell you he is at home wherever he smells the invigorating fragrance of Russia leather. No self-made man feels so. One may, it is true, have all the antecedents I have spoken of, and yet be a boor or a shabby fellow. One may have none of them, and yet be fit for councils and courts. Then let them change places. Our social arrangement has this great beauty, that its strata shift up and down as they change specific gravity, without being

*"Our dear *didascalos*" was meant for Professor James Russell Lowell, now Minister to England. It requires the union of exceptional native gifts and generations of training to bring the "natural man" of New England to the completeness of scholarly manhood, such as that which adds new distinction to the name he bears, already remarkable for its successive generations of eminent citizens.

"Self-made" is imperfectly made, or education is a superfluity and a failure. [Author's note.]

clogged by layers of prescription. But I still insist on my democratic liberty of choice, and I go for the man with the gallery of family portraits against the one with the twenty-five cent daguerreotype, unless I find out that the last is the better of the two.

—I should have felt more nervous about the late comet, if I had thought the world was ripe. But it is very green yet, if I am not mistaken; and besides, there is a great deal of coal to use up, which I cannot bring myself to think was made for nothing. If certain things, which seem to me essential to a millennium, had come to pass, I should have been frightened; but they haven't. Perhaps you would like to hear my

LATTER-DAY WARNINGS

When legislators keep the law,
When banks dispense with bolts and locks,
When berries, whortle—rasp—and straw—
Grow bigger *downwards* through the box,—

When he that selleth house or land
Shows leak in roof or flaw in right,—
When haberdashers choose the stand
Whose window hath the broadest light,—

When preachers tell us all they think,
And party leaders all they mean,—
When what we pay for, that we drink,
From real grape and coffee-bean,—

When lawyers take what they would give,
And doctors give what they would take,—
When city fathers eat to live,
Save when they fast for conscience' sake,—

When one that hath a horse on sale
Shall bring his merit to the proof,
Without a lie for every nail
That holds the iron on the hoof,—

When in the usual place for rips
Our gloves are stitched with special care,
And guarded well the whalebone tips
Where first umbrellas need repair,—

When Cuba's weeds have quite forgot
The power of suction to resist,
And claret-bottles harbor not
Such dimples as would hold your fist,—

When publishers no longer steal,
And pay for what they stole before,—
When the first locomotive's wheel
Rolls through the Hoosac tunnel's bore;*—

*Till* then let Cumming blaze away,
And Miller's saints blow up the globe;
But when you see that blessed day,
*Then* order your ascension robe!

The company seemed to like the verses, and I promised them to read others occasionally, if they had a mind to hear them. Of course they would not expect it every morning. Neither must the reader suppose that all these things I have reported were said at any one breakfast-time. I have not taken the trouble to date them, as Raspail, *père,* used to date every proof he sent to the printer; but they were scattered over several breakfasts; and I have said a good many more things since, which I shall very possibly print some time or other, if I am urged to do it by judicious friends.

I finished off with reading some verses of my friend the Professor, of whom you may perhaps hear more by and by. The Professor read them, he

*This hoped for, but almost despaired of, event, occurred on the 9th of February, 1875. The writer of the above lines was as much pleased as his fellow-citizens at the termination of an enterprise which gave constant occasion for the most inveterate pun on record. When the other conditions referred to are as happily fulfilled as this has been, he will still say as before, that it is time for the ascension garment to be ordered. [Author's note.]

told me, at a farewell meeting, where the youngest of our great historians * met a few of his many friends at their invitation.

Yes, we knew we must lose him,—though
friendship may claim
To blend her green leaves with the laurels
of fame;
Though fondly, at parting, we call him
our own,
'Tis the whisper of love when the bugle
has blown.

As the rider who rests with the spur on
his heel,—
As the guardsman who sleeps in his
corselet of steel,—
As the archer who stands with his shaft
on the string,
He stoops from his toil to the garland
we bring.

What pictures yet slumber unborn in his
loom
Till their warriors shall breathe and their
beauties shall bloom,
While the tapestry lengthens the life-
glowing dyes
That caught from our sunsets the stain
of their skies!

In the alcoves of death, in the charnels
of time,
Where flit the gaunt spectres of passion
and crime,
There are triumphs untold, there are
martyrs unsung,
There are heroes yet silent to speak with
his tongue!

Let us hear the proud story which time
has bequeathed
From lips that are warm with the free-
dom they breathed!
Let him summon its tyrants and tell us
their doom,
Though he sweep the black past like
Van Tromp with his broom!

* "The youngest of our great historians," referred to in the poem, was John Lothrop Motley. His career of authorship was as successful as it was noble, and his works are among the chief ornaments of our national literature. Are Republics still ungrateful, as of old? [Author's note.]

. . . . .

The dream flashes by, for the west-winds
awake
On pampas, on prairie, o'er mountain
and lake,
To bathe the swift bark, like a sea-
girdled shrine,
With incense they stole from the rose
and the pine.

So fill a bright cup with the sunlight
that gushed
When the dead summer's jewels were
trampled and crushed:
THE TRUE KNIGHT OF LEARNING,—the
world holds him dear,—
Love bless him, Joy crown him, God
speed his career!

[ESSAY] II

I really believe some people save their bright thoughts as being too precious for conversation. What do you think an admiring friend said the other day to one that was talking good things,—good enough to print? "Why," said he, "you are wasting merchantable literature, a cash article, at the rate, as nearly as I can tell, of fifty dollars an hour." The talker took him to the window and asked him to look out and tell what he saw.

"Nothing but a very dusty street," he said, "and a man driving a sprinkling-machine through it."

"Why don't you tell the man he is wasting that water? What would be the state of the highways of life, if we did not drive our *thought-sprinklers* through them with the valves open, sometimes?

"Besides, there is another thing about this talking, which you forget. It shapes our thoughts for us;—the waves of conversation roll them as the surf rolls the pebbles on the shore. Let me modify the image a little. I rough out my thoughts in talk as an artist models in clay. Spoken language is so plastic,—you can pat and coax, and spread and shave, and rub out, and fill up, and stick on so easily, when you work that soft material, that there is nothing like it for modelling. Out of it come the shapes which you turn into marble or bronze in your immortal books, if you happen to write such. Or, to use another illustration, writing or printing is like shooting with a rifle; you may hit your reader's mind, or miss it;—but talking is like playing at a mark with the pipe of an engine; if it is within reach, and you have time enough, you can't help hitting it."

The company agreed that this last illustration was of superior excellence, or, in the phrase used by them, "Fust-rate." I acknowledged the compliment, but gently rebuked the expression. "Fust-rate," "prime," "a prime article," "a superior piece of goods," "a handsome garment," "a gent in a flowered vest,"—all such expressions are final. They blast the lineage of him or her who utters them, for generations up and down. There is one other phrase which will soon come to be decisive of a man's social *status,* if it is not already: "That tells the whole story." It is an expression which vulgar and conceited people particularly affect, and which well-meaning ones, who know better, catch from them. It is intended to stop all debate, like the previous question in the General Court. Only it doesn't; simply because "that" does not usually tell the whole, nor one half of the whole story.

—It is an odd idea, that almost all our people have had a professional education. To become a doctor a man must study some three years and hear a thousand lectures, more or less. Just how much study it takes to make a lawyer I cannot say, but probably not more than this. Now, most decent people hear one hundred lectures or sermons (discourses) on theology every year,—and this, twenty, thirty, fifty years together. They read a great many religious books besides. The clergy, however, rarely hear any sermons except what they preach themselves. A dull preacher might be conceived, therefore, to lapse into a state of *quasi* heathenism, simply for want of religious instruction. And, on the other hand, an attentive and intelligent hearer, listening to a succession of wise teachers, might become actually better educated in theology than any one of them. We are all theological students, and more of us qualified as doctors of divinity than have received degrees at any of the universities.

It is not strange, therefore, that very good people should often find it difficult, if not impossible, to keep their attention fixed upon a sermon treating feebly a subject which they have thought vigorously about for years, and heard able men discuss scores of times. I have often noticed, however, that a hopelessly dull discourse acts *inductively,* as electricians would say, in developing strong mental currents. I am ashamed to think with what accompaniments and variations and flourishes I have sometimes followed the droning of a heavy speaker,—not willingly,—for my habit is reverential,—but as a necessary result of a slight continuous impression on the senses and the mind, which kept both in action without furnishing the food they required to work upon. If you ever saw a crow with a king-bird after him, you will get an image of a dull speaker and a lively listener. The bird in sable plumage flaps heavily along his straightforward course, while the other sails round him, over him, under him, leaves him, comes back again, tweaks out a black feather, shoots away once more, never losing sight of him, and finally reaches the crow's perch at the same time the crow does, having cut a perfect labyrinth of loops and knots and spirals while the slow fowl was painfully working from one end of his straight line to the other.

[I think these remarks were re-received rather coolly. A temporary boarder from the country, consisting of a somewhat more than middle-aged female, with a parchment forehead and a dry little "frisette" shingling it, a sallow neck with a necklace of gold beads, a black dress too rusty for recent grief, and contours in basso-rilievo, left the table prematurely, and was reported to have been very virulent about what I said. So I went to my good old minister, and repeated the remarks, as nearly as I could remember them, to him. He laughed good-naturedly, and said there was considerable truth in them. He thought he could tell when people's minds were wandering, by their looks. In the earlier years of his ministry he had sometimes noticed this, when he was preaching;—very little of late years. Sometimes, when his colleague was preaching, he observed this kind of inattention; but after all, it was not so very unnatural. I will say, by the way, that it is a rule I have long followed, to tell my worst thoughts to my minister, and my best thoughts to the young people I talk with.]

—I want to make a literary confession now, which I believe nobody has made before me. You know very well that I write verses sometimes, because I have read some of them at this table. (The company assented, —two or three of them in a resigned sort of way, as I thought, as if they supposed I had an epic in my pocket, and were going to read half a dozen books or so for their benefit.)—I continued. Of course I write some lines or passages which are better than others; some which, compared with the others, might be called relatively excellent. It is in the nature of things that I should consider these relatively excellent lines or passages as absolutely good. So much must be pardoned to humanity. Now I never wrote a "good" line in my life, but the moment after it was written it seemed a hundred years old. Very commonly I had a sudden conviction that I had seen it somewhere. Possibly I may have sometimes unconsciously stolen it, but I do not remember that I ever once detected any historical truth in these sudden convictions of the antiquity of my new thought or phrase. I have learned utterly to distrust them, and never allow them to bully me out of a thought or line.

This is the philosophy of it. (Here the number of the company was diminished by a small secession.) Any new formula which suddenly emerges in our consciousness has its roots in long trains of thought; it is virtually old when it first makes its appearance among the recognized growths of our intellect. Any crystalline group of musical words has had a long and still period to form in. Here is one theory.

But there is a larger law which perhaps comprehends these facts. It is this. The rapidity with which ideas grow old in our memories is in a direct ratio to the squares of their importance. Their apparent age runs up miraculously, like the value of diamonds, as they increase in magnitude. A great calamity, for instance, is as old as the trilobites an hour after it has happened. It stains backward through all the leaves we have turned over in the book of life, before its blot of tears or of blood is dry on the page we are turning. For this we seem to have lived; it was foreshadowed in dreams that we leaped out of in the cold sweat of terror; in the "dissolving views" of dark day-visions; all omens pointed to it; all paths led to it. After the tossing half-forgetfulness of the first sleep that follows such an event, it comes upon us afresh, as a surprise, at waking; in a few moments it is old again,—old as eternity.

[I wish I had not said all this then and there. I might have known better. The pale school-mistress, in her mourning dress, was looking at me, as I noticed, with a wild sort of expression. All at once the blood dropped out of her cheeks as the mercury drops from a broken barometer-tube, and she melted away from her seat like an image of snow; a slung-shot could not have brought her down better. God forgive me!

After this little episode, I continued, to some few who remained balancing teaspoons on the edges of cups, twirling knives, or tilting upon the hind legs of their chairs until their heads reached the wall, where they left gratuitous advertisements of various popular cosmetics.]

When a person is suddenly thrust into any strange, new position of trial, he finds the place fits him as if he had been measured for it. He has committed a great crime, for instance, and is sent to the State Prison. The traditions, prescriptions, limitations, privileges, all the sharp conditions of his new life, stamp themselves upon his consciousness as the signet on soft wax;—a single pressure is enough. Let me strengthen the image a little. Did you ever happen to see that most soft-spoken and velvet-handed steam-engine at the Mint? The smooth piston slides backward and forward as a lady might slip her delicate finger in and out of a ring. The engine lays one of *its* fingers calmly, but firmly, upon a bit of metal; it is a coin now, and will remember that touch, and tell a new race about it, when the date upon it is crusted over with twenty centuries. So it is that a great silent-moving misery puts a new stamp on us in an hour or a moment,—as sharp an impression as if it had taken half a lifetime to engrave it.

It is awful to be in the hands of the wholesale professional dealers in misfortune; undertakers and jailers magnetize you in a moment, and you pass out of the individual life you were living into the rhythmical movements of their horrible machinery. Do the worst thing you can, or suffer the worst that can be thought of, you find yourself in a category of humanity that stretches back as far as Cain, and with an expert at your elbow who has studied your case all out beforehand, and is waiting for you with his implements of hemp or mahogany. I believe, if a man were to be burned in any of our cities to-morrow for heresy, there would be found a master of ceremonies who knew just how many fagots were necessary, and the best way of arranging the whole matter.*

—So we have not won the Goodwood cup; *au contraire,* we were a "bad fifth," if not worse than that; and trying it again, and the third time, has not yet bettered the matter. Now I am as patriotic as any of my fellow-citizens,—too patriotic in fact, for I have got into hot water by loving too much of my country; in short, if any man, whose fighting weight is not more than eight stone four pounds, disputes it, I am ready to discuss the point with him. I should have gloried to see the stars and stripes in front at the finish. I love my country and I love horses. Stubb's old mezzotint of Eclipse hangs over my desk, and Herring's portrait of Plenipotentiary—whom I saw run at Epsom—over my fireplace. Did I not elope from school to see Revenge, and Prospect, and Little John, and Peacemaker run over the race-course where now yon suburban village flourishes, in the year eighteen hundred and ever-so-few? Though I never owned a horse, have I not been the proprietor of six equine females, of which one was the prettiest little "Morgin" that ever stepped? Listen, then, to an opinion I have often expressed long before this venture of ours in England. Horse-*racing* is not a republican institution; horse-*trotting* is. Only very rich persons can keep race-horses, and everybody knows they are kept mainly as gambling implements. All that matter about blood and speed we won't discuss; we understand all that; useful, very,—*of* course,—great obligations to the Godolphin "Arabian," and the rest. I say racing-horses are essentially gambling implements, as much as roulette tables. Now, I am not preaching at this moment; I may read you one of my sermons some other morning; but I maintain that gambling, on the great scale, is not republican. It belongs to two phases of society,—a cankered over-civilization, such as exists in rich aristocracies, and the reckless life of borderers and adventurers, or the semi-barbarism of a civilization resolved into its primitive elements. Real Republicanism is stern and severe; its essence is not in forms of government, but in the omnipotence of public opinion which grows out of it. This public opinion cannot prevent gambling with dice or stocks, but it can and does compel it to keep comparatively quiet. But horse-racing is the most public way of gambling, and with all its immense attractions to the sense and

*Accidents are liable to happen if no thoroughly trained expert happens to be present. When Catharine Hays was burnt at Tyburn, in 1726, the officiating artist scorched his own hands, and the whole business was awkwardly managed for want of practical familiarity with the process. We have still remaining a guide to direct us in one important part of the arrangements. Bishop Hooper was burned at Gloucester, England, in the year 1555. A few years ago, in making certain excavations, the charred stump of the stake to which he was bound was discovered. An account of the interesting ceremony, so important in ecclesiastical history—*the argumentum ad ignem,* with a photograph of the half-burned stick of timber was sent me by my friend, Mr. John Bellows, of Gloucester, a zealous antiquarian, widely known by his wonderful miniature French dictionary, one of the scholarly printers and publishers who honor the calling of Aldus and the Elzevirs. The stake was big enough to chain the whole Bench of Bishops to as fast as the Athanasian creed still holds them. [Author's note.]

the feelings,—to which I plead very susceptible,—the disguise is too thin that covers it, and everybody knows what it means. Its supporters are the Southern gentry,—fine fellows, no doubt, but not republicans exactly, as we understand the term,—a few Northern millionaires more or less thoroughly millioned, who do not represent the real people, and the mob of sporting men, the best of whom are commonly idlers, and the worst very bad neighbors to have near one in a crowd, or to meet in a dark alley. In England, on the other hand, with its aristocratic institutions, racing is a natural growth enough; the passion for it spreads downwards through all classes, from the Queen to the costermonger. London is like a shelled corn-cob on the Derby day, and there is not a clerk who could raise the money to hire a saddle with an old hack under it that can sit down on his office-stool the next day without wincing.

Now just compare the racer with the trotter for a moment. The racer is incidentally useful, but essentially something to bet upon, as much as the thimble-rigger's "little joker." The trotter is essentially and daily useful, and only incidentally a tool for sporting men.

What better reason do you want for the fact that the racer is most cultivated and reaches his greatest perfection in England, and that the trotting horses of America beat the world? And why should we have expected that the pick—if it was the pick—of our few and far-between racing stables should beat the pick of England and France? Throw over the fallacious time-test, and there was nothing to show for it but a natural kind of patriotic feeling, which we all have, with a thoroughly provincial conceit, which some of us must plead guilty to.

We may beat yet.* As an American, I hope we shall. As a moralist and occasional sermonizer, I am not so anxious about it. Wherever the trotting horse goes, he carries in his train brisk omnibuses, lively bakers' carts, and therefore hot rolls, the jolly butcher's wagon, the cheerful gig, the wholesome afternoon drive with wife and child,—all the forms of moral excellence, except truth, which does not agree with any kind of horse-flesh. The racer brings with him gambling, cursing, swearing, drinking, and a distaste for mob-caps and the middle-aged virtues.

And by the way, let me beg you not to call a *trotting match* a *race,* and not to speak of a "thoroughbred" as a "*blooded*" horse, unless he has been recently phlebotomized. I consent to your saying "blood horse," if you like.

*We have beaten in many races in England since this was written, and at last carried off the blue ribbon of the turf at Epsom. But up to the present time trotting matches and base-ball are distinctively American, as contrasted with running races and cricket, which belong, as of right, to England. The wonderful effects of breeding and training in a particular direction are shown in the records of the trotting horse. In 1844 Lady Suffolk trotted a mile in 2:26½, which was, I think, the fastest time to that date. In 1859 Flora Temple's time at Kalamazoo—I remember Mr. Emerson surprised me once by correcting my error of a quarter of a second in mentioning it—was 2:19¾. Dexter in 1867 brought the figure down to 2:17¼. There is now a whole class of horses that can trot under 2:20, and in 1881 Maud S. distanced all previous records with 2:10¼. Many of our best running horses go to England. Racing in distinction from trotting, I think, attracts less attention in this country now than in the days of American Eclipse, and Henry. [Author's note.]

Also, if, next year, we send out Posterior and Posterioress, the winners of the great national four-mile race in 7:18½, and they happen to get beaten, pay your bets, and behave like men and gentlemen about it, if you know how.

[I felt a great deal better after blowing off the ill-temper condensed in the above paragraph. To brag little, —to show well,—to crow gently, if in luck,—to pay up, to own up, and to shut up, if beaten, are the virtues of a sporting man, and I can't say that I think we have shown them in any great perfection of late.]

—Apropos of horses. Do you know how important good jockeying is to authors? Judicious management; letting the public see your animal just enough, and not too much; holding him up hard when the market is too full of him; letting him out at just the right buying intervals; always gently feeling his mouth; never slacking and never jerking the rein;—this is what I mean by jockeying.

—When an author has a number of books out a cunning hand will keep them all spinning, as Signor Blitz does his dinner-plates; fetching each one up, as it begins to "wabble," by an advertisement, a puff, or a quotation.

—Whenever the extracts from a living writer begin to multiply fast in the papers, without obvious reason, there is a new book or a new edition coming. The extracts are *ground-bait*.

—Literary life is full of curious phenomena. I don't know that there is anything more noticeable than what we may call *conventional reputations*. There is a tacit understanding in every community of men of letters that they will not disturb the popular fallacy respecting this or that electro-gilded celebrity. There are various reasons for this forbearance: one is old; one is rich; one is good-natured; one is such a favorite with the pit that it would not be safe to hiss him from the manager's box. The venerable augurs of the literary or scientific temple may smile faintly when one of the tribe is mentioned; but the farce is in general kept up as well as the Chinese comic scene of entreating and imploring a man to stay with you, with the implied compact between you that he shall by no means think of doing it. A poor wretch he must be who would wantonly sit down on one of these bandbox reputations. A Prince-Rupert's-drop, which is a tear of unannealed glass, lasts indefinitely, if you keep it from meddling hands; but break its tail off, and it explodes and resolves itself into powder. These celebrities I speak of are the Prince-Rupert's-drops of the learned and polite world. See how the papers treat them! What an array of pleasant kaleidoscopic phrases, which can be arranged in ever so many charming patterns, is at their service! How kind the "Critical Notices"—where small authorship comes to pick up chips of praise, fragrant, sugary and sappy—always are to them! Well, life would be nothing without paper-credit and other fictions; so let them pass current. Don't steal their chips; don't puncture their swimming-bladders; don't come down on their pasteboard boxes; don't break the ends of their brittle and unstable reputations, you fellows who all feel sure that your names will be household words a thousand years from now.

"A thousand years is a good while," said the old gentleman who sits opposite, thoughtfully.

—Where have I been for the last three or four days? Down at the Island,* deer-shooting.—How many did I bag? I brought home one buck shot.—The Island is where? No matter. It is the most splendid domain that any man looks upon in these latitudes. Blue sea around it, and running up into its heart, so that the little boat slumbers like a baby in lap, while the tall ships are stripping naked to fight the hurricane outside, and storm-stay-sails banging and flying in ribbons. Trees, in stretches of miles; beeches, oaks, most numerous; —many of them hung with moss, looking like bearded Druids; some coiled in the clasp of huge, dark-stemmed grape-vines. Open patches where the sun gets in and goes to sleep, and the winds come so finely sifted that they are as soft as swan's-down. Rocks scattered about,—Stonehenge-like monoliths. Fresh-water lakes; one of them, Mary's lake, crystal-clear, full of flashing pickerel lying under the lily-pads like tigers in the jungle. Six pounds of ditto killed one morning for breakfast. EGO *fecit*.

The divinity-student looked as if he would like to question my Latin. No sir, I said,—you need not trouble yourself. There is a higher law in grammar not to be put down by Andrews and Stoddard. Then I went on.

Such hospitality as that island has seen there has not been the like of in these our New England sovereignties. There is nothing in the shape of kindness and courtesy that can make life beautiful, which has not found its home in that ocean-principality. It has welcomed all who were worthy of welcome, from the pale clergyman who came to breathe the sea-air with its medicinal salt and iodine, to the great statesman who turned his back on the affairs of empire, and smoothed his Olympian forehead, and flashed his white teeth in merriment over the long table, where his wit was the keenest and his story the best.

[I don't believe any man ever talked like that in this world. I don't believe *I* talked just so; but the fact is, in reporting one's conversation, one cannot help *Blair*-ing it up more or less, ironing out crumpled paragraphs, starching limps ones, and crimping and plaiting a little sometimes; it is as natural as prinking at the looking-glass.]

How can a man help writing poetry in such a place? Everybody does write poetry that goes there. In the state archives, kept in the library of the Lord of the Isle, are whole volumes of unpublished verse,—some by well-known hands, and others quite as good, by the last people you would think of as versifiers,—men who could pension off all the genuine poets in the country, and buy ten acres of Boston common, if it was for sale, with what they had left. Of course I had to write my little copy of verses with the rest; here it is, if you will hear me read it. When the sun is in the west, vessels sailing in an easterly direction look bright or dark to one

*The beautiful island referred to is Naushon, the largest of a group lying between Buzzard's Bay and the Vineyard Sound, south of the main land of Massachusetts. It is the noblest domain in New England, and the present Lord of the Manor is worthy of succeeding "the Governor" of blessed memory. [Author's note.]

who observes them from the north or south, according to the tack they are sailing upon. Watching them from one of the windows of the great mansion, I saw these perpetual changes, and moralized thus:—

### SUN AND SHADOW

As I look from the isle, o'er its billows of green,
To the billows of foam-crested blue,
Yon bark, that afar in the distance is seen,
Half dreaming, my eyes will pursue:
Now dark in the shadow, she scatters the spray
As the chaff in the stroke of the flail;
Now white as the sea-gull, she flies on her way,
The sun gleaming bright on her sail.

Yet her pilot is thinking of dangers to shun,—
Of breakers that whiten and roar;
How little he cares, if in shadow or sun
They see him that gaze from the shore!
He looks to the beacon that looms from the reef,
To the rock that is under his lee,
As he drifts on the blast, like a wind-wafted leaf,
O'er the gulfs of the desolate sea.

Thus drifting afar to the dim-vaulted caves
Where life and its ventures are laid,
The dreamers who gaze while we battle the waves
May see us in sunshine or shade;
Yet true to our course, though our shadow grow dark,
We'll trim our broad sail as before,
And stand by the rudder that governs the bark,
Nor ask how we look from the shore!

—Insanity is often the logic of an accurate mind overtasked. Good mental machinery ought to break its own wheels and levers, if anything is thrust among them suddenly which tends to stop them or reverse their motion. A weak mind does not accumulate force enough to hurt itself; stupidity often saves a man from going mad. We frequently see persons in insane hospitals, sent there in consequence of what are called *religious* mental disturbances. I confess that I think better of them than of many who hold the same notions, and keep their wits and appear to enjoy life very well, outside of the asylums. Any decent person ought to go mad, if he really holds such or such opinions. It is very much to his discredit in every point of view, if he does not. What is the use of my saying what some of these opinions are? Perhaps more than one of you hold such as I should think ought to send you straight over to Somerville, if you have any logic in your heads or any human feeling in your hearts. Anything that is brutal, cruel, heathenish, that makes life hopeless for the most of mankind and perhaps for entire races,—anything that assumes the necessity of the extermination of instincts which were given to be regulated,—no matter by what name you call it,—no matter whether a fakir, or a monk, or a deacon believes it,—if received, ought to produce insanity in every well-regulated mind. That condition becomes a normal one, under the circumstances. I am very much ashamed of some people for retaining their reason, when they know perfectly well that if they were not the most stupid or the most selfish of human beings, they would become *non-compotes* at once.

[Nobody understood this but the theological student and the schoolmistress. They looked intelligently at each other; but whether they were thinking about my paradox or not, I am not clear.—It would be natural enough. Stranger things have happened. Love and Death enter boarding-houses without asking the price of board, or whether there is room for them. Alas! these young people are poor and pallid! Love *should* be both rich and rosy, but *must* be either rich or rosy. Talk about military duty! What is that to the warfare of a married maid-of-all-work, with the title of mistress, and an American female constitution, which collapses just in the middle third of life, and comes out vulcanized India-rubber, if it happen to live through the period when health and strength are most wanted?]

—Have I ever acted in private theatricals? Often. I have played the part of the "Poor Gentleman," before a great many audiences,—more, I trust, than I shall ever face again. I did not wear a stage-costume, nor a wig, nor moustaches of burnt cork, but I was placarded and announced as a public performer, and at the proper hour I came forward with the ballet-dancer's smile upon my countenance, and made my bow and acted my part. I have seen my name stuck up in letters so big that I was ashamed to show myself in the place by daylight. I have gone to a town with a sober literary essay in my pocket, and seen myself everywhere announced as the most desperate of *buffos,*—one who was obliged to restrain himself in the full exercise of his powers, from prudential considerations. I have been through as many hardships as Ulysses, in the pursuit of my histrionic vocation. I have travelled in cars until the conductors all knew me like a brother. I have run off the rails, and stuck all night in snow-drifts, and sat behind females that would have the window open when one could not wink without his eyelids freezing together. Perhaps I shall give you some of my experiences one of these days;—I will not now, for I have something else for you.

Private theatricals, as I have figured in them in country lyceum-halls, are one thing,—and private theatricals, as they may be seen in certain gilded and frescoed saloons of our metropolis, are another. Yes, it is pleasant to see real gentlemen and ladies, who do not think it necessary to mouth, and rant, and stride, like most of our stage heroes and heroines, in the characters which show off their graces and talents; most of all to see a fresh, unrouged, unspoiled, high-bred young maiden, with a lithe figure, and a pleasant voice, acting in those love-dramas which make us young again to look upon, when real youth and beauty will play them for us.

—Of course I wrote the prologue I was asked to write. I did not see the play, though. I knew there was a young lady in it, and that somebody was in love with her, and she was in love with him, and somebody (an old tutor, I believe) wanted to interfere, and, very naturally, the young lady was too sharp for him. The play of course ends charmingly; there is a general reconciliation, and all concerned form a line and take each other's hands, as people always do after they have made up their quarrels,—and then the curtain falls,—if it does not stick, as it commonly does at private theatrical exhibitions, in which case a boy is detailed to pull it down, which he does, blushing violently.

Now, then, for my prologue. I am

not going to change my caesuras and cadences for anybody; so if you do not like the heroic, or iambic trimeter brachycatalectic, you had better not wait to hear it.

## THIS IS IT

A Prologue? Well, of course the ladies know;—
I have my doubts. No matter,—here we go!
What is a prologue? Let our Tutor teach:
*Pro* means beforehand; *logus* stands for speech.
'Tis like the harper's prelude on the strings,
The prima donna's courtesy ere she sings.
"The world's a stage,"—as Shakespeare said, one day;
The stage a world—was what he meant to say.
The outside world's a blunder, that is clear;
The real world that Nature meant is here.
Here every foundling finds its lost mamma;
Each rogue, repentant, melts his stern papa;
Misers relent, the spendthrift's debts are paid,
The cheats are taken in the traps they laid;
One after one the troubles all are past
Till the fifth act comes right side up at last,
When the young couple, old folks, rogues, and all,
Join hands, *so* happy at the curtain's fall.
—Here suffering virtue ever finds relief,
And black-browed ruffians always come to grief,
—When the lorn damsel, with a frantic speech,
And cheeks as hueless as a brandy-peach,
Cries, "Help, kyind Heaven!" and drops upon her knees
On the green—baize,—beneath the (canvas) trees,—
See to her side avenging Valor fly:—
"Ha! Villain! Draw! Now, Terraitorr, yield or die!"
—When the poor hero flounders in despair,
Some dear lost uncle turns up millionaire,—
Clasps the young scapegrace with paternal joy,
Sobs on his neck, *"My boy!* MY BOY!! MY BOY!!!"

Ours, then, sweet friends, the real world to-night
Of love that conquers in disaster's spite.
Ladies, attend! While woful cares and doubt
Wrong the soft passion in the world without,
Though fortune scowl, though prudence interfere,
One thing is certain: Love will triumph here!

Lords of creation, whom your ladies rule,—
The world's great masters, when you're out of school,—
Learn the brief moral of our evening's play:
Man has his will,—but woman has her way!
While man's dull spirit toils in smoke and fire,
Woman's swift instinct threads the electric wire,—
The magic bracelet stretched beneath the waves
Beats the black giant with his score of slaves.
All earthly powers confess your sovereign art
But that one rebel,—woman's wilful heart,
All foes you master; but a woman's wit
Lets daylight through you ere you know you're hit.
So, just to picture what her art can do,
Hear an old story made as good as new.

Rudolph, professor of the headsman's trade,
Alike was famous for his arm and blade.
One day a prisoner Justice had to kill
Knelt at the block to test the artist's skill.

Bare-armed, swart-visaged, gaunt, and shaggy-browed,
Rudolph the headsman rose above the crowd.
His falchion lightened with a sudden gleam,
As the pike's armor flashes in the stream.
He sheathed his blade; he turned as if to go;
The victim knelt, still waiting for the blow.
"Why strikest not? Perform thy murderous act,"
The prisoner said. (His voice was slightly cracked.)
"Friend I *have* struck," the artist straight replied
"Wait but one moment, and yourself decide."

He held his snuff-box,—"Now then, if you please!"
The prisoner sniffed, and, with a crashing sneeze,
Off his head tumbled,—bowled along the floor,—
Bounced down the steps;—the prisoner said no more!

Woman! thy falchion is a glittering eye;
If death lurks in it, oh, how sweet to die!
Thou takest hearts as Rudolph took the head;
We die with love, and never dream we're dead!

The prologue went off very well, as I hear. No alterations were suggested by the lady to whom it was sent, so far as I know. Sometimes people criticise the poems one sends them, and suggest all sorts of improvements.* Who was that silly body that wanted Burns to alter "Scots wha hae" so as to lengthen the last line, thus?—

*"Edward!"* Chains and slavery.

Here is a little poem I sent a short time since to a committee for a certain celebration. I understood that it was to be a festive and convivial occasion, and ordered myself accordingly. It seems the president of the day was what is called a "teetotaller." I received a note from him in the following words, containing the copy subjoined, with the emendations annexed to it.

"Dear Sir,—your poem gives good satisfaction to the committee. The sentiments expressed with reference to liquor are not, however, those generally entertained by this community. I have therefore consulted the clergyman of this place, who has made some slight changes, which he thinks will remove all objections, and keep the valuable portions of the poem. Please to inform me of your charge for said poem. Our means are limited, etc., etc., etc.

"Yours with respect."

Here it is,—with the slight alterations.*

**Come! fill a fresh bumper,—for why should we go**
**logwood**
**While the ~~nectar~~ still reddens our cups as they flow!**
**decoction**
**Pour out the ~~rich juices~~ still bright with the sun,**

*I remember being asked by a celebrated man of letters to let him look over an early, but somewhat elaborate poem of mine. He read the manuscript and suggested the change of one word, which I adopted in deference to his opinion. The emendation was anything but an improvement, and in later editions the passage reads as when first written. [Author's note.]

*I recollect a British criticism of the poem "with the slight alterations," in which the writer was quite indignant at the treatment my convivial song had received. No committee, he thought, would dare to treat a Scotch author in that way. I could not help being reminded of Sydney Smith, and the surgical operation he proposed, in order to get a pleasantry into the head of a North Briton. [Author's note.]

dye-stuff
Till o'er the brimmed crystal the ~~rubies~~
shall run.
half-ripened apples
The ~~purple globed clusters~~ their life-dews
have bled;
taste sugar
How sweet is the ~~breath~~ of the ~~fragrance~~
of lead
~~they shed!~~
rank poisons *wines!!!*
For summer's ~~last roses~~ lie hid in the ~~wines~~
stable-boys
That were garnered by ~~maidens who~~
smoking long-nines.
~~laughed through the vines.~~
scowl howl scoff
Then a ~~smile~~, and a ~~glass~~, and a ~~toast~~, and
sneer
a ~~cheer~~,
strychnine and whiskey, and ratsbane
For all ~~the good wine, and we've some of~~
and beer
~~it here~~
In cellar, in pantry, in attic, in hall,
Down, down, with the tyrant that masters
~~Long live the gay servant that laughs for~~
us all!
~~us all!~~

The company said I had been shabbily treated, and advised me to charge the committee double,—which I did. But as I never got my pay, I don't know that it made much difference. I am a very particular person about having all I write printed as I write it. I require to see a proof, a revise, a re-revise, and a double re-revise, or fourth-proof rectified impression of all my productions, especially verse. A misprint kills a sensitive author. An intentional change of his text murders him. No wonder so many poets die young!

I have nothing more to report at this time, except two pieces of advice I gave to the young women at table. One relates to a vulgarism of language, which I grieve to say is sometimes heard even from female lips. The other is of more serious purport, and applies to such as contemplate a change of condition,—matrimony, in fact.

—The woman who "calc'lates" is lost.

—Put not your trust in money, but put your money in trust.

(1857) 1857

# JAMES RUSSELL LOWELL
## (1819–1891)

### I WOULD NOT HAVE THIS PERFECT LOVE OF OURS

I would not have this perfect love of ours
Grow from a single root, a single stem,
Bearing no goodly fruit, but only flowers
That idly hide life's iron diadem:
It should grow always like that Eastern tree
Whose limbs take root and spread forth constantly;
That love for one, from which there doth not spring
Wide love for all, is but a worthless thing.
Not in another world, as poets prate,
Dwell we apart above the tide of things,
High floating o'er earth's clouds on faery wings;
But our pure love doth ever elevate
Into a holy bond of brotherhood
All earthly things, making them pure and good.
(1840) 1841

### TO THE SPIRIT OF KEATS

Great soul, thou sittest with me in my room,
Uplifting me with thy vast, quiet eyes,
On whose full orbs, with kindly lustre, lies
The twilight warmth of ruddy ember-gloom:
Thy clear, strong tones will oft bring sudden bloom
Of hope secure, to him who lonely cries,
Wrestling with the young poet's agonies,
Neglect and scorn, which seem a certain doom:
Yes! the few words which, like great thunder-drops,
Thy large heart down to earth shook doubtfully,
Thrilled by the inward lightning of its might,
Serene and pure, like gushing joy of light,
Shall track the eternal chords of Destiny,
After the moon-led pulse of ocean stops.
(1841) 1841

### AS THE BROAD OCEAN ENDLESSLY UPHEAVETH

As the broad ocean endlessly upheaveth,
With the majestic beating of his heart,
The mighty tides, whereof its rightful part
Each sea-wide bay and little weed receiveth,
So, through his soul who earnestly believeth,
Life from the universal Heart doth flow,
Whereby some conquest of the eternal Woe,
By instinct of God's nature, he achieveth:
A fuller pulse of this all-powerful beauty
Into the poet's gulf-like heart doth tide,

And he more keenly feels the glorious duty
Of serving Truth, despised and crucified, —
Happy, unknowing sect or creed, to rest,
And feel God flow forever through his breast.

1844

## WENDELL PHILLIPS

He stood upon the world's broad threshold; wide
The din of battle and of slaughter rose;
He saw God stand upon the weaker side,
That sank in seeming loss before its foes:
Many there were who made great haste and sold
Unto the cunning enemy their swords,
He scorned their gifts of fame, and power, and gold,
And, underneath their soft and flowery words,
Heard the cold serpent hiss; therefore he went
And humbly joined him to the weaker part,
Fanatic named, and fool, yet well content
So he could be the nearer to God's heart,
And feel its solemn pulses sending blood
Through all the widespread veins of endless good.

1844

## TO THE DANDELION

Dear common flower, that grow'st beside the way,
Fringing the dusty road with harmless gold,
First pledge of blithesome May,
Which children pluck, and, full of pride uphold,
High-hearted buccaneers, o'erjoyed that they
An Eldorado in the grass have found,
Which not the rich earth's ample round
May match in wealth, thou art more dear to me
Than all the prouder summer-blooms may be.

Gold such as thine ne'er drew the Spanish prow
Through the primeval hush of Indian seas,
Nor wrinkled the lean brow
Of age, to rob the lover's heart of ease;
'T is the Spring's largess, which she scatters now
To rich and poor alike, with lavish hand,
Though most hearts never understand
To take it at God's value, but pass by
The offered wealth with unrewarded eye.

Thou art my tropics and mine Italy;
To look at thee unlocks a warmer clime;
The eyes thou givest me
Are in the heart, and heed not space or time:
Not in mid June the golden cuirassed bee
Feels a more summer-like warm ravishment
In the white lily's breezy tent,
His fragrant Sybaris, than I, when first
From the dark green thy yellow circles burst.

Then think I of deep shadows on the grass,
Of meadows where in sun the cattle graze,
Where, as the breezes pass,

The gleaming rushes lean a thousand ways,
Of leaves that slumber in a cloudy mass,
Or whiten in the wind, of waters blue
That from the distance sparkle through
Some woodland gap, and of a sky above,
Where one white cloud like a stray lamb doth move.

My childhood's earliest thoughts are linked with thee;
The sight of thee calls back the robin's song,
Who, from the dark old tree
Beside the door, sang clearly all day long,
And I, secure in childish piety,
Listened as if I heard an angel sing
With news from heaven, which he could bring
Fresh every day to my untainted ears
When birds and flowers and I were happy peers.

How like a prodigal doth nature seem,
When thou, for all thy gold, so common art!
Thou teachest me to deem
More sacredly of every human heart,
Since each reflects in joy its scanty gleam
Of heaven, and could some wondrous secret show,
Did we but pay the love we owe,
And with a child's undoubting wisdom look
On all these living pages of God's book.

1845

## THE PRESENT CRISIS

When a deed is done for Freedom, through the broad earth's aching breast
Runs a thrill of joy prophetic, trembling on from east to west,
And the slave, where'er he cowers, feels the soul within him climb
To the awful verge of manhood, as the energy sublime
Of a century bursts full-blossomed on the thorny stem of Time.

Through the walls of hut and palace shoots the instantaneous throe,
When the travail of the Ages wrings earth's systems to and fro;
At the birth of each new Era, with a recognizing start,
Nation wildly looks at nation, standing with mute lips apart,
And glad Truth's yet mightier man-child leaps beneath the Future's heart.

So the Evil's triumph sendeth, with a terror and a chill,
Under continent to continent, the sense of coming ill,
And the slave, where'er he cowers, feels his sympathies with God
In hot tear-drops ebbing earthward, to be drunk up by the sod,
Till a corpse crawls round unburied, delving in the nobler clod.

For mankind are one in spirit, and an instinct bears along,
Round the earth's electric circle, the swift flash of right or wrong;
Whether conscious or unconscious, yet Humanity's vast frame
Through its ocean-sundered fibres feels the gush of joy or shame;—
In the gain or loss of one race all the rest have equal claim.

Once to every man and nation comes the moment to decide,
In the strife of Truth with Falsehood, for the good or evil side;

Some great cause, God's new Messiah, offering each the bloom or blight,
Parts the goats upon the left hand, and the sheep upon the right,
And the choice goes by forever 'twixt that darkness and that light.

Hast thou chosen, O my people, on whose party thou shalt stand,
Ere the Doom from its worn sandals shakes the dust against our land?
Though the cause of Evil prosper, yet 't is Truth alone is strong,
And, albeit she wander outcast now, I see around her throng
Troops of beautiful, tall angels, to enshield her from all wrong.

Backward look across the ages and the beacon-moments see,
That, like peaks of some sunk continent, jut through Oblivion's sea;
Not an ear in court or market for the low foreboding cry
Of those Crises, God's stern winnowers, from whose feet earth's chaff must fly;
Never shows the choice momentous till the judgment hath passed by.

Careless seems the great Avenger; history's pages but record
One death-grapple in the darkness 'twixt old systems and the Word;
Truth forever on the scaffold, Wrong forever on the throne,—
Yet that scaffold sways the future, and, behind the dim unknown,
Standeth God within the shadow, keeping watch above his own.

We see dimly in the Present what is small and what is great,
Slow of faith how weak an arm may turn the iron helm of fate,
But the soul is still oracular; amid the market's din,
List the ominous stern whisper from the Delphic cave within,—
"They enslave their children's children who make compromise with sin."

Slavery, the earth-born Cyclops, fellest of the giant brood,
Sons of brutish Force and Darkness, who have drenched the earth with blood,
Famished in his self-made desert, blinded by our purer day,
Gropes in yet unblasted regions for his miserable prey;—
Shall we guide his gory fingers where our helpless children play?

Then to side with Truth is noble when we share her wretched crust,
Ere her cause bring fame and profit, and 't is prosperous to be just;
Then it is the brave man chooses, while the coward stands aside,
Doubting in his abject spirit, till his Lord is crucified,
And the multitude make virtue of the faith they had denied.

Count me o'er earth's chosen heroes,—they were souls that stood alone,
While the men they agonized for hurled the contumelious stone,
Stood serene, and down the future saw the golden beam incline
To the side of perfect justice, mastered by their faith divine,
By one man's plain truth to manhood and to God's supreme design.

By the light of burning heretics Christ's bleeding feet I track,
Toiling up new Calvaries ever with the cross that turns not back,
And these mounts of anguish number how each generation learned
One new word of that grand *Credo* which in prophet-hearts hath burned
Since the first man stood God-conquered with his face to heaven upturned.

For Humanity sweeps onward: where to-day the martyr stands,
On the morrow crouches Judas with the silver in his hands;
Far in front the cross stands ready and the crackling fagots burn,
While the hooting mob of yesterday in silent awe return
To glean up the scattered ashes into History's golden urn.

'T is as easy to be heroes as to sit the idle slaves
Of a legendary virtue carved upon our fathers' graves,
Worshippers of light ancestral make the present light a crime;—
Was the Mayflower launched by cowards, steered by men behind their time?
Turn those tracks toward Past or Future, that make Plymouth Rock sublime?

They were men of present valor, stalwart old iconoclasts,
Unconvinced by axe or gibbet that all virtue was the Past's;
But we make their truth our falsehood, thinking that hath made us free,
Hoarding it in mouldy parchments, while our tender spirits flee
The rude grasp of that great Impulse which drove them across the sea.

They have rights who dare maintain them; we are traitors to our sires,
Smothering in their holy ashes Freedom's new-lit altar fires;
Shall we make their creed our jailer? Shall we, in our haste to slay,
From the tombs of the old prophets steal the funeral lamps away
To light up the martyr-fagots round the prophets of to-day?

New occasions teach new duties; Time makes ancient good uncouth;
They must upward still, and onward, who would keep abreast of Truth;
Lo, before us gleam her camp-fires! we ourselves must Pilgrims be,
Launch our Mayflower, and steer boldly through the desperate winter sea,
Nor attempt the Future's portal with the Past's blood-rusted key.

(1844) 1845

## BEAVER BROOK

Hushed with broad sunlight lies the hill,
And, minuting the long day's loss,
The cedar's shadow, slow and still,
Creeps o'er its dial of gray moss.

Warm noon brims full the valley's cup,
The aspen's leaves are scarce astir,
Only the little mill sends up
Its busy, never-ceasing burr.

Climbing the loose-piled wall that hems
The road along the mill-pond's brink,
From 'neath the arching barberry-stems,
My footstep scares the shy chewink.

Beneath a bony buttonwood
The mill's red door lets forth the din;
The whitened miller, dust-imbued,
Flits past the square of dark within.

No mountain torrent's strength is here;
Sweet Beaver, child of forest still,
Heaps its small pitcher to the ear,
And gently waits the miller's will.

Swift slips Undine along the race
Unheard, and then, with flashing bound,

Floods the dull wheel with light and
grace,
And, laughing, hunts the loath drudge
round.

The miller dreams not at what cost
The quivering mill stones hum and
whirl,
Nor how for every turn, are tost
Armfuls of diamonds and of pearl.

But summer cleared my happier eyes
With drops of some celestial juice,
To see how Beauty underlies
For evermore each form of Use.

And more; methought I saw that
flood,
Which now so dull and darkling steals,
Thick, here and there, with human
blood,
To turn the world's laborious wheels.

No more than doth the miller there,
Shut in our several cells, do we
Know with what waste of beauty rare
Moves every day's machinery.

Surely the wiser time shall come
When this fine overplus of might,
No longer sullen, slow, and dumb,
Shall leap to music and to light.

In that new childhood of the Earth
Life of itself shall dance and play,
Fresh blood in Time's shrunk veins
make mirth,
And labor meet delight half-way.

1848

## THE BIRCH-TREE

Rippling through thy branches goes
the sunshine,
Among thy leaves that palpitate forever;
Ovid in thee a pining Nymph had
prisoned,
The soul once of some tremulous inland river,
Quivering to tell her woe, but, ah!
dumb, dumb forever!

While all the forest, witched with
slumberous moonshine,
Holds up its leaves in happy, happy
stillness,
Waiting the dew, with breath and
pulse suspended,
I hear afar thy whispering, gleamy
islands,
And track thee wakeful still amid the
wide-hung silence.

On the brink of some wood-nestled
lakelet,
Thy foliage, like the tresses of a
Dryad,
Dripping round thy slim white stem,
whose shadow
Slopes quivering down the water's
dusky quiet,
Thou shrink'st as on her bath's edge
would some startled Naiad.

Thou art the go-between of rustic
lovers;
Thy white bark has their secrets in its
keeping;
Reuben writes here the happy name of
Patience,
And thy lithe boughs hang murmuring
and weeping
Above her, as she steals the mystery
from thy keeping.

Thou art to me like my beloved
maiden,
So frankly coy, so full of trembly confidences;
Thy shadow scarce seems shade, thy
pattering leaflets
Sprinkle their gathered sunshine o'er
my senses,
And Nature gives me all her summer
confidences.

Whether my heart with hope or sorrow tremble,
Thou sympathizest still; wild and unquiet,

I fling me down; thy ripple, like a river,
Flows valleyward, where calmness is, and by it
My heart is floated down into the land of quiet.

1848

## THE BIGLOW PAPERS [FIRST SERIES]

### NO. I

### A LETTER

FROM MR. EZEKIEL BIGLOW OF JAALAM TO THE HON. JOSEPH T. BUCKINGHAM, EDITOR OF THE BOSTON COURIER, INCLOSING A POEM OF HIS SON, MR. HOSEA BIGLOW

JAYLEM, june 1846.

MISTER EDDYTER:—Our Hosea wuz down to Boston last week, and he see a cruetin Sarjunt a struttin round as popler as a hen with 1 chicking, with 2 fellers a drummin and fifin arter him like all nater. the sarjunt he thout Hosea hed n't gut his i teeth cut cos he looked a kindo 's though he 'd jest com down, so he cal'lated to hook him in, but Hosy wood n't take none o' his sarse for all he hed much as 20 Rooster's tales stuck onto his hat and eenamost enuf brass a bobbin up and down on his shoulders and figureed onto his coat and trousis, let alone wut nater hed sot in his featers, to make a 6 pounder out on.

wal, Hosea he com home considerabal riled, and arter I 'd gone to bed I heern Him a thrashin round like a short-tailed Bull in fli-time. The old Woman ses she to me ses she, Zekle, ses she, our Hosee 's gut the chollery or suthin anuther ses she, do n't you Bee skeered, ses I, he 's oney amakin pottery* ses i, he 's ollers on hand at that ere busynes like Da & martin, and shure enuf, cum mornin, Hosy he cum down stares full chizzle, hare on eend and cote tales flyin, and sot rite of to go reed his varses to Parson Wilbur bein he haint aney grate shows o' book larnin himself, bimeby he cum back and sed the parson wuz dreffle tickled with 'em as i hoop you will Be, and said they wuz True grit.

Hosea ses taint hardly fair to call 'em hisn now, cos the parson kind o' slicked off sum o' the last varses, but he told Hosee he did n't want to put his ore in to tetch to the Rest on 'em, bein they wuz verry well As thay wuz, and then Hosy ses he sed suthin a nuther about Simplex Mundishes or sum sech feller, but I guess Hosea kind o' did n't hear him, for I never hearn o' nobody o' that name in this villadge, and I 've lived here man and boy 76 year cum next tater diggin, and thair aint no wheres a kitting spryer 'n I be.

If you print 'em I wish you 'd jest let folks know who hosy's father is, cos my ant Keziah used to say it 's nater to be curus ses she, she ain't livin though and he 's a likely kind o' lad.

EZEKIEL BIGLOW.

---

Thrash away, you 'll *hev* to rattle
  On them kittle-drums o' yourn,—
'T aint a knowin' kind o' cattle
  Thet is ketched with mouldy corn;
Put in stiff, you fifer feller,
  Let folks see how spry you be,—
Guess you 'll toot till you are yeller
  'Fore you git ahold o' me!

Thet air flag 's a leetle rotten,
  Hope it aint your Sunday's best;—
Fact! it takes a sight o' cotton
  To stuff out a soger's chest:
Sence we farmers hev to pay fer 't,
  Ef you must wear humps like these,
S'posin' you should try salt hay fer 't,
  It would du ez slick ez grease.

'T would n't suit them Southun fellers,
  They 're a dreffle graspin' set,
We must ollers blow the bellers
  Wen they want their irons het;

*Aut insanit, aut versos facit.—H. W.*

May be it 's all right ez preachin',
But *my* narves it kind o' grates,
Wen I see the overreachin'
O' them nigger-drivin' States.

Them thet rule us, them slave-traders,
Haint they cut a thunderin' swarth
(Helped by Yankee renegaders),
Thru the vartu o' the North!
We begin to think it 's nater
To take sarse an' not be riled;—
Who 'd expect to see a tater
All on eend at bein' biled?

Ez fer war, I call it murder,—
There you hev it plain an' flat;
I do n't want to go no furder
Than my Testyment fer that;
God hez sed so plump an' fairly,
It 's ez long ez it is broad,
An' you 've gut to git up airly
Ef you want to take in God.

'T aint your eppyletts an' feathers
Make the thing a grain more right;
'T aint afollerin' your bell-wethers
Will excuse ye in His sight;
Ef you take a sword an' dror it,
An' go stick a feller thru,
Guv'ment aint to answer for it,
God 'll send the bill to you.

Wut 's the use o' meetin'-goin'
Every Sabbath, wet or dry,
Ef it 's right to go amowin'
Feller-men like oats an' rye?
I dunno but wut it 's pooty
Trainin' round in bobtail coats,—
But it 's curus Christian dooty
This 'ere cuttin' folks's throats.

They may talk o' Freedom's airy
Tell they 're pupple in the face,—
It 's a grand gret cemetary
Fer the barthrights of our race;
They jest want this Californy
So 's to lug new slave-states in
To abuse ye, an' to scorn ye,
An' to plunder ye like sin.

Aint it cute to see a Yankee
Take sech everlastin' pains,
All to git the Devil's thankee
Helpin' on 'em weld their chains?
Wy, it 's jest ez clear ez figgers,
Clear ez one an' one make two,
Chaps thet make black slaves o' niggers
Want to make wite slaves o' you.

Tell ye jest the eend I 've come to
Arter cipherin' plaguy smart,
An' it makes a handy sum, tu,
Any gump could larn by heart;
Laborin' man an' laborin' woman
Hev one glory an' one shame.
Ev'y thin' thet 's done inhuman
Injers all on 'em the same.

'T aint by turnin' out to hack folks
You 're agoin' to git your right,
Nor by lookin' down on black folks
Coz you 're put upon by wite;
Slavery aint o' nary color,
'T aint the hide thet makes it wus,
All it keers fer in a feller
'S jes to make him fill its pus.

Want to tackle *me* in, du ye?
I expect you 'll hev to wait;
Wen cold lead puts daylight thru ye
You 'll begin to kal'late;
S'pose the crows wun't fall to pickin'
All the carkiss from your bones,
Coz you helped to give a lickin'
To them poor half-Spanish drones?

Jest go home an' ask our Nancy
Wether I 'd be sech a goose
Ez to jine ye,—guess you 'd fancy
The etarnal bung wuz loose!
She wants me fer home consumption,
Let alone the hay 's to mow,—
Ef you 're arter folks o' gumption,
You 've a darned long row to hoe.

Take them editors thet 's crowin'
Like a cockerel three months old,—
Do n't ketch any on 'em goin',
Though they *be* so blasted bold;

*Aint* they a prime lot o' fellers?
'Fore they think on 't guess they 'll sprout
(Like a peach thet 's got the yellers),
With the meanness bustin' out.

Wal, go 'long to help 'em stealin'
Bigger pens to cram with slaves,
Help the men thet 's ollers dealin'
Insults on your fathers' graves;
Help the strong to grind the feeble,
Help the many agin the few,
Help the men thet call your people
Witewashed slaves an' peddlin' crew!

Massachusetts, God forgive her,
She 's akneelin' with the rest,
She, thet ough' to ha' clung ferever
In her grand old eagle-nest;
She thet ough' to stand so fearless
W'ile the wracks are round her hurled,
Holdin' up a beacon peerless
To the oppressed of all the world!

Ha'n't they sold your colored seamen?
Ha'n't they made your env'ys w'iz?
*Wut* 'll make ye act like freemen?
*Wut* 'll git your dander riz?
Come, I 'll tell ye wut I 'm thinkin'
Is our dooty in this fix,
They 'd ha' done 't ez quick ez winkin'
In the days o' seventy-six.

Clang the bells in every steeple,
Call all true men to disown
The tradoocers of our people,
The enslavers o' their own;
Let our dear old Bay State proudly
Put the trumpet to her mouth,
Let her ring this messidge loudly
In the ears of all the South:—

"I 'll return ye good for evil
Much ez we frail mortils can,
But I wun't go help the Devil
Makin' man the cus o' man;
Call me coward, call me traiter,
Jest ez suits your mean idees,—
Here I stand a tyrant-hater,
An' the friend o' God an' Peace!"

Ef I 'd *my* way I hed ruther
We should go to work an' part,
They take one way, we take t' other,
Guess it would n't break my heart;
Man hed ough' to put asunder
Them thet God has noways jined;
An' I should n't gretly wonder
Ef there 's thousands o' my mind.

(1846) 1846

## NO. III

## WHAT MR. ROBINSON THINKS

[A few remarks on the following verses will not be out of place. The satire in them was not meant to have any personal, but only a general, application. Of the gentleman upon whose letter they were intended as a commentary Mr. Biglow had never heard, till he saw the letter itself. The position of the satirist is oftentimes one which he would not have chosen, had the election been left to himself. In attacking bad principles, he is obliged to select some individual who has made himself their exponent, and in whom they are impersonate, to the end that what he says may not, through ambiguity, be dissipated *tenues in auras*. For what says Seneca? *Longum iter per præcepta breve et efficace per exempla.* A bad principle is comparatively harmless while it continues to be an abstraction, nor can the general mind comprehend it fully till it is printed in that large type which all men can read at sight, namely, the life and character, the sayings and doings, of particular persons. It is one of the cunningest fetches of Satan, that he never exposes himself directly to our arrows, but, still dodging behind this neighbor or that acquaintance, compels us to wound him through them, if at all. He holds our affections as hostages, the while he patches up a truce with our conscience.

Meanwhile, let us not forget that the aim of the true satirist is not to be severe upon persons, but only upon falsehood, and, as Truth and Falsehood start from the same point, and sometimes even go along together for a little way, his business is to follow the path of the latter after it diverges, and to show her floundering in the bog at the end of it. Truth is quite beyond the reach of satire. There is so brave a simplicity in her, that she can no more be made ridiculous than an oak or a pine. The danger of the satirist is, that continual use may deaden his sensibility to the force of language. He becomes more and more liable to strike harder than he knows or intends. He may be careful to put on his boxing-gloves, and yet forget that, the older they grow, the more plainly may the knuckles inside be felt. Moreover, in the heat of contest, the eye is insensibly drawn to the crown of victory, whose tawdry tinsel glitters through that dust of the ring which obscures Truth's wreath of simple leaves. I have sometimes thought that my young friend, Mr. Biglow, needed a monitory hand laid on his arm,—*aliquid sufflaminandus erat.* I have never thought it good husbandry to water tender plants of reform with *aqua fortis,* yet, where so much is to do in the beds, he were a sorry gardener who should wage a whole day's war with an iron scuffle on those ill weeds that make the garden-walks of life unsightly, when a sprinkle of Attic salt will wither them up. *Est ars etiam maledicendi,* says Scaliger, and truly it is a hard thing to say where the graceful gentleness of the lamb merges in downright sheepishness. We may conclude with worthy and wise Dr. Fuller, that "one may be a lamb in private wrongs, but in hearing general affronts to goodness they are asses which are not lions."—H. W.]

Guvener B. is a sensible man;
He stays to his home an' looks arter his folks;
He draws his furrer ez straight ez he can,
An' into nobody's tater-patch pokes;
But John P.
Robinson he
Sez he wunt vote fer Guvener B.

My! aint it terrible? Wut shall we du?
We can't never choose him o' course,—thet 's flat;
Guess we shall hev to come round, (do n't you?)
An' go in fer thunder an' guns, an' all that;
Fer John P.
Robinson he
Sez he wunt vote fer Guvener B.

Gineral C. is a dreffle smart man:
He 's ben on all sides thet give places or pelf;
But consistency still wuz a part of his plan,—
He 's ben true to *one* party,—an' thet is himself;—
So John P.
Robinson he
Sez he shall vote fer Gineral C.

Gineral C. he goes in fer the war;
He do n't vally princerple more 'n an old cud;
Wut did God make us raytional creeturs fer,
But glory an' gunpowder, plunder an' blood?
So John P.
Robinson he
Sez he shall vote fer Gineral C.

We were gittin' on nicely up here to our village,
With good old idees o' wut 's right an' wut aint,
We kind o' thought Christ went agin war an' pillage,
An' thet eppyletts worn't the best mark of a saint;
But John P.
Robinson he

Sez this kind o' thing 's an exploded idee.

The side of our country must ollers be took,
An' President Polk, you know, *he* is our country.
An' the angel thet writes all our sins in a book
Puts the *debit* to him, an' to us the *per contry;*
An' John P.
Robinson he
Sez this is his view o' the thing to a T.

Parson Wilbur he calls all these argimunts lies;
Sez they 're nothin' on airth but jest *fee, faw, fum:*
An' thet all this big talk of our destinies
Is half on it ign'ance, an' t' other half rum;
But John P.
Robinson he
Sez it aint no sech thing; an', of course, so must we.

Parson Wilbur sez *he* never heerd in his life
Thet th' Apostles rigged out in their swallertail coats,
An' marched round in front of a drum an' a fife,
To git some on 'em office, an' some on 'em votes;
But John P.
Robinson he
Sez they did n't know everythin' down in Judee.

Wal, it 's a marcy we 've gut folks to tell us
The rights an' the wrongs o' these matters, I vow,—
God sends country lawyers, an' other wise fellers,
To start the world's team wen it gits in a slough;
Fer John P.
Robinson he
Sez the world 'll go right, ef he hollers out Gee!

(1847) 1847

READER! *walk up at once (it will soon be too late) and buy at a perfectly ruinous rate*

A

## FABLE FOR CRITICS

OR, BETTER,

*(I like, as a thing that the reader's first fancy may strike,*
*an old-fashioned title-page,*
*such as presents a tabular view of the volume's contents,)*

## A GLANCE

AT A FEW OF OUR LITERARY PROGENIES

(*Mrs. Malaprop's word*)

FROM

## THE TUB OF DIOGENES;

A VOCAL AND MUSICAL MEDLEY,

THAT IS,

A SERIES OF JOKES

**By a Wonderful Quiz,**

*who accompanies himself with a rub-a-dub-dub, full of spirit and grace, on the top of the tub.*

Set forth in October, the 31st day,
In the year '48, G. P. Putnam, Broadway.

* * * "There comes Emerson first, whose rich words, every one,
Are like gold nails in temples to hang trophies on,
Whose prose is grand verse, while his verse, the Lord knows,
Is some of it pr— No, 't is not even prose,
I 'm speaking of metres; some poems have welled
From those rare depths of soul that have ne'er been excelled;
They 're not epics, but that does n't matter a pin,
In creating, the only hard thing 's to begin * * *
"But, to come back to Emerson (whom, by the way,
I believe we left waiting),—his is, we may say,
A Greek head on right Yankee shoulders, whose range
Has Olympus for one pole, for t' other the Exchange;
He seems, to my thinking (although I 'm afraid
The comparison must, long ere this, have been made),
A Plotinus-Montaigne, where the Egyptian's gold mist
And the Gascon's shrewd wit cheek-by-jowl coexist;
All admire, and yet scarcely six converts he 's got
To I do n't (nor they either) exactly know what;
For though he builds glorious temples, 't is odd
He leaves never a doorway to get in a god.
'T is refreshing to old-fashioned people like me

To meet such a primitive Pagan as he,
In whose mind all creation is duly respected
As parts of himself—just a little projected;
And who 's willing to worship the stars and the sun,
A convert to—nothing but Emerson.
So perfect a balance there is in his head,
That he talks of things sometimes as if they were dead;
Life, nature, love, God, and affairs of that sort,
He looks at as merely ideas; in short,
As if they were fossils stuck round in a cabinet,
Of such vast extent that our earth 's a mere dab in it;
Composed just as he is inclined to conjecture her,
Namely, one part pure earth, ninety-nine parts pure lecturer;
You are filled with delight at his clear demonstration,
Each figure, word, gesture, just fits the occasion,
With the quiet precision of science he 'll sort 'em,
But you can't help suspecting the whole a *post mortem*.

"There are persons, mole-blind to the soul's make and style,
Who insist on a likeness 'twixt him and Carlyle;
To compare him with Plato would be vastly fairer,
Carlyle 's the more burly, but E. is the rarer;
He sees fewer objects, but clearlier, truelier,
If C. 's as original, E. 's more peculiar;
That he 's more of a man you might say of the one,
Of the other he 's more of an Emerson;
C. 's the Titan, as shaggy of mind as of limb,—
E. the clear-eyed Olympian, rapid and slim;
The one 's two thirds Norseman, the other half Greek,
Where the one 's most abounding, the other 's to seek;
C.'s generals require to be seen in the mass,—
E.'s specialties gain if enlarged by the glass;
C. gives nature and God his own fits of the blues,
And rims common-sense things with mystical hues,—
E. sits in a mystery calm and intense,
And looks coolly around him with sharp common sense;
C. shows you how every-day matters unite
With the dim transdiurnal recesses of night,—
While E., in a plain, preternatural way,
Makes mysteries matters of mere every day;
C. draws all his characters quite *à la* Fuseli,—
Not sketching their bundles of muscles and thews illy,
He paints with a brush so untamed and profuse,
They seem nothing but bundles of muscles and thews;
E. is rather like Flaxman, lines strait and severe,
And a colorless outline, but full, round, and clear;—
To the men he thinks worthy he frankly accords
The design of a white marble statue in words.
C. labors to get at the centre, and then
Take a reckoning from there of his actions and men;

E. calmly assumes the said centre as granted,
And, given himself, has whatever is wanted. * * *

"There is Bryant, as quiet, as cool, and as dignified
As a smooth, silent iceberg, that never is ignified,
Save when by reflection 't is kindled o' nights
With a semblance of flame by the chill Northern Lights.
He may rank (Griswold says so) first bard of your nation
(There 's no doubt that he stands in supreme ice-olation),
Your topmost Parnassus he may set his heel on,
But no warm applauses come, peal following peal on,—
He 's too smooth and too polished to hang any zeal on:
Unqualified merits, I 'll grant, if you choose, he has 'em,
But he lacks the one merit of kindling enthusiasm;
If he stir you at all, it is just, on my soul,
Like being stirred up with the very North Pole.

"He is very nice reading in summer, but *inter*
*Nos,* we do n't want *extra* freezing in winter;
Take him up in the depth of July, my advice is,
When you feel an Egyptian devotion to ices.
But deduct all you can, there 's enough that 's right good in him,
He has a true soul for field, river, and wood in him;
And his heart, in the midst of brick walls, or where'er it is,
Glows, softens, and thrills with the tenderest charities—
To you mortals that delve in this trade-ridden planet?
No, to old Berkshire's hills, with their limestone and granite. * * *

"But, my dear little bardlings, do n't prick up your ears
Nor suppose I would rank you and Bryant as peers;
If I call him an iceberg, I do n't mean to say
There is nothing in that which is grand in its way;
He is almost the one of your poets that knows
How much grace, strength, and dignity lie in Repose;
If he sometimes fall short, he is too wise to mar
His thought's modest fulness by going too far;
'T would be well if your authors should all make a trial
Of what virtue there is in severe self-denial,
And measure their writings by Hesiod's staff,
Which teaches that all has less value than half.

"There is Whittier, whose swelling and vehement heart
Strains the strait-breasted drab of the Quaker apart,
And reveals the live Man, still supreme and erect,
Underneath the bemummying wrappers of sect;
There was ne'er a man born who had more of the swing
Of the true lyric bard and all that kind of thing;
And his failures arise (though he seem not to know it)
From the very same cause that has made him a poet,—
A fervor of mind which knows no separation

'Twixt simple excitement and pure inspiration,
As my Pythoness erst sometimes erred from not knowing
If 't were I or mere wind through her tripod was blowing;
Let his mind once get head in its favorite direction
And the torrent of verse bursts the dams of reflection,
While, borne with the rush of the metre along,
The poet may chance to go right or go wrong,
Content with the whirl and delirium of song;
Then his grammar 's not always correct, nor his rhymes,
And he 's prone to repeat his own lyrics sometimes,
Not his best, though, for those are struck off at white-heats
When the heart in his breast like a trip-hammer beats,
And can ne'er be repeated again any more
Than they could have been carefully plotted before:
Like old what-'s-his-name there at the battle of Hastings
(Who, however, gave more than mere rhythmical bastings),
Our Quaker leads off metaphorical fights
For reform and whatever they call human rights,
Both singing and striking in front of the war
And hitting his foes with the mallet of Thor;
*Anne haec,* one exclaims, on beholding his knocks,
*Vestis filii tui,* O leather-clad Fox?
Can that be thy son, in the battle's mid din,
Preaching brotherly love and then driving it in
To the brain of the tough old Goliath of sin,
With the smoothest of pebbles from Castaly's spring
Impressed on his hard moral sense with a sling?

"All honor and praise to the right-hearted bard
Who was true to The Voice when such service was hard,
Who himself was so free he dared sing for the slave
When to look but a protest in silence was brave. * * *

"Here 's Cooper, who 's written six volumes to show
He 's as good as a lord: well, let 's grant that he 's so;
If a person prefer that description of praise,
Why, a coronet 's certainly cheaper than bays;
But he need take no pains to convince us he 's not
(As his enemies say) the American Scott.
Choose any twelve men, and let C. read aloud
That one of his novels of which he 's most proud,
And I 'd lay any bet that, without ever quitting
Their box, they 'd be all, to a man, for acquitting.
He has drawn you one character, though, that is new,
One wildflower he 's plucked that is wet with the dew
Of this fresh Western world, and, the thing not to mince,
He has done naught but copy it ill ever since;
His Indians, with proper respect be it said,
Are just Natty Bumppo, daubed over with red,
And his very Long Toms are the same useful Nat,

Rigged up in duck pants and a sou'wester hat
(Though once in a Coffin, a good chance was found
To have slipped the old fellow away underground).
All his other men-figures are clothes upon sticks,
The *dernière chemise* of a man in a fix
(As a captain besieged, when his garrison 's small,
Sets up caps upon poles to be seen o'er the wall);
And the women he draws from one model do n't vary,
All sappy as maples and flat as a prairie.
When a character 's wanted, he goes to the task
As a cooper would do in composing a cask;
He picks out the staves, of their qualities heedful,
Just hoops them together as tight as is needful,
And, if the best fortune should crown the attempt, he
Has made at the most something wooden and empty.

"Do n't suppose I would underrate Cooper's abilities;
If I thought you 'd do that, I should feel very ill at ease;
The men who have given to *one* character life
And objective existence are not very rife;
You may number them all, both prose-writers and singers,
Without overrunning the bounds of your fingers,
And Natty won't go to oblivion quicker
Than Adams the parson or Primrose the vicar.

"There is one thing in Cooper I like, too, and that is
That on manners he lectures his countrymen gratis;
Not precisely so either, because, for a rarity,
He is paid for his tickets in unpopularity.
Now he may overcharge his American pictures,
But you 'll grant there 's a good deal of truth in his strictures;
And I honor the man who is willing to sink
Half his present repute for the freedom to think,
And, when he has thought, be his cause strong or weak,
Will risk t' other half for the freedom to speak,
Caring naught for what vengeance the mob has in store,
Let that mob be the upper ten thousand or lower. * * *

"There comes Poe, with his raven, like Barnaby Rudge,
Three fifths of him genius and two fifths sheer fudge,
Who talks like a book of iambs and pentameters,
In a way to make people of common sense damn metres,
Who has written some things quite the best of their kind,
But the heart somehow seems all squeezed out by the mind,
Who—but hey-day! What 's this? Messieurs Mathews and Poe,
You must n't fling mud-balls at Longfellow so,
Does it make a man worse that his character 's such
As to make his friends love him (as you think) too much?
Why, there is not a bard at this moment alive
More willing than he that his fellows should thrive:

While you are abusing him thus, even now
He would help either one of you out of a slough;
You may say that he 's smooth and all that till you 're hoarse,
But remember that elegance also is force;
After polishing granite as much as you will,
The heart keeps its tough old persistency still;
Deduct all you can, *that* still keeps you at bay;
Why, he 'll live till men weary of Collins and Gray.
I 'm not over-fond of Greek metres in English,
To me rhyme 's a gain, so it be not too jinglish.
And your modern hexameter verses are no more
Like Greek ones than sleek Mr. Pope is like Homer;
As the roar of the sea to the coo of a pigeon is,
So, compared to your moderns, sounds old Melesigenes;
I may be too partial, the reason, perhaps o' 't is
That I 've heard the old blind man recite his own rhapsodies,
And my ear with that music impregnate may be,
Like the poor exiled shell with the soul of the sea,
Or as one can't bear Strauss when his nature is cloven
To its deeps within deeps by the stroke of Beethoven;
But, set that aside, and 't is truth that I speak,
Had Theocritus written in English, not Greek,
I believe that his exquisite sense would scarce change a line
In that rare, tender, virgin-like pastoral Evangeline.
That 's not ancient nor modern, its place is apart
Where time has no sway, in the realm of pure Art,
'T is a shrine of retreat from Earth's hubbub and strife
As quiet and chaste as the author's own life. * * *

"There 's Holmes, who is matchless among you for wit;
A Leyden-jar always full-charged, from which flit
The electrical tingles of hit after hit;
In long poems 't is painful sometimes, and invites
A thought of the way the new Telegraph writes,
Which pricks down its little sharp sentences spitefully
As if you got more than you 'd title to rightfully,
And you find yourself hoping its wild father Lightning
Would flame in for a second and give you a fright'ning.
He has perfect sway of what *I* call a sham metre,
But many admire it, the English pentameter,
And Campbell, I think, wrote most commonly worse,
With less nerve, swing, and fire in the same kind of verse,
Nor e'er achieved aught in 't so worthy of praise
As the tribute of Holmes to the grand *Marseillaise*.
You went crazy last year over Bulwer's New Timon;—
Why, if B., to the day of his dying, should rhyme on,
Heaping verses on verses and tomes upon tomes,
He could ne'er reach the best point and vigor of Holmes.
His are just the fine hands, too, to weave you a lyric
Full of fancy, fun, feeling, or spiced with satiric

In a measure so kindly, you doubt if the toes
That are trodden upon are your own or your foes'.

"There is Lowell, who 's striving Parnassus to climb
With a whole bale of *isms* tied together with rhyme,
He might get on alone, spite of brambles and boulders,
But he can't with that bundle he has on his shoulders,
The top of the hill he will ne'er come nigh reaching
Till he learns the distinction 'twixt singing and preaching;
His lyre has some chords that would ring pretty well,
But he 'd rather by half make a drum of the shell,
And rattle away till he 's old as Methusalem,
At the head of a march to the last new Jerusalem."

## THE FIRST SNOW-FALL

The snow had begun in the gloaming,
And busily all the night
Had been heaping field and highway
With a silence deep and white.

Every pine and fir and hemlock
Wore ermine too dear for an earl,
And the poorest twig on the elm-tree
Was ridged inch deep with pearl.

From sheds new-roofed with Carrara
Came Chanticleer's muffled crow,
The stiff rails softened to swan's-down
And still fluttered down the snow.

I stood and watched by the window
The noiseless work of the sky,
And the sudden flurries of snow-birds,
Like brown leaves whirling by.

I thought of a mound in sweet Auburn
Where a little headstone stood;
How the flakes were folding it gently,
As did robins the babes in the wood.

Up spoke our own little Mabel,
Saying, "Father, who makes it snow?"
And I told of the good All-father
Who cares for us here below.

Again I looked at the snow-fall,
And thought of the leaden sky
That arched o'er our first great sorrow,
When that mound was heaped so high.

I remembered the gradual patience
That fell from that cloud like snow,
Flake by flake, healing and hiding
The scar that renewed our woe.

And again to the child I whispered,
"The snow that husheth all,
Darling, the merciful Father
Alone can make it fall!"

Then, with eyes that saw not, I kissed her;
And she, kissing back, could not know
That *my* kiss was given to her sister,
Folded close under deepening snow.

(1849) 1849

## *THE BIGLOW PAPERS, SECOND SERIES*

### THE COURTIN'

God makes sech nights, all white an' still
Fur 'z you can look or listen,
Moonshine an' snow on field an' hill,
All silence an' all glisten.

Zekle crep' up quite unbeknown
  An' peeked in thru' the winder,
An' there sot Huldy all alone,
  'ith no one nigh to hender.

A fireplace filled the room's one side
  With half a cord o' wood in—
There warn't no stoves (tell comfort died)
  To bake ye to a puddin'.

The wa'nut logs shot sparkles out
  Towards the pootiest, bless her,
An' leetle flames danced all about
  The chiny on the dresser.

Agin the chimbley crook-necks hung,
  An' in amongst 'em rusted
The ole queen's-arm thet gran'ther Young
  Fetched back f'om Concord busted.

The very room, coz she was in,
  Seemed warm f'om floor to ceilin',
An' she looked full ez rosy agin
  Ez the apples she was peelin'.

'T was kin' o' kingdom-come to look
  On sech a blessed cretur,
A dogrose blushin' to a brook
  Aint modester nor sweeter.

He was six foot o' man, A 1,
  Clear grit an' human natur',
None could n't quicker pitch a ton
  Nor dror a furrer straighter.

He 'd sparked it with full twenty gals,
  Hed squired 'em, danced 'em, druv 'em,
Fust this one, an' then thet, by spells—
  All is, he could n't love 'em.

But long o' her his veins 'ould run
  All crinkly like curled maple,
The side she breshed felt full o' sun
  Ez a south slope in Ap'il.

She thought no v'ice hed sech a swing
  Ez hisn in the choir;
My! when he made Old Hunderd ring,
  She *knowed* the Lord was nigher.

An' she 'd blush scarlit, right in prayer,
  When her new meetin'-bunnet
Felt somehow thru' its crown a pair
  O' blue eyes sot upon it.

Thet night, I tell ye, she looked *some!*
  She seemed to 've gut a new soul,
For she felt sartin-sure he 'd come,
  Down to her very shoe-sole.

She heered a foot, an' knowed it tu,
  A-raspin' on the scraper,—
All ways to once her feelin's flew
  Like sparks in burnt-up paper.

He kin' o' l'itered on the mat,
  Some doubtfle o' the sekle,
His heart kep' goin' pity-pat,
  But hern went pity Zekle.

An' yit she gin her cheer a jerk
  Ez though she wished him furder,
An' on her apples kep' to work,
  Parin' away like murder.

"You want to see my Pa, I s'pose?"
  "Wal . . . no . . . I come dasignin'"—
"To see my Ma? She 's sprinklin' clo'es
  Agin to-morrer's i'nin'."

To say why gals acts so or so,
  Or do n't, 'ould be presumin';
Mebby to mean *yes*, and say *no*
  Comes nateral to women.

He stood a spell on one foot fust,
  Then stood a spell on t' other,
An' on which one he felt the wust
  He could n't ha' told ye nuther.

Says he, "I 'd better call again;"
  Says she, "Think likely, Mister:"
Thet last word pricked him like a pin,
  An' . . . Wal, he up an' kist her.

When Ma bimeby upon 'em slips,
  Huldy sot pale ez ashes,
All kin' o' smily roun' the lips
  An' teary roun' the lashes.

For she was jes' the quiet kind
  Whose naturs never vary,
Like streams that keep a summer mind
  Snowhid in Jenooary.

The blood clost roun' her heart felt glued
  Too tight for all expressin',
Tell mother see how metters stood,
  An' gin 'em both her blessin'.

Then her red come back like the tide
  Down to the Bay o' Fundy,
An' all I know is they was cried
  In meetin' come nex' Sunday.
(1848) 1848, 1866

## JONATHAN TO JOHN

It do n't seem hardly right, John,
  When both my hands was full,
To stump me to a fight, John,—
  Your cousin, tu, John Bull!
    Ole Uncle S. sez he, "I guess
    We know it now," sez he,
"The lion's paw is all the law,
    Accordin' to J. B.,
    Thet 's fit for you an' me!"

You wonder why we 're hot, John?
  Your mark wuz on the guns,
The neutral guns, thet shot, John,
  Our brothers an' our sons:
    Ole Uncle S. sez he, "I guess
    There 's human blood," sez he,
"By fits an' starts, in Yankee hearts,
    Though 't may surprise J. B.
    More 'n it would you an' me."

Ef *I* turned mad dogs loose, John,
  On *your* front-parlor stairs,
Would it jest meet your views, John,
  To wait an' sue their heirs?
    Ole Uncle S. sez he, "I guess,
    I on'y guess," sez he,
"Thet ef Vattel on *his* toes fell,
    'T would kind o' rile J. B.,
    Ez wal ez you an' me!"

Who made the law thet hurts, John,
  *Heads I win,—ditto tails?*
*"J. B."* was on his shirts, John,
  Onless my memory fails.
    Ole Uncle S. sez he, "I guess
    (I 'm good at thet)," sez he,
"Thet sauce for goose aint *jest* the juice
    For ganders with J. B.,
    No more 'n with you or me!"

When your rights was our wrongs, John,
  You did n't stop for fuss,—
Britanny's trident prongs, John,
  Was good 'nough law for us.
    Ole Uncle S. sez he, "I guess,
    Though physic 's good," sez he,
"It does n't foller thet he can swaller
    Prescriptions signed *'J. B.,'*
    Put up by you an' me!"

We own the ocean, tu, John:
  You mus' n' take it hard,
Ef we can't think with you, John,
  It 's jest your own back-yard.
    Ole Uncle S. sez he, "I guess,
    Ef *thet 's* his claim," sez he,
"The fencin'-stuff 'll cost enough
    To bust up friend J. B.,
    Ez wal ez you an' me!"

Why talk so dreffle big, John,
  Of honor when it meant
You did n't care a fig, John,
  But jest for *ten per cent?*
    Ole Uncle S. sez he, "I guess
    He 's like the rest," sez he:
"When all is done, it 's number one
    Thet 's nearest to J. B.,
    Ez wal ez t' you an' me!"

We give the critters back, John,
  Cos Abram thought 't was right;
It warn't your bullyin' clack, John,
  Provokin' us to fight.

Ole Uncle S. sez he, "I guess
We 've a hard row," sez he,
"To hoe jes now; but thet, some-how,
May happen to J. B.,
Ez wal ez you an' me!"

We aint so weak an' poor, John,
With twenty million people,
An' close to every door, John,
A school-house an' a steeple.
Ole Uncle S. sez he, "I guess,
It is a fact," sez he,
"The surest plan to make a Man
Is, think him so, J. B.,
Ez much ez you or me!"

Our folks believe in Law, John;
An' it 's for her sake, now,
They 've left the axe an' saw, John,
The anvil an' the plough.
Ole Uncle S. sez he, "I guess,
Ef 't warn't for law," sez he,
"There 'd be one shindy from here to Indy;
An' thet do n't suit J. B.
(When 't aint 'twixt you an' me!)"

We know we 've got a cause, John,
Thet 's honest, just, an' true;
We thought 't would win applause, John,
Ef nowheres else, from you.
Ole Uncle S. sez he, "I guess
His love of right," sez he,
"Hangs by a rotten fibre o' cotton:
There 's natur' in J. B.,
Ez wal 'z in you an' me!"

The South says, *"Poor folks down!"* John,
An' *"All men up"* say we,—
White, yaller, black, an' brown, John:
Now which is your idee?
Ole Uncle S. sez he, "I guess,
John preaches wal," sez he;
"But, sermon thru, an' come to *du,*
Why, there 's the old J. B.
A-crowdin' you an' me!"

Shall it be love, or hate, John?
It 's you thet 's to decide;
Aint *your* bonds held by Fate, John,
Like all the world's beside?
Ole Uncle S. sez he, "I guess
Wise men forgive," sez he,
"But not forgit; an' some time yit
Thet truth may strike J. B.,
Ez wal ez you an' me!"

God means to make this land, John,
Clear thru, from sea to sea,
Believe an' understand, John,
The *wuth* o' bein' free.
Ole Uncle S. sez he, "I guess,
God's price is high," sez he;
"But nothin' else than wut He sells
Wears long, an' thet J. B.
May larn, like you an' me!"

1862

## ODE RECITED AT THE HARVARD COMMEMORATION

JULY 21, 1865

I

Weak-winged is song,
Nor aims at that clear-ethered height
Whither the brave deed climbs for light:
We seem to do them wrong,
Bringing our robin's-leaf to deck their hearse
Who in warm life-blood wrote their nobler verse,
Our trivial song to honor those who come
With ears attuned to strenuous trump and drum,
And shaped in squadron-strophes their desire,
Live battle-odes whose lines were steel and fire:
Yet sometimes feathered words are strong,
A gracious memory to buoy up and save

From Lethe's dreamless ooze, the common grave
Of the unventurous throng.

## II

To-day our Reverend Mother welcomes back
Her wisest Scholars, those who understood
The deeper teaching of her mystic tome,
And offered their fresh lives to make it good:
No lore of Greece or Rome,
No science peddling with the names of things,
Or reading stars to find inglorious fates,
Can lift our life with wings
Far from Death's idle gulf that for the many waits,
And lengthen out our dates
With that clear fame whose memory sings
In manly hearts to come, and nerves them and dilates:
Nor such thy teaching, Mother of us all!
Not such the trumpet-call
Of thy diviner mood,
That could thy sons entice
From happy homes and toils, the fruitful nest
Of those half-virtues which the world calls best,
Into War's tumult rude;
But rather far that stern device
The sponsors chose that round thy cradle stood
In the dim, unventured wood,
The VERITAS that lurks beneath
The letter's unprolific sheath,
Life of whate'er makes life worth living,
Seed-grain of high emprise, immortal food,
One heavenly thing whereof earth hath the giving.

## III

Many loved Truth, and lavished life's best oil
Amid the dust of books to find her,
Content at last, for guerdon of their toil,
With the cast mantle she hath left behind her.
Many in sad faith sought for her,
Many with crossed hands sighed for her;
But these, our brothers, fought for her,
At life's dear peril wrought for her,
So loved her that they died for her,
Tasting the raptured fleetness
Of her divine completeness:
Their higher instinct knew
Those love her best who to themselves are true,
And what they dare to dream of, dare to do;
They followed her and found her
Where all may hope to find,
Not in the ashes of the burnt-out mind,
But beautiful, with danger's sweetness round her.
Where faith made whole with deed
Breathes its awakening breath
Into the lifeless creed,
They saw her plumed and mailed,
With sweet, stern face unveiled,
And all-repaying eyes, look proud on them in death.

## IV

Our slender life runs rippling by, and glides
Into the silent hollow of the past;
What is there that abides
To make the next age better for the last?
Is earth too poor to give us
Something to live for here that shall outlive us?
Some more substantial boon

Than such as flows and ebbs with Fortune's fickle moon?
The little that we see
From doubt is never free;
The little that we do
Is but half-nobly true;
With our laborious hiving
What men call treasure, and the gods call dross,
Life seems a jest of Fate's contriving,
Only secure in every one's conniving,
A long account of nothings paid with loss,
Where we poor puppets, jerked by unseen wires,
After our little hour of strut and rave,
With all our pasteboard passions and desires,
Loves, hates, ambitions, and immortal fires,
Are tossed pell-mell together in the grave.
But stay! no age was e'er degenerate,
Unless men held it at too cheap a rate,
For in our likeness still we shape our fate.
Ah, there is something here
Unfathomed by the cynic's sneer,
Something that gives our feeble light
A high immunity from Night,
Something that leaps life's narrow bars
To claim its birthright with the hosts of heaven;
A seed of sunshine that can leaven
Our earthly dulness with the beams of stars,
And glorify our clay
With light from fountains elder than the Day;
A conscience more divine than we,
A gladness fed with secret tears,
A vexing, forward-reaching sense
Of some more noble permanence;
A light across the sea,
Which haunts the soul and will not let it be,
Still beaconing from the heights of undegenerate years.

V

Whither leads the path
To ampler fates that leads?
Not down through flowery meads,
To reap an aftermath
Of youth's vainglorious weeds,
But up the steep, amid the wrath
And shock of deadly-hostile creeds,
Where the world's best hope and stay
By battle's flashes gropes a desperate way,
And every turf the fierce foot clings to bleeds.
Peace hath her not ignoble wreath,
Ere yet the sharp, decisive word
Light the black lips of cannon, and the sword
Dreams in its easeful sheath;
But some day the live coal behind the thought,
Whether from Baäl's stone obscene,
Or from the shrine serene
Of God's pure altar brought,
Bursts up in flame; the war of tongue and pen
Learns with what deadly purpose it was fraught,
And, helpless in the fiery passion caught,
Shakes all the pillared state with shock of men:
Some day the soft Ideal that we wooed
Confronts us fiercely; foe-beset, pursued,
And cries reproachful: "Was it, then, my praise,
And not myself was loved? Prove now thy truth;
I claim of thee the promise of thy youth;

Give me thy life, or cower in empty phrase,
The victim of thy genius, not its mate!"
Life may be given in many ways,
And loyalty to Truth be sealed
As bravely in the closet as the field,
So bountiful is Fate;
But then to stand beside her,
When craven churls deride her,
To front a lie in arms and not to yield,
This shows, methinks, God's plan
And measure of a stalwart man,
Limbed like the old heroic breeds,
Who stands self-poised on manhood's solid earth,
Not forced to frame excuses for his birth,
Fed from within with all the strength he needs.

VI

Such was he, our Martyr-Chief,
Whom late the Nation he had led,
With ashes on her head,
Wept with the passion of an angry grief:
Forgive me, if from present things I turn
To speak what in my heart will beat and burn,
And hang my wreath on his world-honored urn.
Nature, they say, doth dote,
And cannot make a man
Save on some worn-out plan,
Repeating us by rote:
For him her Old-World moulds aside she threw,
And, choosing sweet clay from the breast
Of the unexhausted West,
With stuff untainted shaped a hero new,
Wise, steadfast in the strength of God, and true.
How beautiful to see
Once more a shepherd of mankind indeed,
Who loved his charge, but never loved to lead;
One whose meek flock the people joyed to be,
Not lured by any cheat of birth,
But by his clear-grained human worth,
And brave old wisdom of sincerity!
They knew that outward grace is dust;
They could not choose but trust
In that sure-footed mind's unfaltering skill,
And supple-tempered will
That bent like perfect steel to spring again and thrust.
His was no lonely mountain-peak of mind,
Thrusting to thin air o'er our cloudy bars,
A sea-mark now, now lost in vapors blind;
Broad prairie rather, genial, level-lined,
Fruitful and friendly for all human kind,
Yet also nigh to heaven and loved of loftiest stars.
Nothing of Europe here,
Or, then, of Europe fronting mornward still,
Ere any names of Serf and Peer
Could Nature's equal scheme deface
And thwart her genial will;
Here was a type of the true elder race,
And one of Plutarch's men talked with us face to face.
I praise him not; it were too late;
And some innative weakness there must be
In him who condescends to victory
Such as the Present gives, and cannot wait,
Safe in himself as in a fate.
So always firmly he:
He knew to bide his time,
And can his fame abide,

Still patient in his simple faith sublime,
Till the wise years decide.
Great captains, with their guns and drums,
Disturb our judgment for the hour,
But at last silence comes;
These all are gone, and, standing like a tower,
Our children shall behold his fame,
The kindly-earnest, brave, foreseeing man,
Sagacious, patient, dreading praise, not blame,
New birth of our new soil, the first American.

VII

Long as man's hope insatiate can discern
Or only guess some more inspiring goal
Outside of Self, enduring as the pole,
Along whose course the flying axles burn
Of spirits bravely-pitched, earth's manlier brood;
Long as below we cannot find
The meed that stills the inexorable mind;
So long this faith to some ideal Good,
Under whatever mortal names it masks,
Freedom, Law, Country, this ethereal mood
That thanks the Fates for their severer tasks,
Feeling its challenged pulses leap,
While others skulk in subterfuges cheap,
And, set in Danger's van, has all the boon it asks,
Shall win man's praise and woman's love,
Shall be a wisdom that we set above
All other skills and gifts to culture dear,
A virtue round whose forehead we inwreathe
Laurels that with a living passion breathe
When other crowns grow, while we twine them, sear.
What brings us thronging these high rites to pay,
And seal these hours the noblest of our year,
Save that our brothers found this better way?

VIII

We sit here in the Promised Land
That flows with Freedom's honey and milk;
But 't was they won it, sword in hand,
Making the nettle danger soft for us as silk.
We welcome back our bravest and our best;—
Ah me! not all! some come not with the rest,
Who went forth brave and bright as any here!
I strive to mix some gladness with my strain,
But the sad strings complain,
And will not please the ear:
I sweep them for a pæan, but they wane
Again and yet again
Into a dirge, and die away, in pain.
In these brave ranks I only see the gaps,
Thinking of dear ones whom the dumb turf wraps,
Dark to the triumph which they died to gain:
Fitlier may others greet the living,
For me the past is unforgiving;
I with uncovered head
Salute the sacred dead,

Who went, and who return not.—
Say not so!
'T is not the grapes of Canaan that repay,
But the high faith that failed not by the way;
Virtue treads paths that end not in the grave;
No ban of endless night exiles the brave;
And to the saner mind
We rather seem the dead that stayed behind.
Blow, trumpets, all your exultations blow!
For never shall their aureoled presence lack:
I see them muster in a gleaming row,
With ever-youthful brows that nobler show;
We find in our dull road their shining track;
In every nobler mood
We feel the orient of their spirit glow,
Part of our life's unalterable good,
Of all our saintlier aspiration;
They come transfigured back,
Secure from change in their high-hearted ways,
Beautiful evermore, and with the rays
Of morn on their white Shields of Expectation!

IX

But is there hope to save
Even this ethereal essence from the grave?
What ever 'scaped Oblivion's subtle wrong
Save a few clarion names, or golden threads of song?
Before my musing eye
The mighty ones of old sweep by,
Disvoicèd now and insubstantial things,
As noisy once as we; poor ghosts of kings,
Shadows of empire wholly gone to dust,
And many races, nameless long ago,
To darkness driven by that imperious gust
Of ever-rushing Time that here doth blow:
O visionary world, condition strange,
Where naught abiding is but only change,
Where the deep-bolted stars themselves still shift and range!
Shall we to more continuance make pretence?
Renown builds tombs; a life-estate is Wit;
And, bit by bit,
The cunning years steal all from us but woe;
Leaves are we, whose decays no harvest sow.
But, when we vanish hence,
Shall they lie forceless in the dark below,
Save to make green their little length of sods,
Or deepen pansies for a year or two,
Who now to us are shining-sweet as gods?
Was dying all they had the skill to do?
That were not fruitless: but the Soul resents
Such short-lived service, as if blind events
Ruled without her, or earth could so endure;
She claims a more divine investiture
Of longer tenure than Fame's airy rents;
Whate'er she touches doth her nature share;
Her inspiration haunts the ennobled air,
Gives eyes to mountains blind,
Ears to the deaf earth, voices to the wind,
And her clear trump sings succor everywhere

By lonely bivouacs to the wakeful mind;
For soul inherits all that soul could dare:
Yea, Manhood hath a wider span
And larger privilege of life than man.
The single deed, the private sacrifice,
So radiant now through proudly-hidden tears,
Is covered up erelong from mortal eyes
With thoughtless drift of the deciduous years;
But that high privilege that makes all men peers,
That leap of heart whereby a people rise
Up to a noble anger's height,
And, flamed on by the Fates, not shrink, but grow more bright,
That swift validity in noble veins,
Of choosing danger and disdaining shame,
Of being set on flame
By the pure fire that flies all contact base
But wraps its chosen with angelic might,
These are imperishable gains,
Sure as the sun, medicinal as light,
These hold great futures in their lusty reins
And certify to earth a new imperial race.

X

Who now shall sneer?
Who dare again to say we trace
Our lines to a plebeian race?
Roundhead and Cavalier!
Dumb are those names erewhile in battle loud;
Dream-footed as the shadow of a cloud,
They flit across the ear:
That is best blood that hath most iron in 't.
To edge resolve with, pouring without stint
For what makes manhood dear.
Tell us not of Plantagenets,
Hapsburgs, and Guelfs, whose thin bloods crawl
Down from some victor in a border-brawl!
How poor their outworn coronets,
Matched with one leaf of that plain civic wreath
Our brave for honor's blazon shall bequeath,
Through whose desert a rescued Nation sets
Her heel on treason, and the trumpet hears
Shout victory, tingling Europe's sullen ears
With vain resentments and more vain regrets!

XI

Not in anger, not in pride,
Pure from passion's mixture rude
Ever to base earth allied,
But with far-heard gratitude,
Still with heart and voice renewed,
To heroes living and dear martyrs dead,
The strain should close that consecrates our brave.
Lift the heart and lift the head!
Lofty be its mood and grave,
Not without a martial ring,
Not without a prouder tread
And a peal of exultation:
Little right has he to sing
Through whose heart in such an hour
Beats no march of conscious power,
Sweeps no tumult of elation!
'T is no Man we celebrate,
By his country's victories great,

A hero half, and half the whim of Fate,
But the pith and marrow of a Nation
Drawing force from all her men,
Highest, humblest, weakest, all,
For her time of need, and then
Pulsing it again through them,
Till the basest can no longer cower,
Feeling his soul spring up divinely tall,
Touched but in passing by her mantle-hem.
Come back, then, noble pride, for 't is her dower!
How could poet ever tower,
If his passions, hopes, and fears,
If his triumphs and his tears,
Kept not measure with his people?
Boom, cannon, boom to all the winds and waves!
Clash out, glad bells, from every rocking steeple!
Banners, advance with triumph, bend your staves!
And from every mountain-peak
Let beacon-fire to answering beacon speak,
Katahdin tell Monadnock, Whiteface he,
And so leap on in light from sea to sea,
Till the glad news be sent
Across a kindling continent,
Making earth feel more firm and air breathe braver:
"Be proud! for she is saved, and all have helped to save her!
She that lifts up the manhood of the poor,
She of the open soul and open door,
With room about her hearth for all mankind!
The fire is dreadful in her eyes no more;
From her bold front the helm she doth unbind,
Sends all her handmaid armies back to spin,
And bids her navies, that so lately hurled
Their crashing battle, hold their thunders in,
Swimming like birds of calm along the unharmful shore.
No challenge sends she to the elder world,
That looked askance and hated; a light scorn
Plays o'er her mouth, as round her mighty knees
She calls her children back, and waits the morn.
Of nobler day, enthroned between her subject seas."

XII

Bow down, dear Land, for thou hast found release!
Thy God, in these distempered days,
Hath taught thee the sure wisdom of His ways,
And through thine enemies hath wrought thy peace!
Bow down in prayer and praise!
No poorest in thy borders but may now
Lift to the juster skies a man's enfranchised brow.
O Beautiful! my Country! ours once more!
Smoothing thy gold of war-dishevelled hair
O'er such sweet brows as never other wore,
And letting thy set lips,
Freed from wrath's pale eclipse,
The rosy edges of their smile lay bare,
What words divine of lover or of poet
Could tell our love and make thee know it,
Among the Nations bright beyond compare?

What were our lives without thee?
What all our lives to save thee?
We reck not what we gave thee;
We will not dare to doubt thee,
But ask whatever else, and we will dare!

(1865) 1865

## AUSPEX

My heart, I cannot still it,
Nest that had song-birds in it;
And when the last shall go,
The dreary days to fill it,
Instead of lark or linnet,
Shall whirl dead leaves and snow.

Had they been swallows only,
Without the passion stronger
That skyward longs and sings,—
Woe 's me, I shall be lonely
When I can feel no longer
The impatience of their wings!

A moment, sweet delusion,
Like birds the brown leaves hover;
But it will not be long
Before their wild confusion
Fall wavering down to cover
The poet and his song.

1878

## CREDIDIMUS JOVEM REGNARE

O days endeared to every Muse,
When nobody had any Views,
Nor, while the cloudscape of his mind
By every breeze was new designed,
Insisted all the world should see
Camels or whales where none there be!
O happy days, when men received
From sire to son what all believed,
And left the other world in bliss,
Too busy with bedevilling this!

Beset by doubts of every breed
In the last bastion of my creed,
With shot and shell for Sabbath-chime,
I watch the storming-party climb,
Panting (their prey in easy reach),
To pour triumphant through the breach
In walls that shed like snowflakes tons
Of missiles from old-fashioned guns,
But crumble 'neath the storm that pours
All day and night from bigger bores.
There, as I hopeless watch and wait
The last life-crushing coil of Fate,
Despair finds solace in the praise
Of those serene dawn-rosy days
Ere microscopes had made us heirs
To large estates of doubts and snares,
By proving that the title-deeds,
Once all-sufficient for men's needs,
Are palimpsests that scarce disguise
The tracings of still earlier lies,
Themselves as surely written o'er
An older fib erased before.

So from these days I fly to those
That in the landlocked Past repose,
Where no rude wind of doctrine shakes
From bloom-flushed boughs untimely flakes;
Where morning's eyes see nothing strange,
No crude perplexity of change,
And morrows trip along their ways
Secure as happy yesterdays.
Then there were rulers who could trace
Through heroes up to gods their race,
Pledged to fair fame and noble use
By veins from Odin filled or Zeus,
And under bonds to keep divine
The praise of a celestial line.
Then priests could pile the altar's sods,
With whom gods spake as they with gods,
And everywhere from haunted earth
Broke springs of wonder, that had birth
In depths divine beyond the ken
And fatal scrutiny of men;
Then hills and groves and streams and seas

Thrilled with immortal presences,
Not too ethereal for the scope
Of human passion's dream or hope.

Now Pan at last is surely dead,
And King No-Credit reigns instead,
Whose officers, morosely strict,
Poor Fancy's tenantry evict,
Chase the last Genius from the door,
And nothing dances any more.
Nothing? Ah, yes, our tables do,
Drumming the Old One's own tattoo,
And, if the oracles are dumb,
Have we not mediums? Why be glum?

Fly thither? Why, the very air
Is full of hindrance and despair!
Fly thither? But I cannot fly;
My doubts enmesh me if I try,—
Each lilliputian, but, combined,
Potent a giant's limbs to bind.
This world and that are growing dark;
A huge interrogation mark,
The Devil's crook episcopal,
Still borne before him since the Fall,
Blackens with its ill-omened sign
The old blue heaven of faith benign.
Whence? Whither? Wherefore? How? Which? Why?
All ask at once, all wait reply.
Men feel old systems cracking under 'em;
Life saddens to a mere conundrum
Which once Religion solved, but she
Has lost—has Science found?—the key.

What was snow-bearded Odin, trow,
The mighty hunter long ago,
Whose horn and hounds the peasant hears
Still when the Northlights shake their spears?
Science hath answers twain, I 've heard;
Choose which you will, nor hope a third;
Whichever box the truth be stowed in,
There 's not a sliver left of Odin.
Either he was a pinchbrowed thing,
With scarcely wit a stone to fling,
A creature both in size and shape
Nearer than we are to the ape,
Who hung sublime with brat and spouse
By tail prehensile from the boughs,
And, happier than his maimed descendants,
The culture-curtailed *in*dependents,
Could pluck his cherries with both paws,
And stuff with both his big-boned jaws;
Or else the core his name enveloped
Was from a solar myth developed,
Which, hunted to its primal shoot,
Takes refuge in a Sanskrit root,
Thereby to instant death explaining
The little poetry remaining.
Try it with Zeus, 't is just the same;
The thing evades, we hug a name;
Nay, scarcely that,—perhaps a vapor
Born of some atmospheric caper.
All Lempriere's fables blur together
In cloudy symbols of the weather,
And Aphrodite rose from frothy seas
But to illustrate such hypotheses.
With years enough behind his back,
Lincoln will take the selfsame track,
And prove, hulled fairly to the cob,
A mere vagary of Old Prob.
Give the right man a solar myth,
And he 'll confute the sun therewith.

They make things admirably plain,
But one hard question *will* remain:
If one hypothesis you lose,
Another in its place you choose,
But, your faith gone, O man and brother,
Whose shop shall furnish you another?
One that will wash, I mean, and wear,
And wrap us warmly from despair?
While they are clearing up our puzzles,
And clapping prophylactic muzzles
On the Actæon's hounds that sniff
Our devious track through But and If,
Would they 'd explain away the Devil
And other facts that won't keep level,
But rise beneath our feet or fail,

A reeling ship's deck in a gale!
God vanished long ago, iwis,
A mere subjective synthesis;
A doll, stuffed out with hopes and fears,
Too homely for us pretty dears,
Who want one that conviction carries,
Last make of London or of Paris.
He gone, I felt a moment's spasm,
But calmed myself with Protoplasm,
A finer name, and, what is more,
As enigmatic as before;
Greek, too, and sure to fill with ease
Minds caught in the Symplegades
Of soul and sense, life's two conditions,
Each baffled with its own omniscience.
The men who labor to revise
Our Bibles will, I hope, be wise,
And print it without foolish qualms
Instead of God in David's psalms:
Noll had been more effective far
Could he have shouted at Dunbar,
"Rise, Protoplasm!" No dourest Scot
Had waited for another shot.

And yet I frankly must confess
A secret unforgivingness,
And shudder at the saving chrism
Whose best New Birth is Pessimism;
My soul — I mean the bit of phosphorus,
That fills the place of what that was for us —
Can't bid its inward bores defiance
With the new nursery-tales of science.
What profits me, though doubt by doubt,
As nail by nail, be driven out,
When every new one, like the last,
Still holds my coffin-lid as fast?
Would I find thought a moment's truce,
Give me the young world's Mother Goose
With life and joy in every limb,
The chimney-corner tales of Grimm!

Our dear and admirable Huxley
Cannot explain to me why ducks lay,
Or, rather, how into their eggs
Blunder potential wings and legs
With will to move them and decide
Whether in air or lymph to glide.
Who gets a hair's-breadth on by showing
That Something Else set all agoing?
Farther and farther back we push
From Moses and his burning bush;
Cry, "Art Thou there?" Above, below,
All Nature mutters *yes* and *no!*
'T is the old answer: we 're agreed
Being from Being must proceed,
Life be Life's source. I might as well
Obey the meeting-house's bell,
And listen while Old Hundred pours
Forth through the summer-opened doors,
From old and young. I hear it yet,
Swelled by bass-viol and clarinet,
While the gray minister, with face
Radiant, let loose his noble bass.
If Heaven it reached not, yet its roll
Waked all the echoes of the soul,
And in it many a life found wings
To soar away from sordid things.
Church gone and singers too, the song
Sings to me voiceless all night long,
Till my soul beckons me afar,
Glowing and trembling like a star.
Will any scientific touch
With my worn strings achieve as much?

I do n't object, not I, to know
My sires were monkeys, if 't was so;
I touch my ear's collusive tip
And own the poor-relationship.
That apes of various shapes and sizes
Contained their germs that all the prizes
Of senate, pulpit, camp, and bar win
May give us hopes that sweeten Darwin.
Who knows but from our loins may spring
(Long hence) some winged sweet-throated thing

As much superior to us
As we to Cynocephalus?

This is consoling, but, alas,
It wipes no dimness from the glass
Where I am flattening my poor nose,
In hope to see beyond my toes.
Though I accept my pedigree,
Yet where, pray tell me, is the key
That should unlock a private door
To the Great Mystery, such no more?
Each offers his, but one nor all
Are much persuasive with the wall
That rises now, as long ago,
Between I wonder and I know,
Nor will vouchsafe a pin-hole peep
At the veiled Isis in its keep.
Where is no door, I but produce
My key to find it of no use.
Yet better keep it, after all,
Since Nature 's economical,
And who can tell but some fine day
(If it occur to her) she may,
In her good-will to you and me,
*Make* door and lock to match the key?

1887

## THOREAU

What contemporary, if he was in the fighting period of his life, (since Nature sets limits about her conscription for spiritual fields, as the state does in physical warfare), will ever forget what was somewhat vaguely called the "Transcendental Movement" of thirty years ago? Apparently set astir by Carlyle's essays on the "Signs of the Times," and on "History," the final and more immediate impulse seemed to be given by "Sartor Resartus." At least the republication in Boston of that wonderful Abraham à Sancta Clara sermon on Lear's text of the miserable forked radish gave the signal for a sudden mental and moral mutiny. *Ecce nunc tempus acceptabile!* was shouted on all hands with every variety of emphasis, and by voices of every conceivable pitch, representing the three sexes of men, women, and Lady Mary Wortley Montagues. The nameless eagle of the tree Ygdrasil was about to sit at last, and wild-eyed enthusiasts rushed from all sides, each eager to thrust under the mystic bird that chalk egg from which the new and fairer Creation was to be hatched in due time. *Redeunt Saturnia regna,*—so far was certain, though in what shape, or by what methods, was still a matter of debate. Every possible form of intellectual and physical dyspepsia brought forth its gospel. Bran had its prophets, and the presartorial simplicity of Adam its martyrs, tailored impromptu from the tar-pot by incensed neighbors, and sent forth to illustrate the "feathered Mercury," as defined by Webster and Worcester. Plainness of speech was carried to a pitch that would have taken away the breath of George Fox; and even swearing had its evangelists, who answered a simple inquiry after their health with an elaborate ingenuity of imprecation that might have been honorably mentioned by Marlborough in general orders. Everybody had a mission (with a capital M) to attend to everybody else's business. No brain but has its private maggot, which must have found pitiably short commons sometimes. Not a few impecunious zealots abjured the use of money (unless earned by other people), professing to live on the internal revenues of the spirit. Some had an assurance of instant millennium so soon as hooks and eyes should be substituted for buttons. Communities were established where everything was to be common but commonsense. Men renounced their old gods, and hesitated only whether to bestow their furloughed allegiance on Thor or Budh. Conventions were held for every hitherto inconceivable purpose. The belated gift of tongues, as among the Fifth Monarchy men, spread like a contagion, rendering its victims incomprehensible to all Christian men; whether equally so to the most distant possible heathen or not was unexperimented, though many would have subscribed liberally that a fair trial might be made. It was the pentecost of Shinar. The day of utterances reproduced the day of rebuses and anagrams, and there was nothing so simple that uncial letters and the style of Diphilus the Labyrinth could not turn it into a riddle. Many foreign revolutionists out of work added to the general misunderstanding their contribution of broken English in every most ingenious form of fracture. All stood ready at a moment's notice to reform everything but themselves. The general motto was:—

And we 'll *talk* with them, too,
And take upon 's the mystery of things
As if we were God's spies.

Nature is always kind enough to give even her clouds a humorous lining. I have barely hinted at the comic side of the affair, for the material was endless. This was the whistle and trailing fuse of the shell, but there was a very solid and serious kernel, full of the most deadly explosiveness. Thoughtful men divined it, but the generality suspected nothing. The word "transcendental" then was the maid of all work for those who could not think, as "Pre-Raphaelite" has been more recently for people of the same limited housekeeping. The truth is, that there was a much nearer metaphysical relation and a much more distant æsthetic and literary relation between Carlyle and the Apostles of the Newness, as they were called in New England, than has commonly been supposed. Both represented the reaction and revolt against *Philisterei*, a renewal of the old battle begun in modern times by Erasmus and Reuchlin, and continued by Lessing, Goethe, and, in a far narrower sense, by Heine in Germany, and of which Fielding, Sterne, and Wordsworth in different ways have been the leaders in England. It was simply a struggle for fresh air, in which, if the windows could not be opened, there was danger that panes would be broken, though painted with images of saints and martyrs. Light, colored by these reverend effigies, was none the more respirable for being picturesque. There is only one thing better than tradition, and that is the original and eternal life out of which all tradition takes its rise. It was this life which the reformers demanded, with more or less clearness of consciousness and expression, life in politics, life in literature, life in religion. Of what use to import a gospel from Judæa, if we leave behind the soul that made it possible, the God who keeps it forever real and present? Surely Abana and Pharpar *are* better than Jordan, if a living faith be mixed with those waters and none with these.

Scotch Presbyterianism as a motive

of spiritual progress was dead; New England Puritanism was in like manner dead; in other words, Protestantism had made its fortune and no longer protested; but till Carlyle spoke out in the Old World and Emerson in the New, no one had dared to proclaim, *Le roi est mort: vive le roi!* The meaning of which proclamation was essentially this: the vital spirit has long since departed out of this form once so kingly, and the great seal has been in commission long enough; but meanwhile the soul of man, from which all power emanates and to which it reverts, still survives in undiminished royalty; God still survives, little as you gentlemen of the Commission seem to be aware of it,—nay, will possibly outlive the whole of you, incredible as it may appear. The truth is, that both Scotch Presbyterianism and New England Puritanism made their new avatar in Carlyle and Emerson, the heralds of their formal decease, and the tendency of the one toward Authority and of the other toward Independency might have been prophesied by whoever had studied history. The necessity was not so much in the men as in the principles they represented and the traditions which overruled them. The Puritanism of the past found its unwilling poet in Hawthorne, the rarest creative imagination of the century, the rarest in some ideal respects since Shakespeare; but the Puritanism that cannot die, the Puritanism that made New England what it is, and is destined to make America what it should be, found its voice in Emerson. Though holding himself aloof from all active partnership in movements of reform, he has been the sleeping partner who has supplied a great part of their capital.

The artistic range of Emerson is narrow, as every well-read critic must feel at once; and so is that of Æschylus, so is that of Dante, so is that of Montaigne, so is that of Schiller, so is that of nearly every one except Shakespeare; but there is a gauge of height no less than of breadth, of individuality as well as of comprehensiveness, and, above all, there is the standard of genetic power, the test of the masculine as distinguished from the receptive minds. There are staminate plants in literature, that make no fine show of fruit, but without whose pollen, quintessence of fructifying gold, the garden had been barren. Emerson's mind is emphatically one of these, and there is no man to whom our æsthetic culture owes so much. The Puritan revolt had made us ecclesiastically and the Revolution politically independent, but we were still socially and intellectually moored to English thought, till Emerson cut the cable and gave us a chance at the dangers and the glories of blue water. No man young enough to have felt it can forget or cease to be grateful for the mental and moral *nudge* which he received from the writings of his high-minded and brave-spirited countryman. That we agree with him, or that he always agrees with himself, is aside from the question; but that he arouses in us something that we are the better for having awakened, whether that something be of opposition or assent, that he speaks always to what is highest and least selfish in us, few Americans of the generation younger than his own would be disposed to deny. His oration before the

Phi Beta Kappa Society at Cambridge, some thirty years ago, was an event without any former parallel in our literary annals, a scene to be always treasured in the memory for its picturesqueness and its inspiration. What crowded and breathless aisles, what windows clustering with eager heads, what enthusiasm of approval, what grim silence of foregone dissent! It was our Yankee version of a lecture by Abelard, our Harvard parallel to the last public appearances of Schelling.

I said that the Transcendental Movement was the protestant spirit of Puritanism seeking a new outlet and an escape from forms and creeds which compressed rather than expressed it. In its motives, its preaching, and its results, it differed radically from the doctrine of Carlyle. The Scotchman, with all his genius, and his humor gigantesque as that of Rabelais, has grown shriller and shriller with years, degenerating sometimes into a common scold, and emptying very unsavory vials of wrath on the head of the sturdy British Socrates of worldly common sense. The teaching of Emerson tended much more exclusively to self-culture and the independent development of the individual man. It seemed to many almost Pythagorean in its voluntary seclusion from commonwealth affairs. Both Carlyle and Emerson were disciples of Goethe, but Emerson in a far truer sense; and while the one, from his bias toward the eccentric, has degenerated more and more into mannerism, the other has clarified steadily toward perfection of style,—exquisite fineness of material, unobtrusive lowness of tone and simplicity of fashion, the most high-bred garb of expression. Whatever may be said of his thought, nothing can be finer than the delicious limpidness of his phrase. If it was ever questionable whether democracy could develop a gentleman, the problem has been affirmatively solved at last. Carlyle, in his cynicism and his admiration of force in and for itself, has become at last positively inhuman; Emerson, reverencing strength, seeking the highest outcome of the individual, has found that society and politics are also main elements in the attainment of the desired end, and has drawn steadily manward and worldward. The two men represent respectively those grand personifications in the drama of Æschylus, Βία and Κράτος.

Among the pistillate plants kindled to fruitage by the Emersonian pollen, Thoreau is thus far the most remarkable; and it is something eminently fitting that his posthumous works should be offered us by Emerson, for they are strawberries from his own garden. A singular mixture of varieties, indeed, there is;—alpine, some of them, with the flavor of rare mountain air; others wood, tasting of sunny roadside banks or shy openings in the forest; and not a few seedlings swollen hugely by culture, but lacking the fine natural aroma of the more modest kinds. Strange books these are of his, and interesting in many ways,—instructive chiefly as showing how considerable a crop may be raised on a comparatively narrow close of mind, and how much a man may make of his life if he will assiduously follow it, though perhaps never truly finding it at last.

I have just been renewing my recollection of Mr. Thoreau's writings, and have read through his six volumes in the order of their production. I shall try to give an adequate report of their impression upon me both as critic and as mere reader. He seems to me to have been a man with so high a conceit of himself that he accepted without questioning, and insisted on our accepting, his defects and weaknesses of character as virtues and powers peculiar to himself. Was he indolent, he finds none of the activities which attract or employ the rest of mankind worthy of him. Was he wanting in the qualities that make success, it is success that is contemptible, and not himself that lacks persistency and purpose. Was he poor, money was an unmixed evil. Did his life seem a selfish one, he condemns doing good as one of the weakest of superstitions. To be of use was with him the most killing bait of the wily tempter Uselessness. He had no faculty of generalization from outside of himself, or at least no experience which would supply the material of such, and he makes his own whim the law, his own range the horizon of the universe. He condemns a world, the hollowness of whose satisfactions he had never had the means of testing, and we recognize Apemantus behind the mask of Timon. He had little active imagination; of the receptive he had much. His appreciation is of the highest quality; his critical power, from want of continuity of mind, very limited and inadequate. He somewhere cites a simile from Ossian, as an example of the superiority of the old poetry to the new, though, even were the historic evidence less convincing, the sentimental melancholy of those poems should be conclusive of their modernness. He had none of the artistic mastery which controls a great work to the serene balance of completeness, but exquisite mechanical skill in the shaping of sentences and paragraphs, or (more rarely) short bits of verse for the expression of a detached thought, sentiment, or image. His works give one the feeling of a sky full of stars,—something impressive and exhilarating certainly, something high overhead and freckled thickly with spots of isolated brightness; but whether these have any mutual relation with each other, or have any concern with our mundane matters, is for the most part matter of conjecture,—astrology as yet, and not astronomy.

It is curious, considering what Thoreau afterwards became, that he was not by nature an observer. He only saw the things he looked for, and was less poet than naturalist. Till he built his Walden shanty, he did not know that the hickory grew in Concord. Till he went to Maine, he had never seen phosphorescent wood, a phenomenon early familiar to most country boys. At forty he speaks of the seeding of the pine as a new discovery, though one should have thought that its gold-dust of blowing pollen might have earlier drawn his eye. Neither his attention nor his genius was of the spontaneous kind. He discovered nothing. He thought everything a discovery of his own, from moonlight to the planting of acorns and nuts by squirrels. This is a defect in his character, but one of his chief charms as a writer. Everything grows fresh under his hand. He delved in his mind and nature; he planted them with all manner of native and foreign seeds, and reaped assiduously. He was not merely solitary, he would be isolated, and succeeded at last in almost persuading himself that he was autochthonous. He valued everything in proportion as he fancied it to be exclusively his own. He complains in "Walden" that there is no one in Concord with whom he could talk of Oriental literature, though the man was living within two miles of his hut who had introduced him to it. This intellectual selfishness becomes sometimes almost painful in reading him. He lacked that generosity of "communication" which Johnson admired in Burke. De Quincey tells us that Wordsworth was impatient when any one else spoke of mountains, as if he had a peculiar property in them. And we can readily understand why it should be so: no one is satisfied with another's appreciation of his mistress. But Thoreau seems to have prized a lofty way of thinking (often we should be inclined to call it a remote one) not so much because it was good in itself as because he wished few to share it with him. It seems now and then as if he did not seek to lure others up "above our lower region of turmoil," but to leave his own name cut on the mountain peak as the first climber. This itch of originality infects his thought and style. To be misty is not to be mystic. He turns commonplaces end for end, and fancies it makes something new of them. As we walk down Park Street, our eye is caught by Dr. Winship's dumb-bells, one of which bears an inscription testifying that it is the heaviest ever put up at arm's length by any athlete; and in reading Mr. Thoreau's books we cannot help feeling as if he sometimes invited our attention to a particular sophism or paradox as the biggest yet maintained by any single writer. He seeks, at all risks, for perversity of thought, and revives the age of *concetti* while he fancies himself going back to a pre-classical nature. "A day," he says, "passed in the society of those Greek sages, such as described in the Banquet of Xenophon, would not be comparable with the dry wit of decayed cranberry-vines and the fresh Attic salt of the moss-beds." It is not so much the True that he loves as the Out-of-the-way. As the Brazen Age shows itself in other men by exaggeration of phrase, so in him by extravagance of statement. He wishes always to trump your suit and to *ruff* when you least expect it. Do you love Nature because she is beautiful? He will find a better argument in her ugliness. Are you tired of the artificial man? He instantly dresses you up an ideal in a Penobscot Indian, and attributes to this creature of his otherwise-mindedness as peculiarities things that are common to all woodsmen, white or red, and this simply because he has not studied the pale-faced variety.

This notion of an absolute originality, as if one could have a patent-right in it, is an absurdity. A man cannot escape in thought, any more than he can in language, from the past and the present. As no one ever invents a word, and yet language somehow grows by general contribution and necessity, so it is with thought. Mr. Thoreau seems to me to insist in public on going back to flint and steel, when there is a match-box in his pocket which he knows very well how to use at a pinch. Originality consists in power of digesting and assimilating thoughts, so that they become part of our life and substance. Montaigne, for example, is one of the most original of authors, though he helped himself to ideas in every direction. But they turn to blood and coloring in his style, and give a freshness of complexion that is forever charming. In Thoreau much seems yet to be foreign and unassimilated, showing itself in symptoms of indigestion. A preacher-up of Nature, we now and then detect under the surly and stoic garb something of the sophist and the sentimentalizer. I am far from implying that this was conscious on his part. But it is much easier for a man to impose on himself when he measures only with himself. A greater familiarity with ordinary men would have done Thoreau good, by showing him how many fine qualities are common to the race. The radical vice of his theory of life was that he confounded physical with spiritual remoteness from men. A man is far enough withdrawn from his fellows if he keep himself clear of their weaknesses. He is not so truly withdrawn as exiled, if he refuse to share in their strength. "Solitude," says Cowley, "can be well fitted and set right but upon a very few persons. They must have enough knowledge of the world to see the vanity of it, and enough virtue to despise all vanity." It is a morbid self-consciousness that pronounces the world of men empty and worthless before trying it, the instinctive evasion of one who is sensible of some innate weakness, and retorts the accusation of it before any has made it but himself. To a healthy mind, the world is a constant challenge of opportunity. Mr. Thoreau had not a healthy mind, or he would not have been so fond of prescribing. His whole life was a search for the doctor. The old mystics had a wiser sense of what the world was worth. They ordained a severe apprenticeship to law, and even ceremonial, in order to the gaining of freedom and mastery over these. Seven years of service for Rachel were to be rewarded at last with Leah. Seven other years of faithfulness with her were to win them at last the true bride of their souls. Active Life was with them the only path to the Contemplative.

Thoreau had no humor, and this implies that he was a sorry logician. Himself an artist in rhetoric, he confounds thought with style when he undertakes to speak of the latter. He was forever talking of getting away from the world, but he must be always near enough to it, nay, to the Concord corner of it, to feel the impression he makes there. He verifies the shrewd remark of Sainte-Beuve, "On touche encore à son temps et très-fort, même quand on le repousse." This egotism of his is a Stylites pillar after all, a seclusion which keeps him in the public eye. The dignity of man is an excellent thing, but therefore to hold one's self too sacred and precious is the reverse of excellent. There is something delightfully absurd in six volumes addressed to a world of such "vulgar fellows" as Thoreau affirmed his fellow men to be. I once had a glimpse of a genuine solitary who spent his winters one hundred and fifty miles beyond all human communication, and there dwelt with his rifle as his only confidant. Compared with this, the shanty on Walden Pond has something the air, it must be confessed, of the Hermitage of La Chevrette. I do not believe that the way to a true cosmopolitanism carries one into the woods or the society of musquashes. Perhaps the narrowest provincialism is that of Self; that of Kleinwinkel is nothing to it. The natural man, like the singing birds, comes out of the forest as inevitably as the natural bear and the wildcat stick there. To seek to be natural implies a consciousness that forbids all naturalness forever. It is as easy —and no easier—to be natural in a *salon* as in a swamp, if one do not aim at it, for what we call unnaturalness always has its spring in a man's thinking too much about himself. "It is impossible," said Turgot, "for a vulgar man to be simple."

I look upon a great deal of the modern sentimentalism about Nature as a mark of disease. It is one more symptom of the general liver-complaint. To a man of wholesome constitution the wilderness is well enough for a mood or a vacation, but not for a habit of life. Those who have most loudly advertised their passion for seclusion and their intimacy with nature, from Petrarch down, have been mostly sentimentalists, unreal men, misanthropes on the spindle side, solacing an uneasy suspicion of themselves by professing contempt for their kind. They make demands on the world in advance proportioned to their inward measure of their own merit, and are angry that the world pays only by the visible measure of performance. It is true of Rousseau, the modern founder of the sect, true of Saint Pierre, his intellectual child, and of Chateaubriand, his grandchild, the inventor, we might almost say, of the primitive forest, and who first was touched by the solemn falling of a tree from natural decay in the windless silence of the woods. It is a very shallow view that affirms trees and rocks to be healthy, and cannot see that men in communities are just as true to the laws of their organization and destiny; that can tolerate the puffin and the fox, but not the fool and the knave; that would shun politics because of its demagogues, and snuff up the stench of the obscene fungus. The divine life of Nature is more wonderful, more various, more sublime in man than in any other of her works, and the wisdom that is gained by commerce with men, as Montaigne and Shakespeare gained it, or with one's own soul among men, as Dante, is the most delightful, as it is the most precious, of all. In outward nature it is still man that interests us, and we care far less for the things seen than the way in which they are seen by poetic eyes like Wordsworth's or Thoreau's, and the reflections they cast there. To hear the to-do that is often made over the simple fact that a man sees the image of himself in the outward world, one is reminded of a savage when he for the first time catches a glimpse of himself in a looking-glass. "Venerable child of Nature," we are tempted to say, "to whose science in the invention of the tobacco-pipe, to whose art in the tattooing of thine undegenerate hide not yet enslaved by tailors, we are slowly striving to climb back, the miracle thou beholdest is sold in my unhappy country for a shilling!" If matters go on as they have done, and everybody must needs blab of all the favors that have been done him by roadside and river-brink and woodland walk, as if to kiss and tell were no longer treachery, it will be a positive refreshment to meet a man who is as superbly indifferent to Nature as she is to him. By and by we shall have John Smith, of No. –12–12th Street, advertising that he is not the J. S. who saw a cow-lily on Thursday last, as he never saw one in his life, would not see one if he could, and is prepared to prove an alibi on the day in question.

Solitary communion with Nature does not seem to have been sanitary or sweetening in its influence on Thoreau's character. On the contrary, his letters show him more cynical as he grew older. While he studied with respectful attention the minks and woodchucks, his neighbors, he looked with utter contempt on the august drama of destiny of which his country was the scene, and on which the curtain had already risen. He was converting us back to a state of nature "so eloquently," as Voltaire said of Rousseau, "that he almost persuaded us to go on all fours," while the wiser fates were making it possible for us to walk erect for the first time. Had he conversed more with his fellows, his sympathies would have widened with the assurance that his peculiar genius had more appreciation, and his writings a larger circle of readers, or at least a warmer one, than he dreamed of. We have the highest testimony * to the natural sweetness, sincerity, and nobleness of his temper, and in his books an equally irrefragable one to the rare quality of his mind. He was not a strong thinker, but a sensitive feeler. Yet his mind strikes us as cold and wintry in its purity. A light snow has fallen everywhere in which he seems to come on the track of the shier sensations that would elsewhere leave no trace. We think greater compression would have done more for his fame. A feeling of sameness comes over us as we read so much. Trifles are recorded with an over-minute punctuality and conscientiousness of detail. He registers the state of his personal thermometer thirteen times a day. We cannot help thinking sometimes of the man who

> Watches, starves, freezes, and sweats
> To learn but catechisms and alphabets
> Of unconcerning things, matters of fact,

and sometimes of the saying of the Persian poet, that "when the owl would boast, he boasts of catching mice at the edge of a hole." We could readily part with some of his affectations. It was well enough for Pythagoras to say, once for all, "When I was Euphorbus at the siege of Troy;" not so well for Thoreau to travesty it into "When I was a shepherd on the plains of Assyria." A naïve thing said over again is anything but naïve. But with every exception, there is no writing comparable with Thoreau's in kind, that is comparable with it in degree where it is best; where it disengages itself, that is, from the tangled roots and dead leaves of a second-hand Orientalism, and runs limpid and smooth and broadening as it runs, a mirror for whatever is grand and lovely in both worlds.

George Sand says neatly, that "Art is not a study of positive reality"

*Mr. Emerson, in the Biographical Sketch prefixed to the *Excursions*. [Author's note.]

(*actuality* were the fitter word,) "but a seeking after ideal truth." It would be doing very inadequate justice to Thoreau if we left it to be inferred that this ideal element did not exist in him, and that too in larger proportion, if less obtrusive, than his nature-worship. He took nature as the mountain-path to an ideal world. If the path wind a good deal, if he record too faithfully every trip over a root, if he botanize somewhat wearisomely, he gives us now and then superb outlooks from some jutting crag, and brings us out at last into an illimitable ether, where the breathing is not difficult for those who have any true touch of the climbing spirit. His shanty-life was a mere impossibility, so far as his own conception of it goes, as an entire independency of mankind. The tub of Diogenes had a sounder bottom. Thoreau's experiment actually presupposed all that complicated civilization which it theoretically abjured. He squatted on another man's land; he borrows an axe; his boards, his nails, his bricks, his mortar, his books, his lamp, his fish-hooks, his plough, his hoe, all turn state's evidence against him as an accomplice in the sin of that artificial civilization which rendered it possible that such a person as Henry D. Thoreau should exist at all. *Magnis tamen excidit ausis.* His aim was a noble and a useful one, in the direction of "plain living and high thinking." It was a practical sermon on Emerson's text that "things are in the saddle and ride mankind," an attempt to solve Carlyle's problem (condensed from Johnson) of "lessening your denominator." His whole life was a rebuke of the waste and aimlessness of our American luxury, which is an abject enslavement to tawdry upholstery. He had "fine translunary things" in him. His better style as a writer is in keeping with the simplicity and purity of his life. We have said that his range was narrow, but to be a master is to be a master. He had caught his English at its living source, among the poets and prose-writers of its best days; his literature was extensive and recondite; his quotations are always nuggets of the purest ore: there are sentences of his as perfect as anything in the language, and thoughts as clearly crystallized; his metaphors and images are always fresh from the soil; he had watched Nature like a detective who is to go upon the stand; as we read him, it seems as if all-out-of-doors had kept a diary and become its own Montaigne; we look at the landscape as in a Claude Lorraine glass; compared with his, all other books of similar aim, even White's "Selborne," seem dry as a country clergyman's meteorological journal in an old almanac. He belongs with Donne and Browne and Novalis; if not with the originally creative men, with the scarcely smaller class who are peculiar, and whose leaves shed their invisible thought-seed like ferns.

1865

## ON A CERTAIN CONDESCENSION IN FOREIGNERS

Walking one day toward the Village, as we used to call it in the good old days, when almost every dweller in the town had been born in it, I was enjoying that delicious sense of disenthrallment from the actual which the deepening twilight brings with it, giving as it does a sort of obscure novelty to things familiar. The coolness, the hush, broken only by the distant bleat of some belated goat, querulous to be disburthened of her milky load, the few faint stars, more guessed at yet than seen, the sense that the coming dark would so soon fold me in the secure privacy of its disguise,—all things combined in a result as near absolute peace as can be hoped for by a man who knows that there is a writ out against him in the hands of the printer's devil. For the moment, I was enjoying the blessed privilege of thinking without being called on to stand and deliver what I thought to the small public who are good enough to take any interest therein. I love old ways, and the path I was walking felt kindly to the feet it had known for almost fifty years. How many fleeting impressions it had shared with me! How many times I had lingered to study the shadows of the leaves mezzotinted upon the turf that edged it by the moon, of the bare boughs etched with a touch beyond Rembrandt by the same unconscious artist on the smooth page of snow! If I turned round, through dusky tree-gaps came the first twinkle of evening lamps in the dear old homestead. On Corey's hill I could see these tiny pharoses of love and home and sweet domestic thoughts flash out one by one across the blackening salt-meadow between. How much has not kerosene added to the cheerfulness of our evening landscape! A pair of night-herons flapped heavily over me toward the hidden river. The war was ended. I might walk townward without that aching dread of bulletins that had darkened the July sunshine and twice made the scarlet leaves of October seem stained with blood. I remembered with a pang, half-proud, half-painful, how, so many years ago, I had walked over the same path and felt round my finger the soft pressure of a little hand that was one day to harden with faithful grip of sabre. On how many paths, leading to how many homes where proud Memory does all she can to fill up the fireside gaps with shining shapes, must not men be walking in just such pensive mood as I? Ah, young heroes, safe in immortal youth as those of Homer, you at least carried your ideal hence untarnished! It is locked for you beyond moth or rust in the treasure-chamber of Death.

Is not a country, I thought, that has had such as they in it, that could give such as they a brave joy in dying for it, worth something, then? And as I felt more and more the soothing magic of evening's cool palm upon my temples, as my fancy came home from its revery, and my senses, with reawakened curiosity, ran to the front windows again from the viewless closet of abstraction, and felt a strange charm in finding the old tree and shabby fence still there under the travesty of falling night, nay, were conscious of an unsuspected newness in familiar stars and the fading outlines of hills my earliest horizon, I was conscious of an immortal soul, and could not but rejoice in the unwaning goodliness of the world into which I had been born without any merit of my own. I thought of dear Henry Vaughan's rainbow, "Still young and fine!" I remembered people who had to go over to the Alps to learn what the divine silence of snow was, who must run to Italy before they were conscious of the miracle wrought every day under their very noses by the sunset, who must call upon the Berkshire hills to teach them what a painter autumn was, while close at hand the Fresh Pond meadows made all oriels cheap with hues that showed as if a sunset-cloud had been wrecked among their maples. One might be worse off than even in America, I thought. There are some things so elastic that even the heavy roller of democracy cannot flatten them altogether down. The mind can weave itself warmly in the cocoon of its own thoughts and dwell a hermit anywhere. A country without traditions, without ennobling associations, a scramble of *parvenus,* with a horrible consciousness of shoddy running through politics, manners, art, literature, nay, religion itself? I confess, it did not seem so to me there in that illimitable quiet, that serene self-possession of nature, where Collins might have brooded his "Ode to Evening," or where those verses on Solitude in Dodsley's Collection, that Hawthorne liked so much, might have been composed. Traditions? Granting that we had none, all that is worth having in them is the common property of the soul,—an estate in gavelkind for all the sons of Adam,—and, moreover, if a man cannot stand on his two feet (the prime quality of whoever has left any tradition behind him), were it not better for him to be honest about it at once, and go down on all fours? And for associations, if one have not the wit to make them for himself out of native earth, no ready-made ones of other men will avail much. Lexington is none the worse to me for not being in Greece, nor Gettysburg that its name is not Marathon. "Blessed old fields," I was just exclaiming to myself, like one of Mrs. Radcliffe's heroes, "dear acres, innocently secure from history, which these eyes first beheld, may you be also those to which they shall at last slowly darken!" when I was interrupted by a voice which asked me in German whether I was the Herr Professor, Doctor, So-and-so? The "Doctor" was by brevet or vaticination, to make the grade easier to my pocket.

One feels so intimately assured that one is made up, in part, of shreds and leavings of the past, in part of the interpolations of other people, that an honest man would be slow in saying *yes* to such a question. But "my name is So-and-so" is a safe answer, and I gave it. While I had been romancing with myself, the street-lamps had been lighted, and it was under one of these detectives that have robbed the Old Road of its privilege of sanctuary after nightfall that I was ambushed by my foe. The inexorable villain had taken my description, it appears, that I might have the less chance to escape him. Dr. Holmes tells us that we change our substance, not every seven years, as was once believed, but with every breath we draw. Why had I not the wit to avail myself of the subterfuge, and, like Peter, to renounce my identity, especially, as in certain moods of mind, I have often more than doubted of it myself? When a man is, as it were, his own front-door, and is thus knocked at, why may he not assume the right of that sacred wood to make every house a castle, by denying himself to all visitations? I was truly not at home when the question was put to me, but had to recall myself from all out-of-doors, and to piece my self-consciousness hastily together as well as I could before I answered it.

I knew perfectly well what was coming. It is seldom that debtors or good Samaritans waylay people under gas-lamps in order to force money upon them, so far as I have seen or heard. I was also aware, from considerable experience, that every foreigner is persuaded that, by doing this country the favor of coming to it, he has laid every native thereof under an obligation, pecuniary or other, as the case may be, whose discharge he is entitled to on demand duly made in person or by letter. Too much learning (of this kind) had made me mad in the provincial sense of the word. I had begun life with the theory of giving something to every beggar that came along, though sure of never finding a native-born countryman among them. In a small way, I was resolved to emulate Hatem Tai's tent, with its three hundred and sixty-five entrances, one for every day in the year,—I know not whether he was astronomer enough to add another for leap-years. The beggars were a kind of German-silver aristocracy; not real plate, to be sure, but better than nothing. Where everybody was over-worked, they supplied the comfortable equipoise of absolute leisure, so æsthetically needful. Besides, I was but too conscious of a vagrant fibre in myself, which too often thrilled me in my solitary walks with the temptation to wander on into infinite space, and by a single spasm of resolution to emancipate myself from the drudgery of prosaic serfdom to respectability and the regular course of things. This prompting has been at times my familiar demon, and I could not but feel a kind of respectful sympathy for men who had dared what I had only sketched out to myself as a splendid possibility. For seven years I helped maintain one heroic man on an imaginary journey to Portland,—as fine an example as I have ever known of hopeless loyalty to an ideal. I assisted another so long in a fruitless attempt to reach Mecklenburg-Schwerin, that at last we grinned in each other's faces when we met, like a couple of augurs. He was possessed by this harmless mania as some are by the North Pole, and I shall never forget his look of regretful compassion (as for one who was sacrificing his higher life to the fleshpots of Egypt) when I at last advised him somewhat strenuously to go to the D——, whither the road was so much travelled that he could not miss it. General Banks, in his noble zeal for the honor of his country, would confer on the Secretary of State the power of imprisoning, in case of war, all these seekers of the unattainable, thus by a stroke of the pen annihilating the single poetic element in our humdrum life. Alas! not everybody has the genius to be a Bobbin-Boy, or doubtless all these also would have chosen that more prosperous line of life! But moralists, sociologists, political economists, and taxes have slowly convinced me that my beggarly sympathies were a sin against society. Especially was the Buckle doctrine of averages (so flattering to our free-will) persuasive with me; for as there must be in every year a certain number who would bestow an alms on these abridged editions of the Wandering Jew, the withdrawal of my quota could make no possible difference, since some destined proxy must always step forward to fill my gap. Just so many misdirected letters every year and no more! Would it were as easy to reckon up the number of men on whose backs fate has written the wrong address, so that they arrive by mistake in Congress and other places where they do not belong! May not these wanderers of whom I speak have been sent into the world without any proper address at all? Where is our Dead-Letter Office for such? And if wiser social arrangements should furnish us with something of the sort, fancy (horrible thought!) how many a workingman's friend (a kind of industry in which the labor is light and the wages heavy) would be sent thither because not called for in the office where he at present lies!

But I am leaving my new acquaintance too long under the lamp-post. The same Gano which had betrayed me to him revealed to me a well-set young man of about half my own age, as well dressed, so far as I could see, as I was, and with every natural qualification for getting his own livelihood as good, if not better, than my own. He had been reduced to the painful necessity of calling upon me by a series of crosses beginning with the Baden Revolution (for which, I own, he seemed rather young,—but perhaps he referred to a kind of revolution practised every season at Baden-Baden), continued by repeated failures in business, for amounts which must convince me of his entire respectability, and ending with our Civil War. During the latter, he had served with distinction as a soldier, taking a main part in every important battle, with a rapid list of which he favored me, and no doubt would have admitted that, impartial as Jonathan Wild's great ancestor, he had been on both sides, had I baited him with a few hints of conservative opinions on a subject so distressing to a gentleman wishing to profit by one's sympathy and unhappily doubtful as to which way it might lean. For all these reasons, and, as he seemed to imply, for his merit in consenting to be born in Germany, he considered himself my natural creditor to the extent of five dollars, which he would handsomely consent to accept in greenbacks, though he preferred specie. The offer was certainly a generous one, and the claim presented with an assurance that carried conviction. But, unhappily, I had been led to remark a curious natural phenomenon. If I was ever weak enough to give anything to a petitioner of whatever nationality, it always rained decayed compatriots of his for a month after. *Post hoc ergo propter hoc* may not always be safe logic, but here I seemed to perceive a natural connection of cause and effect. Now, a few days before I had been so tickled with a paper (professedly written by a benevolent American clergyman) certifying that the bearer, a hard-working German, had long "sofered with rheumatic paints in his limps," that, after copying the passage into my note-book, I thought it but fair to pay a trifling *honorarium* to the author. I had pulled the string of the shower-bath! It had been running shipwrecked sailors for some time, but forthwith it began to pour Teutons, redolent of *lager-bier*. I could not help associating the apparition of my new friend with this series of otherwise unaccountable phenomena. I accordingly made up my mind to deny the debt, and modestly did so, pleading a native bias toward impecuniosity to the full as strong as his own. He took a high tone with me at once, such as an honest man would naturally take with a confessed repudiator. He even brought down his proud stomach so far as to join himself to me for the rest of my townward walk, that he might give me his views of the American people, and thus inclusively of myself.

I know not whether it is because I am pigeon-livered and lack gall, or whether it is from an overmastering sense of drollery, but I am apt to submit to such bastings with a patience which afterwards surprises me, being not without my share of warmth in the blood. Perhaps it is because I so often meet with young persons who know vastly more than I do, and especially with so many foreigners whose knowledge of this country is superior to my own. However it may be, I listened for some time with tolerable composure as my self-appointed lecturer gave me in detail his opinions of my country and its people. America, he informed me, was without arts, science, literature, culture, or any native hope of supplying them. We were a people wholly given to money-getting, and who, having got it, knew no other use for it than to hold it fast. I am fain to confess that I felt a sensible itching of the biceps, and that my fingers closed with such a grip as he had just informed me was one of the effects of our unhappy climate. But happening just then to be where I could avoid temptation by dodging down a by-street, I hastily left him to finish his diatribe to the lamp-post, which could stand it better than I. That young man will never know how near he came to being assaulted by a respectable gentleman of middle age, at the corner of Church Street. I have never felt quite satisfied that I did all my duty by him in not knocking him down. But perhaps he might have knocked *me* down, and then?

The capacity of indignation makes an essential part of the outfit of every honest man, but I am inclined to doubt whether he is a wise one who allows himself to act upon its first hints. It should be rather, I suspect, a *latent* heat in the blood, which makes itself felt in character, a steady reserve for the brain, warming the ovum of thought to life, rather than cooking it by a too hasty enthusiasm in reaching the boiling point. As my pulse gradually fell back to its normal beat, I reflected that I had been uncomfortably near making a fool of myself,—a handy salve of euphuism for our vanity, though it does not always make a just allowance to Nature for her share in the business. What possible claim had my Teutonic friend to rob me of my composure? I am not, I think, specially thin-skinned as to other people's opinions of myself, having, as I conceive, later and fuller intelligence on that point than anybody else can give me. Life is continually weighing us in very sensitive scales, and telling every one of us precisely what his real weight is to the last grain of dust. Whoever at fifty does not rate himself quite as low as most of his acquaintance would be likely to put him, must be either a fool or a great man, and I humbly disclaim being either. But if I was not smarting in person from any scattering shot of my late companion's commination, why should I grow hot at any implication of my country therein? Surely *her* shoulders are broad enough, if yours or mine are not, to bear up under a considerable avalanche of this kind. It is the bit of truth in every slander, the hint of likeness in every caricature, that makes us smart. "Art thou *there,* old True-penny?" How did your blade know its way so well to that one loose rivet in our armor? I wondered whether Americans were oversensitive in this respect, whether they were more touchy than other folks. On the whole, I thought we were not. Plutarch, who at least had studied philosophy, if he had not mastered it, could not stomach something Herodotus had said of Bœotia, and devoted an essay to showing up the delightful old traveller's malice and ill-breeding. French editors leave out of Montaigne's "Travels" some remarks of his about France, for reasons best known to themselves. Pachydermatous Deutschland, covered with trophies from every field of letters, still winces under that question which Père Bouhours put two centuries ago, *Si un Allemand peut être bel-esprit?* John Bull grew apoplectic with angry amazement at the audacious persiflage of Pückler-Muskau. To be sure, he was a prince,—but that was not all of it, for a chance phrase of gentle Hawthorne sent a spasm through all the journals of England. Then this tenderness is not peculiar to *us?* Console yourself, dear man and brother, whatever else you may be sure of, be sure at least of this, that you are dreadfully like other people. Human nature has a much greater genius for sameness than for originality, or the world would be at a sad pass shortly. The surprising thing is that men have such a taste for this somewhat musty flavor, that an Englishman, for example, should feel himself defrauded, nay, even outraged, when he comes over here and finds a people speaking what he admits to be something like English, and yet so very different from (or, as he would say, to) those he left at home. Nothing, I am sure, equals *my* thankfulness when I meet an Englishman who is *not* like every other, or, I may add, an American of the same odd turn.

Certainly it is no shame to a man that he should be as nice about his country as about his sweetheart, and who ever heard even the friendliest appreciation of that unexpressive she that did not seem to fall infinitely short? Yet it would hardly be wise to hold every one an enemy who could not see her with our own enchanted eyes. It seems to be the common opinion of foreigners that Americans are *too* tender upon this point. Perhaps we are; and if so, there must be a reason for it. Have we had fair play? Could the eyes of what is called Good Society (though it is so seldom true either to the adjective or noun) look upon a nation of democrats with any chance of receiving an undistorted image? Were not those, moreover, who found in the old order of things an earthly paradise, paying them quarterly dividends for the wisdom of their ancestors, with the punctuality of the seasons, unconsciously bribed to misunderstand if not to misrepresent us? Whether at war or at peace, there we were, a standing menace to all earthly paradises of that kind, fatal underminers of the very credit on which the dividends were based, all the more hateful and terrible that our destructive agency was so insidious, working invisible in the elements, as it seemed, active while they slept, and coming upon them in the darkness like an armed man. *Could* Laius have the proper feelings of a father toward Œdipus, announced as his destined destroyer by infallible oracles, and felt to be such by every conscious fibre of his soul? For more than a century the Dutch were the laughing-stock of polite Europe. They were butterfirkins, swillers of beer and schnaps, and their *vrouws* from whom Holbein painted the all-but loveliest of Madonnas, Rembrandt the graceful girl who sits immortal on his knee in Dresden, and Rubens his abounding goddesses, were the synonyms of clumsy vulgarity. Even so late as Irving the ships of the greatest navigators in the world were represented as sailing equally well stern-foremost. That the aristocratic Venetians should have

> Riveted with gigantic piles
> Thorough the centre their new-catchèd miles,

was heroic. But the far more marvellous achievement of the Dutch in the same kind was ludicrous even to republican Marvell. Meanwhile, during that very century of scorn, they were the best artists, sailors, merchants, bankers, printers, scholars, jurisconsults, and statesmen in Europe, and the genius of Motley has revealed them to us, earning a right to themselves by the most heroic struggle in human annals. But, alas! they were not merely simple burghers who had fairly made themselves High Mightinesses, and could treat on equal terms with anointed kings, but their commonwealth carried in its bosom the germs of democracy. They even unmuzzled, at least after dark, that dreadful mastiff, the Press, whose scent is, or ought to be, so keen for wolves in sheep's clothing and for certain other animals in lions' skins. They made fun of Sacred Majesty, and, what was worse, managed uncommonly well without it. In an age when periwigs made so large a part of the natural dignity of man, people with such a turn of mind were dangerous. How could they seem other than vulgar and hateful?

In the natural course of things we succeeded to this unenviable position of general butt. The Dutch had thriven under it pretty well, and there was hope that we could at least contrive to worry along. And we certainly did in a very redoubtable fashion. Perhaps we deserved some of the sarcasm more than our Dutch predecessors in office. We had nothing to boast of in arts or letters, and were given to bragging overmuch of our merely material prosperity, due quite as much to the virtue of our continent as to our own. There was some truth in Carlyle's sneer, after all. Till we had succeeded in some higher way than this, we had only the success of physical growth. Our greatness, like that of enormous Russia, was greatness on the map,—barbarian mass only; but had we gone down, like that other Atlantis, in some vast cataclysm, we should have covered but a pin's point on the chart of memory, compared with those ideal spaces occupied by tiny Attica and cramped England. At the same time, our critics somewhat too easily forgot that material must make ready the foundation for ideal triumphs, that the arts have no chance in poor countries. But it must be allowed that democracy stood for a great deal in our shortcoming. The Edinburgh Review never would have thought of asking, "Who reads a Russian book?" and England was satisfied with iron from Sweden without being impertinently inquisitive after her painters and statuaries. Was it that they expected too much from the mere miracle of Freedom? Is it not the highest art of a Republic to make men of flesh and blood, and not the marble ideals of such? It may be fairly doubted whether we have produced this higher type of man yet. Perhaps it is the collective, not the individual, humanity that is to have a chance of nobler development among us. We shall see. We have a vast amount of imported ignorance, and, still worse, of native ready-made knowledge, to digest before even the preliminaries of such a consummation can be arranged. We have got to learn that statesmanship is the most complicated of all arts, and to come back to the apprenticeship-system too hastily abandoned. At present, we trust a man with making constitutions on less proof of competence than we should demand before we gave him our shoe to patch. We have nearly reached the limit of the reaction from the old notion, which paid too much regard to birth and station as qualifications for office, and have touched the extreme point in the opposite direction, putting the highest of human functions up at auction to be bid for by any creature capable of going upright on two legs. In some places, we have arrived at a point at which civil society is no longer possible, and already another reaction has begun, not backwards to the old system, but toward fitness either from natural aptitude or special training. But will it always be safe to let evils work their own cure by becoming unendurable? Every one of them leaves its taint in the constitution of the body-politic, each in itself, perhaps, trifling, yet all together powerful for evil.

But whatever we might do or leave undone, we were not genteel, and it was uncomfortable to be continually reminded that, though we should boast that we were the Great West till we were black in the face, it did not bring us an inch nearer to the world's West-End. That sacred enclosure of respectability was tabooed to us. The Holy Alliance did not inscribe us on its visiting-list. The Old World of wigs and orders and liveries would shop with us, but we must ring at the area-bell, and not venture to awaken the more august clamors of the knocker. Our manners, it must be granted, had none of those graces that stamp the caste of Vere de Vere, in whatever museum of British antiquities they may be hidden. In short, we were vulgar.

This was one of those horribly vague accusations, the victim of which has no defense. An umbrella is of no avail against a Scotch mist. It envelopes you, it penetrates at every pore, it wets you through without seeming to wet you at all. Vulgarity is an eighth deadly sin, added to the list in these latter days, and worse than all the others put together, since it perils your salvation in *this* world,—far the more important of the two in the minds of most men. It profits nothing to draw nice distinctions between essential and conventional, for the convention in this case *is* the essence, and you may break every command of the decalogue with perfect good-breeding, nay, if you are adroit, without losing caste. We, indeed, had it not to lose, for we had never gained it. "*How* am I vulgar?" asks the culprit, shudderingly. "Because thou art not like unto Us," answers Lucifer, Son of the Morning, and there is no more to be said. The god of this world may be a fallen angel, but he has us *there!* We were as clean,—so far as my observation goes, I think we were cleaner, morally and physically, than the English, and therefore, of course, than everybody else. But we did not pronounce the diphthong *ou* as they did, and we said *eether* and not *eyther,* following therein the fashion of our ancestors, who unhappily could bring over no English better than Shakespeare's; and we did not stammer as they had learned to do from the courtiers, who in this way flattered the Hanoverian king, a foreigner among the people he had come to reign over. Worse than all, we might have the noblest ideas and the finest sentiments in the world, but we vented them through that organ by which men are led rather than leaders, though some physiologists would persuade us that Nature furnishes her captains with a fine handle to their faces that Opportunity may get a good purchase on them for dragging them to the front.

This state of things was so painful that excellent people were not wanting who gave their whole genius to reproducing here the original Bull, whether by gaiters, the cut of their whiskers, by a factitious brutality in their tone, or by an accent that was forever tripping and falling flat over the tangled roots of our common tongue. Martyrs to a false ideal, it never occurred to them that nothing is more hateful to gods and men than a second-rate Englishman, and for the very reason that this planet never produced a more splendid creature than the first-rate one, witness Shakespeare and the Indian Mutiny. Witness that truly sublime self-abnegation of those prisoners lately among the bandits of Greece, where average men gave an example of quiet fortitude for which all the stoicism of antiquity can show no match. Witness the wreck of the Birkenhead, an example of disciplined heroism, perhaps, the most precious, as the rarest, of all. If we could contrive to be not too unobtrusively our simple selves, we should be the most delightful of human beings, and the most original; whereas, when the plating of Anglicism rubs off, as it always will in points that come to much wear, we are liable to very unpleasing conjectures about the quality of the metal underneath. Perhaps one reason why the average Briton spreads himself here with such an easy air of superiority may be owing to the fact that he meets with so many bad imitations as to conclude himself the only real thing in a wilderness of shams. He fancies himself moving through an endless Bloomsbury, where his mere apparition confers honor as an avatar of the court-end of the universe. Not a Bull of them all but is persuaded he bears Europa upon his back. This is the sort of fellow whose patronage is so divertingly insufferable. Thank Heaven he is not the only specimen of cater-cousinship from the dear old Mother Island that is shown to us! Among genuine things, I know nothing more genuine than the better men whose limbs were made in England. So manly-tender, so brave, so true, so warranted to wear, they make us proud to feel that blood is thicker than water.

But it is not merely the Englishman; every European candidly admits in himself some right of primogeniture in respect of us, and pats this shaggy continent on the back with a lively sense of generous unbending. The German who plays the bass-viol has a well-founded contempt, which he is not always nice in concealing, for a country so few of whose children ever take that noble instrument between their knees. His cousin, the Ph.D. from Göttingen, cannot help despising a people who do not grow loud and red over Aryans and Turanians, and are indifferent about their descent from either. The Frenchman feels an easy mastery in speaking his mother tongue, and attributes it to some native superiority of parts that lifts him high above us barbarians of the West. The Italian *prima donna* sweeps a curtsy of careless pity to the over-facile pit which unsexes her with the *bravo!* innocently meant to show a familiarity with foreign usage. But all without exception make no secret of regarding us as the goose bound to deliver them a golden egg in return for *their* cackle. Such men as Agassiz, Guyot, and Goldwin Smith come with gifts in their hands; but since it is commonly European failures who bring hither their remarkable gifts and acquirements, this view of the case is sometimes just the least bit in the world provoking. To think what a delicious seclusion of contempt we enjoyed till California and our own ostentatious *parvenus,* flinging gold away in Europe that might have endowed libraries at home, gave us the ill repute of riches! What a shabby downfall from the Arcadia which the French officers of our Revolutionary War fancied they saw here through Rousseau-tinted spectacles! Something of Arcadia there really was, something of the Old Age; and that divine provincialism were cheaply repurchased could we have it back again in exchange for the tawdry upholstery that has taken its place.

For some reason or other, the European has rarely been able to see America except in caricature. Would the first Review of the world have printed the *niaiseries* of M. Maurice Sand as a picture of society in any civilized country? M. Sand, to be sure, has inherited nothing of his famous mother's literary outfit, except the pseudonym. But since the conductors of the *Revue* could not have published his story because it was clever, they must have thought it valuable for its truth. As true as the last-century Englishman's picture of Jean Crapaud! We do not ask to be sprinkled with rosewater, but may perhaps fairly protest against being drenched with the rinsings of an unclean imagination. The next time the *Revue* allows such ill-bred persons to throw their slops out of its first-floor windows, let it honestly preface the discharge with a *gare l'eau!* that we may run from under in season. And M. Duvergier de Hauranne, who knows how to be entertaining! I know that *le Français est plutôt indiscret que confiant,* and the pen slides too easily when indiscretions will fetch so much a page; but should we not have been *tant-soit-peu* more cautious had we been writing about people on the other side of the Channel? But then it is a fact in the natural history of the American long familiar to Europeans, that he abhors privacy, knows not the meaning of reserve, lives in hotels because of their greater publicity, and is never so pleased as when his domestic affairs (if he may be said to have any) are paraded in the newspapers. Barnum, it is well known, represents perfectly the average national sentiment in this respect. However it be, we are not treated like other people, or perhaps I should say like people who are ever likely to be met with in society.

Is it in the climate? Either I have a false notion of European manners, or else the atmosphere affects them strangely when exported hither. Perhaps they suffer from the sea-voyage like some of the more delicate wines. During our Civil War an English gentleman of the highest description was kind enough to call upon me, mainly, as it seemed, to inform me how entirely he sympathized with the Confederates, and how sure he felt that we could never subdue them,—" they were the *gentlemen* of the country, you know." Another, the first greetings hardly over, asked me how I accounted for the universal meagreness of my countrymen. To a thinner man than I, or a from a stouter man than he, the question *might* have been offensive. The Marquis of Hartington * wore a secession badge at a public ball in New York. In a civilized country he might have been roughly handled; but here, where the *bienséances* are not so well understood, of course nobody minded it. A French traveller told me he had been a good deal in the British colonies, and had been astonished to see how soon the people became Americanized. He added, with delightful *bonhomie,* and as if he were sure it would charm me, that "they even began to talk through their noses, just like you!" I was naturally ravished with this testimony to the assimilating power of democracy, and could only reply that I hoped they would never adopt our democratic patent-method of seeming to settle one's honest debts, for they would find it paying through the nose in the long-run. I am a man of the New World, and do not know precisely the present fashion of May-Fair, but I have a kind of feeling that if an American (*mutato nomine, de te* is always frightfully possible) were to do this kind of thing under a European roof, it would induce some dis-

*One of Mr. Lincoln's neatest strokes of humor was his treatment of this gentleman when a laudable curiosity induced him to be presented to the President of the Broken Bubble. Mr. Lincoln persisted in calling him Mr. Partington. Surely the refinement of good-breeding could go no further. Giving the young man his real name (already notorious in the newspapers) would have made his visit an insult. Had Henri IV done this, it would have been famous. [Author's note.]

agreeable reflections as to the ethical results of democracy. I read the other day in print the remark of a British tourist who had eaten large quantities of our salt, such as it is (I grant it has not the European savor), that the Americans were hospitable, no doubt, but that it was partly because they longed for foreign visitors to relieve the tedium of their dead-level existence, and partly from ostentation. What shall we do? Shall we close our doors? Not I, for one, if I should so have forfeited the friendship of L. S., most lovable of men. He somehow seems to find us human, at least, and so did Clough, whose poetry will one of these days, perhaps, be found to have been the best utterance in verse of this generation. And T. H., the mere grasp of whose manly hand carries with it the pledge of frankness and friendship, of an abiding simplicity of nature as affecting as it is rare!

The fine old Tory aversion of former times was not hard to bear. There was something even refreshing in it, as in a northeaster to a hardy temperament. When a British parson, travelling in Newfoundland while the slash of our separation was still raw, after prophesying a glorious future for an island that continued to dry its fish under the ægis of Saint George, glances disdainfully over his spectacles in parting at the U. S. A., and forebodes for them a "speedy relapse into barbarism," now that they have madly cut themselves off from the humanizing influences of Britain, I smile with barbarian self-conceit. But this kind of thing became by degrees an unpleasant anachronism. For meanwhile the young giant was growing, was beginning indeed to feel tight in his clothes, was obliged to let in a gore here and there in Texas, in California, in New Mexico, in Alaska, and had the scissors and needle and thread ready for Canada when the time came. His shadow loomed like a Brocken-spectre over against Europe,—the shadow of what they were coming to, that was the unpleasant part of it. Even in such misty image as they had of him, it was painfully evident that his clothes were not of any cut hitherto fashionable, nor conceivable by a Bond Street tailor,—and this in an age, too, when everything depends upon clothes, when, if we do not keep up appearances, the seeming-solid frame of this universe, nay, your very God, would slump into himself, like a mockery king of snow, being nothing, after all, but a prevailing mode, a make-believe of believing. From this moment the young giant assumed the respectable aspect of a phenomenon, to be got rid of if possible, but at any rate as legitimate a subject of human study as the glacial period or the silurian what-d'ye-call-ems. If the man of the primeval drift-heaps be so absorbingly interesting, why not the man of the drift that is just beginning, of the drift into whose irresistible current we are just being sucked whether we will or no? If I were in their place, I confess I should not be frightened. Man has survived so much, and contrived to be comfortable on this planet after surviving so much! I am something of a protestant in matters of government also, and am willing to get rid of vestments and ceremonies and to come down to bare benches, if only faith in God take the place of a general agreement to profess confidence in ritual and sham. Every mortal man of us holds stock in the only public debt that is absolutely sure of payment, and that is the debt of the Maker of this Universe to the Universe he has made. I have no notion of selling out my shares in a panic. It was something to have advanced even to the dignity of a phenomenon, and yet I do not know that the relation of the individual American to the individual European was bettered by it; and that, after all, must adjust itself comfortably before there can be a right understanding between the two. We had been a desert, we became a museum. People came hither for scientific and not social ends. The very cockney could not complete his education without taking a vacant stare at us in passing. But the sociologists (I think they call themselves so) were the hardest to bear. There was no escape. I have even known a professor of this fearful science to come disguised in petticoats. We were cross-examined as a chemist cross-examines a new substance. Human? yes, all the elements are present, though abnormally combined. Civilized? Hm! that needs a stricter assay. No entomologist could take a more friendly interest in a strange bug. After a few such experiences, I, for one, have felt as if I were merely one of those horrid things preserved in spirits (and very bad spirits, too) in a cabinet. I was not the fellow-being of these explorers: I was a curiosity; I was a *specimen.* Hath not an American organs, dimensions, senses, affections, passions even as a European hath? If you prick us, do we not bleed? If you tickle us, do we not laugh? I will not keep on with Shylock to his next question but one.

Till after our Civil War it never seemed to enter the head of any foreigner, especially of any Englishman, that an American had what could be called a country, except as a place to eat, sleep, and trade in. Then it seemed to strike them suddenly. "By Jove, you know, fellahs don't fight like that for a shop-till!" No, I rather think not. To Americans America is something more than a promise and an expectation. It has a past and traditions of its own. A descent from men who sacrificed everything and came hither, not to better their fortunes, but to plant their idea in virgin soil, should be a good pedigree. There was never a colony save this that went forth, not to seek gold, but God. Is it not as well to have sprung from such as these as from some burly beggar who came over with Wilhelmus Conquestor, unless, indeed, a line grow better as it runs farther away from stalwart ancestors? And for our history, it is dry enough, no doubt, in the books, but, for all that, is of a kind that tells in the blood. I have admitted that Carlyle's sneer had a show of truth in it. But what does he himself, like a true Scot, admire in the Hohenzollerns? First of all, that they were *canny,* a thrifty, forehanded race. Next, that they made a good fight from generation to generation with the chaos around them. That is precisely the battle which the English race on this continent has been pushing doughtily forward for two centuries and a half. Doughtily and silently, for you cannot hear in Europe "that crash, the death-song of the perfect tree," that has been going on here from sturdy father to sturdy son, and making this continent habitable for the weaker Old World breed that has swarmed to it during the last half-century. If ever men did a good stroke of work on this planet, it was the forefathers of those whom you are wondering whether it would not be prudent to acknowledge as far-off cousins. Alas, man of genius, to whom we owe so much, could you see nothing more than the burning of a foul chimney in that clash of Michael and Satan which flamed up under your very eyes?

Before our war we were to Europe but a huge mob of adventurers and shopkeepers. Leigh Hunt expressed it well enough when he said that he could never think of America without seeing a gigantic counter stretched all along the seaboard. And Leigh Hunt, without knowing it, had been more than half Americanized, too! Feudalism had by degrees made commerce, the great civilizer, contemptible. But a tradesman with a sword on thigh and very prompt of stroke was not only redoubtable, he had become respectable also. Few people, I suspect, alluded twice to a needle in Sir John Hawkwood's presence, after that doughty fighter had exchanged it for a more dangerous tool of the same metal. Democracy had been hitherto only a ludicrous effort to reverse the laws of nature by thrusting Cleon into the place of Pericles. But a democracy that could fight for an abstraction, whose members held life and goods cheap compared with that larger life which we call country, was not merely unheard-of, but portentous. It was the nightmare of the Old World taking upon itself flesh and blood, turning out to be substance and not dream. Since the Norman crusader clanged down upon the throne of the *porphyro-geniti,* carefully-draped appearances had never received such a shock, had never been so rudely called on to produce their titles to the empire of the world. Authority has had its periods not unlike those of geology, and at last comes Man claiming kingship in right of his mere manhood. The world of the Saurians might be in some respects more picturesque, but the march of events is inexorable, and that world is bygone.

The young giant had certainly got out of long-clothes. He had become the *enfant terrible* of the human household. It was not and will not be easy for the world (especially for our British cousins) to look upon us as grown up. The youngest of nations, its people must also be young and to be treated accordingly, was the syllogism,—as if libraries did not make all nations equally old in all those respects, at least, where age is an advantage and not a defect. Youth, no doubt, has its good qualities, as people feel who are losing it, but boyishness is another thing. We had been somewhat boyish as a nation, a little loud, a little pushing, a little braggart. But might it not partly have been because we felt that we had certain claims to respect that were not admitted? The war which established our position as a vigorous nationality has also sobered us. A nation, like a man, cannot look death in the eye for four years without some strange reflections, without arriving at some clearer consciousness of the stuff it is made of, without some great moral change. Such a change, or the beginning of it, no observant person can fail to see here. Our thought and our politics, our bearing as a people, are assuming a manlier tone. We have been compelled to see what was weak in democracy as well as what was strong. We have begun obscurely to recognize that things do not go of themselves, and that popular government is not in itself a panacea, is no better than any other form except as the virtue and wisdom of the people make it so, and that when men undertake to do their own kingship, they enter upon the dangers and responsibilities as well as the privileges of the function. Above all, it looks as if we were on the way to be persuaded that no government can be carried on by declamation. It is noticeable also that facility of communication has made the best English and French thought far more directly operative here than ever before. Without being Europeanized, our discussion of important questions in statesmanship, in political economy, in æsthetics, is taking a broader scope and a higher tone. It had certainly been provincial, one might almost say local, to a very unpleasant extent. Perhaps our experience in soldiership has taught us to value training more than we have been popularly wont. We may possibly come to the conclusion, one of these days, that self-made men may not be always equally skilful in the manufacture of wisdom, may not be divinely commissioned to fabricate the higher qualities of opinion on all possible topics of human interest.

So long as we continue to be the most common-schooled and the least cultivated people in the world, I suppose we must consent to endure this condescending manner of foreigners toward us. The more friendly they mean to be, the more ludicrously prominent it becomes. They can never appreciate the immense amount of silent work that has been done here, making this continent slowly fit for the abode of man, and which will demonstrate itself, let us hope, in the character of the people. Outsiders can only be expected to judge a nation by the amount it has contributed to the civilization of the world; the amount, that is, that can be seen and handled. A great place in history can only be achieved by competitive examinations, nay, by a long course of them. How much new thought have we contributed to the common stock? Till that question can be triumphantly answered, or needs no answer, we must continue to be simply interesting as an experiment, to be studied as a problem, and not respected as an attained result or an accomplished solution. Perhaps, as I have hinted, their patronizing manner toward us is the fair result of their failing to see here anything more than a poor imitation, a plaster-cast of Europe. And are they not partly right? If the tone of the uncultivated American has too often the arrogance of the barbarian, is not that of the cultivated as often vulgarly apologetic? In the America they meet with is there the simplicity, the manliness, the absence of sham, the sincere human nature, the sensitiveness to duty and implied obligation, that in any way distinguishes us from what our orators call "the effete civilization of the Old World"? Is there a politician among us daring enough (except a Dana here and there) to risk his future on the chance of our keeping our word with the exactness of superstitious communities like England? Is it certain that we shall be ashamed of a bankruptcy of honor, if we can only keep the letter of our bond? I hope we shall be able to answer all these questions with a frank *yes*. At any rate, we would advise our visitors that we are not merely curious creatures, but belong to the family of man, and that, as individuals, we are not to be always subjected to the competitive examination above mentioned, even if we acknowledged their competence as an examining board. Above all, we beg them to remember that America is not to us, as to them, a mere object of external interest to be discussed and analyzed, but *in* us, part of our very marrow. Let them not suppose that we conceive of ourselves as exiles from the graces and amenities of an older date than we, though very much at home in a state of things not yet all it might be or should be, but which we mean to make so, and which we find both wholesome and pleasant for men (though perhaps not for *dilettanti*) to live in. "The full tide of human existence" may be felt here as keenly as Johnson felt it at Charing Cross, and in a larger sense. I know one person who is singular enough to think Cambridge the very best spot on the habitable globe. "Doubtless God *could* have made a better, but doubtless he never did."

It will take England a great while to get over her airs of patronage toward us, or even passably to conceal them. She cannot help confounding the people with the country, and regarding us as lusty juveniles. She has a conviction that whatever good there is in us is wholly English, when the truth is that we are worth nothing except so far as we have disinfected ourselves of Anglicism. She is especially condescending just now, and lavishes sugar-plums on us as if we had not outgrown them. I am no believer in sudden conversions, especially in sudden conversions to a favorable opinion of people who have just proved you to be mistaken in judgment and therefore unwise in policy. I never blamed her for not wishing well to democracy,—how should she?—but Alabamas are not wishes. Let her not be too hasty in believing Mr. Reverdy Johnson's pleasant words. Though there is no thoughtful man in America who would not consider a war with England the greatest of calamities, yet the feeling toward her here is very far from cordial, whatever our Minister may say in the effusion that comes after ample dining. Mr. Adams, with his famous "My Lord, this means war," perfectly represented his country. Justly or not, we have a feeling that we have been wronged, not merely insulted. The only sure way of bringing about a healthy relation between the two countries is for Englishmen to clear their minds of the notion that we are always to be treated as a kind of inferior and deported Englishman whose nature they perfectly understand, and whose back they accordingly stroke the wrong way of the fur with amazing perseverance. Let them learn to treat us naturally on our merits as human beings, as they would a German or a Frenchman, and not as if we were a kind of counterfeit Briton whose crime appeared in every shade of difference, and before long there would come that right feeling which we naturally call a good understanding. The common blood, and still more the common language, are fatal instruments of misapprehension. Let them give up *trying* to understand us, still more thinking that they do, and acting in various absurd ways as the necessary consequence, for they will never arrive at that devoutly-to-be-wished consummation, till they learn to look at us as we are and not as they suppose us to be. Dear old long-estranged mother-in-law, it is a great many years since we parted. Since 1660, when you married again, you have been a step-mother to us. Put on your spectacles, dear madam. Yes, we *have* grown, and changed likewise. You would not let us darken your doors, if you could help it. We know that perfectly well. But pray, when we look to be treated as men, don't shake that rattle in our faces, nor talk baby to us any longer.

Do, child, go to it grandam, child;
Give grandam kingdom, and it grandam will
Give it a plum, a cherry, and a fig!

1869

# GEORGE HENRY BOKER
(1823–1890)

## *From* TO ENGLAND

I

Lear and Cordelia! 'twas an ancient tale
Before thy Shakespeare gave it deathless fame:
The times have changed, the moral is the same.
So like an outcast, dowerless, and pale,
Thy daughter went; and in a foreign gale
Spread her young banner, till its sway became
A wonder to the nations. Days of shame
Are close upon thee: prophets raise their wail.
When the rude Cossack with an outstretched hand
Points his long spear across the narrow sea,—
"Lo! there is England!" when thy destiny
Storms on thy straw-crowned head, and thou dost stand
Weak, helpless, mad, a by-word in the land,—
God grant thy daughter a Cordelia be!
(1851) 1852

II

Stand, thou great bulwark of man's liberty!
Thou rock of shelter, rising from the wave,
Sole refuge to the overwearied brave
Who planned, arose, and battled to be free,
Fell undeterred, then sadly turned to thee;—
Saved the free spirit from their country's grave,
To rise again, and animate the slave,
When God shall ripen all things. Britons, ye
Who guard the sacred outpost, not in vain
Hold your proud peril! Freemen undefiled,
Keep watch and ward! Let battlements be piled
Around your cliffs; fleets marshalled, till the main
Sink under them; and if your courage wane,
Through force or fraud, look westward to your child!
(1851) 1852

## THE FEVER IN MY BLOOD HAS DIED

The fever in my blood has died;
The eager foot, the glancing eye,
By beauty lured so easily,
No more are moved, or turn aside:
My smiles are gone, my tears are dried.

And if I say I love thee now,
'Tis not because my passions burn—
Fair as thou art—to ask return
Of love for love, and vow for vow;
Too dear exchanged for such as thou.

I love thee only as he can
Who knows his heart. I yield in truth,
Not the blind, headlong heat of youth,

That pants ere it has run a span,
But the determined love of man.

And if from me you ask more fire
Than lights my slowly-fading days,—
The sudden frenzy and the blaze,
The selfish clutch of young desire,—
You point where I cannot aspire.

Yet do not bend thy head to weep,
Because my love so coldly shows;
For where the fuel fiercely glows
The flame is brief: in ashes deep
The everlasting embers sleep.

1856

## HERE PART WE, LOVE, BENEATH THE WORLD'S BROAD EYE

Here part we, love, beneath the world's broad eye,
Yet heart to heart still answers as of old;
And though fore'er within my breast I hold
Thy image shut, and ne'er, by look nor sigh,
Betray thy presence to the foes who lie
Ambushed around us, do not deem me cold.
For cowering Love's wide pinions only fold
Closer, to shield him from the storm that's nigh,—
Closer, to warm the fresh and godlike form
That glows with life beneath the shrinking wings,
So my deep love around thee darkly flings
This cloud of coldness, that, beneath it, warm
As the snow-covered currents of the springs,
Our hearts may beat, safe sheltered from the storm.

1856

## ALL THE WORLD'S MALICE, ALL THE SPITE OF FATE

All the world's malice, all the spite of fate,
Cannot undo the rapture of the past.
I, like a victor, hold these glories fast;
And here defy the envious powers, that wait
Upon the crumbling fortunes of our state,
To snatch this myrtle chaplet, or to blast
Its smallest leaf. Thus to the wind I cast
The poet's laurel, and before their date
Summon the direst terrors of my doom.
For, with this myrtle symbol of my love,
I reign exultant, and am fixed above
The petty fates that other joys consume.
As on a flowery path, through life I'll move,
As through an arch of triumph, pass the tomb.

1856

## CAVALRY SONG

Draw your girths tight, boys;
This morning we ride,
With God and the right, boys,
To sanction our side,
Where the balls patter,
Where the shot shatter,
Where the shells scatter
Red death far and wide.

Pause not to think, boys,
Of maidens in tears;
Only this drink, boys,
Let's toss to our dears;
Then O for the battle,
The mad charging rattle,
The foam-snorting cattle,
The victor's wild cheers!

Look to our arms, boys,
Our friends tried and true:
How the blood warms, boys!
The foe is in view!
Forward! break cover!
Ride through them! ride over
Them! baptize the clover
With blood as with dew!

1864

## DIRGE FOR A SOLDIER

IN MEMORY OF GENERAL PHILIP KEARNEY

KILLED SEPTEMBER 1, 1862

Close his eyes; his work is done!
What to him is friend or foeman,
Rise of moon, or set of sun,
Hand of man, or kiss of woman?
Lay him low, lay him low,
In the clover or the snow!
What cares he? he cannot know:
Lay him low!

As man may, he fought his fight,
Proved his truth by his endeavor;
Let him sleep in solemn night,
Sleep forever and forever.
Lay him low, lay him low,
In the clover or the snow!
What cares he? he cannot know:
Lay him low!

Fold him in his country's stars,
Roll the drum and fire the volley!
What to him are all our wars,
What but death bemocking folly?
Lay him low, lay him low,
In the clover or the snow!
What cares he? he cannot know:
Lay him low!

Leave him to God's watching eye,
Trust him to the hand that made him.
Mortal love weeps idly by:
God alone has power to aid him.
Lay him low, lay him low,
In the clover or the snow!
What cares he? he cannot know:
Lay him low!

(1862) 1864

---

## FRANCESCA DA RIMINI

### DRAMATIS PERSONÆ

MALATESTA, *Lord of Rimini*
GUIDO DA POLENTA, *Lord of Ravenna*
LANCIOTTO, *Malatesta's son*
PAOLO, *his brother*
PEPE, *Malatesta's jester*
CARDINAL, *friend to Guido*
RENE, *a troubadour*
FRANÇESCA DA RIMINI, *Guido's daughter*
RITTA, *her maid*
Lords, Ladies, Knights, Priests, Soldiers, Pages and Attendants.

*Scene:* Rimini, Ravenna, and the neighborhood.
*Time:* about 1300 A. D.

### ACT I

SCENE 1. *Rimini. The Garden of the Palace.* PAOLO *and a number of Noblemen are discovered, seated under an arbor, surrounded by* RENE *and other Troubadours, and Attendants.*

PAOLO. I prithee, Rene, charm our ears again
With the same song you sang me yesterday.
Here are fresh listeners.
RENE. Really, my good lord,
My voice is out of joint. A grievous cold— [*Coughs.*]
PAOLO. A very grievous, but convenient cold,
Which always racks you when you would not sing.
RENE. O, no, my lord! Besides, I hoped to hear
My ditty warbled into fairer ears,
By your own lips; to better purpose, too. [*The Noblemen all laugh.*]
FIRST NOBLEMAN. Rene has hit it. Music runs to waste
In ears like ours.

SECOND NOBLEMAN. Nay, nay; chaunt on, sweet Count.

PAOLO [*coughing*]. Alack! you hear, I've caught poor Rene's cough.

FIRST NOBLEMAN. That would not be, if we wore petticoats.

[*The others laugh.*]

PAOLO. O, fie!

FIRST NOBLEMAN. So runs the scandal to our ears.

SECOND NOBLEMAN. Confirmed by all our other senses, Count.

FIRST NOBLEMAN. Witnessed by many a doleful sigh, poured out
By many a breaking heart in Rimini.

SECOND NOBLEMAN. Poor girls!

FIRST NOBLEMAN [*mimicking a lady*]. Sweet Count! sweet Count Paolo! O!
Plant early violets upon my grave!
Thus go a thousand voices to one tune.

[*The others laugh.*]

PAOLO. 'Ods mercy! gentlemen, you do me wrong.

FIRST NOBLEMAN. And by how many hundred, more or less?

PAOLO. Ah! rogues, you'd shift your sins upon my shoulders.

SECOND NOBLEMAN. You'd bear them stoutly.

FIRST NOBLEMAN. It were vain to give
Drops to god Neptune. You're the sea of love
That swallows all things.

SECOND NOBLEMAN. We the little fish
That meanly sculk about within your depths.

PAOLO. Go on, go on! Talk yourselves fairly out.

[PEPE *laughs without.*]

But, hark! here comes the fool! Fit company
For this most noble company of wits!

[*Enter* PEPE, *laughing violently.*]

Why do you laugh?

PEPE. I'm laughing at the world.
It has laughed long enough at me; and so
I'll turn the tables. Ho! ho! ho! I've heard
A better joke of Uncle Malatesta's
Than any I e'er uttered. [*Laughing.*]

ALL. Tell it, fool.

PEPE. Why, do you know—upon my life, the best
And most original idea on earth:
A joke to put in practice, too. By Jove!
I'll bet my wit 'gainst the stupidity
Of the best gentlemen among you all,
You cannot guess it.

ALL. Tell us, tell us, fool.

PEPE. Guess it, guess it, fools.

PAOLO. Come, disclose, disclose!

PEPE. He has a match afoot.—

ALL. A match!

PEPE. A marriage.

ALL. Who?—who?

PEPE. A marriage in his family.

ALL. But, who?

PEPE. Ah! there's the point.

ALL. Paolo?

PEPE. No.

FIRST NOBLEMAN. The others are well wived. Shall we turn Turks?

PEPE. Why, there's the summit of his joke, good sirs.
By all the sacred symbols of my art—
By cap and bauble, by my tinkling bell—
He means to marry Lanciotto!

[*Laughs violently.*]

ALL [*laughing*]. Ho!—

PAOLO. Peace! peace! What tongue dare echo yon fool's laugh?
Nay, never raise your hands in wonderment:
I'll strike the dearest friend among ye all
Beneath my feet, as if he were a slave,
Who dares insult my brother with a laugh!

PEPE. By Jove! ye're sad enough. Here's mirth's quick cure!

Pretty Paolo has a heavy fist,
I warn you, sirs. Ho! ho! I trapped them all; [*Laughing.*]
Now I'll go mar old Malatesta's message [*Aside*]. [*Exit.*]

PAOLO. Shame on ye, sirs! I have mistaken you.
I thought I harboured better friends. Poor fops,
Who've slept in down and satin all your years,
Within the circle Lanciotto charmed
Round Rimini with his most potent sword!—
Fellows whose brows would melt beneath a casque,
Whose hands would fray to grasp a brand's rough hilt,
Who ne'er launched more than braggart threats at foes!—
Girlish companions of luxurious girls!—
Danglers round troubadours and wine-cups!—Men
Whose best parts are their clothes! bundles of silk,
Scented like summer! rag-men, nothing more!—
Creatures as generous as monkeys—brave
As hunted hares—courteous as grinning apes—
Grateful as serpents—useful as lap-dogs—

[*During this, the Noblemen, etc., steal off.*]

I am alone at last! So let me be,
Till Lanciotto fill the vacant room
Of these mean knaves, whose friendship is but breath. [*Exit.*]

SCENE 2. *The Same. A Hall in the Castle.*

[*Enter* MALATESTA *and* LANCIOTTO.]

MALATESTA. Guido, ay, Guido of Ravenna, son—
Down on his knees, as full of abject prayers
For peace and mercy as a penitent.

LANCIOTTO. His old trick, father.
While his wearied arm
Is raised in seeming prayer, it only rests.
Anon, he'll deal you such a staggering blow,
With its recovered strength, as shall convert
You, and not him, into a penitent.

MALATESTA. No, no; your last bout leveled him. He reeled,
Into Ravenna, from the battle-field,
Like a stripped drunkard, and there headlong fell—
A mass of squalid misery, a thing
To draw the jeering urchins. I have this
From faithful spies. There's not a hope remains
To break the shock of his great overthrow.
I pity Guido.

LANCIOTTO. 'S death! go comfort him!
I pity those who fought, and bled, and died,
Before the armies of this Ghibelin.
I pity those who halted home with wounds
Dealt by his hand. I pity widowed eyes
That he set running; maiden hearts that turn,
Sick with despair, from ranks thinned down by him;
Mothers that shriek, as the last stragglers fling
Their feverish bodies by the fountain-side,
Dumb with mere thirst, and faintly point to him,
Answering the dame's quick questions. I have seen
Unburied bones, and skulls—that seemed to ask,
From their blank eye-holes, vengeance at my hand—
Shine in the moonlight on old battle-fields;

And even these—the happy dead, my lord—
I pity more than Guido of Ravenna!

MALATESTA. What would you have?

LANCIOTTO. I'd see Ravenna burn,
Flame into heaven, and scorch the flying clouds;
I'd choke her streets with ruined palaces;
I'd hear her women scream with fear and grief,
As I have heard the maids of Rimini.
All this I'd sprinkle with old Guido's blood,
And bless the baptism.

MALATESTA. You are cruel.

LANCIOTTO. Not I;
But these things ache within my fretting brain.
The sight I first beheld was from the arms
Of my wild nurse, her husband hacked to death
By the fierce edges of these Ghibelins.
One cut across the neck—I see it now,
Ay, and have mimicked it a thousand times,
Just as I saw it, on our enemies.—
Why, that cut seemed as if it meant to bleed
On till the judgement. My distracted nurse
Stooped down, and paddled in the running gore
With her poor fingers; then a prophetess,
Pale with the inspiration of the god,
She towered aloft, and with her dripping hand
Three times she signed me with the holy cross.
'Tis all as plain as noon-day. Thus she spake,—
"May this spot stand till Guido's dearest blood
Be mingled with thy own!" The soldiers say,
In the close battle, when my wrath is up,
The dead man's blood flames on my vengeful brow
Like a red planet; and when war is o'er,
It shrinks into my brain, defiling all
My better nature with its slaughterous lusts.
Howe'er it be, it shaped my earliest thought,
And it will shape my last.

MALATESTA. You moody churl!
You dismal knot of superstitious dreams!
Do you not blush to empty such a head
Before a sober man? Why, son, the world
Has not given o'er its laughing humour yet,
That you should try it with such vagaries.—Poh!
I'll get a wife to teach you common sense.

LANCIOTTO. A wife for me! [*Laughing.*]

MALATESTA. Ay, sir, a wife for you.
You shall be married, to insure your wits.

LANCIOTTO. 'Tis not your wont to mock me.

MALATESTA. How now, son!
I am not given to jesting. I have chosen
The fairest wife in Italy for you.
You won her bravely, as a soldier should:
And when you'd woo her, stretch your gauntlet out,
And crush her fingers in its steely grip.
If you will plead, I ween, she dare not say—
No, by your leave. Should she refuse, howe'er,
With that same iron hand you shall go knock
Upon Ravenna's gates, till all the town
Ring with your courtship. I have made her hand

The price and pledge of Guido's future peace.

LANCIOTTO. All this is done!

MALATESTA. Done, out of hand; and now
I wait a formal answer, nothing more.
Guido dare not decline. No, by the saints,
He'd send Ravenna's virgins here in droves,
To buy a ten days' truce.

LANCIOTTO. Sir, let me say,
You stretch paternal privilege too far,
To pledge my hand without my own consent.
Am I a portion of your household stuff,
That you should trade me off to Guido thus?
Who is the lady I am bartered for?

MALATESTA. Francesca, Guido's daughter.—Never frown;
It shall be so!

LANCIOTTO. By heaven, it shall not be!
My blood shall never mingle with his race.

MALATESTA. According to your nurse's prophecy,
Fate orders it.

LANCIOTTO. Ha!

MALATESTA. Now, then, I have struck
The chord that answers to your gloomy thoughts.
Bah! on your sibyl and her prophecy!
Put Guido's blood aside, and yet, I say,
Marry you shall.

LANCIOTTO. 'Tis most distasteful, sir.

MALATESTA. Lanciotto, look ye! You brave gentleman,
So fond of knocking out poor people's brains,
In time must come to have your own knocked out:
What, then, if you bequeath us no new hands,
To carry on your business, and our house
Die out for lack of princes?

LANCIOTTO. Wed my brothers:
They'll rear you sons, I'll slay you enemies.
Paolo and Francesca! Note their names;
They chime together like sweet marriage-bells.
A proper match. 'Tis said she's beautiful;
And he is the delight of Rimini,—
The pride and conscious centre of all eyes,
The theme of poets, the ideal of art,
The earthly treasury of Heaven's best gifts!
I am a soldier; from my very birth,
Heaven cut me out for terror, not for love.
I had such fancies once, but now—

MALATESTA. Pshaw! son,
My faith is bound to Guido; and if you
Do not throw off your duty, and defy,
Through sickly scruples, my express commands,
You'll yield at once. No more: I'll have it so! [*Exit.*]

LANCIOTTO. Curses upon my destiny! What, I—
Ho! I have found my use at last—What. I.
I, the great twisted monster of the wars,
The brawny cripple, the herculean dwarf,
The spur of panic, and the butt of scorn—
I be a bridegroom! Heaven, was I not cursed
More than enough, when thou didst fashion me
To be a type of ugliness,—a thing
By whose comparison all Rimini
Holds itself beautiful? Lo! here I stand,
A gnarléd, blighted trunk! There's not a knave

So spindle-shanked, so wry-faced, so infirm,
Who looks at me, and smiles not on himself.
And I have friends to pity me—great Heaven!
One has a favorite leg that he bewails,—
Another sees my hip with doleful plaints,—
A third is sorry o'er my huge swart arms,—
A fourth aspires to mount my very hump,
And thence harangue his weeping brotherhood!
Pah! it is nauseous! Must I further bear
The sidelong shuddering glances of a wife?
The degradation of a showy love,
That over-acts, and proves the mummer's craft
Untouched by nature? And a fair wife, too!—
Francesca, whom the minstrels sing about!
Though, by my side, what woman were not fair?
Circe looked well among her swine, no doubt;
Next me, she'd pass for Venus. Ho! ho! ho! *[Laughing.]*
Would there were something merry in my laugh!
Now, in the battle, if a Ghibelin
Cry, "Wry-hip! hunchback!" I can trample him
Under my stallion's hoofs; or haggle him
Into a monstrous likeness of myself:
But to be pitied,—to endure a sting
Thrust in by kindness, with a sort of smile!—
'Sdeath! it is miserable!

*[Enter* PEPE.*]*

PEPE. My lord—

LANCIOTTO. My fool!

PEPE. We'll change our titles when your bride's bells ring—
Ha, cousin?

LANCIOTTO. Even this poor fool has eyes,
To see the wretched plight in which I stand. *[Aside.]*
How, gossip, how?

PEPE. I, being the court-fool,
Am lord of fools by my prerogative.

LANCIOTTO. Who told you of my marriage?

PEPE. Rimini!
A frightful liar; but true for once, I fear.
The messenger from Guido has returned,
And the whole town is wailing over him.
Some pity you, and some the bride; but I,
Being more catholic, I pity both.

LANCIOTTO. Still, pity, pity! *[Aside.]*
*[Bells toll.]* Ha! whose knell is that?

PEPE. Lord Malatesta sent me to the tower,
To have the bells rung for your marriage-news.
How, he said not; so I, as I thought fit,
Told the deaf sexton to ring out a knell. *[Bells toll.]*
How do you like it?

LANCIOTTO. Varlet, have you bones,
To risk their breaking? I have half a mind
To thrash you from your motley coat! *[Seizes him.]*

PEPE. Pardee!
Respect my coxcomb, cousin. Hark! ha, ha! *[Laughing.]*
*[Bells ring a joyful peal.]*
Some one has changed my music. Heaven defend!
How the bells jangle! Yonder graybeard, now,

Rings a peal vilely. He's more used to knells,
And sounds them grandly. Only give him time,
And, I'll be sworn, he'll ring your knell out yet.

LANCIOTTO. Pepe, you are but half a fool.

PEPE. My lord,
I can return the compliment in full.

LANCIOTTO. So, you are ready.

PEPE. Truth is always so.

LANCIOTTO. I shook you rudely; here's a florin. [*Offers money.*]

PEPE. No:
My wit is merchandise, but not my honour.

LANCIOTTO. Your honour, sirrah!

PEPE. Why not? You great lords
Have something you call lordly honour; pray,
May not a fool have foolish honour too?
Cousin, you laid your hand upon my coat—
'Twas the first sacrilege it ever knew—
And you shall pay it. Mark! I promise you.

LANCIOTTO [*laughing*]. Ha, ha! you bluster well. Upon my life,
You have the tilt-yard jargon to a breath.
Pepe, if I should smite you on the cheek—
Thus, gossip, thus—[*Strikes him*] what would you then demand?

PEPE. Your life!

LANCIOTTO [*laughing*]. Ha, ha! there is the camp-style, too—
A very cut-throat air! How this shrewd fool
Makes the punctilio of honour show!
Change helmets into coxcombs, swords to baubles,
And what a figure is poor chivalry!
Thanks for your lesson, Pepe! [*Exit.*]

PEPE. Ere I'm done,
You'll curse as heartily, you limping beast!
Ha! so we go—Lord Lanciotto, look!
[*Walks about, mimicking him.*]
Here is a leg and camel-back, forsooth,
To match your honour and nobility!
You miscreated scarecrow, dare you shake,
Or strike in jest, a natural man like me?—
You cursèd lump, you chaos of a man,
To buffet one whom Heaven pronounces good! [*Bells ring.*]
There go the bells rejoicing over you:
I'll change them back to the old knell again.
You marry, faugh! Beget a race of elves;
Wed a she-crocodile, and keep within
The limits of your nature! Here we go,
Tripping along to meet our promised bride,
Like a rheumatic elephant!—ha, ha!
[*Laughing.*]
[*Exit, mimicking* LANCIOTTO.]

SCENE 3. *The Same. A Room in the Same.*

[*Enter* LANCIOTTO, *hastily.*]

LANCIOTTO. Why do these prodigies environ me?
In ancient Rome, the words a fool might drop,
From the confusion of his vagrant thoughts,
Were held as omens, prophecies; and men
Who made earth tremble with majestic deeds,
Trembled themselves at fortune's lightest threat.
I like it not. My father named this match
While I boiled over with vindictive wrath
Towards Guido and Ravenna. Straight my heart

Sank down like lead; a weakness seized on me,
A dismal gloom that I could not resist;
I lacked the power to take my stand, and say—
Bluntly, I will not! Am I in the toils?
Has fate so weakened me, to work its end?
There seems a fascination in it, too,—
A morbid craving to pursue a thing
Whose issue may be fatal. Would that I
Were in the wars again! These mental weeds
Grow on the surface of inactive peace.
I'm haunted by myself. Thought preys on thought.
My mind seems crowded in the hideous mould
That shaped my body. What a fool am I
To bear the burden of my wretched life,
To sweat and toil under the world's broad eye,
Climb into fame, and find myself—O, what?—
A most conspicuous monster! Crown my head,
Pile Cæsar's purple on me—and what then?
My hump shall shorten the imperial robe,
My leg peep out beneath the scanty hem,
My broken hip shall twist the gown awry;
And pomp, instead of dignifying me,
Shall be by me made quite ridiculous.
The faintest coward would not bear all this:
Prodigious courage must be mine, to live;
To die asks nothing but weak will, and I
Feel like a craven. Let me skulk away
Ere life o'ertask me.

[*Offers to stab himself.*]

[*Enter* PAOLO.]

PAOLO [*seizing his hand*]. Brother! what is this?
Lanciotto, are you mad? Kind Heaven! look here—
Straight in my eyes. Now answer, do you know
How near you were to murder? Dare you bend
Your wicked hand against a heart I love?
Were it for you to mourn your wilful death,
With such a bitterness as would be ours,
The wish would ne'er have crossed you. While we're bound
Life into life, a chain of loving hearts,
Were it not base in you, the middle link,
To snap, and scatter all? Shame, brother, shame!
I thought you better metal.

LANCIOTTO. Spare your words.
I know the seasons of our human grief,
And can predict them without almanac.
A few sobs o'er the body, and a few
Over the coffin; then a sigh or two,
Whose windy passage dries the hanging tear;
Perchance, some wandering memories, some regrets;
Then a vast influx of consoling thoughts—
Based on the trials of the sadder days
Which the dead missed; and then a smiling face
Turned on to-morrow. Such is mortal grief.
It writes its histories within a span,
And never lives to read them.

PAOLO. Lanciotto,
I heard the bells of Rimini, just now,
Exulting o'er your coming marriage-day,
While you conspired to teach them gloomier sounds.
Why are you sad?

LANCIOTTO. Paolo, I am wretched;
Sad's a faint word. But of my marriage-bells—
Heard you the knell that Pepe rang?
PAOLO. 'Twas strange:
A sullen antic of his crabbed wit.
LANCIOTTO. It was portentous. All dumb things find tongues
Against this marriage. As I passed the hall,
My armor glittered on the wall, and I
Paused by the harness, as before a friend
Whose well-known features slack our hurried gait;
Francesca's name was fresh upon my mind,
So I half-uttered it. Instant, my sword
Leaped from its scabbard, as with sudden life,
Plunged down and pierced into the oaken floor,
Shivering with fear! Lo! while I gazed upon it—
Doubting the nature of the accident—
Around the point appeared a spot of blood,
Oozing upon the floor, that spread and spread—
As I stood gasping by in speechless horror—
Ring beyond ring, until the odious tide
Crawled to my feet, and lapped them, like the tongues
Of angry serpents! O, my God! I fled
At the first touch of the infernal stain!
Go—you may see—go to the hall!
PAOLO. Fie! man,
You have been ever played on in this sort
By your wild fancies. When your heart is high,
You make them playthings; but in lower moods,
They seem to sap the essence of your soul,
And drain your manhood to its poorest dregs.
LANCIOTTO. Go look, go look!
PAOLO [*goes to the door, and returns*]. There sticks the sword, indeed.
Just as your tread detached it from its sheath;
Looking more like a blessed cross, I think,
Than a bad omen. As for blood—
Ha, ha! [*Laughing.*]
It sets mine dancing. Pshaw! away with this!
Deck up your face with smiles. Go trim yourself
For the young bride. New velvet, gold, and gems,
Do wonders for us. Brother, come; I'll be
Your tiring-man, for once.
LANCIOTTO. Array this lump—
Paolo, hark! There are some human thoughts
Best left imprisoned in the aching heart,
Lest the freed malefactors should dispread
Infamous ruin with their liberty.
There's not a man—the fairest of ye all—
Who is not fouler than he seems. This life
Is one unending struggle to conceal
Our baseness from our fellows. Here stands one
In vestal whiteness with a lecher's lust;—
There sits a judge, holding law's scales in hands
That itch to take the bribe he dare not touch;—
Here goes a priest, with heavenward eyes, whose soul
Is Satan's council-chamber;—there a doctor,
With nature's secrets wrinkled round a brow
Guilty with conscious ignorance;—and here
A soldier rivals Hector's bloody deeds—

Out-does the devil in audacity—
With craven longings fluttering in a heart
That dares do aught but fly! Thus are we all
Mere slaves and alms-men to a scornful world,
That takes us at our seeming.

PAOLO. Say 'tis true;
What do you drive at?

LANCIOTTO. At myself, full tilt.
I, like the others, am not what I seem.
Men call me gentle, courteous, brave. —They lie!
I'm harsh, rude, and a coward. Had I nerve
To cast my devils out upon the earth,
I'd show this laughing planet what a hell
Of envy, malice, cruelty, and scorn,
It has forced back to canker in the heart
Of one poor cripple!

PAOLO. Ha!

LANCIOTTO. Ay, now 'tis out!
A word I never breathed to man before.
Can you, who are a miracle of grace,
Feel what it is to be a wreck like me?
Paolo, look at me. Is there a line,
In my whole bulk of wretched contraries,
That nature in a nightmare ever used
Upon her shapes till now? Find me the man,
Or beast, or tree, or rock, or nameless thing,
So out of harmony with all things else,
And I'll go raving with bare happiness,—
Ay, and I'll marry Helena of Greece,
And swear I do her honour!

PAOLO. Lanciotto,
I, who have known you from a stripling up,
Never observed, or, if I did, ne'er weighed
Your special difference from the rest of men.
You're not Apollo—

LANCIOTTO. No!

PAOLO. Nor yet are you
A second Pluto. Could I change with you—
My graces for your nobler qualities—
Your strength, your courage, your renown—by heaven,
We'd e'en change persons, to the finest hair.

LANCIOTTO. You should be flatterer to an emperor.

PAOLO. I am but just. Let me beseech you, brother,
To look with greater favor on yourself;
Nor suffer misty phantoms of your brain
To take the place of sound realities.
Go to Ravenna, wed your bride, and lull
Your cruel delusions in domestic peace.
Ghosts fly a fireside: 'tis their wont to stalk
Through empty houses, and through empty hearts.
I know Francesca will be proud of you.
Women admire you heroes. Rusty sages,
Pale poets, and scarred warriors, have been
Their idols ever; while we fair plump fools
Are elbowed to the wall, or only used
For vacant pastime.

LANCIOTTO. To Ravenna?—no!
In Rimini they know me; at Ravenna
I'd be a new-come monster, and exposed
To curious wonder. There will be parade
Of all the usual follies of the state;
Fellows with trumpets, tinselled coats, and wands,
Would strut before me, like vain mountebanks
Before their monkeys. Then, I should be stared

Out of my modesty; and when they look,
How can I tell if 'tis the bridegroom's face
Or hump that draws their eyes? I will not go.
To please you all, I'll marry; but to please
The wonder-mongers of Ravenna—Ha!
Paolo, now I have it. You shall go,
To bring Francesca; and you'll speak of me,
Not as I ought to be, but as I am.
If she draw backward, give her rein; and say
That neither Guido nor herself shall feel
The weight of my displeasure. You may say,
I pity her—

PAOLO. For what?

LANCIOTTO. For wedding me.
In sooth, she'll need it. Say—

PAOLO. Nay, Lanciotto,
I'll be a better orator in your behalf,
Without your promptings.

LANCIOTTO. She is fair, 'tis said;
And, dear Paolo, if she please your eye,
And move your heart to anything like love,
Wed her yourself. The peace would stand as firm
By such a match.

PAOLO [*laughing*]. Ha! that is right: be gay!
Ply me with jokes! I'd rather see you smile
Than see the sun shine.

LANCIOTTO. I am serious,
I'll find another wife, less beautiful,
More on my level, and—

PAOLO. An empress, brother,
Were honoured by your hand. You are by much
Too humble in your reckoning of yourself.
I can count virtues in you, to supply
Half Italy, if they were parcelled out.
Look up!

LANCIOTTO. I cannot: Heaven has bent me down.
To you, Paolo, I could look, however,
Were my hump made a mountain. Bless him, God!
Pour everlasting bounties on his head!
Make Crœsus jealous of his treasury,
Achilles of his arms, Endymion
Of his fresh beauties,—though the coy one lay,
Blushing beneath Diana's earliest kiss,
On grassy Latmos; and may every good,
Beyond man's sight, though in the ken of heaven,
Round his fair fortune to a perfect end!
O, you have dried the sorrow of my eyes;
My heart is beating with a lighter pulse;
The air is musical; the total earth
Puts on new beauty, and within the arms
Of girdling ocean dreams her time away,
And visions bright to-morrows!

[*Enter* MALATESTA *and* PEPE.]

MALATESTA. Mount, to horse!

PEPE [*aside*]. Good Lord! he's smiling! What's the matter now?
Has anybody broken a leg or back?
Has a more monstrous monster come to life?
Is hell burst open?—heaven burnt up? What, what
Can make yon eyesore grin?—I say, my lord,
What cow has calved?

PAOLO. Your mother, by the bleat.

PEPE. Right fairly answered—for a gentleman!
When did you take my trade up?

PAOLO. When your wit
Went begging, sirrah.

PEPE. Well again! My lord,
I think he'll do.

MALATESTA. For what?
PEPE. To take my place.
Once fools were rare, and then my office sped;
But now the world is overrun with them:
One gets one's fool in one's own family,
Without much searching.
MALATESTA. Pepe, gently now.
Lanciotto, you are waited for. The train
Has passed the gate, and halted there for you.
LANCIOTTO. I go not to Ravenna.
MALATESTA. Hey! why not?
PAOLO. For weighty reasons, father. Will you trust
Your greatest captain, hope of all the Guelfs,
With crafty Guido? Should the Ghibelins
Break faith, and shut Lanciotto in their walls—
Sure the temptation would be great enough—
What would you do?
MALATESTA. I'd eat Ravenna up!
PEPE. Lord! what an appetite!
PAOLO. But Lanciotto
Would be a precious hostage.
MALATESTA. True; you're wise.
Guido's a fox. Well, have it your own way.
What is your plan?
PAOLO. I go there in his place.
MALATESTA. Good! I will send a letter with the news.
LANCIOTTO. I thank you, brother. [*Apart to* PAOLO.]
PEPE. Ha! ha! ha!—O! O! [*Laughing.*]
MALATESTA. Pepe, what now?
PEPE. O! lord, O!—ho! ho! ho! [*Laughing.*]
PAOLO. Well, giggler?
PEPE. Hear my fable, uncle.
MALATESTA. Ay.
PEPE. Once on a time, Vulcan sent Mercury
To fetch dame Venus from a romp in heaven.
Well, they were long in coming, as he thought;
And so the god of spits and grid-irons
Railed like himself—the devil. But—now mark—
Here comes the moral. In a little while,
Vulcan grew proud, because he saw plain signs
That he should be a father; and so he
Strutted through hell, and pushed the devils by,
Like a magnifico of Venice. Ere long,
His heir was born; but then—ho! ho!—the brat
Had wings upon his heels, and thievish ways,
And a vile squint, like errant Mercury's,
Which honest Vulcan could not understand;—
Can you?
PAOLO. 'S death! fool, I'll have you in the stocks.
Father, your fool exceeds his privilege.
PEPE [*apart to* PAOLO]. Keep your own bounds, Paolo. In the stocks
I'd tell more fables than you'd wish to hear.
And so ride forth. But, cousin, don't forget
To take Lanciotto's picture to the bride.
Ask her to choose between it and yourself.
I'll count the moments, while she hesitates,
And not grow gray at it.
PAOLO. Peace, varlet, peace!
PEPE [*apart to him*]. Ah, now I have it. There's an elephant
Upon the scutcheon; show her that, and say—
Here's Lanciotto in our heraldry!
PAOLO. Here's for your counsel!
[*Strikes* PEPE, *who runs behind* MALATESTA.]

MALATESTA. Son, son, have a care!
We who keep pets must bear their pecks sometimes.
Poor knave! Ha! ha! thou'rt growing villainous.
[*Laughs and pats* PEPE.]

PEPE. Another blow! another life for that! [*Aside.*]

PAOLO. Farewell, Lanciotto. You are dull again.

LANCIOTTO. Nature will rule.

MALATESTA. Come, come!

LANCIOTTO. God speed you, brother!
I am too sad; my smiles all turn to sighs.

PAOLO. More cause to haste me on my happy work.
[*Exit with* MALATESTA.]

PEPE. I'm going, cousin.

LANCIOTTO. Go.

PEPE. Pray, ask me where.

LANCIOTTO. Where, then?

PEPE. To have my jewel carried home:
And, as I'm wise, the carrier shall be
A thief, a thief, by Jove! The fashion's new. [*Exit.*]

LANCIOTTO. In truth, I am too gloomy and irrational.
Paolo must be right. I always had
These moody hours and dark presentiments,
Without mischances following after them.
The camp is my abode. A neighing steed,
A fiery onset, and a stubborn fight,
Rouse my dull blood, and tire my body down
To quiet slumbers when the day is o'er,
And night above me spreads her spangled tent,
Lit by the dying cresset of the moon.
Ay, that is it; I'm homesick for the camp. [*Exit.*]

## ACT II

SCENE I. *Ravenna. A Room in* GUIDO'S *Palace.*

[*Enter* GUIDO *and a* CARDINAL.]

CARDINAL. I warn thee, Count.

GUIDO. I'll take the warning, father,
On one condition: show me but a way
For safe escape.

CARDINAL. I cannot.

GUIDO. There's the point.
We Ghibelins are fettered hand and foot.
There's not a florin in my treasury;
Not a lame soldier, I can lead to war;
Not one to man the walls. A present siege,
Pushed with the wonted heat of Lanciotto,
Would deal Ravenna such a mortal blow
As ages could not mend. Give me but time
To fill the drainéd arteries of the land.
The Guelfs are masters, we their slaves; and we
Were wiser to confess it, ere the lash
Teach it too sternly. It is well for you
To say you love Francesca. So do I;
But neither you nor I have any voice
For or against this marriage.

CARDINAL. 'Tis too true.

GUIDO. Say we refuse: Why, then, before a week,
We'll hear Lanciotto rapping at our door,
With twenty hundred ruffians at his back.
What's to say then? My lord, we waste our breath.
Let us look fortune in the face, and draw
Such comfort from the wanton as we may.

CARDINAL. And yet I fear—

GUIDO. You fear! and so do I.
I fear Lanciotto as a soldier, though,
More than a son-in-law.

CARDINAL. But have you seen him?
GUIDO. Ay, ay, and felt him, too. I've seen him ride
The best battalions of my horse and foot
Down like mere stubble: I have seen his sword
Hollow a square of pikemen, with the ease
You'd scoop a melon out.
CARDINAL. Report declares him
A prodigy of strength and ugliness.
GUIDO. Were he the devil—But why talk of this?—
Here comes Francesca.
CARDINAL. Ah, unhappy child!
GUIDO. Look you, my lord! you'll make the best of it;
You will not whimper. Add your voice to mine,
Or woe to poor Ravenna!

[*Enter* FRANCESCA *and* RITTA.]

FRANCESCA. Ha! my lord—
And you, my father!—But do I intrude
Upon your counsels? How severe you look!
Shall I retire?
GUIDO. No, no.
FRANCESCA. You moody men
Seem leagued against me. As I passed the hall,
I met your solemn Dante, with huge strides
Pacing in measure to his stately verse.
The sweeping sleeves of his broad scarlet robe
Blew out behind, like wide-expanded wings,
And seemed to buoy him in his level flight.
Thinking to pass, without disturbing him,
I stole on tip-toe; but the poet paused,
Subsiding into man, and steadily
Bent on my face the lustre of his eyes.
Then, taking both my trembling hands in his—
You know how his God-troubled forehead awes—
He looked into my eyes, and shook his head,
As if he dared not speak of what he saw;
Then muttered, sighed, and slowly turned away
The weight of his intolerable brow.
When I glanced back, I saw him, as before,
Sailing adown the hall on out-spread wings.
Indeed, my lord, he should not do these things:
They strain the weakness of mortality
A jot too far. As for poor Ritta, she
Fled like a doe, the truant.
RITTA. Yes, forsooth:
There's something terrible about the man.
Ugh! if he touched me, I should turn to ice.
I wonder if Count Lanciotto looks—
GUIDO. Ritta, come here. [*Takes her apart.*]
RITTA. My lord.
GUIDO. 'Twas my command,
You should say nothing of Count Lanciotto.
RITTA. Nothing, my lord.
GUIDO. You have said nothing then?
RITTA. Indeed, my lord.
GUIDO. 'Tis well. Some years ago,
My daughter had a very silly maid,
Who told her sillier stories. So, one day,
This maiden whispered something I forbade—
In strictest confidence, for she was sly:
What happened, think you?
RITTA. I know not, my lord.
GUIDO. I boiled her in a pot.
RITTA. Good heaven! my lord.
GUIDO. She did not like it. I shall keep that pot

Ready for the next boiling.
[*Walks back to the others.*]
RITTA. Saints above!
I wonder if he ate her! Boil me—me!
I'll roast or stew with pleasure; but to boil
Implies a want of tenderness,—or rather
A downright toughness—in the matter boiled,
That's slanderous to a maiden. What, boil me—
Boil me! O! mercy, how ridiculous!
[*Retires, laughing.*]

[*Enter a* MESSENGER.]

MESSENGER. Letters, my lord, from great Prince Malatesta.
[*Presents them, and exit.*]
GUIDO [*aside*]. Hear him, ye gods!—"from great Prince Malatesta!"
Greeting, no doubt, his little cousin Guido.
Well, well, just so we see-saw up and down. [*Reads.*]
"*Fearing our treachery,*"—by heaven, that's blunt,
And Malatesta-like!—"*he will not send*
*His son, Lanciotto, to Ravenna, but*"—
But what?—a groom, a porter? or will he
Have his prey sent him in an iron cage?
By Jove, he shall not have her! O! no, no;
"*He sends his younger son, the Count Paolo,*
*To fetch Francesca back to Rimini.*"
That's well, if he had left his reasons out.
And, in a postscript—by the saints, 'tis droll!—
"*'T would not be worth your lordship's while, to shut*
*Paolo in a prison; for, my lord,*
*I'll only pay his ransom in plain steel:*
*Besides, he's not worth having.*" Is there one,
Save this ignoble offshoot of the Goths,
Who'd write such garbage to a gentleman?
Take that, and read it.
[*Gives letter to* CARDINAL.]
CARDINAL. I have done the most.
She seems suspicious.
GUIDO. Ritta's work.
CARDINAL. Farewell! [*Exit.*]
FRANCESCA. Father, you seem distempered.
GUIDO. No, my child,
I am but vexed. Your husband's on the road,
Close to Ravenna. What's the time of day?
FRANCESCA. Past noon, my lord.
GUIDO. We must be stirring, then.
FRANCESCA. I do not like this marriage.
GUIDO. But I do.
FRANCESCA. But I do not. Poh! to be given away,
Like a fine horse or falcon, to a man
Whose face I never saw!
RITTA. That's it, my lady.
GUIDO. Ritta, run down, and see if my great pot
Boils to your liking.
RITTA [*aside*]. O! that pot again!
My lord, my heart betrays me; but you know
How true 'tis to my lady. [*Exit.*]
FRANCESCA. What ails Ritta?
GUIDO. The ailing of your sex, a running tongue.
Francesca, 'tis too late to beat retreat:
Old Malatesta has me—you, too, child—
Safe in his clutch. If you are not content,
I must unclose Ravenna, and allow
His son to take you. Poh, poh! have a soul
Equal with your estate. A prince's child

Cannot choose husbands. Her desires must aim,
Not at herself, but at the public good.
Both as your prince and father, I command;
As subject and good daughter, you'll obey.

FRANCESCA. I knew that it must be my destiny,
Some day, to give my hand without my heart;
But—

GUIDO. But, and I will but you back again!
When Guido da Polenta says to you,
Daughter, you must be married,—what were best?

FRANCESCA. 'Twere best Francesca, of the self-same name,
Made herself bridal-garments. [*Laughing.*]

GUIDO. Right!

FRANCESCA. My lord,
Is Lanciotto handsome—ugly—fair—
Black—sallow—crabbed—kind—or what is he?

GUIDO. You'll know ere long. I could not alter him,
To please your taste.

FRANCESCA. You always put me off;
You never have a whisper in his praise.

GUIDO. The world reports it.—Count my soldier's scars,
And you may sum Lanciotto's glories up.

FRANCESCA. I shall be dutiful, to please you, father.
If aught befall me through my blind submission,
Though I may suffer, you must bear the sin.
Beware, my lord, for your own peace of mind!
My part has been obedience; and now
I play it over to complete my task;
And it shall be with smiles upon my lips,—
Heaven only knows with what a sinking heart! [*Exeunt.*]

SCENE 2. *The Same. Before the Gates of the City. The walls hung with banners and flowers, etc., and crowded with citizens. At the side of the scene is a canopied dais, with chairs of state upon it. Music, bells, shouts, and other sounds of rejoicing, are occasionally heard.*

[*Enter* GUIDO, *the* CARDINAL, *Noblemen, Knights, Guards, etc., with banners and arms, etc.*]

GUIDO. My lord, I'll have it so. You talk in vain.
Paolo is a marvel in his way:
I've seen him often. If Francesca take
A fancy to his beauty, all the better;
For she may think that he and Lanciotto
Are like as blossoms of one parent branch.
In truth, they are, so far as features go—
Heaven help the rest! Get her to Rimini,
By any means, and I shall be content.
The fraud cannot last long; but long enough
To win her favor to the family.

CARDINAL. 'Tis a dull trick. Thou hast not dealt with her
Wisely nor kindly, and I dread the end.
If, when this marriage was enjoined on thee,
Thou hadst informed Francesca of the truth,
And said, Now, daughter, choose between
Thy peace and all Ravenna's; who that knows
The constant nature of her noble heart
Could doubt the issue? There'd have been some tears,
Some frightful fancies of her husband's looks;
And then she'd calmly walk up to her fate,

And bear it bravely. Afterwards, perchance,
Lanciotto might prove better than her fears,—
No one denies him many an excellence,—
And all go happily. But, as thou wouldst plot,
She'll be prepared to see a paragon,
And find a satyr. It is dangerous.
Treachery with enemies is bad enough,
With friends 'tis fatal.

GUIDO. Has your lordship done?

CARDINAL. Never, Count Guido, with so good a text.
Do not stand looking sideways at the truth;
Craft has become thy nature. Go to her.

GUIDO. I have not heart.

CARDINAL. I have. [*Going.*]

GUIDO. Hold, Cardinal!
My plan is better. Get her off my hands,
And I care not.

CARDINAL. What will she say of thee,
In Rimini, when she detects the cheat?

GUIDO. I'll stop my ears up.

CARDINAL. Guido, thou art weak,
And lack the common fortitude of man.

GUIDO. And you abuse the license of your garb,
To lessen me. My lord, I do not dare
To move a finger in these marriage-rites.
Francesca is a sacrifice, I know,—
A limb delivered to the surgeon's knife,
To save our general health. A truce to this.
Paolo has the business in his hands:
Let him arrange it as he will; for I
Will give Count Malatesta no pretext
To recommence the war.

CARDINAL. Farewell, my lord.
I'll neither help nor countenance a fraud.
You crafty men take comfort to yourselves,
Saying, deceit dies with discovery.
'Tis false; each wicked action spawns a brood,
And lives in its succession. You, who shake
Man's moral nature into storm, should know
That the last wave which passes from your sight
Rolls in and breaks upon eternity! [*Exit.*]

GUIDO. Why, that's a very grand and solemn thought:
I'll mention it to Dante. Gentlemen,
What see they from the wall?

NOBLEMEN. The train, my lord.

GUIDO. Inform my daughter.

NOBLEMEN. She is here, my lord.

[*Enter* FRANCESCA, RITTA, *Ladies and Attendants.*]

FRANCESCA. See, father, what a merry face I have,
And how my ladies glisten! I will try
To do my utmost, in my love for you
And the good people of Ravenna. Now,
As the first shock is over, I expect
To feel quite happy. I will wed the Count,
Be he whate'er he may. I do not speak
In giddy recklessness. I've weighed it all,—
'Twixt hope and fear, knowledge and ignorance,—
And reasoned out my duty to your wish.
I have no yearnings towards another love:
So, if I show my husband a desire
To fill the place with which he honors me,

According to its duties, even he—
Were he less noble than Count Lanciotto—
Must smile upon my efforts, and reward
Good will with willing grace. One pang remains.
Parting from home and kindred is a thing
None but the heartless, or the miserable,
Can do without a tear. This home of mine
Has filled my heart with two-fold happiness,
Taking and giving love abundantly.
Farewell, Ravenna! If I bless thee not,
'Tis that thou seem'st too blessed; and 'twere strange
In me to offer what thou'st always given.

GUIDO [*aside*]. This is too much! If she would rail a while
At me and fortune, it could be endured.

[*Shouts, music, etc. within.*]

FRANCESCA. Ha! there's the van just breaking through the wood!
Music! that's well; a welcome forerunner.
Now, Ritta—here—come talk to me. Alas!
How my heart trembles! What a world to me
Lies 'neath the glitter of yon cavalcade!
Is that the Count?

RITTA. Upon the dapple-gray?

FRANCESCA. Yes, yes.

RITTA. No; that's his—

GUIDO [*apart to her*]. Ritta!

RITTA. Ay; that's—that's—

GUIDO. Ritta, the pot! [*Apart to her.*]

RITTA. O! but this lying chokes! [*Aside.*]
Ay, that's Count Somebody, from Rimini.

FRANCESCA. I knew it was. Is that not glorious?

RITTA. My lady, what?

FRANCESCA. To see a cavalier
Sit on his steed with such familiar grace.

RITTA. To see a man astraddle on a horse!
It don't seem much to me.

FRANCESCA. Fie, stupid girl!
But mark! the minstrels thronging round the Count!
Ah! that is more than gallant horsemanship.
The soul that feeds itself on poesy,
Is of a quality more fine and rare
Than Heaven allows the ruder multitude.
I tell you, Ritta, when you see a man
Beloved by poets, made the theme of song,
And chaunted down to ages, as a gift
Fit for the rich embalmment of their verse,
There's more about him than the patron's gold.
If that's the gentleman my father chose,
He must have picked him out from all the world.
The Count alights. Why, what a noble grace
Runs through his slightest action! Are you sad?
You too, my father? Have I given you cause?
I am content. If Lanciotto's mind
Bear any impress of his fair outside,
We shall not quarrel ere our marriage-day.
Can I say more? My blushes speak for me:
Interpret them as modesty's excuse
For the short-comings of a maiden's speech.

RITTA. Alas! dear lady! [*Aside.*]

GUIDO [*aside*]. 'Sdeath! my plot has failed,
By overworking its design. Come, come;

Get to your places. See, the Count draws nigh.

[GUIDO *and* FRANCESCA *seat themselves upon the dais, surrounded by* RITTA, *Ladies, Attendants, Guards, etc. Music, shouts, ringing of bells. Enter Men-at-arms, with banners, etc.; Pages bearing costly presents on cushions; then* PAOLO, *surrounded by Noblemen, Knights, Minstrels, etc., and followed by other Men-at-arms. They range themselves opposite the dais.*]

GUIDO. Ravenna welcomes you, my lord, and I
Add my best greeting to the general voice.
This peaceful show of arms from Rimini
Is a new pleasure, stranger to our sense
Than if the East blew zephyrs, or the balm
Of Summer loaded rough December's gales,
And turned his snows to roses.

PAOLO. Noble sir,
We looked for welcome from your courtesy,
Not from your love; but this unhoped for sight
Of smiling faces, and the gentle tone
In which you greet us, leave us naught to win
Within your hearts. I need not ask, my lord,
Where bides the precious object of my search;
For I was sent to find the fairest maid
Ravenna boasts, among her many fair.
I might extend my travel many a league,
And yet return, to take her from your side.
I blush to bear so rich a treasure home,
As pledge and hostage of a sluggish peace;
For beauty such as hers was meant by Heaven
To spur our race to gallant enterprise,
And draw contending deities around
The dubious battles of a second Troy.

GUIDO. Sir Count, you please to lavish on my child
The high-strained courtesy of chivalry;
Yet she has homely virtues that, I hope,
May take a deeper hold in Rimini,
After the fleeting beauty of her face
Is spoiled by time, or faded to the eye
By its familiar usage.

PAOLO. As a man
Who ever sees Heaven's purpose in its works,
I must suppose so rare a tabernacle
Was framed for rarest virtues. Pardon me
My public admiration. If my praise
Clash with propriety, and bare my words
To cooler judgment, 'tis not that I wish
To win a flatterer's grudged recompense,
And gain by falsehood what I'd win through love.
When I have brushed my travel from my garb,
I'll pay my court in more befitting style.

[*Music. Exit with his train.*]

GUIDO [*advancing*]. Now, by the saints, Lanciotto's deputy
Stands in this business with a proper grace,
Stretching his lord's instructions till they crack.
A zealous envoy! Not a word said he
Of Lanciotto—not a single word;
But stood there, staring in Francesca's face
With his devouring eyes.—By Jupiter,
I but half like it!

FRANCESCA [*advancing*]. Father?

GUIDO. Well, my child.

FRANCESCA. How do you like—

GUIDO. The coxcomb!
I've done well!

FRANCESCA. No, no; Count Lanciotto?
GUIDO. Well enough.
But hang this fellow—hang your deputies!
I'll never woo by proxy.
FRANCESCA. Deputies!
And woo by proxy!
GUIDO. Come to me anon.
I'll strip this cuckoo of his gallantry!
[*Exit with Guards, etc.*]
FRANCESCA. Ritta, my father has strange ways of late.
RITTA. I wonder not.
FRANCESCA. You wonder not?
RITTA. No, lady:
He is so used to playing double games,
That even you must come in for your share.
Plague on his boiling! I will out with it. [*Aside.*]
Lady, the gentleman who passed the gates—
FRANCESCA. Count Lanciotto? As I hope for grace,
A gallant gentleman! How well he spoke!
With what sincere and earnest courtesy
The rounded phrases glided from his lips!
He spoke in compliments that seemed like truth.
Methinks I'd listen through a summer's day,
To hear him woo.—And he must woo to me—
I'll have our privilege—he must woo a space,
Ere I'll be won, I promise.
RITTA. But, my lady,
He'll woo you for another.
FRANCESCA. He?—ha! ha! [*Laughing.*]
I should not think it from the prologue, Ritta.
RITTA. Nor I.
FRANCESCA. Nor any one.
RITTA. 'Tis not the Count—
'Tis not Count Lanciotto.
FRANCESCA. Gracious saints!
Have you gone crazy? Ritta, speak again,
Before I chide you.
RITTA. 'Tis the solemn truth.
That gentleman is Count Paolo, lady,
Brother to Lanciotto, and no more
Like him than—than—
FRANCESCA. Than what?
RITTA. Count Guido's pot,
For boiling waiting-maids, is like the bath
Of Venus on the arras.
FRANCESCA. Are you mad,—
Quite mad, poor Ritta?
RITTA. Yes, perhaps I am,
Perhaps Lanciotto is a proper man—
Perhaps I lie—perhaps I speak the truth—
Perhaps I gabble like a fool. O! heavens,
That dreadful pot!
FRANCESCA. Dear Ritta!—
RITTA. By the mass,
They shall not cozen you, my gentle mistress!
If my lord Guido boiled me, do you think
I should be served up to the garrison,
By way of pottage? Surely they would not waste me.
FRANCESCA. You are an idle talker. Pranks like these
Fit your companions. You forget yourself.
RITTA. Not you, though, lady. Boldly I repeat,
That he who looked so fair, and talked so sweet,
Who rode from Rimini upon a horse
Of dapple-gray, and walked through yonder gate,
Is not Count Lanciotto.
FRANCESCA. This you mean?
RITTA. I do, indeed!
FRANCESCA. Then I am more abused—

More tricked, more trifled with, more played upon—
By him, my father, and by all of you,
Than anything, suspected of a heart,
Was ever yet!

RITTA. In Count Paolo, lady,
Perchance there was no meditated fraud.

FRANCESCA. How, dare you plead for him?—

RITTA. I but suppose:
Though in your father—O! I dare not say.

FRANCESCA. I dare. It was ill usage, gross abuse,
Treason to duty, meanness, craft—dishonour!
What if I'd thrown my heart before the feet
Of this sham husband! cast my love away
Upon a counterfeit! I was prepared
To force affection upon any man
Called Lanciotto. Anything of silk,
Tinsel, and gewgaws, if he bore that name,
Might have received me for the asking. Yes,
I was inclined to venture more than half
In this base business—shame upon my thoughts!—
All for my father's peace and poor Ravenna's.
And this Paolo, with his cavalcade,
His minstrels, music, and his pretty airs,
His showy person, and his fulsome talk,
Almost made me contented with my lot.
O! what a fool!—in faith, I merit it—
Trapped by mere glitter! What an easy fool!
Ha! ha! I'm glad it went no further, girl; [*Laughing.*]
I'm glad I kept my heart safe, after all.
There was my cunning. I have paid them back,
I warrant you! I'll marry Lanciotto;
I'll seem to shuffle by this treachery. No!
I'll seek my father, put him face to face
With his own falsehood; and I'll stand between,
Awful as justice, meting out to him
Heaven's dreadful canons 'gainst his conscious guilt.
I'll marry Lanciotto. On my faith,
I would not live another wicked day
Here, in Ravenna, only for the fear
That I should take to lying, with the rest.
Ha! ha! it makes me merry, when I think
How safe I kept this little heart of mine! [*Laughing.*]

[*Exit, with Attendants, etc.*]

RITTA. So 'tis all ended—all except my boiling,
And that will make a holiday for some.
Perhaps I'm selfish. Fagot, axe, and gallows,
They have their uses, after all. They give
The lookers-on a deal of harmless sport.
Though one may suffer, twenty hundred laugh;
And that's a point gained. I have seen a man—
Poor Dora's uncle—shake himself with glee,
At the bare thought of the ridiculous style
In which some villain died. "Dancing," quoth he,
"To the poor music of a single string!
Biting," quoth he, "after his head was off!
What use of that?" Or, "Shivering," quoth he,
"As from an ague, with his beard afire!"
And then he'd roar until his ugly mouth

Split at the corners. But to see me boil—
O! that will be the queerest thing of all!
I wonder if they'll put me in a bag,
Like a great suet-ball? I'll go, and tell
Count Guido, on the instant. How he'll laugh
To think his pot has got an occupant!
I wonder if he really takes delight
In such amusements? Nay, I have kept faith:
I only said the man was not Lanciotto;
No word of Lanciotto's ugliness.
I may escape the pot, for all. Pardee!
I wonder if they'll put me in a bag!
[*Exit, laughing.*]

SCENE 3. *The Same. A Room in* GUIDO's *Palace.*

[*Enter* GUIDO *and* RITTA.]

RITTA. There now, my lord, this is the whole of it:
I love my mistress more than I fear you.
If I could save her finger from the axe,
I'd give my head to do it. So, my lord,
I am prepared to stew.
GUIDO. Boil, Ritta, boil.
RITTA. No; I prefer to stew.
GUIDO. And I to boil.
RITTA. 'Tis very hard, my lord, I cannot choose
My way of cooking. I shall laugh, I vow,
In the grim headsman's face, when I remember
That I am dying for my lady's love.
I leave no one to shed a tear for me;
Father nor mother, kith nor kin, have I,
To say, "Poor Ritta!" o'er my lifeless clay.
They all have gone before me, and 't were well
If I could hurry after them.
GUIDO. Poor child! [*Aside.*]
But, baggage, said you aught of Lanciotto?
RITTA. No, not a word; and he's so ugly, too!
GUIDO. Is he so ugly?
RITTA. Ugly! he is worse
Than Pilate on the hangings.
GUIDO. Hold your tongue
Here, and at Rimini, about the Count,
And you shall prosper.
RITTA. Am I not to boil?
GUIDO. No, child. But be discreet at Rimini.
Old Malatesta is a dreadful man—
Far worse than I—he bakes his people, Ritta;
Lards them, like geese, and bakes them in an oven.
RITTA. Fire is my fate, I see that.
GUIDO. Have a care
It do not follow you beyond this world.
Where is your mistress?
RITTA. In her room, my lord.
After I told her of the Count Paolo,
She flew to have an interview with you;
But on the way—I know not why it was—
She darted to her chamber, and there stays
Weeping in silence. It would do you good—
More than a hundred sermons—just to see
A single tear, indeed it would, my lord.
GUIDO. Ha! you are saucy. I have humored you
Past prudence, malpert! Get you to your room! [*Exit* RITTA.]
More of my blood runs in yon damsel's veins
Than the world knows. Her mother to a shade;
The same high spirit, and strange martyr-wish
To sacrifice herself, body and soul,
For some loved end. All that she did for me;

And yet I loved her not. O! memory!
The darkest future has a ray of hope,
But thou art blacker than the sepulchre!
Thy horrid shapes lie round, like scattered bones,
Hopeless forever! I am sick at heart.
The past crowds on the present: as I sowed,
So am I reaping. Shadows from myself
Fall on the picture, as I trace anew
These rising spectres of my early life,
And add their gloom to what was dark before.
O! memory, memory! How my temples throb! [*Sits.*]

[*Enter* FRANCESCA, *hastily.*]

FRANCESCA. My lord, this outrage —[*He looks up.*] Father, are you ill?
You seem unhappy. Have I troubled you?
You heard how passionate and bad I was,
When Ritta told me of the Count Paolo.
Dear father, calm yourself; and let me ask
A child's forgiveness. 'Twas undutiful
To doubt your wisdom. It is over now,
I only thought you might have trusted me
With any counsel.

GUIDO [*aside*]. Would I had!

FRANCESCA. Ah! well,
I understand it all, and you were right.
Only the danger of it. Think, my lord,
If I had loved this man at the first sight:
We all have heard of such things. Think, again,
If I had loved him—as I then supposed
You wished me to—'twould have been very sad.
But no, dear sir, I kept my heart secure,
Nor will I loose it till you give the word.
I'm wiser than you thought me, you perceive.
But when we saw him, face to face, together,
Surely you might have told me then.

GUIDO. Francesca,
My eyes are old—I did not clearly see—
Faith, it escaped my thoughts. Some other things
Came in my head. I was as ignorant
Of Count Paolo's coming as yourself.
The brothers are so like.

FRANCESCA. Indeed?

GUIDO. Yes, yes,
One is the other's counterpart, in fact;
And even now it may not be—O! shame!
I lie by habit. [*Aside.*]

FRANCESCA. Then there is hope?
He may be Lanciotto, after all?
O! joy—

[*Enter a* SERVANT.]

SERVANT. The Count Paolo. [*Exit.*]

FRANCESCA. Misery!
That name was not Lanciotto!

GUIDO. Farewell, child.
I'll leave you with the Count: he'll make it plain.
It seems 'twas Count Paolo. [*Going.*]

FRANCESCA. Father!

GUIDO. Well.

FRANCESCA. You knew it from the first! [*Exit* GUIDO.] Let me begone:
I could not look him in the face again
With the old faith. Besides, 'twould anger him
To have a living witness of his fraud
Ever before him; and I could not trust—
Strive as I might—my happiness to him,

As once I did. I could not lay my hand
Upon his shoulder, and look up to him,
Saying, Dear father, pilot me along
Past this dread rock, through yonder narrow strait.
Saints, no! The gold that gave my life away
Might, even then, be rattling in his purse,
Warm from the buyer's hand. Look on me, Heaven!
Him thou didst sanctify before my eyes,
Him thou didst charge, as thy great deputy,
With guardianship of a weak orphan girl,
Has fallen from grace, has paltered with his trust;
I have no mother to receive thy charge,—
O! take it on thyself; and when I err,
Through mortal blindness, Heaven, be thou my guide!
Worse cannot fall me. Though my husband lack
A parent's tenderness, he yet may have
Faith, truth, and honour—the immortal bonds
That knit together honest hearts as one.
Let me away to Rimini. Alas!
It wrings my heart to have outlived the day
That I can leave my home with no regret! [*Weeps.*]

[*Enter* PAOLO.]

PAOLO. Pray, pardon me. [*Going.*]
FRANCESCA. You are quite welcome, Count.
A foolish tear, a weakness, nothing more:
But present weeping clears our future sight.
They tell me you are love's commissioner,
A kind of broker in the trade of hearts:
Is it your usual business? or may I
Flatter myself, by claiming this essay
As your first effort?
PAOLO. Lady, I believed
My post, at starting, one of weight and trust;
When I beheld you, I concluded it
A charge of honor and high dignity.
I did not think to hear you underrate
Your own importance, by dishonoring me.
FRANCESCA. You are severe, my lord.
PAOLO. No, not severe;
Say candid, rather. I am somewhat hurt
By my reception. If I feel the wound,
'Tis not because I suffer from the jest,
But that your lips should deal it.
FRANCESCA. Compliments
Appear to be the staple of your speech.
You ravish one with courtesy, you pour
Fine words upon one, till the listening head
Is bowed with sweetness. Sir, your talk is drugged;
There's secret poppy in your sugared phrase:
I'll taste before I take it.
PAOLO. Gentle lady—
FRANCESCA. I am not gentle, or I missed my aim.
I am no hawk to fly at every lure.
You courtly gentlemen draw one broad rule—
All girls are fools. It may be so, in truth,
Yet so I'll not be treated.
PAOLO. Have you been?
If I implied such slander by my words,
They wrong my purpose. If I compliment,
'Tis not from habit, but because I thought

Your face deserved my homage as its due.
When I have clearer insight, and you spread
Your inner nature o'er your lineaments,
Even that face may darken in the shades
Of my opinion. For mere loveliness
Needs inward light to keep it always bright.
All things look badly to unfriendly eyes.
I spoke my first impression; cooler thought
May work strange changes.

FRANCESCA. Ah, Sir Count, at length
There's matter in your words.

PAOLO. Unpleasant stuff,
To judge by your dark brows. I have essayed
Kindness and coldness, yet you are not pleased.

FRANCESCA. How can I be?

PAOLO. How, lady?

FRANCESCA. Ay, sir, how?
Your brother—my good lord that is to be—
Stings me with his neglect; and in the place
He should have filled, he sends a go-between,
A common carrier of others' love;
How can the sender, or the person sent,
Please overmuch? Now, were I such as you,
I'd be too proud to travel round the land
With other people's feelings in my heart;
Even to fill the void which you confess
By such employment.

PAOLO. Lady, 'tis your wish
To nettle me, to break my breeding down,
And see what natural passions I have hidden
Behind the outworks of my etiquette.
I neither own nor feel the want of heart
With which you charge me. You are more than cruel;
You rouse my nerves until they ache with life,
And then pour fire upon them. For myself
I would not speak, unless you had compelled.
My task is odious to me. Since I came,
Heaven bear me witness how my traitor heart
Has fought against my duty; and how oft
I wished myself in Lanciotto's place,
Or him in mine.

FRANCESCA. You riddle.

PAOLO. Do I? Well,
Let it remain unguessed.

FRANCESCA. You wished yourself
At Rimini, or Lanciotto here?
You may have reasons.

PAOLO. Well interpreted!
The Sphinx were simple in your skilful hands!

FRANCESCA. It has become our turn to sneer.

PAOLO. But I
Have gall to feed my bitterness, while you
Jest in the wanton ease of happiness.
Stop! there is peril in our talk.

FRANCESCA. As how?

PAOLO. 'Tis dangerous to talk about one's self;
It panders selfishness. My duty waits.

FRANCESCA. My future lord's affairs? I quite forgot
Count Lanciotto.

PAOLO. I, too, shame upon me! [*Aside.*]

FRANCESCA. Does he resemble you?

PAOLO. Pray, drop me, lady.

FRANCESCA. Nay, answer me.

PAOLO. Somewhat—in feature.

FRANCESCA. Ha!
Is he so fair?
PAOLO. No, darker. He was tanned
In long campaigns, and battles hotly fought,
While I lounged idly with the troubadours,
Under the shadow of his watchful sword.
FRANCESCA. In person?
PAOLO. He is shorter, I believe,
But broader, stronger, more compactly knit.
FRANCESCA. What of his mind?
PAOLO. Ah, now you strike the key!
A mind just fitted to his history,
An equal balance 'twixt desert and fame.
No future chronicler shall say of him,
His fame outran his merit; or his merit
Halted behind some adverse circumstance,
And never won the glory it deserved.
My love might weary you, if I rehearsed
The simple beauty of his character;
His grandeur and his gentleness of heart,
His warlike fire and peaceful love, his faith,
His courtesy, his truth. I'll not deny
Some human weakness, to attract our love,
Harbors in him, as in the rest of us.
Sometimes against our city's enemies
He thunders in the distance, and devotes
Their homes to ruin. When the brand has fallen,
He ever follows with a healing rain,
And in his pity shoulders by revenge.
A thorough soldier, lady. He grasps crowns,
While I pick at the laurel.
FRANCESCA. Stay, my lord!
I asked your brother's value, with no wish
To hear you underrate yourself. Your worth
May rise in passing through another's lips.
Lanciotto is perfection, then?
PAOLO. To me:
Others may think my brother over-nice
Upon the point of honour; over-keen
To take offence where no offence is meant;
A thought too prodigal of human life,
Holding it naught when weighed against a wrong;
Suspicious of the motives of his friends;
Distrustful of his own high excellence;
And with a certain gloom of temperament,
When thus disturbed, that makes him terrible
And rash in action. I have heard of this;
I never felt it. I distress you, lady?
Perhaps I throw these points too much in shade,
By catching at an enemy's report.
But, then, Lanciotto said, "You'll speak of me,
Not as I ought to be, but as I am."
He loathes deceit.
FRANCESCA. That's noble! Have you done?
I have observed a strange reserve, at times,
An over-carefulness in choosing words,
Both in my father and his nearest friends,
When speaking of your brother; as if they
Picked their way slowly over rocky ground,
Fearing to stumble. Ritta, too, my maid,
When her tongue rattles on in full career,
Stops at your brother's name, and with a sigh

Settles herself to dismal silence. Count,
These things have troubled me. From you I look
For perfect frankness. Is there naught withheld?

PAOLO [*aside*]. O, base temptation! What if I betray
His crippled person—imitate his limp—
Laugh at his hip, his back, his sullen moods
Of childish superstition?—tread his heart
Under my feet, to climb into his place?—
Use his own warrant 'gainst himself; and say,
Because I loved her, and misjudged your jest,
Therefore I stole her? Why, a common thief
Would hang for just such thinking! Ha! ha! ha! [*Laughing.*]
I reckon on her love, as if I held
The counsels of her bosom. No, I swear
Francesca would despise so mean a deed.
Have I no honour either? Are my thoughts
All bound by her opinion?

FRANCESCA. This is strange!
Is Lanciotto's name a spell to all?
I ask a simple question, and straight you
Start to one side, and mutter to yourself,
And laugh, and groan, and play the lunatic,
In such a style that you astound me more
Than all the others. It appears to me
I have been singled as a common dupe
By every one. What mystery is this
Surrounds Count Lanciotto? If there be
A single creature in the universe
Who has a right to know him as he is,
I am that one.

PAOLO. I grant it. You shall see,
And shape your judgment by your own remark.
All that my honour calls for I have said.

FRANCESCA. I am content. Unless I greatly err,
Heaven made your breast the seat of honest thoughts.
You know, my lord, that, once at Rimini,
There can be no retreat for me. By you,
Here at Ravenna, in your brother's name,
I shall be solemnly betrothed. And now
I thus extend my maiden hand to you;
If you are conscious of no secret guilt,
Take it.

PAOLO. I do. [*Takes her hand.*]

FRANCESCA. You tremble!

PAOLO. With the hand,
Not with the obligation.

FRANCESCA. Farewell, Count!
'Twere cruel to tax your stock of compliments,
That waste their sweets upon a trammelled heart;
Go fly your fancies at some freer game. [*Exit.*]

PAOLO. O, heaven, if I have faltered and am weak,
'Tis from my nature! Fancies, more accursed
Than haunt a murderer's bedside, throng my brain—
Temptations, such as mortal never bore
Since Satan whispered in the ear of Eve,
Sing in my ear—and all, all are accursed!
At heart I have betrayed my brother's trust,
Francesca's openly. Turn where I will,
As if enclosed within a mirrored hall,
I see a traitor. Now to stand erect,
Firm on my base of manly constancy;

Or, if I stagger, let me never quit
The homely path of duty, for the ways
That bloom and glitter with seductive sin! [*Exit.*]

## ACT III

SCENE 1. *Rimini. A room in the Castle.* LANCIOTTO *discovered reading.*

LANCIOTTO. O! fie, philosophy! This Seneca
Revels in wealth, and whines about the poor!
Talks of starvation while his banquet waits,
And fancies that a two hours' appetite
Throws light on famine! Doubtless he can tell,
As he skips nimbly through his dancing-girls,
How sad it is to limp about the world
A sightless cripple! Let him feel the crutch
Wearing against his heart, and then I'd hear
This sage talk glibly; or provide a pad,
Stuffed with his soft philosophy, to ease
His aching shoulder. Pshaw! he never felt,
Or pain would choke his frothy utterance.
'Tis easy for the doctor to compound
His nauseous simples for a sick man's health;
But let him swallow them, for his disease,
Without wry faces. Ah! the tug is there.
Show me philosophy in rags, in want,
Sick of a fever, with a back like mine,
Creeping to wisdom on these legs, and I
Will drink its comforts. Out! away with you!
There's no such thing as real philosophy! [*Throws down the book.*]

[*Enter* PEPE.]

Here is a sage who'll teach a courtier
The laws of etiquette, a statesman rule,
A soldier discipline, a poet verse,
And each mechanic his distinctive trade;
Yet bring him to his motley, and how wide
He shoots from reason! We can understand
All business but our own, and thrust advice
In every gaping cranny of the world;
While habit shapes us to our own dull work,
And reason nods above his proper task.
Just so philosophy would rectify
All things abroad, and be a jade at home.
Pepe, what think you of the Emperor's aim
Towards Hungary?

PEPE. A most unwise design;
For mark, my lord—

LANCIOTTO. Why, there! the fact cries out.
Here's motley thinking for a diadem!—
Ay, and more wisely in his own regard.

PEPE. You flout me, cousin.

LANCIOTTO. Have you aught that's new?—
Some witty trifle, some absurd conceit?

PEPE. Troth, no.

LANCIOTTO. Why not give up the Emperor,
And bend your wisdom on your duties, Pepe?

PEPE. Because the Emperor has more need of wisdom
Than the most barren fool of wit.

LANCIOTTO. Well said!
Mere habit brings the fool back to his art.
This jester is a rare philosopher.
Teach me philosophy, good fool.

PEPE. No need.

You'll get a teacher when you take a wife.
If she do not instruct you in more arts
Than Aristotle ever thought upon,
The good old race of woman has declined
Into a sort of male stupidity.
I had a sweetheart once, she lectured grandly;
No matter on what subject she might hit,
'Twas all the same, she could talk and she would.
She had no silly modesty; she dashed
Straight in the teeth of any argument,
And talked you deaf, dumb, blind. Whatever struck
Upon her ear, by some machinery,
Set her tongue wagging. Thank the Lord, she died!—
Dropped in the middle of a fierce harangue,
Like a spent horse. It was an even thing,
Whether she talked herself or me to death.
The latest sign of life was in her tongue;
It wagged till sundown, like a serpent's tail,
Long after all the rest of her was cold.
Alas! poor Zippa!

LANCIOTTO. Were you married, fool?

PEPE. Married! Have I the scars upon me? No;
I fell in love; and that was bad enough.
And far enough for a mere fool to go.
Married! why, marriage is love's purgatory,
Without a heaven beyond.

LANCIOTTO. Fie, atheist!
Would you abolish marriage?

PEPE. Yes.

LANCIOTTO. What?

PEPE. Yes.

LANCIOTTO. Depopulate the world?

PEPE. No fear of that.
I'd have no families, no Malatesti,
Strutting about the land, with pedigrees
And claims bequeathed them by their ancestors;
No fellows vaporing of their royal blood;
No one to seize a whole inheritance,
And rob the other children of the earth.
By Jove! you should not know your fathers, even!
I'd have you spring, like toadstools, from the soil—
Mere sons of women—nothing more nor less—
All base-born, and all equal. There, my lord,
There is a simple commonwealth for you!
In which aspiring merit takes the lead,
And birth goes begging.

LANCIOTTO. It is so, in truth;
And by the simplest means I ever heard.

PEPE. Think of it, cousin. Tell it to your friends,
The statesmen, soldiers, and philosophers;
Noise it about the earth, and let it stir
The sluggish spirits of the multitudes.
Pursue the thought, scan it, from end to end,
Through all its latent possibilities.
It is a great seed dropped, I promise you,
And it must sprout. Thought never wholly dies;
It only wants a name—a hard Greek name—
Some few apostles, who may live on it—
A crowd of listeners, with the average dulness
That man possesses—and we organize;
Spread our new doctrine, like a general plague;

Talk of man's progress and development,
Wrongs of society, the march of mind,
The Devil, Doctor Faustus, and what not;
And, lo! this pretty world turns upside down,
All with a fool's idea!

LANCIOTTO. By Jupiter,
You hit our modern teachers to a hair!
I knew this fool was a philosopher.
Pepe is right. Mechanic means advance;
Nature bows down to science' haughty tread,
And turns the wheel of smutty artifice;
New governments arise, dilate, decay,
And foster creeds and churches to their tastes:
At each advance, we cry, "Behold, the end!"
Till some fresh wonder breaks upon the age.
But man, the moral creature, midst it all
Stands still unchanged; nor moves towards virtue more,
Nor comprehends the mysteries in himself,
More than when Plato taught academies,
Or Zeno thundered from his Attic porch.

PEPE. I know not that; I only want my scheme
Tried for a while. I am a politician,
A wrongs-of-man man. Hang philosophy!
Let metaphysics swallow, at a gulp,
Its last two syllables, and purge itself
Clean of its filthy humors! I am one
Ready for martyrdom, for stake and fire,
If I can make my great idea take root!
Zounds! cousin, if I had an audience,
I'd make you shudder at my eloquence!
I have an itching to reform the world.

LANCIOTTO. Begin at home, then.

PEPE. Home is not my sphere;
Heaven picked me out to teach my fellow-men.
I am a very firebrand of truth—
A self-consuming, doomed, devoted brand—
That burns to ashes while I light the world!
I feel it in me. I am moved, inspired,
Stirred into utterance, by some mystic power
Of which I am the humble instrument.

LANCIOTTO. A bad digestion, sage, a bilious turn,
A gnawing stomach, or a pinching shoe.

PEPE. O! hear, but spare the scoffer! Spare the wretch
Who sneers at the anointed man of truth!
When we reached that, I and my followers
Would rend you limb from limb. There!—ha! ha! ha! [*Laughing.*]
Have I not caught the slang these fellows preach;
A grand, original idea, to back it;
And all the stock in trade of a reformer?

LANCIOTTO. You have indeed; nor do I wonder, Pepe.
Fool as you are, I promise you success
In your new calling, if you'll set it up.
The thing is far too simple.

[*Trumpet sounds within.*]

PEPE. Hist! my lord.

LANCIOTTO. That calls me to myself.

PEPE. At that alarm,
All Rimini leaped up upon its feet.
Cousin, your bridal-train. You groan! 'Ods wounds!

Here is the bridegroom sorely malcontent—
The sole sad face in Rimini. Since morn,
A quiet man could hardly walk the streets,
For flowers and streamers. All the town is gay.
Perhaps 'tis merry o'er your misery.
LANCIOTTO. Perhaps; but that it knows not.
PEPE. Yes, it does:
It knows that when a man's about to wed,
He's ripe to laugh at. Cousin, tell me, now,
Why is Paolo on the way so long?
Ravenna's but eight leagues from Rimini—
LANCIOTTO. That's just the measure of your tongue, good fool.
You trouble me. I've had enough of you—
Begone!
PEPE. I'm going; but you see I limp.
Have pity on a cripple, gentle Count. [*Limps.*]
LANCIOTTO. Pepe!
PEPE. A miracle, a miracle!
See, see, my lord, at Pepe's saintly name
The lame jog on.
MALATESTA [*without*]. Come, Lanciotto!
LANCIOTTO. Hark!
My father calls.
PEPE. If he were mine,
I'd go—
That's a good boy! [*Pats* LANCIOTTO'S *back.*]
LANCIOTTO [*starting*]. Hands off! you'll rue it else! [*Exit.*]
PEPE [*laughing*]. Ha! ha! I laid my hand upon his hump!
Heavens, how he squirmed! And what a wish I had
To cry, Ho! camel! leap upon his back,
And ride him to the devil! So, we've had
A pleasant flitting round philosophy!
The Count and Fool bumped heads, and struck ideas
Out by the contact! Quite a pleasant talk—
A friendly conversation, nothing more—
'Twixt nobleman and jester. Ho! my bird,
I can toss lures as high as any man.
So, I amuse you with my harmless wit?
Pepe's your friend now—you can trust in him—
An honest, simple fool! Just try it once,
You ugly, misbegotten clod of dirt!
Ay, but the hump—the touch upon the hump—
The start and wriggle—that was rare! Ha! ha! [*Exit, laughing.*]

SCENE 2. *The Same. The Grand Square before the Castle. Soldiers on guard, with banners, etc. Citizens, in holiday dresses, cross the scene. The houses are hung with trophies, banners, garlands, etc.*

[*Enter* MALATESTA, *with Guards, Attendants.*]

MALATESTA. Captain, take care the streets be not choked up
By the rude rabble. Send to Cæsar's bridge
A strong detachment of your men, and clear
The way before them. See that nothing check
The bride's first entrance into Rimini.
Station your veterans in the front. Count Guido
Comes with his daughter, and his eyes are sharp.
Keep up a show of strength before him, sir;
And set some laborers to work upon
The broken bastion. Make all things look bright;

As if we stood in eager readiness,
And high condition, to begin a war.

CAPTAIN. I will, my lord.

MALATESTA. Keep Guido in your eye;
And if you see him looking over-long
On any weakness of our walls, just file
Your bulkiest fellows round him; or get up
A scuffle with the people; anything—
Even if you break a head or two—to draw
His vision off. But where our strength is great,
Take heed to make him see it. You conceive?

CAPTAIN. Trust me, my lord.

[*Exit with Guards.*]

[*Enter* PEPE.]

PEPE. Room, room! A hall; a hall!
I pray you, good man, has the funeral passed?

MALATESTA. Who is it asks?

PEPE. Pepe of Padua,
A learned doctor of uncivil law.

MALATESTA. But how a funeral?

PEPE. You are weak of wit.
Francesca of Ravenna's borne to church,
And never issues thence.

MALATESTA. How, doctor, pray?

PEPE. Now, for a citizen of Rimini,
You're sadly dull. Does she not issue thence
Fanny of Rimini? A glorious change,—
A kind of resurrection in the flesh!

MALATESTA [*laughing*]. Ha! ha! thou cunning villain! I was caught.
I own it, doctor.

PEPE [*aside*]. This old fool would laugh
To see me break a straw, because the bits
Were of unequal length. My character
Carries more dulness, in the guise of wit,
Than would suffice to break an ass's back.

[*Distant shouts, music, etc.*]

Hark! here comes Jeptha's daughter, jogging on
With timbrels and with dances.

MALATESTA. Jeptha's daughter!
How so?

PEPE. Her father's sacrifice.

MALATESTA [*laughing*]. Ho! ho!
You'll burst my belt! O! you outrageous wretch,
To jest at Scripture!

PEPE. You outlandish heathen,
'Tis not in Scripture!

MALATESTA. Is it not?

PEPE. No more
Than you are in heaven. Mere Hebrew history.
She went up to the mountains, to bewail
The too-long keeping of her honesty.
There's woman for you! there's a character!
What man would ever think of such a thing?
Ah! we of Rimini have little cause
For such a sorrow. Would she'd been my wife!
I'll marry any woman in her case.

MALATESTA. Why, Pepe?

PEPE. Why? because, in two months' time,
Along comes father Jeptha with his knife,
And there's an end. Where is your sacrifice?
Where's Isaac, Abraham? Build your altar up:
One pile will do for both.

MALATESTA. That's Scripture, sure.

PEPE. Then I'm a ram, and you may slaughter me
In Isaac's stead.

MALATESTA. Here comes the vanguard. Where,
Where is that laggard?

PEPE. At the mirror, uncle,
Making himself look beautiful. He comes, [*Looking out.*]
Fresh as a bridegroom! Mark his doublet's fit
Across the shoulders, and his hose!—
By Jove, he nearly looks like any other man!

MALATESTA. You'd best not let him hear you. Sirrah, knave,
I have a mind to swinge you! [*Seizes his ear.*]

PEPE. Loose my ear!
You've got the wrong sow, swineherd! You're unjust.
Being his father, I was fool sufficient
To think you fashioned him to suit yourself,
By way of a variety. The thought
Was good enough, the practice damnable.

MALATESTA. Hush! or I'll clap you in the pillory.

[*Enter* LANCIOTTO.]

PEPE [*sings*].

Ho, ho, ho, ho!—old Time has wings—
We're born, we mourn, we wed, we bed,
We have a devilish aching head;
So down we lie,
And die, and fry;
And there's a merry end of things!

[*Music, etc., within.*]

Here comes Ravenna's eagles for a roost
In Rimini! The air is black with them.
When go they hence? Wherever yon bird builds,
The nest remains for ages. Have an eye,
Or Malatesta's elephant may feel
The eagle's talons.

LANCIOTTO. You're a raven, croaker.

PEPE. And you no white crow, to insure us luck.

MALATESTA. There's matter in his croak.

PEPE. There always is;
But men lack ears.

MALATESTA. Then eyes must do our work.
Old Guido shall be looked to. If his force
Appear too great, I'll camp him out of town.

LANCIOTTO. Father, you are a sorry host.

MALATESTA. Well, well,
I'm a good landlord, though. I do not like
This flight of eagles more than Pepe. 'Sdeath!
Guido was ever treacherous.

LANCIOTTO. My lord,
You mar my holiday by such a thought.
My holiday! Dear saints! it seems to me
That all of you are mocking me.

PEPE. So—so—
Guido was ever treacherous?—so—so!

MALATESTA. So—so! How so?

PEPE. What if this treachery
Run in the blood? We'll tap a vein then—so!

MALATESTA. Sew up your mouth, and mind your fooling, fool!

PEPE. Am I not fooling? Why, my lord, I thought
The fooling exquisite.

LANCIOTTO [*aside*]. This thoughtless knave
Hits near us sometimes with his random shafts.
Marriage for me! I cannot comprehend,
I cannot take it to my heart; the thing
Seems gross, absurd, ridiculous. Ah! well,
My father bears the folly of it all;
I'm but an actor in his comedy.
My part is bad, and I must through with it. [*Retires.*]

[*Shouts, music, etc., within.*]

PEPE. Look! here's the whole parade! Mark yonder knave—

The head one with the standard. Nature, nature!
Hadst thou a hand in such a botch-work? Why,
A forest of his legs would scarcely make
A bunch of fagots. Mark old Guido, too!
He looks like Judas with his silver. Ho!
Here's news from sweet Ravenna!

Malatesta [*laughing*]. Ha! ha! ha!

Pepe. Ah! now the bride!—that's something—she is toothsome.
Look you, my lord—now, while the progress halts—
Cousin Paolo, has he got the dumps?
Mercy! to see him, one might almost think
'Twas his own marriage. What a doleful face!
The boy is ill. He caught a fever, uncle,
Travelling across the marshes. Physic! physic!
If he be really dying, get a doctor,
And cut the matter short. 'Twere merciful.

Malatesta. For heaven's sake, cease your clamor! I shall have
No face to meet them else. 'Tis strange, for all:
What ails Paolo?

Pepe. Dying, by this hand!

Malatesta. Then I will hang you.

Pepe. Don't take up my craft.
Wit's such a stranger in your brain that I
Scarce knew my lodger venturing from your mouth.
Now they come on again.

Malatesta. Stand back!

Pepe [*looking round*]. The bridegroom?
He flies betimes, before the bride shows fight.
[*Walks back, looking for* Lanciotto.]

[*Music, shouts, ringing of bells, etc. Enter Men-at-Arms, with banners, etc.,* Guido, *Cardinal, Knights, Attendants, etc.; then* Paolo, *conducting* Francesca, *followed by* Ritta, *Ladies, Pages, etc., and other Men-at-Arms. They file around the stage, and halt.*]

Malatesta. Welcome to Rimini, Count Guido! Welcome,
And fair impressions of our poor abode,
To you, my daughter! You are well returned.
My son, Paolo! Let me bless you, son. [Paolo *approaches.*]
How many spears are in old Guido's train? [*Apart to* Paolo.]

Paolo. Some ten-score.

Malatesta. Footmen?

Paolo. Double that.

Malatesta. 'Tis well.
Again I bid you welcome! Make no show
Of useless ceremony with us. Friends
Have closer titles than the empty name.
We have provided entertainment, Count,
For all your followers, in the midst of us.
We trust the veterans of Rimini
May prove your soldiers that our courtesy
Does not lag far behind their warlike zeal.
Let us drop Guelf and Ghibelin henceforth,
Coupling the names of Rimini and Ravenna
As bridegroom's to his bride's.

Guido. Count Malatesta,
I am no rhetorician, or my words
Might keep more even with the love I feel:
Simply, I thank you. With an honest hand
I take the hand which you extend to me,
And hope our grasp may never lose its warmth.—

You marked the bastion by the water-side?
Weak as a bulrush.
[*Apart to a* KNIGHT.]
KNIGHT. Tottering weak, my lord.
GUIDO. Remember it; and when you're private, sir,
Draw me a plan.
KNIGHT. I will, my lord.
GUIDO. How's this?
I do not see my future son-in-law.
MALATESTA. Lanciotto!
LANCIOTTO [*advancing*]. I am here, my lord.
FRANCESCA [*starting*]. O! heaven!
Is that my husband, Count Paolo? You,
You then, among the rest, have played me false!
He is— [*Apart to* PAOLO.]
PAOLO. My brother.
LANCIOTTO [*aside*]. Ha! she turns from me.
PEPE [*approaching* LANCIOTTO, *sings*].

Around, around the lady turned,
She turned not to her lord;
She turned around to a gallant, gallant knight,
Who ate at his father's board.

A pretty ballad! all on one string though.
LANCIOTTO. Pepe, go hence!
[PEPE *retires*.]
[*Aside*.] I saw her start and pale,
Turn off with horror; as if she had seen—
What?—simply me. For, am I not enough,
And something over, to make ladies quail,
Start, hide their faces, whisper to their friends,
Point at me—dare she?—and perform such tricks
As women will when monsters blast their sight?
O! saints above me, have I come so low?
Yon damsel of Ravenna shall bewail
That start and shudder. I am mad, mad, mad!
I must be patient. They have trifled with her:
Lied to her, lied! There's half the misery
Of this broad earth, all crowded in one word.
Lied, lied!—Who has not suffered from a lie?
They're all aghast—all looking at me, too.
Francesca's whiter than the brow of fear:
Paolo talks.—Brother, is that well meant?
What if I draw my sword, and fight my way
Out of this cursed town? 'Twould be relief.
Has shame no hiding-place? I've touched the depth
Of human infamy, and there I rest.
By heaven, I'll brave this business out! Shall they
Say at Ravenna that Count Lanciotto,
Who's driven their shivering squadrons to their homes,
Haggard with terror, turned before their eyes
And slunk away? They'll look me from the field,
When we encounter next. Why should not I
Strut with my shapeless body, as old Guido
Struts with his shapeless heart? I'll do it! [*Offers, but shrinks back.*]
'Sdeath!
Am I so false as to forswear myself?
Lady Francesca!
[*Approaches* FRANCESCA.]
FRANCESCA. Sir—my lord—
LANCIOTTO. Dear lady,
I have a share in your embarrassment,
And know the feelings that possess you now.
FRANCESCA. O! you do not.
PAOLO [*advancing*]. My lady—

LANCIOTTO. Gentle brother,
Leave this to me. [PAOLO *retires.*]

FRANCESCA. Pray do not send him off.

LANCIOTTO. 'Tis fitter so.

FRANCESCA. He comforts me.

LANCIOTTO. Indeed?
Do you need comfort?

FRANCESCA. No, no—pardon me!
But then—he is—you are—

LANCIOTTO. Take breath, and speak.

FRANCESCA. I am confused, 'tis true. But, then, my lord,
You are a stranger to me; and Paolo
I've known so long!

LANCIOTTO. Since yesterday.

FRANCESCA. Ah! well:
But the relationship between us two
Is of so close a nature, while the knowledge,
That each may have of each, so slender is
That the two jar. Besides, Paolo is
Nothing to me, while you are everything.
Can I not act? [*Aside.*]

LANCIOTTO. I scarcely understand.
You say your knowledge of me, till to-day,
Was incomplete. Has naught been said of me
By Count Paolo or your father?

FRANCESCA. Yes;
But nothing definite.

LANCIOTTO. Perchance, no hint
As to my ways, my feelings, manners, or—
Or—or—as I was saying—ha! ha!—or— [*Laughing.*]
As to my person?

FRANCESCA. Nothing, as to that.

LANCIOTTO. To what?

FRANCESCA. Your—person.

LANCIOTTO. That's the least of all. [*Turns aside.*]
Now, had I Guido of Ravenna's head
Under this heel, I'd grind it into dust!
False villian, to betray his simple child!
And thou, Paolo—not a whit behind—
Helping his craft with inconsiderate love!—
Lady Francesca, when my brother left,
I charged him, as he loved me, to conceal
Nothing from you that bore on me: and now
That you have seen me, and conversed with me,
If you object to anything in me,—
Go, I release you.

FRANCESCA. But Ravenna's peace?

LANCIOTTO. Shall not be perilled.

GUIDO [*coming behind, whispers her.*] Trust him not, my child;
I know his ways; he'd rather fight than wed.
'Tis but a wish to have the war afoot.
Stand firm for poor Ravenna!

LANCIOTTO. Well, my lady,
Shall we conclude a lasting peace between us
By truce or marriage rites?

GUIDO [*whispers her*]. The devil tempts thee:
Think of Ravenna, think of me!

LANCIOTTO. My lord,
I see my father waits you. [GUIDO *retires.*]

FRANCESCA. Gentle sir,
You do me little honor in the choice.

LANCIOTTO. My aim is justice.

FRANCESCA. Would you cast me off?

LANCIOTTO. Not for the world, if honestly obtained;
Not for the world would I obtain you falsely.

FRANCESCA. The rites were half concluded ere we met.

LANCIOTTO. Meeting, would you withdraw?

FRANCESCA. No. Bitter word! [*Aside.*]

LANCIOTTO. No! Are you dealing fairly?
FRANCESCA. I have said.
LANCIOTTO. O! rapture, rapture!
Can it be that I—
Now I'll speak plainly; for a choice like thine
Implies such love as woman never felt.
Love me! Then monsters beget miracles,
And Heaven provides where human means fall short.
Lady, I'll worship thee! I'll line thy path
With suppliant kings! Thy waiting-maids shall be
Unransomed princesses! Mankind shall bow
One neck to thee, as Persia's multitudes
Before the rising sun! From this small town,
This centre of my conquests, I will spread
An empire touching the extremes of earth!
I'll raise once more the name of ancient Rome;
And what she swayed she shall reclaim again!
If I grow mad because you smile on me,
Think of the glory of thy love; and know
How hard it is, for such an one as I,
To gaze unshaken on divinity!
There's no such love as mine alive in man.
From every corner of the frowning earth,
It has been crowded back into my heart.
Now, take it all! If that be not enough,
Ask, and thy wish shall be omnipotent!
Your hand. [*Takes her hand.*] It wavers.
FRANCESCA. So does not my heart.
LANCIOTTO. Bravo! Thou art every way a soldier's wife;
Thou shouldst have been a Cæsar's! Father, hark!
I blamed your judgment, only to perceive
The weakness of my own.
MALATESTA. What means all this?
LANCIOTTO. It means that this fair lady—though I gave
Release to her, and to Ravenna—placed
The liberal hand, which I restored to her,
Back in my own, of her own free good-will.
Is it not wonderful?
MALATESTA. How so?
LANCIOTTO. How so!
PAOLO. Alas! 'tis as I feared! [*Aside.*]
MALATESTA. You're humble?—How?
LANCIOTTO. Now shall I cry aloud to all the world,
Make my deformity my pride, and say,
Because she loves me, I may boast of it? [*Aside.*]
No matter, father, I am happy; you,
As the blessed cause, shall share my happiness.
Let us be moving. Revels, dashed with wine,
Shall multiply the joys of this sweet day!
There's not a blessing in the cup of life
I have not tasted of within an hour!
FRANCESCA [*aside*]. Thus I begin the practice of deceit,
Taught by deceivers, at a fearful cost.
The bankrupt gambler has become the cheat,
And lives by arts that erewhile ruined me.

Where it will end, heaven knows; but I—
I have betrayed the noblest heart of all!

LANCIOTTO. Draw down thy dusky vapours, sullen night—
Refuse, ye stars, to shine upon the world—
Let everlasting blackness wrap the sun,
And whisper terror to the universe!
We need ye not! we'll blind ye, if ye dare
Peer with lack-lustre on our revelry!
I have at heart a passion, that would make
All nature blaze with recreated light!

[*Exeunt.*]

## ACT IV

SCENE 1. *The Same. An apartment in the Castle.*

[*Enter* LANCIOTTO.]

LANCIOTTO. It cannot be that I have duped myself,
That my desire has played into the hand
Of my belief; yet such a thing might be.
We palm more frauds upon our simple selves
Than knavery puts upon us. Could I trust
The open candor of an angel's brow,
I must believe Francesca's. But the tongue
Should consummate the proof upon the brow,
And give the truth its word. The fault lies there.
I've tried her. Press her as I may to it,
She will not utter those three little words—
"I love thee." She will say, "I'll marry you;—
I'll be your duteous wife;—I'll cheer your days;—
I'll do whate'er I can." But at the point
Of present love, she ever shifts the ground,
Winds round the word, laughs, calls me "Infidel!—
How can I doubt?" So, on and on. But yet,
For all her dainty ways, she never says,
Frankly, I love thee. I am jealous—true!
Suspicious—true! distrustful of myself;—
She knows all that. Ay, and she likewise knows,
A single waking of her morning breath
Would blow these vapors off. I would not take
The barren offer of a heartless hand,
If all the Indies cowered under it.
Perhaps she loves another? No; she said,
"I love you, Count, as well as any man;"
And laughed, as if she thought that precious wit.
I turn her nonsense into argument,
And think I reason. Shall I give her up?
Rail at her heartlessness, and bid her go
Back to Ravenna? But she clings to me,
At the least hint of parting. Ah! 'tis sweet,
Sweeter than slumber to the lids of pain,
To fancy that a shadow of true love
May fall on this God-stricken mould of woe,
From so serene a nature. Beautiful
Is the first vision of a desert brook,
Shining beneath its palmy garniture,
To one who travels on his easy way;
What is it to the blood-shot, aching eye
Of some poor wight who crawls with gory feet,

In famished madness, to its very brink;
And throws his sun-scorched limbs upon the cool
And humid margin of its shady strand,
To suck up life at every eager gasp?
Such seems Francesca to my thirsting soul;
Shall I turn off and die?

[*Enter* PEPE.]

PEPE. Good-morning, cousin!

LANCIOTTO. Good-morning to your foolish majesty!

PEPE. The same to your majestic foolery!

LANCIOTTO. You compliment!

PEPE. I am a troubadour,
A ballad-monger of fine mongrel ballads,
And therefore running o'er with elegance.
Wilt hear my verse?

LANCIOTTO. With patience?

PEPE. No, with rapture.
You must go mad—weep, rend your clothes, and roll
Over and over, like the ancient Greeks,
When listening to the Iliad.

LANCIOTTO. Sing, then, sing!
And if you equal Homer in your song,
Why, roll I must, by sheer compulsion.

PEPE. Nay,
You lack the temper of the fine-eared Greek.
You will not roll; but that shall not disgrace
My gallant ballad, fallen on evil times. [*Sings.*]

My father had a blue-black head,
My uncle's head was reddish—maybe,
My mother's hair was noways red,
Sing high ho! the pretty baby!

Mark the simplicity of that! 'Tis called
"The Babe's Confession," spoken just before
His father strangled him.

LANCIOTTO. Most marvellous!
You struggle with a legend worth your art.

PEPE. Now to the second stanza. Note the hint
I drop about the baby's parentage:
So delicately too! A maid might sing,
And never blush at it. Girls love these songs
Of sugared wickedness. They'll go miles about,
To say a foul thing in a cleanly way.
A decent immorality, my lord,
Is art's specific. Get the passions up,
But never wring the stomach.

LANCIOTTO. Triumphant art!

PEPE [*sings*].

My father combed his blue-black head,
My uncle combed his red head—maybe,
My mother combed my head, and said,
Sing high ho! my red-haired baby!

LANCIOTTO. Fie, fie! go comb your hair in private.

PEPE. What!
Will you not hear? Now comes the tragedy. [*Sings.*]

My father tore my red, red head,
My uncle tore my father's—maybe,
My mother tore both till they bled—
Sing high ho! your brother's baby!

LANCIOTTO. Why, what a hair-rending!

PEPE. Thence wigs arose;
A striking epoch in man's history.
But did you notice the concluding line,
Sung by the victim's mother? There's a hit!

"Sing high ho! your brother's baby!"

Which brother's, pray you? That's the mystery,
The adumbration of poetic art,
And there I leave it to perplex mankind.

It has a moral, fathers should regard,—
A black-haired dog breeds not a red-haired cur.
Treasure this knowledge: you're about to wive;
And no one knows what accident—

LANCIOTTO. Peace, fool!
So all this cunning thing was wound about,
To cast a gibe at my deformity?
[*Tears off* PEPE's *cap.*]
There lies your cap, the emblem that protects
Your head from chastisement. Now, Pepe, hark!
Of late you've taken to reviling me;
Under your motley, you have dared to jest
At God's inflictions. Let me tell you, fool,
No man e'er lived, to make a second jest
At me, before your time!

PEPE. Boo! Bloody-bones!
If you're a coward—which I hardly think—
You'll have me flogged, or put into a cell,
Or fed to wolves. If you are bold of heart,
You'll let me run. Do not; I'll work you harm!
I, Beppo Pepe, standing as a man,
Without my motley, tell you, in plain terms,
I'll work you harm—I'll do you mischief, man!

LANCIOTTO. I, Lanciotto, Count of Rimini,
Will hang you, then. Put on your jingling cap;
You please my father. But remember, fool,
No jests at me!

PEPE. I will try earnest next.

LANCIOTTO. And I the gallows.

PEPE. Well, cry quits, cry quits!
I'll stretch your heart, and you my neck—quits, quits!

LANCIOTTO. Go, fool! Your weakness bounds your malice.

PEPE. Yes:
So you all think, you savage gentlemen,
Until you feel my sting. Hang, hang away!
It is an airy, wholesome sort of death,
Much to my liking. When I hang, my friend,
You'll be chief mourner, I can promise you.
Hang me! I've quite a notion to be hung:
I'll do my utmost to deserve it. Hang! [*Exit.*]

LANCIOTTO. I am bemocked on all sides. My sad state
Has given the licensed and unlicensed fool
Charter to challenge me at every turn.
The jester's laughing bauble blunts my sword,
His gibes cut deeper than its fearful edge;
And I, a man, a soldier, and a prince,
Before this motley patchwork of a man,
Stand all appalled, as if he were a glass
Wherein I saw my own deformity.
O Heaven! a tear—one little tear—to wash
This aching dryness of the heart away!

[*Enter* PAOLO.]

PAOLO. What ails the fool? He passed me, muttering
The strangest garbage in the fiercest tone.
"Ha! ha!" cried he, "they made a fool of me—
A motley man, a slave; as if I felt
No stir in me of manly dignity!
Ha! ha! a fool—a painted plaything, toy—

For men to kick about this dirty world!—
My world as well as theirs.—God's world, I trow!
I will get even with them yet—ha! ha!
In the democracy of death we'll square.
I'll crawl and lie beside a king's own son;
Kiss a young princess, dead lip to dead lip;
Pull the Pope's nose; and kick down Charlemagne,
Throne, crown, and all, where the old idiot sprawls,
Safe as he thinks, rotting in royal state!"
And then he laughed and gibbered, as if drunk
With some infernal ecstasy.

LANCIOTTO. Poor fool!
That is the groundwork of his malice, then,—
His conscious difference from the rest of men?
I, of all men, should pity him the most.
Poor Pepe! I'll be kinder. I have wronged
A feeling heart. Poor Pepe!

PAOLO. Sad again!
Where has the rapture gone of yesterday?

LANCIOTTO. Where are the leaves of Summer? Where the snows
Of last year's Winter? Where the joys and griefs
That shut our eyes to yesternight's repose,
And woke not on the morrow? Joys and griefs,
Huntsmen and hounds, ye follow us as game,
Poor panting outcasts of your forest-law!
Each cheers the others,—one with wild halloos,
And one with whines and howls.—A dreadful chase,
That only closes when horns sound *amort!*

PAOLO. Thus ever up and down! Arouse yourself,
Balance your mind more evenly, and hunt
For honey in the wormwood.

LANCIOTTO. Or find gall
Hid in the hanging chalice of the rose:
Which think you better? If my mood offend,
We'll turn to business,—to the empty cares
That make such pother in our feverish life.
When at Ravenna, did you ever hear
Of any romance in Francesca's life?
A love-tilt, gallantry, or anything
That might have touched her heart?

PAOLO. Not lightly even.
I think her heart as virgin as her hand.

LANCIOTTO. Then there is hope.

PAOLO. Of what?

LANCIOTTO. Of winning her.

PAOLO. Grammercy! Lanciotto, are you sane?
You boasted yesterday—

LANCIOTTO. And changed to-day.
Is that so strange? I always mend the fault
Of yesterday with wisdom of to-day.
She does not love me.

PAOLO. Pshaw! she marries you:
'Twere proof enough for me.

LANCIOTTO. Perhaps, she loves you.

PAOLO. Me, Lanciotto, me! For mercy's sake,
Blot out such thoughts—they madden me! What, love—
She love—yet marry you!

LANCIOTTO. It moves you much.
'Twas but a fleeting fancy, nothing more.

PAOLO. You have such wild conjectures!

LANCIOTTO. Well, to me

They seem quite tame; they are my bed-fellows.
Think, to a modest woman, what must be
The loathsome kisses of an unloved man—
A gross, coarse ruffian!
PAOLO. O! good heavens, forbear!
LANCIOTTO. What shocks you so?
PAOLO. The picture which you draw,
Wronging yourself by horrid images.
LANCIOTTO. Until she love me, till I know, beyond
The cavil of a doubt, that she is mine—
Wholly, past question—do you think that I
Could so afflict the woman whom I love?
PAOLO. You love her, Lanciotto!
LANCIOTTO. Next to you,
Dearer than anything in nature's scope.
PAOLO [*aside*]. O! Heaven, that I must bear this! Yes, and more,—
More torture than I dare to think upon,
Spreads out before me with the coming years,
And holds a record blotted with my tears,
As that which I must suffer!
LANCIOTTO. Come, Paolo,
Come help me woo. I need your guiding eye,
To signal me, if I should sail astray.
PAOLO. O! torture, torture! [*Aside.*]
LANCIOTTO. You and I, perchance,
Joining our forces, may prevail at last.
They call love like a battle. As for me,
I'm not a soldier equal to such wars,
Despite my arduous schooling. Tutor me
In the best arts of amorous strategy.
I am quite raw, Paolo. Glances, sighs,
Sweets of the lip, and arrows of the eye,
Shrugs, cringes, compliments, are new to me;
And I shall handle them with little art.
Will you instruct me?
PAOLO. Conquer for yourself.
Two captains share one honor: keep it all.
What if I ask to share the spoils?
LANCIOTTO [*laughing*]. Ha! ha!
I'll trust you, brother. Let us go to her:
Francesca is neglected while we jest.
I know not how it is, but your fair face,
And noble figure, always cheer me up,
More than your words; there's healing in them, too,
For my worst griefs. Dear brother, let us in. [*Exeunt.*]

SCENE 2. *The Same. A Chamber in the Same.* FRANCESCA *and* RITTA *discovered at the bridal toilet.*

RITTA [*sings*].

Ring high, ring high! to earth and sky;
A lady goes a-wedding;
The people shout, the show draws out,
And smiles the bride is shedding.

No bell for you, ye ragged few;
A beggar goes a-wedding;
The people sneer, the thing's so queer,
And tears the bride is shedding.

Ring low, ring low! dull bell of woe,
One tone will do for either;
The lady glad, and beggar sad,
Have both lain down together.

FRANCESCA. A mournful ballad!
RITTA. I scarce knew I sang.
I'm weary of this wreath. These orange-flowers
Will never be adjusted to my taste:

Strive as I will, they ever look awry.
My fingers ache!

FRANCESCA. Not more than my poor head.
There, leave them so.

RITTA. That's better, yet not well.

FRANCESCA. They are but fading things, not worth your pains:
They'll scarce outlive the marriage merriment.
Ritta, these flowers are hypocrites; they show
An outside gayety, yet die within,
Minute by minute. You shall see them fall,
Black with decay, before the rites are o'er.

RITTA. How beautiful you are!

FRANCESCA. Fie, flatterer!
White silk and laces, pearls and orange-flowers,
Would do as much for any one.

RITTA. No, no!
You give them grace, they nothing give to you.
Why, after all, you make the wreath look well;
But somewhat dingy, where it lies against
Your pulsing temple, sullen with disgrace.
Ah! well, your Count should be the proudest man
That ever led a lady into church,
Were he a modern Alexander. Poh!
What are his trophies to a face like that?

FRANCESCA. I seem to please you, Ritta.

RITTA. Please yourself,
And you will please me better. You are sad:
I marked it ever since you saw the Count.
I fear the splendor of his victories,
And his sweet grace of manner—for, in faith,
His is the gentlest, grandest character,
Despite his—

FRANCESCA. Well?

RITTA. Despite his—

FRANCESCA. Ritta, what?

RITTA. Despite his difference from Count Paolo.—

[FRANCESCA *staggers.*]

What is the matter? [*Supporting her.*]

FRANCESCA. Nothing; mere fatigue.
Hand me my kerchief. I am better now.
What were you saying?

RITTA. That I fear the Count
Has won your love.

FRANCESCA. Would that be cause for fear? [*Laughing.*]

RITTA. O! yes, indeed! Once—long ago—I was
Just fool enough to tangle up my heart
With one of these same men. 'Twas terrible!
Morning or evening, waking or asleep,
I had no peace. Sighs, groans, and standing tears,
Counted my moments through the blessed day.
And then to this there was a dull, strange ache
Forever sleeping in my breast,—a numbing pain,
That would not for an instant be forgot.
O! but I loved him so, that very feeling
Became intolerable. And I believed
This false Giuseppe, too, for all the sneers,
The shrugs and glances, of my intimates.
They slandered me and him, yet I believed.
He was a noble, and his love to me
Was a reproach, a shame, yet I believed.
He wearied of me, tried to shake me off,
Grew cold and formal, yet I would not doubt.
O! lady, I was true! Nor till I saw

Giuseppe walk through the cathedral door
With Dora, the rich usurer's niece, upon
The very arm to which I clung so oft,
Did I so much as doubt him. Even then—
More is my shame—I made excuses for him.
"Just this or that had forced him to the course:
Perhaps, he loved me yet—a little yet.
His fortune, or his family, had driven
My poor Giuseppe thus against his heart.
The low are sorry judges for the great.
Yes, yes, Giuseppe loved me!" But at last
I did awake. It might have been with less:
There was no need of crushing me, to break
My silly dream up. In the street, it chanced,
Dora and he went by me, and he laughed—
A bold, bad laugh—right in my poor pale face,
And turned and whispered Dora, and she laughed.
Ah! then I saw it all. I've been awake,
Ever since then, I warrant you. And now
I only pray for him sometimes, when friends
Tell his base actions towards his hapless wife.
O! I am lying—I pray every night!
[*Weeps.*]

FRANCESCA. Poor Ritta. [*Weeping.*]

RITTA. No! blest Ritta! Thank kind Heaven,
That kept me spotless when he tempted me,
And my weak heart was pleading with his tongue.
Pray, do not weep. You spoil your eyes for me.
But never love; oh! it is terrible!

FRANCESCA. I'll strive against it.

RITTA. Do: because, my lady,
Even a husband may be false, you know;
Ay, even to so sweet a wife as you.
Men have odd tastes. They'll surfeit on the charms
Of Cleopatra, and then turn aside
To woo her blackamoor. 'Tis so, in faith;
Or Dora's uncle's gold had ne'er outbid
The boundless measure of a love like mine.
Think of it, lady, to weigh love with gold!
What could be meaner?

FRANCESCA. Nothing, nothing, Ritta.
Though gold's the standard measure of the world,
And seems to lighten everything beside.
Yet heap the other passions in the scale,
And balance them 'gainst that which gold outweighs—
Against this love—and you shall see how light
The most supreme of them are in the poise!
I speak by book and history; for love
Slights my high fortunes. Under cloth of state
The urchin cowers from pompous etiquette,
Waiving his function at the scowl of power,
And seeks the rustic cot to stretch his limbs
In homely freedom. I fulfill a doom.
We who are topmost on this heap of life
Are nearer to Heaven's hand than you below;
And so are used, as ready instruments,
To work its purposes. Let envy hide
Her witless forehead at a prince's name,
And fix her hopes upon a clown's content.

You, happy lowly, know not what it is
To groan beneath the crownèd yoke of state,
And bear the goadings of the sceptre. Ah!
Fate drives us onward in a narrow way,
Despite our boasted freedom.

[*Enter* PAOLO, *with Pages bearing torches.*]

Gracious saints!
What brought you here?

PAOLO. The bridegroom waits.

FRANCESCA. He does?
Let him wait on forever! I'll not go!
O! dear Paolo—

PAOLO. Sister!

FRANCESCA. It is well.
I have been troubled with a sleepless night.
My brain is wild. I know not what I say.
Pray, do not call me sister: it is cold.
I never had a brother, and the name
Sounds harshly to me. When you speak to me,
Call me Francesca.

PAOLO. You shall be obeyed.

FRANCESCA. I would not be obeyed. I'd have you do it
Because—because you love me—as a sister—
And of your own good-will, not my command,
Would please me.—Do you understand?

PAOLO. Too well! [*Aside.*]
'Tis a nice difference.

FRANCESCA. Yet you understand?
Say that you do.

PAOLO. I do.

FRANCESCA. That pleases me.
'Tis flattering if our—friends appreciate
Our nicer feelings.

PAOLO. I await you, lady.

FRANCESCA. Ritta, my gloves.—Ah! yes, I have them on;
Though I'm not quite prepared. Arrange my veil;
It folds too closely. That will do; retire. [RITTA *retires.*]
So, Count Paolo, you have come, hot haste,
To lead me to the church,—to have your share
In my undoing? And you came, in sooth,
Because they sent you? You are very tame!
And if they sent, was it for you to come?

PAOLO. Lady, I do not understand this scorn.
I came, as is my duty, to escort
My brother's bride to him. When next you're called,
I'll send a lackey.

FRANCESCA. I have angered you.

PAOLO. With reason: I would not appear to you
Low or contemptible.

FRANCESCA. Why not to me?

PAOLO. Lady, I'll not be catechized.

FRANCESCA. Ha! Count!

PAOLO. No! if you press me further, I will say
A word to madden you.—Stand still! You stray
Around the margin of a precipice.
I know what pleasure 'tis to pluck the flowers
That hang above destruction, and to gaze
Into the dread abyss, to see such things
As may be safely seen. 'Tis perilous:
The eye grows dizzy as we gaze below,
And a wild wish possesses us to spring
Into the vacant air. Beware, beware!
Lest this unholy fascination grow
Too strong to conquer!

FRANCESCA. You talk wildly, Count;
There's not a gleam of sense in what you say;
I cannot hit your meaning.

PAOLO. Lady, come!

FRANCESCA. Count, you are cruel! [*Weeps.*]

PAOLO. O! no; I would be kind.
But now, while reason over-rides my heart,
And seeming anger plays its braggart part—
In heaven's name, come!

FRANCESCA. One word—one question more:
Is it your wish this marriage should proceed?

PAOLO. It is.

FRANCESCA. Come on! You shall not take my hand:
I'll walk alone—now, and forever!

PAOLO [*taking her hand*]. Sister!

[*Exeunt* PAOLO *and* FRANCESCA, *with Pages.*]

RITTA. O! misery, misery!—it is plain as day—
She loves Paolo! Why will those I love
Forever get themselves ensnared, and heaven
Forever call on me to succor them?
Here was the mystery, then—the sighs and tears,
The troubled slumbers, and the waking dreams!
And now she's walking through the chapel-door,
Her bridal robe above an aching heart,
Dressed up for sacrifice. 'Tis terrible!
And yet she'll smile and do it. Smile, for years,
Until her heart breaks; and the nurses ask
The doctor of the cause. He'll answer too,
In hard thick Latin, and believe himself.
O! my dear mistress! Heaven, pray torture me!
Send back Giuseppe, let him ruin me,
And scorn me after; but, sweet heaven, spare her!
I'll follow her. O! what a world is this! [*Exit.*]

SCENE 3. *The Same. Interior of the Cathedral.* LANCIOTTO, FRANCESCA, PAOLO, MALATESTA, GUIDO, RITTA, PEPE, *Lords, Knights, Priests, Pages, a bridal-train of Ladies, Soldiers, Citizens, Attendants, &c., discovered before the High Altar. Organ music. The rites being over, they advance.*

MALATESTA. By heaven—

PEPE. O! uncle, uncle, you're in church!

MALATESTA. I'll break your head, knave!

PEPE. I claim sanctuary.

MALATESTA. Why, bridegroom, will you never kiss the bride?
We all are mad to follow you.

PEPE. Yes, yes;
Here was Paolo wetting his red lips
For the last minute. Kiss, and give him room.

MALATESTA. You heaven-forsaken imp, be quiet now!

PEPE. Then there'd be naught worth hearing.

MALATESTA. Bridegroom, come!

PEPE. Lord! he don't like it! Hey!—I told you so—
He backs at the first step. Does he not know
His trouble's just begun?

LANCIOTTO. Gentle Francesca,
Custom imposes somewhat on thy lips:
I'll make my levy. [*Kisses her. The others follow.*] [*Aside.*] Ha! she shrank! I felt
Her body tremble, and her quivering lips
Seemed dying under mine! I heard a sigh,
Such as breaks hearts—O! no, a very groan;
And then she turned a sickly, miserable look
On pale Paolo, and he shivered too!
There is a mystery hangs around her,—ay,

Paolo knows it too.—By all the saints,
I'll make him tell it, at the dagger's point!
Paolo!—here! I do adjure you, brother,
By the great love I bear you, to reveal
The secret of Francesca's grief.

PAOLO. I cannot.

LANCIOTTO. She told you nothing?

PAOLO. Nothing.

LANCIOTTO. Not a word?

PAOLO. Not one.

LANCIOTTO. What heard you at Ravenna, then?

PAOLO. Nothing.

LANCIOTTO. Here?

PAOLO. Nothing.

LANCIOTTO. Not the slightest hint?—
Don't stammer, man! Speak quick! I am in haste.

PAOLO. Never.

LANCIOTTO. What know you?

PAOLO. Nothing that concerns
Your happiness, Lanciotto. If I did,
Would I not tell unquestioned?

LANCIOTTO. Would you not?
You ask a question for me: answer it.

PAOLO. I have.

LANCIOTTO. You juggle, you turn deadly pale,
Fumble your dagger, stand with head half round,
Tapping your feet.—You dare not look at me!
By Satan! Count Paolo, let me say,
You look much like a full-convicted thief!

PAOLO. Brother!—

LANCIOTTO. Pshaw! brother! You deceive me, sir:
You and that lady have a devil's league,
To keep a devil's secret. Is it thus
You deal with me? Now, by the light above,
I'd give a dukedom for some fair pretext
To fly you all! She does not love me? Well,
I could bear that, and live away from her.
Love would be sweet, but want of it becomes
An early habit to such men as I.
But you—ah! there's the sorrow—whom I loved
An infant in your cradle; you who grew
Up in my heart, with every inch you gained;
You whom I loved for every quality,
Good, bad, and common, in your natural stock;
Ay, for your very beauty! It is strange, you'll say,
For such a crippled horror to do that,
Against the custom of his kind! O! yes,
I love, and you betray me!

PAOLO. Lanciotto,
This is sheer frenzy. Join your bride.

LANCIOTTO. I'll not!
What, go to her, to feel her very flesh
Crawl from my touch? to hear her sigh and moan,
As if God plagued her? Must I come to that?
Must I endure your hellish mystery
With my own wife, and roll my eyes away
In sentimental bliss? No, no! until
I go to her, with confident belief
In her integrity and candid love,
I'll shun her as a leper!

[*Alarm-bells toll.*]

MALATESTA. What is that?

[*Enter, hastily, a* MESSENGER *in disorder.*]

MESSENGER. My lord, the Ghibelins are up—

LANCIOTTO. And I
Will put them down again! I thank thee, Heaven,
For this unlooked-for aid! [*Aside.*]

MALATESTA. What force have they?

LANCIOTTO. It matters not,—nor yet the time, place, cause,
Of their rebellion. I would throttle it,
Were it a riot, or a drunken brawl!

MALATESTA. Nay, son, your bride—

LANCIOTTO. My bride will pardon me;
Bless me, perhaps, as I am going forth;—
Thank me, perhaps, if I should ne'er return. [*Aside.*]
A soldier's duty has no bridals in it.

PAOLO. Lanciotto, this is folly. Let me take
Your usual place of honor.

LANCIOTTO [*laughing*]. Ha! ha! ha!
What! thou, a tilt-yard soldier, lead my troops!
My wife will ask it shortly. Not a word
Of opposition from the new-made bride?
Nay, she looks happier. O! accursed day,
That I was mated to an empty heart! [*Aside.*]

MALATESTA. But, son—

LANCIOTTO. Well, father?

PEPE. Uncle, let him go.
He'll find it cooler on a battle-field
Than in his—

LANCIOTTO. Hark! the fool speaks oracles.
You, soldiers, who are used to follow me,
And front our charges, emulous to bear
The shock of battle on your forward arms,—
Why stand ye in amazement? Do your swords
Stick to their scabbards with inglorious rust?
Or has repose so weakened your big hearts,
That you can dream with trumpets at your ears?
Out with your steel! It shames me to behold
Such tardy welcome to my war-worn blade! [*Draws.*]
[*The Knights and Soldiers draw.*]
Ho! draw our forces out! Strike camp, sound drums,
And set us on our marches! As I live,
I pity the next foeman who relies
On me for mercy! Farewell! to you all—
To all alike—a soldier's short farewell! [*Going.*]
[PAOLO *stands before him.*]
Out of my way, thou juggler! [*Exit.*]

PAOLO. He is gone!

## ACT V

SCENE 1. *The Same. The Garden of the Castle.*

[*Enter* PEPE, *singing.*]

PEPE.
'Tis jolly to walk in the shady greenwood
With a damsel by your side;
'Tis jolly to walk from the chapel-door,
With the hand of your pretty bride;
'Tis jolly to rest your weary head,
When life runs low and hope is fled,
On the heart where you confide:
'Tis jolly, jolly, jolly, they say,
They say—but I never tried.
Nor shall I ever till they dress their girls
In motley suits, and pair us, to increase
The race of fools. 'Twould be a noble thing,
A motley woman, had she wit enough
To bear the bell. But there's the misery:
You may make princes out of any stuff;
Fools come by nature. She'll make fifty kings—
Good, hearty tyrants, sound, cruel governors—
For one fine fool. There is Paolo, now,
A sweet-faced fellow with a wicked heart—
Talk of a flea, and you begin to scratch.

Lo! here he comes. And there's fierce crook-back's bride
Walking beside him—O, how gingerly!
Take care, my love! that is the very pace
We trip to hell with. Hunchback is away—
That was a fair escape for you; but, then,
The devil's ever with us, and that's worse.
See, the Ravenna giglet, Mistress Ritta,
And melancholy as a cow.—How's this?
I'll step aside, and watch you, pretty folks.

[*Hides behind the bushes.*]

[*Enter* PAOLO *and* FRANCESCA, *followed by* RITTA. *He seats himself in an arbor, and reads.*]

FRANCESCA. Ritta.

RITTA. My lady.

FRANCESCA. You look tired.

RITTA. I'm not.

FRANCESCA. Go to your chamber.

RITTA. I would rather stay,
If it may please you. I require a walk
And the fresh atmosphere of breathing flowers,
To stir my blood. I am not very well.

FRANCESCA. I knew it, child. Go to your chamber, dear.
Paolo has a book to read to me.

RITTA. What, the romance? I should so love to hear!
I dote on poetry; and Count Paolo
Sweetens the Tuscan with his mellow voice.
I'm weary now, quite weary, and would rest.

FRANCESCA. Just now you wished to walk.

RITTA. Ah! did I so?
Walking, or resting, I would stay with you.

FRANCESCA. The Count objects. He told me, yesterday,
That you were restless while he read to me;
And stirred your feet amid the grass, and sighed,
And yawned, until he almost paused.

RITTA. Indeed
I will be quiet.

FRANCESCA. But he will not read.

RITTA. Let me go ask him.

[*Runs toward* PAOLO.]

FRANCESCA. Stop! Come hither, Ritta.

[*She returns.*]

I saw your new embroidery in the hall,—
The needle in the midst of Argus' eyes;
It should be finished.

RITTA. I will bring it here.—
O, no! my finger's sore; I cannot work.

FRANCESCA. Go to your room.

RITTA. Let me remain, I pray.
'Tis better, lady; you may wish for me:
I know you will be sorry if I go.

FRANCESCA. I shall not, girl. Do as I order you.
Will you be headstrong?

RITTA. Do you wish it, then?

FRANCESCA. Yes, Ritta.

RITTA. Yet you made pretexts enough,
Before you ordered.

FRANCESCA. You are insolent.
Will you remain against my will?

RITTA. Yes, lady;
Rather than not remain.

FRANCESCA. Ha! impudent!

RITTA. You wrong me, gentle mistress. Love like mine
Does not ask questions of propriety,
Nor stand on manners. I would do you good,
Even while you smote me; I would push you back,
With my last effort, from the crumbling edge
Of some high rock o'er which you toppled me.

FRANCESCA. What do you mean?

RITTA. I know.

FRANCESCA. Know what?
RITTA. Too much.
Pray, do not ask me.
FRANCESCA. Speak!
RITTA. I know—dear lady,
Be not offended—
FRANCESCA. Tell me, simpleton!
RITTA. You know I worship you; you know I'd walk
Straight into ruin for a whim of yours;
You know—
FRANCESCA. I know you act the fool. Talk sense!
RITTA. I know Paolo loves you.
FRANCESCA. Should he not?
He is my brother.
RITTA. More than brother should.
FRANCESCA. Ha! are you certain?
RITTA. Yes, of more than that.
FRANCESCA. Of more?
RITTA. Yes, lady; for you love him, too.
I've said it! Fling me to the carrion crows,
Kill me by inches, boil me in the pot
Count Guido promised me,—but O, beware!
Back, while you may! Make me the sufferer,
But save yourself!
FRANCESCA. Now, are you not ashamed
To look me in the face with that bold brow?
I am amazed!
RITTA. I am a woman, lady;
I too have been in love; I know its ways,
Its arts, and its deceits. Your frowning face,
And seeming indignation, do not cheat.
Your heart is in my hand.
PAOLO [*calls*]. Francesca!
FRANCESCA. Hence,
Thou wanton-hearted minion! hence, I say!—
And never look me in the face again!—
Hence, thou insulting slave!
RITTA [*clinging to her*]. O lady, lady—
FRANCESCA. Begone. [*Throws her off.*]
RITTA. I have no friends—no one to love—
O, spare me!
FRANCESCA. Hence!
RITTA. Was it for this I loved—
Cared for you more than my own happiness—
Ever at heart your slave—without a wish
For greater recompense than your stray smiles?
PAOLO [*calls*]. Francesca!
FRANCESCA. Hurry!
RITTA. I am gone. Alas!
God bless you, lady! God take care of you,
When I am far away! Alas, alas! [*Exit weeping.*]
FRANCESCA. Poor girl!—but were she all the world to me,
And held my future in her tender grasp,
I'd cast her off, without a second thought,
To savage death, for dear Paolo's sake!
Paolo, hither! Now he comes to me;
I feel his presence, though I see him not,
Stealing upon me like the fervid glow
Of morning sunshine. Now he comes too near—
He touches me—O heaven!
PAOLO. Our poem waits.
I have been reading while you talked with Ritta.
How did you get her off?
FRANCESCA. By some device.
She will not come again.
PAOLO. I hate the girl:
She seems to stand between me and the light.
And now for the romance. Where left we off?

FRANCESCA. Where Lancelot and Queen Guenevra strayed
Along the forest, in the youth of May.
You marked the figure of the birds that sang
Their melancholy farewell to the sun—
Rich in his loss, their sorrow glorified—
Like gentle mourners o'er a great man's grave.
Was it not there? No, no; 'twas where they sat
Down on the bank, by one impulsive wish
That neither uttered.

PAOLO [*turning over the book*]. Here it is. [*Reads.*] "So sat
Guenevra and Sir Lancelot"—'Twere well
To follow them in that.

[*They sit upon a bank.*]

FRANCESCA. I listen: read.
Nay, do not; I can wait, if you desire.

PAOLO. My dagger frets me; let me take it off. [*Rises.*]
In thoughts of love, we'll lay our weapons by.

[*Lays aside his dagger, and sits again.*]

Draw closer: I am weak in voice today. [*Reads.*]
"So sat Guenevra and Sir Lancelot,
Under the blaze of the descending sun,
But all his cloudy splendors were forgot.
Each bore a thought, the only secret one,
Which each had hidden from the other's heart,
That with sweet mystery well-nigh overrun.
Anon, Sir Lancelot, with gentle start,
Put by the ripples of her golden hair,
Gazing upon her with his lips apart.
He marvelled human thing could be so fair;
Essayed to speak; but, in the very deed,
His words expired of self-betrayed despair.
Little she helped him, at his direst need,
Roving her eyes o'er hill, and wood, and sky,
Peering intently at the meanest weed;
Ay, doing aught but look in Lancelot's eye.
Then, with the small pique of her velvet shoe,
Uprooted she each herb that blossomed nigh;
Or strange wild figures in the dust she drew;
Until she felt Sir Lancelot's arm around
Her waist, upon her cheek his breath like dew.
While through his fingers timidly he wound
Her shining locks; and, haply, when he brushed
Her ivory skin, Guenevra nearly swound:
For where he touched, the quivering surface blushed,
Firing her blood with most contagious heat,
Till brow, cheek, neck, and bosom, all were flushed.
Each heart was listening to the other beat.
As twin-born lilies on one golden stalk,
Drooping with Summer, in warm languor meet,
So met their faces. Down the forest walk
Sir Lancelot looked—he looked east, west, north, south—
No soul was nigh, his dearest wish to balk:
She smiled; he kissed her full upon the mouth."

[*Kisses* FRANCESCA.]

I'll read no more!

[*Starts up, dashing down the book.*]

FRANCESCA. Paolo!
PAOLO. I am mad!
The torture of unnumbered hours is o'er,
The straining cord has broken, and my heart
Riots in free delirium! O, heaven!
I struggled with it, but it mastered me!
I fought against it, but it beat me down!
I prayed, I wept, but heaven was deaf to me;
And every tear rolled backward on my heart,
To blight and poison!
FRANCESCA. And dost thou regret?
PAOLO. The love? No, no! I'd dare it all again,
Its direst agonies and meanest fears,
For that one kiss. Away with fond remorse!
Here, on the brink of ruin, we two stand;
Lock hands with me, and brave the fearful plunge!
Thou canst not name a terror so profound
That I will look or falter from. Be bold!
I know thy love—I knew it long ago—
Trembled and fled from it. But now I clasp
The peril to my breast, and ask of thee
A kindred desperation.
FRANCESCA [*throwing herself into his arms*]. Take me all,—
Body and soul. The women of our clime
Do never give away but half a heart:
I have not part to give, part to withhold,
In selfish safety. When I saw thee first,
Riding alone amid a thousand men,
Sole in the lustre of thy majesty,
And Guido da Polenta said to me,
"Daughter, behold thy husband!" with a bound
My heart went forth to meet thee. He deceived,
He lied to me—ah! that's the aptest word—
And I believed. Shall I not turn again,
And meet him, craft with craft? Paolo, love,
Thou'rt dull—thou'rt dying like a feeble fire
Before the sunshine. Was it but a blaze,
A flash of glory, and a long, long night?
PAOLO. No, darling, no! You could not bend me back;
My course is onward; but my heart is sick
With coming fears.
FRANCESCA. Away with them! Must I
Teach thee to love? and reinform the ear
Of thy spent passion with some sorcery
To raise the chilly dead?
PAOLO. Thy lips have not
A sorcery to rouse me as this spell.
[*Kisses her.*]
FRANCESCA. I give thy kisses back to thee again:
And, like a spendthrift, only ask of thee
To take while I can give.
PAOLO. Give, give forever!
Have we not touched the height of human bliss?
And if the sharp rebound may hurl us back
Among the prostrate, did we not soar once?—
Taste heavenly nectar, banquet with the gods
On high Olympus? If they cast us, now,
Amid the furies, shall we not go down
With rich ambrosia clinging to our lips,
And richer memories settled in our hearts?
Francesca.
FRANCESCA. Love?
PAOLO. The sun is sinking low

Upon the ashes of his fading pyre,
And gray possesses the eternal blue;
The evening star is stealing after him,
Fixed, like a beacon, on the prow of night;
The world is shutting up its heavy eye
Upon the stir and bustle of to-day;—
On what shall it awake?

FRANCESCA. On love that gives
Joy at all seasons, changes night to day,
Makes sorrow smile, plucks out the barbéd dart
Of moaning anguish, pours celestial balm
In all the gaping wounds of earth, and lulls
The nervous fancies of unsheltered fear
Into a slumber sweet as infancy's!
On love that laughs at the impending sword,
And puts aside the shield of caution: cries,
To all its enemies, "Come, strike me now!—
Now, while I hold my kingdom, while my crown
Of amaranth and myrtle is yet green,
Undimmed, unwithered; for I cannot tell
That I shall e'er be happier!" Dear Paolo,
Would you lapse down from misery to death,
Tottering through sorrow and infirmity?
Or would you perish at a single blow,
Cut off amid your wildest revelry,
Falling among the wine-cups and the flowers,
And tasting Bacchus when your drowsy sense
First gazed around eternity? Come, love!
The present whispers joy to us; we'll hear
The voiceless future when its turn arrives.

PAOLO. Thou art a siren. Sing, forever sing;
Hearing thy voice, I cannot tell what fate
Thou hast provided when the song is o'er;—
But I will venture it.

FRANCESCA. In, in, my love!
[*Exeunt.*]

[PEPE *steals from behind the bushes.*]

PEPE. O, brother Lanciotto!—O, my stars!—
If this thing lasts, I simply shall go mad!
[*Laughs, and rolls on the ground.*]
O Lord! to think my pretty lady puss
Has tricks like this, and we ne'er know of it!
I tell you, Lanciotto, you and I
Must have a patent for our foolery!
"She smiled; he kissed her full upon the mouth!"—
There's the beginning; where's the end of it?
O poesy! debauch thee only once,
And thou'rt the greatest wanton in the world!
O cousin Lanciotto—ho, ho, ho!
[*Laughing.*]
Can a man die of laughter? Here we sat;
Mistress Francesca so demure and calm;
Paolo grand, poetical, sublime!—
Eh! what is this? Paolo's dagger? Good!
Here is more proof, sweet cousin Broken-back.
"In thoughts of love, we'll lay our weapons by!"
[*Mimicking* PAOLO.]
That's very pretty! Here's its counterpart:
In thoughts of hate, we'll pick them up again. [*Takes the dagger.*]
Now for my soldier, now for crook-backed Mars!
Ere long all Rimini will be ablaze.

He'll kill me? Yes: what then? That's nothing new,
Except to me; I'll bear for custom's sake.
More blood will follow; like the royal sun,
I shall go down in purple. Fools for luck;
The proverb holds like iron. I must run,
Ere laughter smother me.—O, ho, ho, ho! [*Exit, laughing.*]

SCENE 2. *A camp among the Hills. Before* LANCIOTTO'S *tent.*

[*Enter, from the tent,* LANCIOTTO.]

LANCIOTTO. The camp is strangely quiet. Not a sound
Breaks nature's high solemnity. The sun
Repeats again his every-day decline;
Yet all the world looks sadly after him,
As if the customary sight were new.
Yon moody sentinel goes slowly by,
Through the thick mists of evening, with his spear
Trailed at a funeral hold. Long shadows creep,
From thing beyond the furthest range of sight,
Up to my very feet. These mystic shades
Are of the earth; the light that causes them,
And teaches us the quick comparison,
Is all from heaven. Ah! restless man might crawl
With patience through his shadowy destiny,
If he were senseless to the higher light
Towards which his soul aspires. How grand and vast
Is yonder show of heavenly pageantry!
How mean and narrow is the earthly stand
From which we gaze on it! Magnificent,
O God, art thou amid the sunsets! Ah!
What heart in Rimini is softened now,
Towards my defects, by this grand spectacle?
Perchance, Paolo now forgives the wrong
Of my hot spleen. Perchance, Francesca now
Wishes me back, and turns a tenderer eye
On my poor person and ill-mannered ways;
Fashions excuses for me, schools her heart
Through duty into love, and ponders o'er
The sacred meaning in the name of wife.
Dreams, dreams! Poor fools, we squander love away
On thankless borrowers; when bankrupt quite,
We sit and wonder of their honesty.
Love, take a lesson from the usurer,
And never lend but on security.
Captain!

[*Enter a* CAPTAIN.]

CAPTAIN. My lord.

LANCIOTTO. They worsted us to-day.

CAPTAIN. Not much, my lord.

LANCIOTTO. With little loss, indeed.
Their strength is in position. Mark you, sir.
[*Draws on the ground with his sword.*]
Here is the pass; it opens towards the plain,
With gradual widening, like a lady's fan.
The hills protect their flanks on either hand;
And, as you see, we cannot show more front
Than their advance may give us. Then, the rocks
Are sorry footing for our horse. Just here,
Close in against the left-hand hills, I marked

A strip of wood, extending down the gorge:
Behind that wood dispose your force ere dawn.
I shall begin the onset, then give ground,
And draw them out; while you, behind the wood,
Must steal along, until their flank and rear
Oppose your column. Then set up a shout,
Burst from the wood, and drive them on our spears.
They have no outpost in the wood, I know;
'Tis too far from their centre. On the morrow,
When they are flushed with seeming victory,
And think my whole division in full rout,
They will not pause to scrutinize the wood;
So you may enter boldly. We will use
The heart to-day's repulse has given to them,
For our advantage. Do you understand?

CAPTAIN. Clearly, my lord.

LANCIOTTO. If they discover you,
Before you gain your point, wheel, and retreat
Upon my rear. If your attack should fail
To strike them with a panic, and they turn
In too great numbers on your small command,
Scatter your soldiers through the wood:
Let each seek safety for himself.

CAPTAIN. I see.

LANCIOTTO. Have Pluto shod; he cast a shoe to-day:
Let it be done at once. My helmet, too,
Is worn about the lacing; look to that.
Where is my armorer?

CAPTAIN. At his forge.

LANCIOTTO. Your charge
Must be at sunrise—just at sunrise, sir—
Neither before nor after. You must march
At moonset, then, to gain the point ere dawn.
That is enough.

CAPTAIN. Good-even! [*Going.*]

LANCIOTTO. Stay, stay, stay!
My sword-hilt feels uneasy in my grasp; [*Gives his sword.*]
Have it repaired; and grind the point. Strike hard!
I'll teach these Ghibelins a lesson.
[*Loud laughter within.*]
Ha! What is that clamor?

[*Enter hastily* PEPE, *tattered and travel-stained.*]

PEPE. News from Rimini!
[*Falls exhausted.*]

LANCIOTTO. Is that you, Pepe?
Captain, a good-night!
[*Exit* CAPTAIN.]
I never saw you in such straits before.
Wit without words!

PEPE. That's better than—
O!—O!— [*Panting.*]
Words without wit.

LANCIOTTO [*laughing*]. You'll die a jester, Pepe.

PEPE. If so, I'll leave the needy all my wit.
You, you shall have it, cousin.—O! O! O! [*Panting.*]
Those devils in the hills, the Ghibelins,
Ran me almost to death. My lord—ha! ha! [*Laughing.*]
It all comes back to me—O! Lord 'a mercy!—
The garden, and the lady, and the Count!
Not to forget the poetry—ho! ho!
[*Laughing.*]
O! cousin Lanciotto, such a wife,

And such a brother! Hear me, ere I burst!
LANCIOTTO. You're pleasant, Pepe!
PEPE. Am I?—Ho! ho! ho! [*Laughing.*]
You ought to be; your wife's a—
LANCIOTTO. What?
PEPE. A lady—
A lady, I suppose, like all the rest.
I am not in their secrets. Such a fellow
As Count Paolo is your man for that.
I'll tell you something, if you'll swear a bit.
LANCIOTTO. Swear what?
PEPE. First, swear to listen till the end.—
O! you may rave, curse, howl, and tear your hair;
But you must listen.
LANCIOTTO. For your jest's sake? Well.
PEPE. You swear?
LANCIOTTO. I do.
PEPE. Next, swear to know the truth.
LANCIOTTO. The truth of a fool's story!
PEPE. You mistake.
Now, look you, cousin! You have often marked—
I know, for I have seen—strange glances pass
Between Paolo and your lady wife.—
LANCIOTTO. Ha! Pepe!
PEPE. Now I touch you to the quick.
I know the reason of those glances.
LANCIOTTO. Ha!
Speak! or I'll throttle you! [*Seizes him.*]
PEPE. Your way is odd.
Let go my gullet, and I'll talk you deaf.
Swear my last oath: only to know the truth.
LANCIOTTO. But that may trouble me.
PEPE. Your honour lies—
Your precious honour, cousin Chivalry—
Lies bleeding with a terrible great gash,
Without its knowledge. Swear!
LANCIOTTO. My honour? Speak!
PEPE. You swear?
LANCIOTTO. I swear. Your news is ill, perchance?
PEPE. Ill! would I bring it else? Am I inclined
To run ten leagues with happy news for you?
O, Lord, that's jolly!
LANCIOTTO. You infernal imp,
Out with your story, ere I strangle you!
PEPE. Then take a fast hold on your two great oaths,
To steady tottering manhood, and attend.
Last eve, about this hour, I took a stroll
Into the garden.—Are you listening, cousin?
LANCIOTTO. I am all ears.
PEPE. Why, so an ass might say.
LANCIOTTO. Will you be serious?
PEPE. Wait a while, and we
Will both be graver than a churchyard. Well,
Down the long walk, towards me, came your wife,
With Count Paolo walking at her side.
It was a pretty sight, and so I stepped
Into the bushes. Ritta came with them;
And lady Fanny had a grievous time
To get her off. That made me curious.
Anon, the pair sat down upon a bank,
To read a poem;—the tenderest romance,
All about Lancelot and Queen Guenevra.
The Count read well—I'll say that much for him—
Only he stuck too closely to the text,

Got too much wrapped up in the poesy,
And played Sir Lancelot's actions, out and out,
On Queen Francesca. Nor in royal parts
Was she so backward. When he struck the line—
"She smiled; he kissed her full upon the mouth;"
Your lady smiled, and, by the saints above,
Count Paolo carried out the sentiment!
Can I not move you?

LANCIOTTO. With such trash as this?
And so you ran ten leagues to tell a lie?—
Run home again.

PEPE. I am not ready yet.
After the kiss, up springs our amorous Count,
Flings Queen Guenevra and Sir Lancelot
Straight to the devil; growls and snaps his teeth,
Laughs, weeps, howls, dances; talks about his love,
His madness, suffering, and the Lord knows what,
Bullying the lady like a thief. But she,
All this hot time, looked cool and mischievous;
Gave him his halter to the very end;
And when he calmed a little, up she steps
And takes him by the hand. You should have seen
How tame the furious fellow was at once!
How he came down, snivelled, and cowed to her,
And fell to kissing her again! It was
A perfect female triumph! Such a scene
A man might pass through life and never see.
More sentiment then followed,—buckets full
Of washy words, not worth my memory.
But all the while she wound his Countship up,
Closer and closer; till at last—tu!—wit!—
She scoops him up, and off she carries him,
Fish for her table! Follow, if you can;
My fancy fails me. All this time you smile!

LANCIOTTO. You should have been a poet, not a fool.

PEPE. I might be both.

LANCIOTTO. You made no record, then?
Must this fine story die for want of ink?
Left you no trace in writing?

PEPE. None.

LANCIOTTO. Alas!
Then you have told it? 'Tis but stale, my boy;
I'm second hearer.

PEPE. You are first, in faith.

LANCIOTTO. In truth?

PEPE. In sadness. You have got it fresh.
I had no time; I itched to reach your ear.
Now go to Rimini, and see yourself.
You'll find them in the garden. Lovers are
Like walking ghosts, they always haunt the spot
Of their misdeeds.

LANCIOTTO. But have I heard you out?
You told me all?

PEPE. All; I have nothing left.

LANCIOTTO. Why, you brain-stricken idiot, to trust
Your story and your body in my grasp! [*Seizes him.*]

PEPE. Unhand me, cousin!
LANCIOTTO. When I drop you, Pepe,
You'll be at rest.
PEPE. I will betray you—O!
LANCIOTTO. Not till the judgment day. [*They struggle.*]
PEPE [*drawing* PAOLO'S *dagger*]. Take that!
LANCIOTTO [*wresting the dagger from him*]. Well meant,
But poorly done! Here's my return. [*Stabs him.*]
PEPE. O! beast! [*Falls.*]
This I expected: it is naught—Ha! ha! [*Laughing.*]
I'll go to sleep; but you—what you will bear!
Hunchback, come here!
LANCIOTTO. Fie, say your prayers.
PEPE. Hark, hark!
Paolo hired me, swine, to murder you.
LANCIOTTO. That is a lie; you never cared for gold.
PEPE. He did, I say! I'll swear it, by heaven!
Do you believe me?
LANCIOTTO. No!
PEPE. You lie! you lie!
Look at the dagger, cousin—Ugh!—good-night! [*Dies.*]
LANCIOTTO. O! horrible! It was a gift of mine—
He never laid it by. Speak, speak, fool, speak! [*Shakes the body.*]
How didst thou get it?—speak! Thou'rt warm—not dead—
Thou hast a tongue—O! speak! Come, come, a jest—
Another jest from those thin mocking lips!
Call me a cripple—hunchback—what thou wilt;
But speak to me! He cannot. Now, by heaven,
I'll stir this business till I find the truth!
Am I a fool? It is a silly lie,
Coined by yon villian with his last base breath.
What ho! without there!
[*Enter* CAPTAIN *and Soldiers.*]
CAPTAIN. Did you call, my lord?
LANCIOTTO. Did Heaven thunder? Are you deaf, you louts?
Saddle my horse! What are you staring at?
Is it your first look at a dead man? Well,
Then look your fill. Saddle my horse, I say!
Black Pluto—stir! Bear that assassin hence.
Chop him to pieces, if he move. My horse!
CAPTAIN. My lord, he's shoeing.
LANCIOTTO. Did I ask for shoes?
I want my horse. Run, fellow, run! Unbarbed—
My lightest harness on his back. Fly, fly! [*Exit a Soldier.*]
[*The others pick up the body.*]
Ask him, I pray you, if he did not lie!
CAPTAIN. The man is dead, my lord.
LANCIOTTO [*laughing*]. Then do not ask him! [*Exeunt Soldiers with the body.*]
By Jupiter, I shall go mad, I think! [*Walks about.*]
CAPTAIN. Something disturbs him. Do you mark the spot
Of purple on his brow? [*Apart to a Soldier.*]
SOLDIER. Then blood must flow.
LANCIOTTO. Boy, boy! [*Enter a Page.*] My cloak and riding-staff. Quick, quick!
How you all lag! [*Exit Page.*] I ride to Rimini.
Skirmish to-morrow. Wait till my return—
I shall be back at sundown. You shall see

What slaughter is then!

CAPTAIN. Ho! turn out a guard!—

LANCIOTTO. I wish no guard; I ride alone.

[*Re-enter* Page, *with a cloak and staff.*] [*Taking them.*] Well done!
Thou art a pretty boy.—And now my horse!

[*Enter a* SOLDIER.]

SOLDIER. Pluto is saddled—

LANCIOTTO. 'Tis a damned black lie!

SOLDIER. Indeed, my lord—

LANCIOTTO. O! comrade, pardon me:
I talk at random. What, Paolo too,—
A boy whom I have trotted on my knee!
Poh! I abuse myself by such a thought.
Francesca may not love me, may love him—
Indeed she ought; but when an angel comes
To play the wanton on this filthy earth,
Then I'll believe her guilty. Look you, sir!
Am I quite calm?

CAPTAIN. Quite calm, my lord.

LANCIOTTO. You see
No trace of passion on my face?—No sign
Of ugly humors, doubts, or fears, or aught
That may disfigure God's intelligence?
I have a grievous charge against you, sir,
That may involve your life; and if you doubt
The candor of my judgment, choose your time:
Shall I arraign you now?

CAPTAIN. Now, if you please.
I'll trust my cause to you and innocence
At any time. I am not conscious—

LANCIOTTO. Pshaw!
I try myself, not you. And I am calm—
That is your verdict—and dispassionate?

CAPTAIN. So far as I can judge.

LANCIOTTO. 'Tis well, 'tis well!
Then I will ride to Rimini. Good-night! [*Exit.*]

[*The others look after him, amazedly, and exeunt.*]

SCENE 3. *Rimini. The Garden of the Castle.*

[*Enter* PAOLO *and* FRANCESCA.]

FRANCESCA. Thou hast resolved?

PAOLO. I've sworn it.

FRANCESCA. Ah, you men
Can talk of love and duty in a breath;
Love while you like, forget when you are tired,
And salve your falsehood with some wholesome saw;
But we, poor women, when we give our hearts,
Give all, lose all, and never ask it back.

PAOLO. What couldst thou ask for that I have not given?
With love I gave thee manly probity,
Innocence, honor, self-respect, and peace.
Lanciotto will return, and how shall I—
O! shame, to think of it!—how shall I look
My brother in the face? take his frank hand?
Return his tender glances? I should blaze
With guilty blushes.

FRANCESCA. Thou canst forsake me, then,
To spare thyself a little bashful pain?
Paolo, dost thou know what 'tis for me,
A woman—nay, a dame of highest rank—
To lose my purity? to walk a path
Whose slightest slip may fill my ear with sounds

That hiss me out to infamy and death?
Have I no secret pangs, no self-respect,
No husband's look to bear? O! worse than these,
I must endure his loathsome touch; be kind
When he would dally with his wife, and smile
To see him play thy part. Pah! sickening thought!
From that thou art exempt. Thou shalt not go!
Thou dost not love me!

PAOLO. Love thee! Standing here,
With countless miseries upon my head,
I say, my love for thee grows day by day.
It palters with my conscience, blurs my thoughts
Of duty, and confuses my ideas
Of right and wrong. Ere long, it will persuade
My shaking manhood that all this is just.

FRANCESCA. Let it! I'll blazon it to all the world,
Ere I will lose thee. Nay, if I had choice,
Between our love and my lost innocence,
I tell thee calmly, I would dare again
The deed which we have done. O! thou art cruel
To fly me, like a coward, for thine ease.
When thou art gone, thou'lt flatter thy weak heart
With hopes and speculations; and thou'lt swear
I suffer naught, because thou dost not see.
I will not live to bear it!

PAOLO. Die,—'twere best;
'Tis the last desperate comfort of our sin.

FRANCESCA. I'll kill myself!

PAOLO. And so would I, with joy;
But crime has made a craven of me. O!
For some good cause to perish in! Something
A man might die for, looking in God's face;
Not slinking out of life with guilt like mine
Piled on the shoulders of a suicide!

FRANCESCA. Where wilt thou go?

PAOLO. I care not; anywhere
Out of this Rimini. The very things
That made the pleasures of my innocence
Have turned against me. There is not a tree,
Nor house, nor church, nor monument, whose face
Took hold upon my thoughts, that does not frown
Balefully on me. From their marble tombs
My ancestors scowl at me; and the night
Thickens to hear their hisses. I would pray,
But heaven jeers at it. Turn where'er I will,
A curse pursues me.

FRANCESCA. Heavens! O, say not so!
I never cursed thee, love; I never moved
My little finger, ere I looked to thee
For my instruction.

PAOLO. But thy gentleness
Seems to reproach me; and, instead of joy,
It whispers horror!

FRANCESCA. Cease! cease!

PAOLO. I must go.

FRANCESCA. And I must follow. All that I call life
Is bound in thee. I could endure for thee
More agonies than thou canst catalogue—
For thy sake, love—bearing the ill for thee!

With thee, the devils could not so contrive
That I would blench or falter from my love!
Without thee, heaven were torture!

PAOLO. I must go. [*Going.*]

FRANCESCA. O! no,—Paolo—dearest!— [*Clinging to him.*]

PAOLO. Loose thy hold!
'Tis for thy sake, and Lanciotto's; I
Am as a cipher in the reckoning.
I have resolved. Thou canst but stretch the time.
Keep me to-day, and I will fly to-morrow—
Steal from thee like a thief. [*Struggles with her.*]

FRANCESCA. Paolo—love—
Indeed, you hurt me!—Do not use me thus!
Kill me, but do not leave me. I will laugh—
A long, gay, ringing laugh—if thou wilt draw
Thy pitying sword, and stab me to the heart!

[*Enter* LANCIOTTO *behind.*]

Nay, then, one kiss!

LANCIOTTO [*advancing between them*]. Take it: 'twill be the last.

PAOLO. Lo! Heaven is just!

FRANCESCA. The last! so be it. [*Kisses* PAOLO.]

LANCIOTTO. Ha!
Dare you these tricks before my very face?

FRANCESCA. Why not? I've kissed him in the sight of heaven;
Are you above it?

PAOLO. Peace, Francesca, peace!

LANCIOTTO. Paolo—why, thou sad and downcast man,
Look up! I have some words to speak with thee.
Thou art not guilty?

PAOLO. Yes, I am. But she
Has been betrayed; so she is innocent.
Her father tampered with her. I—

FRANCESCA. 'Tis false!
The guilt is mine. Paolo was entrapped
By love and cunning. I am shrewder far
Than you suspect.

PAOLO. Lanciotto, shut thy ears;
She would deceive thee.

LANCIOTTO. Silence, both of you!
Is guilt so talkative in its defence?
Then, let me make you judge and advocate
In your own cause. You are not guilty?

PAOLO. Yes.

LANCIOTTO. Deny it—but a word—say no. Lie, lie!
And I'll believe.

PAOLO. I dare not.

LANCIOTTO. Lady, you?

FRANCESCA. If I might speak for him—

LANCIOTTO. It cannot be:
Speak for yourself. Do you deny your guilt?

FRANCESCA. No! I assert it; but—

LANCIOTTO. In heaven's name, hold!
Will neither of you answer no to me?
A nod, a hint, a sign, for your escape.
Bethink you, life is centered in this thing.
Speak! I will credit either. No reply?
What does your crime deserve?

PAOLO. Death.

FRANCESCA. Death to both.

LANCIOTTO. Well said! You speak the law of Italy;
And by the dagger you designed for me,
In Pepe's hand,—your bravo?

PAOLO. It is false!
If you received my dagger from his hand,
He stole it.

LANCIOTTO. There, sweet heaven, I knew! And now

You will deny the rest? You see, my friends,
How easy of belief I have become!—
How easy 'twere to cheat me!

PAOLO. No; enough!
I will not load my groaning spirit more;
A lie would crush it.

LANCIOTTO. Brother, once you gave
Life to this wretched piece of workmanship,
When my own hand resolved its overthrow.
Revoke the gift.
[*Offers to stab himself.*]

PAOLO [*preventing him*]. Hold, homicide!

LANCIOTTO. But think,
You and Francesca may live happily,
After my death, as only lovers can.

PAOLO. Live happily, after a deed like this!

LANCIOTTO. Now, look ye! there is not one hour of life
Among us three. Paolo, you are armed—
You have a sword, I but a dagger: see!
I mean to kill you.

FRANCESCA [*whispers* PAOLO]. Give thy sword to me.

PAOLO. Away! thou'rt frantic! I will never lift
This wicked hand against thee.

LANCIOTTO. Coward, slave!
Art thou so faint? Does Malatesta's blood
Run in thy puny veins? Take that!
[*Strikes him.*]

PAOLO. And more:
Thou canst not offer more than I will bear.

LANCIOTTO. Paolo, what a craven has thy guilt
Transformed thee to! Why, I have seen the time
When thou'dst have struck at heaven for such a thing!
Art thou afraid?

PAOLO. I am.

LANCIOTTO. O! infamy!
Can man sink lower? I will wake thee, though:—
Thou shalt not die a coward. See! look here! [*Stabs* FRANCESCA.]

FRANCESCA. O!—O!— [*Falls.*]

PAOLO. Remorseless man, dare you do this,
And hope to live? Die, murderer!
[*Draws, rushes at him, but pauses.*]

LANCIOTTO. Strike, strike!
Ere thy heart fail.

PAOLO. I cannot.
[*Throws away his sword.*]

LANCIOTTO. Dost thou see
Yon bloated spider—hideous as myself—
Climbing aloft, to reach that wavering twig?
When he has touched it, one of us must die.
Here is the dagger.—Look at me, I say!
Keep your eyes from that woman! Look, think, choose!—
Turn here to me: thou shalt not look at her!

PAOLO. O, heaven!

LANCIOTTO. 'Tis done!

PAOLO [*struggling with him*]. O! Lanciotto, hold!
Hold, for thy sake. Thou wilt repent this deed.

LANCIOTTO. I know it.

FRANCESCA [*rising*]. Help!—O! murder!—help, help, help!
[*She totters towards them, and falls.*]

LANCIOTTO. Our honour, boy!
[*Stabs* PAOLO, *he falls.*]

FRANCESCA. Paolo!

PAOLO. Hark! she calls.
I pray thee, brother, help me to her side.
[LANCIOTTO *helps him to* FRANCESCA.]

LANCIOTTO. Why, there!

PAOLO. God bless thee!

LANCIOTTO. Have I not done well?

What were the honour of the Malatesti,
With such a living slander fixed to it?
Cripple! that's something—cuckold! that is damned!
You blame me?

PAOLO. No.

LANCIOTTO. You, lady?

FRANCESCA. No, my lord.

LANCIOTTO. May God forgive you! We are even now:
Your blood has cleared my honour, and our name
Shines to the world as ever.

PAOLO. O!—O!—

FRANCESCA. Love,
Art suffering?

PAOLO. But for thee.

FRANCESCA. Here, rest thy head
Upon my bosom. Fie upon my blood!
It stains thy ringlets. Ha! he dies! Kind saints,
I was first struck, why cannot I die first?
Paolo, wake!—God's mercy! wilt thou go
Alone—without me? Prithee, strike again!
Nay, I am better—love—now—O! [*Dies.*]

LANCIOTTO [*sinks upon his knees*]. Great heaven!

MALATESTA [*without*]. This way, I heard the cries.

[*Enter with* GUIDO, *and Attendants.*]

GUIDO. O! horrible!

MALATESTA. O! bloody spectacle! Where is thy brother?

LANCIOTTO. So Cain was asked. Come here, old men! You shrink
From two dead bodies and a pool of blood—
You soldiers, too! Come here!

[*Drags* MALATESTA *and* GUIDO *forward.*]

MALATESTA. O!—O!—

LANCIOTTO. You groan!
What must I do, then? Father, here it is,—
The blood of Guido mingled with our own,
As my old nurse predicted. And the spot
Of her infernal baptism burns my brain
Till reason shudders! Down, upon your knees!
Ay, shake them harder, and perchance they'll wake.
Keep still! Kneel, kneel! You fear them? I shall prowl
About these bodies till the day of doom.

MALATESTA. What hast thou done?

GUIDO. Francesca!—O! my child!

LANCIOTTO. Can howling make this sight more terrible?
Peace! You disturb the angels up in heaven,
While they are hiding from this ugly earth.
Be satisfied with what you see. You two
Began this tragedy, I finished it.
Here, by these bodies, let us reckon up
Our crimes together. Why, how still they lie!
A moment since, they walked, and talked, and kissed!
Defied me to my face, dishonoured me!
They had the power to do it then; but now,
Poor souls, who'll shield them in eternity?
Father, the honor of our house is safe:
I have the secret. I will to the wars,
And do more murders, to eclipse this one.
Back to the battles; there I breathe in peace;
And I will take a soldier's honour back.—

Honour! what's that to me now? Ha! ha! ha! [*Laughing*.]
A great thing, father! I am very ill.
I killed thy son for honour: thou mayst chide.
O God! I cannot cheat myself with words!
I loved him more than honour—more than life—
This man, Paolo—this stark, bleeding corpse!
Here let me rest, till God awake us all! [*Falls on* PAOLO's *body*.]

1856

# LATE SENTIMENTALISTS

## I. HENRY THEODORE TUCKERMAN
### (1813–1871)

SONNET I

### FREEDOM

Freedom! beneath thy banner I was born,
Oh let me share thy full and perfect life!
Teach me opinion's slavery to scorn,
And to be free from passion's bitter strife;
Free of the world, a self-dependent soul,
Nourished by lofty aims and genial truth,
And made more free by love's serene control,
The spell of beauty and the hopes of youth.
The liberty of nature let me know,
Caught from the mountains, groves, and crystal streams;
Her starry host, and sunset's purple glow,
That woo the spirit with celestial dreams,
On fancy's wing exultingly to soar,
Till life's harsh fetters clog the heart no more!

1843

SONNET VIII

### THE INDIAN SUMMER

The few sere leaves that to the branches cling,
Fall not to-day, so light the zephyr's breath;
O'er Autumn's sleep now plays the breeze of Spring,
Like love's warm kiss upon the brow of death:
Serene the firmament, save where a haze
Of dreamy softness floats upon the air,
Or a bright cloud of amber seems to gaze
In mild surprise upon the meadows bare:
Summer revives, and, like a tender strain
Borne on the night-breeze to the wondering ear,
With tender sighs melts Winter's frosty chain,
And smiles once more upon the dying year:
Thus when we deem Time's frost has chilled the heart,
At Love's sweet call its languid pulses start.

1843

SONNET XXVII

### [LIKE THE FAIR SEA]

My mind's the same
It ever was to you. Where I find worth
I love the keeper, till he let it go,
And then I follow it. —*Old Play.*

Like the fair sea that laves Italia's strand,
Affection's flood is tideless in my breast;
No ebb withdraws it from the chosen land,
Havened too richly for enamored quest;
Thus I am faithful to the vanished grace

Embodied once in thy sweet form and name,
And though love's charm no more illumes thy face,
In memory's realm her olden pledge I claim.
It is not constancy to haunt a shrine
From which devotion's lingering spark has fled;
Insensate homage only wreaths can twine
Around the pulseless temples of the dead:
Thou from thy better self hast madly flown,
While to that self allegiance still I own.

1845

## II. JOHN GODFREY SAXE
(1816–1887)

### SONNET TO A CLAM

*Dum tacent* CLAM*ant*.

Inglorious friend! most confident I am
Thy life is one of very little ease;
Albeit men mock thee with their similies
And prate of being 'happy as a clam!'
What though thy shell protects thy fragile head
From the sharp bailiffs of the briny sea?
Thy valves are, sure, no safety-valves to thee,
While rakes are free to desecrate thy bed,
And bear thee off,—as foemen take their spoil,—
Far from thy friends and family to roam;
Forced, like a Hessian, from thy native home,
To meet destruction in a foreign broil!
Though thou art tender, yet thy humble bard
Declares, O clam! thy case is shocking hard!

1850

### A CHARMING WOMAN

A charming woman, I've heard it said
By other women light as she;
But all in vain I puzzle my head
To find wherein the charm may be.
Her face, indeed, is pretty enough,
And her form is quite as good as the best,
Where Nature has given the bony stuff,
And a clever milliner all the rest.

Intelligent? Yes — in a certain way;
With the feminine gift of ready speech;
And knows very well what *not* to say
Whenever the theme transcends her reach.
But turn the topic on things to wear,
From an opera cloak to a *robe de nuit* —
Hats, basques, or bonnets,— 't will make you stare
To see how fluent the lady can be.

Her laugh is hardly a thing to please;
For an honest laugh must always start
From a gleesome mood, like a sudden breeze,
And hers is purely a matter of art —
A muscular motion made to show
What Nature designed to lie beneath
The finer mouth; but what can she do,
If *that* is ruined, to show the teeth?

To her seat in church — a good half mile —
When the day is fine she is sure to go
Arrayed, of course, in the latest style
*La mode de Paris* has got to show;
And she puts her hands on the velvet pew
(Can hands so white have a taint of sin?),

And thinks — how her prayer book's tint of blue
Must harmonize with her milky skin!

Ah! What shall we say of one who walks
In fields of flowers to choose the weeds?
Reads authors of whom she never talks,
And talks of authors she never reads?
She's a charming woman, I've heard it said
By other women as light as she;
But all in vain I puzzle my head
To find wherein the charm may be.

1875

## III. THOMAS WILLIAM PARSONS
(1819–1892)

### ON A BUST OF DANTE

See, from this counterfeit of him
Whom Arno shall remember long,
How stern of lineament, how grim,
The father was of Tuscan song.
There but the burning sense of wrong,
Perpetual care and scorn, abide;
Small friendship for the lordly throng;
Distrust of all the world beside.

Faithful if this wan image be,
No dream his life was — but a fight;
Could any Beatrice see
A lover in that anchorite?
To that cold Ghibeline's gloomy sight
Who could have guessed the visions came
Of Beauty, veiled with heavenly light,
In circles of eternal flame?

The lips as Cumæ's cavern close,
The cheeks with fast and sorrow thin,
The rigid front, almost morose,
But for the patient hope within,
Declare a life whose course hath been
Unsullied still, though still severe,
Which, through the wavering days of sin,
Kept itself icy-chaste and clear.

Not wholly such his haggard look
When wandering once, forlorn, he strayed,
With no companion save his book,
To Corvo's hushed monastic shade;
Where, as the Benedictine laid
His palm upon the pilgrim guest,
The single boon for which he prayed
The convent's charity was rest.

Peace dwells not here — this rugged face
Betrays no spirit of repose;
The sullen warrior sole we trace,
The marble man of many woes.
Such was his mien when first arose
The thought of that strange tale divine,
When hell he peopled with his foes,
The scourge of many a guilty line.

War to the last he waged with all
The tyrant canker-worms of earth;
Baron and duke, in hold and hall,
Cursed the dark hour that gave him birth;
He used Rome's harlot for his mirth;
Plucked bare hypocrisy and crime;
But valiant souls of knightly worth
Transmitted to the rolls of Time.

O Time! whose verdicts mock our own,
The only righteous judge art thou;
That poor, old exile, sad and lone,
Is Latium's other VIRGIL now:
Before his name the nations bow;
His words are parcel of mankind,
Deep in whose hearts, as on his brow,
The marks have sunk of DANTE's mind.

1841

## IV. THOMAS BUCHANAN READ
(1822–1872)

### DRIFTING

My soul to-day
Is far away,
Sailing the Vesuvian Bay;
My wingéd boat,
A bird afloat,
Swims round the purple peaks remote:—

Round purple peaks
It sails, and seeks
Blue inlets and their crystal creeks,
Where high rocks throw,
Through deeps below,
A duplicated golden glow.

Far, vague, and dim,
The mountains swim;
While on Vesuvius' misty brim,
With outstretched hands,
The gray smoke stands
O'erlooking the volcanic lands.

Here Ischia smiles
O'er liquid miles;
And yonder, bluest of the isles,
Calm Capri waits,
Her sapphire gates
Beguiling to her bright estates.

I heed not, if
My rippling skiff
Float swift or slow from cliff to cliff;—
With dreamful eyes
My spirit lies
Under the walls of Paradise.

Under the walls
Where swells and falls
The Bay's deep breast at intervals
At peace I lie,
Blown softly by,
A cloud upon this liquid sky.

The day, so mild,
Is Heaven's own child,
With Earth and Ocean reconciled;—
The airs I feel
Around me steal
Are murmuring to the murmuring keel.

Over the rail
My hand I trail
Within the shadow of the sail,
A joy intense,
The cooling sense
Glides down my drowsy indolence.

With dreamful eyes
My spirit lies
Where Summer sings and never dies,—
O'erveiled with vines
She glows and shines
Among her future oil and wines.

Her children, hid
The cliffs amid,
Are gambolling with the gambolling kid;
Or down the walls,
With tipsy calls,
Laugh on the rocks like waterfalls.

The fisher's child,
With tresses wild,
Unto the smooth, bright sand beguiled,
With glowing lips
Sings as she skips,
Or gazes at the far-off ships.

Yon deep bark goes
Where Traffic blows,
From lands of sun to lands of snows;—
This happier one,
Its course is run
From lands of snow to lands of sun.

O happy ship,
To rise and dip,
With the blue crystal at your lip!

O happy crew,
My heart with you
Sails, and sails, and sings anew!

No more, no more
The worldly shore
Upbraids me with its loud uproar!
With dreamful eyes
My spirit lies
Under the walls of Paradise!

1860

## V. JAMES MATTHEWS LEGARÉ
(1823–1859)

### HAW-BLOSSOMS

While yesterevening, through the vale
Descending from my cottage door
I strayed, how cool and fresh a look
All nature wore.

The calmïas and golden-rods,
And tender blossoms of the haw,
Like maidens seated in the wood,
Demure, I saw.

The recent drops upon their leaves
Shone brighter than the bluest eyes,
And filled the little sheltered dell
Their fragrant sighs.

Their pliant arms they interlaced,
As pleasant canopies they were:
Their blossoms swung against my cheek
Like braids of hair.

And when I put their boughs aside
And stooped to pass, from overhead
The little agitated things
A shower shed

Of tears. Then thoughtfully I spoke;
Well represent thee maidenhood,
Sweet flowers. Life is to the young
A shady wood.

And therein some like golden-rods,
For grosser purposes designed,
A gay existence lead, but leave
No germ behind.

And others like the calmïas,
On cliff-sides inaccessible,
Bloom paramount, the vale with sweets
Yet never fill.

But underneath the glossy leaves,
When, working out the perfect law,
The blossoms white and fragrant still
Drop from the haw;

Like worthy deeds in silence wrought
And secret, through the lapse of years,
In clusters pale and delicate
The fruit appears.

In clusters pale and delicate
But waxing heavier each day,
Until the many-colored leaves
Drift from the spray.

Then pendulous, like amethysts
And rubies, purple ripe and red,
Wherewith God's feathered pensioners
In flocks are fed.

Therefore, sweet reader of this rhyme,
Be unto thee examples high
Not calmïas and golden-rods
That scentless die:

But the meek blossoms of the haw,
That fragrant are wherever wind
The forest paths, and perishing
Leave fruits behind.

1847

## VI. PHŒBE CARY
(1824–1871)

### NEARER HOME

One sweetly solemn thought
Comes to me o'er and o'er;
I am nearer home to-day
Than I ever have been before;

Nearer my Father's house
  Where the many mansions be;
Nearer the great white throne,
  Nearer the crystal sea;

Nearer the bound of life,
  Where we lay our burdens down;
Nearer leaving the cross,
  Nearer gaining the crown!

But lying darkly between,
  Winding down through the night,
Is the silent, unknown stream
  That leads at last to the light.

Closer and closer my steps
  Come to the dread abysm:
Closer Death to my lips
  Presses the awful chrism.

Oh, if my mortal feet
  Have almost gained the brink;
If it be I am nearer home
  Even to-day than I think;

Father, perfect my trust;
  Let my spirit feel in death,
That her feet are firmly set
  On the rock of a living faith!

1854

## VII. STEPHEN COLLINS FOSTER
(1826–1864)

### OLD FOLKS AT HOME

Way down upon de Swanee ribber,
  Far, far away,
Dere's wha my heart is turning ebber,
  Dere's wha de old folks stay.
All up and down de whole creation,
  Sadly I roam,
Still longing for de old plantation,
  And for de old folks at home.

    All de world am sad and dreary,
      Eb'ry-where I roam,
    Oh! darkeys, how my heart grows
      weary,
    Far from de old folks at home.

All round de little farm I wandered
  When I was young,
Den many happy days I squandered,
  Many de songs I sung.
When I was playing wid my brudder
  Happy was I—
Oh! take me to my kind old mudder,
  Dere let me live and die.

One little hut among de bushes,
  One dat I love,
Still sadly to my mem'ry rushes,
  No matter where I rove.
When will I see de bees a humming
  All round de comb?
When will I hear de banjo tumming
  Down in my good old home?

1851

### MY OLD KENTUCKY HOME, GOOD-NIGHT!

The sun shines bright in the old Kentucky home,
  'Tis summer, the darkies are gay,
The corn top's ripe and the meadow's in the bloom,
  While the birds make music all the day.
The young folks roll on the little cabin floor,
  All merry, all happy and bright:
By 'n by Hard Times comes a knocking at the door,
  Then my old Kentucky Home, good-night!

    Weep no more, my lady! oh! weep no more to-day!
    We will sing one song
    For the old Kentucky Home,
      For the old Kentucky Home, far away.

They hunt no more for the possum and the coon
  On the meadow, the hill, and the shore,
They sing no more by the glimmer of the moon,

On the bench by the old cabin door.
The day goes by like a shadow o'er
the heart,
With sorrow where all was delight:
The time has come when the darkies
have to part,
Then my old Kentucky Home, good-
night!

The head must bow and the back will
have to bend,
Wherever the darkey may go:
A few more days, and the trouble all
will end
In the field where the sugar-canes
grow.
A few more days for to tote the weary
load,
No matter, 'twill never be light,
A few more days till we totter on the
road,
Then my old Kentucky Home, good-
night!

1853

# VIII. DONALD GRANT MITCHELL
## (1822–1908)

## *REVERIES OF A BACHELOR*
### *From* FIRST REVERIE

#### OVER A WOOD FIRE

I have got a quiet farmhouse in the country, a very humble place to be sure, tenanted by a worthy enough man, of the old New-England stamp, where I sometimes go for a day or two in the winter, to look over the farm-accounts, and to see how the stock is thriving on the winter's keep.

One side the door, as you enter from the porch, is a little parlor, scarce twelve feet by ten, with a cosy looking fire-place — a heavy oak floor — a couple of armchairs and a brown table with carved lions' feet. Out of this room opens a little cabinet, only big enough for a broad bachelor bedstead, where I sleep upon feathers, and wake in the morning with my eye upon a saucy colored, lithographic print of some fancy "Bessie."

It happens to be the only house in the world, of which I am *bona-fide* owner; and I take a vast deal of comfort in treating it just as I choose. I manage to break some article of furniture, almost every time I pay it a visit; and if I cannot open the window readily of a morning, to breathe the fresh air, I knock out a pane or two of glass with my boot. I lean against the walls in a very old armchair there is on the premises, and scarce ever fail to worry such a hole in the plastering, as would set me down for a round charge for damages in town, or make a prim housewife fret herself into a raging fever. I laugh out loud with myself, in my big arm-chair, when I think that I am neither afraid of one, nor the other.

As for the fire, I keep the little hearth so hot, as to warm half the cellar below, and the whole space between the jambs, roars for hours together, with white flame. To be sure, the windows are not very tight, between broken panes, and bad joints, so that the fire, large as it is, is by no means an extravagant comfort.

As night approaches, I have a huge pile of oak and hickory placed beside the hearth; I put out the tallow candle on the mantel (using the family snuffers, with one leg broke), then, drawing my chair directly in front of the blazing wood, and setting one foot on each of the old iron fire-dogs (until they grow too warm,) I dispose myself for an evening of such sober, and thoughtful quietude, as I believe, on my soul, that very few of my fellowmen have the good fortune to enjoy.

My tenant meantime, in the other room, I can hear now and then,— though there is a thick stone chimney, and broad entry between,— multiplying contrivances with his wife, to put two babies to sleep. This occupies them, I should say, usually an hour; though my only measure of time, (for I never carry a watch into the country,) is the blaze of my fire. By ten, or thereabouts, my stock of wood is nearly exhausted; I pile upon the hot coals what remains, and sit watching how it kindles, and blazes, and goes out,— even like our joys!— and then slip, by the light of the embers into my bed, where I luxuriate in such sound, and healthful slumber as only such rattling window-frames, and country air, can supply.

But to return: the other evening— it happened to be on my last visit to my farm-house— when I had exhausted all the ordinary rural topics of thought, had formed all sorts of conjectures as to the income of the year; had planned a new wall around one lot, and the clearing up of another, now covered with patriarchal wood; and wondered if the little ricketty house would not be after all a snug enough box, to live and to die in— I fell on a sudden into such an unprecedented line of thought, which took such deep hold of my sympathies— sometimes even starting tears— that I determined, the next day, to set as much of it as I could recall, on paper.

Something— it may have been the home-looking blaze, (I am a bachelor of— say six and twenty,) or possibly a plaintive cry of the baby in my tenant's room, had suggested to me the thought of— Marriage.

I piled upon the heated fire-dogs, the last arm-full of my wood; and now, said I, bracing myself courageously between the arms of my chair,— I'll not flinch,— I'll pursue the thought wherever it leads, though it lead me to the d—— (I am apt to be hasty,)— at least— continued I, softening, until my fire is out.

The wood was green, and at first showed no disposition to blaze. It smoked furiously. Smoke, thought I, always goes before blaze; and so does doubt go before decision: and my Reverie, from that very starting point, slipped into this shape:—

SMOKE — SIGNIFYING DOUBT

A wife?— thought I;— yes, a wife!

And why?

And pray, my dear sir, why not— why? Why not doubt; why not hesitate; why not tremble?

Does a man buy a ticket in a lottery— a poor man, whose whole earnings go in to secure the ticket,— without trembling, hesitating, and doubting?

Can a man stake his bachelor respectability, his independence, and comfort, upon the die of absorbing, unchanging, relentless marriage, without trembling at the venture?

Shall a man who has been free to chase his fancies over the wide-world, without lett or hindrance, shut himself up to marriage-ship, within four walls called Home, that are to claim him, his time, his trouble, and his tears, thenceforward forever-more, without doubts thick, and thick-coming as Smoke?

Shall he who has been hitherto a mere observer of other men's cares, and business — moving off where they made him sick of heart, approaching whenever and wherever they made him gleeful — shall he now undertake administration of just such cares and business, without qualms? Shall he, whose whole life has been but a nimble succession of escapes from trifling difficulties, now broach without doubtings — that Matrimony, where if difficulty beset him, there is no escape? Shall this brain of mine, careless-working, never tired with idleness, feeding on long vagaries and high, gigantic castles, dreaming out beatitudes hour by hour — turn itself at length to such dull task-work, as thinking out a livelihood for wife and children?

Where thenceforward will be those sunny dreams, in which I have warmed my fancies, and my heart, and lighted my eye with crystal? This very marriage, which a brilliant working imagination has invested time and again with brightness, and delight, can serve no longer as a mine for teeming fancy: all, alas, will be gone — reduced to the dull standard of the actual! No more room for intrepid forays of imagination — no more gorgeous realm-making — all will be over!

Why not, I thought, go on dreaming?

Can any wife be prettier than an after dinner fancy, idle and yet vivid, can paint for you? Can any children make less noise, than the little rosy-cheeked ones, who have no existence, except in the *omnium gatherum* of your own brain? Can any housewife be more unexceptional, than she who goes sweeping daintily the cobwebs that gather in your dreams? Can any domestic larder be better stocked, than the private larder of your head dozing on a cushioned chair-back at Delmonico's? Can any family purse be better filled than the exceeding plump one, you dream of, after reading such pleasant books as Münchhausen, or Typee?

But if, after all, it must be — duty, or what-not, making provocation — what then? And I clapped my feet hard against the fire-dogs, and leaned back, and turned my face to the ceiling, as much as to say; — And where on earth, then, shall a poor devil look for a wife?

Somebody says,— Lyttleton or Shaftesbury I think, that "marriages would be happier if they were all arranged by the Lord Chancellor." Unfortunately, we have no Lord Chancellor to make this commutation of our misery.

Shall a man then scour the country on a mule's back, like Honest Gil Blas of Santillane; or shall he make application to some such intervening providence as Madame St. Marc, who, as I see by the Presse, manages these matters to one's hand, for some five per cent. on the fortunes of the parties?

I have trouted, when the brook was so low, and the sky so hot, that I might as well have thrown my fly upon the turnpike; and I have hunted hare at noon, and wood-cock in snow-time,— never despairing, scarce doubting; but for a poor hunter of his kind, without traps or snares, or any aid of police or constabulary, to traverse the world, where are swarming, on a moderate computation, some three hundred and odd millions of unmarried women, for a single capture — irremediable, unchangeable — and yet a capture which by strange metonymy not laid down in the books, is very apt to turn captor into captive, and make game of hunter,— all this, surely, surely may make a man shrug with doubt!

Then, again,— there are the plaguey wife's-relations. Who knows how many third, fourth, or fifth cousins will appear at careless complimentary intervals, long after you had settled into the placid belief that all congratulatory visits were at an end? How many twisted headed brothers will be putting in their advice, as a friend to Peggy?

How many maiden aunts will come to spend a month or two with their "dear Peggy," and want to know every tea-time "if she is n't a dear love of a wife?" Then, dear father-in-law will beg (taking dear Peggy's hand in his,) to give a little wholesome counsel; and will be very sure to advise just the contrary of what you had determined to undertake. And dear mamma-in-law, must set her nose into Peggy's cupboard, and insist upon having the key to your own private locker in the wainscot.

Then, perhaps, there is a little bevy of dirty-nosed nephews who come to spend the holydays, and eat up your East India sweetmeats; and who are forever tramping over your head, or raising the Old Harry below, while you are busy with your clients. Last, and worse, is some fidgety old uncle, forever too cold or too hot, who vexes you with his patronizing airs, and impudently kisses his little Peggy!

— That could be borne, however: for perhaps he has promised his fortune to Peggy. Peggy, then, will be rich: — (and the thought made me rub my shins, which were now getting comfortably warm upon the fire-dogs). Then, she will be forever talking of *her* fortune; and pleasantly reminding you, on occasion of a favorite purchase,— how lucky that *she* had the means; and dropping hints about economy; and buying very extravagant Paisleys.

She will annoy you by looking over the stock-list at breakfast-time; and mention quite carelessly to your clients that she is interested in *such* or such a speculation.

She will be provokingly silent when you hint to a tradesman that you have not the money by you, for his small bill; in short, she will tear the life out of you, making you pay in righteous retribution of annoyance, grief, vexation, shame, and sickness of heart, for the superlative folly of "marrying rich."

— But if not rich, then poor. Bah! the thought made me stir the coals; but there was still no blaze. The paltry earnings you are able to wring out of clients by the sweat of your brow, will now be all *our* income; you will be pestered for pin-money, and pestered with your poor wife's-relations. Ten to one, she will stickle about taste,—"Sir Visto's,"— and want to make this so pretty, and that so charming, if she *only* had the means; and is sure Paul (a kiss) can't deny his little Peggy such a trifling sum, and all for the common benefit.

Then she, for one, means that *her* children shan't go a begging for clothes,— and another pull at the purse. Trust a poor mother to dress her children in finery!

Perhaps she is ugly; — not noticeable at first; but growing on her, and (what is worse) growing faster on you. You wonder why you did n't see that vulgar nose long ago: and that lip — it is very strange, you think, that you ever thought it pretty. And then, to come to breakfast, with her hair looking as it does, and you not so much as daring to say — "Peggy, *do* brush your hair!" Her foot too — not very bad when decently *chaussée* — but now since she 's married, she does wear such infernal slippers! And yet for all this, to be prigging up for an hour when any of my old chums come to dine with me!

"Bless your kind hearts! my dear fellows," said I, thrusting the tongs into the coals, and speaking out loud, as if my voice could reach from Virginia to Paris — "not married yet!"

Perhaps Peggy is pretty enough, only shrewish.

— No matter for cold coffee; — you should have been up before.

What sad, thin, poorly cooked chops, to eat with your rolls!

— She thinks they are very good, and wonders how you can set such an example to your children.

The butter is nauseating.

— She had not other, and hopes you'll not raise a storm about butter a little turned.— I think I see myself — ruminated I — sitting meekly at table, scarce daring to lift up my eyes, utterly fagged out with some quarrel of yesterday, choking down detestably sour muffins, that my wife thinks are 'delicious '— slipping in dried mouthfuls of burnt ham off the side of my fork tines,— slipping off my chair sideways at the end, and slipping out, with my hat between my knees, to business, and never feeling myself a competent, sound-minded man, till the oak door is between me and Peggy!

— "Ha, ha,— not yet!" said I; and in so earnest a tone, that my dog started to his feet — cocked his eye to have a good look into my face — met my smile of triumph with an amiable wag of the tail, and curled up again in the corner.

Again, Peggy is rich enough, well enough, mild enough, only she does n't care a fig for you. She has married you because father, or grandfather thought the match eligible, and because she did n't wish to disoblige them. Besides, she did n't positively hate you, and thought you were a respectable enough young person; — she has told you so repeatedly at dinner. She wonders you like to read poetry; she wishes you would buy her a good cook-book, and insists upon your making your will at the birth of the first baby.

She thinks Captain So-and-So a splendid looking fellow, and wishes you would trim up a little, were it only for appearance's sake.

You need not hurry up from the office so early at night: — she, bless her dear heart! — does not feel lonely. You read to her a love-tale; she interrupts the pathetic parts with directions to her seamstress. You read of marriages: she sighs, and asks if Captain So-and-So has left town? She hates to be mewed up in a cottage, or between brick walls; she does *so* love the Springs!

But, again, Peggy loves you; — at least she swears it, with her hand on the Sorrows of Werther. She has pin-money which she spends for the Literary World and the Friends in Council. She is not bad-looking, save a bit too much of forehead; nor is she sluttish, unless a *negligé* till three o'clock, and an ink stain on the forefinger be sluttish; but then she is such a sad blue!

You never fancied, when you saw her buried in a three volume novel, that it was anything more than a girlish vagary; and when she quoted Latin, you thought innocently that she had a capital memory for her samplers.

But, to be bored eternally about divine Dante and funny Goldoni, is too bad. Your copy of Tasso, a treasure print of 1680, is all bethumbed, and dogs-eared, and spotted with baby gruel. Even your Seneca — an Elzevir — is all sweaty with handling. She adores La Fontaine, reads Balzac with a kind of artist-scowl, and will not let Greek alone.

You hint at broken rest and an aching head at breakfast, and she will fling you a scrap of Anthology — in lieu of the camphor bottle, or chant the *αἰᾶι αἰᾶι*, of tragic chorus.

— The nurse is getting dinner; you are holding the baby; Peggy is reading Bruyère.

The fire smoked thick as pitch, and puffed out little clouds over the chimney piece. I gave the fore-stick a kick, at the thought of Peggy, baby, and Bruyère.

— Suddenly the flame flickered bluely athwart the smoke — caught at a twig below — rolled round the mossy oak-stick — twined among the crackling tree-limbs — mounted — lit up the whole body of smoke, and blazed out cheerily and bright. Doubt vanished with Smoke, and Hope began with Flame. * * *

1849

# NOTES

In these Notes a concise biographical sketch of each author is provided, with selected, annotated bibliographies. For each specimen full details of publication are given, as is also the source of the text. The more difficult allusions are annotated.

## *Lydia Huntley Sigourney (1791–1865)*

Lydia Huntley was born at Norwich, Conn., taught school, and in 1819 married Charles Sigourney. For a half-century, she was one of the most popular poets and editors in America, producing fifty volumes and thousands of uncollected items in prose and verse. Mrs. Sigourney died at Hartford, Conn. An excellent biography is G. S. Haight, *Mrs. Sigourney* (1930).

9. THE ALPINE FLOWERS appeared in *Poems* (1827).

## *Nathaniel Parker Willis (1806–1867)*

Willis was born at Portland, Maine, was graduated from Yale, and established himself as a journalist in New York. Travel in Europe and residence in rural Pennsylvania gave him material for pleasant sketches (*Pencillings by the Way*, 1835; *A L'Abri, or The Tent Pitched*, 1839). Although the American public revered Willis for several decades as one of their major poets and essayists, it was with difficulty that he maintained his organ, the *Home Journal*, from 1846 until his death. The only biography is H. A. Beers, *Nathaniel Parker Willis* (1885).

9. THE WHITE CHIP HAT was published in the *New Mirror*, July 1, 1843, and collected in *Poems of Passion* (1843).

10. UNSEEN SPIRITS was published in the *New Mirror*, July 29, 1843, and collected in *Poems of Passion*.

10. A BREAKFAST WITH CHARLES LAMB. Henry Crabb Robinson (1775–1867), friend of English authors and host at this breakfast with Charles Lamb, recorded the event in his diary on July 19, 1834, describing Willis as a dandy and "one who strives to be genteel." The essay was published in the *New York Mirror*, March 21, 1835; this text follows the first complete edition of *Pencillings by the Way*. ¶11. "*Sketch of Liston.*" Concerning this burlesque biography of the English comedian, John Liston (1776?–1846), Lamb remarked: "Of all the Lies I ever put off, I value this most." ¶12. "*The Journal of Edward* [properly *John*] *Woolman*" had so charmed Lamb that he exclaimed in his *Essays of Elia:* "Get the writings of John Woolman by heart."

## *Charles Fenno Hoffman (1806–1884)*

Hoffman was born in New York, was admitted to the bar but abandoned law for literature, and became the first editor of the *Knickerbocker Magazine*. His journey to St. Louis was recorded in *A Winter in the West* (1835). For several years Hoffman was active as editor and author (*Greyslaer: a Romance of the Mohawk*, 1840, and poems); but in 1849 his mind gave way and he was committed to the state insane asylum at Harrisburg, Pa., where he died. The only biography is H. F. Barnes, *Charles Fenno Hoffman* (1930).

13. WHAT IS SOLITUDE? appeared in the *American Monthly Magazine*, June, 1835. This text is a revision published in *The Echo* for 1844 (pub. 1843).

13. ALGONQUIN DEATH SONG appeared in H. R. Schoolcraft, *Oneóta* (1845). It is a versification of Schoolcraft's literal translation of the Chippewa original. The refrain, *Baim-wa-wa*, means " 'the sound of passing thunders,' a phrase which will convey a just idea of the violence of this figure, and the impossibility of rendering it into English by a single word." [Author's note.]

## *Thomas Holley Chivers (1809–1858)*

Chivers was born in Georgia in 1809 (?), received a doctor's degree in medicine in 1830 but practised little, and produced a play (*Conrad and Eudora; or, The Death of Alonzo*, 1834) and several volumes of verse (*Nachoochee; or the Beautiful Star*, 1837; *The Lost Pleiad*, 1845; *Eonchs of Ruby*, 1851). Chivers died at Decatur, Ga. A sympathetic biography is S. F. Damon, *Thomas Holley Chivers, Friend of Poe* (1930).

14. ISADORE is said to have been published "as early as 1841," four years before Poe's "Raven." (For the most recent discussion of the Poe-Chivers controversy, see Damon.) This text is from *Eonchs of Ruby*.

14. THE SHIP OF DEATH is a portion of "To Shakespeare Dying," included in *The Lost Pleiad*.

14. AVALON appeared in *Eonchs of Ruby*. Certain unfortunate stanzas are here omitted. The poem justifies Poe's description of Chivers as "at the same time one of the best and one of the worst poets in America." Perhaps his most painful effusion is the following:

As an egg when broken, never can be mended,
  but must ever
Be the same crushed egg forever, so shall
  this dark heart of mine
Which, though broken, still is breaking, and
  shall nevermore cease aching,
For the sleep which has no aching—for the
  sleep that now is thine.

## *Edgar Allan Poe (1809–1849)*

Edgar Poe was born in Boston, Jan. 19, 1809, the child of actors. As foster son of John and Frances Allan, he was given an excellent education in Richmond (1813–15), in Great Britain (1815–20), again in Richmond (1820–26), and at the University of Virginia (1826). After a quarrel with Mr. Allan, Poe went to Boston, where he published *Tamerlane and Other Poems* (1827). In 1827–29, he was in the United States army, as Private Edgar A. Perry. During his first residence at Baltimore with his aunt, Mrs. Maria Clemm, he published *Al Aaraaf, Tamerlane, and Minor Poems* (1829). In 1830–31, Poe was a cadet at West Point, where he provoked his discharge from the academy. Before leaving, he arranged to publish *Poems* (1831). While Poe was again in Baltimore with Mrs. Clemm, 1831–35, he was awarded first prize in a short-story contest in the *Baltimore Saturday Visiter* (1833). During 1835–37, he edited and contributed to the *Southern Literary Messenger* in Richmond. In 1835, Poe secretly married his cousin, Virginia Clemm; in 1836, a second and public ceremony was performed. They resided in New York, 1837–38, and in Philadelphia, 1838–44, in great poverty. Poe published *Tales of the Grotesque and Arabesque* (1840), served as assistant editor of *Burton's Gentleman's Magazine* (1839–40), and as editor of and chief contributor to *Graham's Magazine* (1841–42). The family were in New York and Fordham, 1844–49, where Poe wrote for the *Evening Mirror* and became editor and part-proprietor of the *Broadway Journal* (1845–46). *The Raven and Other Poems* (1845) brought the poet considerable notoriety. After his wife's death (1847), Poe steadily declined in health. He died in Baltimore, Oct. 7, 1849.

Bibliographies of Poe are found in the Virginia Edition, XVI, 355–379, and in *CHAL*, II, 452–68. R. W. Griswold edited the first collected edition of Poe's works (1850–56); library editions are those prepared by Stedman and Woodberry (1894–95, 1914) and by J. A. Harrison (1902). T. O. Mabbott has in preparation a definitive edition of Poe. Killis Campbell's one-volume edition of the poems (1917) is indispensable to all students; his single volume of the tales (1927) is also useful. The earliest significant biography of Poe, subsequent to Griswold's notorious sketch, is J. H. Ingram, *Edgar Allan Poe* (1880). J. A. Harrison, *Life and Letters of Edgar Allan Poe* (1903) and G. E. Woodberry, *The Life of Edgar Allan Poe* (1909) are still valuable, although in certain respects antiquated. Valuable new material appears in M. E. Phillips, *Edgar Allan Poe* (1926). Although derivative at times, prejudiced in attitude and erroneous in minor details, Hervey Allen, *Israfel* (1926), is the most inclusive biography yet published. J. W. Robertson, *Edgar Allan Poe, a Psychopathic Study* (1922), and J. W. Krutch, *Edgar Allan Poe* (1926), are inconclusive attempts to apply science to literature. The sources of Poe's early tales are discussed in Margaret Alterton, *Origins of Poe's Critical Theory* (1925). Important is Célestin Pierre Cambiaire, *The Influence of Edgar Allan Poe in France* (1927). Much of Poe's correspondence is now in print, the richest single collection being the Valentine Museum letters, edited by M. N. Stanard (1925). Among many essays, particularly significant are those by L. E. Gates in *Studies and Appreciations* (1900); P. E. More in *Shelburne Essays, First Series* (1904); and W. C. Brownell in *American Prose Masters* (1909).

16. TAMERLANE. The love affair which Poe attributes to Tamerlane is apparently based on the poet's romance with Sarah Elmira Royster of Richmond. The influence of Byron, particularly of his *Manfred* and *The Giaour*, is clearly evident in this immature and uneven composition. The poem was published in

*Tamerlane and Other Poems;* this text appeared in *The Raven and Other Poems.* ¶19. "*Eblis*" was, according to Mohammedans, a devil whose name signified "Despair"; he was originally the angel Azazel.

19. A DREAM WITHIN A DREAM was first entitled "Imitation," probably as an admission of Poe's continued debt to Byron. The poem was published in *Tamerlane and Other Poems;* it is here printed from an extensively revised version in *Flag of Our Union,* March 31, 1849.

19. SONNET—TO SCIENCE was written under the stimulus of Keats (cf. "Lamia," ll. 9–14, 229–38). The poem appeared in *Al Aaraaf;* the present text is that of *The Raven and Other Poems.*

19. AL AARAAF is the title-poem of Poe's second volume; this text is from *The Raven and Other Poems.* For a study of the entire poem, see W. B. Cairns, "Some Notes on Poe's 'Al Aaraaf,'" in *Modern Philology,* XII, 35–44 (1915). This lyric, "'Neath blue-bell or streamer," is sung in Part II of "Al Aaraaf," by a maiden.

20. ROMANCE was perhaps written to express Poe's disagreement with Byron's "To Romance." Of ll. 10–15, Poe declared in 1829, "I am certain that these lines have never been surpassed." First published in *Al Aaraaf,* the poem was repeatedly revised; the present text is from *The Raven and Other Poems.*

21. TO HELEN is, according to Poe, his tribute to Mrs. Jane Stith Stanard of Richmond, described by the poet as "the truest, tenderest of this world's womanly souls, and an angel to my forlorn and darkened nature." The fifteen-year-old Poe was profoundly grieved by her death in 1824 and, according to legend, made nightly visits to her grave. "To Helen" first appeared in *Poems;* this text is from *The Raven and Other Poems.* ¶21. "*Nicean*" is possibly a reference to the "Nyseian isle" of Bacchus, mentioned by Milton, or, more probably, to Niceæ, a city in Asia Minor, commemorated by Catullus. ¶21. "*The glory that was Greece.*" Poe's skill in revision is illustrated by his improvement of these lines, which originally read

To the beauty of fair Greece
And the grandeur of old Rome.

21. ISRAFEL was published in *Poems;* this text is from *The Raven and Other Poems.* The motto is drawn from Sale's *Discourse* on the Koran and Béranger's *Le Rufus.*

22. THE CITY IN THE SEA was published in *Poems* as "The Doomed City," in 1836 as "The City of Sin," in 1845 as "The City in the Sea. A Prophecy." This text is from *The Raven and Other Poems.* Poe has in mind such cities as Sodom, Gomorrah, and Babylon.

22. THE SLEEPER may refer to Mrs. Jane Stanard, Mrs. Frances Allan, or an imaginary love. The poem first appeared in *Poems;* it is here printed from the text of *The Raven and Other Poems.*

23. LENORE was originally printed in alternate tetrameter and trimeter lines; in 1843, it appeared in irregular stanzas; in 1845, it was given its present form. No biographer has demonstrated whether Poe is writing of Mrs. Stanard, Mrs. Allan, Mrs. Elmira Royster Shelton, or a dream-woman. The name may have been taken from Bürger's "Lenore." The poem, published in *Poems,* is here given in the version which appeared in the *Richmond Whig,* Sept. 18, 1849.

24. THE VALLEY OF UNREST was published in *Poems;* this text is from *The Raven and Other Poems.*

24. THE COLISEUM was submitted to the *Baltimore Saturday Visiter* in a poetry competition and was found superior to any other entry. The judges, however, had already awarded first prize in their short-story contest to Poe and they therefore gave only second prize to "The Coliseum." The poem at one time formed a part of Poe's drama *Politian.* "The Coliseum" was published in the *Visiter,* Oct. 26, 1833; the present text is from *The Raven and Other Poems.*

25. TO ONE IN PARADISE was included in Poe's tale, "The Visionary" (later retitled "The Assignation"), published in *Godey's Lady's Book,* Jan., 1834; this revised text is from *The Raven and Other Poems.*

25. SONNET—SILENCE was published in *Burton's Gentleman's Magazine,* April, 1840; this text is from *The Raven and Other Poems.*

26. DREAM-LAND was published in *Graham's Magazine,* June 1, 1844; this revised text is from *The Raven and Other Poems.* ¶26. "*Thule*" is an island in the German Ocean, thought by the ancients to be the most northerly point on the earth.

26. THE RAVEN was probably in Poe's mind for four years. It is believed that the use of a raven was suggested to him by Dickens' *Barnaby Rudge,* which he reviewed in 1841; and an early version of the poem is said to have been in existence in 1842. While the poem was developing, Poe was influenced by such contemporary poets as Thomas Holley Chivers (see his "Isadore," p. 14 above) and Elizabeth Barrett. The actual processes of composition were less conscious and deliberate than Poe would have the reader believe from his clever rationalization of the matter in "The Philosophy of Com-

position" (see pp. 107–116 of text and note, p. 717 below). Completed in 1844, the poem was published in the New York *Evening Mirror*, Jan. 29, 1845. Poe continued to revise "The Raven" until he had produced sixteen versions. The poem is here printed from Griswold's text. ¶28. "*Aidenn*" is a Mohammedan name for Paradise (Eden).

29. ULALUME—A BALLAD. Virginia Poe died in January, 1847; and "Ulalume" was published in the *American Whig Review* in December of the same year. This text follows Griswold.

30. THE BELLS first consisted of eighteen and finally of 113 lines. Probably undertaken in emulation of contemporary verses on bells, the poem was set down on paper in 1848 at the request of Mrs. Mary Shew. It was published in the *Union Magazine*, Nov., 1849, and is here printed from that text.

32. ELDORADO was suggested to Poe by the gold rush of 1849. The poem appeared in *Flag of Our Union*, April 21, 1849, and is here printed from Griswold's text.

32. FOR ANNIE was addressed to Mrs. Annie Richmond of Lowell, Mass. It was published in *Flag of Our Union*, April 28, 1849; the present text follows Griswold.

33. TO MY MOTHER is a tribute to Mrs. Maria Clemm. It was published in *Flag of Our Union*, July 7, 1849, and is here printed from Griswold.

34. ANNABEL LEE is generally thought to be Poe's last poem, written in memory of his wife, Virginia Clemm. It was published in the New York *Tribune*, Oct. 9, 1849, and is here printed from the revised text which appeared in the *Southern Literary Messenger*, Nov., 1849.

34. THE DUC DE L'OMELETTE, the second story now known to have been published by Poe, illustrates his eccentric humor and his early preoccupation with extravagant satire and burlesque. The tale was published anonymously in the Philadelphia *Saturday Courier*, March 3, 1832; it is here printed from Poe's final revision in the *Broadway Journal*, Oct. 1, 1845. ¶34ff. "*L'histoire en est brève*": The story is short. "*Horreur!—chien! . . . servi sans papier!*": Horror!—beast!—Baptiste!—The bird! ah, good God! that modest bird which you have stripped of its feathers, and which you have served without paper! "*Bien comme il faut*": fine as it should be. "*Parmi les nues*": among the clouds. "*C'est vrai . . . beaucoup—mais!*": It is true that he had examined these objects carefully—but! "*Et qui sourit, si amèrement*": and who smiled so bitterly. "*Mais il faut agir*": But it is necessary to act. "*Il avait tué ses six hommes*": he had pinked his six men. "*Il peut s'échapper*": he could escape. "*Mais il joue!*": But you play! "*Que le Diable . . . jeu d'écarté*": that the Devil dares not refuse a game of cards. "*Si je perds . . . soient préparées!*": If I lose, I shall be doubly damned—that is all. If I win, I shall return to my ortolans—let the cards be prepared! "*C'est à vous à faire*": You will deal. "*En presentant le Roi*": in presenting the King. "*Que s'il n'eût pas été . . . d'être le Diable*": that were he not De L'Omelette, he would have no objection to being the Devil.

37. SHADOW—A PARABLE appeared in the *Southern Literary Messenger*, Sept., 1835; this text is from the *Broadway Journal*, May 31, 1845. The setting, Ptolemais, is an ancient city on the Mediterranean.

39. LIGEIA, a reworking of the theme presented in 1835 in "Morella," was considered by Poe to be his finest story. It was published in the *American Museum*, Sept., 1838; the present text is from the *Broadway Journal*, Sept. 27, 1845. ¶39. "*Joseph Glanvill*" was a learned seventeenth-century English divine, more than once mentioned by Poe. ¶40. "*Cleomenes*" was the otherwise unknown sculptor of the Venus de Medici. ¶40. "*The tribe of the valley of Nourjahad.*" The reference is to Mrs. Frances Sheridan, *The History of Nourjahad* (1767). ¶40. "*The well of Democritus.*" This Greek philosopher of the fourth century B.C. is reputed to have retired to a well where he hoped to find truth.

49. THE FALL OF THE HOUSE OF USHER was published in *Burton's Gentleman's Magazine*, Sept., 1839, and is here printed from *Tales*. The motto is from Béranger's *Le Rufus*. ¶55. "*The last waltz of Von Weber . . . reveries of Fuseli.*" Baron Karl von Weber (1786–1826) was a German composer; and John Fuseli (1741–1825), a Swiss artist popular in early nineteenth-century London. ¶57. "*We pored together over such works as . . .*" To appear erudite, Poe alludes to certain authors, with whom he was not in every instance familiar and all of whom did not actually deal in fantasy: Ludwig Tieck, nineteenth-century German Romanticist; Jean Gresset, French satirist, Emanuel Swedenborg, Swedish mystic, Ludwig von Holberg, Danish dramatist—all of the eighteenth century; Robert Fludd, English Rosicrucian, Marian Cureau de la Chambre, French physician, Thommaso Companella, Dominican philosopher—all of the seventeenth century; Niccolo Machiavelli, Italian statesman and satirist of the sixteenth century; Jean D'Indage, abbé and student of astrology of the fifteenth

century; Nicolas Eymeric de Gironne, fourteenth-century Inquisitor General; and Pomponius Mela, first-century Roman geographer. Poe's "forgotten church" was located in Mayence; and copies of its *Vigiliæ Mortuorum* are still preserved. ¶60. "*The Mad Trist of Sir Launcelot Canning*" appear to be a book and an author invented by Poe, as are the extracts read to Usher.

63. THE MURDERS IN THE RUE MORGUE was published in *Graham's Magazine*, April, 1841; this text is from *Tales*. The motto is from *Urn Burial*. ¶67. "*Et id genus omne*": and all that sort of thing. ¶67. "*Chantilly, Orion, Dr. Nichols* [*sic*], *Epicurus, Stereotomy, the street stones, the fruiterer.*" Poe's explanation of this train of thought requires further elucidation. Leaving the fruiterer, Dupin's friend stumbled over certain paving stones, which called to his mind *stereotomy* (pronounced *stereatomy* and here used to describe a certain method of paving), the sound of which word suggested *atomies* (which Poe apparently confused with *atoms* or *atomists*). His thought next passed to the atomic theory of Epicurus, then to the latter's astronomical speculations, and on to John P. Nichol (whose *Architecture of the Heavens* interested Poe). Dupin now observed his friend glancing upward toward the nebula of Orion (formerly Urion?), which suggested changes in names (and an appropriate line of Latin poetry: "The first letter changed the former meaning"). Finally, Orion suggested Chantilly, because the cobbler-actor had altered his name. ¶73. "*Vidocq . . . a good guesser.*" François Eugene Vidocq (1775–1857) was a French adventurer and detective. ¶82. "*Cuvier.*" Poe probably refers to *The Animal Kingdom* by the distinguished French naturalist, Baron Cuvier (1769–1832).

87. ELEONORA appeared in *The Gift* for 1842 (pub. 1841); this text is that of the *Broadway Journal*, May 10, 1845. The motto from Lully is translated, "With the preservation of a specific form, the soul is safe." ¶88. "*The Nubian geographer*" was Claudius Ptolemy. "*Aggressi sunt . . .*" They entered the sea of darkness [the Atlantic], that they might explore what was therein. ¶89. "*Shiraz*" was the home of the twelfth-century Persian poet, Saadi.

91. THE MASQUE OF THE RED DEATH may have been suggested to Poe by a travel-letter from N. P. Willis in the *Mirror*, in which the latter described a grotesque masque of the cholera in Rome. The tale was published in *Graham's Magazine*, May, 1842; it is here printed from the *Broadway Journal*, July 19, 1845. ¶94. "*Hernani.*" The production of Victor Hugo's violently debated play, *Hernani*, in 1830 was a major event in the history of French Romanticism.

96. THE BLACK CAT appeared in the *United States Saturday Post*, Aug. 19, 1843; this text is from *Tales*.

103. HAWTHORNE'S TWICE-TOLD TALES. This text of the review appeared in *Graham's Magazine*, May, 1842, subsequent to the publication of Poe's brief note on the *Tales* in the April issue of the same magazine. He later combined portions of the two articles in *Godey's Lady's Book*, Nov., 1847. ¶104. "*De Béranger.*" Pierre Jean de Béranger (1780–1857) was an extremely popular French lyric poet. ¶104. "*In medio tutissimus ibis*": In the middle course, you go most safely. ¶106. "*John Neal*" was an eccentric American novelist and hack (1793–1876), who early aided Poe and whom the latter gratefully characterized as "second among our men of undisputed genius."

107. THE PHILOSOPHY OF COMPOSITION appeared in *Graham's Magazine*, April, 1846. It is not probable that the actual composition of "The Raven" was so deliberate or so conscious as Poe here attempts to prove. However, before he began to write "The Raven," he had applied to his tales and poems all the doctrines set down in this essay, and he had also given utterance to them in his critical writings. It must be admitted, therefore, that Poe probably employed, now consciously and again unconsciously, all the principles and devices enumerated in "The Philosophy of Composition." That this essay does not tell the whole story of the writing of "The Raven" is evidenced by Poe's failure to record his evident obligations to contemporaries. ¶107. "*Charles Dickens*" had written Poe concerning the latter's ingenious prediction of the outcome of *Barnaby Rudge*, made before the novel was completed by Dickens.

116. THE POETIC PRINCIPLE was delivered as a lecture by Poe in 1848–49, and was published in the *Home Journal*, Aug. 31, 1850. It has here been necessary to omit the poems which Poe quotes to illustrate his points, namely, Shelley, "Serenade"; N. P. Willis, "Unseen Spirits"; Longfellow, "The Day is Done"; Bryant, "June"; E. C. Pinkney, "A Health"; Moore, "Come Rest in This Bosom"; Thomas Hood, "Fair Inez" and "The Haunted House"; Byron, "Stanzas to Augusta"; Tennyson, "Tears, Idle Tears"; and William Motherwell, "The Song of the Cavalier." ¶117. "*The Columbiad . . . Lamartine . . . Pollock* [*sic*]." The French poet and historian, Alphonse Lamartine (1790–1869), was even more volumi-

nous than was Joel Barlow in *The Columbiad;* and, like Barlow, Robert Pollok (1798–1827) was heavily moralistic in *The Course of Time.* ¶119. "*Abbatè Gravina*" was an Italian poet and critic (1664–1718).

## *Ralph Waldo Emerson (1803–1882)*

Emerson was born in Boston, May 25, 1803, and was educated at the Boston Latin School and Harvard College (B. A. 1821). After teaching and desultory attendance at Harvard Divinity School, he was licensed to preach in the Unitarian Church (1826). Ill health took him to South Carolina (1826–27); on his return, he was able to preach only irregularly. After ordination as assistant-pastor of the Second Church of Boston (1829), Emerson was soon made pastor and married Ellen Tucker (died 1831). In 1832, he resigned his pastorate and left Boston, to travel in Italy, France, and England (1833), where he met Wordsworth, Coleridge, and Carlyle. After residence in the Old Manse (1834), he married Lydia(n) Jackson (1835) and purchased a house at Concord, which was his home for the remainder of his life. Emerson was now lecturing as well as preaching. In 1836, he published *Nature* and aided in founding the Transcendental Club; in 1837, he delivered the Phi Beta Kappa oration at Harvard; and in 1838, he gave an address before the Harvard Divinity School. He was a contributor to the *Dial* (1840–44), and for a time its editor (1842–44). He published *Essays* [*First Series*] in 1841, *Essays, Second Series* in 1844, and *Poems* in 1847. Emerson lectured in Great Britain in 1847–48. Later books were *Representative Men* (1850), *English Traits* (1856), *The Conduct of Life* (1860), *May-Day and Other Pieces* (1867), and *Society and Solitude* (1870). During these decades, Emerson lectured extensively in the East, made regular tours through the Middle West, and paid a third visit to Europe. In 1876, he published *Letters and Social Aims.* Emerson died at Concord, April 27, 1882.

The standard bibliography of Emerson is that compiled by G. W. Cooke (1908). More recent material is included in *CHAL*, I, 551–66. Very useful is the admirably edited Centenary Edition (ed. E. W. Emerson, 1903–04). Further material appears in *Uncollected Writings* (ed. C. C. Bigelow, 1912). The *Journals* (ed. E. W. Emerson and W. E. Forbes, 1909–14) are a remarkable record of Emerson's thought; well chosen selections appear in *The Heart of Emerson's Journals* (ed. Bliss Perry, 1926). Emerson's correspondence with Thomas Carlyle, John Sterling, S. G. Ward, and Herman Grimm has been published at various times; an inclusive collection of his letters is now in preparation (ed. R. L. Rusk). The standard biography is J. E. Cabot, *A Memoir of Ralph Waldo Emerson* (1887). Briefer but sound are O. W. Holmes, *Ralph Waldo Emerson* (1885) and G. E. Woodberry, *Ralph Waldo Emerson* (1907). Personal material appears in E. W. Emerson, *Emerson in Concord* (1889). Phillips Russell, *Emerson, The Wisest American* (1929) is at times illuminating; Regis Michaud, *Emerson, The Enraptured Yankee* (1924, 1930) is clever but prejudiced. Significant appreciations are E. L. Cary, *Emerson, Poet and Thinker* (1904), O. W. Firkins, *Ralph Waldo Emerson* (1915), R. M. Gay, *Emerson, a Study of the Poet as Seer* (1928), Bliss Perry, *Emerson Today* (1931), and Van Wyck Brooks, *The Life of Emerson* (1932). Helpful special studies are Emerson Sutcliffe, *Emerson's Theories of Literary Expression* (1923) and F. I. Carpenter. *Emerson and Asia* (1930). Among important essays are those by J. R. Lowell in *My Study Windows* (1871), Henry James in *Partial Portraits* (1888), G. W. Curtis in *Literary and Social Essays* (1894), W. C. Brownell in *American Prose Masters* (1909), and S. P. Sherman in *Americans* (1922). G. S. Hubbell has compiled *A Concordance to the Poems of Ralph Waldo Emerson* (1932). For discussions of Transcendentalism, see O. B. Frothingham, *Transcendentalism in New England* (1876), H. C. Goddard, *Studies in New England Transcendentalism* (1908), and Clarence Gohdes, *The Periodicals of American Transcendentalism* (1931).

The text of Emerson's prose and verse included in the present anthology is that of the Centenary Edition, which incorporates the author's final revisions.

121. JOURNALS. These extracts suggest several of the trends which were evident in Emerson's thinking during the years before he began to publish his meditations.

122. NATURE was the result of at least three years of thought, for Emerson wrote during his voyage from England in 1833: "I like my book about nature." In 1834, he was at work on it in the chamber of the Old Manse where Hawthorne was to write his *Mosses*. When the book was published in 1836, Carlyle wrote to Emerson: "Your little azure-coloured *Nature* gave me true satisfaction." He also praised it as "the true Apocalypse" and "a Foundation and Ground-plan" for a new revelation. The philosophers and men of religion alluded to in *Nature* supply a concise, but by no means a

complete, index to the major sources and stimuli of Emerson's thought: early Greek philosophers, as Xenophanes and Pythagoras of the sixth century B.C.; Plato (one of Emerson's Representative Men) and Aristotle; Neoplatonists, as Plotinus of the third century A.D.; Oriental mystics, as the Manichæns and the Vyassas (compilers of certain Hindu sacred books); English Platonists, as Bacon, Bishop Berkeley, and George Herbert; modern mystics, as Emanuel Swedenborg (another Representative Man) and Coleridge. Emerson's interest in science is revealed by allusions to Carolus Linnæus (1707–1778), Swedish botanist; Comte de Buffon (1707–1788), French naturalist (131); and Leonhard Euler (1707–1783), Swiss physicist (141). In marshaling authorities for the Romantic doctrine of the confusion of the arts, Emerson cites the French Madame de Staël, the German Goethe, and the English Coleridge, all nineteenth-century Romanticists; the Roman engineer, Vitruvius Pollio; and the Italian painter-sculptor, Michael Angelo. ¶129. "*Il più nell' uno*": much in one. ¶137. "*Omne verum vero consonat*": all truth is contained in one truth. ¶141. "*Turgot.*" Robert Jacques Turgot (1727–1781) was a French statesman and economist. ¶147. "*My Orphic poet*" was perhaps Bronson Alcott. ¶147. "*Hohenlohe.*" Leopold Alexander, Prince of Hohenlohe (1794–1849) was a miracle-working Roman Catholic bishop. ¶148. "*Vespertina cognitio . . . matutina cognitio*": twilight knowledge [of man] . . . full-day knowledge [of the Deity].

149. THE AMERICAN SCHOLAR. On this old and seemingly threadbare theme of Phi Beta Kappa orators, Emerson delivered, in the words of Holmes, "our intellectual Declaration of Independence." Older members of his audience at Cambridge, August 31, 1837, were puzzled by the oration; but "the young men went from it as if a prophet had been proclaiming to them, 'Thus saith the Lord.' No listener ever forgot that address, and among all the noble utterances of the speaker it may be questioned if one ever contained more truth in language more like that of immediate inspiration." Carlyle wrote, "Lo, out of the West comes a clear utterance, clearly recognizable as a *man's* voice . . . Miss Martineau tells me, 'Some say it is inspired, some say it is mad.' Exactly so; no *say* could be suitabler. . . . May God grant you strength; for you have a *fearful* work to do." For an admirable account of the occasion, see Bliss Perry, "Emerson's Most Famous Speech," in *The Praise of Folly* (1923). "The American Scholar" was published in 1837.

¶157. "*Flamsteed and Herschel.*" John Flamsteed (1646–1719), William Herschel (1738–1822), and John Herschel (1792–1871) were distinguished English astronomers. ¶161. "*Pestalozzi.*" Emerson's persistent concern with educational reform led him, as a patron of the Temple School in Boston, to commend Alcott's innovations, many of which paralleled the ideas of the famous Swiss educator, Johann Heinrich Pestalozzi (1746–1827).

162. THE DIVINITY SCHOOL ADDRESS was delivered, at the invitation of the graduating class of Harvard Divinity School, on July 15, 1838. Emerson's utterance was at once violently attacked as "the latest form of infidelity" by Andrews Norton and other conservatives; Emerson was supported by George Ripley, Theodore Parker, and other young liberals. When Henry Ware asked Emerson for the arguments underlying his position, he replied in Transcendental fashion: "I could not give account of myself, if challenged. I could not possibly give you one of the 'arguments' you cruelly hint at, on which any doctrine of mine stands. For I do not know what arguments mean in reference to any expression of a thought." The address was published in the year of its delivery. ¶172. "*A devout person, who prized the Sabbath*" is said to have been Mrs. Lydian Emerson. ¶173. "*Wesleys and Oberlins.*" Charles Wesley (1708–1788) and his brother, John Wesley (1703–1791), were leaders in the Methodist revival in England; Jean Frédéric Oberlin (1740–1826) was an Alsatian clergyman famed as a humanitarian, and his brother, Jérémie Jacques Oberlin (1735–1806) was an antiquarian.

175. SELF-RELIANCE. Emerson apparently first thought of writing on this topic in 1832. After touching on self-reliance in various lectures, he spent two years in gathering his material (from lectures and journals) into an essay. It was published in *Essays* [*First Series*]. "Self-Reliance" cannot be understood save in the light of the complementary essay, "The Over-Soul," where Emerson shows how "self-reliance, the height and perfection of man" is grounded in "reliance on God." An apt motto for this essay is the proverb (175), "*Ne te quæseveris extra*": Seek not outside thyself. The range of Emerson's interests is exemplified by his references to Thomas Clarkson (1760–1846), English abolitionist (181); Alexander Scanderbeg (1403–1468), Albanian patriot (182); John Locke (1632–1704) and Jeremy Bentham (1748–1832), notable English philosophers; Antoine Laurent Lavoisier (1743–1794), French chemist; Charles Hutton (1737–1823), English

mathematician (Emerson may refer rather to James Hutton, Scottish geologist of the eighteenth century); and François Charles Fourier (1772–1837), French socialist whose coöperative system attracted the New England liberals (188); Henry Hudson (d. 1611), Vitius Bering (1680–1741), Sir William Parry (1790–1855), and Sir John Franklin (1786–1847), intrepid explorers (191).

192. THE OVER-SOUL is based on passages in Emerson's lectures and journals; it was published in *Essays* [*First Series*]. Here may be observed, perhaps more fully than in *Nature*, Emerson's debts to the ancient Neoplatonists and the English Platonists. (The motto, significantly enough, is from the *Psychozia* of the seventeenth-century Platonist, Henry More.) The emotional nature of Emerson's religion is suggested by his interest in such ecstatic experiences as the trances of Socrates; the visions of Plotinus and Porphyry, Neoplatonists of the third century; the conversion of St. Paul; the revelations of Jacob Behmen, Prussian mystic of the seventeenth century, of George Fox and his Quakers, and of Swedenborg and his New Jerusalem Church; and the religious experiences of the Moravians, the Quietists, and the Methodists (198). Equally significant is Emerson's preference for enthusiasts such as Benedict Spinoza, seventeenth-century pantheist; Immanuel Kant, eighteenth-century champion of reason; and S. T. Coleridge, nineteenth-century Transcendentalist, as compared with such legalists as John Locke, seventeenth-century exponent of the critical philosophy; William Paley, devout but methodical eighteenth-century defender of Christianity; and Sir James Mackintosh and Dougald Stewart, both ethical metaphysicians of the nineteenth century (200). Contemporaries who had misinterpreted "Self-Reliance" naturally failed to understand the mysticism of "The Over-Soul"; and even Holmes dismissed the essay as a poetic rhapsody.

204. THE POET appeared in *Essays, Second Series*. In no single essay does Emerson fully reveal his æsthetic theories or his critical principles; here, he expands and applies to poetry certain ideas already announced in *Nature* and "The Over-Soul." The allusions in this essay are significant: Empedocles and Heraclitus (205) were Greek philosophers of the fifth century B.C.; Iamblichus (208) was a Neoplatonist of the fourth century A.D. and Proclus (209), of the fifth century; Timæus was a Greek historian of the third century B.C. (215); Philippus Paracelsus (1493–1541) and Cornelius Agrippa (1485–1535) were alchemists; Girolamo Cardan (1501–1576) was an astrologist and Johann Kepler (1571–1630) an astronomer; Friedrich von Schelling (1775–1854) and Lorenz Oken (1779–1851) were German philosophers (215).

219. EZRA RIPLEY, D.D. The subject of this sketch was the second husband of Emerson's maternal grandmother, and the resident in the Old Manse at Concord for many years. This kindly portrait of a Calvinist reveals the tolerance and the humor of Emerson. The latter characteristic is exemplified by his allusion to Major Downing (222), the creation of Seba Smith (1792–1868), whose *Life and Letters of Major Jack Downing* (1833) is a notable piece of Yankee wit. Emerson's sketch was delivered as a memorial sermon, published in the Concord *Republican*, Oct. 1, 1841, and collected in *Lectures and Biographical Sketches* (1884). ¶223. "*A Bentley or a Porson.*" Richard Bentley (1662–1742) was a famous English classical scholar, satirized by Pope in the *Dunciad*, and Richard Porson (1759–1808) is remembered for his knowledge of Greek.

224. NAPOLEON; OR, THE MAN OF THE WORLD was one of a series of lectures delivered in the United States and England which, after revision, were published as *Representative Men*. Although Emerson was essentially a prophet and no man of action, his Yankee shrewdness and practicality ("I like people who can do things"), together with his Romantic veneration for the Hero, led him to share, with important reservations, the contemporary admiration of Napoleon. It is clear, however, that the sage of Concord did not here compromise his ideals, for he emphatically condemns Napoleon's moral weakness. To understand Emerson's attitude toward Napoleon (and toward American democracy as well), one must remember that the author's concern is here more social and economic than political. Having defined conservatives as "those who have" and democrats as "those who have not," he is then able to bestow on Bonaparte the surprising epithet of "incarnate Democrat."

232. ENGLISH TRAITS was based on Emerson's observations in England in 1833 and, more particularly, in 1847–48. ¶233. "*Froissart, Voltaire, Le Sage, Mirabeau . . .*" The impressions of Englishmen of Jean Froissart (1339–1410?) are scattered through his *Chronicle;* those of François Marie de Voltaire (1694–1774) are found in his *Lettres Philosophiques sur les Englais;* those of Alain René Le Sage (1688–1747) in his plays; and those of Gabriel Riqueti, Compte de Mirabeau (1749–1791), in his *Mémoires*. ¶233. "*Ses s'amusaient triste-*

*ment, selon la coutume de leur pays*": they amuse themselves sadly, according to the custom of their country. ¶237. "*Dugdales, Gibbons, Hallams, Eldons, and Peels.*" Sir William Dugdale (1605–1686) was an antiquarian; Edward Gibbon (1737–1794) is famous for his *History of the Decline and Fall of the Roman Empire;* Henry Hallam (1777–1859) was likewise a historian; John Scott, Earl of Eldon (1751–1838), was a jurist; and Sir Robert Peel (1788–1850) was a noted statesman.

239. CONCORD HYMN first appeared as a broadside in 1837 and was collected in *Poems.*

239. EACH AND ALL is based upon such experiences as the following, recorded in the *Journals:* "I remember when I was a boy going upon the beach and being charmed with the colors and forms of the shells. I picked up many and put them in my pocket. When I got home I could find nothing that I had gathered—nothing but some dry, ugly mussel and snail shells. Thence I learned that Composition was more important than the beauty of individual forms." The poem was published in the *Western Messenger,* Feb., 1839, and collected in *Poems.*

240. THE HUMBLE-BEE. In 1837, Emerson wrote in his *Journals:* "Yesterday in the woods I followed the fine humble-bee with rhymes and fancies fine. . . . The humble-bee and pine warbler seem to me the proper objects of attention in these disastrous times." The poem was published in the *Western Messenger,* Feb., 1839, and collected in *Poems.*

241. THE RHODORA was composed while Emerson was putting the same thought into prose in *Nature.* The poem appeared in the *Western Messenger,* July, 1839, and was collected in *Poems.*

241. THE PROBLEM was originally entitled "The Priest." Compare this passage in the *Journals* in 1838: "It is very grateful to my feelings to go into a Roman Cathedral, yet I look as my countrymen do at the Roman priesthood. It is very grateful to me to go into an English Church and hear the liturgy read, yet nothing would induce me to be the English priest. . . . I dislike to be a clergyman and refuse to be one. Yet how rich a music would be to me a holy clergyman in my town. It seems to me he cannot be a man, quite and whole; yet how plain is the need of one, and how high, yes, highest is the function." The poem was published in the *Dial,* July, 1840, and collected in *Poems.* ¶242. "*Chrysostom,*" or Golden Mouth, was John of Antioch, a fourth-century Patriarch of the Greek church. ¶242. "[*Jeremy*] *Taylor,*" eloquent English bishop of the seventeenth century, was elsewhere characterized by Emerson as "a Christian Plato."

242. WOODNOTES I was published in the *Dial,* Oct., 1840; it appeared in *Poems* in a revised form, which is here followed. Although Emerson's son insisted that "Woodnotes I" was written before the poet knew Thoreau intimately, the idea persists that the forest seer here portrayed is the hermit of Walden Pond.

244. THE SNOW-STORM. Emerson wrote in the *Journals* in 1832: "Instead of lectures on Architecture, I will make a lecture on God's architecture, one of his beautiful works, a Day. I will draw a sketch of a winter's day. I will trace as I can a rude outline of the far-assembled influences, the contribution of the universe wherein this magical structure rises like an exhalation, the wonder and charm of the immeasurable deep." "The Snow-Storm" was published in *The Dial,* Jan., 1841, and collected in *Poems.*

244. COMPENSATION is the motto for and a summary of the essay, "Compensation," in *Essays* [*First Series*].

245. FORBEARANCE appeared in *The Dial,* Jan., 1842; it was collected in *Poems.*

245. POLITICS is the motto for the essay of the same title in *Essays, Second Series.*

245. CHARACTER is the motto for the essay, "Character," in *Essays, Second Series.*

245. FABLE appeared in the *Diadem* for 1846 (pub. 1845) and was collected in *Poems.*

246. URIEL suggests Emerson's emotions while he was under attack for the Divinity School Address. "Uriel" was published in *Poems.*

246. HAMATREYA was written under the influence of the *Vishnu Purana,* sacred book of the Hindus, from which Emerson transcribed in his journals this germinal passage concerning the sovereigns of the earth: "These, and other kings who with perishable frames have possessed this ever-enduring world, and who, blinded with deceptive notions of individual occupation, have indulged the feeling that suggests 'This earth is mine,—it is my son's,—it belongs to my dynasty,'—have all passed away. So, many who reigned before them, many who succeeded them, and many who are yet to come, have ceased or will cease to be. Earth laughs, as if smiling with autumnal flowers to behold her kings unable to effect the subjugation of themselves. I will repeat to you, Maitreya [Hamatreya], the stanzas that were chanted by Earth." For sovereigns of the Earth, Emerson substitutes early settlers in Concord, including Peter Bulkeley, an ancestor

of Emerson himself. "Hamatreya" was published in *Poems*.

247. ODE, INSCRIBED TO W. H. CHANNING. William Henry Channing, a nephew of the noted Unitarian, William Ellery Channing, and an ardent abolitionist, apparently had urged Emerson to commit himself to more active opposition to slavery. Although Emerson was himself a fearless abolitionist, he here wisely replies that he chooses to battle for the general liberation of the human spirit rather than limit himself to compaigning for a specific group. This sane thought is reiterated in such essays as "The New England Reformers." The "Ode" was published in *Poems*.

248. GIVE ALL TO LOVE is frequently paralleled in Emerson's essays where, for example, he declares: "Life is an ecstacy"; and "We know what madness belongs to love." The poem was published in *Poems*.

249. THE APOLOGY should be compared with Wordsworth's "Expostulation and Reply" and "The Tables Turned." "The Apology" was published in *Poems*.

249. THRENODY. The first portion of the poem voices Emerson's immediate grief over the death of his son, Waldo, in 1842. Two years later, the poet added the portion beginning with l. 176, in which he austerely refuses to yield to the sharp sorrow which, his *Journals* reveal, pursued him until death. "Threnody" was published in *Poems*.

253. DAYS. Emerson was inclined to think that "Days" was perhaps his best poem. The image of divinities waiting on mankind in disguise is often used in his prose and verse. "Days" appeared in the first issue of the *Atlantic Monthly* (Nov., 1857) and was collected in *Selected Poems* (1876).

253. BRAHMA. The unity of the universe, as conceived by Plato, is here restated in the imagery of the Hindu sacred books. Thus the first stanza echoes the *Vishnu Purana*, the *Bhagavad-gita*, and the *Katha-upanishad* ("If the slayer thinks that I slay or if the slain thinks I am slain, then both of them do not know well. The soul does not slay, nor is it slain"). "Brahma" was originally entitled "The Song of the Soul"; Emerson later suggested that puzzled readers might substitute the word "Jehovah" for "Brahma." "The strong gods" whom Emerson mentions (l. 13) are a trinity of Hindu deities absorbed by Brahma; "the sacred Seven" are the Maharshis (superior saints). The poem was published in the *Atlantic Monthly*, Nov., 1857, and collected in *May-Day*.

253. TWO RIVERS was included in *May-Day*.

254. TERMINUS was published in the *Atlantic Monthly*, Jan., 1867, and collected in *May-Day*.

## *Henry David Thoreau (1817–1862)*

Thoreau was born at Concord, Mass., July 12, 1817, was graduated from Harvard College, and for a decade taught and labored with his hands, for a time as a member of the Emerson household. From July 4, 1845, to Sept. 6, 1847, he lived alone at Walden Pond. Although he "travelled much in Concord," Thoreau also made excursions among the White Mountains, along Cape Cod, through the Maine forests, and even into Canada. About 1847, he began lecturing. *A Week on the Concord and Merrimack Rivers* appeared in 1849; *Walden, or, Life in the Woods*, in 1854. In 1859, Thoreau became John Brown's early notable defender. In the last year of his life, Thoreau journeyed westward to Minnesota, seeing for the first time Niagara Falls and the Mississippi River. He died of consumption at Concord on May 6, 1862. Posthumously published were *Excursions* (1863), *The Maine Woods* (1864), *Cape Cod* (1865), *A Yankee in Canada* (1866), and four volumes gleaned from his journals: *Early Spring in Massachusetts* (1881), *Summer* (1884), *Winter* (1888), *Autumn* (1892).

F. H. Allen has compiled a bibliography of Thoreau (1908). A short bibliography appears in *CHAL*, II, 411–15. Standard editions are the Riverside (1894) and the Walden (1906); the latter includes, in fourteen volumes, Thoreau's *Journal* (ed. Bradford Torrey). Useful is *The Heart of Thoreau's Journals* (ed. Odell Shepherd, 1927). The best biography is F. B. Sanborn, *Henry David Thoreau* (1882), later expanded as *The Life of Henry David Thoreau* (1917). W. E. Channing, *Thoreau, the Poet-Naturalist* (1873, 1902) is valuable only for Channing's personal comments. Mark Van Doren, *Henry David Thoreau, A Critical Study* (1916) is sound. Stimulating but at times inconclusive are Léon Bazalgette, *Henry Thoreau, Bachelor of Nature* (trans. 1924) and J. B. Atkinson, *Henry Thoreau, The Cosmic Yankee* (1927). Notable essays on Thoreau are Emerson's in *Lectures and Biographical Sketches* (1884), and Lowell's in *My Study Windows* (see pp. 607–616 of text).

The present extracts from Thoreau's works follow the text of the Riverside Edition; the extracts from his *Journal* are drawn from the Walden Edition.

255. JOURNAL. These passages are samplings, not of Thoreau's minute records of scientific

fact, but of his meditative entries in the early years prior to the publication of *Walden*.

256. CIVIL DISOBEDIENCE was first published as "Resistance to Civil Government" in *Aesthetic Papers* (ed. Elizabeth Peabody, 1849) and was collected in *A Yankee in Canada*. Thoreau here records his break with the church (257), which occurred in or near 1838. In 1846, he was jailed for non-payment of his poll-tax (257). After Thoreau had refused to allow the jailor, Sam Staples, to pay the tax for him, it was paid without Thoreau's knowledge by his Aunt Maria.

260. WALDEN was drawn largely from the *Journal*, not only from the entries made at Walden Pond, but from the matter set down over a period of eight years (1839–1847). Thoreau's interest in Oriental religions is evident in his references to the Harivansa (263), one of the Hindu sacred books, and the sacred Vedas (265).

272. WALKING appeared in the *Atlantic Monthly*, Oct., 1862, and was collected in *Excursions*. The keynote of the essay is "*Ambulator nascitur, non fit*" (273): The walker is born, not made. ¶276. "*Michaux . . . Humboldt . . . Guyot.*" François André Michaux (1770–1855) was a French botanist; Baron Friedrich Heinrich von Humboldt (1769–1859), a German scientist and explorer; Arnold Henry Guyot (1807–1884), a Swiss-American geographer.

277. LIFE WITHOUT PRINCIPLE was taken in large part from the *Journal* (1850–55). The essay was printed in the *Atlantic Monthly*, Oct., 1863, and collected in *A Yankee in Canada*.

284. SIC VITA was written in 1837 for Miss Lucy Brown (who introduced Thoreau to Emerson) and was presented to her with a bunch of violets. "Sic Vita" appeared in the *Dial*, July, 1841, and was reprinted in *A Week on the Concord and Merrimack Rivers*.

285. A PRAYER was quoted in an article by Emerson in the *Dial*, Oct., 1842, and was collected in *A Yankee in Canada*.

285. SMOKE and HAZE were published in the *Dial*, April, 1843; and the former was reprinted in *Walden* and the latter in *A Week on the Concord and Merrimack Rivers*.

286. INSPIRATION appeared in the *Commonwealth*, June 19, 1863, and was collected in *Poems of Nature* (1895).

## *Amos Bronson Alcott (1799–1888)*

Alcott was born on a farm near Wolcott, Conn. After a meager education, he perfected his radical pedagogical theories through practice in several states (1823–33). In 1834, he opened the notable Temple School in Boston. *The Record of a School* (compiled by Elizabeth Peabody, 1835) and *Conversations with Children on the Gospels* (1836, 1837) led conservatives to attack Alcott; and the school was finally closed in 1839. Alcott aided in founding the *Dial* and in 1844–45 maintained the Utopian community of Fruitlands, at Harvard, Mass. Thereafter, he conducted "conversations" from New England to the Mississippi valley. Alcott published *Tablets* (1868), *Concord Days* (1872), and *Table-Talk* (1877). In 1879, he organized the Concord School of Philosophy and directed it until 1882, when he suffered a paralytic stroke. There is no adequate biography of Alcott. Some information may be gathered from F. B. Sanborn and W. T. Harris, *A. Bronson Alcott, His Life and Philosophy* (1893), *Bronson Alcott's Fruitlands* (ed. C. E. Sears, 1915), and a popular volume, H. W. Morrow, *The Father of Little Women* (1927).

287. ORPHIC SAYINGS appeared in the *Dial* during 1840 and 1841. All of the extracts here given were published before Emerson's *Essays [First Series]* came from the press, but not before the latter had recorded similar ideas in his journals.

288. MAN appeared in *Tablets*.

288. MATTER appeared in *Table-Talk*.

## *Frederick Henry Hedge (1805–1890)*

Hedge was born at Cambridge, Mass., studied in Germany, and later was graduated from Harvard College. He was an organizer of the Transcendental Club and a contributor to the *Dial*. As Unitarian clergyman, professor of ecclesiastical history in Harvard Divinity School, and professor of German in Harvard College, he did much to introduce German Transcendentalism to American thinkers.

288. QUESTIONINGS was published in the *Dial*, Jan., 1841.

## *Sarah Margaret Fuller Ossoli (1810–1850)*

Born at Cambridgeport, Mass., and educated under the direction of her father and later with the aid of Henry Hedge, Margaret Fuller early avowed herself a Transcendentalist and feminist. Miss Fuller edited the *Dial* (1840–42) and conducted "conversations," certain of which were published as *Woman in the Nineteenth Century* (1845). From 1844 to 1846 she was literary editor of Horace Greeley's *Tribune*. In 1846 she went to Europe, where she was married to the Marquis d'Ossoli. As supporters of Mazzini, the Marquis and the Marchesa found it necessary to leave Italy in 1850; on their voyage to America, both were lost with their infant in a shipwreck off Fire Island, New York. Early biographers are J. F. Clarke, R. W. Emerson, W. H. Channing, *Margaret Fuller Ossoli* (1852) and Julia Ward Howe, *Margaret Fuller Ossoli* (1883). Most useful is T. W. Higginson, *Margaret Fuller Ossoli* (1884). More recent attempts at interpretations are K. S. Anthony, *Margaret Fuller; A Psychological Biography* (1920) and Margaret Bell, *Margaret Fuller* (1930).

289. WOMAN IN THE NINETEENTH CENTURY was expanded from an article, "The Great Lawsuit. Man versus Men; Woman versus Women," in the *Dial*, July, 1843.

290. ASPIRATION was addressed to the author's brother, R. F. Fuller. The latter portion of the poem (ll. 25 ff.) first appeared in *Woman in the Nineteenth Century;* and these lines, therefore, are to be interpreted as an appeal for the equality of woman (the "Queen") with man (the "King"). The final text of "Aspiration," as here given, was published in *Life Without and the Life Within* (1859).

## *Jones Very (1813–1880)*

Very was born at Salem, Mass., was graduated from Harvard College and Harvard Divinity School, and preached occasionally without being ordained. During a tutorship at Harvard, Very became the victim of mental disorders; soon after, he retired to Salem, where he spent the remainder of his life. Emerson edited Very's *Essays and Poems* (1839).

291. THE PRESENCE and THE DEAD were published in *Essays and Poems.*

291. THE BARBERRY-BUSH was quoted by Emerson in the *Dial*, July, 1841, and was collected in *Poems* (1883).

292. THE LIGHT FROM WITHIN was published in *Poems and Essays* (1886).

## *Christopher Pearse Cranch (1813–1892)*

Born at Alexandria, Va., Cranch studied in Harvard Divinity School, preached before Unitarian congregations in various sections of the country, and finally became a painter, living in Italy, France, New York, and Cambridge. Throughout his life, Cranch continued to write verse, publishing *Poems* (1844) and *Ariel and Caliban, with Other Poems* (1887). He died in Cambridge. The only biography is Leonora Cranch Scott, *The Life and Letters of Christopher Pearse Cranch* (1917).

292. GNOSIS appeared as "Stanzas" in the *Dial*, July, 1840, and was collected in *Poems.*

292. THE PINES AND THE SEA was published in the *Atlantic Monthly*, Dec., 1875, and collected in *Ariel and Caliban.*

## *William Ellery Channing (1818–1901)*

Channing was born in Boston, a nephew of the distinguished Unitarian clergyman after whom he was named. After study at Harvard College, where he took no degree, Channing lived for a time in the Middle West and then returned to Massachusetts. At Concord, Channing became a friend of Emerson, Hawthorne, and Thoreau, and a contributor to the *Dial.* Among his published volumes are *Poems* (1843) and *Poems, Second Series* (1847).

293. CONTENT and SONNET were published in *Poems.*

## *Nathaniel Hawthorne (1804–1864)*

Hawthorne was born in Salem, Mass., July 4, 1804. His boyhood was spent in Salem and on Lake Sebago, Maine. After graduation from Bowdoin College (1825), he resided on Herbert Street, Salem, and Dearborn Street, North Salem, until 1836. Meanwhile, he published *Fanshawe* (1828) and began contributing sketches and tales to gift-books and magazines (from 1829 or 1830 onward). Hawthorne was in Boston in 1836 as editor of the *American Magazine of Useful and Entertaining Knowledge.* At Salem from 1837 to 1839, he published the first series of *Twice-Told Tales* (1837). From 1839 to 1841, he was again in Boston, working in the Boston Custom House, and in 1841–42 he was at Brook Farm. In 1842, Hawthorne published the second series of *Twice-Told Tales,* and in the same year he married Sophia Peabody. In the Old Manse, Concord, from 1842 to 1845, he wrote *Mosses from an Old Manse* (1846). After serving as surveyor in the Salem Custom House, 1846–49, Hawthorne published *The Scarlet Letter* (1850). *The House of the Seven Gables* (1851) was written during his residence at Lenox, Mass. At West Newton, near Brook Farm, in 1851–52, he wrote *The Blithedale Romance* (1852). Hawthorne also published *The Snow-Image, and Other Tales* (1851), *A Wonder Book for Girls and Boys* (1852), and *Tanglewood Tales for Girls and Boys* (1853). In 1852–53, he was in The Wayside, Concord: from 1853 to 1857 he was consul at

Liverpool; and from 1858 to 1860 he was in France, Italy, and England. *The Marble Faun* appeared in 1860. In The Wayside from 1860 onward, he published *Our Old Home* in 1863. Hawthorne died at Plymouth, N. H., May 19, 1864. *Septimius Felton* was published in 1872; *The Dolliver Romance* in 1876; and *Dr. Grimshawe's Secret* in 1883.

A detailed bibliography of Hawthorne has been compiled by N. E. Browne (1905); more concise is the bibliography found in *CHAL*, II, 415–24. The Riverside Edition of Hawthorne (1883) is standard; a few additional items appear in the Old Manse Edition (1904). Of autobiographical significance are the severely edited extracts from Hawthorne's journals and letters published as *Passages from the American Note-Books* (ed. Sophia Hawthorne, 1868), *Passages from the English Note-Books* (ed. Sophia Hawthorne, 1870), and *Passages from the French and Italian Note-Books* (ed. Sophia Hawthorne, 1871). Selections from these volumes are available in *The Heart of Hawthorne's Journals* (ed. Newton Arvin, 1929). *The American Notebooks* are now available in their entirety, published from the original manuscripts (ed. Randall Stewart, 1932). The best biography is Julian Hawthorne, *Nathaniel Hawthorne and His Wife* (1885). Personal memories of Hawthorne are found in J. T. Fields, *Yesterdays with Authors* (1878); G. P. Lathrop, *A Study of Hawthorne* (1876); Horatio Bridge, *Personal Recollections of Nathaniel Hawthorne* (1893); Rose Hawthorne Lathrop, *Memories of Hawthorne* (1897); and Caroline Ticknor, *Hawthorne and His Publisher* (1913). Henry James, *Hawthorne* (1879) is more significant to the student of James than of Hawthorne. G. E. Woodberry, *Nathaniel Hawthorne* (1902), is brief and just. Of recent biographies, Lloyd Morris, *The Rebellious Puritan* (1927) is useful; Herbert Gorman, *Hawthorne, a Study in Solitude* (1927), is inaccurate and misleading; and Newton Arvin, *Hawthorne* (1929), is suggestive as criticism. Among important essays are those by Leslie Stephen in *Hours in a Library* (1874–75); L. E. Gates in *Studies and Appreciations* (1900); W. C. Brownell in *American Prose Masters* (1909); and S. P. Sherman in *Americans* (1922).

The text of the Riverside edition is followed in these selections from Hawthorne.

294. Passages from the American Note-Books. These extracts are representative of Hawthorne's varied entries in his journal prior to the publication of his first tales. Here will be found the germinal ideas for several stories.

295. Sights from a Steeple appeared in *The Token* for 1831 (pub. 1830) and was collected in *Twice-Told Tales* [*First Series*]; it is therefore one of the most immature of Hawthorne's acknowledged writings. ¶296. "*The Limping Devil*" is the title character of Le Sage's *Le Diable Boiteux* (1707). ¶297. "*Old Vicentio . . . of Pisa*" appears in *The Taming of the Shrew* as "a merchant of great traffic through the world." ¶299. "*Thus did Arethusa sink*" as, bathing in the Alpheus, she was pursued by her lover, a river god.

300. Young Goodman Brown is one of the earliest tales in which Hawthorne gave simultaneous expression to his interest in symbolism, allegory, ambiguous supernaturalism, New England history, and human abnormality. The story appeared in the *New England Magazine*, April, 1835, and was later included in *Mosses from an Old Manse*. ¶302. "*Goody Cloyse . . . witch Goody Cory* (303) . . . *Martha Carrier* (307)." Not only were Sarah Cloyse, Martha Corey (or Cory), and Martha Carrier historical personages in the Salem of William and Mary, but each was tried for witchcraft and sentenced to death before Judge John Hathorne in 1692.

309. The White Old Maid reveals Hawthorne's persistent concern with the grotesque, an interest which he early showed in *Fanshawe* and (according to his sister) in the unpublished *Seven Tales of My Native Land*, which he kept well within bounds during the period of his best creative work, and which he finally allowed to escape from control in the last feeble romances (particularly in *Septimius Felton*). This tale was published in the *New England Magazine*, July, 1835, as "The Old Maid in the Winding Sheet," and was reprinted in *Twice-Told Tales, Second Series*. ¶313. "*The shield of arms on the panel*" is that of the ancient Hathorne family in England.

316. The Minister's Black Veil. The tradition that Rev. Joseph Moody covered his face with a black handkerchief in penance for the accidental killing of a youthful friend was widely circulated in New England. Hawthorne, in romanticizing the episode, follows his custom of ignoring the original tragedy, and concentrates on its emotional and spiritual consequences. The story was published in *The Token* for 1836 (pub. 1835) and was reprinted in *Twice-Told Tales* [*First Series*]. ¶324. "*Governor Belcher*," chief executive of Massachusetts and New Hampshire from 1730 to 1741, is a familiar figure in Hawthorne's works.

326. Endicott and the Red Cross. The historical basis of this tale is thus recorded in the *Journal* of John Winthrop: "November 5, [1635]. At the court of the assistants complaint was made by some of the country . . . that

the ensign at Salem was defaced; viz. one part of the red cross taken out. Upon this, an attachment was awarded against Richard Davenport, ensign-bearer, to appear at the next court to answer. Much matter was made of this, as fearing it would be taken as an act of rebellion, or of like high nature, in defacing the king's colors; though the truth were, it was done upon this opinion, that the red cross was given to the king of England by the pope, as an ensign of victory, and so a superstitious thing, and a relique of antichrist." The scene is Town House Square, Salem. "Endicott and the Red Cross" appeared in *The Token* for 1838 (pub. 1837) and was later included in *Twice-Told Tales, Second Series*. ¶326. "[*Governor*] *John Endicott*," although defied to his face by one of Hawthorne's ancestors and disliked as a bigot by the author himself, commanded a degree of respect from Hawthorne, who introduced Endicott in seven other tales and books. ¶327. "*The letter A*" first came to Hawthorne's attention, not while he was collector of customs at Salem from 1846 to 1849 (as is romantically narrated in the preface to *The Scarlet Letter*) but at some time prior to the publication of this tale in 1837. Apparently he was then familiar with a statute of Plymouth Colony, requiring that adulterers should "wear two Capitoll letters viz.: A D cut in cloth and sewed on their uppermost garments."

331. FOOTPRINTS ON THE SEA-SHORE. The germinal idea for this sketch was thus set down in Hawthorne's journal for 1837: "An idle man's pleasures and occupations and thoughts during a day spent at the sea-shore; among them, that of sitting on top of a cliff, and throwing stones at his shadow, far below." Hawthorne's descriptions of a mile-long beach, its wet sands and footprints and other wonders thereon, the ways of beach birds, and the amusement to be had in retracing one's steps along the shore follow closely his detailed entries in the journals, recording an excursion to Phillips Beach, near Salem, on October 16, 1837. The essay appeared in the *Democratic Review*, Jan., 1839, and was collected in *Twice-Told Tales, Second Series*.

336. THE BIRTHMARK. In 1837, Hawthorne entered the theme of the story in his journal in these words: "A person to be in the possession of something as perfect as mortal man has a right to demand; he tries to make it better, and ruins it entirely." "The Birthmark" appeared in the *Pioneer*, March, 1843, and was republished in *Mosses from an Old Manse*. ¶343. "*Albertus Magnus, Cornelius Agrippa, Paracelsus, and the famous friar* [*Roger Bacon*]" are members of "the long dynasty of the alchemists," ranging from the twelfth to the sixteenth century.

348. THE OLD MANSE. The Concord manse had been built in 1765 for a "priest" (349)—Rev. William Emerson (grandfather of Ralph Waldo Emerson)—and from its windows he had watched the fight at Concord bridge (350). He was followed by Rev. Ezra Ripley, who was likewise "the latest inhabitant" (349), the planter of its apple trees (352), and presumably the original owner of the books over which Hawthorne pored (356). The pastor of the parish described as a friend of Whitefield (356) was Rev. Daniel Bliss (predecessor of Rev. William Emerson and maternal great-grandfather of Ralph Waldo Emerson). Whitefield twice preached at Concord at the invitation of Bliss. The ghost of the Manse (356) troubled Mrs. Hawthorne and others, but was never taken seriously by Hawthorne, who found the contemporary cults of spiritism, mesmerism, and hypnotism interesting but insubstantial. The essay was published in *Mosses from an Old Manse*.

360. ETHAN BRAND. During a holiday excursion in and about North Adams, Mass., from July 26 to Sept. 9, 1838, Hawthorne recorded in his journals minute descriptions from which he drew the settings for "Ethan Brand" and likewise its characters. The story was apparently written in 1848 at Salem, was published in the *Dollar Magazine*, May, 1850, and was collected in *The Snow-Image, and Other Tales*. Some idea of the fidelity with which Hawthorne's tales occasionally follow his journals may be gained by comparing the account of the diorama and the dog in "Ethan Brand" (367–68) with the following memoranda in *Passages from the American Note-Books:*

"We left our horse in the shed, and, entering the little unpainted bar-room, we heard a voice, in a strange, outlandish accent, exclaiming, 'Diorama.' It was an old man, with a full, grey-bearded countenance, and Mr. Leach exclaimed, 'Ah, here's the old Dutchman again!' And he answered, 'Yes, captain, here's the old Dutchman,'—though, by the way, he is a German, and travels through the country with this diorama in a wagon, and had recently been at South Adams, and was now returning from Saratoga Springs. We looked through the glass orifice of his machine, while he exhibited the very worst scratches and daubings that can be imagined,—worn out, too, and full of cracks and wrinkles, dimmed with tobacco-smoke and everywise dilapidated. There were none in a later fashion than thirty years since, except some figures that had been cut from tailor's show-bills. There were views of cities and edifices in Europe, of Napoleon's battles and Nelson's sea-fights, in the midst of which would be seen a gigantic, brown, hairy hand (the Hand of Destiny) pointing at the principal points of the conflict, while the old Dutchman explained. He gave a good deal of dramatic effect to his descriptions, but his accent and intonation cannot be written. He seemed to take interest and pride in his exhibition; yet when the utter and ludicrous miserability thereof made us laugh, he joined in the joke very readily. When the last picture had been shown, he caused a country boor, who stood gaping beside the machine, to put his head within it, and thrust out his tongue. The head becoming gigantic, a singular effect was produced.

"The old Dutchman's exhibition being over, a great dog, apparently an elderly dog, suddenly made himself the object of notice, evidently in rivalship of the Dutchman. He had seemed to be a good-natured, quiet kind of dog, offering his head to be patted by those who were kindly disposed towards him. This great old dog, unexpectedly, and of his own motion, began to run round after his not very long tail with the utmost eagerness; and, catching hold of it, growling and snarling with increasing rage, as if one half of his body were at deadly enmity with the other. Faster and faster went he, round and round about, growling still fiercer, till at last he ceased in a state of utter exhaustion; but no sooner had his exhibition finished than he became the same mild, quiet, sensible old dog as before; and no one could have suspected him of such nonsense as getting enraged with his own tail. He was first taught this trick by attaching a bell to the end of his tail; but he now commences entirely of his own accord, and I really believe he feels vain at the attention which he excites."

372. The Love Letters of Nathaniel Hawthorne, 1830–1841. These accounts of life at Brook Farm are drawn from Hawthorne's letters to his fiancée, Sophia Peabody, certain of which were included by her (in a severely edited version) in the posthumous *Passages from the American Note-Books*. They are here given in their original form, from a privately printed edition (1907). It will be observed that one letter (375) was written during a brief absence from Brook Farm.

## *Herman Melville (1819–1891)*

Born in New York in 1819, Melville was educated in public schools and in Albany Academy. After brief experience as a clerk, a farm laborer, and perhaps also as a rural schoolmaster, he shipped in 1837 as a seaman aboard an American merchant ship bound for Liverpool. On his return, he taught school in Massachusetts and New York and tried his hand at writing. In 1841, Melville sailed from New Bedford on the whaler *Acushnet;* in 1842, he deserted the ship with "Toby" Greene in the Marquesas Islands, lived for a time among the cannibal Typees, escaped on an Australian whaler, mutinied, and was set ashore at Tahiti; in 1843, he enlisted on an American frigate at Honolulu, from which he was honorably discharged in 1844 at Boston. Melville then established himself as an author with *Typee* (1846), *Omoo* (1847), *Mardi* (1849), *Redburn* (1849), and *White Jacket* (1850). In 1847, he married Elizabeth Shaw; in 1849, he again visited England; in 1850, he settled at Arrowhead Farm in the Berkshires. There he wrote *Moby Dick* (1851), *Pierre: or the Ambiguities* (1852), *The Piazza Tales* (1856), and *The Confidence Man* (1857). Denied a consular post abroad, Melville finally returned to New York City, where he served as an inspector of customs for twenty years. During this period, he made a voyage to Palestine and another to San Francisco, and published two volumes of verse, *Battle-Pieces* (1866) and *Clarel* (1876). Melville died, not forgotten but generally ignored, in New York in 1891.

Of various editions of Melville's novels, the most valuable are those edited by Raymond Weaver and by R. S. Forsythe. Raymond Weaver, *Herman Melville, Mariner and Mystic* (1921) is the only biography. Sane criticism may be found in John Freeman, *Herman Melville* (1926), and eloquent appreciation, marred by passages of fictitious biography, in Lewis Mumford, *Herman Melville* (1929).

377. Typee. These extracts introduce Melville's host, Marheyo, an elderly Typee; Kory Kory, his son and Melville's bodyguard; and Fayaway, Melville's favorite among the native maidens. The text is that of the unrevised London edition, published under the title, *Narrative of a Four Months' Residence among the Natives of a Valley of the Marquesas Islands.*

383. Mardi. A large part of this fantastic book is devoted to dialogues on religion, public affairs, and other aspects of human activity, which take place among a motley band of comrades who leisurely voyage among the isles of Mardi. The chief speakers are Media (a prince of Mardi), Taji (a dreamer in pursuit of the nymph Yillah), Babbalanja (a witty philosopher), Yoomy (a poet), and Braid-Beard

(a historian), each of whom contributes to a satirical symposium on humanity. In these extracts, they observe and comment on the worship of God (Oro), the doctrines of Christ (Alma), the activities of the King of England (Bello), and the absurdities of the President (Saturnina) and the Senate of the United States (the chiefs of Vivenza). This text is that of the first American edition.

392. Moby Dick. In these scenes aboard the whaleship *Pequod*, appear Captain Ahab, a monomaniac bent on destroying Moby Dick, the white whale; his three mates, Starbuck from Nantucket, Stubb from Cape Cod, and Flask from Martha's Vineyard; three harpooners, Tashtego, an Indian from the Vineyard, Daggoo, a negro, and Queequeg, a South Sea islander; and a crew drawn from all corners of the earth. The final chapters record the fulfilment of a riddling prophecy of Fedallah, a mystic Parsee, who predicted that he himself should die before Ahab, that the latter should see two hearses before meeting death, and that only hemp could kill the Captain. This text is that of the first American edition.

## *William Hickling Prescott (1796–1859)*

Prescott was born at Salem, Mass. At Harvard College, he was handicapped for life when the sight of one eye was destroyed in a student frolic. Thus forced to give up all thought of his chosen profession, the law, Prescott finally turned to history. After long study of English prose, European languages and literature, and Spanish history, he began the writing of the *History of the Reign of Ferdinand and Isabella the Catholic* (1836). Then followed the *History of the Conquest of Mexico* (1843) and the *History of the Conquest of Peru* (1847). After an apoplectic stroke, Prescott attempted to complete his last work, but death intervened. The unfinished *History of the Reign of Philip II* was published in 1855–58. The standard edition of Prescott is the Montezuma (1904). The earliest biography is George Ticknor, *Life of William Hickling Prescott* (1864); more recent but not definitive are Rollo Ogden, *William Hickling Prescott* (1904) and H. T. Peck, *William Hickling Prescott* (1905). Useful is *The Correspondence of William Hickling Prescott* (ed. Roger Wolcott, 1925).

417. History of the Conquest of Mexico. The text is that of the original edition.

421. History of the Conquest of Peru. The text is that of the original edition.

## *Francis Parkman (1823–1893)*

Born in Boston, Parkman was graduated from Harvard College and began the study of law, but soon turned to history. To secure information concerning the Indian and the frontier, Parkman made a journey to the Rocky Mountains in 1846, enduring hardships which permanently weakened his health. His observations were published in *The California and Oregon Trail* (1849). Continuing his study of France in the New World, Parkman made seven journeys to Europe in search of material, while in America he visited the scenes of all the historic events of which he wrote. About 1850, his health gave way, and thereafter his research was prosecuted only with great difficulty. He published *The Conspiracy of Pontiac* in 1851, but not until 1865 was he able to complete *Pioneers of France in the New World*. Then followed *The Jesuits in North America in the Seventeenth Century* (1867), *La Salle; or, the Discovery of the Great West* (1869), *The Old Regime in Canada* (1874), *Count Frontenac and New France under Louis XIV* (1877), *Montcalm and Wolfe* (1884), and *A Half-Century of Conflict* (1892). Parkman's historical works have been collected in the Champlain Edition (1897) and the Library Edition (1902). Biographies are C. H. Farnham, *A Life of Francis Parkman* (1900) and H. D. Sedgwick, *Francis Parkman* (1904).

426. Montcalm and Wolfe. The text of these extracts is that of the first edition.

435. The California and Oregon Trail. In this chapter appear Parkman; his college friend, Quincy Adams Shaw; and their guide, Henry Chatillon, who accompanied them to the Rocky Mountains. The work was serialized in the *Knickerbocker Magazine*, Feb., 1847 to Feb., 1849. This text follows the first collected edition.

## *David Crockett (1786–1836)*

Crockett was born on the Tennessee frontier, attended school for six months at eighteen, and soon after became a hunter. After participating in the Creek War under Andrew Jackson in 1813–14, he was twice elected to the Tennessee legislature and three times to Congress. *A Narrative of the Life of David Crockett of the State of Tennessee, Written by Himself* was published in 1834. Crockett was killed in defence of the Alamo in Texas.

442. A Narrative was probably from the hand of Crockett; but various later works attributed to him are certainly spurious.

## *Augustus Baldwin Longstreet (1790–1870)*

Longstreet was born at Augusta, Georgia, and educated at Yale College. As a country lawyer, he picked up material for humorous newspaper sketches, later collected as *Georgia Scenes* (1835). President of Emory College and later of the University of Mississippi, Longstreet eventually became loath to admit the authorship of these jovial tales. An excellent biography is J. D. Wade, *Augustus Baldwin Longstreet* (1924).

447. THE HORSE SWAP is here printed, with the correction of obvious typographical errors, from the first edition of *Georgia Scenes*.

## *William Gilmore Simms (1806–1870)*

Simms was born of humble parentage in Charleston, S. C. Without adequate education, he vainly sought distinction as poet and as editor. Then turning to romances of adventure, particularly on the Carolina frontier before and during the Revolution, he produced his best books: *The Yemassee* (1835) and *The Partisan* (1835). For some years, he continued to write voluminously on these themes, winning a contemporary reputation in the novel second only to Cooper's. After his second marriage (1836), Simms came to know the Southern plantation, but he never portrayed its genteel life with the vigor which marked his tales of Indians and soldiers. The only biography is W. P. Trent, *William Gilmore Simms* (1892).

453. THE YEMASSEE. The major characters of the novel are Sanutee, a noble chief of the Yemassee, his wife Matiwan, and their son Occonestoga. Occonestoga has betrayed his tribesmen to their white foes and now awaits his death. This extract follows the text of the revised edition of 1853.

## *John Pendleton Kennedy (1795–1870)*

Born in Baltimore, Kennedy was graduated from Baltimore College and was admitted to the bar. He had entered politics when he published *Swallow Barn* (1832), *Horse Shoe Robinson: A Tale of the Tory Ascendancy* (1835), and *Rob of the Bowl* (1838). Kennedy was three times elected to Congress as a Whig; in 1840, he published *Quodlibet*, a satire on Jacksonian Democracy. After serving as Secretary of the Navy, 1852–53, he left public life. An early biography is H. T. Tuckerman, *The Life of John Pendleton Kennedy* (1871). More recent but inadequate is E. M. Gwathmey, *John Pendleton Kennedy* (1931).

463. SWALLOW BARN. These extracts follow the text of the revised edition of 1851.

## *John Caldwell Calhoun (1782–1850)*

Calhoun was born in South Carolina, was graduated from Yale College, and became a lawyer. He was in turn Congressman, Secretary of War, Vice-President, Senator, Secretary of State, and again Senator. From 1832 onward, he was a leading exponent of the doctrine of states' rights. Among biographies are Gaillard Hunt, *John C. Calhoun* (1908), and W. M. Meigs, *The Life of John Caldwell Calhoun* (1917).

468. SPEECH ON THE SLAVERY QUESTION. Calhoun, already stricken with the illness which was soon to cause his death, was present in the Senate chamber on March 4, 1850, while his speech was read by a fellow-member. These extracts follow the original text of 1850.

## *Daniel Webster (1782–1852)*

Webster was born on a farm in New Hampshire, was graduated from Dartmouth College, and became a famed lawyer. As Congressman and Senator, he defended the federal union against Hayne and Calhoun. For some decades, New England considered Webster the greatest American orator. Among numerous biographies are H. C. Lodge, *Daniel Webster* (1883, 1899), F. A. Ogg, *Daniel Webster* (1914), and C. M. Fuess, *Daniel Webster* (1930).

475. SPEECH ON THE CONSTITUTION AND THE UNION was delivered by Webster before the Senate on March 7, 1850, in the presence of Calhoun, who left his sick-bed to hear this reply to his speech of March 4. The abolitionists of New England considered that Webster here betrayed them; for an expression of their righteous anger see Whittier's "Ichabod" (492). These extracts follow the original text of 1850. The satirical reference to abolitionists on p. 477 ("I know many abolitionists in my own neighborhood . . .") was discreetly omitted from collected editions of Webster's speeches.

## *Harriet Beecher Stowe (1811–1896)*

Harriet Beecher was born at Litchfield, Conn., daughter of Rev. Lyman Beecher and sister of Henry Ward Beecher. In 1832, the family removed to Cincinnati, where Lyman Beecher became president of Lane Theological

Seminary and his daughter gained her first direct knowledge of slavery. Here she began to write, and here she was married to Rev. Calvin Stowe. In 1850, they removed to Brunswick, Maine, where Mrs. Stowe wrote *Uncle Tom's Cabin* (1852). To document the book, she published *A Key to Uncle Tom's Cabin* (1853); in 1856, she again handled the problem of slavery in *Dred: A Tale of the Great Dismal Swamp*. Mrs. Stowe's later fiction dealt with New England life: *The Minister's Wooing* (1859), *The Pearl of Orr's Island* (1862), *Oldtown Folks* (1869). Sympathetic biographies are Annie Fields, *Life and Letters of Harriet Beecher Stowe* (1897) and C. E. and L. B. Stowe, *Harriet Beecher Stowe: the Story of Her Life* (1911).

483. UNCLE TOM'S CABIN was serialized in the *National Era*, June, 1851–April, 1852. Only with difficulty did Mrs. Stowe find a publisher for the novel in book form; but within a year it sold 300,000 copies. Even though the comic spinster, Miss Ophelia, is a Yankee and the brutal Legree is a Northern-born planter, Southern readers felt that plantation society had been traduced, and they condemned the novel as vigorously as abolitionists lauded it. These extracts follow the text of the first edition.

## *John Greenleaf Whittier (1807–1892)*

On Dec. 17, 1807, Whittier was born on a farm near Haverhill, Mass., the descendant of a long line of Friends. His boyhood on the homestead was arduous, with much toil and few pleasures. After an apprenticeship in didactic prose and verse and a meagre education, financed by shoemaking and concluded at Haverhill Academy in 1828, Whittier began an active career as journalist and politician. In 1829 he edited the *American Manufacturer* in Boston, in 1830 the *Gazette* in Haverhill, in 1830–31 the *New England Review* in Hartford; in 1831 he published *Legends of New England in Prose and Verse;* in 1833 he committed himself to abolition by writing *Justice and Expediency* and by participating in an anti-slavery convention in Philadelphia; in 1835–36 he was a member of the Massachusetts Legislature; in 1838–40 he edited the *Pennsylvania Freeman;* in 1847–60 he was associated with the *National Era*. Until the close of the Civil War, Whittier continued to be an active abolition agitator, at times suffering mob violence. During these years, slavery was the dominant theme of his verse: *Poems* (1837), *Voices of Freedom* (1846), *Poems* (first collective ed., 1849), *Songs of Labor* (1850), *The Chapel of the Hermits* (1853), and *In War Time* (1864). Sentiment and New England life bulked large in later volumes: *The Panorama and Other Poems* (1856), *Home-Ballads* (1860), *Snow-Bound* (1866), *The Tent on the Beach* (1867), *Among the Hills* (1869), and others. During his last years at Amesbury, Whittier was loved and honored as a sage and patriarch of New England. He died at Hampton Falls, N. H., Sept. 7, 1892.

No complete bibliography of Whittier has been compiled; the bibliography in *CHAL*, II, 436–451, is valuable. The standard edition of Whittier's complete works is the Riverside (1888); and of his poems, the Cambridge (1894). F. H. Underwood, *John Greenleaf Whittier* (1884) is a useful early biography. More complete is S. T. Pickard, *Life and Letters of John Greenleaf Whittier* (1894–1907). Concise biographies are T. W. Higginson, *John Greenleaf Whittier* (1902) and G. R. Carpenter, *John Greenleaf Whittier* (1903). Special studies are S. T. Pickard, *Whittier as a Politician* (1900) and *Whittier-Land* (1904), F. M. Pray, *A Study of Whittier's Apprenticeship as a Poet* (1930), and J. S. Stevens, *Whittier's Use of the Bible* (1930).

The text of these extracts from Whittier is that of the Riverside Edition.

491. THE MORAL WARFARE, written in commemoration of the American Revolution, is one of Whittier's earliest self-dedications to the cause of reform. "The Moral Warfare" was included in *Poems*.

491. SONG OF SLAVES IN THE DESERT was based, according to Whittier, on a Moor's account of a slave song, recorded by James Richardson, the African traveller. "Rubee," in the dialect of Bornou negroes, means "God." The poem was published in the *National Era*, Jan., 1847, and collected in *The Panorama*.

492. PROEM was published as preface to the first collective edition of Whittier's poems.

492. ICHABOD, declared Whittier, "was the outcome of the surprise and grief and forecast of evil consequences which I felt on reading the seventh of March speech of Daniel Webster in support of the 'compromise,' and the Fugitive Slave Law. No partisan or personal enmity dictated it. On the contrary my admiration of the splendid personality and intellectual power of the great Senator was never stronger than when I laid down his speech, and in one of the saddest moments of my life, penned my protest." The title, "Ichabod," is a Hebrew word meaning "inglorious." The poem was published in the *National Era*, May 2, 1850, and collected in *Songs of Labor*. Thirty years

later, Whittier modified but did not withdraw his condemnation of Webster in "The Lost Occasion," which reads in part as follows:

Thou shouldst have lived to feel below
Thy feet Disunion's fierce upthrow;
The late-sprung mine that underlaid
Thy sad concessions vainly made.
Thou shouldst have seen from Sumter's wall
The star-flag of the Union fall,
And armed rebellion pressing on
The broken lines of Washington!
No stronger voice than thine had then
Called out the utmost might of men,
To make the Union's charter free
And strengthen law by liberty.
How had that stern arbitrament
To thy gray age youth's vigor lent,
Shaming ambition's paltry prize
Before thy disillusioned eyes;
Breaking the spell about thee wound
Like the green withes that Samson bound;
Redeeming in one effort grand,
Thyself and thy imperiled land!
Ah, cruel fate, that closed to thee,
O sleeper by the Northern sea,
The gates of opportunity!
God fills the gaps of human need,
Each crisis brings its word and deed.
Wise men and strong we did not lack;
But still, with memory turning back,
In the dark hours we thought of thee,
And thy lone grave beside the sea.

493. Wordsworth was written in the year after the English poet's death, published in the *National Era*, June 12, 1851, and collected in *The Chapel of the Hermits*. The reader will observe allusions to Wordsworth's "She Dwelt among the Untrodden Ways," "Peter Bell," and "I Wandered Lonely as a Cloud."

493. First-Day Thoughts was included in *The Chapel of the Hermits*.

494. Burns. Whittier was introduced to Burns by a wandering Scot and by his first schoolmaster. "One day," wrote Whittier, "we had a call from a 'pawky auld carle' of a wandering Scotchman. To him I owe my first introduction to the songs of Burns. After eating his bread and cheese and drinking his mug of cider he gave us 'Bonny Doon,' 'Highland Mary,' and 'Auld Lang Syne.' He had a rich, full voice, and entered heartily into the spirit of his lyrics." Again Whittier wrote: "When I was fourteen years old, my first schoolmaster, Joshua Coffin, the able, eccentric historian of Newbury, brought with him to our house a volume of Burns's poems, from which he read, greatly to my delight. I begged him to leave the book with me, and set myself at once to the task of mastering the glossary of the Scottish dialect at its close. This was about the first poetry I had ever read (with the exception of that of the Bible, of which I had been a close student), and it had a lasting influence upon me. I began to make rhymes myself, and to imagine stories and adventures." The poem, "Burns," appeared in the *National Era*, Feb. 16, 1854, and was collected in *The Panorama*.

495. The Barefoot Boy is clearly autobiographical. It was included in *The Panorama*.

496. Skipper Ireson's Ride. As a student at Haverhill, Whittier heard an erroneous account of a shipwreck involving Captain Floyd Ireson of Marblehead, on which he based this poem. When a local historian revealed that the crew and not Ireson had been responsible for deserting the ship, Whittier gladly accepted this version of the disaster, adding, "I am glad for the sake of truth and justice that the real facts are given in thy book. I certainly would not knowingly do injustice to any one, dead or living." The refrain and the use of dialect were suggested to Whittier by Lowell. The poem was published in the *Atlantic Monthly*, Dec., 1857, and collected in *Home Ballads*.

498. Telling the Bees, according to Whittier, records a "remarkable custom, brought from the Old Country, [which] formerly prevailed in the rural districts of New England. On the death of a member of the family, the bees were at once informed of the event, and their hives dressed in mourning. This ceremonial was supposed to be necessary to prevent the swarms from leaving their hives and seeking a new home." The poem was written soon after the death of Whittier's mother; the setting is the Whittier homestead, with its stone wall, red-barred gate, cattle-yard, flower-garden, and beehives. "Telling the Bees" was published in the *Atlantic Monthly*, April, 1858, and collected in *Home Ballads*.

499. My Playmate is one of several poems in which Whittier recalled his youthful loves. The setting is on Ramoth Hill and in the woods of Follymill, near his birthplace. The poem was published in the *Atlantic Monthly*, May, 1860, and collected in *Home Ballads*.

500. Laus Deo! As Whittier sat in the Friends' meeting-house at Amesbury in 1865, during the celebration of the passage of a constitutional amendment abolishing slavery, "Laus Deo!", according to the poet, "wrote itself, or rather sang itself, while the bells rang." It was published in the *Independent*,

Feb. 9, 1865, and collected in *National Lyrics* (1865).

500. SNOW-BOUND was dedicated "To the memory of the household it describes." Head of this family was John Whittier, who had died in 1831. "My father when a young man," stated the poet, "had traversed the wilderness to Canada, and could tell us of his adventures with Indians and wild beasts, and of his sojourn in the French villages" (see l. 224). The mother was Abigail Hussey Whittier, a native of "Cocheco town" (l. 259), or Dover, N. H., who told her children tales of "strange people who lived on the Piscataqua and Cocheco." Among these was "Bartram the sorcerer," whose copy of Cornelius Agrippa's *Occult Philosophy* (motto and l. 270) the poet inherited from his mother, who had died in 1857. The uncle, Moses Whittier (l. 307), "was ready with his record of hunting and fishing and, it must be confessed, with stories, which he at least half believed, of witchcraft and superstition." He had died in 1824; and the aunt, Mercy Hussey (l. 350), in 1846. The elder sister, Mary Whittier Caldwell (l. 378), early encouraged her brother in the writing of verse. She had died in 1861; and the younger sister, Elizabeth Whittier (l. 396), in 1864. The schoolmaster (l. 439) was Joshua Coffin, abolitionist and antiquarian, or, more possibly, George Haskell. The other guest referred to (l. 510) was, according to Whittier, "Harriet Livermore, daughter of Judge Livermore, of New Hampshire, a young woman of fine natural ability, enthusiastic, eccentric, with slight control over her violent temper, which sometimes made her religious profession doubtful. She was equally ready to exhort in school-house prayer-meetings and dance in a Washington ball-room, while her father was a member of Congress. She early embraced the doctrine of the Second Advent, and felt it her duty to proclaim the Lord's speedy coming. With this message she crossed the Atlantic and spent the greater part of a long life in travelling over Europe and Asia. She lived some time with Lady Hester Stanhope, a woman as fantastic and mentally strained as herself, on the slope of Mt. Lebanon, but finally quarrelled with her in regard to two white horses with red marks on their backs which suggested the idea of saddles, on which her titled hostess expected to ride into Jerusalem with the Lord. At the time referred to in 'Snow-Bound' she was boarding at the Rocks Village, about two miles from us." This text is Whittier's final revision of "Snow-Bound." ¶503. "*The chief of Gambia's golden shore*" is an allusion to a poem, "The African Chief," by Mrs. Sarah Morton (1759–1846), erroneously attributed to Mercy Otis Warren by Whittier in the first text of "Snow-Bound." ¶504. "*Sewel's ancient tome.*" William Sewel (1654–1720), a Dutch Quaker, wrote *A History of the Quakers* (1717, 1722), a work praised by Charles Lamb in "A Quaker Meeting." ¶504. "*Chalkley's Journal.*" The Anglo-American, Thomas Chalkley (1675–1741), was an eccentric itinerant preacher of the Friends. ¶505. "*Apollonius*" was a Greek philosopher and magician of the first century; "*Hermes*" was also a reputed magician of ancient Greece. ¶505. "*White of Selborne.*" Gilbert White (1720–1793) wrote *The Natural History and Antiquities of Selborne* (1789) in Hampshire, England. ¶507. "*Petruchio's Kate*" appears in *The Taming of the Shrew.* ¶507. "*Siena's saint*" is Saint Catherine, a mystic of the fourteenth century. ¶509. "*Ellwood's meek, drab-skirted Muse.*" Thomas Ellwood (1639–1713), an English Friend, wrote a dreary epic on David and suggested to Milton that he write *Paradise Regained.* ¶509. "*Creeks*" were active in the Indian wars in Florida, 1813–18. ¶509. "*McGregor*" attempted the colonization of Costa Rica in 1821–22. ¶509. "*Ypsilanti*" was a Greek patriot (1792–1828) who led troops from Maina, near Mt. Taygetus, against the Turks.

510. THE ETERNAL GOODNESS was included in *The Tent on the Beach.*

511. THE FRIEND'S BURIAL is a tribute to an old friend, Mrs. Elizabeth Gove. The poem was included in *Hazel Blossoms* (1874).

512. SUNSET ON THE BEARCAMP. In his last years, Whittier spent several summers on the Bearcamp River in New Hampshire. This poem was included in *The Vision of Echard, and Other Poems* (1878).

## *Henry Wadsworth Longfellow (1807–1882)*

Longfellow was born at Portland, Maine, on Feb. 27, 1807, was graduated from Bowdoin College with Hawthorne (1825), and studied modern languages in Europe (1826–29). For six years, he was professor at Bowdoin, in Brunswick, Maine, where he married Miss Mary Potter. Offered a professorship of modern languages at Harvard, Longfellow studied in Scandinavia and Germany (1835–36). Meanwhile, *Outre-Mer: A Pilgrimage beyond the Sea* (1833, 1835) was published; in the latter year his wife died. In 1836, Longfellow took up his duties at Harvard, soon settling in Craigie House where he spent the remainder of his life. *Voices of the Night* and *Hyperion* appeared in

1839. Then followed *Ballads and Other Poems* (1842), *Poems on Slavery* (1842), *The Belfry of Bruges and Other Poems* (1846), and *Kavanagh* (1849). Longfellow's reputation as a narrative poet was established by *Evangeline* (1847), *The Golden Legend* (1851), *The Song of Hiawatha* (1855), and *The Courtship of Miles Standish* (1858). When his income from writing permitted it, Longfellow resigned his professorship (1854). Frances Appleton, who became his wife in 1843, was tragically burned to death in 1861. After her death, he published *Tales of a Wayside Inn* (1863), translated Dante's *Divine Comedy* (1865–67), wrote various verse-tragedies, and experimented with the sonnet. In his last years, Longfellow was revered and honored at home and abroad—the most popular and, in many minds, the greatest of American poets. He died in Cambridge in 1882.

A bibliography of Longfellow has been compiled by L. S. Livingston (1908); more recent and more concise is that in *CHAL*, II, 425–36. The Riverside Edition of Longfellow's complete works (1886) is standard; a convenient edition of his poems is the Cambridge (1893). The most detailed and most adulatory biography is Samuel Longfellow, *Life of Henry Wadsworth Longfellow* (1891). Briefer are G. R. Carpenter, *Henry Wadsworth Longfellow* (1901), and T. W. Higginson, *Henry Wadsworth Longfellow* (1902). Biased but useful is Herbert Gorman, *A Victorian American: Henry Wadsworth Longfellow* (1926). Helpful essays are Bliss Perry, "The Centenary of Longfellow" in *Park Street Papers* (1908); F. L. Pattee, "The Shadow of Longfellow" in *Sidelights on American Literature* (1922); and G. R. Elliott, "Gentle Shades of Longfellow" in *The Cycle of Modern Poetry* (1929).

The text of these extracts from Longfellow is that of the Riverside Edition.

514. A Psalm of Life was described by Longfellow as "a voice from my inmost heart at a time when I was rallying from depression;" the psalmist is neither David nor Solomon, but one aspect of the poet himself. The poem was published in the *Knickerbocker Magazine*, Sept., 1838, and collected in *Voices of the Night*.

514. Footsteps of Angels commemorates the death in 1835 of Longfellow's dear friend and brother-in-law, George W. Pierce, and of the poet's wife, Mary Potter Longfellow. The poem was published in *Knickerbocker Magazine*, May, 1839, and collected in *Voices of the Night*.

515. The Beleaguered City was suggested to Longfellow by the following note which he chanced to see in a copy of Walter Scott's *Border Minstrelsy:* "Similar to this was the *Nacht Lager*, or Midnight Camp which seemed nightly to beleaguer the walls of Prague, but which disappeared upon recitation of certain magical words." The poem was published in the *Southern Literary Messenger*, Nov., 1839, and collected in *Voices of the Night*.

515. Hymn to the Night was written, Longfellow stated, "while sitting at my chamber window, on one of the balmiest nights of the year. I endeavored to reproduce the impression of the hour and scene." The motto, from the *Iliad*, means "Welcome, thrice prayed for." The poem was included in *Voices of the Night*.

516. The Skeleton in Armor. Longfellow stated: "A skeleton had been dug up at Fall River clad in broken and corroded armor; and the idea occurred to me of connecting it with the Round Tower at Newport." Both of these objects were at that time thought to be of Scandinavian origin. The poem was published with marginal glosses as "The Saga of the Skeleton in Armor" in the *Knickerbocker Magazine*, Jan., 1841, and collected in *Ballads and Other Poems*.

518. The Slave's Dream was published in *Poems on Slavery*, a slender volume made up of abolition verses written while Longfellow was confined to his cabin by rough weather, during a voyage from Europe in 1842.

518. The Belfry of Bruges is an expression of Longfellow's delight in the chimes of Bruges, which he described in his journal on May 30 and 31, 1842, while he was lodging at the Fleur-de-Blé. The poem was published in *Graham's Magazine*, Jan., 1843, and collected in *The Belfry of Bruges and Other Poems*.

519. The Arsenal at Springfield. In 1843, Frances Appleton Longfellow and the poet visited the arsenal at Springfield, Mass.; there, she later recalled, "We grew quite warlike against war and I urged H[enry] to write a peace poem." The result was published in *Graham's Magazine*, May, 1844, and collected in *The Belfry of Bruges and Other Poems*.

520. Nuremberg is the poet's tribute to one of the most picturesque centers of the Romantic Movement in Germany. Here Longfellow visited the home and the grave of the sixteenth-century artist, Albrecht Dürer (l. 22), and of his contemporary, the poet Hans Sachs (l. 37); here he examined the work of two Renaissance artists: Peter Vischer, in the church of St. Sebald (l. 17), and Adam Kraft, in the church of St. Lawrence (l. 19). Longfellow alludes also to the writings of a Renaissance poet, Melchior Pfinzing (l. 12). "Nuremberg" was published in *Graham's Magazine*, June, 1844, and collected in *The Belfry of Bruges and Other Poems*.

522. SEAWEED was published in *Graham's Magazine*, Jan., 1845, and collected in *The Belfry of Bruges and Other Poems*.

522. EVANGELINE. Whittier for some time planned to write on the tragedy of the Acadian exiles, but gave up the project when he learned that others were interested. Hawthorne heard an account of "a young couple in Acadie" from Horace Connolly, and in 1838 summarized it in his journal as follows. On the day set for the marriage of the young couple, "all the men of the Province were summoned to assemble in the church to hear a proclamation. When assembled, they were all seized and shipped off to be distributed throughout New England,—among them the new bridegroom. His bride set off in search of him—wandered about New England all her lifetime, and at last, when she was old, found her bridegroom on his death-bed. The shock was so great that it killed her likewise." Longfellow later heard Connolly recount the story, secured Hawthorne's permission to use it, and in 1845 set to work on his "idyll in hexameters." He did not visit Nova Scotia or Louisiana, but drew widely on books of travel and history, particularly for such passages as the opening of Part I, where he describes the village of Grand-Pré ("Grand Meadow") on an arm of the Bay of Fundy.

525. HIAWATHA. As an undergraduate, Longfellow was an enthusiastic champion of the American Indian; in or near 1845, his attention was centered on the legends of western Indians by one of his former students, recently returned from a tour of the prairies; about 1852, the name of Minnehaha and various details of Minnesota scenery were brought to his attention by a daguerreotype of the Falls of Minnehah-hah and by Mary Eastman, *Dahcotah, or Life and Legends of the Sioux around Fort Snelling* (1847); in 1854, he was studying sources and writing the first portion of *Hiawatha*. The metre and several of the episodes, he drew from the Finnish epic, *Kalavala*. Longfellow left this note on the poem:

"This Indian Edda—if I may so call it—is founded on a tradition prevalent among the North American Indians, of a personage of miraculous birth, who was sent among them to clear their rivers, forests, and fishing-grounds, and to teach them the arts of peace. He was known among different tribes by the several names of Michabou, Chiabo, Manabozo, Tarenyawagon, and Hiawatha. Mr. Schoolcraft gives an account of him in his *Algic Researches* . . . ; and in his *History, Condition, and Prospects of the Indian Tribes of the United States* . . . may be found the Iroquois form of the tradition, derived from the verbal narration of an Onondaga chief.

"Into this old tradition I have woven other curious Indian legends, drawn chiefly from the various and valuable writings of Mr. Schoolcraft, to whom the literary world is greatly indebted for his indefatigable zeal in rescuing from oblivion so much of the legendary lore of the Indians."

527. MY LOST YOUTH. On March 29, 1855, Longfellow wrote in his journal: "A day of pain; cowering over the fire. At night as I lie in bed, a poem comes into my mind,—a memory of Portland, my native town, the city by the sea." On the next day, he added: "Wrote the poem; and am rather pleased with it, and with the bringing in of the two lines of the old Lapland song,

A boy's will is the wind's will,
And the thoughts of youth are long,
long thoughts."

Longfellow here recalls a sea-fight witnessed in 1813, during which the American brig *Enterprise* captured the English brig *Boxer* off Portland harbor. Both captains were killed and both lie buried in a Portland cemetery. "My Lost Youth" was published in *Putnam's Monthly*, August, 1855, and collected in *The Courtship of Miles Standish and Other Poems*.

528. TALES OF A WAYSIDE INN was undertaken by Longfellow in 1862 as a series of framed stories. Gathered at the old inn at Sudbury, twenty miles from Cambridge, Mass., a group of six friends entertain each other and their host with tales. "The Saga of King Olaf," originally written in 1859–60 for separate publication, was incorporated in the *Tales* as the narrative of the Musician (identified as Ole Bull, famous Norwegian composer and violinist). Early in the "Saga," Longfellow recounts various feats of King Olaf of Norway, who antagonized his neighbors by his violent temper, by his attempts to christianize his people, and by his many conquests in Scandinavia. In "King Olaf's War-Horns," the conqueror sets forth in his war-boat, the Serpent, with his lieutenants, Ulf the Red and Einar Tamberskelver, against the combined fleets of King Svend of Denmark, the King of Sweden, and Earl Eric of Norway. Episodes of the battle which follows are recounted in "Einar Tamberskelver"; and the final defeat of Olaf is narrated in "King Olaf's Death-Drink."

531. DIVINA COMMEDIA. After the death of his second wife, Longfellow turned for occupation and consolation to the long task of

translating Dante's *Divina Commedia.* While thus occupied, he wrote six sonnets on Beatrice, Dante, and the *Commedia*, five of which sonnets were published in the *Atlantic Monthly* from Dec., 1864, to Nov., 1866. When Longfellow's translation of the *Divine Comedy* appeared, Sonnets I and II prefaced his version of the "Inferno"; III and IV, the "Purgatario"; V and VI, the "Paradiso."

533. CHAUCER, SHAKESPEARE, MILTON, and THE SOUND OF THE SEA (534) were included in "A Book of Sonnets," which was published as a part of *The Masque of Pandora* (1875). ¶533. "*Musagates*": Apollo. ¶533. "*Mœonides*": Homer.

534. THE TIDE RISES, THE TIDE FALLS and NIGHT were included in *Ultima Thule* (1880).

535. KAVANAGH. This extract is a part of Chapter XX.

## *Oliver Wendell Holmes (1809–1894)*

Holmes was born at Cambridge, Mass., Aug. 29, 1809. After graduation from Harvard College (1829), he attended law school (1829–30) and medical school (1830–33) and studied medicine in Paris (1833–35). His youthful verse was collected in *Poems* (1836). In 1840, Holmes married Miss Amelia Jackson. After more than a decade of practice as a physician in Boston, he was made Professor of Anatomy and Physiology in Harvard Medical School (1847), where he was respected as a skilful lecturer and a sound scientist. Locally popular as a familiar poet, Holmes became distinguished as a familiar essayist when he contributed *The Autocrat of the Breakfast Table* (1858) to the early issues of the *Atlantic Monthly.* Then followed *The Professor at the Breakfast Table* (1860), *Elsie Venner* (1861), *Songs in Many Keys* (1862), *The Guardian Angel* (1867), and *The Poet at the Breakfast Table* (1872). After resigning his chair at Harvard (1882), Holmes devoted his last years to literature, publishing a third "medicated novel" (*A Mortal Antipathy*, 1885), biographies, poems, and *Over the Teacups* (1891). Holmes died Oct. 7, 1894, in Boston.

A bibliography of Holmes has been compiled by G. B. Ives (1907); more recent is that in *CHAL*, II, 540–43. The standard edition of Holmes' works is the Riverside (1891) and of his poems, the Cambridge (1895). The standard biography is J. T. Morse, *Life and Letters of Oliver Wendell Holmes* (1896).

These selections from Holmes follow the text of the Riverside Edition.

538. THE HEIGHT OF THE RIDICULOUS was published in July, 1830, in the *Collegian*, a humorous magazine edited by Harvard students, and was collected in *Poems.*

538. THE BALLAD OF THE OYSTERMAN was published in the *Amateur*, July 17, 1830, and collected in *Poems.*

539. OLD IRONSIDES. When in 1830 Holmes learned that the frigate *Constitution*, conqueror of the *Guerrière* during the War of 1812, was to be destroyed in the Charlestown Navy Yard, he dashed off this impassioned poem, which was published in the Boston *Daily Advertiser* on Sept. 16. The lines, widely reprinted in newspapers and as a broadside, so roused public opinion that the *Constitution* was not destroyed. "Old Ironsides" was collected in *Poems.*

539. THE LAST LEAF, describing Major Thomas Melville (1751–1832) of Boston, grandfather of Herman Melville, was published in the *Amateur*, March 26, 1831, and collected in *Poems.*

540. MY AUNT was published in the *New England Magazine*, Oct., 1831, and collected in *Poems.*

540. NON-RESISTANCE was published in *Astrœ* (1850).

541. THE CHAMBERED NAUTILUS was included in an installment of *The Autocrat of the Breakfast Table* in the *Atlantic Monthly*, Feb., 1858.

541. THE LIVING TEMPLE. This "anatomist's hymn" was published in an installment of *The Autocrat* in the *Atlantic Monthly*, May, 1858.

542. THE DEACON'S MASTERPIECE is an allegorical account of the collapse of Calvinistic theology in New England. In writing this "logical story," Holmes doubtless had in mind that masterpiece of orthodox logic, *The Freedom of the Will* by Jonathan Edwards, published in 1754. "The Deacon's Masterpiece" appeared in an installment of *The Autocrat* in the *Atlantic Monthly*, Sept., 1858.

544. THE BOYS is one of a series of poems which, for many years, Holmes annually read at dinners of the class of 1829. Of the members of this class, the "Doctor" (l. 15) was Francis Thomas; the "Judge" (l. 15), George T. Bigelow, Chief Justice of Massachusetts; the "Speaker" (l. 17), Francis B. Crowninshield of the Massachusetts House of Representatives; "Mr. Mayor" (l. 18), G. W. Richardson of Worcester, Mass.; the "Member of Congress" (l. 19), George T. Davis, described by Thackeray as "the most agreeable dinner-companion whom he met in the United States"; " 'Reverend' What's his name" (l. 20), James Freeman Clarke; "that boy with the grave mathematical look" (l. 21), Professor Benjamin Pierce of

Harvard; the "Justice" (l. 28), Benjamin R. Curtis, Chief Justice of Massachusetts; "a nice youngster" (l. 29), S. F. Smith, author of "America"; "that boy laughing" (l. 33), Rev. Samuel May, an amiable abolitionist. The poem was read on Jan. 6, 1859, and published in the following month in an installment of *The Professor at the Breakfast Table* in the *Atlantic Monthly*.

545. A HYMN OF TRUST was published in an installment of *The Professor* in the *Atlantic Monthly*, Nov., 1859.

545. DOROTHY Q is a portrait of Holmes' great-grandmother, Dorothy Quincy. The poem was published in the *Atlantic Monthly*, Jan., 1871, and collected in *Songs of Many Seasons* (1875).

547. AT THE SATURDAY CLUB. This famous dining club met at the Parker House, near King's Chapel, Boston, on the last Saturday of each month. In these lines, Holmes alludes to both deceased and living members: "our POET" (l. 63) was Longfellow (died 1882); "the great PROFESSOR" (l. 85), Louis Agassiz (died 1873); "our Concord Delphi" (l. 122), Emerson (died 1882); and "the great ROMANCER," Hawthorne. The poem was published in the *Atlantic Monthly*, Jan., 1884, and collected in *Before the Curfew* (1888).

550. THE AUTOCRAT OF THE BREAKFAST TABLE. Before Lowell assumed the editorship of the *Atlantic Monthly* at its founding in 1857, he secured from Holmes a promise of regular contributions for the new magazine. The latter responded with *The Autocrat*, which ran from Nov., 1857 to Oct., 1858. As Holmes suggests in his first sentence, these monologues may be viewed as a sequel to his immature essays published under the same title over a quarter of a century before (in the *New England Magazine*, Nov., 1831, Jan., 1832). As is his custom, Holmes here alludes to a varied range of personages. America is represented by William and Washington Irving and their friend, J. K. Paulding, collaborating on *Salmagundi;* the essayist, Gulian Verplanck, William Cullen Bryant, and the poet, Robert C. Sands, collaborating on an annual, *The Talisman* (552); William Pinkney (553), lawyer and statesman of the early nineteenth century; Sylvanus Cobb, Junior (558), sentimental and melodramatic hack-writer of the later nineteenth century; John Smibert (1684–1751), Scottish portrait painter who migrated to Boston, and John S. Copley (1737–1815), Boston portrait painter who migrated to England; Gilbert Stuart (1755–1828), most famous of early American portrait painters, and Edward Malbone (1777–1807), his less distinguished contemporary (560); General William Cumming, a ranting Unionist (562), and William Miller (562), who in 1844 prepared for the immediate ending of the world. England is represented by Martin Tupper (558), best known for his *Proverbial Philosophy* (1838); William Hogarth, eighteenth-century painter and engraver (561); Isaac Barrow and John Tillotson, seventeenth-century theologians and preachers (561); and Eclipse, Revenge, Prospect, and Peacemaker (567), famous race-horses of that day and competitors for the Goodwood Cup, awarded annually in Sussex, England. (Holmes would be interested to know that the present record for trotting a mile is 1:56¾—set in 1922 by Peter Manning.) One pun here perpetrated may require elucidation: Phryne (555), a beautiful Athenian maiden on trial for murder, appealed to her judges by baring her bosom at the command of her lawyer-lover, and was thereupon acquitted.

## *James Russell Lowell (1819–1891)*

Lowell was born at Elmwood, in Cambridge, Mass., on Feb. 22, 1819. After graduation from Harvard (1838), he took a degree in law, considered entering business, and finally settled on a career in letters, publishing *A Year's Life* in 1841, and *Poems* in 1844. He became engaged to Maria White, youthful mystic and radical, in 1840; four years later, they were married. In 1848, Lowell published *Poems, Second Series; The Biglow Papers* [*First Series*]*; A Fable for Critics;* and *The Vision of Sir Launfal*. Lowell and his wife were abroad in 1851–52; in 1853, Maria Lowell died. Appointed Professor of French and Spanish at Harvard, Lowell studied in Europe before taking up his new duties in 1856. In 1857, he married Frances Dunlap; in the same year, he became the first editor of the *Atlantic Monthly*. In 1867, he collected the second series of *Biglow Papers*. From 1863 to 1872, Lowell was associated with the *North American Review*. His critical essays were collected in *Among My Books* (1870), *My Study Windows* (1871), and *Among My Books, Second Series* (1876). Lowell served as Minister to Spain, 1877–1880, and as Minister to Great Britain, 1880–1885. Late volumes of poetry were *Under the Willows* (1868) and *Heartsease and Rue* (1888). Lowell died at Elmwood, Aug. 12, 1891.

G. W. Cooke has compiled a bibliography of Lowell (1906); more recent is that in *CHAL*, II, 544–550. Standard editions of Lowell's works are the Riverside (1890–92) and the

Elmwood (1904); the latter contains four volumes of his letters. The most useful edition of Lowell's poems is the Cambridge (1897). The standard biography is H. E. Scudder, *James Russell Lowell, A Biography* (1901). Excellent also is the briefer Ferris Greenslet, *James Russell Lowell: His Life and Work* (1905). J. J. Reilly, *James Russell Lowell as a Critic* (1915) is iconoclastic; more sympathetic is the chapter on Lowell in Norman Foerster, *American Criticism* (1928).

These extracts from Lowell's writings follow the text of the Riverside edition.

576. I WOULD NOT HAVE THIS PERFECT LOVE OF OURS was written during Lowell's betrothal to Maria White, who encouraged the poet in such dreams of universal brotherhood as appear in this sonnet. The poem was published in *A Year's Life*.

576. TO THE SPIRIT OF KEATS. During these Romantic years, Lowell planned to write a biography of John Keats, and even went so far as to communicate with George Keats. This poem was published in the *Arcturus* for 1842 (pub. 1841) and collected in *Poems*.

576. AS THE BROAD OCEAN ENDLESSLY UPHEAVETH is an expression of the youthful Lowell's mystical faith in an all-pervading Deity. Concerning one ecstatic moment of this period, Lowell declared: "I had a revelation last Friday evening. . . . I never before so clearly felt the spirit of God in me and around me. . . . The air seemed to waver to and fro with the presence of Something, I knew not what. I spoke with the calmness and clearness of a prophet." This sonnet was published in *Poems*.

577. WENDELL PHILLIPS. While Lowell's early humanitarianism was finding its chief outlet in anti-slavery agitation, he maintained a profound admiration for this eloquent abolitionist. The sonnet was published in *Poems*.

577. TO THE DANDELION was published in *Graham's Magazine*, Jan., 1845, and collected in *Poems, Second Series*.

578. THE PRESENT CRISIS was composed in the heat of Lowell's indignation against the proposed annexation of the slave-holding republic of Texas. The poem appeared in the Boston *Courier*, Dec. 11, 1845, and was collected in *Poems, Second Series*.

580. BEAVER BROOK was published as "The Mill" in the *Anti-Slavery Standard*, Jan. 14, 1848, and collected in *Poems* (1849).

581. THE BIRCH-TREE was included in *Poems, Second Series*.

582. THE BIGLOW PAPERS [FIRST SERIES] were published anonymously in the Boston *Courier* and the *Anti-Slavery Standard*, June, 1846, to Sept., 1848, in opposition to the Mexican War. When the poems were collected in 1848, Lowell added the humorously pedantic introduction, notes, glossary, and index—all attributed to an imaginary parson, Homer Wilbur. The first poem voices the protest of Yankee pacifists and abolitionists against attempts to recruit volunteers for service against Mexico. "What Mr. Robinson Thinks" deals with Governor Nixon Briggs of Massachusetts, who, although nominally a Whig, gave aid to the Democrats by issuing, at the beginning of the Mexican War, a proclamation calling for volunteers and thus alienated various members of his party. During the campaign of 1847, John P. Robinson, formerly a Whig, published an open letter explaining why he expected to vote, not for Briggs, but for the Democratic candidate, Brigadier-General Caleb Cushing.

587. A FABLE FOR CRITICS, according to Lowell, "was extemporized, I may fairly say, so rapidly was it written, purely for my own amusement and with no thought of publication. I sent daily instalments of it to a friend in New York, the late Charles F. Briggs. He urged me to let it be printed, and I at last consented to its anonymous publication. The secret was kept till after several persons had laid claim to its authorship." It is therefore no discredit to Lowell that many of his casual estimates, sometimes partaking of caricature, can no longer be accepted as just. ¶589. *"Griswold says so."* Rufus W. Griswold (1815–1857) was a critic and the editor of various anthologies of American literature. ¶591. *"Messieurs Mathews and Poe, you mustn't fling mud-balls at Longfellow so."* Cornelius Mathews was a minor figure in the notorious Longfellow War, which was waged almost single-handed by Poe.

593. THE FIRST SNOW-FALL was written in memory of Lowell's infant daughter, Blanche, who was buried in Mt. Auburn cemetery in 1847. In the same year, another daughter, Mabel, was born. The poem was published in the *Anti-Slavery Standard*, Dec. 27, 1849, and collected in *Under the Willows* (1868).

593. THE BIGLOW PAPERS, SECOND SERIES, were inspired by the Civil War. The separate poems were published in part in the *Atlantic Monthly*, Jan., 1862, to May, 1866. "The Courtin'" originally appeared in the first series of the *Papers*, where it extended only to forty-four lines; it is here printed in the expanded version included in the second series. Lowell left this account of the growth of "The Courtin'": "While the Introduction to the First Series was going through the press, I re-

ceived word from the printer that there was a blank page left which must be filled. I sat down at once and improvised another fictitious 'notice of the press,' in which, because verse would fill up space more cheaply than prose, I inserted an extract from a supposed ballad of Mr. Biglow. I kept no copy of it, and the printer, as directed, cut it off when the gap was filled. Presently I began to receive letters asking for the rest of it, sometimes for the *balance* of it. I had none, but to answer such demands, I patched a conclusion upon it in a later edition. Those who had only the first continued to importune me. Afterward, being asked to write it out as an autograph for the Baltimore Sanitary Commission Fair, I added other verses, into some of which I infused a little more sentiment in a homely way, and after a fashion completed it by sketching in the characters and making a connected story. Most likely I have spoiled it, but I shall put it at the end of this Introduction, to answer once for all those kindly importunings." "Jonathan to John" (595) is the concluding portion of Letter II, entitled "Mason and Slidell; a Yankee Idyll." James Mason, commissioner to Great Britain from the Confederate States, and John Slidell, commissioner to France, in 1861 were taken from an English steamer by an American warship and placed in a federal prison. When the British government demanded their release, it was granted; but reverberations of the affair were heard for several years. This protest of Lowell's against British sympathy for the Confederacy, Lincoln declared, was worth an army of two hundred thousand men.

596. Ode Recited at Harvard Commemoration. Two days before the commemoration service for Harvard men who had fallen in the Civil War, Lowell concluded that he could write no ode. "I had told my friend Child that it was impossible—that I was dull as a door-mat. But the next day something gave me a jog and the whole thing came out of me with a rush. I sat up all night writing it out clear, and took it on the morning of the day to Child. 'I have something, but don't yet know what it is, or whether it will do. Look at it and tell me.' He went a little way apart with it under an elm-tree in the college yard. He read a passage here and there, brought it back to me, and said, 'Do? I should think so! Don't you be scared.' And I wasn't, but virtue enough had gone out of me to make me weak for a fortnight after." The "Ode" was privately printed in 1865 and collected in a revised form in *Under the Willows*. ¶599. "*Our Martyr-Chief.*" This tribute to Lincoln was added after the ode had been delivered. ¶600. "*Dear ones.*" Various relatives of Lowell's, including three nephews, had lost their lives in the war.

604. Auspex was published in *A Masque of Poets* (1878).

604. Credidimus Jovem Regnare was published in the *Atlantic Monthly*, Feb., 1887, and collected in *Heartsease and Rue*. ¶605. "*Lemprière's fables*" are the classi al myths recorded by the English scholar, John Lemprière (*ca.* 1765–1824). ¶605. "*Actæon's hounds*" pursued and destroyed the Grecian hunter, Actæon, after he had been transformed into a stag by Artemis. ¶606. "*The Symplegades*" were, according to the legend of the Argonauts, twin rocks which moved about in the Bosphorus. ¶606. "*Noll . . . at Dunbar.*" Cromwell is supposed to have exclaimed at the Battle of Dunbar: "Now let God arise, and let his enemies be scattered." ¶607. "*Cynocephalus*" was a fabulous race of men with dogs' heads.

607. Thoreau was published in the *North American Review*, Oct., 1865, and collected in *My Study Windows*. Lowell here emphasized his mature rejection of Romanticism by wittily reviving the charges made in the 1840's against the eccentrics of that day (among whom Lowell and Maria White were then numbered) and by repudiating Thoreau's major doctrines. The disillusioned sobriety of post-war America is evident likewise in the sharpness with which Lowell scrutinized European Romantics: Goethe, Heine, Schiller, Schelling, and Novalis in Germany; Wordsworth, De Quincey, and Carlyle in England; and Rousseau, Saint Pierre, and Chateaubriand in France. ¶607. "*Ecce nunc tempus acceptabile!*": Behold now the acceptable time! ¶607. "*Redeunt Saturnia regna*": Now the Saturnian age returns. ¶609. "*Le roi est mort: vive le roi!*": The king is dead: long live the king! ¶610. "Βία and Κράτος": strength and might. ¶613. "*On touche encore à son temps et très-fort, même quand on le repousse*": A man feels his epoch continually and very powerfully, particularly when he resists it. ¶616. "*Magnis tamen excidit ausis*": He fell, however, in a great attempt.

616. On a Certain Condescension in Foreigners was published in the *Atlantic Monthly*, Jan., 1869, and collected in *My Study Windows*. The essay illustrates the range of Lowell's interests. Here he alludes, among American public men, to N. P. Banks, the bobbin-boy who became a general (619); Charles A. Dana of the *Sun* (631); and Charles Francis Adams and Reverdy Johnson, both

Ministers to Great Britain (632). Among Englishmen, he refers to the fourteenth-century adventurer, Sir John Hawkwood (630); the nineteenth-century historian, Henry Thomas Buckle (619); the Marquis of Hartington (627), long a leader of the Liberal party in England; and numerous authors, including three Victorians who had recently visited America: Leslie Stephen, Arthur Henry Clough, and Thomas Hughes (628). Frenchmen mentioned are Montaigne, whose *Travels* (622) were not printed until 1774; Père Dominique Bouhours, seventeenth-century Jesuit (622); Maurice Dudevant, who as a son of George Sand published a novel on American life (*Miss Mary*, 1867) under the pen-name of Maurice Sand (626); and Ernest Duvergier de Hauranne, nineteenth-century commentator on American society (627). Finally, Lowell gracefully unites the New World and the Old in three European-born scholars who served with distinction in American universities: Louis Agassiz at Harvard, Arnold Henry Guyot at Princeton, and Goldwin Smith at Cornell (626). ¶619. "*Hatem Tai*" was a Mohammedan chief of the sixth century, famed for extravagant hospitality. ¶620. "*Gano*," or Ganelon, is a traitor who appears in the "Song of Roland." ¶620. "*Post hoc ergo propter hoc*": After this, therefore because of this—a notorious fallacy. ¶622. "*Si un Allemand peut être bel-esprit?*": Whether a German can be a wit? ¶626. "*Jean Crapaud*," or Johnny Toad, was a satirical English name for Frenchmen. ¶627. "*Gare l'eau*": Look out for the water! ¶627. "*Le Français est plutôt indiscret que confiant*": The Frenchman is more indiscreet than gullible. ¶627. "*Tant-soit-peu*": a tiny bit. ¶627. "*Bienséances*": refinements. ¶627. "*Mutato nomine, de te*": Change the name, and this will apply to yourself.

## *George Henry Boker (1823–1890)*

Boker was born Oct. 6, 1823, in Philadelphia, was graduated from Princeton College, and entered upon a career as man of letters. After publishing *The Lesson of Life and Other Poems* (1848), *The Podesta's Daughter and Other Poems* (1852), and two tragedies, *Anne Boleyn* (1850) and *Leonor de Guzman* (1853), Boker wrote *Francesca da Rimini*, which was published in *Plays and Poems* (1856). During the Civil War, he was an active supporter of the federal government, his *Poems of the War* appearing in 1864. He served as Minister to Turkey (1871–75) and to Russia (1875–78). Boker died in 1890 at Philadelphia.

Boker's published works were collected in 1891. *Sonnets* and *Nydia* (ed. E. S. Bradley, 1929) have recently been printed from the original manuscripts. The definitive biography, with a bibliography, is E. S. Bradley, *George Henry Boker, Poet and Patriot* (1927).

634. To England is a series of seven sonnets included in *The Podesta's Daughter* and *Plays and Poems*.

634. The Fever in My Blood Has Died was included in *Plays and Poems*.

635. Here Part We, Love, Beneath the World's Broad Eye and All the World's Malice, All the Spite of Fate were included in *Plays and Poems*. For an account of Boker's love-affairs in relation to his sonnets, see the introduction to *Sonnets*.

635. Cavalry Song and Dirge for a Soldier (636) were included in *Poems of the War*. Major-General Philip Kearney was killed while reconnoitering near Chantilly, Va., after the second battle of Bull Run.

636. Francesca da Rimini. Boker learned the story of Paola and Francesca from Dante's *Inferno* and from Boccaccio, but he drew the characters of his drama with a free hand. Lanciotto, in particular, is here presented in a new light; and Pepe is entirely of Boker's own invention. The play was first staged at the Broadway Theater, New York, on Sept. 26, 1855.

## *Henry Theodore Tuckerman (1813–1871)*

Born in Boston, Tuckerman travelled extensively before settling in New York. There he devoted himself to authorship, becoming an active editor, biographer, critic, and essayist. His writings include *Thoughts on the Poets* (1846), *Characteristics of Literature* (1849–51), and *Poems* (1851). He died in New York.

700. Sonnets I, VIII, and XXVII were published in the *Democratic Review*, July and Dec., 1843, and April, 1845; they were collected in *Poems*.

## *John Godfrey Saxe (1816–1887)*

Born at Highgate, Vt., Saxe was graduated from Middlebury College and became a successful lawyer. Saxe was also an industrious journalist, lecturer, and writer of light verse. Among his works are *Poems* (1850) and *The Money King and Other Poems* (1860). He died at Albany, N. Y.

701. Sonnet to a Clam was included in *Poems*.

701. A Charming Woman was published in

*Harper's New Monthly Magazine*, March, 1875, and collected in *Leisure-Day Rhymes* (1875).

## *Thomas William Parsons (1819–1892)*

Parsons was born in Boston. During long residences in Europe, he translated Dante's *Inferno* and wrote much verse on Italian themes. Returning to Boston, he entered the profession of dentistry. Parsons died at Scituate, Mass. His work was collected in *Poems* (1893).

702. ON A BUST OF DANTE. Parsons left this note on the poem: "It is told of Dante that, when he was roaming over Italy, he came to a certain monastery, where he was met by one of the friars, who blessed him, and asked what was his desire; to which the weary stranger simply answered '*Pace*.'" The poem was published as "Dante's Portrait" in the Boston *Advertiser and Patriot*, Oct. 7, 1841; it is here printed from the revised text in *Poems* (1854).

## *Thomas Buchanan Read (1822–1872)*

Born in Chester County, Pa., Read became a migratory painter and a prolific poet, publishing *Poems* (1847, 1853, 1860), *The Wagoner of the Alleghanies* (1862), *A Summer Story, Sheridan's Ride and Other Poems* (1865), and *Poetical Works* (1866). Read died in New York.

703. DRIFTING was included in *Poems* (1860).

## *James Matthews Legaré (1823–1857)*

Born at Charleston, S. C., Legaré was an inventor and a poet. He published *Orta-Undis, and Other Poems* in 1847. Legaré died at Aiken, S. C.

704. HAW-BLOSSOMS was included in *Orta-Undis*.

## *Phœbe Cary (1824–1871)*

Phœbe Cary was born near Cincinnati, Ohio, in 1824. With her sister Alice, she removed to New York, where the two, under the patronage of Rufus Griswold and Horace Greeley, were accepted as important literary figures. Together, the sisters published *Poems* (1849) and *Last Poems* (1873). Phœbe Cary died at Newport, R. I. The only biography is Mary Ames, *A Memorial of Alice and Phœbe Cary* (1873).

704. NEARER HOME was included in *Poems and Parodies* (1854); a revised and condensed version published in *Poems of Faith, Hope and Love* (1868) is followed here.

## *Stephen Collins Foster (1826–1864)*

Foster was born at Pittsburgh, Pa., achieved modest fame as a song writer and composer, and died in poverty in New York. A useful biography is H. V. Milligan, *Stephen Collins Foster* (1920).

705. OLD FOLKS AT HOME was published as sheet music in 1851, subtitled "Ethiopian Melody as Sung by Christy's Minstrels." This text follows the original edition.

705. MY OLD KENTUCKY HOME, GOOD-NIGHT! was published as sheet music in 1853. This text follows the original edition.

## *Donald Grant Mitchell (1822–1908)*

Born at Norwich, Conn., Mitchell was graduated from Yale College, studied law, and served as consul at Venice. Mitchell (or "Ik Marvel") was a prolific essayist, best known for *Reveries of a Bachelor* (1850) and *Dream Life* (1851). He died on his farm at Edgewood, Conn.

706. REVERIES OF A BACHELOR. The first Reverie appeared in the *Southern Literary Messenger*, Sept., 1849, and was reprinted in *Harper's New Monthly Magazine*, Oct., 1850; this extract follows the text of the first collected edition. Mitchell's literary allusions here range lightly from Melville's *Typee* through Baron Lyttleton, eighteenth-century politician, and the Earl of Shaftesbury, eighteenth-century moralist (708); Raspe's familiar hoax, *The Adventures of Baron Münchausen* (708) and Goethe's *Sorrows of Werther* (711); Le Sage's *Gil Blas* (711), La Fontaine, seventeenth-century fabulist, La Bruyère, seventeenth-century moralist, and Balzac (711); Dante, Tasso, and the eighteenth-century dramatist Goldoni (711); and on to Seneca and the Greek Anthology (711).

# INDEX

Non-italic numbers refer to pages in text; italic numbers to pages in notes.